ART OF THE NON-WESTERN WORLD

Asia, Africa, Oceania, and the Americas

NANCY L. KELKER

Oxford University Press
New York Oxford

Oxford University Press is a department of the University of Oxford.
It furthers the University's objective of excellence in research, scholarship, and education by publishing worldwide. Oxford is a registered trade mark of Oxford University Press in the UK and certain other countries.

Published in the United States of America by Oxford University Press
198 Madison Avenue, New York, NY 10016, United States of America.

For titles covered by Section 112 of the US Higher Education Opportunity Act, please visit www.oup.com/us/he for the latest information about pricing and alternate formats.

Library of Congress Cataloging-in-Publication Data
Names: Kelker, Nancy L. author.
Title: Art of the non-Western world : Asia, Africa, Oceania and the Americas / Nancy Kelker.
Description: New York : Oxford University Press, [2020] | Includes bibliographical references and index.
Identifiers: LCCN 2019017786 | ISBN 9780190263102 (pbk.)
Subjects: LCSH: Art--History. | Art and society.
Classification: LCC N5300 .K36 2020 | DDC 709--dc23 LC record available at https://lccn.loc.gov/2019017786

9 8 7 6 5 4 3 2 1
Printed by Quad/Graphics, Inc., Mexico

BRIEF CONTENTS

CONTENTS

MAPS

INTRODUCTION

What is non-Western art? Is it really art? Why do I need to know anything about it? These are among the many questions that the author has been asked countless times over the years. Non-Western is a less than satisfactory catch-all term currently used to designate cultures outside of the European or Western tradition. It is a problematic term because it does not tell the reader what it is but rather what it isn't and, in that, resides an implied judgment. Still, it is better than the previously used terms—"tribal" and "primitive," the first of which is inaccurate in most cases and the second, derogatory in all. So, what is this book about? Specifically, *Art of the Non-Western World* surveys the arts—from ancient to modern times—of the indigenous peoples of the Americas, Africa, Asia, and Oceania (Australia and the Pacific Islands).

Why is there a need for such a book? Art History has long given precedence to the Western tradition arising out of the arts of Classical Greece and Rome. Western art and theory have been adopted as the criteria by which all other arts are measured. Unfortunately, this often results in arts from the rest of the world appearing to come up short. For example, in the Western tradition a distinction is made between "fine arts" and "crafts." The "fine arts"—painting, sculpture, and public architecture, form the pinnacle of artistic endeavor. The practice of these arts is believed to require greater intellect and aesthetic sensibility, and to be closely connected to the notion of art for art's sake. "Crafts"—textiles, ceramics, glass arts, metalworking, and woodworking—by contrast are things that can be seen as trades or hobbies, that smack of the utilitarian, or are done primarily by women, and generally are excluded from the consideration of art history. Dismissed as crafts, non-Western objects were not collected by art museums but rather were relegated to ethnography or natural history museums where they were treated as exemplars of cultural practices. The problem with this approach is that critical "art" information was not recorded, for example, the name and biography of the artist. Connections were not made between works made by a single artist, nor was consideration given to the influence of that artist on apprentices or followers—things that make up the basic narrative of Western art history.

The combination of Western artistic biases and Colonialist attitudes gave rise to an art history that has long been both Eurocentric and androcentric. As a result, otherwise well-educated individuals, including more than a few art historians, have been left with the impression that there is no art beyond Western lands, at least "not real art like in the Louvre," as one person once put it to the author. Indeed, such cultural negations were especially important during the late Colonial Era (nineteenth and twentieth centuries) when it was necessary for Europeans to assert cultural superiority over subjugated populations. Evidence of ancient high cultures in a Colonial territory was a significant problem, one that might render invalid or immoral the removal of indigenous populations and the confiscation of their lands. As long as there was no evidence of advanced civilizations, Colonization could proceed smoothly. However, the discovery of monumental architecture or sculpture, particularly in stone, required special elucidation. Thus, for example, the building of North American monumental earthworks and pyramids (diminished as mounds) or African stone circles (*zimbabwe*) was attributed to Atlanteans, Scandinavians, Israelites, or some other more palatable, long-ago, non-native peoples, whose presumed extermination by the local savages could be used as justification for European takeover.

In the second half of the twentieth century some basic art history texts began including short chapters on the Americas, Africa, India, China, Japan, and the Pacific Islands. However, these materials were often presented as a smorgasbord of objects without any apparent rhyme or reason for their selection, except to serve as foils to the arts of the Western tradition. Where the art of the Western world was typically placed in historical and cultural context, enriched with the biographies of the great and not-so-great masters, and the forms and styles of works carefully analyzed, this "other art" was devalued by superficial anthropological or ethnological treatments in which it was presented as the work of a tribal group or as an example of a particular category of object, that is, a "mask" or a "fetish." As a result, it was difficult for students and even instructors to view or talk about non-Western objects as artworks. They remained the "other."

Art of the Non-Western World attempts to bring the standard tools of art history to the study of the arts of the larger world beyond the European tradition. Where possible works are placed in historical, cultural, and religious context; techniques of production are discussed along with form and style; related works are grouped to give students an overview, and where available, information about the artists who created these works and the patrons who commissioned them is provided. Additionally, a special effort has been made to engender both the creators and the art works, particularly in those fields, for example, pre-Columbian art, where the androcentric point of view has resulted in recognizably female rulers being incorrectly identified as males. Obviously, this has been a massive project and while the results may be imperfect, it is the author's hope that it will be a step in the right direction to a better understanding of the arts in a global world.

Many people have contributed to this project through their research as cited in the bibliography. I would especially like to thank the following colleagues and former students who served as readers, provided information, advice, encouragement, and support, or supplied images: Dr. Karen Olsen Bruhns, Dr. Nancy P. Troike, Dr. Virginia Miller, Dr. Billie J. Follensbee, Dr. Rebecca Gonzáles-Lauck, Dr. Debrah Sickler-Voigt, Dr. Kyle D. Stoneman, Susan Sharpe, Virginia B. Kelker, Katherine "Alex" Flanagan, John P. Donovan, Rick Rishaw, Eric Snyder, and Rachael Smith. Additionally, I would like to express my appreciation to the Islamic Center of Murfreesboro, Tennessee, and the Sri Ganesha Temple, Hindu Cultural Center of Nashville, Tennessee, for their assistance and information on the Islamic and Hindu religions respectively.

Finally, I would like to thank the following individuals, galleries, and museums for providing photographic images for the book, either directly or through Wikimedia licenses: Peju Alatise, Jenny Ellerbe, Gulay Semercioglu, Alfonso Bouchot, Diego Delso, Jack Hynes, Jorge Pérez de Lara, Greg Willis, Raymond Ostertag, Tato Grasso, Jan Harenburg, Alejandro Linares Garcia, Arian Zwegers, Miguel Alvarez, Martin St-Amant, Ingo Mehling, Karolyn Aroca, Eric Ewing, Herb Roe, Hieronymous Rowe, W. V. Bailey, David Coulson, Francesco Raffaele, Max Gattringer, Jon Bodsworth, Ricardo Liberato, Olaf Tausch, Ad Meskens, Alexander Baranov, Philip Pikart, Ron Van Oens, Ondřej Žváček, Bernard Gagnon, Janice Bell, Dirk Bakker, A. Parrot, Einsamer Schütze, Mark Szarejko, Andy Gilham, Richard T. Bryant, Reinhard Dietrich, Marie Lan Nguyen, Radomir Vrbovsky, Andrew Shiva, Jean Pierre Bazard, Patrick Ringgenberg, Saqib Qayyum, Amit Nimade, Biswarup Ganguly, Kevin Standage, C. S. Gautham, Dennis Jarvis, Afifa Afrin, Suraj Rajiv, Jakub Hatun, Bjorn Christian Torrissen, Gerd Eichmann, Mark Alexander, Krzysztof Golik, Hartmann Linge, Gunawan Kartapranata, Caitriana Nicholson, Jan S. Peterson, Marcin Konsek, Professor Gary Lee Todd, Marcin Biatek, Daniel Case, J. T. Williams, Richard Fabi, John Gollings, Marius Fenger, E. K. Silverman, C. T. Snow, and Arian Zwegers. The Jack Shainman Gallery, New York, New York; Metropolitan Museum of Art; Brooklyn Museum; Museum of Fine Arts, Boston; Art Institute of Chicago; Parque Museo de La Venta, Villahermosa, Tabasco, Mexico; Neuberger Museum of Art, Purchase College, State University of New York; Sam Noble Oklahoma Museum of Natural History, University of Oklahoma, Norman; Cleveland Museum of Art; British Museum; National Museum of Scotland; Museo Tumbas Reales de Sipán and Bruning Archaeological Museum, Lambayeque, Peru; New Orleans Museum of Art; Poverty Point Station Archaeology Program; FEMA and the State of Louisiana; Louisiana State University CADGIS Research Laboratory, Baton Rouge; Ohio History Connection; Field Museum, Chicago; National Park Service; Smithsonian Institution, National Museum of the American Indian;

State Museum of Namibia; Trust for African Rock Art (TARA); LatinAmericanStudies.org; Fondazione Passaré; Museum of Egyptian Antiquities, Cairo; United Nations Educational, Scientific and Cultural Organization; Nigerian National Museum, Lagos; Museo Nazionale Preistorico e Etnografico Luigi Pigorini, Rome; Museum of Ankara, Turkey; National Museum of Iraq, Baghdad; University of Pennsylvania Museum of Archaeology and Anthropology, Philadelphia; Freer Gallery of Art and Arthur M. Sackler Gallery Archives, Smithsonian Institution, Washington, DC; Shirazi Art Gallery PTY LTD, Melbourne; National Museum, New Delhi; Archaeological Museum of Sarnath; Victoria and Albert Museum, London; National Gallery of Modern Art, New Delhi; Myanmar National Museum; Changsha Hunan Provincial Museum; Shunya.net; National Palace Museum, Taipei, Taiwan; Tokyo National Museum; Zhejiang Provincial Museum in Hangzhou; C. C. Wang Collection, New York; Nelson-Atkins Museum of Art, Kansas City; Asian Art Museum, San Francisco; National Museum of Korea; Kagami Jinja Temple, Karatsu, Japan; Ho-Am Art Museum; Gansong Art Museum, Seoul; National Museum of Modern and Contemporary Art, Seoul, South Korea; Ministry of Land, Infrastructure, Transport and Tourism, Japan; Tokugawa Art Museum; Tokyo National Museum; University Art Museum, Tokyo University of the Arts; Musée due Quai Branly; National Gallery of Australia; Holmes à Court Collection, Heytesbury, Estate of Clifford Possum Tjapaltjarri; Tropenmuseum Amsterdam; Denver Art Museum; and the Glasgow Museum of Art.

ART OF THE NON-WESTERN WORLD

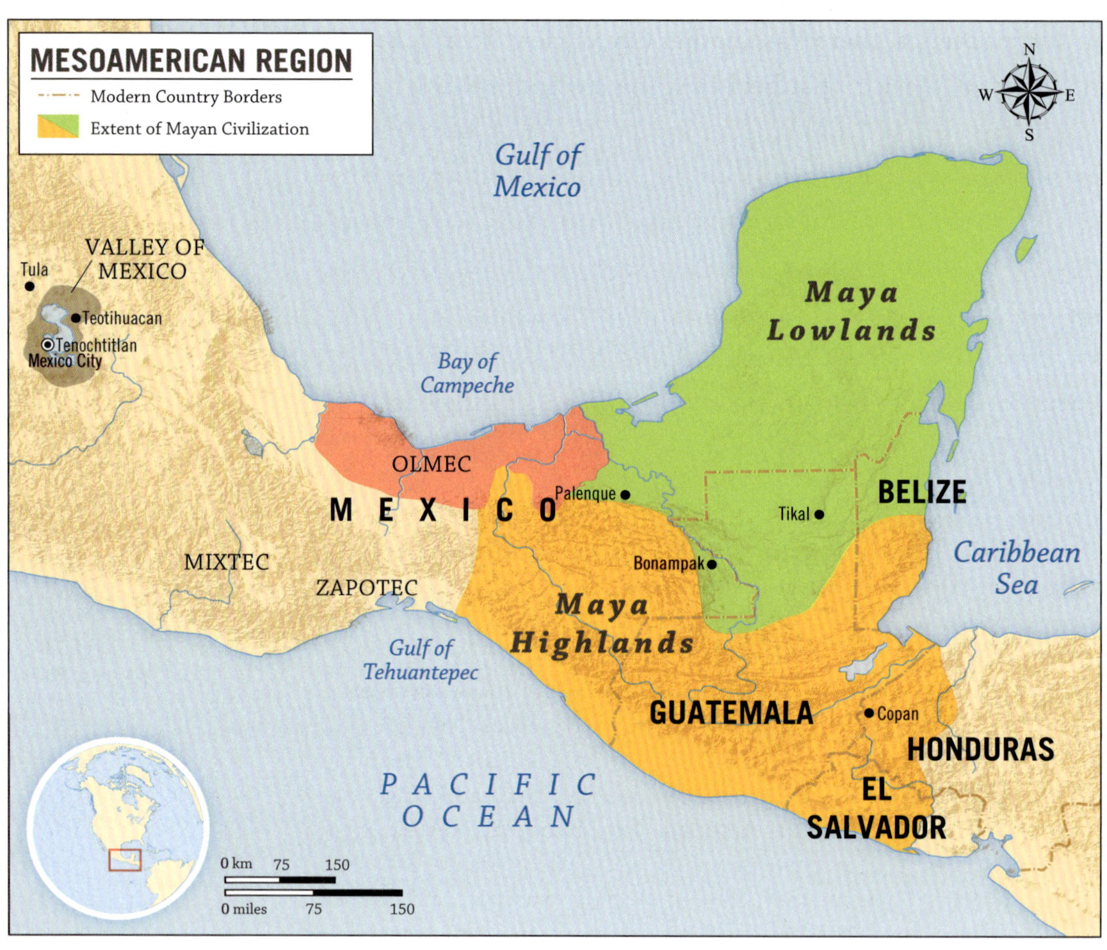
MESOAMERICAN REGION
Modern Country Borders
Extent of Mayan Civilization
N
W
E
S
Gulf of Mexico
VALLEY OF MEXICO
Tula
Teotihuacan
Tenochtitlan
Mexico City
Maya Lowlands
Bay of Campeche
OLMEC
MEXICO
Palenque
Tikal
BELIZE
Caribbean Sea
MIXTEC
ZAPOTEC
Bonampak
Maya Highlands
Gulf of Tehuantepec
GUATEMALA
Copan
HONDURAS
EL SALVADOR
PACIFIC OCEAN
0 km 75 150
0 miles 75 150

Mesoamerica

1

Brief Overview

Long before New York City became the acknowledged art capital of North America, there was another city, ancient Teotihuacan in the Valley of Mexico, that held that title for more than six hundred years. Artists and craftspersons from across Mesoamerica came to the city to work in its ateliers. The artworks produced at Teotihuacan were not only appreciated locally but collected by foreign elite as far away as modern-day Honduras. Teotihuacan was also a great exporter of culture; its religious ideology provided the theological underpinnings, including the gods Tlaloc and Quetzalcoatl, for many subsequent Mesoamerican religions.

While Teotihuacan was an art center of international significance, there were many other important regional centers, among the Olmec, Maya, Mixtec, Zapotec, Huastec, Toltec, and Aztec. In their capitals, amazingly engineered works of monumental architecture were built; magnificent state sculpture and paintings were created, and a variety of beautiful and useful crafts from jewelry, textiles, lapidary, papermaking, and pottery to more exotic feather and flower mosaics were made.

The designation "Mesoamerica" for this New World region is of fairly recent origin, having been coined by the German-Mexican anthropologist Paul Kirchhoff in 1943 to identify an area of "high cultures" within larger Middle America. In Kirchhoff's system high cultures were defined by their use of stone for architecture, 365- and 260-day calendar cycles, hieroglyphic writing systems, and certain agricultural practices. Kirchhoff's Mesoamerica, geographically speaking, runs from just north of the Valley of Mexico (where Mexico City is today) down to the western part of Honduras. However, it should be understood that the term is an invention; none of Kirchhoff's high cultures, or low ones for that matter, recognized any pan-regional concept such as "Mesoamerica." They would have self-identified with their community or kingdom.

Like the term itself, Mesoamerica as a field of research is relatively new; the first studies of Mesoamerican civilizations began only in the nineteenth century. It was not until 1821 when Mexico and

Chapter Objectives

1. Understand that art production began in Mesoamerica early in the second millennium BCE with the rise of civic and ceremonial centers such as La Venta and San Lorenzo in the Olmec region where the first monumental stone sculptures were carved to commemorate rulers and the first earthen pyramids were created. Realize that the artistic progress of Mesoamerican peoples continued unabated until the Spanish Conquest.
2. Recognize different cultural styles within Mesoamerican art and architecture and understand how they reflect religious and political concerns of the peoples who created them and how they influenced others.
3. Understand the impact of the Spanish Conquest and Christianization on Mesoamerican civilizations, both for their citizens and their art.
4. Explore the work of Indigenous artists in the nineteenth and early twentieth centuries.

other Latin American nations achieved independence that explorers, adventurers, and gentleman-scholars, including John Lloyd Stephens, Frederick Catherwood, Claude-Joseph-Désiré Charnay, Alfred Percival Maudslay, and others, began traveling through Mexico and Central America, discovering ancient cities hidden in their jungles, collecting artifacts, and writing the first descriptions of them.

In formulating the first chronologies for Mesoamerica, in particular the Maya, nineteenth-century scholars turned to ancient Greece for a model. Greece, with the help of European nations, had just achieved its independence and things Hellenistic were immensely popular in the West. To these first scholars the model seemed appropriate as the Maya were seen as Greek-like in their art; the Aztecs at this same time were equated with the Romans for their skills in running a vast empire. As a result, Mesoamerican chronologies followed a Classical model, resulting in three main periods: The Pre-Classic, the Classic, and the Post-Classic. While the names of these epochs are problematic for some modern scholars, the organization of pre-Columbian cultures, those before the arrival of Columbus, into Early (2000 BCE–250 CE), Middle (100–900 CE), and Late (900–1550 CE) periods still works and in original and adjusted formats remains in standard use.

The Early or Pre-Classic Period (c. 2000 BCE–100 CE)

The first great Mesoamerican civilizations evolved during the Pre-Classic period. Among these were Cuicuilco and Teotihuacan in the Valley of Mexico, the Olmec in Tabasco and Veracruz, the Zapotec in Oaxaca, and the Maya in Chiapas and the Petén. Although the tendency has been to treat these cultures as though they developed in isolation, that is not the case. The early Mesoamerican cultures not only traded with each other but with other developing civilizations to the north and south. As is the case with kingdoms elsewhere, they also formed alliances with each other against common enemies, and sealed those agreements with gifts and through marriages.

The Olmec (c. 1500–400 BCE)

The Olmecs inhabited an area along the Mexican Gulf Coast in what are today the states of Veracruz and Tabasco. Since these people did not have a written language, what they called themselves is not known. The name "Olmec" is derived from "Olman," meaning "Rubber Country," a designation given some three millennia later by the Aztecs, who knew it as the source for natural rubber.

LA VENTA, MESOAMERICA'S FIRST ART CENTER (1200–400 BCE)

La Venta in the state of Tabasco was founded around 1200 BCE on a sandy island in the middle of a coastal mangrove swamp, some 10

timeline

DATE	TYPE	EVENT
		BCE
c. 6000	Art	Burgos Cave paintings in northeast Mexican state of Tamaulipas
c. 5000	Art	Baja California cave paintings
c. 2700	History	Corn domesticated in the Valley of Mexico
c. 2000	History	Calendar invented
c. 1400	History	Start of Formative or Pre-Classic period
	Art	Cuicuilco founded in the Valley of Mexico
	Art	Olmec San Lorenzo, founded Veracruz
c. 1200	Art	Olmec La Venta, founded in Tabasco
c. 1000	Art	Olmec carve colossal heads
	Art	Great Pyramid of La Venta began
c. 900	History	San Lorenzo destroyed
c. 800	History	Maya Tikal settled in Guatemala
c. 600–500	Culture	Zapotecs at Monte Alban, Oaxaca invent writing
c. 500	History	Maya Palenque settled in Chiapas
c. 400	History	Teotihuacan settled in the Valley of Mexico
	History	La Venta abandoned
c. 300	Culture	Maya invent writing and mathematics with zero as place holder
c. 100	History	Cuicuilco abandoned
		CE
c. 100	Art	Pyramid of the Sun constructed at Teotihuacan
	Art	Construction of first stage of Pyramid of the Moon
	Art	First frescoes painted at Teotihuacan
c. 200	Art	Pyramid of Quetzalcoatl and adjoining palaces constructed
c. 250	History	Start of Classic Period in the Maya area
c. 300	Art	First stuccoed vessels at Teotihuacan
c. 350	Art	Adosados added to Quetzalcoatl, Sun, and Moon pyramids; Temple of Quetzalcoatl burned
378	History	Yax Nuun Ahiin I (First Crocodile) arrived at Tikal
426	History	Arrival of K'inich Yax K'uk Mo at Maya city of Copan

(Continued)

timeline *continued*

DATE	TYPE	EVENT
		CE
431	History	Palenque's Royal dynasty established by K'uk' Bahlam
445	Art	Stele 31 erected by Siyaj Chan K'awiil II at Tikal
c. 450	Art	Seventh enlargement of the Pyramid of the Moon at Teotihuacan
c. 500	Art	Teotihuacan's Golden age of fresco painting began
562	History	Tikal attacked by Caracol and Calakmul; - the Hiatus begins at Tikal
599	History	Palenque sacked by Calakmul
c. 600	History	Birth of K'inich Janaab Pakal at Palenque
611	History	Palenque sacked a second time by Calakmul
615	History	Pakal assumed the throne of Palenque
c. 620	History	Chiik Nahb Structure Sub 1–4 murals painted at Calakmul
c. 650	History	Teotihuacan burned and abandoned
672	Art	Temple XIII built for Lady Tz'akbu Ajaw at Palenque
c. 675	Art	Temple of Inscriptions at Palenque began
682	History	Accession of Jasaw Chan K'awiil I to the throne of Tikal
686	History	Hiatus ended at Tikal
c. 700	History	Maya city of Uxmal founded
	History	Xochicalco founded in central highlands
c. 703	Art	Lady 12 Macaw dies; Temple II built at Tikal
c. 732	Art	Construction of Temple I at Tikal began
c. 790	History	Yajaw Chan Muwann II installed as King at Bonampak
	Art	Murals painted in the Temple of the Murals, Bonampak
c. 900	History	Start of the Post-Classic Period
	History	Toltec city of Tula founded in the Valley of Mexico
c. 935–947	History	Ce Acatl Topiltzin Quetzalcoatl born at Tula
c. 1170	History	Tula destroyed
	History	Toltecs resettled at Chapultepec on the west shore of Lake Texcoco
c. 1200	History	Mexica (Aztecs) arrived in the Valley of Mexico
1325	History	Mexica city of Tenochtitlan founded

DATE	TYPE	EVENT
CE		
1376	History	Acampichtli became Mexica Tlatoani
1481	Art	Tizoc laid foundation stone for enlargement of the Templo Mayor
1487	Art	Templo Mayor rededicated in Tenochtitlan by Ahuitzotl
1519	History	Hernando Cortes landed in Yucatan and Veracruz
1520	History	Moctezuma Xocoyotzin killed in Tenochtitlan
	History	Spaniards flee city (Noche Triste)
1521	History	Cuauhtemoc surrendered to Cortes
1539	Art	*The Mass of St. Gregory* made for Pope Paul III
c. 1550	Art	Mural painted at Church of San Miguel Arcangel, Ixmilquilpan
1552	Culture	Bartolome de Las Casas published his *Brief Relations of the Destructions of the Indies* detailing the barbarous treatment of Native Peoples by the Spanish
1790	Art	Coatlicue statue unearthed in the Zócalo in Mexico City
1810	History	War of Independence from Spain began
1821	History	Mexico achieved independence from Spain
1832	Art	Hermenegildo Bustos born in Guanajuato State
1846	History	War with United States, northern territories lost
1899	Art	Rufino Tamayo born in Oaxaca
1910	History	Mexican Revolution began
1923	History	Obregon became president of Mexico
	Art	Mexican Mural Movement began
1978	Art	Coyolxauhqui found near the Zócalo in Mexico City
2010	Art	Tlaltecuhtli discovered near the Templo Mayor in Mexico City

miles (15 km) inland from the Gulf. By 800 BCE it had a population estimated at 20,000 and was one of the most important centers, especially in terms of art production, in early Mesoamerica. To date, some ninety monumental works have been found at the site, including Colossal Heads, sculptures-in-the-round, altars, and stelas, all of which were integrated into a vast ceremonial center. Around 400 BCE, for unknown reasons, the city was abandoned.

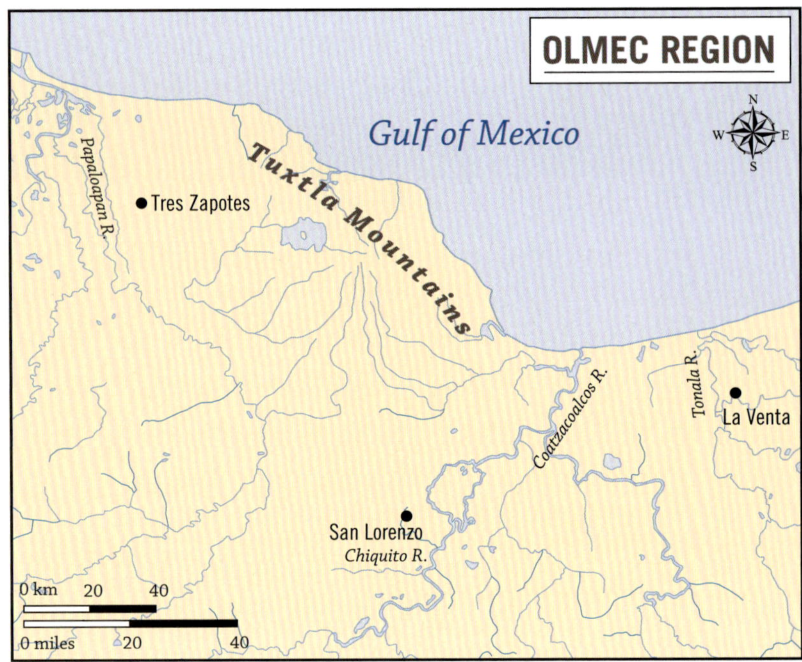

MONUMENTAL ARCHITECTURE AT LA VENTA

The ceremonial core of the city featured nine distinct groups of monumental earthen pyramids. These mound groups were originally platforms for temples, administrative buildings, and elite residences. All of the mounds were aligned on a north-south axis and positioned in straight rows that formed the borders for broad avenues, large plazas, and smaller courts. This arrangement suggests that early on, Mesoamericans had already devised a system of urban planning that paired mass and space.

The Great Pyramid of La Venta Standing in the center of ancient La Venta is the massive earthen mound known as the Great Pyramid (Figure 1.1). It is the largest architectural construction at the site, standing some 100 feet (30 m) high, and is one of the earliest known Mesoamerican pyramids. It sits on a square base-platform, measuring approximately 420 feet (128 m) by 374 feet (114 m), with a 26 foot (8 m) wide extension in the center of the base on the south side. Aligned with this tab-like extension was a 30 foot wide stair, which provided access to the summit and presumably to any temple that once stood there. The massive structure was constructed of local clay and sandy soils, with bits of broken pottery and stone tool fragments intermixed. To stabilize the mass of the pyramid, rough limestone blocks, sometimes vertically and sometimes diagonally oriented, were randomly embedded into the structure as buttresses; archaeologists working at the site

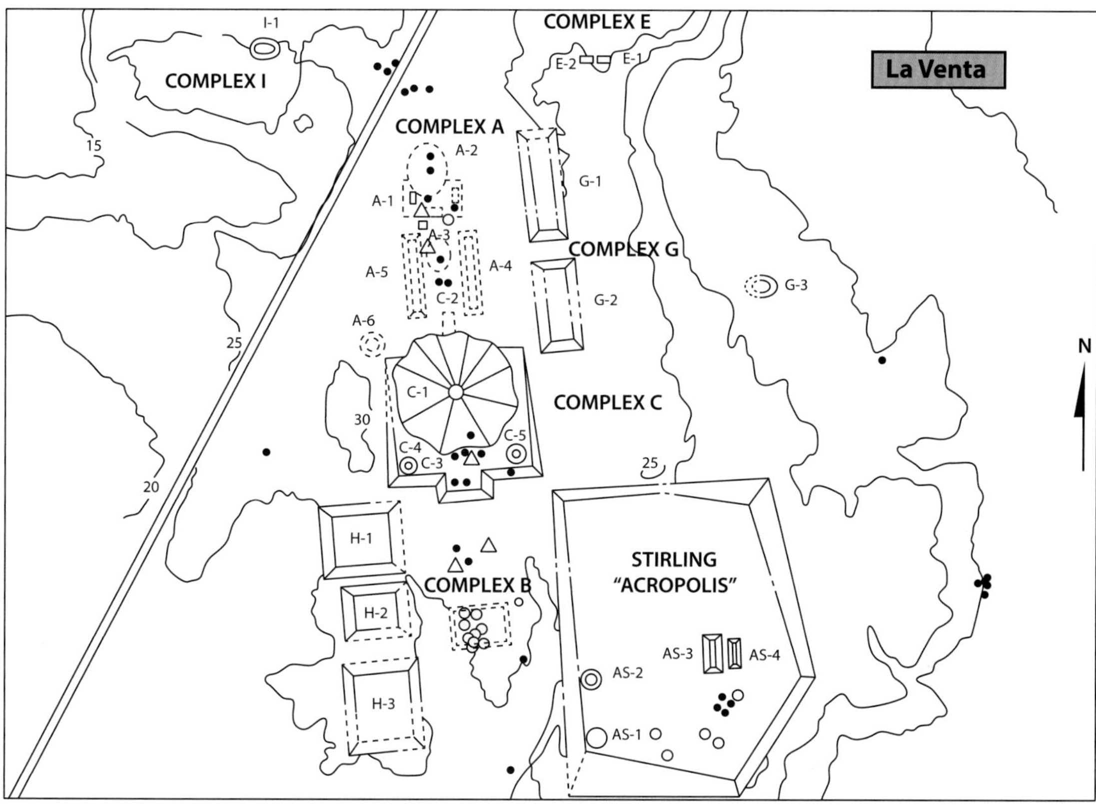

have yet to discern any pattern for the placement of these limestone blocks (Gonzáles Lauck 1997, 81–85).

The exact original shape of the Great Pyramid is a matter of considerable speculation and often fanciful reconstruction. In the three millennia since the construction of the pyramid, its earthen mass has been considerably eroded by the heavy coastal rainfall. In addition to changes caused by water erosion and slumping, windblown sand and humus from tropical vegetation have accumulated over the original surface. Further damage resulted from clearing the mound and from bulldozing parts of the platform to provide soil for a private landing strip. The effect today is that the pyramid appears as a flat-topped conical mass with undulating sides. Recent archaeological work has only explored a section of basal area on the south side of the pyramid, showing it to recede, on each side of the south access, toward curved corners (Gonzáles Lauck email to author, August 18, 2015,). Based on information from the excavation, aero-topographical maps, and accounting for erosion, the most probable form for the pyramid as originally built was a rectangle (slightly longer north to south) with broadly rounded corners. The pyramid was situated on a rectangular platform, approximately 30 feet larger on at least three sides, and some 10 to 15 feet (3 to 4 m) high depending upon terrain.

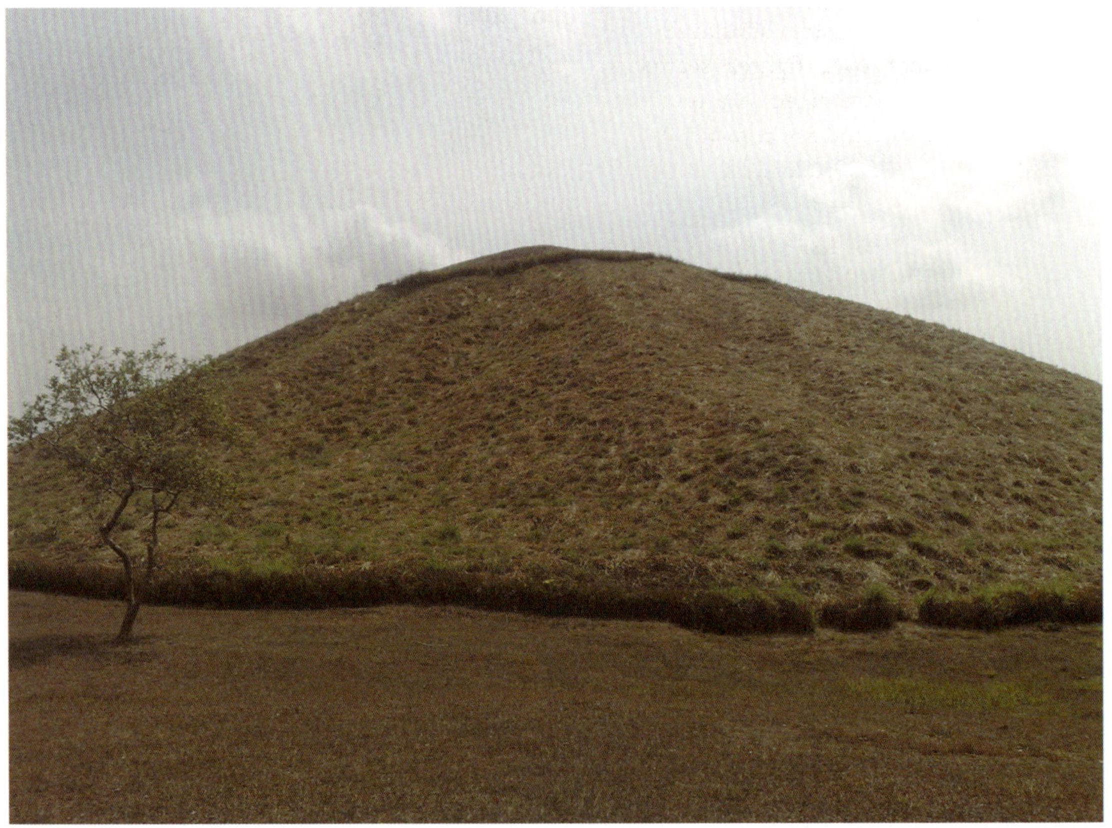

▲ 1.1 La Venta, Great Pyramid (Mound C-1), viewed from base platform, c. 1200–900 bce. 100 ft. high.

This earthen mound is one of the earliest in Mesoamerica and was constructed entirely of fill material brought in one basketload at a time.

EARLY OLMEC SCULPTURE

Olmec monumental basalt sculpture was political in function, depicting rulers of dynastic lineages and commemorating important historical events. Traditionally, it has been assumed that the figures depicted on stelas and altars or rendered as Colossal Heads were male even when there was physical evidence to the contrary. As documented in the art, many Mesoamerican civilizations had ruling queens as well as kings. Discerning the difference between male and female in ancient Mesoamerica is not difficult because clothing and hairstyles were gender specific. Olmec ladies wore wrapped skirts, usually low on the hips, and the men wore loincloths. Both sexes adorned themselves with jewelry, which sometimes varied in form according to gender (Bruhns 1999, 169).

La Venta Stela 1 La Venta Stela 1(Figure 1.2) is a deeply carved stone slab some 8 feet (2.5 m) tall that features a high relief female figure standing within a rectangular niche. Despite the fact that the figure is obviously feminine with rounded breasts, narrow waist, full hips and thighs, and long female hair, the piece was often referred to as male in the early literature on La Venta. She wears a pleated skirt hanging low on the hips in female fashion, a helmet-like headdress with a central U-shaped band and pendant forms, and drop earrings. The block above the niche is incised with a design interpreted as a supernatural feline or the Earth Monster ; similar designs sometimes appear over figures seated in niches, where they are often interpreted as representing a cave, and are associated with accession (Bruhns 1999, 171–172).

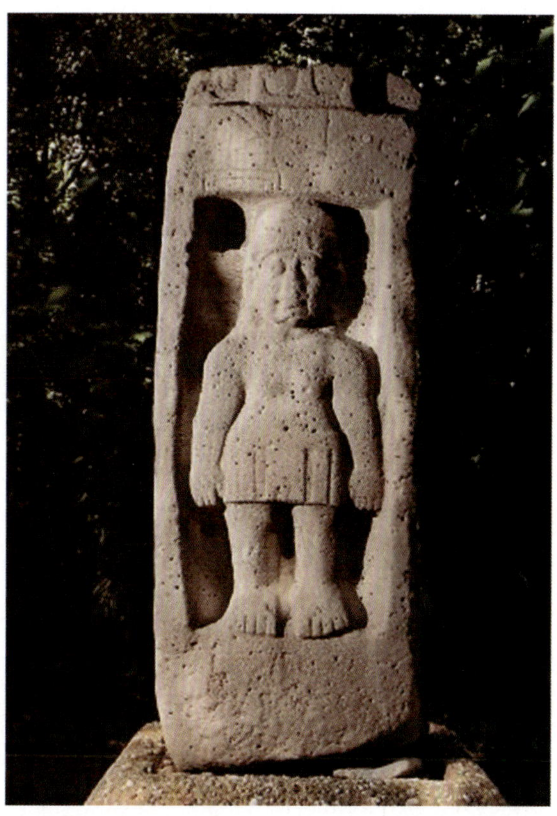

▲ La Venta Stela 1, c. 900–400 bce. Basalt, 8.2 ft. × 3.21 ft. × 2.29 ft.

The high relief figure standing inside of a niche marked the accession of an early Olmec queen.

La Venta Monument 1 Four Colossal Heads are known from La Venta; three (Monuments 4, 2, and 3) were found all in a row, north of Complex A and facing north. The fourth one, Monument 1 (Figure 1.3), was located in the plaza to the south of the Great Pyramid and faced south toward Complex B (Clewlow et al. 1967, 19). La Venta Monument 1 was carved from a 24-ton basalt boulder brought down from the Tuxtla Mountains, some 50 miles (80 km) to the west. Since it was difficult to move such large stones overland, it is believed that the Olmec loaded the stones onto rafts, floated them downriver to the gulf and finally maneuvered them upriver to La Venta. The off-loaded boulders were moved on log rollers to their final location and carved in place. Standing almost 8 feet (2.41 m) high and measuring 6.8 feet (2.08 m) wide by 6.4 feet (1.95 m) deep, La Venta Monument 1 was conceived and executed as sculpture-in-the-round, but with particular emphasis given to the features. The greatest depth of relief and degree of naturalism is found in the facial core of nose, eyes, and mouth. As the Olmec sculptors moved outward the carving often became shallower and the forms more schematically rendered.

La Venta Monument 1 is unusual in its considerable refinement and softer, less angular treatment of the face compared to the other Colossal Heads at the site. The eyes are well-proportioned and the eyelids protrude over them to give a sense of roundness to the form of the eyeball underneath. The nose is broad, flat, and rounded at the tip. The lips are full, the upper one bow-shaped and the lower one plump, with both turning downward at the corners. Under the lips is a W-shaped depression, which adds emphasis to the rise of the chin boss. The prominent nasolabial folds found on many male heads are missing, giving a sense of fullness, youthfulness, and perhaps, femininity to the face. Two elements seem to tie Monument 1 to the figure in Stela 1: the U-shaped element in the helmets and the drop earrings; it is possible that the same individual is represented by both monuments, or at the very least individuals of the same gender. Recognizably male heads wear ear flares represented either frontally or in profile view.

Stela 1 and Monument 1 are good examples of Olmec stone working techniques. Olmec artisans did not possess metal tools; their

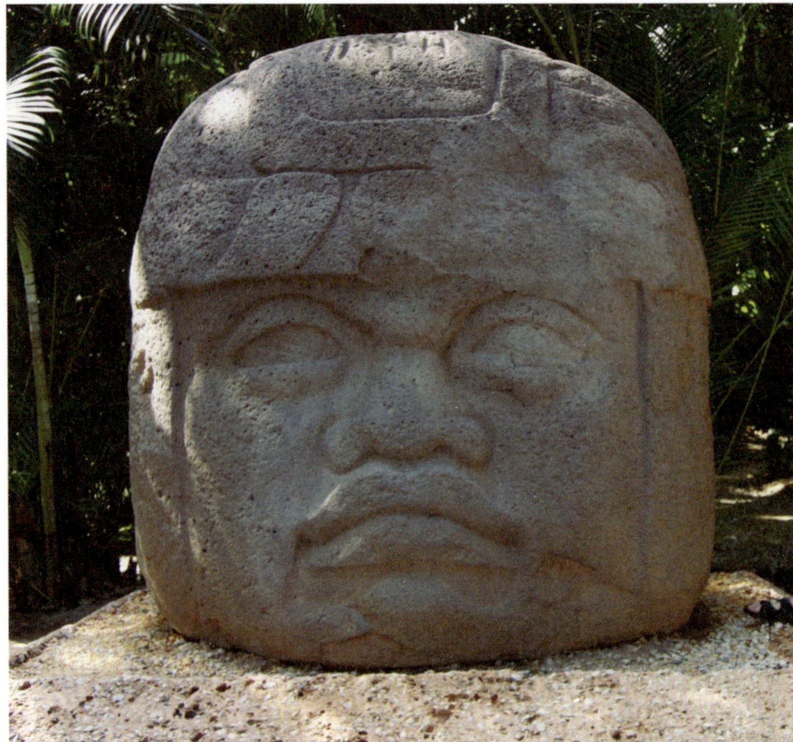

▶ **1.3** La Venta, Monument 1, c. 1200–900 bce. Basalt, 7.9 ft. × 6.8 ft. × 6.4 ft.

Olmec Colossal Heads are known from several sites in the Olmec heartland. Although their identities are unknown, the distinctive elements of their headgear suggest they represent specific individuals in the royal dynasties of the sites where they were found.

sculptor's tool box contained sharpened hard stone chisels, hammer stones for rough and fine work, and drills, consisting of various diameter hollow tubes filled with sand or quartz. The final grinding down and smoothing of the surface was done with fine abrasives, perhaps stuck to a hard surface for use like a file. A careful examination of the face of Monument 1 shows circular drill marks at the outer corners of the eyes, mouth, and possibly the nostril and chin areas. Drill marks can also be identified in the corners of the niche on Stela 1. Using drills to open an area to the correct depth, Olmec stoneworkers then chiseled outward to separate the background from the raised forms.

LATE OLMEC SCULPTURE

Excavations along the south side of the Great Pyramid unearthed several large stone stelas that were arranged as a tableau. A single radiocarbon date (394 BCE ±36) places these works toward the end of the Olmec occupation of La Venta and some five hundred years after the carving of the Colossal Heads, Stela 1 and Altar 4. Whereas La Venta's early sculptural style was highly naturalistic, with modeled low relief surfaces and high relief approaching sculpture-in-the-round, the late style is executed in a very shallow relief, often with a flat planar surface. The human figures on these late reliefs lack the naturalism of earlier works. Still they are interesting for their historical context: they show meetings between elite individuals and may commemorate state events, possibly a reception or parley of foreign

VISUAL COMPARISON

La Venta Altar 4 and San Lorenzo Monument 14

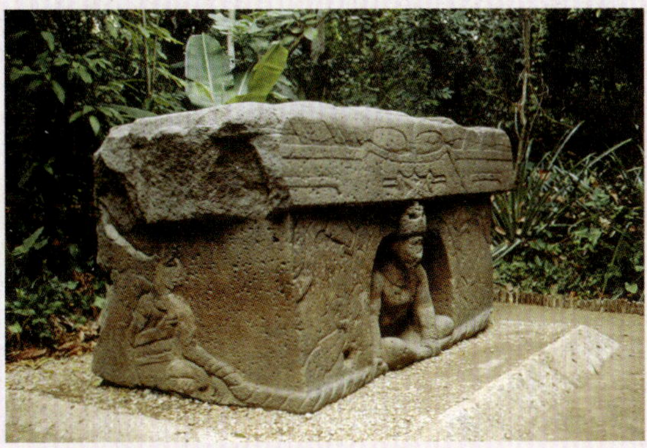

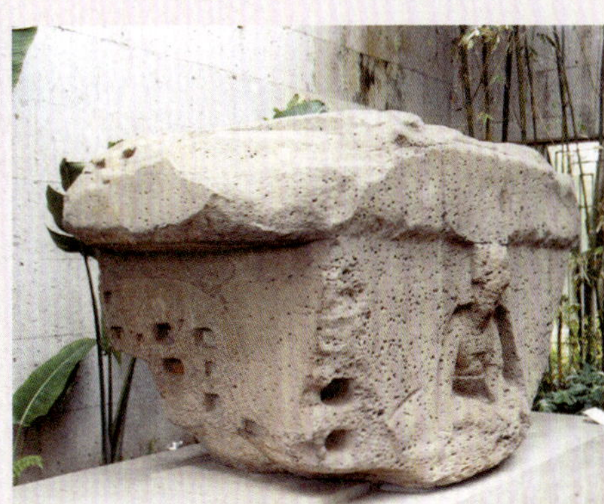

▲ **1.4** La Venta Alta 4 (left); San Lorenzo Monument 14 (right), c.1000-600 BCE, Basalt, Altar 4: 5.24 ft. × 10.41 ft. × 6.23 ft; Monument 14: 6 ft. × 11.33 ft × 5 ft.

These two table-top thrones, similar in scale, design, and style, may be the work of a single master and his atelier.

A feature of many Olmec sites are large rectangular stone blocks, termed "altars" but now thought to be tabletop ceremonial thrones. Although these "altars" can vary widely in size and design within and between sites, two very similar works, La Venta Altar 4 and San Lorenzo Monument 14, are intriguing in that they are so remarkably alike in scale, style, technique, and iconography that an argument could be made for their being the work of the same master artist and his atelier. It is probable that Olmec master artists, like some in later Mesoamerican eras, and many others around the world, were itinerant to some degree, traveling among the various Olmec centers for commissions. The artist's approach to the carving of these thrones follows that of the Colossal Heads. The front panel figures are carved in very high relief, with that on Altar 4 approaching sculpture-in-the-round, while lateral figures are rendered in bas-relief. However, unlike some of the Colossal Heads, there is no lessening of the naturalism or evidence of abstracted forms in these side panels.

The fronts of both altars are occupied by seated figures leaning forward with their heads extending out from niche-like openings as they reach forward to grasp a rope-like form along the base of the altar. Both figures wear elaborate headdresses, necklaces, and wide-belted loincloths indicating they are male. The figures occupying the niches are presumably the rulers, or perhaps important lineage ancestors. The lateral figures of both altars were carved in low relief and rendered in twisted perspective with the head and extremities profile and the torso frontal. In each case, one of the side figures remains, and one was defaced. Luckily, opposite sides were destroyed on both. On Altar 4, a female figure is preserved on the proper right side. Although she is carved in low relief, there is definite modeling of the anatomy, with contour lines used to add definition, as in the sagging jowl of the jawline, the swell of flesh above the arm bands, the folded-back fingers, and the rounded, middle-aged torso. The figure's extended left arm is overlapped by the end of the twisted "rope" held by the niche figure. The right arm is folded across her chest, covering her breasts, and the right hand is shown

(Continued)

palm-out with all but the index finger closed over the palm; this pointing gesture directs the viewer back to the niche figure, in whose direction the lady faces.

Monument 14 has the proper left preserved and it shows a seated male figure, who wears a wide-belted loincloth, conical hat, tubular ear ornaments, and a wide necklace with a irregularly shaped pendant. His pose is similar to that of the female on Altar 4. It is possible, based on the remaining lateral images, that both monuments had female and male figures on the sides, which were connected by a "rope" to the central niche figure. Because of the presence of what looks like a rope, these figures have been intrepid as captives to be sacrificed; however, it is equally possible that the rope is an umbilical cord and the figures constitute a parentage statement legitimizing the ruler. Such parentage statements are found in the later art of the Maya and in the Mixtec codices where parents and children are connected by painted umbilical cords.

dignitaries. However, Stela 5 and Stela 3 are most fascinating for what they show about artistic development during the late first millennium BCE.

▼ **1.5** La Venta, Stela 3, c. 600–394 BCE. Basalt, 14 ft. × 6.6 ft. × 3 ft.

Stela 3 records what appears to be a historical meeting between two dignitaries and their attendants. The figure on the proper right is female and the other is male.

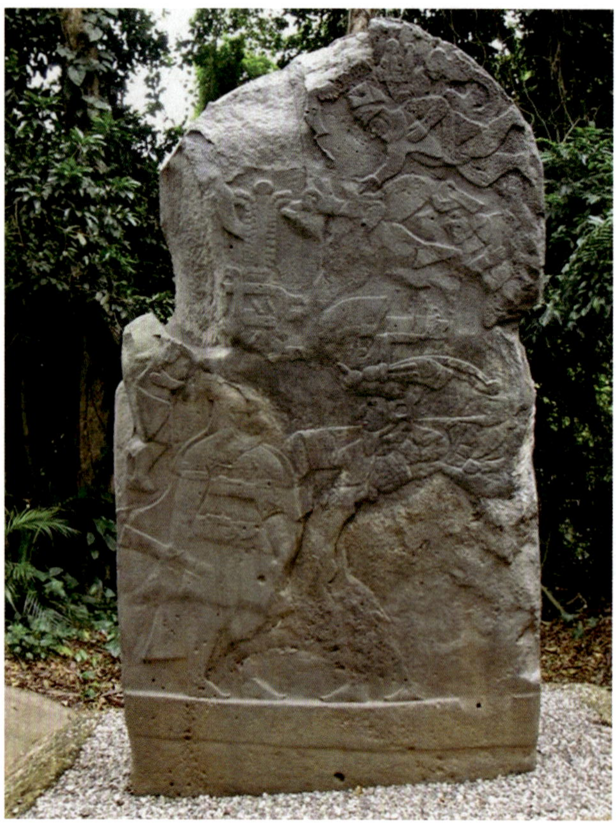

La Venta Stela 3, c. 600–394 BCE Stela 3 (Figure 1.5) was carved on an enormous block of basalt. It stands 14 feet (4.2m) high, is 6 feet 6 inches (2 m) wide, and 3 feet (91 cm) thick and weighs 28.66 tons. The only carving is on the face of the stela and that was done in an especially shallow and flat relief that has suffered substantial weathering. The bodies are stiffer and less life-like than those on earlier works such as Altar 4. Stela 3 depicts a multi-figural scene anchored by a common ground-line. Two life-size personages (5 ft. 7 in. tall) stand left and right in the foreground; they appear to be the protagonists of the scene, based on their elaborate headdresses, elite attire, and composite view rendering (Heizer 1967, 29). Behind these two are several smaller figures who appear to be the attendants of these two dignitaries. The figure on the proper right is dressed in a long cape and a long skirt cinched by a wide belt and wears and elaborate pectoral and other ornaments. Based on this attire and bodily characteristics this figure is believed to be female (Follensbee 2014, 231). The other figure's attire and beard mark him as male. The male and female protagonists of Stela 3 are joined by a several smaller figures that form their respective retinues. Those behind the female elite include another female and two figures too worn to identify with absolute certainty but probably are male; the bottom two figures stand in a stacked position while the third, lacking sufficient room for an upright stance has been rotated 90° so that his feet are at the edge of the stela. The three secondary figures behind the dominant male figure are all male and all are rotated 90° as well. The rotated figures have been described as "floating" and assumed by scholars to be supernatural beings, as if the gods were in attendance at the meeting. Such descriptions are problematic. Prior to the invention of one-point perspective, artists often struggled with showing relative distance between groups of people. A common solution was to use height of placement to show distance. In such a system those figures placed highest on the wall or stela were farther away than lower figures. The "floating" figures on the proper left and right of Stela 3 are not actually flying as has been suggested but rather, the artist having run out of space, has simply turned the ground line at a right angle and run it up the side of the stone, placing the male's entourage figures along it as space allowed. A similar spatial solution is found on Stela 5, which depicts another multi-figure reception scene and has a single "floating" background figure.

The Middle or Classic Period (c. 100–900 CE)

After the decline of the Olmec, many of the cultures who had been their trading partners, including Teotihuacan, the Maya, and the Zapotecs, achieved political and artistic prominence during the first centuries of the Common Era. Unfortunately, the traditional Maya-based formulation for the Classic Period as c. 250–300 to 900 CE does not take into account early developments at Teotihuacan in the Valley of Mexico or Monte Albán in Oaxaca which made important contributions to Classic period culture. The period is characterized by the widespread use of the 260-day ritual calendar and a 365-day solar calendar divided into eighteen months of twenty days each plus five unlucky days. The Classic marks the end of Mesoamerican prehistory with the development of pictographic and hieroglyphic writing systems among the Maya, Mixtec, and Zapotec, and the recording of the first New World histories. It was also an era of advanced vigesimal or base 20 mathematical systems with the independent invention in Mesoamerica of zero as a placeholder. The period saw advances in the sciences as New World astronomers tracked and recorded the cycles of the sun, moon, stars, and planets, especially that of Venus. Mesoamerican peoples also made advances in engineering, devising new structural support systems for their monumental pyramid platforms, formulating new mortars and cements, and inventing new methods of wall and vault construction. It was also a time when the arts of sculpture, painting, lapidary, and ceramics flourished across the region.

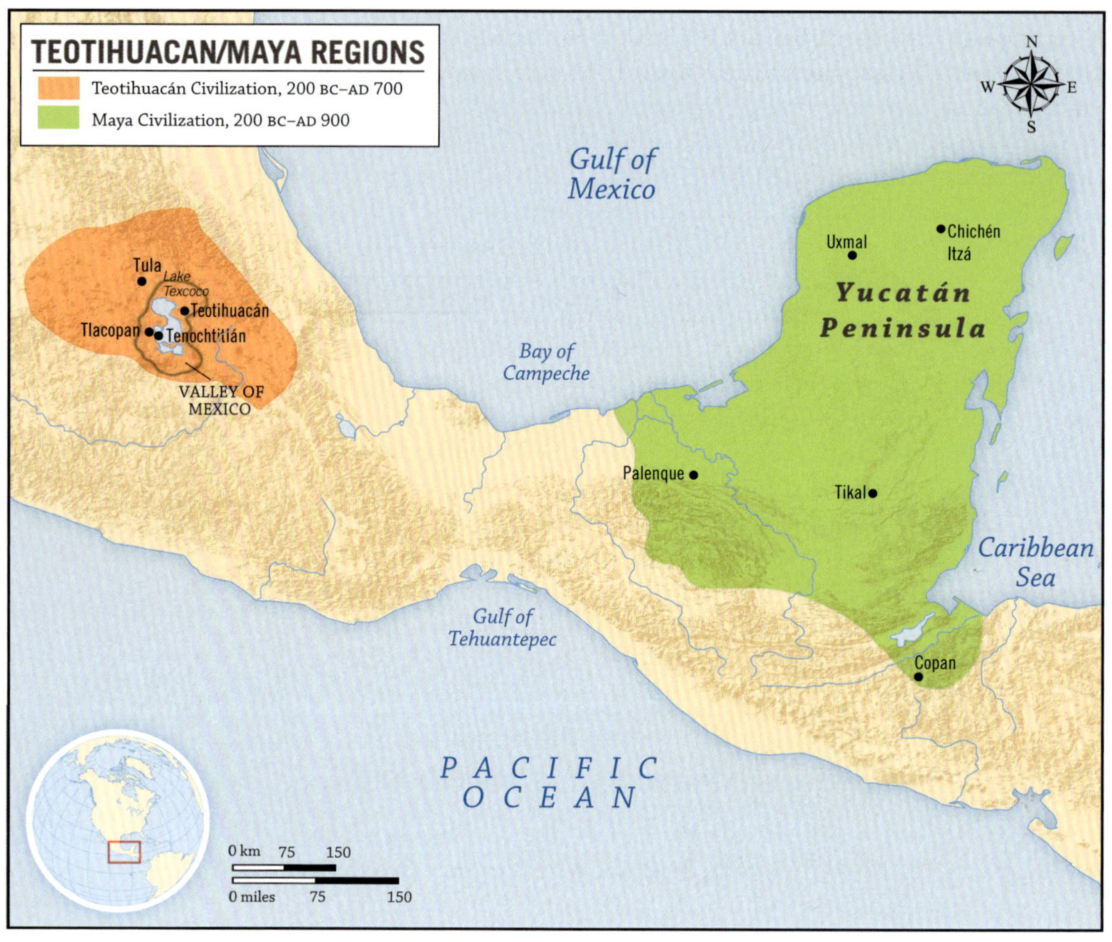

Teotihuacan (c. 400 BCE–750 CE)

Teotihuacan, the first metropolis of the New World, began as a small farming community at the north end of the Valley of Mexico around 400 BCE. Prior to the draining of the Valley's five lakes after the Spanish Conquest, Teotihuacan sat about ten miles inland from the brackish waters of Lake Xaltocan, at an altitude of 7,200 feet (2,200 m). In the distance the inhabitants of Teotihuacan had views of higher mountains and volcanoes, the most famous being the snow-capped Ixtacihuatl, meaning "White Woman" and the active volcano Popocatepetl or "Smoking Mountain." From these modest beginnings Teotihuacan grew into the largest city in the Americas and the sixth largest in the world in its time. The name Teotihuacan, meaning "place where the gods were born," was given to it by the Aztecs, who arrived in the Valley of Mexico some five hundred years after Teotihuacan was abandoned and burned. The immense scale of the ruins they encountered so impressed the Aztecs that they thought the city must have been built by giants (Sahagún 1961: X, 191–192). Ultimately,

Teotihuacan became embedded in Mexica mythology as the place where the gods had come together to create the world, and thus where time began.

MONUMENTAL ARCHITECTURE AND CITY PLANNING

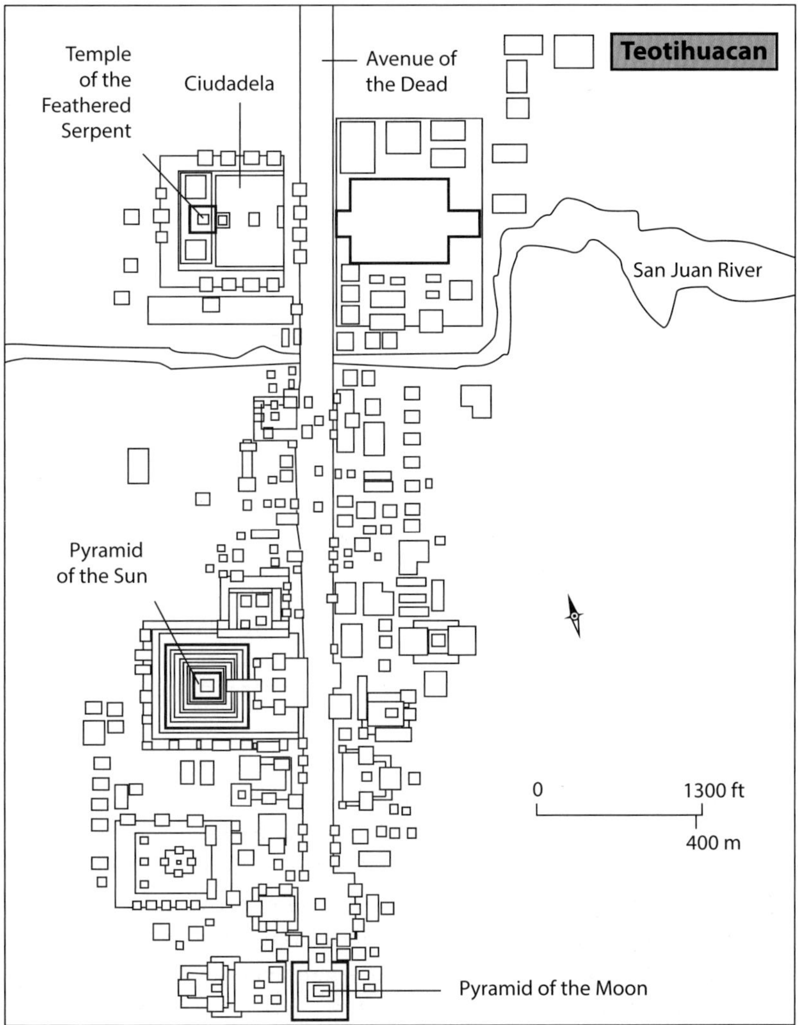

Teotihuacan was a cosmopolitan city; among its residents were artisans and traders from other parts of Mesoamerica, who were drawn there by the city's cultural and economic power. The city was laid out on a grid plan, with its main north-south axis being the so-called "Avenue of the Dead." This main axis was crossed by a secondary east-west road toward the southern end of the avenue, near the Ciudadela. Located along the Avenue were Teotihuacan's three most important structures: The Pyramid of the Moon at the north extreme, the Pyramid of Quetzalcoatl on the southern end, and the Pyramid of the Sun, on the east side.

The Pyramid of the Sun, c. 150 CE In the first century CE, Teotihuacan entered into a period of explosive growth and its architecture took on a monumental scale. The first major construction was the Pyramid of the Sun (Figure 1.6). The pyramid rises to 204.75 feet (63 m), making it one of the tallest structures in the Western Hemisphere until the mid-nineteenth century. Its basal area is only slightly smaller than that of the Great Pyramid of Khufu in Egypt. Originally the pyramid rose in four stages with a broad stair in the center of the west façade. Its current five levels and variable width stair are the result of an unfortunate misreconstruction in the early twentieth century by Leopoldo Batres, who, inexplicably, added the strange band-like structure near the top. Each of the four original sections of the pyramid was a rectangular platform with sloping sides or ***taluds*** and a flat deck area, giving it a profile similar to that of an Egyptian mastaba. Each successive level was diminished in size from its predecessor, creating a stepped pyramid structure. Later, circa the fourth century CE, a four-tiered platform, known as an ***adosada***, was added to the west façade; this, too, has suffered from clumsy restoration.

The Pyramid of the Sun was built in a single phase of construction. The core of the pyramid is a fill mound of soil and ground ***tepetate*** (tuff), mixed with silty sand and, in places, broken pottery. The volume of the Pyramid of the Sun is estimated at some 41.5 million cubic feet (1,175,000 m^3) of material (Cowgill 2015, 62; Millon et al. 1965, 12). Remarkably, the builders of the Pyramid of the Sun do not seem to have used any type of interior reinforcing system to stabilize the fill, as they did with later constructions at the site. Instead, the mass of the Pyramid of the Sun is contained and protected from weather-induced erosion primarily by its exterior sheathing. When the earthen mass of each section had reached its desired height, it was partially encased in a layer of adobe blocks, followed by a veneer of

▼ **1.6** Teotihuacan, Pyramid of the Sun, looking east from the Avenue of the Dead, c. 150 ce. 204.75 ft. high.

Built in a single construction of earth and rubble fill and encased in layers of adobe and stone veneer, this was one of the tallest structures in the Americas until the twentieth century.

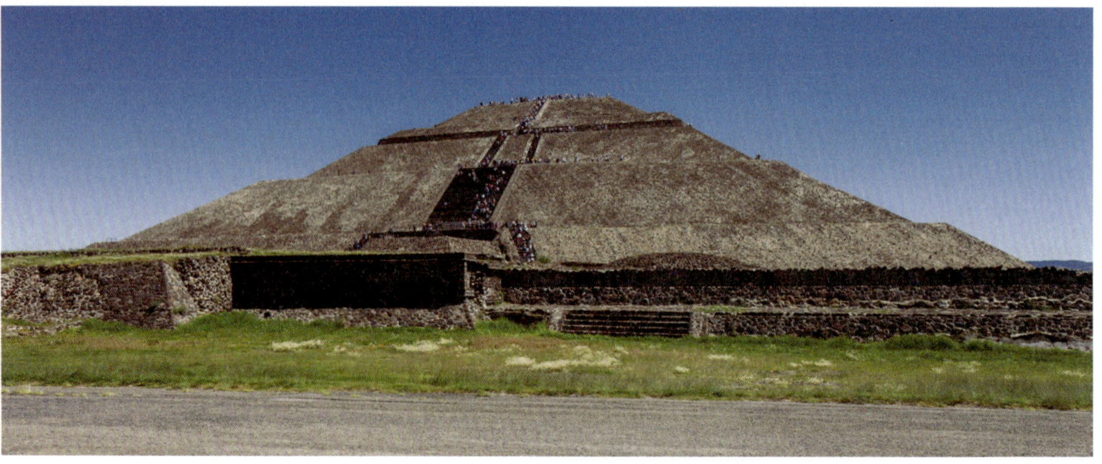

flat, unworked stones bound together with ***aplanado*** or "Teotihuacan cement," made with mud, pea-gravel-size crushed scoria, and sand. The final stage was the application of a coat of lime plaster and paint, usually a solid red; this was the most common color for architecture in Mesoamerica.

The Avenue of the Dead, c. 200 CE The Avenue of the Dead (Figure 1.7) is not an avenue in the usual sense of the word. Rather it is a multi-level series of broad plazas connected by transverse stairs. At its southern end, where the terrain is relatively flat, south of the San Juan River and the Ciudadela, the avenue is some 290 feet (90 m) wide. Once it crosses north of the river, the width of the avenue's plazas shrinks to only 129 feet (40 m) until it broadens into the Plaza of the Moon at its northern extreme. The name "Avenue of the Dead" is derived from the Aztec "Miccaotli," meaning "Way of the Dead." The name came from the Aztec belief that the ancient Teotihuacanos had enshrined the mummy bundles of their ancestors in the temples that once lined the plazas along the route.

The Pyramid of the Moon, c. 100–400 CE At the northern terminus of the Avenue of the Dead is Teotihuacan's second largest structure, the Pyramid of the Moon (Figure 1.8). The pyramid is a four-level, stepped platform, which rises to a height of 149.5 feet (46 m). Access to its summit is provided

▼ 1.7 Teotihuacan, Avenue of the Dead, from the top of the Pyramid of the Moon looking south, 200 CE.

The center of this level section of the plaza has been paved with asphalt in modern times for the convenience of tourists but the area from wall to wall was originally an open plaza; notice farther to the south the avenue is broken into small plazas of differing heights.

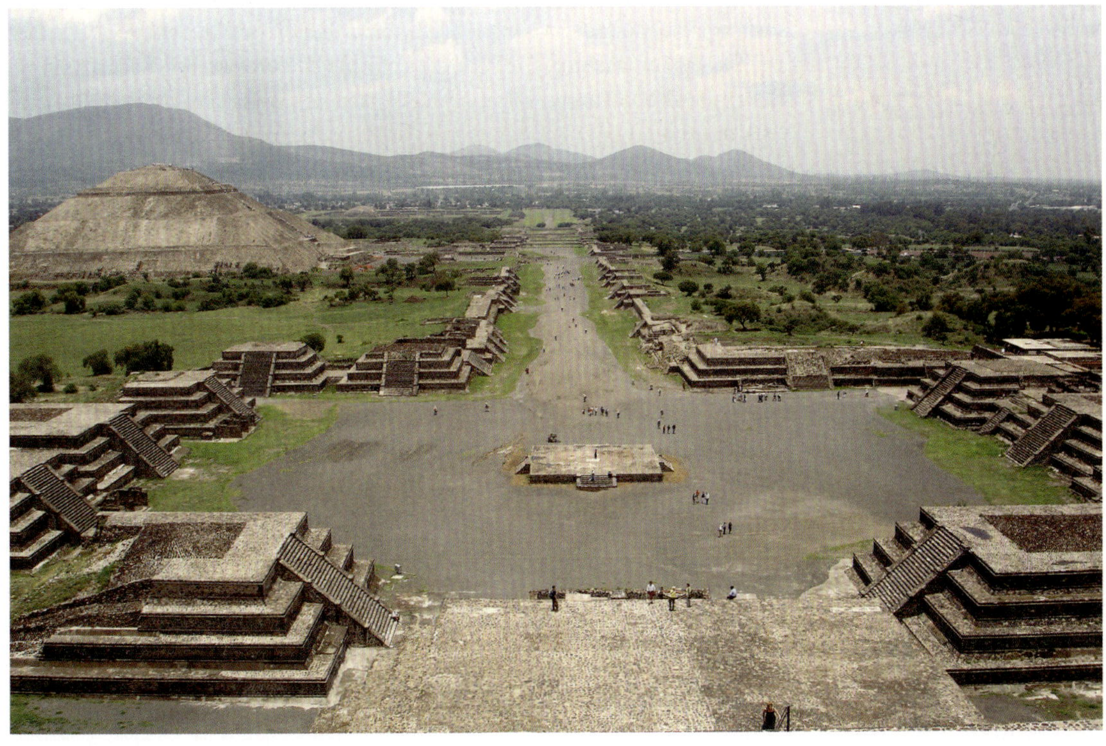

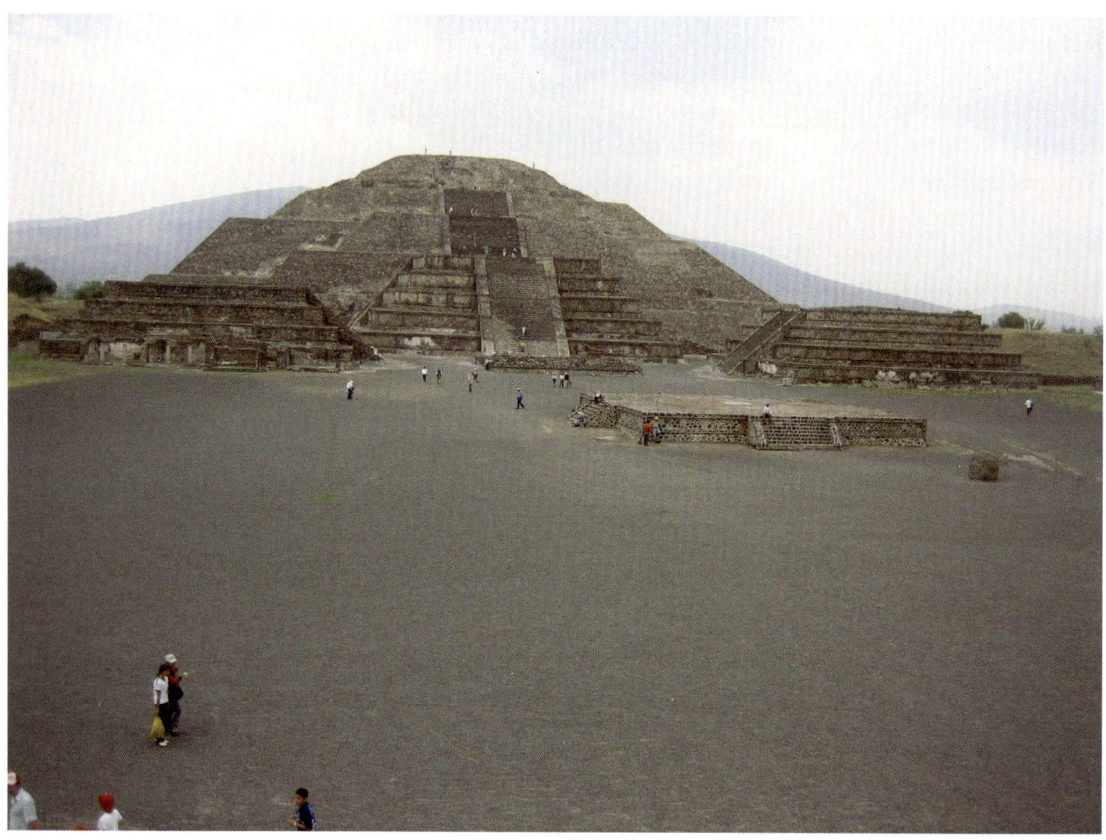

▲ **1.8** Teotihuacan, Plaza and Pyramid of the Moon, c. 100–400 CE. 149.5 ft. high.

Unlike the Pyramid of the Sun that was built all at one time, the Pyramid of the Moon started out as a small structure and was enlarged seven times to reach its current height and width.

by a single, wide stair, as is typical of most Mesoamerican pyramids. Unlike the Pyramid of the Sun, the Moon Pyramid was not constructed in a single phase but was enlarged seven times between approximately 100 CE and 450 CE. It began as a modest structure and did not achieve monumental scale until its fourth enlargement around 200 CE (Sugiyama, Sugiyama, and Sarabia 2013, 412). The Pyramid of the Moon began as a stepped pyramid with a square base, measuring approximately 76.37 feet (23.5 m) per side, and veneered with cut stones of a pinkish hue set with mud plaster. This earliest pyramid was encapsulated within three successive pyramids by 200 CE and, in the process its footprint had grown to 290 feet (98.2 m) by 289 feet (88.9 m).

Successive alterations consisted of partial enlargements of the structure. Phase Five saw the north façade of the pyramid expanded and the adosada added to the south façade, increasing the north-south dimensions to more than 338 feet (104 m), while the east-west measurements remained constant. Further, modifications in the sixth and seventh phases created the pyramid observed today with its four-stage sloped platform, the baroque step-out of the intermediate platform, and then the five-tiered adosada platform with talud and ***tablero*** or "table" design. This final enlargement was completed around 400–450 CE and brought its basal measurement to 550 feet (168 m) by 490 feet

TAKE A CLOSER LOOK

Talud-Tablero Construction

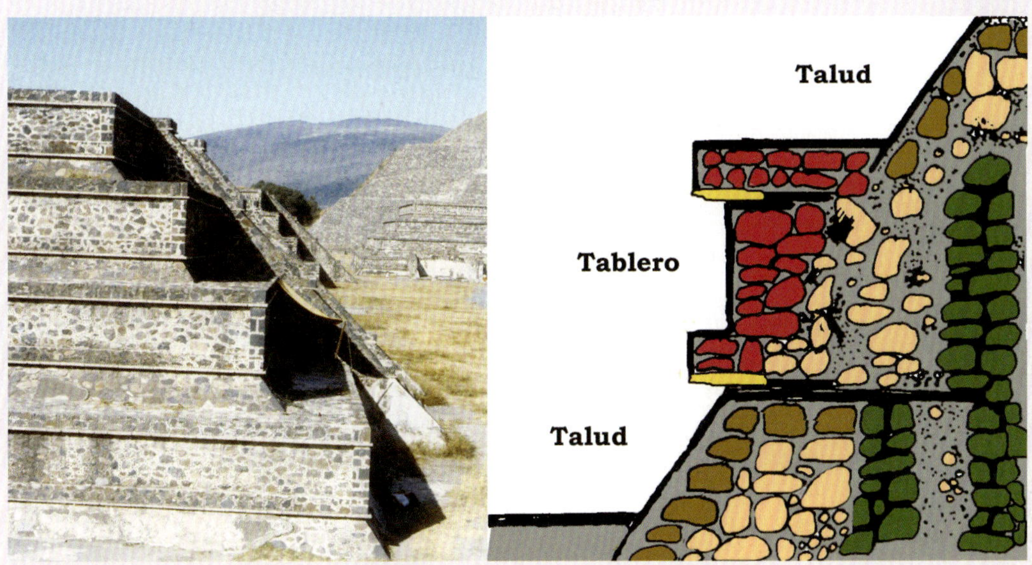

▲ **1.9** Teotihuacan, Left: Detail showing the Talud-Tablero of one of the platforms along the Avenue of the Dead; Right: Drawing showing the Talud-Tablero construction and parts.

The pyramid of Quetzalcoatl was one of the first to use a battered or sloping base wall, known as a talud, to support and progressively step back an upright segment, called a tablero or "table." It is an interesting new take on the concept of the pyramid as mountain, possibly inspired by mountain talus slopes, which are sloping piles of rock that accumulate at the base of cliffs. This new architectural profile was made possible by advances in building techniques such as the pier and cell construction used in the Quetzalcoatl pyramid to stabilize the fill mass. While the taluds and tableros of the Quetzalcoatl were covered in relief sculpture, those of later pyramids were plain forms with only the cornice frame of the tablero to relieve the flatness of the surfaces. Originally these would have been covered with plaster and painted decoration. From Teotihuacan the talud-tablero style spread to other regions of Mesoamerica where the forms were adapted to suit local materials and aesthetics.

(149 m), giving the Pyramid of the Moon a more rectangular footprint than that of the Pyramid of the Sun.

The Pyramid of Quetzalcoatl, c. 200 CE About a mile to the south of the Pyramid of the Sun stands Teotihuacan's third major pyramid, the Pyramid of Quetzalcoatl or Feathered Serpent (Figure 1.10). It is

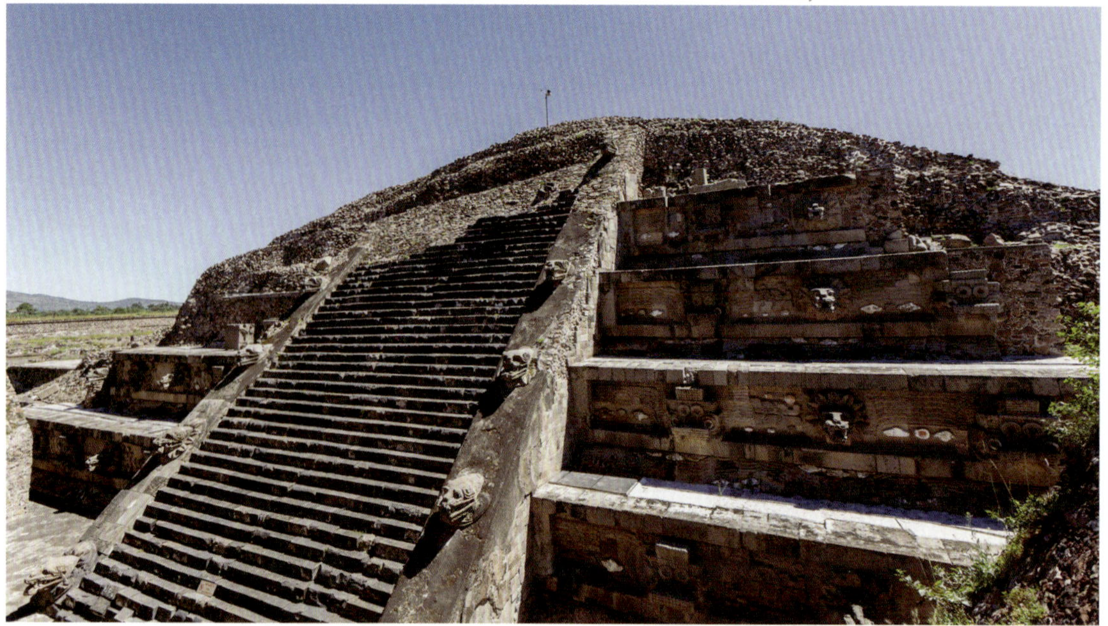

▲ 1.10 Teotihuacan, Pyramid of Quetzalcoatl, c. 200 ce. 72 ft. high.

Originally all four sides of this pyramid platform were decorated with relief carvings and painted in red, blue, and green; however, the only section of the original sculpture that was preserved is this section that was buried under the adosada platform.

located at the rear of an enclosed thirty-eight-acre plaza, thought to be capable of holding the entire population of the city, perhaps some 85,000 individuals, more or less (Cowgill 2015, 142–143). The 72 foot (23 m) high pyramid and its temple superstructure were built about 200 CE and continued in use until the mid-fourth century, when the temple was burned, and the exposed sculptures torn off. The destruction of the temple and the defacement of the pyramid are believed to signal a dramatic shift in religious and political authority, perhaps as a consequence of a long period of severe drought.

The Pyramid of Quetzalcoatl was groundbreaking in its use of a new compartmentalized pier and fin-wall (cell) construction system, and the new talud-tablero architectural profile. On the Pyramid of Quetzalcoatl, the tablero is framed by rows of cantilevered stones, creating a shadow-box-like cornice. Both the taluds and tableros of the Pyramid of Quetzalcoatl were decorated with high and low relief friezes that continued around all four sides of the structure; it is the only pyramid platform at Teotihuacan now known to have had sculptural relief. The smaller scale taluds are decorated with profile images of Quetzalcoatl, his feathered body undulating like ocean waves between clusters of bivalves and conch shells. Quetzalcoatl, in low relief, also stretches across the upright tableros, but his head and the Tlaloc masks near his tail are carved in high relief. Oddly two different carving techniques were used for the heads. The massive Tlaloc heads were carved from stones that were cantilevered out as they were laid up in the façade, while the serpent heads were carved separately and **tenoned** into the façade.

The variations of color and texture in the stone and the joints did not present an aesthetic problem for the pyramid's architects and masons as it might for modern builders. Once the carving was completed, the entire surface of pyramid was covered with **tezantle**, a plaster-like material, and painted. Based on traces of remaining pigment and paint flakes collected by Manuel Gamio in 1917, when he excavated the trench through the back of the adosada, the Tlaloc heads were a bluish-green; the body and feathered ruff of Quetzalcoatl were green while his rattles were yellow; the backgrounds, cornice frame, and interiors of shells were red, and the exteriors of the shells were lime white.

Teotihuacan's artists went to great lengths to indicate sound in their fresco paintings (see Take a Closer Look: The Art of Fresco Painting for discussion and example). It is unlikely that they would have expected the façade of the Pyramid of Quetzalcoatl to be mute. However, three-dimensional works present different problems for an artist trying to indicate emanating sound; there is no place to paint a speech scroll on a projecting head. If the components of the Quetzalcoatl figures are considered carefully, they are far from silent. The rainy season in the Valley of Mexico coincides with the mating season of large wild felids such as jaguar and puma as well as crocodilians, whose respective roaring and booming sounds have often been associated with the sound of thunder. The feathers of Quetzalcoatl's body could be read as emitting a rustling sound as he moved, like the sound of the wind before an approaching storm, and of course, the rattles on his tail, following the Tlaloc image, make the sound of falling rain. In this way the façade could be read as an elegant visual kenning, each part of the amalgamated Quetzalcoatl and the composite Tlaloc describing not only the nature of these deities but also the natural phenomenon that signal their approach. The adosada's talud-tablero decoration is simpler than that of the Pyramid of Quetzalcoatl, having been covered with polychrome frescoes. The construction of the platform is more haphazard as well; only a few embedded wooden poles were used to stabilize its loose earth and rubble core (Cowgill 2015, 146).

PALACES AND APARTMENTS

Intermixed with the pyramids and platforms of the Avenue of the Dead, and expanding outward from this central axis, were impressive structures commonly referred to as "palaces." However, this term is somewhat misleading; it refers simply to multi-room or sometimes multi-story buildings, some of which were elite residences while others served administrative or religious purposes. The Quetzalpapalotl Palace, for example, was not a residence.

The majority of Teotihuacanos lived in less ornate surroundings than those of the Quetzalpapalotl. Domestic architecture in ancient Teotihuacan is represented by the more than 2,000 apartment compounds identified to date. The compounds were grouped together into neighborhoods or barrios. Some of these barrios were organized around trades or ethnicities. Ancient Teotihuacan was a cosmopolitan center with a significant foreign population. At least two foreign barrios, the Oaxaca barrio and the "Merchants' barrio" have been identified. Although only a few of these compounds have been excavated, they show Teotihuacan apartments to be one-story buildings with flat roofs arranged as multi-family units around a central patio. The only breaks in the often meter-thick stone or adobe exterior walls were doorways. Apartments were usually painted red, but more elaborate structures sometimes had polychrome murals.

The Quetzalpapalotl Palace, c. 200 CE As with most of the palace and apartment buildings at Teotihuacan, the Quetzalpapalotl or "Quetzal-butterfly" Palace (Figure 1.11) was organized around a square courtyard or patio. The palace takes its name from the images of birds carved on its stone pillars, which early scholars thought were composite bird/butterfly creatures. The massive pillars support the

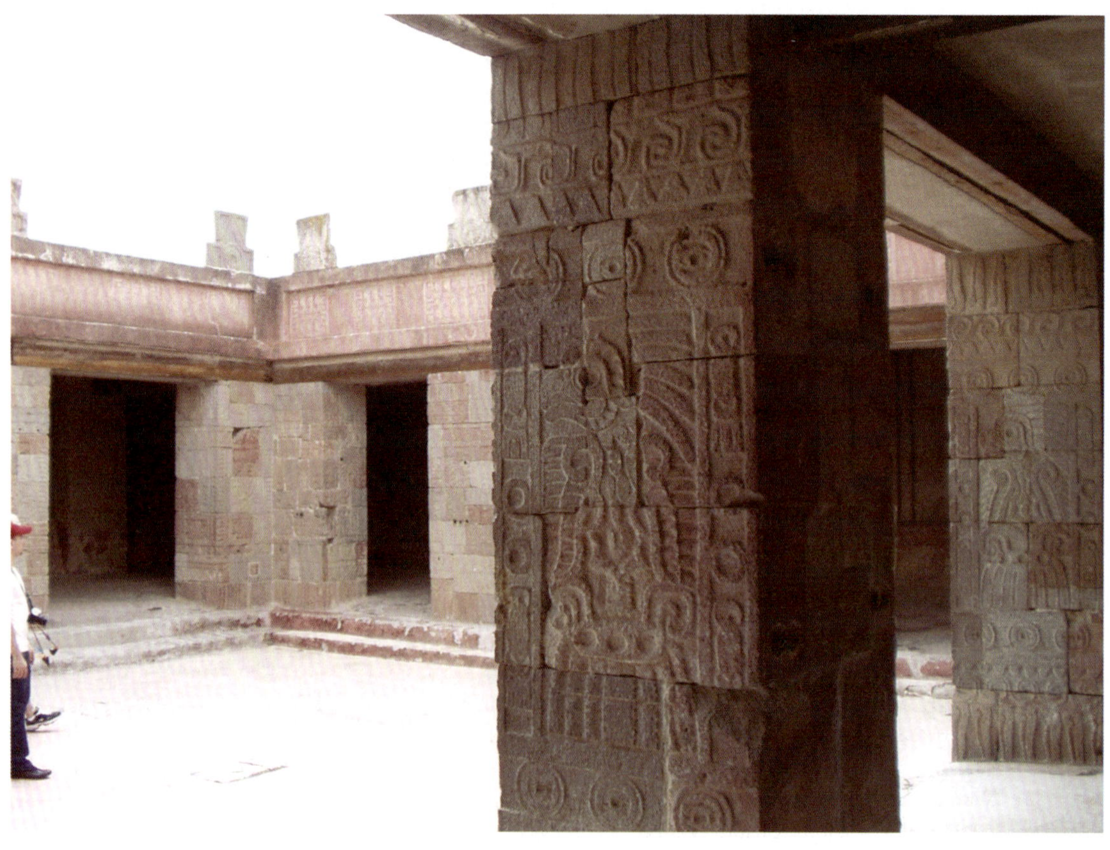

▼ 1.11 Teotihuacan, Court of the Quetzalpapalotl Palace, c. 200 CE.

The building takes its name from the creature depicted on its pillars. Originally thought to be Quetzalpapalotl or quetzal (feathered) butterflies; now believed to be owls and associated with warriors, priests, and ruling elite of the city. Notice that the bird's eyes and some of the circular elements around him have been inlaid with dark stone.

TAKE A CLOSER LOOK
The Art of Fresco Painting

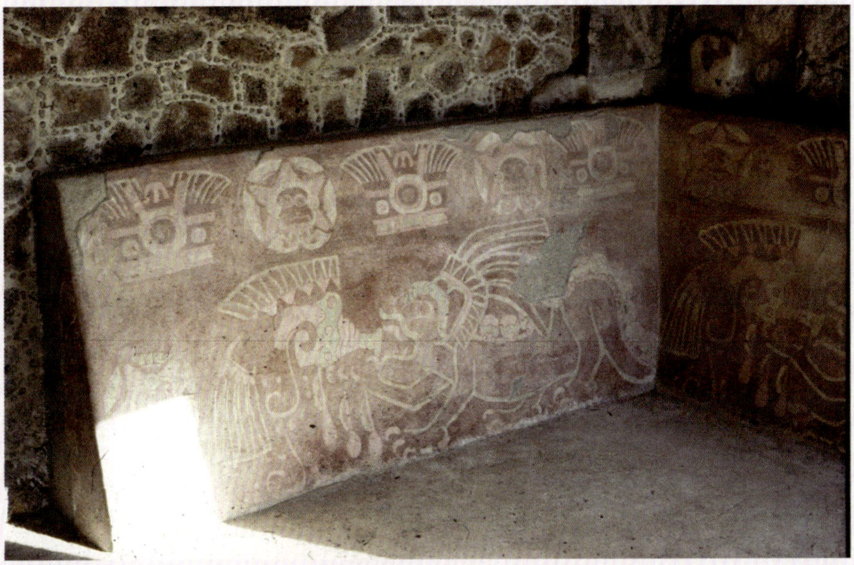

▲ **1.12** Teotihuacan, Jaguar Blowing Conch Shell, Palace of the Jaguars, c. 450-500 CE, Fresco. Image is labeled to show the fresco process: A. Rough stone wall with chinking pebbles set in mortar; B. Layer of aplanado or "Teotihuacan cement;" C. Red wash coat; D. Talud section of lower wall, and E. In-painted color.

This fresco of a large wild feline, possibly a jaguar or puma, blowing a conch trumpet is part of a talud mural in the Palace of Jaguars. Water drips from the bottom of the conch suggesting both its sea origins and the purpose of blowing it to summon the rains, an idea reinforced by the Tlaloc images in the border above the animal. That the conch is sounding is indicated by the scrolls dropping from its large open end. The scrolls are commonly known as "speech scrolls" and were used in Teotihuacan frescoes to show that humans were talking or chanting, and that animals, insects or things were making sounds.

The fresco process began with the application of "Teotihuacan cement" over a rough stone or adobe wall (A). This was followed by a "brown coat" or *aplanado* of "Teotihuacan cement"—plaster mixed with kaolin and fine quartz sand (B). The final painting surface was a fine, smooth coat of lime plaster, applied thinly, in some cases being less than a millimeter thick. The actual painting was done in a mix of **buon fresco** or wet application, **fresco secco** or dry application, and **mezzo fresco** or re-wetted techniques.

Once the final coat of plaster was applied, several workers rapidly applied a thin red "wash coat"(C) Then the design was outlined in red or black and the areas established by the contour lines were filled in with colors (E). Most Teotihuacan murals were either polychrome or red monochrome, the latter becoming dominant after about 500 CE for reasons that may have religious or political significance. The Teotihuacan artist's paint box contained seven basic colors: two reds—hematite (red iron oxide) and cinnabar (red mercuric sulfide), malachite green, azurite blue, yellow limonite (iron oxide), carbon black, and lime white. A range of tints, shades, and tones could be achieved through the addition of lime and carbon black; for example, seven distinct reds have been identified in the monochrome frescoes, ranging from pale pink to deep blood red. After the colors were painted in, the red or black outlines were often redrawn, presumably to cover any errors in the application of the paint.

tablero-style lintels of a continuous, flat-roofed veranda around the four sides of the patio. With the exception of the east side, which abuts the back of a temple platform facing the Avenue of the Dead, windowless rooms opened off the patio. The patio provided light and air to the interior rooms as well as access to an under-pavement drainage system running beneath the patio. Interior walls were rubble set in, and surfaced with, "Teotihuacan concrete" and then finished with a thin coat of white plaster. The profile of the interior walls is reminiscent of the talud-tablero arrangement of platform construction. Beginning about a meter up from the floor, the base of the wall steps out to form a narrow ledge and then inclines, talud-fashion, to the floor; in effect, turning the upper surface of the wall into a monumental tablero. Both the talus and flat upper wall were often decorated with frescoes.

The Teotihuacan frescoes present a complex iconography that is still poorly understood. Decoding these pictorial texts is made more difficult by their fragmentary nature, and by the fact that the language spoken in ancient Teotihuacan is unknown. For this reason, interpretations based on the belief systems or linguistics of later populations, are speculative. However, this does not mean the murals are beyond comprehension; art is, after all, a visual language. The Teotihuacan artists seem to have worked in two stylistic canons: one formal, used for the depiction of religious and political ceremonies, supernatural beings, and elite personages, and the other a vernacular style, used to depict non-elites in commonplace activities.

TEOTIHUACAN CERAMICS

Ceramic artisans working at Teotihuacan produced a wide variety of wares ranging from simple utilitarian pieces to elaborate painted and inlaid incense-burners with appliqued, mold-made elements. However, the form most closely associated with the site was a slab-footed tripod of slightly incurving cylindrical form with a lid. These typically brown-bodied vessels were embellished with incised, relief-carved, or stuccoed and painted decoration, the latter done in a fresco technique similar to that of mural painting.

Painted stucco is one of the rarer forms of ceramic decoration due to its fragility. The first vessels to be stucco-painted were previously decorated pots, or thin-orange trade wares that were later jazzed up with stucco decoration. However, by at least 550 CE, the clay bodies of stuccoed vessels show evidence of the intention to stucco them from the start (Fletcher 2002, 142). The process began with scoring the surface of the clay vessel. After bisque firing, the porous ceramic body was dampened and a thin coat of white plaster or a cream-colored plaster-kaolin mix was applied as the intonaco.

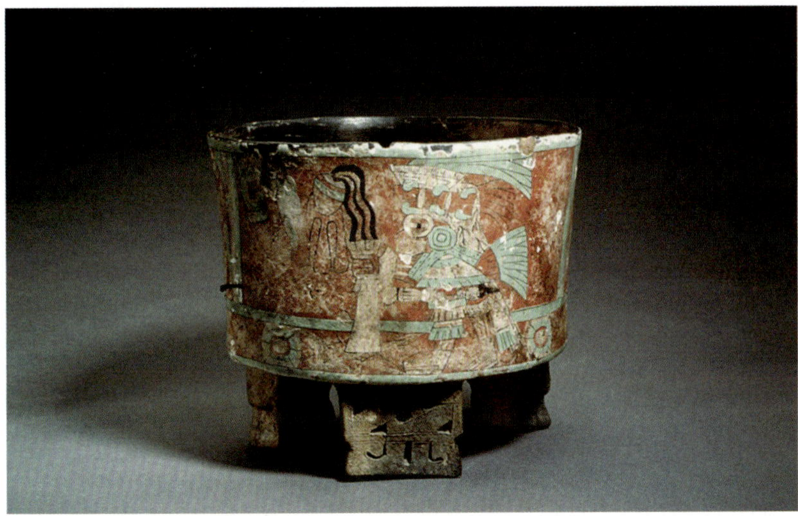

◀ 1.13 Teotihuacan, Stuccoed Tripod Vase, c. 300–500 CE.

The vessel depicts a priest in the guise of a Tlaloc impersonator.

The vessel was then painted in the same manner as a wall fresco, with a background wash and red outlining of forms; finally, color was applied. Chemical analysis of the pigments used on the painted vases shows them to be the same as those used in wall painting with the exception that cinnabar was not found. The final step in the process was the application of the black outlines. To control and contain the flow of this critical last application of paint, contour lines were first incised into the existing pigment and ground layers (Fletcher 2002, 143–146).

Stuccoed Tripod Vase, c. 300–500 CE This early Classic period tripod vase (Figure 1.13) is a good example of the stucco technique. The vessel was plastered and then given a red wash coat. This background was divided by blue bands into what reads as the tablero and talud format of Teotihuacan architecture, suggesting an interior space. The talus of this wall is decorated with blue shield-like elements. The striding protagonist of the scene is rendered in profile, suggesting he is a human rather than a deity who would be depicted frontally. The elaborately dressed figure holds a bundle in one outstretched hand and carries a copal bag over the other, marking him as a priest. The details of the ornaments, goggle-eye, costume and headdress were defined with an extremely fine and even black outline. Indeed, the line is so thin that it must have been painted using a brush containing only two or three soft hairs.

The Maya Realms (250–900 CE)

Among Teotihuacan's trading partners were the Maya kingdoms, which occupied a contiguous territory far to the southeast of the Valley of Mexico, in the modern states of Chiapas, Tabasco, Campeche, Yucatan, and Quintana Roo, and the neighboring nations of Guatemala, Belize, El Salvador and western Honduras. Numerous finds of Teotihuacan ceramics and obsidian in elite burials across the Maya region, as well as evidence of Maya residents in the foreign quarters of Teotihuacan, point to the close relationship between Teotihuacan and many Maya states. The Maya territories were organized into autonomous kingdoms of diverse scale. Some, such as Tikal, controlled vast stretches of territory, including vassal states, while others, for example Palenque, were more modest in size. The Maya kings were not dissimilar from their counterparts in Africa, Asia, or Europe. They made alliances, fought wars, performed state rituals, supported the sciences, patronized the arts, commissioned great architecture, and ordered the recording of dynastic histories in books and inscriptions.

TIKAL, GUATEMALA (C. 800 BCE–850 CE)

The site of Tikal is, perhaps, the best known of all Maya cities due, in part, to its brief appearance as a rebel outpost in the 1977 movie, *Star Wars Episode IV: A New Hope*. As is evident from the movie, Tikal is set in a dense tropical jungle that obscures all but the tops of the city's tallest temples. The terrain in this part of the Petén is hilly with seasonal wetlands in low lying areas. Tikal was founded around 800 BCE on a high ridge that over time was terraced into a series of platforms and plazas which supported temples and palace complexes.. For more than half a millennium this ridge, the North Acropolis, remained the locus of construction at Tikal; its original structures being encapsulated by newer ones, and stelas and altars added to commemorate dynastic rulers.

TIKAL STYLE STELAS

More than forty carved stela and thirty associated altars have been found at Tikal. The stelas were erected to commemorate important events in the reigns of Tikal's ruling dynasty. The earliest is thought to be Stela 29, which bears a hieroglyphic inscription dating it to 292 CE. Tikal stelas are carved in a distinct representational style that remained consistent throughout the more than five-hundred-year period in which they were erected at the site. Tikal stelas are carved in low relief on typically slender stone shafts. Figures of the ruler, are rendered in composite view with frontal torso and profile head and legs on the wide face of the stone, but there may also be secondary profile figures on the two sides. While the body is often obscured by complex and elaborate regalia, the anatomy is treated naturalistically.

Stela 31, 445 CE One of the more interesting early monuments is Stela 31 (Figure 1.14), a celt-shaped, flat-surfaced monument that is almost 8 feet (2.43 m) tall. This stela was erected in 445 CE by Siyaj Chan K'awiil II, a king of Tikal, nicknamed "Stormy Sky" (r. 411–456). The monument commemorates events that occurred sixty-seven years earlier when a contingent of nobles from Teotihuacan arrived in the city to oversee the installation of his father, Yax Nuun Ahiin I or "First Crocodile" (formerly "Curl Snout") on the throne of Tikal. "First Crocodile" (r. 379–404?) is thought to have been a son of the Teotihuacan lord, "Spearthrower Owl," and his ascension, most likely, was through a strategic dynastic marriage.

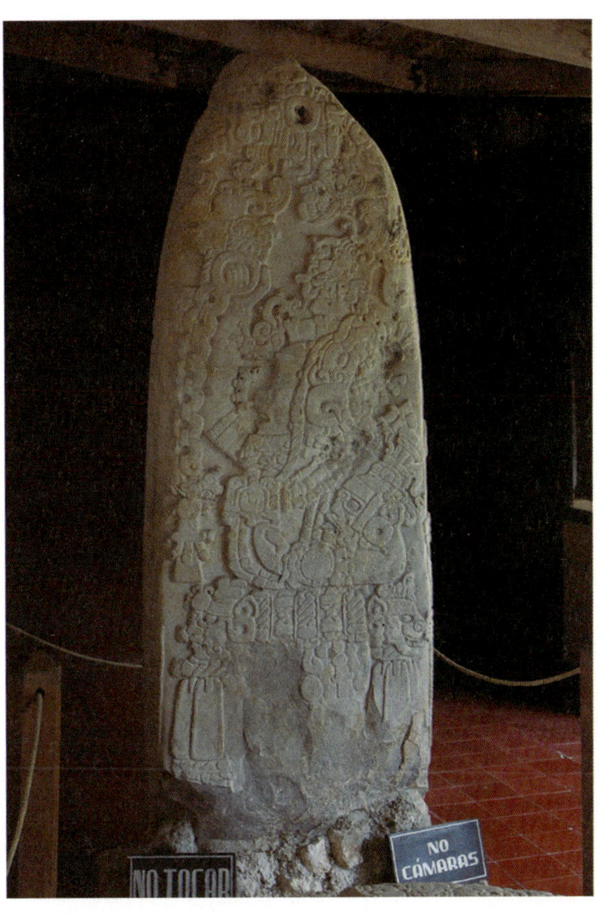

▲ 1.14 Tikal, Stela 31, c. 445 CE.

Depicted on the front of this monument is the king "Stormy Sky" in full ceremonial regalia. He holds aloft a headdress referencing his grandfather Spearthrower Owl's arrival from Teotihuacan sixty-seven years earlier.

In a break from the strictly frontal arrangement of images on stelas, Stela 31 folds its scene across three faces of the stone shaft. On the front, "Stormy Sky" is depicted as a left-facing profile figure, while on the two sides are the left and right profiles of a single attendant figure (Clancy 1992, 108). The three images are rendered on the planar surfaces in bas-relief. However, there is a remarkable illusion of spatial depth that has been established through the use of progressively shallower carving toward the background and the overlapping of forms. "Stormy Sky" is depicted in the opulent regalia of a Maya king, every detail of which has been finely engraved. In his raised hand, "Stormy Sky" holds aloft a second headdress from which hangs the emblem of "Spearthrower Owl," as a reference to his Teotihuacan lineage. The statement is echoed by the ancestor figure with crocodilian attributes, and an owl in its mouth that floats above the king. On the two sides of the stela, "Stormy Sky's" parentage statement is repeated, yet again, through full figure depictions of "First Crocodile," represented as he was on his own monuments (Stelas 4 and 18) in classic Teotihuacan attire, carrying a shield bearing the image of the goggle-eyed Tlaloc and holding a spear (actually dart) throwing weapon (Harrison 1999, 79–81).

LORD JASAW CHAN K'AWIIL AND THE TIKAL STYLE OF ARCHITECTURE

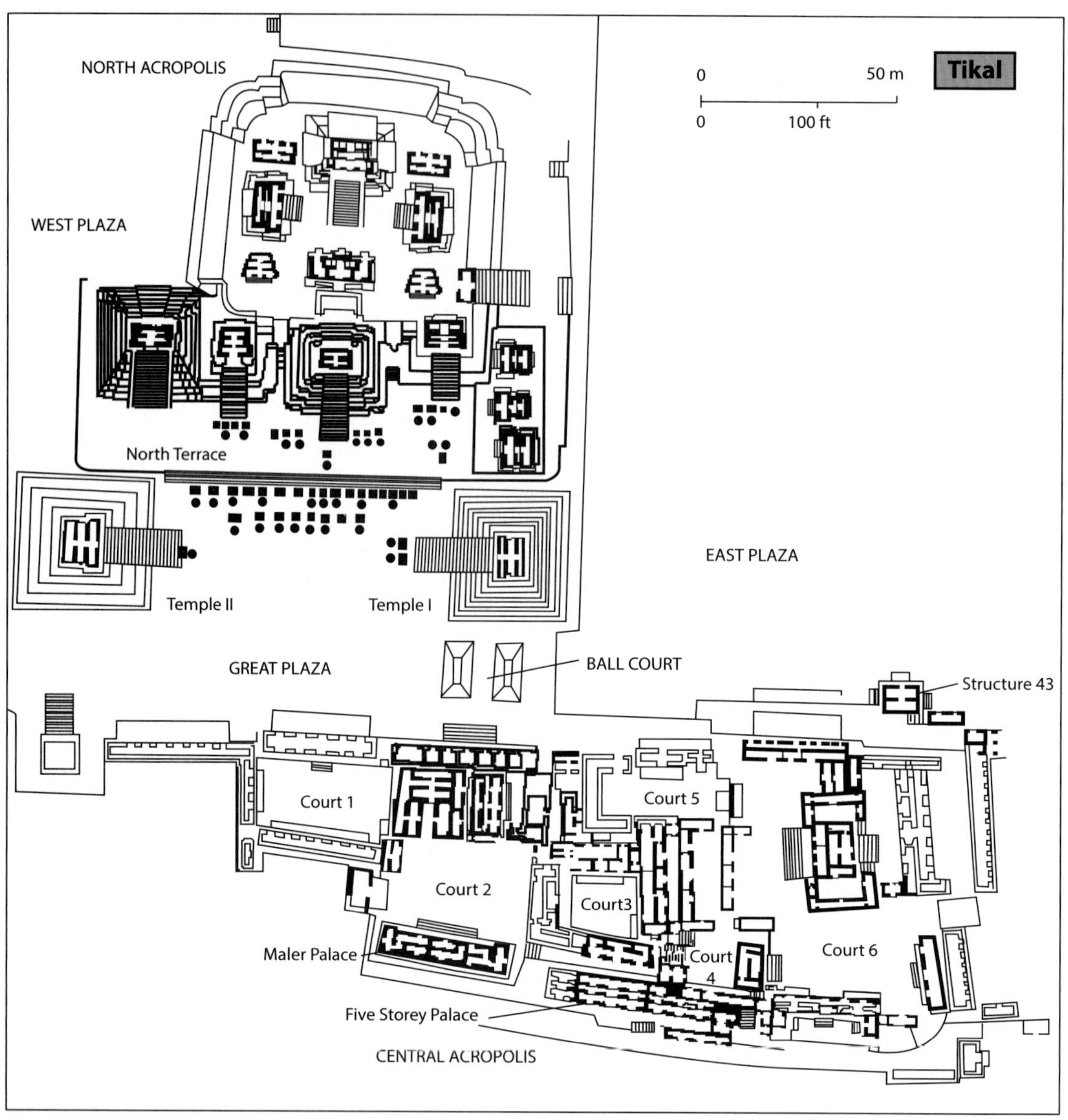

During the early Classic period, Tikal grew increasingly powerful through alliances with other regional states until ultimately it came into conflict with Calakmul, a belligerent state to its north. In 562 CE, the allied armies of Caracol and Calakmul captured and sacrificed Tikal's king. This defeat, coupled with a prolonged drought, plunged the city into a "dark age." This period is called the *Hiatus*," and for the next 124 years, no inscriptions were carved and no monuments were erected. It was not until the ascension of the twenty-sixth king, Jasaw Chan K'awiil I or "Sky Rain," nicknamed "Ah Cacao" or "Lord Chocolate," in 682 CE that the historical record was resumed and new temples were again erected (Martin and Grube 2008, 44–47). Several temple structures are associated with the reign of Jasaw Chan K'awiil I (r. 682–734) and they introduced what came to be known first as the "Tikal Style," and later as the "Petén Style," of architecture. The best-known examples of this style are Temple II, built as a monument to Jasaw Chan K'awiil's wife, and Temple I, his own funerary temple. Buildings in the Tikal style are characterized by austere, emphatically vertical, stepped platforms, often having false corners. The summit temples have a single doorway and are crowned by heavy, carved stone roof crests (or "combs") positioned toward the back (Wernecke 2005, 135).

Temple II, after 703 CE The east-facing Temple II (Figure 1.15) was constructed as a monument to Lady Lachan Unen Mo', known as Lady "Twelve Macaw," Jasaw Chan K'awiil's queen, who died in 703 CE. The lady was never interred in Temple II; in fact, excavations of the pyramid failed to find any burials. It is thought she was buried first at Topoxte, her birthplace, but when that town came under the control of an enemy city, Calakmul, her remains were exhumed and reburied elsewhere to prevent their desecration (Martin and Grube 2008, 46).

The pyramid platform of Temple II rises in three stages to a height of 59 feet (18 m). The chamfered corners of this and other Petén style pyramids created an architecture not only of mass and space but also of light and shadow. The corner channels are broken vertically by stepped-out masonry "shadow planes" which cast a pattern-play of light and shadow across the pyramid with the movement of the sun (Harrison 1999, 108–109). On the summit of the pyramid sits a single level base-platform that supports the temple. The two platforms, together with the temple and its soaring roof crest, bring the overall height of the structure to 125 feet (38 m). This temple base-platform was originally decorated with stucco masks, hence the alternate name, "Temple of the Masks."

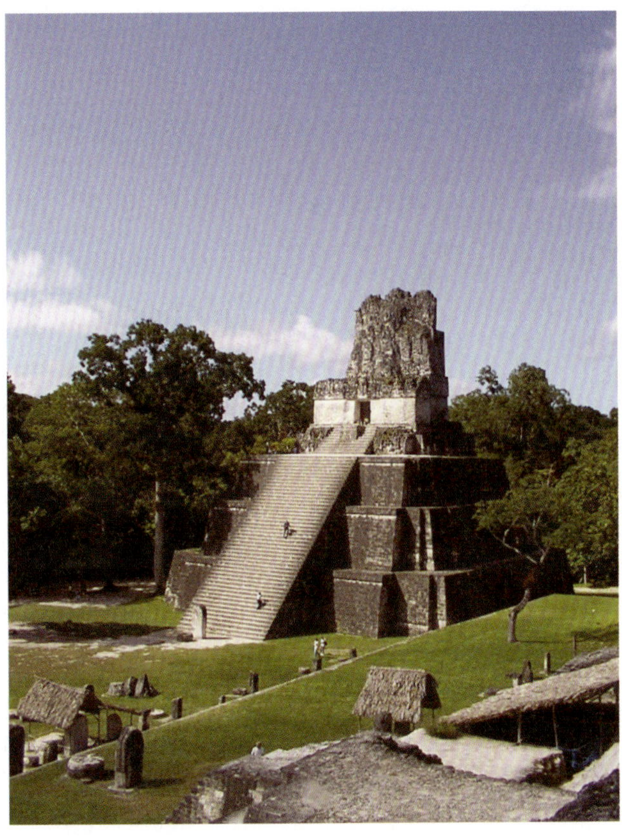

▼ **1.15** Tikal, Temple II, after 703 CE. 59 ft. high.

Although she was buried elsewhere, Temple II was built as a monument to Lady Lachan Unen Mo' or "Lady 12 Macaw," wife of Jasaw Chan K'awiil I, who died in 703 CE.

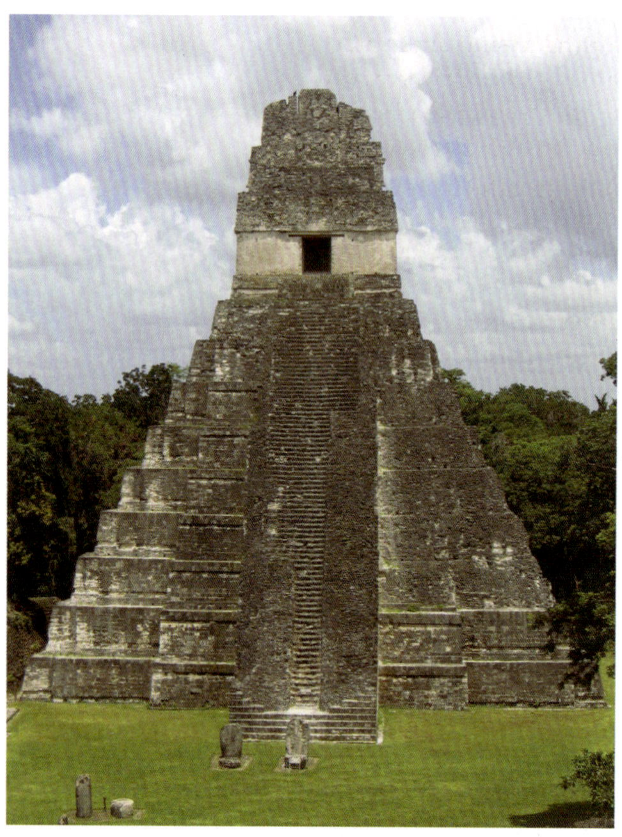

▲ 1.17 Tikal, Temple I, c. 732 ce. 154 ft. high.

As indicated by its nine-level platform base, Temple I was built as Jasaw Chan K'awiil I's funerary temple.

Temple II contained three narrow rooms, their doorways spanned by lintels constructed from multiple planks of sapodilla, an extremely hard and durable tropical wood. Of these, only Lintel 2 was carved; it shows a woman presumed to be Lady "Twelve Macaw" (there is no glyphic inscription). She wears ceremonial garb consisting of a beautiful brocaded huipil and over-mantle, jade collar, and elaborate feathered headdress, all rendered in exquisite detail. Like Stela 31, the carving style of Lintel 2 is executed in a variable depth low relief with overlapping elements that gives a sense of the figure in three dimensions.

Temple I, c. 732 CE Facing Temple II at the west end of the Great Plaza is, perhaps, the building most closely associated with the Tikal style, Temple I (Figure 1.16). Also known as the "Temple of the Great Jaguar", it was built to serve as the funerary temple of Jasaw Chan K'awiil I. Together the temple and pyramid form a structure that rises in nine levels to a height of about 154 feet (57 m). In the Maya area, nine level pyramids are thought to reference the nine levels of the underworld and thus indicate a funerary function. Pyramid construction techniques in the Maya region differ from those of Teotihuacan and La Venta. While clay was sometimes used in construction to consolidate fill, it was more commonly employed in vernacular rather than monumental architecture. Although some particulars of construction varied according to the skill of local craftsmen or quality of local materials, the construction techniques employed in building the Temple I pyramid are fairly typical across most of the region. The structural core of the pyramid is an aggregate of cobble, rough stone, and other fill items consolidated with lime-mortar, or in some areas **sascab**, a decomposing limestone that, when mixed with water, hardens like concrete and remains so as long as it is kept dry (Wernecke 2005, 21). This core material was laid down in courses and then covered with a nonstructural veneer of dressed stone.

The same basic, mortared-rubble-core and stone-veneer construction was employed in building Maya temples and palaces. Since the Maya, except in a few cases, did not build interlocked masonry structures, the sequencing of construction tasks was not always approached in the same manner. In some buildings the long walls were constructed, one at a time, to the point of the vault spring; then the vaults were constructed and the upper façade added, before the end walls and tympanums were set into place. In others, all of the walls of the room were completed before the vaulting work began; but even in these buildings, the walls are rarely bonded at the corners. The autonomous nature of the building parts is particularly evident in vault construction. Maya vaults are often described as corbelled vaults. However, corbelling in masonry construction requires that the weight of each succeeding course anchors the cantilevered stones of the previous one. Although the Maya vault stones appear from the surface to be corbelled, they are not laid in courses but rather stacked, one on top of the other, and supported by the mortar bed of the masonry core. This results in each half of the vault forming a self-supporting, monolithic unit with its wall; the two halves of the vault are joined only in the sense that they both support the capstones that close the vault. Thus, it is not unusual to see a Maya ruin in which one half of a vault has collapsed and yet its partner still stands (Staneko 1996, 135–156). The final stage of construction was the coating of the walls, inside and out, with a layer of lime plaster. The purpose of the lime coat was to protect against moisture penetration weakening the walls, however, multiple applications of lime plaster were sometimes used to disguise irregularities in vault construction.

Temple I is similar in presentation to its companion across the Great Plaza, Temple II. Both were raised above the summits of their pyramids by single stage base-platforms; each was entered by means of a single, centrally placed doorway and each supported a massive roof crest. The exterior mass of each building is substantial while the interior space is minimal, due to the thick walls necessary to support the weight of the roof combs.

Temple I Roof Crest Crowning Temple I is a massive roof comb or roof crest that rises to a height of 50.21 feet (14.5 m) from the rear of the temple and pushes forward to the midpoint of the roof. These heavy superstructures functioned as signboards, describing in image and sometimes in hieroglyphic text, the glorious achievements of the rulers who built these temples. In actuality, the Tikal roof combs are not always as weighty as they appear. Unlike other constructions, they rarely contained mortar and rubble cores; most were constructed of shaped stone, mortared together, and stuccoed, and often contained significant interior voids to lessen the load on the roof. The Temple I crest presents, as its centerpiece, the colossal, high relief image of Jasaw Chan K'awiil. This is his ultimate statement of triumph; he is arrayed in his royal raiment and seated on a throne in a formal frontal pose that suggests his enduring presence, much as did the pharaonic images of ancient Egypt.

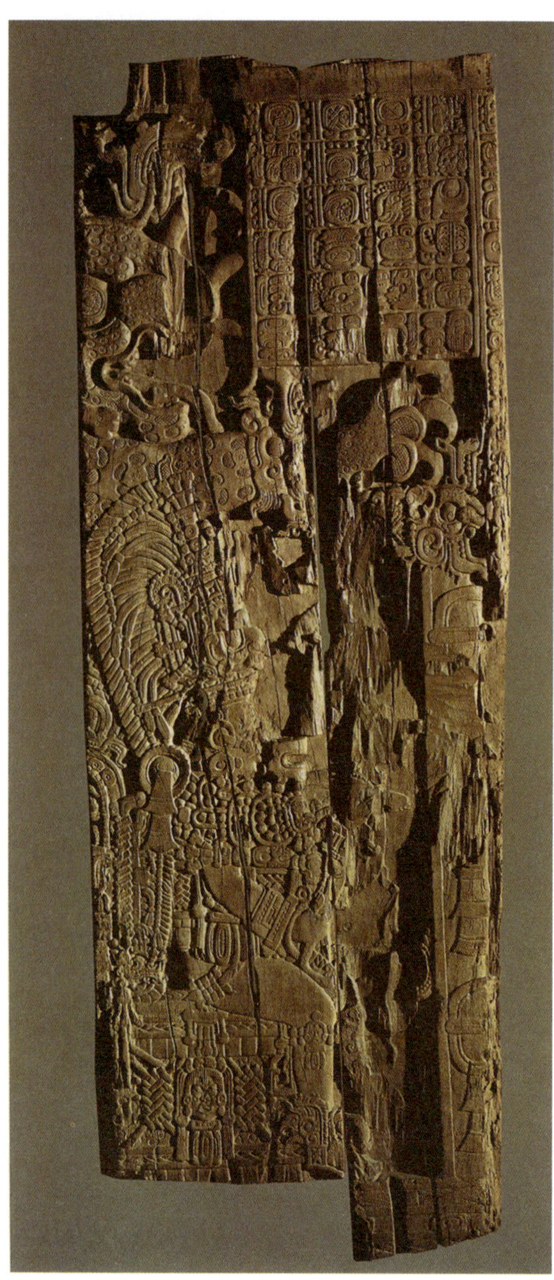

▲ 1.17 Tikal, Temple I, Lintel 3, sapodilla wood, c. 735 CE.
This lintel commemorates events that occurred September 14, 695, when the king was seated on the sacred palanquin of Calakmul.

Temple I, Lintel 3, c. 735 CE Temple I has three parallel, high-vaulted galleries, of differing overall dimensions, but each aligned on the central doorway axis. Each of the three doorways originally had a planked sapodilla wood lintel. The exterior doorway lintel was undecorated, but the second and third were carved with celebratory images of Jasaw Chan K'awiil.

Lintel 3 (Figure 1.17) records ceremonies that took place forty days later on September 14, 695 CE. As shown in the image and detailed in the lintel's hieroglyphic text, these were the seating of the Tikal king on the sacred palanquin of Calakmul; a ritual blood-letting performed by the king, and finally, a dedication ceremony. Although the text does not state what was dedicated, it was most likely Temple 33, which Jasaw Chan K'awiil built as a funerary monument to his father, entombing Stela 31 within it. On this lintel, a large jaguar reaches protectively over the king, who is arrayed in ceremonial regalia reminiscent of that worn by "Stormy Sky" on the face of Stela 31.

PALENQUE, CHIAPAS, MEXICO

Palenque, in the Mexican state of Chiapas, lies about 150 miles (253 km) west of Tikal. Very little is known about Palenque before the founding of its royal lineage in 431 CE but the first settlers may have arrived in the area as early as 500 BCE. Palenque's first king, K'uk' Bahlam or "Quetzal Jaguar," is described in the hieroglyphic records as "Toktahn Ajaw," a title suggesting that he came from the more prominent city of Toktahn[1], to serve as the ruler of Palenque. His ascension to the throne of Palenque coincides with the reign of Siyaj Chan K'awiil II at Tikal and dominant Teotihuacan influence in that region (Martin and Grube 2008, 156). It may well be that Teotihuacan was also instrumental in the seating of the Palenque dynasty.

[1] The site of Toktahn has not yet been identified with any known Maya archaeological site.

PAKAL THE GREAT AND THE PALENQUE ARCHITECTURAL STYLE

Except for their names, titles, and dates of birth, accession, and death, very little is known about Palenque's early kings or its first reigning queen, Lady Yohl Ik'nal. It is not until the seating of Palenque's ninth king, K'inich Janaab Pakal, or "Radiant (?) Shield," in 615 CE that a broader picture begins to emerge. Pakal came to the throne at the age of 12 after a chaotic period in which the city was attacked and sacked twice by Calakmul (599 and 611 CE). His early reign must have been concerned with military matters as Pakal did not begin construction of the monuments for which he is famous until his thirty-fifth year as ruler.

The Palencano style architecture that developed, during the reign of Pakal the Great and his sons, was very different from that of Tikal both in construction and design. Where the temples of Tikal soared to tower above the jungle, those of Palenque were lower and the emphasis was on the horizontal. Tikal's temples were entered through a single door, which was the central axis for a series of stacked rooms. At Palenque, most buildings consisted of two parallel galleries, the first in essence a portico formed by three or five portals, and the second divided by curtain walls into three or more small chambers.

In comparison to the masonry work at Tikal, that at Palenque seems slip-shod. Palencano wall construction was less massive and often lacked the mortar core that made Tikal walls monolithic. Palencano walls were frequently not laid up in courses; instead, random-thickness limestone blocks were crudely stacked and the gaps between them were filled with chinking stones. These rough walls were then covered, inside and out, with thick layers of plaster stucco. While these thinner walls allowed for more interior space, they were also less stable, leading Palencano masons to devise ingenious ways to lighten the load of the vaults, such as the use of cross-vault systems and key-hole-shaped voids, used like coffering to reduce the mass of the vault. Another solution to the weight problem was the invention of inward-sloping "mansard-style" roofs. Roof crests were also lighter at Palenque, being open, double-walled trellis-frames that were covered in stucco ornamentation. Moved forward and centered over the interior wall of the temple, Palencano roof combs rarely achieved the heights of those at Tikal.

The Palace Group, c. 654–750 CE Pakal commissioned a number of structures that transformed the city and defined the Palencano style of architecture. One of his first projects was the renovation of the royal palace complex. The Palenque Palace Group (Figure 118), like the palaces of Teotihuacan, was probably more of an administrative and ceremonial center than a royal residence. The initial phase of Pakal's new construction included the addition of a second terrace, running from the middle to the south end of the original platform. This brought the height of the palace platform to 33 feet (10 m), and in the process,

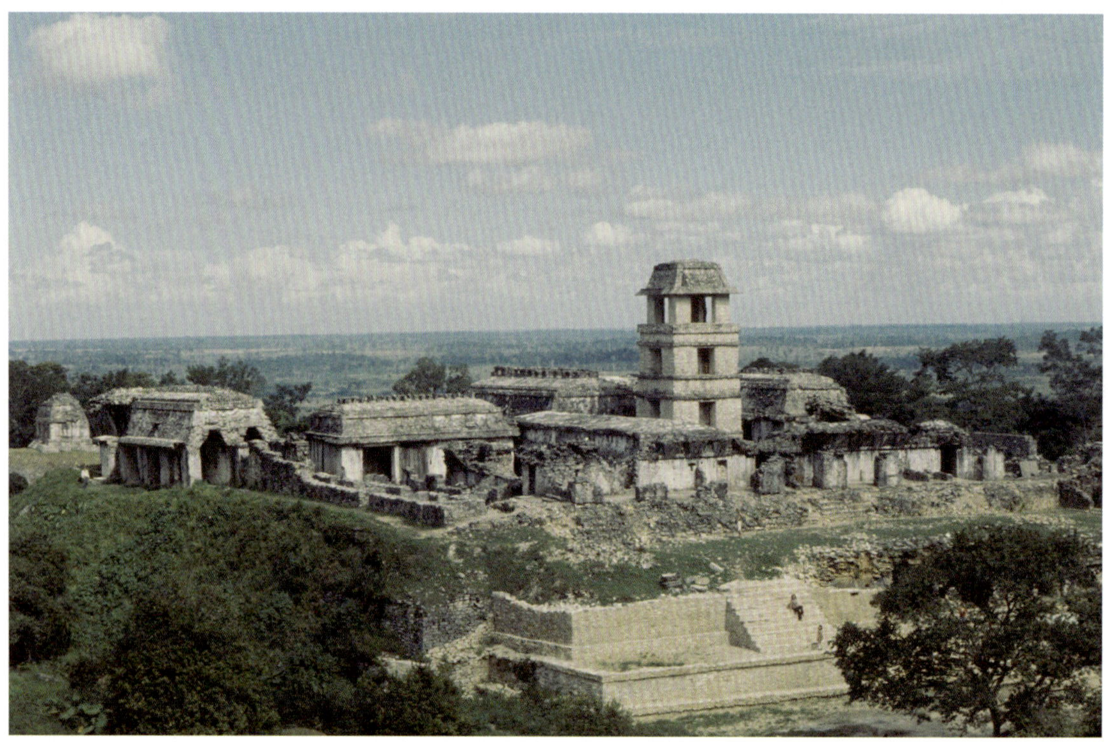

▲ 1.18 Palenque, Palace Group, c. 564–750 CE.

During the reign of Pakal the Great, the previous buildings were buried in the enlarging and leveling of the platform and new structures built.

buried existing structures at the southern end of the original platform, converting them into subterranean galleries.

House E was the first of the thirteen buildings to be commissioned by Pakal and his successors. Dedicated in 654 CE, it served as Pakal's throne room. It is a unique structure, having a nearly vertical façade and a white exterior, rather than the more usual deep red ocher . Indeed the official name of the structure was "Sak nuk naah" or "White Skin House" (Stuart and Stuart 2008, 156). House E consisted of two parallel galleries, divided into three main rooms and a stair hall that provided access down to the southern subterranean galleries. Three doorways opened from the Tower Court and also from the Southeast Court, while two doorways in the interior wall provided communication between the galleries.

House E: Oval Palace Tablet, c. 654 CE Palencano style sculpture is also distinct from that of Tikal. Where Tikal's rulers frequently erected stone stelas and companion altars to commemorate important events and period endings, stelas and altars are rarely found at Palenque. This, again, is due to the quality and softness of the available limestone in the Palenque area. Yucatan limestone is exceptionally fine-grained and easy to carve, but too soft to be durable in outdoor use. Most of the stone reliefs at Palenque were created as bas-relief tablets set into the walls of palace buildings and temples, although occasionally they are found on the exterior as foundation panels for some of the Palace structures.

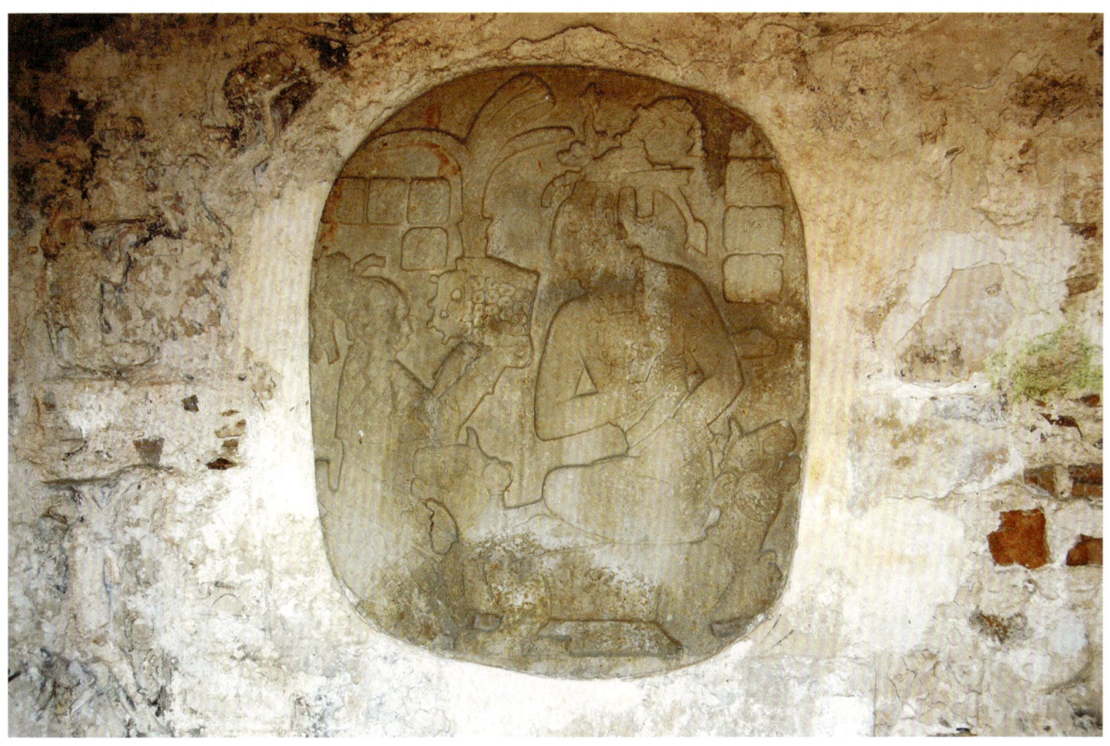

▲ **1.19** Palenque, Oval Palace Tablet, limestone relief, c. 654 CE.

This is the first monument connected to Pakal the Great and although it was done long after the actual event, it shows his accession to the throne in 615 CE. Pakal's throne was placed beneath this tablet.

The first sculpture associated with the reign of Lord Pakal is the Oval Palace Tablet (Figure 1.19). The approximately 45-inch (114-cm) by 36-inch (91-cm) limestone bas-relief panel was embedded into the back wall of House E and originally framed with a border of stucco relief. Pakal's throne once stood beneath it. The tablet commemorates Pakal's accession in 615 CE. It shows Pakal, dressed in a simple hip cloth and wearing jade ornaments: ear flares, pectoral, cuffs, and belt, seated cross-legged on a throne ornamented with carved feline heads; his lower body is twisted toward his mother, while his torso is rendered frontally. His mother, Lady Zak K'uk ("Resplendent Quetzal"), dressed in the regalia of a queen, offers the jade-beaded "drum-major" headdress of Palenque to an adult, not adolescent, Pakal. The Oval Palace Tablet, with its symbolic transfer of the "crown" from mother to son, established the prototype for accession statements in which power was symbolically passed from parents to child. In Pakal's case, his father is not present, suggesting that the line of royal descent was through his mother. Lady Zak K'uk's status is conveyed by her ceremonial attire of bead netting skirt and capelet, garments that constituted royal robes and were worn only on the most formal occasions (Bruhns 1988, 106).

The Temple of Inscriptions, c. 685 CE The death of Pakal's wife of forty-six years, Lady Tz'akbu Ajaw (formerly Lady Ahpo Hel), in 672 CE,

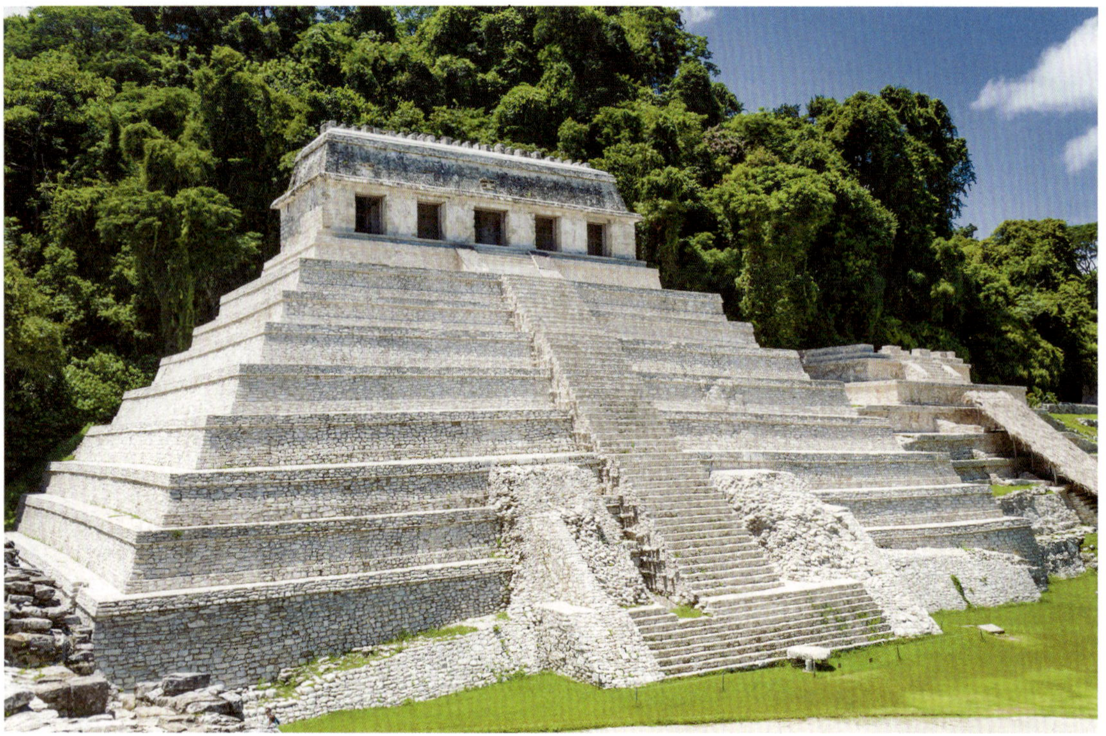

▲ 1.20 Palenque, Temple of Inscriptions, c. 685 CE. 89.2 ft. high.

Pakal the Great began work on his funerary temple, The Temple of Inscriptions in 672 CE when he was already in his seventies; the burial chamber beneath the plaza and his sarcophagus were completed first and the building constructed above. It was completed after his death by Pakal's son and heir Chan Bahlum II.

and the necessity of constructing an appropriate funerary monument for her, Temple XIII, may have prompted the seventy-year-old king to commence construction of his own tomb, the Temple of Inscriptions (Figure 1.20). Pakal's temple was situated next to Temple XIII and was terraced into the crest of a natural hill so that the overall height of the temple and its platform is 89.2 feet (27.2 m), making it one of the taller buildings in the city. The temple is a long rectangular structure measuring 76 feet (23.31 m) by 25 feet (7.65 m) that is accessed through five portals. It derives its name from the hieroglyphic text panels set into the rear walls of the second gallery's chambers. This long inscription, the second longest after Copan's hieroglyphic staircase, details the dynastic successions through that of Pakal and recounts actual military, political, and ritual-offering events as well as incidents occurring in the mythical past and future (Stuart and Stuart 2008, 167–169).

The first phase of construction began around 675 CE and saw the excavation of the 22.75 foot (7 m) by 12.18 feet (3.75 m) tomb chamber and the setting of the solid limestone sarcophagus base and its lid into position within that space prior to the building of the vaults. Once the chamber was completed, the pyramid, stair, and finally the temple were constructed above it. When Pakal died in 683 CE, the temple was unfinished, but his tomb chamber and sarcophagus were ready. It was a simple matter to transport his body down the stairs and place it in the hollowed-out space in the sarcophagus base, then slide the lid into position.

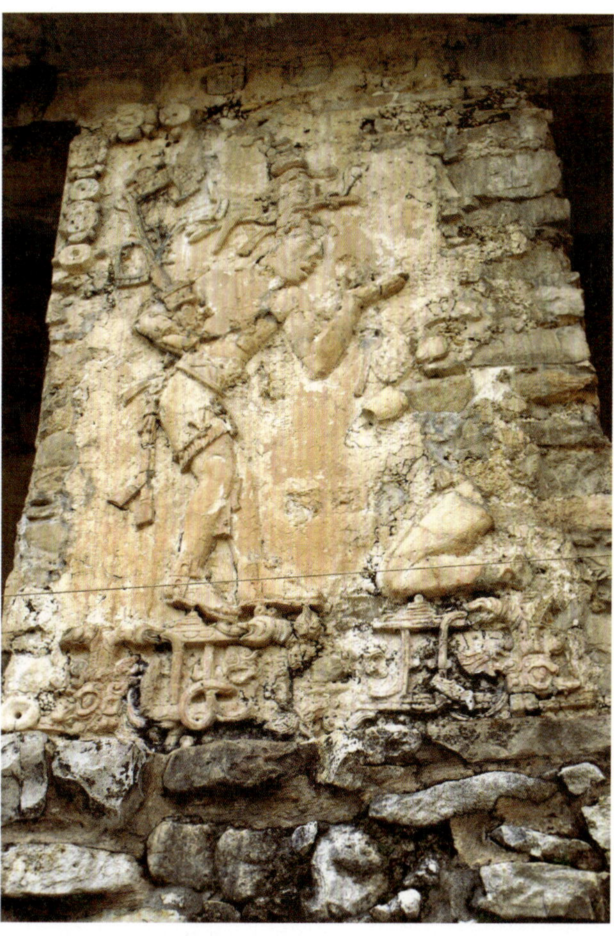

▲ 1.21 Palenque, Palace of Inscriptions, detail stucco relief on one of the piers, c. 685 CE.

The stucco work at Palenque rivals the finest stone carving in quality but it was modeled onto the stone armature rather than carved.

Stucco Reliefs of the Temple of Inscriptions, c. 685 CE The exterior piers of the Temple of Inscriptions were decorated with fine stucco relief panels (Figure 1.21). The stucco work at Palenque rivals the finest limestone carving in its finished form. However, unlike the bas-relief carvings, it is an additive rather than reductive process. The remains of stucco tablets that originally adorned buildings of the Palace Group as well as the Temple of Inscriptions have provided clues to the process used to create the Palenque stucco tablets. Stucco artisans worked under the direction of a master, whose job it was to ensure that the figures adhered to an established canon of proportions. In one case, a wrist broken off a figure on Pier C of House A showed a fully formed, but apparently too narrow, wrist beneath it that was corrected by the overlay of a wider, more properly scaled one (Robertson in Miller and Martin 2004, 247–249).

The process began with the creation of a cartoon or template for each figure. This template could be adjusted along the length of the torso to create a figure appropriate to the available space. The image was transferred to the plaster coat either by incising the cartoon or, in some cases, quickly sketching onto the surface using red or black paint. After this, the successive layers of plaster were applied in a sequence that followed the order of dressing an actual human being: underwear, hip cloths, jaguar skirts, loincloths, ornaments, and feather headdresses. Each garment was applied as a layer of stucco and painted the appropriate color even if it would be concealed by the next garment. In some cases, the heavy stucco layers were reinforced with an armature of large flat stones set into the surface of the wall. The stomach, chest, arms, and thigh areas often were created utilizing such armatures (Robertson in Miller and Martin 2004, 247–249).

The Sarcophagus of Pakal the Great, c. 672 CE In Maya hieroglyphic inscriptions it is not unusual for there to be a pattern of redundancy and elaboration of information. The sarcophagus lid (Figure 1.22) follows this repetition in visual form. Pakal's is depicted at the moment of

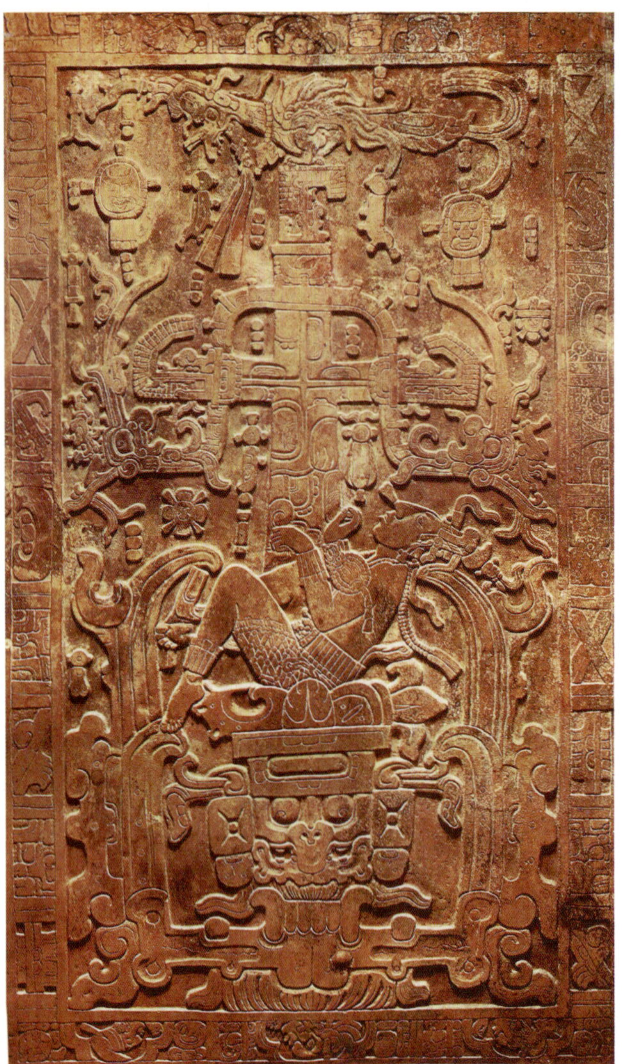

▲ 1.22 Palenque, Temple of Inscriptions, Sarcophagus Lid of Pakal the Great, c. 675 CE.

The carving on the sarcophagus lid depicts the moment of Pakal's death and transformation into an ancestor as he falls down the world tree into the jaws of the Quadripartite Monster.

his transformation from a living lord to a sacred ancestor; he is literally suspended between life and death, heaven and the underworld of Xibalba, and darkness and light, represented by the sky-bands with sun and moon on the left and right edges of the lid. Behind him is the World Tree, the Maya axis mundi, which connects the celestial, terrestrial, and underneath realms. The trunk of the tree is marked with signs for "wood," "brightness," "sacredness," "blood," and "blood-letting." Perched at the top of the tree is the Celestial Bird, while at its base is the Quadripartite Monster (the sun), which will carry Pakal on his journey through the nine levels of the underworld to his resurrection into the celestial realm when the sun rises again into the heavens. Around the sides of the lid are ten named ancestors of Pakal, representing six generations of Palenque kings and queens. Each is shown regenerated, emerging from a crack in the earth along with a fruiting tree (Schele and Miller 1986, 282–285).

MAYA MURAL PAINTING

The Maya excelled at the art of fresco painting but unfortunately, at many sites, including Palenque, most of the mural painting has been lost. The technique used by the Maya was similar to that of Teotihuacan. Once the intonaco had been applied, figures and hieroglyphs were outlined in red ocher and the background color painted around them. Figures were then dressed and adorned in color and the final touch was the addition of a black outline.

Bonampak Murals, c. 790 CE In 1946 the most famous of all Maya murals (Figure 1.23) were discovered in Bonampak Structure 1, known as the Temple of the Murals. Bonampak, in the state of Chiapas, was a small kingdom that was a dependency of its more powerful neighbor Yaxchilan. About 790 CE, Yaxchilan's king, Itzamnaaj Bahlam IV or "Shield Jaguar" oversaw the installation of Yajaw Chan Muwaan II ("Lord of the Sky Hawk") as king of Bonampak.

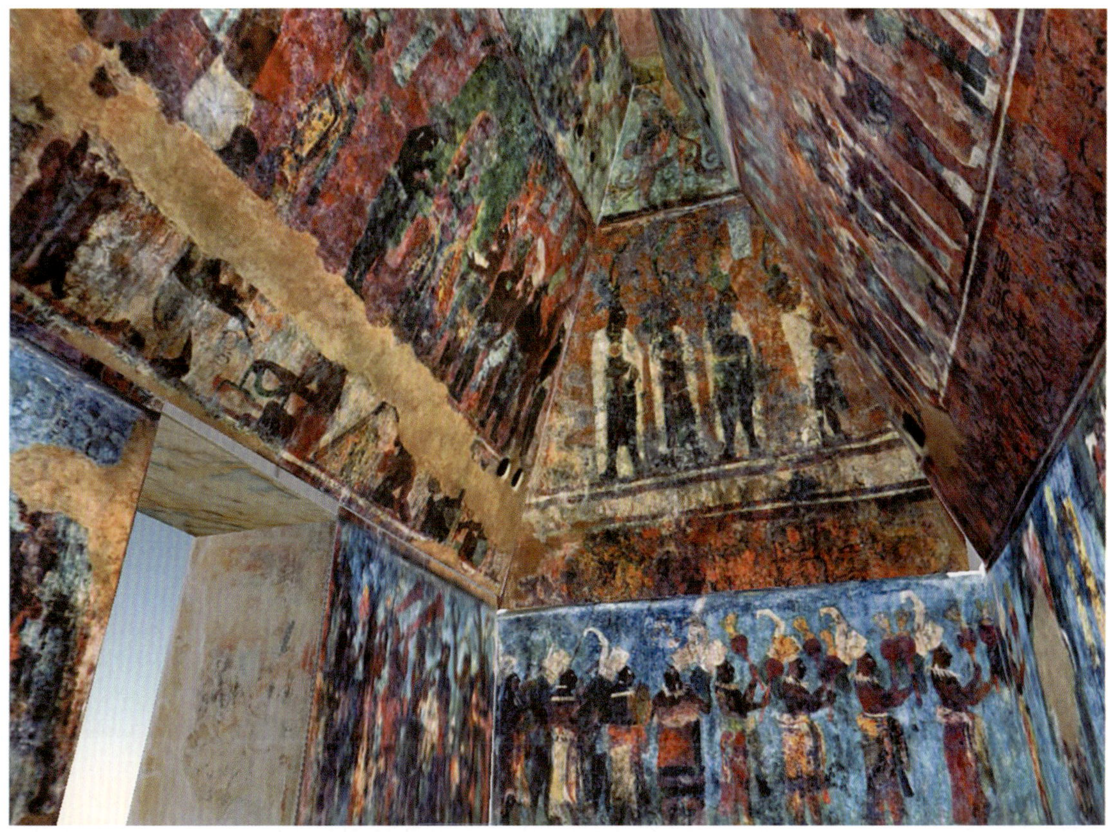

▲ 1.23 Bonampak, Temple 1, Room I Murals, c. 790 CE.

The scenes painted on the walls and vaults of this room detail the preparations for a ceremony designating king Chan Muwaan II's son as heir. In the bottom register musicians play while lords dress for the celebration and assemble for the ritual in the upper registers.

To commemorate his installation Chan Muwaan commissioned the building of the Temple of the Murals and brought artists from Yaxchilan to paint its frescoes. The temple's three rooms are painted from floor to capstone with scenes showing celebrations, ritual warfare, and the sacrifice of captives. The first room shows the preparation and celebration of the designation of Chan Muwaan's son as successor to the throne of Bonampak. The first register shows musicians playing while in the second row Maya nobles dress in their ceremonial regalia. The upper level shows the child, accompanied by his parents, being presented to assembled lords. The walls of the second room show a fierce battle in which Chan Muwaan and his nobles capture enemy warriors, who are then tortured and sacrificed as part of the rituals surrounding the designation of Chan Muwaan's heir. The third room shows another celebration, following sacrifice of the captives, where members of the court let blood as the final event of the heir designation rituals (Martin and Grube 2008, 135–136).

Calakmul Murals, c. 620–700 CE The murals at Bonampak present the panorama of royal pageantry, courtly ritual, and military exploits that were elements of noble life among the Maya. A rare depiction of everyday life for Maya craftspersons and commoners comes from scenes

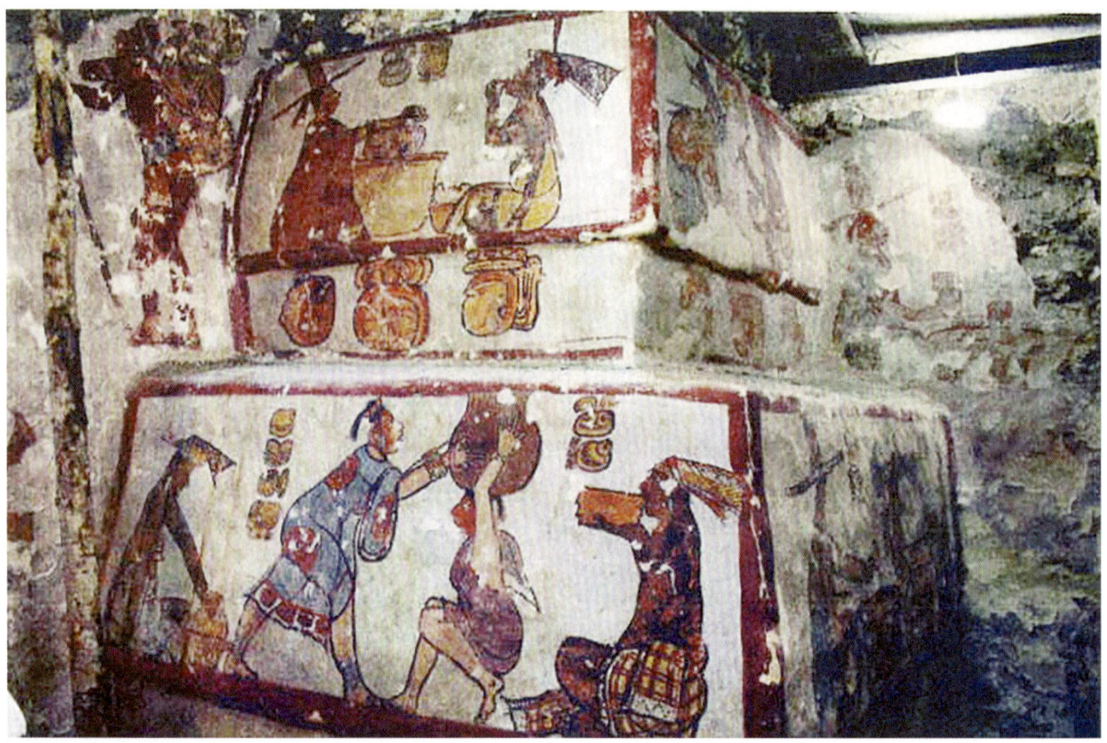

▲ **1.24** Calakmul, Building Sub 1–4, southeast corner mural, c. 620–700 CE.

The murals of Sub 1–4 are unusual in that they show the life of Maya commoners rather than elites. The scenes appear to show the activities of a Maya market with people buying and selling beer and food stuffs.

painted on the pyramid of Chiik Nahb, Structure Sub 1–4, at the site of Calakmul. The site was first discovered in 1931 but the murals were only recently revealed during government sponsored excavations on the Chiik Nahb complex. The surface structure was the last in a program of temple refurbishment that saw the construction of a new temple over an earlier structure. In each reconstruction, the previous temple was completely enclosed within the new construction; this was a common practice among Mesoamerican peoples, particularly the Maya and Mexica (Aztec). When archaeologists tunneled through the third overbuilt layer, they found a structure, which was designated Sub 1–4 to indicate that it was the fourth structure buried within building 1. This building was square, measuring 36 feet (11 m) on a side, and it rose in three tiers to a remaining height of 15 feet (4.7 m). Four cardinally oriented staircases provided access to the top of the structure, which unfortunately had been destroyed by the subsequent rebuilding. The Sub 1–4 structure was an exceptional find in that its exterior surface was covered with painted murals that had been preserved by the overbuilt layers. In fact, it appears that the builders of Sub 1–3 had taken care to pack a layer of mud and small stones over the painted surfaces in an effort to prevent damage; this level of care is unusual in the overbuilding process (Carrasco Vargas et al. 2009, 19245).

The murals (Figure 1.24), covered all the levels of the structure as well as the sidewalls of the stairs, and consisted of genre scenes, showing what appear to be activities at a market, with males and females carrying loads; serving customers various food stuffs identified in accompanying glyphic captions as "atole" (maize beer), tamales, beans, and salt; dispensing medicinal tobacco; and vending ceramic housewares including chocolate pots and other items (Martin 2012, 61–80).

The visible murals constituted the second repainting of the structure; archaeologists discovered earlier murals underneath, which depicted similar themes but in fewer colors by a less adept painter. Stylistically, the second murals were the work of a different artist than the painter of the first. Both were painted in the mezzo fresco technique. The figures of the surface layer were drawn onto the wall surfaces using red outlining, filled in with sixteen different colors, and given a final outline in black. In each stage outlines were painted as continuous, rapidly-applied fluid lines, indicating that the artist possessed significant skill as a draftsman. The artist also seems to have had a good understanding of human anatomy, proportion, and natural movement that contrasts dramatically with the more formal stances of the Bonampak painting. Certain scenes such as that on the southeast corner of Sub 1–4, showing a standing woman steadying a large olla as another woman rises to carry it, have strong, anatomically correct, figural outlines that suggest a working method similar to that of Italian Renaissance masters such as Michelangelo, who often sketched his figures in as nudes and then painted on the clothing.

The Late or Post-Classic Period (900–1450 CE)

The Post Classic begins toward the end of the ninth century with the collapse, due to prolonged drought, of the Maya kingdoms of the southern highlands. In the Valley of Mexico, the process had begun even earlier with the fall of Teotihuacan and the resulting influx of new peoples into Central Mexico. The period is often portrayed as a decadent phase in which militaristic themes are dominate in the arts. Such interpretations present an overly simplistic picture of the era. While apparently more war-like civilizations, the Toltecs and Mexica, did arise in the area around the Basin of Mexico, in the northern lowlands of the Yucatan Peninsula, Maya kingdoms, initially less affected by the drought conditions, continued to flourish and develop new architectural styles and techniques.

Post-Classic Maya

During the Post-Classic, cities in the Puuc region of the Yucatan invented a new architectural style, termed "Puuc style." The word "Puuc" translates as "a range of hills" and designates a roughly triangular region running from northern Campeche across central Yucatan to western Quintana Roo. Water sources in the Puuc region, primarily

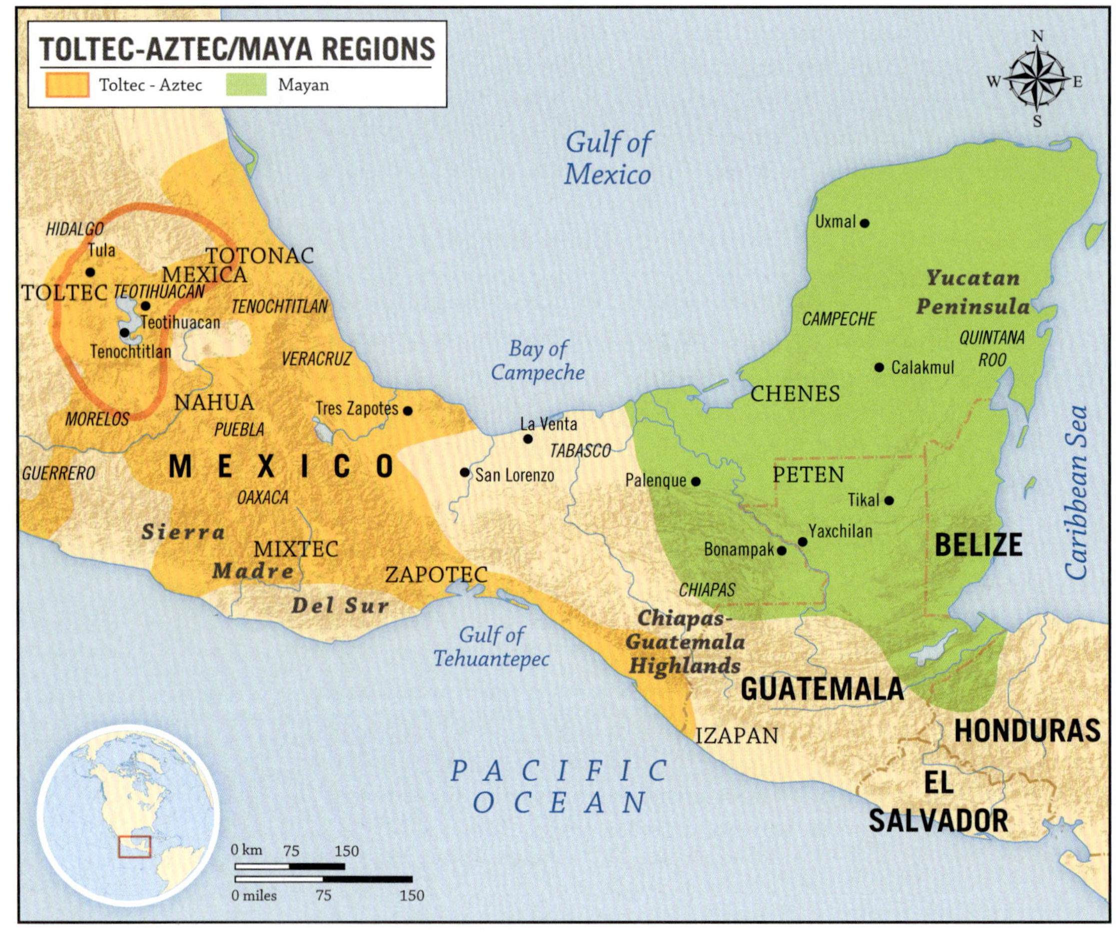

cenotes (wells formed by sinkholes), underground lakes, and *chultunes* or cisterns, allowed Puuc communities to survive the recurring drought conditions longer, but by 1450 CE many of the Yucatan cities had been abandoned.

THE PUUC STYLE IN ARCHITECTURE

The first examples of the Puuc style appear in the Late or Terminal Classic period (c. 700 CE) and the last Puuc monuments were built around the end of the first millennium CE. Puuc architecture is the technical culmination of advances in mortar construction developed during the Classic Period. Instead of building walls with thick mortar beds set between load-bearing limestone facings, Puuc architects developed a lime-based concrete that allowed them to create cast-in-place walls. Since these cast walls were able to support their loads based on the strength of their mass, Puuc designers were free to create decorative architectural veneers that had no load-bearing function (Staneko 1996, 66).

Puuc buildings range from single-room structures to those of more than seventy rooms and are typically single-story structures. The effect of multistoried buildings of as many as five levels was achieved by progressively stepping back supporting platforms as elevation increased; the result being stair-stepped structures that were perceived as a single visual unit. The lower wall surfaces of Puuc buildings are usually unadorned. Embellishment was reserved for the upper wall and usually consisted of a mosaic frieze made up of thousands of cut limestone blocks, most about 8 inches (20 cm) square and just a few centimeters thick. While larger elements might be morticed into the wall, most of these veneer pieces were simply cemented to the core. Puuc veneers were constructed using pre-fabricated blocks, carved in relief, to form X- or T-shapes, step-frets, round and serrated disks, stepped pyramids, diamonds, and other elements, which could be quickly assembled to form geometric patterns such as latticework, step-frets, or stylized Chac masks. Instead of the more substantial roof combs of Classic Maya architecture, Puuc buildings had free-standing "flying facades" positioned over the front wall of the building and extending for the entire length of the façade.

UXMAL, YUCATAN (700–1100 CE)

The city of Uxmal was founded around 700 CE but by 900 CE it had grown into one of the largest Puuc cities, with a central area of 150 acres and subsidiaries at Kabah, Sayill, and Labna. Uxmal was connected to these smaller towns by sacbes or "white roads"; the road connecting Uxmal to Kabah was inaugurated at both ends through a monumental portal vault that was free-standing like a triumphal arch. The dynastic history of Uxmal is murky. Very few of its surviving hieroglyphic texts have been studied by **epigraphers**. Much of what we know about the history of the city is derived from Post Classic and Colonial era manuscripts. These sources point to Hun-Uitzil-Chac, nicknamed "Lord Chac," as the founder of the city and the royal dynasty of Xiu. An inscription on Uxmal Altar 10 seems to name Chac-Uinal-Kan as his successor; beyond this, little is currently known. The Chac component in the names of these early rulers is a reference to the Maya god of storms, lightning, and rain. The preponderance of his imagery, usually in the form of architectural masks, indicates the high level of concern over water resources at Uxmal, which depended on rainwater collected in chultunes for its survival.

The Nunnery Quadrangle, c. 800–900 CE The majority of Uxmal's buildings were constructed during the ninth and tenth centuries when the city was an ascendant regional power. As elsewhere in Mesoamerica, the architecture of Uxmal is organized around plazas; however, at Uxmal plazas take the form of quadrangular courts, defined by architecture. The best known of these is the Nunnery Quadrangle

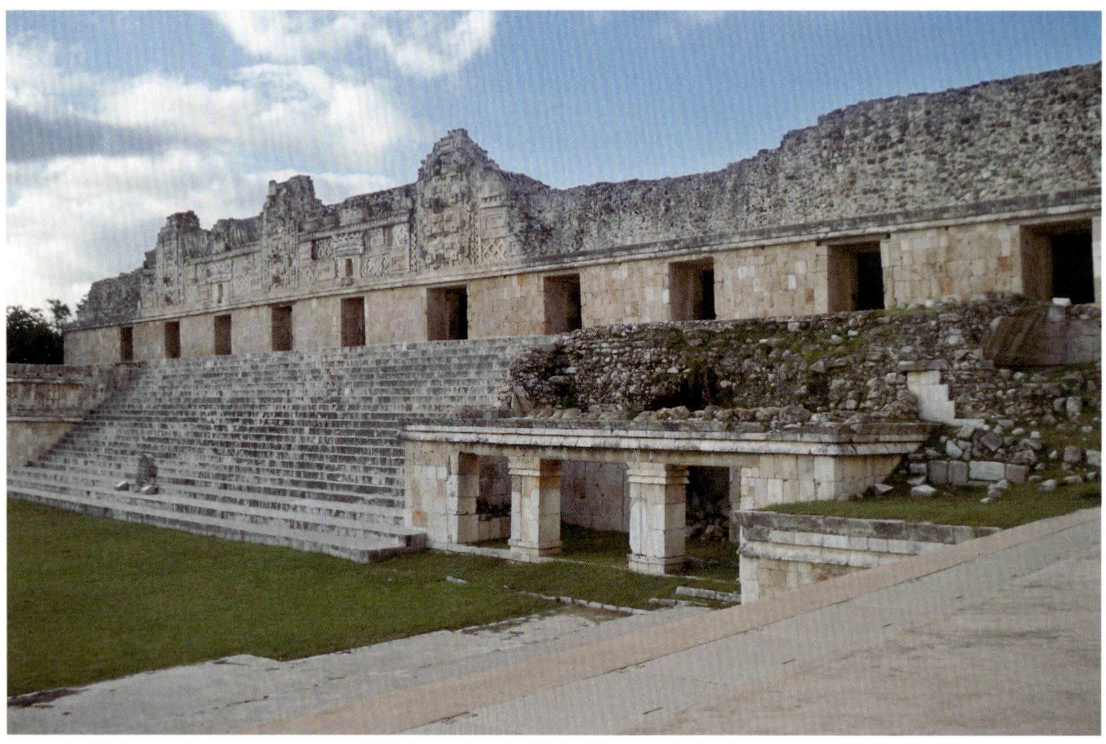

▲ 1.25 Uxmal, Nunnery Quadrangle, North Building, c. 800–900 CE.

Puuc architecture is exception for its uses of pre-fabricated tiles, which could be arranged into layers of design as on the upper façade of this structure.

(Figure 1.25), so named by the Spanish colonists because of its layout's similarity to that of Catholic convents in Spain.

The four buildings of the Nunnery Quadrangle define a large rectangular court, measuring roughly 208 feet(64 m) by 146 feet (45 m). The structures were built at different times, the first being the North Building, a long rectangular structure, situated atop an almost 22 foot (6.7 m) high platform that was accessed by means of a broad processional stair. The main façade of the building faced the plaza, and, following Puuc conventions, consisted of a plain lower wall pierced by eleven doorways, and an elaborately decorated upper frieze band, ornamented with frets, serrated lattice panels, huts surmounted by serpents, and vertical stacks of Chac masks. These last elements extended well above the upper cornice segments, giving the effect of a crenelated roof crest running the length of the building. The arrangement of motifs on the frieze bands was layered. Latticework elements serving as a background, while frets, serpent bars, Chac masks, and almost fully round sculptural elements stepped out progressively farther from the frieze ground, creating a play of pattern on pattern. The other buildings in the complex were all set lower than the North Building, especially the South Building (second constructed) which provided, in the form of a monumental vault-way, the primary access to the court. Although similar in design and construction, each building features a different combination of motifs in their individual frieze bands.

The Toltecs (c. 900–1168 CE)

After the collapse of Teotihuacan, nomadic peoples began migrating into Central Mexico from the arid lands to the north and west and establishing themselves in the Valley of Mexico and along the plateau. These groups were generally considered to be barbarians by the long-settled inhabitants. Among the first to arrive, around 600 CE, were the Toltecs, who initially may have settled at Tulancingo in Hidalgo, before founding the city the Aztecs called "Tollan" or "place of reeds." That city, better known as Tula, was the dominant military power in Central Mexico for almost three centuries. Like Teotihuacan, Tula was at the heart of a vast trading empire that extended as far to the south as Costa Rica and north into the American Southwest.

The power vacuum created by the destruction of Tula around 1170 CE and the dispersal of Toltec refugees around the five lakes brought a flood of new migrants into the Valley, among them the Chichimecs, Tepanecs, Acolhua, and finally the Mexica. This last group, popularly known as the Aztec, created the last great Central Mexican Empire. Although Tula fell long before the founding of Aztec Tenochtitlan, the Mexica revered the Toltecs as the fathers of agriculture, medicine, and the arts. Thus, in Post-Classic central Mexico, to be a descendant of the Toltecs was, in effect, to be civilized.

TULA

Tula on the Central Mexican plateau, to the north of Teotihuacan and the Valley of Mexico, was founded around 900 CE. Although population estimates for the Toltec capital have exceeded 60,000 inhabitants, the civic-ceremonial district or "Tula Grande" was compact compared to those of Teotihuacan or the larger Maya states. The main structures were organized around a rectangular plaza, some 394 feet (120 m) by 459 feet (140 m), that was filled in places to create a level space (Mastache and Cobean 2000, 100). Two pyramids were the focus of civic and ceremonial life, Pyramid B and Pyramid C. An L-shaped colonnade created a sheltered pathway that connected the two pyramids to the pillared halls of the Quemado or "Burnt palace." The remaining space was defined by a ball court and Coatepantli or "serpent wall" on the west and Building K on the south. In the center of the plaza was a low altar known as the *adoratorio*. A second, sunken ball court stood to the north of the plaza and Pyramid B.

Today these structures seem austere and spartan, a condition that reinforces the concept of the Toltecs as a warlike people. However, as indicated by the stone bracing remaining on the taluses of the two pyramids, Tula's buildings were once covered with stone reliefs assembled into great friezes, and painted in bright colors. Many of the sculptures and relief plaques were stripped from the site by the Aztecs who patterned their own art and architecture after that of the Toltecs.

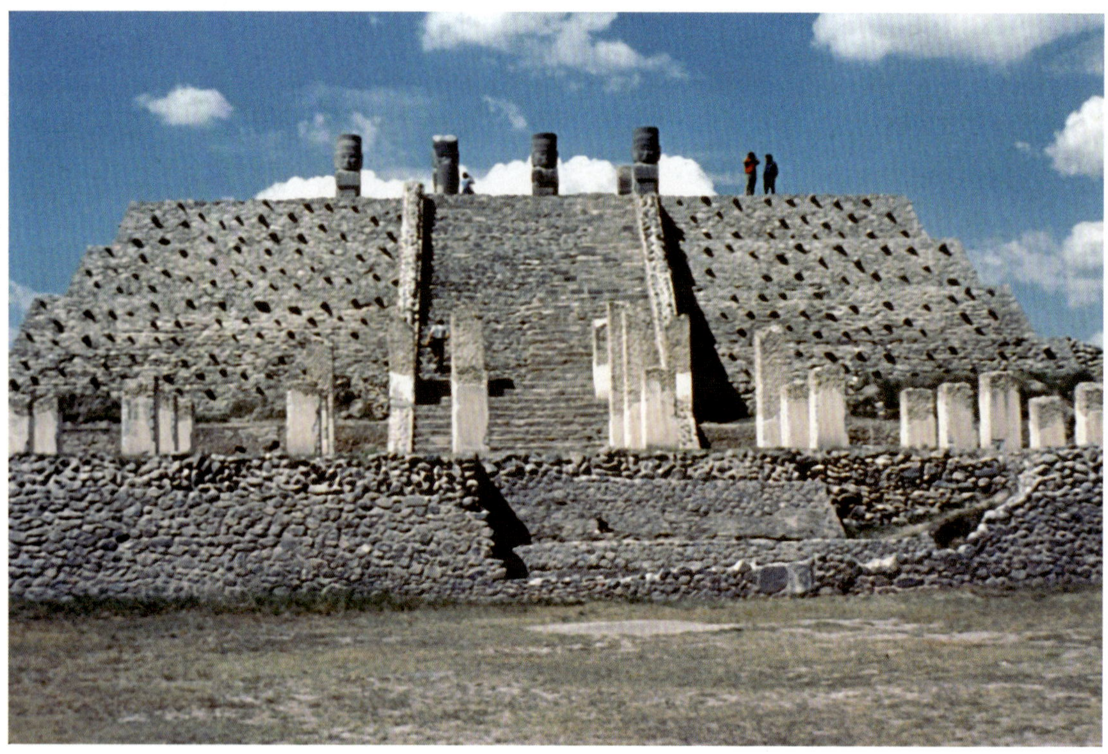

▲ 1.26 Tula, Pyramid B or Pyramid of Quetzalcoatl as Tlahuizcalpantecuhtli, c. 1100 CE. 32 ft. high.

The façades of this platform pyramid were once covered with painted relief plaques. The structure on its summit was made of perishable materials.

Pyramid B, c. 1100 CE Pyramid B (Figure 1.26) was dedicated to Quetzalcoatl in his aspect as Tlahuizcalpantecuhtli or "Lord of the House of Dawn." It is a square pyramid, measuring approximately 124 feet (38.2 m) on a side and rising in five terraces to a height of almost 32 feet (9.8 m). Brightly painted stone reliefs once decorated its sides; only a few were found intact on the east wall of the pyramid. The reliefs form a procession of jaguars and coyotes across the top register, while in the lower are eagles eating human hearts and an image of Tlahuizcalpantecuhtli. The prowling felids, canids, and raptors are reminiscent in style of similar processions in the murals of Teotihuacan, which were likely known to the Toltec artists who carved these reliefs.

The Atlantes, c. 1100 CE Pyramid B originally supported a structure that may have functioned as an audience hall or council chamber. Except for its piers, columns, and ***Atlantes*** or Atlantean figures (Figure 1.27), the structure was constructed of perishable materials, which were destroyed when the city was burned around 1170 CE. The most spectacular of these supporting members were the four Atlantes figures, each 15 feet (4.6 m) tall and representing high-ranking Toltec warriors, armed with ***atlatl*** or dart-thrower and darts. Each figure wears a tall, cylindrical feather headdress, large "butterfly" pectoral, apron-like garments, and a dorsal ornament. The Atlantes were constructed from four drum-like sections, secured by means of a pin and socket.

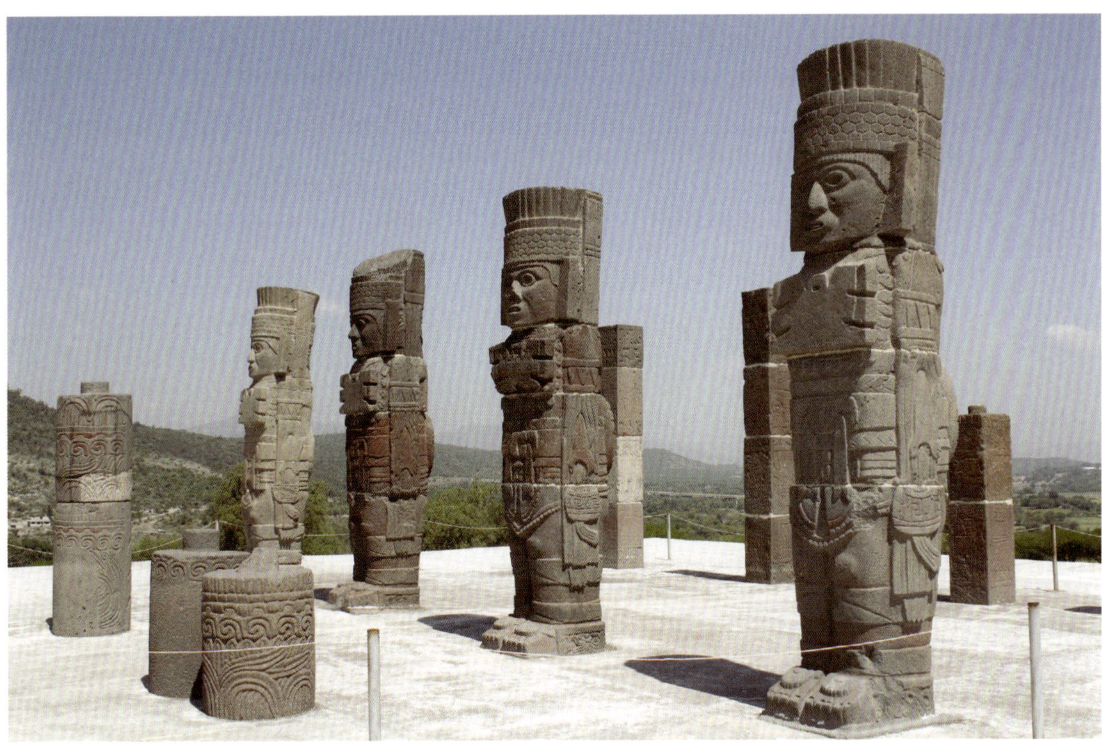

▲ 1.27 Tula, Pyramid B, Atlantes, c. 1100 CE.

The roof of the summit structure was supported by columns carved as feathered serpents, four atlantes in the form of Toltec warriors armed with darts and atlatls. The piers behind them are carved with what are thought to be Toltec kings. All were originally painted.

Remaining traces of red pigment show that these figures were originally painted. Behind them were four square stone piers, decorated with reliefs thought to represent Tula's kings.

The Mexica or "Aztecs" (1100–1521 CE)

Around 1100 CE, one of the last nomadic Nahua tribes, the Mexica, arrived in the Basin of Mexico. Several Colonial manuscripts tell the story of the Nahua migration from their homeland, known as Aztlán ("the place of cranes"). Current scholarly opinion holds that Aztlán was somewhere in western Mexico, perhaps in the states of Nayarit, Michoacán or Guanajuato. The popular designator "Aztec" is derived from Aztlán and was first used by Alexander von Humboldt in 1810 to distinguish the Mexicans of his day from those of the pre-Columbian era. However, the people conquered by Hernando Cortes in 1521 would have identified as "Mexica."

When the Mexica finally arrived in the Valley, the best lands were already occupied by descendants of the Toltecs and by other migrating groups that had arrived earlier. The Mexica were forced to continue their nomadic existence for a time, their reception by the various states around the lakes being hostile. Ultimately, they settled at Chapultepec (Grasshopper Hill) and became vassals of Culhuacan, a state established by refugees from Tula. The warlike nature of the Mexica did not sit well with their neighbors and there was constant talk among the more settled groups of driving the Mexica barbarians from Chapultepec. Ultimately, the Mexica asked Achitometl, lord of Culhuacan, for the

RELIGION AND PHILOSOPHY
Aztec Gods

Although each civilization had its own pantheon of gods, there are some deities, apparently of great antiquity, who were shared, sometimes under different names, by many Mesoamerican peoples. Chief among these ancient gods were Tlaloc, the goggle-eyed rain god, and the "Plumed Serpent" Quetzalcoatl, both of which originated at Teotihuacan. Others with a long history included Huehuetéotl, the old god, and Xiuhtecuhtli, the fire god. In addition to these, there were creator gods and goddess, gods personifying the forces of nature, the sun, moon, and planets; gods who oversaw the human condition, diseases, and manner of death; gods who were patrons of occupations and crafts, and gods who were cultural or local guardians, such as the Aztec tutelary god Huitzilopochtli.

At the time of the Conquest, the Spanish chronicler López de Gómara claimed there were more than 2,000. However, like the medieval Catholic saints the Spanish would have known, most pre-Columbian gods are represented with some attribute that makes them readily identifiable in their anthropomorphic and zoomorphic forms. Here's a list of a few of the more commonly encountered ones in Mexica art:

Coatlicue (Koh-aht-lee-kway) is an earth goddess. Her name translates as "She of the serpent skirt." She is identifiably by her braided serpent skirt, necklace of human hearts and hands with a pendant skull, and her serpent face. She is the mother of the sun, moon and stars.

Coyolxauhqui (Koi-yohl-shauw-kee) is the moon goddess. She is recognizable by the copper clam-shell bells on her cheeks; her name is often translated as "face painted with bells." She is the daughter of Coatlicue and the sister of Huitzilopochtli as the sun.

Huehuetéotl (Way-way-tay-oht) is an ancient fire god known as the "old god." He is depicted as a wrinkled and emaciated old man often with a disk-like headpiece.

Huitzilopochtli (Weeze loh-poch-tlee) was the Aztec god of the sun and war. His name translates as "Hummingbird on the left." He is often shown with what looks like a hooked weapon; it is his xiuhcoatl or "turquoise snake," possibly a solar ray. He can appear as a hummingbird or an eagle and his anthropomorphic form may have eagle feathers at the wrists.

Quetzalcoatl (Ket-sal-ko-aht) is known as the feathered serpent. He has snake fangs and jaguar teeth with a forked tongue. In anthropomorphic form he often has feathers or snakes as an identifier. He is associated with rain, wind, and fertility.

Tlahuizcalpantecuhtli (Tla-weeze-kal-pan-tee-koo-tlee) or "Lord of the House of Dawn" was the personification of Venus as morning star and as such was considered to be a potentially dangerous god.

Tlaloc (Tlah-lokh) is known as the old "goggle-eyed rain god." He has ringed eyes, fangs, jaguar teeth, a forked tongue, and is blue or green. He is god of rain, fertility, lightning, and hail.

Tlaltecuhtli (Tlal-teh-koo-tlee) are a class of earth gods/goddesses, recognizable by clawed hands and feet.

Xiuhtecuhtli (Shee-tay-koo-tlee) or the "Turquoise Lord" was the Aztec god of fire and creation and is often conflated with Huehuetéotl.

hand of his daughter in marriage to their lord Huitzilopochtli, whose name means "Hummingbird on the left." Thinking his daughter would start a new royal line, the lord agreed. When the Culhua nobles arrived for the wedding feast, they found that the princess had been sacrificed and her flayed skin was being worn by a Mexica priest. In the ensuing battle, the Mexica were driven from Chapultepec onto a small island in the reed beds of Lake Texcoco. There they saw an eagle, perched on a nopal cactus, eating a serpent; in Aztec mythology this was the sign the god Huitzilopochtli had given them so they would know when they had arrived at the land he had promised to them.

TENOCHTITLAN

The founding of Tenochtitlan, occurred in the Aztec calendrical year Two House or 1325 CE. From these inauspicious beginnings on a muddy island, Tenochtitlan grew into a great city, laid out on a grid system that was divided into four quarters. These districts were further subdivided into wards for different clans as well as for artisans of various crafts. Movement through the city was facilitated by networks of roads and canals. Food for Tenochtitlan's residents was grown in the ***chinampas*** or "floating gardens," a system of artificial islands that ringed the city. Causeways connected Tenochtitlan to the mainland and an aqueduct brought fresh water from the springs of Chapultepec.

THE SACRED PRECINCT AND TEMPLO MAYOR, 1487 CE

At the heart of the city, next to the Palace of Moctezuma, was the Sacred Precinct, a walled plaza measuring approximate 1140 feet (347.47 m) by 990 feet (301.75 m), within which stood temples to the most important Aztec gods. The main temple was the Huey Teocalli ("Great House of the Gods") or Templo Mayor, where Huitzilopochtli and Tlaloc were the focus of devotion. Surmounting this large, square, terraced pyramid, were the twin Temples of Tlaloc (north side) and Huitzilopochtli (south end). Each temple was conceived as standing on a separate mountain platform; thus, each had a separate staircase on the west face of the pyramid. Tlaloc's side was his mountain of life, while Huitzilopochtli's temple stood on Coatepetl (Serpent Mountain). The Templo Mayor was enlarged seven times between the construction of the first perishable temples around the time of the city's founding and 1487 CE, when the last ritual enlargement occurred. The renewal of an Aztec pyramid involved the enclosing of the temple, sculptures, and platform within the new structure; in essence, each new structure becoming a sort of reliquary preserving the remains of the previous one. Unfortunately, the Spanish Conquistadors leveled the Templo Mayor and buried it under the main city square, the Zócalo.

Coatlicue, c. 1470–1500 CE In 1790, during a resurfacing of the Zócalo, workers unearthed the monumental 11.6 feet (3.5 m) tall basalt

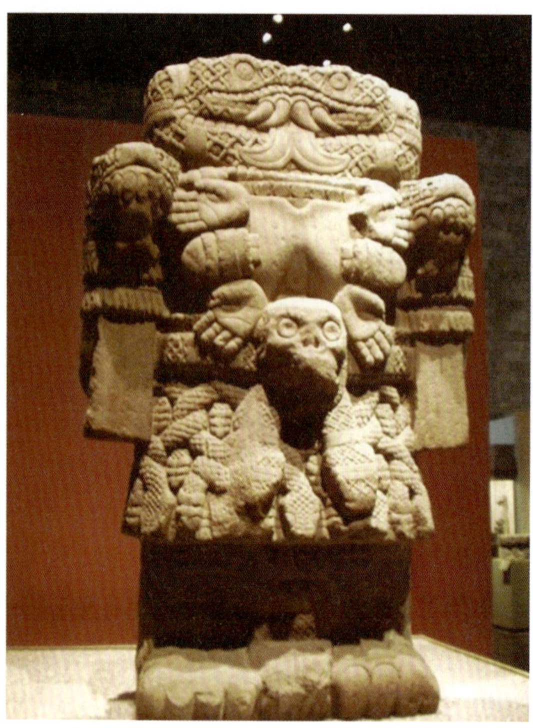
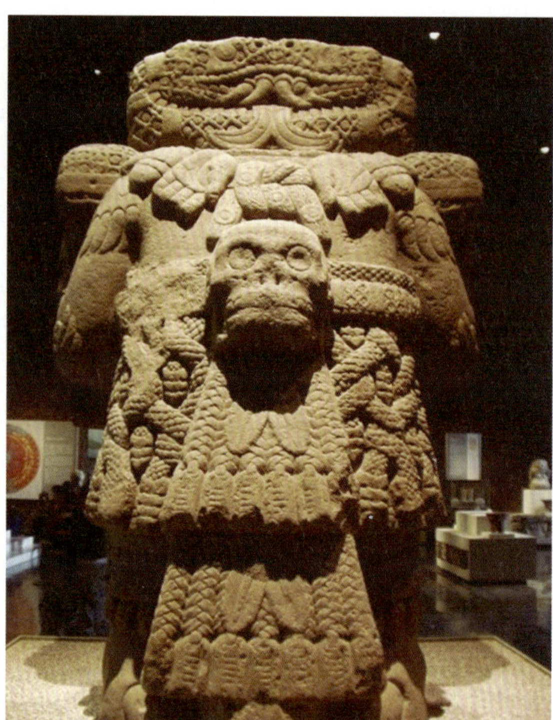

▲ **1.28** Tenochtitlan, Templo Mayor, Aztec goddess Coatlicue (left front, right rear), c. 1470–1500 CE. 11.6 ft. high.

As mother of Huitzilopochtli, Coatlicue originally stood atop the Templo Mayor but was pulled down and buried by the Spanish.

statue of Coatlicue (Figure 1.28), which stood atop the Templo Mayor. Coatlicue was an ancient earth goddess who, like the Hindu Lord Shiva, was both a creative and destructive force. She is associated with fertility, had power over life, death, and rebirth and was the mother of the sun-and-war god Huitzilopochtli, the moon goddess Coyolxauhqui, and the Four Hundred Huiztnaua, or Southern stars. In Aztec myth, she is a priestess of a temple on Coatepetl (Serpent Mountain) who is impregnated by a ball of down falling from the heavens. When Coyolxauhqui learns that her mother Coatlicue is pregnant, she is outraged and plots with the Huiztnaua to kill her. However, the child Coatlicue is carrying, Huitzilopochtli, vows to protect her. When his siblings arrive, he emerges from his mother's womb, fully grown and armed with a Xiuhcoatl or fire-serpent, to slay them.

The statue is a horrific representation of Coatlicue's dual nature as creator and destroyer. Her head is conceived as two confronting rattlesnakes, which in a Gestalt shift can also be read as a single frontal snake head. It has been suggested that the serpents represent flowing blood from decapitation but that interpretation is not consistent with the myth. Rather they represent the terrible beauty of this powerful earth goddess; monstrous faces, claws, and skull or serpent joints are frequent attributes of earth deities. Snakes, in particular, are associated with the fertility and the regenerative cycle of the earth because of their habit of shedding their skin after hibernation. Her skirt is formed from intertwined black king snakes, while her belt, bustle, and loincloth are marked as rattlesnake. Coatlicue's maternal role is expressed by sagging breasts and rolls of flesh around her midsection that show she has given birth. Her necklace of human hearts, hands, and a skull pendant expresses her role as eater of the dead.

Despite her fearsome aspect, the Coatlicue is a wondrous work. She is carved on all sides, including the bottom, which bears an image of Tlaltecuhtli. Aztec artists frequently carved the bottom of sculptures, even if they would not be seen. Coatlicue was sculpted as a figure in-the-round but she has not been liberated from her block. Although Mexica stone carvers were capable of producing sculptures that broke free, they rarely did so when the work was intended to reinforce state ritual or myth; this may be a legacy of the civic art of Tula and the desire of the Mexica to claim Toltec heritage. In the case of Coatlicue, her monumental blockiness and multitude of serpents create a visual metaphor for Coatepetl. The fine detail of the carving and variable depth of relief are extraordinary, especially considering that the work was done with stone tools and abrasives. Originally, Coatlicue was painted to further enhance the effect, but no traces of color remain.

Coyolxauhqui Disc, c. 1487 The remarkable Coyolxauhqui disk (Figure 1.29) was discovered in 1978 by electrical workers excavating

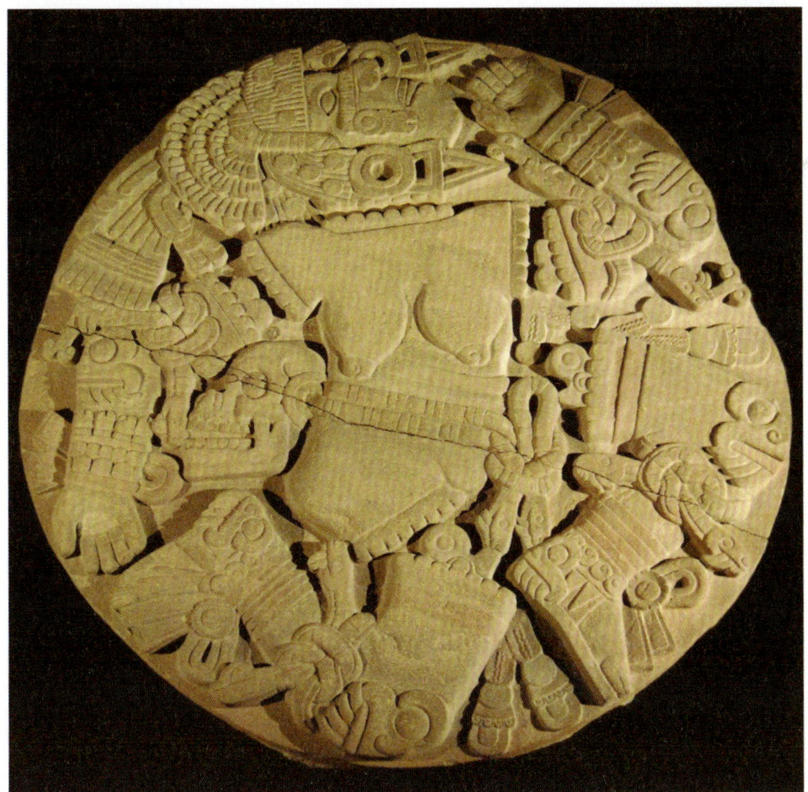

◀ **1.29** Tenochtitlan, Templo Mayor, Coyolxauhqui Disc, c. 1487 CE. 11 ft. diameter.

The disk was originally located at the foot of the Templo Mayor as if she were a sacrificial victim cast off of the pyramid. She is shown as dismembered by her brother Huitzilopochtli; it is both a reference to the story of his birth and a metaphor for the sun conquering the night.

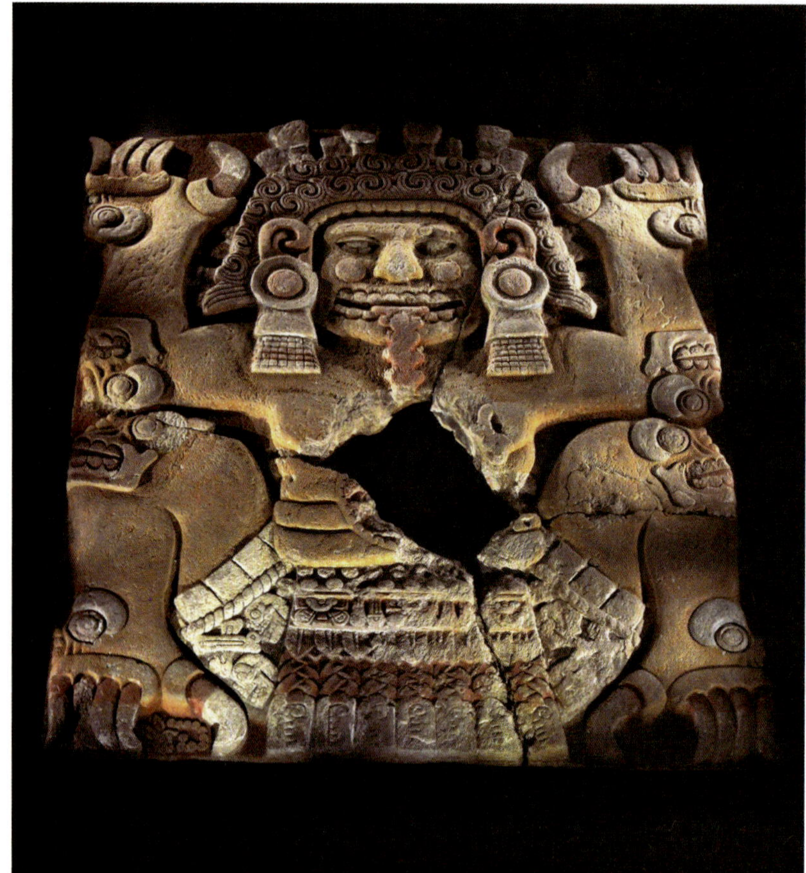

▶ **1.30** Tenochtitlan, near the Templo Mayor, Tlaltecuhtli Slab, c. 1500–1520 ce. 13.61 ft. × 11.76 ft.

Tlaltecuhtli was a monstrous earth goddess who would not bear fruit unless fed with the blood of human sacrifices. This remarkable sculpture is one of the few to still have its original paint.

near the Zócalo. The circular stone measures almost 11 feet (3.3 m) in diameter and was found in situ at the base of the Templo Mayor; its discovery actually enabled archaeologists to locate the foundations of the pyramid. Coyolxauhqui or "Bells on her cheeks" is shown on the disk naked and dismembered by her brother Huitzilopochtli; bones stick realistically out of her severed limbs. Despite the graphic and gruesome nature of the depiction, the work is a masterpiece of Aztec carving. Coyolxauhqui is rendered on this planar relief in highly detailed manner; great attention has been paid to the form of the torso, the pendulous breasts, and rolls of flesh around the midsection.

Tlaltecuhtli Slab, c. 1500–1520 ce In 2010 a remarkable 12-ton stone relief, measuring 13.61 feet(4.19 m) by 11.76 feet (3.62 m) was discovered near the Templo Mayor. The huge monolith (Figure 1.30), carved with an image identified as Tlaltecuhtli, is unique in that it is the only known Aztec sculpture that retains its original pigments. The relief dates from the reign of Ahuitzotl or perhaps Moctezuma II and shows a full-length, yellow-ocher squatting figure with upraised arms, clawed hands and feet, and skulls as joints. Skull and crossed-bone motifs decorate its garments which are highlighted in white pigment. Extending from the bottom of the deity's tongue is a red zigzag representing blood (from sacrifices) flowing into its mouth, signaling its acceptance of the offering. Similar red, yellow, and white color schemes may have once heightened the impact of the Coatlicue and Coyolxauhqui.

The Colonial Period: Native Artists in Mexico (1533–1821 CE)

In August 1521, after the surrender of Cuauhtemoc, the last ruler of the Mexica, Cortes ordered the destruction of the Sacred Precinct as the first stage in the construction of a new, European-style city. Stone from the Aztec temples and even sculptures, were repurposed, some as materials for the new Cathedral and other colonial buildings; others consigned as fill for the new main plaza of Mexico City, the Zócalo. The Indigenous artists, who had created the glories of Tenochtitlan, were put to work by the mendicant orders, creating art to aid in the conversion of newly conquered peoples to Christianity. Working in traditional methods and materials they created murals, feather mosaics, and sculptures in wood and stone to further evangelization efforts.

The Christian-Indigenous Style

One of the first art ateliers was organized by Fray Pedro de Gante, a Franciscan missionary, at San Jose de los Naturales in Mexico City in the years immediately following the conquest. There, Indigenous artists working in traditional media created religious images based on engravings in books the friars had brought with them from Europe. One of the workshops at San Jose de los Naturales was devoted to feather arts, an elite craft among the Aztecs. The Tribute Rolls of Moctezuma show vast numbers of tropical bird feathers collected by the Aztecs from their vassal states.

▼ **1.31** Diego de Alvarado Huanitzin, *The Mass of St. Gregory*, 1539 CE.

This feather mosaic on a wooden support was made under the direction of Fray Pedro de Gante at San Jose de los Naturales as an offering to the Pope Paul III.

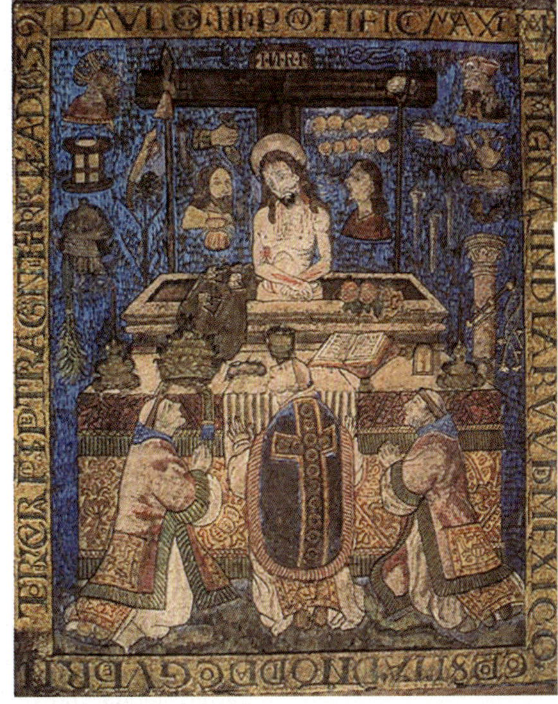

Diego de Alvarado Huanitzin,* The Mass of St. Gregory, *1539 CE *The Mass of St. Gregory* (Figure 1.31) is the oldest surviving example of a Christian-Indigenous feather mosaic. It depicts the miraculous mass of Pope Gregory the Great in 595 CE, during which Christ appeared on the altar. A Latin inscription

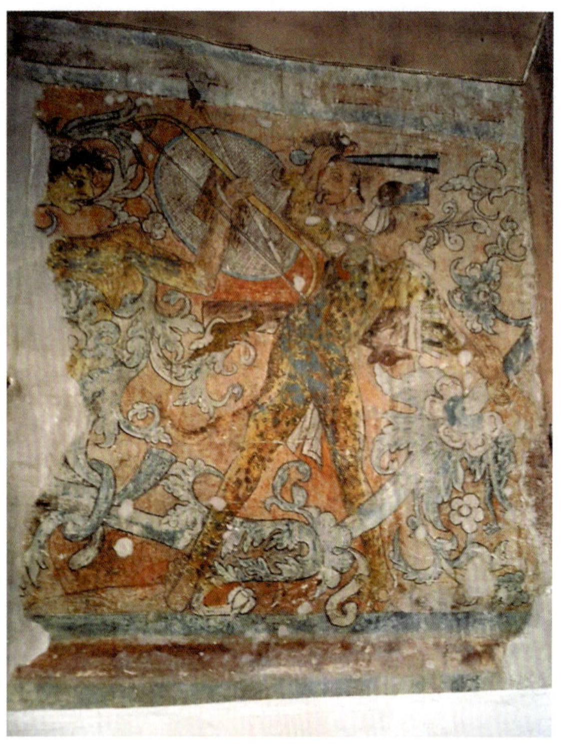

▲ **1.32** Ixmilquilpan, Hidalgo, Church of San Miguel Arcángel, detail of mural in the entrance, c. 1550 CE.

The mural, meant to explain the stories of the Bible to newly converted Aztecs, shows St. Michael as an Aztec jaguar warrior, wearing the turquoise tiara of an Aztec Tlatoani.

around the border identifies Pedro de Gante and the reigning pope, Paul III. The work is thought to have been made at San Jose de los Naturales as an offering to the Pope. The work has been connected to Don Diego de Alvarado Huanitzin, brother-in-law of Cuauhtemoc, as patron or perhaps artist. Feather-working was an art often practiced by Aztec nobles. The image is composed entirely of bits of bird feathers adhered with a binder to a wooden support.

The Church of San Miguel Arcángel in Ixmilquilpan, Hidalgo, c. 1550 CE The Church of San Miguel Arcángel in Ixmilquilpan was founded in the mid-sixteenth century by Augustinian friars. Decoration of the church and cloisters was done by local Native artists. Most of the surviving frescoes are European images: religious paintings and borders of Renaissance designs. However, something very different was discovered in the church under several layers of yellow paint. The walls of the church were divided, like a painted pre-Columbian manuscript, into registers. The top register featured paintings of eagles and jaguars reflecting the pre-Hispanic warrior classes of the Mexica. The lower band is filled with battles between Native armies intertwined with stylized foliage. One scene shows a jaguar warrior, identified as the archangel Michael (Figure 1.32), wearing the turquoise tiara of the Aztec **Tlatoani** or "Great Speaker," with flowery speech scrolls emanating from his mouth. In another Lucifer appears as a monstrous white centaur armed with bows and arrows. The scenes are unusual for their pre-Conquest context, particularly in a church. The frescoes were likely an attempt to portray the Biblical battle between good and evil in terms readily understood by a Native audience. In this case, as a battle between Aztecs and conquistadors.

Indigenous Artists in the Modern Era (1821–1950 CE)

By the mid-sixteenth century, immigrant artists from Europe had arrived in sufficient numbers to establish the first New World guilds. In Mexico the guilds were used to exclude Indigenous artists from access to training and from competition for commissions. Pushed into the background, often autodidactic, and working in provincial cities and towns far from major art centers, relatively few Indigenous artists achieved recognition in the nineteenth and early twentieth centuries.

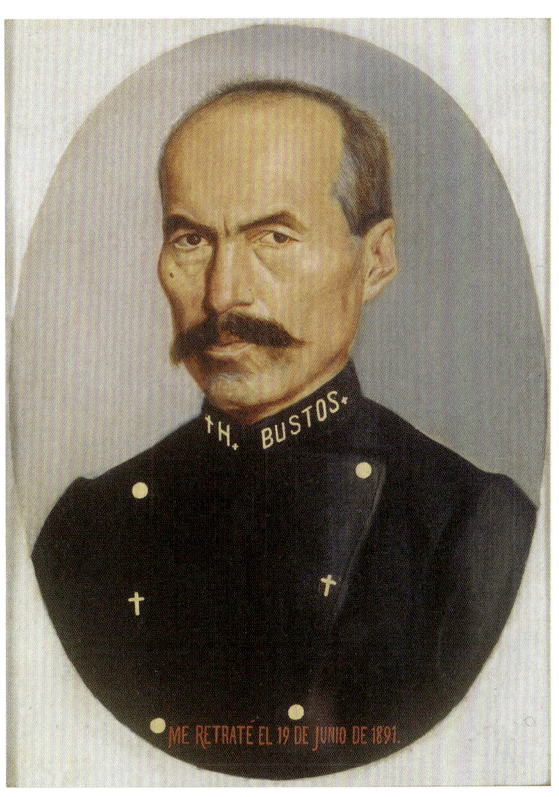

▲ 1.33 Hermenegildo Bustos, *Self-Portrait*, 1891.

Bustos was a highly talented but largely self-taught artist who approached his subjects with unflinching realism.

Hermenegildo Bustos (1832–1907),* Self-Portrait, *1891 Bustos was an Indigenous artist born in the village of Purisima del Rincon in the state of Guanajuato. He described himself as "Indian" in the inscription on the back of his self-portrait. He made his living as an ice-cream vendor, doing paintings on the side. Although highly talented, he considered himself to be an amateur. He was largely self-taught, having only had a few months of instruction under Juan Nepomunceno Herrera, a provincial painter in the nearby town of Leon. He painted for the local market, creating still-lives, **ex-votos** or religious offering paintings, and portraits of his friends and neighbors.

Bustos' portraits and self-portraits are characterized by an unflinching realism. He painted exactly what he saw in minute detail without flattering his sitters or improving upon nature. His portraits depict sober, hardworking provincials, who gaze with intensity at the viewer. In his self-portrait (Figure 1.33), he presents himself in the same hard-eyed manner. His image is modeled with a minimum of light and shadow but still achieves dimensionality. He has disguised his signature as collar insignia and an inscription in red across the bottom identifies the work as his portrait of June 19, 1891.

Rufino Tamayo (1899–1991),* Woman Spinning, *1943 Rufino Tamayo, a Zapotec, was born in Oaxaca de Juarez, Mexico. He attended art school for a time at the Escuela Nacional de Artes Plasticas in Mexico City but left after his third year because of dissatisfaction with the academic style of instruction. From that point on he was largely self-taught. He worked for a time as a draftsman at the National Museum of Archeology where he became interested in the pre-Hispanic art of Mexico.

The influences of both pre-Columbian and folk art are evident in his use of strong color contrasts, monumental form, and often grotesque imagery. He was also aware of modernist movements

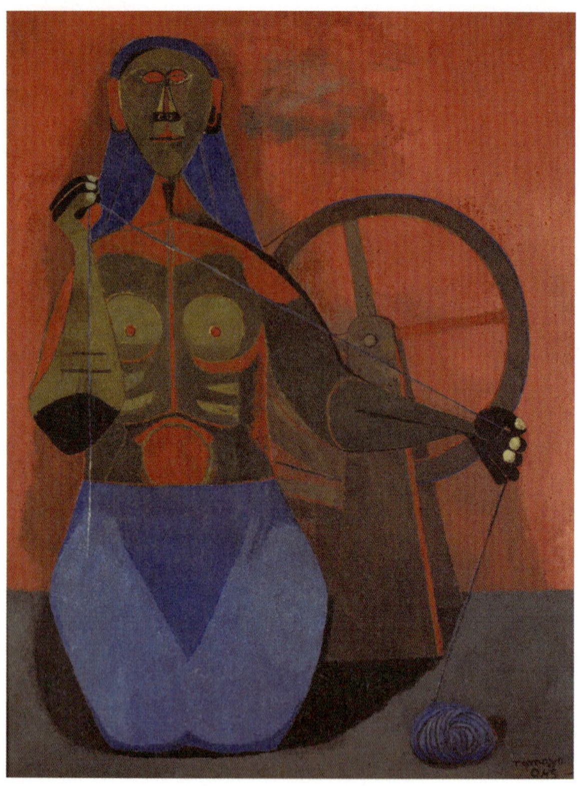

▲ 1.34 Rufino Tamayo, *Woman Spinning*, 1943.

Tamayo's paintings often draw inspiration from works of pre-Columbian art that he became familiar with while working at the National Museum of Archaeology as well as from his own experiences growing up as a Zapotec in Oaxaca.

such as Cubism, Expressionism, and Surrealism, and his work is indebted to those as well. Non-political, Tamayo was often harshly criticized and dismissed as an easel painter by the communist and socialist Tres Grandes (Diego Rivera, José Clemente Orozco, and David Alfaro Siqueiros), the mural painters who dominated Mexican art during the first half of the twentieth century. As a result, Tamayo spent most of his career abroad, working in New York and Paris. His *Woman Spinning* (Figure 1.34) draws heavily on the genre tradition of pre-Columbian Ameca-style ceramics from Jalisco. Like those ancient female forms, she sits back on her heels and wears only a simple skirt, leaving her torso bare. Her long face with long nose, ears, and blank eyes echo those of ancient figures.

Chapter Quick Review

The Early or Pre-Classic Period (c. 2000 BCE–100 CE)

- The Olmec are generally described as the "mother culture" of Mesoamerica because they built the first earthen pyramids, created monumental sculptures, figural and utilitarian pottery, and carved jade.
- Olmec monumental sculpture appears to have been raised to memorialize their kings and queens and to commemorate important historical events such as accords between peoples.

The Middle or Classic Period (c. 100 to 900 CE)

- This period is characterized by large-scale constructions in stone, the carving of stone stelas and relief tablets, use of ornamental stucco work, the use of a 365-day solar calendar and a 260-day ritual calendar, and the development of pictographic and hieroglyphic forms of writing. It was also a time of advances in mathematics, science, and engineering.
- In the Valley of Mexico, Teotihuacan grew to be the largest city in the New World and a leading center for the arts. Its influence was spread by trade and through the insertion of its elite into the founding dynasties of many Maya kingdoms.
- At this time several Maya kingdoms, including Tikal, Palenque, Copan, Yaxchilan, and others were producing great funerary temples, and carving stelas or tablets according to the quality of the local stone, to commemorate their rulers and record their mythical and actual histories.

The Late or Post-Classic Period (900–1450 CE)

- Beginning around 600 CE or perhaps earlier in some locations, many Mesoamerican civilizations experienced prolonged periods of unremitting drought that caused the collapse of Teotihuacan and ultimately, of the Maya kingdoms.
- In the Yucatan subterranean water sources allowed some of the Maya states to survive longer but most had succumbed to conditions by 1450 CE. During this late period Maya architects in the Puuc region developed concrete wall systems covered over by thin stone veneer tiles that could be mass-produced and assembled into decorative patterns on architecture.
- In the Valley of Mexico, the Toltec civilization rose to prominence after the fall of Teotihuacan. Its capital was at Tula, known to the later Aztecs as Tollan. Although the Toltec state is thought to have been militaristic, it drew its wealth from its vast trading empire.
- The architecture at Tula featured four- and five-level pyramid platforms, many of which were covered with carved and painted stone panels. The structures crowning these platforms were often constructed of perishable materials supported by stone columns, carved piers, and anthropomorphic columnar figures known as Atlantes.
- Although the Mexica or Aztecs arrived late in the Valley of Mexico by 1325, they had founded their capital of Tenochtitlan on an island in Lake Texcoco and began a program of conquest that brought much of Central Mexico under their control.
- The Aztecs claimed descent from the Toltecs and modeled their state art after that of Tula, even going so far as to strip reliefs and other portable works from the site to bring back to Tenochtitlan.
- When not intended for the state, Aztec sculptors could produce works of incredible naturalism. One unique feature of Aztec sculpture, whether state or vernacular, was that every surface, even those not seen, was carved.

The Colonial Period: Native Art in Mexico (1533–1821 CE)

- In the early years after the conquest of the Mexica in 1521, Indigenous artists were employed by the mendicant friars to create works of art which would promote the conversion of Indigenous Peoples.
- Fray Pedro de Gante opened a school for Native artists at San Jose de los Naturales in Mexico City. Many Indigenous art forms were used during these early years, including feather mosaics in which images, usually woodblocks, illustrating religious books brought to the New World by the friars, were reproduced using colored bird feathers.
- By 1550 sufficient numbers of artists had emigrated from Europe that the guild system was installed in Mexico City. Membership in the guild was restricted to those of European descent and Indigenous artists were unable to gain access to training or commissions.

Indigenous Artists in the Modern Era (1821–1950 CE)

- Native American artists in Mexico during this period were often self-taught or might study with a provincial artist for a few months. While out of the mainstream many of these artists produced works of great imagination and unflinching realism as amateur painters.

- One of the few Indigenous artists to achieve international status in the early years of the twentieth century was Rufino Tamayo; however, to do so, he had to live and work abroad.

Chapter Questions

1. Explain Paul Kirchhoff's criteria for defining the "High Cultures" of Mesoamerica. What characteristics was he looking for?
2. Why were the Olmec termed the "mother culture" of Mesoamerica? Describe some examples of Olmec art and how our understanding of them has changed in recent years.
3. Maya art is often generalized as if it was consistent across the Maya region. Describe the characteristics of its three main styles of architecture and sculpture. How did the local environment influence these styles?
4. Describe how the Spanish Conquest impacted the arts in Mexico after the Conquest. What impact did it have on Indigenous artists and the media they used? How did their telling of Christian stories use Indigenous sources to make them appeal to a converted population?

Key Terms and Figures

Key Terms

Adosada: Spanish term used to describe the platform pyramids attached "back-to-front" on the pyramids of the Sun, Moon, and Quetzalcoatl at Teotihuacan.

Aplanado: Teotihuacan cement made with mud, pea-gravel-size crushed scoria, and sand and used as a base coat over the stone veneer on pyramid platforms.

Atlantes: A column sculpted in the form of a standing warrior; four sit atop Pyramid B at Tula.

Atlatl: A stick-like device with a hook at one end and finger holes at the other that was used in Mesoamerica to throw darts, generalized as "spears," which increases the thrower's leverage and increases the distance the projectile will travel.

Buon fresco: "True fresco" process in which water-based pigment is applied while the plaster is still fresh or wet. As the pigments are drawn into the wet surface, the work must be done quickly. The advantage of this process is that it is more resistant to damage, being protected by a coat of calcium carbonate that forms as the plaster dries.

Chinampas: Aztec "floating gardens"; a system of artificial islands built in the shallow lake beds of the Valley of Mexico that were used to grow food.

Epigrapher: A person who studies and interprets ancient inscriptions such as Maya hieroglyphic writing.

Ex-voto: Christian images made as offerings to a saint, the Virgin, God in fulfillment of a vow, usually in gratitude for healing or deliverance from danger.

Fresco secco: A dry fresco process in which the pigments are applied after the plaster has dried. This process allows for finer details but is not as durable as buon fresco.

Mezzo fresco: A fresco process in which the unpainted plaster wall is re-wetted prior to the application of pigment to each new section.

Sascab: A deteriorated limestone that when mixed with water forms a concrete-like product that remains hard so long as it stays dry.

Tenon: A projecting piece of stone, often on the back of a carved head, that is held in place by insertion into a corresponding pocket called a mortise.

Tepetate: A type of volcanic tuff rock formed of compressed ash.

Tezantle: At Teotihuacan the plaster-like material used as a top coating on architecture.

Tlatoani: "Great Speaker"; the title given to the ruler of a town as well as to the Aztec emperor.

Tres Grandes: A name used to group the Mexican mural painters—Diego Rivera, José Clemente Orozco, and David Alfaro Siqueiros.

Key Figures

Ahuitzotl—Eighth Aztec emperor who expanded the empire and dedicated the last rebuilding of the Templo Mayor in 1487.

Cuauhtemoc—Nephew and son-in-law of Montezuma II; last Aztec emperor who was captured, tortured, and executed by Cortes.

Diego de Alvarado Huanitzin—Nahua noble and nephew of Montezuma II; presumed artist of the St. Gregory feather mosaic.

Fray Pedro de Gante—founder of San Jose de los Naturales, a school for Native artists.

Hun-Uitzil-Chac—founder of the Maya city of Uxmal.

Itzamnaaj Bahlam IV—King of Yaxchilan (r. 752–768 CE), who oversaw the installation of Yajaw Chan Muwaan II at Bonampak.

Jasaw Chan K'awiil I—eighth century King of Tikal who built Temple I and Temple II.

K'inich Janaab Pakal—King of Palenque who rebuilt the Palace, Temple XIII, and the Temple of Inscriptions.

Kirchhoff, Paul—German-Mexican anthropologist who coined the term "Mesoamerica" to describe the advanced cultures of Middle America.

K'uk' Bahlam—Fourth century founder of the Palenque dynasty.

Lachan Unen Mo'—Maya queen, also known as Lady 12 Macaw; wife of Jasaw Chan K'awiil who built Temple II as her commemorative monument.

Moctezuma II—Ninth ruler of the Aztecs, who believed Cortes was the returning Toltec god-king Quetzalcoatl and tried, unsuccessfully, to bribe the Spanish with gold to go away. His death in 1520 precipitated the Noche Triste when the Spanish fleeing Tenochtitlan were attacked by the Aztec.

Siyaj Chan K'awiil II—"Stormy Sky" was a fifth century ruler of Tikal who is memorialized by Stela 31.

Spearthrower Owl—Name derived from his glyphic representation of an owl holding an atlatl, he may have been a fourth- or fifth-century ruler of Teotihuacan, who seems to have been involved in the seating of dynasties at Tikal, Yaxchilan, Uaxactun, El Peru, and Tonina; he is depicted on the sides of Stela 31.

Yajaw Chan Muwaan II—Eighth century king of Bonampak, who commissioned the three rooms of murals in the Temple of the Murals, Bonampak.

Yax Nuun Ahiin I—Fourth century king of Tikal, who was a son of Spearthrower Owl.

Bibliography

Adams, Richard E. W. *Prehistoric Mesoamerica.* Little, Brown and Company, 1977.

Ades, Dawn. *Art in Latin America.* New Haven, CT: Yale University Press, 1989.

Álvarez-Sandoval, Brenda A., Linda R. Manzanilla, Mercedes González-Ruiz, Assumpico Malgosa, and Rafael Montiel. "Genetic Evidence Supports the Multiethnic Character of Teopancazco, a Neighborhood Center of Teotihuacan, Mexico (AD 200–600)." *PLoS ONE* 10, no. 7 (2015): e0132371. doi:10.1371/journal.pone.0132371.

Benson, Elizabeth, and Beatriz de la Fuente. *Olmec Art of Ancient Mexico.* Washington, DC: National Gallery of Art, 1996.

Berlo, Janet Catherine, editor. *Art, Ideology, and the City of Teotihuacan.* Washington, DC: Dumbarton Oaks Research Library and Collection, 1988.

Bernal, Ignacio. *The Olmec World.* Berkeley: University of California Press, 1969.

Berrin, Kathleen, and Esther Pasztory. *Teotihuacan: Art from the City of the Gods.* Thames and Hudson, 1993.

Blanton, Richard E., Stephen A. Kowalewski, Gary M. Feinman, and Laura M. Finsten. *Ancient Mesoamerica: A Comparison of Change in Three Regions.* 2nd edition. Cambridge and New York: Cambridge University Press, 1993.

Boone, Elizabeth Hill. *Stories in Red and Black: Pictorial Histories of the Aztecs and Mixtecs.* Austin: University of Texas Press, 2000.

Broda, Johanna, David Carrasco, and Eduardo Matos Moctezuma. *The Great Temple of Tenochtitlan: Center and Periphery in the Aztec World.* Berkeley: University of California Press, 1987.

Bruhns, Karen Olsen.

"The Olmec Queens," YUMTZILOB, 11.2/1999, pp. 163–189.

"Yesterday the Queen Wore...An Analysis of Women and Costume in the Public Art of the Late Classic Maya." In V.E. Miller (editor), The Role of Gender in Precolumbian Art and Architecture, Lanham: University Press of America, 1988, 105–134.

Bruhns, Karen Olsen, and Karen E. Stothert. *Women in Ancient America.* Norman: University of Oklahoma Press, 1999.

CarrascoVargas, Ramon, Veronica A. Vazquez Lopez, and Simon Martin. "Daily Life of the Ancient Maya Recorded on Murals at Calakmul, Mexico." *PNAS* 106, no. 46 (November 2009): 19245–19249. ww.pnas.org_cgi_doi_10.1073_pnas.0904374106.

Clewlow, C. William, Richard A. Cowan, James F. O'Connell, and Carlos Benemann. "Colossal Heads of the Olmec Culture." *Contributions of the University of California Archaeological Research Facility*, no. 4 (October 1967).

Cowgill, George L. *Ancient Teotihuacan: Early Urbanism in Central Mexico.* New York: Cambridge University Press, 2015.

"An Update on Teotihuacan," *Antiquity* 82 (2008): 962–975.

Davies, Nigel. *The Ancient Kingdoms of Mexico.* New York: Penguin, 1982.

The Aztec Empire. Norman: University of Oklahoma Press, 1987.

Davis, Whitney. "So-Called Jaguar-Human Copulation Scenes in Olmec Art." *American Antiquity* 43, no. 3 (July 1978): 453–457.

Diehl, Richard A. *The Olmecs: America's Frist Civilization.* London: Thames and Hudson, 2004.

Drucker, Philip. "Excavations at La Venta, Tabasco, 1955." *Smithsonian Institution Bureau of American Ethnology Bulletin* 170 (1959).

Edwards, Emily. *Painted Walls of Mexico: From Prehistoric Times until Today.* Austin: University of Texas Press, 1966.

Evans, Susan Toby. *Ancient Mexico & Central America: Archaeology and Culture History.* London: Thames and Hudson, 2008.

Fash, William L., and Leonardo Lopez Lujan, editors. *The Art of Urbanism: How Mesoamerican Kingdoms Represented Themselves in Architecture and Imagery*. Washington, DC: Dumbarton Oaks Research Library and Collections, 2009.

Fletcher, Jessica M.

"Stuccoed Tripod Vessels from Teotihuacan: An Examination of Materials and Manufacture." *Journal of the American Institute for Conservation*, 41, No. 2 (Summer, 2002): 139–154.

Follensbee, Billie J. A. "Formative Period Gulf Coast Ceramic Figurines: The Key to Identifying Sex, Gender, and Age Groups in Gulf Coast Olmec Imagery." In *Mesoamerican Figurines: Small-Scale Indices of Large-Scale Social Phenomena*, edited by Cristina T. Halperin, 77–118. Gainesville: University of Florida, 2009.

"Unsexed Images, Gender-Neutral Costume and Gender-Ambiguous Costume in Formative Period Gulf Coast Cultures." In *Wearing Culture: Dress and Regalia in Early Mesoamerica and Central America*, edited by Heather Orr and Matthew Looper, 207–252. Boulder: University Press of Colorado, 2014.

Fuente, Beatriz de la. "Olmec Sculpture: The First Mesoamerican Art." Symposium Papers XXXV: Olmec Art and Archaeology in Mesoamerica, *Studies in the History of Art* 58 (2000): 252–263.

Gill, Richardson B. *The Great Maya Droughts: Water, Life, and Death*. Albuquerque: University of New Mexico Press, 2000.

Gillespie, Susan D. *The Aztec Kings*. Tucson: University of Arizona Press, 1989.

"Archaeological Drawings as Re-Presentations: The Maps of Complex A, La Venta, Mexico." *Latin American Antiquity* 22, no. 1 (March 2011): 3–36.

Golden, Charles, Stephen Houston, and Joel Skidmore, editors. *Maya Archaeology 2*. San Francisco, CA: Precolumbia Mesoweb Press, 2012.

Gonzáles Lauck, Rebecca B. "The Architectural Setting of Olmec Sculpture Clusters at La Venta, Tabasco." Original manuscript version submitted to *The Place of Sculpture in Mesoamerica's Preclassic Transition: Context, Use and Meaning*, edited by Julia Guernsey, John Clark, and Barbara Arroyo. March 2008.

"Acerca de pirámides de tierra y seres sobrenaturales: observaciones preliminares en torno al edificio C-1, La Venta, Tabasco." *Arqueología*, 2ª. época, no.17 (1997): 79–97.

Graham, John A. "Studies in Ancient Mesoamerica, IV." *Contributions of the University of California Archaeological Research Facility*, no. 41 (December 1979).

Halperin, Christina T., Katherine A. Faust, Rhonda Taube, and Aurore Giguet, editors. *Mesoamerican Figurines: Small-Scale Indices of Large-Scale Social Phenomena*. Gainesville: University of Florida, 2009.

Hammond, Norman. *Ancient Maya Civilization*. New Brunswick, NJ: Rutgers University Press, 1988.

Harrison, Peter D. *The Lords of Tikal: Rulers of an Ancient Maya City*. London: Thames and Hudson, 1999.

Heizer, Robert F. "Analysis of Two Low Relief Sculptures from La Venta." *Contributions of the University of California Archaeological Research Facility*, no. 3 (August 1967): 25–55.

Heizer, Robert F., John A. Graham, and Lewis K. Napton. "The 1968 Investigations at La Venta." *Contributions of the University of California Archaeological Research Facility*, no. 5. 127–154.

Heizer, Robert F., Tillie Smith, and Howel Williams. "Notes on Colossal Head no. 2 from Tres Zapotes." *American Antiquity* 31, no. 1 (July 1965): 102–104.

Heyden, Doris. "An Interpretation of the Cave Underneath the Pyramid of the Sun in Teotihuacan, Mexico." *American Antiquity* 40, no. 2 (April 1975): 131–147.

Heyden, Doris, and Paul Gendrop. *Pre-Columbian Architecture of Mesoamerica*. New York, NY: Harry N. Abrams, Inc., 1975.

Marken, Damien B., editor. *Palenque: Recent Investigations at the Classic Maya Center.* Lanham, MD: Altamira Press, 2007.

Martin, Simon. "Hieroglyphs from the Painted Pyramid: The Epigraphy of Chiik Nahb Structure Sub 1–4, Calakmul, Mexico." In *Maya Archaeology 2*, 60–81. San Francisco, CA: Precolumbia Mesoweb Press, 2012.

Martin, Simon, and Nikolai Grube. *Chronicle of the Maya Kings and Queens: Deciphering the Dynasties of the Ancient Maya.* 2nd edition. London: Thames and Hudson, 2008.

Marquina, Ignacio. *Arquitectura Prehispanica.* Instituto Nacional de Antropologia e Historia Secretaria de Educacion Publica, Mexico, 1964.

Mastache, Alba Guadalupe and Robert H. Cobean

"Ancient Tollan: The Sacred Precinct." *RES: Anthropology and Aesthetics*, no. 38 (Autumn 2000): 100–133.

Miller, Arthur G. *The Mural Painting of Teotihuacan.* Washington, DC: Dumbarton Oaks, 1973.

Miller, Mary and Simon Martin. *Courtly Art of the Ancient Maya.* New York: Thames and Hudson, 2004.

Millon, Rene, and Bruce Drewill. "Earlier Structures within the Pyramid of the Sun at Teotihuacan." *American Antiquity* 26, no. 3 (January 1961): 371–380.

Millon, Rene, Bruce Drewill, and James A. Bennyhoff. "The Pyramid of the Sun at Teotihuacan: 1959 Investigations." *Transactions of the American Philosophical Society* 55, Part 6 (1965).

Molina-Montes, Augusto. "Archaeological Buildings: Restoration or Misrepresentation." In *Falsifications and Misreconstructions of Pre-Columbian Art*, edited by Elizabeth H. Boone. Washington DC: Dumbarton Oaks, 1978.

Navarrete, Carlos. "The Olmec Rock Carvings at Pijijiapan, Chiapas, Mexico and Other Olmec Pieces from Chiapas and Guatemala." *Papers of the New World Archaeological Foundation*, no. 35 (1975).

Nicholson, H. B., and Eloise Quiñones Keber. *Art of Aztec Mexico: Treasures of Tenochtitlan.* Washington, DC: National Gallery of Art, 1983.

Orr, Heather, and Matthew G. Looper, editors. *Wearing Culture: Dress and Regalia in Early Mesoamerica and Central America.* Boulder: University Press of Colorado, 2014.

Parmington, Alexander. *Space and Sculpture in the Classic Maya City.* Cambridge University Press, 2011.

Pasztory, Esther. *Teotihuacan: An Experiment in Living.* Norman: University of Oklahoma Press, 1997.

"The Iconography of the Teotihuacan Tlaloc." The Iconography of the Teotihuacan Tlaloc. *Studies in Pre-Columbian Art and Archaeology*, no. 15 (1974): 1–22.

Pool, Christopher A. "From Olmec to Epi-Olmec at Tres Zapotes, Veracruz, Mexico." Symposium Papers XXXV: Olmec Art and Archaeology in Mesoamerica. *Studies in the History of Art* 58 (2000): 136–153.

Olmec Archaeology and Early Mesoamerica. Cambridge University Press, 2007.

Porter, James B. "Olmec Colossal Heads as Recarved Thrones: 'Mutilation,' Revolution, and Recarving." *Anthropology and Aesthetics* 18, no. 1 (Spring–Autumn, 1989): 22–29.

Robertson, Merle Greene. *The Sculpture of Palenque.* Volumes I–IV. Princeton, NJ: Princeton University Press, 1985.

Robertson, Merle Greene, editor. *Sixth Palenque Round Table, 1986.* Norman: University of Oklahoma Press, 1991.

Sahagún, Bernadino de.

General History of the Things of New Spain: Florentine Codex, 1579. 13 volumes. Translated by Arthur J.O. Anderson and Charles F. Dibble. Santa Fe: School of American Research, 1961.

Sandweiss, Daniel H., and Jeffrey Quilter, editors. *El Niño: Catastrophism, and Culture Change in Ancient America.* Washington, DC: Dumbarton Oaks Research Library and Collection, 2008.

Schele, Linda, and David Freidel. *A Forest of Kings: The Untold Story of the Ancient Maya*, New York: Quill William Morrow, 1990.

Schele, Linda, and Mary Ellen Miller. *The Blood of Kings: Dynasty and Ritual in Maya Art.* Fort Worth, TX: Kimbell Art Museum, 1986.

Schuster, Angela M. H. "New Tomb at Teotihuacan." *Archaeology.* December 4, 1998. archive.archaeology.org/online/features/mexico/.

Staller, John E. "Lighting in Mesoamerica: Manifestations and Transformations." April 4, 2013. http://www.mexicolore.co.uk/aztecs/home/lightning-in-mesoamerica.

Staneko, Justine Cecilia

Peeking at the Puuc: New Views on the Design, Engineering, and Construction of Ancient Maya Architecture from Yucatan and Northern Campeche, Mexico. Berkeley: University of California. Dissertation. 1996.

Stephens, John L. *Incidents of Travel in Central America, Chiapas and Yucatan.* 2 Volumes, New York: Dover

Publications, 1969.

Stierlin, Henri. *The Maya Palaces and Pyramids of the Rainforest.* Cologne: Taschen, 2001.

Stirling, Matthew W.

Stone Monuments of Rio Chiquito, Veracruz, Mexico, Smithsonian Institution: Bureau of American Ethnology, Bulletin 157, Anthropological Papers, No. 43, Washington: U.S. Government Printing Office, 1955.

Stuart, David, and George Stuart. *Palenque: Eternal City of the Maya.* London: Thames and Hudson, 2008.

Sugiyama, Saburo, and Ruben Cabrera Castro. "The Moon Pyramid Project and the Teotihuacan State Polity." *Ancient Mesoamerica* 18 (2007): 109–125.

Sugiyama, Nawa, Saburo Sugiyama, and Alejandro Sarabia G. "Inside the Sun Pyramid at Teotihuacan, Mexico: 2008–2011 Excavations and Preliminary Results." *Latin American Antiquity* 24, no. 4 (2013): 403–432.

Toussaint, Manuel. *Colonial Art in Mexico.* Translated and edited by Elizabeth Wilder Weismann. Austin: University of Texas Press, 1967.

Townsend, Richard F. *The Aztecs.* London: Thames and Hudson, 1992.

Vela, Enrique, editor. *Olmecs.* Arqueologia Mexicana, INAH, Mexico, D.F. 1996.

Wernecke, Daniel Clark

A Stone Canvas: Interpreting Maya Building Materials and Construction Technology. Austin:University of Texas. Dissertation. 2005.

Williams, Howel, and Robert F. Heizer. "Sources of Rocks Used in Olmec Monuments." *Contributions of the University of California Archaeological Research Facility*, no. 1 (September 1965).

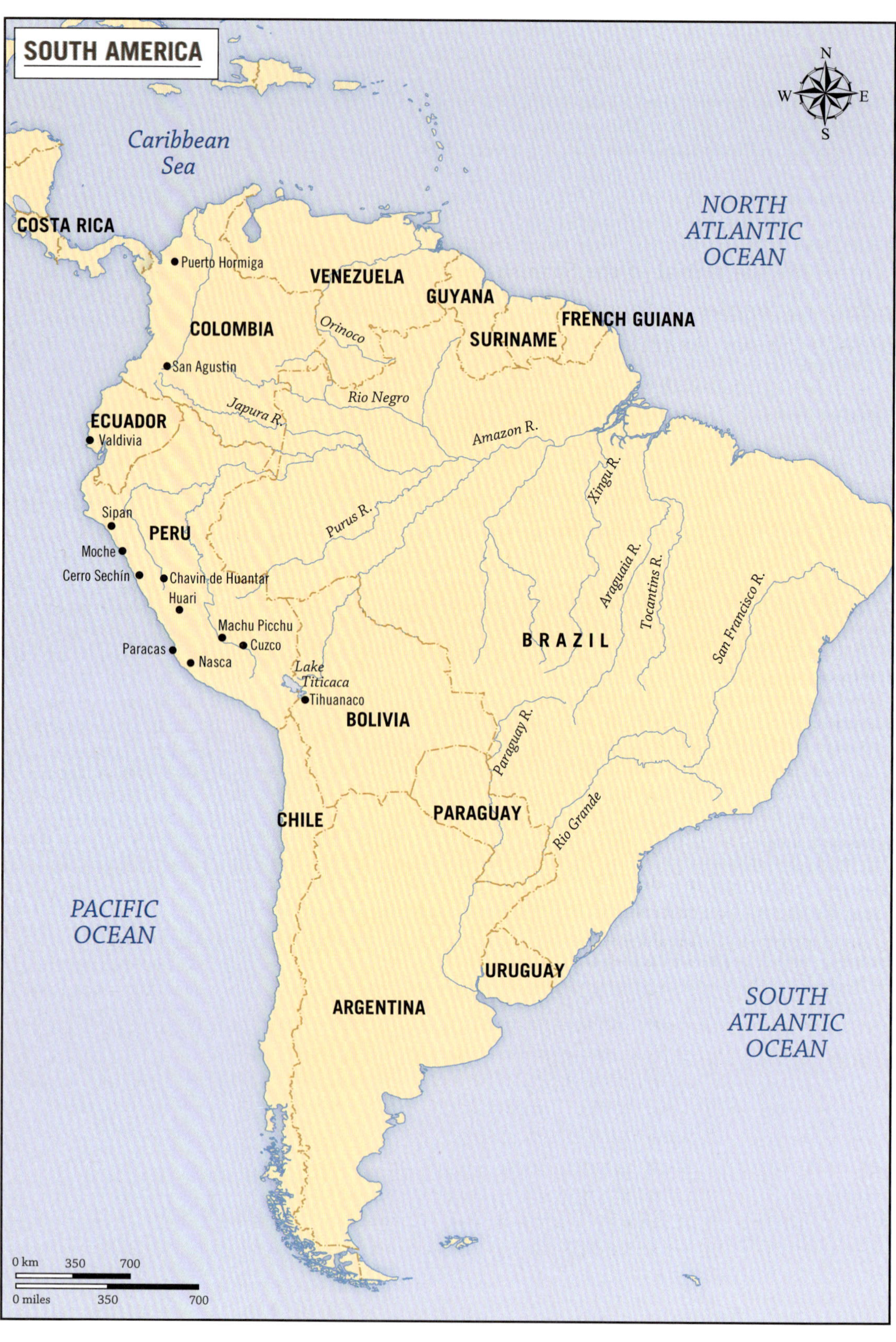

SOUTH AMERICA
N
W
E
S
Caribbean Sea
NORTH ATLANTIC OCEAN
COSTA RICA
Puerto Hormiga
VENEZUELA
GUYANA
FRENCH GUIANA
SURINAME
COLOMBIA
Orinoco
San Agustin
Rio Negro
Japura R.
ECUADOR
Valdivia
Amazon R.
Xingu R.
Sipan
Purus R.
PERU
Moche
Araguaia R.
Tocantins R.
Cerro Sechín
Chavin de Huantar
San Francisco R.
Huari
Machu Picchu
BRAZIL
Paracas
Cuzco
Nasca
Lake Titicaca
Tihuanaco
BOLIVIA
Paraguay R.
PARAGUAY
CHILE
Rio Grande
PACIFIC OCEAN
URUGUAY
ARGENTINA
SOUTH ATLANTIC OCEAN
0 km
350
700
0 miles
350
700

South America

2

Brief Overview

Long before the arrival of the Spanish in the New World, the Indigenous Peoples of South America built great ceremonial centers with monumental architecture, vast highway systems, and immense earthworks. South American artists created dimensional wall murals that recounted historical and mythical events, made painted and modeled pottery, worked silver, gold, and copper alloys into beautiful objects, carved relief sculpture, and wove astonishing textiles from native cotton and camelid fibers. Their farmers domesticated corn, tobacco, potatoes, peanuts, sweet potatoes, pineapples, and manioc, and used a variety of medicinal and ritual plants such as coca and hallucinogenic cacti.

Unfortunately, much of South America outside of the Andean zone, along the western edge of the continent, is not well known. Some areas, for example, the Amazonian region, are just now receiving archaeological attention, spurred by discovery of massive earthworks in the form of geometric trenches in the Bolivian and Brazilian rainforests. In the next few decades, the picture of South America as a zone of Andean high cultures surrounded by a vast wilderness of virtually unoccupied tropical forest may well change dramatically and in exciting new ways.

After the Spanish Conquest, South America was organized into the Viceroyalty of Peru, with its administrative capital at Lima. Later a second viceroyalty of New Granada was formed to serve what are now the countries of Colombia, Ecuador, Panama and Venezuela. During the Colonial Period the production of many traditional crafts declined or in some cases ceased altogether as Native Peoples were encouraged to accept Spanish dress, religion, and culture. The main focus of artistic production during this time was on religious items to advance the Catholic Church's mission of converting conquered peoples to Christianity. Many Indigenous artists in the Cuzco

Chapter Objectives

1. Understand how the development of Andean art and architecture was uniquely tied to the environments in which people lived.
2. Recognize how early Andean artists, such as the Chavín, used artistic techniques such as modular width, figurative elaboration, and contour rivalry in their art, and how these techniques and some motifs were adopted and refined by succeeding cultures.
3. Understand how the Inca affinity for stone as something inherently sacred influenced the way they used it in their art and architecture, especially in the capital of Cuzco and at royal estates such as Machu Picchu.
4. Explain how the Spanish Conquest impacted the arts and artists of the Andean region and the role of "Indian" as a symbol in the post-Independence nations of South America.

area became members of the painter's guild and worked alongside Europeans to produce religious works. The names of a few Indigenous painters, such as Diego Quispe Tito, are known but it is often difficult to identify their surviving works since most did not sign them. One of the more popular Cuzqueño subjects of this era are the wonderful paintings, glittering with gold, of archangels dressed in the fashionable livery of Spanish gentlemen and carrying the fifteenth century long guns known as arquebuses. In addition to paintings and sculptures, some incredible examples of metalwork, in the form of liturgical vessels, were made in Colombia during the Colonial Period. These include three works considered to be the most valuable items made in the Western Hemisphere: the Crown of the Andes, the Custodia of San Ignacio, Bogota, known as "La Lechuga" or "lettuce" because of its encrustation of emeralds, and the Custodia Grande de Santa Clara, Tunja.

After Independence in 1821, Latin American artists influenced by the Romantic movement in Europe turned to the "Indian" as a motif for expressing the history of their newly independent nations. The "Indian" became the symbol of an American Golden Age in the time before colonization. Among the more iconic images of this type are Francisco Laso's *The Indian Potter*, 1855, and José Sabogal's *The Indian Mayor of Chincheros: Varayoc*, 1925.

During the twentieth century few Indigenous artists achieved prominence in the Andes. However, in many traditional communities today, Indigenous artisans continue to make ceramics and other crafts, following the same techniques used by their ancestors; some of which are marketed to tourists as the reproductions they are, but others are not. The revival of this cottage industry may have been inspired in part by increased archaeological work, conducted in the Andes, during the late nineteenth and twentieth centuries that inspired a popular interest in antiquities.

Over the course of the last century several cultural chronologies have been proposed for different Andean cultures, zones, and regions. The most commonly used divides the coast and highlands into three zones each and establishes a chronology, similar to that for ancient Egypt, of three Horizon Periods when certain cultures were politically dominant across regions and three Intermediate Periods when no group was ascendant. While this system may be meaningful for the archaeologist, it is somewhat unwieldy for the study of art history. For that reason and in an effort to create a manageable and comparable system, this chapter will group the Andean cultures into three chronological units, roughly paralleling the divisions established for Mesoamerica: Early Cultures (2200–200 BCE), Middle Cultures (100 BCE–1000 CE), and Late Cultures (1200–1550 CE).

timeline

DATE	TYPE	EVENT
		BCE
c. 3500	Art	Valdivia, Ecuador, ceramic tradition began
c. 3100	Art	Puerta Hormiga, Colombia, ceramic industry
	History	Sechín and Casma Valleys occupied
c. 2200	Art	Cerro Sechín founded
c. 2140	Art	Ceramics made at Monagrillo in Panama
c. 1800	Art	First pottery made in Peru
c. 1200	Art	Chavín de Huántar ceremonial site established in the highlands
	Art	Lanzón sculpture erected in Old Temple at Chavín de Huántar
c. 900	Art	New Temple at Chavín de Huántar, Black and White Portal, Circular Plaza reliefs, and Raimondi Stela
c. 500	History	Construction ceases at Chavín de Huántar
c. 400	History	Paracas culture evolves along the South Coast
c. 200	History	Nasca culture evolves, Cahuachi ceremonial center
	Art	First Paracas/Nasca geoglyphs created
	Art	Tiahuanaco established south of Lake Titicaca in Bolivia
		CE
c. 50	History	Moche culture evolves
c. 100	Art	San Augustin ceremonial site established in Colombia
c. 200	History	Paracas ended
	Art	Huaca del Sol and Huaca de la Luna began at Moche
c. 600	History	Huari expansion began in south central Andes of Peru
c. 650	History	Nasca ended
c. 800	Art	Diquis culture of Costa Rica and Panama
	History	Moche ceremonial center abandoned
c. 850	History	Moche culture collapsed
c. 900	History	San Agustin culture ended
c. 1000	History	Incas arrived in the Valley of Cuzco
	History	Tiahuanaco culture collapsed
	History	Huari Empire ended
c. 1200	History	Manco Capac became first Sapa Inca

DATE	TYPE	EVENT
		CE
1438	History	Pachacuti fended of Chanca attack on Cuzco and became Sapa Inca
	Art	Pachacuti laid out redesign of Cuzco
c. 1450	History	Machu Picchu and Ollantaytambo established
c. 1463	History	Incas conquered Chimu Empire
1487	History	Northern (second) Inca capital established in Quito
1527	History	Sapa Inca Huayna Capac dies of smallpox in Quito without naming a successor, civil war erupts between his sons Huascar and Atahualpa
1530	History	Atahualpa murders Huascar and takes the throne
1531	History	Francisco Pizarro lands in Peru
1532	History	Pizarro captures Atahualpa and holds him for ransom
1533	History	Atahualpa pays, is freed, arrested for the murder of his brother,
		baptized and executed
	History	Cuzco is sacked by the Spanish
1534	History	Church of Santo Domingo built over the Koricancha in Cuzco
1542	History	Viceroyalty of Peru established
1572	History	Sapa Inca Tupac Amaru captured and executed by the Spanish
1611	Art	Diego Quispe Tito born in Cuzco
1633	Art	Church of Santo Domingo consecrated in Cuzco
1780	History	Inca uprising under Tupac Amaru II
1799	History	Alexander von Humboldt explored Venezuela
1801	History	Humboldt explored the Andes
1821	History	General Jose de San Martin proclaimed Peruvian independence
1825	History	Peru achieved independence
1855	Art	Francisco Laso (Peruvian) painted *The Indian Potter*
1866	History	War with Spain
1879	History	Pacific War with Chile began
1925	History	Jose Sabogal (Peruvian) painted *The Indian Mayor of Chincheros*: Varayoc

The Early Cultures (2200 BCE–200 CE)

In many parts of the world the appearance of pottery-making is an indicator of the rise of agrarian societies with permanent settlements and developing social hierarchies. While pottery does appear very early in northern South America, beginning around 4640–4500 BCE at Real Alto and Valdivia in Ecuador, and around 3800 BCE on the north coast of Colombia at Puerto Hormiga, none of these sites had ritual centers or large architectural works. In the Peruvian pre-ceramic era are found the beginnings of state-level polities with the ability to command labor, sometimes on a regional level, for the construction of ceremonial centers with pyramid platforms and temples. There is also significant evidence of craft production, including twinned and woven textiles, pyro-engraved gourds, repoussé metalworking, and elaborate stone relief carving, but until 1800 BCE no pottery was made. The slow start of Peruvian ceramics was not due to lack of cultural development but to the scarcity of sufficient fuel resources in the harsh climates of the coastal desert and Andean highlands, pointing up the importance of environmental resources in the development of the arts in any specific location.

Cerro Sechín (2200–1600 BCE)

The Casma and Sechín valleys of Peru offer some very early examples of monumental buildings. Several sites are known from the two valleys, some of which are thought to date from the fourth millennium BCE. One of the larger, if not the oldest, of these sites is Cerro Sechín.

THE CENTRAL STRUCTURE

The focus of the ceremonial district of the city was the Central Structure, a quadrangular, three-tiered platform with rounded corners and a staircase on the northern side (Figure 2.1). The wide stair led up to a multi-room building, consisting of a main chamber on the south,

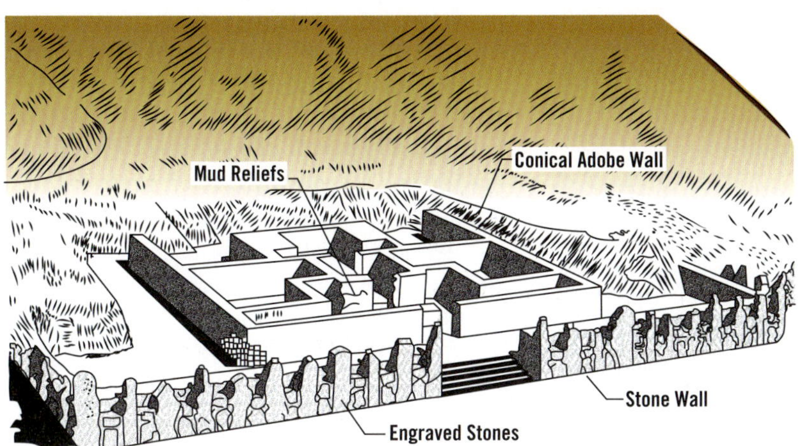

◀ **2.1** Reconstruction drawing of the Central Structure at Cerro Sechín showing mud reliefs on the adobe temple and the outer stone relief wall.

The relief images on the wall surrounding the temple are unusual in their public display of ritual sacrifices.

and several side chambers, which were accessed through a long central atrium. The building was constructed with cone-shaped adobes, set in mud mortar and plastered over to create a smooth wall surface. The inside walls of the chambers were painted blue-gray while those of the atrium and the building exterior were pink. The two walls flanking the entrance to the structure were decorated with murals of wild felines, most likely pumas, painted with a bold black contour line; the beasts had white-tipped red claws and yellow ocher paws (Fuchs and Patzschke 2013, 80–81).

In later periods the platform was enlarged to form a two-tiered base that measured 171 feet (53 m) on a side. The walls of the enlarged platform were again painted pink but the new reliefs featured realistic fish that were almost 12 feet (3.6 m) long and painted a contrasting blue-green. Additional images of open-mouthed fish and falling human figures adorned the walls of the new temple structure. The scene has been interpreted as a narrative of human sacrifice, perhaps by casting victims off a cliff into the ocean.

▼ 2.2 Cerro Sechín, Central Structure, Stone Relief of a Warrior, c. 2000 BCE. Approx. 13 ft. high.

Carved as a sunken relief this image depicts one of the victorious Sechín warriors, who stands between smaller stone reliefs depicting dismembered body parts.

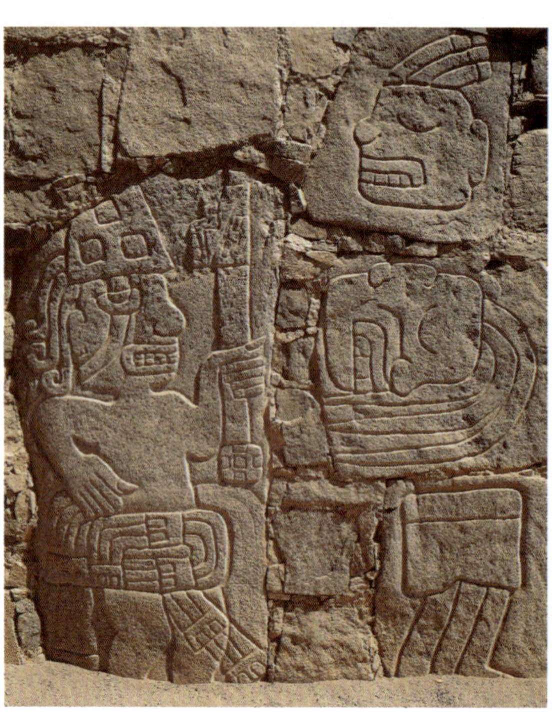

Stone Reliefs, c. 2000 BCE Sometime after 2000 BCE, the base platform of the Central Structure was surrounded by a stone wall approximately 13 feet (4 m) high. The most prominent feature of this wall is its approximately three hundred carved granite monoliths set with clay mortar. The granite slabs are carved with figures who appear to be taking part in rituals that include a victory procession of the Cerro Sechin military and other dignitaries, the sacrifice of captives, and the display of war trophies. The larger slabs are carved with striding figures of warriors, who are divided into two processional lines by the central stairs. Smaller blocks, stacked up along the wall, depict the gruesome trophies of war, including severed heads with gouged-out eyes, amputated arms, legs and feet, disemboweled intestines, and human eyeballs laid out in neat rows (Onuki 2013, 83). The blocks are carved in **sunken relief**, meaning that the surface of the image does not project beyond that of the ground. The figures are formed by sharply incised contour lines, angled so as to create a shadow line around the image. Full figures are rendered in **composite view** with head and limbs shown in profile and the torso frontal.

The striding warriors (Figure 2.2) wear fez-like hats, marked with three rectangular elements, from which three long strands of hair, feathers, or cloth streamers extend;

and loincloths with similar streamer-like elements at the front and rear. Faces are marked with a wide band of face paint extending from the hair line, over one eye, and ending beneath the ear; their mouths are drawn back in fierce expressions. Although no traces of pigment remain, it is probable that the reliefs were originally colored. In addition to the victorious warriors, there are images of what appear to be the enemy rendered in a fully frontal manner; some of these are dressed in tunics with scalloped hems while others are nude. Most of these figures show signs of mutilation or bisection suggesting that they have been sacrificed.

The Cerro Sechín reliefs are unusual not only in the brutality of the depictions in this historical narrative but in their placement. Scenes of sacrifice are often set within the confines of a sacred precinct as in the sea sacrifice scene on the walls of the Central Structure, since human sacrifice is usually a ritual act, intended to propitiate the gods. The Cerro Sechín reliefs are placed in what appears to be public space, suggesting they are a historical narrative rather than a sacred one.

Chavín de Huántar (1200–500 BCE)

The Chavín Culture, named for the site of Chavín de Huántar, is comprised of several stylistically related sites, which seem to have shared a common iconography during the late second and first millenniums BCE. There is some evidence to suggest that Chavín may have been rooted in earlier Sechín, Nepeña Valley, and Kotosh cultures. Chavín influence was so widespread across the highland and coastal areas that it is considered to be Peru's first **Horizon Style,** meaning a style that dominated a widespread area across cultures. Chavín sites are known for their monumental stone and adobe architecture, finely carved stone sculpture, modeled clay friezes, repoussé gold work, painted textiles, and ceramics.

The type site of Chavín de Huántar is located at the foot of a high mountain valley in the Cordillera Blanca range of the Andes. It sits far above the tree line, at an altitude of 10,335 feet (3,180 m), on a 17-acre plot of land where the Mosna and Huachecsa Rivers come to confluence.

EARLY ARCHITECTURE

The architecture of Chavín de Huántar consists of connected platform mounds, originally with crowning structures and stairs, and associated terraces and sunken plazas. These constructions were built, enlarged, buried, and built-over several times during the occupation of the site. Based on the analysis of seams in the buildings, fifteen different phases of construction have been postulated (Kembel 2001, IV). Unlike Mesoamerican pyramids, which were solid, many of the mound structures at Chavín de Huántar include interior galleries and shrines.

The Old Temple, c. 1200 BCE The earliest structures at Chavín de Huántar are part of the complex originally designated as the "Old Temple" (Figure 2.3). In its final form, the temple appears as a U-shaped structure, formed by three rectangular masonry platforms of unequal height and size, which originally supported shrines. While the platforms have substantial cores of rubble fill, they are not solid as in the case of Mesoamerican pyramids. The platforms are honeycombed with galleries, ventilation ducts, and drainage channels, all of which appear to have been designed as part of the original phases of construction. Since the platforms were not the same height, steep staircases were added to provide access to the structures on top. Recent research at Chavín de Huántar shows a complex pattern of building stages for the Old Temple, beginning in the late second millennium BCE with the erection of the Lanzón platform and the larger one to its south. In subsequent phases the original Lanzón platform and its summit structure were encased within a new mound, making what was once an above-ground shrine into a subterranean one. In the later construction phases that followed, care was taken to preserve access, through a series of galleries, to the original Lanzón shrine.

The various additions to the Old Temple brought the walls of its highest section up to a height of 39 feet (12 m) in its final configuration. To unify the sections visually, the temple was covered with a stone veneer laid in courses and set with clay mortar; the walls were **battered** (sloped backwards) as they rose for greater stability. The stones used in the earliest parts of the structure are rougher, being unworked local quartzite, but those of later phases, particularly after 900 BCE, utilized cut granite, sandstone, and limestone, some of which

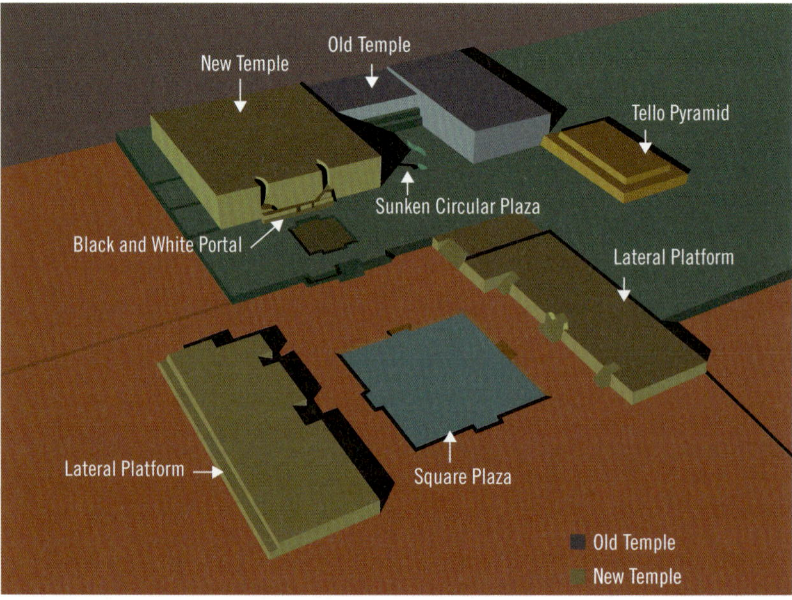

▶ **2.3** Chavín de Huántar, Plan showing the Old/New Temple Complex and Plazas, c. 1200–900 BCE.

The main temple complex at Chavín began as a complex of three platforms and their temple structures arranged in a U-shape. During the time that the site was occupied, the temple platforms were repeatedly enlarged, sometimes encapsulating earlier structures, and the areas around processional courts were built up creating the effect of "sunken" plazas.

were brought to the site from considerable distances (up to 24 miles or 40 km) and higher elevations.

Chavín masons created a visual richness to the wall surface by laying up the courses in a rhythmic two-over-one pattern, consisting of two courses of thin slabs followed by a single row of thick blocks. Toward the top, the walls were adorned with more than a hundred tenon heads, carved in the round, representing human, feline, and composite half-human and half-animal beings. Capping the walls was an overhanging cornice of large stones incised with figures of humans, animals, and hybrid beings all marching in procession (Rick 2013, 150–165).

The Lanzón, c. 1200 BCE The Lanzón (Figure 2.4) is a roughly triangular shaft of white granite with a notched, haft-like top that stands more than 14 feet (4.53 m) tall and depicts across its surface the Primary Deity of the Old Temple. The sculpture was named, in the early twentieth century, by the Peruvian archaeologist Julio C. Tello, who saw its triangular shape as similar to that of a lance. The monolith sits in the center of a small cruciform-chamber capable of accommodating only two or three people at a time. Initially installed in the shrine atop the

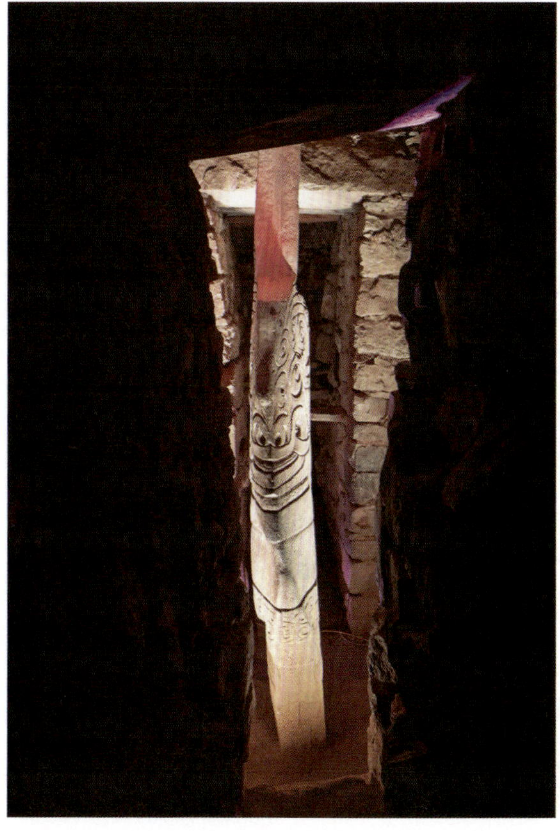

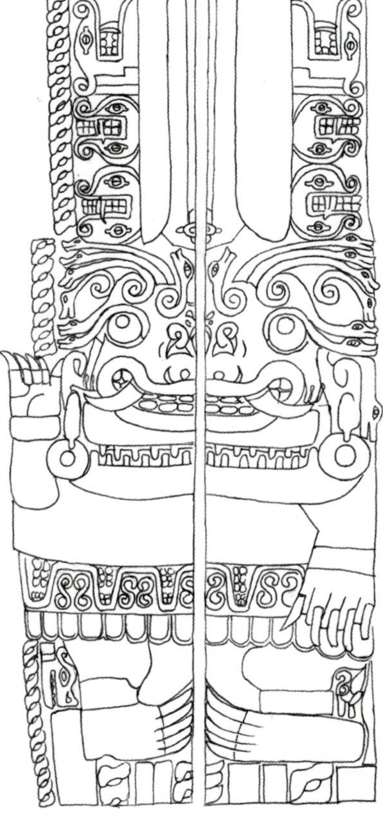

▼ 2.4 Chavín de Huántar, Old Temple Lanzón Gallery, Lanzón Monolith, c. 1200 BCE.

The sculpture consists of two profile images that merge along the narrow edge of the shaft to create a frontal image of the Chavín Primary Deity, sometimes called the "Smiling God."

earliest phase of construction, the sculpture is now buried deep within several subsequent enlargements of the platform. Its foot is sunk below the floor of the chamber and the top of its shaft passes through the ceiling into what was once an upper gallery. Because the Lanzón is irremovably integrated into its building, it is one of the few examples of an Andean sculpture still in its original location.

Depicted across the two faces of the Lanzón is the being known as the Primary Deity, or "Smiling God". The image of this god appears in a wide variety of media from across the Chavín horizon. While taking an overall anthropomorphic form, the god is adorned with zoomorphic elements. The animal parts are **visual kennings** or metaphors, intended to give a nuanced reading of his characteristics; this is sometimes referred to as figurative elaboration.

In depicting the Primary Deity on the Lanzón, its Chavín carver is not only providing a poetic description of the divine being but is also attempting to show the deity from all sides at once. The two long sides of the shaft are carved as the left and right profiles of the being, which, when viewed along its narrowest point, merge to create a frontal image, rendering him as both frontal and profile at the same time. This is most easily seen in roll-out rubbings of the sculpture.

Although the sculpture is monumental in scale, the figure is rendered in a squat, 1-to-3 ratio of proportion and, except for the opposing hand positions, is bilaterally symmetrical. A groove has been cut into the narrow part of the upper shaft. This groove seems to have been a channel for fluid offerings poured over the image from the upper chamber. The fluids would have collected in the cruciform well in the top of the deity's head and then overflowed to bathe the image. The deity wears a tunic with a scalloped fringe and decorated neckline, partially visible under his collar ornament and his waist is encircled by a belt decorated with mirror image feline heads. He wears plain cuffs, anklets, and simple pendant earrings with a dangling hoop. It has been suggested that the notched portion of the shaft represents the god's headdress as it is marked with the same motif as the belt. The face of the god is fearsome, the most prominent feature being the upturned and fanged mouth; he has flaring nostrils, upward looking eyes, and snakes for hair and eyebrows. Despite its frightening aspect, the Lanzón has some remarkably naturalistic detail; for example wrist, palmar, and digital joint creases, as well as nail folds, are all clearly incised on the upraised hand of the deity.

The Lanzón deity is rendered in a hard, linear style across the largely unworked surface of the monolith; no attempt seems to have been made to create a planar surface before carving the stone. Indeed, the irregularities of the stone were ignored in its carving, the design being continued across areas of loss such as on the thigh and belt of the right profile figure. Much of the image is shallowly incised into the surface but a few areas such as the inside of the left arm, top and bottom of the belt, wristlets, shoulder cape and outer circumference of the earring hoop show the deeper, angled cuts of sunken relief, suggesting its artist was aware of the possibilities for the movement of light and shadow over the image. Luis G. Lumbreras (2013, 179) suggested that a now-collapsed shaft, built into the structure, once provided light and air to the Lanzón gallery and that on the winter solstice light from the shaft could have raked the face of the statue. In this case, the deeper carving would have given the image greater contrast when hit by the beam of sunlight.

BLACK AND WHITE PHASE

The final and most expansive building phase at Chavín de Huántar began around 900 BCE and continued until the collapse of the city four hundred years later. The period is known as the "Black and White" phase because of the frequent use in construction of black and white stones in oppositional arrangements that emphasized the contrast of color. It was at this time that the majority of Chavín de Huántar's remaining structures, sunken plazas, and planar relief sculptures were constructed.

The New Temple and Black and White Gateway During this period the original south platform of the Old Temple and its summit structures were considerably enlarged, and as a result, early scholars designated this enlarged south platform the "New Temple" (Figure 2.5). Its main processional approach was through the large principal plaza, measuring approximately 341 (105 m) by 276 feet (85 m), and then continuing through a second sunken court, 162 feet (50 m) squared, and ending at the Black and White Portal, a massive free-standing stone gateway that originally gave access to the main stair of the new construction. The portal's dark stone columns are decorated with shallow relief images of male and female beings with avian and feline characteristics.

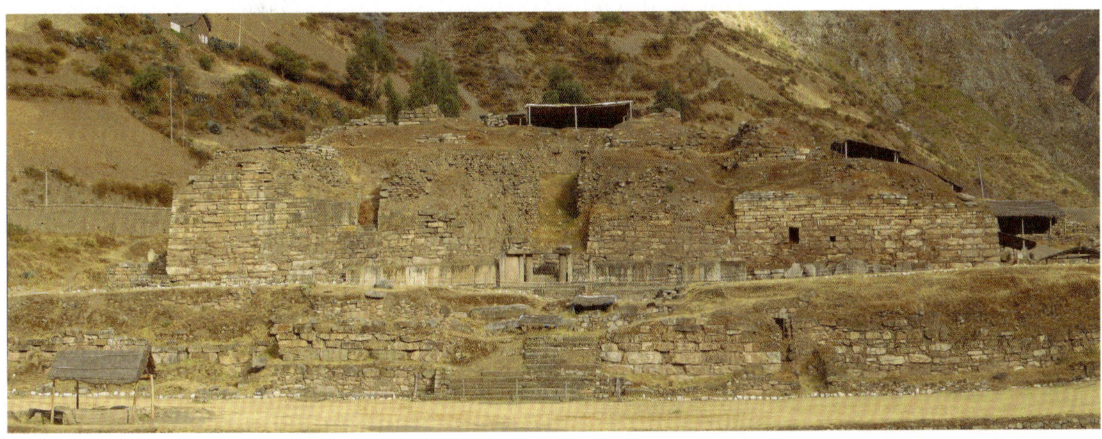

▼ **2.5** Chavín de Huántar, View of New Temple addition and Black and White Portal, c. 900–500 BCE.

The south leg of the original U-shaped structure was considerably enlarged during this period. A characteristic of this period was the use of black and white contrasting stone such as in the gateway in the center of the structure.

LATE CHAVÍN SCULPTURE

The sculptures of the Black and White period show Chavín artists to have made considerable technical advances in carving compared to the relatively rough preparatory work done on the Lanzón shaft before it was carved. By the late Chavín period, sculptors were producing monolithic stone panels of regular format that had highly polished surface finishes. The bas-relief sculptures of this period have significantly cutback grounds and planar images to which further details were added by incision. The figures on these panels exhibit **contour rivalry**, a technique in which an image appears to be one thing when viewed one way and an altogether different thing when the work is flipped or rotated. Chavín sculptures may also exhibit **modular width**, meaning that the elements of the composition are arranged in equal width bands as though they had been laid out on a grid. Additional, figural elements are reduced to basic components such as lines, curves, and scrolls. A new motif that appears in the art of the late Chavín is the agnathic mouth in which the lower jaw is missing; this motif sometimes appears as a substitute for other body parts, especially joints.

Although the "New Temple" seems to have been the primary focus of construction during the Black and White period, the "Old Temple" was also improved during this time with the addition of a circular plaza set into its square atrium. Originally described as a sunken plaza, new research (Rick 2013, 155) suggests that plaza was not excavated but rather built up as part of a new addition to the atrium platform. The new construction increased the platform height by some 8 feet (2.5 m), causing the circular plaza to appear sunken.

The Circular Plaza is bisected by two stairs aligned with its east-west axis. The walls of each half of the plaza were decorated with two courses of bas-relief friezes separated by a double row of thin, finely cut stone blocks. The lower frieze is composed of rectangular slabs, horizontally oriented and carved with matched pairs of profile felines, moving toward the west staircase leading up to the Old Temple. All of the felines depicted at Chavín de Huántar are generically identified in the literature as "jaguars." However, the pelage patterns shown in the Circular Plaza reliefs are not uniform, suggesting that different species of wild felids are being represented. Among these appear to be the pampas or Geoffroy cat, and the Andean mountain cat; the latter is still offered as a ritual sacrifice in the Andes today.

The upper frieze consists of vertically oriented slabs carved with anthropomorphic figures representing warriors holding weapons, musicians blowing conch-shell trumpets, Spondylus shell bearers, deity impersonators carrying hallucinogenic San Pedro cacti, and supernatural beings. Like the Cerro Sechín reliefs, these processional figures are rendered in composite view and are paired with an identical figure on the opposite side of the Circular Plaza. These reliefs seem to reference rituals that may have been enacted in the plaza prior to entering the Lanzón gallery.

***The Raimondi Stela**, c. 900–500 BCE* The Raimondi stela (Figure 2.6) is named for Antonio Raimondi (1826–1890), a nineteenth century Italian-born Peruvian academician, geographer, and scientist who discovered the bas-relief panel that bears his name. Unfortunately, the stela's initial location is not known, but its panel format and Black and White period style suggest it was originally a wall tablet, most likely associated with the New Temple.

The polished granite slab is considered a masterpiece of late Chavín lithic art. The stela is carved in bas-relief with the image of the Chavín Primary Deity, wearing an elaborate headdress and holding what may be two flowering San Pedro cactus stems. Finely incised into the polished surface are the complex details of the god's clothing and headdress of agnathic animal mouths and looped serpents. Comprehension of the image is difficult not only because of the stela's polished surface but also because of the use of an artistic technique known as "contour rivalry." In the case of the Raimondi stela, the technique of contour rivalry allows the viewer to recognize the human-like face of the god as the dominant image when the stela is in the upright position. However, when inverted, the lines that formed the original image present as the snout of a caiman with a feline face on top. It is unlikely that a granite stela, measuring 6.4 feet (1.98 m) by 29.13 inches (74 cm) by 6 inches (17 cm), would have been moved since its weight would have been significant, so such alternate interpretations must have been read on some level by the initiated just as were the kenning descriptors of the deity.

▼ **2.6** Chavín de Huántar, Raimondi Stela, c. 900–500 BCE. 6 ft. 4 in. high.

The original location of this stela is unknown but its format suggests that it was a wall panel and probably associated with the New Temple construction.

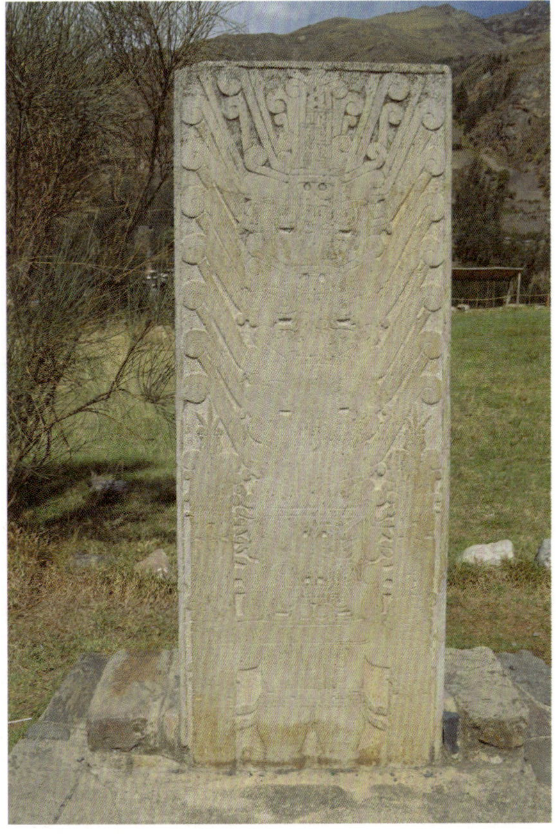

Paracas (400 BCE–200 CE)

Sometime after 500 BCE construction stopped at Chavín de Huántar but Chavín art and technology continued to exert a substantial influence on cultures in the northern and central highlands and those of the Peruvian coast for several centuries. One of those initially influenced by Chavín was Paracas, which went on to evolve its own unique art style. The Paracas Peninsula is a small point of land that juts out into the cold waters of the Pacific between the Pisco and Ica river valleys of the South Coast. Its name derives from the strong winds blowing onshore from the ocean and the frequent sandstorms they stir up.

Like other coastal civilizations, the Paracas people built their cities, towns, and ceremonial centers in the river valleys, where agriculture was possible. Paracas ritual centers included mound structures with earthen cores enclosed by mud-mortared adobe block or fieldstone walls. The finished walls were plastered with an adobe mixture then decorated with incised or painted designs, generally interpreted as representing supernatural beings. Unfortunately, Paracas architecture has been little studied and poorly published.

TEXTILES AND MUMMY BUNDLES

The arid Paracas peninsula served as a necropolis for the elite dead from the nearby valley communities. The cemeteries around the slopes of Cerro Colorado were first excavated during 1925 through 1927 field seasons by Julio Tello (1880–1947) and Toribio Mejia Xesspe (1896–1983) in response to the sudden market-flood of looted textiles that were said to be from Paracas. The archaeologists excavated three tomb sites, the most spectacular of which was the Necropolis of Wari Kayan, a large underground burial precinct containing some 429 mummy bundles in three sizes: large, medium, and small. The differing bundle sizes and their associated offerings seemed to reflect a hierarchy of status in the society (Tello 1929, 131).

At the core of each bundle, regardless of size, was a coiled basket containing the body of the decedent, legs and arms drawn up to the chest and secured in place. The basket would be packed with reeds and then wrapped with several meters of plain-weave cotton cloth. Elaborately embroidered ritual garments, animal hides, and other offerings would be placed in successive layers over the core, until all would be sealed within a plain cotton outer cloth. Some bundles were further enhanced with red or brown painted mummy masks, showing features or sometimes a full figure rendered in a linear style.

Paracas garments were untailored lengths of plain-weave cloth that were either wrapped as mantles, kilts, loincloths, and turbans or were folded over and stitched to form tunics and ponchos. While the plain wrapping cloths were typically woven from native cottons and left natural, the more elaborate textiles utilized camelid (Alpaca) fibers because wool absorbs dye more readily than cotton fiber. Paracas dyers utilized natural plant and insect sources to produce a wide range of reds, blues, greens, and yellows as well as purple, brown, and white. The catalogue of textile motifs is fairly limited: spotted cats, birds, killer whales, dancers, avian impersonators, and a deity known as the Oculate Being because of his large, staring eyes.

Paracas Mantle, 1–100 CE Among the more spectacular Paracas textiles are the rectangular mantles, which were worn over the shoulders shawl-style and were often quite large. In 1931 a particularly fine Paracas mantle (Figure 2.7) was acquired by the Boston Museum of Art. The large mantle features a deep red field with navy, bracket-shaped borders at the top and bottom; both the field and borders are plain-weave cloth. The mantle is decorated with 180 colorful, block-style figures done in stem-stitch embroidery. The figures are arranged in nineteen vertical rows with a single horizontal row on the top and bottom borders. The embroidered images represent a ritual procession of dancers, moving across the red field of the mantle in a **boustrophedon** pattern or an up and down movement like that of oxen plowing a field. Some dancers in each field line turn left while others go right. The border figures appear to be dancing in a circle around the perimeter of the field.

The figures wear face and body paint, pectoral ornaments, short kilts, and embroidered ankle bands probably decorated with Conus shells. They all carry dance wands and either a feather fan or a triangular-bladed knife. The dance appears to be an active one; knees flexed, each dancer seems to be performing some sort of head-rolling gyratory movement of the upper body. Many of the items that dancers and ritual impersonators are depicted as wearing or holding on the Paracas textiles have been found in mummy bundles (Bruhns email to author, July 11, 2016).

PARACAS CERAMICS

Paracas potters crafted a wide range of vessel forms, from bowls, jars, and bottles to distinctive double-spout-and-bridge forms. These ceramics were frequently included as offerings in and around mummy bundles. Although plain wares have been found, fine Paracas wares are highly prized for their incised, post-fire painted, and resist or negative-painted decoration. Incised decoration was cut into the

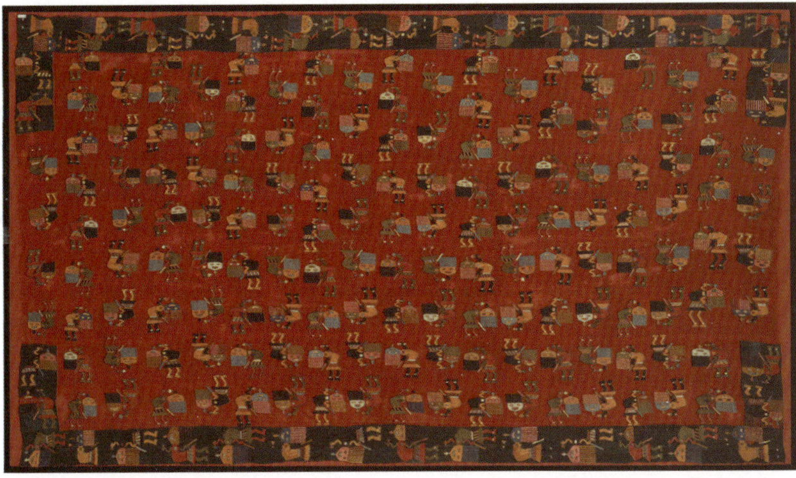

◀ **2.7** Paracas, South Coast, Embroidered Mantle, c. 1–100 CE. 55.87 in. × 94.87 in.

This large mantle was decorated with 180 embroidered figures who appear to be taking part in some sort of processional dance. The brilliance of its color after two millennia is the result of natural dyes.

leather-hard surface of the vessel prior to firing and frequently served as a cartoon for post-fire paint application. Paracas artists made water-soluble paints by mixing mineral pigments with gum from the native acacia tree. The basic Paracas palette included whites, greens, reds, golds, and blacks; they also knew how to make tints and shades of each of these colors. When thinned with a small amount of hot water, the paint had good flow control, reducing the likelihood of bleeds and obvious brushwork. Painted decoration included geometric designs and animal, human, and composite forms, among which the most common is the Oculate Being, recognizable by his large staring eyes formed by concentric circles.

Paracas Bowl with Oculate Deity, c. 300–301 BCE This Oculate Deity bowl (Figure 2.8) from the Ica Valley of Peru features incised and post-fire painted decoration on both its interior and exterior surfaces. The outside of the bowl features a large red ground framed at top and bottom by narrow bands of gold, much in the manner of a Paracas textile. Moving across the red ground in a clockwise direction are supernatural felines, rendered with profile bodies, frontal heads, and large circular eyes, colored green or gold. These grinning felids may well be an animal variant of the Oculate Being. Both the interior and exterior designs were incised into the clay body of the bowl prior to firing. The incised lines not only served as a guide for painting but also functioned as contour lines defining the painted fields.

▼ **2.8** Paracas, Rattle Bowl with Oculate Deity, c. 300–1 BCE, 6.75 in. diameter.

The image of the Oculate Deity is painted on the ceramic after firing with pigments mixed with a water-soluble gum binder.

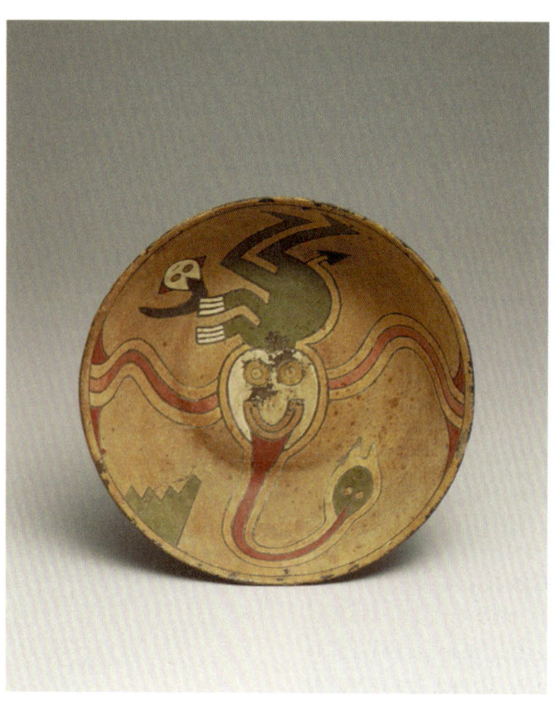

Depicted on the inside of the bowl is a large image of the Oculate Being who, like his feline companions, has a profile body and a frontal face. The Oculate Being's green body, while human, crouches in a catlike posture. In his right hand he holds a trophy head by a long hank of hair. A second head seems to be suspended at the end of a long red appendage issuing from below the Oculate Being's mouth; whether this element represents his tongue or blood being sucked into the mouth of the Being is unclear. A gold band runs from the Being's left shoulder around his head and the appendage, where it forms a beaked profile, and then continues down his back to end in a tail with a triangular head. Yellow and red bands fly out from either side of the Oculate Being's face as he moves toward a stepped platform near the rim of the bowl. The taking of trophy heads appears to have been an important part of Paracas rituals associated with agricultural fertility.

RELIGION AND PHILOSOPHY
Andean Pantheons

Identifying deities in Andean religion presents some considerable challenges as none of these societies left written records of their beliefs. Their art is filled with images of supernatural beings with fangs (a deity indicator), whose repeated appearances across time and geography offer some certainty that they were important deities. However, the names of these gods are unknown and their functions surmised; it is only with the coming of Spanish missionaries that any records of pre-Hispanic belief systems, and then, primarily, those of the Inca were recorded. The following are the deities who appear most frequently in early Andean pre-Columbian art.

- Chavín "Primary Deity" or "Smiling God" appears first at the site of Chavín de Huántar on the Lanzón and Raimondi Stelas. He is a fanged being with snakes for hair and clawed hands and feet. He sometimes has feline or caiman elements and may hold staffs with plant elements. His function seems to be as an agricultural deity.
- Moche "Rayed Deity" or "Decapitator God" may have an X-shaped arrangement of rays coming from his body, especially on gold ornaments and fine-line ceramics. He is typically shown holding a ceremonial knife with a crescent-shaped blade and a long handle in one hand and a decapitated human head known as a "trophy head" in the other.
- Paracas "Oculate Being" is identifiable by his large staring eyes. He is a frequent motif on Paracas textiles and ceramics. Generally, he holds one or more trophy heads.
- Nasca "Anthropomorphic Mythical Being" is similar to the Oculate Being in that he also has large staring eyes. He is often shown wearing a gold mouth mask with whisker-like appendages and carries a trophy head.
- Tiahuanaco "Staff God" as seen on the Sun Gate is a being with a rayed headdress who holds a staff in each hand. He is usually accompanied by avian attendants. He also appears in the art of the Huari.

The Spanish chroniclers recorded that the Incas kept the idols of the peoples they had conquered in their temple in Cuzco along with the images of their own gods. Their gods were typically represented in anthropomorphic form. The Inca pantheon included gods who represented natural phenomena such as mountains, lakes, rain, and thunder and lightning as well as the sun and moon. Chief among them were Viracocha the creator of the heavens and earth who taught mankind the arts of civilization; Pachamama the earth goddess, and Inti, the sun god.

The Middle Period Cultures (200–1000 CE)

The end of the early period in the Andes saw the influence of the Chavín tradition waning in most regions of the Andes. Following the decline of Chavín, localized traditions evolved along the coast and in the highlands. Early in the Middle Period, the south coast saw the rise of the Nasca culture in the Rio Grande drainage and the Ica valley, while in the north the Moche spread out from its namesake valley to dominate the coast from the Huarmey to the Piura River. By 600 CE both the Nasca and Moche civilizations were in decline, possibly as a result of climatic changes. In the northern highlands and Titicaca Basin the Huari (also Wari) and Tiahuanaco cultures entered expansive phases during which they spread out to influence large portions of the Peruvian coast and highlands. Farther north along the coast of Ecuador and in the southern mountains of Colombia, cultures were evolving that produced spectacular ceramics and sculpture.

Nasca (200 BCE–650 CE)

About one hundred air miles southeast of the Paracas Peninsula is the heartland of the Nasca civilization, which may well have its roots in the earlier Paracas culture. Nasca centers are found in the Ica Valley as well as those of the Rio Grande de Nazca[1] drainage. Nasca is best known for its **geoglyphs** or desert lines, but the culture also wove marvelous textiles, utilizing a variety of techniques, made fine, slip-painted ceramics, and built ceremonial centers featuring numerous earthen mounds that supported buildings.

NASCA ARCHITECTURE

Like most of the coastal cultures, the Nasca built their cities and towns in the river valleys where there was water for agriculture. Their houses were constructed of small conical, rounded-block adobes or *quincha* walls.[2] In addition to residential areas they also constructed ceremonial centers. These centers featured stepped pyramids that incorporated natural hills, large plazas and temple precincts. One of the largest ceremonial centers was Cahuachi in the Nazca Valley.

Cahuachi, c. 100 BCE–400 CE Cahuachi (Figure 2.9) was an important pilgrimage center early in the first millennium CE. Scattered across the site are some forty mounds of varying sizes and shapes. Many of these are natural hills that were truncated over the millennia by wind and sand erosion. The Nasca enlarged these naturally pyramid-form features, as needed, with adobes and layers of fibrous plant matter; the resulting hybrid structures were encapsulated within conical adobe walls. These platform mounds and their crowning temples would have been finished with mud plaster and incised decoration. The mounds were associated with open plazas, and walled precincts, called *kanchas* (Silverman and Proulx 2002, 158). Cahuachi's population seems to have abandoned the city in the fourth century CE; afterward it served primarily as a mortuary center.

---

[1] When spelled as Nasca, the word refers to the ancient culture; Nazca is used to refer to the geographic area.

[2] A wattle and daub type construction employing a cane or stick framework covered by mud.

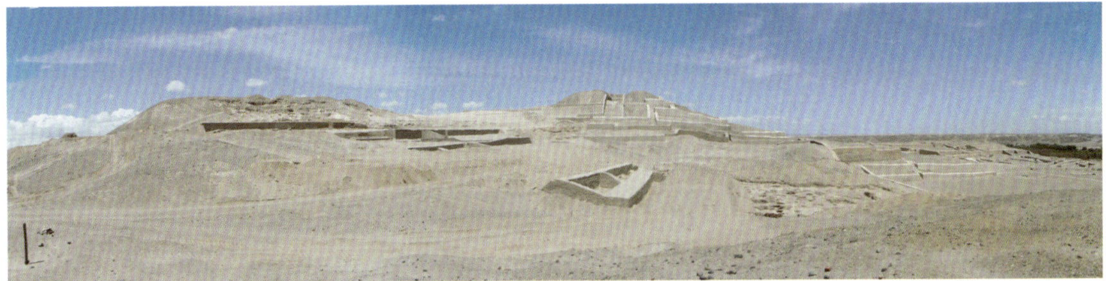

▲ **2.9** Cahuachi, Nazca Valley, c. 1–500 CE.

Cahuachi was an important pilgrimage center, featuring more than forty platform mound and associated structures and plazas. From the top of Cahuachi's taller platforms some of the Nasca lines would have been visible.

GEOGLYPHS: NASCA DESERT LINES AND ZOOMORPHS (C. 500 BCE–500 CE)

The Nasca lines were first mentioned in 1553 by the Spanish Conquistador and chronicler, Pedro Cieza de Leon (c.1518–1554), who mistook them for trail markers. More than four centuries later the function of the lines and geoglyphs is still a matter of scholarly debate, as is also the identity of the cultures that made them. Originally, the desert drawings on the pampas of Jumana were thought to be solely the work of the Nasca people, but recent discoveries have dated some figures to the earlier Paracas culture. This suggests that the lines spread across some 280 square miles (400 square km) of desert were not all made at the same time, or by the same people, or perhaps even for the same purpose.

Fueled by popular fiction and pseudo-documentaries, there are a lot of misconceptions about the lines. One of the most common is that the lines can only be seen from the air; the earliest geoglyphs (Paracas period) were placed on hillsides where they could be seen from the pampa and the later (Nasca) pampa ones could be viewed from the tops of pyramids and surrounding hillsides without the necessity of the Nasca inventing hot air balloons, spaceships, or other flying contraptions. Equally convoluted theories exist about the difficulty of creating the geoglyphs without aerial direction. The straight lines, geometric forms, zigzags, spirals, plant forms, figures, animals, and insects depicted across the Nazca desert could have been constructed with relative ease, using string lines and stakes, and the labor of relatively few workers, even though some of the constructions extend for several kilometers. A few of the earliest (Paracas period) geoglyphs were done in an additive technique, specifically piling up surface rocks to create the design. However, most were done in a subtractive method in which the oxidized surface pebbles would be brushed aside to reveal the lighter material underneath; the surface material was often used as an edging along the line.

The Condor Geoglyph, c. 1–500 CE A good example of a figurative geoglyph created using a reductive technique is the desert drawing popularly termed "the Condor" (Figure 2.10), although it is in all likelihood not a member of the vulture family; its long, thin beak is more in

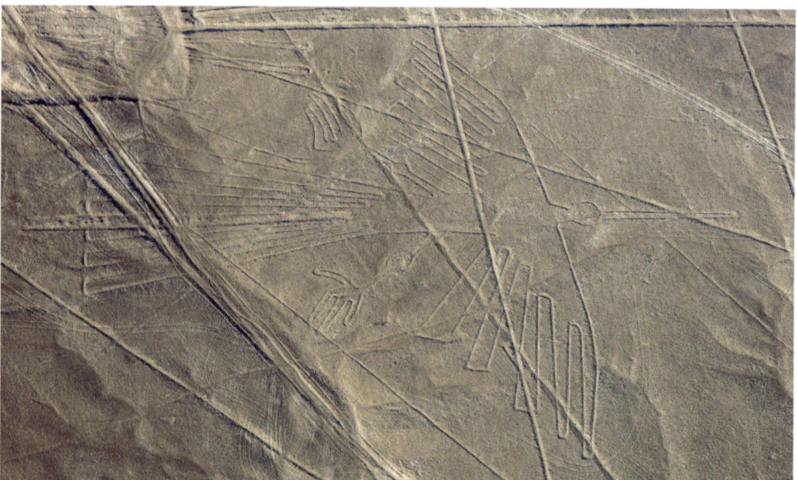

▶ 2.10 Nazca Valley, Condor Geoglyph, c. 1–500 CE.

Although the bird has been given the name "Condor" after the culturally important vulture, the image is more likely a woodpecker or coastal waterfowl.

keeping with a hummingbird or some variety of coastal waterfowl. The "condor" is one of the larger drawings, measuring 440 feet (134 m) from the point of its beak to the tip of its tail feathers. The body of the bird is constructed with a single continuous contour line, formed by removing the oxidized surface material or **desert varnish** and piling it up alongside the line as a low berm. Nowhere along the entirety of the design does the line cross over itself or even vary in width. As a single-line drawing it would be a simple matter for the artists creating it to step over the line, without damaging it, to work either inside or outside of the design.

NASCA CERAMICS

Nasca ceramics evolved, over a period of a thousand years, out of the Paracas pottery of the Ica Valley. The earliest Nasca ceramics continued the Paracas technique of incising the designs into the clay body. Paracas vessel forms, in particular the double-spout-and-bridge bottle, as well as decorative motifs such as the killer whale, fish, fox, falcon, and feline persist into the Nasca. Recent studies of Paracas and Nasca genetic material in the Ica Valley show them to be a single population group with no new admixtures until the arrival of the Huari and later Inca in the region (Silverman and Proulx 2002, 15–16).

The main distinctions between the ceramics of the Paracas and Nasca appear to be technological. Where Paracas ceramics were decorated with a post-fire application of pigments in a water-soluble gum or "resin" binder, the Nasca developed clay slips, which were applied to the ceramics pre-firing, resulting in permanent, waterproof colors. Another advance was the incorporation of organic tempers into Nasca clay bodies, which facilitated the production of extremely thin-walled and lightweight vessels. The Nasca created a wide range of bowl, beaker, and spouted vessel forms as well as effigy vessels and figurines. Several decorative styles have been identified for the Nasca but it is not entirely clear as to whether these styles represent regional variations, sequential phases, or were simultaneously produced.

Double-Spout-and-Bridge Bottle with Anthropomorphic Mythical Being, c. 100–300 CE Nasca subject matter has been categorized as either secular or religious based on whether the depiction seems to represent things of the world, for example plants and animals, or things of a spiritual nature such as mythical beings. To assume that any representation, no matter how seemingly ordinary, is completely devoid of religious meaning is problematic. Nasca artists, as did those of the Chavín and some Mesoamerican cultures, often elaborated the symbolic content through the use of visual kennings (Proulx 2006, 17–18).

Depicted on the Double-Spout-and-Bridge Bottle (Figure 2.11), is one of the more frequently depicted motifs in Nasca art, the Anthropomorphic Mythical Being (AMB). This mythical being appears on textiles and ceramics from the earliest to latest phases of Nasca art and may well have been a continuation from Paracas. The AMB is a ritual performer who wears the headdress, mask, and regalia of the deity he impersonates. The AMB's most notable feature is a bewhiskered mouth-mask through which his tongue sometimes protrudes. He wears an animal pelt headdress over his hair, which is bound with circular ornaments in two long hanks, a spondylus shell necklace, a crest-like forehead ornament, a short tunic and loincloth. He may carry a dance fan or a club as well as trophy heads suspended on cords. Similar items from looted tombs are known from museum collections (Townsend 1985, 131; Proulx 2006, 62). To this basic configuration of elements for the AMB are often added other signifiers for felines, killer whales, birds, snakes, and so on, which may reference particular attributes of the deity or recount events in his myths; however, since the Nasca lacked writing, it is impossible to know with certainty the narrative content they were intended to convey.

▼ 2.11 Nasca, Double-Spout-and-Bridge Bottle, c. 100–300 CE. 6.25 in. high and wide.

The figure depicted on this vessel is the Anthropomorphic Mythical Being, who wears a mouth mask and carries trophy heads.

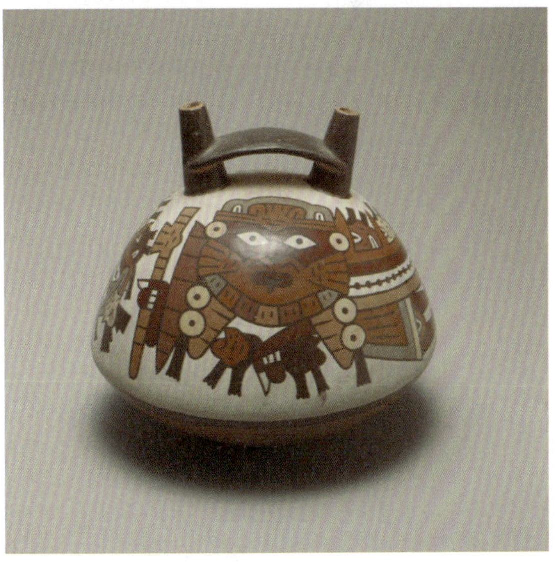

The Nasca potter approached the application of painted decoration in a manner reminiscent of that used for wall painting in Mesoamerica. After the vessel surface had been burnished to remove imperfections, ground color, often white or red, would be applied. The design would then be painted in as many as eight to twelve colors, including hues, tints, and shades of black, white, purple, red, orange, yellow, gray, violet, pink, and blue. Colors would be applied in a considered manner to create an alternating visual rhythm, as seen in the gray, orange, brown, yellow, brown, orange, gray sequence of the AMB's necklace, as well as to create color balance. As in the case of fresco painting, the final step was to outline the forms with an even-width black line; this served to define the forms as well as to cover any irregularities in the original painted edges. Although so shallow as to be easily misread as flat, Nasca painters attempted to show visual depth in their work through the overlapping of forms. For example, the AMB's hair ornaments overlap the hank of hair, which overlaps the sleeve covering the arm and hand grasping the hair of a trophy head (Proulx 2006, 16–17).

▼ **2.12** Nasca, Coyungo Valley, Sampler, c. 1–200 CE. Cotton and camelid fiber embroidery on cotton plain weave, 23.62 x 14.87 in.

This textile features five rows of assorted bird motifs on a blue plain-weave cotton cloth ground. The birds were outlined in white and filled in with colored threads to show plumage details.

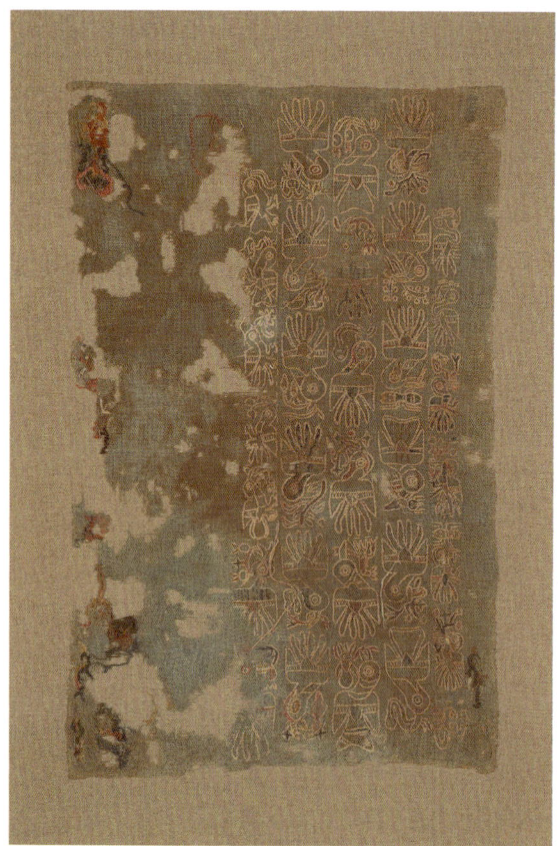

NASCA TEXTILES

As in the case of the ceramics, Nasca textiles evolved from earlier Paracas forms and techniques. Nasca garments were decorated in a number of techniques, including painting, embroidery, and featherwork as revealed by a cache of early Nasca women's dresses and shawls excavated at the site of Cahuachi in 1998. Common Nasca needlework textiles include simple samplers stitched in one or two colors of thread and multicolor block embroideries worked on plain weave cloth. The embroidered fields were often enclosed by elaborately worked tabbed, cross-knit, and fringed borders. Many of the motifs found in Paracas are continued in Nasca but often have a geometric appearance and may be presented in a variety of views: frontal, dorsal, and profile. A proliferation of secondary elements such as hooks, rays, and trophy heads often complicate the reading of figures.

Nasca Sampler, Coyungo, Nazca Valley, c. 1–200 CE This blue-colored, plain-weave cotton sampler (Figure 2.12) is embroidered with five rows of assorted bird motifs outlined in white cotton and camelid wool threads; bird heads, beaks, and plumage details are suggested by area of colored fill embroidery. The birds are arranged in three rows of large motifs, presented in alternating frontal and dorsal views, and set between two rows of smaller, profile birds. The birds hold plants, snakes, spiders, crustaceans, insects, and fish in their beaks. The remains of an elaborate embroidered border appear down the left side of the sampler.

Moche (c. 200–850 CE)

Moche kingdoms dominated the north coast of Peru from the Piura Valley, near Ecuador, to the Huarmey River in the south, an area of some 310 miles (500 km). Because the cold waters of the Humboldt Current flow close to the coast, this region is one of the driest on earth; it is a hyperarid desert with an average annual rainfall of less than eight inches. As a result the Moche located their settlements and ceremonial centers in the river valleys, where it was possible to irrigate the rich soils of the flood plains and practice agriculture. Their penetration into these valleys was seldom greater than 50 miles (80km) inland from the coast. Moche occupation of this region was not uniform and today scholars recognize that the Moche were not a monolithic empire as previously thought but were divided into two core zones, one to the north and the other south of the Pampa de Paiján. The two regions offer distinct patterns of urbanism, architecture, and ceramic production (Pillsbury 2001, 11–12).

THE HUACAS OF MOCHE

The name given to this civilization is derived from the site of Moche which lies at the foot of Cerro Blanco on the south bank of the Moche River about 3 miles (5 km) inland from the Pacific coast. The ceremonial center is dominated by two massive, multilevel platform complexes, known as the Huaca de la Luna and the Huaca del Sol. These two adobe brick structures are separated by some 1625 feet (500 m). To the south was a labyrinthine area, which appears to have had residential and manufacturing compounds. Archaeologists have found the remains of what appear to be ceramics and textile workshops, suggesting the area may have been organized according to craft specialties.

Huaca del Sol, c. 200–560 CE The now heavily damaged Huaca del Sol or "Shrine of the Sun" (Figure 2.13) anchored the western end of Moche's great plaza; the structure is believed to have been the site of civic rituals and ceremonies, and to have held royal residences and tombs. It was built entirely of adobe blocks; some 130 to 143 million are estimated to have been used to bring the shrine to its final measurement of 1,132 feet (345 m) long, 525 feet (160 m) wide and more than 135 feet (40 m) high. Each of the blocks bore marks, which are thought to have identified the community or workshops that produced them. Approximately one hundred such marks have been catalogued, suggesting that several communities provided materials for the construction of the shrine.

In its final form, circa 450 CE, the Huaca del Sol consisted of four adjoined platforms of differing heights and scales. The tallest unit was in the center of the shrine; it was flanked on the northeast by a single square platform and on the southwest by two unequal rectangular mounds. The Huaca del Sol was enlarged eight times during the occupation of the site, presumably to accommodate royal burials. Along

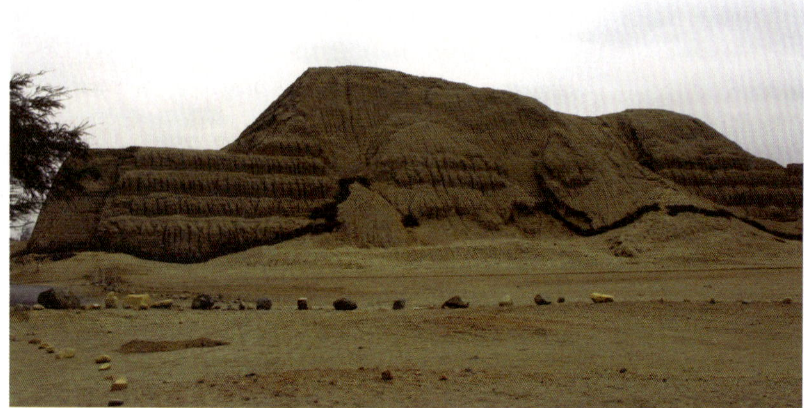

▶ **2.13** Moche, Huaca del Sol, c. 200–560 CE. 1,132 ft. × 525 ft. × 135 ft.

Built entirely out of adobe bricks, the "Shrine of the Sun" consisted of four adjoined platforms of differing heights and to have been the civic and ritual center of the community.

the front and southwest side of the shrine the remains of terraced levels are apparent. Originally, these levels of the Huaca were decorated with painted murals or perhaps painted reliefs, but that decoration has eroded away. Access to the different levels was provided by ramps. Around 560 CE, the structure was damaged by an El Niño–triggered flash flood and subsequently repaired; however, not long afterward, sand dunes began invading the site and the Huaca de la Luna at the opposite end of the plaza became the focus of ritual and ceremonial activities at the site. The Huaca del Sol suffered further depredation at the hands of Spanish treasure hunters. In 1602, Colonial era looters diverted the waters of the Moche River to facilitate looting of the Huaca tombs by eroding away a significant portion of the mound. Approximately two thirds of the structure was destroyed at this time.

Huaca de la Luna, c. 200–800 CE The Huaca de la Luna or "Shrine of the Moon" (Figure 2.14) sits at the foot of Cerro Blanco on the eastern side of the great plaza. The Huaca de la Luna is a complex consisting of three adobe platform mounds connected by four plazas and accessed by ramps. After the abandonment of the Huaca del Sol, it became the principal shrine of the city. The scale of construction was more modest, the compound measuring only 690 feet (210 m) by 950 feet (290 m), including platforms and plazas, and requiring only an estimated 50 million adobe bricks. The largest of the Huaca mounds is Platform I, measuring 311 feet (95 m) on each side and rising to a height of 105 feet (32 m). Its summit was divided into an upper and a lower level, separated by 16 feet (5 m) of elevation. The upper level supported a four-room structure that was decorated inside and out with murals.

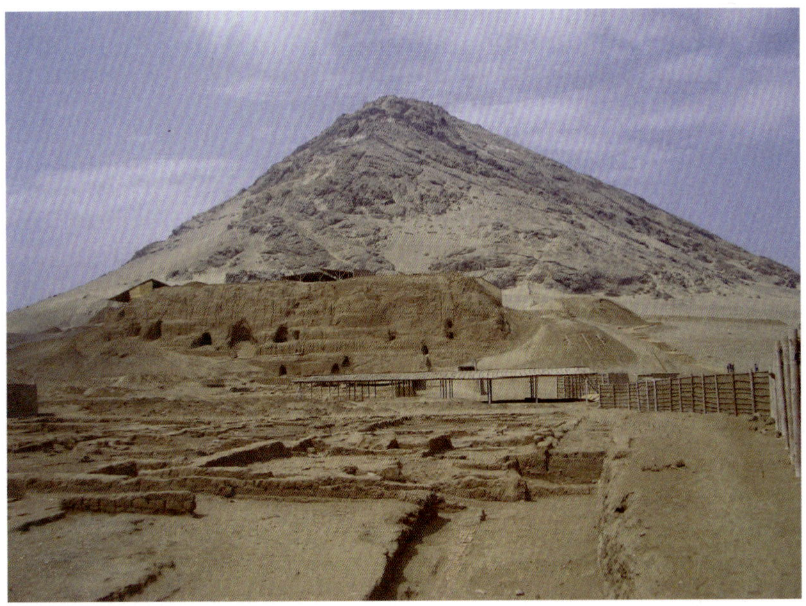

◀ **2.14** Moche, Huaca de la Luna at the foot of Cerro Blanco, c. 200–800 CE. 690 ft. × 950 ft. × 105 ft.

This complex consisted of three adobe platform mounds connected by four plazas. The Huaca de la Luna was the principal shrine of the city and is famous for its painted mud reliefs.

The plaza to the east of the platform served as the locus of human sacrifice rituals. Warfare and human sacrifice were important themes in Moche iconography and are frequently depicted in painted murals and on painted pottery.

Huaca de la Luna, Platform I, North Façade Relief Murals, c. 200–800 CE The sides of Platform I were stepped and each level was ornamented with a band of painted, low-relief mud sculptures (Figure 2.15). The bottom register featured a procession of Moche warriors, represented in composite view. Standing against a white ground, they wear short, fringed tunics over loincloths and carry shields and clubs. Suspended from their clubs are captured shields, clubs, and the tunics of their defeated advisories. Nude captives, bound together by ropes around their necks, trail behind the victorious warriors; they were brought into the city to be sacrificed. The second level shows a line of Moche wearing longer tunics and elaborate headdresses, who dance together with joined hands, presumably as part of a victory celebration. The third level is decorated with images of the "Decapitator Spider" framed within a yellow border. These spiders carry trophy heads. The Moche and other Andean peoples were apparently aware that in some species of spiders, the female bites off the head of the male after mating, and saw this practice as akin to their own taking of trophy heads. The fourth through seventh rows represented mythical, often composite beings, such as "Sea Twin" (fourth row), a marine deity who has fisherman and sea lion hunter attributes; the "Mythical/Lunar Being" (fifth row), an iguana with a feline head on its tail, who carries a trophy head; a large undulating serpent flanked by the fanged face of a sea deity; and

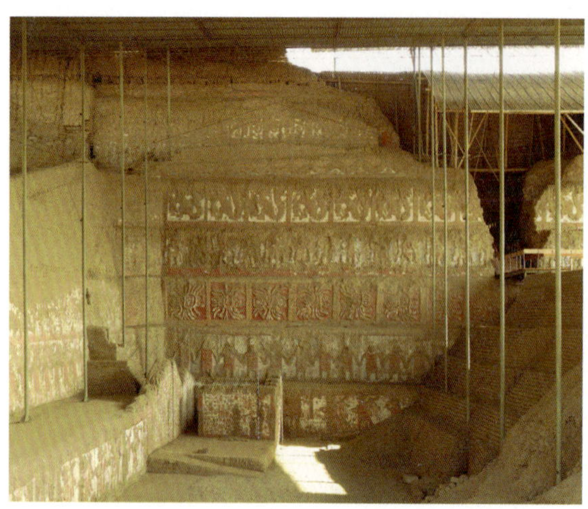

then finally an image of the "Decapitator God" holding a ceremonial knife and trophy head. Although only red, yellow, black, and white pigments are discernable on the platform terraces, the Moche palette consisted of seven basic colors: green (chrysocolla), white (calcite), black (charcoal), a bluish-gray (charcoal and calcite), red (red ocher), yellow (yellow ocher), and a pink that was probably a tint of red ocher (Scott, Doughty, and Donnan 1998, 177). These pigments were mixed with the sap of the hallucinogenic San Pedro cactus as a binder.

▲ **2.15** Moche, Huaca de la Luna, Platform I, Murals on the North Façade, c. 200–800 CE.

Painted mud reliefs depict (bottom to top) victorious warriors, dancers, decapitator spiders, and mythical creatures.

MOCHE FINELINE PAINTED CERAMICS

Archaeologists have found evidence of ceramic workshops at a number of Moche sites, including the type-site of Moche itself. However, as an estimated 95 percent of all known Moche vessels in museums and collections worldwide were looted, it has been difficult to identify particular styles or themes with specific sites (Donnan and McClelland 1999, 18). The Moche produced both modeled and painted ceramics, which appear judging from wear, breakage, and repairs to have been used in daily life and not made exclusively as grave offerings. Everyday use is further supported by ceramic motifs showing people carrying them on a sling around their necks or by the stirrup spout.

Moche fineline painted ceramics appear to have developed first among the northern Moche, evolving out of the pottery traditions of earlier Salinar people of the North Coast. Early fineline vessels were constructed by coiling the body and stirrup-spout separately and then, joining the pieces together. Later, the Moche developed fired-clay, two-part molds, which allowed them to make their vessels more quickly. The Moche used two types of clays for the production and decoration of fineline vessels. The first of these was a local red "terracotta" that was used to form the vessels and also diluted as a red slip, and the second was a cream-colored clay, thought to have been brought from the highlands. This was used to slip coat the vessels before painting. When the clay body was leather hard, the Moche artist would sketch his design on the vessel by scratching it into the clay with a sharp tool. The depth of incision seems to have varied, some things being light enough to be obscured by the slip, while at other times it was deep enough to remain visible as a contour line after the vessel was painted. The vessel would then be coated with white and using the sketch lines as a guide, the red slip would then be added. The majority of Moche fineline vessels are painted red-on-white but a few examples of white-on-red as well as polychrome painted ceramics are known. Once the vessel had dried, it was burnished with smooth stones and then it was pit-fired (Donnan and McClelland 1999, 28–37; 305).

The earliest fineline vessels (c. 50–400 CE) had a limited repertoire of motifs, primarily images of the "Decapitator God," spiders, crustaceans, birds, snakes, gastropods, and mammals. Later vessels display a number of complex painted scenes often involving several human, animal, and supernatural actors. A number of themes have been identified on the pots that may have religious aspects such as warfare, the capture and presentation of prisoners, ritual runners, deer hunting scenes, journeys by reed boat, burial scenes, curing ceremonies, and occasionally, erotic activities.

Very little is known about the artists who painted these scenes; however scholars researching Moche fineline-painted pottery have identified approximately fifty different Moche painters. Each of these anonymous artists had distinctive representational characteristics, such as depicting figures with long torsos, short legs, big noses, or thin lips that were peculiar to them stylistically, or the painters specialized in depicting certain themes.

Cleveland Painter, Vessel with Running Figures, c. 450–550 CE One of the Moche specialist artists was the "Cleveland Painter," so designated because one of the vessels attributed by style to this artist is in the collection of the Cleveland Museum of Art. The Cleveland painter seems to have specialized in the depiction of ritual runners, a prominent theme in Moche art. The running figures on the Cleveland Museum vessel (Figure 2.16) wear short loincloths, held up by ornamented belts, dark stockings with light toes, and elaborate headdresses consisting of feline head and pelts, and gold crests. The faces and kneecaps of the runners are painted and they carry bags filled with beans like those in the background. It is thought that the beans were used as mnemonic devices similar to the way knots were used on later Inca quipus.

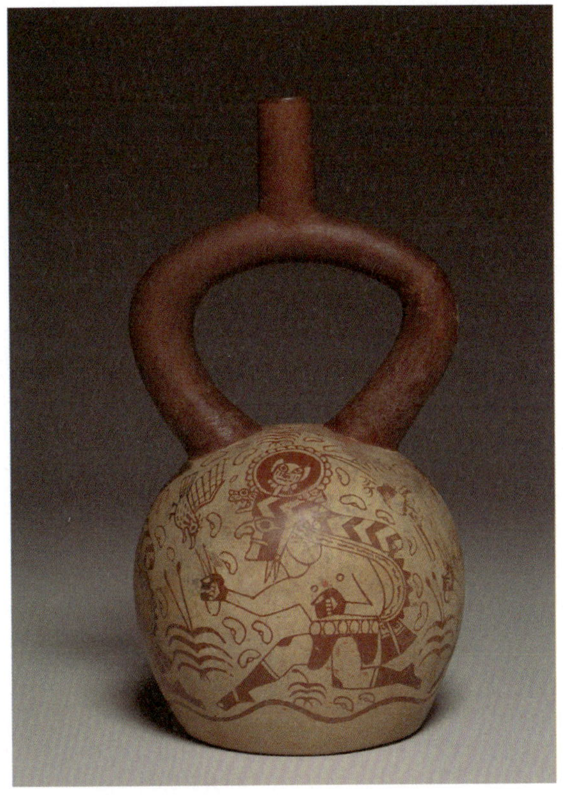

▼ **2.16** Moche, Cleveland Painter, Vessel with Running Figures, c. 450–550 CE. 11.37 in. × 6.12 in.

The vessel depicts a ritual runner who is carrying a bag from which beans seem to be dropping. The falling beans have attracted the attention of a swooping bird.

The style in which these figures are depicted is close to that of two other artists dubbed the "Chicago Painter" and the "Dipper Painter." However, the Cleveland Painter's work is distinguished by the unique treatment of the nose, slit-like mouths, tear-shaped eyes, and by the absence of wrist bands (Donnan and McClelland 1999,

202–206). In the Andes crafts, especially ceramics, tend to be made by family groups, often several generations of the same family will work together to produce "signature" styles. In the case of ceramics workshops, labor was divided along gender lines. Men usually dug the clay and acquired materials for which travel was required. Women made and decorated the pots. The close similarity in style between the Cleveland, Chicago, and Dipper painters and a fourth unnamed artist whose work is in the collection of the British Museum may well result from their having participated in the same ceramics atelier together.

MOCHE MODELED CERAMICS

Both the northern and southern Moche groups made modeled zoomorphic, botanical, and human effigy vessels as well as portrait head bottles. The distinction between the northern and southern groups appears to have been in the degree of realism. Northern vessels tend to be more generic, while those produced in the south are often so highly realistic as to be portraits of specific individuals. As with the fineline painted vessels, the earliest modeled pottery was hand-built, but by 450 CE, if not before, they were produced modeled pots using two part molds.

The production of a portrait mold was a more complex process than that used to create a simple pottery vessel because it required the production of an "original" to serve as a matrix. A clay vessel of the appropriate size was created and then modeled with the features and headdress details of the subject individual; this was divided into front and back parts by an incised groove, and then allowed to dry leather-hard. The original was covered with fresh clay, and sectioned following the groove already established in the matrix. When the fresh clay "mold" had dried sufficiently to separate it from the matrix, it was fired. The bottoms of these molds were typically left open; after duplicate vessels were taken out of the mold, they would be sealed with clay coils to create a flat base (Donnan 2004, 21–33).

Modeled Portrait Vessel, c. 450–550 CE The modeled Portrait Vessel (Figure 2.17) stands 13 inches (33 cm) high, and depicts a high-ranking, middle-aged Moche personage. His face is sensitively modeled to show prominent cheekbones, straight nose, even lips, and a strong jaw. Wrapped twice around his head is a narrow tapestry headband that has been overlapped and tied in back. His elite status is shown by his prominent ear spools. The dark brown color of his face is the result of fire-clouding. This can occur when pieces are placed too closely together or the fuel does not burn completely during firing (Donnan 2004, 39). Multiple copies of some portrait vessels, in one case forty examples, are known and some are so similar that they appear to be produced from the same mold. Typically, portraits of the same individual will exhibit some differences in details, for example in textile patterns or face paint. The existence of multiple copies of elite portrait vessels is intriguing. It is possible that they were produced as a type of state art to commemorate significant events or important rituals performed by Moche lords. Multiple portrait vessels of captives were also produced, presumably to memorialize their having been sacrificed.

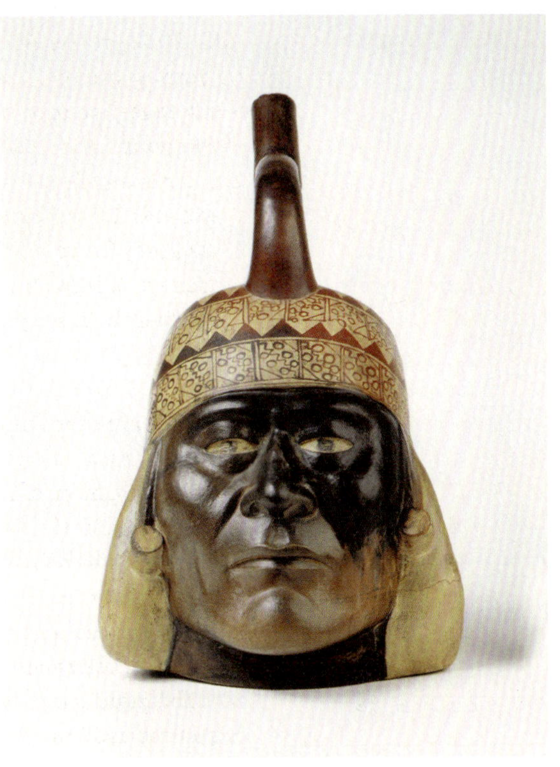

▲ 2.17 Moche, Modeled Portrait Vessel, c. 450–550 CE. 13 in. high.

This mold-made vessel depicts a high-ranking Moche man. Such pots were often produced in multiples and may have been distributed in elite exchanges.

MOCHE METALLURGY

Metallurgy seems to have begun in the Andes around four thousand years ago and to have spread northward into the Isthmus, arriving in Mesoamerica only in the Post-Classic. The earliest gold artifact currently known is a gold and turquoise bead necklace excavated from a burial at Jiskairumoko, in the Lake Titicaca basin, which dates from the period between 2155 and 1936 BCE. The discovery of gold foil and a metal working tool kit at Waywaka suggest metalworking was being practiced in the Andes even before the rise of the Chavín civilization. What is distinctive about Andean metallurgy is that it does not seem to have been connected to the production of either weapons or agricultural tools. Rather, from the earliest times gold items seem to have been tied to the display of status or rank.

Andean metalworkers had a good understanding of the properties of the metals they used. The most common were gold, copper, and silver, although platinum was worked in the Tumaco–La Tolita region of the Colombian and Ecuadorian Pacific coasts. Using stone hammers, anvils, and chisels, they hammered gold nuggets into sheets, which were decorated with ritually significant imagery using both **repoussé** (reverse hammering) and **chasing** (front working) techniques. They were well aware that gold becomes brittle when it is hammered and so they **annealed** (heating the metal and then quenching it in water) the gold sheets during the hammering process. The pieces they created were joined by soldering, assembled using wire, or with slots and bent tabs. They also knew techniques for lost wax casting (although this was rarely used in Peru due to difficulties in obtaining beeswax), metal casting using stone and ceramic molds, granulation, alloying, depletion and foil gilding, and mosaic inlay.

Moche Articulated Warrior Ear Ornament, Lord of Sipan Tomb, c. 50–300 CE

In 1986, a royal tomb in the 60 foot (18 m) high mound known as Huaca Rajada at the north coast site of Sipán was plundered by Samuel and Ernil Bernal. Over the course of several nights the Bernals destroyed

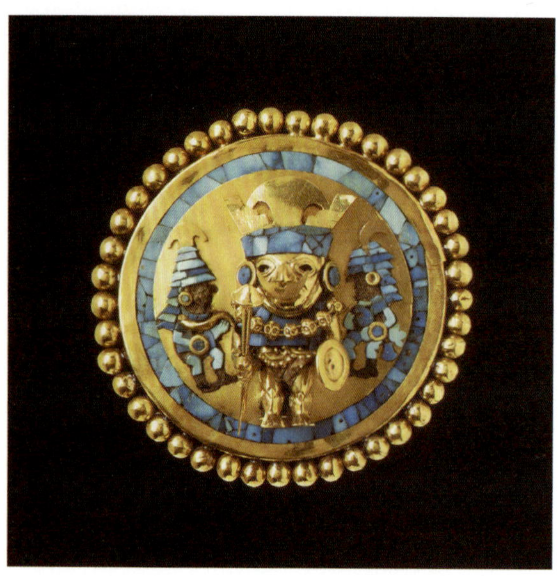

▲ 2.18 Moche, Huaca Rajada, Sipan, Articulated Warrior Ear Ornament, c. 50–300 CE.

This ear spool showing the figure of a warrior and two profile attendants is a marvelous piece of kinetic art. The central figure is composed of individually attached parts that are capable of moving.

hundreds of ceramic offerings and scattered human remains in their haste to collect gold objects from the burial. Artifacts from the tomb were transported over the Andes to Bolivia and from there trafficked to Europe and North America. When these artifacts began appearing on the art market, Peruvian archaeologist Walter Alva launched a rescue operation to recover artifacts from other tombs in Huaca Rajada before they were lost to looters.

One of the remarkable finds uncovered by Alva was an incredible pair of articulated gold and turquoise ear ornaments (Figure 2.18), which are about 3.5 inches (9 cm) in diameter. The central figure of the frontal is a diminutive warrior with shield and club, flanked by two profile turquoise and gold warriors. The warrior's face is a single unit consisting of a gold mask with a dangling crescent-shaped gold nose ornament and turquoise ear flares and crowned by a gold crescent headdress. Around his neck the warrior figure wore a necklace of individually strung owl-head beads and suspended from his belt were tiny crescent-shaped bells. The anatomical details of the warrior's hammered gold arms and legs were exactingly reproduced with muscles, knee caps, and the knuckles of the hand all indicated (Alva and Donnan 1993, 83–87).

The First Andean Empires (200 BCE–1000 CE)

During the late sixth century CE, environmental and climate changes along the southern coast of Peru prompted the northward movement of the southern Moche. The Moche valley and those to its south were vacated. In the wake of the Moche abandonment of their southern zone, two new states expanded to exert control over the south, Tiahuanaco[3] and Huari (also "Wari"). The Tiahuanaco homeland was south of Lake Titicaca in what is now Bolivia, while the Huari arose in the Ayacucho region of Peru. The nature of the relationship between these two states and their interaction over time is not well understood. The arts of these two states appear to have a common religious iconography centered on a frontally depicted Staff God, and styles that are similar enough to have been derived from a single source.

---

[3] In recent literature the spelling Tiwanaku has become popular; however, serious scholarship continues to use the traditional spelling. The argument against the new spelling has been made by several eminent linguists including John H. Rowe and more recently, Rodolfo Cerrón- Palomino, who have argued that the new spelling is linguistically incorrect (see Protzen and Nair 2014, vii).

TIAHUANACO (200 BCE–1000 CE)

Despite the cold climate of the Titicaca basin, it was settled during the second millennium BCE by the Chiripa Culture (1500–200 BCE). Chiripa seems to have been a progenitor state for Tiahuanaco, on the south side of the lake, and Pucara (100 BCE–100CE) on the north and, through Tiahuanaco, for the Huari and Inca cultures of Peru. Chiripa's contributions include the architectural prototypes for a system of artificial mounds and semi-subterranean temples, and a style of low-relief stone sculpture, termed Yayamama after the Chiripa religious tradition. Yayamama sculpture typically features a prominent ray-headed being as well as male and female human and animal pairs.

Ancient Tiahuanaco lies about 15 miles (25 km) to the southwest of Chiripa. It sits at an elevation of approximately 12,600 feet (3840 m) and covers an area of approximately 2.31 square miles (6 square km) on the treeless altiplano. The ceremonial core of the city encompasses the Akapana, the Semi-Subterranean Temple, the Kalasasaya, and the courtyards of the Puntuni, and the Kerikala. A secondary area about a kilometer to the southwest is the site of the temple mound known as the Pumapunku. Understanding of these structures has been seriously impacted by rampant depredation at the site beginning in Colonial times and continuing into the modern era. In the sixteenth century the Spanish used stone from the ruins to build the nearby town of Tiahuanaco and its church, and some of the stone was even hauled to La Paz for use in buildings there. During the same era, looters dug through the Akapana looking for gold. In the first years of the twentieth century a railroad line was run through the site and more of its stones were taken and dynamited to provide rock for the roadbed (Protzen and Nair 2014, xvi).

The Semi-Subterranean Temple The Semi-Subterranean Temple at Tiahuanaco (Figure 2.19) takes the form of a scalene trapezoid, measuring approximately 94 by 85 feet (28.57 by 26.05 m). The lower walls of temple were restored during the early 1960s. The temple's four unequal length walls were constructed of sandstone and andesite blocks laid in horizontal courses without mortar, and buttressed at intervals by upright monolithic stones. Many of these stones extend above the current wall levels, suggesting that in ancient times, before the building was mined for its materials, the walls were considerably higher. Around the base of the wall are two rows of tenon heads, staggered in a triangular arrangement. Piles of additional tenon heads discovered in the court during excavation suggest that there may have been additional rows of tenon sculptures in the upper walls. The heads depict Yayamama-style flat faces with large staring eyes, heavy brows set atop a chisel-shaped nose to form a "T," and rectangular mouth; some heads appear to be wearing a hat or head-cloth.

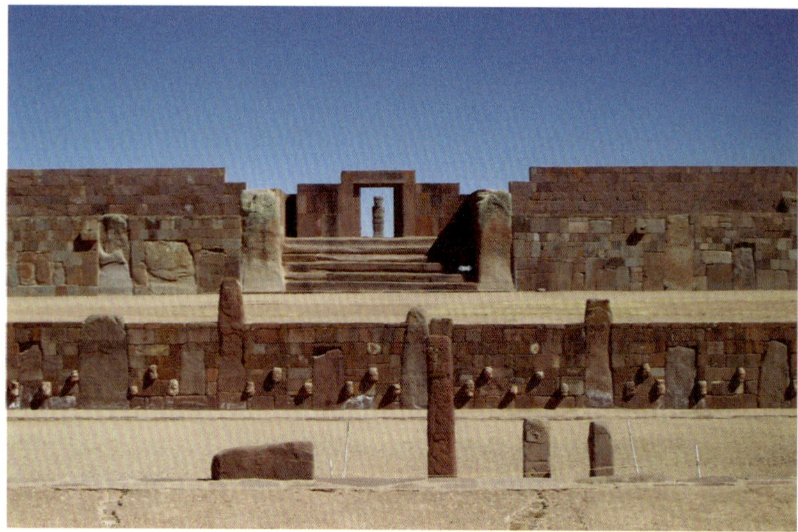

▶ **2.19** Tiahuanaco, Semi-Subterranean Temple with Yayamama Stela in center of the sunken court and the Kalasasaya in the background, c. 200 BCE–1000 CE.

The stone walls of the Semi-Subterranean Temple may have been higher in ancient times; they are decorated with two rows of tenon heads arranged in a repeating triangular format.

Yayamama Stela Standing in the center of the Semi-Subterranean Temple is a monumental stone stela (see in Figure 2.19) carved with a figure dressed in a short kilt decorated with pumas. The carving on this and the two smaller stelas nearby was done in the Yayamama style, which suggests the Semi-Subterranean Temple may have been the first structure built at the site and that the stela may have been its original cult image. The figure's face is rendered in the same manner as the tenon heads; its proper right arm reaches across the chest toward the left shoulder while the left- hand rests upon the stomach. Undulating forms, possibly serpents, are carved into the sides of the stela.

The Akapana, c. 200 BCE–1000 CE The Akapana (Figure 2.20) overlooks the Semi-Subterranean Temple and the Kalasasaya. It is such a large structure, measuring almost 700 feet (200 m) on each side and rising to a height of 56 feet (17 m), that for a long time it was thought to be a modified natural hill. However, it is actually an artificially constructed terraced platform mound that rose in six or seven steps. The levels of the platform were contained by dry-laid sandstone walls that repeated the Semi-Subterranean Temple's pattern of large upright stones bracketing horizontal courses, but with additional stair-stepped buttresses. The structure has been considerably damaged by looters and stone-thieves but it seems to have been roughly shaped like the letter "T" crossed by a second shorter arm. The summit of the platform shows the remains of several structures and what some scholars believe to have been a sunken court but may simply be the result of looters digging down from the top of the mound and tossing the soil over the side.

Gateway of the Sun The best-known monument of Tiahuanaco is the Gateway of the Sun, which stands in the northeast corner of

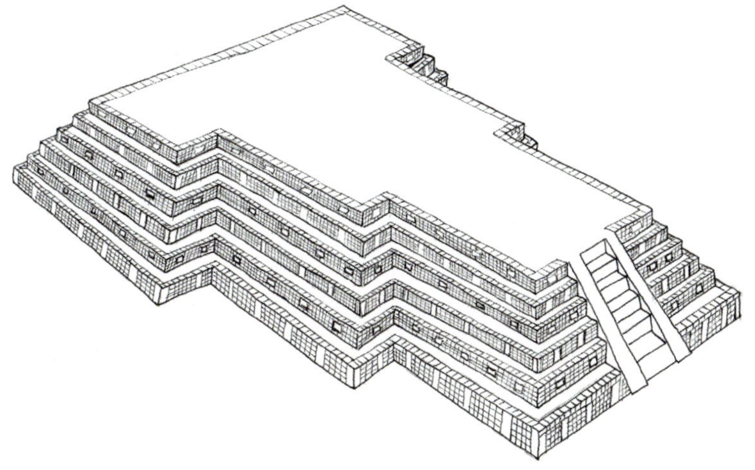

◀ **2.20** Tiahuanaco, Reconstruction drawing of the Akapana Pyramid, c. 200 BCE–1000 CE.

Until very recent times the Akapana was mined for its stones and since Colonial times has been a target of looters. This reconstruction shows the basic shape of the pyramid platform with its terraced walls. Opinions differ as to the nature of the structures that originally topped the platform.

the Kalasasaya, a bi-level court immediately adjacent to the Semi-Subterranean Temple; but this may not have been its original location. One theory is that it was relocated in ancient times and cracked during the move. It is one of three surviving monumental gateways at the site; the others being the so-called Gateway of the Moon, and the Sandstone Gateway. Fragments of several more are known from the Pumapunku. All were monolithic structures, meaning they were carved from a single massive block of stone rather than constructed from large individual stones using a post and lintel system, as is more common in world architecture.

The andesite Gateway of the Sun (Figure 2.21) stands 9.35 feet (2.85 m) high, 12.53 feet (3.82 m) wide, and is more than 20 inches (0.50 m) thick. The front of the gateway features a relief frieze with a

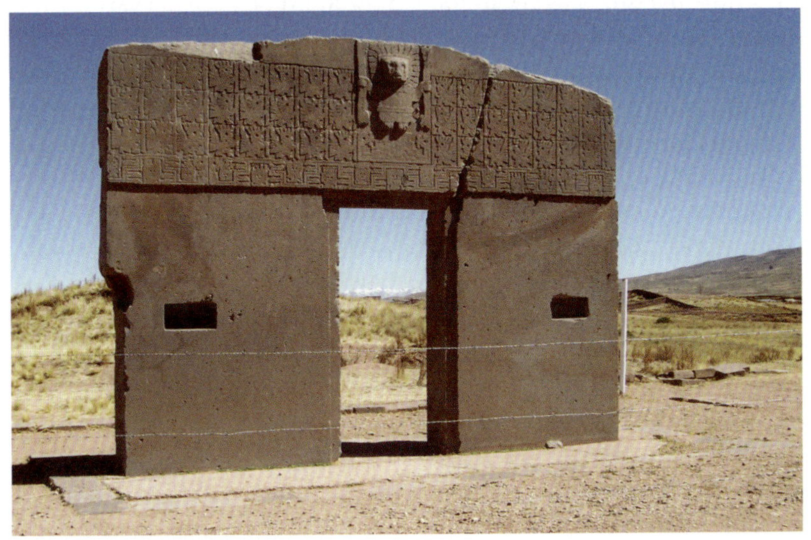

◀ **2.21** Tiahuanaco, Kalasasaya Temple, Gateway of the Sun, c. 200 BCE–1000 CE. 9.35 ft. x 12.53 ft. x 1.8 ft.

This monumental gateway was carved from a single block of andesite. The decorated band across its top features a high relief Staff God and bands of low relief attendant figures.

central, frontal image of a Staff God wearing a rayed headdress with appendages ending in puma heads and circular beads. The deity figure stands out in higher relief than the background attendant figures. His body and staffs are in low relief while his head projects sufficiently to be high relief. The face continues the Yayamama style with large eyes, in this case carved as a depression, chisel-shaped nose, and rectangular mouth. On either side of the main figure are blocks of avian and masked human attendants, each holding a staff and genuflecting toward the Staff God. They are arranged in three horizontal rows of eight figures each in a manner reminiscent of block embroidery on textiles. At the base of the frieze is a meander pattern with inset rayed heads. The carving of the attendant figures and meander band are interesting in that careful examination of the forms suggests that two, possibly three, different artists of unequal skill levels worked on the frieze.

Cut into the plain sides of the front of the Gate of the Sun are a pair of rectangular pockets intended for the attachment of other building blocks to the gate; typically, these would have been secured with copper or arsenic-copper alloy cramps. The molten metal would have been poured into cramp sockets cut into the stones. The back of the gateway features two large niches on either side of the doorway and paired niches in the upper corners of the frieze level. It is possible that these vertical recesses were used for the attachment of more than one building block (Protzen and Nair 1997, 154–162). Framing the doorway on the back are stepped cornice bands. The gateway shows modifications that suggest it was worked on for a considerable period of time and was, in fact, still unfinished when Tiahuanaco collapsed.

HUARI (600–1000 CE)

The Huari Empire spread out from its capital Huari, in Ayacucho, to control a vast state; its southern border with Tiahuanaco was in the Moquegua Valley, and its northern boundary was near modern Lima, a distance of approximately 800 miles. To administer their Empire the Huari built roads and established administrative centers of uniform plan. It is the regularity of the design of these outlying cities that has enabled archaeologists to map the extent of the Huari Empire. They were square, laid out on a grid plan, and protected by rough stone perimeter walls, sometimes reaching heights of 40 feet (12 m); Huari buildings appear to have been multi-storied, but in most cases all that remains are the foundations of these structures.

Huari Tunic with Sacrificer, c. 600–1000 CE The Huari are best known for their exquisite camelid and cotton fiber tapestry weave textiles, which often feature motifs derived from Tiahuanaco such as the Staff God and the winged attendant figures. The signature Huari garment was the male tunic. Like most Andean garments, tunics were not tailored but rather constructed from identical panels of cloth, usually measuring about 20 inches wide by 80 inches in length (50 by 200 cm). The panels were seamed together in the center, allowing an opening at midpoint large enough for the head. The sewn panels were then folded in half and the sides stitched leaving an opening for the arms. When worn the tunics would hang down to the typical Huari man's knees; as indicated from depictions of tunic wearers in a variety of media, the tunics were sometimes cinched at the waist by a woven belt.

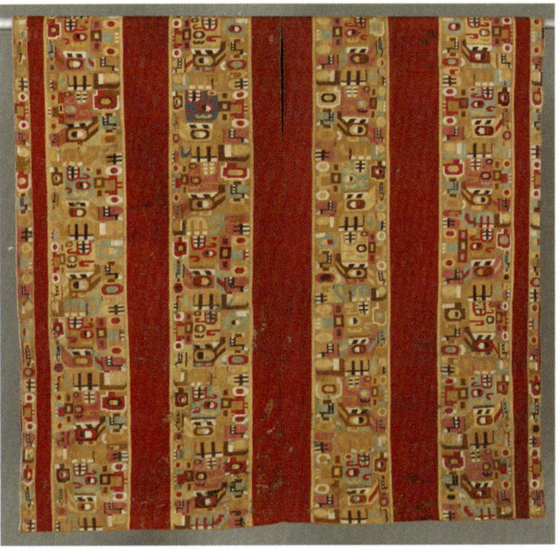

▲ **2.22** Huari, Sacrificer Tunic, c. 600–1000 CE. Camelid and cotton, 79.75 x 44.06 in.

Although tunics were standard male attire, this example was not an everyday item. Garments with such complex designs worked in several colors were reserved for ritual use by elite individuals.

Typically, Huari tunics have one to three vertical bands of discontinuous warp and weft tapestry separated by plain weave bands of a single color. The number of motifs used in Huari and Tiahuanaco textiles is fairly limited, although the designs range from relatively simple profile-faces and stepped-frets (these look like a stair with an attached scroll) to more complex figural patterns. Regardless of the complexity of the pattern, the imagery on each tunic consists solely of a single repeating motif. Given the limited number of patterns used, it is likely that the more complex patterns were the privilege of certain official or religious ranks. Other status indicators include the colors used and yarn count (the number of weft or horizontal threads). Tunics with the highest weft counts, rare colors like dark inky blues, and elaborate patterns consisting of multiple small motif elements, such as in the Sacrificer Tunic (Figure 2.22), and are more time-consuming to weave, suggest a garment belonging to an individual of the highest rank. Less complex patterns such as the more common profile-face- and stepped-fret patterns, executed in more readily available colors such as reds, browns and yellows, and with lower weft counts, may indicate lower status owners. Huari weavers manipulated their tapestry motifs in a number of ways including expanding and contracting image widths, elimination and substitution of elements, inverted orientation of forms, and color variations, among others.

Colombia and the Isthmus (c. 100–1200 CE)

During the first millennium CE, a tradition of monumental stone sculpture, often with a funerary context, developed to the north of Peru in the southwestern Colombian Andes and to a lesser extent on the isthmus in Panama and Costa Rica. The most spectacular and largest numbers of sculptures come from a series of related sites in Colombia,

TAKE A CLOSER LOOK
Seeing the Form in Huari Textiles

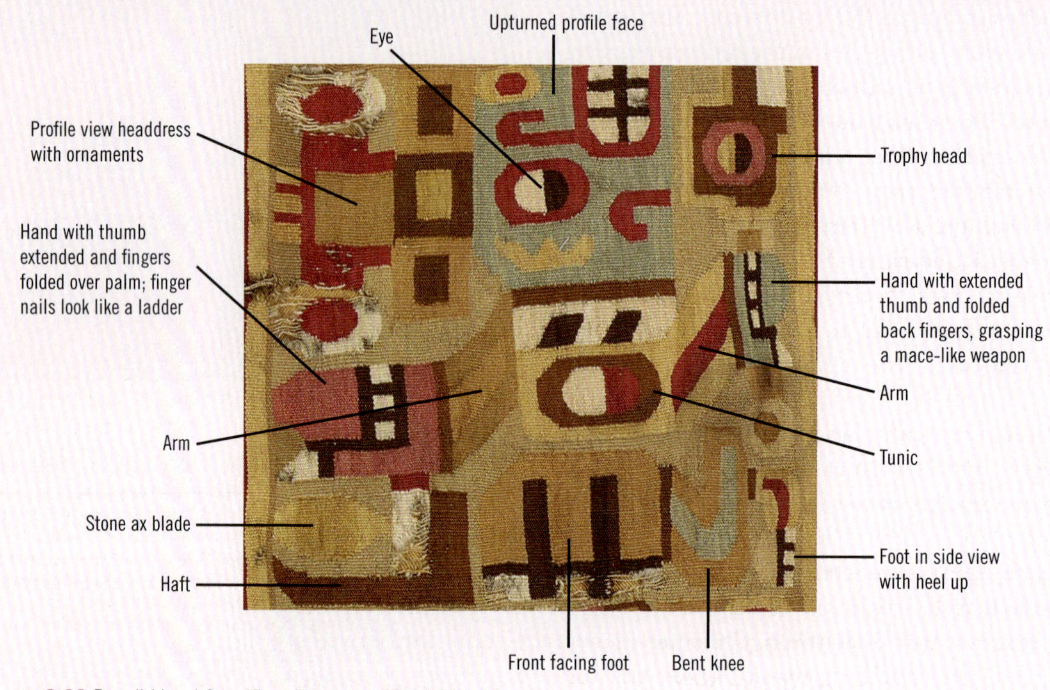

▲ **2.23** Detail Huari Sacrificer Tunic, c. 600-1000 CE
Detail showing the parts of the base motif.

Simple two-color weaving patterns, such as profile-faces and stepped-frets are fairly easy to learn to recognize. More complex patters, with additional elaborations and manipulations, can be much harder to see and comprehend, especially when confronted with textile bands that seem to be entirely filled with complex multicolor patterns. The first thing to remember is that even the most complex designs repeat a single motif, often in blocks of four. Look for color repeats that allow the identification of a block. Once the block is identified, it is easier to separate out a single motif. Below (Figure 2.23) is a single figural motif isolated from the Sacrificer Tunic (Figure 2.22) with the parts labeled.

One key to unraveling a figural motif such as in the Sacrificer Tunic is to look for a divided, football-shaped eye. Normally, there is only one. However, this element has been multiplied in the elaboration of the Sacrificer Tunic, and there are three things that look like eyes: the largest appearing on the figure's tunic, a second serving as the being's eye, and a third found on the trophy head finial of his staff. In this case, it may be easier for some to find a second possible key element: the typical Huari tooth-filled mouth; in this example, it is in the center of the top edge because the Sacrificer has tilted his head backwards. The Huari frequently focus on dentition, often adding fangs to supernatural beings. Once the head has been located it is possible to see that the being wears an elaborate headdress (upper left), holds a staff in one hand (right edge) and an axe in the other (bottom left), and that he balances on one large foot (bottom center) while the other leg and foot are in a kneeling position (bottom right).

located around the municipality of San Agustín. At the same time in Panama massive alignments of basalt columns were erected at El Caño, while in Costa Rica figurative sculpture was produced in the Nicoya, Atlantic Watershed, Linea Vieja, and Diquis regions.

SAN AGUSTÍN, COLOMBIA (100–900 CE)

Today, the sites of San Agustín, Alto de los Ídolos, and Alto de Las Piedras compose the San Agustín archaeological park. Some six hundred individual stone sculptures, ranging in size from as small as 20 inches (50 cm) to more than 13 feet (4 m) tall, have been found in association with large burial mounds that were connected by paths, terraces, and raised causeways. The sculptures, carved from tuff and volcanic rock, depict supernatural beings, human males and females, and a variety of animals. They functioned as sarcophagus covers, tomb markers, and as guardian figures.

Female Supernatural, El Purutal, San Agustín Supernatural beings identifiable, as in Peru, by their fanged mouths, make up the largest number of sculptures, followed by humans, including the doubled guardians, and animals. The carvings range from highly stylized and even schematic representations to more naturalistic interpretations of the human form. Even the most lifelike of the San Agustín sculptures, typically those functioning as relief-carved sarcophagus lids or grave markers depicting the decedent, lack realistic ratios of proportion. Heads are often exaggerated in size while the trunk and limbs of the figures are compressed. Also, the statues have an overall blockiness resulting from the carver's approach to the stone as a four-sided relief rather than a true work in the round. As shown by the Female Supernatural from El Purutal (Figure 2.24), the visual impact of these sculptures was originally heightened with red, yellow, and black pigments.

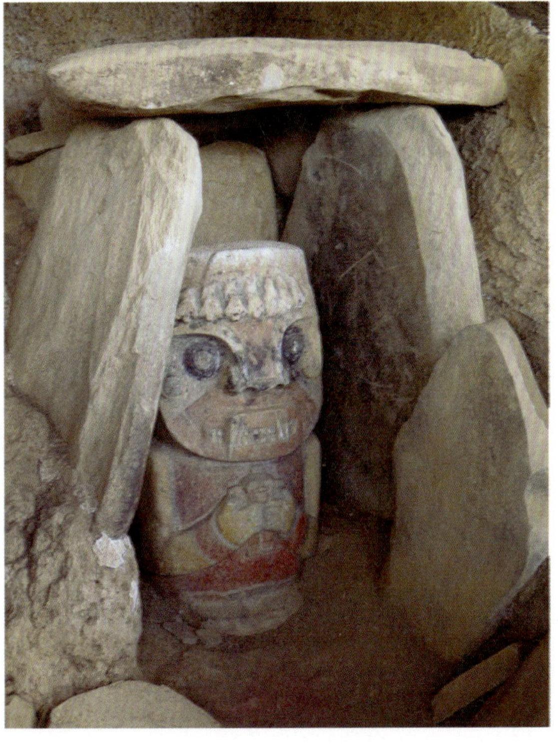

▼ **2.24** San Agustín, Colombia, El Purutal, Female Supernatural with Child, c. 100–900 CE.

Most of the San Agustín sculptures have lost their original pigments but all were once brightly painted as is this figure from El Purutal.

COSTA RICA (500–1200 CE)

The tradition of carving stone sculpture began in ancient Costa Rica early in the first millennium CE, perhaps earlier in some regions. Ancient stone workers created perfectly spherical stone balls, some weighing as much as 15 tons and measuring over 6 feet (2 m) in diameter, fashioned large ornamented metates, and carved figurative sculptures,

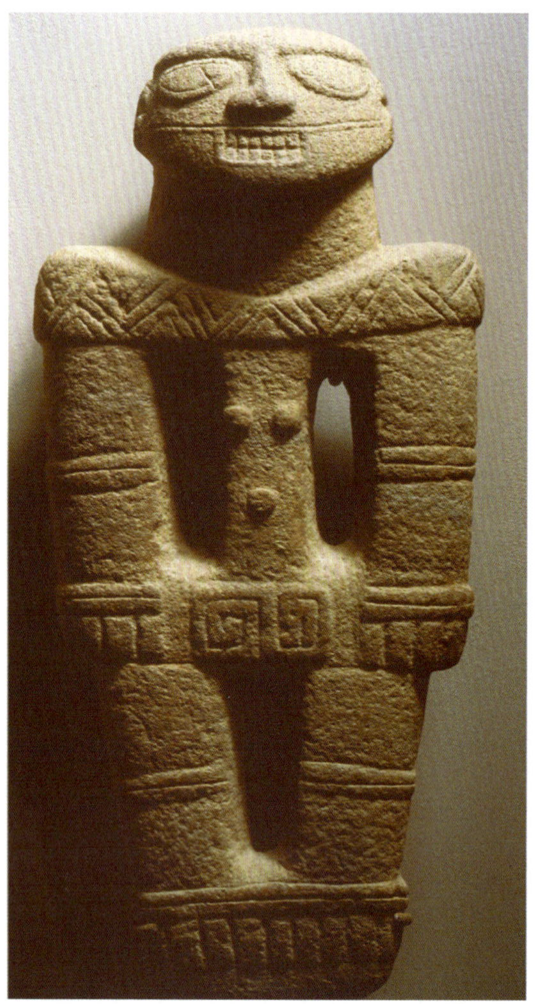

▲ **2.25** Diquis, Costa Rica, Peg-Based Female Figure, c. 800–1550 CE. 21 in. high.

This statue was probably a grave marker for an elite woman since it displays female sexual characteristics and dress.

ranging from less than 2 feet to more than 5 feet in height. The style of figurative carving varies widely from region to region and even within regions over time. Sculptures tend to be freestanding, sometimes with a pegged foot to facilitate their insertion into the ground. As at San Agustín, the Costa Rican sculptures are thought to have been associated with funerary mounds and cemeteries. However, since few works have been scientifically excavated it is difficult, in many cases, to know their specific context or even formulate an accurate chronology.

Diquis Peg-Based Female Figure, c. 800–1550 CE This 21 inch (55 cm) tall, pierced slab-like figure from the Diquis Delta (Figure 2.25) was probably a grave marker for an elite female since it displays female sexual characteristics: breasts and extended belly button often associated with pregnancy and perhaps intended to show that the woman has given birth. She wears a short skirt marked with a scroll pattern, ligature ornaments at the wrists, elbows, knees, and ankles; the designs on her shoulders probably represent a beaded collar. The eyes are large and tear-shaped, the brow and nose form a single T-element and the mouth is drawn back to reveal the teeth in a death grimace.

The Late Period (1200–1550 CE)

When Francisco Pizarro Gonzáles (c.1471–1541) landed in Peru in 1533, the Inca (also Inka) emperor ruled a territory that ran from southern Colombia through Ecuador and Peru down to central Chile, a distance of some 2,500 miles (4,023 km) north to south, and continued eastward to include parts of Bolivia and northwestern Argentina. This empire, known to the Inca as the *Tahuantinsuyu* or "Land of the Four Quarters," absorbed numerous highland and lowland peoples who had more often been adversaries than allies. The Inca state had been founded in the early thirteenth century by Manco Cápac, who led his small ayllu to settle in the Cuzco Valley.

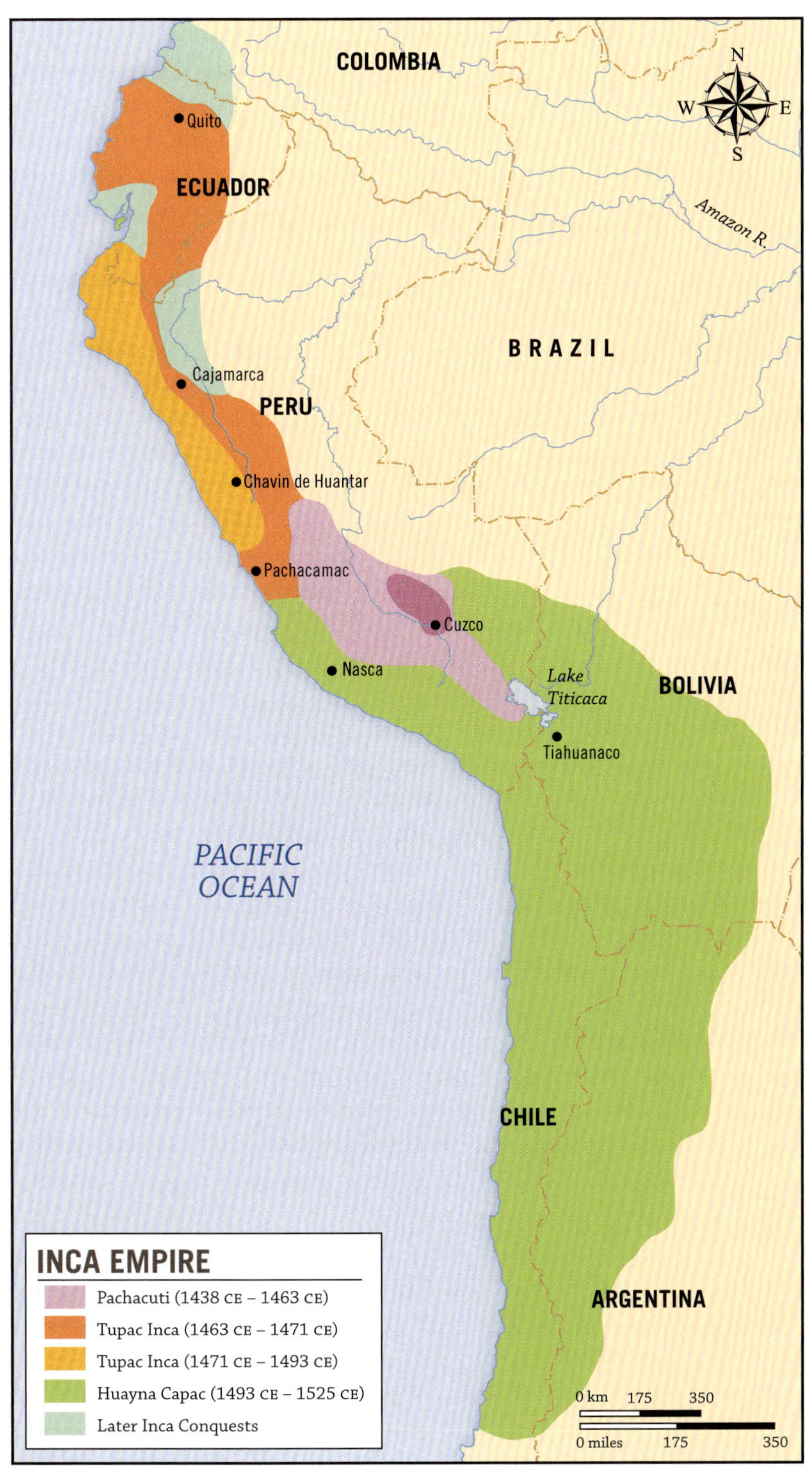
COLOMBIA
N
W
E
S
Quito
ECUADOR
Amazon R.
BRAZIL
Cajamarca
PERU
Chavin de Huantar
Pachacamac
Cuzco
Nasca
Lake
Titicaca
BOLIVIA
Tiahuanaco
PACIFIC
OCEAN
CHILE
ARGENTINA
INCA EMPIRE
Pachacuti (1438 CE – 1463 CE)
Tupac Inca (1463 CE – 1471 CE)
Tupac Inca (1471 CE – 1493 CE)
Huayna Capac (1493 CE – 1525 CE)
Later Inca Conquests
0 km 175 350
0 miles 175 350

The Inca Empire (c. 1438–1533 CE)

In the early fifteenth century the Inca were a group of farmers living in the Cuzco valley under the leadership of Hatun Tupaq who took the name Wiracocha (1410–1438 CE) when he came to the throne as the eighth ***Sapa Inca*** or "unique king" of the Kingdom of Cuzco. Wiracocha launched a campaign of conquest that saw the Inca move into the Urubamba Valley and then into the Titicaca basin. However, in 1438 Cuzco was attacked by the Chancas who were also trying to expand their territory. Determining that Cuzco was not defensible, Wiracocha and his designated heir abandoned the city, leaving its fate to his third son, Kusi Yupanqui. After defeating the Chancas, Kusi took the throne, as Pachacuti (r.1438–1471 CE), a name meaning "earth shaker." Pachacuti expanded the Inca state into southern Peru and northward into Ecuador. He is credited with re-designing Cuzco in the form of a puma with Saqsawaman as the head, the Rio Tullumayo as its spine, the main plaza as its belly, and its tail where the land narrows as the city's two rivers come to confluence. Pachacuti also founded a number of royal estates, including Ollantaytambo and Machu Picchu.

INCA ARCHITECTURE IN CUZCO

The Inca are justly famous for their extraordinary cyclopean architecture at sites such as Sacsahuaman, overlooking Cuzco, and Ollantaytambo, a royal estate some 37 miles (60km) northwest of Cuzco. Using stone tools, hoisting grips (drill holes through which ropes were threaded), gravity, and friction, Inca masons fitted massive, irregularly shaped granite blocks, some weighing as much as 100 tons, into walls so tight that the gap between blocks is measured in fractions of a millimeter. Important temples, such as the Koricancha (Qorikancha) in Cuzco, and royal palaces were built of regular blocks of ashlar masonry, laid up without mortar. However, non-elite structures having no religious or governmental functions and simple residences were often built of mud-bonded rough stone. In areas of the empire where suitable stone was not available, for example Tambo Colorado near the coast, the pragmatic Inca built using traditional adobe blocks.

Koricancha The city's most sacred shrine was the Koricancha meaning "Golden Enclosure," which lay in the root of the Puma Chupan or "Puma's Tail." Within the walls of the Koricancha were shrines to the Sun God Inti, the Creator god Viracocha, the Moon, Venus, and the Pleiades as well as those that held the gods of the peoples conquered by the Inca. The complex was enclosed by granite walls which, according to Garcilasco de la Vega (1539–1616), were covered with sheets of gold; those were quickly looted by the Spanish. After the conquest, the Spanish destroyed much of the Inca city and built a European-style one on its ruins. The remaining walls of the Koricancha (Figure 2.26)

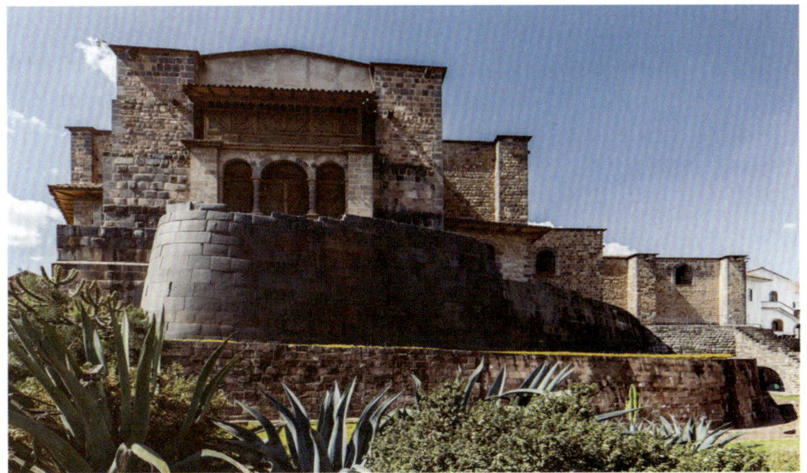

◀ **2.26** Inca Cuzco, Koricancha and Church of Santo Domingo, 1100–1550 CE.

After the Conquest the Spanish stripped the gold plate from the walls of the Koricancha and using some of its stone, built a church atop the ruins. The curving, dark granite wall was laid up without mortar; the stones were fitted to each other by abrading.

serve as a foundation under the Colonial Church and Monastery of Santo Domingo. This curving section of the Koricancha was constructed using fine dark gray granite which still stands today despite the region's numerous earthquakes. Inca masons constructed battered walls, which were trapezoidal in cross-section so that the stones were self-bracing; the same principle resulted in trapezoidal-form doorways and windows, which have withstood repeated shaking by tremors over the centuries.

MACHU PICCHU (C. 1450 CE)

In the mid-fifteenth century the Sapa Inca Pachacuti began building a new royal estate (Figure 2.27) on a narrow ridge between the mountains known as Machu Picchu and Huayna Picchu. The site sits in a three-sided bend of the Urubamba River at an elevation of 8,040 feet (2450 m). Because of its lower elevation and close proximity to the equator, Machu Picchu was warmer and milder than the capital, and when conditions in Cuzco were cold and unpleasant the Inca and his retinue would make the journey to Machu Picchu, swelling the population to as many as 1,500 individuals. The permanent population of the estate was fairly small, probably fewer than five hundred persons whose job it was to maintain the site and grow crops on the terraced hillsides. Unlike Cuzco and other major cities made over in Spanish style after the conquest, Machu Picchu, while known to the Spanish, was never occupied by them so it remained largely as it had been during Inca times.

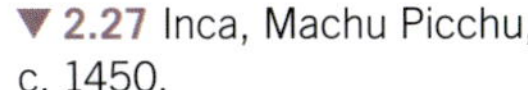

▼ **2.27** Inca, Machu Picchu, c. 1450.

Pachacuti built several royal estates including Machu Picchu. The city's temples, palaces, and residences accommodated some 1,500 people when the Inca was in residence; food for all these people was grown in the terraced beds along the mountain sides as well as in fields along the Urubamba below.

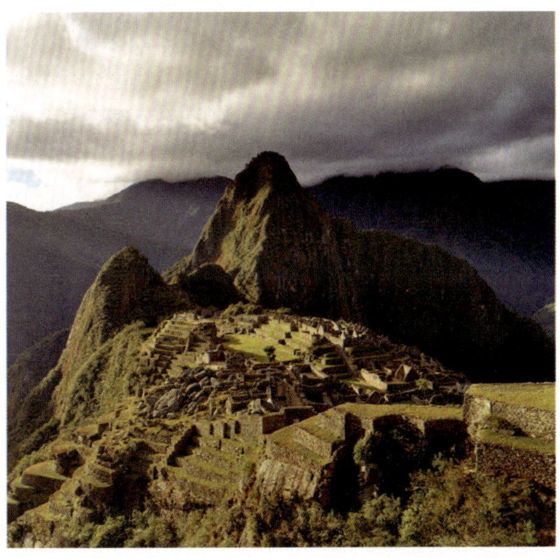

Machu Picchu is a much more impressive site than is conveyed by the standard shots of the "city center." It covers more than 80,000 acres, including more than six hundred terraces that were built, for agricultural purposes, down the slopes of the mountain all the way to the Urubamba River some 1,500 feet below. The terraces at Machu Picchu are a marvelous feat of engineering. The retaining walls, built of locally quarried stone, were battered for stability and then backed with smaller stones, gravel, sand, and then filled with soil brought up from the river valley. The terraces were designed in this fashion to provide for the careful drainage of rainwater downward through each planting level, eliminating the need for irrigation. By terracing the mountainsides, the Inca were able not only to utilize the steep slopes but also to extend their growing seasons through the changes in altitude.

The entrance to the city was through a gateway in the west wall that framed a view of Huayna Picchu. The city was organized around a central plaza and divided into sectors of royal and religious structures and residential neighborhoods, all constructed of local stone. Most of Machu Picchu's residential buildings were rectangular in design with gabled ends supporting wood beam and thatch roofs. Houses were typically one room with a single trapezoidal shaped doorway. In some cases buildings constructed on slopes might have two levels and guard houses often had one long wall left open. Exceptions to this were religious and royal structures, which might have circular or U-shaped walls and multiple doorways and windows. Gravity-fed water from a spring in the north face of the mountain was supplied to Machu Picchu's residents by a water distribution system consisting of stone canals and fountains positioned throughout the city.

Torreon or Temple of the Sun, c. 1450 CE The exception to the usual rectangular building plan at Machu Picchu is the Torreon (Figure 2.28) or "tower." The Torreon is a P-shaped building, consisting of a segment of straight wall to which was added a half-round section. The round section frames a portion of the granite outcrop upon which the structure was constructed. Indeed, it is the marriage of built wall and living rock that makes the Torreon remarkable. This blending is particularly apparent in the small cavern beneath the tower where the Inca carved a series of steps into the rock and then built a wall with blocks carefully contoured to the shape of the native outcrop.

The Inca seem to have had an appreciation of stone as more than building material. Some Inca legends, such as that of the stones on the battlefield rising up to assist Pachacuti in defeating the Chancas, hint at animistic or numinous beliefs, meaning that certain mountains, stones, or rock outcrops were considered to have spiritual essence, to be *huacas* or shrines in a sacred geography. Such sacred rocks were often distinguished in various ways, such as being framed by, within, or contoured by masonry architecture. Machu Picchu is replete

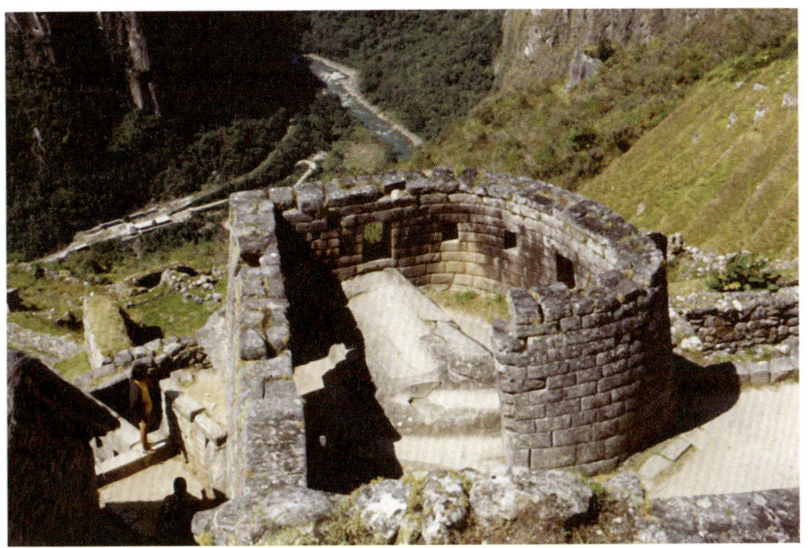

◀ **2.28** Inca, Machu Picchu, Torreon or Temple of the Sun, c. 1450 CE.

The Torreon is a P-shaped building that frames the top of the granite outcrop over which it was built. The building's trapezoidal windows frame views of distant mountains considered to be sacred by the Inca.

with examples of this practice, including the Torreon. The Torreon's windows frame views of the surrounding mountains, its walls are contoured to the living rock, and its circular section surrounds or "frames" a natural rock outcrop. The Torreon has also been proposed to be a sun temple or solar observatory as a ray from the rising sun on the day of the winter solstice (June in the southern hemisphere) is said to bisect the stone inside the structure. Similarly the cavern beneath the Torreon is also said to be aligned to the rising sun on the day of the winter solstice.

Intiwatana Stone Atop the terraced hill that forms the so-called Intiwatana pyramid, the highest point of the city, is the carved rock, popularly known as the "hitching-post of the sun" or Intiwatana Stone (Figure 2.29); the popular idea being that such structures helped to "anchor" the sun in its travels. The name for the stone at Machu Picchu is borrowed from that given by locals to a circular nub rising from a table rock at Pisac, which Ephraim George Squier visited in the 1860s and decided was a "sundial." When Hiram Bingham saw the square stone rising from a relatively uneven platform stone atop the hill at Machu Picchu, he conclude it was also a sundial. Both Squier and Bingham were incorrect in their assumptions about their respective Intiwatana stones. Approached from the western steps of the platform the Intiwatana stone aligns with and echoes the shape and shadow patterns of Huayna Picchu behind it. The Intiwatana's four faces are oriented toward the cardinal directions, and surrounding sacred mountains. Other "echo" stones at Machu Picchu include the 25 foot (7.6 m) long "Sacred Rock" in the eastern sector of the city, which replicates the silhouette of Mount Yanantin to the east of the city.

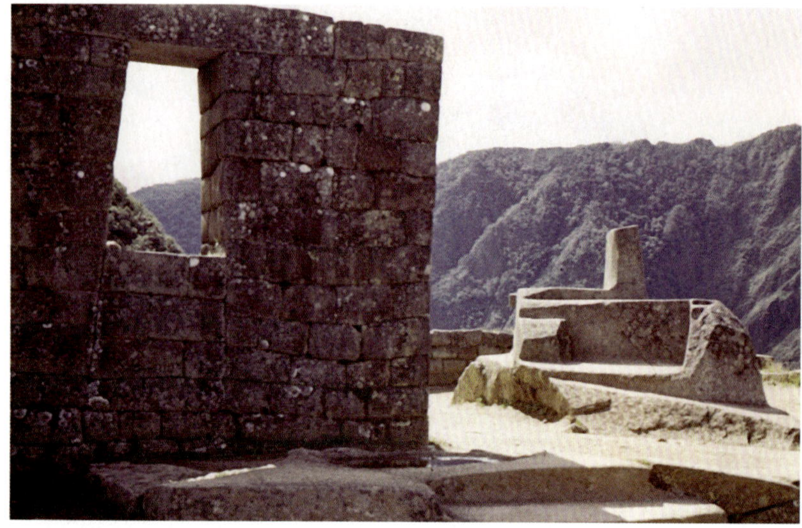

▶ **2.29** Inca, Machu Picchu, Intiwatana Pyramid, Intiwatana Stone, c. 1450 CE.

Popularly conceived as a sundial or hitching post for the sun, the four faces of the Intiwatana Stone orient to the cardinal directions and surrounding sacred mountains.

INCA ROCK CARVING

In addition to stones carved to reference sacred mountains, the Inca distinguished inherently sacred rocks, such as the Kenko and Sayhuite stones, with carving. Such embellishments often included step designs, platform shapes, terraces, **cupules** (cup-shaped depressions), and channels for the flowing of liquids over the stone. In a few cases zoomorphic elements were also carved.

The Sayhuite Stone The Sayhuite (also Saywite) Stone (Figure 2.30) is a large andesite boulder, about 13 feet (4 m) in diameter and more than 8 feet (2.5 m) tall at its highest point. Its upper portion is carved with some two hundred geometric and zoomorphic forms. The animals depicted are felines, serpents, frogs or toads, lizards, felines, monkeys, and birds. The animals are spread across a landscape of mountains, water channels, ponds, steps, terraces, platforms, and rectangular basins. The summit of the stone contains a well with channels running from it to various areas of the stone; when filled with water, the overflow follows the carved channels and ultimately, spills over the carved edge of the boulder. Over the years there have been a number of theories proposed as to the purpose of these carved landscape stones, including that they were design models for cities or hydraulic models for building irrigation and drainage systems. While these seem reasonable, there are no Inca towns that align with the layout of either the Kenko or Sayhuite stones, nor any known water systems that correspond. What is more likely is the carvings were done to embellish and facilitate the bathing with liquid of a stone that was considered sacred. This is basically a more elaborate version, for a larger stone, of the shaft channel and reservoir atop the head of the Lanzon, which when filled from above, flowed liquid over the statue of the "Smiling God."

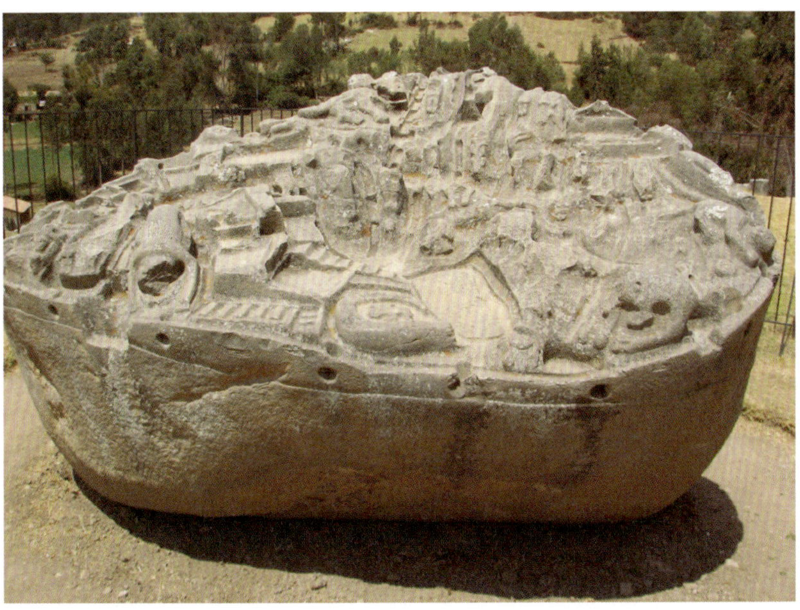

◀ **2.30** Inca, Abancay Province, Sayhuite Stone, c. 1440–1520 CE. 13 ft. diameter.

This huge granite bolder was carved with animals and mountains, steps, terraces, platforms, and water reservoirs and channels. Stones that were inherently sacred were often decorated and offerings of water or beer poured over them.

INCA CERAMICS

The classic Inca style of ceramics, sometimes termed "Imperial Inca", developed in the Cuzco region around 1400 CE and continued in production until the Spanish Conquest. The Inca genius for organization is evident in the standardization of vessel types across the empire. The potters who worked under the Inca produced around fourteen different vessel forms, which were made in a range of sizes to suit various needs. Among the common forms were the *keros* or "beakers," which could be either ceramics or wood, the *urpu* or bulbous jar used for storing maize, flat dishes, the *paccha***,** which was a foot-plow shaped funnel used to pour maize beer as an offering to the earth, and the ***aryballo***, a vessel with a cylindrical flaring-rimmed neck, broad body, and a pointed foot, used for storing liquids.

▼ **2.31** Inca Aryballo, c. 1400–1532 CE. 8.62 in. × 7.37 in. × 5.75 in.

Inca potters made certain standard vessel forms in a range of sizes to suit a range of uses; this is a fairly small example of its type. These classic forms were often copied across the empire and embellished with local decorative motifs. Aryballo were used for storing liquids.

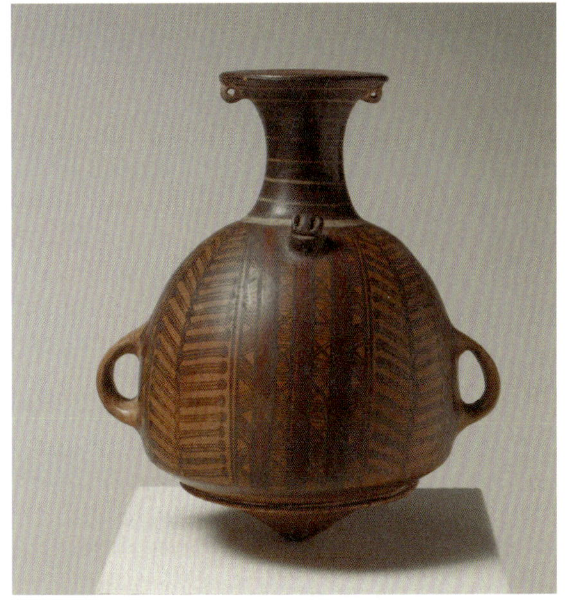

Classic Inca Aryballo, c. 1400–1532 CE The vessel most closely identified with the Inca culture is the aryballo (Figure 2.31), whose Spanish name derives from the vessel's similarity to the Greek pyriform aryballos. The Inca aryballo was a practical vessel used for carrying water and storing maize beer. To facilitate these functions, the Inca potters added handles and a lug in the form of a llama head to the shoulder of the vessel so it could be carried on the back with a tumpline. The pointed foot allowed the aryballo to stand upright in sandy soil. However, most also have a natural balance point somewhere on the body, which allows them to be positioned on their sides with the neck angled up, this facilitated the tipping of larger vessels for pouring.

Painted decoration on aryballos in the Cuzco area, consisted of vertical bands of geometric designs such as zigzags, linear X-and-band motifs, and Quipu patterns, painted in red and black slip on a cream ground. From the distribution of the Cuzco style vessels across the Inca Empire, it appears they may have been presented as gifts to local administrators and others who had served the empire. In the provinces these high status ceramics were often replicated in form but decorated with local motifs and patterns.

INCA TEXTILES

As in earlier Andean civilizations, textiles played an important role in the Inca Empire. The production of the finest cloth, particularly that worn by the Sapa Inca, was the task of the "Chosen Women" or "Virgins of the Sun," who, from a young age, lived chastely in the temple compounds, where among their duties was the weaving of a fine double-tapestry cloth known as ***kompi***. The wearing of tunics made from this exceptional cloth was a privilege controlled by the state and the Sapa Inca often rewarded service with gifts of textiles. Other elite and ordinary textiles were woven on the local level with some communities paying their taxes to the state in cloth. Such garments would be redistributed as part of administrative and military pay.

▼ **2.32** Inca, Tunic with Diamond Band, c. 1460–1540. Camelid hair and cotton, 29 in. × 35 in.

Finely woven textiles such as this tunic were known as kompi and were highly prized by Inca elites. Unlike earlier tunics that were woven as two lengths of cloth and sewn together down the center, this is a single length of cloth with the neck opening woven into the middle.

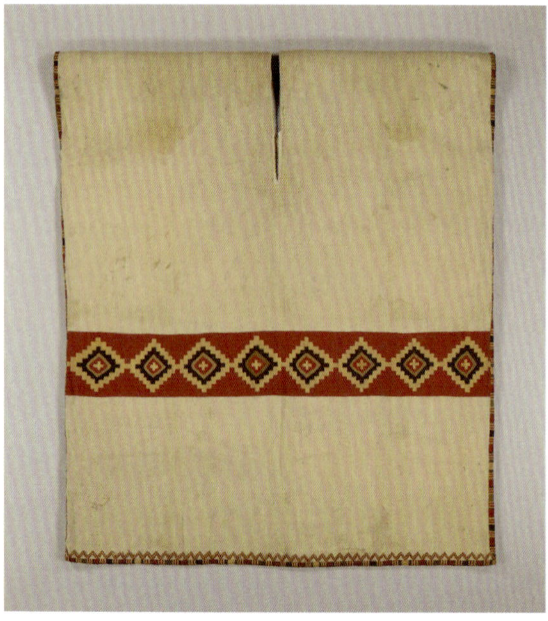

Tunic with Diamond Band, c. 1460–1540 CE

Many of the surviving Inca period tunics or "*unku*" were military uniforms as was the Tunic with Diamond Band from the Ica region (Figure 2.32). In contrast to earlier "square" tunics, those made by the Inca were longer than they were wide so that the garment hung down to the knees. Inca tunics were also different from those of earlier cultures in that they were made from a single length of cloth instead of being seamed together. To create a neck opening in the cloth Inca weavers strung their looms sideways. Typically warp threads run vertically through the length of the cloth and the weft threads are horizontal, going from side to side. By reversing this arrangement it was possible to create an opening using discontinuous warp threads. When finished, the length of cloth was simply folded over and the sides stitched together. This tunic is an example of kompi and is extremely practical in that it is reversible, the pattern being the same inside and out and front to back. The design consists of a single red belt at the waist ornamented with a pattern of stepped diamonds in white, black, green, and red with central crosses in white. The hem and sides of the garment are embellished with embroidery in the same colors. Similarly to ceramics, gifts of fine textiles often inspired locally woven examples that followed Inca construction techniques but were decorated with locally significant motifs.

The Colonial Period

When Francisco Pizarro Gonzales landed on the coast of Peru, he found the Inca Empire in disarray. Huayna Capac (r. 1493–1524) had contracted smallpox and died in Quito and a civil war over the succession had erupted between Capac's surviving sons Huascar (1503–1532) and Atahualpa (1502–1533). Just before Pizarro arrived Atahualpa murdered his brother and ascended the throne. In 1532 Pizarro captured Atahualpa and demanded a ransom that required filling a large room with gold and then twice again with silver. It took several months for sufficient gold and silver objects to arrive to fill the room but as soon as the ransom demand was met, Pizarro released Atahualpa only to arrest him for the murder of his brother. He was executed on July 26, 1533, effectively bringing the Inca Empire to an end.

In the first years after the Spanish Conquest of the Andes, Indigenous artisans—silversmiths, weavers and painters—continued to work as they always had, particularly in the more isolated areas. As the work of conquest and conversion progressed, the populations of the Andes became more or less Catholic, although there was often a fusion of the old beliefs with those of the new religion. As elsewhere in Latin America, much of the art created during the Colonial era was made for the Church.

Painting in the Colonial Andes

As early as the 1540s the first European artists began arriving in Peru, Colombia, and Ecuador, bringing with them the guild system. In South America the guild system was receptive to Indigenous artists; many were brought into the guild, where they received training in European styles, media, and techniques, often working together with European artists. One of the early Colonial art centers was Cuzco, where from the sixteenth through eighteenth centuries a group of Inca and European artists worked together, producing paintings for the various mendicant churches tasked with converting the Native Peoples. They created both easel paintings and murals that sometimes included astonishing transformations of Christian themes, such as the archangels Michael and Uriel dressed in the finery of Spanish gentlemen and carrying arquebuses

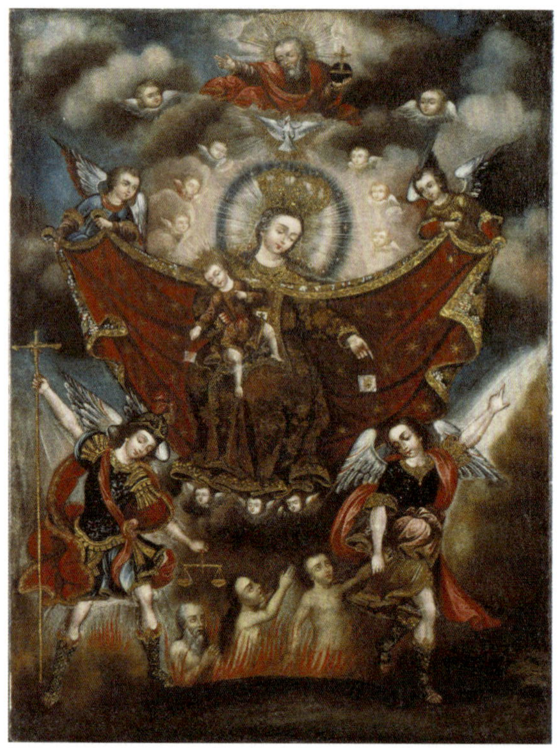

▲ **2.33** Cuzco School, Circle of Diego Quispe Tito (1611–1681) *Virgin of Carmel Saving Souls in Purgatory*, late seventeenth century CE. Oil on canvas, 41 in. × 29 in.

This painting shows the Madonna and Child holding out scapulars as a sign of the Virgin's promise to deliver early from Purgatory those who wear the scapular.

(rifles). Unfortunately the names of most of the Indigenous artists working in the Cuzqueño style are unknown.

Circle of Diego Quispe Tito (1611–1681),* Virgin of Carmel Saving Souls in Purgatory, *seventeenth century One exception to the general anonymity of Native painters in the Andes is Diego Quispe Tito. Quispe Tito was descended from Incan nobility and was born in Cuzco. His earliest documented work dates from 1627 when he was sixteen years old. He spent his working life in the community of San Sebastian not far from Cuzco. Nothing concrete is known about his training, although one popular story has him studying under the Italian Jesuit painter Bernardo Bitti (1548–1610); but Bitti died before Quispe Tito was born. It is probable, however, that Quispe had studied Bitti's works in Cuzco, where the Friar-painter was active in the late sixteenth century. Another tale has Quispe Tito traveling to study in Italy and Spain. A more likely influence on his work would be Flemish engravings brought by the mendicant friars to aid in the work of conversion. Often the illustrations in those books, used as examples of the type of image required, were directly copied. Among Quispe Tito's models are designs gleaned from the Wierix brothers, Jan Sadler, Cornelis Galle, and Johannes Stradanus, which Tito interspersed in his paintings along with Andean motifs (Bailey 2011, 297).

Attribution of Spanish Colonial paintings is often a difficult task as many are unsigned and church archives do not always contain records of commissions or contracts, particularly in the case of Indigenous artists. The *Virgin of Carmel Saving Souls in Purgatory* (Figure 2.33) is one such unsigned work, but stylistically consistent with the work of Quispe Tito. It is a smallish painting, measuring 41 (104.1 cm) by 29 inches (73.7 cm). According to Carmelite tradition, the order's brown scapular was presented to St. Simon Stock in 1251 by the Virgin Mary, who appeared to him with it in her hand and promised that those who wear the scapular and remain faithful in their devotion will be delivered early from Purgatory. The painting shows the Virgin Mary in the center in her role as Queen of Heaven with the Christ Child seated on her lap, the Holy Spirit and God the Father centered above her. Angels spread open her cloak in a gesture of protection for the souls being released from Purgatory by two archangels. Both the Virgin and Christ Child hold out small scapulars as a sign of the Virgin's promise. The influence of Jerome Wierix's engraving of the *Holy Trinity with Archangels*

(c. 1586–1600) is evident in Quispe Tito's figures of God the Father, the Holy Spirit, and the Archangel holding the staff and balance scales.

Circle of the Master of Calamarca,* Archangel with Arquebus, *Salamiel Paxdei, late seventeenth century One of the more popular subjects of the Cuzco School was that of the soldier archangel often carrying an arquebus. These paintings were widely distributed and inspired similar works in Bolivia and Argentina. One such painting comes from the Titicaca School in Bolivia (Figure 2.34) and is attributed to the anonymous painter known as the Master of Calamarca for the two Archangels he painted for the colonial church there. The popularity of archangels derives from their role in Catholicism as representing the spiritual functioning of the Cosmos, and for Aymara and Quechua converts whose traditional religion had venerated the sun, moon, and stars, such beings could be extrapolated as Andean deities such as Ilyapa, Inti, and Viracocha.

Tapestries and Weaving in the Colonial Andes

Prior to the Conquest, the weaving of fine textiles was considered a high art. The wearing of clothing was not simply a practical matter but was part of the political strategy of the empire. The type of garment, the quality of its weaving, and the designs used in its decoration identified the wearer's rank, status, and community or regional affiliation. The wearing of Inca style garments, especially by Inca noble families, continued after the Conquest despite the efforts of Spanish officials and the Church to persuade them to adopt Spanish dress. Inca-style garments of the early Colonial Period, while made in the traditional style, often incorporated Spanish decorative motifs and materials such as silk and metallic threads.

▼ 2.34 Lake Titicaca School, Circle of the Master of Calamarca, *Archangel with Arquebus*, Salamiel Paxdei, late 17th century CE. Oil on cotton, 42.50 in. × 31 in.

Native painters in Cuzco and elsewhere were fond of depicting Christian archangels in fancy Spanish costume and carrying long guns.

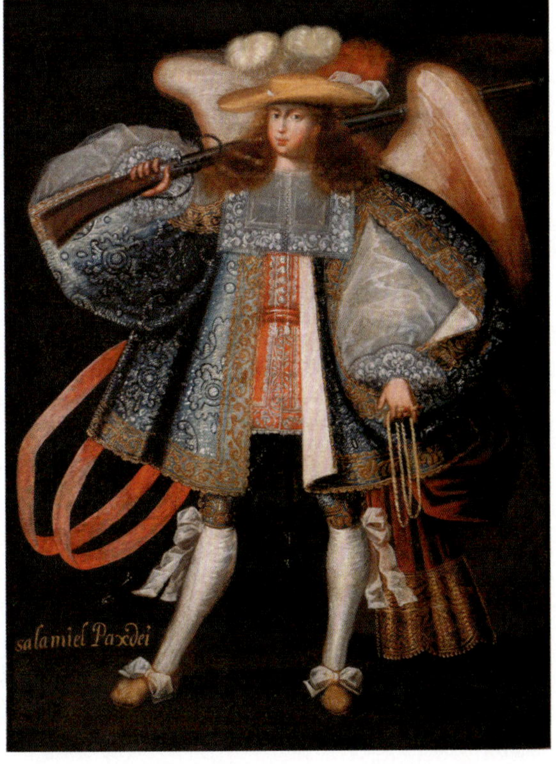

Woman's Anacu, Late sixteenth century The traditional Inca woman's dress or *anacu* (Figure 2.35) was a single length of cloth that was wrapped around the body and secured at the shoulder with two copper, silver, or gold straight pins known as *topo*. The garment was cinched at the waist with belts. Very few examples of women's garments have survived and among those even fewer are complete. In contrast to male garments, which had vertically oriented and symmetrical decorative patterns, the decorative bands of women's garments were horizontal and asymmetrical. The upper band features a variety of floral and faunal motifs including butterflies, goats, birds, and double-headed birds; the last motif

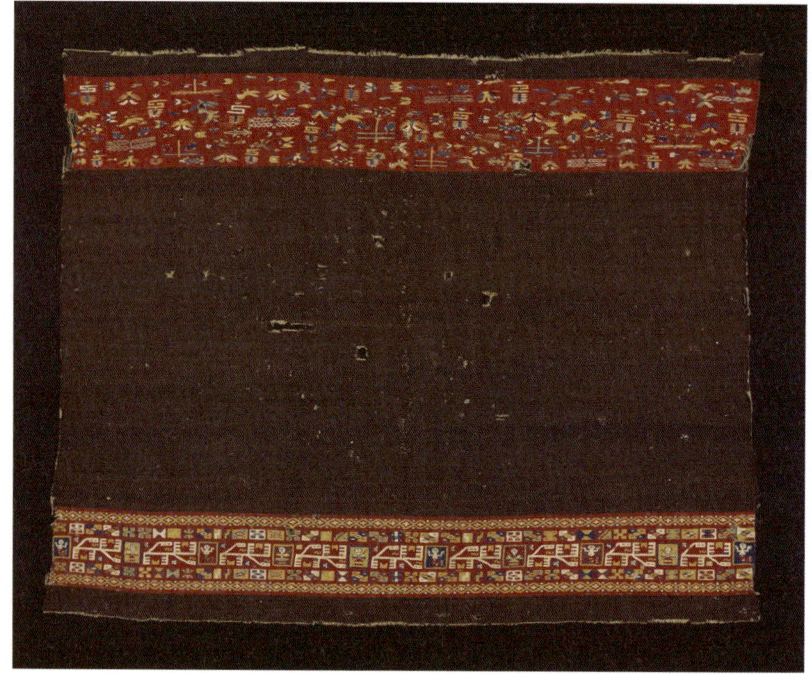

▶ **2.35** Colonial Inca Woman's Anacu or Dress, late sixteenth century CE. Camelid fiber and cotton with embroidered edge-stitching, 56 in. × 67.50 in.

The garment was wrapped around the body, secured at the shoulder with topo pins, and cinched with a belt at the waist. The dissimilar decorative panels feature native and colonial motifs.

may be derived from the Hapsburg Eagle. The lower band is decorated with geometric motifs, stylized lions, and blocks of alternating mermaids and women in traditional Inca dress.

Contemporary Indigenous Artists

The end of Spanish rule in 1825 brought new challenges to the former South American viceroyalties; among these was the task of creating a national identity not bound to their former colonial status. The answer for many countries, particularly those with significant Indigenous populations, was to focus on the pre-Columbian past as a sort of Arcadian age. Latin American Independence was achieved during the height of the Romantic movement in the arts. Romanticism (c.1800–1860) with its focus on the exotic, nature, and heroic themes was particularly suited to the task of recreating an epic American past. An example of such a work is Francisco Laso's *The Indian Potter* from 1855. Unfortunately, the search for national roots rarely did anything to elevate the status or condition of the Native Peoples of South America, whose ancestry was co-opted for political expediency.

A century after Independence, socially liberal artists in Peru and other nations again made the "Indian" the focus of the movement known as *Indigenismo* (c. 1910–1940), which advocated for a social and political advancement for Native Peoples in those countries where they constituted a dominant portion of the population. Once again, the "Indian" became the focus of painters of European descent and a symbol of the unrealized need for political and social change. In Peru, the movement's leading painter was José Sabogal, whose *The Indian*

Mayor of Chincheros: Varayoc, 1925 is in many ways an update of Laso's theme. Ironically, despite the importance of the "Indian" as a symbol of nationalism or as a rallying point for social justice, very few persons of Indigenous ancestry have come to prominence as Contemporary artists. One exception is the Bolivian artist Roberto Mamani Mamani.

Roberto Mamani Mamani (b.1962), Wiphala Murals El Alto, La Paz, Bolivia, 2015 Mamani Mamani was born to Aymara parents in Cochabamba, Bolivia, a predominately Quechua area. As a small child, he was sent to Tiahuanaco to live with his grandparents, who taught him about his heritage and encouraged him to draw and paint. He attended the University of San Andrés in La Paz, where he studied agriculture and law but had difficulty reconciling Western culture with his Aymara values. As a way of dealing with this internal conflict he began drawing on newspapers, not having the money to purchase proper art materials. Even today, as a successful artist, Mamani Mamani continues to sketch on newspapers as a way of remembering his roots.

Mamani Mamani's paintings tell stories drawn from Aymara beliefs and culture and from the history of the Spanish Conquest and Catholic Conversion of his people. Inspired by traditional Aymara weavings, Mamani Mamani assigns specific meanings and cultural references to his pigments, which he makes himself rather than purchasing commercial paints. Certain colors and shapes in his work are engendered: Yellow suns are male while blue moons are female; pointed mountains are male and rounded ones are female.

For the Wiphala housing project in El Alto, Bolivia, a city with a majority Aymara population, Mamani Mamani was commissioned by Evo Morales, Bolivia's first Indigenous president, to create fourteen monumental murals on seven, twelve-story block apartment buildings (figure 2.36). The murals draw on Aymara myths, concepts, and

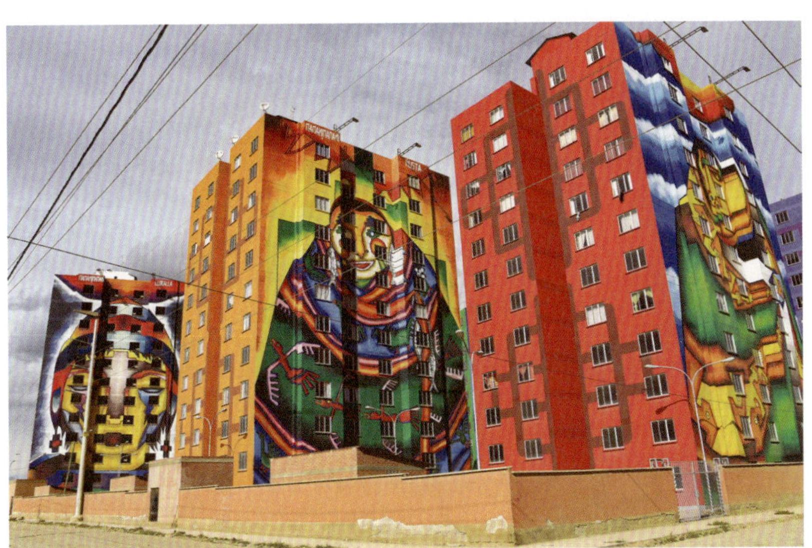

◀ **2.36** Roberto Mamani Mamani (b. 1962) Wiphala Murals, El Alto, La Paz, Bolivia, 2015.

The murals draw on Aymara myths, concepts, and imagery to provide the apartment buildings' Aymara residents with a sense of community and identity.

imagery, including among others la Pachamama (Andean earth goddess), the condor (associated in myth with the sun), the *lloq'alla* (niño or child), *amauta* (the wise one or teacher), and *mallku* (prince or leader). The idea behind the murals was to provide each building's residents with a sense of community and identity.

Chapter Quick Review

The Early Cultures (2200 BCE–200 CE)

- Although ceramics appear early in northern South America, the first ceramics do not appear in Peru before 1800 BCE, long after complex societies, ceremonial centers, and monumental architecture.
- At Cerro Sechin the base of the tri-level platform and building, known as the Central Structure, was enclosed by a wall of stone slabs which were carved with image of victorious warriors, captives, and stacks of body parts.
- In the Peruvian Highlands the site of Chavín de Huántar was an important ritual center, composed of platforms and their structures arranged around plazas. These structures were enlarged many times during the occupation of the city.
- The main cult image at Chavín de Huántar is a lance-shaped monolith carved with profile images that form a composite frontal view of a deity known as the Primary Deity or Smiling God. His image was found on stone reliefs, ceramics, goldwork, and textiles across the Chavín Horizon.
- After the decline of the Chavín, new polities arose in the south of Peru that retained some Chavín influence in their arts. Among these was Paracas, known for its embroidered textiles and post-fire painted bowls.

The Middle Period Cultures (200–1000 CE)

- The Nasca culture of the Ica Valley and the Rio Grande drainage was the successor culture to the Paracas on the South Coast. They built a ritual center at Cahuachi that consisted of 40 mounds, buildings, and walled precincts.
- The Nasca continued the Paracas practice of creating geoglyphs on the pampa, some of which were visible from Cahuachi's platform mounds.
- The Nasca improved earlier Paracas pottery by adding grits that lightened the weight and by inventing true slip decoration that was permanent when fired.
- The Moche culture occupied the Peruvian coastal valleys from the Huarmey in the south to the Piura in the north; within this region the Pampa de Paiján marked the division between the northern and southern Moche areas.
- The Moche built large adobe brick platform pyramids and buildings that were decorated with painted relief murals. Remain murals show scenes of warriors and captives and ritual sacrifice.
- Similar themes are found on Moche fineline painted ceramics and in some case, participants in ritual themes were depicted on Moche modeled pottery. Moche pottery appears to have been produced in familial workshops, much like those found in the Andes today. Researchers have been able to identify some fifty distinct painters' styles in the corpus of Moche fineline pottery.

- The Moche were also impressive metalworkers, creating a wide variety of repoussé ornaments, including some works that were articulated, such as a magnificent pair of earspools excavated at the site of Sipan.
- During this era, the Tihuanaco and Huari cultures rose in the high altiplano south of Lake Titicaca and the Peruvian Andes respectively. These cultures extended their influence along the south coast after the abandonment of the southern Moche sites. Both produced ceramics and textiles with very similar forms and motifs.
- In northern South America and lower Central America, various peoples were creating large ritual sites with stone sculpture, including reliefs and sculpture-in-the-round. These cultures were also producing lost-wax cast gold and gilded copper ornaments and fine polychrome and modeled pottery.

The Late Period (1200–1550 CE)

- In the fifteenth century the Inca began a program of expansion from their homeland in the Cuzco Valley. Their empire ultimately included all the lands between southern Colombia and northern Chile as well as parts of Bolivia and northwestern Argentina.
- The Inca took a pragmatic approach to administering their empire that was echoed in the state sponsored production of crafts such as pottery and weaving.
- Inca architecture was designed along a hierarchical system that used tightly fitted stone for ritual and royal structures, mortared field stone for common structures, and adobe blocks in areas where stone was not available.

The Colonial and Contemporary Periods

- Much of the art of the Colonial Period was produced to facilitate religious conversion. Unlike Mexico where Native artists were quickly frozen out of the guild system, Native artists worked together with European artists in the Cuzco guild.
- Still only a few of these Native painters are known because of the practice of artists not signing paintings and as well as the fact records in church archives rarely name the artists commissioned to do religious paintings.
- After Latin American Independence, Indigenous Peoples were a frequent and romanticized subject of painters of European descent, but few Indigenous artists are known from this era.
- Today relatively few persons of Indigenous descent are working as Contemporary artists in the Andes.

Chapter Questions

1. In many parts of the world the invention of ceramics is one of the first indicators of evolving, agriculture-based communities. Why doesn't the Early Period in Peru follow this pattern?
2. Citing specific works as examples, list and discuss the characteristics of the Chavín sculptural style. How did these change over time? What role did Chavín play in the development of Andean art?
3. The Moche were master potters. Describe the techniques they used to create their pottery forms and the advantages or disadvantages of each? What are some of the common themes found on Moche pottery? What do differences in several pots depicting the same theme potentially tell us?

4. During the Colonial Period, Indigenous artists worked in the Cuzco guild system alongside European artists. What sorts of works did they produce and for whom? How did Indigenous painters reinvent some of the traditional images of European religious art?

Key Terms and Figures

Key Terms

Annealing: A process in which metal is heated to increase its pliability and reduce hardness, making it easier to work.

Aryballo: An Inca vessel with a pointed foot, wide body, and cylindrical neck meant for carry water or storing beer.

Batter In architecture a receding or inward sloping wall.

Boustrophedon: A back and forth or up and down reading order or design arrangement; the name describes the plowing pattern followed by oxen pulling a plow.

Chasing: A metalworking technique in which the metal is worked from the front by hammering to raise or depress surface areas.

Composite view: Also composite pose; figures shown in composite view usually appear with their feet, legs, and hips in profile while the torso is shown facing to the front.

Contour rivalry: An image that can be viewed in one position and be recognized as one design, then rotated, usually 180°, and appear as something completely different.

Cupules: Cup-shaped marks that were drilled into stone or cave walls.

Desert varnish: A dark colored surface oxidation of stones in desert or arid environments.

Geoglyph: Large designs or lines created on the surface of the earth, either by removing an oxidized top layer or by piling up stones.

Horizon style: In Andean art a style such as that of the Chavín, Huari, or Inca which is widespread over several regions.

Modular width: An arrangement of elements in an image in equal width bands as if they had been laid out on a grid.

Repoussé: A metalworking technique in which the metal is hammered out from the back side to create a raised relief on the front; the opposite of chasing.

Sapa Inca: Unique King; the ruler of the Inca Empire.

Sunken or Sunk Relief: A type of relief in which the image is cut deeply into the stone so that the highest point of the image is below the original surface.

Visual kenning: Also called figurative elaboration, the addition of elements, often zoomorphic to figures to convey metaphoric information about a deity.

Key Figures

Atahualpa—Last Sapa Inca, executed by Pizarro in 1533.

Cieza de Leon, Pedro—Spanish conquistador and chronicler whose Crónocas del Perú provide some of the best accounts of Inca Peru.

De la Vega, Garcilaso—Writer and chronicler of early Peru; son of a conquistador and an Inca noblewoman, wrote *Comentarios Reales de los Inca*, a cultural history of the Inca based on the stories of his Inca relatives.

Hatun Tupaq—Also known as Wiracocha, eighth Sapa Inca who began expansion of the empire but abandoned Cuzco in the face of the Chanca advance on the city.

Huascar—Brother of Atahualpa who took the throne after the death of their father and fought a bloody civil war with his brother; executed by Atahualpa in 1532.

Huayna Capac—Twelfth Sapa Inca, father of Huascar and Atahualpa.

Manco Capac—First Sapa Inca.

Pachacuti—Ninth Sapa Inca who defended Cuszo and began conquests that became the basis of the empire.

Pizarro Gonzales, Francisco—Spanish conqueror of Peru; assassinated 1541.

Raimondi, Antonio—Italian-Peruvian archaeologist who discovered the Chavín stela that bears his name.

Tello, Julio—Pioneering Peruvian Indigenous archaeologist who excavate the Paracas culture.

Xesspe, Mejia—Peruvian archaeologist who worked on Paracas with Tello and then went on to study the Nasca lines.

Bibliography

Ades, Dawn. *Art in Latin America.* New Haven, CT: Yale University Press, 1989.

Alva, Walter, and Christopher B. Donnan. *Royal Tombs of Sipán.* Fowler Museum of Cultural History, 1993.

Bailey, Gauvin Alexander. *Art of Colonial Latin America.* London and New York: Phaidon, 2011.

Bawden, Garth. *The Moche.* The Peoples of America Series. Malden, MA: Blackwell Publishers, 1996.

Bergh, Susan E. *Wari: Lords of the Ancient Andes.* London: Thames and Hudson, 2013.

Bonavia, Duccio. *Mural Painting in Ancient Peru.* Bloomington: Indiana University Press, 1985.

Boone, Elizabeth Hill, editor. *Andean Art at Dumbarton Oaks.* Volumes I and II. Washington, DC: Dumbarton Oaks, Research Library and Collection, 1996/

Bruhns, Karen O. *Ancient South America.* Cambridge World Archaeology. Cambridge University Press, 1994.

Burger, Richard L. *Chavín and The Origins of Andean Civilization.* London: Thames and Hudson, 1995.

Cahlander, Adele, with Suzanne Baizerman. *Double-Woven Treasures from Old Peru.* St. Paul, MN: Dos Tejedoras, 1985.

Chavez, Karen L. Mohr. "The Significance of Chiripa in Lake Titicaca Basin Developments." *Expedition* 30, no. 3 (2016): 17–26

Conklin, William J., and Jeffrey Quilter, editors. *Chavín: Art, Architecture, and Culture.* Monograph 61. Los Angeles: Cotsen Institute of Archaeology Press, 2008.

D'Harcourt, Raoul (Grace G. Denny and Carolyn M. Osborne, editors). *Textiles of Ancient Peru and their Techniques.* University of Washington Press, 1962.

Donnan, Christopher B. *Moche Art of Peru.* Los Angeles: Museum of Cultural History, 1978.

Moche Portraits from Ancient Peru. Austin: University of Texas Press, 2004.

Donnan, Christopher B., and Donna McClelland. "The Burial Theme in Moche Iconography." *Dumbarton Oaks: Studies in Precolombian Art and Archeology*, no. 21 (1979).

Moche Fineline Painting: Its Evolution and Its Artists. Los Angeles: UCLA Fowler Museum of Cultural History, 1999.

Frame, Mary. "Nasca Sprang Tassels: Structure, Technique, and Order." *Textile Museum Journal* 25 (1986).

"What the Women Were Wearing: A Deposit of Early Nasca Dresses and Shawls from Cahuachi, Peru." *Textile Museum Journal* 42–43 (2003–2004).

Fuchs, Peter R. and Renate Patzschke

"Early Monumentalism in the Central Andes: The Origins of Monumental Architecture in the Casma Valley." In Peter Fux (editor), *Chavín: Peru's Enigmatic Temple in the Andes. Zurich: Scheidegger & Spiess/ Museum Rietberg. 2013 : 71-85.*

Fux, Peter, editor. *Chavín: Peru's Enigmatic Temple in the Andes.* Zurich: Scheidegger & Spiess/ Museum Rietberg, 2013.

Kembel, Silvia Rodriguez

Architectural Sequence and Chronology at Chavín de Huántar Peru, Dissertation, Stanford University, 2001.

King, Mary Elizabeth. *Textiles and Basketry of the Paracas Period, Ica Valley, Peru.* Dissertation. University of Arizona, 1965.

Lumbreras, Luis G. *The Peoples and Cultures of Ancient Peru.* Washington, DC: Smithsonian Institution Press, 1974.

"Religious Rituals in Chavín and their Supraregional Significance." In Peter Fux (editor), *Chavín: Peru's Enigmatic Temple in the Andes. Zurich: Scheidegger & Spiess/ Museum Rietberg. 2013 :177-189.*

McEwan, Gordon F., editor. *Pikillacta: The Wari Empire in Cuzco.* Iowa City: University of Iowa Press, 2005.

Nieves, Ana Cecilia. *Between the River and the Pampa: A Contextual Approach to the Rock Art of the Nasca Valley (Grande River System, Department of Ica, Peru).* Dissertation. Austin: University of Texas, 2007.

Phipps, Elena, Johanna Hecht, and Cristina Esteras Martin. *The Colonial Andes: Tapestries and Silverwork, 1530–1830.* New York: Metropolitan Museum of Art, 2004.

Pillsbury, Joanne, editor. *Moche Art and Archaeology in Ancient Peru.* Washington, DC: National Gallery of Art, 2001.

Protzen, Jean-Pierre, and Stella Nair. "Who Taught the Inca Stonemasons Their Skills? A Comparative Study of Tihuanaco and Inca Cut-Stone Masonry." *Journal of the Society of Architectural Historians* 52, no. 2 (1997): 142–167.

The Stones of Tihuanaco: A Study of Architecture and Construction. Monograph 75, Second Printing. Los Angeles: Cotsen Institute of Archaeology Press, 2014.

Proulx, Donald A. *A Sourcebook of Nasca Ceramic Iconography.* Iowa City: University of Iowa Press, 2006.

Quilter, Jeffrey. *The Ancient Central Andes.* Routledge World Archaeology Series. New York: Routledge, Taylor & Francis, 2014.

Rick, John W.

"Architecture and Ritual Space at Chavín de Huántar." In Peter Fux (editor), *Chavín: Peru's Enigmatic Temple in the Andes. Zurich: Scheidegger & Spiess/ Museum Rietberg. 2013 :151-167*

Rowe, Ann Pollard, editor. *The Junius B. Bird Conference on Andean Textiles.* Washington, DC: The Textile Museum, 1984.

Costumes & Featherwork of the Lords of Chimor: Textiles from Peru's North Coast. Washington, DC: The Textile Museum, 1984.

Rowe, John Howland. "Form and Meaning in Chavín Art," Anthropology Emeritus Lecture Series at U.C. Berkeley, 1967. http://www.lib.berkeley.edu/ANTH/emeritus/rowe/pub/chavin/index.html

Rowe, John H., and Patricia J. Lyon. "On the History of the Nasca Sequence" in *Nawpa Pacha: Journal of Andean Archaeology* 30, no. 2 (December 2010): 231–241. http://www.jstor/stable/24413786

Sandweiss, Daniel H., and Jeffery Quilter, editors. *El Niño: Catastrophism, and Culture Change in Ancient America.* Harvard University Press, 2008.

Sawyer, Alan R. *Early Nasca Needlework*. London, UK: Laurence King Publishing, 1997.

Scott, David A, Douglas H. Doughty and Christopher B. Donnan

"Moche Wallpainting Pigments from La Mina, Jequetepeque, Peru." Sudies in Conservation, 43, no. 3 (1998): 177-182.

Scott, John F. *Latin American Art: Ancient to Modern*. Gainesville: University Press of Florida, 1999.

Silverman, Helaine

Cahuachi: An Andean Ceremonial Center, Dissertation, The University of Texas at Austin, 1986.

"The Formative Period on the South Coast of Peru: A Critical Review," *Journal of World Prehistory*, vol 10, 2 (June 1996):95-146.

Silverman, Helaine, and Donald A. Proulx. *The Nasca*. Malden, MA: Blackwell Publishers, 2002.

Silverman, Helaine, and William H. Isbell, editors. *Handbook of South American Archaeology*. Springer, 2008.

Tello, Julio C.

Antiguo Perú:Primera Época. Lima: Comisión Organizadora del Segundo Congreso Sudamericano de Turismo, 1929.

Townsend, Richard

Deciphering the Nazca World: Ceramic Images from Ancient Peru. Chicago: The Art Institute of Chicago Museum Studies 11 (2), 1985: 117-139.

Wolfe, Elizabeth Farkass. "The Spotted Cat and the Horrible Bird: Stylistic Change in Nasca 1–5 Ceramic Decoration." *Nawpa Pacha: Journal of Andean Archaeology*, no. 19 (1981): 1–62. http://www.jstor.org/stable/27977717

Wright, Ruth M., and Dr. Alfredo Valencia Zegarra. *The Machu Picchu Guidebook*. Boulder, CO: Johnson Books, 2004.

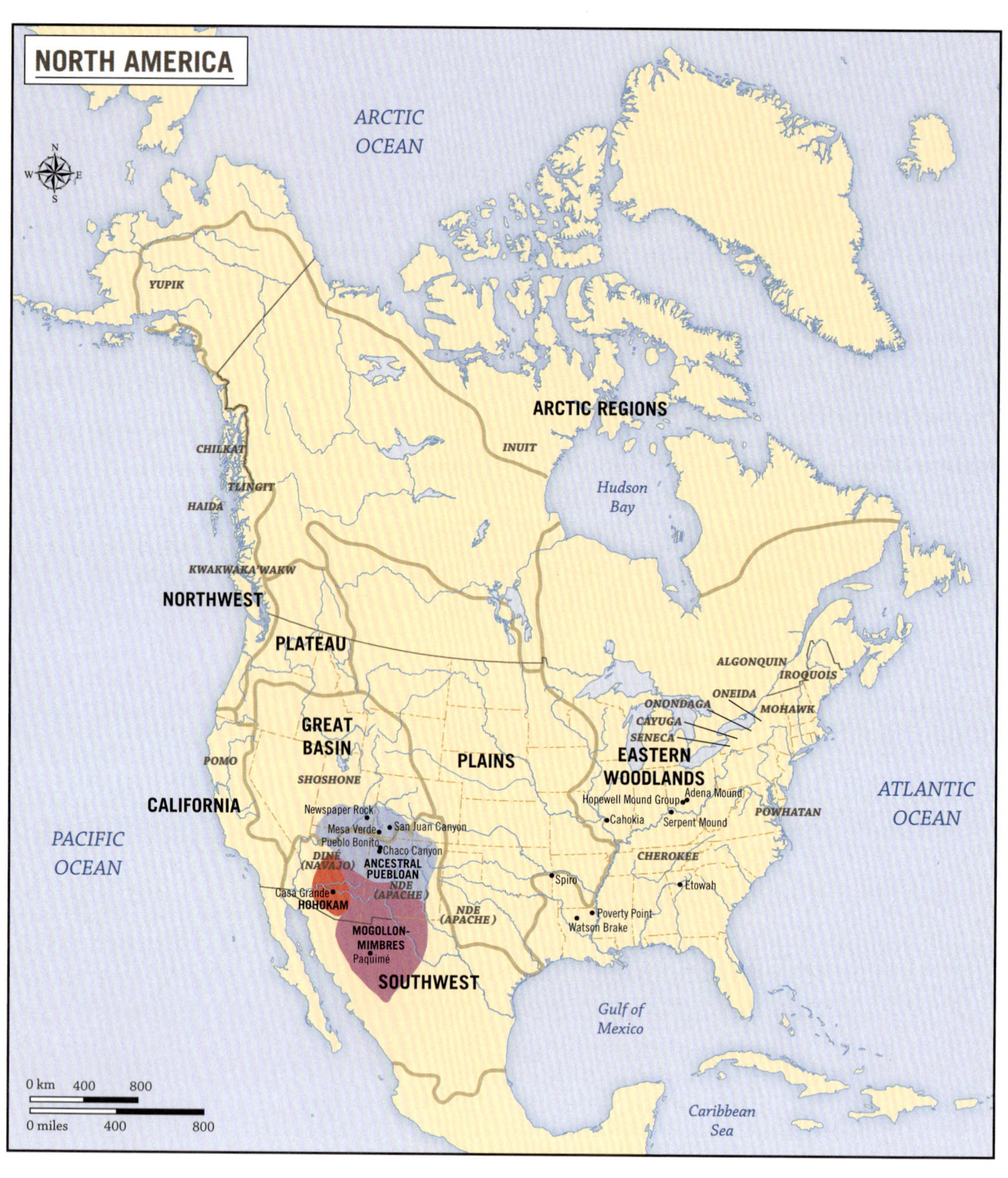
NORTH AMERICA
ARCTIC OCEAN
N
W
E
S
YUPIK
ARCTIC REGIONS
INUIT
CHILKAT
TLINGIT
HAIDA
Hudson Bay
KWAKWAKA'WAKW
NORTHWEST
PLATEAU
ALGONQUIN
IROQUOIS
ONEIDA
ONONDAGA
MOHAWK
CAYUGA
SENECA
GREAT BASIN
PLAINS
EASTERN WOODLANDS
POMO
SHOSHONE
CALIFORNIA
ATLANTIC OCEAN
Hopewell Mound Group
Adena Mound
Newspaper Rock
Cahokia
Serpent Mound
POWHATAN
Mesa Verde
San Juan Canyon
Pueblo Bonito
Chaco Canyon
PACIFIC OCEAN
DINÉ (NAVAJO)
ANCESTRAL PUEBLOAN
CHEROKEE
NDE (APACHE)
Spiro
Etowah
Casa Grande
HOHOKAM
Poverty Point
Watson Brake
NDE (APACHE)
MOGOLLON-MIMBRES
Paquimé
SOUTHWEST
Gulf of Mexico
0 km 400 800
0 miles 400 800
Caribbean Sea

North America

3

Brief Overview

The pre-Columbian art history of North America is at least as long as those of Mesoamerica and South America, but considerably less well-understood and less valued by mainstream America. Indigenous Peoples independently invented pottery-making, stone and shell lapidary, and metalworking in copper. A millennium before the first Mesoamerica (or Egyptian) pyramid was even begun, First Nations peoples in the lower Mississippi Valley were already building earthen pyramids, some of impressive scale, with platform bases, ramps, and associated earthworks.

In the Common Era, Native Americans living in the Eastern Woodlands created large ceremonial and burial sites, and marked significant locations with effigy mounds, while those in the Southwest were constructing multi-storied, environmentally responsive buildings in stone and adobe and covering their walls with painted murals. All across the continent First Nations artists were engaged in producing works according to local resources. Some were making modeled or painted ceramics, carving figural pipes, making cutout ornaments in copper and mica, working stone and shell into pendants and pectorals, weaving textiles, baskets, and wampum belts, or recording their histories on bison hides. In the twentieth century Native Americans often had to overcome obstacles, from within and from outside of their communities to acquire training and to achieve success as artists. Despite these difficulties, First Nations artists working in a wide range of media and in traditional and modernist styles have garnered international acclaim for their work.

Despite the long history and cultural richness of Native American art, relatively little is known about the cultures that produced art, monumental architecture, and earthworks before the arrival of Europeans, or even much about those living on the continent at that time. This is in large part due to the political realities of colonization, which requires the devaluation of Indigenous achievement and displacement of original peoples to legitimize the appropriation of their lands, usually followed by restricted territorial use and some degree of coercive

Chapter Objectives

1. Understand the independent and early development in North America of monumental architecture and earthworks to define ritual centers as areas of mass and space.
2. Recognize the importance of long-distance trade, including with Mesoamerica, played in the development of the arts and agriculture in both the American Southwest and Southeast.
3. Explain how contact with Europeans affected Indigenous American cultures and how the political necessities of colonization shaped the perceived history of First Nations peoples.
4. Understand the role of non–Native American teachers and traders in defining authenticity in nineteenth and twentieth century Native American art.

assimilation. It is a pattern that has been repeated many times around the world since the sixteenth century.

Early European accounts of encounters with Indigenous Americans either depict them as childlike in their simplicity or, when it suited larger nationalist objectives, as brutish savages standing in the way of progress. One of the first such propagandist depictions was the 1804 painting by John Vanderlyn, *The Death of Jane McCrea*, which showed the moment before the woman was scalped with a tomahawk. In the 1840s, a period of rapid westward expansion and the dislocation of many First Nations peoples, the popular art print firm, Currier and Ives, revisited the McCrea story in one of the first prints they issued. At about this same time, the first Native monumental architectural sites, including Cahokia, Adena, Hopewell, and Serpent Mound were discovered and mapped; however, there were many at the time who dismissed the possibility that such works could have been made by Native Americans, attributing the works, instead, to a whole range of immigrant Eurasian groups. Some of the more popular theories of the time proposed North American pyramids and earthworks to have been built by peoples from Atlantis, Israel, Egypt, or Scandinavia. The fact that there was no evidence of these peoples having been in the Americas was explained away by the assumption that they had been displaced by the primitive tribes encountered by the first colonists. Such rationalizations were politically expedient: if the "Indians" could be viewed as having destroyed previous, preferably white civilizations, then the annihilation of these "interloper" populations and the destruction of their cultural works seemed justified. Even in the twenty-first century the many ancient sites are still being threatened by development and energy exploration.

For art history the end result of this ingrained cultural bias is that the study of the pre-Columbian art of North America is hampered by cultural loss and in many areas, lack of professional archaeological work having been done. At present, a good comprehensive chronology that considers the continent as a whole across time remains to be written. Therefore, in an attempt to provide an interregional view of cultural development in North America, this chapter will continue the approach of the two previous and use overarching periods: Early, Middle, Late, Colonial, and Modern eras to provide a framework.

The Early Period (4000–1000 BCE)

During the fourth millennium BCE, in what archaeologists term the Middle Archaic, the first ceramics and works of monumental architecture appeared in the lower southeastern region, particularly in Florida and Louisiana. More than thirty early, seasonally-occupied sites with monumental earthen structures have been identified in northern

timeline

DATE	TYPE	EVENT
BCE		
c. 8000	History	Northwest Coast settled
c. 4000	History	Inuit settled in subarctic North America
c. 3880	Art	Mound A (Gentry Mound) began at Watson Brake
c. 2800	History	Watson Brake abandoned
c. 2000	Art	First Plank Houses built along Northwest Coast
c. 1730	History	Poverty Point seasonal settlement
c. 1700	Art	Crescent-shaped earthworks constructed at Poverty Point
c. 1550	Art	Construction of mounds at Poverty Point began
c. 700	History	Poverty Point abandoned
c. 500	History	Adena culture evolved in Scioto Valley
c. 381	Art	Serpent Mound constructed in Adams County, Ohio
c. 250	Art	Grave Creek Mound built
c. 200	History	Hopewell culture developed in southern Ohio
c. 100	Art	Construction of Adena mound began; Human effigy pipe carved
	Art	Hopewell Mound Group developed east of Chillicothe; Mica silhouettes
CE		
c. 50	History	Ancestral Puebloan established in Southwest
	Art	San Juan Canyon Rock Art Style
c. 200	History	Hohokam settled in Sonoran Desert of Arizona
c. 650	History	Mesa Verde settled
c. 1000	History	Mimbres communities established along the Mimbres River
	History	Nde and Diné arrived in the Southwest
c. 1050	Art	Cahokia in Illinois became a major city
	Art	Monks Mound construction began
c. 1130	History	Mimbres culture declined
c. 1190	Art	Construction of Cliff Palace, Mesa Verde, began
c. 1250	Art	Work began on Craig's Mound, Spiro, Oklahoma
	Art	Etowah mounds built, and marble sculptures created
c. 1350	History	Cahokia abandoned

(Continued)

timeline *continued*

DATE	TYPE	EVENT
CE		
	Art	Casa Grande construction began in Coolidge, Arizona
c. 1450	History	Casa Grande abandoned
1513	History	Juan Ponce de León claimed Florida for Spain
1539	History	Hernando de Soto marched through the Southeast
1540	History	Francisco Vasquez de Coronado marched north from Human effigy pipe carved
1542	History	Juan Rodríguez Cabrillo explored California coast
1565	Art	St. Augustine founded
1580	History	Iroquois League formed against the Huron
1584	History	The Secotan welcomed the English at Roanoke Island
1598	History	Don Juan Oñate claimed Hopi lands (Arizona) for Spain
1607	History	Jamestown established in Virginia
1616	History	Smallpox epidemic decimated tribes in the northeast
1632	History	First description of Iroquois False Face mask use in the *Relations des Jésuites de la Nouvelle-France*
1646	History	Powhatan chief Opechancanough captured and executed by
		colonists in Virginia
1648	History	Iroquois League drove the Huron to Great Lakes
1675	History	King Philip's War began between colonists and First Nations peoples in New England
1680	History	Great Pueblo Revolt
1709	History	Wall Street (New York) slave market sold Africans and Native Americans into slavery
1741	History	Vitus Bering explored Alaska and makes first contact with the Inuit
1750	History	Great Plains Peoples acquired horses
1756	History	Governor Robert Morris (Pennsylvania) signed "Scalp Act" placing a bounty on the scalps of Native men, women, and children
1758	History	First Native American reservation established by New Jersey Colonial Assembly
1769	History	Spanish Franciscans established Mission San Diego de Alcala, first mission in California
1770–1782	History	Arikara (Nebraska) and the Piegan Blackfeet (Montana and Alberta) suffered massive losses from smallpox and measles

DATE	TYPE	EVENT
		CE
1804	History	Lewis and Clark Expedition
1823	Art	Tlingit weaver Anisalaga born
1830	History	Indian Removal Act signed by Andrew Jackson
1835–1842	History	Seminole Wars
1838	History	Trail of Tears—removal of the Cherokee; Trail of Death— removal of the Potawatomi
1850	Art	Navajo weaving tradition began
1851	History	Indian Appropriations Act established Oklahoma as "Indian Territory"
1866	Art	Cotsiogo born; Shoshone relocated to Wind River
1867	History	Alaska Purchase
1884	History	Carving of Totem Poles and celebration of Potlaches by Northwest Coast Peoples outlawed
c. 1900	Art	Negakfok Mask carved by the Yupik
1904	History	Sun Dance outlawed
1934	History	Indian Reorganization Act
1940–1960s	History	Indian Termination Policy implemented to force assimilation of Native Americans
1990	History	Native American Graves Protection and Repatriation Act

Louisiana, Mississippi, and Arkansas. The oldest of these is Watson Brake, near Monroe, Louisiana. The reliable dating of these early sites to a pre-agricultural period has run counter to the general assumption that monumental architecture was a hallmark of sedentary, agrarian societies, but this was definitely not the sequence in archaic era North America.

Watson Brake (c. 3500–2800 BCE)

Watson Brake[1], located in Ouachita Parish, Louisiana, was discovered in 1967 after the land had been clear-cut. The site is located on the flood plain of the Ouachita River in northern Louisiana. It is the earliest

[1] A brake is an area of marshland or swamp that is typically overgrown with a single type of plant. In Louisiana, such areas are often the habitat of cypress trees.

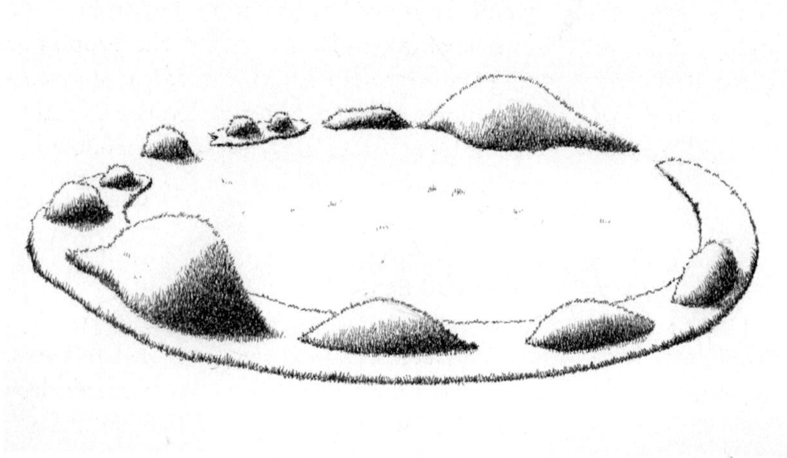

▶ **3.1** Reconstruction Watson Brake Mounds and Embankments, c. 3500–2800 BCE.

Watson Brake in Louisiana is the earliest known site in North America to have significant monumental architecture and earthworks.

known site in North America to have significant monumental architecture. Radiocarbon dated to the fourth millennium BCE, Watson Brake features eleven earthen pyramid platforms in an oval arrangement, which were connected by earthen embankments to enclose a central area, measuring some 787 feet (240 m) by 984 feet (300 m). The site is one of the first examples in the Americas of the conceptualization of architecture as consisting of both mass and space, in that its mounds surround an oval "plaza" area.

Gentry Mound, c. 3880 BCE Construction appears to have begun sometime after 3880 BCE with the large pyramid designated "Mound A" or Gentry Mound, on the northeast side of the complex. The conical structure rises to a height of 25 feet (7.5 m) and is roughly 165 feet (50 m) in diameter. The structure consists of layers of humus mixed with refuse built up over a gravel base. It seems to have grown by accretion over time in contrast to some of the other structures that were the work of a single season. The next highest is on the southwest side and is termed "Mound E"; it stands 16 feet (5 m) high but has a significantly larger basal diameter at almost 200 feet (60 m). The remaining nine structures vary in height from 4 feet (1.2 m) to about 13 feet (4 m). Once the main structures had been established they were connected by wide artificial ridges less than 6.6 feet (2 m) in height but up to 66 feet (20 m) wide; these embankments and some of the pyramids show evidence of domestic occupation including the remains of a lithic workshop operating near Mound A.

Among the more unusual artifacts uncovered in excavations at the site are fired clay cubes, rectangles, and balls. These fired clay forms were local substitutes for the cooking stones found at early occupation sites in lithic rich areas, which Louisiana is not. Prior to the advent of ceramic vessels, foods would be cooked by dropping hot stones into water-tight baskets. These "cooking balls" show that the peoples at Watson Brake were taking the first steps toward developing ceramics. Watson Brake was abandoned after 2800 BCE when the Ouachita changed course, and for the next thousand years, no monumental earthen architecture was constructed until work began on the pyramids and embankments of Poverty Point.

Poverty Point (c. 1730–1100 BCE)

Poverty Point is a 500-acre ceremonial site (Figure 3.2) in West Carroll Parish, Louisiana that seems to have been occupied and built up over a period of more than six hundred years. Its name derives from the antebellum plantation that occupied the area when the ancient earthworks were first discovered in the 1840s. The plantation, five pyramids, and almost 0.75 mile (1.2 km) long earthworks all sit on the edge of Maçon Ridge, a 5 mile (8 km) wide plateau that rises 25 feet (7.6 m) above the Mississippi flood plain. The first archaeological exploration of the site was undertaken in 1873 by Samuel Lockett, but the true scale of Poverty Point, and the existence of its massive earthworks, was not revealed until the first aerial photographs of the site were taken in 1938.

Bird Mound, c. 1450–1300 BCE The largest of the Poverty Point pyramids is Bird Mound (Figure 3.3), a roughly T-shaped pyramid built between 1450 and 1300 BCE. It rises to the west of the earthwork semi-circles at

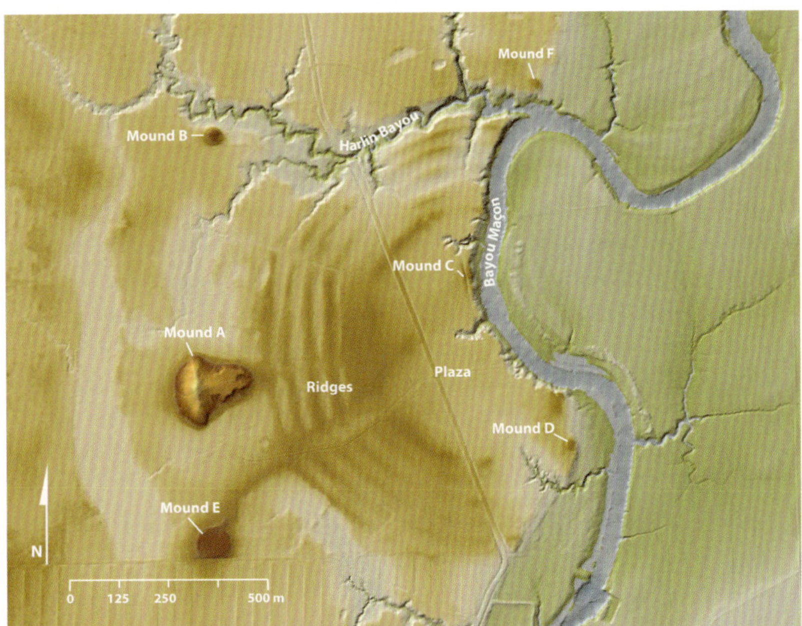

◀ 3.2 LIDAR of Poverty Point Site.

Poverty Point's earthworks, six concentric embankments are most visible from the air. Bird Mound (Mound A) is the trapezoidal pyramid immediately to the left of the embankments.

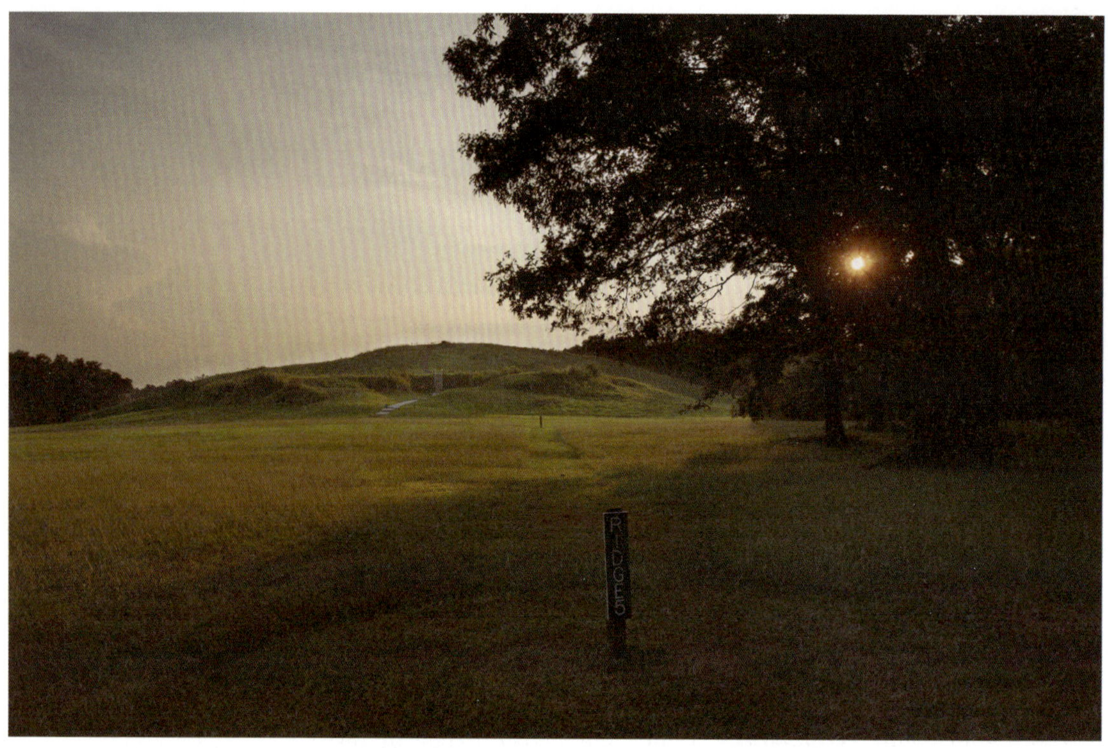

▲ 3.3 Poverty Point Bird Mound, c 1450–1300 BCE. 72 ft. high.

Bird Mound was a roughly T-shaped, two-level (platform and base) pyramid with a long connecting ramp.

the end of the main east-west alley through the ridges. The structure has three component parts: rectangular pyramid, platform, and connecting ramp. The shape of the pyramid and platform is seen by some as a bird in flight, the rectangular western pyramid as the outstretched wings and the lower eastern platform as a tail, thus the popular name "Bird Mound." The structure rises to a height of 72 feet (21 m), making it the second largest[2] surviving prehistoric monument in North America.

Poverty Point Earthworks, c. 1700 BCE Poverty Point's earthworks (Figures 3.4) are unique in the Americas. Six concentric crescent, east-facing ridges were built to the west of the 43 acres eastern plaza and structures C and D. Construction is thought to have begun on the embankments around 1700 BCE and may have continued for several generations. The embankments are divided into six unequal sectors by four broad aisles and a 295 foot (90 m) long causeway on the southwest which runs westward almost to the platform mound known as the Ballcourt Mound.

---

[2] The Great Mound, a three-tiered pyramid at Jonesboro in Central Louisiana, originally held the title of second largest with a height of 80 feet but was damaged by trenching during the Civil War and flattened afterward.

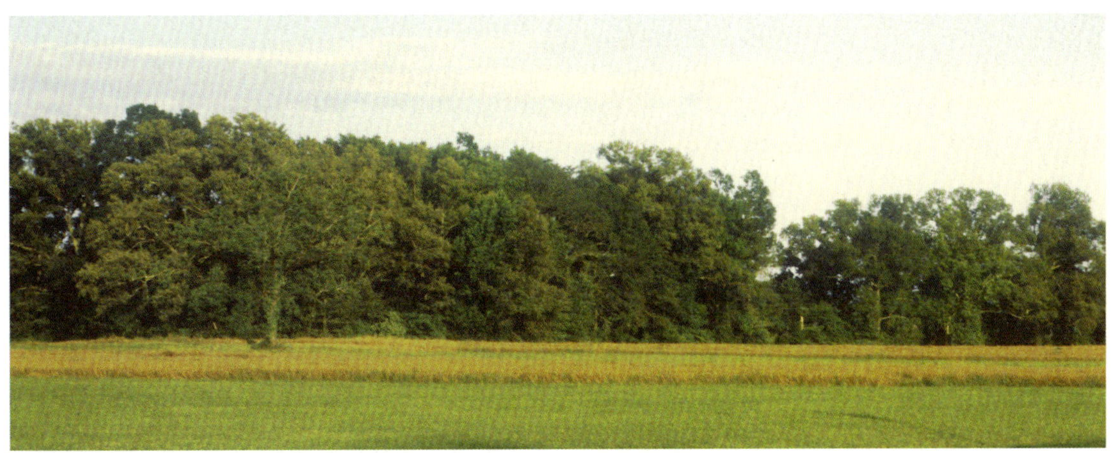

▲ 3.4 Poverty Point Earthworks, detail embankments, 1999.

Centuries of erosion and agricultural use have worn the Poverty Point embankments down from their original 5- to- 6-foot heights to around 2 feet high.

Although the original heights and widths of the ridges have been reduced by centuries of agricultural use and by the construction of Louisiana Highway 577, it is thought they once were at least 5 feet (1.5 m) high and 45 to 105 feet (14 to 32 m) wide, and were separated by broad ditches, some 65 to 100 feet (20 to 30 m) across. The current height is generally about one meter, more or less. Excavations conducted on the embankments found the remains of postmolds at various places, suggesting that wooden structures might have been built on top of the earthworks. Fire pits, household refuge, worked stone and pottery fragments, and figurines have been found, suggesting the earthworks may have been residential platforms. This certainly would have been a practical urban planning solution to seasonally rising water levels in what is thought to have been an ancient lake on the edge of the plateau where Bayou Maçon now flows.

The Middle Period Cultures (c. 1000 BCE–500 CE)

After the decline of Poverty Point, the focus of pyramid and earthwork building shifted to the Scioto River Valley of Ohio. There Early Woodlands cultures devised new pyramid forms as well as effigy and geometric earthworks. Based on differences in the design of mortuary structures and the types of funerary offerings, two distinct cultural traditions were proposed: Adena and Hopewell.

During this same period in the Southwest, the ancient ancestors of the Hopi, Zuni, Acoma, Laguna and other Puebloans were making the transition from hunting and gathering to agriculture and a sedentary way of life. They located their communities in shallow caves and rock shelters where they constructed semi-subterranean pit houses. During this early period the Ancestral Puebloan peoples had yet to develop ceramics so the term "Basketmaker" is often applied to this phase because of the extraordinarily well-made baskets found in the excavations of their habitation sites. In the far Northwest the ancestors of the Tlingit, Tsimshian, Kwakiutl, and Haida were beginning to construct plank houses.

Adena Culture (500 BCE–500 CE)

The Adena Culture derives its name from the estate of Thomas Worthington (1773–1827) near Chillicothe, Ohio, in the Scioto Valley. Worthington was a Virginian who settled in Ohio in the 1790s and became a wealthy and prominent citizen, who served as governor and senator of the new state. His 5,000-acre estate on the western side of the valley took its name from the Hebrew word "Adena," meaning "places remarkable for the delightfulness of their situations" (Woodward and McDonald 2002, 217). To the east of a small lake on the estate was a large conical earthen structure standing 27 feet (8.3 m) high, 140 feet (43 m) in diameter, and surrounded by a circular embankment. The conical pyramid on the Worthington estate is a typical example of the Adena type. Hundreds of similar ones, a few like the Grave Creek Mound (c. 250–150 BCE), at 70 feet (21.5 m) were considerably larger but most were modest in scale, standing only 6 feet (1.5 m) high.

At the heart of many Adena mounds was a circular or rectangular mortuary chamber. These crypts were constructed with log floors, roofs, and walls, the last being formed of paired logs set upright into the earth. Circular structures also had four central posts, forming a square bay, to support the peak of the roof. A few structures also had a second inner row of posts and exterior posts flanking the entrance. Once these original crypts had been filled, additional burials were often added to the mound at various levels; periodically the entire structure would be given a dirt cap to maintain a conical shape.

Adena Mound, c. 100 BCE–40 CE The Adena Mound (Figure 3.5) was one of the first to be scientifically excavated instead of being plundered for artifacts. In 1901 William C. Mills (1860–1928) excavated the structure under the auspices of the Ohio Archaeological and Historical Society. Mills' careful documentation of the work showed that it was constructed in two stages. The first of these created an earthen structure some 20 feet (6.15 m) high and 90 feet (27.69 m) in diameter. This initial conical mound was built over a rectangular log tomb chamber, measuring 13 feet (4 m) by 11 feet (3.4 m), sunk 7 feet (2.15 m) below ground level and containing the remains of twenty-one individuals. Sometime after the first section

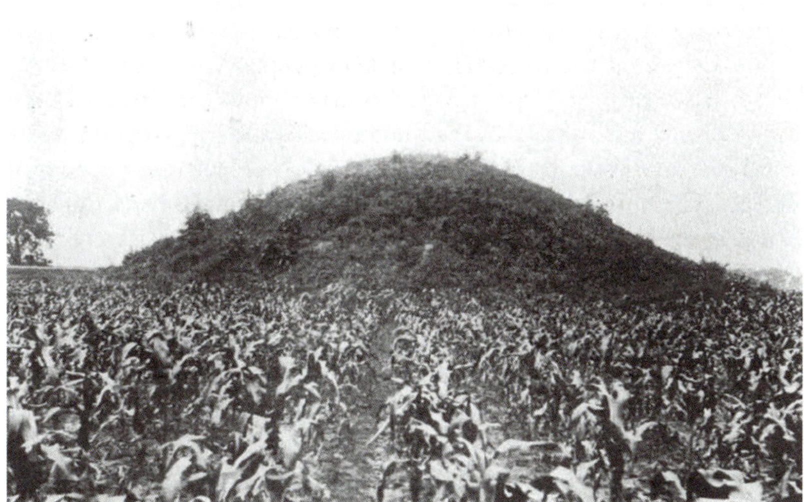

◄ **3.5** Adena Mound, Chillicothe, Ohio, c. 100 BCE to 40 CE. 27 ft. high.

Adena was a conical burial mound built over a log chamber. This photograph was taken prior to excavation of the mound in 1901. Today, the site has been leveled and a subdivision built over it.

was closed, work began on the second stage in which it was enlarged, growing another 7 feet (2.15 m) higher and 50 feet (15.4 m) in diameter. The second layer contained 12 later burials, placed throughout the new construction rather than in a tomb chamber or under bark coverings (Woodward and McDonald 2002, 217–218). Unfortunately, at the time Mills excavated at Adena, radiocarbon dating had not yet been invented. Recently, however, samples of black locust tree bark and a fragment of a woven textile from the Mills excavation were radiocarbon dated, showing that Adena and its artifacts date from the period between 100 BCE and 40 CE.

▼ **3.6** Adena Effigy Pipe, c. 100 BCE–40 CE. Pipestone, 8 in. high.

This pipe is one of the earlier examples of an anthropomorphic figure pipe in North American art. The figure wears large ear spools, apron ornamented with a serpent, and a dance bustle.

Adena Effigy Pipe, c. 100 BCE–40 CE During excavation of the earliest section of the Adena Mound, Mills found a unique human effigy pipe (Figure 3.6) near the left hand of one of the buried individuals. Made of Ohio pipestone, it is considerably more ornate than the plain tubular stone pipes commonly found at Adena sites. The upper body of the figure is fully in the round, while the slightly flexed legs are rendered in high relief on either side of the pipe tube. The piece is remarkable in the depiction of anatomical details and understanding of the mechanics of the body. From the front, the tapering torso clearly shows the edge of the ribcage and the fold lines at the elbows and wrists. The hands are sensitively done with the finger lengths differentiated and the nails clearly

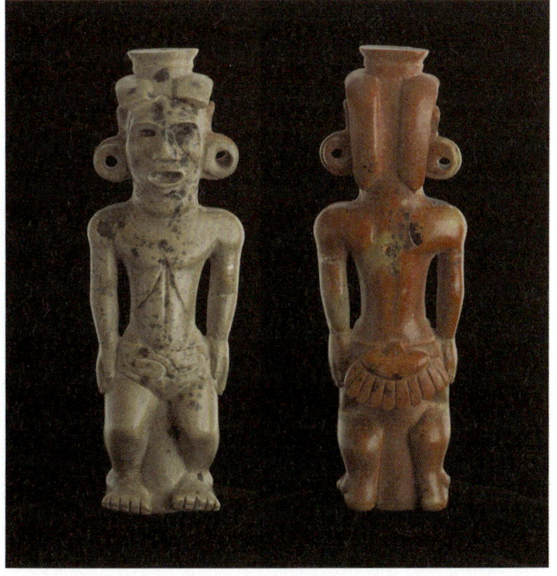

indicated. The back view shows the shoulder blades and the indention of the spine continuing into the buttocks. The figure's head is disproportionately large and blocky, a fact which led Mills to misidentify the figure as a "dwarf," not realizing that many non-Western cultures give prominence in scale to the head. The mouthpiece sits atop the figure's divided hair style, which continues down the back of the head and neck of the figure. On either side of the head with its open mouth are large yo-yo-shaped ear spools. The 8-inch (20 cm) figure wears a loincloth with an apron-like front that is decorated with a serpent motif and a dance bustle–like element in the back. The pipe is extraordinary in its high polish, three-dimensional carving and pierced-work as well as its evidence of the artist's anatomical understanding. The ritual use of tobacco (first domesticated in the Andean region) seems to have been introduced to eastern North America during this period, most likely from Mesoamerica.

Great Serpent Mound, Adams County, Ohio, c. 381–344 BCE The Great Serpent Mound (Figure 3.7) was first reported by Ephraim George Squier (1821–1888) and Edwin Hamilton Davis (1811–1888), in their *Ancient Monuments of the Mississippi Valley* (1848). Investigating reports of a defensive embankment—an all-too-common assumption about earthwork constructions—Squier and Davis discovered a huge sinuous embankment in the form of a serpent with an oval at the northwest end. The 120 foot (37 m) by 60 foot (18.5 m) oval has been variously interpreted as the serpent's head, its eye, or an egg that the serpent is swallowing.

The crescent-shaped spur of land on which the earthwork is located is part of an ancient meteor impact crater. The resulting rock formations are somewhat suggestive of a snake's head and undulating form and may have inspired the shape of the structure. Squier and Davis surveyed the length of the mound, along a straight line through

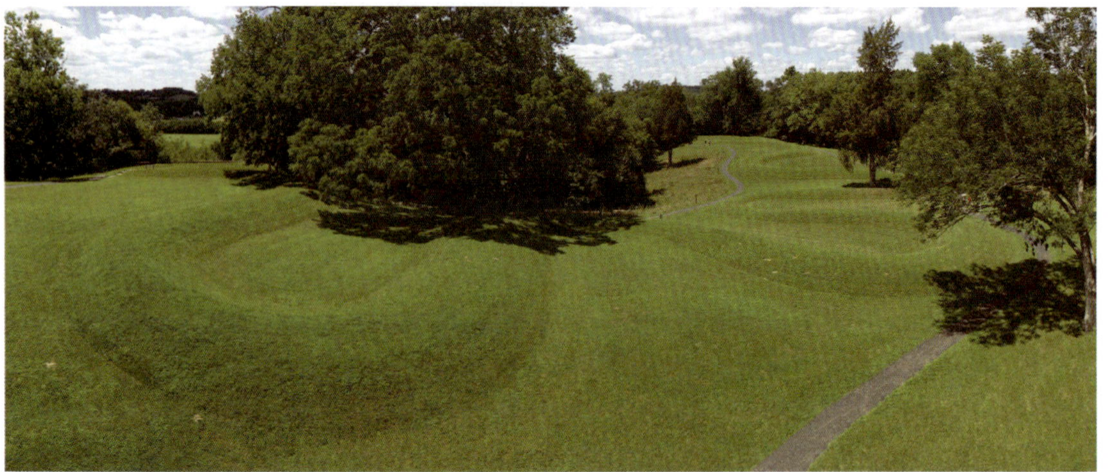

▼ 3.7 Great Serpent Mound, Adams County, Ohio, c. 381–344 BCE. 1,420 ft. long.

This immense earthwork, first reported in 1848, has not suffered the destruction that befell many other early Native American earthworks and mounds. At the head of the long serpent is an oval, in the center of which was, originally, a burnt stone circle.

the coils, as 700 feet but its actual length, following the coils, is 1,420 feet (433 m) with a height ranging from 4 to 5 feet (1.2–1.5 m). One particularly interesting point in the Squier and Davis description is their report of a burnt stone circle in the center of the oval. They lament that the stones had been pulled down and scattered about, presumably by "some ignorant visitor, under the prevailing impression probably that gold was hidden beneath them" (Squier and Davis 1848, 97). Like the Nazca lines of the Peruvian desert, the function of the Great Serpent Mound and other animal **effigy mounds** built by Native Americans is much debated and theories, often conflicting, abound.

The Hopewell Culture (c. 200 BCE–400 CE)

Also in the Chillicothe area is the Hopewell Mounds site, which was first explored by Squier and Davis when the property was owned by W.C. Clark. It was published it in their survey as "Clark's Works." In the late nineteenth century, the property was in the possession of Mordecai C. Hopewell. Since he was the owner when the first excavations occurred, it was his name that was applied to the culture. During the 1891 – 1892 field season, Warren K. Moorehead (1866–1939) excavated several mounds on the Hopewell farm to supply artifacts for display at the 1893 World Columbian Exposition in Chicago.

Initially, Hopewell was thought to be a successor culture to the Adena; however, recent radiocarbon dates from some Hopewell sites show the culture to have been contemporaneous with Adena. The difference in the design of their monumental architecture, earthworks, pipes, and other elite items is more likely a result of cultural distinctions and access to a larger trade network.

Mound 25, Hopewell Mound Group, c. 100 BCE–400 CE As mapped by Squier and Davis, the Clark's Works, or Hopewell Mound Group, consisted of twenty-nine pyramids set within a 111-acre, roughly rectangular enclosure, with a rounded corner on the northwest side, and a smaller, 16-acre square on the east end. Both the larger and smaller enclosures are surrounded by earthen embankments some 6 feet (1.8 m) high. Within the larger enclosure were secondary enclosures, one a circle, measured by Squier and Davis at 350 feet (107 m) in diameter and the other a semicircular enclosure, 2000 feet (610 m) in circumference (Squier and Davis 1848, 27). Although Squier and Davis assumed the embankments were defensive works, this is unlikely. It is more probable that the circle and square earthworks found at Hopewellian sites across the Midwest were intended to define sacred spaces for ceremonial or ritual purposes.

Within the circular enclosure were seven structures, three of which were elliptical in form and joined end-to-end to form the massive Mound 25 (Figure 3.8), which is approximately 34 feet (9 m) high,

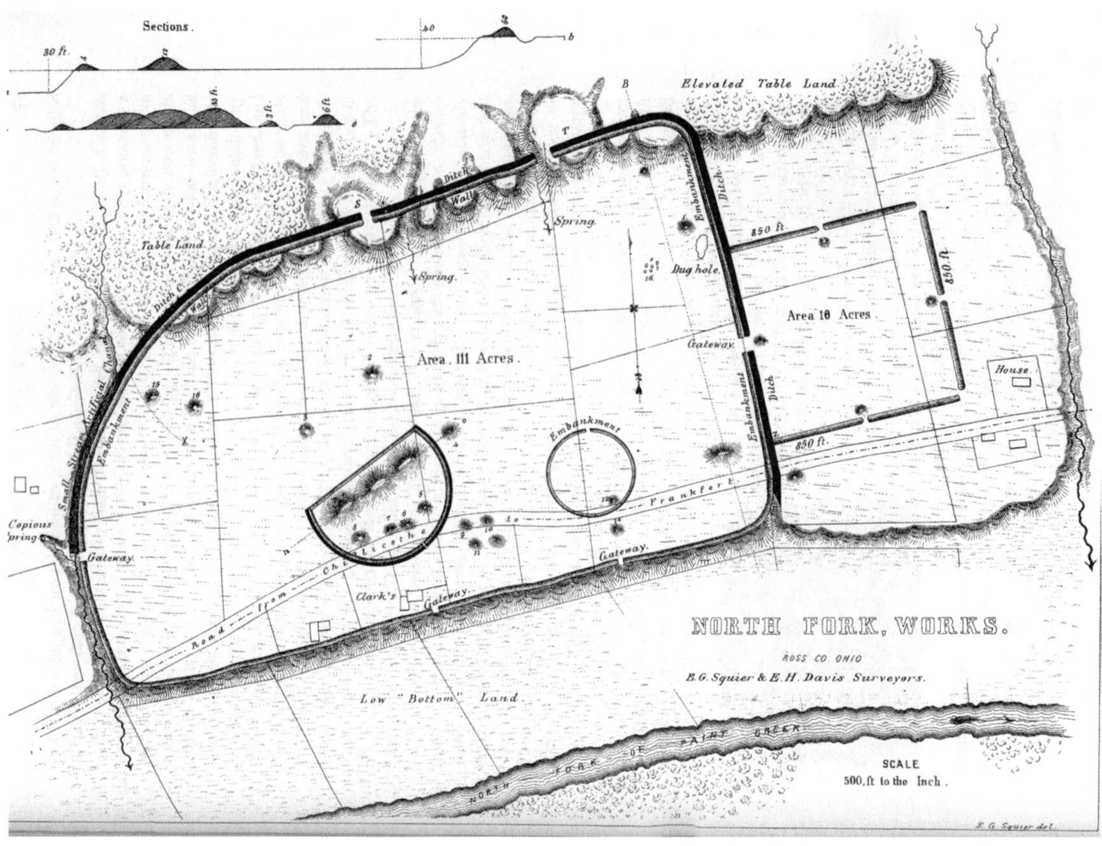

▲ **3.8** Clark's Work or Hopewell Mound site, North Fork of Paint Creek, Chillicothe, Ohio, Squier and Davis, Plate X, 1848.

The Hopewell Mound groups were excavated in 1891–1892 to provide exhibits for the 1893 World Columbian Exposition. Unfortunately, this site has since been leveled.

500 feet (152 m) long, and 180 feet (55 m) wide. The excavation of Mound 25, done with teams of horse-drawn scrapers in 1891, revealed the remains of several domed chambers where wooden mortuary structures had endured long enough for the clay to harden into an arched chamber.

More recent, less destructive excavations have shown that some Hopewellian mounds contained extensive "Great Houses"; the Tremper Mound, near Portsmouth, Ohio, had a mortuary or **charnel house** that was 200 feet long. These houses often had several rooms, which may have reflected different functions or simply the expansion of the charnel house over time. When the houses reached capacity, they were either burned and the ashes covered with a layer of fresh soil before a new house was constructed, or the structure was left intact and buried under a layer of earth.

The structures within Mound 25, according to Moorehead (1922, 105), were made of bent saplings, some 2 or 3 inches in diameter. Accompanying the 102 bodies were various artifacts and ornaments often brought from considerable distances, such as copper from the Great Lakes region, obsidian from Wyoming and Utah, and mica from North Carolina.

Mica Silhouette of a Human Hand from Mound 25, c. 100–400 CE Among the more unusual artifacts excavated from Mound 25 are four sheet mica cutouts or silhouettes in the form of a hand (Figure 3.9), a bird's claw, and two headless human torsos, one of which had severed arms, while the other had all limbs dismembered. Mica is a translucent mineral, sometimes called isinglass, that is easily separated into thin sheets. The mineral was not locally sourced but brought in from North Carolina where there are mica deposits. Mica is easily cut with an obsidian blade but the fluidity of design and accuracy of anatomical detail is extraordinary considering it was done with stone tools. The Mica Hand measures approximately 11 inches (29 cm) high by 7 inches (16 cm) wide. The artistry of the hand, its large scale, as well as the scarcity and fragility of the medium suggest that it and the other pieces were funerary offerings for an elite individual.

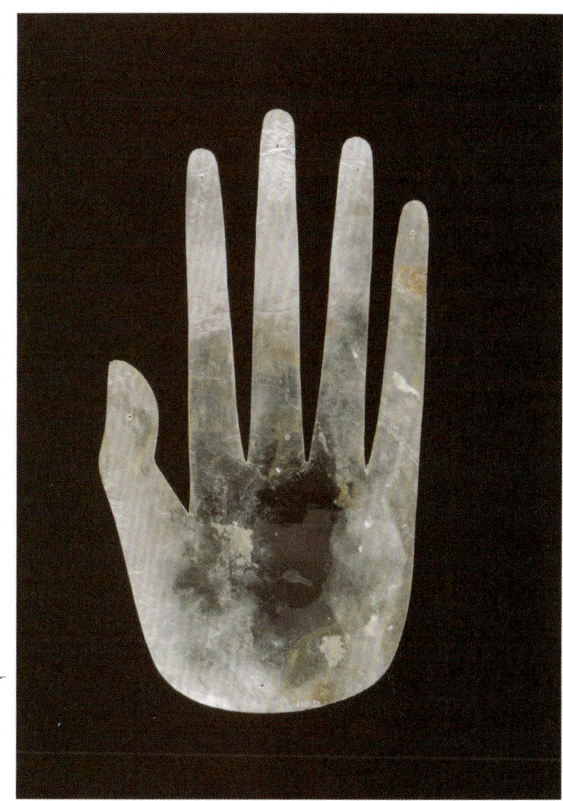

▲ 3.9 Hopewell Mound 25, Mica Human Hand, c. 100–400 CE.

This elegant hand was cut from translucent mineral mica; small holes in the palm, thumb, and fingers suggest it may have been attached to a garment.

Ancestral Puebloan (50–400 CE)

During the Middle Period, the Ancestral Puebloans established communities in the four corners region of the American Southwest. These peoples are sometimes called Anasazi in the archaeological literature; "Anasazi" is a Navajo (Diné) word meaning "enemy ancestors" and its use has fallen out of favor. The Ancestral Puebloans, the probable antecedents of the Hopi, Zuni, Acoma and Laguna, moved into the Southwest region around 6000 BCE but did not begin to practice agriculture until the Basketmaker II phase. During this period they began building pithouses, which were often tucked into shallow caves or beneath dry rock shelters, where they also stored their corn harvest in bins or cysts. The Basketmaker designation derives from the well-made baskets, sandals, and cordage often found in their habitation sites.

Newspaper Rock, Utah, 50–1750 CE During the Basketmaker II–III periods, the Ancestral Puebloans created petroglyphs on the stone walls of canyons in southern Utah and northern Arizona. Some rock art sites, such as Newspaper Rock in Utah (Figure 3.10), seem to have been in use for several hundred years with new images added by succeeding generations and groups of Native Peoples. The first of several hundred images were pecked into the surface of the rock wall

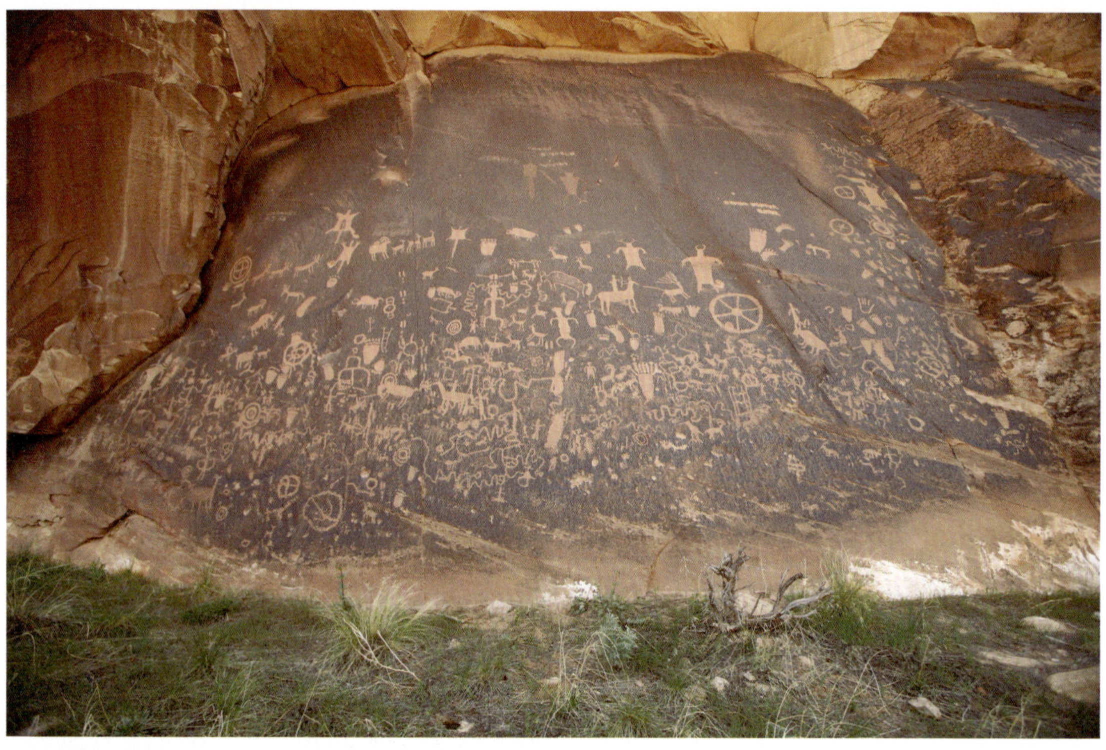

▲ 3.10 Ancestral Puebloan, Puebloan, Diné, Newspaper Rock, Utah, c. 50–1750 CE.

Petroglyphs continued to be produced in the Southwest from the Archaic through Historic Periods. Newspaper Rock has one of the largest collections of images produced over a span of almost two millennia.

sometime in the first century CE by Ancestral Puebloans. The earliest images on the rock wall are more difficult to see due to ongoing patination of the rock surface. More recent designs, added by Pueblo, Diné, and much later Anglo settlers are lighter in color. Ancestral Puebloan peoples created rock art designs using solid-fill and outline techniques; both styles are present on Newspaper Rock. Commonly depicted anthropomorphic motifs in Ancestral Puebloan art include figures with wide shoulders and stout bodies but stick-like arms and legs, sometimes wearing bird headdresses and armed with atlatls, later with bows and arrows. Animals on Newspaper Rock include bighorn sheep, birds, deer, buffalo, and horses and riders. Interspersed throughout the scenes are miscellaneous motifs such as quartered circles or wheel designs, human foot- and hand-prints, animal tracks, and some abstract forms.

The Late Period Civilizations (c. 700–1550 CE)

During the second half of the first millennium CE, maize- and bean-based agriculture allowed peoples living in both the Mississippi river basin and the Southwest to develop more complex urban societies. Pyramid building reached its zenith during this period in the

Mississippian and Caddoan[3] kingdoms. In the Southwest, the communities that flourished during this era are termed "Puebloan," derived from the Spanish word *pueblo* or "town," used to describe their multistory communal structures. Included under this designation are the Ancestral Pueblo, the Hohokam, and the Mogollon cultures.

Mississippian Cultures (800–1600 CE)

In the 1960s the application of system theory to the Late Period societies of the Mississippi Valley resulted in a monolithic view of Mississippian peoples as monumental and homogenized, ignoring distinctions of region and scale. Some Mississippian societies, for example the Cahokia, did achieve a level of sophistication on a par with those of Post-Classic Mesoamerica, forming hierarchical states with vassal polities, engaging in long distance trading networks that extended beyond North America, and building impressive urban centers with large ceremonial precincts containing upwards of one hundred earthen pyramids. However, few states reached such high levels; more common were large towns with between five and fifty structures such as Spiro, and even smaller towns with fewer than five pyramids, such as Etowah.

CAHOKIA (1050–1350 CE)

The largest city north of the Valley of Mexico was Cahokia, a ritual and administrative center located in the fertile flood plain of the Mississippi some 10 miles (16 km) east of St. Louis, Missouri, in East St. Louis, Illinois. At its height, the city encompassed an area of some five square miles (13 square km) and had an urban population estimated at 15,000 with an affiliated regional population of perhaps 50,000 or more. The layout of Cahokia is reminiscent of Mesoamerican city plans, with a central ritual district surrounded by residential areas that were organized according to craft production, including bead and shell pendant lapidary, weaving, pottery-making, and weapons manufacture. The central focus of the city was a large pyramid, known as "Monks Mound." On each of its four sides, aligned to the cardinal directions, were four plazas, the largest being the Great Plaza on the south.

Additional pyramids were located within the ritual district as well as in the suburbs; these included truncated platforms, terraced pyramids, conical and oval forms, and ridgetop or "hayrick" structures. Platform and conical pyramids were often associated with plaza-like

---

[3] The primary distinction between Mississippian and Caddoan cultures is one of geography. Those located east of the Mississippi River are termed "Mississippian" while those to the west are "Caddoan."

spaces but could also be solitary structures; the long, rectangular-based and narrow summit ridgetop "hayrick" structures are thought to have been boundary markers of some type. In all some 120 earthen structures once stood within the confines of Cahokia; unfortunately only about forty of these have escaped flattening by farmers, urban sprawl, and interstate highway construction. In addition to pyramids and plazas, the remains of four wooden circles or **henges** have been located west of the central ceremonial district; these are thought to have been used to track solstices and equinoxes.

Monks Mound, c. 950–1200 CE Monks Mound (Figure 3.11) was a terraced earthen pyramid which rises to a height of 100 feet (30 m), making it the largest pyramid north of the Valley of Mexico. The moniker "Monks Mound" comes from Henry Brackenridge (1786–1871), who published the first description of the Cahokia pyramid, and named it in honor of the Trappist monks who had established a chapter at the site in 1809. They did not build on the pyramid but did use it to grow wheat and vegetables.

Monks Mound has an unusual multi-terraced design with platforms of different sizes and heights; it rises from a 40 foot (11.7 m) high, long rectangular base platform that measures 790 feet (241 m) by 1040 feet (317 m). Earthen ramps on the south and possibly east sides, may have provided access to the second level but the existence of these ramps is a matter of some scholarly debate. The second level stands about 25 feet (7.7 m) higher than the base. A third platform added

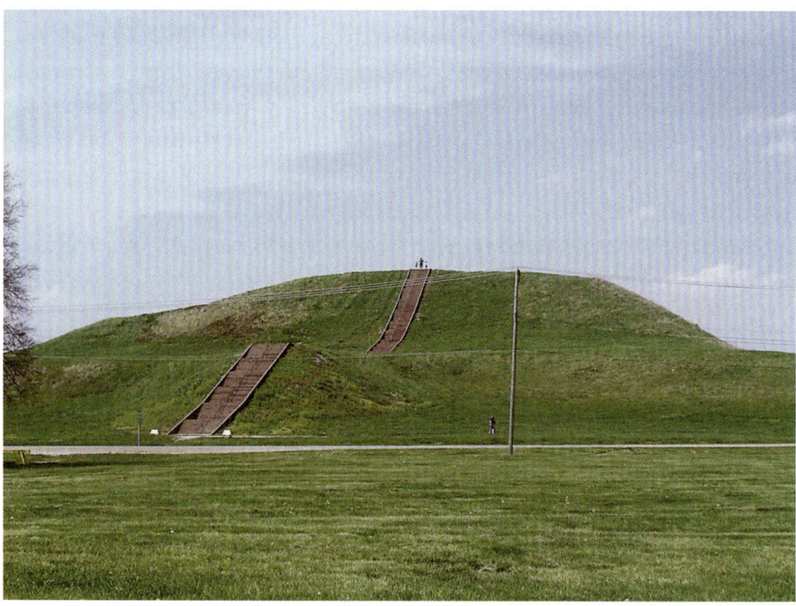

▶ 3.11 Cahokia, Monks Mound, East St. Louis, IL, c. 950–1200 CE.

Cahokia's main earthen pyramid rose in four terraces to a height of 100 ft., making it the largest pyramid north of the Valley of Mexico.

another 30 feet (9.2 m) to the overall height of the structure. The third level was placed slightly off-center so that a long, narrow platform opened on its west side. In the southeast corner of the third terrace stood a conical structure, estimated to have been about 10 feet (3 m) high. Behind this rose the fourth level, which originally supported a wooden temple or other structure, surrounded by a **palisade** or a wall made of tree trunks set upright into the ground. Unfortunately, the original height of the fourth level is unknown as the area was disturbed by the monks' farming activities on the summit. When the fourth level was built, a small platform addition was built onto the southwest corner of the base.

Unlike many Mesoamerican pyramids that were protected by veneers of stone and had their mass stabilized with interior posts, stone piers and retaining walls, or the occasional well-placed boulder, Monks Mound is built entirely of layers of clays and soils. The clays are especially problematic because they swell when wet and shrink when dry, a process that could ultimately lead to the failure of the pyramid. The architects of Monks Mound seemed to have been aware of the problem and took steps to counteract it, incorporating layers of limestone cobbles to improve drainage within the structure. They attempted to improve water resistance by building interior and exterior clay-coated retaining walls and buttresses. Traces of puddled clay on the exterior suggest that the structure originally may have been coated with this water-resistant material.

Monks Mound overlooked the 47-acre Great Plaza to the south and the sixteen considerably smaller pyramids located within the plaza space. The plaza, smaller pyramids, and Monks Mound were enclosed by a tall, six-sided, palisade with towers set every 70 feet (21 m) along the eastern side. The wall served to define Cahokia's sacred precinct, and like the palisade on the uppermost level of Monks Mound, screened sacred rituals from the uninitiated. Pragmatically, it also could operate defensively in times of war.

SPIRO (950–1400 CE)

Spiro was located on the far western periphery of the Eastern Woodlands near the junction of the Poteau and Arkansas Rivers in Le Flore County, Oklahoma. Compared to Cahokia, with which it seemed to have carried on an extensive trade, Spiro was a medium-size town of twelve major earthen structures, and a Caddoan-speaking population of perhaps 10,000 individuals. The earthen structures consisted of six platform pyramids; three were mortuary structures, including Craig's Mound, and three mounds enclosing earthen-walled buildings.

Unlike Cahokia, where destruction of the site by agriculture began in the early nineteenth century, Spiro remained intact and unmolested until 1933. In that year a group of six treasure hunters, operating as the Pocola Mining Company, took a two-year lease on the property with the intention of digging the mounds for antiquities. Working at first with picks and shovels, the men began tunneling into the pyramids. In the process they unearthed and quickly sold off hundreds of artifacts ranging from ceramic vessels, effigy pipes, beads, tools, and weapons; the miners did not consider the textiles and feathers they found to be valuable, and tossed them aside.

Craig's Mound, c. 1250–1400 CE In the summer of 1935, with only a few months before their lease was up and with increasing pressure from the University of Oklahoma, which was trying to stop the destruction, the Pocola miners attacked the last undisturbed structure, "Craig's Mound." The company hired more workers and when the digging did not move quickly enough, they began using dynamite to speed up the process. The earthen pyramid contained 1,100 skeletons, which the miners loaded up into wheelbarrows and dumped outside the tunnel entrance. When everything of value had been removed from the mortuary chamber, the miners dynamited their tunnels.

Craig's Mound (Figure 3.12) was a 350 foot (107.69 m) long pyramid consisting of four conjoined structures, each of which contained an earthen-walled building. The tallest of the four peaks rose to a height of 33 feet (10 m) and enclosed the "Great Mortuary" chamber,

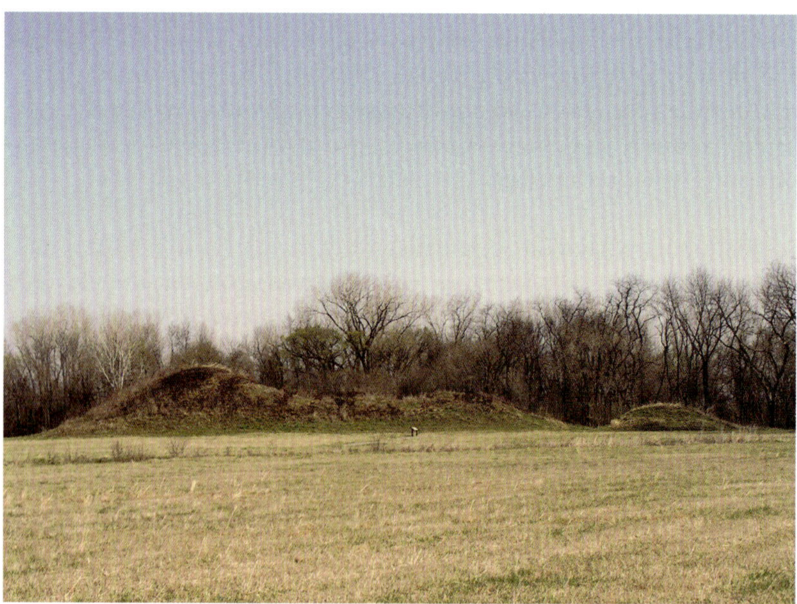

▶ **3.12** Spiro, Craig's Mound, Oklahoma, c. 1250–1400 CE. 33 ft. × 350 ft.

The four conjoined structures of Craig's Mound contained earthen walled structures that served as a cremation basin and mortuary chambers for 1,100 individuals. The site was systematically looted by the Pocola Mining Company in 1935.

a circular earthen-walled building measuring 115 feet in diameter. The three smaller peaks to the south were 20 feet (6 m) high and about 80 feet (25 m) across. Immediately to the south of the "Great Mortuary" was a cremation basin followed to the south by burial chambers.

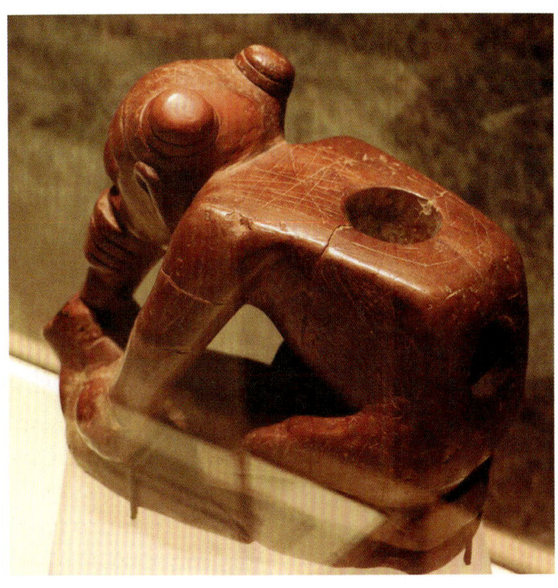

▲ **3.13** Spiro, Human Effigy Pipe Smoker Pipe, c. 1100 CE, Red Fireclay, 10 in. × 5 in. × 8.5 in.

This humorous smoking man pipe was carved at Cahokia, which was a center for pipe carving, and traded to Spiro; it was one of the many items removed from Craig's Mound in the 1930s.

Human Effigy, Pipe Smoker, c. 1100 CE The "Great Mortuary" served as a treasury for thousands of offerings of beads, textiles, tools, weapons, engraved shell cups, copper ear spools and cut outs, and effigy pipes. These elite goods showed Spiro, despite its peripheral location, was an important trading center. Among the more interesting items reputed to have been found in the Spiro pyramids are large flint clay (stone) effigy pipes, which were brought as high status items from Cahokia, where they had been made around 1100 CE.

The Cahokian pipes are incredible works of three-dimensional sculpture, which given their size and weight, must have been intended for ceremonial use items. The red fireclay Human Effigy Pipe (Figure 3.13), found in Craig's Mound, depicts a nude male figure bending to smoke from a frog effigy pipe, illustrating exactly, and humorously, how the pipes were used. The anatomical details of the crossed-legs and arms bent at the elbow are well rendered, as is the expressive face of the figure. The pipe stands 10 inches (25.4 cm) high, 8.5 inches (21.5 cm) wide and is 5 inches (12.7 cm) deep. There are two openings in the back of the figure, the upper one being the bowl and the lower the opening for the wooden stem that would be inserted when the pipe was smoked.

Raccoon Dancers Shell Gorget, c. 1000–1400 CE Other offerings found in Craig's Mound included copper repoussé plaques, whelk shell cups, and shell gorgets. The numerous fragments and reworked pieces found at the site, suggest Spiro may have been a significant center of shell-working. Spiro gorgets were cut using stone tools and string saws. Facial and costume details were incised with fine lines. While the shell cups were engraved on the outside, gorgets utilized the smooth, slightly concave interior surface of the shell, which was easier to carve especially when the shell was fresh. Gorgets at Spiro included both solid and fenestrated forms, the latter featuring pierced and cut-out areas that defined the forms of the design, sometimes

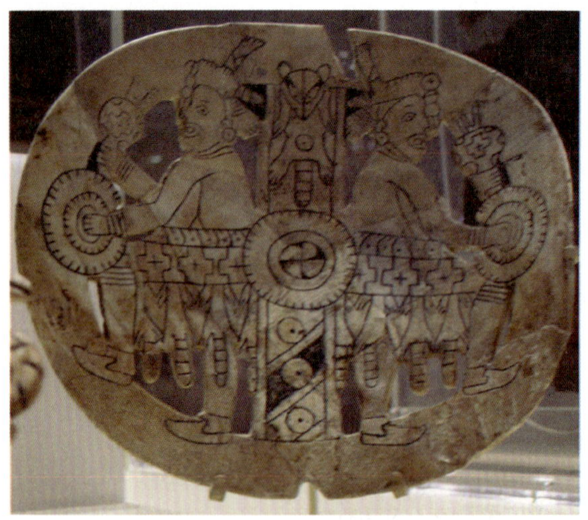

▲ 3.14 Spiro, Craig's Mound, Raccoon Dancers Shell Gorget, c. 1000–1400 CE.

Although shell gorgets have been found at several Mississippian sites, the raccoon dancers motif is unique to Spiro.

resulting in an almost lace-like effect. These pieces were widely traded throughout the Southeastern region (Sievert, Rogers and Urcid, 2011, 127–139).

The ovoid Raccoon Dancers Gorget (Figure 3.14), found in Craig's Mound, is a unique piece and depicts a motif that has been identified only at Spiro. Two **addorsed** (back-to-back) dancers with rattles and circular dance fans stand on either side of a central post. The post is decorated with a raccoon pelt, shell disc, and circular dance fan and it is wrapped diagonally with strips of cloth to which more shell discs have been attached. The two high-stepping figures wear caps with tall plume elements, copper earrings, bib-like chest ornaments, wrist and knee bands, moccasins, and kilts of raccoon pelts suspended from belts marked with cross motifs. The artist of the Raccoon Dancers Gorget attempted to show space through the overlapping of forms such as the layering of the hands over fans over legs.

ETOWAH, GEORGIA (C. 950–1550 CE)

Etowah, located in Northwestern Georgia, near Cartersville, is one of the best-preserved sites in the southeast, having been spared the depredations of Spiro and Cahokia. As yet, only a tenth of the site has been excavated. Etowah was a relatively small Mississippian town with three main truncated pyramid structures; the largest of these, Mound A, was a residential platform 63 feet (19 m) high that faced a clay-surfaced plaza on its east side. Access from the plaza to the summit was provided by an earthen ramp. There may have been a two-stepped terrace on the south end of this main structure. Two other significant pyramids stood to the southeast, Mound B, and to the southwest, Mound C. The southeastern platform stands 35 feet (10.7 m) high, while the southwestern one was only 20 feet (6 m) tall. Mound C was a burial structure constructed in five discernable phases. Its summit supported a mortuary or charnel house. The pyramid contained some 350 burials along with ritual offerings. Three more small, 10-foot (3 m) pyramids were located to the northeast of the primary structure. Etowah's semicircular ceremonial district was enclosed by a palisade wall with towers at 80-foot (24 m) intervals. Outside the walls was a moat that joined the Etowah River at each end, so that the site was completely encircled.

Seated Male and Female Figures, c. 1250–1375 CE Among the items found during the excavation of Mound C were two marble sculptures representing a seated male and female (Figure 3.15). Fragments of seated figures in wood and stone have been found across the Southeast from Oklahoma to Georga, but few have survived intact and as pairs. The figures appear to have been hastily buried when Etowah was abandoned; they were found one on top of the other and damaged. The nude male measures 24 inches (61 cm) high and is seated in a cross-leg pose with hands on knees; he wears a head covering and his hair is twisted into a knot in back. The female at 22 inches (55.9 cm) is slightly smaller than her companion figure. She wears a skirt, belt, and turban-like head cloth, and sits with her legs folded under her. Her hair hangs down her back. Both figures exhibit a typical, non-Western one-to-three ratio of proportion, with priority given to the heads of the figures, which are slightly overlarge. While the faces are detailed and expressive, the bodies are more generalized and do not show a lot of anatomical detail; arms, legs, and torsos are tubular rather than tapering. Remaining traces of pigment show that the figures were originally enlivened with color. The ears, mouths, and garments were painted with red ocher, and carbon black was used to create a band across the face. The chests of both figures are encrusted with a copper-based greenish-black pigment. Given the mortuary context of the figures they may represent primordial ancestors of the Etowah people.

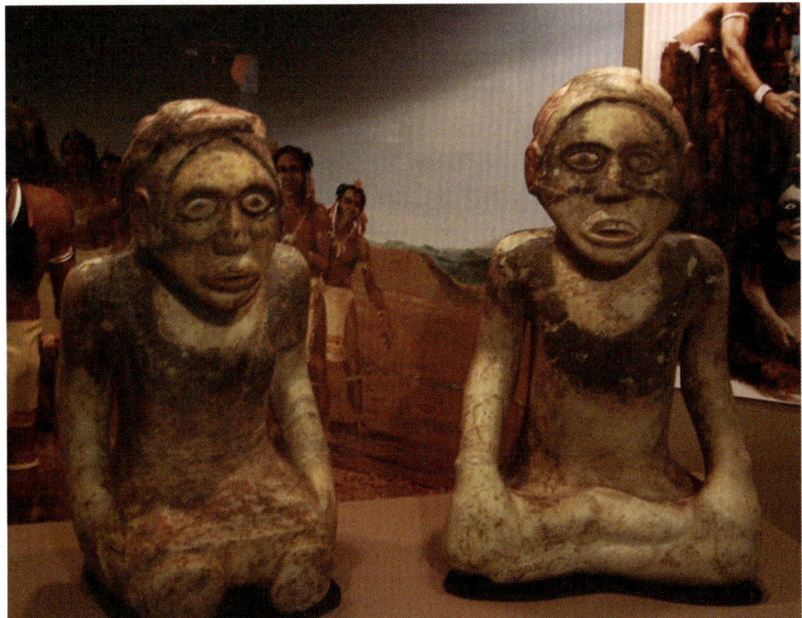

◀ **3.15** Etowah, Seated Male and Female Figures, C. 1250–1375, marble, 2 ft. high.

These figures were excavated from Mound C, which covered a charnel house that held some 350 individuals. The statues were original enlivened with red ocher, a carbon black band across the face, and a copper-green pigment on the chests.

Peoples of the Southwest (500–1300 CE)

About the same time that the Mississippian and Caddoan peoples were building complex states, populations in the desert Southwest were forming hierarchical and centralized political structures of their own. The Ancestral Puebloans, Hohokam, and Mogollon established permanent, agriculturally-based communities in the early centuries of the Common Era. The Ancestral Puebloans moved onto the Colorado Plateau around 650 CE and by the twelfth century were constructing large multistoried "Great Houses" in Mesa Verde canyon wall alcoves. In the Sonoran Desert of Arizona, the Hohokam built great cities at Casa Grande and Snaketown with Mesoamerican-style ball courts, platform pyramids and multistoried buildings. During the same era, the Mogollon of eastern Arizona, New Mexico, and Chihuahua built communities at Gila in New Mexico and Paquimé (Casas Grandes) in Chihuahua. Paquimé offered its citizens ball courts, stone veneered mounds, and multi-story adobe buildings. To grow crops in these arid and semiarid regions, the Hohokam and Mogollon developed extensive water collection and irrigation systems, some of which still function today.

ANCESTRAL PUEBLOAN (650–1285 CE)

Around 650–750 CE the Ancestral Puebloan peoples had begun farming and establishing towns or "pueblos" on the mesa tops. However, in the mid-twelfth century, the Ancestral Puebloans, while continuing to farm the mesas, moved their communities to canyon alcoves, hundreds of feet above the canyon floor. The alcove or cliff houses were constructed in the same manner as the mesa top structures had been, using hand-cut sandstone blocks set in adobe or "mud" mortar. Most of the canyon alcoves are quite small, accommodating houses of five or fewer rooms; the average room size being 6 feet (1.8 m) by 8 feet (2.4 m), although smaller storage rooms were also built to utilize the available cave spaces. In selecting alcoves for building, the Ancestral Puebloan peoples preferred south- or southwest-facing caves that received warming sunshine on winter days.

Cliff Palace, Mesa Verde, c. 1190–1260 CE Mesa Verde is a sandstone plateau some 15 miles (24 km) long by 8 miles (12.9 m) wide, which sits at an elevation of 8,500 feet (2,600 m) above sea level. It takes its name, "Green Table," from the scrub juniper and piñon pine growing on it. Over the last few million years stream erosion has sliced through the plateau, creating a series of deep canyons between narrow ribbons of tableland; rushing monsoonal flood waters over the same period hollowed out alcoves, some quite large, into these canyon walls.

The largest of all the Mesa Verde alcove communities, Cliff Palace (Figure 3.16), was discovered and named in 1888 by Richard Wetherill

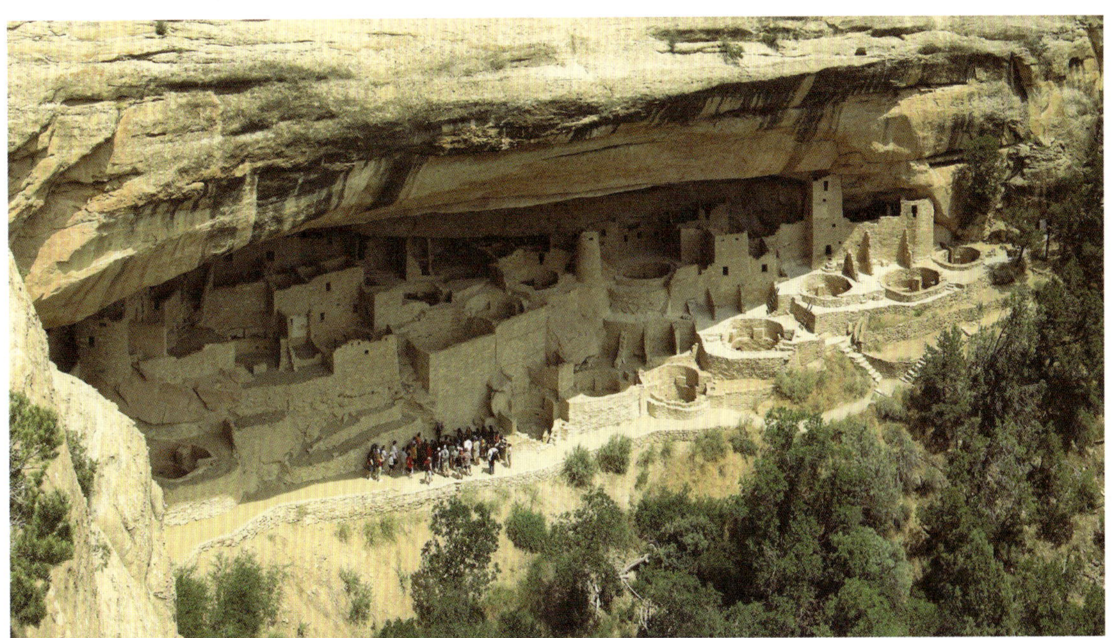

▲ **3.16** Ancestral Puebloan, Mesa Verde, CO, Cliff Palace, c. 1190–1260 CE.

Cliff Palace is the largest of all the Mesa Verde alcove communities; it has 217 rooms and 23 kivas.

and Charlie Mason, who were tracking stray cattle through Cliff Canyon. The city was built into an enormous cliff cavity some 300 feet (91 m) long, almost 100 feet (30 m) deep, and between 50 and 100 feet (15–30 m) high; the space was large enough to accommodate 217 rooms and 23 kivas.

Building in this large sandstone cavern presented difficulties beyond the movement of materials up some 200 feet (61 m) from the canyon floor. The cavern floor was sloping and littered with fallen boulders too large to be moved so they had to be incorporated into the architecture. Cliff Palace's builders began by establishing the location of the ritual spaces or kivas in the gaps among the boulders. When the kiva walls had been constructed, the floor of the cavern was terraced around them and leveled with fill dirt, making the kivas into semi-subterranean structures. The remaining area of the cavern was filled with multi-story apartment structures and storage facilities. Every available space was utilized, including a narrow ledge near the roof of the cave, which was walled in and used for seed storage.

Two of the more interesting structures are the round and square towers. The round tower is the smaller of the two, at only two stories high, but it is impressive in that every stone used had to be individually shaped to create a perfectly smooth round wall. The square tower rises in four stories to almost touch the cave roof. Access to the upper levels of Cliff Palace dwellings was provided by wooden ladders. The use of these ladders inspired one of the unique features of Puebloan architecture, the T-shaped doorway. The upper level of the square tower has one of these T-shaped portals. These were designed to allow persons carrying burdens on their backs to enter the rooms without having to remove their loads.

Long House, Kiva, c. 1190–1260 CE Among modern Pueblo peoples, **kivas** are subterranean ritual and communal spaces that belong to individual clans or kin groups. It is probable that the Ancestral Puebloan kivas served similar purposes. At Mesa Verde and Chaco Canyon kivas are generally circular spaces in contrast to modern kivas, which are often square. The circular design of the early kivas is thought to derive from the earlier circular-form Basketmaker pit house.

Cliff Palace has twenty-two kivas within the main cavern and a twenty-third a slight distance away; twenty are typical circular structures, while three are unusual square-form chambers with rounded corners. Typically, Mesa Verde kivas, like that at Long House in the western part of the mesa, (Figure 3.17) are small structures, about 12 feet (3.7 m) to 13 feet (4 m) in diameter, but deep enough that a man could stand upright beneath the cribbed roof. In creating a **cribbed roof**, wooden beams were laid between pilasters, built into the kiva wall, so that they formed a polygonal framework around the top of the wall. As each layer of posts was added the polygon was shifted slightly so that the corners met in the center of one of the beams of the previous layer. The cribbing continued until the only opening was the central smoke and access hole. The shelves created by the polygons were covered with shakes, bark, and then the whole thing covered with a layer of earth to form a small plaza-like space on top of the kiva.

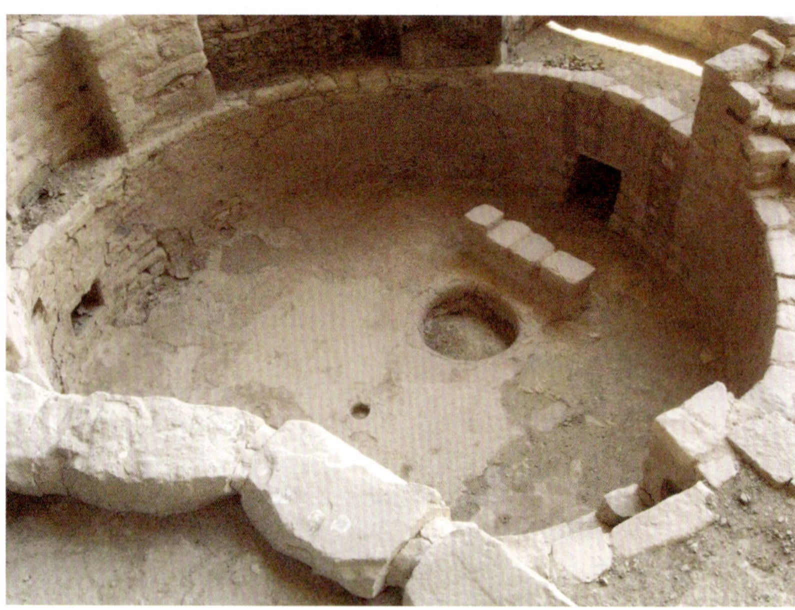

▶ **3.17** Ancestral Puebloan, Mesa Verde CO, Longhouse, Kiva, c. 1190–1260 CE.

Kivas were subterranean ritual and communal spaces that belonged to individual clans or kin groups. They are typically round with a bench or shelf from which rise piers that supported the cribbed roof; in the floor is a small sipapu, firepit, stone deflector, and vent shaft.

Set into the floor of each chamber were a firepit and a second, smaller hole called a ***sipapu***. The sipapu is a symbolic portal commemorating the opening through which the first ancestors of the Puebloan peoples emerged into this world. Fresh air was supplied by a ventilator shaft, usually set in a side wall and separated from the fire by a stone deflector. Running entirely around the circular room, a few feet up from the floor, was a stone bench. At intervals along the bench were five or six stone pilasters, which supported the roof beams.

Square Tower Wall Paintings, c. 1190–1260 CE Traces of adobe plaster and color have been found on both exterior and interior walls of Mesa Verde buildings, suggesting that the cliff dwellings may have originally been painted in red and white, colors that would have made them more visible against the muted tones of the sandstone walls. The Ancestral Puebloan peoples used a fairly simple technique for fresco painting that was not too dissimilar from that found earlier in the Valley of Mexico. The first step was to smooth the stone walls with a thick "rough coat" of sandy, yellow-brown adobe. This base coat was followed by a thin intonaco or smooth coat of white gypsum plaster. The designs, often the same geometric patterns used to decorate Mesa Verde pottery, were painted in red derived from hematite or red ocher. Incised lines and hatch marks were sometimes used to create tonal variations. Some of the kiva walls show up to six alternating layers of rough coat and intonaco, suggesting that the rooms may have been repainted when the original designs became worn or were no longer ritually relevant.

At Cliff Palace a large fragment of fresco (Figure 3.18) remains on two walls of the third-floor room of the square tower. The lower portion of the wall is painted red and appears to show what may be a landscape scene of low hills between triangular mountains. The upper

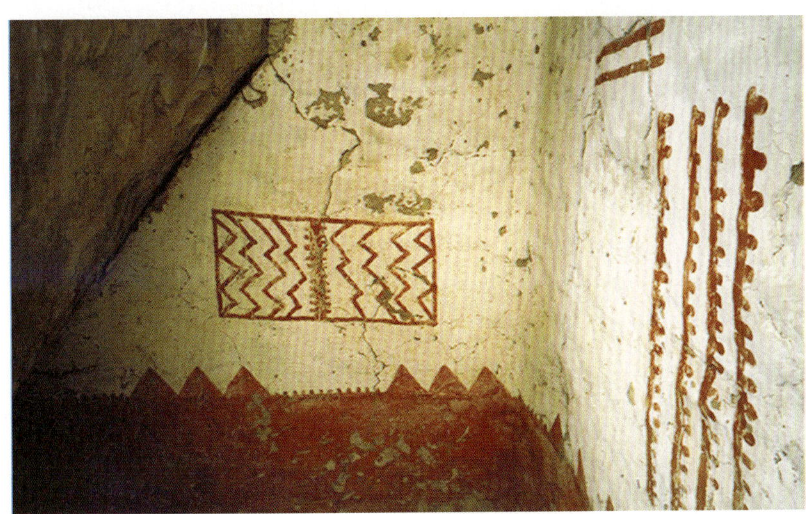

◀ **3.18** Ancestral Puebloan, Mesa Verde, Cliff Palace, Square Tower, Third Floor Mural, c. 1190–1260 CE.

Traces of pigment found on the buildings at Mesa Verde show that they were originally painted both inside and out. This mural is a combination of geometric and linear patterns and what appears to be a landscape with mountains.

portion of the wall is white with red painted patterns of lines, dots, and zigzags; the meaning of these geometric designs is unknown. Similar designs appear on Ancestral Pueblo pottery.

Mesa Verde was abandoned at the end of the thirteenth century after a prolonged period of drought that had lasted for almost twenty-five years. The inhabitants of Cliff Palace and other Mesa Verde communities moved south into what is now Arizona and New Mexico, where they came into closer contact with the Hohokam and Mogollon.

Mesa Verde Ceramic Bowl, c. 1100–1300 CE At Mesa Verde and other Ancestral Puebloan sites, potters made elegant black on white ceramic bowls, pitchers, jars, and other storage containers. These vessels were beautifully formed by coiling; then scraped and given a final polishing with stones. Surface decoration of the cream clay body was done using black paints made from both mineral and organic sources depending upon the area. Where available, iron-rich hematite was crushed and mixed to create preparations which produced a shiny black color when fired. In areas lacking hematite resources, Ancestral Puebloan potters boiled Rocky Mountain beeweed (*Cleome serrulata*) down to the consistency of thick syrup, known to Hopi potters, as ***guaco*** (Shepard 1980, 33). Although almost transparent when applied, the guaco turned a flat black when fired.

The Mesa Verde bowl (Figure 3.19) is the work of a master potter who took care to create a regular form with consistently thin walls. Only the inside surface of the bowl was decorated. The artist created a

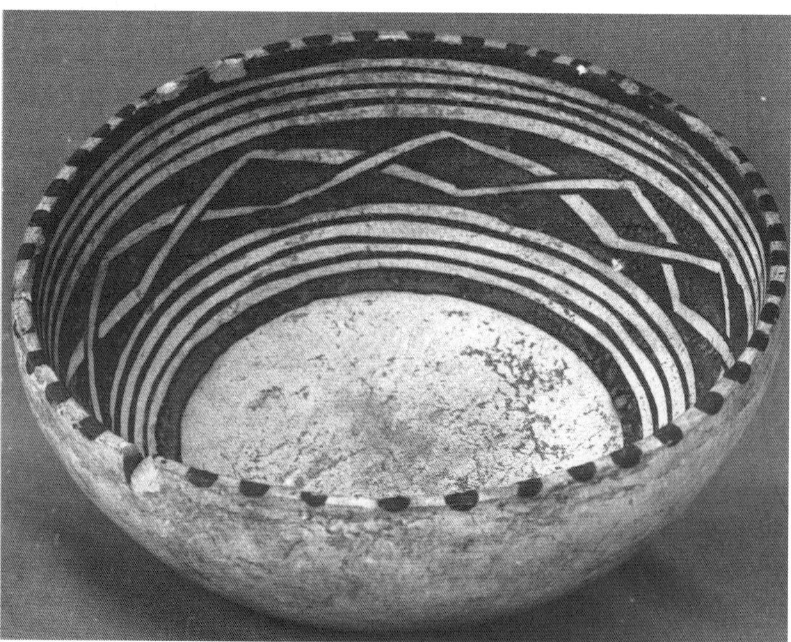

▶ **3.19** Ancestral Puebloan, Mesa Verde, Black-on-White Painted Bowl, c. 1100–1300 CE. 2.62 in. × 6.37 in.

Mesa Verde potters created elegant black and white painted wares using mineral and plant-based pigments that turned black when fired.

simple but elegant free-hand pattern of four stripes above and below a wider band featuring a chained or twined design, using a negative painting technique. The combination of pattern band with stripes is reminiscent of textile designs used in historic times by the Hopi and may well have been derived from Ancestral Puebloan textile patterns.

HOHOKAM (1150–1450 CE)

The Hohokam settled in the Sonoran Desert of central and southern Arizona, along the Gila and Salt Rivers, around 200 CE. They were able to make this semiarid region productive with an extensive irrigation system that brought water from the river to their fields of corn, cotton, tobacco, agave, and amaranth. In addition to farming, the Hohokam were engaged in the trade of commodities such as salt, shell, carved stone, and macaw feathers. They participated in long-distance trade networks that extended north into the Great Plains, west to California, and southward into various parts of Mexico. Among the things the Hohokam acquired from their Mesoamerican trading partners were, apparently, architectural prototypes for ball courts and platform pyramids.

Casa Grande, Coolidge, Arizona, c. 1350–1450 CE Set within a large walled enclosure measuring approximately 420 feet (128 m) by 260 feet (79 m) were several multiroom structures, including a tall rectangular building known as the Casa Grande (Figure 3.20) or "Big House." Casa Grande is a three-story-tall rectangular structure, with a 58.5 feet (18 m) by 43 feet (13 m) footprint, which sits atop a 6-foot (1.8 m) platform, now mostly buried by desert sands. It was built around 1350 CE and used for about a century before the Hohokam abandoned the site. The various

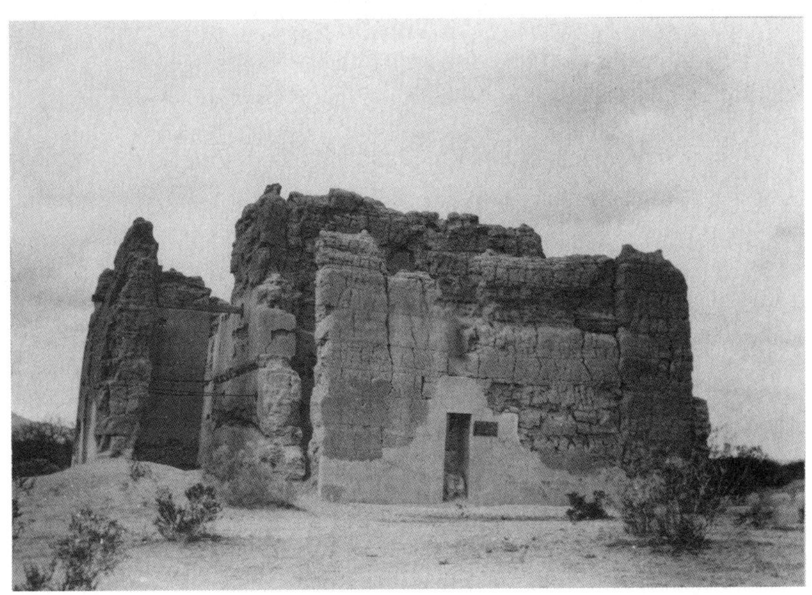

◀ **3.20** Hohokam, East side of the Casa Grande, Coolidge, AZ, c. 1350 CE (photo c. 1900 CE).

Constructed from local caliche, the Casa Grande was a three-story structure that was aligned for viewing the rising and setting of the sun on the solstices and equinoxes and for tracking the minimum and maximum extreme of the setting moon over its 18.5-year cycle.

functions of the building are unknown but there is some evidence that it was aligned for viewing solstice and equinox sunrises and sunsets as well as for tracking the minimum and maximum extreme of the setting moon over its 18.5-year cycle. Calendars based on solar and lunar cycles are also known to have been used by the Ancestral Puebloan peoples of Chaco Canyon.

Casa Grande was built in one period of construction from local caliche. **Caliche** is a type of calcium carbonate–encrusted soil or sedimentary rock deposit that when mixed with water forms a natural concrete. To build Casa Grande, the Hohokam piled up the caliche as a continuous row around the building about 2 feet (61 cm) high. As each row solidified, another was added until the walls reached the desired height for the first floor; then spruce and fir beams were then set in place and the caliche work continued up to the next floor level. The trees used for the floor beams do not grow locally and were brought in from forests some 50 miles distant. Casa Grande's caliche walls are almost 5 feet thick at the bottom and tapered inward as they rise to a terminal thickness of about 3 feet (1 m). The first two levels of the building had five rooms each. These were two long ones on the northern and southern ends that were oriented east-west; three north-south oriented rooms were set between the two outer rooms. Circulation was around the perimeter of the building, but the room at the center was accessible only from an eastern door. The top floor had only a single large room.

The walls of Casa Grande would have been smoothed on the interior and exterior with a plaster coat and painted. None of the Hohokam murals have survived the six hundred years of abandonment and weather, but several early visitors described seeing wall paintings. When Jesse Walter Fewkes (1850–1930) surveyed the site in 1908, he recorded seeing a fragment of a mural in the "Clan House," one of the other buildings in the compound with Casa Grande. He described the mural as figures of "birds and other animals, painted in red" (Fewkes 1914-1924/1993, 108).

THE MIMBRENOS-MOGOLLON PEOPLE (C. 1000–1130 CE)

The Mimbrenos or Mimbres were a branch of the Mogollon culture who occupied the Mimbres River valley in southwestern New Mexico. During the 130 years or so that they lived in the area, they constructed single-story apartment blocks, usually arranged around plazas. They also built rectangular plan Great Kivas for community use. Unfortunately, very little legitimate archaeological work has been done in the Mimbres valley, but every known Mimbres site has been looted, often with mechanized destruction, by pot hunters seeking the highly desirable classic Mimbres black-on-white wares. The Mimbres people typically buried their dead in a squatting position beneath their house floors. The bowls, many of which show prior use, were ritually "killed" by punching a hole in the bottom, and placed over the head of the deceased.

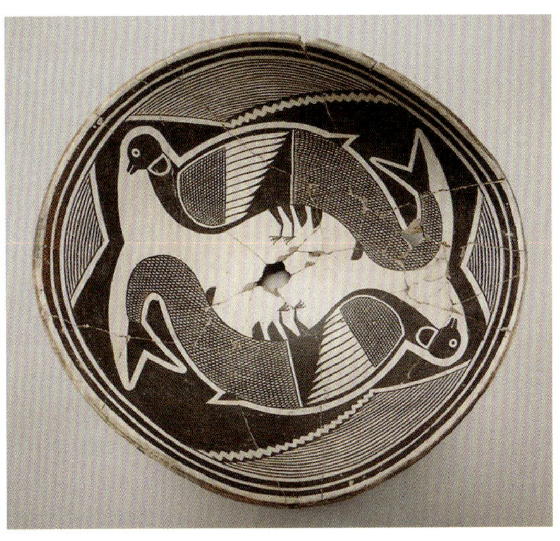

▲ 3.21 Mogollon-Mimbres Bowl with Avian-Fish Design, c. 1000–1130 CE.

Mimbres designs often exhibit a sense of humor or whimsy as in these composite bird-fish creatures. The hole in the center of the bowl shows that it was ritually "killed" as a funerary offering.

Mimbres Black on White Bowl with Avian-Fish Design, 1000–1130 CE During the eleventh and early twelfth centuries the Mimbres people began producing an exceptional black-on-white pottery with representational forms and complex geometric designs that are much admired by collectors. Prior to this time the pottery produced along the Mimbres differed little from other Mogollon plain wares. What inspired the Mimbres women potters to create this new style is unknown.

Mimbres ceramics were made by coiling and smoothing but the forms are sometimes imperfectly round. Bowls were only decorated on the insides; exteriors show the plain brown clay body. The designs, painted in black-on-white are most frequently geometric and bear some resemblance to the geometric designs of Ancestral Puebloan black-and-white pottery, but are local inventions. What distinguishes Mimbres geometric painting is a sense of visual movement as if the bowls were intended to be turned in the hands to appreciate the graphic imagery. The designs, such as composite bird-fish creatures on the bowl (Figure 3.21) are often whimsical.

In addition to geometric patterns, human, animal, and insect forms appear as single images, inverted pairs, and quartered designs. The images, while often realistic, are presented with a whimsy that makes them highly desirable. Many vessels are painted with **genre scenes**, showing everyday activities, including hunting parties or women, recognizable by their string aprons or anatomical features, tending children or training macaws. The Mogollon imported the birds from farther south and raised them for their highly prized scarlet feathers.

The Colonial Period (c. 1540–1900 CE)

Unlike Mexico and Peru where the beginning of the Colonial era can be pegged to the arrival of a single Spanish Conquistador, be he Cortes or Pissarro, the Colonial era in North America occurred in a piecemeal fashion with several European nations staking claims to different parts of the continent at different times. The first to arrive were the Spanish, who made incursions into the Southeast in the 1530s and the Southwest in the next decade; they were quickly followed by the French, English, Dutch, Swedes, and Russians. With few exceptions the arrival of European explorers and settlers was often an apocalyptic event for First Nations peoples, bringing disease, famine, enslavement, displacement, cultural disruption, and forced conversion to Christianity.

The Southwest

The last peoples to settle in the Southwest were the Athapascan-speaking groups known as the **Diné** (Navajo) and Nde (Apache). Originally from the far northwest in what is today Canada, these groups of Athapascan speakers began migrating southward around 1000 CE and arrived in the Four Corners region around 1400 to 1525 CE, although advance groups may have entered the region in the twelfth century. The Puebloans referred to the Athapascan groups as Apachü-Navajo, meaning "enemy," because of their raids on pueblo communities. However, they refer to themselves as Diné or Nde each meaning "the people." Ultimately, the Diné made peace with the Puebloans and engaged in trade with them. When the Spanish instituted the reconquest of New Mexico after the Great Pueblo Revolt of 1680, many Puebloans fled the harsh reprisals and resettled among the Nde and Diné on the Great Plains.

DINÉ (NAVAJO) WEAVING

From the Puebloans, the Diné learned to raise sheep and to weave. The first Diné weavings were blankets; rugs were produced later in response to the tourist market. They created three types of blankets: long serapes patterned after those of Mexico, saddle blankets, and wide mantles worn like a shawl and pinned in front, which were commonly known as wearing or "chief's blankets." The term "chief's blanket" references their popularity with chiefs of the Plains Nations who traded for the weavings; the Diné did not have chiefs as such.

▲ **3.22** Diné, Wearing or "Chief's" Blanket, NM, c. 1840–1860. Wool, 60 in. × 71 in.

This brown, white, and blue striped blanket is an example of a First Phase weaving; the brown and white are natural wool colors and the blue was produced with indigo dye.

Diné, Wearing or "Chief's" Blanket, c. 1840–1860 CE The earliest or "First Phase" Navajo weavings were simple brown, black, and white banded blankets similar to those of the Pueblo weavers (Figure 3.22). The colors were those natural to the churro sheep. Blue stripes were added by coloring white wool with indigo dyes imported from Mexico. Deep cochineal reds were obtained by unraveling *bayeta* (baize) cloth brought into the region by Mexican traders and recycling the yarn into their weavings. Later, in 1863, when the Diné were forcibly removed to Bosque Redondo and their sheep killed by the U.S. Army, Diné weavers unraveled army uniforms, long johns, and army blankets to make their weavings.

By the mid-nineteenth century Diné weavers had added yellows and greens to their color palette and had begun layering red rectangles over striped grounds. These "Second Phase" geometrically patterned blankets typically had twelve elements. In the "Third Phase" the number of elements was reduced to nine and expanded to include squares, diamonds, and triangles, often with interior patterns of crosses, bands, and zigzags.

After five years' incarceration in Bosque Redondo, the Diné were allowed to return to their traditional lands in 1868. The establishment of trading posts and the arrival of the railroad created a boom market for Native arts, especially "Navajo" blankets and rugs. However by the 1880s the classic period of Navajo weaving was over as Germantown yarns and less permanent aniline dyes came into use in weavings produced for the burgeoning tourist market.

California

The first Spanish explorer, Juan Rodriguez Cabrillo, sailed up the California coast in 1542, going as far as present-day Mendocino. For the most part the people Rodriguez Cabrillo encountered were hunters and gatherers who exploited the rich marine and land resources without the need to resort to intensive farming. The Spanish saw the aboriginal Californians as primitive and unsophisticated because their communities lacked monumental architecture, highly stratified social hierarchies, and the skilled armies that had so impressed the Spanish during the conquest of Mexico. Seeing even less to exploit, more than two centuries passed before the first Spanish friars and soldiers arrived in California.

POMO BASKETS

Among the peoples Rodriguez Cabrillo saw in the lands to the north of present-day San Francisco were the Pomo; the name refers to seven linguistically-related groups who were renowned for their twined and fine woven baskets. Both Pomo men and women made baskets. The men twining fishing weirs and bird traps. The finest baskets were made by women. These included sturdy coiled baskets for cooking and finer baskets made as ritual items; the latter were often decorated with shell and magnesite beads and a variety of bird feathers.

Jenny Hughes, **Girl's Dowry** *or* **Puberty Basket,** *late nineteenth century*

Among the Pomo, especially talented basket weavers, such as Jenny Hughes, achieved widespread recognition. Hughes's *Girl's Dowry* or *Puberty Basket* (Figure 3.23) was made by coiling with willow or sedge root used for the warp and sedge and bulrush root as the weft. The basket features a repeating stepped flag design in contrasts of brown against a beige ground. Special ritual baskets such as this one often incorporated topknot feathers from woodpeckers and quail into the

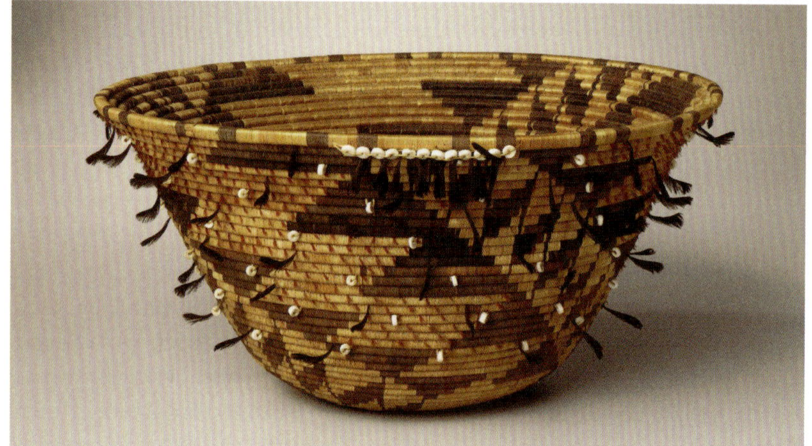

▶ **3.23** Pomo, Jenny Hughes, *Girl's Dowry* or *Puberty Basket*, late nineteenth century. Willow, sedge, and bulrush root, feathers, and shell disks.

Baskets such as this were once part of coming-of-age rituals for Pomo girls.

design; the feathers were worked under the fabric of the basket as it was woven. Sometimes as in the Hughes basket the feathers were used singly, on the exterior of the basket, to add visual dimension to the design. Feathers of various colors were occasionally used to cover the entire surface of the basket. Other ornamentation on the Hughes basket was provided by disc-shaped beads made from the shells of the *olivella biplicata*, a type of sea snail. Conical baskets of this type were once part of coming-of-age rituals for Pomo girls, but when the Hughes basket was collected in the late nineteenth century, those rituals were no longer practiced by the Pomo, although traditional baskets continued to be made for sale.

The Great Plains

Prior to the seventeenth century, the Great Plains were sparsely occupied by small bands of hunter-gatherers, and a few sedentary agriculturalists in the river valleys. This changed radically with the acquisition of horses by Plains peoples. Horses were introduced into the Southwest by the Spanish in the sixteenth century but after the Pueblo Revolt of 1680 CE, horses were traded to the Navajo, Apache, and Ute and from them to other groups in the Plains; by 1750 CE, horses were being kept by groups as far north as the Canadian borderlands. Horses dramatically changed Plains culture, allowing Native Americans to more efficiently exploit natural resources, especially, the most important of all resources, bison.

BUFFALO HIDE PAINTINGS

The Plains peoples used every part of the bison; in addition to meat it provided the raw materials for weapons, utensils, clothing, ritual paraphernalia, war shields, and battle armor. Tanned buffalo and elk hides were used to record personal histories, document winter counts, battles, and important ceremonies. The earliest surviving hide paintings, collected during the Lewis and Clark expedition, date to around 1800 CE, but the practice of making these paintings is certainly much older. With the forced removal of Plains tribes to reservations, many were unable to hunt bison and elk, but they continued to record their histories using muslin yard goods and later, surplus accounting ledger books.

Cotsiogo "Cadzi Cody" (c. 1866–1912 CE), Elk Hide Robe Painting of the Sun Dance, c. 1890–1900 CE One of the more prolific and commercially successful hide painters was the Eastern Shoshone artist Cotsiogo, who was also known by his Anglicized name, Cadzi Cody. Cotsiogo was one of several sons of Chief Washakie who was a renowned hide painter and tribal leader. Cotsiogo began painting hides around 1885. As the railroads brought more white tourists seeking authentic experiences of the American West, and mementos of those experiences, Cotsiogo began to paint scenes designed to appeal to this market, often combining elements from different narrative scenes in one painting.

When Cotsiogo was a small child, the Eastern Shoshone were relocated to the Wind River reservation. By the time he painted this hide painting (Figure 3.24), many of the traditional ways of life depicted on it were little more than memories. The great herds of bison that had once roamed the plains had been nearly exterminated by railroad hunters who shot the animals for sport. The Sun Dance ceremonials depicted in the center of the hide had been actively discouraged for several years by the U.S. government, which ultimately banned it in 1904. The dances, held at the time of the summer solstice, focused on spiritual renewal and the regeneration of the earth, but some groups also had vision quest rituals that included chest piercing, a practice that white authorities considered abhorrent. Cotsiogo seems to have been aware of the official sentiment surrounding the Sun Dance and in this painting has tried to lessen the impact by adding in elements of the more acceptable Wolf Dances.

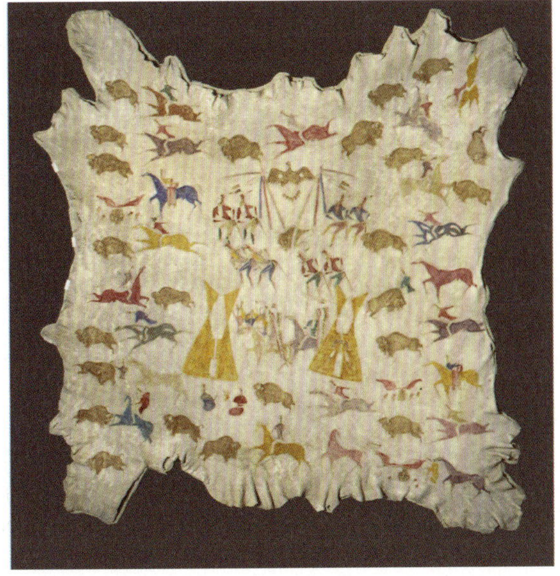

▼ **3.24** Shoshone, Cotsiogo "Cadzi Cody" (1866–1912), Elk Hide Robe Painting of the Sun Dance, c. 1890–1900 CE. 81 in. × 78 in.

A Sun Dance ritual is depicted in the center between two camps, while hunting scenes appear around the sides.

The Shoshone camp is indicated by the two tipis just below the center point of the elk hide. Two warriors with long war bonnets, a reference to the Wolf or War Dance, ride into the camp while women sit above and below the camp. The Sun Dance occupies the center of the hide where eight dancers move around a symbolic sun tree upon which hangs a bison head; above the tree an eagle flies. The eagle and bison represent the body (bison) and spirit (eagle) coming together in harmony. Around the center scenes revolves a hunting scene in which hunters armed with bows and arrows chase after the buffalo. Some have dismounted and are shown butchering and skinning the animals; they carefully pile up all the parts, wasting nothing. Although traditional hide paintings would have been done with natural pigments, Cotsiogo was successful enough that he could buy commercial paints. Close examination of the human and animal forms reveals that Cotsiogo used a combination of stenciling and freehand drawing to create this painting.

The Northwest Coast

At the time of the first European contacts in the sixteenth century, the narrow strip of land between mountains and ocean along the Pacific Northwest (including coastal Oregon, Washington, British Colombia, and southern Alaska) was one of the most densely occupied regions of North America. During the historic period, the area was home to some thirty nations, each with its own language and distinct culture. The ancestors of these peoples are thought to have established themselves in the region perhaps as early as 8000 BCE. However, as the majority of their arts were created in wood and other perishable materials, as were their communal houses, there are very few examples of Northwest Coast art and architecture that date back more than two or three centuries.

CEDAR PLANK HOUSES

The tradition of building cedar plank houses (Figure 3.25) seems to have been established in the Pacific Northwest by the end of the second millennium BCE, if not before. Plank houses or longhouses were built in the primary winter villages, which were typically occupied from fall through spring of each year. Some of these communities were quite large with upwards of eighty houses arranged in rows, houses of greatest

PLATE 89

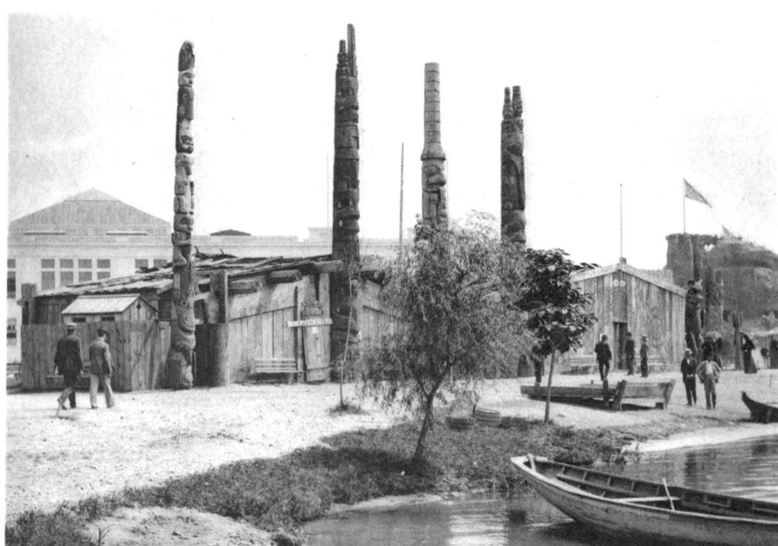

HOUSES AND TOTEM POLES OF ALASKAN INDIANS.

▶ **3.25** World's Columbian Exposition 1893, Houses and Totem Poles of Alaskan Indians, C. D. Arnold and H. D. Higinbotham photographers.

This photograph shows the different styles of cedar plank houses and totem poles from the Northwest Coast Peoples.

prominence facing the ocean and those of lesser status in rows behind them. The largest houses, typically found in the milder southern coast regions, were as much as 60 feet (18.46 m) square and could shelter one hundred residents; those in the colder areas tended to be smaller, about 35 feet (10.66 m) square. The individual houses were led by a "house chief" who was usually a noble and the ultimate authority over the commoners and slaves who also occupied the house; village chiefs, as such, were rare.

World's Columbian Exposition, 1893, Houses and Totem Poles of Alaskan Indians Plank houses were built in two distinct styles. In the colder northern coast, the houses had gable roofs while in the south they typically had simple, single-pitch shed roofs, and were sometimes built as modular units that were joined up lengthwise to create structures that measured as much as 150 feet (46 m) long. Regardless of the style, the houses were designed so the cedar planks could be taken down and carried to the summer camps, leaving only the post and beam frame intact until the community returned to their winter camp and reassembled the house. This was accomplished by tying the planks together or by slotting them between poles; the planks forming the roof were held in place with rocks or halved logs as weights.

The interiors were typically arranged around a central common area with a firepit that was used by all the families. The common area was surrounded by a two-tiered plank floor; the lower level served as a seating area and the upper platform served as family sleeping and storage areas. In the partitioning of the house, the "house chief" was afforded the largest area against the back wall, and the remainder of the perimeter space was apportioned to the families. Individual family areas were established with decorated plank screens, or woven cedar bark mats that served as partition walls. Interior decoration varied among the groups, some had elaborately carved house posts and beams featuring stylized human and animal forms that referenced house lineages and histories.

TOTEM POLES AND POTLATCHES

The art form most closely associated with the Northwest Coast peoples is the totem pole. The poles are visual representations of family lineages and histories, rendered in a symbolic and stylized form. The animals and humans depicted on them constituted family crests and reference events in family histories, functioning as mnemonic devices rather than as narratives. While some figures are drawn from myths such as those of Raven[4], which would be generally known by members

[4] In addition to being a clan totemic ancestor, Raven is one of the more important characters in Northwest Coast mythologies. He is a trickster and transformer, credited with creating the land and the first men, stealing the sun, moon and stars to light the world, and bring fire to mankind.

of all clans, others would only be understood by those who knew the family's history. Traditionally totem poles were erected as part of a potlatch ceremony and were intended to validate the status and privileges held by the sponsoring family. The most common form is the freestanding pole erected in front of the longhouse but some houses also had carved frontal poles that were attached to the midpoint of the façade, often with an opening in the base through which people entered and exited the house.

Tlingit Kiks.ádi Clan, K'alyaan Totem Pole, 2005 Totem poles averaged between 10 feet (3 m) and 65 feet (20 m) in height but the Haida and Tsimshian are known to have carved some poles that reached heights of 100 feet (30 m). While the carving and painting of totem poles is an ancient art, the number of poles carved increased dramatically in the nineteenth century when European traders brought metal tools to the region. In addition to crest poles, totem poles were also carved to serve mortuary and social purposes. Mortuary poles, typically among the tallest, both commemorated the individual and served as his tomb; the remains were placed within a grave box carved into the pole. Such poles can also be carved in commemoration; the 35 foot (10.66 m) tall K'alyaan Totem Pole (Figure 3.26), for example, was erected for the bicentennial of the Battle of Sitka, to honor the warriors who died fighting the Russians in 1804.

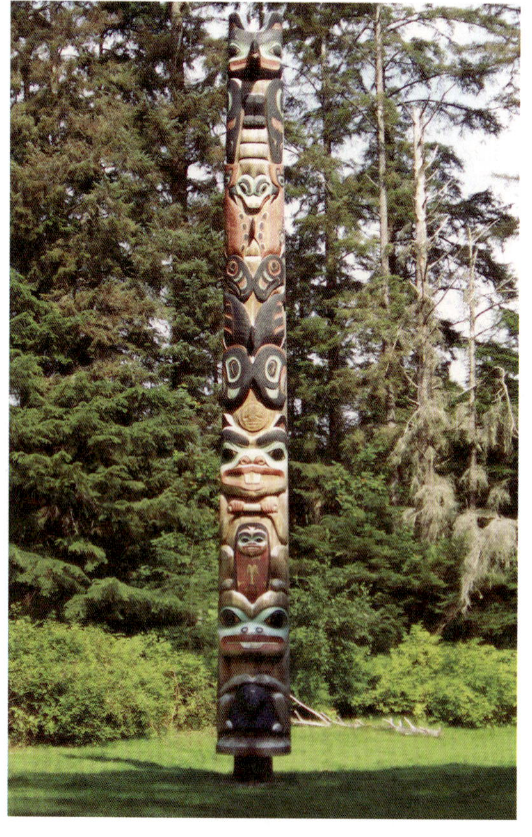

▼ 3.26 Tlingit Kiks.ádi Clan, K'alyaan Totem Pole, 2005.

This totem pole was erected to commemorate the Tlingit warriors who fought against the Russians in the Battle of Sitka in 1804.

Another type of pole was carved as a means of influencing social behavior; known as a "shame pole," these carvings were intended to ridicule individuals or neighboring groups who owed unpaid debts. The poles remained standing as long as the debt was unpaid. One famous example of such a pole was erected in the 1880s to shame Secretary of State William Seward, who visited Tongass Village in 1869 and was honored with a potlach by Chief Ebbits of the Taant'a kwáan Teikweidí. When Seward did not reciprocate in a reasonable period of time the pole was erected to remind him of the debt. Since the obligation has never been repaid, the pole remained standing until it deteriorated, and the original replaced by a replica.

The carving of totem poles and holding of potlatches and other ceremonies was outlawed in Canada in 1884 as part of an attempt to force First Nations peoples to assimilate and adopt Christianity. Culturally ignorant Euro-American missionaries and government officials saw the poles as heathen idols and encouraged their destruction. Poles were removed from villages by the authorities and sold off to museums and collectors. The carving of totem poles by Canadian groups did not resume until the law was rescinded in 1951. Today, many First Nations are actively seeking the return of poles taken during the nineteenth and early twentieth centuries.

Kwakwaka'wakw Potlatch with Masked Dancers, c. 1914 CE All of the Northwest Coast Nations carved wooden masks; these were used in ceremonies celebrating family and clan lineages, performances that recounted histories, and myths, as well as in shamanistic rituals. These masks ranged from simple humanoid face masks to elaborate articulated animal masks with moveable wings, fins, and mouths, and transformation masks that opened up to reveal the inner human face of the totemic spirit they represented. Masks were frequently danced during potlatches or "gifting ceremonies" held by many Pacific Northwest peoples. Potlatches, sometimes lasting for weeks, were held to celebrate births and weddings, memorialize the dead, mark important events, or to restore or raise the social status of the sponsoring house. In addition to feasting, guests received gifts according to their rank, including food supplies, canoes, blankets, slaves, ornamental coppers, titles, songs, and rights to exploit resources such as berries or hunting and fishing lands.

The masks in Edward S. Curtis's circa-1914 photo (Figure 3.27) of a Kwakwaka'wakw (formerly Kwakiutl) potlatch, represent mythical ancestral animals such as the bear, killer whale, eagle, and raven and were danced as a reiteration of the hosts' genealogy, describing the family's descent from a supernatural ancestor. The larger masks were often

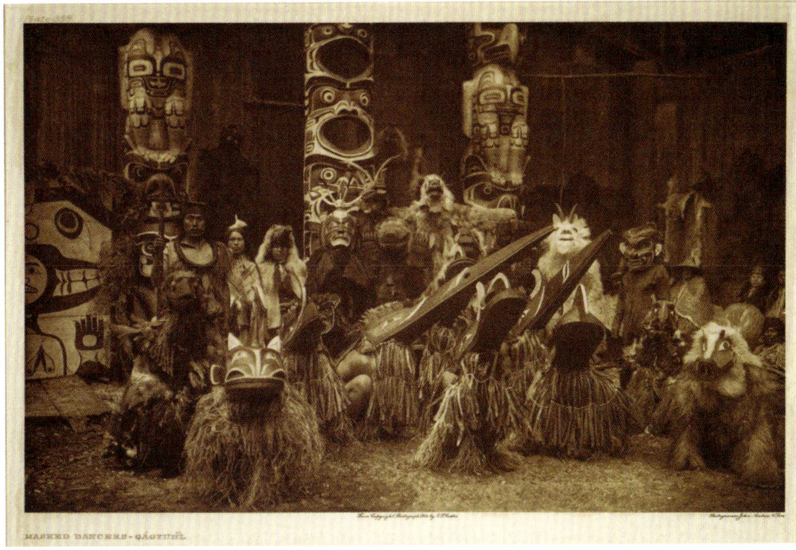

3.27 Kwakwaka'wakw Potlatch with Masked Dancers, c. 1914, photographed by Edward S. Curtis.

This photo shows a group of dancers with articulated masks representing ancestral animal spirits; in the background are carved house posts and divider panels. The house chief is the man on the left wearing the cedar ring collar.

made up of several pieces of cedar to create moveable parts, which were controlled by cords that the dancer could pull to animate the mask. Masks, totem poles, and other carvings were often painted; black, red, blue, and green were the most commonly used colors, but how they were applied varied among Northwest Coasts groups.

CHILKAT BLANKETS

Chilkat dance blankets were worn by chiefs at potlatches and were among the high-status gifts that might be given to especially honored guests. The Chilkat, a band of the Tlingit Nation, were renowned as weavers. Weaving of blankets is thought to have begun with the neighboring Tsimshian Nation and spread to the Tlingit, among whom the best weavers were the Chilkat women. The weaving was a joint process between the sexes. The men hunted the sheep, made the looms, and painted the pattern boards, while the women removed the wool from the sheep hide, hand-spun it, dyed it and then did the weaving on a warp-weighted single bar loom.

This type of loom consists of two upright poles supporting a crossbar from which the wool and yellow cedar-bark warp threads were hung. The ends of the warp threads were tied into bundles and weighted with stones to give tension to the yarn. The weft threads were wool, sometimes with dog hair added. The weaving was done entirely with the fingers, and two or more weft threads would be twisted around the warps. The long fringe was created by leaving a length of warp yarns and the sides were finished by braiding the selvages. Prior to the introduction of commercial aniline dies in the 1890s, the blankets were limited in color, being primarily natural white, yellow, black, and blue. Wolf-moss lichen provided the yellow, and the blue-green was produced by boiling copper ores in urine.

The weaving of a single blanket took from six months to a year and thus only the wealthy could afford to own them. Used as mantles, the Chilkat blankets were wide rectangles with the bottom tapering to a V-shape. The tripartite designs featured on the blankets represented clan totem animals. The abstract quality of the image is the result of the animal being seen from more than one perspective at the same time.

Anisalaga "Mary Ebbets Hunt" (1823–1919), Chilkat Dowry Blanket, c. 1880

The daughter of a Tlingit chief, Anisalaga or Mary Ebbets, married Robert Hunt, a Hudson Bay trader, and settled with him in the Kawkwaka'wakw Nation at Fort Rupert. She is known to have woven a Chilkat blanket for each of her thirteen children. This particular blanket (Figures 3.28) was woven as a dowry item for one of Anisalaga's daughters. The blanket disappeared a century ago but was recently offered for sale at a Paris auction house. When it did not sell, the Kawkwaka'wakw raised the funds to recover their cultural treasure.

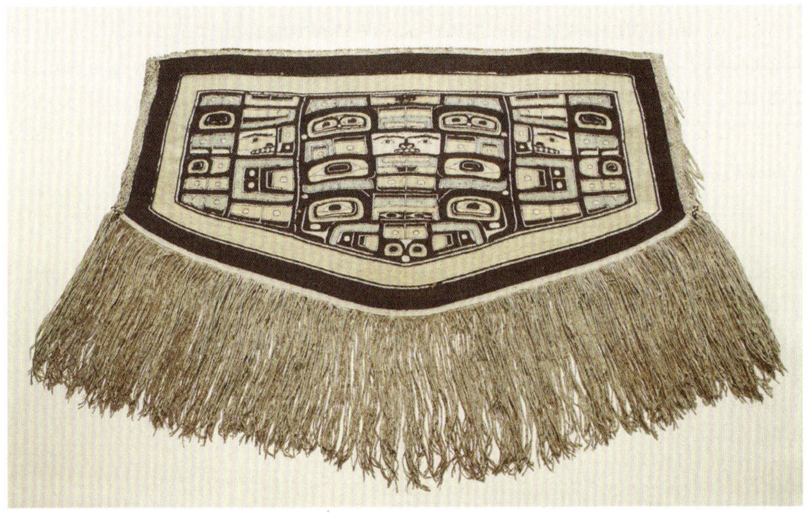

◀ **3.28** Anisalaga "Mary Ebbets Hunt" (1823–1919), Chilkat Dowry Blanket, c. 1880. Wool and cedar bark.

Chilkat blankets were worn by chiefs and presented as high-status gifts. Anisalaga is known to have woven thirteen Chilkat blankets, one for each of her children. This blanket was woven for one of her daughters.

Anisalaga's daughter is shown wearing the blanket and a mask in an Edward Curtis photograph, circa 1880 (Figure 3.29).

In this blanket Anisalaga depicts the Raven in frontal and profile views. The center panel is divided into upper and lower views with the upper section being a close-up, large-scale view of the face of the animal. The lower center section shows the bird in frontal view, the human face of the spirit at the top of the panel flanked by profile views of the animal head as though the face were being revealed by the opening of a transformation mask. The body extends down from the head and the wings bracket the sides as if the raven were flying toward the viewer. A second head with stylized wings fills in the bottom of the panel. The side panels feature the same elements in profile. Eye elements and small circles, representing ball and socket joints, are used to fill the empty spaces.

▼ **3.29** Anisalaga's daughter wearing the Chilkat blanket made for her dowry, photography by Edward S. Curtis, c. 1880.

The blanket worn in this photograph disappeared in the early twentieth century and was recently reclaimed by the Kwakwaka'wakw when it appeared for sale in a Paris auction house.

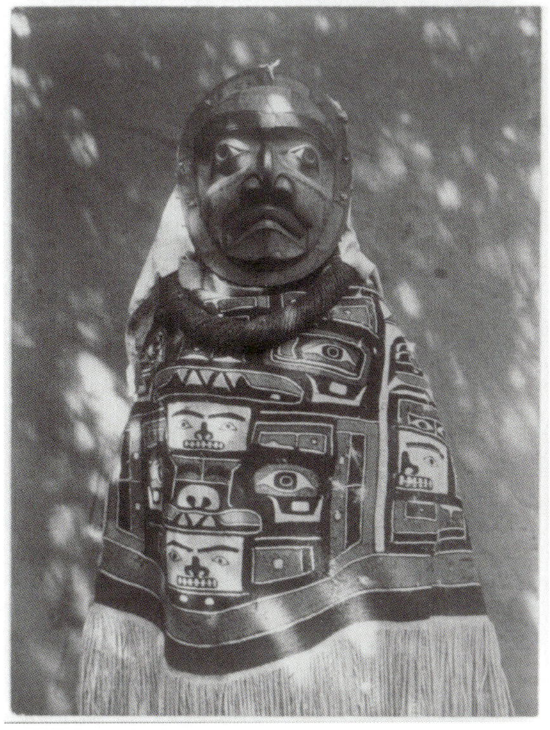

The Inuit

The barren, treeless subarctic and arctic regions of Alaska, Canada, and Greenland are home to the Inuit. In Alaska the term Eskimo, considered pejorative by some, is still used but in Canada the preferred term is *Inuit*, meaning "the people." Despite the difficulties of the environment, people are believed to have inhabited the Arctic regions as early as 10,000 to 4000 BCE. The North American Inuit had little contact with Europeans before the eighteenth

TAKE A CLOSER LOOK

Reading Panel Design in Chilkat Blankets

As in the case of the Huari textile in Chapter 2, woven Chilkat Blanket, or dance robe, designs can be difficult to read. Most blankets can be divided vertically into three parts: a frontal view in the central panel and two symmetrical side panels with the left and right profiles of the blanket animal. This arrangement is the result of the artist trying to show multiple perspectives at the same time, much in the same way that analytical cubism tried to show multiple views of the same object. Additionally, the blankets can be divided horizontally into three sections: head (usually at the bottom in the V), body (center), and tail (usually top). The key to making the horizontal divisions is finding the body section, which looks like an anthropomorphized face, and may represent the animal's hidden human face.. In the central panel the body face will be frontal and in the side panels it will be rendered in profile. Identifying the particular totem animal depicted requires the identification of a characteristic element such as a beak and wings for a raven, claws and ears for the bear, or, in the case of the example above, fins and tail for the whale. In many blankets, animal eye-motifs are used as space fillers and the proliferation of these irrelevant anatomical motifs can be confusing. Although the side panels generally use the same motifs, their positioning can be more random as if the animal had been disarticulated and the parts tossed onto the blanket.

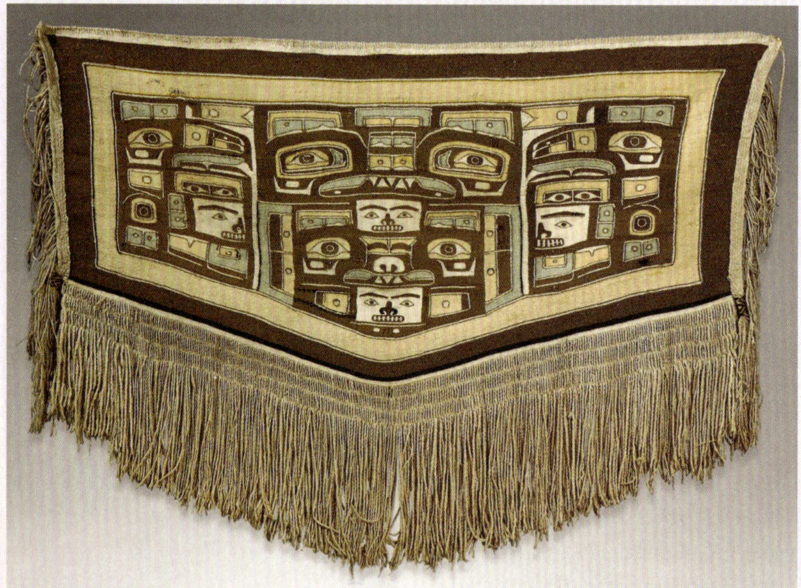

▲ **3.30** Chilkat Blanket , Haida Gwaii, c. 1900, Wool and cedar, 68.50 x 35.43 in. (174 x 90 cm).

Chilkat dance blankets designs can be divided vertically into three panels; a central panel showing a frontal view of the totem animal and two side panels offering profile images of the animal.

century when Russian fur traders established outposts in the Aleutian Islands. In the nineteenth century, traders and whalers established bases in Inuit territory; they were followed by Moravian missionaries. Contact with Europeans was a mixed blessing for the Inuit peoples; it brought disease and depletion of whale stocks, but also metal tools and other goods. The one advantage that the Inuit had over other Indigenous populations was that their land was not attractive to European settlers.

YUPIK WINTER CEREMONIALS: QASGIQS AND MASKED DANCES

The Yupik people live in the western, southwestern and southcentral parts of the Alaskan mainland just to the north of Alaskan Peninsula and the easternmost parts of Russia. They moved seasonally between summer fish camps and permanent winter villages, where contrary to the popular conception of Eskimo architecture as the snow hut or igloo, the Yupik built wood and sod houses. At the time of European contact, each winter village contained one or more ***qasgiqs*** or men's ceremonial houses and ***enas*** or women's houses. The qasgiq and ena typically stood side by side and were sometimes connected by a tunnel. Both houses were constructed using driftwood poles set into the ground palisade-style to form the walls; these posts also supported cribbed beams that held up the rafters and planks of the low, domed roof. The entire structure was covered with an insulating layer of sod; winter snowfall provided additional insulation. In the center of the structure was a firepit and corresponding smoke hole in the roof. The qasgiq was the larger of the two structures, serving as a ceremonial house for winter festivals that featured storytelling, masked dances, and shamanistic rituals.

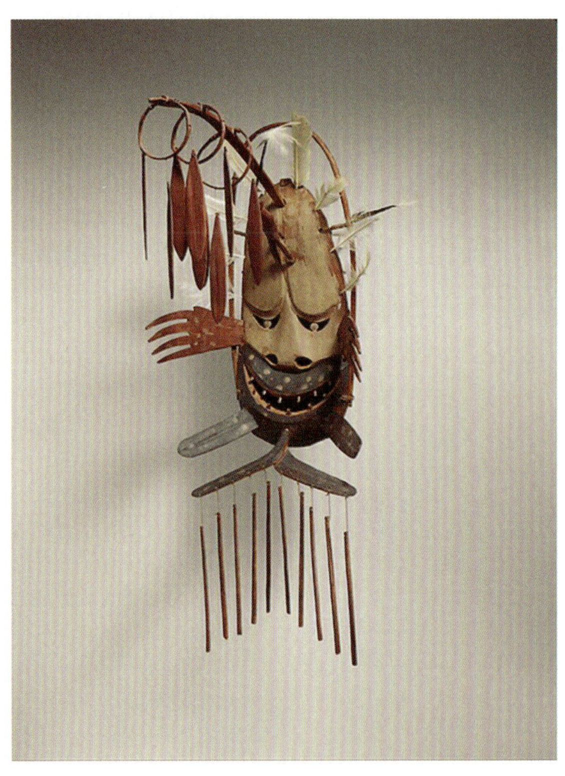

▲ **3.31** Yupik, AK, North Wind or "Negakfok" Mask, c. 1900 CE. Wood, paint, feathers, 45.25 in. × 21.37 in. × 17.87 in.

Yupik dancers performed these masks during the winter ceremonials held in the qasgiq. These dances were unusual in that the dancers only moved their upper body and arms.

North Wind or "Negakfok" Mask, c. 1900 CE

During the long Arctic winter, ceremonial cycles, designed to keep the human, animal, and spiritual worlds in harmony, were performed in the qasgiq. At these ceremonies, costumed dancers performed with masks that transformed them into the spirits of animals such as owl and raven, and natural forces such as the north wind. The driftwood and feather masks (Figure 3.31) were carved and danced in pairs. Yupik dances were unusual in that they remained stationary, moving only their arms and upper body.

The Negakfok mask (the name means "spirit that likes cold and stormy weather") represents the spirit of the north wind, whose cold breath signals the start of the Arctic winter. The masks carved around 1900 may reference the extremely cold winter of 1899. The white spots around the mouth, fins and tails represent snow. The wooden danglers projecting from the top and tail of the mask, clacking against each other, replicate the sound of the winter storms. The arrival of Christian missionaries in the late nineteenth century resulted in the suppression of the winter ceremonials and masked dances as idolatry, and the end of qasgiq building.

Eastern Woodlands

The peoples first encountered by Europeans along the Atlantic coast from Nova Scotia down to North Carolina and inland along the St. Lawrence River and Great Lakes were speakers of Algonquin languages. They and their Iroquoian neighbors and enemies in western New York and Ontario lived in longhouse communities where they exploited natural resources and grew crops. The bark-covered, pole-frame longhouses, some reaching 400 feet (122 m) in length, provided shelter for several families of the same lineage as well as space for ceremonies and rituals. In response to the encroachment of Europeans, the Algonquian Powhatans organized a confederacy, uniting to resist the expansion of Virginia settlers. In the late sixteenth century the Iroquois nations offered a similar response to European expansion, organizing the Cayuga, Mohawk, Oneida, Onondaga, and Seneca into the Iroquois or Haudenosaunee Confederation. Tradition credits the formation of the league to Dekanawidah, a Huron known as the Great Peacemaker, and the Onondaga chief Hiawatha. The Iroquois Nations were united under the Great Law of Peace, a constitution, recorded on wampum belts. **Wampum** were woven belts of different colored shell beads, arranged as a form of writing, and used as mnemonic devices; they were created for the ratification of treaties. The constitution provided for an intertribal governing council, making it one of the first representative forms of government in North America.

IROQUOIAN FALSE FACE SOCIETIES

The arrival of Europeans and their Old World diseases devastated many of the Native American peoples living in the Eastern Woodlands, depopulating some communities entirely. In the century following the first European contacts, historians estimate that the Native American populations were reduced by almost 80 percent (Berlo and Phillips 1998, 86). Among the Iroquoians, treating illness and disease was the province of medicine societies which specialized in different types of sicknesses. When the efforts of the curing societies failed, the False Face society would be summoned. The wooden False Faces (*Gagöhsa'*) and related Husk Faces (*Gajesa*), made of braided corn husks, are considered to be supernatural spirits who have the power to heal. The False Face societies appear to be of great antiquity; the earliest accounts of the use of False- and Husk-Faces are found in the 1636 annual of the *Relations des Jésuites de la Nouvelle-France* (1632–1673). These were reports sent back by the Jesuit missionaries of New France to the superiors of their order (Ritzenthaler 1969, 14).

The origin of the False Faces derives from the creation myths that tell of a contest between the Creator of the World and the First False Face, each of whom claimed to have created the world. They decided to settle the dispute with a mountain moving contest; the victor would be determined to be the actual creator. The First False Face, known as the Great Defender or Great Doctor, turned his back to the mountain, shook his rattle, and summoned it but the mountain only came half way. The Creator then turned his back, summoned the mountain and it came up so close behind the First False Face that when he turned around he smashed his nose and face. The Creator decided the First False Face could stay in the world, if he would agree to help the people the Creator was about to fashion. He agreed that when the people summoned him by creating a mask in his image, he would use his power to protect people from storms and to heal the sick.

Traditionally the creation of a mask began with the selection of a living tree; basswood (linden) was preferred but magnolia, poplar, white pine, willow, and maple have been used. Prior to beginning the carving, prayers and offerings of tobacco would be made to the tree and the False Face spirits. Then the tree would be notched and the mask carved into its wood. The finished face, considered to be a living representation of a spirit, would be cut free of the tree and the back side hollowed out so that the face could be worn. The face would then be painted, usually all black or all red but sometimes vertically divided half black and half red. After painting, the face might be adorned with deer hide eyebrows, sheet tin around the eyes, a horsehair wig, and pouches of tobacco or miniature faces on the forehead. There are different types of False Faces. Some represent the Great Doctor, with broken noses and crooked or spoon-shaped blower mouths, while others represent forest-dwelling spirits seen in dreams; these latter are termed "Common-faces." The Iroquois consider the faces to be living and sacred and not to be put on display or photographically reproduced. They have successfully applied for the repatriation of these and other items deemed sacred from museums in the United States and Canada.

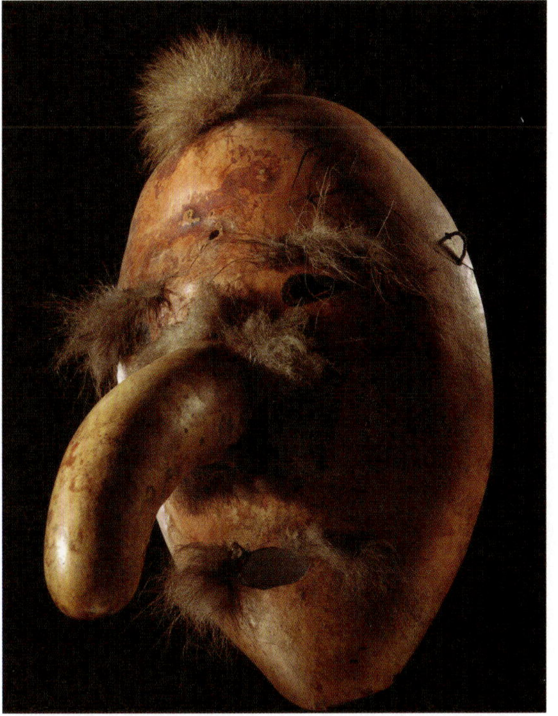

▲ 3.32 Eastern Band of the Cherokee, Booger Mask, c. 1910. Gourd, fox fur, cordage, 11.41 in. × 6.69 in. × 6.69 in.

The Booger masks represent outside forces, often Anglos, that disrupted tribal life, brought disease and death, and took tribal lands.

Eastern Band of the Cherokee, Booger Mask, c. 1910 In the southern Appalachians, the Cherokee of eastern Tennessee and western North Carolina, distant relations of the Iroquois, also had a tradition of mask-making but unlike the Iroquois False Faces, the Cherokee masks were not considered to be sacred. The masks (Figure 3.32) were performed in the Booger Dances held during midwinter ceremonials. The grotesque Booger masks represented enemy tribes, whites, and other strangers, who were perceived as being the cause of illness and negative forces within the community. The boisterous, often ribald, dances were a type of clown dance intended to provoke humor and relieve anxiety. The dances were regularly held until the 1880s when many types of Native American dances, especially clown dances, were suppressed by missionaries and government authorities.

Cherokee masks were carved from basswood or pine wood, created from dipper gourds, or fashioned from hollowed-out hornets' nests. The gourd masks often had the neck or handle of the gourd cut off and reattached as long, phallic noses. The masks were sometimes painted and adorned with animal fur to create eyebrows and other facial hair for the mask characters.

The Contemporary Period Toward the end of the nineteenth century and well into the twentieth century, the art of Native American peoples was complicated not only by separation from traditional media but also by Anglo-American attempts to define what was authentic Indian art. As part of a program to further assimilation, and, as Teddy Roosevelt put it, "to break up the tribal mass," the federal government established boarding schools for Native American students, where they were removed from their own cultures and immersed in that of the West. The exception, in some cases, was in art classes. Under the tutelage of Indian School teachers such as Ester B. Hoyt at San Ildefonso, and Elizabeth DeHuff and Dorothy Dunn (1903–1992) at Santa Fe, students were encouraged to paint scenes drawn from their cultural traditions, such as mythic subjects, dances, and other ceremonials. Instruction in the basics of Western art, such as perspective and figure drawing, was kept to a minimum; the prevailing theory of the time being that Indians were innately creative and care must be taken not to pollute authentic expression with too much Western training. Native American art students were taught to paint in a flat-style that featured areas of bright, opaque watercolor defined by heavy outlining. The style, known as **Studio Style** was thought to be based on Puebloan painted pottery, ancient rock art, and Plains hide paintings, and as such was considered the only authentic style for Native artists to follow.

The preference for a flat, untutored style of painting was established earlier by anthropologists such as Jesse Walter Fewkes who was working in the Southwest at the time. On one occasion Fewkes hired four Pueblo men to paint images of the sacred ancestral spirits, known as **Kachinas**; he provided them with paper, pencils, and watercolors. In the end he rejected the work of one man, who had been sent to a boarding school in Kansas, as being too much contaminated by

TAKE A CLOSER LOOK
The Santa Fe Indian School and Studio Style

Since the founding of the first Indian boarding school in Carlisle, Pennsylvania, by Richard Pratt in 1879, the 150 schools, to which Native American children were forcibly removed, had worked to assimilate their charges into Western culture, disallowing native dress, languages, and arts. The philosophy of these schools toward their students was, as Pratt expressed it, to "Kill the Indian in him, and save the man." However, in 1930, at the start of the Great Depression, the Bureau of Indian Affairs suddenly reversed its decades' old policy of prohibiting the teaching of traditional Native arts. The turnaround at the bureau was not the result of sudden cultural enlightenment, but its directors who, possibly based on success of Thomas Keams and other trading post entrepreneurs in selling Native crafts, had come to the realization that encouraging the "Indian" to produce traditional arts and crafts made good economic sense.

The Santa Fe Indian School was one of the first to benefit from the relaxing of the bureau's anti-indigenous arts prohibition. In 1932 Dorothy Dunn arrived there and opened the first art studio at the school. Dunn, a graduate of the Art Institute of Chicago, was careful to avoid tainting her students with Western art

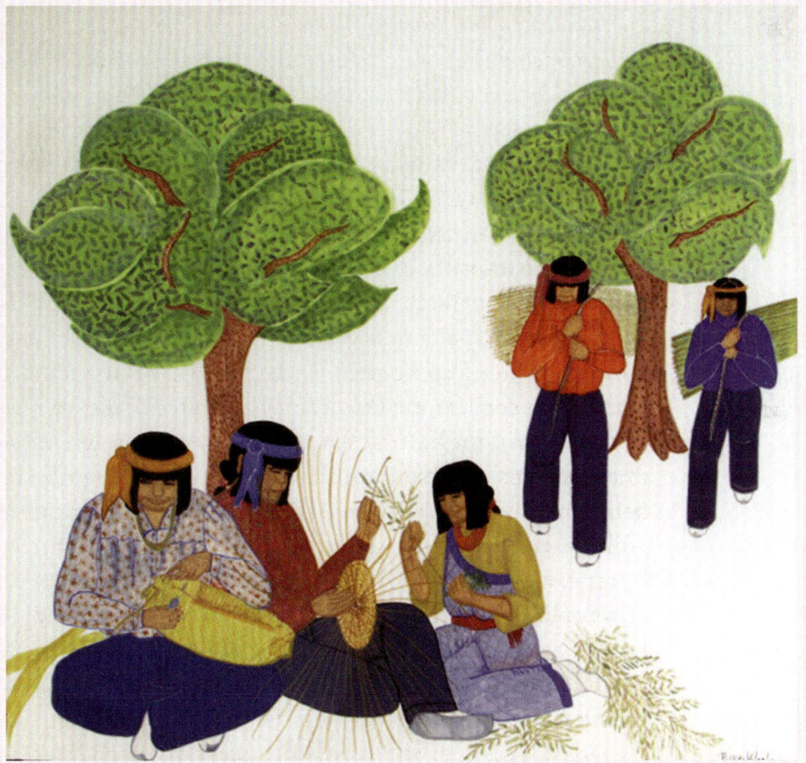

▲ **3.33** Tse Tsan "Pablita Velarde" (1918-2006), Basketmaking, 1940, casein paint on board, 11.5 x11.125 in (28.3x 28.25 cm).

The Tewa artist Pablita Velarde attended the Santa Fe Indian Scheel where she was encouraged by Dorothy Dunn to paint, traditionally considered to be a male activity.

(Continued)

theory, perspective, or history, instead bringing in non-Native American experts to teach the students about their tribal histories and crafts. Initially students were given watercolors and paper, but these were soon replaced with lessons in making mineral pigments, using pulverized earths, water, and Elmer's white glue; the idea was to give students the tools to make more traditional artworks. Dunn instilled in her students a set of what she believed were universal design principles and standards of originality. This resulted in a homogenous style, termed "Studio Style".

One of the more successful of Dunn's students was the Tewa artist Tse Tsan, whose anglicized name was "Pablita Velarde" (1918–2006). Velarde was born at the Santa Clara Pueblo and sent off to the St. Catherine Indian School at age six. In seventh grade she transferred to the Santa Fe Indian School where she and her sister Rosita were Dorothy Dunn's first female students. Dunn encouraged her to paint the daily activities of her pueblo, which was a radical thing for Pueblo women to do at the time. Women were expected to be wives and mothers and if they wanted to make something, acceptable crafts for women were pottery, weaving, and embroidery; painting was considered to be a man's occupation. Velarde's paintings, such as *Basketmaking*, narrate the daily lives of the people whom she saw around her in the pueblo. The painting features four men and a woman working in the shade of two pointillist trees that establish an ambiguous space. Velarde included a remarkable degree of flat detail in her works from the patterning of the men's shirts to the leaves on the willow stems being stripped for the baskets.

instruction. The same preferences were exhibited by trading post entrepreneurs, such as Thomas Varker Keams (1842–1904), who bought Hopi and Navajo pottery, arts, and crafts for resale to collectors, and to railroad tourists, coming to the region for an "authentic" experience of the Old West. Keams' records show that he sold pieces replicating historic pottery styles for the highest prices. The standards of authenticity set by Fewkes, Keams, the Indian School teachers, and art collectors continued to define the market for Native American arts through the first half of the twentieth century. Artists whose styles evolved beyond the expected often found their works rejected as not being sufficiently illusionistic and traditional, basically meaning not "Indian" enough.

Fritz Scholder, **The American Indian,** *1970* Fritz Scholder (1937–2005 CE), was one-quarter Luiseno, a California nation. His father worked for the Bureau of Indian Affairs, so he grew up around Native American peoples on the reservations to which his father was assigned. However, Scholder did not want to be marginalized as an "Indian artist" and there were times in his career when he swore he would never paint "Indians". Scholder was raised in the Midwest and Plains regions. He attended high school in Pierre, South Dakota, where he studied with Oscar Howe, a Yankton Sioux artist who was one of the first artists to reject Studio Style in favor of modernism. After his freshman year at Wisconsin State University, Scholder moved with his family to Sacramento where he studied with pop artist Wayne Thiebaud. Scholder earned his MFA from the University of Arizona at Tucson, and then took a teaching post at the Institute of American Indian Arts (IAIA) in Santa Fe.

Despite his determination not to paint Indians, Scholder was inspired to begin working on a series of Native American images by his IAIA students' awkward handling of the same subject. Scholder's Indians represented a radical departure from the usual romanticized and homogenized notions of Native Americans as some sort of mythical beings. His Indians are real people, not clichés or figures cloaked in a veil of history; he painted them with American flags, cans of Coors beer, cats, and beach umbrellas. Although Scholder was working on his Indian series during the heyday of the American Indian Movement, he did not intend his paintings as protest works. Painting for Scholder was primarily an exploration of color and paint; subject matter was of secondary importance.

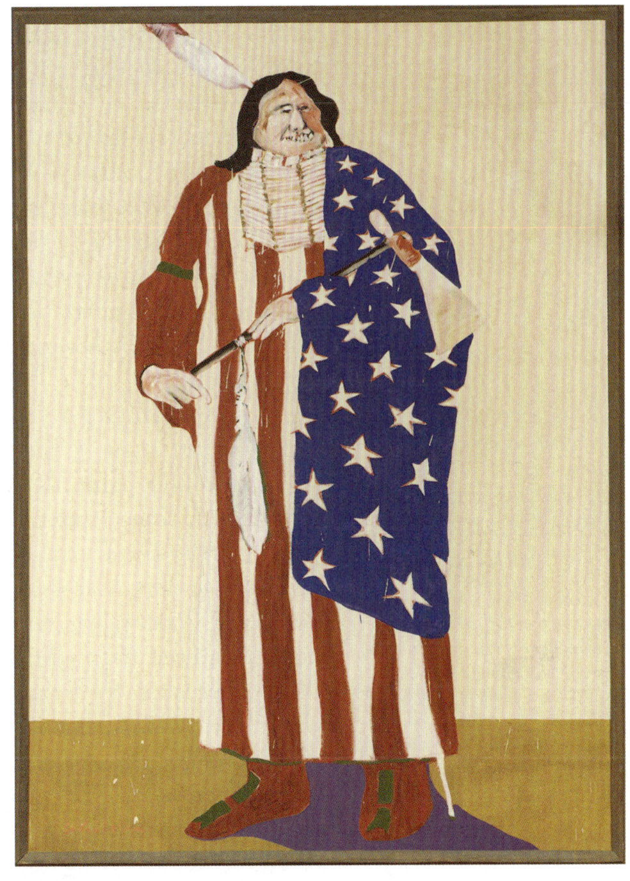

▲ **3.34** Fritz Scholder (1937–2005), *The American Indian,* 1970, Oil on linen.

This depiction of an American Indian is a departure from the romanticized and mythic images of Native Americans that were popular in movies and advertising during the 1970s.

Scholder's *The American Indian* (Figure 3.34) depicts a standing Native American in an ambiguous indoor space. He is dressed in a long war shirt that was created out of an American flag and wears a hair pipe breastplate, single eagle feather in his hair, and beaded moccasins, and carries a tomahawk peace pipe. The face of the man is distorted as though it is being forced into a shape that is not natural. The eyes are small, dark, and set closely on either side of a large nose that seems to recede into the face rather than project from it. The mouth is disturbing; it is jagged like that of a jack-o'-lantern and it is filled with a jumble of teeth. The angularity of the face and its pale coloration make it reminiscent of a skull.

Jaune Quick-to-See Smith,* State Names, *2000 Jaune Quick-to-See Smith (b. 1940) was born at the St. Ignatius Indian Mission in Montana and is an enrolled Salish member of the Confederated Salish and Kootenai Tribes of the Flathead Nation. From an early age she knew she wanted to be an artist. Her father did little drawings on scraps of paper and when he gave them to her she would carry them around in her pocket. In high school she decided she wanted to go to college and study art. Then, she was called into her teacher's office and told that she needed to find a different major because women did not become artists.

Undeterred, Smith went on to earned an associate of arts degree from Olympic College in Bremerton, Washington in 1960, a BA in art education in 1976 from Framingham State College, and an MA in art from the University of New Mexico in 1980. In contrast to Scholder, who professed an apolitical stance, Smith's paintings are political and didactic. She considers herself to be a cultural arts worker and often addresses Native American and women's issues, human rights, and ecology in her works.

Smith's painting *State Names* (Figure 3.35) presents an abstract expressionist map of the United States covered with drips of red, white, and blue paint. Closer examination reveals that the artist has stenciled in some state names while obliterating others; the distinction between those that remain and those that are disappeared is in their derivation. States such as Louisiana, Virginia, Maryland, New York, and Washington, with European-origin names, have had their names painted over while those such as Arkansas, Tennessee, and Illinois, which came from the names of First Nations remain. In this work Smith is focusing on the idea of maps as being political, in that they mark boundaries between peoples, and historical, in that they record the movement of peoples through time. Maps of North America,

▼ **3.35** Jaune Quick-to-See Smith (b. 1940), *State Names*, 2000. Oil, collage, and mixed media on canvas, 48 in. × 72 in.

In this painting the map of the United States is covered with drips of paint in the colors of the American flag. While all the forty-eight contiguous states are represented, some have had their names obliterated, leaving only those with Native American derived names; it is a reminder that the continent was already occupied when Europeans arrived.

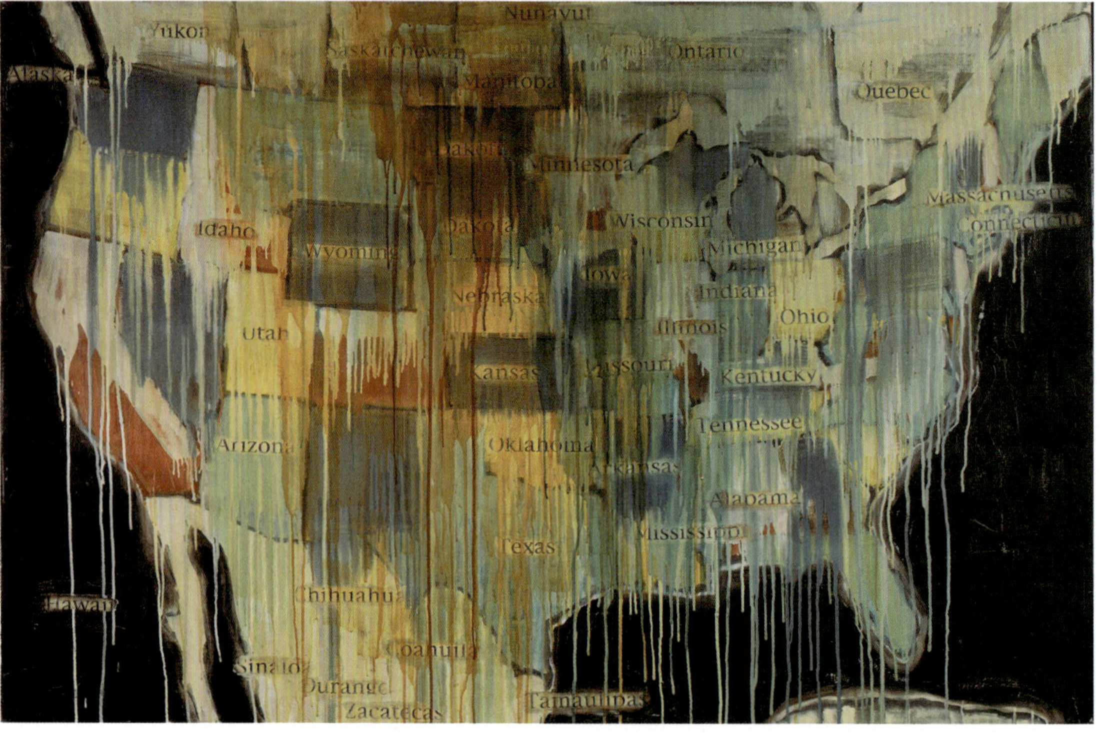

by their nature, are historical documents; they can tell mythologized stories of discovery and progress while at the same time telling the uncomfortable truths of the destruction of the land's original occupants, through disease, invasion, colonization, and cultural appropriation.

Chapter Quick Review

The Early Period (4000–1000 BCE)

- During the fourth millennium BCE the first sites with monumental earthen architecture began to be built in the Mississippi River drainage. The earliest of these was Watson Brake in Louisiana; it was a seasonally occupied site consisting of several low pyramids arranged around a central plaza and connected by embankments.
- Later at the site of Poverty Point, monumental earthworks in the form of concentric embankments were built around an open plaza on the edge of Maçon Ridge. The embankments appear to have supported domestic residences and workshops. Aligned east and west of the embankments were five pyramids, the largest being the T-shaped "Bird Mound."

The Middle Period Cultures (c. 1000 BCE–500 CE)

- The contemporaneous Adena and Hopewell cultures of Ohio built large charnel houses in which the bodies of the dead and offerings were laid. Funerary offerings included ceramics, textiles, stone platform and effigy pipes, carved shell and stone ornaments, and mica cutouts.
- Hopewell pyramids were often enclosed by earthen walls to form large complexes. A third type of structure appeared during this period, the animal effigy mound. Although effigy mounds continued to be built into the Late Period, the best known is Serpent Mound, a more than 1,400-foot-long (427 m) embankment in the form of a snake in Adams County, Ohio.
- At the same time in the Southwest, the Ancestral Puebloan peoples were building pit houses on mesa tops in the Four Corners Region and creating petroglyphs and pictographs on canyon walls. The images were of both humans and animals, sometimes showing domestic or hunting scenes.

The Late Period Civilizations (c. 700–1550 CE)

- The Mound-Builder cultures of the Eastern Woodlands built cities and towns along the Mississippi River and its tributaries. Central features of these settlements were platform and burial pyramids, often enclosed by palisades.
- Mississippian artisans produced pottery and textiles and worked shell into cups and engraved gorgets that were decorated with images of falcon and raccoon dancers and various cultural symbols.
- The largest of the Mississippian centers was Cahokia in Illinois, with 122 pyramids and associated plazas. The main ceremonial was the Great Plaza in which stood Monks Mound, the largest pyramid north of the Valley of Mexico.
- Cahokia was also a center for ceramics and pipe-making. Cahokian fireclay pipes were widely traded as elite objects in the Mississippian and Caddoan communities.

- In the Southwest, Ancestral Puebloans built communities in rock shelter sites that consisted of multi-story stone buildings and semi-subterranean kivas. Fragments of surviving murals suggest that the walls of dwellings and kivas were often plastered and painted with geometric designs and what may be landscape scenes. They also made beautifully decorated black-on-white pottery.
- The Hohokam of Arizona were making the arid lands arable by building complex irrigation systems, sometimes bringing water from sources miles away. They also build large multi-room structures of adobe bricks, such as the three-story Casa Grande, which were originally decorated with mural paintings, but none of those have survived into modern times.
- The Mimbres-Mogollon peoples of New Mexico also practiced agriculture with the aid of irrigation systems. They are renowned for their black-on-white painted pottery bowls, which were placed over the heads of the dead and which often featured humorous human and animal images.

The Colonial Period (c. 1540–1900 CE)

- The first contacts with Europeans began in the 1530s when the Spanish sent explorers into the Southeast and Southwest.
- Contact and resulting exposure to European diseases such as smallpox and measles were often devastating to Native American populations; some areas of the east coast were almost totally depopulated after the initial contacts with Europeans.
- In response to the arrival of Europeans and their appropriation of native lands, members of the Iroquois and Algonquin peoples formed associations of mutual assistance and defense; among the Iroquois these treaties were recorded on Wampum belts.
- To deal with European diseases, Iroquoian False Face and Husk Face societies were formed to treat the sick. In the South, the Cherokee created Booger Masks, to deal with the anxiety and negativity within their communities brought on by Europeans.
- The arrival of the Spanish in the Southwest was marked by the enslavement of Puebloan peoples, resulting in the bloody Pueblo Uprising of 1680. The Spanish introduced horses into the Southwest, which the Puebloans traded to the Plains Nations, dramatically altering how the peoples of the Great Plains lived.
- Buffalo were the primary resource of the Plains Nations, providing food, tools, clothing, and the support for paintings depicting tribal and personal histories.
- During this period the Diné adopted sheepherding and weaving through contact with their Hopi neighbors. During the nineteenth century, when they were forced onto reservations and their sheep were killed by the U.S. Army, they had to resort to unraveling garments and Mexican blankets to produce their weavings. Later these Diné blankets and rugs became popular with tourists visiting the Southwest.
- The Spanish settlement of California came late, as initial explorations did not reveal the same sorts of complex societies the Spanish had encountered in Mexico. The first missions were not established in the eighteenth century.
- The first peoples arrived in the Northwest Coast around 8000 BCE or earlier. They constructed large communal plank houses, which held several families and their slaves, and served as the site of winter ceremonials, including masked performances, and potlatches or ritual exchanges.
- Totem Poles were erected in front of plank houses as visual displays of clan lineages and histories. Totem poles traditionally were erected as

part of potlatch ceremonials. Potlatches were outlawed by the Canadian government in 1884 and many poles were removed from communities by the government and sold to collectors and museums.
- The Chilkat, a band of the Tlingit Nation, were renowned weavers, producing woven blankets for use by chiefs and as gifts to important guests during potlatch ceremonies.
- Northwest Coast peoples are also known for their large articulated cedar plank masks, which could be opened and closed during performances.
- The Inuit peoples of the subarctic region also made masks but they were usually much smaller due to the scarcity of wood. Since the performance spaces were also smaller, Inuit performers moved only their arms and upper bodies.
- The nineteenth and early twentieth centuries were devastating times for many Native Peoples as the United States government evicted them from their lands and forced them to move to reservations in less desirable agricultural locations such as the Oklahoma territory. In policies of forced assimilation, children were removed from their parents and sent to boarding schools for Western-focused education and Christian indoctrination.

The Contemporary Period

- The coming of railroads to the Southwest in the late nineteenth century inspired many reservation trading post operators to commission "Indian arts and crafts" according to European formulations of authenticity, resulting in the rise of the "studio style" of watercolor painting, and to a modern ceramics movement loosely based on archaeological examples.
- Some Native American artists, like Post-Colonial artists elsewhere, have chosen to use Western media and modes of expression to express the contemporary concerns of First Peoples and other minority groups.

Chapter Questions

1. Identify the two types of pyramids found in North America and describe how each was used.
2. Using the Spiro Smoker Pipe as an example, discuss the ritual use of tobacco in North America and describe some of the different styles of pipes that evolved in the region.
3. Discuss the impact of European colonization on Native American peoples of North America. Explain how the political realities of the United States government colored the way Native Americans were depicted in historical accounts as well as in twentieth century popular culture.
4. Explain how Jesse Walter Fewkes, Thomas Keams, and Dorothy Dunn contributed to the creation of the Studio Style and how it became the measure of authenticity in Native American art.

Key Terms and Figures

Key Terms

Addorsed Figures that stand back-to-back.

Ancestral Puebloans Ancient peoples who lived in the Four Corners area, ancestors of the Hopi; formerly "Anasazi."

Caliche A sedimentary rock composed of calcium carbonate that was mixed with sand and water, and used as natural cement for building by cultures in the Southwest.

Charnel house A building in which the dead were stored.

Cribbed roof A kiva roofing system used by the Ancestral Puebloans in which roof beams were laid around the perimeter in layers of rotating polygonal configurations to form a domed space.

Diné Self-designation for the Athapascan speaking peoples commonly called Navajo.

Effigy mound Earthworks in the shape of animal or human forms.

Enas Women's houses among the Yupik.

Genre scene In art, scenes of everyday activities.

Guaco A black pigment used by Ancestral Puebloan and Hopi potters that is made by boiling down Rocky Mountain beeweed to a thick syrup.

Henge A prehistoric monument composed of stone or wooden posts arranged in a circle.

Kachina Hopi ancestral spirits.

Kiva Ancestral Puebloan and Puebloan semi-subterranean ceremonial structure that may be either round or square in form.

Nde Self-designation for the Athapascan speaking peoples commonly called Apache

Palisade A palisade is a wall constructed of wooden tree trunks, set vertically, side-by-side into the ground; such walls, also known as stakewalls or palings, were used to screen ceremonial spaces as well as for defensive purposes.

Platform mound A truncated, flat-topped pyramid that served as a foundation for a residence or temple.

Qasgiqs Yupik men's ceremonial house.

Sipapu A hole in the floor of a kiva that represents the portal through which the ancestors of the Puebloan peoples emerged into the world.

Studio style A flat style of painting in watercolor advocated by Dorothy Dunn that was theoretically derived from pottery and buffalo hide painting; seen as an "authentic" Native American painting style.

Wampum Woven belts of white and purple shell beads, used by Northeastern Peoples as a form of gift exchange, cementing treaties and alliances.

Key Figures

Brackenridge, Henry—Lawyer and amateur historian who found Cahokia in 1810 and gave the name "Monks Mound" to the primary pyramid there.

Davis, Edwin Hamilton—Archaeologist and physician who worked with Squier to survey Native American mound sites for *Ancient Monuments of the Mississippi Valley*, 1848.

DeHuff, Elizabeth—Art teacher and wife of the superintendent of the Santa Fe Indian School; among her students were important early twentieth century Native American artists such as Fred Kabotie, Otis Polelonema, and Velino Shije Herrera.

Dunn, Dorothy—Art teacher at the Santa Fe Indian School during the 1930s; advocated for a flat painting style termed "studio style" after the studio in which she taught.

Fewkes, Jesse Walter—Anthropologist who worked in the Southwest, supervising the excavations of Casa Grande and Mesa Verde, also worked on the Mimbres.

Hopewell, Mordecai C.—Owner of the Hopewell Group property for whom the culture was named.

Keams, Thomas—Hopi reservation trading post owner who sold Indian crafts to tourists.

Mills, William Corless—Archaeologist and pharmacist who excavated the Adena Mound and several other Adena sites.

Moorehead, Warren King—Archaeologist who excavated at the Hopewell mound site.

Squier, Ephraim George—Engineer and antiquarian who collaborated with Davis on *Ancient Monuments of the Mississippi Valley*, 1848.

Worthington, Thomas—Ohio governor (1814–1818) and owner of the Adena estate in Ohio

Bibliography

Ambler, J. Richard. *The Anasazi.* Museum of Northern Arizona, 1977.

Ames, Kenneth M., and Herbert D.G. Maschner. *Peoples of the Northwest Coast: Their Archaeology and Prehistory.* London: Thames and Hudson, 1999.

Anderson, David G., and Robert C. Mainfort, Jr. *The Woodland Southeast.* Tuscaloosa: University of Alabama Press, 2002.

Berlo, Janet C., and Ruth B. Phillips. *Native North American Art.* New York: Oxford University Press, 1998.

Brody, J. J. *Pueblo Indian Painting: Tradition and Modernism in New Mexico, 1900–1930,* Santa Fe, NM: School of American Research Press, 1997.

Brody, J. J., Catherine J. Scott, and Steven A. LeBlanc. *Mimbres Pottery: Ancient Art of the American Southwest.* New York: Hudson Hills Press, 1983.

Brose, David S., James A. Brown, and David W. Penney. *Ancient Art of the American Woodlands Indians.* New York: Harry N. Abrams, Inc., 1985.

Dickens, Jr., Roy S. *Of Sky and Earth: Art of the Early Southeastern Indians.* Georgia Department of Archives and History, 1982.

Elliot, George. *Sculpture/Inuit.* Canadian Eskimo Arts Council. Toronto: University of Toronto Press, 1971.

Fagan, Brian M. *Ancient North America: The Archaeology of a Continent.* 4th edition. London: Thames and Hudson, 2005.

Feder, Norman. *Two Hundred Years of North American Indian Art.* New York: Praeger Publishers, 1971.

Feest, Christian F. *Native Arts of North America.* London: Thames and Hudson, 1980.

Fewkes, J. Walter. *The Mimbres Art and Archaeology.* Albuquerque, NM: Avanyu Publishing Inc., Original work published 1914-1924/ reprint1993..

Fish, Suzanne K., and Paul R. Fish. *The Hohokam Millennium.* Santa Fe, NM: School for Advanced Research Press, 2008.

Frink, Douglas S. "OCR Carbon Dating of the Watson Brake Mound Complex." Paper presented at the symposium "An Overview of Research at Watson Brake: A Middle Archaic Mound Complex in Northeast Louisiana," 53rd Annual Meeting of the Southeastern Archaeological Conference, Birmingham, AL, 1997.

Fundaburk, Emma Lila, and Mary Douglass Fundaburk Foreman. *Sun Circles and Human Hands: The Southeast Indians Art and Industries.* Fairhope, AL: American Bicentennial Museum, 1968.

Furst, Peter T., and Jill L. Furst. *North American Indian Art.* New York: Rizzoli, 1982.

Gibson, Jon L. *Ancient Mounds of Poverty Point*. Gainesville, FL: University Press of Florida, 2001.

"Navels of the Earth: Sedentism in Early Mound-Building Cultures in the Lower Mississippi Valley." *World Archaeology* 38, no. 2 (June 2006): 311–329.

Herrman, Edward W., et al. "A New Multistage Construction Chronology for the Great Serpent Mound, USA." *Journal of Archaeological Science* 50, no. 1 (2014): 117–125. http://www.sciencedirect.com/science/article/pii/S0305440314002465

Holm, Bill. *Northwest Coast Indian Art: An Analysis of Form*. Seattle: University of Washington Press, 1970.

Hudson, Charles. *The Southeastern Indians*. Knoxville: University of Tennessee Press, 1976.

Jacka, Lois Essary. *Enduring Traditions: Art of the Navajo*. Northland Publishing, 1994.

LeBlanc, Steven A. *Painted by a Distant Hand: Mimbres Pottery from the American Southwest*. Cambridge, MA: Peabody Museum Press, 2004.

Lee, Molly, and Gregory A. Reinhardt. *Eskimo Architecture: Dwelling and Structure in the Early Historic Period*. Fairbanks: University of Alaska Press, 2003.

Lekson, Stephen H. *The Architecture of Chaco Canyon, New Mexico*. Salt Lake City: University of Utah Press, 2007.

Mera, H.P. *Navajo Textile Arts*. Santa Barbara and Salt Lake: Peregrine Smith, Inc., 1975.

Milner, George R. *The Moundbuilders: Ancient Peoples of Eastern North America*. London: Thames and Hudson, 2004.

Morgan, William N. *Precolumbian Architecture in Eastern North America*. Gainesville: University Press of Florida, 1999.

Narciso, Dean. "Carbon Dating Used to Date Adena Mound Culture: Strip of Bark Saved a Century Ago Helps Archaeologists Better Understand Ancient People." *Columbus Dispatch*. January 12, 2014. http://www.dispatch.com/content/stories/science/2014/01/12/1-carbon-dating-the-adena-culture.html

Pauketat, Timothy R. *The Oxford Handbook of North American Archaeology*. Oxford: Oxford University Press, 2012.

Pauketat, Timothy R., and Diana DiPaolo Loren, editors. *North American Archaeology*. Malden, MA: Blackwell Publishing, 2005.

Penney, David W. *North American Indian Art*. London: Thames and Hudson World of Art, 2004.

Phillips, Philip, and James A. Brown. *Pre-Columbian Shell Engravings from the Craig Mound at Spiro, Oklahoma*. Part 1. Cambridge, MA: Peabody Museum Press, 1978.

Quinlan, Angus R., editor. *Great Basin Rock Art: Archaeological Perspectives*. Reno and Las Vegas: University of Nevada Press, 2007.

Rees, Mark A., editor. *Archaeology of Louisiana*. Baton Rouge: Louisiana State University Press, 2010.

Ritzenthaler, Robert. "Iroquois False-Face Masks." *Publications in Primitive Art* 3 (1969).

Samuel, Cheryl. *The Chilkat Dancing Blanket*. Norman: University of Oklahoma Press, 1982.

Sassaman, Kenneth E. "Poverty Point as Structure, Event, Process." *Journal of Archaeological Method and Theory* 12, no. 4, Part 2 (December 2005): 335–364.

Saunders, Joe W., Thurman Allen, and Roger T. Saucier. "Four Archaic? Mound Complexes in Northeast Louisiana." *Southeastern Archaeology* 13, no. 2 (Winter 1994): 134–153.

Saunders, Joe W., et al. "A Mound Complex in Louisiana at 5400–5000 Years Before the Present," *Science* 277, no. 5333 (September 19, 1997), 1796–1799. http://www.Jstor.org/stable/2893835

Shepard, A. O. *Ceramics for the Archaeologist*. Reprinted Ann Arbor: Braun-Brumfield, 1980. Originally published as Publication 609 Washington, DC: Carnegie Institution of Washington, 1956.Sievert, April K., J. Daniel Rogers, and Javier Urcid

Artifacts from the Craig Mound at Spiro, Oklahoma. Washington D.C.: Smithsonian Institution Scholarly Press, 2011.

Sofaer, Anna. *Chaco Astronomy.* Santa Fe, NM: Ocean Tree Books, 2008.

Squier, Ephraim G., and Edwin H. Davis. *Ancient Monuments of the Mississippi Valley.* Originally published 1848. Smithsonian Classics of Anthropology. Washington, DC: Smithsonian Books, reprint 1988.

Steponaitis, Vincas P. *Ceramics, Chronology, and Community Patterns: An Archaeological Study at Moundville.* Tuscaloosa: University of Alabama Press, 2009.

Stewart, Joe D., Karen R. Adams, Graham J. Borradaile, and Allan J. MacKenzie. "Investigations of Paints on Ancestral Puebloan Black-on-White Pottery Using Magnetic and Microanalytic Methods," *Journal of Archaeological Science* 29 (2002): 1309–1316.

Sturtevant, William C., editor. *Handbook of North American Indians, Volume 9: Southwest.* Washington, DC: Smithsonian Institution, 1979.

Sullivan, Lynne P. "Dates for Shell Gorgets and The Southeastern Ceremonial Complex in the Chickamauga Basin of Southeastern Tennessee." McClung Museum, University of Tennessee. March 1, 2001. http://mcclungmuseum.utk.edu/shell-gorgets/

Wheat, Joe Ben. "Mogollon Culture Prior to A.D. 1000." *American Antiquity* 20, no. 4, Part 2 (April 1955).

Woodward, Susan L., and Jerry N. McDonald. *Indian Mounds of the Middle Ohio Valley.* Blacksburg, VA: McDonald and Woodward Publishing Co., 2002.

Young, Biloine Whiting, and Melvin L. Fowler. *Cahokia: The Great Native American Metropolis.* Urbana and Chicago: University of Illinois Press, 2000.

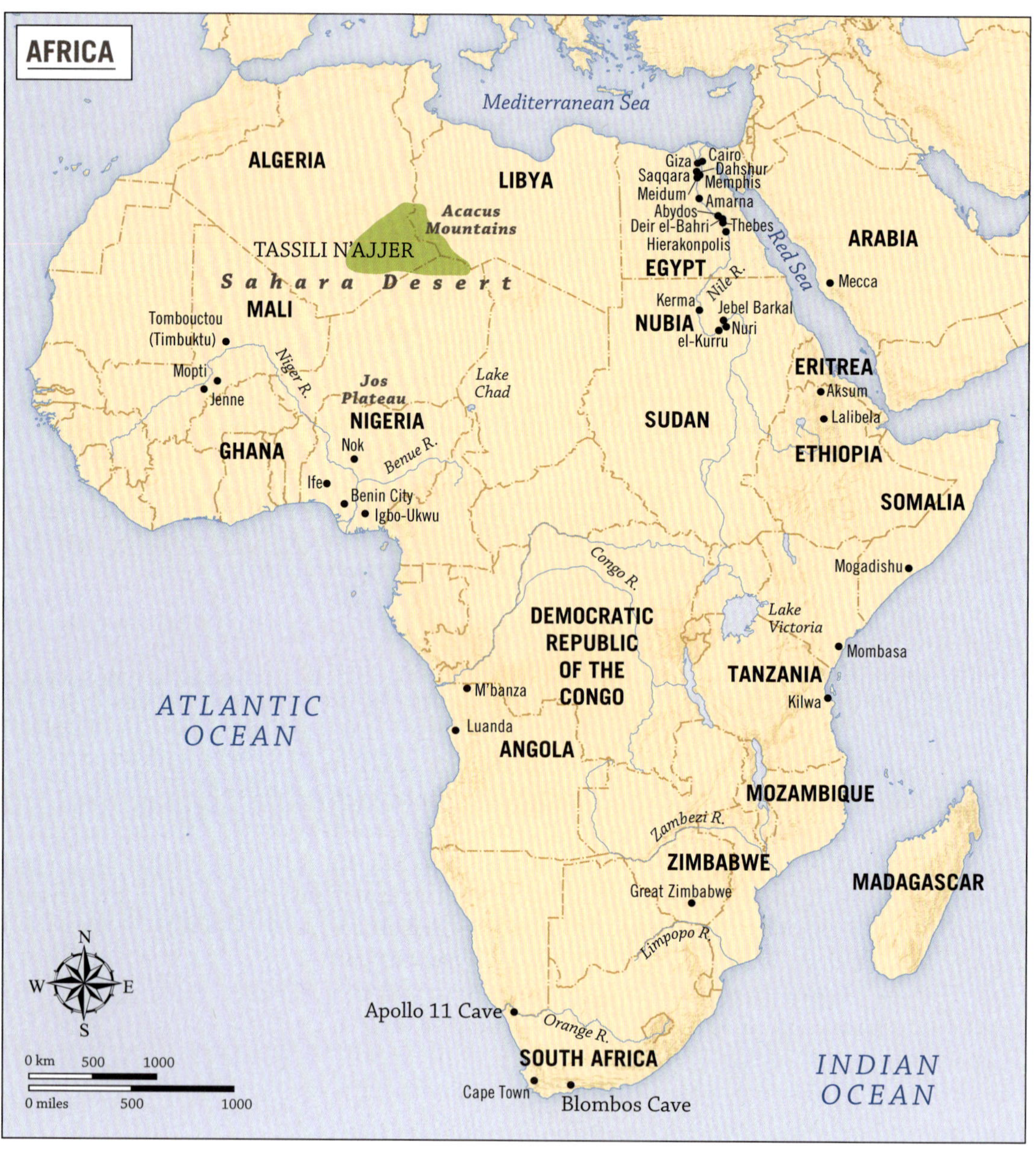
AFRICA
Mediterranean Sea
ALGERIA
LIBYA
Acacus Mountains
TASSILI N'AJJER
Sahara Desert
MALI
Tombouctou (Timbuktu)
Mopti
Jenne
Niger R.
Jos Plateau
Lake Chad
NIGERIA
GHANA
Nok
Benue R.
Ife
Benin City
Igbo-Ukwu
Giza
Cairo
Dahshur
Saqqara
Memphis
Meidum
Amarna
Abydos
Deir el-Bahri
Thebes
Hierakonpolis
EGYPT
Nile R.
Red Sea
ARABIA
Mecca
Kerma
NUBIA
Jebel Barkal
Nuri
el-Kurru
ERITREA
Aksum
Lalibela
SUDAN
ETHIOPIA
SOMALIA
Mogadishu
Congo R.
DEMOCRATIC REPUBLIC OF THE CONGO
Lake Victoria
Mombasa
TANZANIA
Kilwa
M'banza
Luanda
ANGOLA
ATLANTIC OCEAN
MOZAMBIQUE
Zambezi R.
ZIMBABWE
Great Zimbabwe
MADAGASCAR
Limpopo R.
N
W
E
S
Apollo 11 Cave
Orange R.
SOUTH AFRICA
Cape Town
Blombos Cave
INDIAN OCEAN
0 km 500 1000
0 miles 500 1000

Art of Africa

4

Brief Overview

The history of art on the African continent starts around 500,000 BCE, when early humans began to recognize faces and animal forms in pebbles, and to collect them. These naturally occurring objects are known as geofacts, and are considered a type of found art. The earliest proof of humans engaged in making art comes from Blombos Cave on the South African coast, where some 100,000 years ago the first paint manufactory was mixing colored clays with charcoal and pulverized bone to make a range of shades and tints.

Despite the early discovery of pigments, the oldest currently known African paintings, from the Apollo 11 Cave in Namibia, date only to about 27,500 years ago, and there is a gap of almost 18,000 years before the next known works, petroglyphs and pictographs, appear in the Tassili n'Ajjer region. These large jumps in time between known works point up one of the major problems in studying African art: the record is woefully incomplete with frequent periods from which no works appear to have survived. This is due, in some instances, to a lack of professional archaeological work having yet been done, and in others, is simply the result of the art having been made in perishable media.

The first great African civilizations arose along the Nile River, in what are today Egypt and the Sudan. During the fourth millennium BCE, the first monumental architecture in brick and stone was constructed, the first colossal stone sculpture was carved, pottery was invented, the art of metal casting discovered, a hieroglyphic form of writing devised, and the first stylistic canons in African art formulated.

In the first millennium CE two major religions, Christianity and Islam, were introduced into Africa, inspiring new modes of artistic expression. In Ethiopia, Christianity's crowning achievements are the numerous rock-cut Coptic churches and monasteries, the most famous being the eleven churches carved out of tufa in the ancient city of Lalibela. As Islam spread across North Africa in the seventh century, it

Chapter Objectives

1. Understand how local resources used by artists in various parts of Africa not only determined the types of art and architecture that would be produced but also whether or not those works would be lost to history.
2. Recognize that the early civilizations in Egypt, Kush, and Aksum were part of an ongoing African development, not exceptions to that process.
3. Understand that prior to the arrival of the Portuguese in the fifteenth century that African traders had long been in contact with the Mediterranean, West Asia, India, and China.
4. Explain how contact with other cultures both enriched and disadvantaged African peoples and created negative perceptions of African arts and artists.

brought a new type of building, the mosque. Among the most impressive examples of African mosques are the Great Mosque of Kairouan and the Great Friday Mosque of Djenné.

Since ancient times the riches of Africa have lured traders and explorers from the Mediterranean world and from West, South, and East Asia. In the fifteenth century CE, the search for a new route to India brought the Portuguese to West Africa. Trade with the West brought prosperity to Africa, while at the same time opening one of the darkest chapters in African history, the slave trade. The Portuguese were followed into Africa by other European states in the sixteenth and seventeenth centuries, including the Dutch, Danes, French, Germans, and British. In the late nineteenth century's "Scramble for Africa", the continent was divided up among them.

African artists responded to the arrival of Europeans by producing what must be the world's first tourist art made for a specific market. Among the great artists of the early colonial era was a remarkable West African carver known only as the "Master of the Symbolic Execution." Unfortunately, history makes no mention of this artist or of the many others who worked in Africa during the Colonial era. In many cases, the Europeans who collected and even commissioned works from African artists kept no records because they did not view the items as art. Instead, the works were considered curiosities of savage primitives who lived in a nonrational world filled with demonic spirits and barbarous rituals; regrettably, some of the early ethnography conducted on the continent also reflects this bias.

The realization that African art *was* art occurred in the early twentieth century, when European artists such as Pablo Picasso, George Braque, and Henri Matisse discovered African art and began to appropriate its forms in their own work. Today, artists from across the continent are achieving international acclaim for their work in both traditional and modern styles, and in a wide range of media. Much of the art that is produced is provocative, speaking to the painful political, social, and economic realities of Africa's colonial past and often complicated present.

Early Africa (100,000–1000 BCE)

Human history and art-making both began in Africa. The story of how humans came to make art may begin with our earliest ancestors around 500,000 BCE. It was around this time that our early human ancestors began to recognize human and animal forms in natural formations or in small objects or geofacts. One of these early items of found art, the Makapansgat pebble, bears a crude resemblance to a face. This similarity was recognized and the pebble picked up and carried some twenty miles from its geologic source to the South African cave where it was discovered. The next major event in African art history occurred around 100,000 BCE, when early Africans began manufacturing pigments.

Paleolithic to Neolithic Art (c. 70,000 – 10,000 BCE)

In 1991, South African archaeologist Christopher Henshilwood discovered Blombos Cave, in a rock cliff overlooking the ocean about 187 miles (300 km) east of Cape Town. Ongoing excavations at the site have revealed the remains of a paint-making workshop. Archaeologists unearthed all the necessary tools: stone hammers, grindstones, bone spatulas, and abalone shells used for mixing pigments. Also found were two rectangular blocks of ocher with incised geometric designs. **Ocher** is a principle component of ancient paints around the world. It is obtained from iron oxide rich clays and can be either red or yellow in color. The ochers obtained from the Blombos Cave site were dated to 70,000 BCE by Optically Stimulated Luminescence (OSL), a technique which measures the time that has elapsed since the mineral's last exposure to sunlight. In the case of the Blombos ochers, this would have been when the clays were brought into the cave.

While the incised ocher plaques may seem unremarkable as artworks, what they show is that some 100,000 years ago, humans were purposely manufacturing and storing paints and presumably creating art works with them. It is possible that the pigments were used for body painting, decoration on objects, or cave wall paintings, although cave conditions in southern Africa are not conducive to the long preservation of exposed rock art.

Apollo 11 Cave Painted Plaque, c. 25,500–23,500 BCE The earliest surviving rock paintings were found in the Apollo 11 Cave located in the Huns Mountains of southwest Namibia. Buried in the occupational debris of the cave were seven quartzite plaques. Painted on the stones in charcoal, ocher, and kaolin (white clay) were images of animals, including rhinoceros, zebra, and a strange feline-like animal (Figure 4.1). The creature is rendered in profile with a frontal eye, in the manner of animals depicted in the better known European Paleolithic caves, and like those animals, care has been taken to show that the animal has two horns (barely discernable on the head), four legs, a tail, and a male sexual organ. Some scholars see the hind legs of the animal as human, and propose that the creature is a **therianthrope**, a supernatural being that is part human and part animal. It is also possible that the figure represents a human actor wearing the pelt of the animal as part of a ritual or hunting activity. Charcoal deposits excavated with the plaques, in 1969, produced a radiocarbon date of 25,500–23,500 BCE but more recent testing, by the Smithsonian Institution of materials from the cave layer in which the plaques were found, has resulted in a

timeline

DATE	TYPE	EVENT
		BCE
c. 70,000	Art	Blombos Cave, South Africa, paint manufactory
c. 25,500	Art	Apollo 11 Cave, Namibia, painted slabs
c. 10,000	Art	Tassili n'Ajjer incised elephant
c. 8000	Art	First settlements and early pottery appeared in Sudan
c. 5500	History	First settlements along the Nile
c. 5200	Art	Tassili n'Ajjer painted camp scene
c. 4000	History	Hieroglyphic writing invented in Egypt
c. 3500	Art	Hierakonpolis necropolis, Tomb 100 murals painted
	Art	Nubian "A-Group" pottery made in Sudan
c. 3100	History	Unification process began in Egypt
c. 3000	Art	Papyrus paper invented
c. 2950	Art	Narmer offered votive palette at Temple of Horus, Hierakonpolis
c. 2686	History	Beginning of the Old Kingdom
	Art	Imhotep began work on the Stepped Pyramid of King Djoser
c. 2613	Art	Nefermaat began first of King Sneferu's three pyramids
c. 2589	History	Khufu becomes pharaoh
	Art	Hemiunu began work on the Great Pyramid of Giza
c. 2558	Art	Khafre began pyramid and Great Sphinx
c. 2532	Art	Menkaure began work on Valley Temple and pyramid
c. 2300	History	Kerma established as trading center in Kingdom of Yam (Sudan)
	Art	"C-Group" pottery appeared; Deffufas built in Kerma
c. 2160	History	First Intermediate Period; Egypt dissolved into separate states
c. 2055	History	Mentuhotep II reunited Egypt, beginning Middle Kingdom Period
	Art	Funerary Complex of Mentuhotep II at Deir el-Bahri
c. 2050	History	Kerma became capital of First Kingdom of Kush
c. 1500	History	Second Kingdom of Kush
c. 1473	History	Hatshepsut began reign as Pharaoh
	Art	Construction of Djeser-Djeseru began at Deir el-Bahri
c. 1352	History	Akhenaten became pharaoh
	Art	Construction of first Aten Temple at Karnak

DATE	TYPE	EVENT
		BCE
c. 1348	Art	Akhenaten established new capital at Akhetaten (Amarna)
	Art	Thutmose of Amarna created his bust of Queen Nefertiti
c. 1200	Art	Temple of Amun constructed at Jebel Barkal, Kingdom of Kush
c. 1000	History	Bantu People migrated into Southern Africa from West Africa
c. 760	History	Kushite rule began in Egypt
c. 591	History	Kushite capital moved to city of Meroe
c. 500	Art	Nok Culture began in Northern Nigeria
	History	Aksumites settled in northeastern Ethiopia
305	History	Ptolemaic rule began in Egypt
c. 300	Art	Royal funerary pyramids built at Meroe
c. 250	Art	Djenne-Djeno established in Mali
c. 30	History	Egypt became a Roman province
		CE
c. 100	History	Kingdom of Aksum established in Northern Ethiopia
c. 200	History	Nok culture ended
c. 300	History	Soninke empire of Ghana established
c. 330	History	Meroe fell to Aksum
	Art	Aksumite Steles erected
	Culture	King Ezana converted to Christianity
c. 500	History	Ilé-Ifé became a prominent urban center in Nigeria
c. 700	History	Aksum declined
	History	Islam advanced in Africa
c. 800	Art	Igbo-Ukwu bronze working culture began in southern Nigeria
c. 900	History	Zagwe dynasty established in Ethiopia moves capital to Roha
c. 1000	History	Prince Oranmiyan founded a new royal dynasty at Benin
	History	Mali Empire founded
c. 1100	History	Shona established kingdoms on Zimbabwean Central Plateau
	Art	Tradition of bronze memorial heads began at Ilé-Ifé
1190	Art	King Lalibela built rock-cut churches at Roha
c. 1275	Art	Great Zimbabwe established
c. 1300	Art	Master metal caster Igueha went to Benin

(Continued)

timeline *continued*

DATE	TYPE	EVENT
CE		
1324–1325	Culture	Emperor of Mali, Mansa Musa, made a pilgrimage to Mecca
1400	History	Swahili Coast became important trading center
1489	History	Portuguese arrived along the Benin coast; slave trade began
1652	History	Dutch established a colony in South Africa
1717	History	Asante Empire of the Akan established
1795	History	British take South Africa from the Dutch
1871	History	"Scramble for Africa" began; Europeans claimed colonies
1884–1885	History	Berlin Conference divided Africa among the European Powers
1897	History	British Punitive Expedition against Benin
1951–1976	History	Decolonization of Africa

date range of approximately 58,051-- 38,051 BCE ("Apollo 11 Plaque," 2016). The plaques are interesting in that they do not appear to have originated in the cave. Geological evidence suggests the stones were brought in from elsewhere, making them an early example of what is known as ***art mobilier*** or "moveable art."

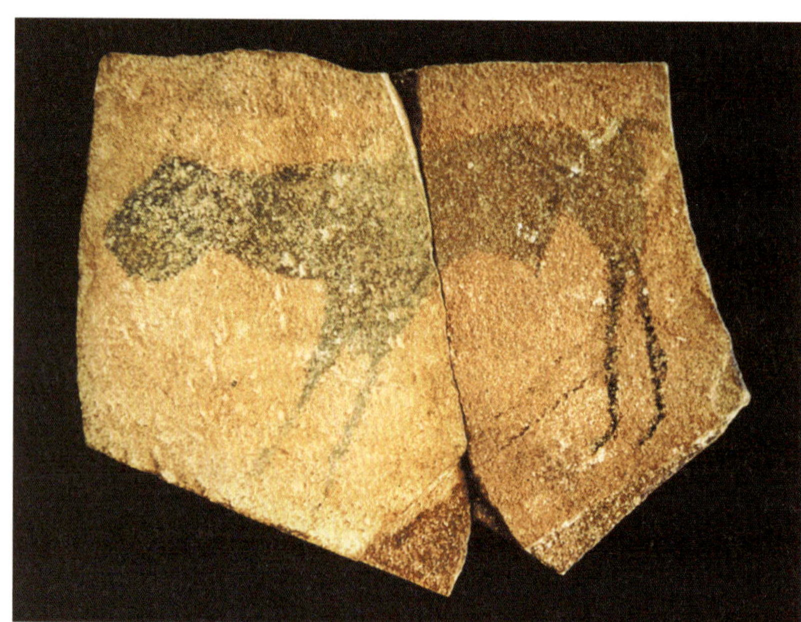

▶ 4.1 Apollo 11, Namibia, Cave Painted Plaque, c. 25,500–23,500 BCE.

The animal on this plaque is one of the earliest surviving works of art, especially *art mobilier*, in Africa. The creature may be a *therianthrope*, a half-human-half-animal supernatural being.

Rock Shelter Art in Africa (c. 10,000 BCE–1000 CE)

Petroglyphs (images cut into rock) and **pictographs** (paintings on rock) have been found in rock shelters across Africa but most have been little studied or published. One exception is the Tassili n'Ajjer region of North Africa. Today, much of North Africa is an inhospitable desert but that was not always the case. Between 10,000 and 5,000 BCE, the Sahara was a temperate grassland, dotted with lakes and crossed by ancient rivers. Herds of giraffe, elephants, antelopes, and extinct aurochs (wild cattle) roamed the region along with prides of ostriches and lions. The Sahara's lakes supported fish, crocodile, hippopotami, and water fowl. The abundance of game attracted early hunter-gatherers, and many settled in the Algerian highlands, known as Tassili n'Ajjer and the adjacent Tadrart Acacus area of Libya. Over several millennia, these peoples left behind rock engravings and paintings that record the changing parade of life in the Sahara.

Elephant with Two Giraffes, Wadi Mathendous, Libya, c. 10,000–7,000 BCE The earliest works from the Tassili region were produced during this wetter period. In art, this time is known as the *Large Wild Fauna Period*. The designation is not based on the size of the animals that roamed the Sahara then, but rather on the scale of the carved images themselves. For example, a Large Wild Animal Period rhino cut into a rock wall at Wadi Djerat measured 26 feet (7.9 m) long, or twice the length of the largest rhinoceros species.

The Neolithic artists working in the Tassili and other areas had only rudimentary stone tools and natural mineral abrasives to use but still created thousands of remarkable images. The process of creating a petroglyph began with sketching an image onto the rock, either with charcoal or by scratching into the surface of the stone. The image would then be enhanced by pecking an outlining groove into the rock face; the resulting grooves were often smoothed or "polished" to create clean lines. Several styles of petroglyphs have been found in the Sahara. Some are highly detailed, showing wrinkles, folds, and pelage patterns of the animals depicted; others are simple outline figures, and still others were cut as **sunken reliefs**, in which the highest point of the image does not extend beyond the original surface of the stone.

The Elephant with Two Giraffes petroglyph (Figure 4.2) is one of the more detailed images. The spot patterns, mane, ears, and horns of the two giraffes have been carefully rendered as well as the form of the elephant with them. The artist seems to have had a keen understanding of the habits of the animals depicted; the giraffes stand in characteristic poses, one holds its head aloft while the other stretches out as though to browse low vegetation. The elephant is positioned behind the giraffes so most of its body is obscured other than its head and legs; however, the details of its expression are particularly

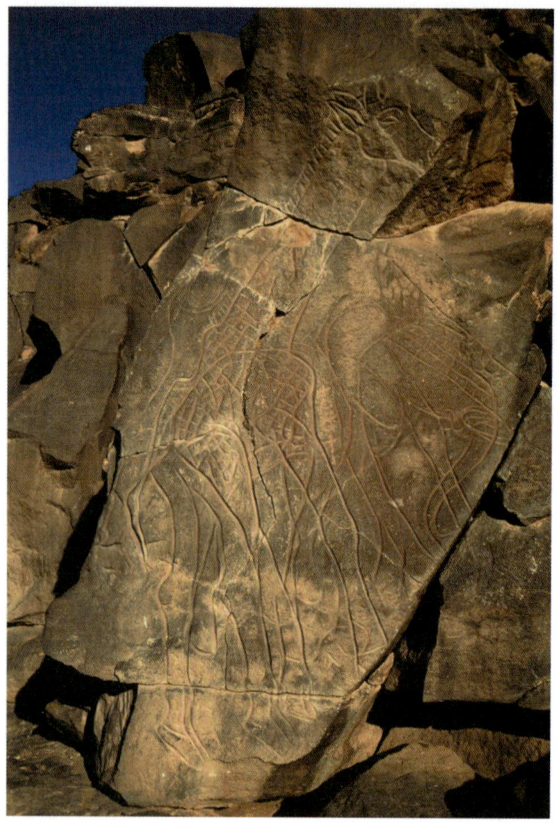

▲ 4.2 Wadi Mathendous, Libya, Elephant with Two Giraffes, c. 10,000–7,000 BCE.

Rendered in the outline-polished style these animals show careful depictions of pelage patterns and natural behaviors.

interesting. The parted lips of the animal have been emphasized in what might be a flehmen response. Flehmening is a behavior in which an animal opens its mouth, sometimes curling its upper lips to reveal teeth, in order to investigate smells using auxiliary scent organs in the roof of its mouth. This reaction is often triggered by pheromone-containing substances.

Tassili n'Ajjer, Camp Scene, Pastoral Period, c. 5200–2000 BCE Around 5000 BCE the Sahara entered a drier phase, during which the switch from hunting and gathering to cattle herding seems to have occurred. This phase in the Tassili is known as the *Pastoral Period*. Pictographs are usually red-filled and painted with brushes, showing realistic depictions of human and domesticated animals, including cattle, basenji-like dogs, and occasionally wild animals, such as aoudad or "mountain sheep." The specificity of the human depictions in dress, hairstyles, and in a few case the use of black in addition to red pigments, has led some scholars to propose that the Tassili populations during the Pastoral Period included both African and Mediterranean stock (Coulson and Campbell 2013, 11). The Camp Scene (Figure 4.3), from the Pastoral Period shows men and women engaged in a variety of activities: herding cattle, hunting with bow and arrow and dogs, and women seated together working, giving the scene a **genre** or "everyday life" quality. By 2000 BCE, the progressive desertification of the Saharan region caused many of these early pastoralists to begin migrating out of the region. Some went north to the coastal areas of Morocco, Algeria, and Tunisia, known as the Maghreb. Others migrated south into the sub-Saharan Sahel, or east to the fertile lands along the Nile.

Egypt (c. 7000 BCE–1070 BCE)

Egypt, as the Greeks called it, was settled around 7000–6000 BCE, when it like the Tassili was much wetter and cooler than it is today. As the wide swath of land extending across North Africa, the Arabian Peninsula, the Levant and into Mesopotamia became progressively dryer and inhospitable, the Nile Valley received an influx of climate refugees, many from Africa but potentially also from adjacent areas of West Asia. The new settlers were drawn by the rich black soils that

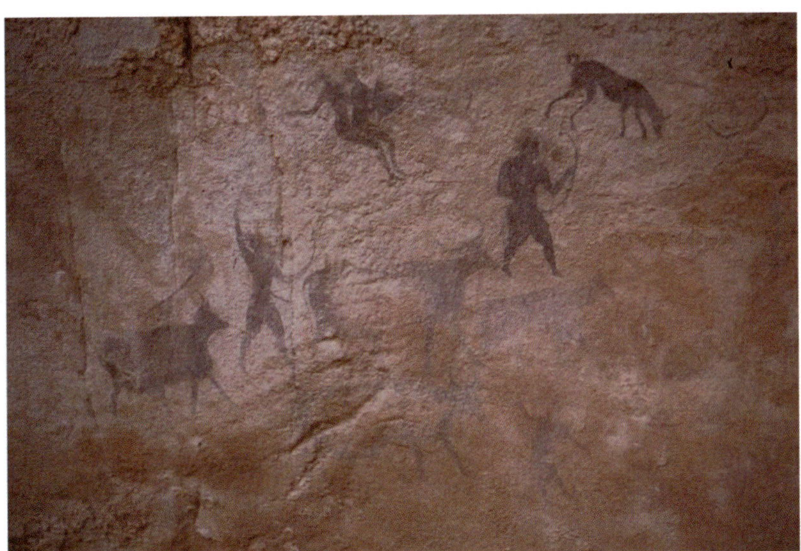

◀ 4.3 Tassili n'Ajjer, Algeria, Camp Scene, c. 5200–2000 BCE.

This pictograph shows a genre scene of seated women working, cattle being herded, and a hunter with his basenji-type dog.

gave the land its name, *Kemet* or "Black Lands" and the Nile's reliable water resources. It is thought that agriculture was imported, along with the cereal grains at this time, perhaps brought by migrating farming peoples. Over the next several millennia, peoples living along the river would coalesce into more complex states in Upper and Lower Egypt, and ultimately would form a single nation. The Egyptians are credited with a number of firsts and inventions. They built the first monumental architecture and sculpture, invented hieroglyphic writing and the papyrus paper to record it on, devised a system of mathematics that included whole numbers and fractions, developed a 365-day calendar, constructed the papyrus boats, pioneered eye makeup (kohl) for men and women, perfumes, breath mints and door locks, among other things.

The Early Nile Cultures (c. 5500–3100 BCE)

In his *History*, Herodotus (1971: 50) observed that "Egypt to which the Greeks go in their ships is an acquired country, the gift of the river." This statement became the basis for the truism that Egypt is the gift of the Nile. Certainly, without the narrow green belt of the Nile, this great African civilization probably would not have arisen. The importance of the Nile to agriculture, animal husbandry, and trade is illustrated in murals from a pre-Dynastic period tomb, known as the "Painted Tomb" or Tomb 100 excavated in the late nineteenth century at Hierakonpolis.

Hierakonpolis Tomb 100 Mural, c. 3500 BCE The walls of Tomb 100 at Hierakonpolis (Figure 4.4) were plastered and painted with **fresco secco** (dry fresco) scenes of people, animals, and boats on the river. Five of these boats are white and have a similar crescent design, but the

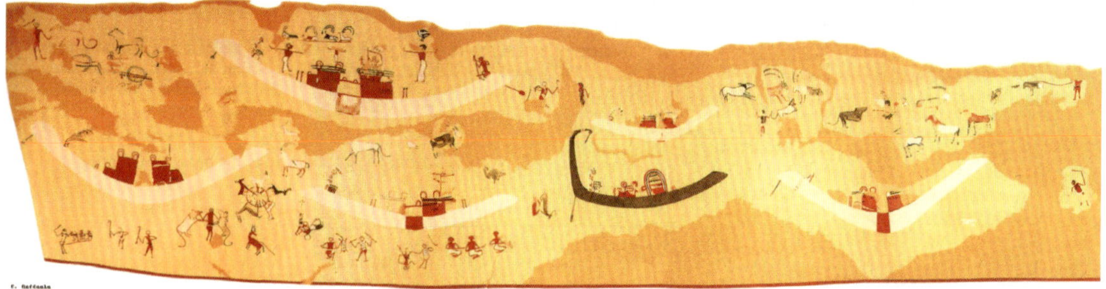

▲ 4.4 Hierakonpolis, Egypt, Fragment of a Painting from Tomb 100, c. 3500 BCE.

This fresco secco mural shows five papyrus boats and a wooden ship moving on the Nile, while on the shore people are engaged in various domestic and military activities.

sixth is black and has a high recurvate prow. The light-colored vessels probably represent the papyri-form boats that were used for local transport of goods and travel, as well as for daily activities and religious ceremonies. Papyrus boats typically had a central deck cabin, sometimes two, as do the white vessels in the fresco. For heavier loads such as stone building blocks and for sea travel the Egyptians also had wooden boats made of Lebanese cedar with up-curved ends. The use of black for the sixth ship is intended to show it was a wooden craft, but its atypical design suggests this may be a foreign trading ship. On the shore groups of figures, rendered in a style similar to that of the Saharan paintings, are engaged in various activities: hunting, combat, and the display of prisoners; in one of these a mace-wielding man subdues three adversaries. Some figures seem to strike heraldic poses, such as in the lower left where a figure stands between two lions. This "Master of Animals" stance, also found in early Mesopotamian and Iranian art (see the inlay panel on Figure 5.9 for a Mesopotamian example of this motif) sets the pattern for later displays of power in Africa in which a ruler is shown with leopards as symbols of his prowess.

The Early Dynastic Period and the Old Kingdom (c. 3100–2160 BCE)

The unification of Upper and Lower Egypt into one kingdom inaugurates the Early Dynastic Period. Traditionally, the unification is attributed to a king recorded as Menes or Meni, in the Abydos Tablet, the Turin Royal Canon, and by the third century BCE Egyptian historian, Manetho. All these records are from considerably later periods, the first two from the New Kingdom and the last from the Ptolemaic period, leading some to question whether the Two Lands were united by a single conqueror, and if so by whom, or through a much longer process of consolidation. A votive palette, given in offering at the Temple of Horus in Hierakonpolis, by a king named Narmer from Abydos, is often read as a statement of the unification of Egypt under Menes. However, the narrative can also be read as a record of one king's contributions to a much longer process of nation-building.

Palette of Narmer, c. 2950 BCE The Palette of Narmer (Figure 4.5) and an accompanying mace were found in a cache of sacred objects excavated at the temple of Horus at Hierakonpolis in 1898 (Quibell et al 1900-1902). The palette is very large, measuring 25 inches (63.5 cm) long, a size not practical for daily use; common make-up palettes were small-scale items that could be held easily in one hand. Inscriptions placed inside a serekh or palace façade on both the obverse (front) and reverse (back) of the palette give the donor's name, Narmer, written phonetically with the catfish (nir) and chisel (mr) glyphs. The inscriptions on the Narmer Palette mark it as one of the earliest examples of the use of hieroglyphic writing. It is as well one of the earliest expressions of a formal **canon**, or set of rules for representation, in Egyptian art. The relief carvings on both sides of the palette are ordered by registers to form a coherent narrative of conquest and victory. The importance or insignificance each actor is indicated by the use of hierarchical scale and view. Significant personages—kings, priests, and court officials, are larger and shown in **composite view**: frontal torso and eye with the head and limbs in profile; while inconsequential figures are small and rendered in strict profile.

This conquest narrative is found on the reverse of the palette, where the story begins in the upper register. Narmer is shown wearing the *hedjet* —the tall, white, bowling-pin-shaped crown of Upper Egypt— a royal beard, and a linen kilt with a belt from which hangs a bull's tail, and a row of pendants in the shape of the head and horns of cattle (Wengrow 2001, 94). Narmer enacts the capture ritual by seizing the enemy king by the hair and preparing to smite him with the mace he wields in his other hand. Above the captive, the papyrus symbol of

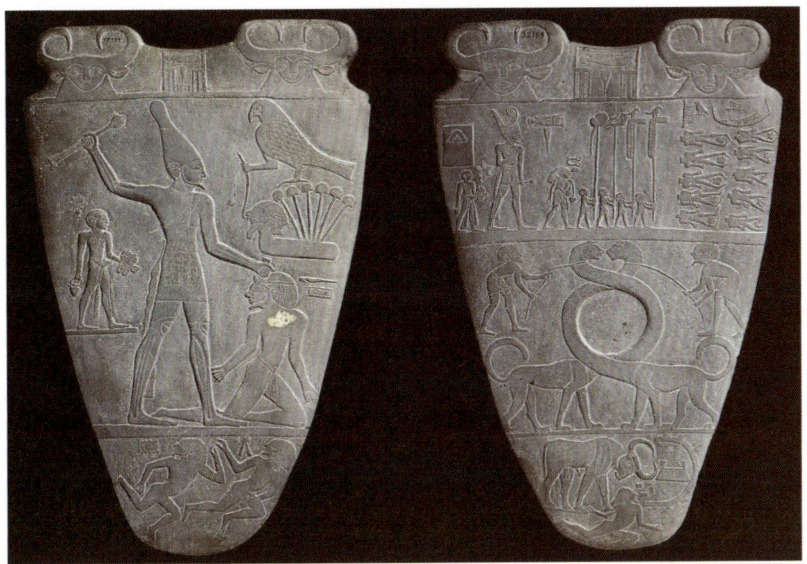

◀ 4.5 Hierakonpolis, Egypt, Palette of Narmer, c. 2950 BCE. 25 in. long (obverse right, reverse left).

The inscriptions on the palette mark it as one of the earliest examples of hieroglyphic writing in Egypt. The palette narrates the story of military conquests by a king named Narmer from Abydos.

Lower Egypt is held captive by the falcon-god Horus, divine protector of the pharaoh. The importance of Narmer's captive is demonstrated by the inclusion of his hieroglyphic name, *Wash*, and by his size relative to Narmer. Kneeling he comes almost to Narmer's waist and were he standing, the captive would be nearly as tall, thus reiterating the significance of Narmer's conquest as his defeat of an equal.

The front of the palette is a victory statement divided into three registers; Narmer appears in the uppermost band, wearing the *deshret* —the red, rear-peaked crown with a curlicue of Lower Egypt— and holding his mace in a lowered, nonaggressive posture. In his other hand he holds a fly whisk, a symbol of royal authority. In this instance, Narmer walks in a victory procession, preceded by a priest and four standard-bearers carrying *sepat* banners. Sepat, or *nome*, were originally autonomous states that became administrative districts after unification. The display of banners in this case may be a reference to city-states ruled by, or allied with, Narmer. The objective of the procession seems to be a review of the enemy dead who have been laid out in two rows of five bodies each shown in aerial perspective. All the prisoners have been decapitated and their severed heads placed between their feet. The dead here may represent vanquished towns brought under Narmer's control during the military campaign. Depicted above the bodies are a wooden boat (perhaps a reference to trade in this instance) and the hawk god Horus grasping a banner in its talons. In the second register a pair of mythical "serpopards" or serpent-necked felines, variously identified as leopards or lions, intertwine their necks around the well for mixing pigment. The two beasts are generally interpreted as representing the unification of the Two Lands. The bottom register shows a large bull, a metaphor for the power of the king, which butts his head against a walled city as a final reiteration of victory.

ARCHITECTURE IN THE OLD KINGDOM (C. 2780–2280 BCE)

Although the average Egyptian probably would have noticed little difference as a new dynasty took control in Memphis, historians mark the ascension of Djoser, first king of the Third Dynasty, as the beginning of a new period termed the Old Kingdom. The three kingdom periods—Old, Middle, and New—represent times when the nation was unified under a centralized government capable of marshaling the labor and resources necessary for the construction of monumental state architectural projects such as temples and pharaonic tombs. The intermediate periods mark times in Egyptian history when a ruling dynasty failed and the country reverted to a collection of small regional states.

The earliest Egyptian royal tombs, beginning in the pre-dynastic period, were trapezoidal mud-brick structures known as *mastabas*; the term is derived by the Arabic word for "bench." The ancient Egyptians placed great importance on the preservation of the body as a dwelling place for the ***Ka*** (life force) in the afterlife. As a result, great emphasis was put on permanence of tomb structures, known locally as "Houses of Eternity" or as "House of a Million Years" because the Ka, after death, was expected to dwell there for all time. For the Egyptians of the Old Kingdom, permanence in architecture was equated with mass. This was possibly the result of the bulk of the mastaba being interpreted as a way to protect the remains of the dead from predation by animals and potentially, from grave robbers. The manufacture of mud-bricks and the construction of these massive tombs was a lengthy process and most rulers began construction of their tombs early in their reigns. To facilitate interment at the appropriate time, a shaft was built into the center of the mastaba for lowering of the remains.

Imhotep, the Stepped Pyramid of Djoser, c. 2686–2648 BCE The pioneering architect of the Old Kingdom Period was a man named Imhotep. He served Djoser as vizier, architect, scribe, sculptor, medical doctor, and high priest of Heliopolis, this last being an honor that according him a share of the income of the temple. King Djoser's "House of Eternity" was originally conceived as a standard mastaba but instead of using sun-dried brick, Imhotep chose to use stone, a material that had not been used previously in Egyptian funerary architecture. As Imhotep began to realize the structural potential of this new material, he redesigned and enlarged the building, changing it from a simple mastaba into a stepped pyramid (Figure 4.6) with six levels, each essentially a mastaba stacked upon the last. Djoser's pyramid rose to a height of 204 feet (62 m) and had a basal area measuring 358 feet (109 m) by 411 feet (125 m). The pyramid was originally covered with a veneer of fine limestone that would have increased the height by another 3 to 4 feet.

The Stepped Pyramid was part of a larger complex, enclosed by a stone wall almost 35 feet (10.6 m) high, which included Djoser's mortuary temple, the Heb Sed court, the House of the North (its columns

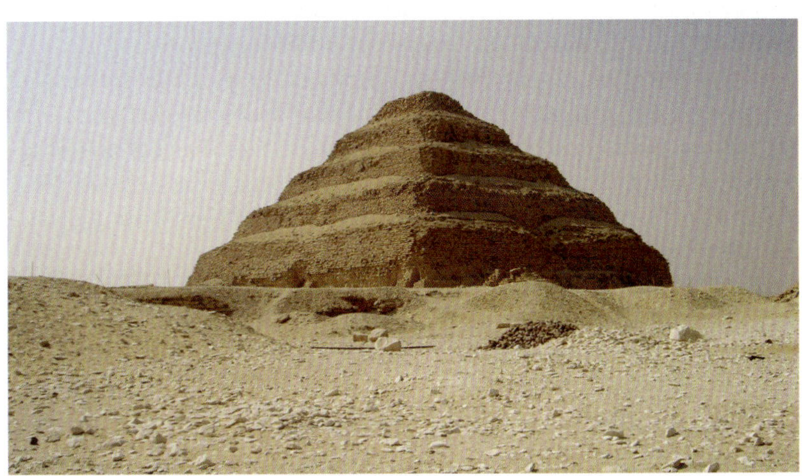

◀ **4.6** Saqqara, Egypt, Imhotep, Pyramid of Djoser, c. 2686–2648. 204 ft. high.

This pyramid was the first use of stone in Egyptian tombs; prior to this time most tombs had been brick. The structural properties of stone allowed Imhotep to stack several mastaba forms to create this first pyramid.

decorated with papyrus capitals symbolizing Lower Egypt), the House of the South (its columns decorated with lotus capitals for Upper Egypt), colonnade, Southern court, and South Tomb. With the exception of the Mortuary Temple, most of the buildings were symbolic rather than functional. The North and South Houses had elaborate façades with doors but no interior space, being entirely solid construction. The Heb Sed court was the focus of activity during the lifetime of the king. This was the location for the enactment of the Heb Sed ritual during which the king would race back and forth between the symbolic representations of Upper and Lower Egypt to demonstrate his strength and vitality and readiness to rule both lands. This ritual was generally celebrated during the king's thirtieth year of rule and was followed by a festival.

Sneferu's Red Pyramid, Dahshur, c. 2613–2589 BCE One of the more ambitious builders of the Fourth Dynasty was its first ruler Pharaoh Sneferu. He is credited with two pyramids at Dahshur, south of Saqqara, and possibly a third at Meidum, although some scholars believe that pyramid was constructed for his predecessor, Huni, who the Egyptian historian Manetho, writing in the third century BCE, listed as the last king of the Third Dynasty, although he may have been Sneferu's father. Whether or not Sneferu is credited with the Meidum pyramid, it does show that by the end of the Third Dynasty, Egyptian architects were working toward creating a true pyramid. The Meidum pyramid was constructed as a stepped structure like Djoser's and then the spaces between the steps were filled in to create the effect of a smooth-sided pyramid; however, flaws in the construction caused the structure to collapse.

The first attempts to build a true pyramid from the start were at Dahshur. It is not certain who served as the architect of the Dahshur pyramids; it may well have been Sneferu's son and vizier, Nefermaat, and it is likely as vizier that he might have played a role in overseeing the construction. Interestingly, it is Nefermaat's son, Hemiunu, who served as vizier and architect to Khufu. Building a pyramid-form tomb from the start was a bold move as no one had ever built one before. Again, the first attempt was not successful as problems with the foundation and the initial too-steep angle of ascent required a radical alteration of the design in mid-construction to prevent another total collapse. The structure was saved but the end result was a pyramid with a broken profile, known as the Bent Pyramid.

Undeterred by his two previous failures, Sneferu began construction of a third pyramid (Figure 4.7) about a mile to the north of the Bent Pyramid. A reddish-hued limestone was used for the core of the structure, giving the new pyramid the popular designation the "Red Pyramid." The pyramid had several engineering changes that made it successful. The horizontal arrangement of stone lintels that

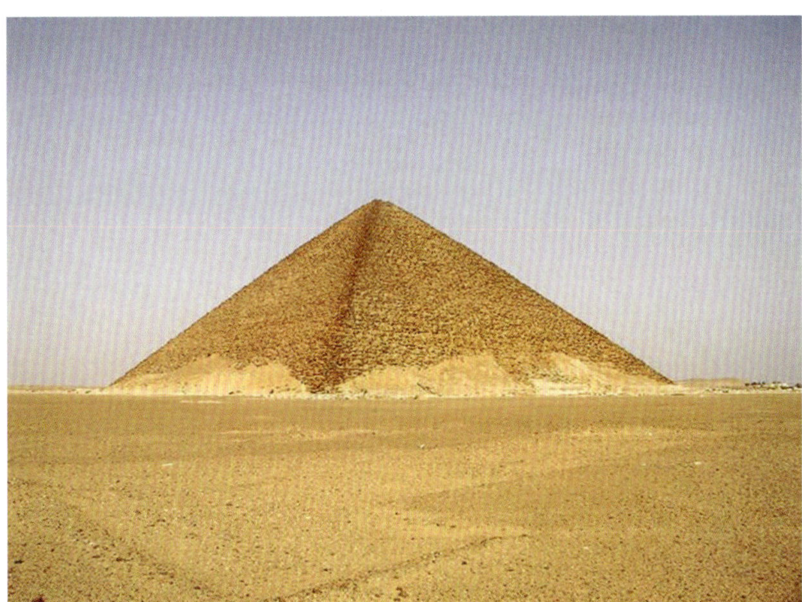

◀ **4.7** Dahshur, Egypt, Sneferu's Red Pyramid, c. 2613–2589 BCE. 344 ft. high.

This first true pyramid takes its name from the reddish hued limestone used for its core. Originally, it was covered with a veneer of white limestone.

had roofed tomb chambers in the earlier pyramids, beginning with Djoser's, was replaced with a new corbelled vaulting system that provided greater structural integrity (Lehner 1997, 98). The pyramid was also given a broader foundation of 715 square feet (220 m^2) and a less radical 43-degree angle of ascent was used. These changes eliminated the structural problems encountered in the previous pyramids. When the pyramid was completed, it had a sheathing of fine white limestone, which was scavenged during later eras, leaving its red sandstone core.

Hemiunu, the Great Pyramid of Khufu at Giza, c. 2551–2528 BCE Sneferu's son and heir, Khufu following his father's example, commissioned the best known and largest of the Egyptian pyramid tombs, The Great Pyramid at Giza (Figure 4.8). The architect of the project was Khufu's vizier, Hemiunu. Remarkably, Khufu's pyramid has a footprint only 32 square feet larger than that of the Red Pyramid but its steeper 51 degree angle allows it to rise to a height of 481 feet (146.5 m). It was constructed using an estimated 2.3 million massive limestone blocks, some of which weighed as much as 16 tons. These blocks were maneuvered into place using ropes, pulleys, and levers to move them up earthen ramps and into position. Like the Red Pyramid, the Great Pyramid had an inner structure of more roughly cut and laid limestone blocks held together with gypsum mortar and an outer shell of more precisely cut white Tura limestone. Unfortunately, its outer casing was also stripped from the pyramid during the Middle Ages and ferried across the Nile to build the rising city of Cairo.

Within the pyramid were three chambers: a box-like, beam-roofed subterranean chamber, a gable-roofed "Queen's chamber," and the pink granite, corbel-vaulted "King's chamber" in the center of the structure,

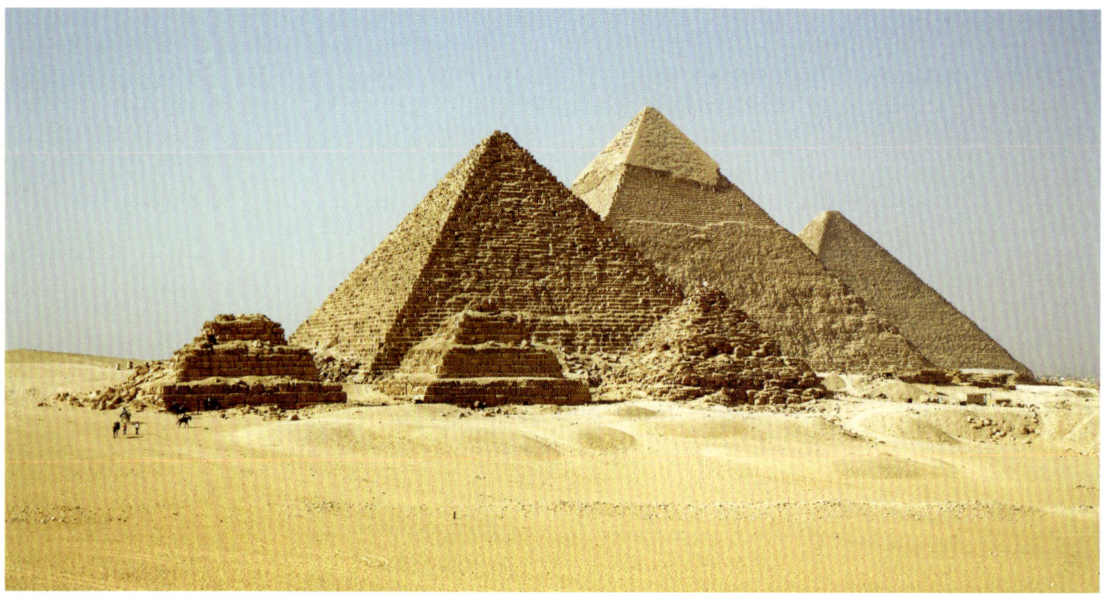

▲ **4.8** Giza, Egypt, (L–R) Pyramids of Menkaure, Khafre, and Khufu, c. 2551–2472 BCE.

Khufu's architect, and nephew, Hemiunu, used the lessons learned at Dahshur to construct the 481 ft. high pyramid of Khufu.

which held the pharaoh's red granite sarcophagus. The chambers were accessed by a series of passageways or galleries equipped with blocking systems to deter thieves. Recently, scientists, using cosmic ray imaging that produces results akin to x-rays, discovered a large void in the pyramid above the grand gallery that may be a previously unknown fourth chamber.

The Great Pyramid was part of a massive funerary complex surrounded by a stone wall 26 feet (7.9 m) high, which connected to Khufu's pillared mortuary temple on the east side. From the court of the mortuary temple a long paved causeway ran down to Khufu's valley temple. The causeway was still standing in Herodotus' time. He described it as running 5 furlongs (3300 ft; 1006 m) long, being ten fathoms (60 ft; 18.2 m) wide and eight fathoms (48 ft; 14.6 m) at its highest point; built all of polished stone covered with carvings of animals (Herodotus 1971, 75). Outside the walls, Khufu had five wooden funerary boats buried: two on the east and south and one on the north side. The boats on the east and south were for the king's travels in the afterlife to the four directions, while the boat on the north is thought to have been the vessel that ferried the king's mummified body to the burial site. On the east, south of the causeway, stand three identical small pyramids, popularly known as the Queens' Pyramids. These are thought to have once contained the burials of three Egyptian queens, including Khufu's own mother, Hetepheres, and the mothers of his two sons, Djedefre and Khafre (Verner 2001, 208–212). West of the Great Pyramid was a large necropolis, containing the mastaba tombs of Hemiunu and other high courtiers.

SCULPTURE IN THE OLD KINGDOM

Egyptian sculpture, like architecture, was concerned with mass and permanence according to rank, and tended to be very conservative, seldom veering from the established canons. The result was that the highest levels of sculpture, those created for the rulers as Ka statues, tended to be formal, frontal, blocky, and unchanging from one dynasty to the next. Since the image of the Pharaoh was closely associated with the strength and power of the nation, he is always idealized as youthful and vigorous regardless of his actual age or physical condition. His physical appearance was largely dictated by a canon of proportion that specified the length and breadth of each body part in relation to other parts. For example, the ideal length of the foot was three times the width of the palm. Rulers were typically portrayed as seated or standing in a static pose, giving them a timeless quality. No attempt is made to show action since movement in space offered the potential for breakage of unsupported appendages.

The process of carving these most important images was as unbending as the resulting images themselves. Sculptors using copper chisels and stone tools addressed each face of the block independently of those adjoining it. On the face of the stone, a frontal view of the image would be chalked; then lateral views would be added to each side, and the back to the rear of the block. Then the carver's assistants would begin working on each surface of the block simultaneously until they reached the core. At this point the master would take over and work the sculpture into a consistent whole. This would be followed by polishing with progressively finer abrasives, depending upon the stone. Pharaonic images were often worked in hard stones, which would take a fine polishing. Those of lesser status, such as various royal half-siblings and more distant royal relations, might have their portraits carved in softer stones such as limestone, which did not polish to a high sheen. In these cases, the sculptures were often painted to make them appear more lifelike.

Sculptures in stone and wood of nonroyals, such as scribes and other court officials, were often carved fully in the round, sometimes with a seemingly lifelike quality not seen in pharaonic images. However, there were conventions of representation for lesser ranks as well. For example, scribes and court officials such as Hemiunu, Khafre's chief minister, are often shown as corpulent, soft-bodied individuals, no matter how they actually looked, as a means of showing that these persons did not do manual labor. Depending upon the medium, these statues might also be painted and the eyes inlaid with rock crystal to make them more lifelike.

Commoners are rarely depicted in three-dimensional works although they are often shown as attendants in reliefs, for example, the banner carriers in the Palette of Narmer. The exception is a category of small-scale sculptures of male and female servants that were placed in tombs so that they could continue to serve the decedent in the next life.

Great Sphinx of Giza, c. 2520–2494 BCE The first colossal sculpture of the ancient world, the Great Sphinx (Figure 4.9) stood near the lower end of the causeway that ran from the Mortuary Temple and Pyramid of Khafre to his valley temples. The sphinx is a hybrid creature with the body of a couchant lion and a human head. The face of the sphinx is, traditionally, thought to be that of the Pharaoh Khafre as it stands in front of his pyramid at Giza, and because it wears the pharaonic *nemes* striped head cloth, representing the flaring hood of the cobra goddess Wadjet. The sculpture may have at one time had a fake beard; pharaohs wore these as a sign of their status as living gods. The identification of the sculpture with the pharaoh is also suggested by its Egyptian designation of *shesep-ankh* or "living image." However, some Egyptologists believe the sphinx to have been cut during the reign of Khufu or an even earlier pharaoh.

The immense sculpture measures 240 feet (73 m) long, 20 feet wide (6 m), and 66 feet (20 m) high, and was carved out of the limestone bedrock of the Giza plateau and sits at the bottom of an excavated court, created as blocks for Khafre's pyramid and temples were excavated in a U-shaped ditch around the rock outcrop. The Giza limestone is a sedimentary rock that was laid down in three distinct strata.

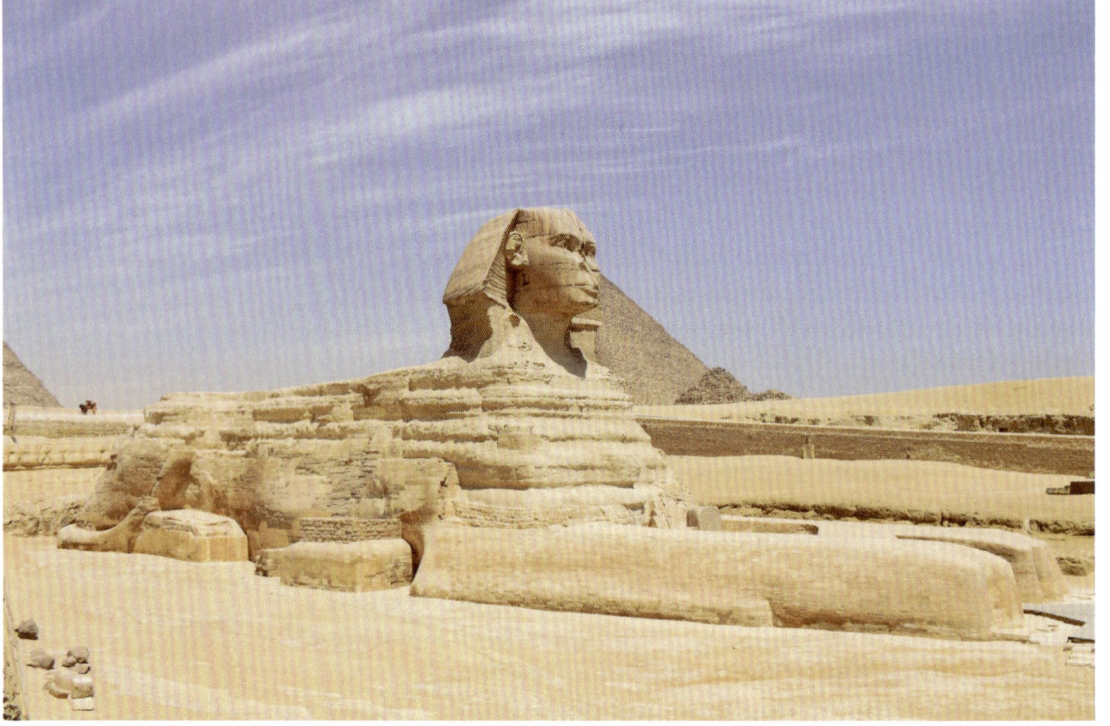

▼ 4.9 Giza, Egypt, Great Sphinx, c. 2520–2494 BCE. 240 ft. × 20 ft. × 66 ft.

Khafre's Great Sphinx, the first colossal sculpture of the ancient world, was carved from a limestone outcrop near the end of the causeway leading to his valley temple. It was originally encased in limestone masonry to protect the soft core of the sculpture.

These layers are evident in the color and hardness changes from the soft yellow of the sphinx's lower body to the hard gray stone at the level of the head. Possibly because the sphinx's sculptors realized that the softer limestone core was prone to weathering, it was originally sheathed in masonry. The casing that remains around the base of the sculpture is a mixture of original stones and later repairs. The first recorded restoration was during the reign of Thutmose IV (r. 1401–1391 BCE), who had the desert sand cleared away and the fallen casing stones replaced. The sphinx's beard may have been added at this time to stabilize the head and the sculpture may have been painted. Traces of pigment found on the sphinx, and on what is believed to be a portion of its beard, now in the British Museum, show that the face and, probably the body, were red; the nemes head cloth was yellow with blue stripes, and the eyebrows and beard were blue to suggest the lapis lazuli beards of gods. Around 500 BCE a new layer of masonry was added to the upper part of the sphinx's body, tail, and headdress. In Roman times, masonry was added to the paws and sides of the Sphinx.

Menkaure, Goddess Hathor, and the Deified Hare Nome, c. 2490–2472 BCE

Khafre's successor Menkaure made no attempt to outshine his father and grandfather in architecture, electing to build the modest red and white westernmost pyramid at Giza. His greater interest seems to have been in sculpture. The centerpiece of his mortuary temple was a monumental white alabaster sculpture in the traditional seated pose, fragments of which were excavated by George Reisner during the 1908–1910 Harvard University Museum of Fine Arts expedition. The head of the sculpture shows it to have been detailed in black to define hair at the temples, eyebrows, mustache, the kohl around his eyes, and the straps that hold his fake beard. Most Egyptian sculpture was heightened to some degree with paint, with the exception of some of the darker diorite and graywacke sculptures.

The Harvard group also excavated Menkaure's valley temple, discovering the famous double statue of Menkaure and his queen, Khamerernebty, four intact triad sculptures, and fragments of two more. The triad relief sculptures are small in scale, 33.25 inches (84.5 cm) tall and were carved in the coarse gray sandstone, known as graywacke. Three show Menkaure in hierarchical scale and highest relief, standing between the figures of Khamerernebty and a male or female nome deity; nome deities personified the administrative districts of Egypt.

The fourth triad (Figure 4.11) showed a seated figure of the goddess Hathor, flanked by smaller figures of Menkaure and the Hare or Hermopolite Nome. Menkaure stands to the proper left of the seated goddess, who wraps one arm around the king's waist and touches his forearm with her other in a gesture reminiscent of the Menkaure and Khamerernebty double statue. He wears a pleated kilt and the crown of Upper Egypt. Both he and the smaller deified Hermopolite Nome

VISUAL COMPARISON
Conventions of the Ka Statue

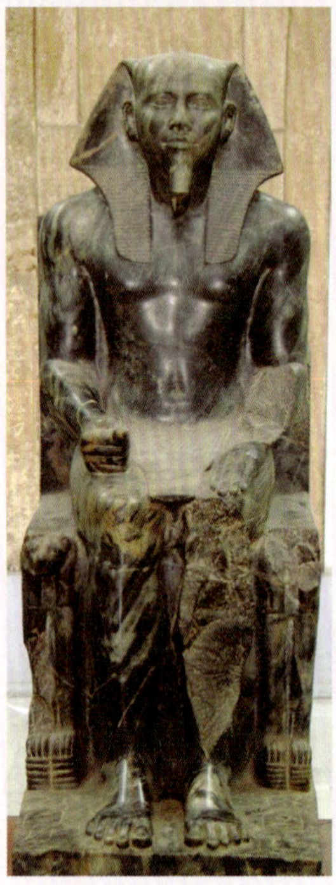
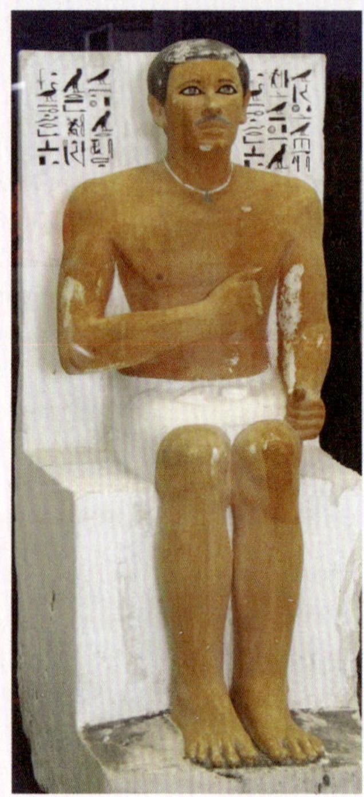
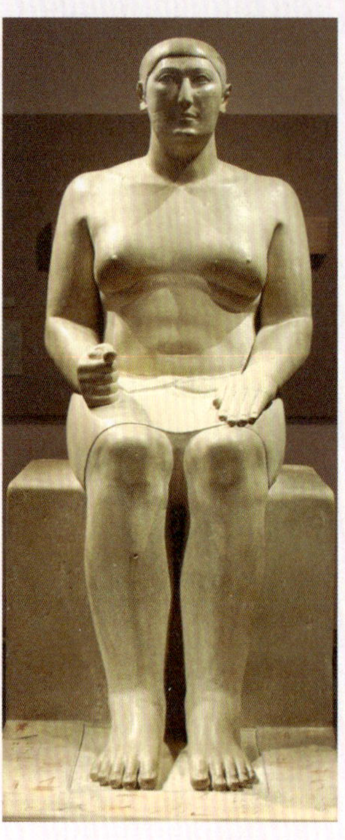

▲ 4.10 Egypt, Ka statues L-R: Pharaoh Khafre, Prince Rahotep, and Vizier Hemiunu, *(c. 2575–c. 2465 BCE) L: diorite; others: limestone.*

Ka statues of pharaohs, royals, and high court officials adhered to the established canons and materials for their rank.

The Egyptians believed that humans and gods had a ka, a spiritual "double" or life essence, which continued to live on after death, residing in the physical body; hence the need for mummification. If for some reason the body decomposed or otherwise became corrupted, the ka could dwell in a carved image or even a bas relief. The ancient Egyptians took great care to provide one or more alternate locations for the ka because without a place to reside, it would die and immortality would be lost.

The pharaoh had his Ka statue carved out of the hardest stones, diorite being especially favored as it took a high polish. Those of lower status, including various lesser royals and more distant relatives, might have their images carved in limestone. Officials of lowest rank and least means might have statues of wood or just a head carved in stone. Because permanence was the paramount consideration, stone ka statues often depict the individual seated on a throne or bench with legs together and arms tight against the body. There is no attempt to show movement in space, not only because timelessness is the desired quality, but also because any element cut free from the block was susceptible to damage, making the sculpture unsuitable as a dwelling place for the ka.

The rank and occupation of the decedent determined not only the choice of materials used in the creation of the ka statue but also how the individual was depicted. The pharaoh was always idealized as youthful and vigorous, even when this was not the case in real life. For example, Khafre's diorite Ka statue depicts the ruler at the peak of physical condition, with muscular arms, firm chest, flat abdomen, and a youthful face. He wears a linen kilt, false beard, and nemes headdress as insignia of his rank. This representation was intended to show the pharaoh as a potent divine king whose service, on behalf of Egypt, would continue for eternity. It was not a realistic portrait of Khafre, a man in his eighties when he died. Pharaonic depictions were further constrained by a canon of proportion that specified the length and breadth of each body part in relation to other parts. For example, the ideal length of the foot was three times the width of the hand.

Prince Rahotep, a son of Pharaoh Snefru, and priest of Ra, as a lesser ranking royal, had his ka statue carved in limestone. He is depicted wearing only a linen kilt and a bead necklace. Since limestone would not take a high polish, the finished carving was painted to give it a more natural appearance and to add details such as the prince's mustache and jewelry. In Rahotep's case, the eyes were inlaid with rock crystal to give them a glassy living quality.

While statues of court officials were often carved fully in the round and possess a seemingly lifelike quality, these too were idealized. After Imhotep, Hemiunu was the second great genius of the Old Kingdom. He was an architect, engineer, and mathematician as well as serving as Khufu's vizier. He was also a prince of Egypt being both Sneferu's grandson and Khufu's nephew but he is not depicted with the trim, athletic body of a prince, as was his uncle Rahotep. Instead, Hemiunu's Ka statue depicts him as obese, with a sagging chest, round belly, and heavy limbs. At first it might seem that Hemiunu has been rendered as a true portrait, but corpulent figures were a convention in images of court officials from the vizier to the king's scribe. It is thought that the stout bodies were a statement of the relatively comfortable lives led by court officials who did not engage in manual labor.

are shown in a striding pose but the actual mechanics of human movement are not present. There is no weight-shift (contrapposto) or counter-positioning of the hips and shoulders, both in horizontal alignment. The suggestion of movement was accomplished by lengthening the advancing leg. This nome represented the city of Hermopolis on the border between Upper and Lower Egypt. Its designation as the "Hare" Nome derives from the naturalistic rabbit shown crouching on top of the standard that rises behind the head of the nome.

Except for their scale the two female figures are quite similar; both wear the same helmet-shaped wigs and long, tight dresses that reveal the navel and nipples. The similarity is a result of the figures' adherence to the standard canon of idealized beauty. Likewise, the figure of Menkaure conforms to the stylistic canons for pharaonic representation.

The Middle Kingdom (c. 2055–1650 BCE)

During the Sixth Dynasty, Egypt saw the decline of the power of the central government in Memphis and an increase in that of the regional administrators or nomarchs. This shift in the balance of

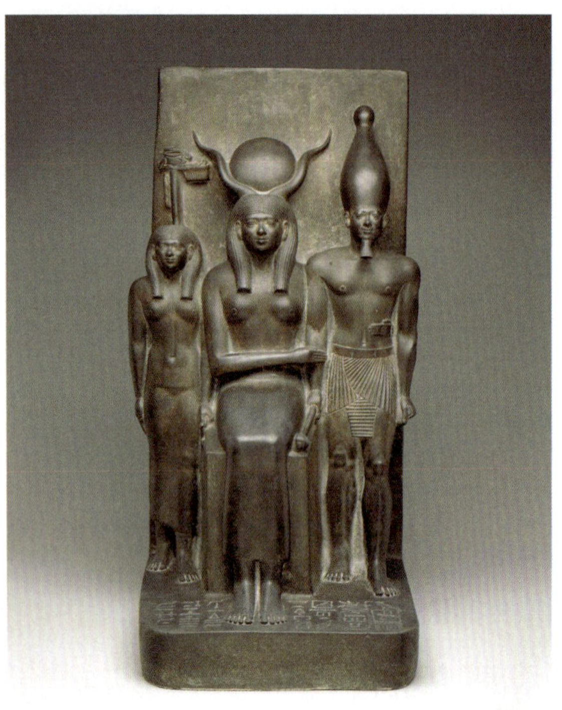

▲ 4.11 Menkaure, the goddess Hathor, and deified Hare Nome, c. 2490–2472 Greywacke, 17.12 x 33.25 x 19 in.

The seated goddess is flanked by Menkaure (proper left) wearing the white crown of Upper Egypt and the Hare Nome (proper right) identifiable by the rabbit in the standard rising behind her head.

power is reflected in the changing burial practices of these provincial officials. In earlier times they would have been buried in the mastaba necropolises associated with the pharaoh's mortuary complex, but by the end of the dynasty, they were not only building their tombs in their nomes but these tombs were often more elaborate than those built around Memphis. After the death of Pepy II, the last pharaoh of the dynasty, Egypt entered a transitional period, termed the First Intermediate Period (c. 2181–2055 BCE). The kings of the Seventh and Eighth Dynasties continued to rule from Memphis but had little power beyond the capital, the priests of Ra and nomarchs having usurped some of the powers traditionally held by the ruling dynasty in the capital. The pharaohs of the ninth and tenth dynasties moved the capitol to Herakleopolis, prompting the nomarch at Thebes to assert power as the first ruler of the Eleventh Dynasty, effectively dividing the country.

It was not until the thirty-ninth year of the reign of the Theban Mentuhotep II (c. 2055–2004 BCE) that Egypt was reunited, and monumental royal tombs again were constructed. Mentuhotep selected Deir el-Bahri, a deep bay in the Theban Hills, well back from the Nile, for his royal mortuary complex. Rather than resume building the pyramids of the Old Kingdom, Mentuhotep II created an entirely new type of funerary monument. Earlier Theban rulers had carved ***saff*** or row tombs into the escarpment at el-Tarif in the northern end of the Theban necropolis, but these had been simple affairs only slightly larger than the local private tombs (Arnold in Shafer 1997, 74). Mentuhotep II's temple was the prototype for several later temples of similar type, including the neighboring Eighteenth Dynasty temple of Hatshepsut.

Temple of Mentuhotep II at Deir el-Bahri, c. 2046–1995 BCE Compared to the simple Theban saff tombs of the First Intermediate Period, the Temple of Mentuhotep II (Figure 4.12) was an immense architectural monument, rivaling those of the Third and Fourth Dynasties in scale and complexity. Like the Old Kingdom complexes at Saqqara and Giza, Mentuhotep II's featured two temples, one in the valley (later destroyed), and a second one at the foot of the escarpment. The

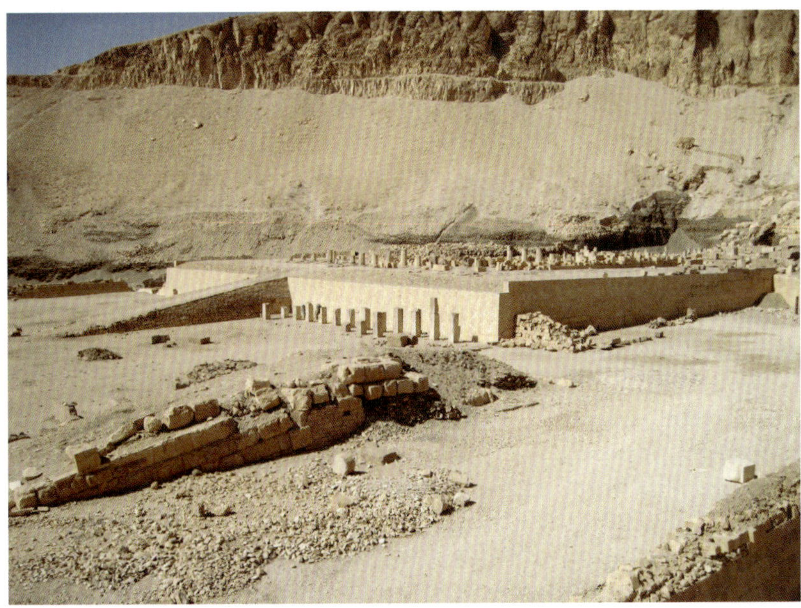

◀ 4.12 Deir el-Bahri, Egypt, Temple of Mentuhotep II, c. 2046–1995 BCE.

This temple was the first large-scale mortuary complex built since the Old Kingdom. It included a valley temple and second one at the foot of the escarpment; the two were connected by a wide causeway lined with statues of the pharaoh. The first court featured a grove of tamarisk and sycamore trees.

two structures were connected by a 150 foot (46 m) wide processional way that was lined with statues of the pharaoh, those on the south side wearing the white crown of Upper Egypt and those on the north, the red one of Lower Egypt.

As the causeway entered the vast court at the foot of the upper temple, it ran through a grove of fifty-four tamarisks and eight sycamores. Tamarisk trees had a funerary connotation, being connected in legend to the god Osiris, whose coffin became embedded in one when it washed ashore in Byblos. Sycamore trees, however, were associated with the sun and creator god Ra. The two different species of trees reflected the dual functions of Mentuhotep II's temple. It served as his mortuary, but it also contained a sanctuary to Montu-Ra, the Theban supreme god, who represented the scorching rays of the sun. Mentuhotep II's regnal name meant "Montu is in peace."

At the west end of the courtyard garden were a pillared hall and a ramp leading to a colonnaded second terrace. In the center of this upper level was a walled court, containing a **hypostyle hall** (many-columned hall) and a natural mound, which symbolized benben. In some versions of the Egyptian creation myth, the benben was a mound that rose out of the primordial waters and upon which Atum created himself as the first god. Beyond this was another court containing the entrance to Mentuhotep's burial chamber, a hypostyle hall, a sanctuary to the sun god with a statue of Amun-Ra, and at the far end, a niche cut into the bedrock of the cliff that once housed a monumental painted limestone statue of Mentuhotep II, rendered in the archaicizing style of Thebes.

The New Kingdom (c. 1570–1070 BCE)

The Second Intermediate Period was another interval of weak centralized rule. During the Thirteenth Dynasty the town of Avaris in the far north of Egypt became an important trading center that drew Semitic peoples from the Sinai and Palestine as well as a group termed Hyksos by the Greeks. The Hyksos took control of Lower Egypt, ruling for 108 years until driven out by Ahmose I. Having chased the Hyksos into Syria, Ahmose I turned his attention to the south, engaging militarily with the kingdom of Kush, to secure that border. Ahmose I established buffer zones around Egypt and fortified frontier cities to prevent further foreign incursions.

Under the pharaohs of the Eighteenth, Nineteenth, and Twentieth Dynasties, the New Kingdom was a time of great prosperity for Egypt. Ahmose I (r. 1539–1514 BCE) and his successors built an empire, which, at its greatest extent, included Libya, Syria, Nubia, and part of northwestern Assyria. The riches that poured in from these territories, especially gold from Nubia, financed one of the most creative eras in Egyptian art. Architecture flourished as old temples were renovated and enlarged, and new mortuary complexes were built and new sanctuaries were constructed to honor gods other than Amun. In the arts, the new media of glass-making was discovered by makers of Egyptian ***faience*** (sintered quartzite ceramics). The New Kingdom Period saw the relaxing of the old representational canons, resulting in dynastic sculptures that were slenderer and sometimes executed fully in the round. Ultimately, an entirely new, somewhat androgynous, representational style appeared, inspired by Akhenaten's short-lived experiment with monotheism, the worship of the Aten, or life-giving solar disk.

Hatshepsut: Queen and King of Egypt

One of the more interesting pharaohs of the eighteenth Dynasty was Hatshepsut. She was the daughter of Thutmose I, the half-sister of Thutmose II, and his chief or "Great Royal Wife." Since the First Dynasty, Egyptian Pharaohs had claimed to be living gods by virtue of their descent from divine ancestors. To ensure the continuance of their divine bloodlines, the pharaohs engaged in intra-familial marriages, taking their sister, first cousin, or even their daughter as their chief wife. When these incestuous unions were fruitful, they tended to result in female offspring; male children were more likely to be produced by unrelated minor wives. The laws of succession in ancient Egypt specified that the throne be passed down to the eldest male heir produced by the Great Royal Wife;" but if there was none, then it went to the eldest son by a minor wife. Hatshepsut and Thutmose II produced only daughters; the heir, Thutmose III, was the child of a minor wife. When Thutmose II died, his son was too young to take the throne, so Hatshepsut initially served as regent for her nephew-stepson. After serving as regent for a few years, Hatshepsut, with the backing of the priests of Amun, claimed the throne for herself as the issue of Thutmose I by his sister-wife.

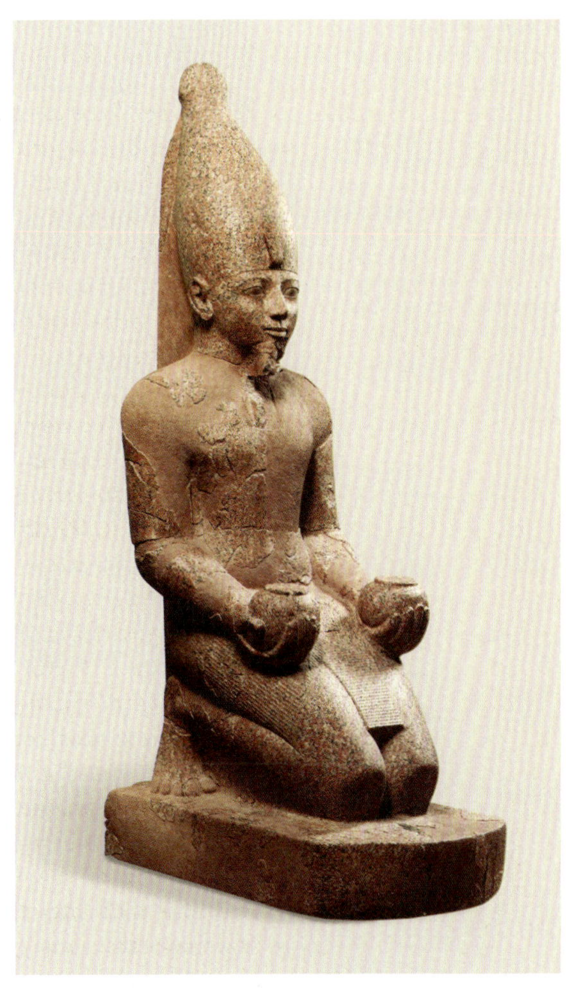

▲ **4.13** Deir el-Bahri, Egypt, Large Kneeling Statue of Hatshepsut with Offering Jars, c. 1479–1458 BCE. Granite, 116.50 in. × 32 in. × 57.25 in.

After taking the title of Pharaoh, Hatshepsut was depicted in masculinized form and described with masculine terms in inscriptions.

Large Kneeling Statue of Hatshepsut with Offering Jars, c. 1479–1458 BCE Hatshepsut was only the second woman in the history of Egypt to rule as Pharaoh. The first was Sobeknfru (r. 1785–1782 BCE), who had taken the throne after her brother-husband died without issue, because she was the last surviving member of her line. Her death, after only three years of rule, brought the Middle Kingdom to an end and paved the way for the conquest of Lower Egypt by the Hyksos. With such an inauspicious precedent, Hatshepsut seems to have had to work doubly hard to prove herself. The earliest images of Hatshepsut as a ruler, created during her regency, showed her as a very feminine queen. However, once she claimed the throne for herself, her depictions are often masculinized. *Hatshepsut with Offering Jars* (Figure 4.13) is an example of such a masculinized image. It was one of more than two hundred statues carved fully in the round for display at her mortuary temple in Deir el-Bahri. The statue shows a flat-chested Hatshepsut wearing the white crown of Upper Egypt, pleated linen kilt, and false beard. The inscriptions on the sculpture refer to her in masculine terms as "king." Other images show her performing typically male activities such as conducting state rituals, spearfishing, and smiting enemies (Roth in Roehrig et al. 2005, 9). In adopting masculine representational conventions, Hatshepsut is attempting to show herself the equal of Egypt's male rulers, and perhaps to reassure her subjects of the stability, continuity, and permanence of the state during her reign. Although her successor, Thutmose III, attempted to obliterate her name from Egyptian history, Hatshepsut's reign was a time of peace and prosperity in Egypt.

Senmut, Hatshepsut's Djeser-Djeseru at Deir el-Bahri, c. 1473–1458 BCE Shortly after her accession, construction of her mortuary temple, known as the Djeser-Djeseru or "Holy of Holies" (Figure 4.14) began at Deir el-Bahri. Inscriptions at the temple identify Hatshepsut's steward, Senmut, as the architect of the temple. Like Imhotep, Senmut was a commoner. The site selected was to the north of the

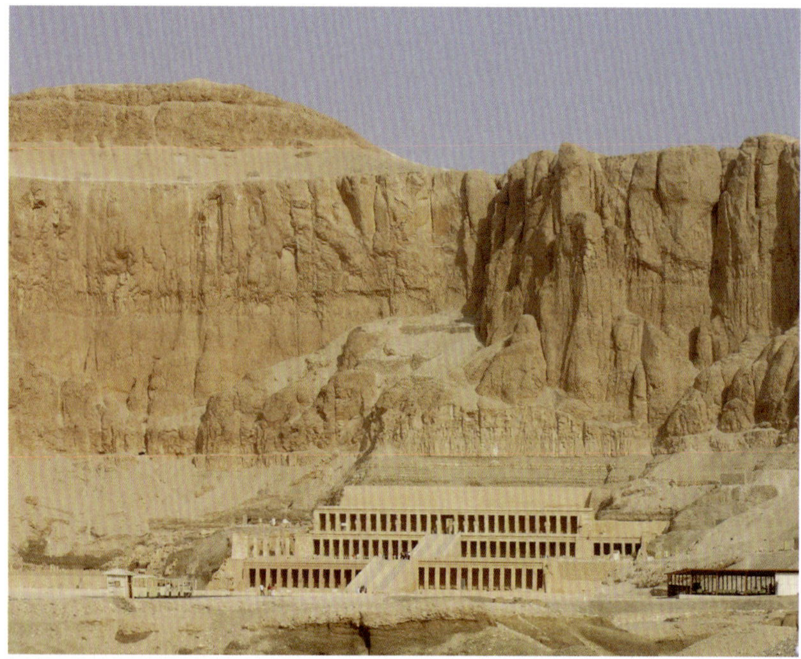

▶ 4.14 Deir el-Bahri, Egypt, Senmut, Djeser-Djeseru Mortuary Temple of Hatshepsut, c. 1473–1458 BCE.

Hatshepsut selected a site to the north of Mentuhotep II's Temple Complex for her temple and had her architect and steward, Senmut, build a much grander version of the earlier structure. The first court was planted with fragrant trees brought back by her expedition to Punt.

then-almost-six-hundred-year-old temple complex of Mentuhotep II. It was a difficult building site, filled with massive rock falls from the escarpment. Senmut solved the problem by designing an even grander version of the Mentuhotep temple that rose in three colonnaded courts to a height of 97 feet (30 m) above the valley floor. The pillared porticos provided wall space for relief panels detailing the accomplishments of Hatshepsut's reign. The third level was distinguished by Osirian statues of Hatshepsut, of which only a few remain. This portico opened onto a court containing shrines to Hatshepsut and Thutmose I and a temple to Amun, from whom Hatshepsut claimed divine birth.

The temple was approached along a 121 foot (37 m) wide processional way that ran from Hatshepsut's valley temple to her mortuary temple and sanctuary. A **pylon gate** or monumental gateway (now destroyed) marked the entrance to the first court. This lower court, like that of Mentuhotep, featured a temple garden. Hatshepsut's was planted with exotic frankincense and myrrh trees that would have filled the air with their perfume.

Relief Showing Expedition to Punt, c. 1473–1458 BCE The proper left portico of the second level of Hatshepsut's temple featured bas-reliefs, depicting the return of the expedition to Land of Punt (Figure 4.15). Egyptian bearers carry the frankincense and myrrh trees that were planted in the temple garden. Painted reliefs reach their pinnacle during the New Kingdom. Both sculptures-in-the-round and raised reliefs were commonly painted. The process began with artisans establishing a grid by snapping a line covered in pigment dust across the surface of the wall

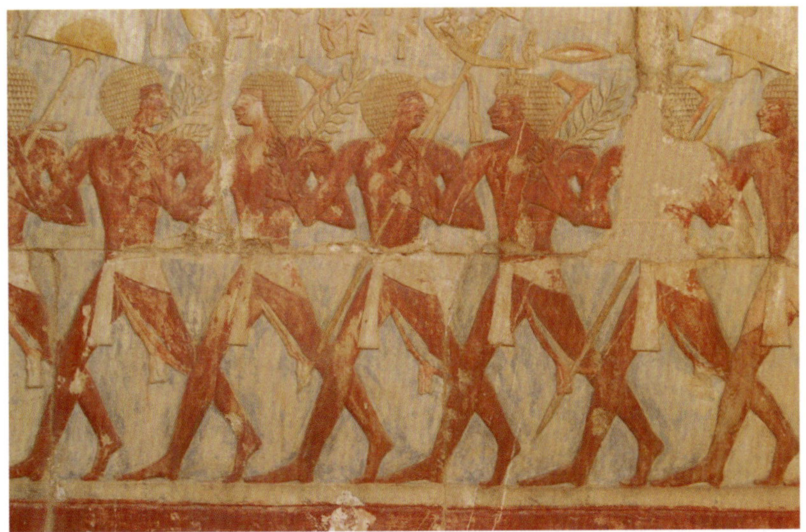

◀ **4.15** Deir el-Bahri, Egypt, Painted Relief Panel from the Mortuary Temple of Hatshepsut, c. 1473–1458 BCE. This relief shows soldiers returning from the expedition to Punt carrying the frankincense and myrrh trees that were planted in Hatshepsut's temple garden.

or panel; the grid helped the artists to properly proportion and align figures and other elements in the scene. Following the sketches drawn on the stone, carvers worked in the details of figures and cut away the background. When the carving was completed, the relief was covered with a coat of fine plaster and painted. As seen in the Hatshepsut relief, red was used for flesh tones; other common colors were black, yellow, green, blue, and white.

Akhenaten and the Amarna Revolution (c. 1352–1336 BCE)

Akhenaten, tenth ruler of the Eighteenth Dynasty, was a second son who was not originally destined for the throne. However, after the death of his elder brother Thutmose, he became crown prince and successor to his father Amenhotep III. During his reign Amenhotep III had been concerned about the growing power of the priests of Amun-Ra, seeing them as a threat to the continuation of the monarchy. As a countermeasure he had commissioned shrines and statues to other traditional gods and promoted their worship. When Akhenaten came to the throne as Amenhotep IV, initially he was a traditional ruler; building temples to Amun at Karnak. However, he soon made a radical break, changing his name to Akhenaten, moving the capital to the new city of Akhetaten (Amarna), and declaring the supremacy of the Aten over all other gods. The Aten was the personification of the solar disk, which unlike other Egyptian gods did not have an anthropomorphic form. Akhenaten and his Great Royal Wife Nefertiti were not only the high priest and priestess of the Aten, but also the living embodiments, son and daughter, of the Aten, whom they worshiped on behalf of the people. In promoting the religion of the Aten, Akhenaten built new open-air temples, and inspired the abandonment of millennia-old artistic canons and conventions in favor of a strange new art that was

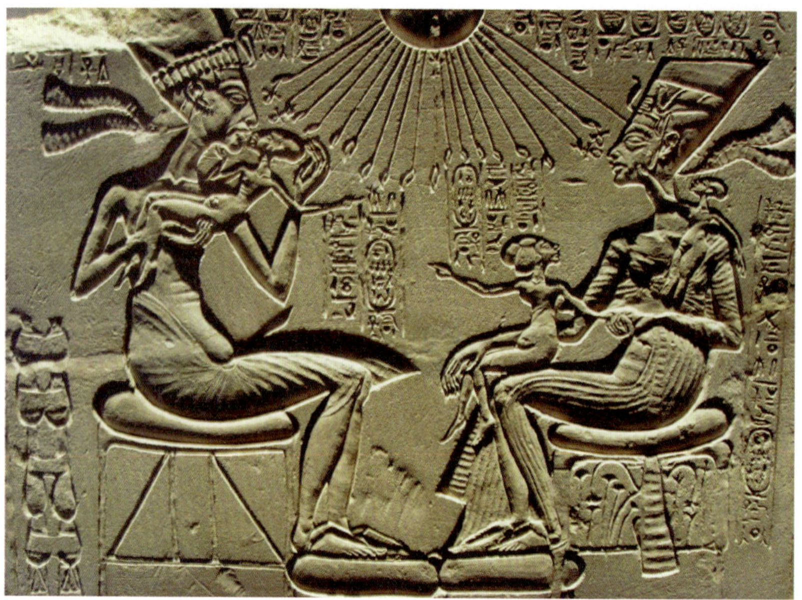

▶ 4.16 Amarna, Egypt, Akhenaten, Nefertiti, and their three daughters, c. 1353–1335. Limestone, 12.25 in. × 15.25 in.

The panel shows the royal couple and their children seated in the light of the Aten. The scene is unusual in its depiction of the natural and affectionate interaction of parents and children.

both highly stylized and symbolic. The era in Egyptian art history is known as the Amarna Period after Akhenaten's capital.

Akhenaten, Nefertiti, and Their Three Daughters, c. 1353–1335 BCE The sunken relief panel from Amarna (Figure 4.16) shows Akhenaten, Nefertiti, and three of their daughters, seated in an open-air pavilion in the light of the Aten. The king and queen cuddle and caress their children, creating a natural and loving family portrait that was unprecedented in Egyptian art. But what is more striking is the physical depiction of Akhenaten; his face is extremely long, his cheek bones overly prominent, and his jaw sharply pointed. While his and Nefertiti's bodies are still depicted in the composite view first seen on the Palette of Narmer, the pharaoh's body is far from vigorous or idealized. It is abnormally proportioned for a male, with a narrow waist, sagging belly, broad feminine hips and thighs, and scrawny arms, narrow torso, and a long neck.

In his *Hymn to Aten*, Akhenaten describes himself as living in ***maat***, meaning "order, truth, and righteousness." This declaration has been used to suggest Akhenaten chose to be depicted as he actually appeared, without the usual idealization. This assumption has led to speculation that the pharaoh suffered from a wide range of genetic maladies, which have symptoms not in evidence in Akhenaten's history. Although seeming to be lifelike, Egyptian state art was symbolic, not veristic. In his hymns to the Aten, Akhenaten invokes the solar disk as the "maker of all things" and as the "nurse who suckles creation". These descriptors suggest the Aten has both a male and female nature. As the living representative of the Aten, Akhenaten may have chosen an androgynous form as a means of conveying the masculine and feminine duality of the deity and of creation itself. Akhenaten and Nefertiti nurturing their children can be read as a mirroring of the "parental" role of the life-giving Aten.

The importance of these male and female roles may also be reflected in the decision to depict the royal couple as equal in scale and seated on thrones of the same height. While Egyptian women had greater autonomy than many in the ancient world, their status, during the Amarna Period, seems to have been especially high. Not only is Nefertiti Akhenaten's equivalent in that she is the daughter of the Aten, but in the latter part of Akhenaten's reign, he appointed her his co-regent under the name Neferneferuaten (van Dijk in Shaw 2002, 278). Although earlier rulers had sometimes shared rule with their son-successors, the elevation of Nefertiti, rather than his son, as co-ruler is highly unusual.

Thutmose of Amarna, Bust of Nefertiti, c. 1353–1336 Among the artists at the Amarna court was a master sculptor named Thutmose. While Thutmose of Amarna may not be a well-known name, his life-size portrait bust of Queen Nefertiti (Figure 4.17 is world famous as the archetype of feminine beauty. After carving, the limestone bust was covered with a layer of gypsum plaster and painted. The sculpture is believed to have been an artist's working model for the creation of other works rather than being intended for display.

Discovered in the 1912 excavations of Thutmose's house and studio at Amarna were an additional twenty-two plaster heads depicting various members of the royal family, including Akhenaten, as well as persons who may have been prominent members of the Amarna court. These, too, may have been artist's models. These workshop portraits are remarkable in their intense realism; it is without parallel in the second millennium BCE. They include images of older women who bear the weight of their years in wrinkles, heavy eyelids, and sagging jowls, and an image believed to be Akhenaten that shows none of the strange distortions of the early Amarna style. Still, Thutmose could flatter his sitter when required. CT scans of the Nefertiti bust revealed that the original carved limestone portrait hidden by the plaster layer depicted a much older Nefertiti with sunken cheekbones, wrinkled cheeks and a bump on her nose (Ireland 2013; Moan 2009).

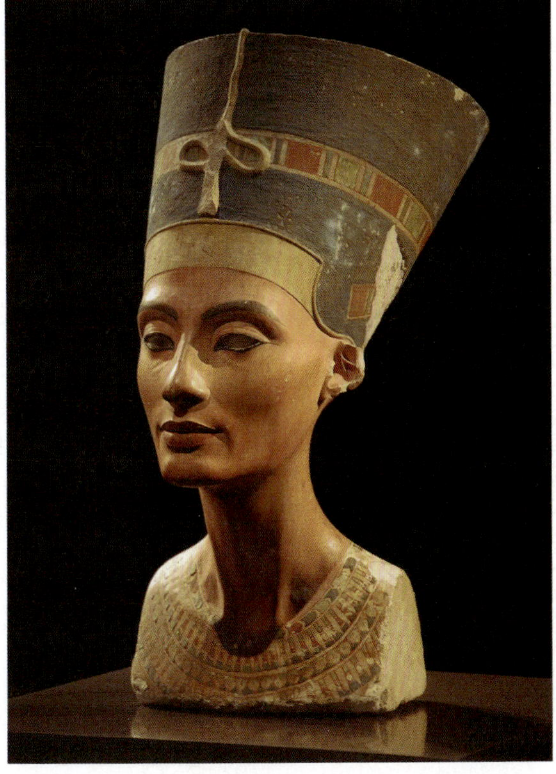

▼ 4.17 Amarna, Egypt, Thutmose, Bust of Nefertiti, c. 1353–1335 BCE. Painted limestone, 20 in. high.

Thutmose's bust of Nefertiti is a classic icon of feminine beauty but recent scientific examinations reveal that the limestone bust under the paint and plaster show a much older version of the queen that was improved in the final version.

The Land of Kush (3100 BCE–339 CE)

To the south of Egypt, along the middle reaches of the Nile, was the Land of Kush. The Romans knew it as Nubia; today, the nations of Sudan and South Sudan occupy the area. In ancient times Kush had a complex relationship with neighboring Egypt; it was a trading partner, a sometimes vassal state, and for a brief period, an overlord. Kush began at the first cataract or waterfall of the Nile, at what is now Aswan, and followed the river southward to the confluence of the Blue and White Niles at Khartoum. Egypt saw Kush as a source for exotic goods, especially gold and copper, both highly prized by the Egyptian Pharaohs.

Art production in the form of ceramics has a long history in the region. Some of the earliest African pottery, the Incised Wavy Line and Impressed Wavy Line types, c. 8000 BCE, was found around Khartoum. In later times Kush became a center for iron-working and the dissemination point for early pyrogenic technologies, such as ceramics and metalworking, into sub-Saharan Africa (Gillion 1991, 55).

Nubian "A-Group" Conical Eggshell-Ware Bowl, c. 3100–3000 BCE In 1907, archaeologist George Reisner excavated a group of prehistoric cemeteries located between the first and second cataracts of the Nile. This early culture flourished between 3500 and 2900 BCE before disappearing, presumably under pressure from Egypt. Although these people were cattle herders rather than agriculturalists, they produced especially fine ceramics in a process that simultaneously combined reduction and oxygenated firing techniques. Reisner gave them the designation Nubian "A-Group." The generic name resulted from the A-Group peoples having been pre-literate so they left no record of what they called themselves. They were also not mentioned in Egyptian texts from the period even though the presence of Egyptian goods in some A-Group burials shows they were trading with Egypt.

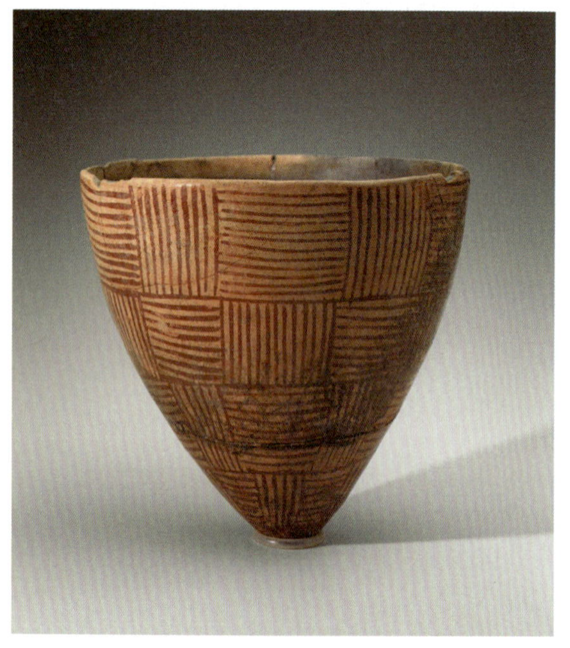

▼ 4.18 Near Egeba, Sudan, Nubian A-Group, Conical Eggshell-Ware Bowl, c. 3100–3000 BCE.

These fine eggshell thin wares feature shiny black interiors and orange paste exteriors with red ocher painted designs.

The A-Group potters produced very fine, pit-fired ceramics that were unlike those of early Egypt. Typical A-Group wares (Figure 4.18) were eggshell-thin, had shiny black interiors and rims, and orange paste exteriors. These two-toned vessels were created by inverting the pot over a mound of organic matter such as chaff, sawdust, or powdered dung during firing (Williams 1986, 25). This created an oxygen-deprived but carbon-rich environment inside the pot. The basket weave pattern on the exterior of this vessel was painted with red ocher pigments.

The First and Second Kingdoms (2500 BCE–339 CE)

Around 2500 BCE a powerful state, known to the Egyptians as Kush, arose at Kerma near the third cataract. Kerma was a wealthy trading center with workshops that produced faience, metal, and other goods. The city was protected by massive earthen walls and deep moats; at its center were palaces and a royal audience hall, elite residences, and an enormous temple, known as a Deffufa. The Deffufa was a rectangular mud-brick structure 62 feet (19 m) high, 170 feet (52 m) wide and 87 feet (26.5 m) deep. Kushite expansion to the north ultimately brought them into conflict with Egypt. After repeated battles along the border, Thutmose I conquered Kush in 1500 BCE and for the next 431 years Egypt controlled all the lands along the Nile as far south as the fourth cataract.

The death of Ramesses XI, the last ruler of the Twentieth Dynasty, in 1070 BCE marked the end of the New Kingdom and Egyptian rule in Kush. The restored kingdom of Kush grew powerful in the absence of a strong Egypt. In 750 BCE, the Kushite King Kashta marched northward into Egypt as far as Thebes, where he took the throne as the first Pharaoh of the Twenty-Fifth Dynasty. Kushite Kings reigned over Upper Egypt until 663 BCE when they were driven out by the Assyrians.

The long period of Egyptian rule in Kush had prompted many Kushite elite to adopt Egyptian dress, customs, religion, and burial practices. Nubian kings and queens built elaborate funerary complexes at el-Kurru, Nuri, and Jebel Barkal that included pyramids, mortuary temples with pylon gates called *bekhenet*, and underground burial chambers decorated with Egyptian style mural paintings. Many of the Kushite pyramids have been destroyed or heavily damaged, but those that have survived show that they tended to be much smaller in scale with steeper angles of assent (68 degrees or more) than those of Egypt. The largest of the Nubian pyramids is that of King Taharqa (r. 690–664 BCE) at Nuri; it has a basal area of 170 feet (51.75 m) square and rose, originally, to a height exceeding 131 feet (40 m). Most, however, like those at Meroe (Figure 4.19)

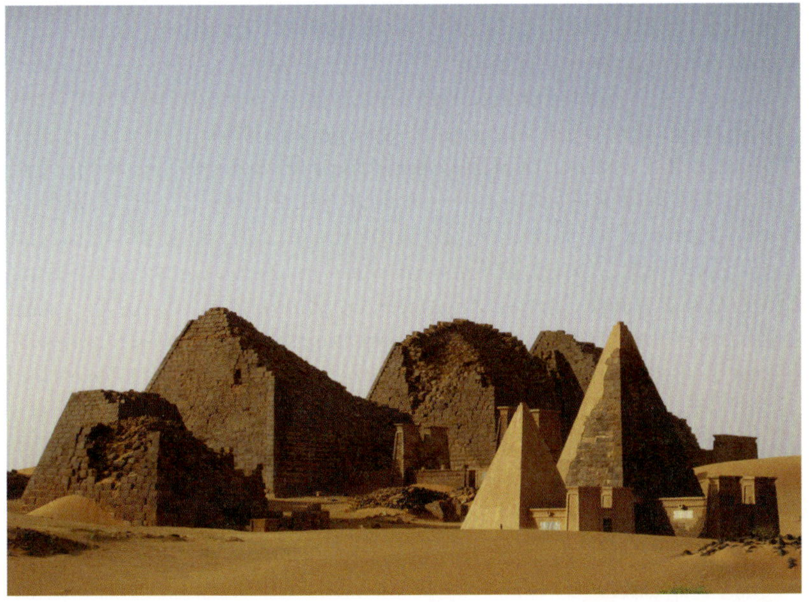

◀ **4.19** Meroe, Sudan, Pyramids of Meroe, c. 720 BCE–350 CE.

Kushite kings and queens built steep-sided pyramids at several sites in ancient Kush. The stone pyramids were often covered with lime plaster and painted. Many were crowned by gold capstones.

were only about 40 feet (13 m) tall with footprints of about 80 feet (25 m) square. Construction was in cut stone or fired brick around a rubble core; the stone pyramids at Nuri were stepped and the corners framed with bands of stone. Others were covered with a layer of lime plaster and then brightly painted; some are thought to have been crowned with gold capstones, long since lost (Yellen in Fisher et al. 2012, 264–265).

Ancient Ethiopia (c. 500 BCE–1270 CE)

To the south of Kush, in the Horn of Africa, archaeologists have discovered some of the earliest evidence of human occupation; the remains of the first human ancestor, "Lucy," were found here. Since ancient times this region, now occupied by Ethiopia, Eritrea, and Somalia, has been a crossroads between Africa and the Arabian Peninsula. The close proximity of the two, facilitated not only the migration of peoples but in later times made Ethiopia the marketplace of Africa. Based on analysis of embalmed baboons from Egyptian tombs, some scholars believe that the ancient Land of Punt, to which Hatshepsut sent an expedition in the fifteenth century BCE, may have been in this area (Perlman 2010). The first recorded kingdom, D'mt, arose in northern Ethiopia and Eritrea around 800 BCE; its traders sold myrrh, frankincense, gold, ivory, rhinoceros horn, and grains such as barley, millet, and wheat. D'mt went into decline around 500 BCE just before the city of Aksum was founded. Aksum came to prominence in the first centuries CE as the seat of a rising empire that would ultimately control not only Kush, but also parts of the Arabian Peninsula. The wealth of Aksum, like D'mt, was based on trade. From their Red Sea port of Adulis (near modern Massawa), the Aksumites supplied salt, ivory, iron, and other products to their trading partners in Persia, the Roman Empire, India, and possibly points farther east.

The Kingdom of Aksum (c. 500 BCE–940 CE)

Worshiping a number of cult gods, among which was the moon god Almaqah, the early Aksumites were polytheists. They buried their dead in underground tombs and marked them with tall stone stelae carved as houses for the dead. The last of these stelae was erected by King Ezana (r. 330–360 CE), before he converted to Coptic, or Alexandrian Rite, Christianity in 341 CE, and made it the official religion of Ethiopia. It was during his reign that the translation of the Bible into Ge'ez was begun. In the eighth century Christianity became a source of political identity and stability for Ethiopia as it was isolated by the Muslim conquest of North Africa. The kingdom went into a long period of economic decline as its access to the Nile trade routes and the Red Sea were cut off. In the early tenth century, power shifted to the Zagwe dynasty, and the capital was moved south to the city of Roha.

Obelisk of Aksum, c. 300 CE Among the more unusual relics of the early Aksumite kingdom are the soaring stone stelae, often inaccurately described as obelisks. The stelae were carved from single blocks of nepheline syenite, a native granite-like stone that when freshly quarried reveals a glittering blue surface (Phillipson 2014, 47). The stelae were erected as markers over the subterranean tombs of early kings and nobles and represented symbolic residences of the dead. Most of the stelae appear to have doors in the base but these, and the windows of the upper levels, are blind. The stelae are interesting in that they replicate in carved stone the vernacular Aksumite building practice of the time, which alternated layers of stone and wood construction. Every few courses as the stone was laid up, pairs of heavy wooden timbers, running the length of the wall, were set in, and the stonework resumed. These timbers were braced at intervals along their span by shorter transverse logs, notched to hold the main beams in place. The circular elements on the façades of stelae imitate the projecting ends of these shorter timbers, known as "monkey heads."

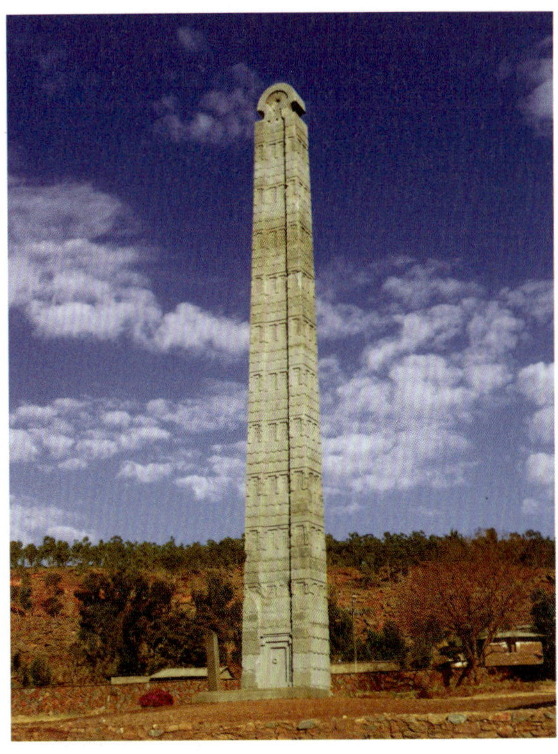

▲ 4.20 Aksum, Ethiopia, the Obelisk of Aksum, c. 300 CE. Nepheline syenite, 80 ft. high.

These monumental stelae served as markers over the subterranean tombs of early Aksumite kings and queens. They are carved to replicate the construction used in Ethiopian vernacular architecture of the period.

This architectural decoration covered the front and sides of the stelae, but the back was usually left plain. Some of the stelae rose to remarkable heights considering they were carved from a single block of stone. The tallest known, the Great Obelisk, stood 108 feet (33 m) high before it toppled and broke. The tallest now standing is the 80 foot (24.6 m) Obelisk of Aksum (Figure 4.20), commonly called the "Rome Stele", because it was carted off to Rome in 1937 by Mussolini's soldiers, during Italy's brief colonial adventure in Ethiopia. The stele was finally repatriated in 2005. Its façade is divided into ten stories, which is something of an architectural exaggeration since the tallest Aksumite buildings only reached four stories. The top of the stele is carved into a tall crescent-shaped finial, thought to represent the moon.

The Zagwe Dynasty (c. 940–1270 CE)

The decline of the Aksumite kingdom provided an opportunity for the rise of the Zagwe dynasty. The Zagwe were part of the Agew ruling class from the central and northern highlands of Ethiopia. They based their claim to the throne on their first king, Mara Takla Haymanot, having married the daughter of the last Aksumite king. The Zagwe rulers were zealous Christians who built numerous churches across Ethiopia.

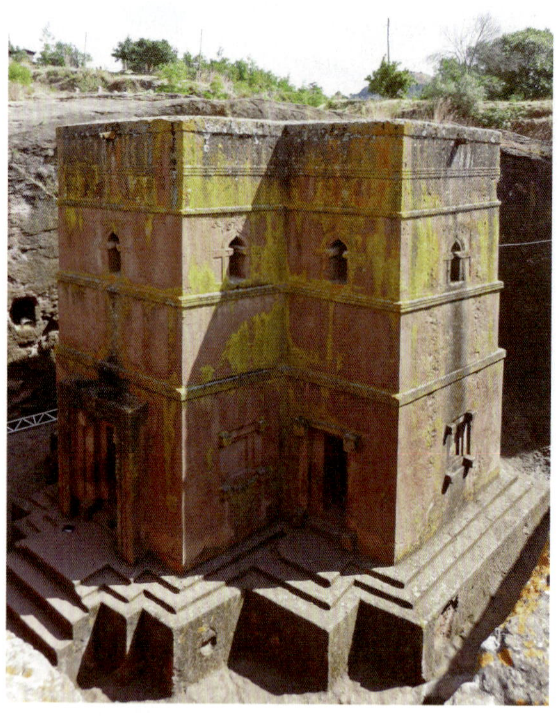

▲ 4.21 Lalibela, Ethiopia, West Façade of Bet Giyorgis, c. 1180–1220 CE. Rock-hewn tuff, 41 ft. × 41 ft. × 35 ft.

Both the church and its surrounding court were hewed down into the native rock so that the roof of the church sits slightly below ground level. Certain elements such as the brackets at the corners of windows and doors are derived from vernacular architecture.

The best known of all the Zagwe kings was Gebre Mesquel Lalibela (r. 1181–1221 CE). He is credited as patron of eleven rock-hewn churches in the city of Roha. The Zagwe dynasty ended in 1270 CE, when its last king was killed by a challenger to his succession, Yekuno Amlak. Amlak's accession marked the beginning of Ethiopia's third royal line, the Solomonic dynasty. The name is based on the claim that the line of kings descended from Menelik I, the son of the Queen of Sheba by King Solomon. The Solomons ruled Ethiopia until 1974, when the last king, Haile Selassie, was overthrown.

Bet Giyorgis, Lalibela, c. 1200 CE King Lalibela is described as a man of great piety who tried to remake Roha into the New Jerusalem. After his death the city was renamed Lalibela after him. The jewels of the city are its eleven rock-cut churches. Six of these, including Beta Madhane Alam, formed a cluster north of the partially canalized stream, called the Yordanos (Jordan), in keeping with the Jerusalemic symbolism of the city. Four more stood south of the river. The eleventh, Bet Ghiorgis (Figure 4.21), was built far to the southwest of the first cluster. While Lalibela was certainly the patron of some of the churches, differences in design and craftsmanship indicate that some were begun long before Lalibela came to the throne and may have only taken their final shape during his reign. Originally the churches were connected by underground passageways, some of which are now collapsed or blocked (Phillipson 1998, 133).

Bet Giyorgis, or the "House of St. George," a Greek plan cruciform church, is thought to have been begun during the latter part of King Lalibela's reign, circa 1200 CE. It was hewn from a single block of red tuff 41 feet (12.5 m) long and wide and 35 feet (10.6 m) high that sits atop a 6 foot (1.8 m) high podium. **Tufa** or **tuff** is compressed volcanic ash and takes its color from the minerals it contains; the streaks of yellow seen in some of the churches are sulphur deposits. Tuff rocks have the advantage of being soft and easy to carve when freshly exposed, but over time, the rock becomes concrete-hard.

To create Bet Giyorgis and the other rock-cut churches, stone masons began at ground level by clearing away the soil and leveling the area. The blank for the church, its surrounding court, and access ramps would then be laid out and the carvers would begin working down from the roof, carving both the outside and inside simultaneously. The progressively lowered court area served as the scaffolding for the workers.

The windows of the upper level were the initial points of entry and portals for debris removal as the interior was carved. Although the churches have piers, columns, lintels, domes, arches, and buttresses, they are giant works of sculpture rather than the constructed buildings they replicate in form (Gerster 1970, 86).

Bet Giyorgis has three doorways on the west side. Only the main portal has a stair; the side doors must be accessed along the narrow podium. Because of its small footprint the interior space is much reduced, consisting of a central square crowned by a shallow dome (visible only on the interior) and four short transept arms. Some of the Lalibela churches were decorated with frescoes but Bet Giyorgis has no ornamentation other than the carved architectural moldings and an oil-on-linen painting of Saint George on horseback slaying a dragon.

Southeastern Africa (1100–1550 CE)

Around 1100 CE the ancestors of the Shona established kingdoms across the Central Plateau of what is today the Republic of Zimbabwe. A characteristic feature of many of these communities was the construction of stone circle enclosures, generically termed **zimbabwe**. The name derives from the Shona root word *dzimbabwe,* which can refer to the court, home, or grave of a chief (Huffman 1985a). In all some 250 stone enclosures have been identified in Zimbabwe, Botswana, Mozambique, and northern South Africa.

Great Zimbabwe (c. 1275–1550 CE)

Great Zimbabwe on the southern plateau is the largest of all the stone circle sites. It was discovered by Karl Mauch in 1871, who believed it to be the location of King Solomon's mines and a palace of the Queen of Sheba. Other early European researchers proposed that the site had been built by the Portuguese, Phoenicians, Arabs, or just about anyone other than African peoples.

Great Zimbabwe actually dates to the thirteenth century CE, when it was the seat of a powerful Shona kingdom. The Shona city was the seat of a long-distance trading empire whose partners included Persia and China, to whom they supplied gold, copper, tin, and iron as well as agricultural and forest products. Archaeologists digging at the site in the early twentieth century discovered a cache of trade goods that included Persian and Chinese ceramics, and Near Eastern glass beads (Reader 1998, 320). The city was abandoned after 1550 CE but continued to serve as a religious pilgrimage site for the Shona well into the twentieth century.

The Great Enclosure or Valley Complex, c. 1275 CE Great Zimbabwe's stone ruins include two major centers, known as the "Hill Complex" and the "Valley Complex." In between the two were densely packed

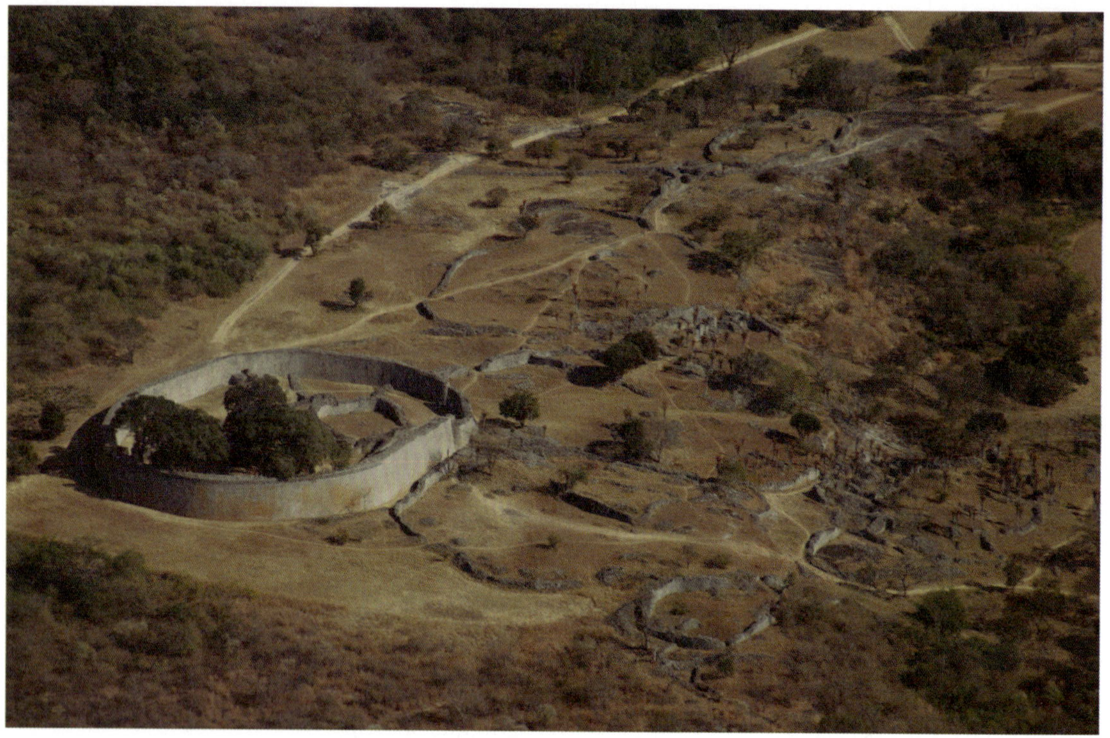

▲ **4.22** Great Zimbabwe, Valley Complex, Great Enclosure, c. 1275–1550 CE. Stacked granite, 290 ft. diameter.

Great Zimbabwe was the seat of a powerful Shona kingdom that traded with partners in West Asia and the Far East. The largest component of the Valley Complex was the Great Enclosure thought to be the residence of the king's senior wife.

neighborhoods of mud huts, known as *daga*, which were occupied by commoners. The Hill Complex sits atop a granite outcrop; it was the residence of the king, and also held a temple in its eastern interior enclosure. The main structure of the Valley Complex is the Great Enclosure (Figure 4.22), which the Shona identify as the residence of the King's Senior Wife. However, it may have had an entirely different, perhaps economic, function.

The Great Enclosure is impressive in scale, being the largest prehistoric structure in sub-Saharan Africa (Garlake 1973, 27). Its perimeter wall runs some 793 feet (244 m) to enclose a circular court that is 290 feet (89 m) in diameter; this large space was further divided by interior walls, creating separate compounds. The outer wall rises to a height of 32 feet (10 m) and is approximately 16 feet (5 m) thick at the base. Both the hill and valley temples were constructed of granite blocks, dry stacked in regular courses to form walls and, in the valley temple, two tall conical granary towers for the storage of locally grown rice and millet. Granite is abundant on the plateau and, in areas exposed to the weather, tends to spall from the rock face in thin slabs that can be broken into roughly uniform blocks through firesetting, a process of fire heating followed by water quenching to fracture the stone (Matenga 1998, 14). The walls of the most important buildings were embellished with stones laid in chevrons, dentil, and herringbone patterns or with bands of dark stone to provide visual contrast.

The Niger River and the Cultures of West Africa (500 BCE–1900 CE)

In West Africa the Niger River plays a role as vital to the economy as that of the Nile in Egypt and Sudan. From its source in the Tingi Mountains of Guinea and Sierra Leone, the river winds some 2,600 miles (4200 km) through sub-Saharan West Africa before emptying its waters into the Bight of Biafra. As the desertification of the Saharan region progressed, some of its pastoralists moved southward into the Niger River region. By the second millennia BCE, several artistically and technologically advanced cultures had begun appearing along the reaches of the Niger River, making this region one of the most artistically dense areas of the continent.

Nok (c. 500 BCE–200 CE)

The first artifacts of an early iron and ceramics working culture were discovered in 1928 near the village of Nok, in Kaduna State, Nigeria, when a tin mining operation unearthed fragments of terracotta sculpture including human and monkey heads along with stone tools. The Nok culture was the first in West Africa to produce nearly life-size figural sculptures in clay and also the earliest in the sub-Saharan region to engage in iron-smelting.

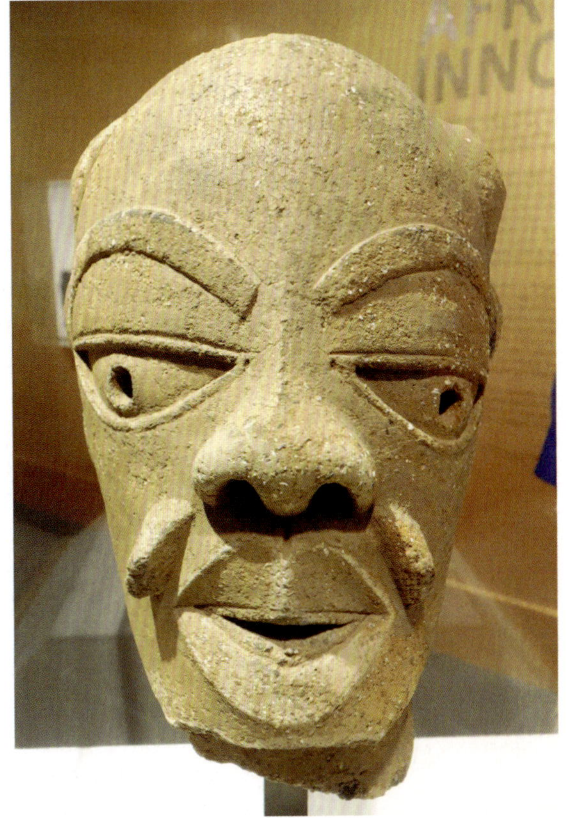

▼ 4.23 Nok Culture, Nigeria, Male Head, c. 500–50 BCE. Terracotta.

This head shows the triangular eyes with pierced irises, broad flat nose, and open mouth characteristic of Nok style. These openings served the practical purpose of venting moisture during firing.

Male Head, Kaduna or Nassarawa State, c. 500–50 BCE The Nok made a range of sculptures that included small-scale figurines, engaged in a variety of activities from simply sitting to riding horses, and large, nearly life-size figures, of which only fragments have been found. The male head (Figure 4.23), is from one of the large-scale sculptures. While each Nok head seemed to be individualized, there are some stylistic elements they all share; these are large triangularly shaped eyes with perforated irises, broad flat noses with open nostrils, and full lips that are shown parted on the hollow pieces. Nok figures were formed in the same manner as utilitarian pottery, being built up by coiling. The coils were thick enough to allow facial features to be shaped reductively by cutting or carving into the clay rather than being modeled onto the form. Finer details such as eyebrows and mustaches were created by appliquéing thin fillets of clay. Hairstyles are often quite elaborate.

Microscopic analysis of the clay used in Nok sculptures shows that a single clay source was used; this suggests that there may have been centralized workshops engaged in the production of pottery forms. This may account for the consistent and ingenious use of facial orifices: mouth, nostrils, ear canals, and pierced irises, as vents for escaping steam during the firing process.

Igbo-Ukwu (c. 800–900 CE)

The archaeological site of Igbo Ukwu, in southeastern Nigeria near the town of Onitsha, is located in the traditional homelands of the Igbo people. The first finds of early metal artifacts were made by Isaiah Anozie, while digging a cistern to store water, in 1939. He found several items of copper and leaded bronze, including a ram's head pendant, a human head pendant with scarification marks on the face, a bowl in the form of a half calabash; a knotted copper manilla or cuff-type wristlet, and a copper support rod for a leather scabbard. Anozie dutifully reported the find to the government but it was another twenty years before excavations began on Anozie's and neighboring properties. The site was a burial complex consisting of a storehouse for ritual objects, the tomb of an elite personage accompanied by four attendant burials, and an associated shrine. The tomb's elite occupant had been interred seated on a stool and dressed in elaborate ceremonial regalia. The tomb was extraordinarily rich, with more than seven hundred metal objects in copper, bronze, and iron, several carved ivory tusks, ceramics, and glass beads produced at Fustat in Egypt. The tomb was radiocarbon dated to 850 CE, meaning that metalworking begins earlier at Igbo Ukwu than at Ilé-Ifè. The presence of the glass beads shows that Igbo Ukwu was also part of a long-distance trading network that extended into the Nile Valley.

▼ **4.24** Igbo Ukwu, Nigeria, Pot on Stand with Rope Netting, c. 800–900 CE. Leaded bronze, 12.68 in. high.

This remarkable vessel was lost-wax cast in stages and the parts joined together by brazing.

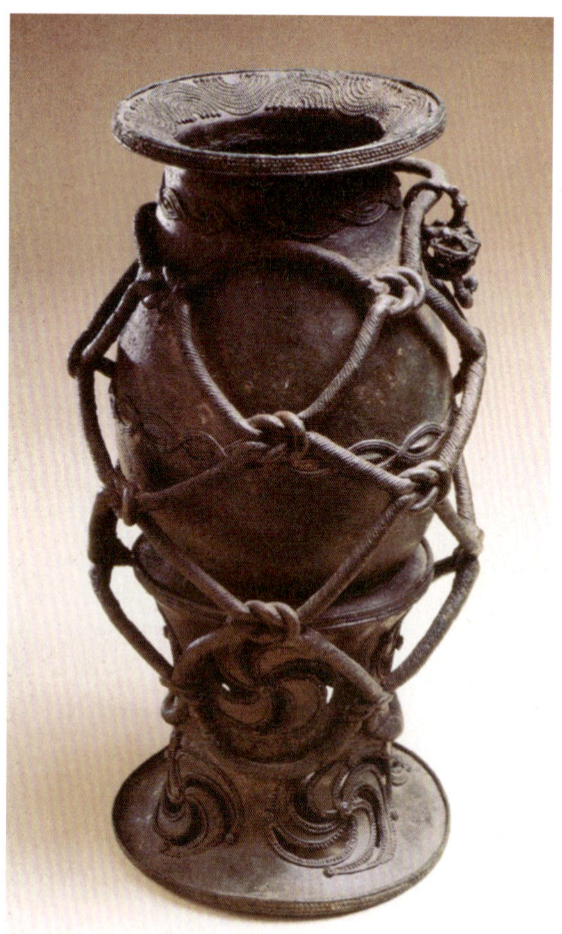

Cast Bronze Vessel with Stand, c. 800–900 CE

Igbo Ukwu metalsmiths created a variety of personal and ritual items in copper and bronze, using the lost wax casting techniques and ores mined in the Benue Valley a short distance north of the settlement (Garlake 2002, 118). These ores contain a high percentage of silver as well as copper, tin, and especially lead, making them distinct from those used at Ilé-Ifè and Benin. One of the more sophisticated pieces was a foot-high (0.3 m) water vessel on a stand bound with rope-work netting (Figure 4.24). The piece was cast in several stages and the resulting parts joined together by **brazing** or burning in more bronze. The ornamental designs on many Igbo Ukwu vessel appear to replicate pyro-engraving on calabashes. The decoration on these is so refined that some scholars believe natural latex rather than the usual beeswax was used in the casting (Garlake 2002, 118). Others show a kind of humorous naturalism by added images of ubiquitous African flies that appear to have just alighted on the vessel.

Sacred Ilé-Ifè (c. 500–1500 CE)

Ilé-Ifè, whose name means "the place of expansion," is the sacred city of the Yoruba descendants of the Ifè. In their mythology, it is the place where the world was created when the god Oduduwa climbed down from heaven, threw a lump of clay into the primordial waters, and set a rooster upon it to spread out the land. History suggests that the area of Ilé-Ifè was originally occupied by the Igbo, who were driven east, in the first centuries CE, by migrating peoples from the north. Yoruba legend has these peoples led by a warrior named Oduduwa. This Oduduwa became the first Ifè king and his sons and grandsons founded the sixteen Yoruba kingdoms.

However Ilé-Ifè came to be founded, by the twelfth century CE it had grown into a substantial city with large royal compounds, residential areas, shrines, and streets paved with potsherds. It had also become an important center for the arts. Ifè artists made utilitarian items and figural sculpture in a variety of media, carving hard stones such as granite, modeling terracotta figures, casting in bronze and copper, and making glass beads. What sets Ifè art apart is its refined elegance and portrait-like naturalism. Indeed, Ifè artworks are so lifelike that colonial historians argued that they must have been produced by the ancient Greeks or Egyptians; it was, unfortunately, a consistent response to African achievements in the nineteenth and early twentieth centuries.

▼ **4.25** Wunmonije Compound, Ife, Nigeria, Memorial Head of an Oni, c. 1100–1400 CE. Brass, 13.77 in. × 4.9 in. × 5.9 in.

The head is thought to commemorate an early, perhaps foreign, king of Ife because of the facial abaja marks.

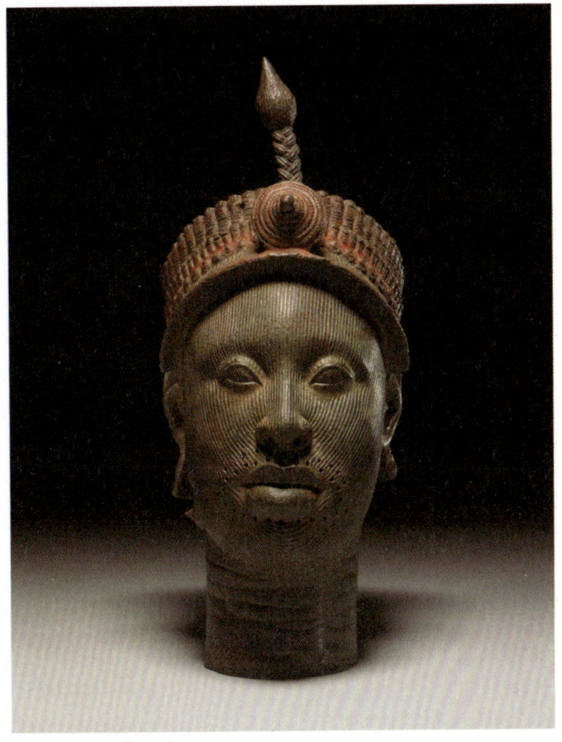

Memorial Head of an Oni, c. 1100–1400 CE The Memorial Head of an Oni (Figure 4.25) depicts an early king of Ifè. The striated oval face is sensitively modeled with full lips, almond-shaped eyes, and prominent fleshy-tipped nose. Ifè memorial heads are divided into two general types: plain and striated.

The striations are thought to represent *abaja* or facial scarification marks; however, the rulers of Ilé-Ifè were not known to have worn facial marks in historical times. It has been suggested that the striated portrait heads belong to an earlier line of kings associated with Oduduwa while the unmarked ones represent later kings who retook power from the foreigners (Adepegba 1986, 85–87). Both types of heads are punched around the hairline for the attachment of a headdress or wig, except in those cases where one was modeled on as part of the original piece. Some figures were also punched around the mouth for the addition of facial hair. Additionally, some heads show traces of pigment, and in one case gilding, indicated that some may have been painted to make them more lifelike.

The Kingdom of Benin (c. 1000–1897 CE)

The cultural influence of Ilé-Ifè extended far beyond the Yoruba, exerting a major influence on the development of the Kingdom of Benin in southeastern Nigeria. According to the oral histories of both peoples, the Edo of Benin after a long period of dissatisfaction with the rule of a mythical first dynasty, known as the Ogiso, appealed to the Oni Oduduwa to send a prince to rule over them, and to found a new royal dynasty. Prince Oranmiyan was sent to Benin and his son Eweka, by an Edo woman, is considered to have been the first **oba** or king of Benin.

The Benin also received knowledge of metal casting from Ilé-Ifè. The introduction of metalworking to Benin is credited to the fourteenth century Oba Oguola. According to tradition, he sent an emissary to the Oni of Ifè requesting a master metal caster be sent so that the Benin could make memorials to record important events. The oni granted the request, sending a master named Igueha to Benin. Prior to this time memorial brasses had been made for the Benin rulers by artisans in Ilé-Ifè (Egharevba 1960, 12).

Head of an Oba, Benin, sixteenth century CE Since metal casting was believed to have been brought to Benin from Ilé-Ifè, scholars have long assumed that the earliest works are the most naturalistic and thinnest walled in imitation of the Ifè prototypes. This assumption may not be completely accurate, as some oral traditions suggest that the Benin already had a tradition of metal casting long before the reign of Oguola. It may simply be that a new type of cast object was inaugurated under Oguola (Ben Amos 1980, 17–18).

However, the arrival of the Portuguese in 1485 CE was the catalyst for the dramatic changes in Benin metal casting. Prior to the arrival of the Portuguese, the number and scale of objects cast in brass (copper and zinc alloy) was limited by the local scarcity of metal ores. Trade with Europeans not only made the kingdom wealthy but also provided an abundance of raw materials. It is likely that the increased availability of metals inspired the creation of larger and thicker-walled pieces, simply because the casters did not have to be so careful with the metal.

The cast-brass *Head of an Oba* (Figure 4.26) is an idealized portrait of a Benin king in the prime of his life. He wears a cap of coral beads and several coral necklaces. Compared to Ifè style memorial heads, this one is considerably more stylized; the features have an abstract quality, the eyes are large and linear, the nose is flatter and more angular, and the lips have a harder quality. The straightforward gazing eyes, which would have included iron inlays, possess the ability to see into the other world, communicating the divine power of the oba to survey his kingdom. The beaded coral headdress and collar are depictions of the king's royal regalia. To the Edo, coral had particular importance because of its associations with the ancestral realms of the sea and immense wealth of the oba gained through maritime trade with Europe. The opening in the top of the head would have held an ivory tusk. Such tusks were carved with human figures that referenced significant events in the kings reign or with animals that symbolized his power.

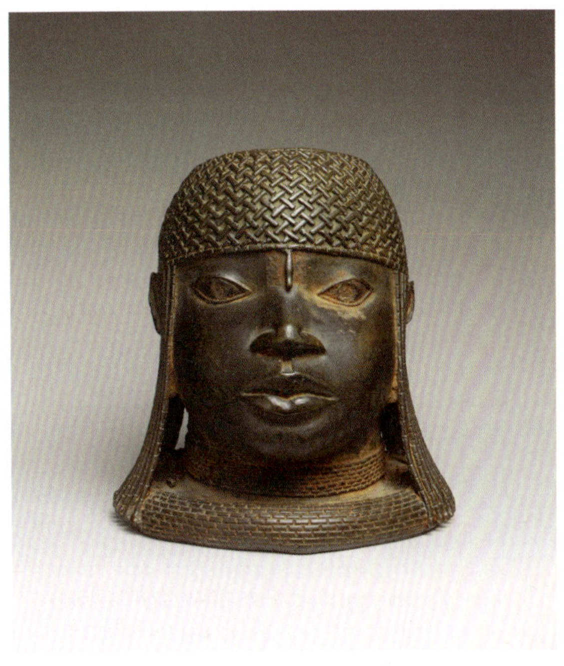

▲ **4.26** Benin, Nigeria, Head of an Oba, c. sixteenth century. Brass, 9.25 in. × 8.62 in. × 9 in.

Upon the death of the Oba, a commemorative head, such as this one, would be cast. Although naturalistic the work is idealized, like Egyptian Ka portraits, to show the king as youthful and vigorous.

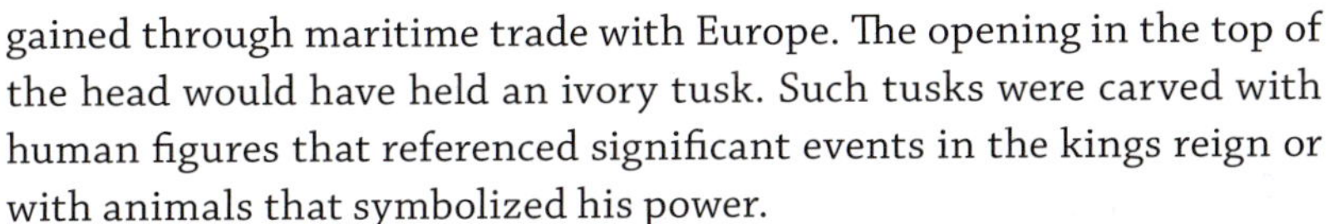

The relatively minor amount of brass used to make this casting and the minimal amount of regalia depicted indicate that the head was created during the earlier half of the sixteenth century. Art historians have suggested that over the centuries, as greater quantities of brass became available, casters had less incentive to be economical with the material, and the trappings of office worn by the kings of Benin became more ostentatious.

The Arts in Colonial Africa (1800–1976)

The first European traders began arriving in Africa in the fifteenth century, but it was not until four hundred years later, in the "Scramble for Africa", that the continent was parceled out among colonial powers without the assent of any African. The administrators, explorers, and missionaries, who arrived during the Colonial Period to administer and Christianize these lands, collected works of "Tribal Art," especially masks and sculptures, primarily as curiosities of savage races. These collections filled private curio cabinets, before ultimately ending up in ethnography museums. Europeans viewed most African sculpture, ceramics, and textiles in the light of their own culture's distinctions between fine art and craft, and notions of "art for art's sake"—concepts that did not exist in Africa. African artists viewed art as skillful execution without

VISUAL COMPARISON

Islam in Africa: A Comparison of the Mosques of Kairouan and Djenné

Islam was first introduced into Africa from the Arabian Peninsula, when early followers of the Prophet Muhammad, fleeing persecution in Mecca, crossed the Red Sea and took refuge in Eritrea. Following the death of the Prophet, the Rashidun caliphs began the conquest of North Africa, wresting Egypt and Libya from the Byzantine Empire and continuing westward into Tunisia. The Islamization of the North was completed under the Umayyad caliphs when Arab armies reached the Atlantic in 706 CE. The spread of Islam southward into sub-Saharan Africa occurred more gradually, being carried primarily by traders along the caravan routes into the interior. Many rulers in the Sudano-Sahelian region did not convert until the fourteenth century CE or later.

The first African mosque was built by the Arab general Uqba ibn Nafi at the center of the city of Kairouan, which he founded in 670 CE. It was known as the Great Mosque of Kairouan. That first mosque was destroyed twenty years later when Berbers captured the city. The earliest parts of the current mosque date from the mid-ninth century CE, when it was rebuilt by the Emir of Ifriqiya, Abou Ibrahim Ahmad.

The Great Mosque of Kairouan is an Arab-plan mosque, a type principally built by the Umayyad and Abbasid caliphs (see Chapter 5). These mosques are usually rectangular in layout with a flat-roofed hypostyle prayer hall and an enclosed, arcaded courtyard. The Great Mosque's hypostyle hall features repurposed Roman and Byzantine stone columns that support horseshoe

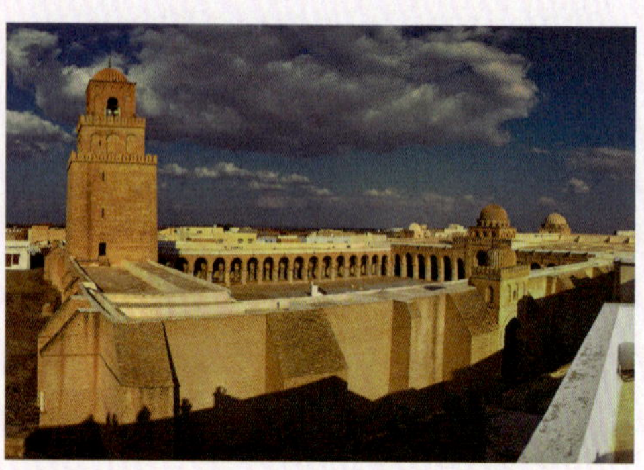

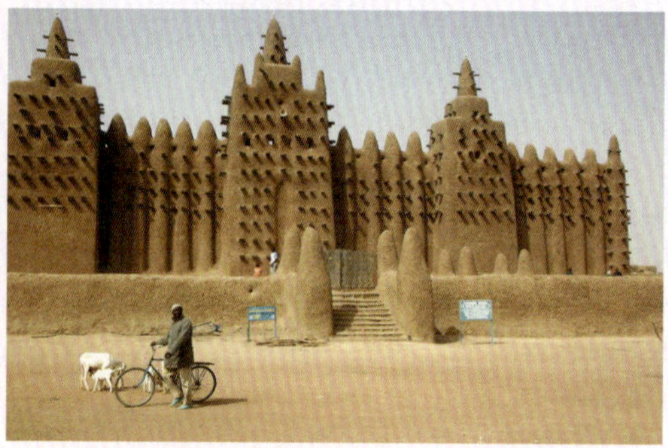

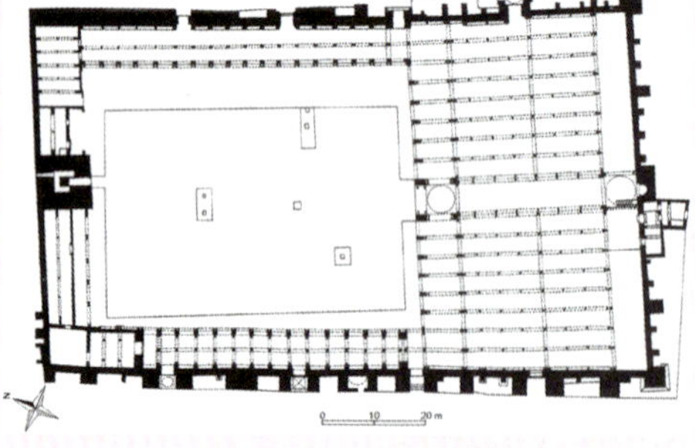

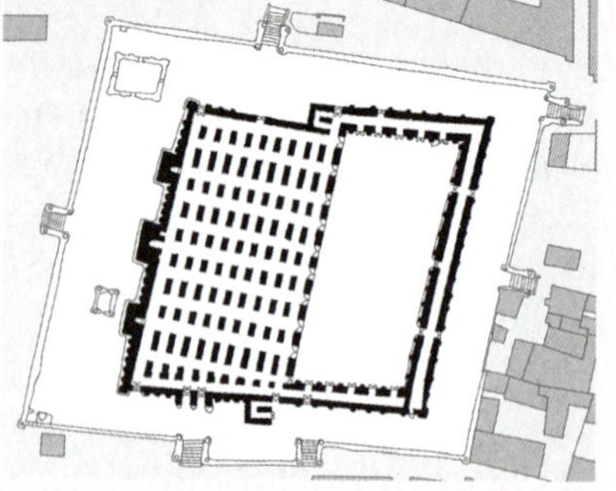

▲ 4.27 L: Great Mosque of Kairouan, Tunisia, c.863 CE; R: Great Friday Mosque, Djenné, Mali, 1907 CE.

The first African mosque at Kairouan established the Arab-style mosque in Africa. This mosque-type followed the spread of Islam in the continent with some adjustments due to location and available materials.

arches; Kairouan's arches are one of the first instances of the use of this type of arch in Islamic architecture. The Great Mosque of Kairouan was an important pilgrimage center for African Muslims unable to make the hajj to Mecca, a fact which may have influenced later mosque design such as the Great Friday Mosque of Djenné in Mali.

The Great Friday Mosque in Djenné, according to tradition, was originally the palace of Koy Konboro, the twenty-sixth king of Djenné. When he converted to Islam around 1300 CE, he gave his palace to be the first mosque. The name "Friday Mosque," or *masjid-I jami`* in Arabic, means that the Djenné mosque is a congregational mosque, large enough to hold the community for prayers on Friday, the Islamic holy day. Konboro's transformed palace was used for almost six hundred years until the city fell to the Fulani under Sekou Amadou in the early nineteenth century. Amadou considered it too ornate to be a proper mosque and allowed it to fall into ruin. The current structure was rebuilt, in 1907, on the platform and foundations of the fourteenth century mosque but it is not an exact replica of Konboro's original. The rebuilding was done with financial assistance from the colonial government of French Sudan (Mali). The mosque was designed by Ismaila Traore, head of the mason's guild in Djenné. Traore was experienced with traditional adobe architecture and worked in the generic neo-Sudanese style preferred by colonial administrators (Cotter 2012). The mosque sits on a 9 foot (3 m) high platform because of its location between two rivers.

The Great Friday Mosque was built in a modified Arab plan; its modifications, necessitated because the platform is skewed to the northeast, make the building more of a parallelogram than a true rectangle. It has a pillared, rather than columned, hall that can accommodate three thousand worshipers, and an arcaded courtyard that can accommodate many more. The location of the ***qibla*** or prayer wall is indicated on the exterior by three 36 foot (11 m) high towers; each of these is topped by ostrich egg finials, associated in the local tradition with fertility and the cosmos (Visona et al. 2008, 111). The ***mihrab*** or prayer niche is set into the base of the central tower.

Like much of the local vernacular architecture, the Great Friday Mosque is constructed of adobe blocks, some 2 feet thick at the base and gradually tapering to 16 inches at the top of the wall. The walls are further stabilized with palm trunk beams, called ***torons***. The torons also serve as scaffolding for the annual re-mudding of the building. One traditional feature missing in the Great Friday Mosque is a minar or minaret due to the potential instability of a tall, freestanding adobe tower. The interior of the building is plain with unembellished mud-plastered walls and piers, and a bare earthen floor that is covered with prayer rugs used by the faithful.

distinctions of media; one work was not more important than another because it was carved in wood or cast in bronze. Unlike European "fine art," all art in Africa was functional. Masks were made for funerals, initiations, and other rituals; sculptures were carved to communicate with the spirits; everything was created for a purpose. European perceptions of African art colored the way this art was written about; objects were categorized by culture and purpose rather than as the works of particular artists, even though that information was, in many cases, available. It was not until European Modernists, among them Picasso, Vlaminck, and Matisse, discovered the "primal power" of these works that the shift of artifact to art occurred in the Western mind.

The acceptance of African art *as art* and its movement from natural history and ethnography museums into art museums did little to

TAKE A CLOSER LOOK

Afro-Portuguese Ivories: The First Tourist Art

Tourist art or works made by indigenous artisans to appeal to a market of foreign visitors, was generally thought to be a post–World War II phenomenon in Africa, when increased air travel encouraged Western tourism to the continent. However, the earliest tourist art works were produced centuries earlier by enterprising West African artists who, beginning in the fifteenth century CE, saw a promising new market for ivory carvings in the arrival of European explorers and traders. These works are often designated as "Sapi," a term that is essentially meaningless as the Portuguese used it indiscriminately to refer to a variety of peoples they encountered in West Africa, particularly in what is now Sierra Leone.

The term "tourist art" generally carries a negative connotation, implying that the works are of lesser quality than those indigenous craftsmen would have made for use within their own communities; again, reflecting Western notions of "traditional" artworks being more "authentic" than those carved for markets. This idea, of course, ignores the fact that pre-Colonial African artists usually made works for specific clients and purposes. Certainly, the Afro-Portuguese ivory carvings illustrate the highest levels of artistry and craftsmanship. Ivory carving was an elite craft in Africa; works

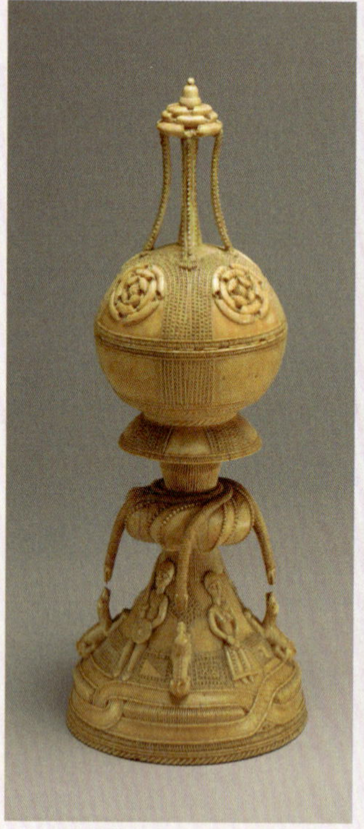

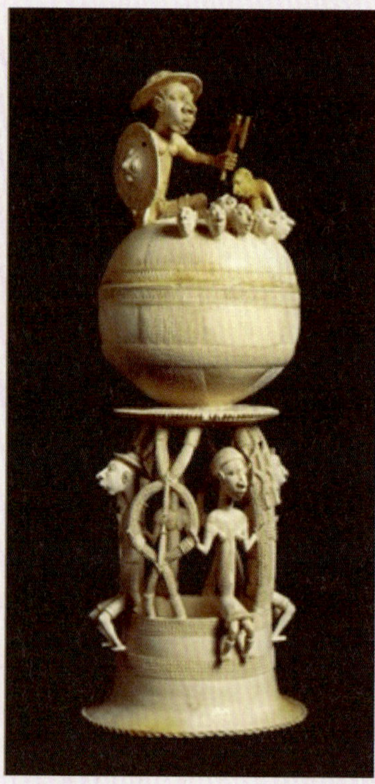

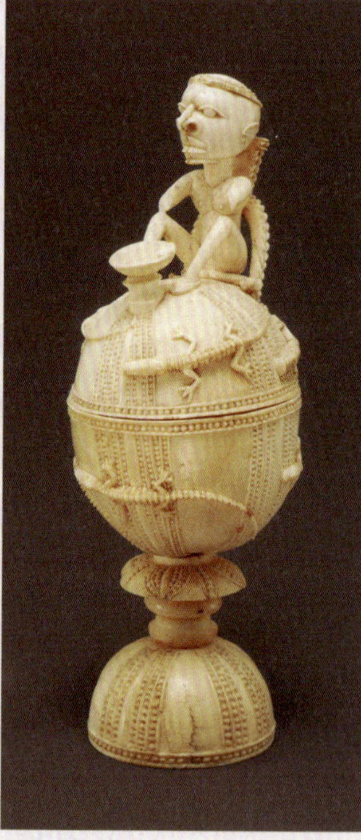

▲ **4.28** Sapi-Portuguese Salt Cellars, Sierra Leone, 15th-16th CE, ivory, Left: 11.75 in. (29.8 cm); Center: "Master of the Symbolic Execution," 16.87 (42.84 cm); Right: 8.12 in. (20.63 cm).

Ivory salt containers such as these were made for the European market often incorporated native and Portuguese figures, the latter recognizable by their short pants and helmets.

in ivory were commissioned only by kings, so the carvers who would have access to ivory and who had the skill to work it, were among the upper ranks of master carvers. The ivories—salt cellars, spoons, hunting horns—were also elite items in Europe, affordable only by the wealthiest individuals. These items often combined elements of both European and African origin. Many of the hunting horns, for example, bear the crests of European noble families and motifs derived from Renaissance decoration. These three cellars show African and Portuguese persons, each identifiable by their clothing; African women wear skirts and bear scarification marks, while the Portuguese wear breeches, helmets, and carry shields and weapons. Animals are also represented including snakes, crocodiles, and dogs which have various meanings in African and European cultures. The center cellar is attributed to the Master of the Symbolic Execution, an extraordinary master carver, whose name results from his treatment of the execution scene displayed on the lid of the cellar in which a Portuguese soldier prepares to decapitate a native man, while on the base, an audience of native women and Portuguese soldiers alternate around the rim of a well.

change the anthropological way in which it was discussed, or how it was labeled—"Primitive," "Tribal," or "Traditional." Each of these terms presented problems and each was more descriptive of European attitudes than of the art itself. "Primitive" was used to refer to people who were at a preindustrial level of development; they had tools but not machines, and created art that provoked in the mind images of horrid rites, fertility rituals, and superstition (Price 1989, 2). "Tribal" was considered less to be Eurocentric than the term "primitive" but "tribal" still suggested a lesser level of cultural and technical development in contrast to that of "non-tribal or civilized" peoples. Even the seemingly innocuous "traditional" suggests an art that is rooted in the past and frozen in time, and artists who are constrained by society and unable to innovate or create freely.

In the minds of collectors and museum curators, the subtext of these terms constituted a standard of authenticity. Works that were made in response to new markets or represented evolving forms were often dismissed as inauthentic and branded "tourist art." Still, some efforts were made to start recording the names of the artists who made specific works; they were known in their communities, of course, but they were not lionized in the same way as Western artists, a fact that also created problems for historians and curators trying to write new histories of African art.

The Dogon

The Dogon of Mali are a good example of the impact of Eurocentrism on the perception of African artworks. In the fourteenth century CE, they moved to the Bandiagara escarpment of central Mali, fleeing subjugation by the Mossi Empire. On the way they were joined by other groups also forced out by the Mossi. When they arrived in the Bandiagara, the area was already occupied by a people whom the Dogon called "Tellem," meaning "We found them there." These people, too, seem to have been

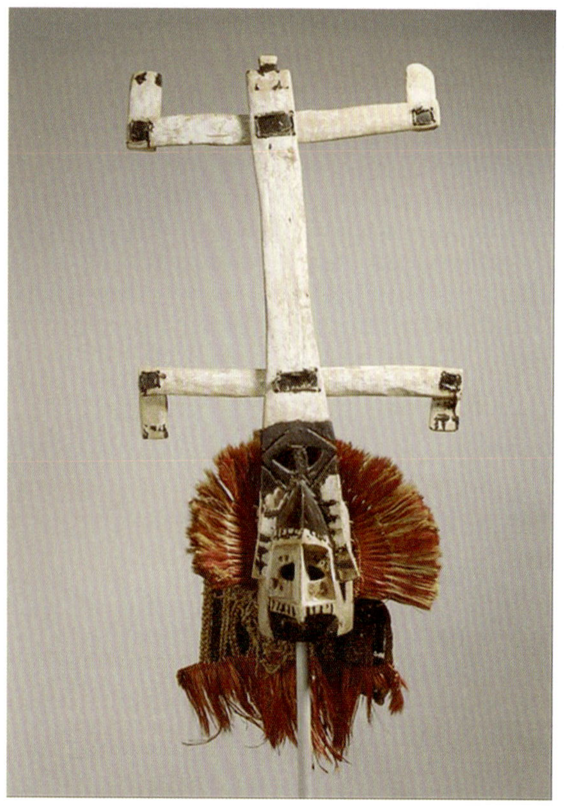

▲ **4.29** Dogon Peoples, Mali, Kanaga Mask, twentieth century CE. Wood, fiber, hide, and pigment, 21.12 in. × 38.25 in. × 6.25 in.

Kanaga Masks were danced during the dama funerary rituals intended to help the souls of the dead leave the village.

assimilated by the Dogon. The merging of these cultures enriched the art of the Dogon as did subsequent contact with other peoples, including Europeans, because Dogon art is a living art.

Unknown Dogon Artist, Kanaga Mask, twentieth century CE In the first half of the twentieth century Marcel Griaule identified seventy-eight distinct types of Dogon masks, each with its own function and mythology. But in the Western view, only one of these is truly "authentic" and that is the stick-figure-like Kanaga mask (Figure 4.29). The face mask of the Kanaga is the head of a figure sometimes described as human or as a flattened lizard; the body is the vertical post and the crosspieces represent the arms, two of which point downward toward the earth while the other two point upward toward the sky. Missing from most of the masks displayed in museums are the cloth hood that covered the dancer's head, and the costume, consisting of a black and red cloth vest decorated with cowrie shells and dangling beads, dark indigo trousers, and skirts of sanseveria fibers. The masks were typically painted in red, white, and black with black rectangles marking the "joint" of the mask armature.

In the late nineteenth and early twentieth centuries Kanaga masks were danced in the funerary ritual known as the *dama*. The dama was intended to assist the souls of the dead in transitioning from the village into the realm of spirits. During the dama, the Kanaga dancers rotated the masks in wide circle to open a symbolic bridge to the afterlife; occasionally they bent low enough to touch the mask to the ground for the soul to cross over.

The Dogon explanations of the meaning of the Kanaga mask vary according to the audience's level of understanding. Children and the uninitiated are told that the mask represents a bird, an insect that planted the first seed, or a fox. Those who have been initiated into greater levels of understanding within the mask society understand the mask to represent *Amma*, the sky and creator god, who brought all things into existence. It is said that afterward *Amma* rested with his right hand pointing to the sky and his left hand pointing to the earth.

The dama is still performed in Dogon villages. However, the Kanaga mask is seldom danced, having been supplanted by newer masks, representing rabbits, antelope, monkeys, foreign anthropologists, and their

Fulani neighbors, among others, all characters that have relevance in the contemporary life of the community. The old Kanaga masks appear primarily in performances staged for tourists who come by the busload to see "authentic" masks danced.

The Yoruba

Yoruba communities are spread across the nations of Benin, Nigeria, Togo, Ghana, and Sierra Leone. During the early Colonial Period, the power of Ilé-Ifè declined, although it still remained important as a religious center. In its place other Yoruba kingdoms, particularly the Oyo, grew in wealth due to their participation in the slave trade. The British Blockade of the Slave Coast in the early nineteenth century ended the transatlantic slave trade, and precipitated the collapse of the Oyo Empire in 1817. This was followed by intermittent periods of civil war in Yorubaland that lasted until late in the nineteenth century when Ghana, Nigeria, and Benin came under British Rule.

During the British occupation order was restored in the Yoruba kingdoms and the production of commissioned artworks resumed. At that time some Yoruba artists were itinerant, traveling among the various Yoruba kingdoms, where they created works associated with the royal courts. Some of these were ceremonial and ritual items but there were also carvers who specialized in architectural work, creating palace doors, veranda columns, thrones, and other items. One of these artists was Olowe of Ise.

Olowe of Ise (c. 1873–1938), Equestrian Veranda Post, c. 1890–1938 CE Olowe of Ise was born in Efon-Alaiye but raised in nearby Ise. Little is known about his life or artistic training, although presumably he must have apprenticed with a Yoruba master carver who taught him his craft. His career as a professional carver seems to have begun under the patronage of the Oba Arinjale of Ise. The sculptures Olowe produced there made him highly sought after as a carver by other kings in Yorubaland and as a teacher to young Yoruba carvers who apprenticed in his workshop.

Olowe is well-known for his carved veranda posts (Figure 4.30). These figural columns supported the porches in the palace

▼ **4.30** Nigeria, Olowe of Ise (1873–1938) Veranda Post with Equestrian Figure and Caryatid, early twentieth century. Wood and pigment, 71 in. × 11.24 in. × 14 in.

This figure is one of the many veranda posts carved by Olowe of Ise for the palaces of Yoruba kings.

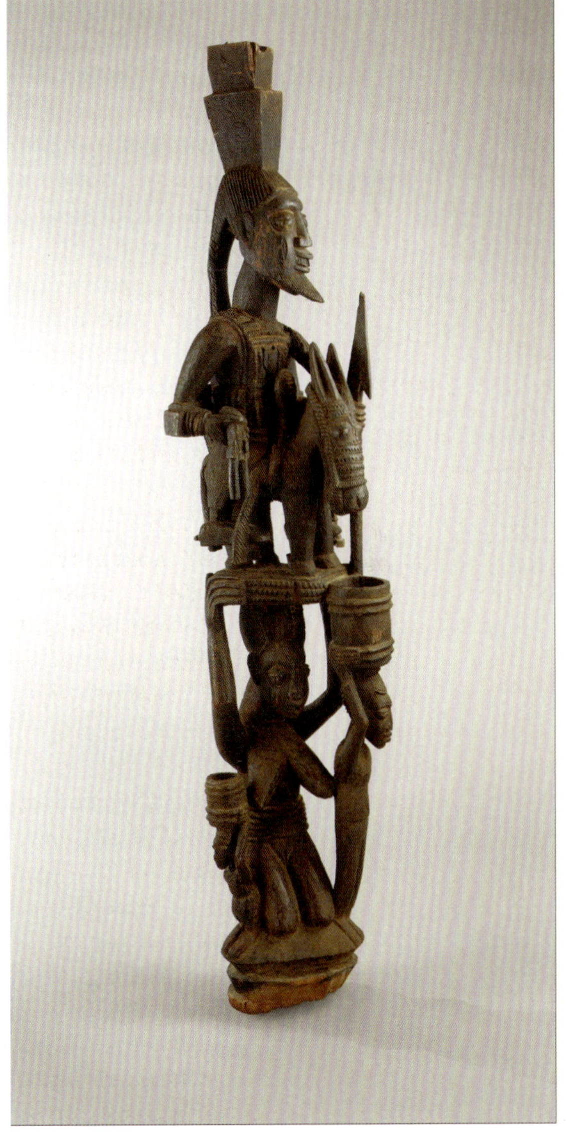

courtyard where the king would sit in state. In African art, equestrian images are associated with kings and warriors, and at least three examples of this theme by Olowe are known. The horseman and other figures on this veranda post feature disproportionately large heads and elongated necks, which is characteristic of traditional Yoruba carving. More unusual is Olowe's treatment of figural proportions and scale relationships between figures. The horseman, for example, shows a progressive, downward shortening of the body so that the figure's legs are only two-thirds the length of the torso, but even with the addition of his mount he does not exceed the height of the kneeling female figure who supports him.

In many of Olowe's carvings female figures exceed the scale of their male counterparts, even when the male figures are more significant in the hierarchy. At Ikere Palace, the figures of women on the veranda posts dwarf the male figures, including that of the king. In this way the artist is both evoking and describing the importance of women's power and supportive role in Yoruba society (Visona et al 2008, 240–241). The importance of the women is further emphasized by the positioning and scale of the two male bearer figures, which raise powder kegs above their heads but do not directly support the equestrian figure. Olowe's primary figures wear elaborate coiffures, and their surfaces are further embellished with relief carving suggesting a brocaded fabric tunic for the warrior and fancy bridle and saddle for his horse; the back of the female figure is decorated with an intricate scarification pattern. The secondary figures are unadorned. Originally, this and other of Olowe's sculptures would have been painted.

The Asante

The Asante or Ashanti, one of the ethnic Akan groups, settled along the Guinea coast between the eleventh and thirteenth centuries, in what are, today, the nations of Ghana and Côte d'Ivoire. This particular stretch of the West African coast was known from the fifteenth century on as the "Gold Coast" because the Akan peoples did an active gold trade with the Songhay Empire (Mali), the Hausa (Nigeria), and various European nations. The Asante are renowned as goldsmiths, potters, sculptors, and weavers who produce brightly colored Kente cloth. In the twentieth century one of the great masters of Asante carving was Osei Bonsu.

Osei Bonsu (1900–1977), Linguist's Staff Finial, c. 1945–1960 CE Osei Bonsu was born in the Asante capital, Kumasi, Ghana. His grandfather was the Asante king Mensah Bonsu (r. 1874–1883) and his father Kwaku Bempah was a drummer who had learned to carve from court artists at the palace. Bonsu's training was provided by his father, who took him on as an apprentice when he reached the age of ten. While he was still in his teens, he began receiving commissions from both Asante and non-Asante chiefs across the Akan region (Ross 1984, 30). In the 1930s, 1940s, and 1950s he worked at several colonial schools in the capital, and in the cities of Accra and Cape Coast. During the 1960s he spent six years, without ever being tried, as a political prisoner after falling out of favor with

Ghana's authoritarian first president, Kwame Nkrumah. After his release, he returned to work as an educator, teaching carving at the University of Science and Technology in Kumasi until shortly before his death in 1977.

Bonsu had a distinctive carving style that set him apart from other sculptors in the Akan region. Instead of the oversized, round, flat faces with stylized eyebrows and nose forming a "T," common to many Asante carvings, Bonsu created three-dimensional, egg-shaped heads with naturalistic facial features. His bodies are well proportioned, rather than stick-like, and show an understanding of basic human and animal anatomy. Many of his works give visual form to the Asante proverbs. One theme that he carved in at least three versions was a Linguist's Staff. The staff (Figure 4.31) is carried by the king's linguist who speaks on behalf of the king, particularly in situations where there may be a challenge to royal authority. The gilded head of the staff shows two men seated at a table with a food bowl between them; one dips his hand into the food bowl while the other watches, gesturing to his mouth or stomach to signal his hunger. The figures illustrate the proverb "Food is for the man who owns it and not for the man who is hungry" (Berns 2014). Food in this case is a metaphor for royal power, suggesting that the office of king or chief belongs to the rightful heir, not to someone who simply wants it.

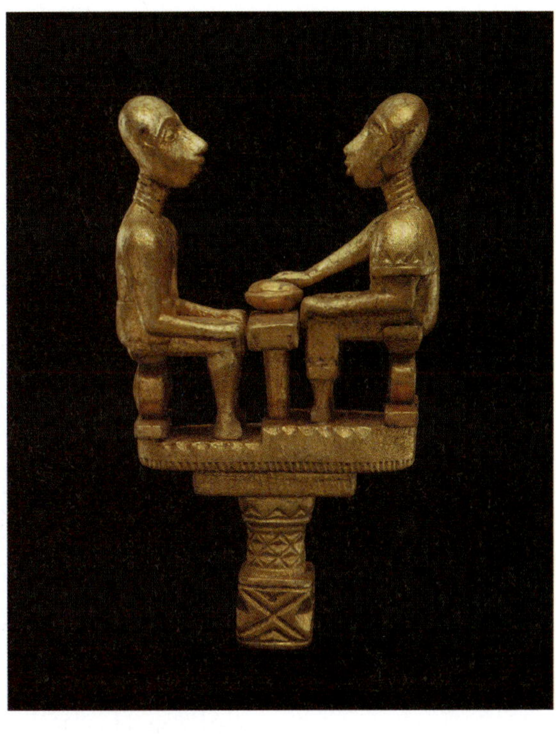

▲ **4.31** Ghana, Osei Bonsu (1900–1977), Linguist's Staff Finial, c. 1945–1960 CE. Wood and gold leaf, 14 in. high.

The two figures seated at a table reference an Asante proverb that states food (power) is for its rightful owner as a warning to would-be usurpers.

Modern Africa (1976–)

Between 1903 and 1937, Western style art schools were founded in Egypt, Ghana, Lagos, Nigeria, and Uganda. Most of these institutions were under the direction of European artists who taught Western Modernist techniques and media. Some African artists also went abroad to attend art academies in Europe and the Americas.

With a few exceptions the decolonization of Africa did not begin until the end of the Second World War. As the former African colonies began to gain their independence, their artists were faced with some of the same challenges encountered by their colleagues in other post-colonial nations. Chief among these was how to define themselves and their art in the new political realities of independence. Some artists supported incorporating Western media, styles, and techniques to express African concepts and concerns while others advocated for indigenous African materials and sources. Still others continued to produce art in traditional, pre-colonial styles. As a result, contemporary African art is diverse, expressing the particular concerns of each individual artist and the community in which they live and work; there is no overarching theme, common medium, or standard style.

El Anatsui (b. 1944), New World Map, 2009–2010 El Anatsui was born in the coastal town of Anyako in the Volta region of Ghana. He was the youngest of thirty-two children. He showed an interest in art at an early age and eventually went to study at the University of Science and Technology in Kumasi, where, because of the university's affiliation with the University of London and Goldsmiths, he received training based in the European academic model. Anatsui moved to Nigeria in 1975 to teach at the University of Nigeria, Nsukka. As an artist and teacher, Anatsui impresses upon his students that they do not have to spend money on expensive art supplies and tools. Instead he encourages them to look for things in their environment that can be made into art. Indeed, many of his works are made from discarded items: bottle caps and milk tin lids, which he sometimes combines with organic materials, including driftwood, clay, and plant materials.

Although Anatsui never practiced weaving, growing up he saw his father and older brothers weave during the off-season. In many of his works, he draws upon that element of his remembered personal history to create tapestry-like works that recall the strip construction of the Kente cloth produced in Ghana. Like Kente cloth, his works carry a meaning in their designs. The massive *New World Map* (Figure 4.32) is

▼ **4.32** Ghana, El Anatsui (b. 1944), *New World Map,* 2009. Aluminum and copper wire, 133.87 in. × 196.87 in.

The artist's materials, often discarded objects and organic items, are selected to reflect the history and environment of Africa, while the concept of the map is in itself a political statement, referencing the arbitrary divisions of land and peoples during the European Colonial era.

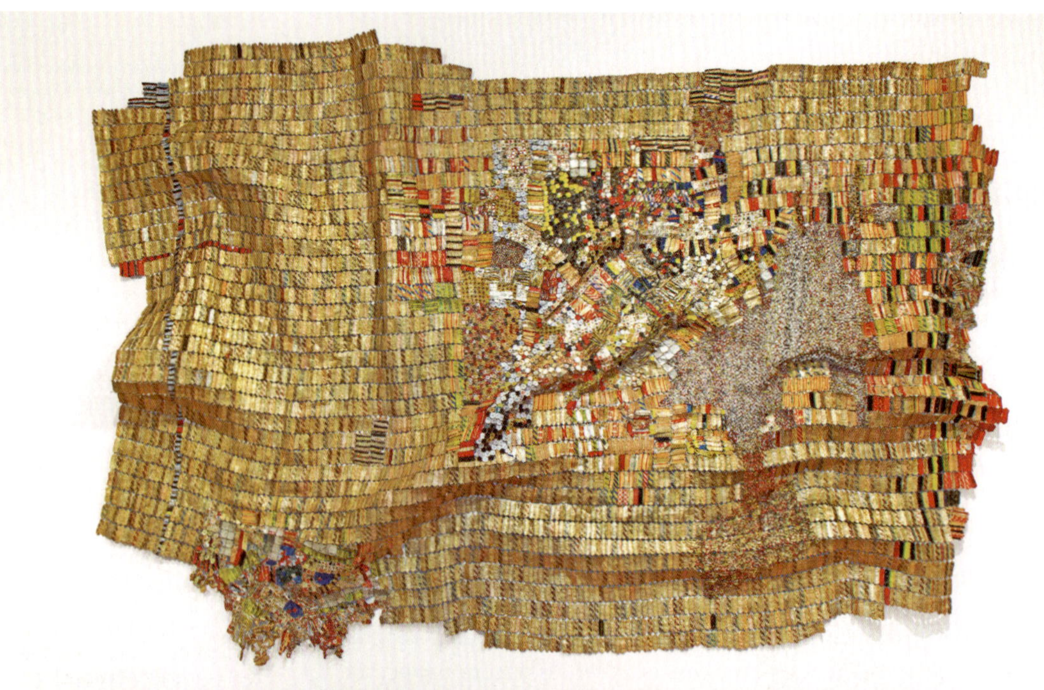

a shimmering tapestry made from copper and aluminum wire and disparate bits of found metal. It is a commentary on the colonial history of Africa, when Europeans redrew the political and cultural boundaries, dividing and recombining diverse peoples. The discarded whiskey bottle caps Anatsui uses to form his map are intended to evoke a particular historical context: the exchange of African slaves for European whiskey (Leciézio 2013). *New World Map* reflects as well on the erosion of traditional arts and culture first under colonialism, and again, by foreign media, advertising, and consumer goods in a post-Colonial world.

Peju Alatise (b. 1975), High Horse, 2014–2015 Peju Alatise was born in a Yoruba community in Nigeria and still lives and works in that country. Her interest in drawing and painting began when she was about four years old; however, her family encouraged her to seek a profession, so in college she studied architecture. Alatise is also an accomplished poet and novelist as well as a visual artist. She works in a variety of media, creating pieces that frequently combine painting, sculpture, and fabric collage.

Alatise frequently gives her works humorous or punning titles; she explains this by saying that Nigerians like to laugh even at the most serious subjects. The societal problem referenced by *High Horse* (Figure 4.33) is the continuing abduction of young girls in Nigeria. The kidnapping of 276 girls from their Chibok school by Boko Haram in 2014 caught the

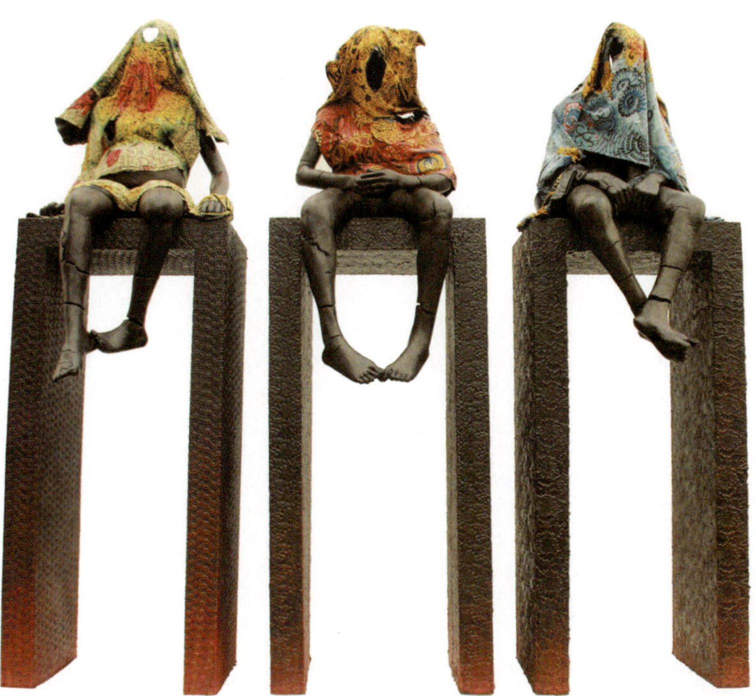

◀ **4.33** Nigeria, Peju Alatise (b. 1975), *High Horse* (Triptych), 2014–2015. Wood, textile, resins, fiberglass, acrylic paints, 92 in. × 27 in. each piece.

This work is a response to the ongoing abduction and sexual abuse of thousands of young girls in Nigeria. The seemingly humorous title for such a serious subject is intended to describe the arrogance of government officials who have done little to stop the practice of sexual kidnapping.

attention of the world but this was not a singular event in Nigeria. In 2013 some 3,600 girls were kidnapped in Nigeria and in the first four months of 2014, almost 2,300 were also taken (Chalabi 2014). The country has no laws prohibiting the marriage of girls as young as eight or nine to men many times their age. Nigeria is fourth among the world's nations for the human trafficking of young girls into sexual slavery. The seemingly humorous title describes the arrogance and contempt of Nigerian officials, who have done little to address these problems. At the same time it also references the artist's activism on behalf of women in her country; since the term derives from medieval descriptions of warhorses, it suggests someone going to battle.

The sculpture shows three semi-nude girls, between the ages of twelve and sixteen, sitting on tall stools; their faces and upper bodies are covered by bright printed Nigerian cloths. One of the girls is obviously pregnant. In Nigeria the designs printed on cloth and the colors used are a symbolic language understood by the groups that produce and wear the cloth as wrappers. Alatise draws on that history and uses the wrappers in this work as a metaphor for the secret miseries and shame suffered by the violated girls. She takes care to cover the female bodies, not only because of her Muslim sense of propriety but also because Alatise sees her works as living beings with feelings.

Chapter Quick Review

Paleolithic to Neolithic Art (100,000–1000 BCE)

- Evidence of art production is in Africa begins around 70,000 BCE with the manufacture of pigments at Blombos Cave, but the earliest existing examples are the much later painted plaques from the Apollo 11 Cave.
- The largest body of early art works, petroglyph and pictographs, is found in the Tassili n'Ajjer region which illustrate the changing conditions in the times before the Sahara became a desert.

Egypt

- Some populations fleeing the desertification of North Africa and West Asia settled along the Nile River, eventually evolving into independent states that coalesced into two polities, Upper Egypt and Lower Egypt.
- The unification of the Two Lands marks the beginning of the Dynastic Period in Egypt. Although people living in Egypt would not have noticed the change, historians divide Egypt into periods of strong government and high art production, called Kingdoms, and periods of lesser cohesion and artistic production, designated Intermediate Periods.
- The development of the first pyramid, the Stepped Pyramid of Djoser, is attributed to Imhotep, the first recorded architect in history. His designs were improved upon by Sneferu's and Khufu's architects, who built the first true straight-sided pyramids.
- Sculpture and painting in Egypt adhered to strict representational canons that ordered two-dimensional figures according to their importance by hierarchical scale and composite view. Three-dimensional works were often

idealized according to concepts of rank and movement was constrained by the need for permanence.
- Under the Pharaoh Akhenaten, the Amarna Period saw the development of new temple forms and idealized androgynous representations of the human form in state art inspired by the worship of the Aten. The first attempts at realism in art appeared during this time in the work of Thutmose of Amarna.

The Land of Kush

- The earliest African ceramics, dating to 8000 BCE appeared along the Middle Nile in what is now Sudan.
- The rulers of the Kingdom of Kush were influenced by the long Egyptian presence in their land and adopted many elements of Egyptian culture and religion including pyramid-form funerary monuments. Kushite pyramids tend to be smaller and steeper than Egyptian prototypes. They were built of cut stone or brick, covered with a coat of plaster and brightly painted.

Ancient Ethiopia

- The pre-Christian Aksumites buried their elite dead in underground tombs and marked them with tall stone stelae carved as houses for the dead. The largest of these stelae reached over 100 feet in height and replicated details of contemporary architectural practices.
- Under the Zagwe dynasty in the tenth to twelfth centuries CE rock-hewn churches were cut around the city of Roha as part of a plan to make the city into the New Jerusalem.
- The Zagwe were replaced by a Solomonic dynasty, claiming descent from King Solomon, that ruled Ethiopia until the 1970s, when the last Ethiopian Emperor, Haile Selassie, was overthrown.

Southeastern Africa

- Stone architecture, in the form of circular compounds or zimbabwe,was built by the Shona kingdoms during the thirteenth century CE. These zimbabwe were the seats of states that traded with the Middle East and the Far East.
- Later colonialist denied these structures were the work of Africans, preferring to attribute their construction to the Phoenicians, Portuguese, Arabs, or the biblical King Solomon.

The Niger River and the Cultures of West Africa

- Peoples moving south from the Sahara brought the arts of ceramics and metalworking into the Niger River area.
- The Nok Culture was one of the earliest in West Africa to smelt iron; they are known for their hollow figural ceramics, some of which were nearly life-size. Nok ceramic heads from larger figures are characterized by prominent triangular eyes with pierced irises, broad flat noses, open mouths and elaborate hair styles.
- Bronze casting appeared around 850 CE at the site of Igbo Ukwu in southeastern Nigeria. The Igbo metal casters made ornaments and ritual item

out of bronze and copper; many of these were found in an elaborate elite burial at the site.
- Around 1100 CE, the Ifè people began casting copper and bronze memorial figures and heads of their kings and queens. The lifelike works showed persons both with plain and striated (scarified) faces. It is thought the distinction may represent two lines of kings.
- The people of Benin appealed to the Ifè Oni for a prince to start a new royal dynasty and for a master metal caster to teach them to make memorial portrait heads. Benin heads are more stylized than their Ifè prototypes and are often larger and heavier due to greater access to metal ores through trade with the Portuguese.

The Arts in Colonial Africa (1800–1976)

- In the Scramble for Africa the continent was divided into colonies assigned to various European states. The Europeans were primarily interested in exploiting the resources of Africa and Christianizing its peoples.
- While missionaries and colonial administrators did collect African artworks, they were not initially viewed as art in the European sense. This resulted in works being treated as cultural artifacts rather than art.
- The names of a handful of African artists who worked in this era were recorded, but their works have been little studied in art history. Two prominent artists of this era are Olowe of Ise and Osei Bonsu.

Modern Africa (1976–)

- Prior to World War II, some colonial powers established Western-style art academies in their African colonies. African artists also began studying abroad in Europe and the Americas at this time.
- As the African nations achieved independence after the war, artists in these countries faced the challenge of creating a new art reflecting their new status. Some artists opted to return to pre-Colonial practices while others embraced modernism as a key to defining Africa's place in a new global world.

Chapter Questions

1. What are some of the issues art historians have encountered in trying to reconstruct the history of art in Africa?
2. In many treatments of African art, early Egypt is not included. How does this affect our understanding of the greater development of art on the African continent? What were the reasons for the removal of Egypt and its placement with West Asia?
3. What are some of the conventions of Egyptian art and how were they applied to individuals of different ranks? How did these change during the Amarna Period? Do you recognize other canons of style in the arts of later African peoples such as the Nok, Ife, or Benin?
4. How did the arrival of Europeans as traders and colonizers impact the development of African art in the Colonial and Modern periods? Be sure to cite specific works as examples.

Key Terms and Figures

Key Terms

Art mobilier "Portable art"; a category of small, moveable works of art.

Canon A set of rules, principles, or standards governing the depiction of the human form in art at particular times, such as in Old Kingdom Egypt; canon is also used to refer to the body of basic knowledge in a field, as in the "canon of art history."

Composite view Also composite pose; figures shown in composite view usually appear with their feet, legs and hips in profile while the torso is shown facing to the front.

Faience Sometimes called "Egyptian Faience"; a type of ceramic containing large amounts of sintered (heat compacted) quartz which produces a brightly colored vitrified surface.

Fresco secco "Dry fresco"; a mural or wall painting technique in which pigments are mixed with a binder and applied after the plaster has dried.

Genre scene A type of art depicting people engaged in the activities of daily life.

Hypostyle Hall A type of post and lintel construction in which the roof is supported by closely spaced columns.

Ka In Egyptian religion one of the parts of the soul, sometimes described as the "life essence," sometimes as a spiritual double that remains after the death of the physical body and continues to occupy the mummified remains or an image made to be its dwelling, such as a Ka statue.

Kente A type of cloth woven in narrow strips and sewn together into larger sections; Kente is woven by men of the various Akan peoples; the colors and designs have particular meanings.

Maat An expression of the cosmic order of the universe as truth, harmony, and justice; personified by the winged goddess Maat.

Oba Among the Edo and Yoruba peoples, the title of king.

Ocher A mineral clay pigment containing iron oxide, producing a range of red, brown, and yellow colors

Petroglyph A rock carving made by pecking or engraving into the stone.

Pictograph A drawing or painting on a rock wall.

Pylon gate Monumental Egyptian gateway consisting of two tapering wall sections with the entrance set between them.

Saff tomb Rock-cut tombs of the eleventh Dynasty in Egypt that were cut in rows into the hillside.

Sunken or Sunk Relief A type of relief in which the image is cut deeply into the stone so that the highest point of the image is below the original surface.

Therianthrope Mythical beings which are part human and part animal.

Tufa Tufa or tuff is a type of rock formed from compressed volcanic ash.

Zimbabwe A circular stone enclosure found in parts of southeast Africa, which contained elite compounds.

Key Figures

Akhenaten—Tenth pharaoh of the Eighteenth Dynasty in Egypt, who proclaimed his devotion to the Aten and initiated a new Amarna style in Egyptian art.

Amozie, Isaiah—Discoverer of the Igbo Ukwu site.

Djoser—Second king of the Third Dynasty of Egypt.

Hatshepsut—Fifth pharaoh of the Eighteenth Dynasty in Egypt and the second woman to rule as pharaoh.

Hemiunu—Architect of the Great Pyramid of Khufu at Giza; son of Nefermaat and grandson of Sneferu.

Henshilwood, Christopher—Archaeologist who excavated Blombos Cave.

Imhotep—Pharaoh Djoser's vizier, architect, scribe, sculptor, medical doctor, and high priest; architect of Djoser's stepped pyramid.

Khafre—Son and heir of Khufu and builder of the second pyramid at Giza.

Khufu—Heir of Sneferu and second pharaoh of the Fourth Dynasty; builder of the first and largest Giza pyramid.

Lalibela—Twelfth century king of the Ethiopian Zagwe Dynasty, credited with building the rock-hewn churches of Roha.

Manetho—An Egyptian priest who lived during the Ptolemaic era in the third century BCE; believed to have written a history of Egypt.

Menes or Meni—According to Manetho, Menes was the ruler who united the Two Lands.

Menkaure—Son and successor of Khafre; builder of the third and smallest Giza pyramid and Great Sphinx.

Mentuhotep II—First pharaoh of the Middle Kingdom who reunited Egypt after the First Intermediate Period.

Narmer—King of Abydos who gave the palette and mace that bear his name to the Temple of Horus at Hierankonpolis.

Nefertiti—Great Wife and co-regent of Akhenaten during the Amarna Period.

Oduduwa—In Yoruba myth a god who created the earth; also, the name of a foreign warrior who became king of Ilé-Ifè.

Oranmiyan—Son of Oduduwa who went to Benin to establish a new royal line for the Edo people.

Reisner, George—Archaeologist who worked in Egypt and the Sudan in the early twentieth century; excavated the valley and mortuary temples of Menkaure and the cemeteries of the A and C Groups in Sudan.

Senmut—Vizier and architect of Hatshepsut's mortuary temple at Deir el Bahri.

Sneferu—First pharaoh of the Fourth Dynasty; father of Khufu; grandfather of Hemiunu.

Sobeknfru—Last pharaoh of the Twelfth Dynasty and first woman to rule as pharaoh.

Taharqa—Nubian fourth pharaoh of the Twenty-Fifth Dynasty of Egypt.

Thutmose of Amarna—Court artist to Akhenaten who pioneered a new realism in art.

Bibliography

Anon.

"Apollo 11 Plaque" The Smithsonian Institution's Human Origins Program, (March 29, 2016) http://humanorigins.si.edu/evidence/behavior/art-music/rock-art/apollo-11-plaque

Adepegba, Cornelius O. "The Descent from Oduduwa: Claims of Superiority among Some Yoruba Traditional Rulers and the Arts of Ancient Ife." *International Journal of African Historical Studies* 19, no. 1 (1986): 77–92.

Adams, William Y. "Post-Pharaonic Nubia in Light of Archaeology. I." *Journal of Egyptian Archaeology* 50 (December 1964): 102–120.

"Post-Pharaonic Nubia in Light of Archaeology. II." *Journal of Egyptian Archaeology* 51 (December 1965): 160–178.

Amer, Amin A.M.A. "Wentawat, Viceroy of Nubia, and His Family." *Studien zur Altägyptischen Kultur*, Bd. 27 (1999): 27–31.

Badawy, Alexander M. "Askut: A Middle Kingdom Fortress in Nubia." *Archaeology* 18, no. 2 (June 1965): 124–131.

Ben Amos, Paula. *The Art of Benin*. London: Thames and Hudson, 1980.

Berns, Marla C. *World Art, Local Lives: The Collections of the Fowler Museum at UCLA*. Los Angeles: Fowler Museum, 2014.

Bondarenko, Demitri M. "Advent of the Second (Oba) Dynasty: Another Assessment of a Benin History Key Point." *History in Africa* 3 (2003): 63–85.

Bourgeois, Jean-Louis. "The History of the Great Mosques of Djenne." *African Arts* 20, no. 3 (May 1987): 54–64, 90–92.

Burstein, Stanley M. "When Greek Was an African Language: The Role of Greek Culture in Ancient and Medieval Nubia." *Journal of World History* 19, no. 1 (March 2008): 41–61.

Chalabi, Mona. "Kidnapping of Girls in Nigeria Is Part of a Worsening Problem." Updated May 6, 2014. http://fivethirtyeight.com/datalab/nigeria-kidnapping/

Clarke, John Henrik. "The Kongo Nation and Kingdom." www.africafederation.net.

Connah, Graham. *African Civilizations: An Archaeological Perspective*. 2nd edition. Cambridge: Cambridge University Press, 2001.

Cotter, Holland. "A Tribute to Islam, Earthen but Transcendent." *New York Times*. April 18, 2012.

Coulson, David, and Alec Campbell. "Rock Art of the Tassili n Ajjer, Algeria." 2013. http://africanrockart.org/wp-content/uploads/2013/11/Coulson-article-A10-proof.pdf

De Grunne, Bernard. *Djenne-Jeno: 1000 Years of Terracotta Statuary in Mali*. New Haven, CT: Mercatorfonds, 2014.

Dieterlen, Germaine. "Mythology among the Dogon." *African Arts* 22, no. 3 (May 1989): 34–43, 87–88.

Drewal, John Henry, and Enid Schildkrout. *Dynasty and Divinity: Ife Art in Ancient Nigeria*. Museum for African Art, Fundación Marcelino Botín, 2009.

Edwards, David N. "The Archaeology of Sudan and Nubia." *Annual Review of Anthropology* 36 (2007): 211–228.

Egharevba, Jacob. *A Short History of Benin*. Ibadan, Nigeria: Ibadan University Press, 1960.

Fisher, Marjorie M., Peter Lacovara, Salima Ikram, and Sue D'Auria, editors. *Ancient Nubia: African Kingdoms on the Nile*. Cairo: American University in Cairo Press, 2012.

Freeborn, Odiboh. "The Crisis of Appropriating Identity for African Art and Artists: The Abayomi Barber School Responsorial Paradigm." Ann Arbor, MI: MPublishing, 2005. http://hdl.handle.net/2027/spo.4761563.0002.103

Garlake, Peter. *Early Art and Architecture of Africa*. Oxford: Oxford University Press, 2002.

Great Zimbabwe (New Aspects of Archaeology), New York: Stein & Day Pub. 1973

Gerster, Georg

Churches in Rock: Early Christian Art in Ethiopia. London: Phaidon, 1970.

Gillion, Werner. *A Short History of African Art*. New York: Penguin Books, 1991.

Gratien, Brigitte. "The Small Seals of the Fortress of Askut." *Journal of Egyptian Archaeology* 84 (1998): 201–205.

Hale, Sondra. "Africa in Antiquity: The Arts of Ancient Nubia and the Sudan." *African Arts* 12, no. 2 (February 1979): 75–76.

Herodotus (George Rawlinson, translator)

The History of Herodotus, London: William Benton Publisher, 1971

Huffman, Thomas N.
"The Soapstone Birds from Great Zimbabwe," *African Arts*, vol 18, 2 (May, 1985): 68 -73 + 99 - 100.
Ireland, Corydon
"The Queen and the Sculptor," Harvard Gazette, October 2, 2013
https://news.harvard.edu/gazette/story/2013/10/the-queen-and-the-sculptor/
Jarus, Owen
"Baboon Mummy Analysis Reveals Eritrea and Ethiopia as Location of Land of Punt," *Independent,* April 26, 2010. https://www.independent.co.uk/life-style/history/baboon-mummy-analysis-reveals-eritrea-and-ethiopia-as-location-of-land-of-punt-1954547.html
Kamil, Jill. *Sakkara and Memphis: A Guide to the Necropolis and the Ancient Capital.* 2nd Edition. New York: Longman Inc. 1985.
Killick, David. "Cairo to Cape: The Spread of Metallurgy Through Eastern and Southern Africa." Modeling Early Metallurgy II. *Journal of World Prehistory* 22, no. 4 (December 2009): 399–414.
Kirwan, L.P. "The Oxford University Excavations in Nubia, 1934–1935." *Journal of Egyptian Archaeology* 21, no. 2 (December 1935): 191–198.
Lacovara, Peter. "An Incised Vase from Kerma." *Journal of Near Eastern Studies* 44, no. 3 (July 1985): 211–216.
Lagamma, Alisa. "The Recently Acquired Kongo Mangaaka Power Figure." *Metropolitan Museum Journal* 43 (2008): 210–210.
Leciézio, Mélissa. "El Anatsui: From Local Colours to International Splendour." *The Culture Trip*, 2013. http://theculturetrip.com/Africa/Ghana/articles/el-anatsui-from-local-colours-to-international-splendour/
Lehner, Mark. *The Complete Pyramids.* London: Thames and Hudson, 2001.
McIntosh, Susan Keech, and Roderick J. McIntosh. "Jenne-Jeno: An Ancient African City." *Archaeology* 33, no. 1 (January–February 1980): 8–14.
Matenga, Edward
The Soapstone birds of Great Zimbabwe: Symbols of a Nation. Harare: African Publishing Group, 1998
Moan, Rebekah
"CT Reveals Queen Nefertiti's Nose Job," *Modern Medicine Network.* April 8, 2009. https://www.diagnosticimaging.com/ct/ct-reveals-queen-nefertitis-nose-job
Mercier, Jacques, and Claude Lepage. *LaLibela: Wonder of Ethiopia.* Ethiopian Heritage Fund. London: Paul Holberton Publishing, 2012.
Morris, James and **Blier, Suzanne Preston.** *Butabu: Adobe Architecture of West Africa.* New York: Princeton Architectural Press, 2004.
Ogundiran, Akinwumi O. "Ceramic Spheres and Regional Networks in the Yoruba-Edo Region, Nigeria, 13th–19th Centuries A.C." *Journal of Field Archaeology* 28, no. 1–2 (Spring–Summer, 2001): 27–43.
"Filling a Gap in the Ife-Benin Interaction Field (Thirteenth–Sixteenth Centuries AD): Excavations in Iloyi Settlement, Ijesaland." *African Archaeological Review* 19, no. 1 (March, 2002): 27–69.
"Four Millennia of Culture History in Nigeria (ca. 2000 B.C.–A.D. 1900): Archaeological Perspectives." *Journal of World Prehistory* 19, no. 2 (June 2005): 133–168.
Pankhurst, Richard. "A Far-Off Country." *Minerva* 26, no. 3 (May–June 2015).
Pearlman, David
"Scientists Zero in on Ancient Land of Punt," SFGATE May 8, 2010,
https://www.sfgate.com/hdn/hrlm/p/callback.html
Phillipson, David W. *Ancient Ethiopia.* London: British Museum Press, 1998.
Foundations of an African Civilisation: Aksum and the Northern Horn 1000 BC–AD 1300. Addis Ababa, Ethiopia: Addis Ababa University Press, 2012/paperback edition 2014.
Price, Sally
Primitive Art in Civilized Places, Chicago: University of Chicago Press, 1989

Quibell, James Edward, F.W. Green and William Matthew Flinders Petrie
Hierakonpolis, Publications of the British School of Egyptian Archaeology, vols. 4-5, London: B. Quaritch, 1900-1902.
Radiological Society of North America.
"Hidden Face In Nefertiti Bust Examined With CT Scan." ScienceDaily. ScienceDaily, 8 April 2009. <www.sciencedaily.com/releases/2009/03/090331091246.htm>.
Reader, John
Africa: A Biography of the Continent, New York: Vintage Books, 1997.
Roehig, Catherine H., editor with Renée Dreyfus and Cathleen A. Keller
Hatshepsut from Queen to Pharaoh, New Haven: Yale University Press, 2005
Rifkin, R. F., Prinsloo, L. C., Dayet, L., Haaland, M. M., Henshilwood, C. S., Diz, E. Lozano., Moyo, S., Vogelsang, R. & Kambombo, F.
"Characterising pigments on 30000-year-old portable art from Apollo 11 Cave, Karas Region, southern Namibia." Journal of Archaeological Science: Reports, 5 (2016): 336-347.
Romer, John. *Ancient Egypt Revisited.* Cambridge: Cambridge University Press, 2007.
Ross, Doran H. "The Art of Osei Bonsu." *African Arts* 17, no. 2 (February 1984): 28–90.
Roth, Ann Macy
"Models of Authority: Hatshepsut's Predecessors in Power." In Roehig et al, *Hatshepsut from Queen to Pharaoh,* New Haven: Yale University Press, 2005: 9-14.
Shafer, Byron E., editor. *Temples of Ancient Egypt.* Ithaca: Cornell University Press, 1997.
Shaw, Ian, editor. *The Oxford History of Ancient Egypt.* Oxford: Oxford University Press, 2000.
Sooke, Alastair. "Akhenaten: Mad, Bad, or Brilliant?" *The Telegraph* (January 9, 2014). https://www.telegraph.co.uk/culture/art/10561090/Akhenaten-mad-bad-or-brilliant.html
Thurman, Christa C. Mayer. "Archaeological Textiles from Nubia." *Bulletin of the Art Institute of Chicago (1973–1982)* 73, no. 3 (May–June, 1979): 12–14.
Van de Mieroop, Marc. *A History of Ancient Egypt.* Chichester, West Sussex: Wiley-Blackwell, 2011.
Van Dijk, Jacobus
"The Amarna Period and Later New Kingdom (c. 1352-1069 BC)." In Shaw, editor, *The Oxford History of Ancient Egypt.* Oxford: Oxford University Press, 2000:272-313.
Verner, Miroslav. *The Pyramids: The Mystery, Culture, and Science of Egypt's Great Monuments.* New York: Grove Press, 2001.
Visona, Monica Blackmun, Robin Poynor, and Herbert M. Cole. *A History of Art in Africa.* 2nd Edition. Upper Saddle River, NJ: Pearson/Prentice Hall, 2008.
Vogel, Susan Mullin. "Art and Politics: A Staff from the Court of Benin, West Africa," *Metropolitan Museum Journal* 13 (1979): 87–100.
Wengrow, David
"Rethinking `Cattle Cults' in Early Egypt: Towards a Prehistoric Perspective on the Narmer Palette," *Cambridge Archaeological Journal*, vol. 11, part 1 (2001):91-104.
Wilkinson, Richard H. *The Complete Temples of Ancient Egypt.* London: Thames and Hudson, 2000.
Williams, Bruce. "The Lost Pharaohs of Nubia." *Archaeology* 33, no. 5 (September–October 1980): 12–21.
Excavations Between Abu Simbel and the Sudan Frontier, Part I: The A-Group Royal Cemetery at Qustul: Cemetery L. Oriental Institute of the University of Chicago, 1986.
"Forebears of Menes in Nubia: Myth or Reality?" *Journal of Near Eastern Studies* 46, no. 1 (January 1987): 15–26.
Willett, Frank. *Ife in the History of West African Sculpture.* New York: McGraw-Hill Book Company, 1967.
Wright, William. "The Whitewash of Egypt: Identifying Egypt and Nubia." *African Arts* 27, no. 4 (Autumn 1994): 10, 12, 14, 16.

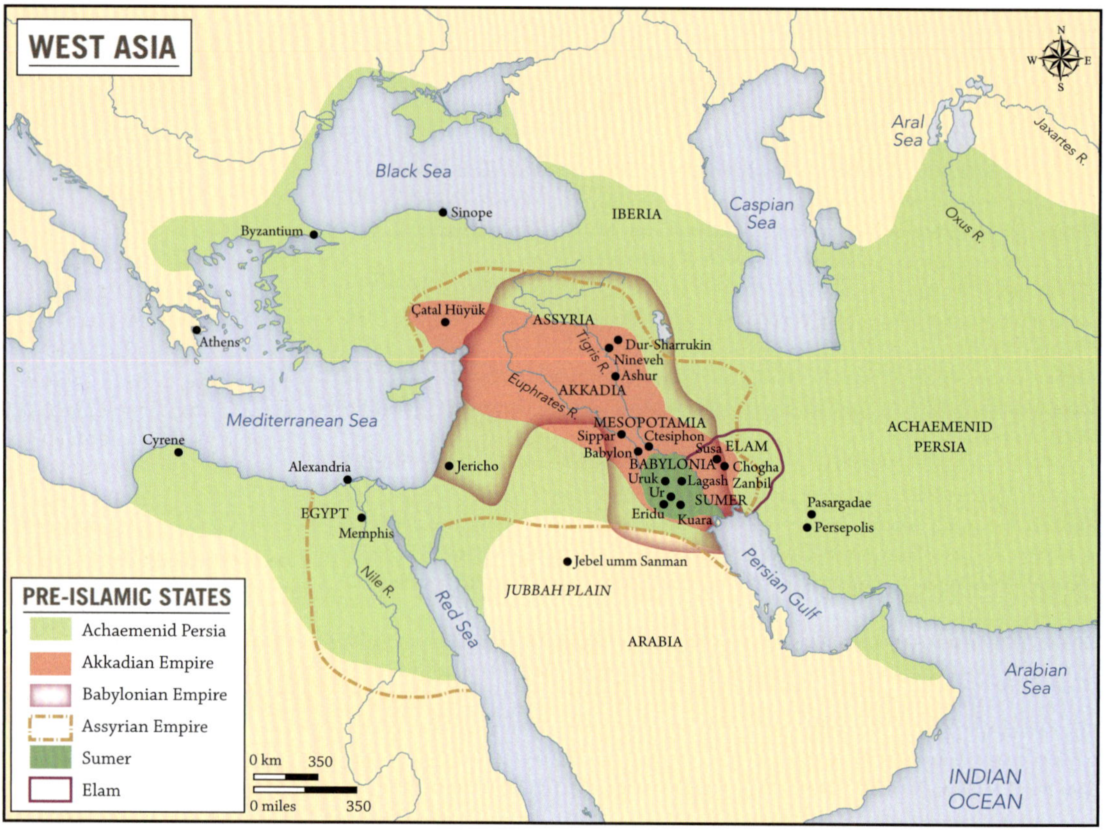

WEST ASIA

Black Sea
Sinope
Byzantium
IBERIA
Caspian Sea
Aral Sea
Jaxartes R.
Oxus R.
Çatal Hüyük
ASSYRIA
Athens
Tigris R.
Dur-Sharrukin
Nineveh
Ashur
AKKADIA
Euphrates R.
Mediterranean Sea
MESOPOTAMIA
Sippar
Ctesiphon
Babylon
Susa
ELAM
ACHAEMENID PERSIA
Cyrene
Alexandria
Jericho
BABYLONIA
Chogha Zanbil
Uruk
Lagash
Ur
SUMER
Eridu
Kuara
Pasargadae
Persepolis
EGYPT
Memphis
Jebel umm Sanman
Nile R.
Red Sea
JUBBAH PLAIN
Persian Gulf
ARABIA
Arabian Sea
INDIAN OCEAN

PRE-ISLAMIC STATES

Achaemenid Persia
Akkadian Empire
Babylonian Empire
Assyrian Empire
Sumer
Elam

0 km 350
0 miles 350

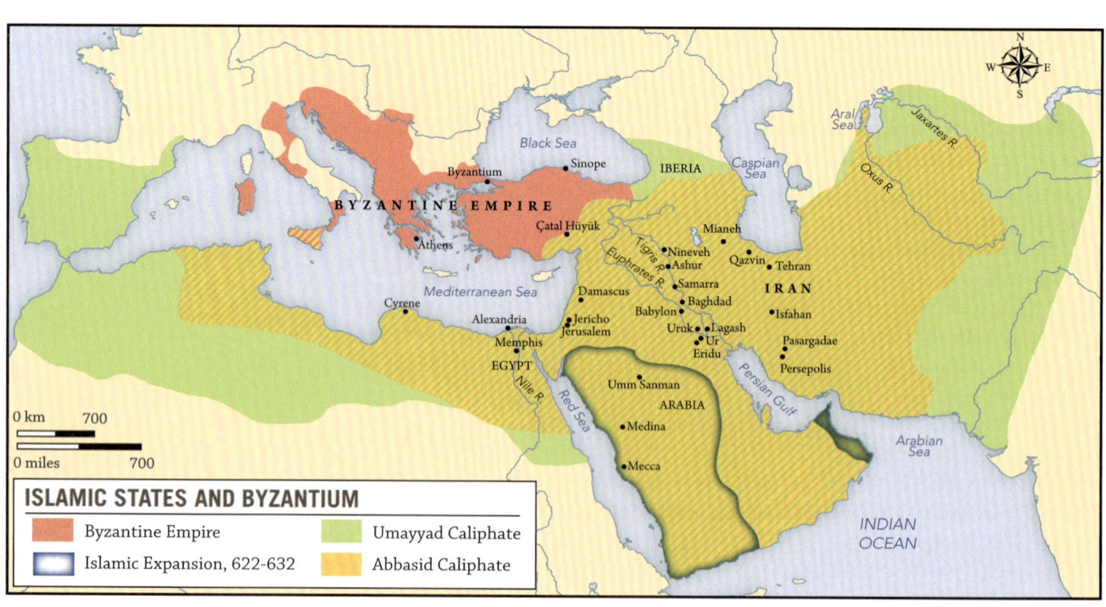

West Asia

5

Brief Overview

West Asia is a wide swath of land abutting the European and African continents at the eastern end of the Mediterranean. The region, sometimes with the addition of Egypt or near parts of Central Asia, has been known from the political perspective of Europe as the Near East or in more recent times as the Middle East. The importance of West Asia lies in its having been one of the early cradles of the arts, civilization, and religion. The world's first cities, Jericho and Çatal Hüyük, were founded very early in the Neolithic Period. Within their walls arose the arts of architecture, portraiture, landscape painting, and sculpture.

By the end of the sixth millennium BCE the first theocratic city states arose in southern Mesopotamia along the shores of the Persian Gulf. These Sumerian cities were theocracies that built towering ziggurats crowned by shrines to their patron gods; they filled those temples with rich offerings, including alabaster vessels carved with the earliest known examples of narrative relief in the region. A succession of nation states and empires followed the Sumerians in Mesopotamia, each enriching their cities with temples and palaces filled with relief carvings and sculptures. Among the great achievements of the early Mesopotamians was the creation of the first royal library by the Assyrian king Assurbanipal; in this collection were preserved some 30,000 clay tablets, including king lists for various city states as well as works of literature such as the *Epic of Gilgamesh*.

Ancient West Asia was also the birthplace of several major religions including the three great monotheisms of Judaism, Christianity, and Islam. The last of these has had a profound impact on the art and architecture of the region from the sixth century CE to the present. The various Islamic caliphates and dynasties that ruled in West Asia built mosques, libraries, hospitals and madrassas, promoted the sciences and sponsored the translation of classical texts into Arabic, and encouraged both secular and religious arts. Painting flourished under the Ottoman sultans, especially during

Chapter Objectives

1. Understand how figurative representation evolved from the earliest times in West Asia and understand the conventions that developed for the representations of gods and kings in anthropomorphic form. Describe how such representations were used to create historical and religious narratives on artworks of various kinds from Sumerian offering vessels to the staircases of grand palaces to the miniature paintings of the Ottoman court.
2. Recognize how city planning developed from simple beginnings in early Neolithic cities into much more complex forms with specific functions expressed in their design. Explore some of the architectural styles that evolved in the ancient Near East.
3. Describe how indigenous styles rooted in earlier religious practice were interpreted by Islamic architects. Understand how Islamic rulers used architecture to make political and religious statements in the areas brought under their rule.

timeline

DATE	TYPE	EVENT
		BCE
c. 8500	History	Settlers arrived in the lower Jordan Rift Valley; Jericho founded
c. 7500	Art	Over-modeled skulls at Jericho and other sites in the Levant
	History	*Çatal Hüyük* settled (Turkey)
c. 7000	Art	Rock art of the Jubbah plain (Saudi Arabia)
c. 6200	Art	First landscape painted at *Çatal Hüyük*
c. 5400	History	Eridu (Tell Abu Shahrein) settled in Sumer, southern Mesopotamia (Iraq)
c. 5000	Art	First temple to Enki built at Eridu
	History	City of Ur founded (Iraq)
c. 4000	History	Susa founded (Iran)
c. 3750	History	Uruk founded (Iraq)
c. 3517	Art	Construction began on the White Temple of Uruk
c. 3300	Art	Warka Vase arrived at the Temple of Inanna in Uruk
c. 3000	Art	Priest King of Uruk Votive figure carved
	Art	Votive figures offered at Temple of Abu in Eshnunna
c. 2600	History	Queen Puabi buried in Royal Cemetery of Ur
	History	City of Ashur (Qalat Sherqat) founded in northern Mesopotamia
c. 2500	History	Enmebaragesi of Kish (Iraq) conquered Elam (Iran)
c. 2400	History	Babylon is founded as a Sumerian administrative center (Iraq)
c. 2334	History	Sargon I established Akkadian rule; conquered Sumer
c. 2285	History	Enheduanna served as High Priestess at Ur
c. 2220	Art	Victory Stele of Naram-Sin placed in his temple at Sippur (Iraq)
c. 2154	History	Akkadian Empire collapsed
c. 2025	History	Amorites (Syrian) migrated into Mesopotamia
c. 2112	History	Ur-Nammu, Third Dynasty of Ur, created Neo-Sumerian Empire
	Art	Great Ziggurat of Ur
c. 2004	History	Third Dynasty of Ur fell to the Elamites
c. 1894	History	Amorites seized Babylon

DATE	TYPE	EVENT
BCE		
c. 1792	History	Hammurabi took the throne of Babylon
	Art	Stele of Hammurabi
c. 1764	History	Hammurabi conquered Ashur, Eshnunna, and Elam
c. 1750	History	Elam conquered Ur
c. 1595	History	Hittites sacked Babylon
c. 1570	History	Kassites took control of Babylon
c. 1454	History	Mitanni conquered Assyrians
c. 1353	History	King Ashur-Ubalit I took the Assyrian throne
c. 1275	History	Untash-Napirisha took the throne of Elam
c. 1250	Art	Untash-Napirisha began Dur-Untash and its ziggurat
c. 1000	History	Nomadic Persians began settling in Iran near Lake Urmia
c. 912	History	Assyrian King Adad Nirari II began territorial expansion
c. 721	History	Sargon II took the imperial Assyrian throne;
	Art	Work began on a new capital at Dur-Sharrukin (Khorsabad)
c. 669	History	Assurbanipal began reign;
	Art	Assurbanipal built North Palace in capital of Nineveh
c. 647	History	Susa destroyed
c. 645	History	North Palace reliefs showing Assurbanipal hunting lions and bulls
c. 626	History	Assurbanipal dies; Nabopolassar seized Babylon throne
c. 612	History	Nineveh abandoned
c. 605	History	Nebuchadnezzar II took the throne of the Neo-Babylonian
c. 575	Art	Ishtar Gate built as part of Babylon city walls
c. 559	History	Cyrus II established the Achaemenid Persian Empire (Iran)
c. 546	Art	Cyrus II began work on new capital at Pasargadae (Iran)
c. 539	History	Persian conquest of Babylon
c. 522	History	Darius I took the Persian throne
c. 518	Art	Darius I began construction of new capital at Persepolis
c. 334	History	Alexander the Great conquered Persia
c. 330	History	Alexander the Great sacked Persepolis

(Continued)

timeline *continued*

DATE	TYPE	EVENT
c. 305	History	Seleucid Kingdom established in Persia
c. 247	History	Parthian Empire conquered Seleucids
		CE
224	History	Parthian Empire fell
	History	Sassanid Empire founded in Persia
570	Culture	Birth of the Prophet Muhammad in Mecca (Saudi Arabia)
610	Culture	"Night of Destiny"; Gabriel appeared to Muhammad
621	Culture	Prophet Muhammad's Night Journey and Mir'aj in Jerusalem
622	Culture	The Hijrah: Prophet Muhammad went to Medina (Saudi Arabia)
	Culture	Islamic calendar began; dates are After Hijrah (AH)
632	Culture	Mecca is conquered and the Kaaba cleansed
	Culture	Death of the Prophet Muhammad
637	History	Islamic conquest of Jerusalem
651	History	Sassanid Empire fell to the Islamic Rashidun Caliphate
661	History	Rashidun Caliphate ended
	History	Islam divided into Sunni and Shi'ite sects
	History	Muawiya I established the Umayyad Caliphate
687	Art	Abd al-Malik commissioned Dome of the Rock
691–692	Art	Dome of the Rock completed in Jerusalem
706–715	Art	Al-Walid I built the Great Mosque of Damascus (Syria)
	Art	Barada Mosaics completed
750	History	Umayyad dynasty conquered by Abbasid Caliphate
762	Art	Caliph Al-Mansur constructed Baghdad as new Abbasid capital
786	History	Caliph al-Ma'mum built House of Wisdom (Bayt al-Hikma)
836	Art	Caliph Al-Mu'tasim laid out new capital at Samarra (Iraq)
849	Art	Caliph al-Mutawakkil began Great Mosque and Minar of Samarra
1258	History	Mongol conquest of Abbasid Baghdad
1416	Art	Earliest surviving Ottoman miniatures painted
1299	History	Osman Gazi founded Ottoman state (Turkey)

DATE	TYPE	EVENT
CE		
1453	History	Ottoman conquest of Constantinople
	Art	Ottoman Academy of Greek Painters established
1501	History	Safavid Dynasty began rule in Iran
1550	Art	Sinan began work on the Süleymaniye Mosque in Constantinople
1575	Art	Divan of the poet Mahmud 'Abd al-Baqi painted
1597	History	Safavid capital moved to Isfahan
1611	Art	Work began on the Masjid-I Imam (Masjid-I Shah) in Isfahan
1827	Art	Western art added to curriculum of Ottoman military academies
1867	History	Sultan Abdülaziz became the first Ottoman ruler to visit Western Europe
1873	History	Shah Näser od-Din became first Iranian ruler to visit Europe
1914	History	Ottoman Empire entered World War I
1922	History	Ottoman Empire partitioned

the reign of Mehmet II, who had a keen interest in the advances of the Renaissance and even sent Ottoman artists to study in Italy. He founded the first art academies and his successors saw courses in European-style painting added to the curriculum of Ottoman military schools. After the dissolution of the Ottoman Empire, West Asia was divided into its current configuration of states under French and British protectorates. For many of these new nations this was a time of increasing Western educational and cultural influence. In the years since the ending of French and British rule most of these nations have developed active art scenes with galleries, world-class art museums, and artists working in a wide variety of traditional Islamic and Western styles.

Neolithic West Asia (9000–1500 BCE)

The modern image of West Asia as an arid territory was not always so; at the beginning of the Neolithic, approximately 11,000 years ago, the climate was much cooler and wetter than it is today. Satellite data shows that the Arabian Peninsula and the adjacent lands of Iraq and Iran were once crisscrossed by ancient rivers, dotted with lakes, or inundated by higher seas. As was the case in North Africa, many of these water courses dried up as the region underwent a long period of desertification. The changing climate of West Asia is reflected in its ancient rock art. In the Arabian Peninsula alone some two thousand rock art sites have been mapped. These sites, like those of Tassili n'Ajjer in Africa, reflect the process of climate change in the variety of animals depicted in the petroglyphs pecked into the walls of stone outcrops. The earliest pictographs at Jubbah and Shuwaymas depict the range of wild animals that once inhabited the land, including large predators such as cheetah, leopards, lions, Arabian wolves, and hyena. Prey animals such as gazelle, ibex, onager, oryx, ostrich, as well as wild goats and cattle also cover the rock walls. Later as the climate warmed and became dryer, depictions of wild animals are replaced by scenes of humans with domesticated cattle and hunting dogs, and finally, around 4,000 years ago, images of desert-adaptable horses and camels appeared.

Rock Art of the Jubbah Plain (c. 7000–1500 BCE)

To the northwest of the city of Ha'il is one of the earliest known rock art sites in Saudi Arabia: Jubbah. Today, the 10 mile (16 km) long Jubbah plain is surrounded by the shifting red sands of the Nafud Desert, but in ancient times it was occupied by a large, shallow lake. The oasis of Jubbah is a remnant of those ancient waters. Lining the shores of the ancient lakebed are several rock-faced mountains: Jebel umm Sanman, Jebel Katefeh, Jebel Qattar, and Jebel Gattar, which served as canvases for Neolithic and later artists. The earliest Jubbah images, thought to date to the tenth millennium BCE, are highly naturalistic, and often life-size in scale. They are also deeply incised into the rock, creating sunken reliefs with distinct shadow lines. Subjects include humans, and sometimes dogs, engaged in herding domesticated cattle whose characteristics of coat pattern and horns are rendered with remarkable detail. Later these engraved images were replaced with more shallowly pecked designs of camels and horses that required the contrasting color of fresh stone to heighten visibility. Although it is notoriously difficult to date rock art, these images are considered to be chronologically later not only because of the difference in execution but also because they often overlap the earlier motifs. This last phase, thought to date from the late first millennium BCE into the Common Era, shows a stylistic devolution from the early naturalism to a more schematic form in which humans are rendered as simple stick figures. These final pictographs are often accompanied by ancient north Arabian (Thamudic) inscriptions, some of which are thought to be **wusum** or tribal signs.

The "King" Petroglyph, Jebel umm Sanman, Saudi Arabia, c. 5500 BCE One of the more unusual pictographs (Figure 5.1) from the Jubbah area is located high up on Jebel umm Sanman where it is illuminated by the morning sun. The local Bedouin tribesmen refer to it as "malik" or the "king." It is also possible that the large figure may have been a deity image. The full-size, deeply engraved anthropomorph is depicted in a composite view with a frontal torso and profile face and limbs. He looks and gestures toward a smaller, nude male figure whose posture suggests supplication. The larger figure wears a cloth belt wrapped around his waist, a large circular pectoral on his chest and a tall spear appears to rest against his extended arm. Most unusual for the period is the attempt to render facial features on the large figure. The "king" is the only Jubbah figure to be rendered with this level of detail. Behind the two figures the stone has been scored horizontally to suggest that the figures interact within an enclosed space.

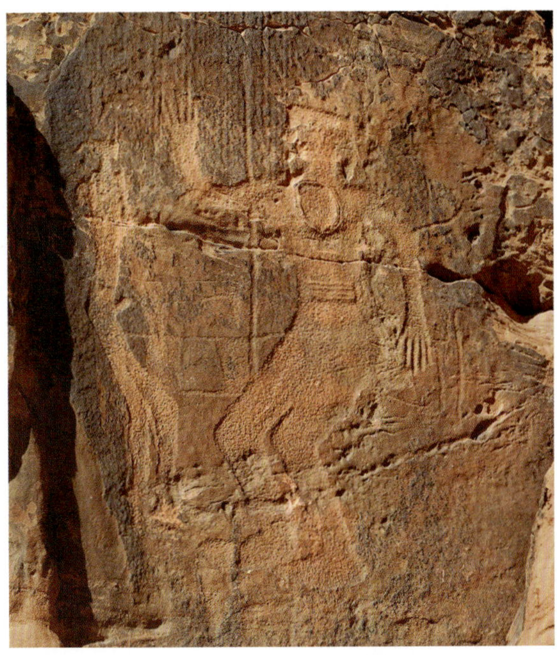

▲ 5.1 Saudi Arabia, Jebel umm Sanman, "King" Petroglyph, c. 5500 BCE.

The local Bedouin tribesmen refer to this large figure as the "king" but might have been created as an image of a deity. The "king" is unusual in that an attempt was made to show ornaments and facial details in contrast to the more simply pecked forms of the smaller attendant.

Ancient Jericho (Tell es-Sultan), Palestine (c. 8500–6000 BCE)

The first settlers arrived at Jericho in the lower Jordan Rift Valley around 8500 BCE during a period when the climate in the region was much milder and wetter than it is today, offering an ideal environment for cereal agriculture. With highlands on the east and west and the Dead Sea to the south, the site offered natural protection, fertile soil, and Ain es-Sultan, a vigorous perennial spring that even in today's drier climate produces over 1,000 gallons of fresh water per minute. Major trade routes passed nearby, providing access to markets along the Levantine coast and into the Fertile Crescent of Mesopotamia. Jericho is considered to be the world's oldest and first walled city; it also holds the distinction of being the world's lowest city as it sits at an elevation of more than 800 feet (250 m) below sea level. The desirability of Jericho's location is shown by its almost 10,000 year history of occupation, during which the city and its fortifications were rebuilt or enlarged several times, possibly as a result of successive occupiers. Ancient Jericho or Tell es-Sultan is an oval mound, measuring approximately 1,312 (400 m) by 590.5 feet (180 m), and rising to a height of 70 feet (21.3 m) above the valley floor. The height of the mound is a result of a pattern of accumulative occupation in which the city was built over many times by successive inhabitants. The site was sporadically excavated during the twentieth century and, as of yet, the full extent of the archaeological ruins from any given period is a matter of speculation.

Round Tower and Town Walls, c. 8000–7000 BCE The fertile soils of the Jordan Valley made Neolithic Jericho prosperous and able to support a population estimated at 2,000 inhabitants. In what may have been the first communal public works project in history, the people of Jericho surrounded their town with fortifications consisting of an outer ditch 27 feet (8.2 m) wide and 9 feet (2.7 m) deep, and a massive inner wall that included at least one round, stone watch tower. The wall systems not only protected the citizens but their agricultural surpluses, clustered around the tower, are several deep storage silos. The tower (Figure 5.2) survives to a height of 25.42 feet (7.75 m) and is almost 28 feet (8.5 m) in diameter; it adjoins remaining sections of the city wall that are 19 feet (5.75 m) high. Although it stands at the beginning of architectural history, the tower reflects surprisingly advanced building techniques for the time. It was constructed of undressed stones, some more than 5 feet (1.5 m) across, and river cobbles laid in mud mortar. The exterior surface was smoothed with a thick layer of mud and like other structures in the city, finished with a burnished plaster coat, usually cream or pink in color. An interior stone stair provided access to the top of the tower. The technology used in the city wall adjoining the tower shows the adaptive nature of Jericho's builders. Perhaps because some of the larger stones used in the tower had to be brought from locations up to a half-mile away, the wall builders opted for locally available and more easily worked building materials. The walls were constructed of unfired, lozenge-shaped mud bricks that were keyed on the flat sides with a thumb-worked herringbone pattern to increase adhesion with the mud setting mortar (Kenyon 1954, 103–106).

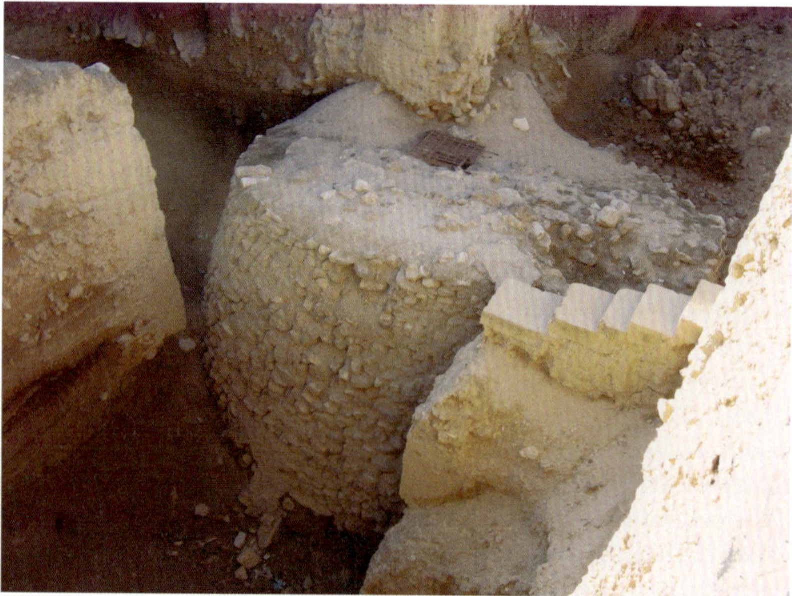

▶ **5.2** Palestine, Jericho (Tell es-Sultan), detail of round tower and wall, c. 8000–7000 BCE. Tower is 25.42 ft. high and 28 ft. diameter.

The towers and walls of Jericho were originally covered with a mud plaster, burnished, and painted.

Jericho's Over-Modeled Skulls, c. 7500–6000 BCE In addition to initial examples of architecture, Jericho offers what maybe the first portraits in human history. Although earlier human images are known from the Paleolithic and Mesolithic eras, they cannot be definitively identified as representing specific individuals. In the rare cases when features are shown, they are highly abstracted, often with little more than a couple of lines to suggest the eyes and nose. The practice of portraiture begins at Jericho in the custom of over-modeling facial features on to the defleshed skulls of select individuals.

During the Neolithic period at Jericho the dead were commonly buried under the floors of their houses. In the case of certain individuals, the bodies were disinterred after sufficient time had passed for the flesh to decompose. At this point the skulls were disarticulated from the bodies; their cavities filled with mud, and clam or cowrie shells from the Red Sea were inserted into the ocular orbit. Over this base the decedent's features: ears, eyebrows, nose, lips, cheeks, and eyelids were carefully modeled in plaster to create a lifelike expression. A final "skin-layer" of plaster, tinted with iron oxide, was then applied and facial hair, including mustaches and beards, was painted on. One over modeled skull also had brown paint applied to the top of the skull to suggest hair or a headdress. In some cases the bottom of the skulls were plastered, presumably to facilitate their display in the home. Thirty-three over-modeled skulls, deposited in six caches, have been excavated at Jericho and additional examples are known from several contemporaneous sites in Syria, Jordan, and as far away as Çatal Hüyük in Turkey. Anthropologists have suggested that these skulls represent the beginnings of an ancestor cult.

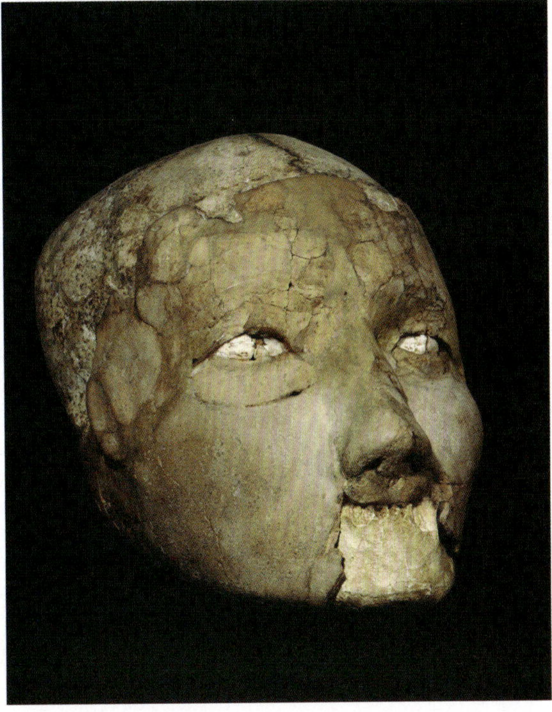

▼ **5.3** Palestine, Jericho, Over-modeled Human Skull, c. 7500–6000 BCE. Plaster and pigment.

Over-modeled human skulls may represent one of the first attempts at portraiture as well as reflecting the beginnings of an ancestor cult.

Among the skulls excavated by Kathleen Kenyon in the mid-twentieth century is one currently in the Jordan Museum that best illustrates the artistry of the Neolithic portraitist. The large skull (Figure 5.3) is thought to belong to an adult male, who was between thirty and forty years of age at the time of death. The skull is complete, remarkably well preserved, and shows no evidence of the crushing suffered by many of the Jericho skulls under the weight of the successive layers of occupation. The facial mask was modeled with extraordinary attention to detail. Particularly impressive is the treatment of the upper and lower eyelids, which overlap the shell inlay of the eyes in a naturalistic manner; the nose with nostrils, cheeks, and brow ridge are also realistically handled to create what is a unique image. The small upper lip remains but the skull sustained injury to the lower lip and chin, resulting in the loss of the plaster coat. The damage shows an interesting element: the tooth sockets of both the upper and lower jaw are empty. Because the plaster coat would have protected from post-mortem tooth loss, it is probable that the teeth were removed prior to the modeling of the face (Strouhal 1973, 238–240).

Çatal Hüyük, Turkey (c. 7500 BCE–5700 BCE)

A thousand years after the founding of Jericho, and some 700 miles to the north in southern Anatolia, another important Neolithic city, Çatal Hüyük, arose on the Konya Plain. The site's name literally translates from Turkish as "forked mound" and refers to the fact that the large city was spread across two accretion mounds: the first one on the east and a second later mound to the west, with the Çarşamba River once flowing between them. At its largest the population of Çatal Hüyük is estimated to have been as many as eight thousand persons. The city seems to have grown by aggregation rather than by design; for example, there were no streets or footpaths through the town and people moved about across the flat roofs of the houses.

ARCHITECTURE IN ÇATAL HÜYÜK

All of the buildings at Çatal Hüyük (Figure 5.4) were constructed of mud bricks, sometimes reinforced with clay-covered wooden piers or columns, and wooden ceiling beams. Differences in the size and color of the bricks used suggest that each family made its own as needed. Despite the homespun nature of the building materials, the houses are remarkably uniform, consisting of a large rectangular main room, approximately 20 feet (6 m) by 13 feet (4 m) that provided areas around the perimeter for cooking and working, benches for sitting and platforms for sleeping, and two smaller rooms thought to have been used for storage. The walls, floors, and platforms were covered with a coat of fine lime plaster. The houses were one story but floor and ceiling heights sometimes varied from room to room as new houses were constructed over fill from the collapsed walls of earlier structures. Access to the houses was through an opening in the flat roof that generally allowed a ladder to be let down into the cooking area of the main room. This arrangement also allowed the opening to serve as the vent for smoke from cooking and oven fires.

The main room of almost every house at Çatal Hüyük was decorated. Some of the houses are more elaborately ornamented than others and the distinction may be one of economics. Some houses had simple monochrome painting on the walls and platforms that featured geometric designs, landscapes, or scenes of wild animals or

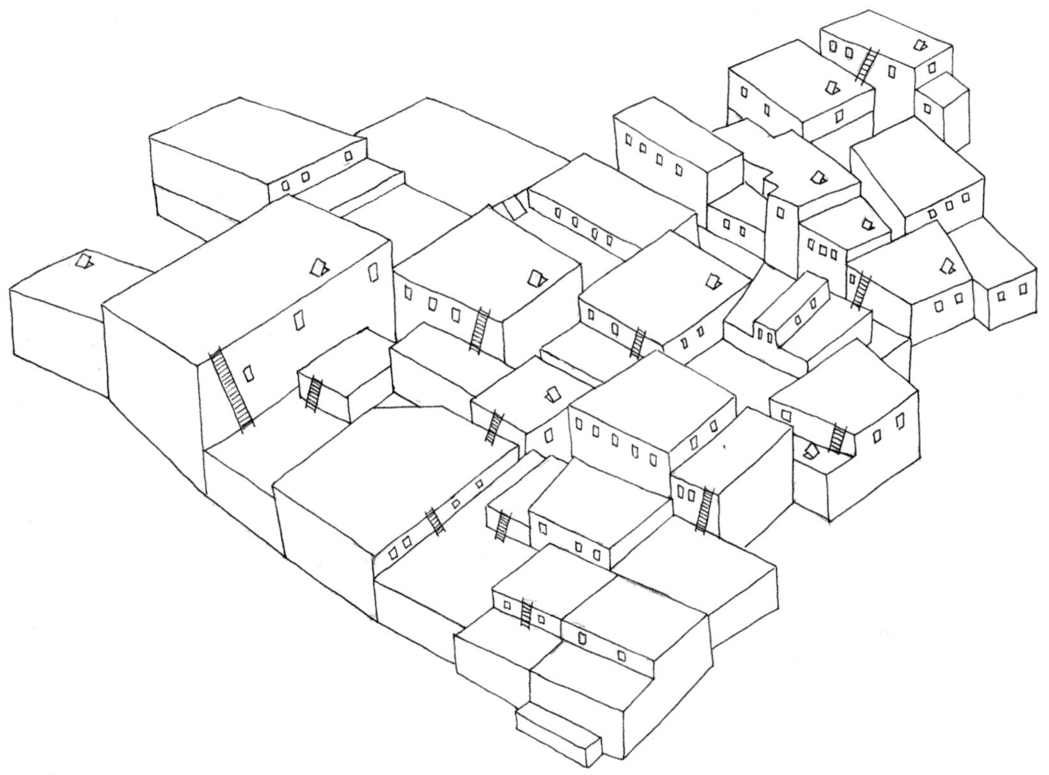

▲ 5.4 Turkey, Çatal Hüyük, Reconstruction of the Ancient City.

The city had no exterior walls or streets; instead people moved over the rooftops.

of humans and animals. Others featured painted plaster wall reliefs, representing bears with outstretched legs or pairs of facing Anatolian leopards, while others were decorated with mounted boar and auroch (wild cattle) skulls or cut-out clay silhouettes of skulls. Some had walls that were inset with boar tusks or the claws of leopards and bears. The animal skulls, tusks, claws, and horns would be plastered and painted with iron oxide pigment (Twiss 2006, 5).

Çatal Hüyük Landscape, c. 6200 BCE One of the more interesting murals at Çatal Hüyük shows what may be either the earliest known landscape painting or the first map (Figure 5.5). Across the bottom of the red-on-white plaster painting are some eighty rectangular cells laid out in a pattern remarkably similar to that of the main rooms of houses excavated at Çatal Hüyük. In the distance is a double-peaked form, thought to represent Hasan Daği, a stratovolcano visible to the northeast of the site; it last erupted around 6900 BCE (Schmitt 2014).

SCULPTURE IN ÇATAL HÜYÜK

The artisans at Çatal Hüyük carved small-scale, portable sculptures out of a variety of stones as well as modeling figures out of clay. Some

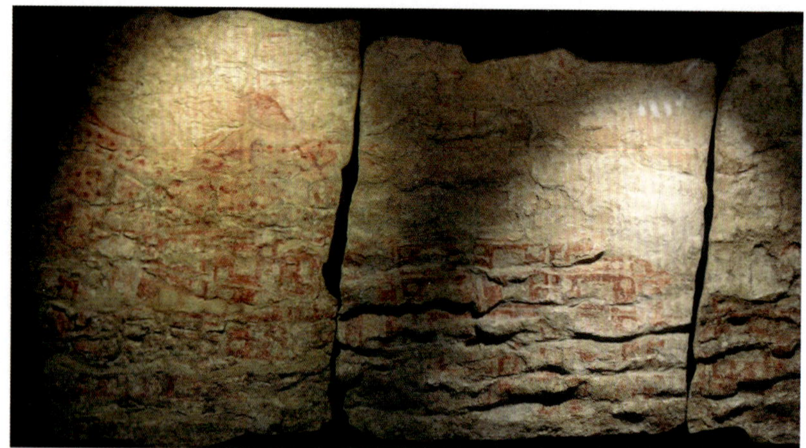

▶ **5.5** Turkey, Çatal Hüyük, Fragment of a Wall Mural Showing a Landscape, c. 6200 BCE.

This mural may well be the world's first landscape painting, or, perhaps, the first known map. It appears to show a double-peaked mountain in the distance and the houses of Çatal Hüyük in the foreground.

two thousand figurines have been excavated so far at Çatal Hüyük; the majority of these are zoomorphic forms, followed by lesser numbers of anthropomorphic, geometric, and schematized pieces. The human figures are the best known and most mythologized of the sculptural corpus.

Woman Seated on a Feline bench, c. 6000 BCE In 1961, just as the feminist movement was building in the West, James Mellaart found a handful of small, mostly headless figures at Çatal Hüyük that depicted corpulent women with pronounced bellies and buttocks. One figure, in particular, a statuette of an obese woman seated on a bench with leopard sides (Figure 5.6), inspired a sensational theory of Çatal Hüyük culture that assumed it was matriarchal and focused on a Mother Goddess fertility cult. The head of the figure and one of the felines has been restored; however, an image of the figure as found shows that the head was cleanly cut off not broken (Mellaart 1963, 30).

Two important facts were overlooked in the rush to matriarchy: first, not all corpulent figures are clearly female, many lack gender-specific signifiers, and those that are identifiably female are not necessarily pregnant; this corpulent body type—sagging belly and pendulous breasts—is characteristic of women who have previously given birth, and also of post-menopausal women. Second, the removal of the figures' head was in many cases intentional, rather than accidental; some of the stone and clay figures show cut marks and subsequent polishing of the sawn area (Meskell 2008, 379–380). The treatment of these figures seems to parallel Çatal Hüyük mortuary practices. The people of Çatal Hüyük buried their dead under the floors, hearths, and platforms in the main rooms of their houses, and as at Jericho, certain decedents, both male and female, were later disinterred, their skulls disarticulated, over-modeled, and displayed within the home. These figures may reference the practice of skull disarticulation and the veneration of the skulls of important ancestors; indeed, the proper right foot of Mellaart's "goddess" is resting on a skull in the pre-restoration photo.

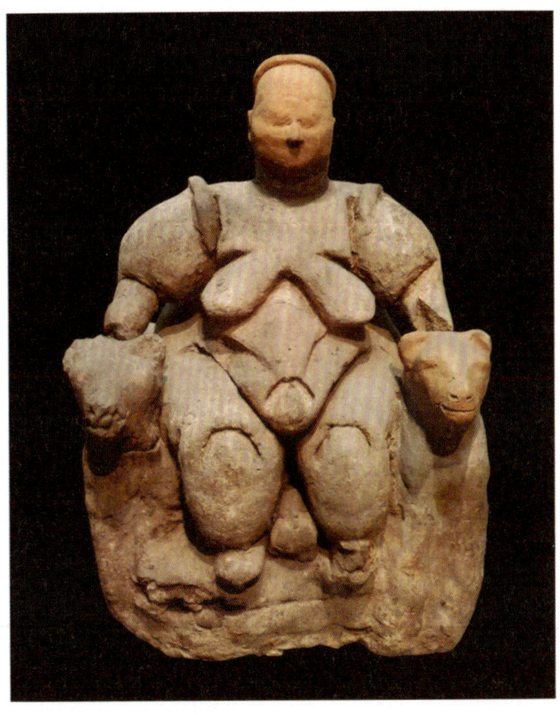

▲ 5.6 Turkey, Çatal Hüyük, Woman Seated on a Feline Bench, c. 6000 BCE.

This figure was found with its head purposely removed and missing the proper left feline head. Traditionally, the figure has been identified as a "mother goddess" and it is evident that she has previously given birth. Some scholars now believe that the figure may have referenced the practice of disarticulating the skulls of important ancestors similar to that at Jericho.

Ancient Mesopotamia (5500–500 BCE)

Mesopotamia, meaning "land between two rivers," was the name given by the Classical era Greeks to the rich alluvia plain lying between the Euphrates and Tigris Rivers in Syria and northern Iraq. Today the term is applied to a much larger area extending along the entire length of the river systems from their sources in the Anti-Taurus Mountains of Turkey to their deltas in the Persian Gulf. Long before the Greeks knew of it, the region was home to a succession of cultures, beginning in the south with Sumer around 5400 BCE. The civilizations of ancient Mesopotamia are credited with inventing the wheel, systems of writing, the recording of history, literature, canons of law, organized religion, and beer, among other achievements.

Sumer (c. 5400–2350 BCE)

Southern Mesopotamia's first settlers, the non-Semitic Sumerians, arrived in the sixth millennium BCE at a time when the waters of the Persian Gulf extended about 60 miles (100 km) farther inland than now. The first Sumerian cities, Eridu, Ur, Kuara, and Lagash, were built on the coast. Later cities were established inland along the courses of the Euphrates, Tigris, and their tributaries. The Sumerians spoke a common language and shared the same pantheon of gods and goddesses, although each city was dedicated to one particular god or goddess; for example, Eridu was the home of Enki, god of waters, wisdom, and magic; Ur was dedicated to Nanna, the moon god, and Lagash to Ningirsu, the god of rain and farming. The attributes of the Sumerian gods are a reflection of the concerns and accomplishments of the Sumerian people. They devised a system of writing, known as cuneiform, and used it to record hymns of praise to their gods, lists of kings, and the first law codes with prescribed penalties for specific offenses against persons and property. They built levees to control flooding, dug canals to irrigate their fields, and invented the plow. Although the Sumerian cities might form temporary alliances in times of war, they

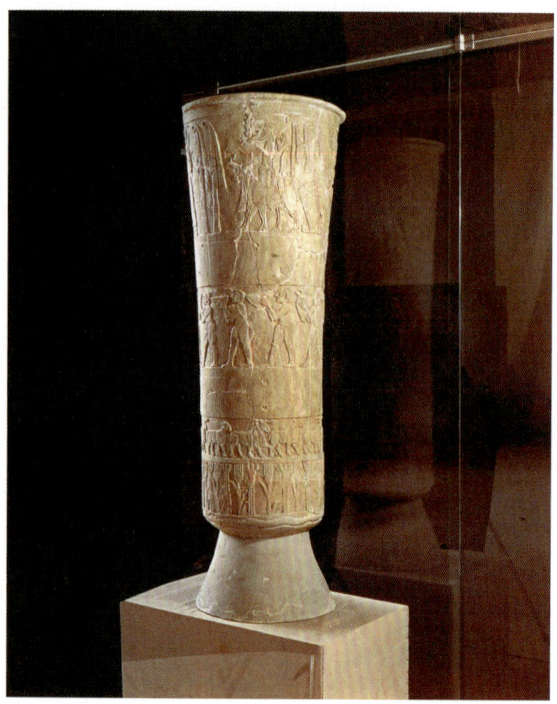

▲ 5.7 Iraq, Uruk, Warka Vase, 3300–3000 BCE. Alabaster, 36.35 in. high.

The vase was an offering at the Temple of Inanna in Uruk and narrates the story of the annual harvest and procession of offerings to the goddess.

did not unite into an organized confederation. Each Sumerian city was an independent theocratic state, ruled by dynasties of priest-kings who also officiated in the temple of the local god, for whom all labor in the city was performed.

The focal point of every Sumerian city was the temple to its patron deity. The earliest known Sumerian temple was built at Eridu (Tell Abu Shahrein), Sumer's first city, around 5000 BCE. It was a simple mud brick building about 10 feet square that offered enough space within its walls for an altar niche and an offering table. This first temple was rebuilt eighteen times, with each new construction being built upon the remains of the previous temple. Successive reconstructions of the temple resulted in the accumulation of a high debris mound and the elevation of the originally ground-level temples to the tops of steep-walled, stepped platforms known as **ziggurats** (Lloyd and Müller 2004, 12–13, 19). The building of a temple was a massive undertaking not just in the scale of its architecture but also in its decoration and temple furnishings.

The Warka Vase, Uruk, c. 3300–3000 BCE The Warka[1] or Uruk Vase (Figure 5.7) is an impressive example of an item that would have been presented as a temple offering in the fourth millennium BCE. The vessel was discovered broken in pieces during the 1930s excavations at the ruins of the temple to Inanna in Uruk. Restored, the vessel stands slightly more than 36 inches (96 cm) tall and weighs 600 pounds (272 kg). It was carved out of alabaster, a translucent form of gypsum that is easy to work. The face of the Warka Vase is ornamented with three registers of bas-relief carving, which combine to narrate the story of the annual harvest and procession of offerings to be presented to the goddess. The lowest register displays the fertility of the land and livestock with depictions of grains, reeds, sheep, and cattle. The center band presents a procession of nude, male bearers who carry baskets and offering jars to the temple. The large upper band shows the figure of a priest-king, his wrapped skirt held up by a long belt, followed an attendant who carries the tasseled ends of the belt; both watch as the first bearer presents a basket to a female figure who is perhaps the high

[1] The name Warka is derived from the modern town of Warka.

priestess of the temple. Behind her is a tall pair of reed-bundle gateposts, which in early Sumerian art and text was the icon of the goddess Inanna (Frankfort 1939, 15; Black and Green 1992, 108). To the right of the bundle-posts, the received offerings, including a pair of vases similar in form to the Warka Vase, have been gathered into the temple stores.

The relief figures on the Warka Vase are rendered with an interesting mix of naturalism, stylization, and hierarchical scale, similar to that found on the slightly later Egyptian Palette of Narmer. As on the Narmer palette (see Chapter 4), the scale, position, and individualization of the figures appears to indicate relative rank and importance. The largest figure in the upper register is that of the ruler who is rendered in the composite view familiar from Egyptian art: head and legs in profile pose while the torso is depicted frontally, followed in scale by the priestess who is also depicted in twisted perspective. The remaining figures are smaller in scale and nude with the exception of the king's attendant who wears a short wrap skirt. Although the nude figures are so generalized as to suggest they are intended to represent a type or category rather than individuals, the attention given to their anatomy, particularly the musculature of the legs, is astonishing for such an early work.

During the Second Gulf War in 2003, the Warka Vase along with hundreds, if not thousands, of other items was looted from the Iraq National Museum. The thieves snapped off the vessel's base when they broke its display case. The vase was later recovered but it had suffered significant damage.

Statuette of a Priest King, Uruk, c. 3300–3000 BCE In addition to state ceremonies of offering, such as those depicted on the Warka Vase, individual devotees might present statues of themselves to the temple. These figures allowed the worshiper to be continually present in adoration of the divine. Such votive offerings are known from both Sumerian and Neo-Sumerian temple sites. The figures show a great deal of stylistic variety, ranging from blocky naturalism to schematized abstraction, which most likely represent local aesthetics rather than any sort of developmental sequence. Typically the figures show individuals standing, or occasionally sitting, with their arms folded at the elbow and their hands either resting or folded on their chests in an attitude of supplication.

The bearded votive figure, possibly representing a priest king (Figure 5.8), is one of three similar works found at Uruk, during the same excavations that unearthed the Warka Vase. Carved in limestone, the nude figure represents a male, whose full head of hair and full beard suggest he may be a "priest-king." The king's face is a youthful one with full lips and round cheeks. Particular attention has been given to the wide-open eyes. The king stands with his arms folded at the elbows and his hands on his chest in a position that suggests prayer. The lower

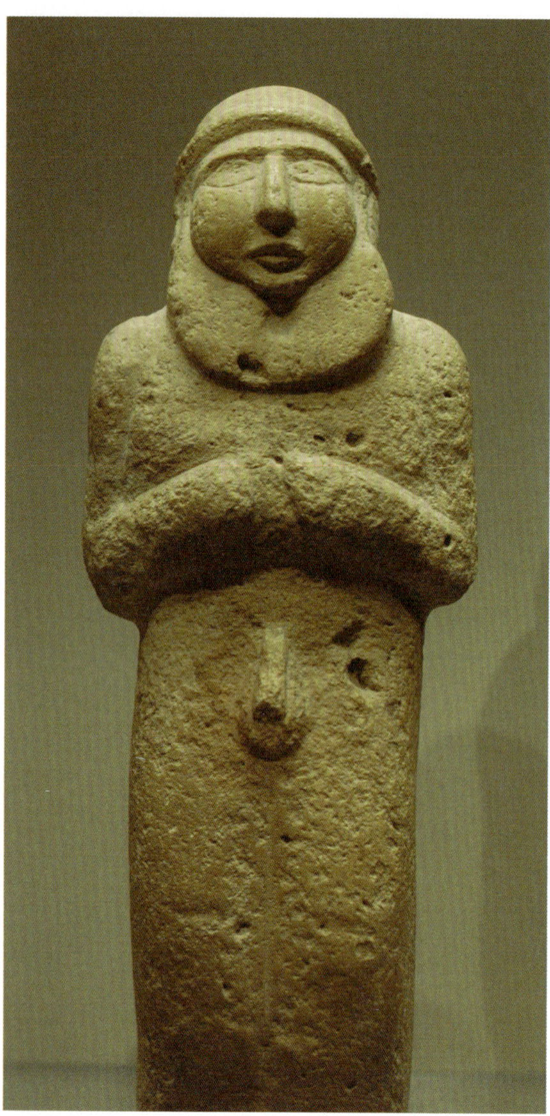

▲ **5.8** Iraq, Uruk, Statuette of a Priest King, c. 3300 BCE. Limestone, 12 in. × 4 in. × 2.7 in.

The figure's full beard and hair, bound by a circlet or cap, suggests that he is a "priest king" whose votive image stands in perpetual adoration of the divinity.

portions of the figure are more schematized with a single groove suggesting the division between the legs. Although the work has an overall feeling of blockiness, it is an important first step in the process of creating sculpture in the round.

Tomb of Queen Puabi, Royal Cemetery of Ur, c. 2600 BCE During the 1927–1928 field season, five years into his work in the ancient cemetery at Ur, the British archaeologist Charles Leonard Woolley (1880–1960) excavated a deep shaft tomb and, at its bottom, found a limestone and mud brick crypt, approximately 14.27 feet (4.35 m) by 9.18 feet (3.8 m) , which housed a royal burial. The find was remarkable, first, in that the burial offerings were intact (many of Ur's tombs had been looted in antiquity), and second, because the burial was that of a woman. Three cylinder scrolls, decorated with banqueting scenes, were found near her shoulder; they bore cuneiform inscriptions, which identified her as a queen named Puabi, meaning "word of my Father" in Akkadian. Women in ancient Mesopotamia were usually identified in the context of a male relative, either husband or father; however the inscriptions on the scrolls do not identify a husband for Puabi. It is possible; therefore, that she may have been a queen in her own right. Puabi's skeletal remains suggest she was a small woman, less than five feet tall and about forty years old when she died. Her tomb was filled with everything she would have needed in the afterlife including cosmetics, jewelry, gold and alabaster vessels, oxen and carts, retainers and handmaidens, and musical instruments.

Bull Lyre, Tomb of Queen Puabi, Ur, c. 2550–2450 BCE The remains of two large standing lyres were found in Queen Puabi's tomb and while the wooden parts had rotted away, Woolley was able to make plaster casts of their impressions in the soil as a model for reconstructing the eleven string instrument. One of these, Bull Lyre (Figure 5.9), now in the British Museum, has been restored and stands 44.29 inches (112.5 cm) high. The front of the lyre is decorated with inlaid panels of lapis lazuli, shell, gold, and silver set in **bitumen** (natural tar) and is crowned by a three dimensional gold bull's head with a carved lapis lazuli beard. The meaning of the four scenes on the front of the sound box is unclear but may reference early versions of stories that later formed the Epic of Gilgamesh. From top to bottom they show a lion-head eagle between gazelles, addorsed bulls and foliage, a human-headed bull holding leopards by the hind legs, and a fight between a lion and a bull.

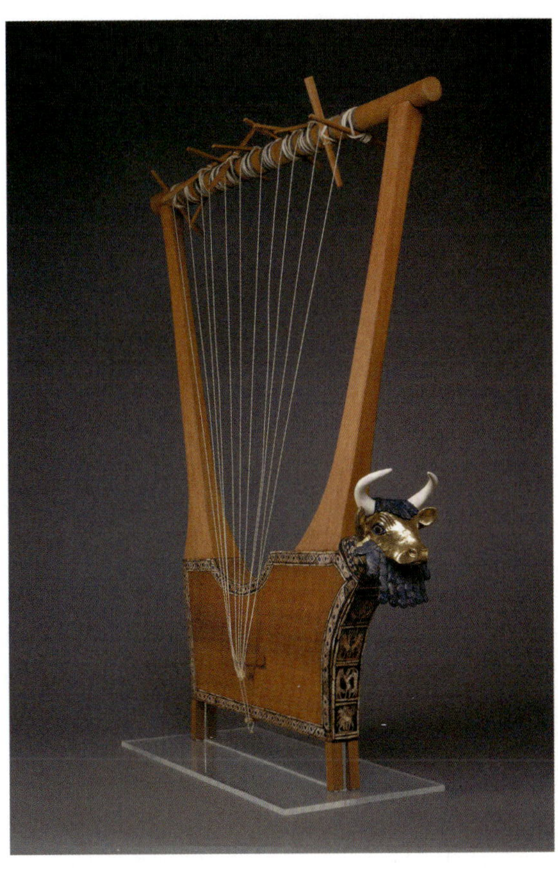

▲ 5.9 Iraq, Ur, Tomb of Queen Puabi, Bull Lyre, c. 2550–2450 BCE. Lapis lazuli, shell, and red limestone mosaic set in bitumen with gold bull head (wood, strings, and horns are restored), 44.29 in. × 28.7 in. × 2.7 in.

The two lyres placed in the tomb as offerings may have been played as part of the funerary rituals.

Akkadian Empire (c. 2334–2154 BCE)

The Akkadians were a Semitic people who established themselves in the northern Sumerian city of Kish sometime before 2300 BCE and, in time, Semitic-sounding names began to appear in the king list of that city. The greatest of these Semitic rulers was Sargon I (r. 2334–2279), also known as Sargon the Great, who came to power after usurping the throne of Kish. Sargon made his capital at Agade, which is thought to have been somewhere to the south of the modern city of Baghdad, and from there launched a campaign of conquest that brought all of Mesopotamia under Akkadian rule. His sons, grandson, and great-grandson ruled the empire for only 180 years before it collapsed.

Votive Disk of Enheduanna, Ur, c. 2300–2275 BCE Sargon sent his daughter, Enheduanna (c. 2285–2250 BCE), to serve as high priestess at the Temple of Nanna, the Moon god at Ur. Her service there was marked by the dedication of an alabaster disk (Figure 5.10) with a relief band on its face that echoes elements of the much earlier Warka Vase at Uruk. The scene shows a procession toward the four-level Great Ziggurat at the left. Immediately before the ziggurat is a tall offering vase similar in design to the Warka Vase that the first figure, a nude male bearer, has apparently just set into place. Behind him stands Enheduanna, in layered skirt, followed by two attendant priestesses. On the reverse a cuneiform inscription identifies Enheduanna as wife of Nanna, daughter of Sargon, and the patron of an altar to the god. Despite her role as priestess at Ur, Enheduanna had a particular devotion to the goddess Inanna in whose praise she wrote the *Ninmesarra* ("Exaltation of Inanna") and the *Inninsagurra* ("Hymn to Inanna"). The fact that Enheduanna is known

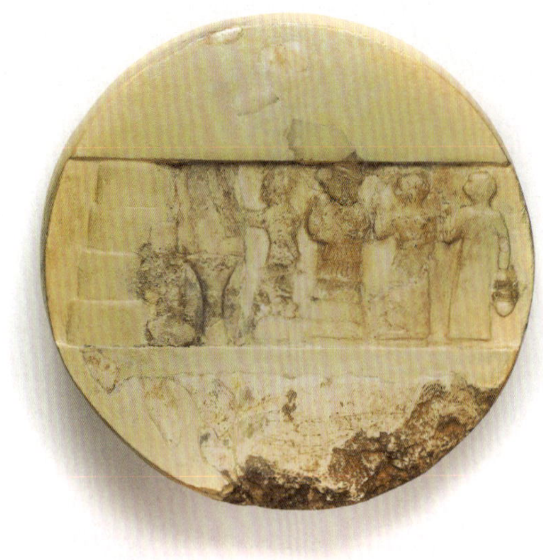

▲ **5.10** Iraq, Akkad, Disk of Enheduanna, c. 2300–2275 BCE. Alabaster, 10 in. (25.6 cm) diameter.

The disk shows Enheduanna in a layered skirt in procession behind a bearer who has put down an offering vase similar to the Warka Vase.

as the author of these works makes her the first poet whose name was recorded in history. The slightly more than 10 inch (25.6 cm) diameter disk was discovered in 1927 during excavations of the temple precinct.

Victory Stele of Naram-Sin, Sippar, c. 2220–2184 BCE Discovered in the excavations at Susa in 1901 is one of the masterpieces of Akkadian sculpture, the Victory Stele of Naram-Sin (Figure 5.11). Originally the **stele** stood in the Temple of Naram-Sin at Sippur, but it was plundered by the Elamite king Shutruk-Nahhute in the twelfth century BCE. Naram-Sin (r. 2254–2218 BCE) was the grandson of Sargon I and the fourth king of Akkad. He was also the first Mesopotamian ruler to self-deify as a god-king as attested in the stele's inscription where the king's name is written with a divine determinant.

The stele celebrates Naram-Sin's victory over the Lullubi of the eastern Zagros Mountains. The work is an extraordinary break from the format of earlier Mesopotamian celebratory monuments, which ordered scenes in horizontal registers. Instead, kilted Akkadian soldiers battle nude Lullubi as they climb the steep slopes of a mountain landscape. At the top of the composition towers the heroic figure of Naram-Sin, god-king as signified by his horned helmet; he appears to read the inscription carved into the conical peak behind the pleading figure of the Lullubi leader. The two stars shining down upon Naram-Sin represent other gods in the Akkadian pantheon. Naram-Sin and his soldiers are shown in the formulaic composite view used to represent important or elite figures in Mesopotamian and Egyptian art. As a result they have a stiff quality compared to the Lullubi who fall, cower, die, and are trampled upon with exacting naturalism; even the trees have been carefully rendered to conform to types that grow in the Zagros.

Neo-Sumerian Empire (c. 2112–2004 BCE)

Around 2350 BCE the Sumerian city-states were conquered and incorporated into the Akkadian Empire by Sargon the Great. For the next two hundred years the expansionist Akkadians ruled over northern and southern Mesopotamia until their state collapsed around 2180 BCE. Under the leadership of Ur-Nammu, first king of the Third Dynasty of Ur, and, with that city as its capital, the city-states of old Sumer were revived and organized into a single polity known as the Neo-Sumerian Empire. Ur-Nammu is credited with rebuilding several Sumerian ziggurats and with writing the Code of Ur-Nammu, the oldest surviving Mesopotamian law code.

Ur-Nammu, The Great Ziggurat of Ur (Tell al-Muqayyar), c. 2100 BCE Among the many ziggurats restored by Ur-Nammu (r. 2112–2095 BCE) was the Great Ziggurat of Ur. It is today the best preserved and most restored example of Sumerian ziggurat design. A temple to the Moon God, Nanna, once stood on the ziggurat's summit. Unfortunately, the temple and the upper levels of the platform have been lost. The ziggurat, as originally built, had a solid core of sun-dried bricks, buffered with layers of reeds between courses, and enclosed within a veneer of baked bricks. The surface bricks were almost a foot square and 3 inches thick; each weighed around 30 pounds (13.6 kg). These face bricks were set in bitumen for water resistance. The Ur ziggurat (Figure 5.12) measures 209 feet (64 m) by 150 feet (46 m) and rose in three levels to a height thought to be around 70 feet (21 m). Its four corners, rather than its façades, were oriented to the cardinal directions. The next rebuilding of the Great Ziggurat was undertaken by the Babylonian king Nabonidus (r. 555–539), who may have had little to work with beyond the first stage. His reconstruction brought the ziggurat to seven levels with a height that may have been as much as 100

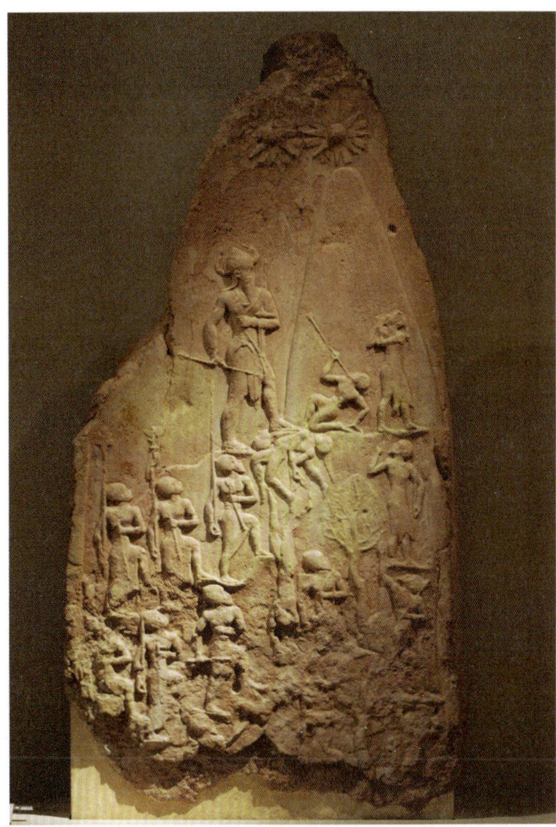

▲ **5.11** Iraq, Akkad, Sippar (found Susa), Victory Stele of Naram-Sin, c. 2220–2184 BCE. Sandstone, 79 in. high.

The stele celebrates the victory over Lullubi of the eastern Zagros Mountains. The god-king and his soldiers trample the nude Lullubi as they ascend under stars representing the Akkadian gods.

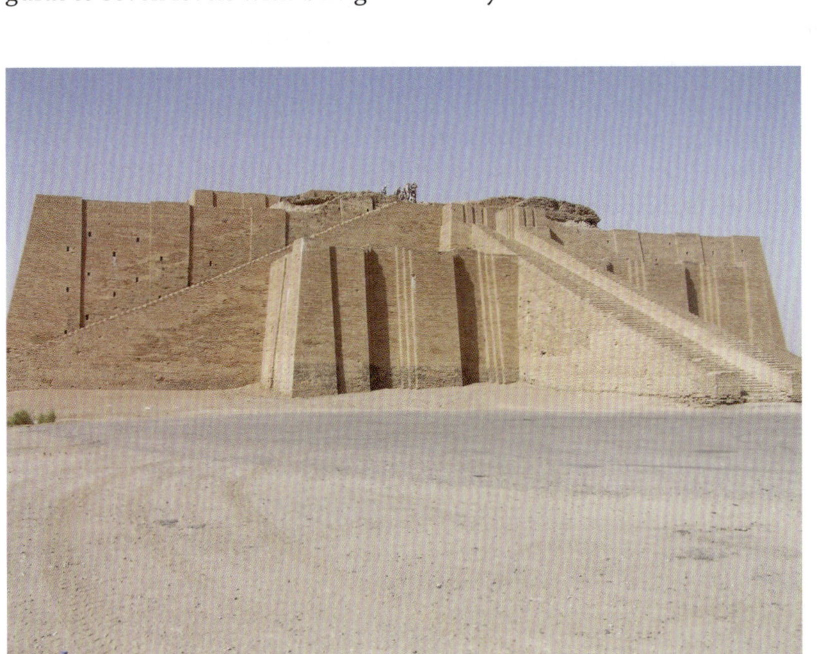

◀ **5.12** Iraq, Neo-Sumerian, Ur-Nammu, The Great Ziggurat of Ur (Tell al-Muqayyar), c. 2100 BCE. Sun-dried brick and baked brick set in bitumen, 209 ft. × 150 ft. × 70 ft.

This ziggurat has been restored at least three times in its history, the first being the reconstruction by Ur-Nammu. Its summit held a temple to the Moon God Nanna.

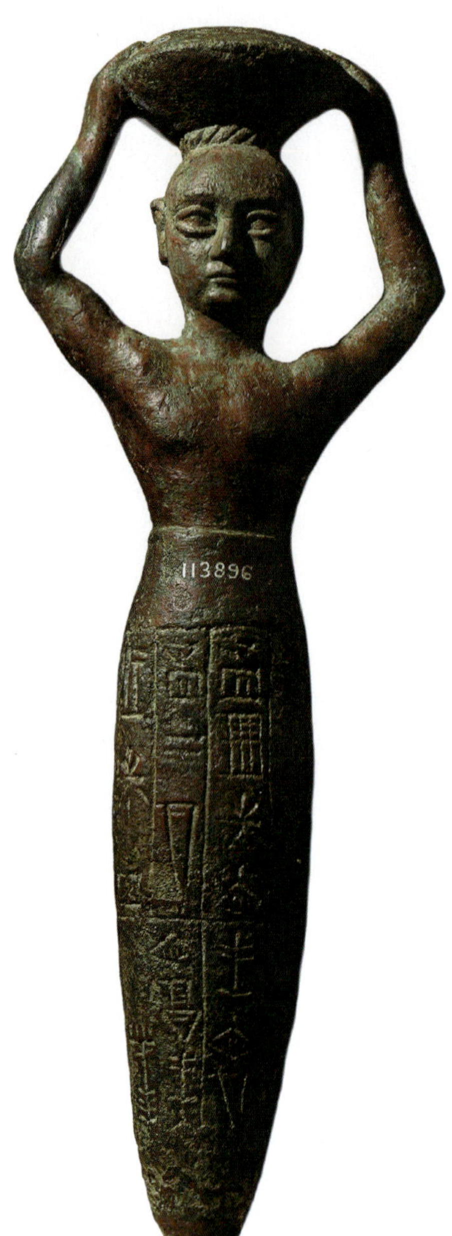

▲ 5.13 Iraq, Neo-Sumerian, Foundation Figure of Ur-Nammu, c. 2112–2095 BCE. Copper alloy, 10.75 in. (27.3 cm) high.

Ur-Nammu took an active role in the building of temples, actually setting the foundation pegs that marked the boundaries of the building. The peg depicts the king carrying a basket of clay to make the first brick for the temple.

feet (30 m). Access to the top of the first platform was provided by a triple staircase (restored by Saddam Hussein in the 1980s) on the northeast face.

Foundation Figure of Ur-Nammu Holding a Basket, c. 2112–2095 BCE One of the chief responsibilities of Sumerian and Neo-Sumerian priest-kings was the building and renovation of temples. Rather than simply commanding the work these rulers appear to have taken an active role in the rituals that inaugurated construction. It was the king who laid out the temple, establishing the lines of the foundation by setting the temen or "foundation pegs." These pegs often were cast in the image of the ruler, a god, or sometimes an animal. The pegs would be covered in cloth and placed upright in foundation boxes of baked brick sealed with bitumen that marked the corners of walls or other significant parts of the structure. After the pegs had been set, the king would carry a basket of excavated clay, water, and a brick mold, and with his own hands make the first brick. Ur-Nammu's participation in these rituals is documented by a few surviving foundation pegs associated with the ziggurats he rebuilt.

One of these, Foundation Figure of Ur-Nammu holding a Basket (Figure 5.13), is a cast copper alloy statuette of Ur-Nammu as a canephore or "basket-carrier." Ur-Nammu is shown with face and head shaven and his upper torso bare and unadorned. He wears only a long wrap skirt and a wide belt. The skirt provides the surface for the cuneiform inscription that identifies him as the builder of a temple to Inanna. The features of Ur-Nammu's face have been naturalistically rendered and show an impressive attention to detail; for example, the upper and lower eyelids have been carefully modeled over the orb of the eye rather than simply indicated by a heavy outline as is common. This is particularly impressive given the peg is only 10.75 inches (27.3 cm) high.

Old Babylon (c. 1792–1595 BCE)

The city of Babylon was founded as a regional Sumerian administrative center and Euphrates port town sometime in the twenty-fourth century BCE, but it does not figure prominently in ancient texts until the Akkadian period when Sargon I claimed to have built temples in the city. Babylon briefly came back under Sumerian control during the Third Dynasty of Ur but after the Neo-Sumerian Empire fell to the Elamites, it became an independent city state. In 1894 BCE, the Amorites took control of Babylon and established a kingdom under Sumuabum (r. 1894–1877 BCE). Under the Amorite dynasty kings, most notably the sixth, Hammurabi (r. 1792–1750), Babylon became a wealthy city with many temples and palaces enclosed within tall city walls.

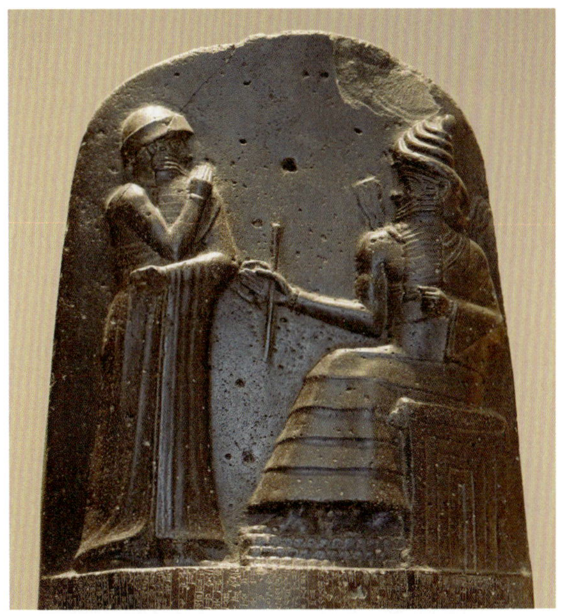

▲ **5.14** Iraq, Babylon, Stele of Hammurabi, c. 1760 BCE. Basalt, 88 in.

The king stands before the mountain throne of Shamash, from whom he receives the authority to make the laws inscribed on the shaft of the stele.

The Stele of Hammurabi, c. 1760 BCE Under Hammurabi the Babylonian state expanded to include all of southern Mesopotamia. In order to govern these diverse subjects, Hammurabi devised a code of some three hundred laws that governed all manner of civil and criminal offenses ranging from disputes over property or the quality of beer to marital infidelity, bodily injury, and murder; the "eye for an eye" concept of justice is found in Hammurabi's Code. The best-preserved example of the Hammurabi canon of laws is the *Stele of Hammurabi* (Figure 5.14), a more than 7 foot (2.23 m) black basalt monolith found in 1901 by French archaeologists excavating at the ruins of Susa (Iran). The stele, along with other Mesopotamian treasures, had been taken as plunder by the Elamite king Shutruk-Nahhunte (r. 1185–1155 BCE) after his victory over Babylon. The introductory inscriptions on the stele relate that it originally stood before a statue of Hammurabi in the Temple of Marduk at Babylon (Lyon 1904, 266); however, it is probable that Hammurabi had similar stelae set up in the main temples of all the cities under his rule as a means of assuring his diverse subjects of the righteousness of his justice.

The bas-relief panel at the top of the stele shows King Hammurabi standing, his right arm raised in a gesture of reverence, before the imbricated mountain[2] throne of Shamash, the Babylonian sun god. Shamash was invoked as the god of justice because the sun in his journey across the sky saw and illuminated all things below. The scene makes the statement that the code inscribed on the stele as well as the power to enforce it has been given by the god of justice to Hammurabi; the rod and ring held by the king are symbols of this divine authority. However, the close scale of the two figures suggests an almost coequal status of Shamash and Hammurabi not only as lawgivers but also as god and divine king. In the preamble to his code, Hammurabi states:

---

[2] The scale pattern beneath Shamash's throne first appears as a mountain attribute in early Akkadian seals, circa 2300 CEBCE; see Metropolitan Museum of Art no. 41.160.192 for an example.

"I am the Sun of the city of Babylon, who spreads light over the lands of Sumer and Akkad" (Roth 1995, 80).

In addition to breaking hierarchical norms, the artist of the Hammurabi Stele pushes, if sometimes tentatively, standard conventions of space and the representation of the bodies of elite and divine beings. Instead of presenting the standard composite view the artist is subtly pushing against the formula to try to create an illusion of a third dimension. The lateral movement of Hammurabi's raised arm gesture breaks the strict frontality of the torso, creating a three-quarter pose. Likewise the dropping of Shamash's left shoulder and backward thrust of the same arm suggests both an attempt at contrapposto and at foreshortening. Other efforts to create a sense of receding space are also evident in the progressive overlapping of figural elements—Hammurabi's arm over beard over necklace over neck, and in the corresponding diminishment of carving depth. Although presumably unfinished—notice the differing treatment of Hammurabi's beard from cheek to chest as compared to that of Shamash—the work has a greater plasticity of form than previously evident in Mesopotamian relief sculpture.

Ashur and the Assyrian Empires (c. 2400–609 BCE)

The ancient city of Ashur or Assur (modern Qalat Sherqat) took as its patron deity the Mesopotamian god of war, Ashur. According to ancient accounts, the city was founded by Sargon I of Akkad as a provincial outpost in the third millennium BCE. Located along the northern reaches of the Tigris, the city was an important stop on the trade route to Anatolia and as a result grew rich. This wealth allowed Ashur to expand its territory and defeat the invading Amorites but it also made it a target for conquest. The city fell to Babylon during the reign of Hammurabi. Although Hammurabi treated its citizens justly, he did divert its Anatolian trade to Babylon and Ashur languished economically under the Babylonian curtailment. After the death of Hammurabi and the collapse of the Old Babylonian state, Ashur became an unwilling vassal of the Mitanni. In the fourteenth century BCE, Ashur regained its independence under the leadership of Ashur-Ubalit I (1353–1318 BCE) but it was not until the reign of Adad Nirari II (r. 912–891 BCE) that the Assyrian state began expanding into an empire that would ultimately control Mesopotamia, Anatolia, the Levant, and Egypt. The period beginning with the rule of Adad Nirari II until the fall of the empire in 612 BCE is known as the Neo-Assyrian Empire.

The Palace of Sargon II, Khorsabad, c. 720 BCE Unlike the art of earlier Mesopotamian civilizations, which was produced for the veneration of their gods, Assyrian art had an earthly purpose, the glorification of Assyrian power. The primary venue for this display was not in the temples of patron gods, but on the walls of the royal palace-temple-fortresses of the Assyrian divine-kings. Every major Assyrian king either built a new palace or enlarged an existing one as a statement of his power. The most extensively researched of these is the palace of Sargon II (r. 721–705 BCE) at Dur Sharrukin (modern Khorsabad), which was first excavated during the mid-nineteenth century and again in the second and third decades of the twentieth century.

Sargon II began work on his new palace at Dur-Sharrukin shortly after he ascended to the throne, but the palace, still unfinished at his death, was abandoned when his successor moved the capital to Nineveh. The city of Dur-Sharrukin was roughly square in plan and surrounded by high, mud-brick walls. Access to the city was provided by seven monumental gateways: two each on the east, north, and south, and one on the west near the palace. Assyrian palaces were set on two-tiered platforms and enclosed within citadel walls that were set along, and sometimes broke the main city wall (Winter 1975, 31). The upper level held the palace, royal temples, and armory while administrative buildings occupied the lower. Assyrian palaces were massive structures with large-scale rooms arranged around open courts, the largest of which reached 300 feet (90 m) square.

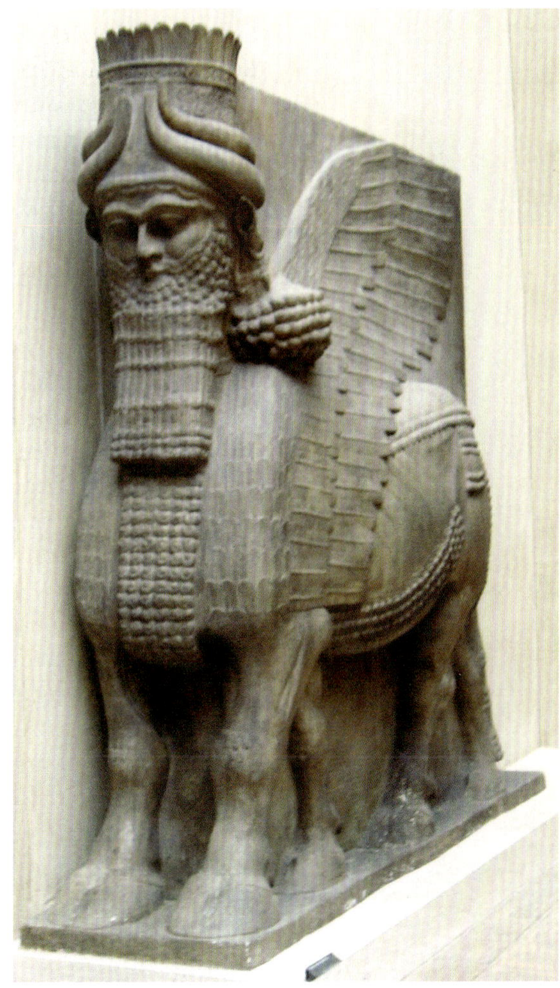

▲ 5.15 Iraq, Assyrian, Palace of Sargon II, Dur-Sharrukin (Khorsabad), Lamassu, c. 721–705 BCE. Gypsum alabaster, 13.77 ft. × 14.30 ft. × 3.18 ft.

The hybrid lamassu are visual metaphors for the power of the Assyrian god-kings.

Lamassu* from *Dur-Sharrukin, Neo-Assyrian, c. 721–705 BCE Assyrian sculpture fully in the round is extremely rare; one of the few known examples being a votive statue of King Ashurnasirpal II (r. 883–859 BCE), excavated from the Ishtar temple at Nimrud in 1850. Individualized sculptural reliefs, single images not intended as part of a larger narrative, are also infrequent in Assyrian art. Among these uncommon types are a group of hybrid creatures having the head of a man, wings of a bird, and the body of a bull or lion that were known as **lamassu**. During the roughly 250 year period between the reigns of Ashurnasirpal II and Assurbanipal (r. 669–626 BCE), lamassu were set in place on either side of palace gateways as guardian figures. Each one carved out of a single block of native alabaster,[3] the figures were monolithic in scale. The Lamassu from Dur-Sharrukin (Figure 5.15), for example, measures 13.78 by 14.30 by 3.18 feet (4.20

[3] Some museum examples appear to be made up of separate blocks as a result of the works having been cut up in the nineteenth century to facilitate shipping.

by 4.36 by 0.97 m) and weighs almost 28 tons, and it is not even the largest of the known examples.

The *lamassu* are interesting in that while highly detailed and naturalistic in their rendering of the component parts, for example the patterns of hair and beard and the fine barbs of the feathers, the artist appears unable to approach the figure as an integrated form rather than as the sum of its planes. Close examination reveals that the creature has five legs and is both stationary and moving at the same time. Approached from the front, the high relief figure stands at attention and in some examples, the head is fully in the round; however, move into a position parallel with the side and the beast is trotting along with wing raised as though it is being carried along by the force of alighting. The lamassu can be interpreted as metaphoric representations of the power of the Assyrian god-kings: the intelligence of man, swiftness of the eagle, and the strength of the bull or lion.

Assurbanipal Hunting Lions, North Palace at Nineveh, c. 645–640 BCE As was the case with much of the architecture of Mesopotamia, Assyrian palaces were constructed primarily of mud-brick, a plentiful, if inelegant, material. During the Neo-Assyrian period, the lower portions of palace walls were often faced with large slabs of gypsum, which completely covered the rough walls, sometimes to heights of 15 feet (4.6 m). While panels featuring a single figure in bas-relief have been found, the most common compositional scheme divided the panels into three horizontal registers depicting continuous narratives that recounted the king's military campaigns, hunting expeditions, and occasionally less bloody activities such as the reception of emissaries in his palace.

This panel (Figure 5.16) is one of several that once lined the walls of Room S in the North Palace at Nineveh. Its three registers show a portion of a larger narrative of Assurbanipal Hunting Lions. Lion hunts were far from sporting events in ancient Assyria; rather they

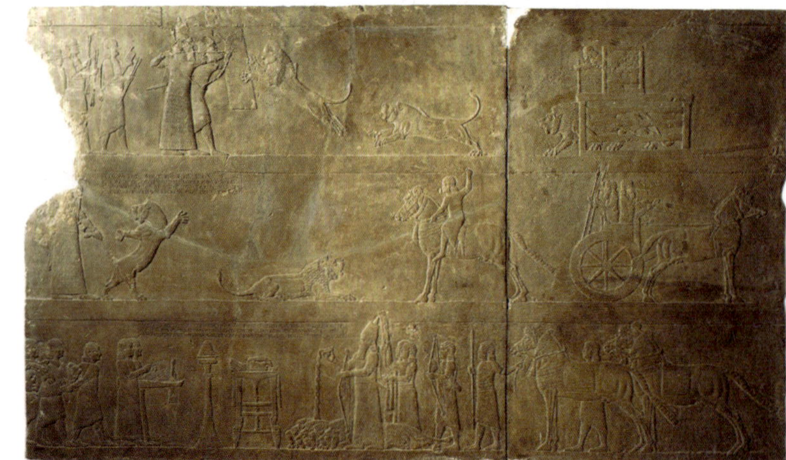

▶ **5.16** Iraq, Nineveh, North Palace, Detail Assurbanipal Hunting Lions, c. 645–640 BCE. Gypsum, 63 in. × 66 in. × 6.7 in.

The three registers of the panel show the king hunting lions as a statement of his power and protection. The hunts were staged events with animals released from cages along the course of the hunt.

were political statements of the king's power and reminders to his people of his protection. The narrative is read from right to left and top to bottom and begins with a lion (upper right) being released from its cage. The hunts were staged with lions being rounded up well in advance of the hunt and then released individually for the king to dispatch with bow and arrow, spear, sword, or sometimes a mace. Once free the lion charges toward a soldier who deflects him with a shield while the king draws his bow. Behind the king, the court eunuchs ready more arrows. The center panel shows a man on horseback distracting a lion while spearmen in a chariot stand ready. With the lion distracted, the king, mace raised to strike, moves in behind and grabs the beast's tail. The bottom panel shows the conclusion of the hunt with the king, according to the inscription, pouring a libation of wine over the bodies of four lions, while to the left stands a table with food, a tall incense burner, musicians, and servants with fans and towels.

Other sections of the relief show the extreme brutality of these ritual hunts, often detailing the awful suffering of lions wounded and left to die. The empathy that the modern viewer feels for these animals was probably not a concern for the Assyrians, who saw the lions as something evil and dangerous. Still the works show the artists' remarkable understanding of animal anatomy, personality, and raw pain.

The Neo-Babylonian Empire (c. 626–539 BCE)

In 626 BCE, just a year after the death of Assurbanipal, one of his former army commanders, a Chaldean named Nabopolassar, declared himself king of Babylon. Together with his Mede and Scythian allies he attacked the Assyrian Empire, which after more than a decade of fighting collapsed in 612 BCE, ending more than six centuries of vassalage for Babylon. Nabopolassar's son, Nebuchadnezzar II (r. 605–562 BCE), founded a new Babylonian Empire, termed "Neo-Babylonian" or "Chaldean" to distinguish it from the earlier Babylonian Empire of Hammurabi. This resurgent Babylonian state lasted 70 years before falling to the Persian armies of Cyrus II in 539 BCE.

NEBUCHADNEZZAR'S BABYLON

Nebuchadnezzar II was the longest reigning of the Neo-Babylonian monarchs and much of what remains of Neo-Babylonian art and architecture dates from his period of rule. Nebuchadnezzar II used the wealth from the empire he built to restore the temples of Babylon and build a great palace that included one of the wonders of the ancient world, the hanging gardens, built to make Nebuchadnezzar's Median princess wife feel more at home. Babylon was a large city; its ruins cover more than 2,200 acres, only a small portion of which has been excavated. The royal palace of Nebuchadnezzar was almost as large as those occupied by the great Assyrian kings and, in many respects, was of similar design with its rooms being arranged around five open

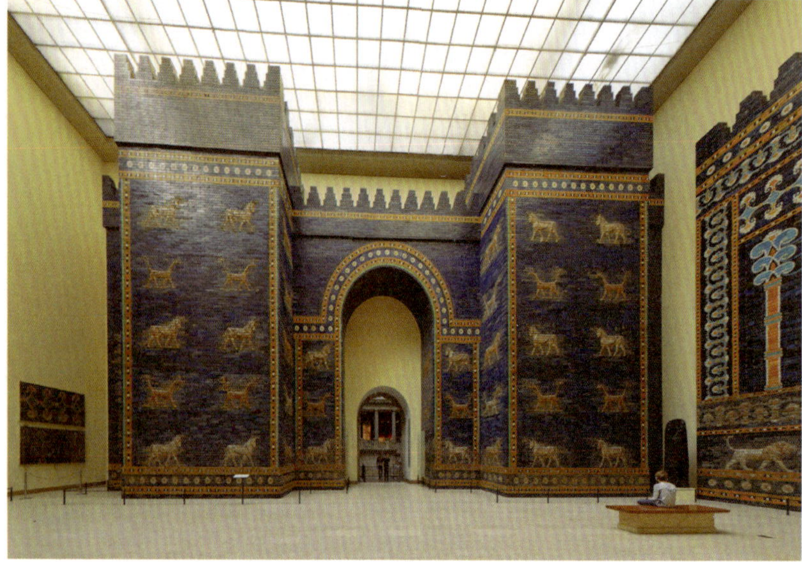

▶ 5.17 Iraq, Babylon, Ishtar Gate (restored), c. 575 BCE. Brick relief.

Nebuchadnezzar's Babylon featured a main processional way with walls and gates covered with glazed and molded brick reliefs.

courtyards. The walls of the palace were constructed in the traditional manner with sun-dried bricks but lacked the veneer of gypsum relief panels found in Assyrian palaces. Instead, they were faced with fired and glazed bricks and ornamented with modeled brick reliefs of bulls, lions, and dragons all striding in slow procession. These animals were associated with primary Babylonian deities: the bulls with Adad the storm god, lions with Ishtar, goddess of love, and the dragons with Marduk, the patron of Babylon.

THE ISHTAR GATE, c. 575 BCE Raised molded brick relief was also used to decorate the processional ways and the city walls of Babylon. According to Herodotus (1971,178–179) the city was laid out on a square plan, surrounded by a wide moat, and enclosed by a protective double wall system that ran 14 miles (22.5 km) on a side. The space between the inner and outer walls was filled with rubble. Eight major double-gateways provided access to the city. One of these city gates, the Ishtar Gate (Figure 5.17) was unearthed by German archaeologists in the early twentieth century, and its broken brick fragments painstakingly pieced back together. In its original location, the gate opened onto Babylon's Processional Way, which connected the royal palace with the city's main temples. The façades of the Ishtar Gate were decorated with modeled reliefs of bulls and dragons aligned in vertical rows against a blue ground, while the walls of the Processional Way held some 120 lion reliefs. Each relief was the same as every other of its species. This suggests that special brick molds were used to create standardized blocks that were assembled into the modeled reliefs. After bisque firing, details were outlined in black, the appropriate color glazes applied, and the tiles fired a second time. (King 1915, 250).

Ancient Iran (4000–330 BCE)

The little that is known about the early peoples of Iran comes almost exclusively from Mesopotamian sources. Sumerian, Babylonian, and Akkadian cuneiform tablets and art works of the third and second millennia BCE recount repeated campaigns against marauders from the Zagros Mountains along Mesopotamia's eastern border. The first Iranian peoples mentioned by the Sumerians were the Elamites living to the southeast of Sumer. According to the King List, Enmebaragesi, First Dynasty King of Kish, conquered the lands of Elam around 2500 BCE. Later rulers of Mesopotamia would battle against the Elamites, Lullubi, Kassites, Guti, and Medes until the Persian conquest of the Neo-Babylonian Empire in 539 brought an end to Mesopotamian independence.

Elam (c. 1400–1100 BCE)

Susa, capital of Elam, was founded around 4000 BCE, in southwest Iran, in what is today Khuzistan Province. Long before contact with Sumer gave the Elamites knowledge of writing and inspired a tradition of state art and architecture, Susa was an early center of pottery production and metal-working, particularly in silver. However, the golden age of Elamite art came late in the second millennium BCE with the rise of the independent Elamite Igihalkid Dynasty. The greatest of the seven Igihalkid kings was Untash-Napirisha (r. c. 1275–1240 BCE), who restored the temples and cities of Elam and built an entirely new capital at Dur-Untash (modern Chogha Zanbil) southeast of Susa. Dur-Untash was a walled city that contained three palaces and a large temple complex including a great ziggurat dedicated to the Elamite national god, Inshushinak. Judging from the stores of unused building materials at the site, the building program at Dur-Untash seems to have ended abruptly with the death of Untash-Napirisha, although the city was not abandoned entirely. Ultimately, the city and its ziggurat were destroyed by the Assyrian king Assurbanipal in 640 BCE.

Untash-Napirisha, Ziggurat of Inshushinak, Chogha Zanbil, c. 1250 BCE

When the ruins of the Dur-Untash ziggurat (Figure 5.18) were discovered in 1936, the underlying structure had been completely covered over by alluvial sand deposits and looked like an oddly shaped hill. *Chogha*

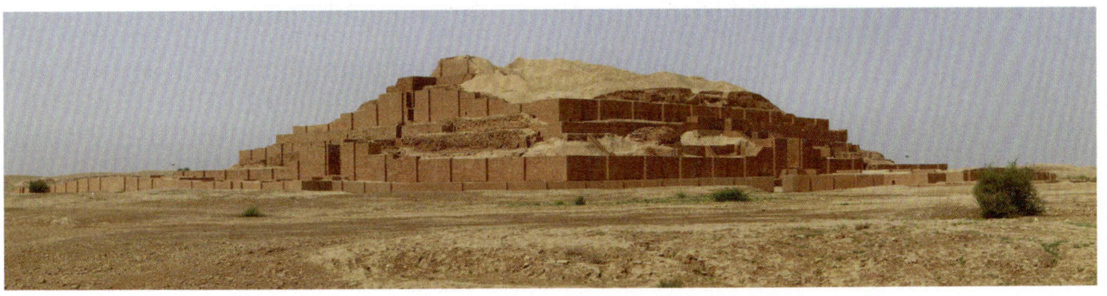

▼ **5.18** Iran, Elam, Untash-Napirisha, Ziggurat of Inshushinak, Chogha Zanbil, c. 1250 BCE, 82 ft. restored height.

Unlike the solid ziggurats of Ur, this structure incorporated earlier temples and storerooms into its levels. Access to the summit was via an interior stair.

Zanbil, meaning "upside-down-basket," was the name given in description of the ziggurat hill. Excavation and restoration of the ziggurat and its two, walled enclosures began in the 1950s. Even in its ruined state, the scale of the structure is impressive; its square base measures 344 feet (105 m) in length on each side. As the ziggurat at Ur had been, the four corners of Chogha Zanbil are aligned to the cardinal directions. Currently the ziggurat has been restored to a height of 82 feet (25 m) but it is believed to have exceeded twice that height when its four levels and crowning temple were intact. Access to the summit was provided by a staircase enclosed within the façade on the southwest side.

Unlike the Sumerian ziggurats that rose from the ground up, Chogha Zanbil incorporates an earlier square temple built around a court into its base. The mud-brick core of the ziggurat was laid down in the open temple court and as construction progressed some of the rooms of the original temple were closed off; however others remained in use as storerooms and were accessed via a stair that descended from the first terrace (Ghirshman 1966, 39–45). The core and temple rooms were encased in a thick skin of fired bricks set in bitumen. Every eleventh course of bricks bears Elamite inscriptions that invoke a curse on any who would damage the temple or steal its property. Such protective curses were frequently inscribed on Mesopotamian temples and sculptures to protect them from defacement.

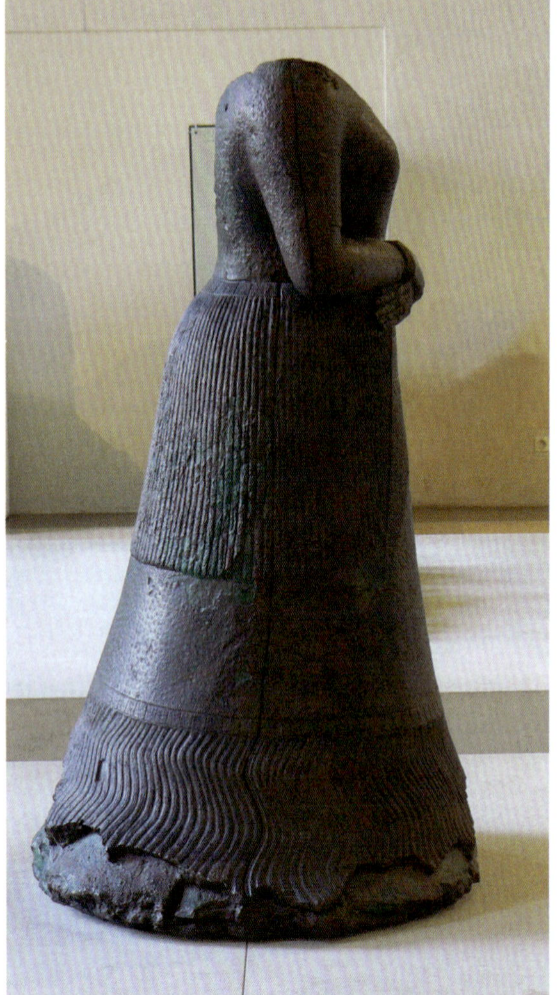

▼ **5.19** Iran, Elam, Statue of Queen Napirasu, c. 1250 BCE. Bronze and copper.

This life-sized sculpture may have been a votive offering in the temple at Dur-Untash and later moved to Susa. The queen was the wife of Untash-Napirisha.

Statue of Queen Napirasu, c. 1250 BCE Although it was excavated in 1903 from the ruins of Susa, the life-size statue of Untash-Napirisha's queen, Napirasu (Figure 5.19) was probably a votive offering in the temple at Dur-Untash that was removed to the capital when construction on the ziggurat ceased. Despite the head and proper left arm of the statue being damaged, the work is a remarkable example of Elamite metal-working and was produced using an unusual casting process. As is revealed in the damaged areas of the queen's fringed skirt, the statue was cast in two sections. Because this statue seems to have been planned from the start as a bimetal sculpture, the Elamite metalworkers inserted crossed metal rods through the core and wax layer at the base and waist of the statue. The investment was then added and the statue cast using the lost wax process. The resulting hollow copper statue was then filled with molten bronze (alloy of copper and tin). This two-stage casting process was successful because the addition of tin reduced the melting temperature of the core below that required to damage the copper skin. Adhesion of the two metals was further enhanced with additional connecting pins, which are visible on the exterior. The surface of the statue was most likely gilded or silvered but that layer has been lost (Meyers 2000, 11–18). The heavy metal weight of the sculpture, at more than 3,850 pounds (1,750 kg), may have contributed more to its preservation than the Elamite curse inscribed on the queen's fringed skirt.

Achaemenid Persia (c. 775–330 BCE)

In the second millennium BCE the Persians were one of the many nomadic tribes moving into Iran. They settled first in northern Iran near Lake Urmia. By the ninth century BCE, the Persian kingdom of Parsua was under increasing pressure from the Biainili (Urartu), Medes, and Assyrians. Led by Teispes, son of Hakhamanish (Achaemenes to the Greeks), the Persians migrated to the southern Zagros region, and established the kingdom of Parsa (Persis) to the south of Elam. As the political climate shifted, the Persians found themselves first vassals of Elam, then the Assyrians, and finally the Medes before Cyrus II, also known as Cyrus the Great (r. 559–530 BCE), threw off the Median yoke and established an empire that would rule over all of Iran, Asia Minor, Mesopotamia, and ultimately Egypt.

CYRUS II'S PASARGADAE

Cyrus II drew on the resources of his empire to build a new capital at Pasargadae on the Murghab plain. Construction of the city began in 546 BCE and continued for sixteen years It was an enormous project, the city ran almost a mile and a quarter (2 km) from north to south, and contained two palaces, columned audience halls, formal gateways, a sacred precinct, the Zenden tower, the Tall-I Takht citadel, and Cyrus II's tomb. Pasargadae's design, buildings, and construction methods broke radically with traditional practices in the region. Where much of the architecture of Mesopotamia and Iran had been constructed using a combination of mud- and fired-bricks and timber columns, Cyrus II's new capital was built primarily of finely cut limestone blocks joined together with dovetailed metal cramps. As there was no local custom of building in this manner, Cyrus II brought in architects and artisans from his Lydian and Ionian territories where there was a long tradition of building in stone. In some cases conventional building types were not just replicated in stone but reinterpreted. For example, the eastern palace gateway, Gate R, reinvents the old Mesopotamian style gate as a freestanding propylaeum; one of the earliest examples known of the type. Today, the ruins of the city are a stark white but in ancient times the buildings and limestone reliefs would have been enlivened with pigment. Additional color would have been provided by the city's progression of gardens including a palace garden that may be the first example of the Persian charbagh or four-part garden divided by water courses.

DARIUS I'S PERSEPOLIS (TAKT-E JAMSHID)

When Cyrus II's son and successor Cambyses II died in Syria on his way back from conquering Egypt, a distant cousin, Darius I (r. 522–486 BCE), seized the throne. Following the example of Cyrus II, Darius early in his reign determined to construct a new capital city and ceremonial center. He selected a site at the foot of Kuh-e Rahmat Mountain for the city he called Pärsa but which is better known in the West by its Greek designation of Persepolis, meaning "city of the Persians." Its contemporary name of Takt-e Jamshid comes from early Muslim scholars' mistaken belief that the city had been built by King Solomon.

Darius's city had a smaller footprint than Pasargadae but it was a more ambitious project with buildings that were larger, grander, and more richly ornamented. Construction began with the terracing and filling of the foot of the mountain to create a platform measuring 1476 feet (450 m) by 984 feet (300 m). The platform was protected by a system of towers and fortified walls. Situated within these walls were the apadana or audience hall, a throne hall, a treasury, and the palaces of Darius and Xerxes. The architecture was a mixture of traditional Mesopotamian and Elamite building practices with the new ideas of stone architecture brought in from Ionia, Lydia, and other Greek-influenced parts of the Persian realm.

Darius and Xerxes, Apadana, c. 518–465 BCE The grandest of the buildings of Persepolis was the large hypostyle apadana or audience hall (Figure 5.20) begun by Darius I and completed by his son Xerxes I (r. 486–465 BCE). The hall was used for ceremonial occasions such as

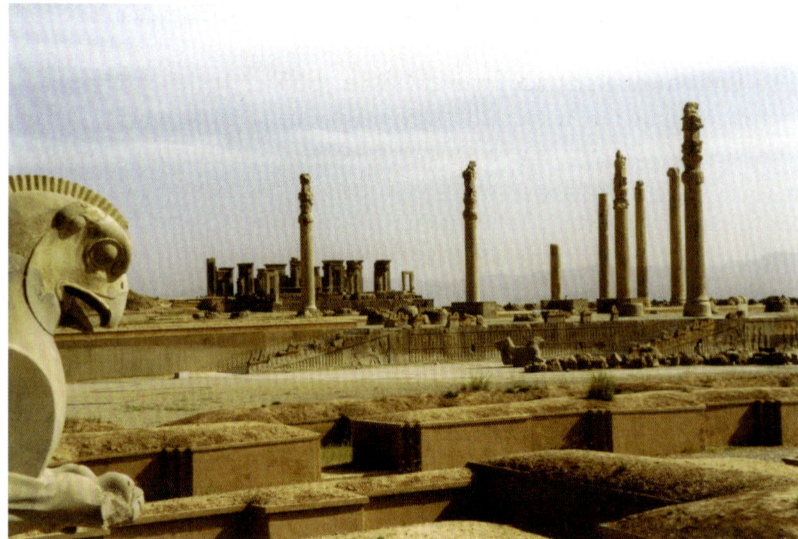

▶ **5.20** Iran, Persepolis, View toward Grand Stair, Apadana and Throne Hall, c. 518–465 BCE.

The grandest building at Persepolis was the immense Apadana or audience hall begun by Darius and completed by his son Xerxes. Access was provided by two staircases which featured reliefs of bearers bringing offerings for the Nowruz festival.

receiving representatives from the various nations of the empire and for the Nowrūz (New Year) festival on the day of the spring equinox, when tribute was received by the emperor. The building was immense; it is estimated to have been capable of accommodating as many as 10,000 people. The central audience hall was 197 feet (60 m) square and its gypsum-plastered mud-brick walls stood some 72 feet (22 m) high. Thirty-six stone columns originally stood in the main hall; the several columns still complete and standing measure 66 feet (20 m) high. Each column had a capital in the form of addorsed bulls which held the massive cedar timbers that supported the roof. On the south side the audience hall abutted the palace of Darius but on the other three sides, porticos of a dozen columns each opened up additional space.

Access to the hall was provided by wide, double-reversed staircases on the northern and eastern sides of the apadana podium. The side walls of the stairs were ornamented with three registers of bas-relief profile figures representing a procession of guards, standard-bearers, and tribute-bearers carrying offerings or leading animals. The center wall is divided into two registers: a smaller upper band with a winged disk between sphinxes, and a larger lower register with alternating Median and Persian soldiers. The slanting stair walls on either side are ornamented with scenes of lions attacking bulls. The apadana reliefs are reminiscent of Neo-Assyrian style carving but lack the fine detail that characterized the earlier art. At Persepolis this sort of detail was provided by pigment rather than the sculptor's chisel. Recent examinations of some early reliefs excavated in the 1930s revealed that they were originally painted in reds (cinnabar and hematite), green (malachite), yellows (yellow ocher and sulfur), blue (cuprorivaite aka "Egyptian Blue"), white (calcite), and black (copper oxide). Work continued on the buildings of Persepolis for almost two hundred years until the last Persian emperor, Darius III, was defeated by Alexander the Great. Although Alexander had left other capitals unharmed, he sacked and burned Persepolis in 330 BCE.

The Sasanian Persian Empire (224–651 CE)

The death of Alexander in 323 BCE ushered in a period during which Mesopotamia and Persia were ruled by a succession of unstable states beginning with the Seleucid Empire (312–63 BCE) of Seleucus I Nicator, one of Alexander's generals. Seleucus expanded his empire to include all of Alexander's eastern conquests but his successors were unable to hold the state together, losing all of their territories east of the Euphrates River in the second century BCE to the Arsacid Parthians (247 BCE to 224 CE). Indigenous rule was restored in 224 CE when the Sassanids under Ardashir I overthrew the Parthians and established their Sassanid Empire.

Taq Kisra, Ctesiphon, Iraq, c. 250/540 CE Ardashir I made his winter capital at Asbānbar just to the south of the old Parthian city of Ctesiphon. Asbānbar (New Ctesiphon) stood on the east bank of the Tigris about

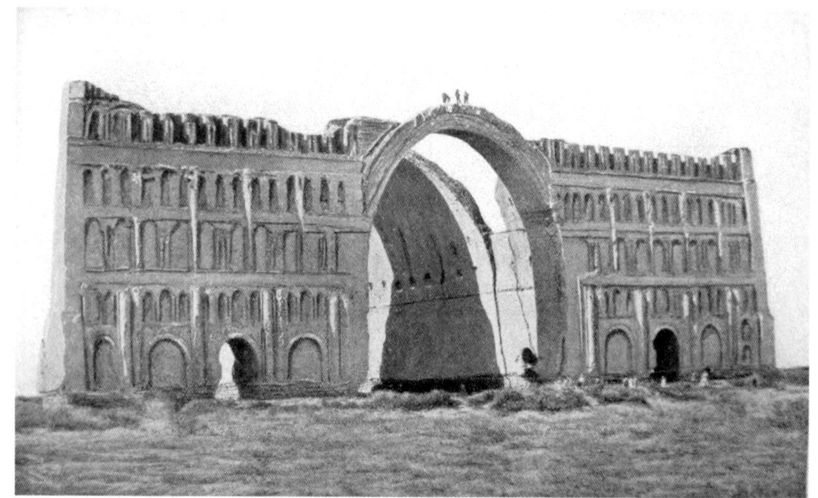

▶ **5.21** Iraq, Sasanian Persian, Ctesiphon, Taq Kisra, c. 250/540 CE. Photograph 1864 prior to partial collapse of the structure.

The Taq Kisra was an iwan-form vaulted audience hall that was built without centering using. It was flanked on each side by 114 ft.-high façade wall segments.

22 miles (35 km) south of modern Baghdad. The centerpiece of the Sasanian capital was the royal palace audience hall known as Taq Kisra (Figure 5.21). Traditionally, Shapur I (r. 241–272 CE) has been credited with building the palace but some authorities have placed construction of the audience hall as late as 540 CE.

Taq Kisra takes the form of an ***iwan*** or a barrel vaulted rectangular room, walled on three sides with the fourth left open to an outside court. The audience hall is an immense space, measuring 158 feet (48 m) deep, 84 feet (25.5 m) wide, and rising to a height of 122 feet (37 m), making it the largest freestanding brick vault in the world. The vault springs from the top of walls 23 feet (7m) thick at the base, which taper and corbel slightly inward as they rise, considerably lessening the space that the vault must span. The construction of the vault in the upper third of the structure was an incredible feat, having been done without centering; to accomplish this, the Taq Kisra masons devised a system of slanting courses in which the bricks were laid up on edge.

Flanking the iwan on the north and south were two segments of blind façade,[4] each 114 feet (35m) tall. The façades were divided into four registers of diminishing scale. The largest band was the base, which featured large arches topped by triple arcuated niches and set between paired monolithic columns. The next level linked pairs of arches with slender engaged columns. Each arch and column unit was bracketed by monumental columns extending through the next level, where they separated units of three arches and two pairs of columns. The fourth band was ornamented with a simple running arcade. All of the façade features were constructed of brick and originally would have been smoothed over with plaster. The brick iwan became a staple of Sasanian and later Iranian architecture, being used in mosques, hospitals, palaces, and schools.

---

[4] The south façade and a portion of the vault were washed away in the 1888 flooding of the Tigres; restoration of the south façade began in 2013.

RELIGION AND PHILOSOPHY
Islam

Islam is one of the three Abrahamic monotheisms that arose in ancient West Asia. The word Islam is often defined as meaning "submission to God," but its root is in the Arabic "Salam," meaning "Peace." Thus, the peace of Islam comes from the surrender of the individual to the will of Allah. The religion was promulgated by Abū al-Qāsim Muḥammad ibn 'Abd Allāh ibn 'Abd al-Muṭṭalib ibn Hāshim, known as the Prophet Muhammad, who was born around 570 CE in Mecca. At the time of the Prophet's birth, many Arabs were polytheists. In adulthood Muhammad worked as a merchant, taking caravans of goods to Syria. When Muhammad was about forty years old, he went into the mountains near Mecca to pray. One night while sleeping in a cave on Jabal al-Nur (the Mountain of Light), he was visited by the archangel Gabriel, who revealed that Muhammad's destiny was to be a prophet of God. Muhammad continued to receive revelations over the next twenty-three years, which were written down in the Qur'an, the sacred text of Islam.

Islam had much in common with the Judaic and Christian religions of that time. Indeed, Muhammad saw Islam not as an entirely new religion but the correction and completion of the two earlier ones. Islam recognizes a number of Old Testament figures including Moses and Abraham as well as Jesus from the New Testament as prophetic precursors to Muhammad, the final prophet. All three religions required the acknowledgment of only one true God, established times for daily prayer, periods of fasting, the making of pilgrimages to holy sites, and the practice of tithing or giving alms. In Islam these tenets laid down in the Qur'an are known as the Five Pillars of Islam and they are the religious duties of every Muslim:

1. *Shahada, the daily profession of faith that there is no God but Allah and that Muhammad is His prophet;*
2. *Salat, prayer five times a day at dawn, midday, afternoon, sunset, and evening;*
3. *Zakat, the duty to pay the alms tax;*
4. *Sawm, the dawn-to-dusk fast during the month of Ramadan;*
5. *Hajj, the duty for those who are physically and fiscally able to make a pilgrimage to Mecca at least once in their lives during the month of Dhu al-Hijja (the twelfth lunar month of the Islamic Hijri calendar).*

The two main sects of Islam are the Sunni (about 85 percent of all Muslims) and Shi'a (about 15 percent of the Muslim population). The two groups broke apart over the question of who was the rightful successor to the Prophet as leader of the young Islamic state. The majority believed that the Prophet had named as his successor, Abū Bakr, and that he should be caliph. A smaller group believed that the Prophet had named his son-in-law and cousin, Alī ibn Abī Tālib, as the keeper of his legacy and therefore, Ali, and those of his line, should be caliph. When Ali did become the fourth caliph, his failure to punish those who had assassinated his predecessor led to the *First Fitna* or Islamic Civil War.

While there are some doctrinal differences between the two groups, both agree on the basic tenets of the religion and accept the Qur'an. In addition to the two sects of Islam, there is Sufism. Sufism is not a sect but a spiritual and acetic practice within Islam; its adherents can be either Sunni or Shi'a.

The Islamic Caliphates (632–1258 CE)

While the Sassanian state was strong enough to thwart Roman and Byzantine expansion into Iran, it fell, in 651 CE, to Islamic Arab forces and was incorporated into the short-lived Rashidun Caliphate

(632–661 CE). The caliphate was established after the death of the Prophet Muhammad when Abū Bakr (r. 632–634 CE) became the first ***caliph*** or "successor." Abū Bakr was the only one of the four Rashidun caliphs to die a natural death. The last Rashidun caliph was Alī ibn Abī Tālib who was selected after the murder of the third caliph but his refusal to punish those responsible for the death of his predecessor led to the division of Islam into the Sunni and Shi'ite sects and the First Fitna ("discord"), a civil war, which brought the Umayyad dynasty to power.

The Umayyad Dynasty (661–750 CE)

The first Umayyad caliph, Muawiya I, was only distantly related to the Prophet through a common ancestor some five generations back. A dispute over inheritance after the death of that ancestor had made the two clans bitter enemies and the Umayyad were late converts to Islam. As governor of Syria under the Rashiduns, Muawiya had built a large army which was victorious in the civil war, and he was installed as caliph. The Umayyads were effective secular rulers, expanding the caliphate into Central Asia, northwestern India, across North Africa, and into the Iberian Peninsula. They also left a rich architectural legacy of mosques and palaces. But they were also criticized by both Sunni and Shi'ite sects for acting as temporal rulers rather than religious leaders following the edicts of Islam. The dynasty was overthrown in 750 CE by the Abbasids.

Yazid Ibn Salam and Raja Ibn Haywah, Dome of the Rock, Jerusalem, 691–692 CE

Although Damascus was the seat of the Umayyad Caliphate, the dynasty's first major building projects were undertaken in Jerusalem. In 691 CE the fifth caliph, Abd al-Malik (r. 685–705 CE) chose the highest point in the old city, Mt. Moriah, to build the shrine known as the Dome of the Rock. The site overlooked Christian, Jewish, and Muslim neighborhoods and was theologically significant to all three monotheistic religions. The mountain had long been revered in Judaism as the place where Abraham had prepared to sacrifice Isaac and as the location of Solomon's Temple, and for Christians as the site of the second temple from which Jesus had cast out the merchants and money-changers. In the Qur'an (Surah 17.1), Jerusalem is identified as the site of the farthest mosque to which Muhammad was taken on his Night Journey, the *Isra'*, circa 621 CE. That farthest mosque is commonly identified as the Al-Aqsa Mosque, built first as a simple wooden prayer house under the Rashidun caliph Umar ibn al-Khattab, shortly after his conquest of the city in 637 CE. The Dome of the Rock (Figure 5.222) was built nearby to enshrine a large rock in the Haram al-Sharif or "Noble Sanctuary" that is believed to be the place from which Muhammad ascended into heaven on the winged steed al-Buraq. Symbolically, in identifying a site of such importance to Christians and Jews with significant events in the new religion of Islam, Abd al-Malik was making a statement to the adherents of the two other monotheisms that in Islam is their correction and completion.

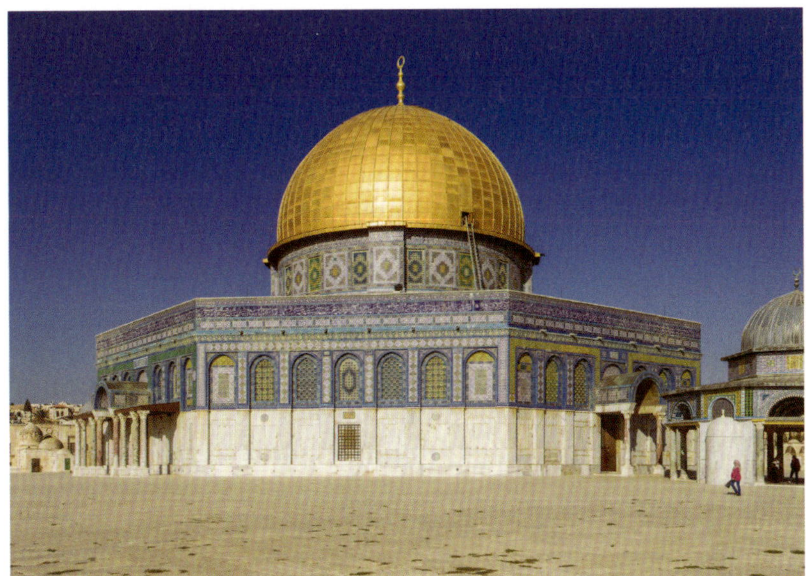

◄ **5.22** Israel, Jerusalem, Dome of the Rock, 691–692 CE.

The Dome of the Rock encloses the rock outcrop from which the Prophet Muhammad is believed to have ascended into heaven on the steed al-Buraq. The Mt. Moriah site is also sacred to Christians and Jews as the location of Solomon's Temple.

While the Dome of the Rock or *Qubbat As-Sakhrah* has been restored and refurbished over the years, its design has not been significantly altered since the time of Abd al-Malik. The prototypes for the Dome of the Rock are thought to be the Christian martyrium and rotunda or central-plan church as the building is without precedent in Islamic architecture. Indeed, the first Church of the Ascension, c. 390 CE and the first Church of the Holy Sepulchre, c. 335 CE may have provided inspiration for the architects/master-builders, Yazid Ibn Salam and Raja Ibn Haywah, charged by Abd al-Malik with construction of the shrine. However, the Dome of the Rock is far from a slavish copy of the earlier building types.

The Dome of the Rock is an immense building, a fact often lost in aerial views of the exterior. For example, each of the eight façades is 60 feet (18 m) wide and 36 feet (11 m) high. The focal point of the shrine is it gilded dome. Together the dome and its drum reach a height of approximately 67 feet (20.4 m) and have a diameter of 65 feet (20 m). Instead of masonry, the dome is constructed of wooden panels that have been stuccoed and then decorated with inscriptions and floral **arabesques** rendered in paint and gilt. The dome and drum are supported by twelve monolithic stone columns, set in groups of three, between four massive piers. Surrounding the dome are two octagonal ambulatories, divided by an arcade of sixteen columns and eight piers, and accessed through doorways on the four cardinal façades of the building. The idea of circumambulation suggested by the two aisles recalls the devotions during the Hajj in Mecca, specifically the counterclockwise ambulation around the Kaaba and its *al-Hajaru al Aswad* or "Black Stone."

Interior illumination was originally provided by stained glass windows set into the drum and exterior walls of the ambulatory. Islamic windows are made using a different technique than is commonly practiced in the West. Instead of joining the pieces of colored glass together with lead strips, the creation of an Islamic window begins with the manufacture of a wooden window frame of the exact size needed for the opening. The frame is then filled with a soft gypsum plaster. When the plaster has hardened, the intricate grille design is traced onto the gypsum blank and carved out using hand tools. While soft and easy to carve, the gypsum is strong enough to support the weight of the glass inlay. Each piece of glass is individually hand cut to fit the grille and then anchored with wet plaster. In the higher windows the glass is usually set into the frame at a 45 degree angle to facilitate the passing of the light into the building.

Remarkably, the Dome of the Rock retains much of its original interior mosaic, faience, and marble ornamentation. These adornments were added at different times as successive Islamic rulers enriched and restored the shrine. In addition to calligraphic Qur'anic inscriptions, decorative patterns worked into the glass tile mosaics include floral arabesques and repeating geometric patterns or **tessellations**. The original mosaic exterior decoration was replaced during the reign of the Ottoman Sultan Suleiman the Magnificent (r. 1520–1566 CE) with blue under-glazed painted Izink ceramic tiles.

Al-Walid I, Great Mosque of Damascus, Damascus, Syria, 706–715 CE In the first year of his reign, al-Walid ibn Abd al-Malik (r. 705–715 CE), began construction of a Great Mosque (Jama Masjid) in Damascus (Figure 5.23). The location selected for the new mosque , in the center of the old city, had a long history of religious use. Originally, a temple to the Aramaic god of storms, Hadad, stood on the site, but in 64 BCE the Romans replaced it with a temple to Jupiter, and in the fourth century CE, the ancient temple was converted into the Church of St. John the Baptist. After the Muslim conquest in 635 CE, the temple compound was shared amicably by Christians and Muslims for seventy years. However, by the time al-Walid I acceded to the throne, the Muslim community had outgrown their space in the compound. The caliph purchased and razed the old church, and in its place, built one of the largest mosques of its time.

By tradition the basic components of the mosque are taken from the layout of the Prophet's house in Medina; where the courtyard or ***sahn*** served as the first ***masjid*** (place for bowing down) with a section of roof, marking the ***qibla*** or direction for prayer, and a raised platform, called a ***minbar***, providing a space for the Prophet to address the faithful. As Islam spread the design of mosques also responded to local architectural traditions; the hypostyle prayer hall, for example, appears to have been inspired by Mesopotamian and Persian columned audience halls. In Syria and parts of the Levant, Roman and Byzantine building practices were adapted to the needs of the Islamic community as evidenced in the design of the Great Mosque of Damascus.

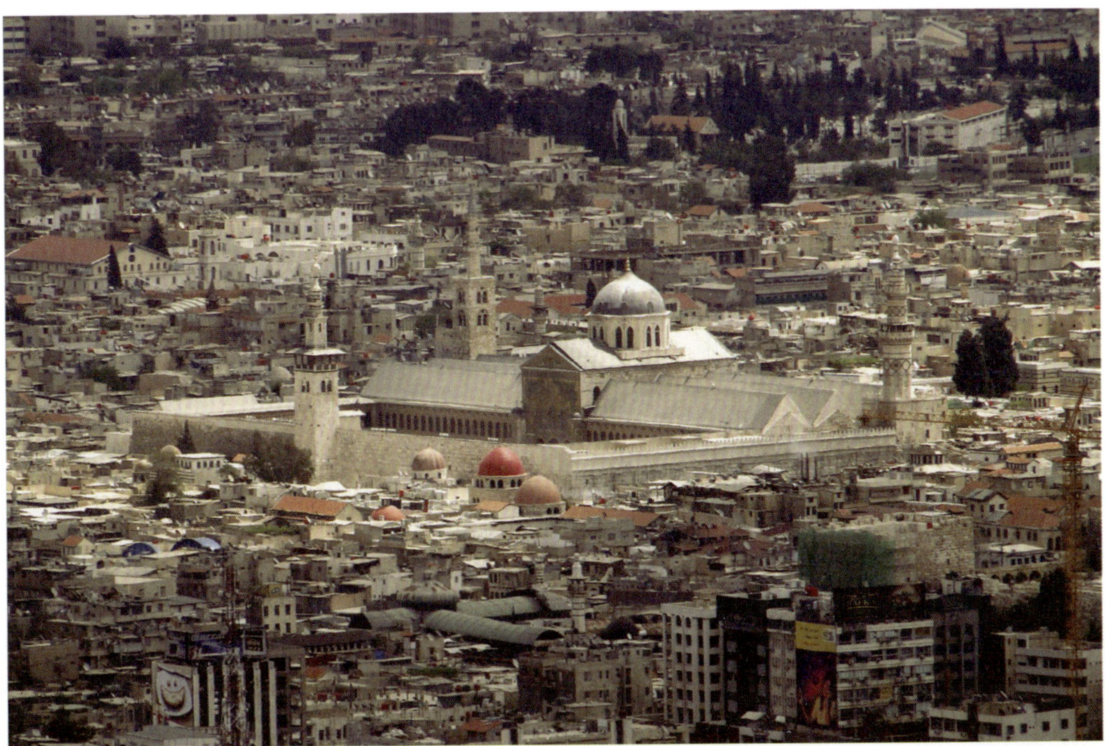

▲ 5.23 Syria, Damascus, Great Mosque of Damascus, 706–715 CE.

In the first year of his reign the Umayyad caliph al-Walid built this three-aisle mosque, using local laborers trained in the Byzantine style.

The old Roman temple perimeter walls defined a rectangular space measuring approximately 318 feet (97 m) by 512 feet (156 m). The caliph's architects divided the space along the horizontal axis, giving the northern part over to the sahn. The main architectural feature of this courtyard is its arcade with joins up with that of the sanctuary. Originally it was a continuous arcade supported by pairs of repurposed, mostly Corinthian order columns set between masonry piers; an earthquake in the eighteenth century destroyed the northern leg of the arcade and it was rebuilt without columns. Three gateways open into the court arcade on the east, west, and north sides.

The southern portion of the precinct is taken up entirely by the tripartite prayer hall, which runs 446 feet (136 m) from east to west and 121 feet (37 m) north to south. The principal section of the hall is a three-bay nave some 66 feet (20 m) wide, with a north facing gabled façade and a dome that rises 118 feet (36 m) over the central bay. Flanking this nave are two large transverse halls. Both side halls are divided into three equal aisles by ***riqaqs*** or double-stacked arcades paralleling the southern qibla wall.

Gable Mosaic Murals, Great Mosque of Damascus, Damascus, Syria, c. 715 CE

Medieval Arabic visitors to the Great Mosque wrote effusively of the splendor of the mosaic decoration that graced the sanctuary of the Great Mosque of Damascus, but unfortunately most of the Umayyad period mosaics were destroyed in the repeated fires suffered by the

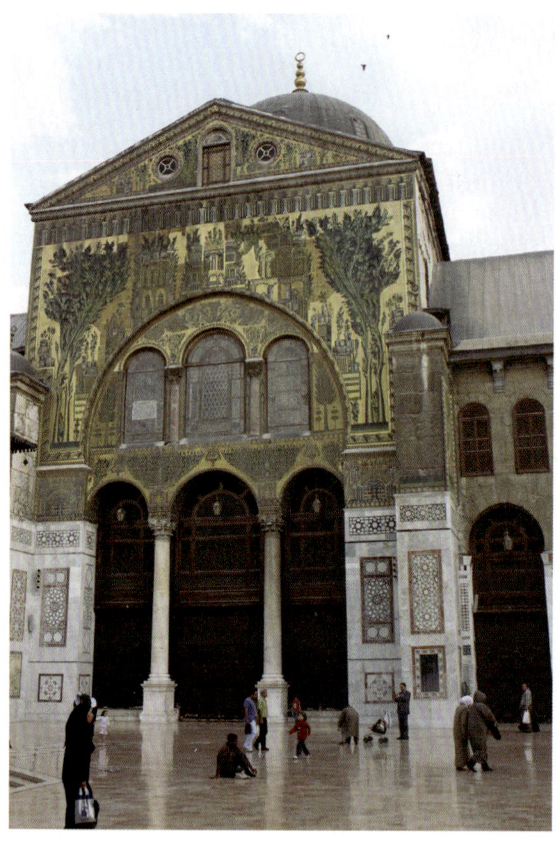

▲ 5.24 Syria, Damascus, Great Mosque of Damascus, detail gable mosaic murals 706–715 CE.

The exterior of the gable and arcades of the courtyard were richly decorated with mosaic scenes of the houses and gardens of paradise as described in the Qur'an.

mosque. However, exterior renovation work undertaken in 1929 uncovered fragments of the original mosaics, hidden beneath several layers of whitewash, on the gabled façade (Figure 5.24), the western arcade walls, and on the sides of the octagonal treasury (*khazna*) in the courtyard. The remaining sections on the gable and part of the western arcade, dubbed the "Barada Panel" after the river that runs through Damascus, depict scenes of houses, large and small, set into treed gardens. Early scholars believed these urban scenes represented the cities and towns ruled by the Umayyad Caliphate. More recent interpretations, based on Qur'anic sources (Surah 29.58), which describes dwellings and rivers in Paradise, propose that the decorative scheme was a vision of the heavenly realm promised to the faithful (Rabbat 2003, 82–86).

The mosaics offer views into panoramic landscapes that alternate between rustic and palatial. There are scenes of rural villages with block-like houses climbing the slopes of rocky hills, often reduced in scale as if attempting to show them at a distance. Larger, presumably foreground, images show richly detailed Roman-style palaces, tholos temples, towers, and curving columned porticos. These habitations are set against an ethereal gold sky, reminiscent of Byzantine work. Large green trees, rendered with subtle chiaroscuro, frame scenes and separate the landscape into distinct sections. The landscapes seem all the more otherworldly in their lack of figures even though the labors of man, in the buildings and limbed-up trees, are clearly evident. The absence of human and animal forms is drawn from the teachings of the Hadith, which discourage making images of sentient beings.

The style of the mosaics has long been attributed to that of the Byzantine Empire and it has often been suggested that they were the work of Byzantine artisans brought from Constantinople. Fanciful accounts of requests for workers by the caliph or offers of workers extended by the Byzantine Emperor appear in some later Arab histories and are often cited as evidence. However, there would have been little need for al-Walid to import workers from the Byzantine Empire. Mosaic decoration had been known in the Levant since at least the fourth century BCE and had a long history of use by Romans and Christians in Syria, Jordan, and Palestine. If skilled workers were scarce in Damascus, it would have been a simple matter to bring artisans from

Jerusalem where only twenty years earlier the Dome of the Rock had been enriched with mosaic decorations.

The Abbasid Caliphate (750–1258 CE)

The last years of Umayyad rule were marked by revolts against the dynasty, particularly from eastern Persia. Dissident leaders characterized the caliphate as impious, corrupt, and biased in favor of Arabs to the detriment of other ethnicities. They backed the rise of leaders whose family ties to the Prophet were closer than those of the Umayyads. In 750 CE, rebel forces under the Persian general Abu Moslem defeated the Umayyad army at the Battle of Great Zab River (Iraq) and the Abbasid caliphate inaugurated. The Abbasids were descendants of Al-'Abbas ibn 'Abd al-Muttalib, the paternal uncle of the Prophet Muhammad, and their promise to rule in accordance with Islamic law earned them the support of both Sunni and Shi'ite Muslims.

The Abbasid Caliphs ushered in an Islamic golden age in the arts, literature, and science. The caliph Harun al-Rashid (r. 786–809) founded the Bayt al-Hikma "House of Wisdom" where scholars using logic and scientific methods of inquiry made advances in mathematics, medicine, chemistry, optics, and astronomy. The House of Wisdom also housed an extensive library where works of Greek philosophy and science were translated into Arabic and preserved for posterity. Literature, especially poetry, flourished at the courts where entertainments included poems about hunting, love, and wine. It was during this period that collections of stories such as the *Arabian Nights* and *Kalila and Dimna* were compiled. The Abbasid caliphs had great enthusiasm for architecture, building several garrison towns and new capitals at Madinat-as-Salem ("City of Peace") and Surra Man Ra'a (He who sees it rejoices.)

▼ **5.25** Circular Plan of Madinat-as-Salem (Bagdad), c. 782 CE.

The city was laid out with double mud-brick outer walls, residential rings, four main arteries leading to the center plaza with the main mosque, caliph's palace, and police facilities.

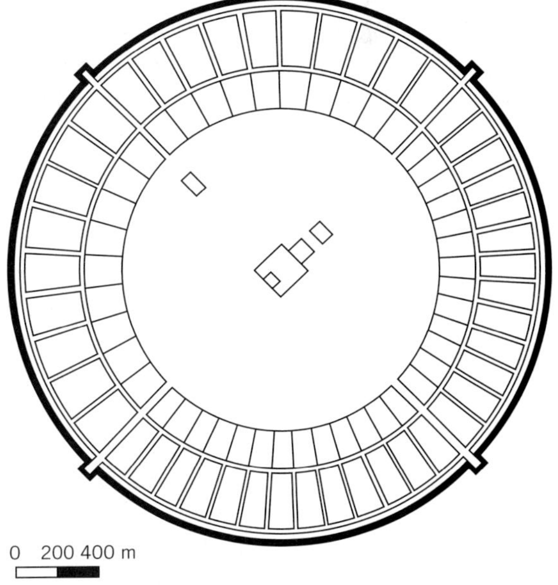

ABBASID CITY DESIGN: BAGHDAD AND SAMARRA

In 762, after four years of planning, the second Abbasid caliph, Al-Mansur (r. 754–775), began construction of a new capital, Madinat-as-Salem (modern Baghdad) on the banks of the Tigris in central Iraq. Built of traditional mud- and fired-brick, nothing remains of the original city. What is known about it comes from the Geography of Ahmad al-Ya'qubi (d. 897), who describes the city as a circle some 5,000 feet (1600 m) in diameter and surrounded by double mud-brick walls (Figure 5.25). At the intercardinal points the walls were broken by massive gates that opened onto four wide avenues leading to the center of the city. In this innermost ring were the palace with its gardens, the main mosque, and facilities for the guards and police. Surrounding the core were administrative offices and residences for government officials, army officers, and soldiers. Outside the walls of the city, on both sides of the Tigris, were the unfortified suburbs occupied by commoners. As described by al-Ya'qubi, early Baghdad seems to be an attempt to apply the logic of geometry to urban design. Another attempt can be seen in the octagon of Qadisiyya near Samarra, begun before 796 CE by Harun al-Rashid, but never finished.

Al-Ya'qubi also wrote about the city of Surra Man Ra'a (Samarra), the new capital founded by Caliph al-Mu'tasim, in 836 CE, near one of his favorite hunting preserves. The move to a new capital after only 75 years was prompted by increasing resentment and violence in Baghdad between locals and the caliph's army of ***mamluks*** (Central Asian Turkish slave-soldiers), who were seen as insufficiently devout. The new city stood on the eastern bank of the Tigris and ultimately grew to encompass some 30 miles (50 km) along the river. Included in the city were government buildings, palaces and gardens, mosques, three race tracks, and orthogonally planned neighborhoods, all of which were connected by seven major avenues running the length of the city. The palaces and elite residences were beautifully decorated with stucco reliefs of vegetal motifs and friezes of glazed tiles. In 892 CE caliph al-Mu'tadid moved the capital back to Baghdad and the city was largely abandoned by the mid-tenth century. During the Mongol invasions of the thirteenth century, which brought down the caliphate, much of Samarra and its mosques were destroyed by the armies of Hulagu Khan.

The Great Mosque of Samarra (Mosque of al-Mutawakkil), 849–852 CE The second caliph to rule from Samarra, al-Mutawakkil (r. 847–861) began construction of what was then the largest congregational or "Friday Mosque" in the Islamic world. The huge congregational mosque measured 784 feet (239 m) by 512 feet (156 m) and was set within a walled compound enclosing some 40 acres. Al-Mutawakkil's Great Mosque of Samarra (Figure 5.26) is an austere structure compared to those built during the Umayyad period. The 34 feet (10.5 m) high exterior walls were laid up in fired brick set in gypsum mortar and buttressed with brickwork half-columns; larger three-quarter diameter buttresses were used to stabilize the corners. A simple relief of brick and stucco decorated the top of the mosque wall.

Sixteen entrances opened into the sahn which was enclosed by a triple colonnade of brick piers that supported a flat wooden roof. The hypostyle prayer hall had seventeen aisles and the interior walls were decorated with marble panels and glass tesserae mosaics. The qibla wall featured a rectangular niche or ***mihrab*** to designate the direction of prayer. The niche was flanked by a pair of marble columns and paneled with gold glass. Doors on either side of the mihrab provided access to

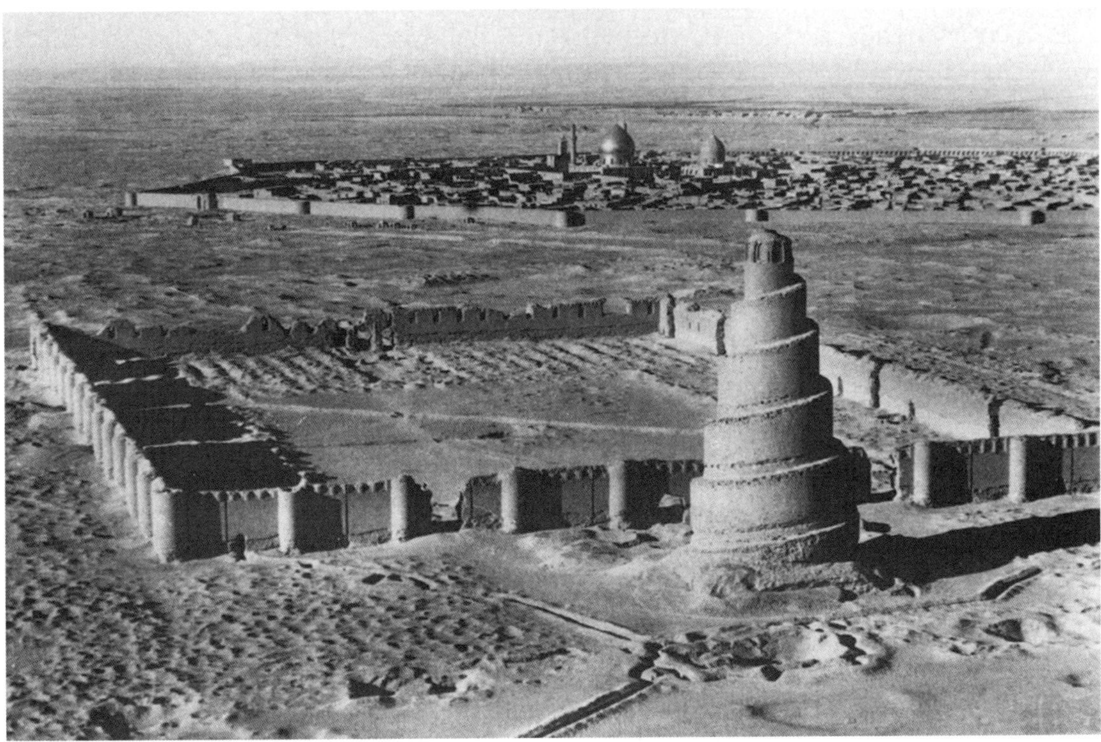

▲ 5.26 Iraq, Samarra, Mosque of al-Mutawakkil, 849–852 CE. Photo: Ernst Herzfeld, 1918.

In 836 CE the Abbasid Caliph al-Mu'tasim moved the capital to the new city of Samarra and began construction of the largest congregational mosque in the Islamic world at that time. An unusual feature of this and another of the caliph's mosques was the spiraling 170 ft.-high minar.

a small structure on the south side of the mosque, thought to include storage, a residence for the ***imam***, and a place for the caliph to rest after prayers.

On the north side of the mosque was the Malwiya minar from which the faithful were called to prayer. The sandstone minar was originally accessed by a bridge that connected it to the mosque. The design of the minar is an unusual spiral shape, hence its name meaning "snail shell." The minar stands approximately 170 feet (52 m) high and is 108 feet (33 m) in diameter at the base. Access to the top of the minar was provided by a steeply curving ramp. The caliph later built a second, shorter spiral minar at the Abu Dulaf Mosque a short distance north of the city.

Ottoman Empire (1299–1922 CE)

After the Mongol invasions of the thirteenth century, the Abbasid caliphate splintered into a number of Mongol and Turkic sultanates, khanates, and tribal kingdoms. In Anatolia about 1300 CE, Osman Gazi (r. 1299–1324 CE), the *bey* or local chief of a small Turkman tribe on the eastern border of the Byzantine Empire, declared an Ottoman state. The dynasty and state that Osman I founded became a sultanate that conquered the Byzantine Empire in the fifteenth century. Ultimately, the Ottoman Empire expanded northwest into Europe, advancing to the gates of Vienna, southward into Iraq, Syria, and Palestine, west into Egypt and across North Africa, and east to the Caspian Sea.

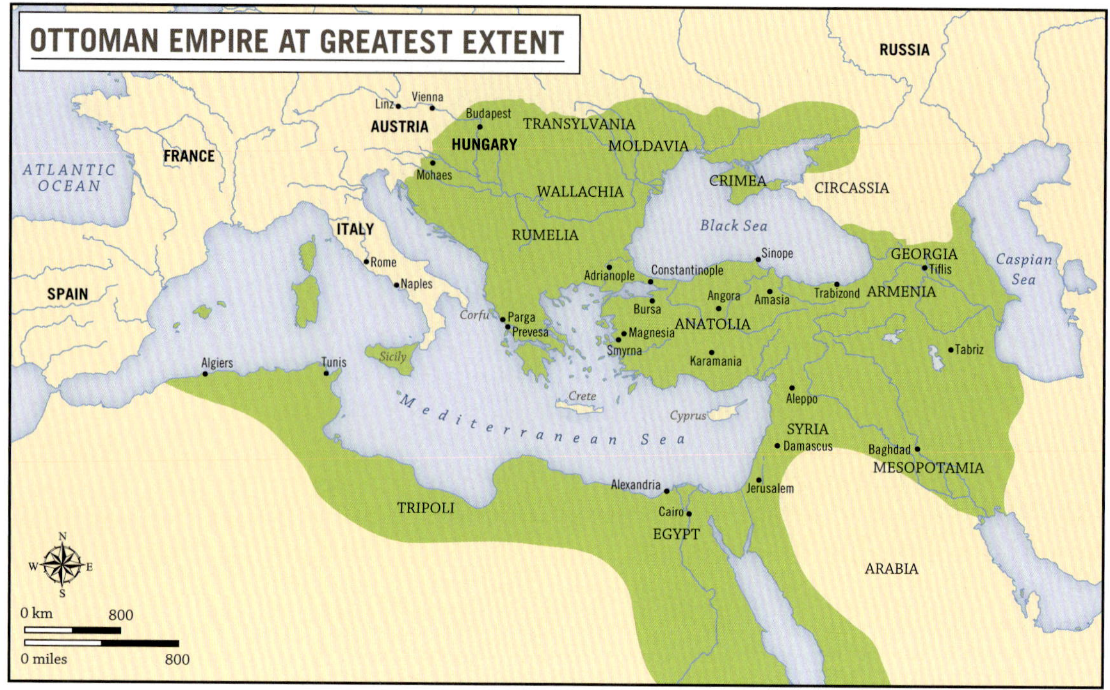

Ottoman Architecture

Under the tenth Ottoman sultan, Suleiman I (r. 1520–1566 CE), the empire reached its greatest extent. Suleiman, who had himself trained as a goldsmith, was a demanding patron of the arts, often personally inspecting the progress of his commissioned works. The sultan appointed Koca Mimar Sinan as his chief royal architect and head of a ***has*** or workshop that employed some forty to seventy architects. Sinan's first important royal commission from Suleiman was a mausoleum and mosque, the Sehzade, built in Constantinople[5] as a memorial to his eldest son, Crown Prince Mustafa, who died in 1543 CE. In all Sinan is credited with building or overseeing the design of more than 450 buildings, including 79 mosques, erected during the reigns of Suleiman I, his son Selim II (r. 1566–74 CE), and his grandson Murad III (r. 1574–1595).

KOCA MIMAR SINAN (C. 1489/90–1588 CE)

Contemporary Turkish sources, including the *Tezkiret-ul Bunyan*, a biography by Sinan's friend Sai Mustafa Celebi, suggest that the future "Great Architect" Sinan, born Joseph, was the son of Armenian or Greek Orthodox Christian parents from the town of Agirnas in central Anatolia. The future architect's early training was provided in his father's workshop where he learned carpentry and stonemasonry. In

[5] Constantinople will be used for consistency because the city was not renamed "Istanbul" until 1930.

1512 he was drafted into the Ottoman army under the Devshirme or "blood tax" in which the sons of Christians were enslaved, converted to Islam, and trained to serve the sultan as military or civil servants. He was sent to Constantinople for training as an artillery officer and architect. He served in several campaigns under Selim I (r. 1512–1520 CE) and Suleiman I, which took him to Austria, Egypt, and Iraq. In addition to blowing up enemy structures, Sinan also built bridges and fortifications for the Ottoman army. In 1539, he was appointed chief royal architect to Suleiman I and spent the rest of his fifty-year career serving Suleiman and his successors by designing and overseeing the construction of public works projects, including mosques, mausoleums, hospitals, public kitchens, schools, roads, bridges, and aqueducts.

Süleymaniye Mosque, Istanbul, 1550–1557 CE The best known of Sinan's architectural master works is the Süleymaniye Mosque (Figure 5.27), set on a hillside overlooking the entrance to the Golden Horn, where the old Saray-i Atik-i-Amire palace had stood. As the chief architect Sinan was also in charge of city planning for Constantinople and so, in selecting this site for the imperial mosque, he was very much aware of the impact the mosque would have on the city's silhouette. Clustered around the mosque on its 25-acre compound were madrassas (Islamic schools), a hospital and medical college, mausoleums for Suleiman and for his wife Hurrem Sultan (Roxelana), a soup kitchen, an asylum, a bath house, a caravansary, and a hospice for travelers.

The Süleymaniye mosque was modeled on Hagia Sophia, Constantinople's great Byzantine cathedral, overlooking the Bosporus, which was built by Justinian I in the sixth century CE. After the conquest of the city, Sultan Mehmet II (r. 1451–1481 CE) ordered Hagia Sophia's conversion into a mosque; at that time its mosaics were plastered over

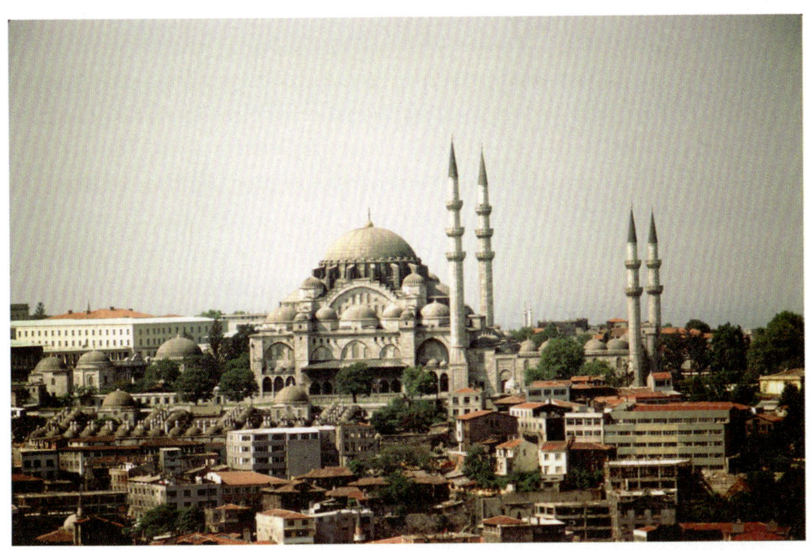

◀ **5.27** Turkey, Istanbul, Koca Mimar Sinan (1489/90–1588 CE), Süleymaniye Mosque, 1550–1557 CE.

The Süleymaniye was modeled after the Byzantine cathedral of Hagia Sophia.

and the mihrab along with the first of four towering pencil minarets were added. Following the mathematic principles pioneered by Hagia Sophia's builders, Isidore of Miletus and Anthemius of Tralles, Sinan designed a large central dome flanked by half-domes on the north and south, and windowed walls on the east and west, to create a large, well-lit oval space for prayer. The central mass of the building is a symmetrically balanced series of curving forms that flow into each other as domed exedra, towers, and appended octagonal and dodecagonal rooms. These forms function not only to give the building an elegant geometry but also serve to dissipate the thrust of the dome through the building. Four pencil minarets marked the corners of the sahn.

The building of the Süleymaniye was spread over seven years, not because of lack of funds or skilled workers but Sinan was interested designing a building able to withstand the major earthquakes that had repeatedly damaged Hagia Sophia. The Ottoman records relating to expenditures for buildings often indicate periods when construction activities were minimal; Sinan is known to have left foundations for major buildings such as the Süleymaniye to settle before continuing construction and to have included reinforcement of the foundation with staves, special cements, and lead isolation layers to make sure that buildings could absorb the shock of quakes. He also designed drainage systems to protect the foundation and reduce the build-up of moisture within the mosque as well as airflow systems to remove smoke and soot, and balance the cool and warm air. Unfortunately, the mosque suffered a fire in 1660 and a misguided attempt in the nineteenth century at renovation in the Baroque style, so other than architectural elements, very little of the original interior ornamentation remains from the time of Sinan. From the account books of the expenditures on the mosque we know the quantities of pigments, gold leaf, ceramic tile, and stained glass that went into the building but little about how it was used by the master.

Miniature Painting under the Ottomans

Papermaking, a Chinese invention, was introduced into the Islamic world in the eighth century CE as a result of the Abbasid defeat of the Tang armies at Battle of Talas River in Central Asia. The ancient Turkic city of Samarkand (Uzbekistan) was one of the first to produce fine paper, but within a century paper was being manufactured in Damascus, Baghdad, and at several towns in Khorasan (Iran). Prior to the introduction of papermaking, books in the Islamic world, primarily the Qur'an, were copied on vellum (animal hide) which had to be laboriously prepared to accept ink and pigments for illumination. Exactly when the first illustrated books were made in the Islamic world is not known with certainty as nothing remains from before the Mongol invasions of the thirteenth century. In addition to destroying the cities of the caliphate, the Mongols attacked libraries. In the city of Baghdad, which, with its famed House of Wisdom, had become a great center of learning, the Mongols are said to have thrown so many books into the Tigris that the water was black with ink (Frazier 2005).

The earliest surviving Turkish miniatures are found in the Bibliothèque Nationale's copy of the *Iskendername of Ahmedi*, a manuscript dated in the colophon to 1416 (Atil 1973, 106). However, the golden age of Ottoman miniature painting begins three decades later with the reign of Sultan Mehmet II. Prior to the Muslim conquest, Constantinople had been a leading art center for more than a millennium, and despite the declining fortunes of the Byzantine Empire the arts had continued to flourish in the city. Byzantine imperial artists who survived the fall of the city were brought into Mehmet II's court and organized as the *Nakkashane-i-Rum* or "Academy of Greek (Christian) Painters." Later the *Nakkashane-i-Irani or* "Academy of Persian Painters" was established for Islamic artists who came to the court as a result of Ottoman victories against the Egyptian Mamluks and Safavid Persians. Mehmet II had a keen interest in the cultural and scientific developments of the Italian Renaissance. He sent Turkish artists to Italy to study and invited European scholars and artists to his court; the most famous of these visitors was the Venetian master, Gentile Bellini, who painted a portrait of the Sultan in 1480. Under Mehmet II and his successors Ottoman miniature painting developed an eclectic style that uniquely synthesized East and West.

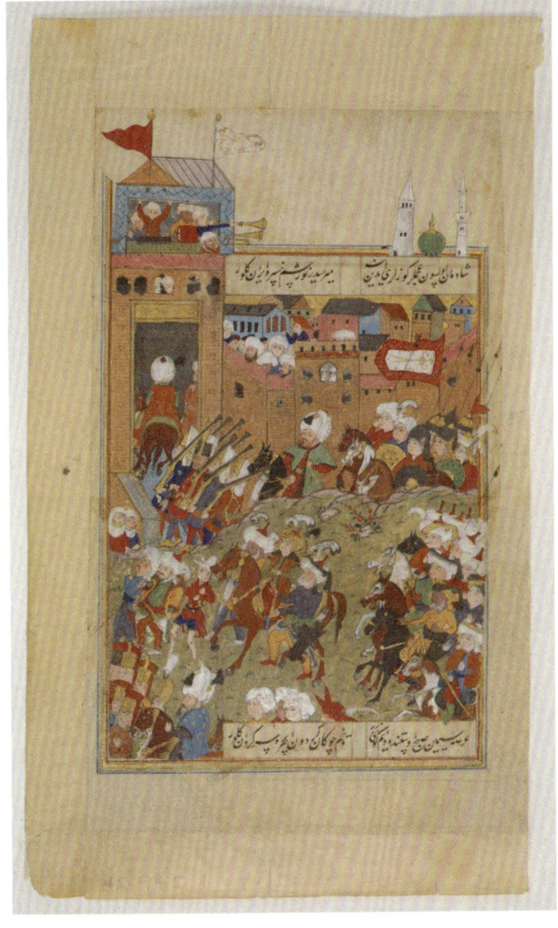

▼ 5.28 Unknown Artist, *Ottoman Army Entering a City*, Folio from a Divan of Mahmud 'Abd al-Baqi (1526–1600 CE). Ink, opaque watercolor, and gold on paper, 10.25 in. × 6.31 in.

The painting depicts the hostage Safavid prince Haidar Mirza arriving at the Ottoman court as required by the terms of a treaty between the warring states.

Ottoman Army Entering a City, ***Divan of the poet Mahmud 'Abd al-Baqi, Turkey, c. 1575–1600 CE***

Ottoman court artists, known as ***nakkas***, meaning "artist/designers," often worked closely with calligraphers; their images intended to enrich the written accounts. In addition to providing illustrations for literary and translated works, artists were charged with chronicling the daily life of the sultan by rendering scenes of his military victories, the visits of foreign dignitaries, and court ceremonials according to established protocol. Unfortunately, the nakkas rarely signed or dated their works unless they had been the sole artist of the painting. The usual process was for the head painter to lay down the composition with a very fine red line, after which other artists, using opaque watercolors, painted in the parts, outlines, applied border designs, and added the gold leaf. The Ottoman nakkas worked quickly and flatly to sketch in his scenes, avoiding illusionistic conventions such as one-point perspective or light and shadow effects on forms. This is particularly evident in the miniature of *Ottoman Army Entering a City* (Figure 5.28), in which the viewer can still see the red underlining in places as well as the buildup of opaque color, one layer over the last. Still closer examination reveals an unexpected wealth of detail in horse trappings, clothing patterns, feather fronds, and blades of grass.

The scene illustrates a poem in praise of Sultan Murad III (r. 1574–1595 CE) in the Divan of Mahmud 'Abd al-Baqi, a Turkish judge and poet. It shows the arrival, in 1590, of the ten-year-old Safavid prince Haidar Mirza to the Ottoman court. The prince, in a gold turban, rides on horseback between walking attendants. A short distance away on a prancing black horse is Mahdi Quli Khan Shamlu, a Turkman military officer sent by the Safavid Shah 'Abbas to accompany the prince. The young prince is bringing gifts, including twenty illuminated books, on the occasion of the circumcision of one of the last of Sultan Murad III twenty-one sons. The young Persian prince would remain at the Ottoman court as a hostage to guarantee peace between the two empires.

▼ **5.29** Unknown Ottoman artist, *Portrait of a Painter*, c. 1444–1481 CE. Ink, watercolor, and gold on paper.

In this miniature one of the Sultan's court artists is at work on a portrait, perhaps of the sultan himself.

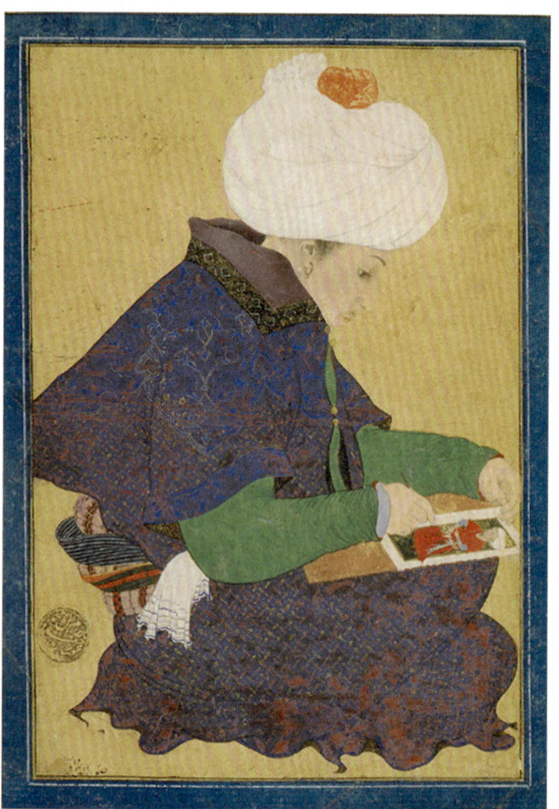

***Portrait of a Painter*, c. 1451–1481 CE, Turkey** The tradition of realistic portraiture began during the reign of Mehmet II and was rooted in his cultural engagement with the Venetian Renaissance. In addition to Bellini, the sultan was painted several times by his own court artists, and in the manner of European princes, he sent the portraits to other monarchs as diplomatic gifts. The practice was continued by Mehmet's successors and ultimately the portraits evolved into individual, full-sheet works that were collected into albums for viewing. In the early seventeenth century the Moghul rulers of India adopted the practice of portraiture from the Ottomans.

While most of the portraits were of the sultans, high officials, or members of the royal family, the *Portrait of a Painter* (Figure 5.29), thought to date from Mehmet's reign, is a full-scale profile image of one of the Sultan's nakkas who, oblivious to the viewer's gaze, is at work on a standing male portrait, perhaps the sultan. The influence of Western art can be seen in the subtle shading defining the bridge of the nose and the shadow at the outer edge of the nostril. The artist wears a richly embroidered kaftan and a patterned woven sash around his waist. No attempt is made to place the figure in a defined space; rather he seems to float against the neutral ground of the paper.

VISUAL COMPARISON
Mosque Layouts

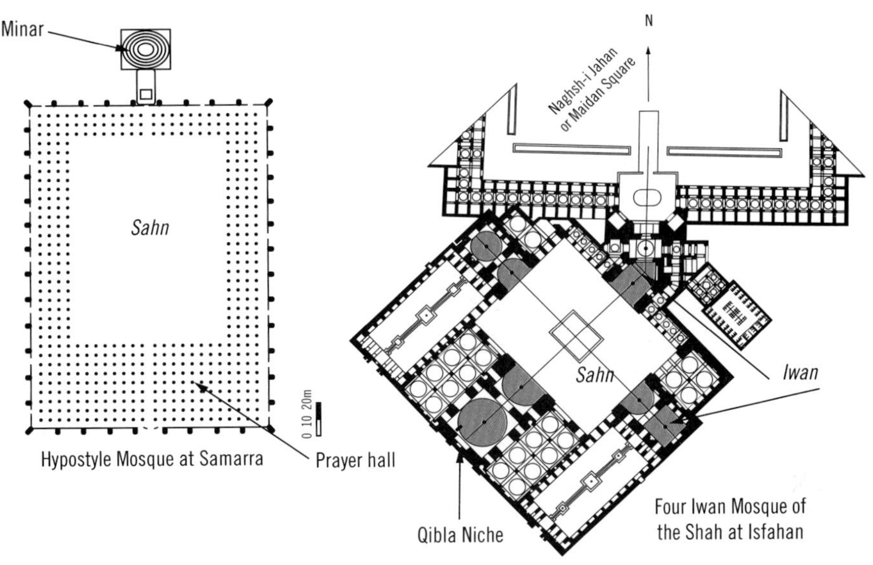

▲ **5.30** Basic Mosque Plans: Hypostyle and Iwan.
The hypostyle or Arab plan mosque was modeled after the layout of the Prophet's house in Medina. As Islam spread into Iran, a new mosque design, the four iwan, appeared based on earlier building practices in the area.

Adjacent to his house in Medina, the Prophet built the first masjid which served as the prototype for many later mosques. The Prophet's Mosque was a simple mud-brick structure, constructed like much of the domestic architecture of the time around a rectangular courtyard, measuring about 98 feet (30 m) by 114 feet (35 m), where the faithful worshiped in the open air. Covered colonnades were set up on two sides with a series of rooms opening off a third wall. The prayer direction (qibla) at that time was to the north toward Jerusalem; when it was later changed to Mecca, the mosque was reoriented to the south. A small raised platform (minbar) provided a space for the Prophet to speak to those gathered.

As Islam spread the design of mosques incorporated local architectural traditions; the hypostyle prayer hall, as seen in plan of the Great Mosque of Samara, appears to have been inspired by Mesopotamian and Persian columned audience halls. When the Prophet's Mosque was rebuilt under the Umayyad Dynasty, it was converted into a hypostyle mosque.

In the Levant, Roman and Byzantine building practices were adapted to the needs of the local Islamic community and early mosques, for example, the Great Mosque of Damascus incorporate features such as a three-aisle arrangement, derived from the Roman basilica. Although not a mosque, the Dome of the Rock in Jerusalem owes its arrangement to Byzantine central plan churches. Later Ottoman mosques were also inspired by Byzantine forms, particularly the Church of Hagia Sophia.

The Iranian Four-Iwan mosque is an architectural descendant of the pre-Islamic Sassanid Persian monumental iwan or brick audience hall; the Palace of Ardashir Pāpakan, in Dezh Dokhtar (Fars), Iran (c. 224 CE), and the Taq Kisra at Ctesiphon, Iraq (c. 250 CE), being two surviving early examples of these arched barrel vaulted halls.

Safavid Persia (c. 1501–1722 CE)

Shah Abbas's surrendering of the young prince, his nephew, as a hostage to Sultan Murad III brought a temporary end to hostilities between the Ottoman Empire and Safavid Persia. The Safavids had come to power in Iran in 1501 CE after almost three centuries of foreign rule by Mongols and Timurids. The dynasty descended from Safi al-Din, the leader of a mystic Sufi order in the northwestern city of Ardabil. Originally Sunni Muslims, the Safavids became Shi'ites at the end of the fourteenth century CE, expediently claiming a connection to Ali, the son-in-law of the Prophet. Under the Safavids Shi'itism became the official state religion.

Ustad 'Ali Akbar Isfahani, with Badi' al-Zaman Tuni and Muhibb 'Ali Beg, Masjid-I Shah, Isfahan, 1611–1638 CE In 1597 Shah Abbas (r. 1571–1629 CE) moved his capital from the northern city of Qazvin to the more centrally located city of Isfahan, effectively making it less of an Ottoman target. Almost immediately, he began transforming the old city, building new mosques, madrassas, palaces, pavilions, public baths, caravansaries, public squares and tree-lined boulevards. During his reign the Isfahan school of painting and calligraphy was established; Chinese masters were brought in to enhance ceramic pottery and tile production, and the manufacture of fine carpets was encouraged.

The Shah's greatest architectural monument was his large imperial mosque, the Masjid-I Shah (Figure 5.31), renamed Masjid-I Imam after the Iranian Revolution. The Masjid opens onto the south end of the Naghsh-I Jahan ***Maidan***, an immense ceremonial plaza. The architect of the mosque, according to inscriptions on the building was Ali Akbar Isfahani but nothing is known about him, the designer, Badi' al-Zaman Tuni, or the master builder, Muhibb 'Ali Beg, who worked with him. In designing the mosque Master Isfahani had to resolve a

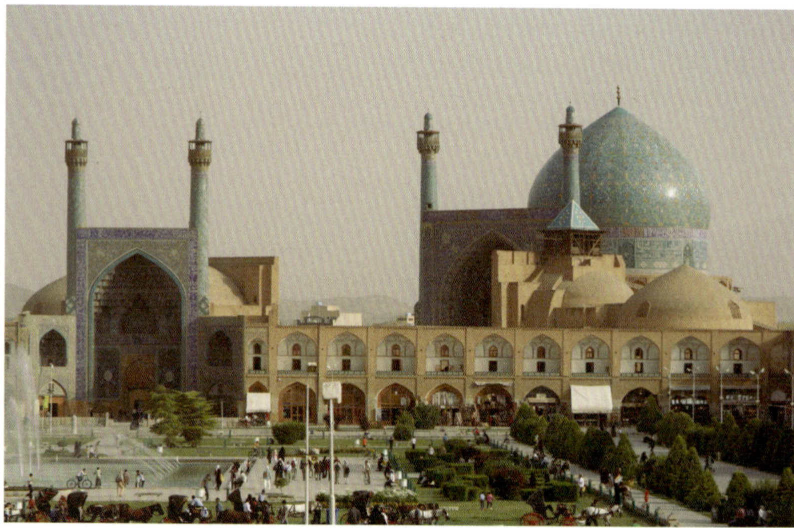

▶ **5.31** Iran, Isfahan, Ustad 'Ali Akbar Isfahani, Naghsh-I Jahan Maidan and entrance Iwan of the Masjid-I Shah, 1611–1638.

The Masjid-I Shah was renamed Maszid-I Imam after the Revolution. Its blue tiled iwan opens onto the south end of the maidan; its other iwans and domes can be seen beyond the row of shops.

conflict between the orientation of the existing city space and the need to align the mosque with the direction of prayer. His solution was to line up the main entrance with the maidan arcade and then to bend the connecting north hall 45 degrees to the southwest so that the mosque qibla faces toward Mecca.

The Masjid-I Shah is a four-iwan plan mosque, a design that originated in pre-Islamic Iran. As is typical in such designs, the Masjid-I Shah's iwans are centered in the four sides of the sahn and connected by a two story arcade. Each iwan consists of a domed chamber with a vaulted end and a fronting monumental gateway known as a ***pishtaq***. The vaults of the entrance and the southwest prayer hall iwan are ornament with ***muqarnas*** work, giving the effect of a tiered honeycomb, and framed by pairs of tall, pencil minarets. The muqarnas decoration consists of cantilevered rows of miniature squinches that have a scalloped front edge. Muqarnas are not structural so they can be carved into almost any surface; the upper vaults of the arcade and the base of the minaret pavilions are also decorated with muqarnas elements.

The main prayer hall is covered by a double-shell dome, some 82 feet (25 m) in diameter. The dome is set on a high drum, from which it rises to a height of 42 feet (14 m). Smaller domes rise from the other *iwans*. Adjacent to the main prayer hall on the east and west sides are two large enclosed winter prayer halls, each crowned by eight low hemispherical domes. Moving outward from the winter halls are two open madrassas.

The results of Shah Abbas' patronage of the arts, particularly calligraphy, illumination, textiles, and ceramic tile, can be seen in the rich ornamentation of the Masjid-I Shah that borrows from each of these traditions. Inside and out its walls are decorated, not with the expensive mosaics and marble panels that enriched Umayyad and Abbasid mosques but with more economical ***haft rang*** (seven color) ceramic tiles (Figure 5.32). While the resulting surface is not as luminescent

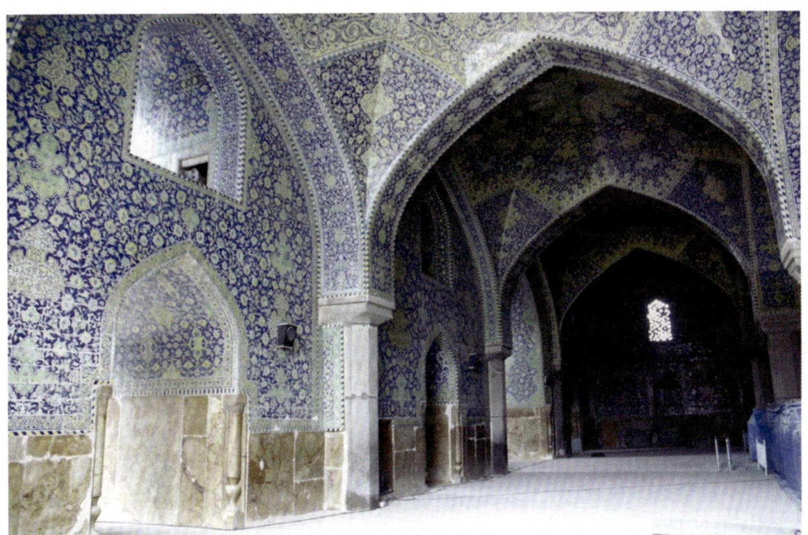

◀ **5.32** Iran, Isfahan, Ustad 'Ali Akbar Isfahani, Masjid-I Shah, 1611–1638. Interior of the Winter Prayer hall with half rang tilework.

Isfahan was a center of tile-making under the Safavids and specialized in the creation of haft rang or seven color tile which was used to create carpet-like patterns.

as glass mosaics and thus does not perform as well in low light, the tiles allowed the Shah's artisans to create a densely patterned surface filled with intricate floral arabesques and bands of fine calligraphy on a multi-toned ground.

The haft rang process begins with firing a white surface glaze on the tiles, then the tiles are laid out as needed for a particular space. A paper pattern bearing the larger design is laid across the tile set and the individual color glazes (green, brown, turquoise, violet, blue, and yellow) are applied and black lines added to separate the colors. The tiles are then numbered and fired to set the overglaze colors. The predominately blue tones used in the mosque's tilework visually heighten and lighten the spaces with an effect that is reminiscent of the finest Persian carpets.

Contemporary Islamic Art

While Iran under the Qajar, and Iraq and Turkey under the Ottomans, managed to avoid colonization in the nineteenth century, they did not escape Western artistic influence. As early as 1827, Western easel painting courses were included in the curriculum of Ottoman military academies. The students who trained in these academies brought this knowledge to the cities in Egypt, Lebanon, Syria, and Iraq to which they were posted. Ottoman and Qajar engagement with the West increased in the second half of the century when Sultan Abdülaziz (r. 1861–1876) and Shah Näser od-Din (r. 1848–1896 CE) became the first rulers of their nations to visit Western Europe. Both rulers and their successors promoted programs of modernization in the arts and sciences and opened schools and academies that offered Western-style instruction.

▼ **5.33** Iran, Ali Ajali (b. 1939), *Untitled* 2005, acrylic.
Ajali is works in a style known as Naqqashi-Khat or script-painting that is based in traditional calligraphic forms but his work is less about text than the beauty of script forms.

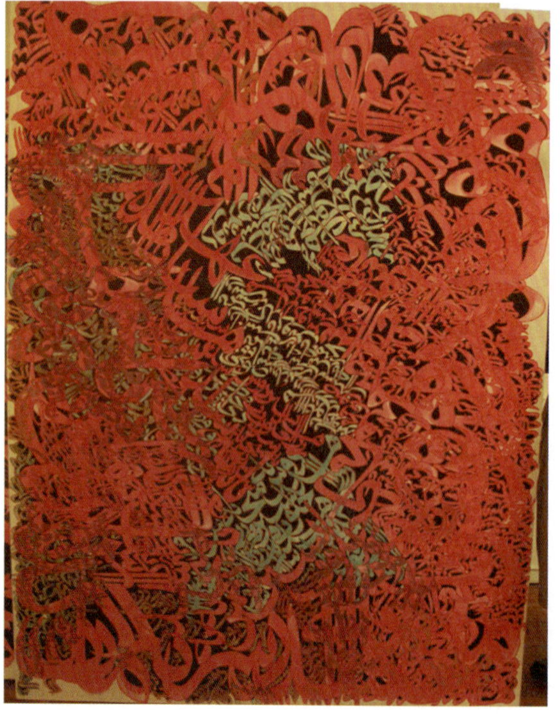

Despite the enlightened attitude of the Ottomans toward art and culture, they spent most of the nineteenth century at war with other nations or with the various ethnic groups within the empire. Their entry into World War I on the side of the Triple Alliance with a surprise attack on their long-time adversary, Russia, was the undoing of the empire. At the close of the war, Constantinople was occupied by British and French forces, and under the mandate of the League of Nations, the Ottoman Empire was partitioned along ethnic lines to create the current configuration of West Asian states. These new nations had disparate attitudes towards the arts. Countries such as Turkey, Syria, Lebanon, and Iraq that had millennia-long traditions of art-making, had enjoyed state support under the Ottomans, and had art facilities in place, fared better in the new nationalist cultural climate. Those states established in regions historically underpopulated, with few economic or institutional resources, and little in the way of artistic traditions, found the path to forging national cultural identities and building institutions more challenging. Yet, by the time the British and French withdrew from the last of these states in the 1970s, most had developed vibrant art scenes.

Ali Ajali (b. 1939), Untitled, 2009 In the 1960s, a group of young Iranian artists responding to the criticism being directed against Westernized art started the movement known as *Naqqashi-Khat* (script-painting). Naqqashi-Khat drew inspiration from the traditional art form of Islamic calligraphy, which had been practiced in Iran for more than a thousand years. The appeal of calligraphy was not in its ability to communicate text but in its visual form.

One of the artists participating in the Naqqashi-Khat movement is Ali Ajali. Ajali was born in Mianeh in north eastern Iran. He was educated in Tehran at the Lycée Français, and went on to study interior design and architecture at the College of Design, also in Tehran. After graduation he decided to pursue training in traditional calligraphy, entering a journeyman period when he studied with several Iranian master calligraphers. His contribution to the field was a new dense and overlapping style of calligraphy called *Gol Gasht*. Calligraphy constitutes the main element of Anjali's large acrylic paintings such as *Untitled*, 2009 (Figure 5.33); individual letters and words, selected for their formal and aesthetic properties, are repeated hundreds of times, building a heavy tangle of thick and thin ribbons, and often painted in a single color.

▼ **5.34** Turkey, Gulay Semercioglu (b. 1968), *The Golden Wings*, 2013. Wire, screws, wood, 15.7 in. × 15.7 in.

Semercioglu's works look like subtle chalk drawings but are actually done with very fine gage wires that she weaves in layers to achieve the gossamer effect of wings.

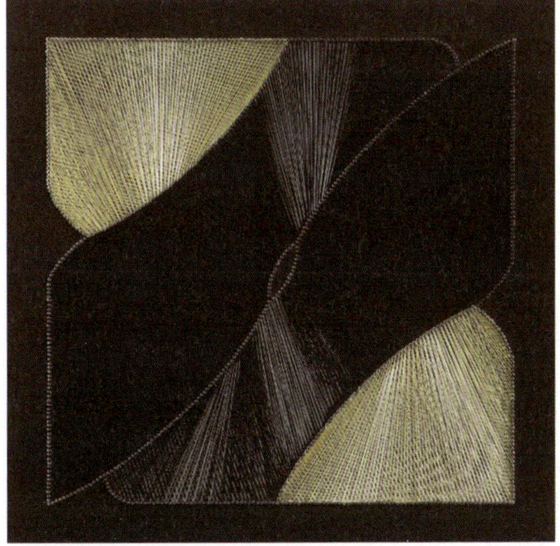

Gulay Semercioglu (b. 1968), The Golden Wings, 2013 Gulay Semercioglu is a native of Istanbul. She studied painting at Mimar Sinan University, receiving a BA in 1994 and then earned an MA from the university's Institute of Social Science (1998). Trained as a traditional painter, she was inspired to begin working with industrial metallic wires when, while strolling through the Persembe Bazaar, she discovered a display of hardware wire and noticed how the different wires reflected light. In 2004, Semercioglu began constructing metal pieces, weaving hair-thin colored wires, in multiple layers, around

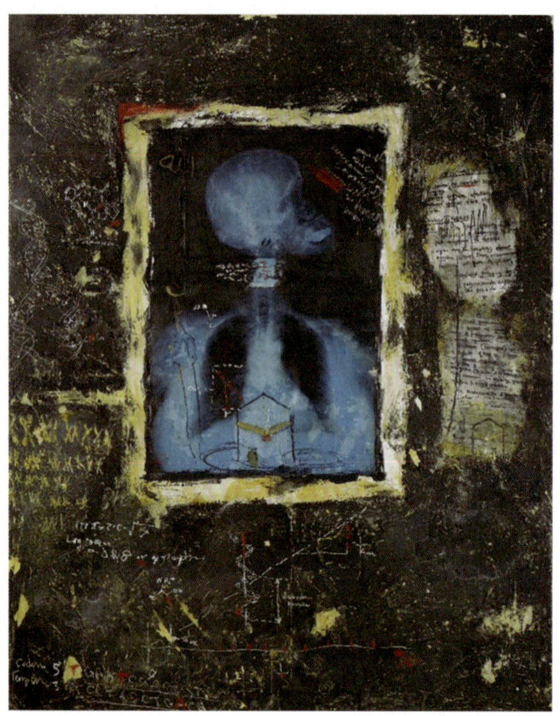

▲ **5.35** Saudi Arabia, Ahmed Mater al-Ziad Aseeri (b. 1979), *X-Ray*, 2003. Mixed media and x-ray on canvas, 53 in. × 41 in.

A physician, Dr. Aseeri creates intimate interior portraits, using his medical knowledge and discarded x-ray films.

screws set in a wooden plank, to create a shimmering mesh. Viewed from a distance her works look like painted minimalist abstractions; it is only upon close examination that the delicacy of the medium in pieces like *The Golden Wings* (Figure 5.34) is revealed.

Ahmed Mater al-Ziad Aseeri (b. 1979), X-Ray, 2003 Ahmed Mater Al-Ziad Aseeri was born in rural Rujal Al-Ma's in the Aseer (Asir) region of southwestern Saudi Arabia near the Yemen border. He studied medicine in the provincial capital of Abha and works as a physician at the local hospital. In works such as *X-ray* (Figure 5.35), Mater draws on his medical knowledge and the products of his practice, using x-ray films that were blurred or otherwise unusable for diagnosis, as a springboard for his works. *X-ray*, although a large scale work, is reminiscent of the tradition of Ottoman portrait miniatures, but in this case the "sitter" is revealed more intimately. Drawing on the film, he adds in the double helix strings of DNA, chromosome karyotypes, resonance structure diagrams, and medical notes to suggest the question: "Is it simply our DNA that makes us human or is there something more?"

Chapter Quick Review

Neolithic West Asia (9000–1500 BCE)

- The earliest art in West Asia dates from around 9,051 years BCE when the region was much wetter than today. Thousands of rock art sites with pictographs are known in the region; the earliest show wild animals such as cheetahs, leopards, hyenas, and ostriches. Later, as the region became drier, the scenes show humans with cattle and hunting dogs.
- Around 8500 BCE Jericho was founded in the Lower Jordan Rift Valley where there was a perennial spring. Jericho was a walled city with towers set into the walls at intervals. The first attempts at memorial portraiture appear at Jericho when human skulls were overmodeled with clay to make them more lifelike.
- Another early city, Çatal Hüyük, arose in Anatolia around 7500 BCE; they also practiced overmodeling of human skulls, modeled figures in clay, and painted the first recognizable landscape around 6200 BCE.

Ancient Mesopotamia (5500–500 BCE)

- The first city states arose in the lands between the Euphrates and Tigris Rivers in what is today Iraq and Syria. The first of these was Sumer in southern Iraq; its major cities: Eridu, Ur, Kuara, and Lagash were on the shores of the Persian Gulf. Each city was dedicated to a patron god, whose temple on a ziggurat stood at the center of the community. The city's economy was managed for the god and, as shown on the Warka Vase from the temple of Inanna in Uruk, there were annual processions of offerings to the temple.

- The Akkadians established themselves to the north of Sumer, ultimately conquering all of Mesopotamia. The Akkadian kings recorded their military victories on stone stele such as the Victory Stele of Naram-sin, which celebrates Naram-sin's victory over the Lullubi.
- Around 2112 BCE, Ur-Nammu, first king of the Third Dynasty of Ur resurrected the old Sumerian state under his rule. He is credited with rebuilding many of the old ziggurats and with writing the Code of Ur-Nammu, the earliest Mesopotamian law code.
- After the Neo-Sumerian state fell to the Elamites, Babylon became an independent state. Its best-known ruler was Hammurabi, who had his law code inscribed upon a stone stele.
- After the death of Hammurabi, the Assyrians began building the first Mesopotamian Empire. The Assyrians decorated their palaces with carved stone reliefs intended to show the power of the Assyrian king. They also set up gate guardian figures, known as *lamassu,* hybrid human-headed, winged bulls rendered as both frontal and profile views in the same work.
- After the fall of the Assyrian Empire Babylon once again became an independent state. Its great king Nebuchadnezzar rebuilt the old city and its temples, lining the main processional way with glazed brick walls and double gateways decorated with lions, bulls, and dragons in molded brick.

Ancient Iran (4000–330 BCE)

- Much of what is known about the ancient Iranian states comes from accounts written on Sumerian, Babylonian, and Akkadian cuneiform tablets.
- Susa, the capital of Elam, was an early center for pottery making and silver working. In the late second millennium BCE, King Untash-Napirisha moved the capital to Dur-Untash and built a great ziggurat to the god Inshushinak. Offerings at the temple included a life-size copper and bronze statue of Queen Napirasu that was moved to Susa after the abandonment of Dur-Untash.
- The Persians moved into Iran in the second millennium BCE and ultimately settled in the southern Zargos and founded the kingdom of Parsa. In the sixth century BCE, Cyrus the Great established the Persian Empire, which expanded to include Iran, Asia Minor, Mesopotamia, and Egypt. The genius of the Persians was in city design and architecture; the last great Persian capital was Persepolis.
- After the death of Alexander the Great, Iran was ruled by a succession of states, including the Seleucid Empire, the Arsacid Parthians, and the Sassanid Empire.

The Islamic Caliphates (632–1258 CE)

- In 632 CE the twenty-nine-year rule of the Rashidun Caliphate began. The first caliph or "successor to the Prophet" was Abū Bakr. The Caliphate ruled over Egypt, the Arabian Peninsula, Mesopotamia, and much of Iran. During this period Islam split into Sunni and Shi'ite factions.

- In 661 CE the Umayyad Dynasty succeeded the Rashidun Caliphate, expanding Islamic rule into Central Asia and across North Africa into the Iberian Peninsula. The Umayyads enriched their cities with great works of architecture including the *Dome of the Rock* and the *Great Mosque of Damascus*.
- In 750 CE the Abbasid established their caliphate and ushered in an Islamic golden age with the founding of the "House of Wisdom" where scholars using logic and scientific methods of inquiry made advances in mathematics, medicine, chemistry, optics, and astronomy. The Abbasids were also supporters of the arts and especially architecture, founding new cities and building great mosques.

Ottoman Empire (1299–1922 CE)

- The Mongol invasions of the thirteenth century caused the Abbasid Caliphate to splinter into regional sultanates, khanates, and tribal kingdoms. One of these, founded by Osman I, grew to overtake the Byzantine Empire and became known as the Ottoman Empire.
- The Ottoman rulers were often enthusiastic patrons of the arts and architecture, establishing royal painting workshops and sponsoring the building of magnificent mosques. One of the great Ottoman architects was Koca Mimar Sinan who designed the *Süleymaniye* mosque.
- Miniature painting flourished under the Ottoman sultans; painters who survived the conquest of the Byzantine Empire were gathered into Academy of Greek Painters and later Islamic painters from the Egyptian Mamluks and Safavid Persian courts were organized into the Academy of Persian Painters. The first Western-style painting schools were established in Ottoman military academies in 1828.

Safavid Persia (c. 1501–1722 CE)

- After two centuries of Mongol and Timurid rule, Iran gained its independence under the Safavid Dynasty. Shi'itism became the official state religion.
- Under the Safavids a new style of mosque, the four-iwan mosque, was developed. One of the greatest examples of this style was the Masjid-I Imam, Isfahan. Safavid mosques were characterized by monumental entrance pishtaqs and surfaces inside and out were embellished with multicolor haft rang tile work.

Contemporary Islamic Art

- At the end of World War I the Ottoman Empire was partitioned by the League of Nations due to its participation in the war on the side of the Triple Alliance. The new states were administered by British and French forces over a period of years, ending in the 1970s.
- Some of these states had long traditions of art and architecture; others did not. The path to forging new nationalistic art was different for each nation but today most have built exciting art scenes and impressive systems of museums and galleries.

Chapter Questions

1. West Asia has a long history of relief sculpture beginning in the Neolithic period, much of it describing the actions of kings. Pick three works and discuss how these were used to record important events or show the power of the state.
2. The various Islamic caliphates and empires built mosques and shrines as political and religious statements in the lands they conquered. These varied in significant ways. Describe how mosque design evolved from the time of the Prophet's house in Media through the building of the Great Mosque of Damascus, the Süleymaniye, and the Masjid-I Imam. What were some of the influences that inspired these developments? Do research on mosque design in the United States. How do modern mosques follow or break with these building traditions?
3. Pick two works of religious architecture constructed during the caliphates and describe how their interiors were ornamented. Identify and describe the motifs used.
4. Although the depiction of living beings is not allowed in the context of religious art, Islamic secular art has a long tradition of the figure. Select an example of a figurative work in miniature painting and compare it with a contemporary work that explores human anatomy. How are the approaches similar and different?

Key Terms and Figures

Key Terms

Arabesques A flowing, interlaced linear design commonly used in Islamic decoration.

Bitumen A naturally occurring tar-like petroleum product, usually obtained from seepage areas.

Canephore A sculptural figure, most often female, carrying a basket on her head.

Haft rang A seven color over-glazed tile used in Safavid architecture.

Has Under the Ottomans a has was a government workshop of forty to seventy architects.

Imam The prayer leader in a mosque.

Iwan A rectangular vaulted hall with an open end commonly found in Safavid architecture.

Lamassu In Assyrian art a hybrid guardian figure, having a human head, the body of a bull or lion, and wings of a bird, often flanking portals.

Madrassa An Islamic religious school, often associated with a mosque.

Mamluks Slave soldier in many Muslim armies, ultimately rising to positions of leadership in many Islamic states.

Masjid A "place for bowing down" or another term for a mosque.

Mihrab A niche set into the qibla of a mosque to designate the direction of prayer.

Minbar The pulpit in a mosque used by the imam to deliver sermons.

Muqarnas A form of ornamentation in which a vault or squinch is geometrically divided into miniature segments resulting in a "honeycomb" effect.

Nakkas Artist/designers who often worked with calligraphers to produce miniature paintings for manuscripts.

Pishtaq A monumental gateway often used to mark the entrance to an iwan.

Qibla The direction that should be faced by Muslims in prayer; in architecture it is often marked by a niche.

Riqaqs A double stacked arcade in Islamic architecture.

Sahn A courtyard; often a feature of mosque architecture.

Stele Also stela; an upright slab often with a carved or inscribed face that was often a commemorative marker.

Tesselation A decorative pattern of repeating geometric shapes arranged closely and without overlapping.

Wusum Tribal symbols, usually geometric designs, used in Saudi Arabia in preliterate and modern times.

Ziggurat A rectangular structure stepped tower, usually surmounted by a temple and constructed of mud brick in ancient Mesopotamia and the Elamite kingdom of Iran.

Key Figures

Abd al-Malik—Caliph of the Umayyad Dynasty who built the Dome of the Rock.

Abū Bakr—Successor of the Prophet as the first caliph of the Rashidun Caliphate.

Assurbanipal—Seventh century BCE king of Assyria, who assemble a cuneiform library at his palace in Ninevah.

Cyrus II—Sixth century BCE Persian king who founded the Achaemenian Empire.

Darius I—Late sixth to fifth century BCE ruler of the Persian Empire who founded the capital of Persepolis.

Enheduanna—Daughter of Sargon I, priestess and first known poet.

Hammurabi—Sixth king of the first Babylonian dynasty who had his laws inscribed on the stele bearing his name.

Kenyon, Kathleen—British archaeologist who excavated at Jericho in the 1950s.

Mellaart, James—British archaeologist who discovered the site of Çatal Hüyük.

Napirasu—Wife of Elamite king Untash-Napirisha; she was immortalized in a 3,850 pound bi-metallic statue.

Naram-Sin—Grandson of Sargon I, first to declare as a god-king.

Nebuchadnezzar II—Second Chaldean king of Babylonia who was responsible for rebuilding the city of Babylon.

Raja Ibn Haywah—Architect of the Dome of the Rock.

Sargon I—Founder of the Akkadian Empire.

Sargon II—Eighth century BCE Assyrian king.

Shah Abbas—Sixteenth century CE Safavid ruler who moved the capital to Isfahan and constructed the Masjid-I Imam.

Sinan, Koca Mimar —Sixteenth century architect, born Greek Orthodox, who was drafted into the Ottoman army and became chief architect of the empire under Suleiman the Magnificent, Selim II, and Murad III; he is credited with more than 450 buildings.

Untash-Napirisha—King of Elam who built the city of Dur-Untash and raised a ziggurat to Inshushinak.

Ur-Nammu—First king of the Third Dynasty of Ur who established the Neo-Sumerian state.

Woolley, Charles L.—British archaeologist who excavated the Sumerian city of Ur during the 1920s and 1930s.

Xerxes I—Son of Darius I who completed construction of Persepolis.

Yazid Ibn Salam—Architect of the Dome of the Rock.

Bibliography

Anon. "Art Treasures of Turkey." *Metropolitan Museum of Art Bulletin* 26, no. 5 (January 1968).

"Islamic Art." *Metropolitan Museum of Art Bulletin* 36, no. 2 (Fall 1978).

"The Ottoman Empire." *Metropolitan Museum of Art Bulletin* 26, no. 5 (January 1968): 204–224.

Ali, Wijdan. "The Status of Islamic Art in the Twentieth Century." *Muqarnas* 9 (1992): 186–188.

Aqrawi, Adnan A. M. "Stratigraphic Signatures of Climatic Change During the Holocene Evolution of the Tigris-Euphrates Delta, Lower Mesopotamia," *Global and Planetary Change* 28 (2001): 267–283.

Atil, Esin. "Ottoman Miniature Painting under Sultan Mehmed II." Freer Gallery of Art Fiftieth Anniversary Volume. *Ars Orientalis* 9 (1973): 103–120.

Bailey, Martin. "Ancient Nimrud Ziggurat Bulldozed by Isil: Islamic Extremists Razed Massive 2,900-Year-Old Assyrian Structure to the Ground." *Art Newspaper*, November 14, 2016.

Banning, E. B. "The Neolithic Period: Triumphs of Architecture, Agriculture, and Art." *Near Eastern Archaeology* 61, no. 4 (December 1998): 188–237.

Bates, Ülkü Ü. "Two Ottoman Documents on Architects in Egypt." *Muqarnas* 3 (1985): 121–127.

Black, Jeremy, and Anthony Green. *Gods, Demons, and Symbols of Ancient Mesopotamia. An Illustrated Dictionary.* University of Texas Press, 1992.

Bonfioli, Mara. "Syriac-Palestinian Mosaics in Connection with the Decorations of the Mosques at Jerusalem and Damascus." *East and West* 10, nos. 1–2 (March–June 1959): 57–76.

Briggs, Martin S. "Newly Discovered Syrian Mosaics." *Burlington Magazine for Connoisseurs* 58, no. 337 (April 1931): 180–181, 183.

Brown, Brian A., and Marian H. Feldman, editors. *Critical Approaches to Ancient Near Eastern Art.* Boston and Berlin: Walter De Gruyter, Inc., 2014

Cerasi, Maurice. "Late-Ottoman Architects and Master Builders." *Muqarnas* 5 (1988): 87–102.

Charpin, Dominique. "I Am the Sun of Babylon: Solar Aspects of Royal Power in Old Babylonian Mesopotamia." In *Experiencing Power, Generating Authority: Cosmos, Politics, and the Ideology of Kingship in Ancient Egypt and Mesopotamia.* University of Pennsylvania Press, 2013.

Choksy, Jamsheed K. "Gesture in Ancient Iran and Centralk Asia II: Proskynesis and the Bent Forefinger." *Bulletin of the Asia Institute* 4 (1990): 201–207.

Creswell, K. A. C. The Legend that Al-Walid Asked for and Obtained Help from the Byzantine Emperor: A Suggested Explanation." *Journal of the Royal Asiatic Society of Great Britain and Ireland*, nos. 3–4 (October 1956): 142–145.

Dayton, John. "The Problem of Climatic Change in the Arabian Peninsular." *Proceedings of the Seminar for Arabian Studies*. Vol. 5, Proceedings of the Eight Seminar for Arabian Studies held at the Oriental Institute, Oxford, on July 3–5, 1975 (1975): 33–60.

DeMarco, Emily. "What Ancient Rock Art Reveals about a Wetter Arabia." *Inside Science*. July 7, 2016. https://www.insidescience.org/news/what-ancient-rock-art-reveals-about-wetter-arabia

Diez, Ernest. "The Mosaics of the Dome of the Rock at Jerusalem." *Ars Islamica* 1, no. 2 (1934): 235–238.

Eigner, Saeb. *Art of the Middle East: Modern and Contemporary Art of the Arab World and Iran*. London and New York: Merrell, 2010.

Engel, Max, Helmut Bruckner, Anna Pint, Kai Wellbrock, Andreas Ginau, Peter Voss, Matthias Grottker, Nicole Klasen, and Peter Frenzel. "The Early Holocene Humid Period in NW Saudi Arabia—Sediments, Microfossils and Palaeo-Hydrological Modelling." *Quaternary International* 266 (2012): 131–141.

Ertug, Zeynep Tarim. "The Depiction of Ceremonies in Ottoman Miniatures: Historical Record or a Matter of Protocol?" *Muqarnas* 27 (2010): 251–275.

Erzen, Jale. "Sinan as Anti-Classicist." *Muqarnas* 5 (1988): 70–86.

Foster, Benjamin R. *The Age of Agade: Inventing Empire in Ancient Mesopotamia*. London and New York: Routledge: Taylor & Francis Group, 2016.

Frankfort, H. *Cylinder Seals: A Documentary Essay on the Art and Religion of the Ancient Near East*. London: MacMillan, 1939.

Frazier, Ian. "Invaders: Destroying Baghdad." *New Yorker*. April 25, 2005, http://www.newyorker.com/magazine/2005/04/25/invaders-3

Ghirshman, Roman. *Tchoga Zanbil (Dur-Untash) Vol I. La ziggurat*. MDAFI 39, Paris, 1966.

Tchoga Zanbil (Dur-Untash) Vol II. Temenos, temples, palais, tombes. MDAFI 40, Paris, 1968.

Goodwin, Godfrey. *A History of Ottoman Architecture*. London: Thames & Hudson, 1987 (reprint 2003).

Sinan: Ottoman Architecture and its Values Today. London: Saqi Books, 1993.

Goodwin, Jason. "The Glory That Was Baghdad." *Wilson Quarterly* (1976–) 27, no. 2 (Spring 2003): 24–28.

Groucutt, Huw S., and Michael D. Petragua. "The Prehistory of the Arabian Peninsula: Deserts, Dispersals, and Demography." *Evolutionary Anthropology* 21 (2012): 113–125.

Guralnick, Eleanor.

"Sargonid Sculpture and the Late Assyrian Cubit." *Iraq* 58 (1996): 89–103.

Hamzeh, Mohammad Ali, Mohammad Hosein Mahmudy Gharaie, Hamid Alizadeh Ketek Lahijani, Morteza Djamali, Reza Moussavi Harami, and Abdolmajid Naderi Beni. "Holocene Hydrological Changes in SE Iran, a Key Region Between Indian Summer Monsoon and Mediterranean Winter Precipitation Zones, as Revealed from a Lacustrine Sequence from Lake Hamoun." *Quaternary International* 408 (2016): 25–39.

Harper, Prudence O., JoanAruz, and Françoise Tallon, editors. *The Royal City of Susa: Ancient Near Eastern Treasures in the Louvre*. New York: Metropolitan Museum of Art, 1993.

Harrigan, Peter. "Art Rocks in Saudi Arabia." *Saudi Aramco World* 53, no. 2 (March–April) 2002: 36–47.

Helbaek, Hans. "Textiles from Çatal Hüyük." *Archaeology* 16, no. 1 (March 1963): 39–46.

Hemming, Henry. "Ahmed Mater Al-Ziad Aseeri," *Nafas Art Magazine* (November 2008). http://u-in-u.com/en/nafas/articles/2008/ahmed-mater/

Herodotus (George Rawlinson, translator)

The History of Herodotus, London: William Benton Publisher, 1971

Hilâlî, Muhammad Taqî-ud Dîn and Muhammad Muhsin Khân (translators)

The Noble Qur'an in the English Language, Madinah: King Fahid Complex for the Printing of the Holy Qur'an, n.d.

Hillenbrand, Robert. *Islamic Architecture: Form, Function and Meaning.* New York: Columbia University Press, 1994.

Hodder, Ian (Director), et al. Çatalhöyük Archive Report, 2004–2016. www.Catalhoyuk.com

Hoffman, Eva R. "Between East and West: The Wall Paintings of Samarra and the Construction of Abbasid Princely Culture." *Muqarnas* 25 (2008): 107–132.

Holakooei, Parviz. *Technological Study of the Seventeenth Century Haft Rang Tiles in Iran with a Comparative View to the Cuerda Seca Tiles in Spain.* PhD dissertation Università degli Studi di Ferrara, 2012.

Holakooei, Parviz, Flavia Tisato, Carmela Vaccaro, and Ferruccio Carlo Petrucci. "Haft rang or cuerda seca? Spectroscopic Approaches to the Study of Overglaze Polychrome Tiles from Seventeenth Century Persia." *Journal of Archaeological Science*, no. 41 (2014): 447–460.

Ismail, Osman S. A. "The Founding of a New Capital: Samarra." *Bulletin of the School of Oriental and African Studies* 31, no. 1 (1968): 1–13.

Jennings, Richard P., Ceri Shipton, Abdulaziz Al-Omari, Abdullah M. Alsharekh, Remy Crassard, Huw Groucutt, and Michael D. Petraglia. "Rock Art Landscapes Beside the Jubbah palaeolake, Saudi Arabia." *Antiquity* 87 (2013): 666–683.

Kaaki, Lisa. "Gulay Semercioglu: The Line of Life." *Arab News.* June 20, 2012. http://www.arabnews.com/gulay-semercioglu-line-life

Kenyon, Kathleen M. "Jericho." *Archaeology* 20, no. 4 (October 1967): 268–275.

"Excavations at Jericho." *Journal of the Royal Anthropological Institute of Great Britain and Ireland* 84, no. 1/2 (January–December 1954): 103–110.

King, L. W. "Excavations at Babylon." *Burlington Magazine for Connoisseurs* 26. no. 144 (March 1915): 244–245, 248–250.

Kolay, İlknur Aktuğ, and Serpil Çelik. "Ottoman Stone Acquisition in the Mid-Sixteenth Century: The Suleymaniye Complex in Instanbul." *Muqarnas* 23 (2006): 251–272.

Koppes, Clayton R. "Captain Mahan, General Gordon, and the Origins of the Term 'Middle East.'" *Middle Eastern Studies* 12, no. 1 (January 1976): 95–98.

Le Mière, Marie. "The Earliest Pottery of West Asia: Questions Concerning Causes and Consequences." In *The Emergence of Pottery in West Asia*, 9–16. Oxbow Books, 2017.

Leoni, Francesca. *Power and Protection: Islamic Art and the Supernatural.* Ashmolean Museum, Oxford, 2016.

Lewis, Bernard. *The Middle East: A Brief History of the Last 2,000 Years.* New York: Scribner, 1995.

Lloyd, Seton. *The Archaeology of Mesopotamia: From the Old Stone Age to the Persian Conquest.* London: Thames and Hudson, 1978.

The Art of the Ancient Near East. London: Thames and Hudson, 1961.

Lloyd, Seton and Hans Wolfgang Müller

Ancient Architecture (History of World Architecture), London: Phaidon, 3rd edition, 2004

Lyon, David G. "Notes on the Hammurabi Monument." *Journal of the American Oriental Society* 25 (1904): 266–278.

MacGinnis, John. "Herodotus' Description of Babylon." *Bulletin of the Institute of Classical Studies*, no. 33 (1986): 67–86.

McLerran, Dan. "Researchers Discover Prehistoric Human Habitation Sites in the Nefud Desert." *Popular Archaeology* 11 (October 2014). http://popular-archaeology.com/issue/june-2013/article/researchers-discover-prehistoric-human-habitation-sites-in-the-nefud-desert

Mellaart, James. "Excavations at Çatal Hüyük: First Preliminary Report, 1961." *Anatolian Studies* 12 (1962): 41–65.

"Excavations at Çatal Hüyük, 1962: Second Preliminary Report." *Anatolian Studies* 13 (1963): 43–103.

"Excavations at Çatal Hüyük, 1963: Third Preliminary Report." *Anatolian Studies* 14 (1964):39–119.

"Excavations at Çatal Hüyük, 1965: Fourth Preliminary Report." *Anatolian Studies* 16 (1966): 165–191.

"Deities and Shrines of Neolithic Anatolia: Excavations at Catal Huyuk, 1962." *Archaeology* 16, no. 1 (March 1963): 29–38.

Meskell, Lynn. "The Nature of the Beast: Curating Animals and Ancestors at Çatalhöyük." *World Archaeology* 40, no. 3 (September 2008): 373–389.

Meyers, Peter"The Casting Process of the Statue of Queen Napir-Asu in the Louvre." From *The Parts to the Whole*, Acta of the 13th International Bronze Congress Held at Cambridge, Massachusetts, May 28–June 1, 1996, Ed. C. C. Mattusch et al. *Journal of Roman Archaeology* I (2000): 11–8.

ichell, George, editor. *Architecture of the Islamic World: Its History and Social Meaning*, London: Thames and Hudson, 1978.

Muscarella, Oscar White. *Bronze and Iron: Ancient Near Eastern Artifacts in the Metropolitan Museum of Art*. New York: Metropolitan Museum of Art, 1988.

Naef, Silvia. "Reexploring Islamic Art: Modern and Contemporary Creation in the Arab World and Its Relation to the Artistic Past." *RES: Anthropology and Aesthetics*, no. 43 (Spring 2003): 164–174.

Necipoğlu, Gülru. "Creation of a National Genius: Sinan and the Historiography of 'Classical' Ottoman Architecture." *Muqarnas* 24 (2007): 141–183.

Necipoğlu-Kafadar, Gülru. "The Süleymaniye Complex in Istanbul: An Interpretation." *Muqarnas* 3 (1985): 92–117.

Nigro, Lorenzo. "Tell es-Sultan 2015: A Pilot Project for Archaeology in Palestine." *Near Eastern Archaeology* 79, no. 1 (March 2016): 4–17.

Northedge, Alastair. "The Racecourses at Samarra." *Bulletin of the School of Oriental and African Studies* 53, no. 1 (1990): 31–56.

Northedge, Alastair, and Derek Kennet. *The Samarra Archaeological Survey*. http://community.dur.ac.uk/derek.kennet/samarra.htm

Ornan, Tallay. "The Bull and its Two Masters: Moon and Storm Deities in Relation to the Bull in Ancient Near Eastern Art." *Israel Exploration Journal* 51, no. 1 (2001): 1–26.

Onat, Sema. *Islamic Art of Illumination: Classical Tazhib from Ottoman to Contemporary Times*. Clifton, NJ: Blue Dome Press, 2015.

Petersen, Andrew. *Dictionary of Islamic Architecture*. London and New York: Routledge, 1999.

Preston, G. W., A. G. Parker, H. Walkington, M. J. Leng, and M. J. Hodson. "From Nomadic Herder-Hunters to Sedentary Farmers: The Relationship Between Climate Change and Ancient Subsistence Strategies in South-Eastern Arabia." *Journal of Arid Environments* 86 (2011).

Rabbat, Nasser. "The Dialogic Dimension of Umayyad Art." *RES: Anthropology and Aesthetics*, no. 43 (Spring 2003): 78–94.

Rawlinson, George, translator. *The History of Herodotus*. Great Books Series, Encyclopaedia Britannica, 1971.

Riehl, Simone. "Climate and agriculture in the Ancient Near East: A Synthesis of the Archaeobotanical and Stable Carbon Isotope Evidence." *Veget Hist Archaeobot* 17 (2008) (Suppl 1): S43–S51.

Rose, Jeffery I. "New Light on Human Prehistory in the Arabo-Persian Gulf Oasis." *Current Anthropology* 51, no. 6 (December 2010): 849–883.

Roth, M. *Law Collections from Mesopotamia and Asia Minor.* Writings from the Ancient World. Volume 6. Atlanta: Society of Biblical Literature, 1995.

Roux, Georges. *Ancient Iraq.* 3rd edition, London: Penguin Books, 1992.

Rutz, Matthew, and Piotr Michalowski. "The Flooding of Esnunna, the Fall of Mari: Hammurabi's Deeds in Babylonian Literature and History." *Journal of Cuneiform Studies* 68 (2016): 15–43.

Sakisian, A. "Turkish Miniatures." *Burlington Magazine for Connoisseurs* 87, no. 510 (September 1945): 224, 226–232.

Schlossman, Betty L. "Portraiture in Mesopotamia in the Late Third and Early Second Millennium B.C. Part II: The Early Second Millennium." *Archiv für Orientforschung* 28 (1981/1982): 143–170.

Schmitt, A.K. et al. "Identifying the Volcanic Eruption Depicted in a Neolithic Painting at Çatalhöyük, Central Anatolia, Turkey." *PLoS ONE* 9, no. 1 (2014): e84711. doi: 10.1371/journal.pone.0084711

Shahbazi, A. Shapur. "Persepolis." *Encyclopædia Iranica*, 2012. http://www.iranicaonline.org/articles/persepolis

Stordeur, Danielle. "Domestication of Plants and Animals, Domestication of Symbols?" In *The Development of Pre-State Communities in the Ancient Near East*, 123–130. Oxbow Books, 2010.

Stronach, David, and Hilary Gopnik. "Pasargadae." *Encyclopaedia Iranica*. 2009. http://www.iranicaonline.org/articles/pasargadae

Strouhal, Eugen. "Five Plastered Skulls from Pre-Pottery Neolithic B Jericho: Anthropological Study." *Paleorient* 1, no. 2 (1973): 231–247.

Tanindi, Zeren. "Additions to Illustrated Manuscripts in Ottoman Workshops." Muqarnas 17, no. 1 (2000): 147–161. https://archnet.org/system/publications/contents/5129/original/DPC1862.pdf?1384788412.

Taha, Hamdan, and Ali Qleibo. *Jericho a Living History: Ten Thousand Years of Civilization.* Palestinian Ministry of Tourism and Antiquities, 2010.

Tosi, Maurizio. "The Emerging Picture of Prehistoric Arabia." *Annual Review of Anthropology* 15 (1986): 461–490.

Twiss, Katheryn C. "A Modified Boar Skull from Çatalhöyük." *Bulletin of the American Schools of Oriental Research*, no. 342 (May 2006): 1–12.

Van de Mieroop, Marc. "Hammurabi's Self-Presentation." *Orientalia* 80, no. 4 (2011): 305–338.

"Reading Babylon." *American Journal of Archaeology* 107, no. 2 (April 2003): 257–275.

Winter, Irene J. "Seat of Kingship/A Wonder to Behold: The Palace as Construct in the Ancient Near East." *Ars Orientalis* 23 (1993): 27–55.

Yarshater, Ehsan, editor. "Čogā Zanbīl." *Encyclopaedia Iranica* [electronic resource], Columbia University Center for Iranian Studies, New York, 1996.

Zarins, Juris. "The Early Settlement of Southern Mesopotamia: A Review of Recent Historical, Geological, and Archaeological Research." *Journal of the American Oriental Society* 112, no. 1 (January–March 1992): 55–77.

Zeder, Melinda A. "The Origins of Agriculture in the Near East." *Current Anthropology* 52, no. S4 (October 2011): S221–S235.

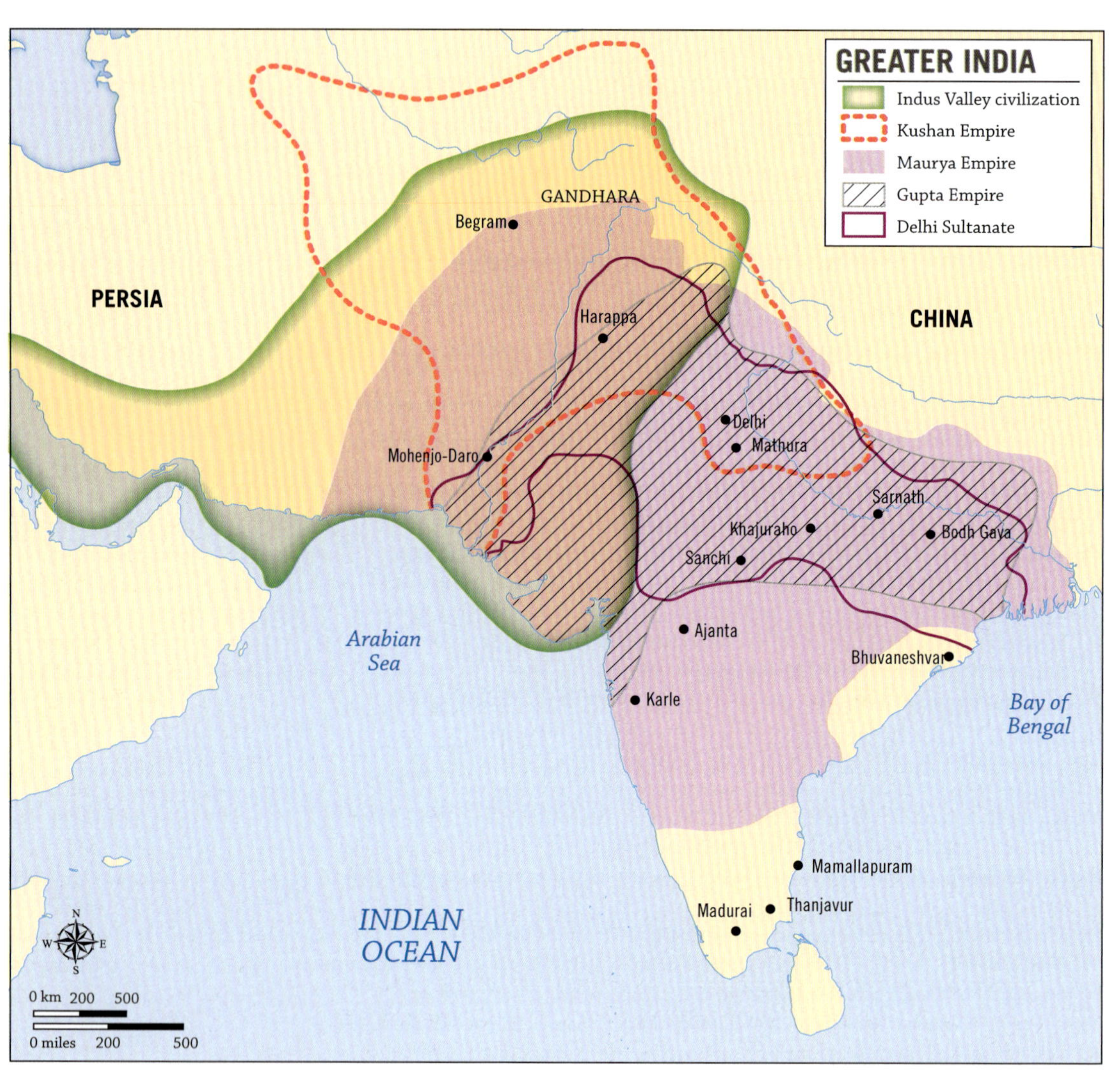

GREATER INDIA
Indus Valley civilization
Kushan Empire
Maurya Empire
Gupta Empire
Delhi Sultanate
GANDHARA
Begram
PERSIA
CHINA
Harappa
Delhi
Mathura
Mohenjo-Daro
Sarnath
Khajuraho
Bodh Gaya
Sanchi
Ajanta
Arabian Sea
Bhuvaneshvar
Karle
Bay of Bengal
Mamallapuram
Madurai
Thanjavur
INDIAN OCEAN
N
W
E
S
0 km 200 500
0 miles 200 500

India

6

Brief Overview

The first humans moved onto the Indian subcontinent at least 290,000 years ago, registering their presence with enigmatic meanders and cupules left in the rock walls of Auditorium Cave at Bhimbetka, the Daraki-Chattan rock shelter, and other sites in Central India. However, it is not until the Paleolithic Period, circa 30,000 BCE, that the first petroglyphs and paintings appear at the Bhimbetka caves; many of these were depictions of local fauna, including peacocks, monkeys, elephants, rhinoceros, and tigers rendered in a linear style using pigments made from charcoal, hematite, and manganese. These caves were used by successive groups of people for thousands of years and represent a record of cultural development from early hunter-gatherer and agricultural societies into the historic period.

Chapter Objectives

1. Recognize and describe significant artworks, styles, media, and technologies from key periods in Indian art history, including the Indus Valley, Maurya, Gupta, and Mughal Empires. Explain how India's greatest rulers shaped the course of art during their reigns.
2. Understand and be able to provide examples of how indigenous religious and philosophical beliefs, such as Hinduism and Buddhism, and later arrivals, such as Islam and Christianity, influenced, and continue to shape, the development of Indian art.
3. Explain the impact of the period of British rule on the art and culture of pre-and-post independence India in terms of specific works, artists, and contemporary directions.

During the third millennium BCE, the first Indian civilization arose along the course of the Indus River in northwestern India. The more than one thousand cities and towns that have been identified in the Indus Valley civilization were organized on a grid plan, offered multistory fired brick architecture, advanced water and drainage systems, ritual baths, and elevated storage granaries. The artisans of the Indus Valley produced a wide range of pottery for utilitarian purposes, made terracotta figurines, cast bronze and copper using the lost wax process, and carved highly naturalistic figurative sculptures in the round and as intaglios on stone seals. These images appear to set the aesthetic approach to the human form that is seen throughout the long history of Indian art. Concepts of the divine in art and literature appear in this period when the Hindu Vedas and Upanishads were written and the prototypical depictions of what may well be Lord Shiva appear on Indus seals and small sculpture.

By the first millennium BCE two additional indigenous religions, Jainism and Buddhism appeared in India; both, along with Hinduism, made significant contributions to the development of

Indian art and architectural forms. The same architectural, sculptural, and painting styles were often shared by all three religions but the motifs adapted to meet the devotional needs of each particular faith. This can be seen in sites such as Ellora Caves, which contain works by Hindu, Jain, and Buddhist artists, and the Hindu paintings in the ambulatory of Rajarajeshwara Temple, but which follow the same painting practices and artistic conventions found in the much earlier Buddhist caves of Ajanta.

The most profound changes to Indian art occurred with the arrival of Islam in the early eighth century CE and the British East India Company in the seventeenth century CE. Both were responsible for introducing foreign forms, practices, and materials into Indian architecture and painting that often merged with native styles to produce exciting new hybrid forms. The richness of Indian art continued into the modern era, where art played a critical role in defining the new Indian and Pakistani nations after independence was achieved by both in 1947. Today, many artists from the subcontinent, working in a wide range of media, have achieved international recognition for the quality and originality of their art.

The Indus Valley Civilization (3300–300 BCE)

The first major Indian civilization arose in the fertile Indus Valley and along the coast before the third millennium BCE. Known as the Harappan civilization, after Harappa, the first of its cities to be discovered, or as the Indus civilization, after its major river, it covered an area roughly equivalent to that of Western Europe. Harappa was first explored in 1826 by James Lewis, a British army deserter and travelogue writer. Although he published an account of the site, it was not formally excavated until the 1920s. During that interval, Harappa suffered considerable destruction; in the 1850s, its structures were mined for bricks used to build the local section of the Sind and Punjab Railway. The Indus civilization's second major city, Mohenjo-Daro was not discovered until 1922. Since that time archaeologists have identified more than a thousand Indus cities along the river and in coastal regions from the Gulf of Oman to the Gulf of Cambay and in the Ghaggar-Hakra and upper Yamuna valleys, which suggest a much longer timeline for the civilization.

The Indus civilization presents a number of striking differences in comparison with other early civilizations. Archaeological excavations show Indus cities did not have identifiable palaces, temples, or fortifications, and their art does not show scenes of military victories or persons identifiable as rulers, themes so common in the art of Egypt and Mesopotamia. Several theories have been proposed to explain this unusual situation. One suggests that each urban center was governed by a committee composed of merchants, landholders, or spiritual leaders

timeline

DATE	TYPE	EVENT
		BCE
c. 9000	Art	Bhimbetka rock shelter paintings
c. 5000	History	Indus Valley culture began
c. 4500–2000	Culture	Vedas composed
c. 3000	History	Harappa and Mohenjo-Daro became leading cities
c. 2800	Culture	Cremation replaced burial for dealing with the dead
c. 2600	Art	Great Bath constructed at Mohenjo-Daro
c. 2300	History	Seals used to identify property
c. 1700	History	Harappa and Mohenjo-Daro suffered decline
c. 1000	Culture	Upanishads composed
c. 600	Art	India divided into sixteen Great Kingdoms
c. 599	Culture	Mahavira, founder of Jainism, born
c. 563	Culture	Siddhartha Gautama, founder of Buddhism, born
c. 518	History	Darius I of Persia conquered states of Sindh and Punjab
c. 500	Culture	*Ramayana* (Rama's Journey) composed by Valmiki
339	History	Alexander the Great established city of Alexandria Escate
326	History	Alexander the Great pushed into India
321	History	Chandragupta Maurya founded Maurya Empire
c. 300	Culture	*Mahabharata* composed
	History	Megasthenes, the Greek ambassador, visited Maurya Empire
c. 273	History	Ashoka acceded to the Maurya throne
c. 261	History	Ashoka fought Battle of Kalinga
c. 250	Culture	Third Buddhist Council convened
	Art	Ashokan column erected at Sarnath
	Art	Great Stupa at Sanchi commissioned by Ashoka
c. 200	Art	First caves carved at Ajanta
c. 185	History	Shunga Dynasty established
	Art	Great Stupa enlarged and veneered
c. 135	History	Kushan nomads arrived in Bactria
c. 100	History	Silk Route established from China to the Mediterranean

(Continued)

timeline *continued*

DATE	TYPE	EVENT
		BCE
	Culture	Buddhism split into Theravada and Mahayana forms
c. 73	Art	Great Stupa's Four Toranas added by the Andhra rulers
c. 29	Culture	First Fourth Buddhist Council in Sri Lanka: Pali Canon written
		CE
c. 50	History	Andhra Dynasty collapsed
	Art	Excavation began on the Chaitya hall at Karli
c. 100	History	Spice trade with Romans reached its zenith
	History	First Indian Buddhist Missionaries sent to China
	Culture	Second Fourth Buddhist Council held in Kashmir
c.120	History	Kanishka I acceded to the Kushan throne
c. 131	Art	Bodhisattva of Monk Bala
c. 240	History	Sri Gupta founded Gupta Dynasty
c. 320	History	Chandragupta Gupta founded Gupta Empire
	History	Pallava Empire established
399–412	History	Chinese Buddhist monk Faxian (337–c. 422) visited India
c. 400	Culture	*Mahabharata* and *Ramayana* written down
	Culture	*Kama Sutra* composed
c. 465	Art	*Seated Buddha Preaching the First Sermon* carved
c. 480	Art	Major period of cave carving began at Ajanta
c. 630	Art	Carving of the Five Rathas began at Mammallapuram
c. 650	Art	Parashurameshvara Temple built in Bhuvaneshvar
c. 800	History	Chandella dynasty founded
c. 850	History	Imperial Chola dynasty founded by Vijayataya
c. 897	History	Pallava dynasty ended
998	History	Mahmud of Ghazni invades the Sind and Punjab
985	History	Rajaraja I acceded to the Chola throne
1002	Art	Vishvanatha Temple completed in Khajuraho
	Art	Rajarajeshwara Temple began in Thanjavur
1010	Art	Rajarajeshwara Temple consecrated
1175	History	Muhammad of Ghur invaded India

DATE	TYPE	EVENT
CE		
1199	Art	Quwwat- ul-Islam and Qutb Minar began in Delhi
1206	History	Qutb al-din Aibek established Delhi Sultanate
1310	History	Temple of Meenakshi-Sundareswarar in Madurai destroyed
c. 1400	History	Guru Nanak founded Sikhism
1526	History	Zahir-ud-din Muhammad Babur founded Mughal Empire
c. 1540	History	Akbar the Great born
1555	History	Akbar acceded to the Mughal throne
c. 1562	Art	Akbar commissioned the *Hamzanama* and *Akbarnama*
1559	History	Nayak dynasty founded
1572	Art	Tomb of Humayun completed
1600	History	British East India Company founded in London
1605	History	Jahangir succeeded his father as emperor
1615	History	Sir Thomas Roe visited Mughal Court
1623	Art	Nayaks began reconstruction of Meenakshi Temple
1627	History	Shah Jahan began reign as Mughal Emperor
1631	Art	Construction began on the Taj Mahal
1657	History	Aurangzeb killed his brothers, deposed his father
1736	History	Fall of the Nayak Dynasty
1819	Art	Ajanta caves discovered by British officer, John Smith
1826	Art	James Lewis discovered Harappa
1856	History	Harappa mined for bricks for Railway
1857	History	Great Rebellion (Great Mutiny)
1858	History	British Rule (Raj) began
1869	History	Mohandas Gandhi born
1871	Art	Abanindranath Tagore born
1876	History	Queen Victoria became Empress of India
c. 1880	Art	Narsingh painted the Portrait of Jaswant Singh
1885	History	Indian National Congress founded
1915	Art	Maqbool Fida Husain born
1922	Art	Mohenjo-Daro discovered
1947	History	India and Pakistan achieved independence from Britain

(Kenoyer 2003, 71), or by the heads of senior lineages in the community (Sen 1992, 35–36).

Indus Architecture

Indus Valley cities were laid out on a grid plan with major avenues, some 40 feet (12.2 m) wide, oriented to the cardinal directions. These main thoroughfares were intersected by secondary streets that provided access to residential neighborhoods. Buildings were multi-storied, constructed of uniform, kiln-fired clay bricks, and featured amenities such as bathing houses and latrines. They were equipped with water wells and highly sophisticated sewer systems that brought the sludge out to the agricultural fields where it served as fertilizer (Kenoyer 2003, 71). Many Indus cities had "citadels" raised on brick embankments that may have served as places of refuge during periods of river flooding. At Mohenjo-Daro, the citadel stands 43 feet (13.1 m) above the city and supports a cluster of public buildings, including a granary and a structure known as the Great Bath.

The Great Bath, c. 2600–1900 BCE The importance of the Great Bath (Figure 6.1) is shown by its placement atop the elevated citadel. It is a brick-lined pool that was originally surrounded by a colonnade and a paved court. The pool is an impressive 39 feet (12 m) long, 23 feet (7 m) wide, and 8 feet (2.4 m) deep, with steps at each end to facilitate entrance and exit.. The Great Bath was made watertight by coating the brick joints with **bitumen**, a naturally occurring petroleum tar. It was probably not a recreational swimming pool or public bath, but a place

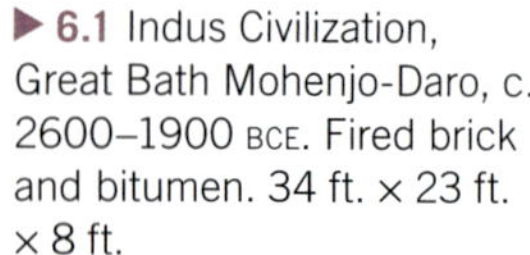

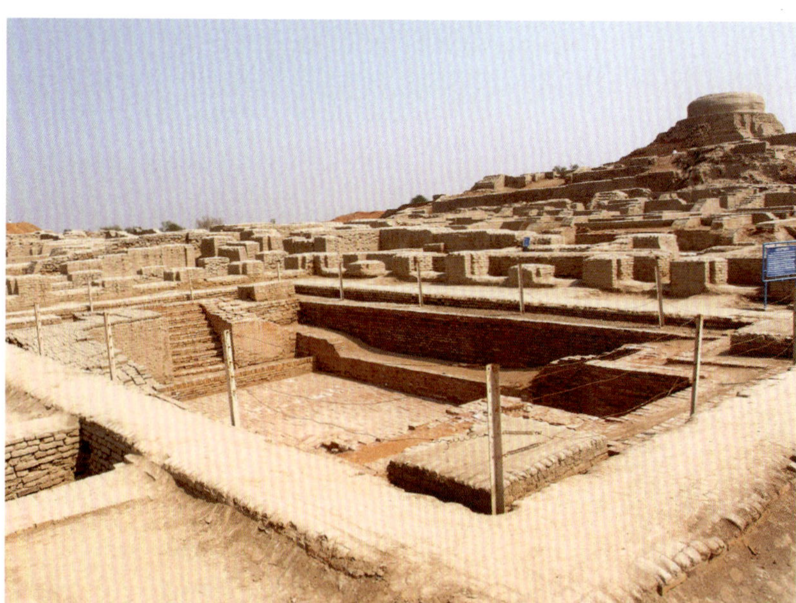

▶ **6.1** Indus Civilization, Great Bath Mohenjo-Daro, c. 2600–1900 BCE. Fired brick and bitumen. 34 ft. × 23 ft. × 8 ft.

Located atop the citadel, the Great Bath was a ritual purification pool for use in religious rituals.

for ritual purification. This suggests that the concepts of pollution and purification through bathing in sacred pools or rivers, so elemental in Hinduism, were already present in the religious practices of the Indus Valley people.

Indus Sculpture

The artisans of the Indus Valley created highly realistic sculpture in metal, stone, and clay but none of these reached the sometimes monumental scale of other early cultures in Africa or West Asia.. Harrapan sculptures were small-scale works, usually less than 10 inches (25 cm) tall. They included human, divine, and animal forms all worked in exacting detail regardless of medium. Again, Indus Valley art is distinct from its contemporaries in that it lacks the monuments glorifying rulers or depicting the great military conquests so common in the art of other cultures.

Young Dancer from Mohenjo-Daro, c. 2500 BCE One of the better known Indus Valley sculptures is the small figure, only 4.25 inches (10.8 cm) high, of a nude young woman (Figure 6.2). She is commonly identified as a dancer because of her active pose, sweeping hair, and multiple bangles (bracelets) of a type still worn today by traditional Indian dancers. The figure's nudity and bent arm and leg pose seem to suggest she is the ancestress of the voluptuous ***Yakshi***, the female fertility and nature spirit, commonly depicted in later Hindu and Buddhist art. The Young Dancer was solid-cast in bronze using the *cire perdu* or lost wax method, a technology which seems to have appeared in the Indus Valley around 4000 BCE (Thoury et al 2016).

▼ **6.2** Indus Civilization, Mohenjo-Daro, Young Dancer from Mohenjo-Daro, c. 2500 BCE, bronze, 4.25 in. high.

This lost-wax cast figure is highly animated and strikes a pose that is consistent with later images of Yakshi nature spirits in Buddhist and Hindu art.

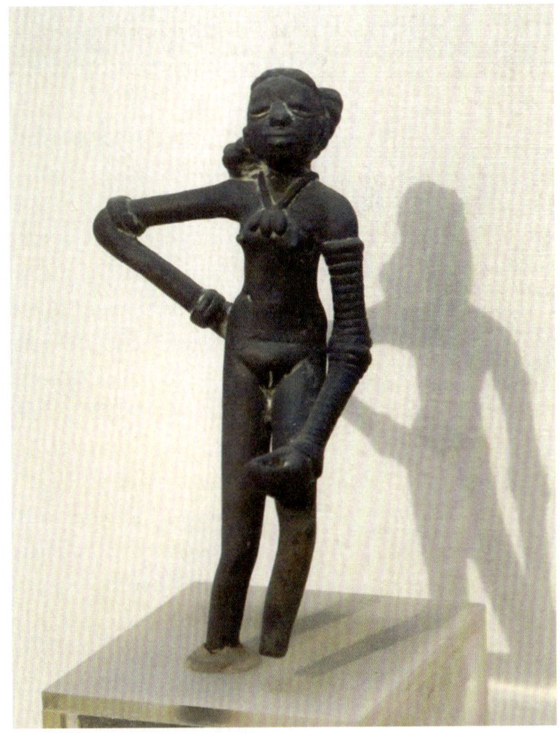

Red Sandstone Male Torso from Harappa, c. 2000–1900 BCE Another notable small-scale work from the Indus Valley is the red sandstone Nude Male Torso (Figure 6.3), found at Harappa. Although the sculpture is less than 4 inches (8.86 cm) high, it possesses a presence normally seen in monumental works of art; it seems as if it should be much larger than it is. Because the figure was found under a few feet of surface debris at Harappa, some scholars have challenged its attribution to the Indus Valley civilization, suggesting it is a later work reflecting Greek naturalism. However, its smooth,

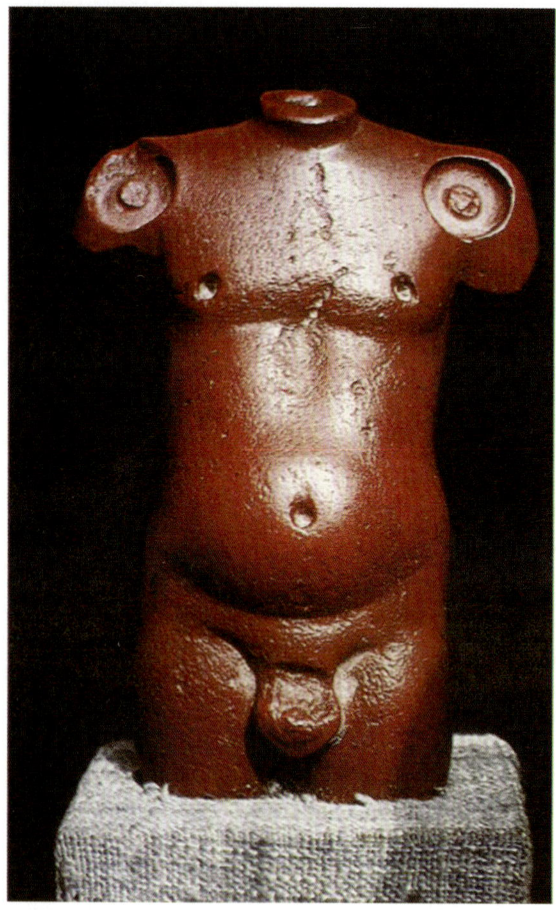

▲ **6.3** Indus Civilization, Red Sandstone Male Torso from Harappa, c. 2000–1900 BCE. 3.5 in.

This tiny figure shows the rounded body type and prana characteristic of later Indian sculpture. The head was pegged into the neck and the drilled areas in the shoulders may have been attachment points for additional arms, a signifier of divinity in Indian art.

rounded forms and its yogic ***prana*** pose (the figure's belly is extended with breath) show it to be clearly Indian in design and concept. Like the Young Dancer from Mohenjo-Daro, this torso seems to be the prototype for a later Indian form, the ***Yaksha***, a male nature and fertility spirit. The drill-hole in the neck of the figure with its smooth rim indicates that the head was a separate piece that was attached to the body by means of a tenon; this arrangement could have allowed the head to be turned. The drill marks in the shoulders are particularly interesting. They may indicate that the figure was reworked at some point, perhaps for the insertion of a second set of arms, multiple arms being an indicator of the supernatural power of the gods in Indian art. If this was, indeed, done originally or as an alteration made during the Indus Valley period, it may be one of the earliest divinity figures in Indian art. Indeed, the **ithyphallic** position (having an erect phallus) implied by the damage to the figure's genital area suggests that it may be an early prototype for the Hindu god, Shiva (see Religion and Philosophy: Santana Dharma or Hinduism); similar depictions are found on some Indus Valley steatite seals.

INDUS VALLEY SEALS

Thousands of carved steatite (soapstone) seals have been found at Harappa, Mohenjo-Daro, and other Indus sites. These stamp-type seals are quite tiny, the largest being about an inch and a half square (3.81 cm) with a knob or boss on the back that is drilled so the seals can be suspended. Given their miniscule size, the degree of observed detail found in their images is astonishing. The designs were carved into the surface of the stone, a process known as **intaglio**, so that when the seal was pressed into the wet clay, it produced an embossed or raised relief image. The completed seals were given a coating of **alkali** (a soluble mineral salt), and then fired to produce a smooth white surface. The writing on these seals has yet to be deciphered, but the variety of the text suggests the inscriptions were personal for the most part, rather than religious, because devotional texts would most likely repeat. The seals feature a wide variety of animals: Brahma bulls, buffalo, rhinoceros, elephants, hares, antelope, and composite animals, all carefully observed and rendered with character. Human figures are known but infrequent.

The Pashupati Seal, c. 2300–1750 BCE The Pashupati Seal (Figure 6.4) shows an ithyphallic figure seated in a yogic position, surrounded by a deer, tiger, elephant, rhinoceros, and buffalo, and what may be two human figures. The yogic figure may represent Lord Shiva as Pashupati or Lord of Animals, and if so, may be one of the earliest depictions of this important Hindu deity. The figure wears a large horned headdress, typically a divinity indicator, and has multiple faces, three visible and a presumed fourth in back. In the Hindu triad, Brahma (the Creator) and Shiva (the Destroyer) both have manifestations that look to the cardinal directions.

THE EVOLUTION OF INDUS CIVILIZATION

The archaeological record suggests that a shift in power occurred during the late second millennium BCE when cities such as Mohenjo-Daro and Harappa, which had been dominant in the earlier eras, entered a period of decline. The failure of Indus cities may have resulted from different factors in different regions. For some, such as Harappa, the fall may have resulted from political or economic collapse. Excavations at the site show that during the six-hundred-year period from 1900–1300 BCE, the city suffered from overcrowding and the decay of its infrastructure due to lack of maintenance. In other regions, natural disasters such as massive flooding, the drying up of major rivers, or earthquake may have caused the downfall. The waning of the Indus Civilization was not a universal phenomenon, nor was it the result of outside invasion. Indeed, cities in some areas, such as the Ganga and Yamuna Valleys, continued to thrive well into the late first millennium BCE. What the archaeological record reveals is the history of continuous occupation from ancient times onward, during which the religious, social, cultural, and artistic practices rooted in the Indus civilization evolved and flourished (Frawley 1996).

▼ **6.4** Indus Civilization, Pashupati Seal, c. 2300–1750 BCE. Steatite, 1.50 in.

These miniature sculptures, about the size of a postage stamp, show incredible detail. The image was cut into the stone so that the resulting impression was raised.

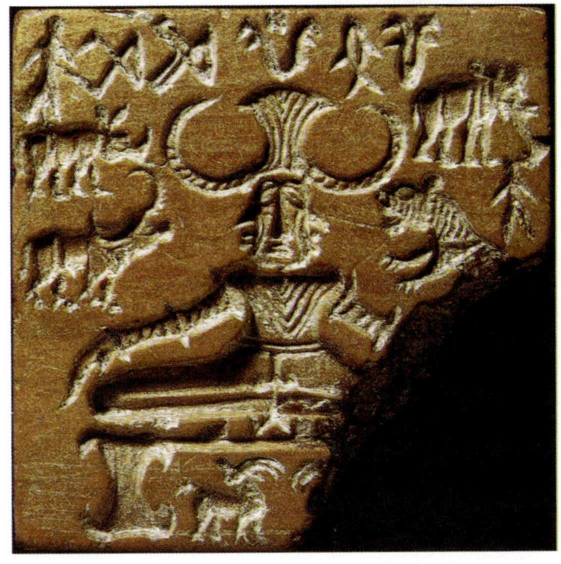

The Maurya Empire (322 BCE–185 CE)

The Maurya Empire was founded by Chandragupta Maurya. Very little is known with certainty about Chandragupta. Legend says he was a guerrilla warrior who fought against the invading armies of Alexander

RELIGION AND PHILOSOPHY

Santana Dharma or Hinduism

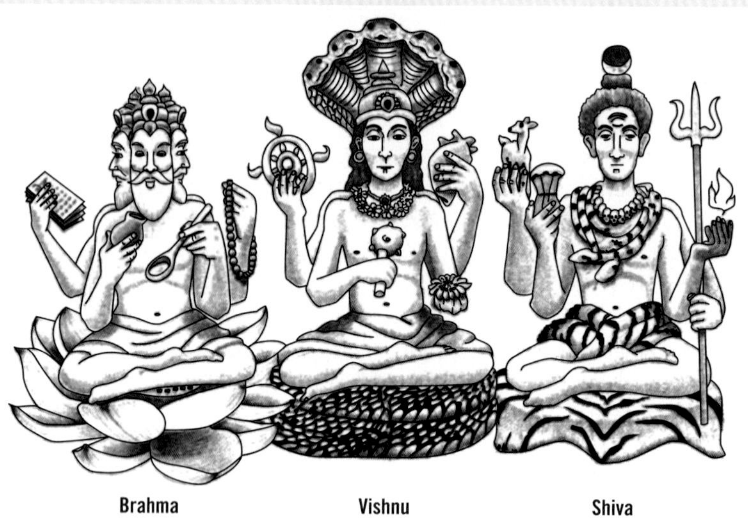

▲ 6.5 Hindu Triad: Brahma the creator, Vishnu the protector, and Shiva the destroyer.

Each of the Hindu gods is considered to be a manifestation of the one God Brahman while additionally having their own avatars.

In order to understand the **iconography** (or meaning of images) in Indian art, it is important to know the basic tenets of the religious and philosophical beliefs that developed during each period. The first of these was **Santana Dharma**, meaning "the Eternal Way," commonly called **Hinduism**. The name Hinduism is derived from the Sanskrit word *Sindhu* or river. When the Achaemenid Persians conquered the Indus region in 518 BCE, they pronounced the river's name as "Hindu" and referred to the area as "Hindustan," and the people as "Hindus." The first use of "Hinduism" in reference to a belief system is thought to be in the *Great Tang Record of the Western Regions*, an account of the travels of the Chinese Buddhist monk Xuanzang who visited India in the seventh century CE

Santa Dharma has its roots in the Indus Valley and a set of four Sanskrit poetic texts known as the **Vedas**. These were the Rig, Sama, Yajur, and Atharva Vedas and together they are the foundational scriptures of Hinduism. In Sanskrit the word Veda means "knowledge." In the nineteenth century Sir William Jones and Max Müller, believing that the stories in the Bible were historical fact, used Biblical chronology to date the writing of the four Vedas to the period between 1500 and 500 BCE. However, more recently scholars using techniques of archaeoastronomy have suggested that the oldest of these texts, the Rig Veda, dates to 4000 BCE or even earlier.

Hinduism did not begin as a religion in the traditional sense; it has no known founder, no spiritual leader, and no required orthodoxy. Rather it might be better described as a philosophy of living based in the four **Purusarthas** or aims of human life. These are described in the Vedas as

1. *Dharma*: Values and duties that are in accord with the natural order of the universe

2. *Artha*: Livelihood or wealth that allows a person to uphold dharma
3. *Kama*: Fulfillment of life and sexual love in accordance with dharma
4. *Moksha*: Liberation from ignorance and the illusions ("Maya") of the world

The utmost goal of Hinduism is to escape the endless cycle of reincarnation and to become one with the formless essence of the divinity.

Hinduism is said to have 33 million (some say 333 million) gods and yet, at the same time, it is the world's oldest monotheism. This seeming contradiction is best explained by the saying, "Truth is eternal but there are many paths to it." In Santana Dharma, there is one God, Brahman, who is present in all things animate or inanimate; however, Brahman has an infinite number of qualities that are presented as the various gods of the Hindu pantheon. These diverse manifestations allow the individual to connect to the divine in the way that is most suited to their level of spiritual sophistication. The form of God that a person connects with emotionally is known as his Ishta-Deva or "cherished god." Put simply, the gods are the tools that help people to achieve the ultimate goal of **nirvana**, the union with the Brahman. There are three main sects within Hinduism, which are defined by the particular god that group has selected as the supreme godhead. In Vaishnavism the supreme god is Vishnu, the Preserver; in Shaivism it is Shiva, the Destroyer, and in Shaktism it is the "Great Goddess", Devi, an ancient Mother Goddess. While the gods are reflections of the attributes of Brahman, they also have manifestations or avatars of their own, for example, Vishnu can appear as Krishna, Rama, Parashurama, the Buddha, and in animal and animal-human hybrid forms, among others.

the Great in 326 BCE. What can be taken as fact is that when Alexander retreated from India, Chandragupta saw an opportunity to build his own empire. He overthrew the last Nanda dynasty ruler of Pataliputra and made that city his capital. From this base in northeastern India, Chandragupta and his successors launched a series of conquests that ultimately brought most of the subcontinent under Maurya rule. The greatest of the Maurya rulers was Chandragupta's grandson, Ashoka (r. 273–232 BCE). By the time Ashoka succeeded to the throne the only territory left to conquer was the small southeastern state of Kalinga that he attacked in 261 BCE. Although victorious Ashoka was disheartened by the destruction and realized rule by conquest was senseless. Ashoka converted to Buddhism on the spot and determined to rule according to the laws of Dharma.

Lion Capital at Sarnath, c. 250 BCE To promulgate the new law, Ashoka had monolithic limestone columns inscribed with his edicts, in several languages, erected across the empire. These Ashokan columns stood some 40 feet (12 m) to 60 feet (18 m) high and were topped by polished sandstone capitals. Only seven complete capitals have survived from antiquity but they show that two distinct designs were used. The first featured a single crowning animal; surviving examples include a bull,

RELIGION AND PHILOSOPHY
Theravada and Mahayana Buddhism

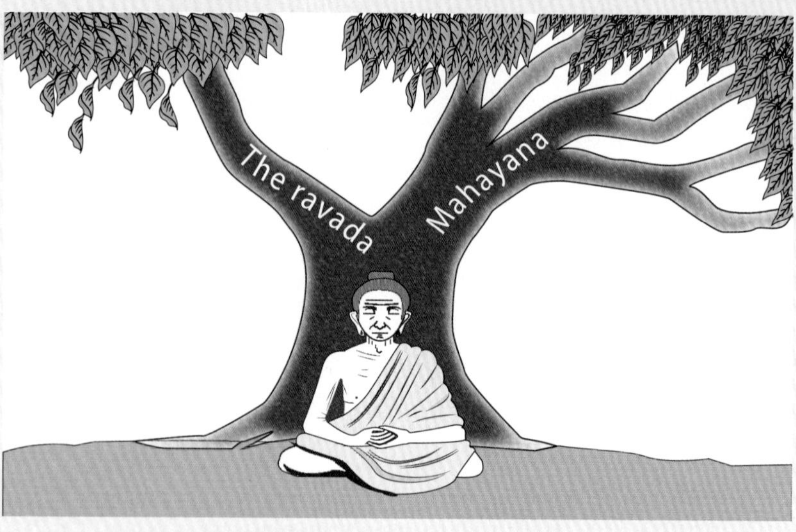

▲ **6.6** Buddhism's Family Tree.

The first form of Buddhism as taught by the Buddha was Theravada "Way of the Elders" that focused on the historical Buddha Siddhartha Gautama. Around the beginning of the Common Era, a less strenuous form of Buddhism, known as Mahayana "Greater Vehicle" , emerged, offering numerous Buddhas of the past, present and future and a class of compassionate beings called bodhisattvas.

The second major religion to evolve on the subcontinent and to have a profound impact on Indian art was Buddhism. Its founder, Siddhartha Gautama, was a prince of the Shakya clan, born in what is now Nepal. The date of his birth is a matter of debate, ranging from 624 BCE to 450 BCE. What is agreed upon is that he lived for eighty years. After achieving enlightenment around the age of thirty-five, the Buddha (the Awakened One) spent the remainder of his life helping others to achieve their own awakening. The Buddha's own path to enlightenment was spurred by a desire to understand the causes of human suffering and by his compassion for those who suffered. After meditating for forty-nine days and nights under the Bodhi tree at Bodh Gaya, Siddhartha achieved Buddhahood; he awakened to the truth. The Buddha preached his first sermon in the Deer Park at Sarnath and shared his understanding by expounding the Four Noble Truths:

1. *Dukkha*: Life is suffering.
2. *Samudaya*: Suffering is caused by desire.
3. *Nirodha*: Desire can be overcome and extinguished.
4. *Magga*: The way to overcome desire is by following the Eightfold Path or Middle Way: Right View, Right Intention, Right Speech, Right Action, Right Livelihood, Right Effort, Right Mindfulness, and Right Concentration.

After the Buddha's **parinirvana** (nirvana-after-death), his followers collected his sermons and saying into the Sutras, which were first communicated orally and later written down. The teachings of the Buddha as communicated by his disciples became known as **Theravada**, meaning "Way of the Elders." In Theravada Buddhism, liberation is achieved through one's own efforts, focusing on meditation and concentration, and through living a monastic life. Even so, only a few people achieve Buddhahood. Around the first century CE or perhaps before, a new school known as **Mahayana** or "Greater Vehicle" arose in opposition to Theravada, which was sometimes referred to by Mahayana followers as Hinayana or "Lesser Vehicle." While Mahayana accepts the teachings of Theravada, it offers the promise that everyone can become a Buddha if they achieve right mindfulness and right action. Whereas Theravada focused on the historic or Shakyamuni Buddha, Mahayana offered a plethora of Buddhas of the past, present, and future, and their attendant Bodhisattvas or "Buddhas-to-be."

elephant, and several lions. The second type was more elaborate and seems to have been connected to significant pilgrimage or monastery sites; it featured four addorsed (back-to-back) lions supporting the wheel of Dharma. Both single and addorsed animals stood on either square or circular abaci (the flat slab at the top of the capital) supported by a single inverted lotus blossom.

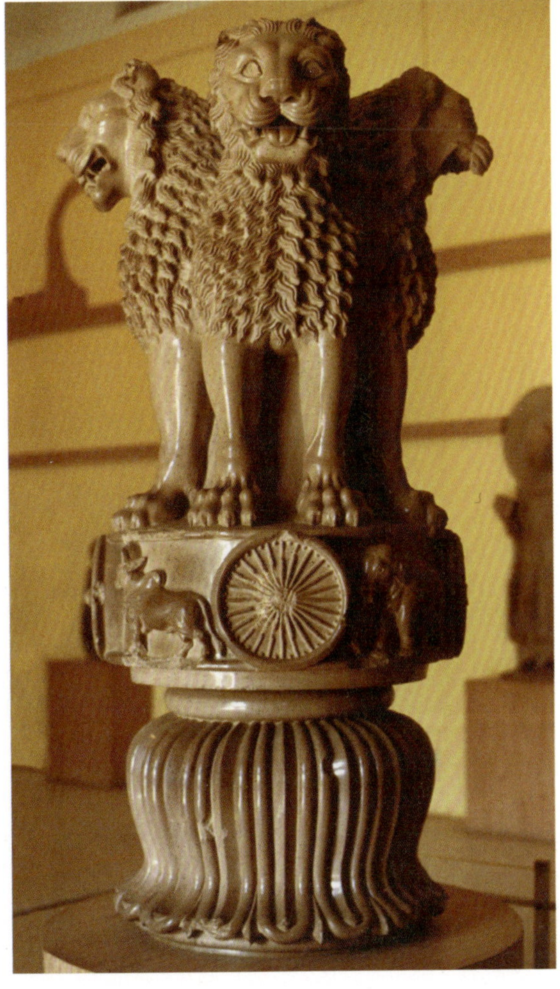

▼ **6.7** Lion Capital from Sarnath, c. 250 BCE. Polished sandstone.

This is one of the more elaborate surviving Ashokan capitals. The four lions once supported a large wheel, symbolizing the Buddha setting the wheel of Dharma into motion with his teaching in the Deer Park.

The best preserved of the surviving Ashokan capitals is an addorsed lion capital from Sarnath (Figure 6.7), the city where the Buddha, in preaching his First Sermon in the Deer Park, set the wheel of Dharma into motion. The decorative elements of this capital were based on a long tradition of emblematic values originating in Hindu cosmology. The lotus was an ancient symbol of purity and divinity. The four animals—bull, elephant, lion, and horse—on the abacus represent the four rivers that flow down from Mount Meru, the World Mountain. The four wheels between them suggest the cardinal directions and the four divisions of the solar year. The four lions once supported a large wheel, referencing the wheel of law set into motion by the Buddha. Additionally, lions signified the Buddha's royal birth and—as an ancient sun sign because of their coloration, they suggest the Buddha Illuminating the spirit with his teachings (La Plant 1992, 13).

The Great Stupa at Sanchi, Madhya Pradesh, c. 250 BCE As an act of devotion Ashoka built hundreds of stupas throughout his empire. Stupas were first constructed as burial mounds sometime in the third millennium

BCE when cremation became the preferred method of dealing with the remains of the dead. In keeping with Hindu and Buddhist practice, when the Buddha died his body was cremated. His ashes were gathered into eight portions, and divided among the cities where significant events in his life had occurred. There they were enshrined in stupas. Ashoka had the original ashes unearthed and divided among additional stupas. However, as such relics are finite, in time the stupa form itself, whether in two- or three-dimensions, came to symbolize the body of the Buddha and was venerated as such.

The selection of Sanchi as a site for a major stupa and monastery complex seems an unusual one as the city was not associated with Buddha's life or ministry. According to the *Chronicles of Sri Lanka* (Ceylon), Ashoka built the monastery in tribute to his son Mahendra, a Buddhist monk, who stopped at the site on his way to bring Buddhism to the people of Ceylon. Mahendra chose to break his journey there because his mother's hometown was nearby.

In Ashoka's time the Great Stupa (Figure 6.8) was a solid brick structure with a cut brick surface enclosed by a wooden railing. After the assassination of the last Maurya emperor, the monastery may have been damaged during a wave of anti-Buddhist violence in the reign of Pushyamitra Shunga (c. 185–149 BCE), or at least allowed to fall into disrepair due to lack of royal patronage. Subsequent Shunga rulers, even though Hindus, seemed to have taken a more benevolent stance toward Sanchi, doubling the size of the stupa and encasing it in a veneer of dressed stone. They also added the double staircase, **harmika** (square enclosure at the top of the stupa) and the drum balustrades. The four monumental gateways or ***toranas*** were added under the Andhra dynasty around 73 BCE.

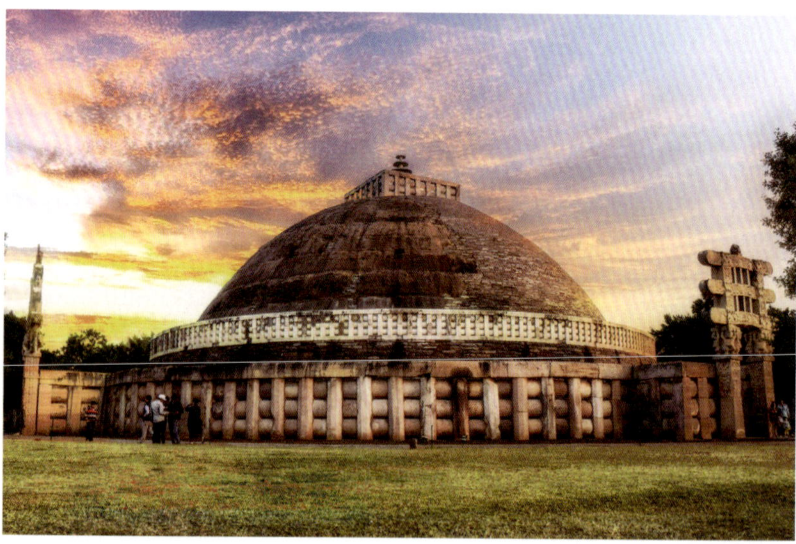

▶ **6.8** Great Stupa at Sanchi, Madhya Pradesh c. 250 BCE.

Built by Ashoka, the Great Stupa was embellished by later rulers with a veneer of fine sandstone, railings, fence, and four triple-lintel torana gateways.

The dome of the Great Stupa rises 50 feet (15 m) from the top of the drum for an overall height of 70 feet (21 m). The diameter of the drum is greater than that of the dome to allow the faithful to perform the ***pradaksina*** or circumambulation on both the ground and drum levels. There is no access to the harmika at the top of the dome. While the four toranas are placed at the cardinal points, they are offset, each

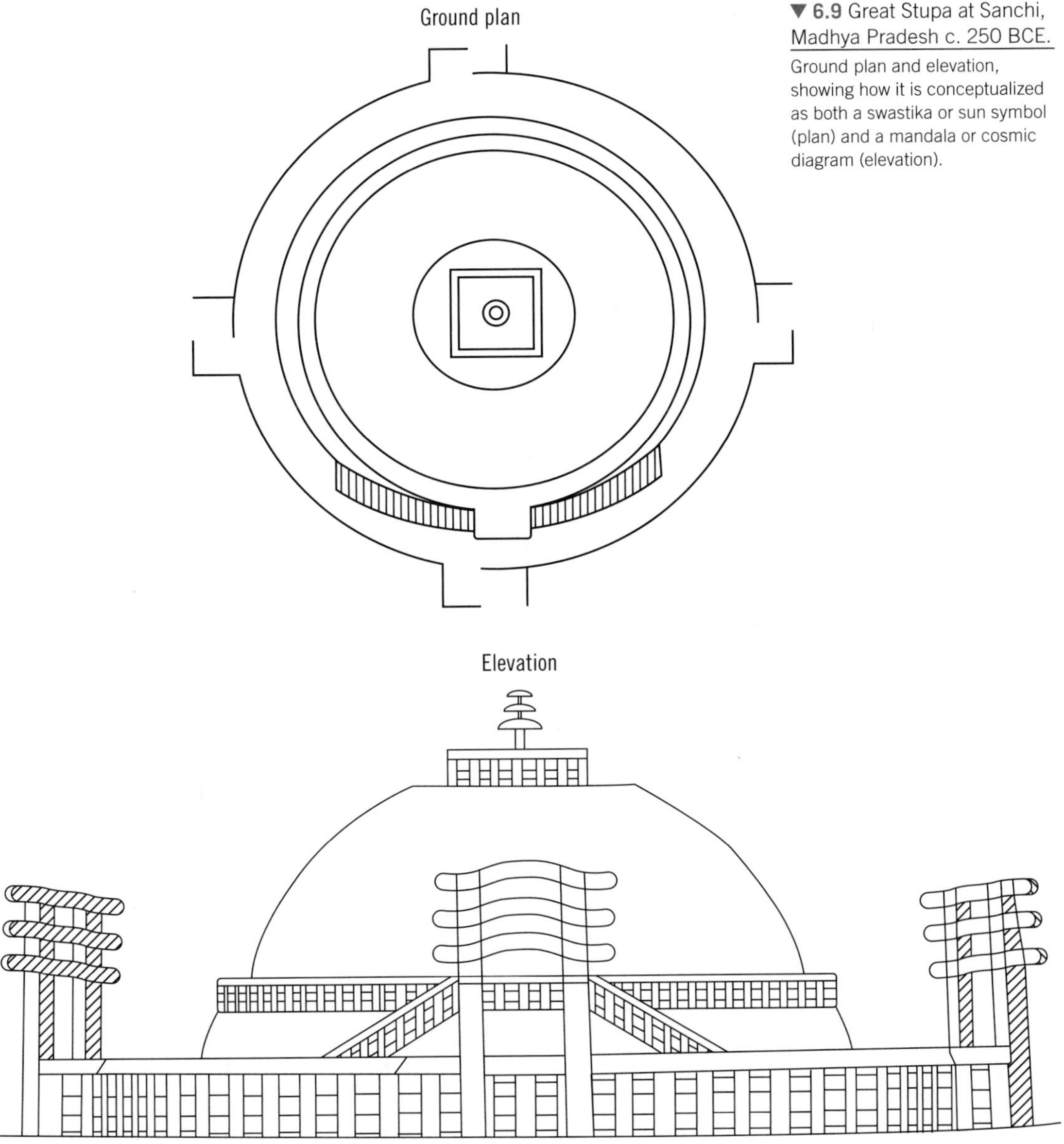

▼ **6.9** Great Stupa at Sanchi, Madhya Pradesh c. 250 BCE.

Ground plan and elevation, showing how it is conceptualized as both a swastika or sun symbol (plan) and a mandala or cosmic diagram (elevation).

forming a wing of a ***swastika*** and conceptually turning the stupa into an ancient solar symbol (Figure 6.9). Cosmologically, the Great Stupa is conceived as a three-dimensional diagram of the universe or ***mandala***. The mast that rises from the center of the dome represents the ***axis mundi*** (cosmic column) running through the levels of the stupa just as does the pillar rising from the center of Mount Meru to align the three levels of the universe.

This tripartite arrangement defines not only cosmic levels but also those of human existence: sense, form, and idea. In Buddhist teaching, it is our perception of the world as reality that keeps the individual soul trapped in the cycle of ***samsara*** or reincarnation. The two levels of circumambulation, ground and drum, represent the senses and matter or bodily form. The third level, the hamika, represents nirvana, a state of pure joy and bliss, of enlightenment, resulting from the unbinding of the mind from ignorance and illusion of the physical world.

North Torana, c. 73 BCE–50 CE The Andhras were sophisticated, Buddhist rulers who grew rich from the spice trade with the Roman Empire. The influence of their contact with Rome can be seen in the relief carvings of the Great Stupa's four monumental toranas. The bas-reliefs on the piers and lintels of the gateways show the shallow, crowded spatial arrangements, and compressed body types common in vernacular Roman sculpture. The scenes recount ***Jataka tales*** or stories from the past lives of the Buddha. Although these stories recount the Buddha's histories, he is not depicted in human form. Instead, his presence is indicated metaphorically by the lotus, wheel, footprint, tree, lion, throne, and stupa.

Although each gateway has the same form, the decorative and narrative scheme of each torana is unique. The East Torana, for example has a surviving lintel bracket in the form of voluptuous Yakshi, very much descended from the Young Dancer of the Indus Valley, while her male companion, the Yaksha, occupies the same position on the North Torana (Figure 6.10). The incorporation of these sensuous Hindu nature spirits as decorative elements on the torana of a Buddhist shrine might seem out of place, given Buddhism's renunciation of worldly things. Their use here is an example of a practice known as **syncretism** in which symbols from an older religion (Hinduism) are reinterpreted and used in a new faith (Buddhism).

The Chaitya Hall at Karli, 50–70 CE During the Maurya period, Buddhists built wooden **chaitya halls** as places of worship. These buildings are reminiscent of Roman basilicas. They are long, columned, barrel-vaulted buildings with a rounded apse at one end, and the entry and its crowning window at the opposite. In the center of the apse was usually a small stupa for circumambulation. All of the wooden Chaitya Halls have been lost but their form has been preserved in a dozen or

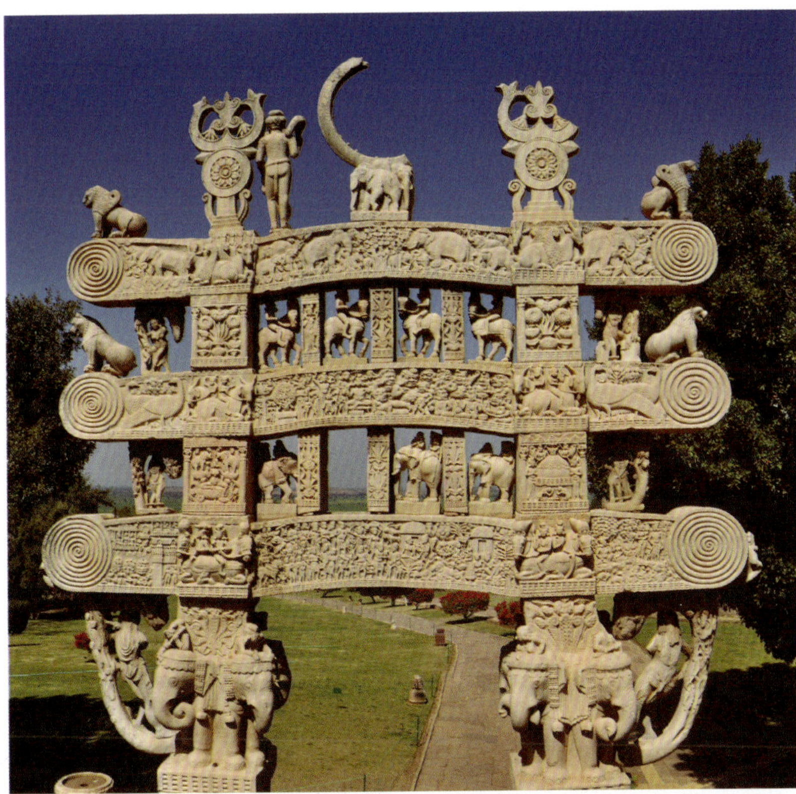

◀ **6.10** North Torana (Reverse) at Sanschi, c. 73 BCE–50 CE.

This gateway features male Yaksha brackets in contrast to the female Yakshi on the eastern gate. The lions, thrones and partial wheel all reference the Buddha. The scenes on the lintels illustrate stories of the Buddha's past lives.

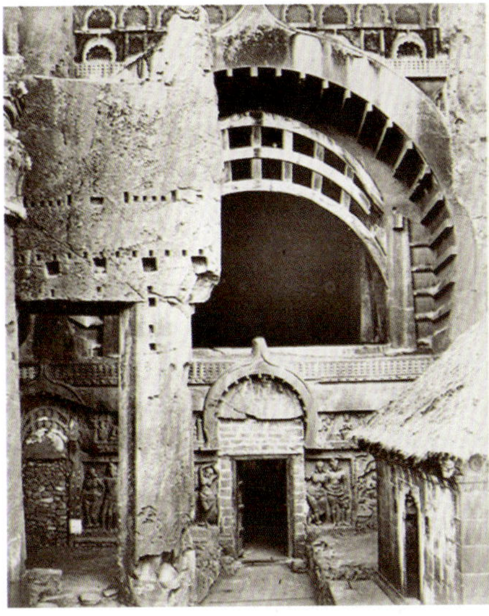

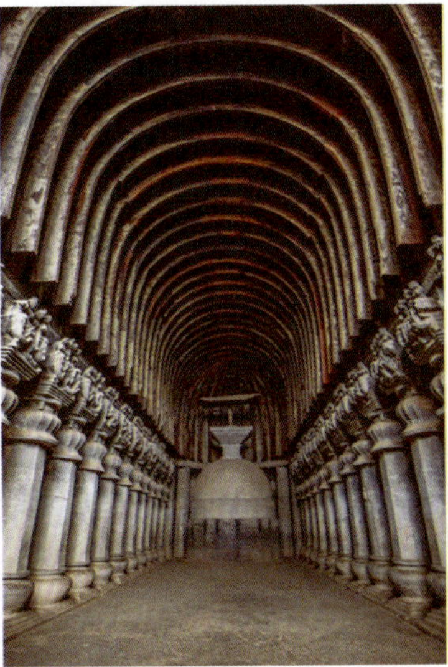

◀ **6.11** Chaitya Hall at Karli, Left Entrance, Right Interior, c. 50–70 CE.

Indian rock-cut caves are archives of early Indian architecture, replicating in stone the components of contemporaneous wooden buildings. Inside the ribs of the barrel vault and the umbrella of the stupa are wood.

so rock-cut sanctuaries that closely replicated all of the details of the wooden originals.

The largest of these rock-cut halls was carved during the first century CE at the site of Karli in the Maharashtra district. The Karli hall (Figure 6.11) measures 124 feet (37.79 m) long and 45 feet (13.71 m) high and wide. The hall was carved directly into the cliff. Workers would have tunneled into the rock and excavated the vaults first. From the ceiling, work continued downward to the double row of columns and side walls; the kneeling elephant and inverted lotus capitals would have been carved first, then the shafts, and finally the water pot bases. Because the process here is a reductive (carving out) rather than constructive (building up), work proceeded in the reverse order from normal built-construction. In wooden chaitya halls, the rows of columns would have been structural, but at Karlie they are not. At the same time as work progressed on the colonnade, sculptors would have carved the stone stupa in the apse in the same reductive manner. The final stage of carving was the smoothing of the floor. Not all elements at Karli are carved into the living rock. Certain details such as the ribs of the vault, the umbrella of the stupa, and the window screen are carved from teak wood.

The approach to the Karli chaitya hall is today partially obscured by a modern Hindu shrine to the right of its entrance. Originally the cave was approached through a columned portico (entrance) with a heavy lintel that marked the front of the rock outcropping; this outer wall is now partially destroyed. In front of the remains of this wall, on the left, stands an Ashokan-style pillar surmounted by four lions. This column is 38 feet (11.58 m) high, which gives a sense of the immense scale of the façade. Three doors are set into the façade, the central one being the entrance into the hall. Each door is covered by a carved horseshoe arch with supporting rafters and ridge cap, replicating the thatched roofing system of the original wooden buildings. Above the central door and extending to the inner edge of the side doors is a large half-moon-shaped chaitya window that provided the only illumination for the interior.

The façade and side walls of the portico are elaborately carved. Panels on either side of the entry doors feature pairs of Yakshi and Yaksha who form ***mithuna*** or "happy couples." Mithuna are found in both Hindu and Buddhist contexts, and are often shown in gymnastic amorous poses. Although in some cases these images would seem to be a celebration of life's corporal pleasures, the meaning here is metaphorical, expressing the longing of the soul for union with the divine in nirvana. The recessed space behind the projecting chaitya window is decorated with bands of repeating chaitya windows and doors carved in bas-relief. This motif appears in four registers on the upper side walls of the portico. The bottom panel on each side is the same height as the Mithuna of the main façade but instead of happy couples, a trio of high relief elephants carrying Buddhas completes the narrative scheme.

The Kushan Empire (135 BCE–280 CE)

The Kushan were nomadic Central Asian horsemen, known to the Han Chinese as the Yuezhi. They were driven west by the Xiongnu tribes and by 135 BCE had established themselves in the Alexandrian kingdom of Bactria (Tajikistan and northwest Afghanistan). From their Bactrian base, the Kushan expanded into northern India, bringing the Ganges region under their control. The Silk Road—the trade route between China and the Roman Empire—ran through Kushan territory and they grew wealthy from this long distance trade. The ancient trade route not only facilitated the exchange of goods but also of ideas and art styles. The Kushans recruited artists and artisans from the Roman colonies of Asia Minor to enrich their summer capital at Peshhawar, resulting in a local style that was strongly influenced by the Greco-Roman tradition. The Kushan established a winter capital in Mathura, south of Delhi. The artists in their Mathura atelier, without the direct influence of the Mediterranean, continued to work in an indigenous Indian style rooted in the art of the Indus Valley.

Kanishka Casket, 127 CE Chinese Buddhist sources describe Kanishka I (r. 127–151 CE) as a tolerant ruler who converted to Buddhism. He was a great patron of the arts, having built the world's largest stupa in Peshawar, according to the Chinese monk and pilgrim Faxian, who visited India in the fifth century CE. In his *Record of Buddhistic Kingdoms*, Faxian described the stupa as 394 feet (120 m) high and covered with precious substances. During excavations carried out at the ruins in the early twentieth century, a small, 7.5 inch (19 cm) tall, bronze reliquary was discovered; it contained three bits of bone thought to have been remains of the Buddha.

Known as the Kanishka Casket (Figure 6.12), the reliquary bears an inscription identifying Kanishka as the donor in 127 CE, the first year of his reign. The lid of the casket bears three dimensional images of the Buddha with two attendant figures, the Hindu gods Indra and Brahma, who later will be transformed into Buddhist guardian figures. Although these figures are only an inch and a half tall (3.81 cm), they are remarkably detailed. The Buddha's robe, for example, has the nesting U-shape folds that are the hallmark of the Gandharan sculptural style.

▼ 6.12 Peshawar, Kanishka Casket, 127 CE. Cast bronze, 7.5 in. high.

An inscription on the casket gives its date and identifies its patron as Kanishka, the Kushan ruler. The work blends elements from Greco-Roman art with Buddhist imagery.

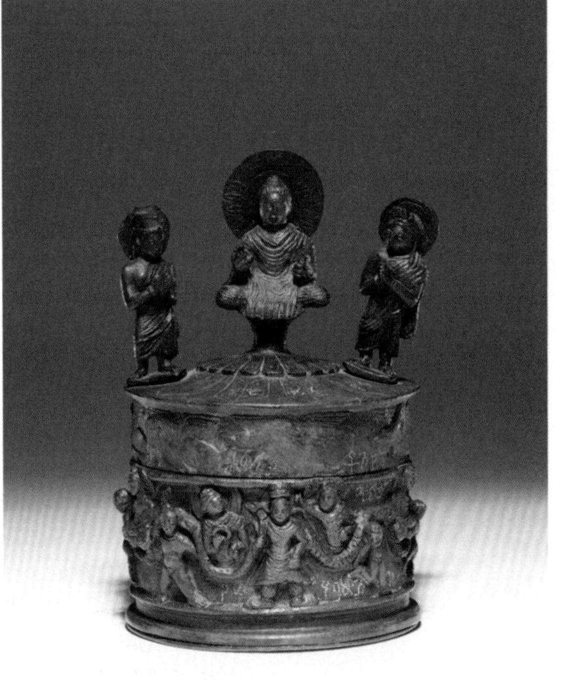

The piece is thought to have been cast in Peshhawar or the secondary Kushan summer capital of Taxila.

The casket was cast in pieces: the base, cylinder, and the two flanking figures on the lid were created separately, while the Buddha on his pedestal was cast in one piece with the lotus lid. The cylinder is decorated with a garland held up by nude infants, an obvious borrowing from the Roman world, while above the garland are images of Buddhas, and a standing figure, identifiable by his helmet, breastplate, flaring kilt, and padded boots as Kanishka himself. Flanking the emperor are figures representing the sun and the moon (Myer 1966, 396–403).

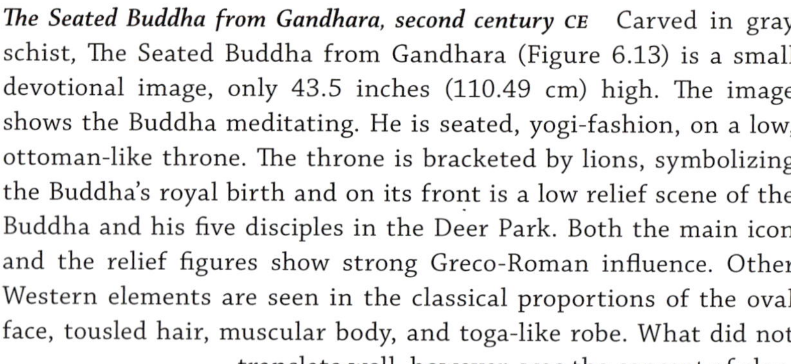

▼ **6.13** Seated Buddha from Gandhara, c. 100–200 CE. Hornblende schist, 43.5 in. high.

This image of Gautama Buddha, and many similar ones produced in Gandhara, reflect Greco-Roman influence in their proportions, facial and hair types, and the toga-like treatment of the sanghati.

The Seated Buddha from Gandhara, second century CE Carved in gray schist, The Seated Buddha from Gandhara (Figure 6.13) is a small devotional image, only 43.5 inches (110.49 cm) high. The image shows the Buddha meditating. He is seated, yogi-fashion, on a low, ottoman-like throne. The throne is bracketed by lions, symbolizing the Buddha's royal birth and on its front is a low relief scene of the Buddha and his five disciples in the Deer Park. Both the main icon and the relief figures show strong Greco-Roman influence. Other Western elements are seen in the classical proportions of the oval face, tousled hair, muscular body, and toga-like robe. What did not translate well, however, was the concept of classical drapery. Instead of the soft doublings natural to cloth, the Gandharan artist has rendered the folds in a more stylized linear manner; this is especially evident in the nested U-shaped pattern of the hem of the garment hanging down in front. The torso of the Buddha has been cut free of the block, suggesting that this sculpture was made to be placed against the wall at the base of Chaitya-Hall stupas or in **Viharas** (Buddhist monasteries). These types of sculptures were often painted and gilded.

Bodhisattva of Monk Bala, 131 CE A second major center of Buddhist sculpture evolved at the Kushan winter capital of Mathura. The school that developed there, while showing some influence from Gandhara, adhered strongly to indigenous Indian traditions. Standing more than 8 feet (2.4 m) tall, the red sandstone image, commissioned according to the inscription by a Buddhist monk named Bala in 131 CE, is one of the first monumental images of the Buddha. The inscription identifies the image as a Bodhisattva. In early

Buddhism, the Buddha during his period of teaching after his enlightenment but before his entry into nirvana was referred to as a Bodhisattva. Later as the Mahayana form of Buddhism emerged, Bodhisattvas became a class of semi-divine beings who assist others in achieving enlightenment.

Stylistically, the Bodhisattva of Monk Bala (Figure 6.14) combines the boneless quality of early Indian art with elements derived from the Gandharan imitation of Greco-Roman art. His body, like those of Yaksha figures, is soft, rounded, and the belly swells with prana. The Bodhisattva wears his sanghati (robe) in "open" fashion with the end thrown over one shoulder and arm. In contrast to the more natural and organic treatment of the body, the garment folds are rendered in an arbitrary manner that reveals the artist is copying the linear patterning of his Gandharan contemporaries but he does not fully understand it.

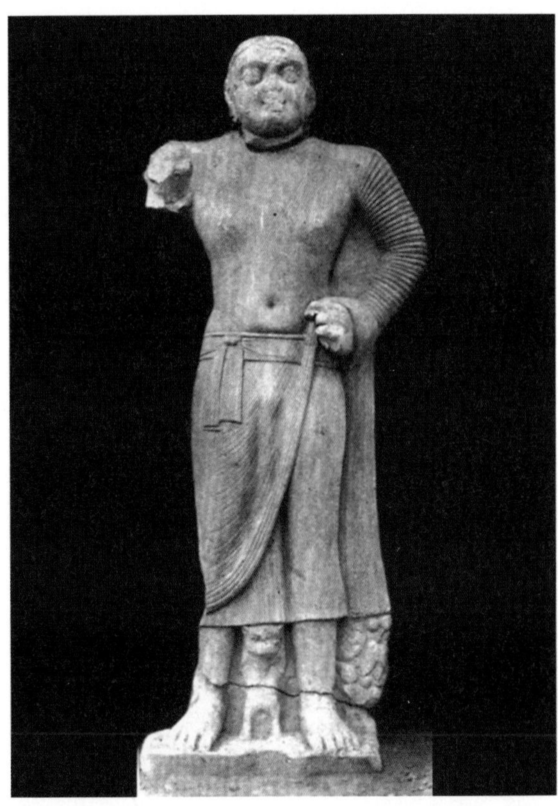

▲ **6.14** Sarnath, Bodhisattva of Bala, 123 CE. Red sandstone, 92 in. high.

This sculpture, commissioned by the Monk Bala, was one of the first images of the Buddha in human form. The small animal between his legs is a lion, a reference to the Buddha's royal birth.

The Gupta Dynasty (320–486 CE)

In 320 CE Chandragupta Gupta ascended the throne of the small state of Magadha in north central India. Chandragupta I (r. 320–335 CE) was a great warrior who set about to conquer the other small kingdoms that had arisen in northern India after the fall of the Maurya Empire. Through marital alliances and military conquest, Chandragupta I and his successors brought all of northern India under Gupta control. The period is marked by great achievements in the arts, literature, mathematics, astronomy, and medicine. Gupta mathematicians invented the decimal system, the concepts of zero and infinity, and calculated the value of *pi* to the fourth decimal. Gupta astronomers independently advanced the theory that the earth was round, not flat. When Faxien visited the Gupta kingdom during the reign of Chandragupta II (r. 375–414 CE), he described the empire as having beautiful cities, fine hospitals, and universities.

Seated Buddha Preaching the First Sermon from Sarnath, c. 465–485 CE. The Gupta rulers were Hindu but they took a secular approach to governing, tolerating all but patronizing no religion. During the Gupta period, a new school of Buddhist sculpture arose at Sarnath. Seated Buddha Preaching the First Sermon from Sarnath (Figure 6.15) shows the refinements of this new style. In this work the Buddha takes on

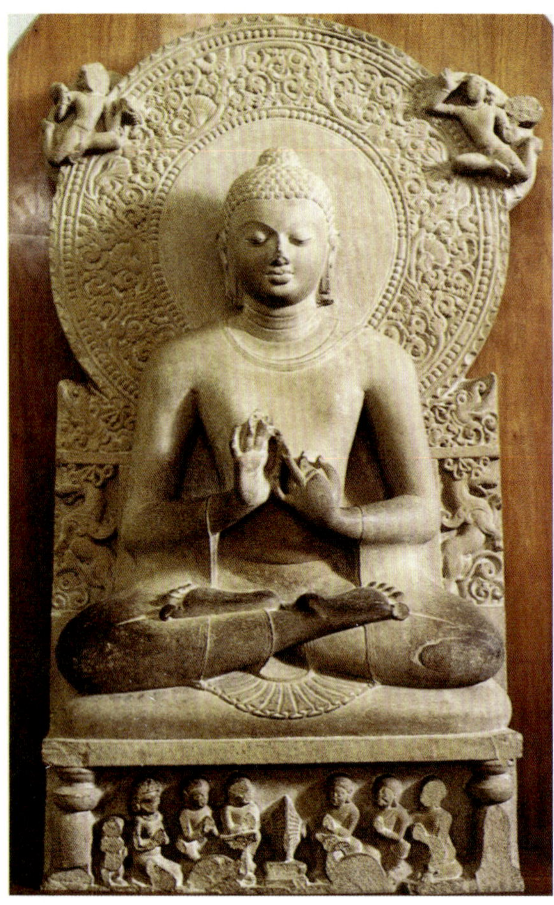

▲ **6.15** Seated Buddha Preaching First Sermon, Sarnath, c. 465–485 CE. Sandstone, 63 in. high.

Gupta sculptors at Sarnath refined and streamlined the representation of the Buddha to emphasize his spiritual aspect, while creatively embellishing his halo and throne.

an androgynous and ageless character. He is shown in an attitude of teaching, his hands forming the Dharmachakra or "Turning the Wheel of the Law" mudra. In the front panel of his throne, the Buddha appears again with a wheel and his five companions, who received this first teaching. At the far left are the figures of a woman and child, perhaps a reference to the wife and child the Buddha left behind when he first set out to seek the truth.

Although the Sarnath style is an offshoot of the Mathuran school, it features more attenuated proportions, with figures growing taller and slimmer, and anatomical detail, particularly genitalia, suppressed. This lessening of attention to the body was intended to emphasize the divine nature of the Buddha in keeping with the evolving Mahayana form of Buddhism. The Sarnath style is also recognizable by the elimination of almost all drapery detail. In the Sarnath Buddha, the sanghati is indicated only as hems at the neck, wrists, ankles, and by the fan of folds between the feet. New in the Sarnath style is the treatment of the Buddha's hair as a covering of tight corkscrew curls. These curls are often ascribed to Persian influence but are more probably the result of a greater adherence to the description of the Buddha's **lakshana** or "signs" detailed in the Pali Canon. This collection of Buddhist teachings was compiled and written down following the Fourth Buddhist Council, circa 29 BCE. The twelfth lakshana describes the Buddha's hair as arranged in soft, right-spun curls, commonly called scorpion-sting curls.

The one element of the Sarnath style that runs counter to this drive for reduction and simplification is in the treatment of the Buddha's halo. Sarnath halos are at least twice the size of those seen in Gandharan and Mathuran works of the Kushan period, and they now have wide borders of complex floral patterning. The codification of the characteristics of the Buddha and his new status as a divine figure made it inappropriate to deviate from the accepted depiction of his person. The only opportunity that the Gupta carver had to show his creativity was in the patterning of the halo.

Ajanta Caves, c. 480–650 CE The first Buddhist rock-cut caves, both chaitya halls and viharas, were excavated at Ajanta around 200 BCE,

RELIGION AND PHILOSOPHY

The Lakshana of the Buddha

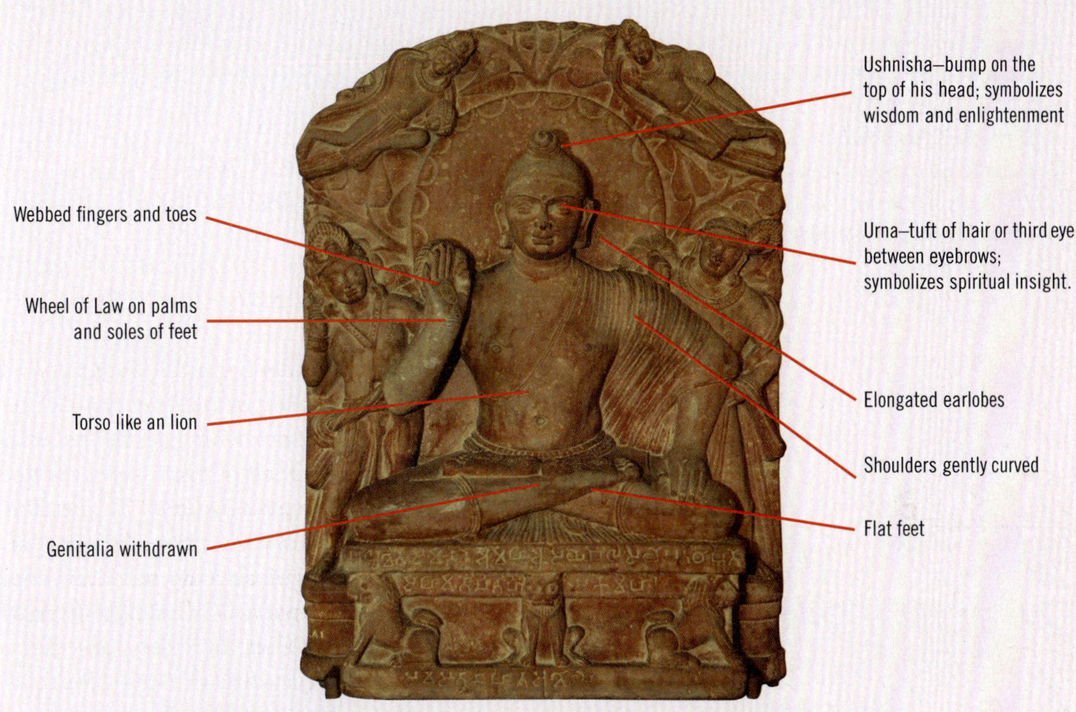

▲ **6.16** Lakshana of the Buddha.

The physical characteristics of the Buddha, known as Lakshana were codified in the Pali Canon at Fourth Buddhist Council in 29 BCE. There are thirty-two major marks and eighty minor ones.

Prior to the first century BCE, the teachings of the Buddha had been transmitted orally. Tradition has it that during the life of the Buddha, certain of his most devout and dedicated monks immediately committed to memory all of his sermons, discourses, and sayings. In 29 BCE the first of two Fourth Buddhist Councils was convened in Ceylon; the harvests were poor that year and many monks died. The survivors, realizing that the Buddha's teachings would have been lost if they all had died, decided it was necessary to write them down. Over the next three years the basic texts of Buddhism were transcribed onto palm leaves and the leaves placed into one of three baskets or *pitaka*, reflecting three categories of knowledge:

1. *Vinaya* or "Discipline" containing rules for Buddhist monks and nuns
2. *Sutta* or "Sutras" containing sermons, discourses, poetry, and jataka stories
3. *Abhidhamma* or "Doctrine" containing analysis and commentaries on the sutras

Because they were placed in these three baskets, the texts are known as the ***Tripitaka***, and because they were written down in the Pali language, they are also known as the **Pali Canon**.

Among the thousands of documents in the Pali Canon are the ***lakshana*** or descriptions of physical characteristics of the Buddha, presented as thirty-two major and eighty

(*Continued*)

minor signs of the "Great Man." These lakshana provided the template for representations in painting and sculpture during the second century CE when the first images of the Buddha in human form were made. The lakshana spell out, often in analogous descriptions (e.g., "lower legs like an antelope's") every bodily element of the Buddha down to the number of teeth he had and how they were spaced in his mouth.

In general the Buddha was described as having an elongated body with especially long arms reaching to his knees, long hands, and long webbed fingers, flat feet, a torso like a lion's, round shoulders, thick neck, an elongated head with a prominent bump or ***ushnisha***, a well-formed nose, long ears, forty very white teeth, deep Sapphire blue eyes, white tuft of hair or ***urna*** (third eye) between his eyebrows, black curly hair, gold-toned skin, and the marks of the Wheel of Law on the soles of his feet and palms of his hands.

but the majority of the twenty-nine caves date from the Gupta period. The complex sits in the bend of the Waghora River and consists four devotional chaitya halls and twenty-five viharas, which served as living quarters for monks and pilgrims. Originally all of the caves were decorated but paintings have only survived in caves 1 and 17. These paintings show scenes densely packed with figures, which give a glimpse into life during the Gupta period. There are figures of Yogis, warriors, commoners, merchants, and princely figures dressed in richly patterned textiles and wearing ornate crowns, necklaces, bracelets, and heavy earrings. These paintings form important records of Gupta court life because, as Hindus, they would have cremated their dead, leaving no tombs for archaeologists to excavate.

The paintings were done in a fresco technique in which the rock walls were smoothed with a clay "skim coat," and subsequently covered with a lime coat that was kept moist to better absorb the pigment. Figures would be outlined in red before being filled in with color. When the paintings had dried, the whole surface of the wall was burnished to a high gloss. The Ajanta painters showed regression into space by stacking the figures on the wall; the highest being farthest away. Most of the figures in the scene are presented frontally or in three-quarter poses. The relative importance of individual figures is indicated through the use of hierarchical scale and variations in color. At the top of the Hindu caste system were the Brahmins, described in the Vedas as "light," meaning "pure." In the Ajanta paintings, Brahmin figures such as the princely Bodhisattvas are often lighter than those of the lower castes around them. Both human and animal forms are subtly modeled in light and shadow to give them a remarkably three-dimensional quality.

Bodhisattva of Cave 1, fifth century CE A beautiful scene in Cave 1 shows the figure of the Bodhisattva Avalokitesvara (Figure 6.17), whose name means "the Lord who looks down in compassion." Because of his vow to be reincarnated until all humans achieve nirvana, this Bodhisattva is viewed as the personification of divine mercy and ultimate compassion. In the painting, he wears a jeweled tiara, a pearl necklace with a sapphire clasp, and a strap of seed pearls diagonally across his chest, marking him as a Brahmin. In his right hand, the Bodhisattva holds a blue lotus flower, indicating his manifestation as Padmapani, "the holder of the blue lotus." The proliferation of Bodhisattvas in Mahayana Buddhism seemed to satisfy an emotional need for more accessible figures than the divine Buddhas, who, having achieved Nirvana, were beyond mortal concerns.

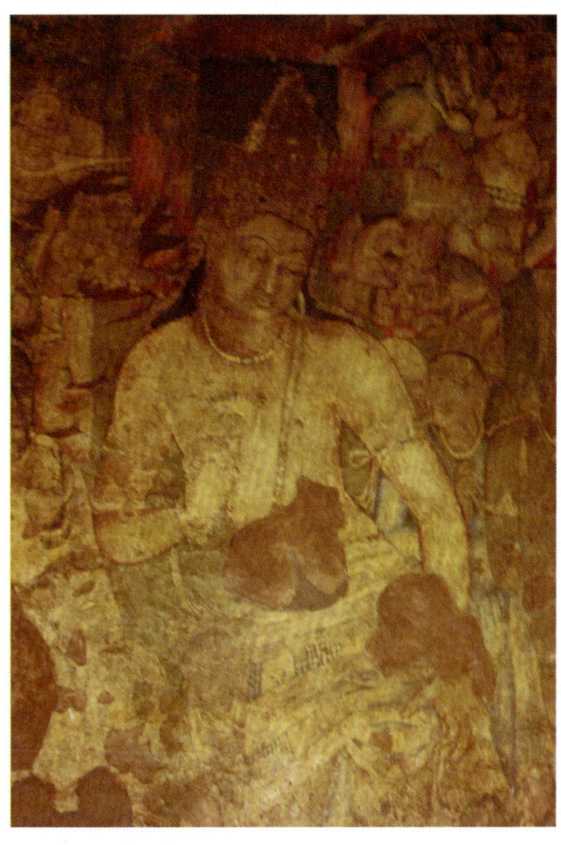

▲ **6.17** Ajanta Cave I, Detail of Bodhisattva Padmapani, 450–500 CE.

The holder of the blue lotus is the Bodhisattva of Infinite Compassion, one of the more popular Mahayana Buddhist figures. The Gupta period artist have used a subtle chiaroscuro to give dimension the Bodhisattva's form.

The Hindu Temple (600–1665 CE)

The construction of brick and stone temples seems to have begun late in the Gupta period and flowered after the collapse of the dynasty. The new kingdoms that arose in India were ardent patrons of Hinduism. Prior to this time, the First Hindu temples were probably rock-cut caves. In the first millennium BCE free-standing temples evolved as simple mud-walled and thatch-roofed structures, and later as wooden buildings. In post-Gupta India, stone temples were erected to patron deities as acts of religious piety. In the process, two distinct regional styles of Hindu temple evolved: Dravida or southern and Nagara or northern.

Dravida or Southern Style Temples

The southern or Dravida style temple developed in the Deccan plateau of peninsular South India. The southern temple is characterized by its distinctive ***Vimana*** or pyramidal-form tower, composed of successive stacked stories, each smaller than the previous, and crowned by an octagonal capstone or ***stupika***. In more elaborate temples, the sanctuary is preceded by one or two flat roofed columned halls known as ***mandapas***. The temple precincts are often surrounded by an outer wall, broken by cardinally oriented gateways or ***gopuras***.

Pallava Dynasty, Five Rathas, Mamallapuram, c. 630–850 CE None of the early mud-walled or wooden temples have survived, but these early temple designs are preserved at Mamallapuram in a group of sculpto-architectural shrines begun under the Pallavas king Narasimhavarman

I (r. 630–670 CE). The project included nine temples and a large relief scene, with engineered waterfall, the Descent of the Ganges. Among these are a set of five shrines, known as the *Five Rathas* (Figure 6.18), all carved from a single massive granite boulder. The name ***rathas*** or "carts" was inspired by the alignment of the temples, four in a row with the fifth running along the side like carts in a procession. The individual temples are named for the sons of King Pandu in the *Mahabharata* (one of the major Hindu epic poems written down during the Gupta period), but this reflects later local tradition, not the original names or presiding deities of the temples.

The scale of the rathas is a result of the natural slope of the granite boulder. At the high end is the Dharmaraja Ratha, standing 42.25 feet (12.87 m) tall, while at the low end is the small Draupadi shrine at 18 feet (5.5 m). A careful examination of the shrines reveals the working process of their creation. In all cases the upper parts of the shrines are the most complete and refined, while lower portions become progressively rougher, indicating that the temples were worked from the top down. In most the lower colonnades and sanctuary remain unfinished because the project was abandoned before any of the shrines were completed and consecrated.

The Five Rathas lay out the progression of southern temple designs from the first mud-walled and thatched shrines (the Draupadi) to the more elaborate wooden buildings with stepped pyramidal towers replicated in the Arjuna and Dharmaraja rathas. The vimanas of these two temples are the architype of the southern style. Each level of the tower rests on a stringcourse set with chaitya-style windows through which faces peer. Standing on this course are miniature shrines and deities in their various manifestations. The tower is topped by an octagonal stupika, and had the shrines been consecrated, this capstone would have been crowned with the "water pot" ***kalasha*** finial, symbolizing the primordial water from which all creation flows. Some early temple

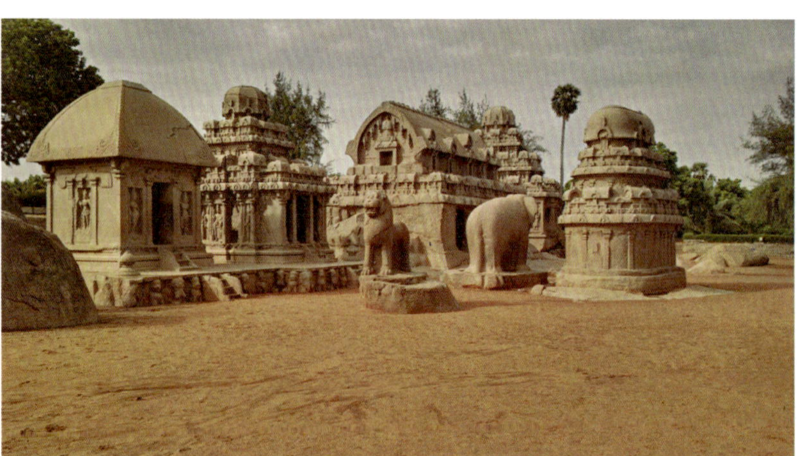

▶ **6.18** Mamallapuram, Rock-cut Rathas, c. 650–700 CE. L–R: Draupadi, Arjuna, Bhima, Dharmaraja rathas, and far right, the rounded Nakula Sahadeva ratha.

These five temples and the associated animal sculptures were all carved out of one immense granite boulder, working from the top down. The project was abandoned before any of the temples were completed and consecrated. The stepped vimanas of the Arjuna and Dharmaraja became the prototype for later southern temple towers.

variants, apparently discarded during the conversion from carved to constructed stone temples, are also preserved in the chaitya hall-like form of the Sahadeva ratha and the Conestoga wagon-like roofline of the Bhima ratha. This last design became the model for the monumental southern style temple gateway known as a ***gopura***.

Chola Dynasty, Rajarajeshwara Temple, Thanjavur, 1010 CE In 897 CE the last Pallava king fell in battle against the Chola. The expanding Chola Empire would ultimately rule all of south India as well as Ceylon, the Maldives, and the Laccadive Islands. The greatest of the Chola kings was the ninth, Rajaraja I (r. 985–1014 CE). A devout Hindu, Rajaraja I sponsored the construction of many temples and shrines in Ceylon and on the mainland. His greatest architectural achievement was the granite temple, known as the Raharajeshwara and decicated to Lord Shiva, that he built in his capital city of Thanjavur.

Constructed, rather than carved out of the rock, the monumental Rajarajeshwara Temple (Figure 6.19) was completed in only seven years. Each stone was carefully fitted and joined without mortar. Although the temple was conceived on a grand scale, the stylistic features are unchanged from those of the Mamallapura rathas. The "Big Temple," as it is known locally, sits on a granite outcrop that serves as a foundation for the temple's tall plinth or base. The temple is aligned on an east-west axis with its entrance porch on the east end. Devotees move from the porch into a large, flat-roofed, columned hall or mandapa and then through a second larger "great mandapa" or ***mahamandapa*** to the cave-like garbhagriha or sanctuary. The focus of the sanctuary is a 13 foot (3.96 m) tall Shiva ***linga*** (also lingam), a

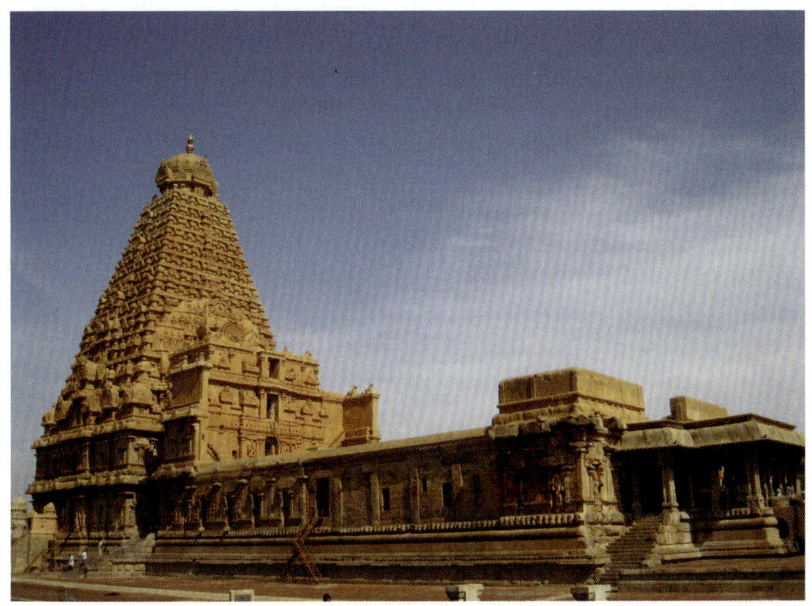

◀ **6.19** Thanjavur, Rajarajeshwara Temple, c. 1010 CE. 216 ft. high.

Unlike its prototypes at Mamallapuram, this monumental southern-style temple was constructed of dry laid stone blocks and features two flat-topped halls or mandapas through which the sanctuary is accessed.

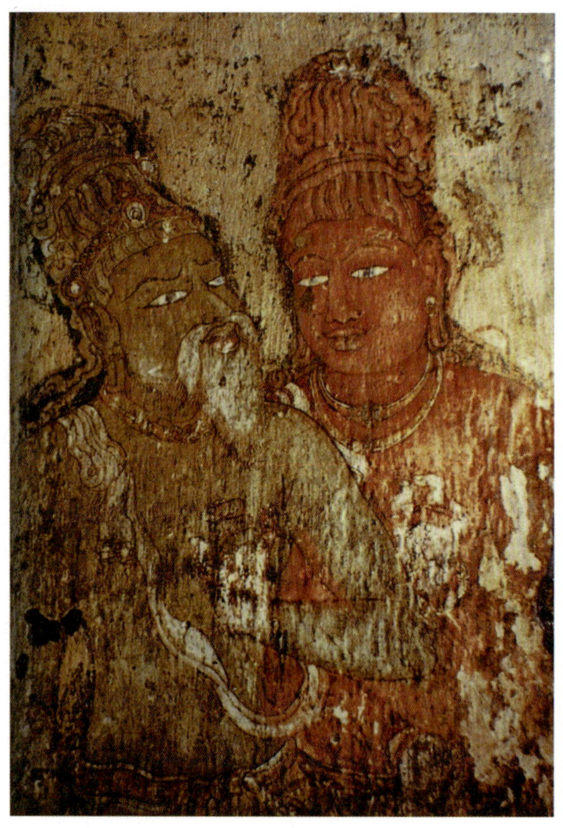

▲ 6.20 Thanjavur, Rajarjeshwara Temple, Ambulatory Mural, c. 1010 CE.
This portrait of King Rajaraja I and his teacher, the Hindu guru Karuvur Thevar are the earliest known surviving examples of Chola painting. In the use of a fine classical outline and subtle chiaroscuro, these painting are similar to the earlier Gupta Period paintings at Ajanta.

representation of the potency of Lord Shiva conceptualized as a cosmic pillar or sometimes taking the form of a phallus. From the garbhagriha, the vimana rises to a height of 216 feet (65.83 m), making it the tallest in South India. Just like its Dharmaraja prototype, the Rajarajeshwara vimana is a pyramidal structure with levels that are defined by chaitya-window stringcourses, which support miniature shrines intermingled with figures. The granite blocks of the tower are held in place by their own weight and, occasionally, by iron cramps. The tower is crowned by a massive stupika some 25 feet (7.62 m) high and carved from a single block weighing 80 tons; since the temple was consecrated, the stupika is crowned by a gilded copper kalasha.

Rajaraja I and his Teacher The ambulatory around the Rajarajeshwara's sanctuary was originally decorated with frescos of the Hindu gods. These original murals were discovered in the 1930s under later works from the Nayak dynasty; one painting (Figure 6.20) shows the Temple's patron, Rajaraja I, in the company of his teacher, the Hindu guru Karuvur Thevar. The Rajarajeshwara frescoes are rare surviving examples of Chola painting, but their style has strong affinities with the earlier Gupta period images at Ajanta. The figures were executed in the same manner as at Ajanta, being drawn first in red and then the color added. The fully frontal bodies are softly modeled in light and dark and they exude the same sense of inner tranquility that characterized the image of the Bodhisattva from Ajanta Cave 1 (see Figure 6.17).

Western Gopura, Rajarajeshwara Bodhisattva The Rajarajeshwara temple stands in the center of a sacred space measuring 1137 feet (346.5 m) square and is enclosed by a wall with gateways aligned with the temple on an east-west axis. Of its two gopuras, the western (Figure 6.21) is the better preserved. This monumental gateway stands 78.74 feet (24 m) high and wide and retains much of the style of its Bhima ratha prototype. Although Indian builders may have been aware of the keystone or Roman arch, it was not used in either Hindu or Jain construction. Careful examination of the central arch of the Rajarajeshwara gopura shows an obvious asymmetry in the arcs of the opening. When an arched opening was required, it would either be cut into a monolithic lintel or formed by cutting the cantilevered end blocks of a corbelled arch to shape. **Corbelled arches** and **vaults** could be fashioned by progressively narrowing the gap between the cantilevered blocks in masonry courses until the remaining space could be closed by a single stone.

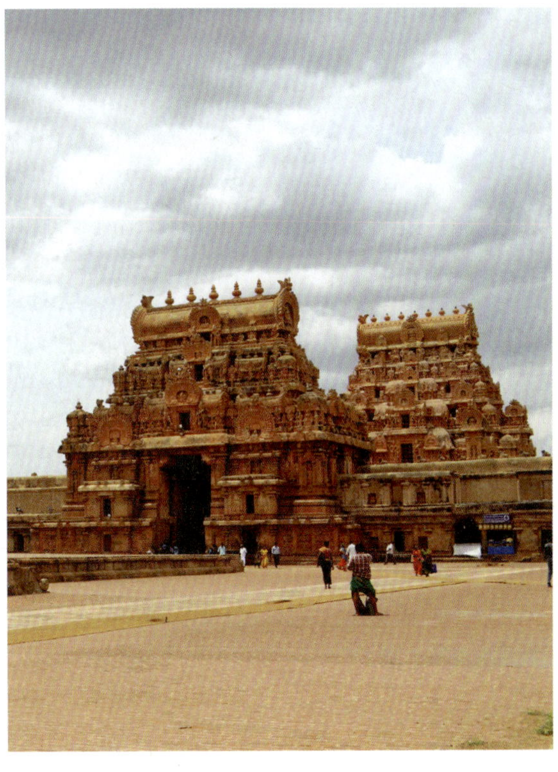

▲ **6.21** Thanjavur, Rajarajeshwara Temple Gopuram, c. 1010 CE. 78.74 ft. high.

The Bhima Ratha at Mamallapuram, with its stacked levels of shrines and Conestoga wagon-like roof, provided the prototype for the southern-style gopura.

Nayak Dynasty, Outer Gopuras at Meenakshi-Sundareswara Temple, Madurai, c. 1623–1655 CE

In the far south of India at Madurai the Nayak ruler Tirumalai (1623–1659), created the ultimate examples of the southern-style monumental gopura. The Nayaks had been governors of Madurai under the Vijayanagar dynasty but broke away in 1559. The main temple of this ancient sacred city was the Meenakshi-Sundareswarar, dedicated to Lord Shiva as Sundareswarar (Beautiful Lord) and his consort Parvati, reincarnated as Meenakshi. The temples had been destroyed during the 1310 incursion by the Delhi Sultanate. When Tirumalai came to the throne he restored the temples and enriched them with new mandapas, a water tank, a thousand-pillared hall, and four outer gopuras, which brought the number associated with the compound to twelve.

The four Nayak gopuras (Figure 6.22) rise in nine distinct stages and are crowned by ***sala*** or "wagon" roofs in the style of the Bhima ratha. The towers rise to heights of between 160 feet (48.7m) and 170 feet (51.8 m), the South Gopura being the tallest. In comparison to the Western Gopura of the Rajarajeshwara, Nayak style gopuras are considerably taller, having more and higher stories. They also appear to be slenderer because their height is greater than their width. While

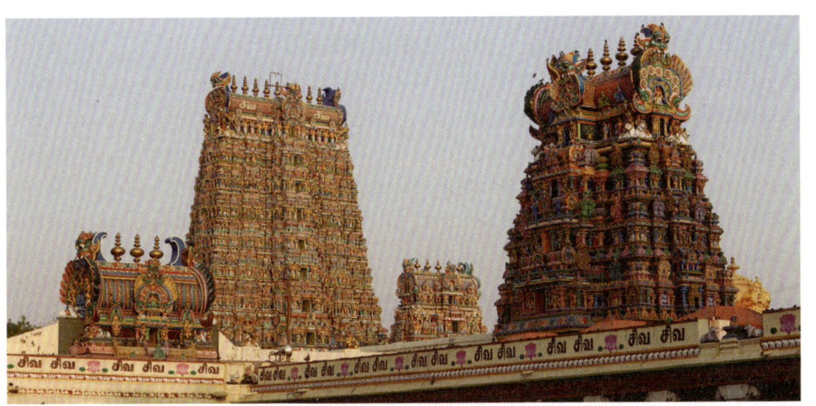

◀ **6.22** Madurai, Meenakshi-Sundareshwara Temple, Gopuram, seventeenth century.

The ultimate baroque expression of the southern-style gopura was executed by the Nayak Dynasty when they added four outer gopuras to the Temple Complex bringing the number of gopuram to twelve. The tallest of these is 170 ft. high. The temple and gopuram are repainted in bright primary colors every twelve years.

the Rajarajeshwara gopura has single figures of the Hindu gods arranged between the shrines on its five stories, the nine levels of the Nayak gopuras are filled with a baroque exuberance of thousands of stucco figures representing the Hindu gods in all their manifestations, mithunas, mythical animals, and demons, all painted in bright red, green, yellow, and blue. Every twelve years the stucco work is repaired before the temples and gopuras are repainted and re-consecrated.

HINDU TEMPLE SCULPTURE: CHOLA BRONZES

While many Shiva temples had linga as the focus of veneration, Chola sculptors also created cast bronze images of Shiva and other gods for devotional and processional purposes. Chola bronzes were always solid cast and thus tend to be of modest size, weight alone making life-size images impractical. Because the images were sometimes carried in procession, holes were designed into the base of the sculpture for the insertion of poles so that the heavy images could be lifted and carried by bearers.

In creating deity images, Hindu craftsmen took care to portray the god or goddess as youthful, beautiful, and graceful; it was necessary for the image to be pleasing to the deity for the god or goddess to manifest in it. To create pleasing forms, the Hindu artist relied on a set of texts known as the ***Shilpa-shastras*** contained in the *Sthapatya Veda*. The *Shilpa-shastras* dealt with the manual arts, among them painting, sculpture, and architecture as well as the rules of Hindu iconography. Bodily proportions for the figure were described through analogy to the form of certain plants and animals. For example, the male torso was likened to the shape of a bull's head: broad at the shoulders and tapering at the waist like the bovine muzzle. The result was not anatomical realism but an idealized form worthy of the divine presence. The belief that the deity could inhabit his cult image resulted in these statues being treated as if they were alive. The images would be bathed and dressed (in the temple they are never shown unclothed), bejeweled, and given offerings of food. They would be entertained with music and dance and taken on outings

Lord Shiva as Nataraja, c. 950–1000 CE Temple statues were more than beautiful images in which the gods might dwell; they were didactic instruments, "visual sermons" for the devotees of the god or goddess. One of the more iconic images of Lord Shiva is his avatar as Shiva Nataraja (Figure 6.23) or "Lord of the Dance." As Nataraja, Shiva is engaged in a cosmic dance of creation and destruction for both the universe and the individual. The dance, called *Anandatandava*, or "Dance of Bliss," is usually depicted by the Chola bronze sculptors as a frenetic one; the god's hair and sash fly out, suggesting the speed with which he spins as he dances.

The power of the god is represented by his multiple arms, which also reference the cardinal directions. As he dances he keeps rhythm with an hourglass-shaped drum in his upper right hand. The drum beat sets the rhythm of the cosmic cycle of creation and destruction as well as the human cycle of birth, death, and rebirth. The universe is symbolized by the ring in which Lord Shiva dances and through his dance it is simultaneously being created and destroyed, as signified by its flames. The tongue of fire Lord Shiva holds in his rearmost left hand represents the promise of the destruction of samsara for the individual. The god's lower right hand is raised in the *abhaya* or "Have no fear" mudra, a gesture of the god's protection. The fingers of Lord Shiva's lower left hand form the *gaja hasta* pose, suggesting an elephant's trunk, and point to the god's raised left foot. Lord Shiva's rising foot is another promise of release from the cycle of samsara.

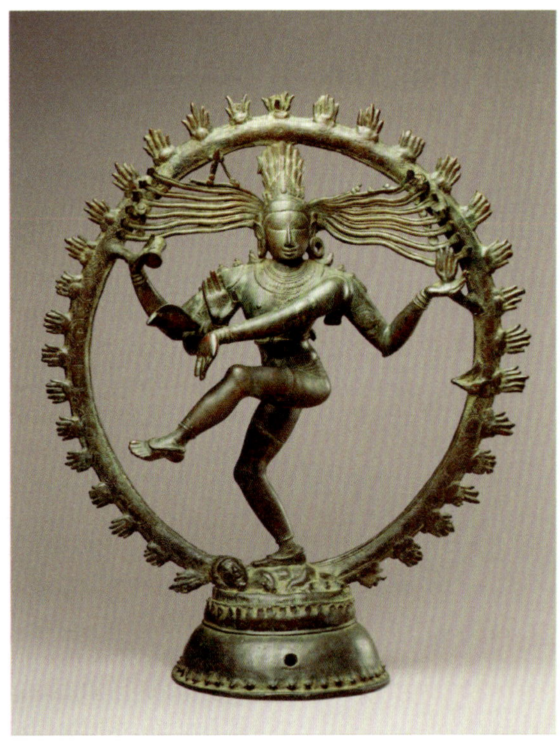

▲ **6.23** Chola, Shiva as Nataraja, c. 1000 CE. Bronze, 26.87 in. × 22.25 in.

As Nataraja or Lord of the Dance, Shiva engages in a furious dance of creation, destruction, and rebirth, both on a cosmic and individual level. He balances on the figure of a dwarf representing the ignorance that prevents release from the cycle of reincarnation.

In many depictions of Shiva as Nataraja, he is shown with deadly cobras uncoiling from his legs or left arm. These serpents and the dwarf Apasmara-purusha (man of forgetfulness) upon which Shiva dances refer to a legend. In it, a group of heretical sages sent the serpents and demon-monster, in the form of a dwarf, to attack the god and interrupt his dance. Shiva draped the serpents around himself like garlands and, with his foot, broke the back of the dwarf. The monstrous dwarf is the embodiment of ignorance, complacency, indifference, and laziness—the qualities that keep mankind trapped in the cycle of reincarnations—and he is often depicted holding a cobra in his hand, symbolizing egotism. Thus, in dancing upon the back of this demon, Shiva is stamping out ignorance and making possible his promise of enlightenment. In Shiva's crown are a skull and also a crescent moon, alluding to the god's phased presence in the cosmos. In his hair are jewels, ashes of the cremated dead, and often the figure of Ganga, the personification of the Ganges River, whose waters Shiva received on his head when they were let down from the heavens. Finally, the base of the sculpture takes the form of a lotus, representing the creative force of the universe.

The Nagara or Northern Style Hindu Temple

North of the Deccan plateau a very different style of temple evolved during the sixth century CE. The northern or Nagara style temple is characterized by a solid, rectilinear tower or ***shikhara*** often with a curving profile as it nears the summit; the mass of the tower consists of compressed levels known as ***bhumis***. On larger temples it may be buttressed by smaller shikharas, and there are often shikharas over the pillared mandapas. The Shikhara is crowned by a low, cushion-like ***amalaka*** or "sunburst."

Ganga Dynasty, Parashurameshvara Temple, Bhuvaneshvar, Orissa, c. 650 CE
Although the Ganga kings were Jains, they sponsored the building of several Hindu temples in Bhuvaneshvar, a city sacred to Lord Shiva. One of these was Parashurameshvara Temple (Figure 6.24). The temple's early date makes it contemporaneous with the Dharma Rathas of Mammallapuram and like the Dharmaraja ratha, it is a modest structure. The temple has a distinctive shikhara (locally called a "deul"), which rises as a block over the sanctuary and curves inward toward its pinnacle at 41 feet (13 m), making it roughly the same height as the Dharmaraja Ratha. The tower is subdivided into compressed levels called bhumis. The top of the tower is crowned by an amalaka and kalasha water pot finial. Adjoining the sanctuary is the temple's tiered-roof mandapa, which measures 29.33 feet (8.9 m) by 28.58 feet (8.7 m). The attachment of the mandapa to the tower, however, is not entirely satisfactory; the two parts of the building remain visually separate units instead of forming an integrated whole. The exterior walls of the temple are decorated with relief carvings of the various Hindu gods, figures of lions and elephants, floral elements, and arch motifs. This part of the temple has two doorways and lattice-work windows on three sides.

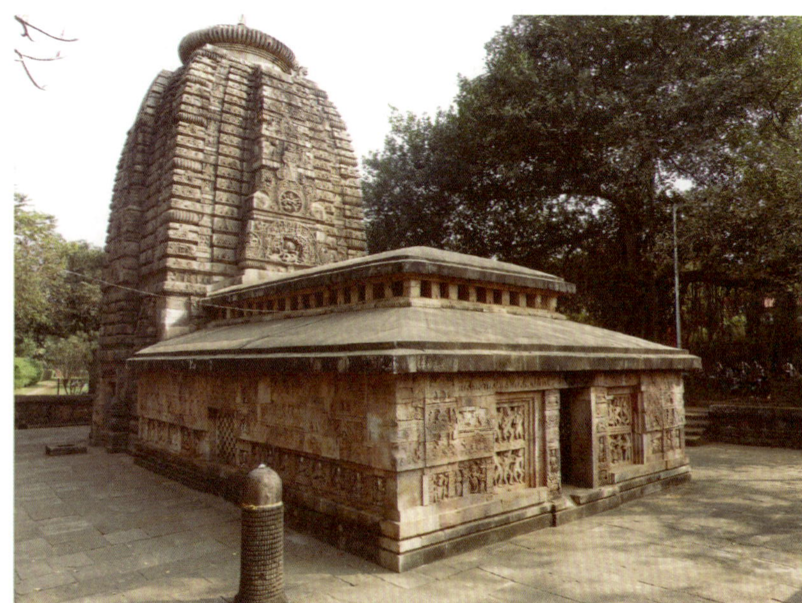

▶ **6.24** Bhuvaneshvar, Parashurameshvara Temple, c. 650 CE.

This small temple is one of the early examples of the northern style, being roughly contemporaneous with the Rathas of Mamallapuram. It has a distinctive curving tower block or shikhara crowned by a flat disk-like amalaka.

Chandella Dynasty, Vishvanatha Temple, Khajuraho, 1002 CE As the Nagara style reached maturity around 1000 CE, towers became considerably taller, their profiles slimmer, and the low, mandapa roof type seen at Parashurameshvara evolved into more dramatic, multi-tiered pyramidal forms that created more pleasing transitions between tower and mandapa. Also, unlike Parashurameshvara, which sat on the ground, the monumental temples were raised up on tall plinths. Some of the best examples of this style were built by the Chandella rulers at Khajuraho over the course of a century beginning in 950 CE. Local tradition claims that the Chandella kings built some eighty to eighty-five shrines, both Hindu and Jain. Unfortunately, only twenty-five temples survive today. One of the finest of these is the Vishvanatha Temple (Figure 6.25) built by King Dhanga and dedicated to Shiva as Lord of the Universe.

Like all the Khajuraho temples, Vishvanatha sits on a granite bedrock base. However, the temple that rises from this natural stone foundation was constructed entirely of fine buff-pink sandstone that was suitable for highly detailed carving. Like the Rajarajeshwara, the Vishvanatha is a more complex structure than earlier temples. The sanctuary is approached through a high entry pavilion, mandapa, and mahamandapa," all in an east-west alignment with the garbhagriha, so that the devotee can see straight into the inner sanctum from the entry porch.

Observed from the side, Vishvanatha's roofline rises as a series of four towers running from the entry porch to the shikhara over the sanctuary, each tower rising higher than its predecessor, with the summit of the shikhara reaching a height of 131.23 feet (40 m). These towers are buttressed by subsidiary shikhara-like elements rising from porches opening off the ambulatory that circles the perimeter of the mahamandapa and garbhagriha. The effect when viewed from a distance is of a mountain range rising to its pinnacle. This was intentional

▼ 6.25 Khajuraho, Vishvanatha Temple, c. 1002 CE.

The Chandella architects solved the problem of the uncomfortable union between the mandapa and the sanctuary in earlier northern temples here by creating a series of progressively taller shikaras rising from the porch to that of the sanctuary. The mountain range effect was a reference to the cosmic mountain Mt. Meru.

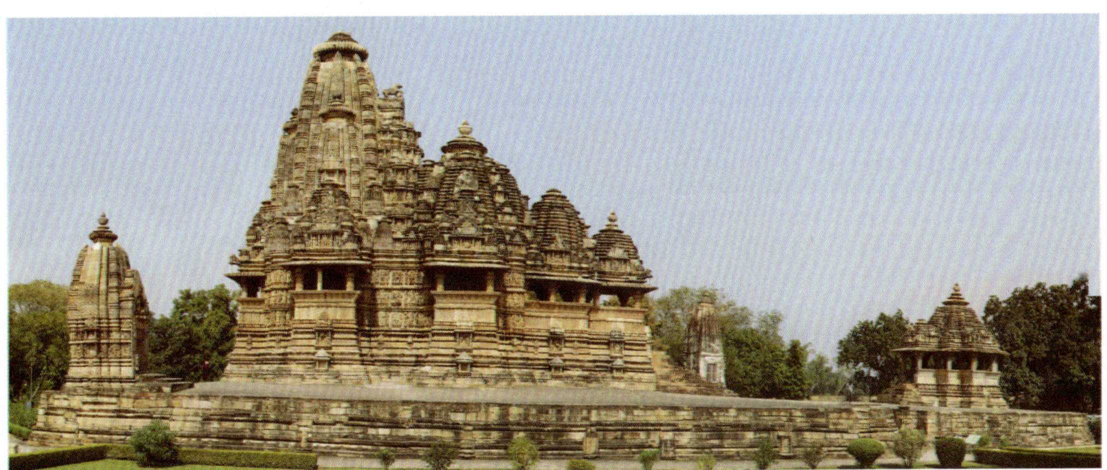

because the Hindu temple is, like the Buddhist stupa, conceived as a microcosm, a miniature Mount Meru, standing as axis of the universe. This sacred mountain concept is apparent, as well, in the eastern entry, which functions as a cave mouth leading back to the dark recesses of the garbhagriha or "womb room" where the stone Shiva linga, symbolizing Lord Shiva's cosmic energy, is enshrined. This effect is enhanced by the temple's long, narrow footprint; it measures 87 feet (26 m) front to back but is only 46 feet (14 m) at its widest point. The temple's proportions were carefully composed based on the ideal mathematical ratios enumerated in the shastras. This striving for perfection in form and execution was based on the belief that the god would only inhabit the temple if it were pleasing to him.

Relief Sculpture, Vishvanatha Temple, Khajuraho, 1002 CE The Hindu and Jain temples of Khajuraho have long been famous for their sculptural reliefs (Figure 6.26). The exterior platform walls are ornamented with scenes of the gods, mortals, and animals engaged in a variety of activities, some of which are of a sexually explicit nature. In 1838, the Khajuraho temples were visited by Captain T. S. Burt, a British officer and Victorian gentleman. In his journals, Burt recorded that he had been thoroughly scandalized by the overt eroticism of the images, which show couples performing sexual acts, sometimes with multiple partners and animals. While the Khajuraho temples are known for their graphic imagery, it should be noted that such scenes make up a very small portion of the thousands that typically decorate these temples.

While there is a long tradition in Hindu art of fertility spirits (Yakshis and Yakshas) personified as voluptuous and virile figures,

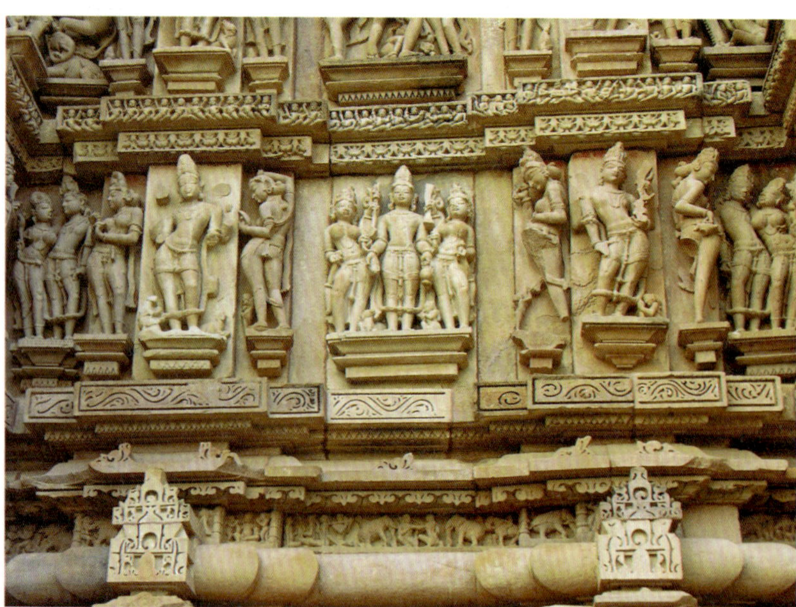

▶ **6.26** Khajuraho, Vishvanatha Temple, Detail of the exterior wall reliefs, c. 1000 CE.

The exterior platform walls are ornamented with scenes of the gods, mortals, and animals engaged in a variety of activities, some of which are of an erotic nature reflecting esoteric currents in Hinduism in that era.

individually and as Mithuna, these are relatively chaste depictions compared to some of the images that appear on the Visvanatha and some other medieval temples. The emphasis on what appears to be erotic art seems to be the result of the influence of Tantric Hinduism, ancient texts such as the *Atharva Veda* and the *Vatsyayana Kamasutra* attributed to Mallanaga Vatsyayana. The *Kamasutra*, in keeping with the shastras or ancient books of knowledge, was intended as a scientific and scholarly study of human sexuality in terms of the Hindu *purusharthas* or goals of life (see Religion and Philosophy: Santana Dharma or Hinduism). These images of sexual congress are always depicted on the exterior walls of the temple, not in the sanctuary, and as such mark the distinction between profane (human) and sacred (divine) spaces. In the religious sense, they are instructional metaphors for the creative oppositions that are basic in the design of the cosmos.

Muslim India (1175–1707 CE)

By 650 CE the countries to India's west had been incorporated into the Umayyad Caliphate (see Chapter 5). Nevertheless, the first Islamic incursions into India did not come until 712 CE. In that year, the Umayyad caliph, Walid bin Abdul Malik, sent Muhammad bin Qasim and an army of six thousand men to conquer the Sindh, bringing it under Umayyad control. Muslim rule of the Sindh was tolerant of Hinduism and Buddhism, although Buddhism declined under the influence of Islam. For hundreds of years those wishing to escape the bonds of the Hindu caste system, which did not allow social mobility, had converted to Buddhism. However, with the arrival of Islam, particularly the more mystical Sufi form, those looking to escape the caste system or the demands of an austere Buddhism converted to the Muslim faith (Tschannen 2013).

The Delhi Sultanate (1206–1526 CE)

The wealth of India made it attractive to Turkish regional lords (former caliphate governors who had established independent kingdoms). Mahmud of Ghazni (Afghanistan) launched seventeen raids into India between 1000 and 1030 CE. While most of these were sacking and pillaging missions against Hindu and Jain temples, he did add several Hindu frontier states in the Punjab to his territory. However, it was not until the twelfth century CE that any Islamic ruler attempted to consolidate and expand Muslim control in India. In 1175, Muhammad of Ghur, after campaigns in Afghanistan and Persia, entered India and attacked Gujarat, sacking the capital, before being repulsed by Indian forces. Undeterred, he attacked the Ghazavid governors of the former Hindu Sindh and brought those regions under his rule. Muhammad of Ghur continued his push eastward into India, ultimately, conquering much of northern India. When he was assassinated in 1206 CE, rule of his Indian territories fell to his trusted general Qutb al-din Aibek. A mamluk or Turkish slave soldier, Aibek established a dynasty that would rule the Delhi Sultanate until 1290 CE, when they were succeeded by Khalji dynasts. The power and territory of the Delhi Sultanate was greatly reduced after the incursion of Timur-e Lang (Tamerlane) who sacked Delhi at the end of the fourteenth century.

Quwwat-ul-Islam, Delhi, c. 1192-1316 CE Soon after the establishment of the Delhi Sultanate, Aibek ordered the building of the Sultanate's first mosque, Quwwat-ul-Islam, meaning "strength of Islam." The site chosen for the masjid had previously been occupied by Delhi's largest Hindu temple. To expedite construction, he ordered that temple as well as another twenty-six Hindu and Jain temples be taken down to provide building materials. Because Islamic craftsmen were not available, he conscripted an army of local Hindu stonemasons to work on the mosque. Reusing the carved elements from the local temples posed problems in the construction of the mosque. They were shorter than needed so the masons double-stacked them to achieve the necessary height (Figure 6.26). However, the most significant difficulty, given the Islamic prohibition against the use of human or animal images in a sacred context, was presented by the original Hindu and Jain carvings on the columns. The masons' solution was to plaster over the stone columns and cover the new surface with geometric designs. Exposure to weather, after the abandonment of the mosque, has caused this plaster coat to crumble and fall away, revealing the original state of the columns.

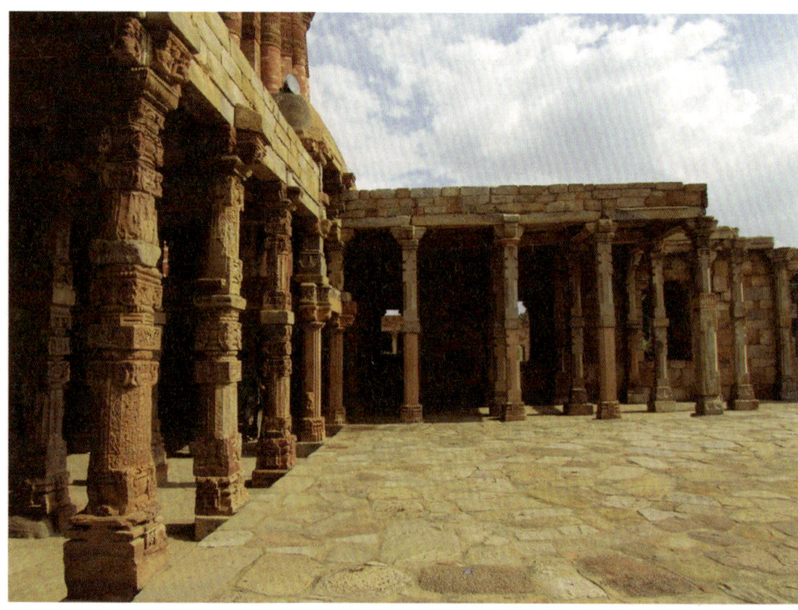

▶ **6.27** Delhi, Quwwat-ul-Islam, Detail columns from first mosque, c. 1199.

To build the first mosque of the Delhi Sultanate, Qutb al-din Aibek tore down more than two dozen Hindu and Jain temples and reused their materials. Since representations of living beings were prohibited, his workers altered the sculptural works and concealed offending images under a coating of plaster.

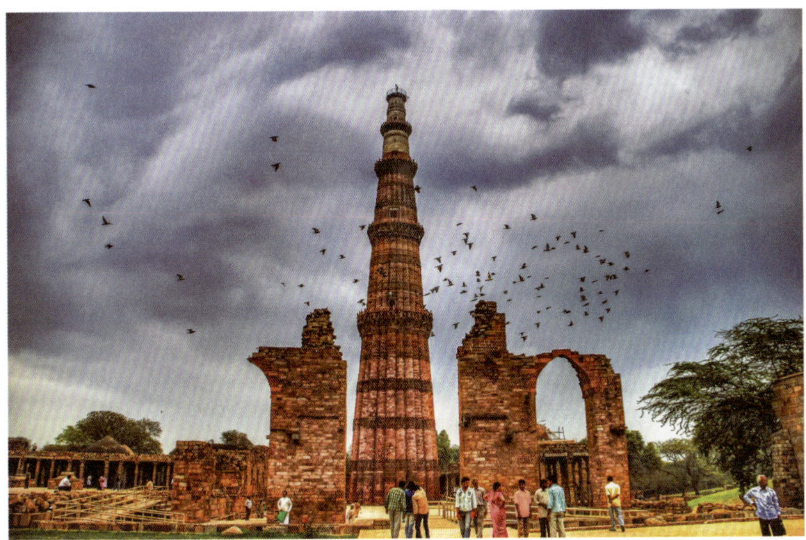

◀ 6.28 Qutb Minar and outer walls of the early mosque, c. 1100 CE. Red sandstone and white marble, 238 ft. high.

Only the first level had been completed when Qutb al-din Aibek died. The next three levels were added by his successor Shams al-Din Iltutmish and the final one by Firuz Shah Tughlaq in the fourteenth century.

Qutb Minar, Delhi, c. 1192-1220 CE Qutb al-din Aibek was succeeded by his son-in-law Shams al-Din Iltutmish in 1211 CE. Sultan Iltutmish continued to improve the mosque during his reign, expanding the prayer hall screen by three arches and finishing the minar begun by Aibek in 1192 CE. Only the first section of the Qutb Minar (Figure 6.28) had been completed before the death of Aibek; Iltutmish added three more stories to the tower. The tower stands 238 feet (72.58 m) tall, suggesting a larger purpose beyond calling the faithful to prayer. The rulers of the new sultanate intended the structure to be a symbol of Islamic power in Delhi and the surrounding area; indeed, an inscription on the tower states its purpose: "to cast the long shadow of Allah over the conquered city of the Hindus" (Craven 2006, 195).

The minar was carved from red- and buff-sandstone by local stonemasons. Each level of the tower is distinct. The base is approximately 47 feet (14.32 m) in diameter and is decorated with twenty-four alternating round and triangular sections cut in buff stone and crossed by three horizontal bands of red sandstone, bearing Kufic inscriptions. The second level features rounded columns bundled by two red sandstone bands. The third story has all angular sections. In the mid-fourteenth century CE, the fourth story was repaired, enlarged, and given a sheathing of white marble, and a new fifth story was added by Firuz Shah Tughlaq.

The Mughal Empire (1526–1707 CE)

Zahir-ud-din Muhammad Babur, prince of Ferghana, founded the Mughal Empire in 1526, after defeating Ibrahim Lodi, the last Sultan of Delhi at the battle of Panipat. The Mughals were Turks, descended on the paternal side from Timur-e Lang, the Turkman conqueror, and on the maternal side from Genghis Khan; they were also distantly related to the Safavids of Persia.

The designation "Mughal" was a Persian pejorative for the barbarian Mongols who had devastated Iran in the thirteenth century. Despite the insulting term, the Mughal dynasty that ruled over northern India for the next 181 years produced some of India's most enlightened rulers and greatest patrons of the arts. They were themselves often poets, writing in Persian or Chaghatai Turkish, painters or calligraphers, musicians and singers, and garden designers and architects, as well as capable warriors. The Mughals were also collectors of paintings, books, rare plants and exotic animals.

THE MUGHAL SCHOOL OF MINIATURE PAINTING

Three distinct painting styles evolved within the Mughal School, each defined by the needs and interests of the rulers for whom the images were created. The first of these was the Akbari style developed during the reign of Abu'l-Fath Jalal ud-din Muhammad Akbar (r, 1556.1605). Sources differ as to Akbar's age at the time of his accession, some making him as young as twelve or as old as fifteen or sixteen. While growing up at the Persian court during his father's exile, Akbar had taken drawing lessons from Mir Sayyid Ali and had developed a great appreciation of painting, poetry, and music; he was also passionately interested in philosophy and religion. Akbar was a brilliant man but he never learned to read. He commissioned painted serializations of works of Persian and Indian mythology so that he could visually "read" the stories. In addition to two masters, Mir Sayyid Ali and Khwaja Abdus Samad, brought from the Safavid Persia, when his father, Humayun, reclaimed his throne, Akbar recruited more than one hundred Hindu and Jain artists to work in his court atelier. The result was a fusion of Persian and Indian styles, termed the "Akbari Style."

The Akbari style is characterized by highly dramatic and brilliantly colored scenes that convey the adventure of the stories they illustrate. In 1580 contact between the Mughal court and Europe began with a Jesuit mission to India. The Jesuits presented Akbar with copies of European prints and paintings. Intrigued, Akbar had his artists copy European art works such as the illustrations in the copy of Plantyn's Royal Polyglot Bible gifted to him by the Jesuits.

The second style is known as the Jahangiri style and it originated in the court of Nur ud-Din Salim Jahangir (r. 1605–1627 CE). He succeeded his father Akbar as emperor of India in 1605 at the age of thirty-seven. He shared his father's love of painting and while still a young prince had established his own independent atelier in Allahabad, headed by the Persian artists, Aqa Riza and his son Abu Hasan. Jahangir preferred portraits and natural history subjects as well as paintings that documented the events of his reign. It was during this period that contact between England and the Mughal court began. Many Jahangiri paintings show a strong European influence.

The third style is the Jahani style developed during the reign of Shah Jahan. While miniature painters continued to work at the Mughal court during this time, Shah Jahan was primarily interested in architecture. The Jahani style is a continuation of that of Jahangir but the execution is colder and more rigid. Major themes in the style are lovers and entertainments. When Shah Jahan's son Aurungzeb usurped the throne, he banished the painters, poets, and musicians from his court. Most of these found work at the Hindu Rajput courts, in central and northern India, where they enriched art, literature, and music with elements derived from Mughal tradition.

Basawan (active c. 1560–1600 CE) and Chetar Muni (active c. 1580–1600 CE), Akbar and the Elephant Hawai, c. 1590–1595 CE Among the first works Akbar commissioned, about 1586, was the *Akbarnama*, the official chronicle of his reign, written by Abul Fazl (1551–1602) and illustrated by at least forty-nine artists; it took his artists seven years to complete. One innovation found in the Akbarnama was the use of actual portraits of the emperor and prominent members of his court. Akbar's history was illustrated with 116 paintings, rendered in an opaque watercolor using gum Arabic as a binder. Each painting was first laid out on its leaf in black chalk, then painted and burnished. On the verso or back of each sheet is Abul Fazl's text explaining the event detailed in the painting.

The painting of *Akbar and the Elephant Hawai* was a joint work by two of Akbar's court artists, Basawan who drew the image, and Chetar Muni who colored it. Akbar encouraged his artists to work collaboratively on paintings done in his atelier. The painting (Figure 6.29) depicts an incident that occurred when the emperor was about nineteen or twenty years old. Like many young men he participated in sporting activities. The sport shown here is elephant baiting, in which two wild bull elephants were pitted against each other in battle; Akbar rides the victorious elephant Hawai. When the second elephant fled in defeat, Hawai, with Akbar still on his back, charged after it across a pontoon bridge. The rhythm of the bounding elephants sets the bridge to

▼ **6.29** Basawan (a. 1560–1600) and Chetar Muni (a. 1580–1600), *Akbar and the Elephant Hawai*, ca. 1590–1595 CE. Opaque watercolor and gold on paper.

The painting illustrates Emperor Akbar participating in the sport of bull elephant baiting when he was about nineteen years old. His ability to control the wild elephant Hawal is a metaphor for his ability to rule a diverse Indian empire.

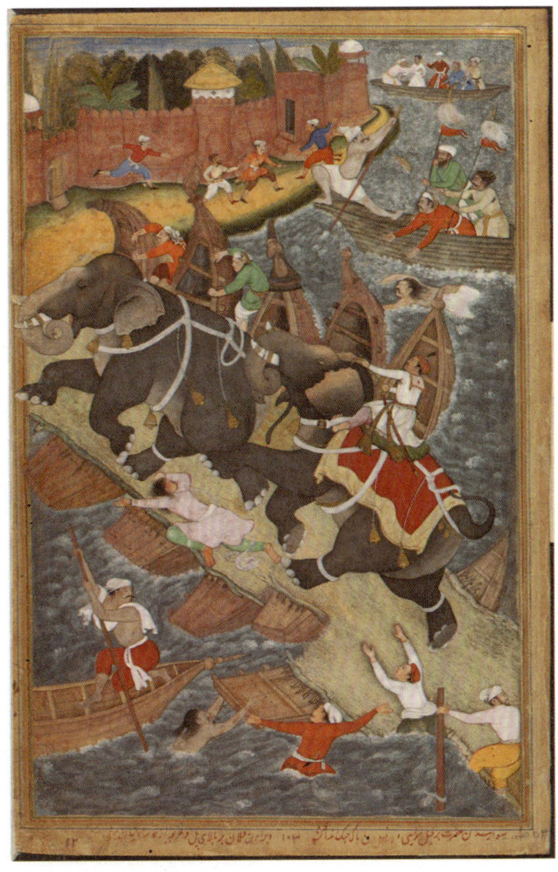

rocking violently, capsizing the boats supporting it and sending pedestrians into the water. Akbar on the back of the enraged elephant seems unperturbed; indeed, he was able to bring the elephant under control and to dismount safely. Abul Fazl makes this incident into an allegory of Akbar as ruler who, even as a young man, is able to govern an unruly empire of combative factions.

Ustad Mansur (active 1590–1624), Zebra, 1621 Unlike his father, who had encouraged his artists to collaborate on works, Jahangir encouraged his painters to work independently, to specialize and to develop their personal styles. Some concentrated on court scenes and official portraits, while others found their niches in genres such as botanical or zoological studies (Jain 2004). Jahangir was an avid collector, not only of art, but of exotic plants and animals, which he gathered into his gardens and menageries. He had his artists paint what he collected as well as recording things that he could not acquire. One of the artists who frequently accompanied Jahangir on his travels around the Mughal Empire was an exceptional painter named Ustad Mansur (Master Mansur), who recorded the animals and plants that caught the emperor's interest. His paintings of birds, plants, and animals, such as his *Zebra* (Figure 6.30) show him to be a preeminent realist who depicted his subjects without emotion or flights of fancy. Indeed, the degree of precision and objectivity found in his renderings has made them extremely valuable for scientific study. His watercolor of the dodo bird, which went extinct due to overhunting by Europeans in 1681, is considered to be the only accurate drawing made from a living specimen. So amazing was his skill in his own time that Jahangir bestowed the title *Nadir-ul-'Asr* meaning "Miracle of the Age" upon him.

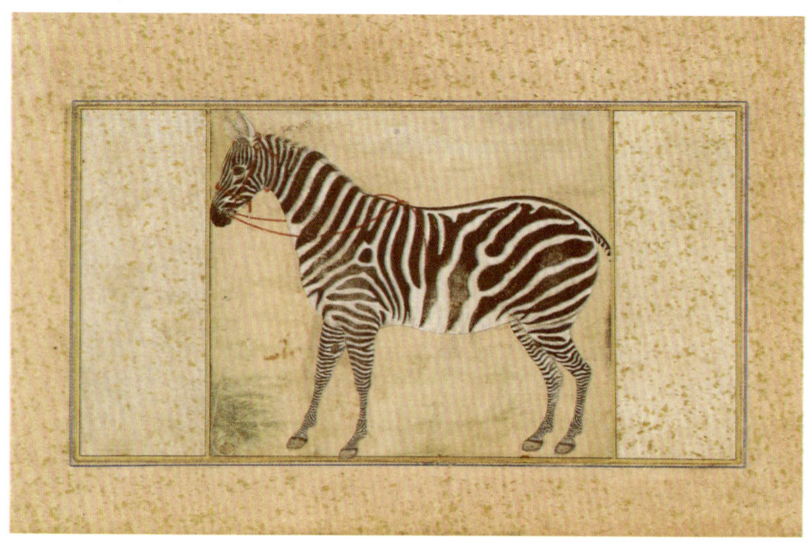

▶ **6.30** Usted Mansur, Zebra, c. 1621. Opaque watercolor on paper, 7.43 in. × 10.62 in.

Mansur frequently traveled with Emperor Jahangir, recording exotic animals, plants, and even foreign visitors for his master. His approach was one of direct realism without the flights of fancy sometimes seen in contemporary European depictions of exotic animals.

Bichitr (active c. 1615–1660 CE), Jahangir Preferring a Sufi Shaykh to Kings, c. 1615 CE

Another artist greatly favored by Jahangir was the Hindu painter Bichitr, whose work shows strong European influence. His use of Western perspective, chiaroscuro modeling, and motifs such as cherubs and cupids are thought to derive from his study of European artworks. As a portraitist, Bichitr possessed great observational skill, resulting in likenesses of exacting detail, precisely drawn and brilliantly colored. However, his court portraits of Jahangir often take on an unusual allegorical quality.

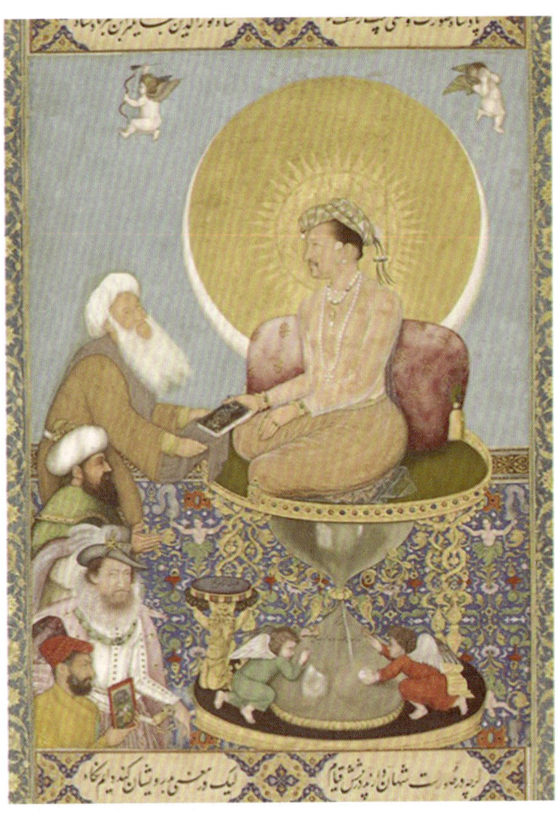

▲ 6.31 Bichitr, Jahangir Preferring a Sufi Shaykh to Kings, c. 1615–1618. Opaque watercolor, ink, and gold on paper.

Bichitr, shown holding a miniature painting at bottom left, was strongly influenced by European works of art coming into Jahangir's court, indicated by the cherubs and cupids depicted above and below the emperor.

In *Jahangir Preferring a Sufi Shaykh to Kings* (Figure 6.31), painted about 1615, Bichitr shows Jahangir seated on a throne in the form of an hourglass through which the sands of time are rapidly shifting. In Northern European vanitas paintings of this era, which featured symbols of the inevitability of change and death, hourglasses were commonly used as *memento mori* or reminders of death. In this case, the hourglass is a particularly apt reminder of Jahangir's limited time on earth and his throne. Jahangir's fondness for opium-laced wine had taken a toll on his health when this work was painted. Indeed, on either side of the hourglass are a pair of cherubs who frantically try to slow the falling sands, writing on the glass, "O Shah may the span of your life be a thousand years" (Craven 2006, 208).

Behind Jahangir, flanked by cupids, is a huge golden nimbus (halo), in which appear the sun and the crescent moon, a reference to night and day and again to the passage of time. Moreover, they may signify the title Nur ud-Din, meaning "Light of Faith," which Jahangir took when he ascended the throne, representing that Jahangir favors religion over the things of the world. This is further illustrated by the interaction between Jahangir and the Sufi Shaykh Husain, the religious leader to whom Jahangir hands a book, a precious object in the Mughal court. Husain was responsible for the Ajmer Sharif Dargah, an important Sufi pilgrimage site frequented by the Mughal rulers. Jahangir looks only at the cleric as a symbol of the religious source of his power, ignoring the two contemporaneous rulers, the Ottoman Sultan (possibly Ahmet I) and King James I of England, who stand in line behind the Shaykh. An inscription—"although to all appearances kings stand before him, he looks inwardly toward the dervishes" (a dervish is a Sufi holy man)—seems to bear out this interpretation. The importance of the religious figure is emphasized by his scale, which is closer to that of Jahangir than any of the other figures. The presence of the Ottoman sultan and King James do not a record of an actual audience but a bit of artistic fiction, intended to show the greatness of Jahangir as a "world ruler." The source for the image of the English king was likely a state portrait presented to the Mughal emperor by Sir Thomas Roe in 1615. The third figure is not a prince or potentate but Jahangir's court artist Bichitr. While European artists had a long tradition of including their self-portraits in commissioned works, this was unusual at the Mughal Court. Bichitr's inclusion of his own image is an honor bestowed upon him by Jahangir, just as were the gifts of an elephant and two horses shown in the miniature the artist holds.

MUGHAL ARCHITECTURE

The golden age of Mughal architecture is a period of less than a century in duration. It begins with Akbar's construction of a tomb for his father, Humayun, in 1564, and ends with the completion of the Taj Mahal in 1653. The uniqueness of Mughal architecture, like Mughal painting, lies in its skillful blending of traditional Central Asian and Safavid Persian forms of Islamic architecture with those of Hindu India. Although Aurungzeb patronized the construction of several mosques during his reign, none compare with the exceptional works built by his father and great-grandfather.

Mirak Mirza Ghiyath, Tomb of Humayun, Delhi, 1572 CE Akbar selected the Persian architect Mirak Mirza Ghiyath to build his father's mausoleum along the banks of the Jumna in Delhi. Ghiyath had worked widely in Persia and Central Asia before coming to India. His travels would have given him familiarity with earlier Islamic tombs such as the tenth century CE Mausoleum of the Samanids, a canopy tomb (open through on all four sides) in Bukhara, where he had worked for the Shaybanid rulers, and the Gur Emir (see Figure 6. 32) in Samarkand, where he had also worked before being called to India. The Gur Emir was the mausoleum of Timur-e Lang, founder of the Timurid Dynasty. Certainly Ghiyath would have understood the importance of Timur as an ancestor of the Mughal rulers. Indeed, many elements found in the Tomb of Humayun (see Figure 6.32) appear to have been derived from the Gur Emir, in particular the use of ***pishtaqs***, arcuate façade niches, and the double dome on a high drum.

Ghiyath set the Tomb of Humayun in a long Persian ***charbagh*** or garden divided into four parts by watercourses and pathways. Common in Persia, the charbagh was based on the description in the Qur'an of the paradisiacal garden. Originally, the gardens surrounding the mausoleum would have been planted with fragrant shrubs and plants, as scent and the sound of water are two important aspects in the design of the charbagh. Within the garden the mausoleum is raised on a square platform, almost 23 feet (7 m) above ground level. The four faces of the platform are softened by a running arcade of red sandstone inlaid with white marble in geometric patterns.

In plan, the massive red sandstone mausoleum is a square, 298.55 feet (91 m) on a side, whose corners have been chamfered to soften the block-like quality of the building. Recessed into the center of each façade is a 52 foot (16 m) high monumental gateway. Each pishtaq features a large pointed arch set into a box-like frame known as an ***alfiz*** or "container" because it contains or frames the arch. Between the arch and alfiz are two triangular squinches done in a contrasting color and ornamented with a circle and star motifs, a common decorative motif in Samarkand. Centered in the face of the façade on either side of the monumental gateway is a tall alcove arch, replicating the design of the main pishtaq but with curved niches on two levels. The surface area of the façade around the secondary archways is decorated with blind niches framed in white marble inlay, while functional niches are stacked in the chamfered side walls.

The central core of the building is crowned by bulbous double-shell dome on a high drum. The outer shell is faced with white marble so that it seems to visually soar over the red sandstone drum upon which it sits. Beneath the dome, in the center of the octagonal chamber is the marble **cenotaph** (tomb monument) of Humayun; his actual internment is in the crypt directly below the cenotaph. Opening to the west is a mihrab pointing in the direction of Mecca. Surrounding the main hall are four additional rooms, on two floors, which contain the cenotaphs of other members of the Mughal dynasty. In all some 150 persons are buried in the tomb, earning it the nickname "Dormitory of the Mughals."

Although Ghiyath's mausoleum is largely influenced by Persian tradition, he also incorporated some Hindu elements into the design. Surrounding the dome are large and small-scale pillared cupolas, known as ***chattri***. In India chattri were Hindu garden pavilions, open on all sides and covered by a domed roof. The chattri roofs on the Tomb of Humayun were covered originally in blue, green, and yellow tiles. Rising as extensions over each exterior and interior angle of the façade are the shaft-like pinnacles known as ***guldasta***; they are another element derived from Hindu architectural tradition.

Ustad Ahmad Lahauri (chief architect), Taj Mahal, 1631–1653 CE The undisputed masterpiece of Mughal architecture is the Taj Mahal (see Figure 6.32), built by Shah Jahan as a mausoleum for himself and for his wife "Mumtaz Mahal" (Arjumand Banu Begu). Although Shah Jahan had other wives, he was deeply in love with Mumtaz and the two were inseparable in life; she even accompanied him on military campaigns. Construction of the Taj Mahal or "Crown Palace" began in 1631 after Mumtaz Mahal died giving birth to her fourteenth child.

Shah Jahan brought in architects and artisans from all over the Islamic world to collaborate on the project. Thirty-seven different architects are mentioned in the court histories as having worked on the Taj Mahal, but its principal designer and chief architect seems to have been Ustad Ahmad Lahauri (1580–1649). Prior to starting work on the Taj Mahal, Lahauri had worked on several projects for Shah Jahan. In addition to architects, there were calligraphers, lapidaries, and goldsmiths among the twenty thousand or so workers who labored for twenty-two years to build the mausoleum. The cost of the project was 32 million rupees, an astronomical sum, especially considering that the Taj Mahal's prototype, the Tomb of Humayun, had cost 1.5 million rupees to build (ASI 2011).

The Taj Mahal has much in common with its Akbari prototype in its blend of Muslim and Hindu elements. It, too, is set on a high podium in a charbagh, has the same chamfered-square form crowned by a double-shelled dome, a similar surface pattern of monumental pishtaqs and arcuate niches, and it is also ornamented with Hindu chattri and guldastras. The most obvious distinctions are the larger scale, allover use of the more expensive white marble veneer, and the addition of the four towering minarets rising from the corners of the podium to heights of 130 feet (40 m). Other refinements are evident in the higher double dome and drum, the use of *pietra dura* (stone inlay) decoration on the pishtaqs, and the Qur'anic inscriptions in Kufic calligraphy framing the alfizes, a feature not found on the Tomb of Humayun. The importance given to calligraphy is indicated by the fact that the calligrapher, Amanat Khan (Abdu I-Haq), was allowed the rare honor of signing his name in the inscription on the south pishtaq. As in the Tomb of Humayun the octagonal chamber under the dome contains the cenotaphs of Mumtaz Mahal and Shah Jahan; their actual burials are in the crypt directly below. Surrounding the central chamber, in the same manner as in the Tomb of Humayun, are secondary chambers meant to hold the cenotaphs of future Mughal rulers; however, this did not come to pass.

The British Raj (1858–1947)

The British came to India first as traders under the auspices of the Governor and Company of Merchants of London Trading into the East Indies (1600–1708), a stock company chartered by Queen Elizabeth on December 31, 1600. The merchants of the East India Company, as it was commonly known, were seeking a piece of the lucrative spice and exotic goods (tea, silk, cotton, indigo and opium) trade with the East. The charter gave them a monopoly on trade with India, China, and Southeast Asia. Company ships arrived at the port of Surat in 1608 and during the reign of the Mughal emperor Jahangir were allowed to establish a trading post at Gujarat. Treaties were negotiated

VISUAL COMPARISON

Gur Emir, Tomb of Humayun, and Taj Mahal

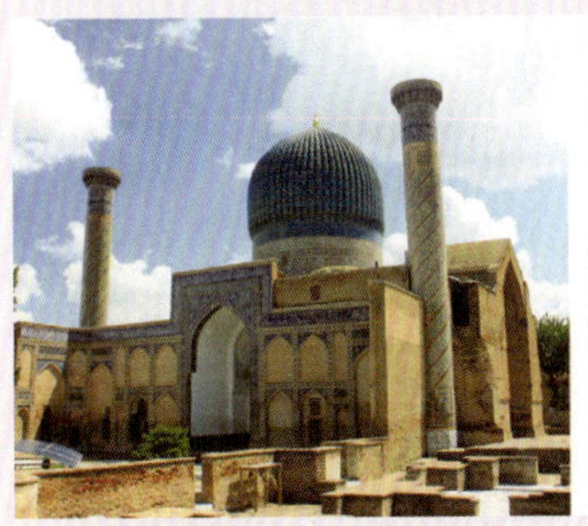

Gur Emir, Samarkand

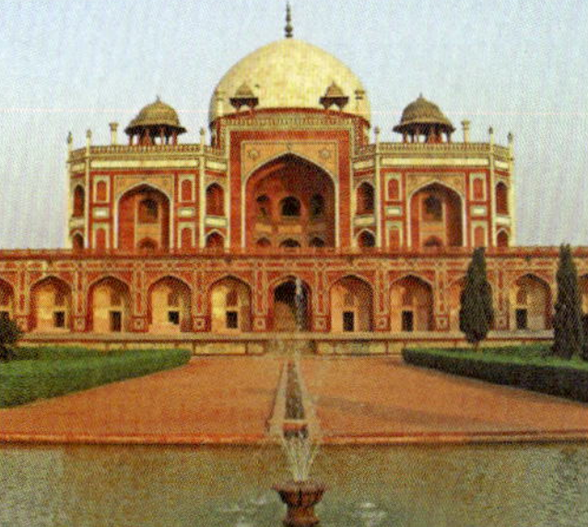

Tomb of Humayun, Delhi

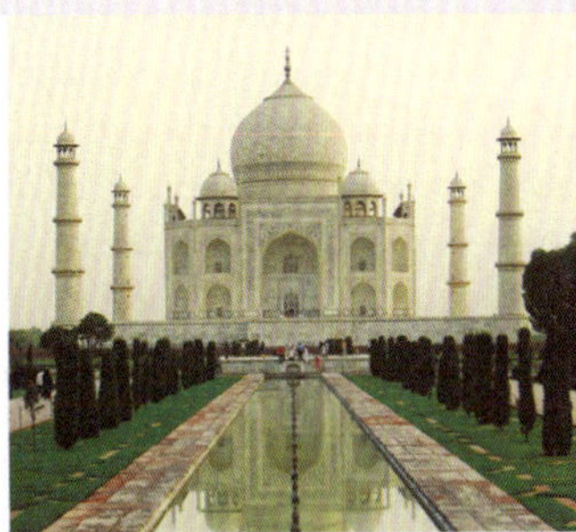

Taj Mahal, Agra

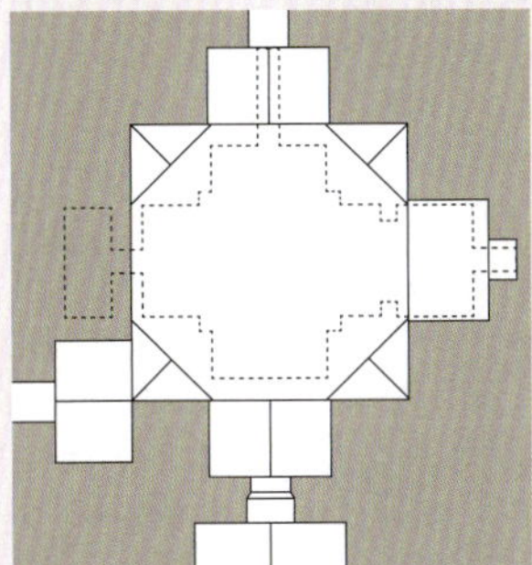

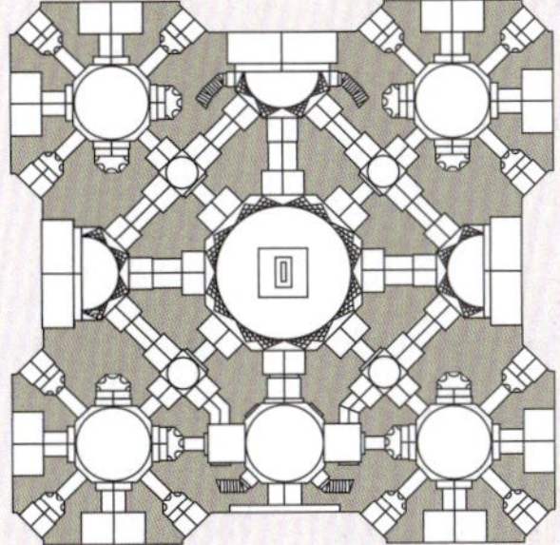

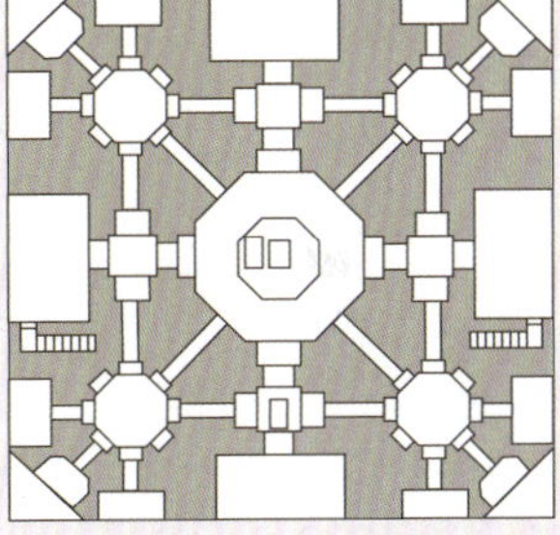

▲ **6.32** Gur Emir, Samarkand, Tomb of Humayun, Delhi, and Taj Mahal, Agra.

Although based on ideas derived from the Gur Emir, the tomb of the Mughal ruler's ancestor, the two Indian mausoleums incorporated Indian and Persian elements.

Shah Jehan's Taj Mahal is the undisputed pinnacle of Mughal architecture. The gleaming white marble hall would seem to represent a unique architectural vision but many of its features were derived from two earlier dynastic mausoleums. These were the Gur Emir in Samarkand (Uzbekistan), belonging to the emperor's sixth great grandfather Timur-e Lang, and his great-grandfather Humayun's Tomb in Delhi.

The first of these, the Gur Emir, was begun in 1403 as a simple block structure, enlarged by an axial arrangement of projecting iwans, which opened off the building instead of a court as was the pattern in Safavid Persia. Typical of the Timurid style is the tall, ribbed dome set on a high cylindrical drum and the use of tile work on the exterior. The blind façade of the building was decorated with a repeating pattern of double-stacked niches set between tall arches. The corners of the building were originally anchored by four minarets, two of which were toppled by earthquakes. The complex was later enlarged to include a madrassa, a khanqah or Sufi meeting house, and several other structures.

It is likely that the Persian architect Mirak Mirza Ghiyath, selected by Akbar to build his father's tomb, knew the Gur Emir. The Timurids of Samarkand had been among Ghiyath's many Central Asian patrons before he arrived in India. The use of design elements from the Gur Emir to ornament the Tomb of Humayun makes a strong political statement on behalf of the Mughal dynasty. It not only reiterates the

(Continued)

Mughals' descent from Timur-e Lang, the Turco-Mongol conqueror of much of Central Asia, but also serves to legitimize Humayun's and, by inference Akbar's, rule over India. Humayun's throne had been usurped by the Afghan general Sher Shah, and even though Mughal rule had been restored with the help of the Safavids, there were still some in the Afghan Sur dynasty that wished to reassert control over India.

The most obvious of Ghiyath's references to the Gur Emir are the high drum, tall double-shell dome, and prominent pishtaq entry into the primary iwan. Likewise he borrows the niche-arch rhythm of the Gur Emir and uses it to create an undulating pattern of arched iwans set between niched side walls. There are also differences. Where the Gur Emir sits on the ground, the Tomb of Humayun has been made more prominent by being raised on a high arcaded platform. Other differences are adaptations from local Hindu architecture and this as well can be read as a political promise of equal treatment under Akbar, who abolished taxes on non-Muslims and appointed Hindus to high positions in his government. These Hindu elements include the use of local red sandstone trimmed with white marble, the pavilion-like chattri, and the guldasta pinnacles that mark the segments of the façade. Lastly, he adds a Persian element, again perhaps to be read as an acknowledgment of the Mughals' familial connections to Safavid Persia, by placing the monument at the end of an elaborate quadrilateral charbagh with watercourses.

In turn, Ustad Ahmad Lahauri, selected by Shah Jehan as chief architect of the Taj Mahal, based his design on those of the Tomb of Humayun and the Gur Emir. Lahauri simplifies and refines the masses of the Delhi mausoleum by subtly altering several key elements. Most importantly he constructs the building entirely of white marble, creating a more tranquil surface without the push-pull of contrasting colored materials. Next he places the building on a lower platform ornamented with a blind arcade, and increases the height of the drum and dome. Lahauri's design seems to revert to a more standard cubic mausoleum form by removing Ghiyaths secondary pishtaqs and connecting the narrower niched side walls. At the same time he softens the block of the building by chamfering its corners. Other refinements include fewer but larger chattri, a wider water channel in the charbagh, and the addition of four towering minarets to the corners of the platform; this last feature was likely inspired by the Gur Emir as minarets are an atypical feature of Islamic mausoleum architecture.

with other Indian rulers and by 1835 the company controlled vast areas of the subcontinent. Indeed, the expanse of territory managed by the company was so great that it could mandate English as the official language of India. Through inequitable alliances or military conquest when necessary, the company continued to expand not only in the subcontinent but eastward into Burma (Myanmar) and Thailand. By the mid-nineteenth century, Indian Hindus and Muslims began to fear that the next company edict to be imposed might dictate their conversion to Christianity. At about this same time a rumor swept through the company's Indian regiments that the new shipment of rifle cartridges had been greased with lard and beef tallow, an insult to both Muslims and Hindus. This fueled a rebellion that lasted for little more than a year before being quelled. As a result of the "Great Mutiny" a British governor-general was appointed for India, instituting the British Raj or "British Rule." Queen

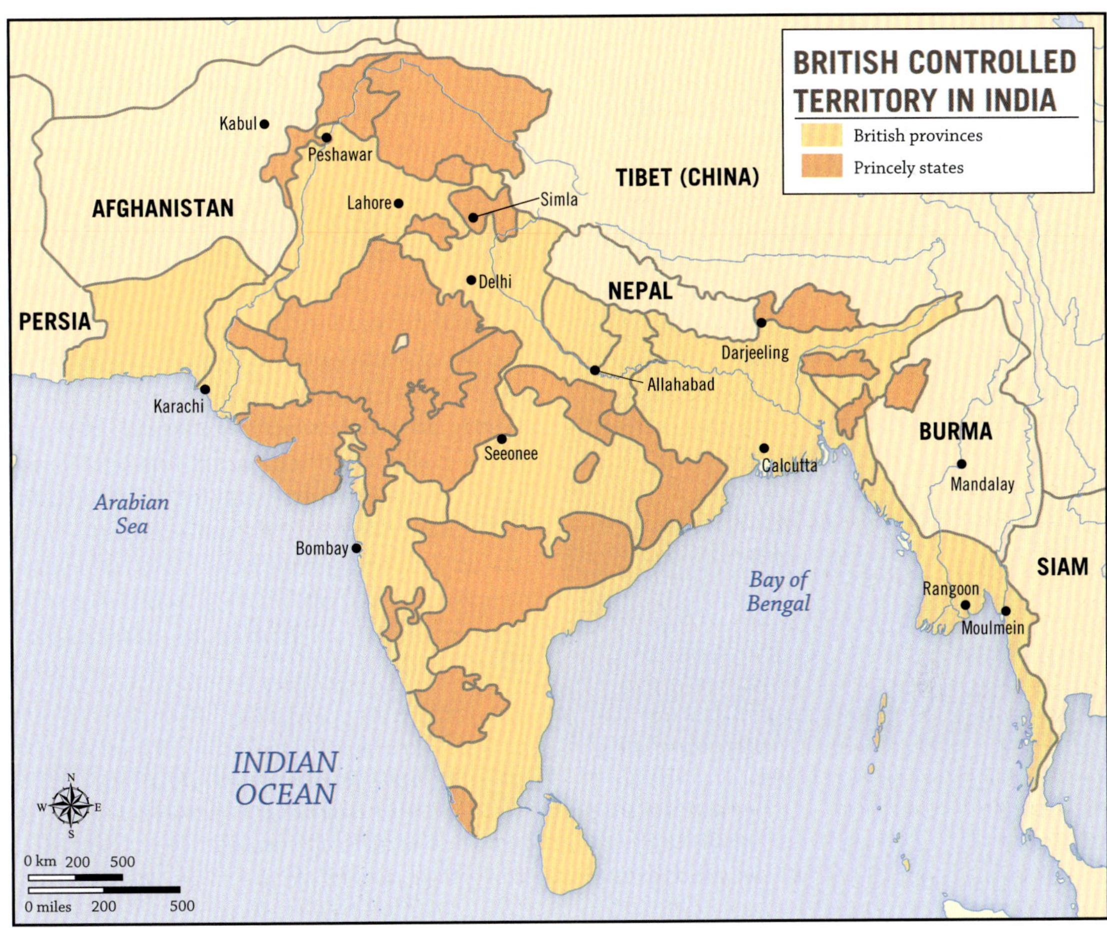

Victoria, later Empress of India, promised her Indian subjects that her government would work to better their lives. Practically speaking this meant bringing education, industry, and railroads to India to make the colony more profitable by more efficiently exploiting its resources and labor.

Narsingh, Portrait of Maharaja Sir Jaswant Singh II of Marwar, c. 1880 Under the British Raj, the first European-style art academies were founded in Madras and Calcutta. Western styles of painting, particularly portraiture, were popular not only with the British in India, but also with the local rajas. Many local rulers and educated upper-class Indians found it expedient, when dealing with the British authorities, to take on some of the trappings of the British gentry. A miniature portrait (Figure 6.33), circa 1880, of the Maharaja Sir Jaswant Singh II of Marwar, attributed to the painter Narsingh, reflects the growing taste for Western forms during the British Raj as well as the influence of photography—one of the scientific advancements brought to India by the British. Narsingh's

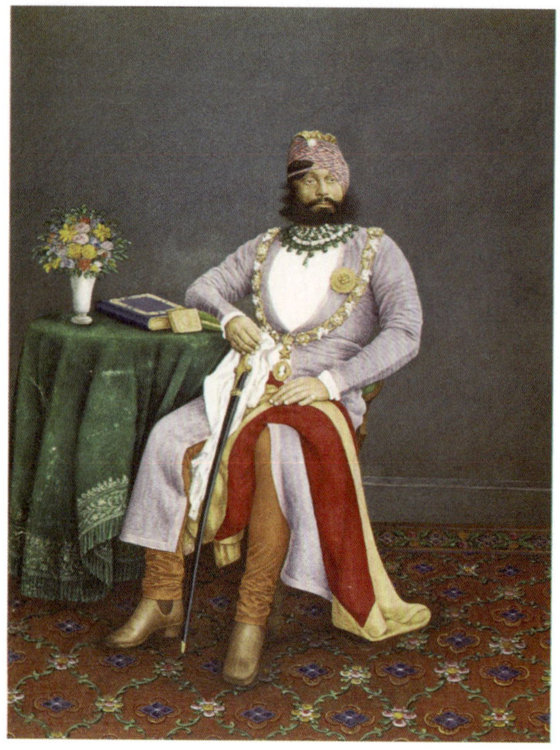

▲ 6.33 Attrib. Narsingh, Portrait of Maharaja Sir Jaswant Singh II of Marwar, c. 1880. Opaque watercolor on paper.

The Maharaja is shown in a Westernized manner, seated in a chair beside a cloth-covered table with books and flowers and against a neutral backdrop, all standard in Victorian portraiture. His dress is a meeting of East and West as are his titles and ornaments. He wears a bib of emeralds and the collar of a knight commander.

painting is based on a hand-colored photograph of the Maharaja.[1] The same photo was also used for a number of other portraits that show the Maharaja in more traditional garb and poses.

In this opaque watercolor portrait, presumably intended for an English audience, Sir Jaswant wears English boots and jodhpurs under his *angarhka* or long coat. Instead of being seated on a dais and throne, he is seated next to a table covered with a green cloth, in what looks very much like the corner of a Victorian parlor. The books and flowers are intended to show the Maharaja as an educated, cultured gentleman and thus as an enlightened, modern ruler. He holds a *shamshir* or curved hunting sword, suggesting an affinity for hunting, the favorite pastime of the English gentry. The ornaments he wears reflect his position in two worlds: India and England. He wears the emerald bib of the Hindu maharaja and the gold collar of the Knight Commander of the Most Exalted Order of the Star of India, an honor conferred, along with a knighthood, by Queen Victoria, whose silhouette adorns the collar.

Indian Art after Independence (1947–)

Since the Great Revolt of 1857, discontent with British rule had been building. In 1885 the Indian National Congress Party was founded to lobby for reform. Initially, the Congress Party was a moderate group but over time some of its members became radicalized and splintered into the *Swaraj* or "Home Rule" party. In 1903 British officials decided to partition Bengal province along religious and linguistic lines, creating Hindu West Bengal and Muslim East Bengal. The stated reason was that the province was too large to administer effectively but the division was actually an attempt to weaken the growing nationalist movement in the province. In response the party launched the *Swadeshi* (self-sufficiency) movement and called for the boycott of British goods, encouraging people to use only Indian products. In the 1920s and 1930s under the leadership of Mohandas (Mahatma) Gandhi, the

---

[1] A hand-colored photo of the Maharaja, showing him seated at the same table, is in the collection of the Metropolitan Museum of Art in New York. https://www.metmuseum.org/art/collection/search/60050744?rpp=20&pg=2&ao=on&ft=india&pos=25

Congress Party advocated for nonviolent noncooperation, including nonpayment of taxes, and acts of civil disobedience such as the Salt March,[2] to protest British rule. When India was brought into World War II without consulting Indian leaders, the Congress Party organized mass acts of civil disobedience under the Quit India Movement, declaring that India would not support the war effort unless it was immediately granted full independence. The British responded by jailing Gandhi and keeping him imprisoned until May 1944.

The Raj was brought down very quickly at the end of the war in response to growing sectarian violence that began in Calcutta during the summer of 1946 and spread across the country. Not having the resources after the devastation of World War II to put down the unrest in India, Britain agreed to the partitioning of India along sectarian lines into the states of India and Pakistan, separated into West Pakistan and East Pakistan (now Bangladesh). Pakistan achieved independence on August 14, 1947, and India, the next day.

In such a highly politicized climate, it is not surprising that India's Post-Colonial art scene was also politically charged. Artists sought to redefine themselves and their nation in the wake of independence and the partitioning of their country. In India, the artistic debate revolved around the use of Western media and modes of expression versus indigenous materials and styles. Two camps were defined: the Nationalists, who advocated a return to traditional Indian arts in an effort to formulate an indigenous modern style, and the Progressives, who espoused the belief that Western modernism could be used to express the concerns of the new Indian nation.

Abanindranath Tagore (1871–1951), The Journey's End, 1913 The leader of the Nationalist movement was Abanindranath Tagore. He was born into a multi-generational family of artists. Tagore grew up and attended art school under the British Raj. In 1890, he enrolled in the Calcutta School of Art, where he studied oil painting with the British artist, Charles Palmer, and pastels and watercolor with the Italian artist, Olindo Ghilardi. He left art school fully proficient in Western techniques and modes of expression, but at the same time he was fascinated by traditional Mughal and Rajput painting. Around the turn of the century he became acquainted with Japanese wash techniques through a demonstration by visiting Japanese artists Yokoyama Taikan and Hishida Shunso. After this Tagore's work took on a dreamlike, atmospheric quality and often featured nostalgic subject matter.

After independence Tagore sought to create an indigenous style that would respond to Mahatma Gandhi's call for swadeshi or Indian

[2] Under British Indians were not allowed to produce salt but forced to buy heavily taxed British salt.

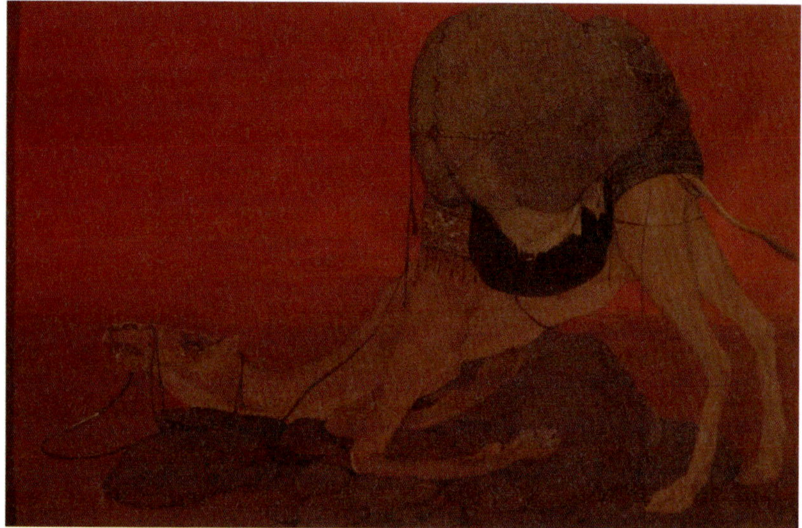

▶ **6.34** Abanindranath Tagore (1871–1951), *The Journey's End*, 1913. Wash and tempera on paper, 8.25 in. × 5.90 in.

An artistic nationalist, Tagore drew on native arts such as the Ajanta Caves and Indian miniature painting to formulate an art for newly independent India.

self-sufficiency. For this he drew on traditional Indian sources, such as Ajanta cave murals, and Indian miniatures. As a counter to the influence of Western colonialism in art, Tagore founded the "Indian Society of Oriental Art," which promoted the development of a modern pan-Asian style, expressing a common Eastern aesthetic. Ultimately, this group of artists coalesced into the *Bengal School*.

Tagore's *The Journey's End* (Figure 6.34) illustrates a wistful yearning for an earlier, Pre-Colonial India. A camel is in the ungainly process of lowering itself to the ground so that the load it carries can be unpacked. Camels were the main beasts of burden on the Silk Road that wound across northern India as it made its way from the Mediterranean to China. The painting reflects the ending of a long historic journey and an ancient era of Indian greatness with the use of a deep red wash, suggesting the sunset. The shallow space, the use of classical line, and the bold color are characteristics derived from Pre-Colonial Indian painting.

Maqbool Fida Husain, (1915-2011), Mother and Child: A Tribute to Mother Theresa, the Great Humanist of our Time, 1980 Not all Indian artists shared the Bengal School's enthusiasm for traditional Indian art and rejection of western modernism. Artists who believed that modernism had a role in creating an inherently Indian, yet contemporary art formed the organization known as the Progressive Artists Group. Among its founding members was M.F. Husain. Husain was born into a working-class Muslim family in Pandharpur, Maharashtra state. In 1935, he moved to Bombay where he enrolled in the Sir. J.J. School of Art. To support himself he worked as a cinema billboard painter for Bollywood movies; payment was by the square foot and usually amounted to only a few rupees even for a large signboard. For a time, he also worked in a toy factory.

Husain's style was strongly influenced by the expressionist and cubist movements, earning him the appellation, "The Picasso of India." He is known for his narrative series of paintings illustrating themes in Indian life, history, and literature, such as the lives of Mahatma Gandhi and Mother Theresa, Hindu epics including the Ramayana and Mahabharata, and the histories of the Maurya, Mughal, and British Empires. Although his work received many honors from the Indian government, it was not without controversy. Conservative Hindus were often offended by his painting Hindu goddesses in the nude, which they considered blasphemous, especially since he was a secular Muslim. After several nuisance lawsuits and death threats, Husain left India in 2006, eventually taking up residence in London.

In 1980, Husain began a series of paintings and lithographic prints which took as their subject the work of the Albanian nun, Mary Teresa Bojaxhiu, popularly known as Mother Teresa (1910-1997). She was the founder of an order of nuns, the Missionaries of Charity, dedicated to serving the poorest of the poor worldwide. During her lifetime Mother Teresa was a controversial figure. She was awarded the Nobel Peace Prize (1979), and ultimately, canonized as a Catholic saint (2017), for her ministry among the destitute and dying and her care for abandoned children, but she was also criticized for the lack of sanitary conditions and questionable medical care in her facilities, mismanagement of the money her charity received, and her problematic friendships with dictators.

Husain's lithograph, *Mother and Child: A Tribute to Mother Theresa, the Great Humanist of our Time,* (figure 6.35), shows three nuns, in the distinctive sari-habit of the Missionaries of Charity, and three Indian children. While the children, as personifications of destitute children and orphans, are not individualized by facial features, they are recognizably human in form. In contrast, the nuns who tend to them read

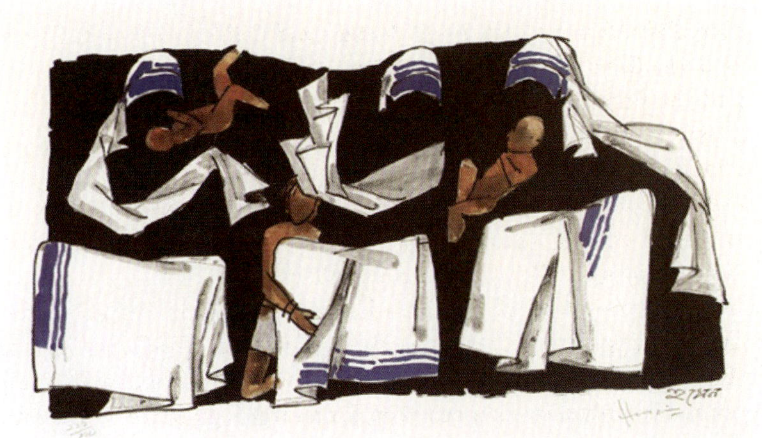

◀ **6.35** M. F. Husain, *Hindu Triad,* 2008–2011.

Husain was a progressive artist and believed that a modernist idiom could be used to create a uniquely Indian and contemporary art. In this painting he presents the Hindu Trimurti as three faces connected by overlapping elements from the Hindu myths.

only as voids; their forms hinted at by the edges of the garments. The sisters are rendered as part of the black background as a way of focusing attention on the needs of the poor rather than on the women themselves. .

Subodh Gupta (1964–), Dada, 2014 The political and religious divides of post-Independence India had forced some artists, such as M.F. Husain and Francis Newton Souza, cofounder of the Progressive Movement, to seek refuge abroad. The decade of the 1960s continued to offer political and economic challenges, some brought on by a disastrous war with China over the North East Frontier Area. Subodh Gupta, born in 1964, is one of a post-partition generation of artists who have chosen to remain and work in India.

Gupta grew up in rural Khangaul, Bihar, in northeast India; his family worked for the local railroad and expected him to follow that same path in life. As a child his mother took him to local theater productions and he was inspired to become an actor, a career choice which his family refused to support. He joined a theater company and discovered his talent for the visual arts when he was asked to make posters advertising the company's productions. He went on to study art at the local College of Art and Craft in Patna, earning a BFA in painting.

In his paintings and sculptures, Gupta explores his childhood memories and rituals, often nostalgically incorporating items and humble materials (e.g., cow pats, tools, and kitchen utensils) from everyday life. Ultimately, stainless steel pails, pans, and lunch buckets, the ubiquitous products of Indian steel manufactory, became his signature form. Using these materials Gupta creates enormous works that sometimes replicate landscape environments. His *Dada* (Figure 6.36) is a banyan tree constructed of stainless steel pails, milk containers,

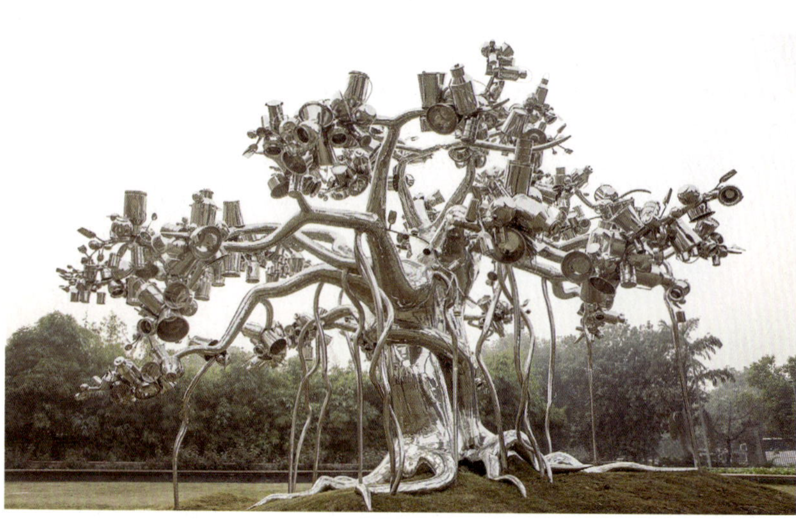

▶ **6.36** Subodh Gupta (b. 1964), *Dada*, 2014. Stainless steel utensils, and tubing.

Gupta paints and creates sculptures from common everyday industrial items, such as lunch pails, not only because of the intrinsic beauty of the items but also to express nostalgia for a simpler time in India.

pans, and utensils that sprout from a stainless trunk and root system. The name is derived from the Hindi term of address for one's grandfather, giving the work the context of a family tree to suggest the importance of roots and origins.

Pakistani Art after Independence (1947–)

Pakistan also faced many difficulties in the decades after independence including repeated military dictatorships, tension with India, and policies of forced Islamization under the Zia regime, as well as everyday problems resulting from the two halves of the country being divided by the 1,000-mile expanse of India. However, the post-partition climate in Pakistan was more favorable for artists who embraced modernism. Not only were early Pakistani artists unhindered by established stereotypes but modernism was seen as representing change and economic possibilities. The movement was pioneered in Pakistan by artists such as Zubeida Agha (1922–1997), who first exhibited her abstract paintings in Lahore in 1949, and Shakir Ali (1914–1975), painter and teacher, whose work explored Cubism and also the painterly aspects of traditional Islamic calligraphy.

Rashid Rana (1968–), Veil Series, 2004

Rashid Rana is one of Pakistan's most important contemporary artists. He was born in the city of Lahore, a little more than two decades after the nation achieved independence. Although Rana trained as a painter, he works in a variety of media, including sculpture, photography, and video. Photography has offered Rana a means of exploring traditional ideas about two-dimensionality and abstraction, and how both can be used to create illusions of space.

Rana often draws his subject matter from popular culture and current politics; a recurrent theme in his work has been "sex and violence," which he translated into a series of works based on elements of "flesh and blood." Working with micro-scale photos as pixels, Rana creates macro-scale pictures that may seemingly contradict their component images. The micro images used for the element of "flesh" are drawn from popular media advertisements, fashion magazines, pornography, and his own photography, while those representing "blood" are derived from slaughterhouses and medical journals as well as his own work. Rana sees the elements of flesh/sex and blood/violence as connected.

His *Veil Series* (Figure 6.37) presents three women covered by Islamic burqas. Mandated in extremist regimes, the wearing of Islamic head coverings is traditionally a display of faith and modesty. However, since 9/11 the wearing of the burqa in the West has been met with suspicion and the presumption of potential violence. A close examination of the component images reveals that the veils covering the women's flesh are "flesh." In this work, the shuttlecock-like garments

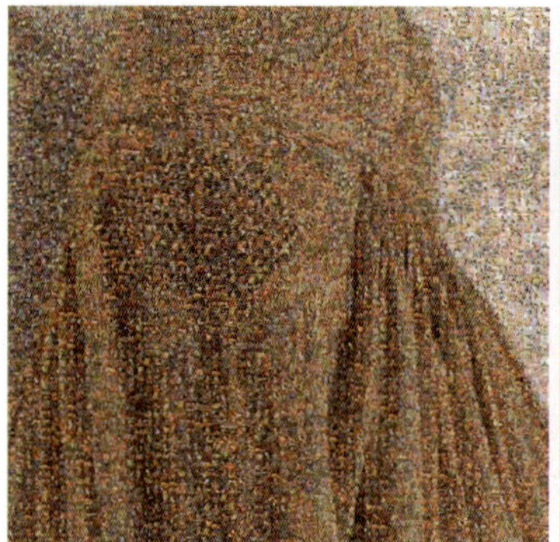
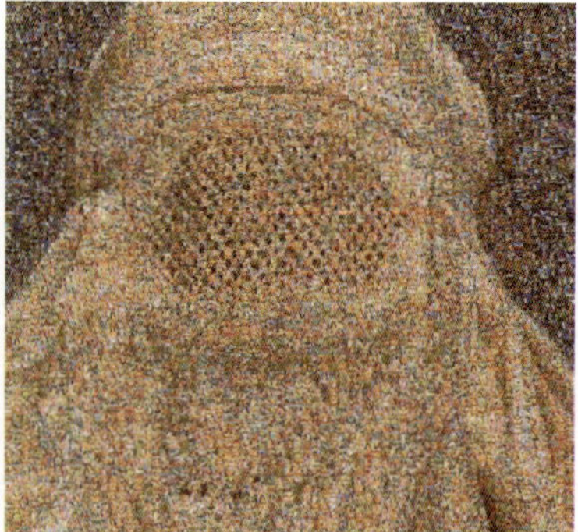
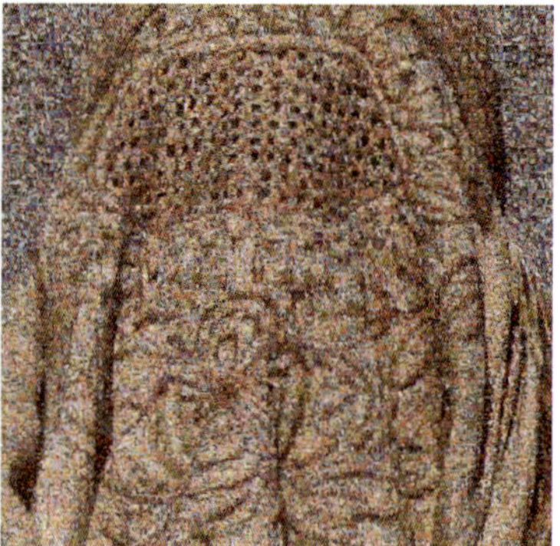

▲ 6.37 Rashid Rana (b. 1968), *Veil Series I. II. III*, 2004. Photo-collage.

Rana uses micro-scale photos as individual pixels in his macro-pictures. The images he selects for his pixels are drawn from popular media and his own photographs to create a subtext for his images.

are comprised of thousands of individual photographic "pixels," each one a tiny image of a nude woman. Some of the nude images are explicitly sexual stills from erotic and pornographic movies. Rana adds an element of social commentary in that he has created his pixels from cinema images. By their nature, these images are projected onto a screen, which receives the image but is powerless to change it. Here, Rana makes the burqa into a "screen" onto which is projected Islamic society's attitudes toward women as seductive, immoral, dangerous, and sexually voracious beings. In the end, one wonders if it is women's modesty that is protected by the burqa, or men's.

Chapter Quick Review

The Indus Valley Civilization (3300–300 BCE)

- The Indus Valley Civilization was the first to evolve in India. It offered cities with wide avenues, advanced water and sewer systems, fired-brick architecture and ritual pool sealed with bitumen, and an economy based on agriculture and long-distance trade.
- The Indus arts included pottery and small-scale sculptures in clay, stone, and cast bronze, and intaglio carved seals.
- The world's oldest religion, Hinduism, has its roots in the Indus civilization. The Vedas, Hindu sacred texts, were first written down during this period.

The Maurya Empire (322 BCE–185 CE)

- Buddhism came to prominence during the reign of the third Maurya Emperor, Ashoka, who converted to the faith after the Battle of Kalinga and decided to rule according to the laws of Dharma.
- Buddhism was founded by Siddhartha Gautama in the last half of the first millennium BCE. He defined the Four Noble Truths and Eight-Fold Path to assist others in achieving enlightenment and nirvana.
- Ashoka built numerous stupas, including the Great Stupa at Sanchi, and erected Ashokan columns to promulgate the new faith. The stupas were large brick or stone veneered hemispherical mounds set atop drums, which were circumambulated to venerate the Buddha.

The Kushan Empire (135 BCE–280 CE)

- Around 100 BCE Buddhism split into Theravada and Mahayana forms, the latter growing in popularity with the introduction of multiple Buddhas of the past, present, and future, and a class of compassionate beings known as Bodhisattvas.
- The first images of the Buddha in human form appear during the Kushan period. Two styles of representation developed in the Kushan capitals of Peshawar in Gandhara (Pakistan), formerly part of Alexander's Hellenistic kingdoms, and Mathura in India. The Gandharan style was influenced by Greco-Roman art, while Mathura continued native Indian styles that had been developing since the Indus Civilization.

The Gupta Dynasty (320–486 CE)

- The Gupta period was a time of great advancements in the arts, literature, mathematics, astronomy, and medicine.
- During this period Gupta artists developed a new school at Sarnath. Sarnath-style works featured more attenuated proportions, with figures growing taller and slimmer, and details of the Buddha's robes becoming highly simplified and appearing to be skin-tight.
- The oldest surviving examples of Indian painting date from this period and are found in the Buddhist murals of the Ajanta Caves. The works are highly advanced, showing fine classical line drawing, modeling in light and dark, unified light sources, and an attempt to show distance by vertical placement.

The Hindu Temple (600–1665 CE)

- The Gupta rulers were Hindus but practiced tolerance toward all religions. In the years after the fall of the Gupta, rising kingdoms in the north and south of India built new temples that defined regional Davidian and Nagara Styles.
- The Dravidian style is characterized by a stepped Vimana while the Nagara style has a parabolic Shikhara with compressed levels. After 1000 CE both northern and southern temple builders created new monumental forms with towers that rose more than 100 feet high.
- The sanctuaries of the southern-style Chola kingdom temples often held solid-cast bronze devotional images of the patron deity of the temple. The exterior walls of temples were often decorated with high relief sculptures of gods, goddesses, and mithuna.

Muslim India (1175–1707)

- The first Muslims came to India as traders around 650 CE. They were followed by sporadic invasions led by regional Islamic governors seeking plunder.
- The first permanent Islamic state was the Delhi Sultanate, founded by Qutb al-din Aibek. Aibek who established the first mosque in Delhi, the Quwwat-ul-Islam and began construction of the adjacent Qutb Minar.
- In 1526 the Delhi Sultinate was conquered by the Mughals who established one of the great Empires of India. The Mughal rulers were great

patrons of architecture, building the Tomb of Humayun, the Red Fort at Agra, and the Taj Mahal among other buildings.
- The art of miniature painting flourished under the Mughals, with the emperors assembling ateliers of Persian and Hindu artists to record the events of their reigns.

The British Raj (1858–1947)

- The British entered India as traders under the auspices of the "East India Company" wishing to gain a piece of the highly lucrative spice and exotic goods trade. The company was chartered by Queen Elizabeth I in 1600.
- The first contact with the Mughal court occurred during the reign of Jahangir. The company went on to establish posts along both coasts and expanded inland through negotiated concessions from various rulers or by military force when the native rulers were not sufficiently agreeable to British demands. After the Great Revolt of 1857, a viceroy was appointed to replace company rule in India.
- Under British Rule efforts were made to modernize roads and build railroads in India. Art academies were established which offered training in Western media and techniques. Photography was also introduced to India and contributed significantly to the modernization of the arts.

Indian Art after Independence (1947–)

- In 1885 the Indian National Congress was formed to lobby for reform and home rule. Beginning in the 1920s the Congress Party was led by Mahatma Gandhi, who urged nonviolent noncooperation and demonstration against British Rule.
- After World War II increasing sectarian violence resulted in the partitioning of India into two nations: Hindu India and Muslim Pakistan.
- Artists in post-partition India were divided over the role of modernism in defining a new Indian art. Nationalist groups such as Tagore's Bengal School advocated for a return to traditional forms of paintings, while the Progressive Artists Group, led by F. M. Husain and F. N. Souza, argued that modernism could be used to express Indian concerns.

Pakistan after Independence (1947–)

- For Muslim Pakistan, partition meant not only separation from India but also from half of the nation. Pakistan was divided into West and East Pakistan with India between them.
- There were few stylistic divisions among artists in the new nation of Pakistan. While some artists chose to work in traditional Islamic forms, others embraced modernism in general and abstraction in particular, seeing modernism as progressive and as a means to greater economic opportunity.

Chapter Questions

1. In what ways did the Indus Valley civilization shape the direction of later Indian art? How, for example, does the Yakshi bracket figure on the East Torana at Sanchi, or the Yakshi on the Outer Gopuram at Madurai, reflect an inheritance from the Indus Valley Young Dancer?

2. What were the shilpa shastras and how were they used in the creation of Hindu deity sculptures and temples? Why was the perfection of form and proportion so important in the creation of such works?
3. What are the stylistic sources for the Akbari style of Moghul miniature painting? How did each influence the development of this court style? How do the paintings of his atelier differ from those produced in the workshops of his son Jahangir?
4. How does Narsingh's *Portrait of Maharaja Sir Jaswant Singh II* seek to appeal to a European rather than an Indian audience? What messages about the Maharaja do the objects in the painting convey?
5. Citing examples of specific artworks, compare and contrast the Bengal and Progressive Schools' approaches to crafting the art of a newly independent India. How did attitudes about the arts differ in post-partition Pakistan?

Key Terms and Figures

Key Terms

Alkali A whitish coating, derived from soluble mineral salts, used on Indus Valley seals.

Amalaka The cushion-like "sunburst" capstone topping a northern style Hindu temple tower.

Bhumis The horizontal compressed layers of a northern style Hindu temple tower.

Bodhisattva In Mahayana Buddhism, bodhisattvas are compassionate beings who have achieved enlightenment, who delay their own entry into nirvana in order to help others achieve enlightenment.

Buddha A fully awakened being; one who is fully aware of the illusions of the world (ignorance) and has achieved release from the cycle of reincarnation (suffering).

Cenotaph An empty tomb monument erected to honor a person buried elsewhere

Chaitya Hall A Buddhist assembly or prayer hall, featuring a stupa at one end.

Charbagh A Persian term meaning "four gardens" based on the division of a garden into four equal parts by two watercourses and four walkways; in concept, it represents the gardens of Paradise in the Islamic religion.

Chattri In Hindu architecture chattri were garden pavilions, sometimes having a memorial purpose; this form was adopted by Mughal architects as rooftop ornaments on forts, palaces, mausoleums, and other important buildings.

Corbelling A means of creating an arch or vault by progressively cantilevering the ends of masonry courses into an opening until the remaining gap can be closed with a single stone.

Garbhagriha The sanctuary of a Hindu temple, housing the cult image occupied by the deity.

Gopura A monumental gateway tower entrance to a Dravidian Hindu temple precinct.

Harmika A square railing that encloses the top of a stupa.

Intaglio A design sunk well-below the surface of stone or metal so the resulting impression is a raised relief.

Ithyphallic An image of a deity having an erect penis.

Jataka tales Stories of the past lives of the Buddha Shakyamuni

Kalasha The water pot finial placed on the tower of a consecrated Hindu temple.

Lakshana The thirty-two major physical characteristics of the Buddha as recorded in the Pali Cannon.

Linga The potency of Lord Shiva symbolized as a cosmic pillar; lingam often serve as cult images in Shaivite Hindu temples.

Mandala A ritual and spiritual diagram in Hinduism and Buddhism representing the cosmos.

Mandapa A columned or pillared outdoor hall, often occupying the intermediate space between the temple entrance and the garbhagriha.

Mithuna Male-female (Yaksha/Yakshi) couples, often termed "Happy" or "Loving" couples in Hindu art.

Nirvana The ultimate goal of the Buddhist, a transcendent state of pure joy and bliss in which the soul is released from karma and samsara.

Pishtaq In Islamic architecture a monumental arched gateway entrance, often decorated with bands of Kufic calligraphy, geometric patterning, or tilework.

Pradaksina In Buddhism and Hinduism, the rite of circumambulation around sacred places, for example, a stupa.

Prana "Life force" visualized in Hindu art as a slight swelling of the lower abdomen, indicating a being filled with the breath of life.

Ratha In Sanskrit the word means a temple chariot or cart but in Hindu architecture, it can also refer to a vertical offset in the wall of a temple sanctuary or tower.

Samsara The eternal cycle of reincarnation from which Buddhist and Hindu adherents seek ultimate release.

Shikhara A Sanskrit word meaning "Mountain Peak" used to identify the tower over the sanctuary in northern-style Hindu temple architecture.

Shilpa shastras Hindu texts laying out the elements of design and standards of practice for each of the arts and crafts.

Stupa A solid bell- or dome-shaped structure, containing relics of the historical Buddha, past Buddhas, or Buddhist monks and nuns.

Stupika "Little Stupa" refers to the octagonal capstone crowning the vimana of a southern-style Hindu temple.

Syncretism The adoption and merging of the beliefs of one religion or philosophy by another; in art this may include the absorption and reinterpretation of symbols used in one religion by another.

Torana Monumental gateway in Buddhist architecture consisting of two posts and three lintels.

Vimana The stepped-pyramidal tower of a southern-style Hindu Temple; consists of a decorative horizontal band (stringcourse) marked by chaitya windows, which supports miniature shrines and figures of Hindu divinities and mithuanas.

Yaksha In Hinduism and Buddhism, a class of male nature spirits.

Yakshi A female nature spirit frequently represented in Hindu and Buddhist art.

Key Figures

Abu'l-Fath Jalal ud-din Muhammad Akbar—Also known as Akbar the Great, third ruler of the Mughal Empire.

Ashoka Maurya—Third ruler of the Maurya Empire who converted to Buddhism, ruled according to the laws of dharma, and convened the Third Buddhist Council c. 250 BCE.

Bodhisattva Padmapani—In Mahayana Buddhism the Bodhisattva of Infinite Compassion; also known as Avalokitésvara, Lokesvara, Guanyin, and Kannon. He is often represented as an androgynous figure.

Kanishka I—Third King of the Kushan Dynasty, a devout Buddhist, he is credited with convening the Fourth Buddhist Council. The first representation of the Buddha in human form appeared during his reign.

Nur ud-Din Salim Jahangir—Son of Akbar and fourth Mughal ruler.

Qutb al-din Aibek—Founder of the Delhi Sultanate and initiator of Muslim rule in India.

Shah Jahan (Shahab-ud-din Muhammad Khurram)—Son of Jahangir and fifth Mughal ruler, who commissioned the Taj Mahal in memory of his favorite wife.

Shams al-Din Iltutmish—Successor and son-in-law of Qutb al-din Aibek; completes the Qutb Minar.

Siddhartha Gautama—The historic Buddha Shakyamuni.

Bibliography

Al-Jafri, Nazim Husain. "From Harappa to Cemetery-H: Fifty Years after the Wheeler Hypothesis." *Proceedings of the Indian History Congress* 60 (1999): 1064–1068.

Bharne, Vinayak and Krupali Krusche

Rediscovering the Hindu Temple: The Sacred Architecture and Urbanism of India, Newcastle on Tyne: Cambridge Scholars Publishing, 2012.

Archaeological Survey of India (ASI), Indian Ministry of Culture. http://asi.nic.in/about-us/

Branfoot, Crispin. "'Expanding Form': The Architectural Sculpture of the South Indian Temple, ca. 1500–1700." *Artibus Asiae* 62, no. 2 (2002): 189–245.

Bruneau, Laurianne. "L'architecture bouddhique dans la vallée du Haut Indus: un essai de typologie desreprésentations rupestres de stūpa." *Arts Asiatiques* 62 (2007): 63–75.

Buchthal, Hugo. "The Monuments of Sanchi." *Burlington Magazine for Connoisseurs* 81, no. 476 (November 1942): 278–279, 281.

Carr, Tarini. "The Harappan Civilization." *Archaeology Online*, 2011. http://archaeologyonline.net/artifacts/harappa-mohenjodaro

Coomaraswamy, Ananda. "A Yaksi Torso from Sanchi." *Bulletin of the Museum of Fine Arts* 27, no. 164 (December 1929): 90–94.

Craven, Roy C. *Indian Art: A Concise History*. London: Thames and Hudson World of Art, 1997/reprinted 2006.

Czuma, Stanislaw. "Kushan Sculpture: Images from Early India." *Archaeology* 38, no. 6 (November–December 1985): 54–57.

Eaton, Natasha. "'Swadeshi' Color: Artistic Production and Indian Nationalism, ca. 1905–ca. 1947." *The Art Bulletin* 95, no. 4 (December 2013): 623–641.

Frawley, David

Myth of the Aryan Invasion of India, HinduNet.org, (1996) https://hindunet.org/srh_home/1996_1/msg00614.html

Grewal, Jagtej Kaur. "Representations of Royalty: Photographic Portraiture in Princely Punjab." *Proceedings of the Indian History Congress* 73 (2012): 729–736.

Hirsh, Marilyn. "Mahendravarman I Pallava: Artist and Patron of Māmallapuram." *Artibus Asiae* 48, no. 1–2 (1987): 109–123, 125–130.

Hoag, John D. The Tomb of Ulugh Beg and Abdu Razzaq at Ghaszni, A Model for the Taj Mahal." *Journal of the Society of Architectural Historians* 27, no. 4 (December 1968): 234–248.

Iyengar, P. T. Srinivas. "The Myth of the Aryan Invasion of India." *Journal of the Royal Society of Arts* 60, no. 3113 (July 19, 1912): 841–846.

Jain, P.C

"Mughal Miniature Painting – An Alternative Source of History," ExoticIndianArt, (July 2004) https://www.exoticindiaart.com/article/mughal/

Kaimal, Padma. "Shiva Nataraja: Shifting Meanings of an Icon." *Art Bulletin* 81, no. 3 (September 1999): 390–419.

Karashima, Noboru. *A Concise History of South India: Issues and Interpretations*. New York: Oxford University Press, 2014.

Kenoyer, Jonathan. "Uncovering the Keys to Lost Indus Cities." *Scientific American* 289, no. 1 (July 2003): 66–75.

Koch, Ebba. "The Taj Mahal: Architecture, Symbolism, and Urban Significance." *Muqarnas* 22 (2005): 128–149.

Kroger, Jens. "On Mahmud B. Ishaq al-Shihabi's Manuscript of 'Yūsuf va Zulaykhā' of 964 (1557)." *Muqarnas* 21 (2004): 239–253.

La Plante, John D. *Asian Art*. 3rd edition. McGraw Hill, 1992.

Lowry, Glenn D. "Humayun's Tomb: Form, Function, and Meaning in Early Mughal Architecture." *Muqarnas* 4 (1987): 133–148.

Majewski, Lawrence J. "Report on Examination of Murals of Ajanta Caves in India." *Bulletin of the American Institute for Conservation of Historic and Artistic Works* 16, no. 1 (Winter 1975–1976): 57–59.

Meister, Michael W. "Maṇḍala and Practice in Nāgara Architecture in North India." *Journal of the American Oriental Society* 99, no. 2 (April–June 1979): 204–219.

Menon, Sadanand. "M. F. Husain: When the Nation Loses Its Own Narrative." *Economic and Political Weekly* 46, no. 25 (June 18–24, 2011): 13–15.

Myer, Prudence R. "Again the Kanishka Casket." *Art Bulletin* 48, no. 3–4 (September–December 1966): 396–403.

Padmanabha, K. "The Buddha Image in Sculptural Arts of India." *The Tibet Journal* 20, no. 4 (Winter 1995): 93–98.

Parodi, Laura E. "Taj Mahal: Geometria, Progetto, Simbolo." *Rivista degli studi orientali* 68, Fasc. 3–4 (1994): 311–338.

Pradhan, Shrikant A. "Painted Decorative Motifs in the Ajanta Caves." *Bulletin of the Deccan College Research Institute* 56–57 (1996–2997): 129–134Rajaram, Navaratna S. "Aryan Invasion—History or Politics?", Archaeology online,

http://archaeologyonline.net/artifacts/aryan-invasion-history

.

Rezavi, Syed Ali Nadeem. "Antiquarian Interests in Medieval India: The Relocation of Ashokan Pillars By Firuzshah Tughluq." *Proceedings of the Indian History Congress* 70 (2009–2010): 994–1010.

Samvartha "Sahil." "M.F. Husain: The Sufi Painter." *Indian Literature* 55, no. 3 (263) (May–June 2011): 138–142.

Sankalia, H. D. "Antecedents of the Harappan Art or Beginning of Art in the Indus Valley." *Bulletin of the Deccan College Research Institute* 40 (1981): 145–148.

Schofield, Katherine Butler. "Mughal/Mughlai." In *Key Concepts in Modern Indian Studies*, edited by Gita Dharampal-Frick et al, NYU Press, 2015.

Seid, Betty. *New Narratives: Contemporary Art from India*. India: Mapin Publishing, 2007.

Sen, Rahul. "Formation of State and the Indus Valley Civilization." *Indian Anthropologist* 22, no. 1 (June 1992): 25–40.

Singh, Abhay Kumar. "Ashoka's Perception of Nature and Man: A Study in Art and Attitude." *Proceedings of the Indian History Congress* 65 (2004): 131–138.

Srinivasan, Sharada. "Shiva as 'Cosmic Dancer': On Pallava Origins for the Nataraja Bronze." *World Archaeology* 36, no. 3 (September 2004): 432–450.

Tartakov, Gary Michael. "The Beginning of Dravidian Temple Architecture in Stone." *Artibus Asiae* 42, no. 1 (1980): 39–99.**Thoury, M. *et al.***

"High spatial dynamics-photoluminescence imaging reveals the metallurgy of the earliest lost-wax cast object." *Nature Communications.* **7**, article no. 13356 doi: 10.1038/ncomms13356 (2016).

Tschannen, Rafiq A.

"How Islam Spread in India," The Muslim Times, (2013) https://themuslimtimes.info/2013/08/07/how-islam-spread-in-india/

Vajpeyi, Ananya. "Abanindranath Tagore: Samvega, the Self's Shock." In *Righteous Republic*, 127–167. Cambridge, MA: Harvard University Press, 2012.

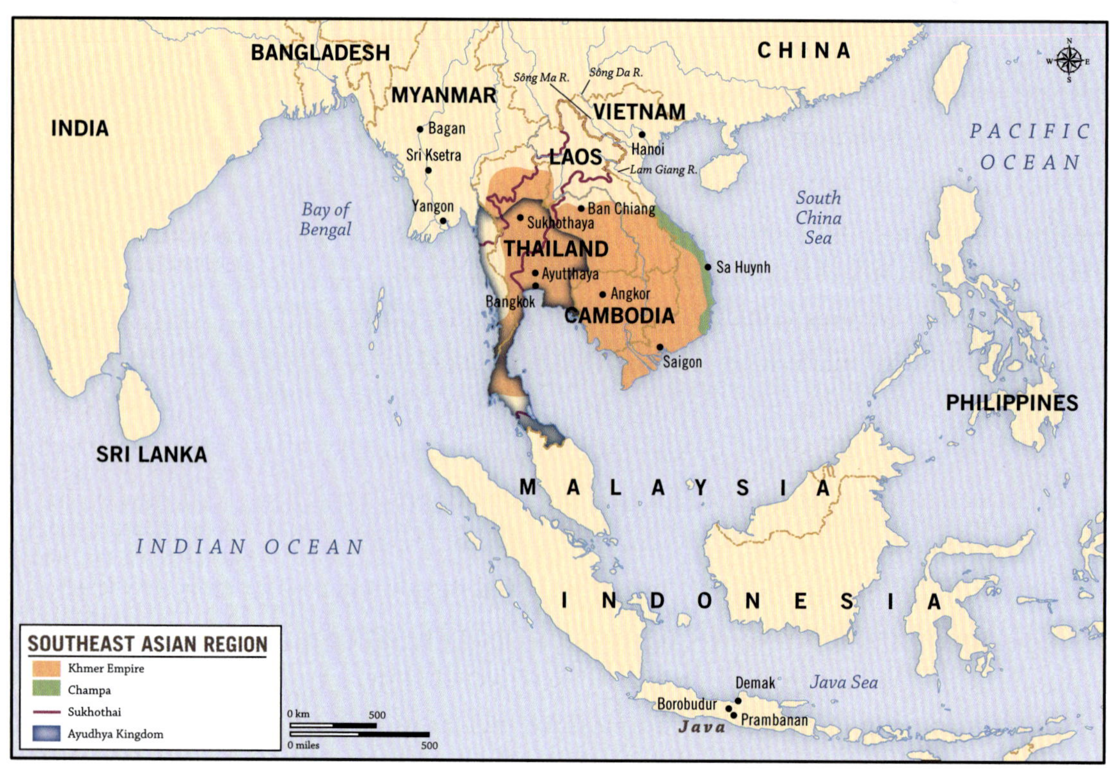
BANGLADESH
CHINA
INDIA
MYANMAR
Sông Ma R.
Sông Da R.
VIETNAM
Bagan
Hanoi
Sri Ksetra
LAOS
Lam Giang R.
PACIFIC OCEAN
Bay of Bengal
Yangon
Ban Chiang
South China Sea
Sukhothaya
THAILAND
Sa Huynh
Ayutthaya
Bangkok
Angkor
CAMBODIA
Saigon
PHILIPPINES
SRI LANKA
MALAYSIA
INDIAN OCEAN
INDONESIA
SOUTHEAST ASIAN REGION
Khmer Empire
Champa
Sukhothai
Ayudhya Kingdom
0 km 500
0 miles 500
Demak
Java Sea
Borobudur
Prambanan
Java

Southeast Asia

7

Brief Overview

The rich diversity of the arts in Southeast Asia—Cambodia, Laos, Myanmar (Burma), Thailand, Vietnam, Malaysia, and Indonesia—reflects the region's long history as a cultural crossroads. The first settlers arrived some forty thousand years ago and were followed by successive waves of immigrants well into the second millennium CE. Available archaeological data shows that pottery-making and metalworking developed independently at several sites, including Ban Chiang, Phung Nguyen, Sa Huynh, and Dong Son in the first three millennia BCE. Shortly before the beginning of the Common Era, Southeast Asian cultures were enriched artistically and culturally by traders and missionaries from India who spread Buddhism and Hinduism and associated art and architectural styles across Southeast Asia. At about the same time, China exerted its cultural and military influence in northern Vietnam. In historic times the kingdoms and empires of Southeast Asia built cities resplendent with towering temples and images of devotion rendered in dynamic art styles including those of the Khmer, Sukhothai, and Ayutthaya. In the fifteenth and sixteenth centuries the spread of Islam and the arrival of European traders introduced new religious beliefs and artistic practices.

The concept of Southeast Asia as a geographic and political unit dates from the Second World War when the region was lumped together under the South East Asia Command, the military body overseeing Allied operations in the Southeast Asian Theater. Before the war, the region had been a patchwork of Colonial states designated as Further India, Ultraindia, Cochin China, and Indochina, reflecting British, Dutch, and French territorial interests and assumptions. As suggested by these colonial descriptors, the long prevailing view of Southeast Asian culture was one of Indianization or Sinification, attributing the development of its art and architecture largely to Indian and Chinese influence.

Chapter Objectives

1. Recognize and describe key artworks, regional styles, and important technologies used in the art and architecture of Southeast Asia, including those of the Khmer Empire, the kingdoms of Bagan, Sukhothai, Ayutthaya, Rattanakosin, Sailendra, and the Demak Sultanate.
2. Understand and be able to provide examples of how the introduction of Buddhism and Hinduism influenced the development of art and architecture as well as constructs of kingship and state in the various Southeast Asian nations. Additionally, be able to discuss the impact of the arrival of Islam on the arts and architecture of maritime Southeast Asia.
3. Explain the impact of colonial rule on the art and culture of pre- and post-independence Southeast Asian nations in terms of specific works, artists, and contemporary directions.

timeline

DATE	TYPE	EVENT
		BCE
c. 3600	Art	Ban Chiang pottery (Thailand)
c. 2000	Art	Phung Nguyen bronze (Vietnam)
c. 1000	Art	Sa Huynh pottery (Vietnam)
c. 600	Art	Dong Son bronzes (Vietnam)
c. 250	Culture	Ashoka sent Buddhist missionaries into Southeast Asia
221	History	Qin Chinese established outpost in northern Vietnam
c. 200	History	Pyu people arrived in Irrawaddy Valley
		CE
c. 100	Culture	Hindu traders brought Hinduism to Southeast Asia
	History	Hindu Funan kingdom established (Cambodia)
	History	Tai began migrating southward from Hunan, China
c. 500	Art	Bawbawgyi Pagoda began in Sri Ksetra (Myanmar)
	Art	Shwedagon Pagoda began Yangon (Myanmar)
	History	Mon Kingdom of Dvaravati established (Thailand)
c. 541	Art	Tan Quoc Pagoda began in Hanoi (Vietnam)
c. 725	History	Sailendra dynasty founded (Java)
c. 778	Art	Borobudur began (Java)
802	History	Khymer Empire (Cambodia) founded
c. 849	History	Bagan founded (Myanmar)
850	Art	Borobudur abandoned after volcanic eruption
c. 856	Art	Chandi Prambanan built (Central Java)
c. 931	Art	Nathlaung Kyaung Temple, Bagan (Myanmar)
939	History	Vietnam gained independence from China
c. 1000	History	Tai people arrived in northern Thailand
c. 1050	History	Pyu states conquered by Burman peoples
	History	Muslim traders arrived in Southeast Asia
c. 1091	Art	Ananda Temple in Bagan began
c. 1113	History	Suryavarman II began reign as Khmer king
	Art	Construction of Angkor Wat began (Cambodia)

DATE	TYPE	EVENT
CE		
1145	Art	Angkor Wat completed
1177	History	Cham of Vietnam attacked Angkor Wat
c. 1181	History	Jayavarman VII acceded to the Khmer throne
	Art	Construction of Angkor Thom began (Cambodia)
c. 1190	Art	Bayon Temple, Angkor Thom
1238	History	Sri Intraditya founded Kingdom of Sukhothai (Thailand)
1277	History	Mongol invasion of Bagan kingdom
1283	History	Second Mongol invasion of Bagan
1292	Art	Wat Mahathat "Old Relic" built in Sulhothai
1297	History	Bagan Empire collapsed
1351	History	Kingdom of Ayutthaya (Thailand) founded
1369	Art	Wat Phra Ram built in Ayutthaya
1431	History	Khmer conquered by Ayutthaya
1434	Art	Emerald Buddha discovered at Wat Pa Yia (Thailand)
1466	Art	Masjid Agung Demak (Java)
1471	History	Dai Viet defeated the Cham in Vietnam
1511	History	Portuguese captured Malacca
1552	Art	Emerald Buddha taken to Luan Prabang (Laos)
1605	History	First traders from the Dutch East India Company arrived
1641	History	Portuguese colony of Malacca captured by the Dutch
1689	Culture	Luang Prasoet Chronicles of Siam written
1749	History	Khmer lost Mekond Delta to the Dai Viet
1778	Art	Emerald Buddha returned to Thailand
1782	History	Rattanakosin dynasty established (Thailand)
1785	Art	Wat Phra Kaew built (Thailand)
1863	History	French protectorate of Cambodia established
1886	History	British annexed Burma
1887	History	French created Indochina (Annam, Tonkin, Cochinchina)
1893	History	French added Laos

(Continued)

timeline *continued*

DATE	TYPE	EVENT
		CE
1897	Art	U Ba Nyan born in Myanmar
1913	Art	French art school opened in Saigon
	Art	Burma Art Club founded in Rangoon
1923	Art	École de Beaux-Arts d'Indochine opened in Hanoi
1925	Art	Sithu U Tin, Yangon City Hall
1947	History	Burma gained independence
	History	Laotian independence
1949	History	Indonesia gained independence from the Dutch
1953	History	Cambodian independence
1954	History	Vietnam divided
1961	History	Vietnam War began
1973	History	United States withdrew from Vietnam
1975	History	Vietnam reunified

The end of colonial rule after the Second World War plunged many Southeast Asian countries into the chaos of civil wars, foreign interventions, Communist takeovers, military dictatorships, and genocide. Only Thailand, which had never ceded its sovereignty to European control, managed to avoid the considerable turmoil of the post-war era. It has been only in recent years that conditions in some countries have allowed the resumption of archaeological and art historical research, now conducted by native scholars. Yet, despite the adversities of independence, the arts, both traditional and contemporary, continue to thrive in Southeast Asia.

Neolithic Southeast Asia (4000 BCE–300 CE)

The earliest evidence of human presence in Southeast Asia, a partial human skull dated to 60,000 BCE, was discovered in 2009, by archaeologists working at the Tam Pa Ling or "Cave of the Monkeys" site in northern Laos. Elsewhere across the region stone tools, dating back even farther in history, have been found. While human occupation in Southeast Asia is quite ancient, the first settled villages, ceramics, and metal objects do not appear before the introduction of rice agriculture in the third millennium BCE.

Ban Chiang Culture (c. 3600 BCE–200 CE)

Southeast Asia's most spectacular Neolithic era ceramics were discovered near the village of Ban Chiang in 1966. Stephen Young, an American university student, had been hiking through the area in northeastern Thailand when he tripped over a tree root and landed on a vessel partially buried in the roadbed. His discovery spurred investigation of what ultimately became a 20-acre archaeological site. Excavations revealed that Ancient Ban Chiang was first settled during the fourth millennium BCE by rice farmers and was continuously occupied for almost four thousand years. In addition to ceramics dating back to 3600 BCE, Ban Chiang artisans were also casting bronze and working iron by 1500 BCE, making Ban Chiang one of the earliest Bronze Age societies outside of the West Asia.

Ban Chiang Footed Vessel with Incised and Painted Decoration, c. 1000–300 BCE The earliest Ban Chiang pottery consisted of globular, pedestal-footed earthenware vessels crafted from local clays, by coiling; the walls were thinned and smoothed using a paddle and anvil technique. Decoration included cord-marking, rocker-stamping, applique, combing and incised designs with some vessels showing evidence of reduction firing. During the last millennium BCE, red ochre-slip painting on buff clay vessels was introduced. Motifs tend to be geometric or organic shapes, consisting of single and double spirals, circles, triangles, and concentric ovoid designs. Ban Chiang artists created more complex vessel forms as separate units, in this case the bowl and pedestal stem, which were joined together before firing. In some cases, the decoration of each of the separate parts, although compatible, is distinct. A careful examination of the footed vessel (Figure 7.1) shows that the bowl was embellished with a wide band of floral (palm leaf?) motifs followed by an area of triangular elements while the bottom is decorated with interlocking and running scroll motifs over a band of short vertical stripes.

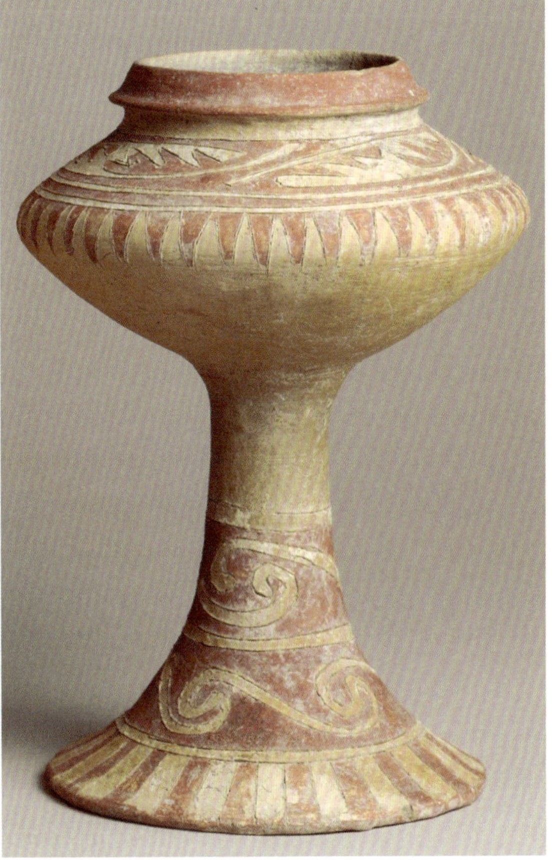

▼ 7.1 Thailand, Ban Chiang, Earthenware with buff slip and incised and painted decoration, c. 1000–300 BCE. 9.5 in. × 6.87 in.

Over a period of more than three thousand years the Ban Chiang artists made beautifully decorated vessels in a range of forms. The bowl and foot were created separately then joined to create the pedestal vase.

Sa Huynh Culture (1000 BCE–200 CE)

During the first millennium BCE, the Sa Huynh Culture appeared along the central Vietnamese coast. In 1909 French archeologists discovered some two hundred urn burials grouped into clusters and interred beneath the sand dunes near Sa Huynh in Quang Ngai province. In addition to the bones, the painted jars contained stone beads, ear ornaments, and items of bronze, iron, and glass. Ritually broken ceramic offering jars were also discovered in the pits.

Sa Huynh Bicephalous Ear Ornament, c. 500 BCE–300 CE The Sa Huynh carved **bicephalous** (double-headed) zoomorphic ear ornaments (Figure 7.2) out of stones that were suspended from the ear by a C-shaped hook. The animals appear to be deer-like with long ears and slightly bulging eyes. The mouth of one head maybe shown open with the tongue extended while the other is closed. By the first century CE, the Sa Huynh began making their ornaments out of glass; the technology was most probably introduced from China or India, both of which had earlier glass traditions. These signature ear ornaments have been found as far away as Thailand, the Philippines, and Indonesia.

Dong Son Culture (c. 600 BCE–200 CE)

Contemporaneous with the Sa Huynh was the Dong Son culture, which arose in the first millennium BCE in the Song Ma and Lam Giang River basins of northern Vietnam. The first excavation of a Dong Son burial site occurred in the 1920s near the village which lent its name to the culture. Only one Dong Son habitation site has been excavated and that was at Co Loa about 10 miles (17 km) north of Hanoi. Co Loa appears to have been a fortified city that was protected by three rammed-earth walls and two outer moats. Like the Sa Huynh, the

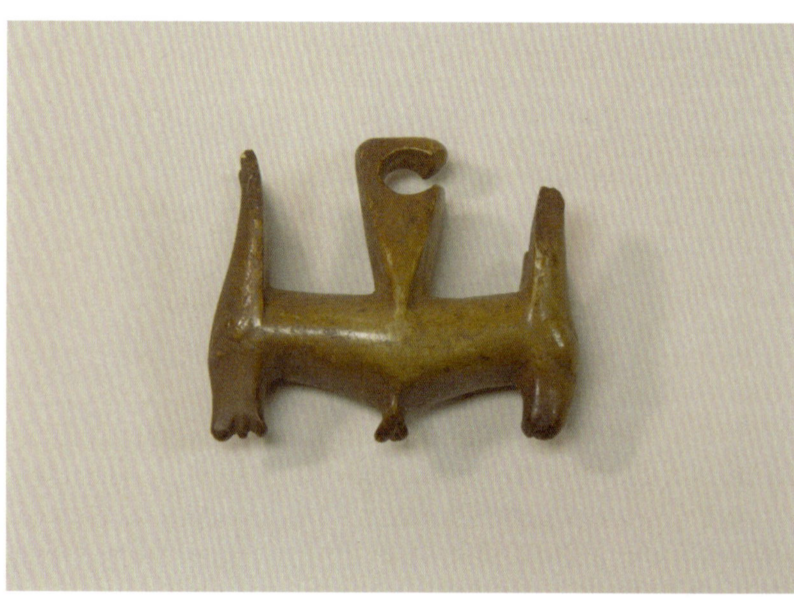

▶ 7.2 Vietnam, Sa Huynh, Bicephalous ear ornament, c. 500 BCE–300 CE. Stone, 1.75 in. × 0.75 in. × 2 in.

Two animal heads, possibly deer, decorate this carved stone ornament. Despite the small scale there is a remarkable degree of detail.

Dong Son were talented metalworkers who engaged in long-distance sea trading.

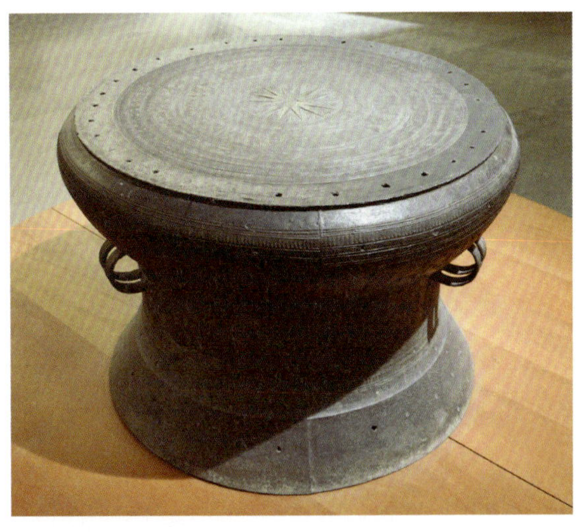

▲ 7.3 Vietnam, Sông Da, Dong Son Bronze Drum, c. 500 BCE.

Bronze drums were cast in a range of sizes using piece-mold and lost wax casting techniques. The drums were suspended over a pit for playing. The center of the tympanum is typically decorated with a slightly raised eight-pointed star motif.

Dong Son Bronze Drum, Sông Da, Vietnam, c. 500 BCE The Dong Son made a variety of bronze objects, including daggers, bells, tools, and ornaments but they are renowned for their bronze drums, identifiable by their characteristic "star" in the center of the tympanum. Hundreds of such drums have been found, primarily in burials, across Vietnam, southern China, in Cambodia, the Indonesian archipelago, the Philippines, and on the Malaysian peninsula. The drums were lost-wax cast in a single piece and come in a variety of sizes with the largest weighing as much as 220 pounds (100 kg) and standing more than 3 feet (1 m) high. The drums were played while suspended over a pit in the ground, which served as a resonating chamber. The earliest drums have a mushroom-shaped profile divided into three well-defined sections, while later drums are more cylindrical. Typically, the drums, including the Sông Da drum (Figure 7.3), feature a central eight-pointed star design on the tympanum, which is surrounded by concentric bands of humans, animals, or birds moving in procession. Decoration often continues down the shoulders and bell of the drum. Four cord-marked loop handles extend from the bell of the drum on each side.

Indianization and Sinification in Medieval Southeast Asia (c. 500–1500)

Indian cultural influence in Southeast Asia begins during the reign of the Mauryan emperor Ashoka in the last centuries BCE. After his conversion to Buddhism, Ashoka sent missionaries to the four directions to spread the teachings of the Buddha; it was at this time that Buddhism was introduced to Burma. Slightly later, in the first century CE, Hinduism was brought to Southeast Asia by seafaring Hindu traders who established trading posts both on the mainland and in the Indonesian archipelago. The early influence of Hinduism is widespread in the arts but the religion did not survive long in most areas; only the island of Bali still has a significant Hindu presence. The period of Indian interaction continued through the end of the Gupta dynasty in the fifth century CE, by which time Buddhism had been established in Cambodia and the Malay Peninsula. During the subsequent medieval period Indian prototypes became the basis for the development of local styles of art and architecture.

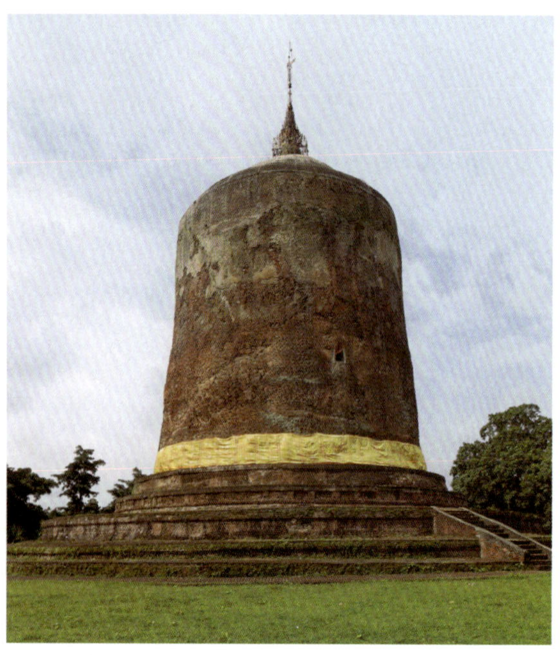

▲ 7.4 Myanmar, Sri Ksetra (pyay), Bawbawgyi Pagoda.

Burma was one of the first areas in Southeast Asia to receive Buddhism. This early stupa is an example of the "heap-of-paddy" type of stupa set on a high drum. It is twice as high as the Great Stupa at Sanchi.

Bawbawgyi Pagoda, Sri Ksetra, Myanmar, c. 500–600 CE The Buddhist missionaries sent east by the Mauryan Emperor Ashoka would have traveled along the overland route from India to China, known as the Silk Road. This trade route ran through the Pyu city states in north central Myanmar, where some of the earliest surviving examples of Indianized architecture can be found. In the ancient Sri Ksetra (modern Pyay) stands the Bawbawgyi Pagoda. Bawbawgyi (Figure 7.4) is the best-preserved example of the ancient Pyu style stupa and served as the prototype for later Burman pagodas. In contrast to the Indian hemispherical-dome-on-a-drum stupas, Bawbawgyi sits on a five-tiered circular terrace from which it rises as a plain solid brick cylinder with a conical top and a hollow mast in the center. At a height of 153 feet (47 m), Bawbawgyi is more than twice the Great Stupa at Sanchi's 70 feet (21 m).

The Shwedagon Pagoda, Yangon, Myanmar, c. 500–900 CE In the old Mon city of Yangon (ancient Dagon) is one of Myanmar's most revered Buddhist shrines, the Shwedagon Pagoda. The original stupa is thought to have been built sometime between the sixth and tenth centuries, although it is claimed in *The Great Glass Palace Chronicle*, complied in the 1830s, that the stupa is 2,500 years old. Its name Shwedagon or "Reliquary of the Four" is derived from the belief that its vault contains relics from three Buddhas of the past: Kahusandha, Kassapa, and Konagamana along with three hairs from the head of the historic Buddha, Gautama.

In its earliest form, Shwedagon (Figure 7.5) was a simple, solid brick stupa, most likely bell or cylindrical in shape, standing about 27 feet (8.22 m) tall. Beginning in the fourteenth century various Mon kings showed their Buddhist devotion through the restoration and enlargement of Shwedagon. The first of these was King Banya U (r. 1353–1385) who raised the pagoda to a height of 60 feet (18 m). In the mid-fifteenth century, Queen Shinsawbu (r. 1453–1472) again enlarged Shwedagon, more than doubling its height and creating the large, paved terrace on top of the hill; she also donated her weight in gold to the gilding of the stupa. King Hsinbyushin (r. 1763–1776) brought the brick structure to its current configuration and height of 326 feet (99 m).

Shwedagon sits atop a more than 20 foot (6 m) high square platform, which is ringed by sixty-four small, gilded pagodas, each housing

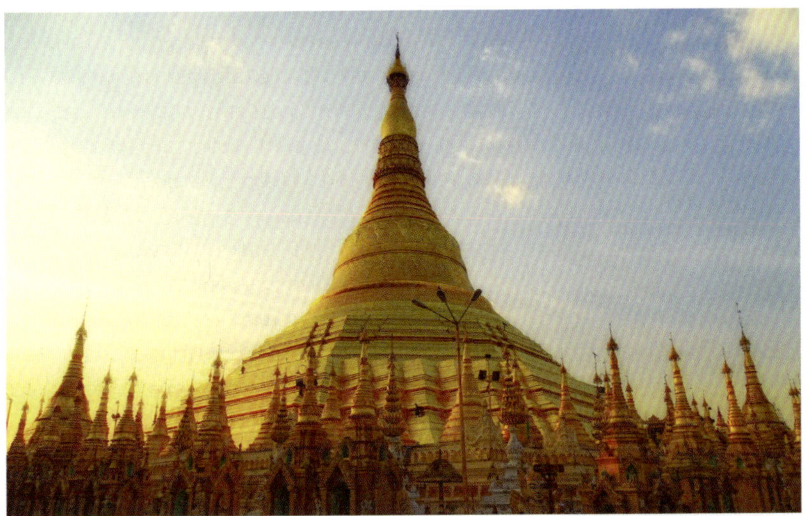

◀ **7.5** Myanmar, Yangon, Shwedagon Pagoda, c. 500–900 CE. Brick, gold plate, gold leaf, and jewels.

At the heart of this structure is the original sixth century solid brick stupa that stood 27 ft. high; it has been enlarged several times over the centuries to reach its current height of 326 ft.

a Buddha image; larger ones mark the cardinal points with medium-size pagodas at the corners of the plinth. Rising from the platform are a series of octagonal terraces leading to a bell capped by an inverted alms bowl; these two elements form the dome of the stupa. Continuing upward from the bowl is a ringed steeple of the Singhalese type, which is topped by lotus petals, banana bud, crown, weathervane, and orb elements. The weathervane and orb are encrusted with more than two thousand carats of diamonds along with more than a thousand rubies and sapphires. At the pinnacle of the spire is a single 76-carat diamond. The placement of a crystal or jewel at the top of the spire is intended to symbolize the "light of truth."

▼ **7.6** Myanmar, Bagan, Nathlaung Kyaung Temple, c. 931 CE.

This is one of the few Hindu temples that has survived in Burma. It is a Gu or "cave temple" type. Earthquakes destroyed its mandapa and have damaged its shikhara.

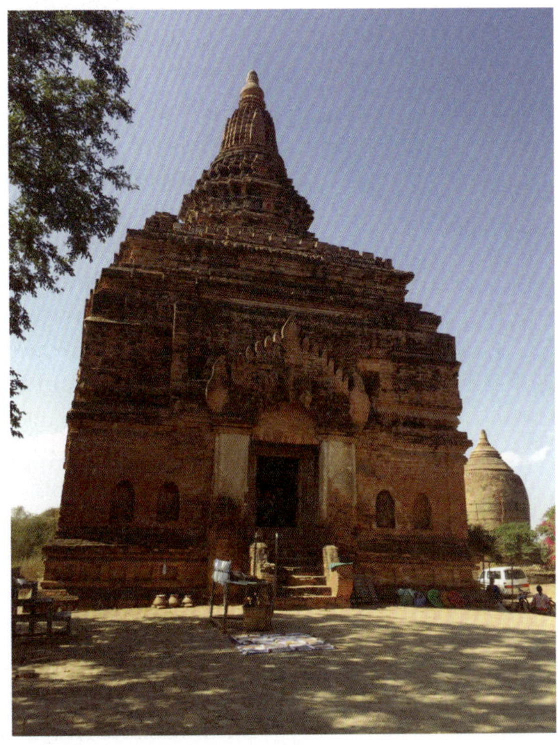

Nathlaung Kyaung Temple, Bagan, Myanmar, c. 931 CE Very few early Hindu temples have survived in Myanmar; one exception is the Nathlaung Kyaung Temple. The Nathlaung Kyaung (Figure 7.6) is attributed to King Taunghthugyi (r. 931–964), an early Hindu king of Bagan (also Pagan). The temple has suffered considerable damage over the centuries from earthquakes and neglect, resulting in the loss of its mandapa and the crumbling of its shikhara. Nathlaung Kyaung is an early, single-face ***Gu*** or "cave temple." *Gu* temples were intended as artificial caves for meditation, and rituals of devotion. The temple is entered through a small vestibule leading to a remarkably small rectangular sanctuary. Although from the exterior the

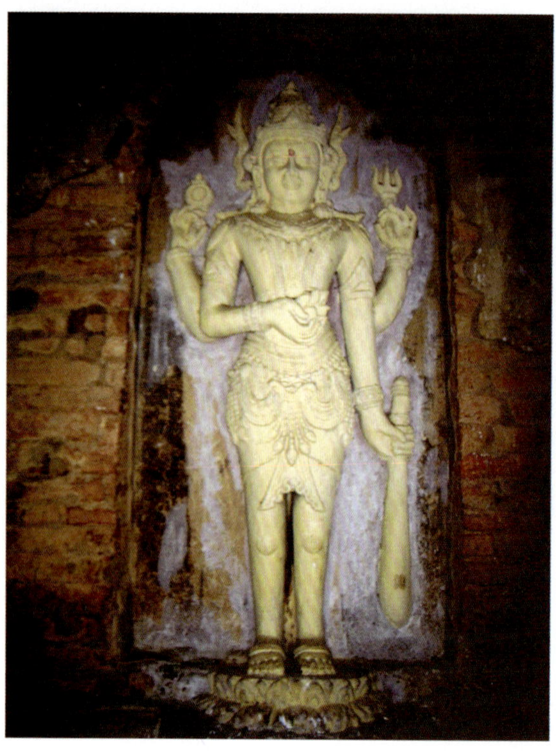

▲ 7.7 Myanmar, Bagan, Nathlaung Kyaung Temple, *Harihara*, c. 931 CE. Brick, stucco, and pigment.

Harihara is a composite or dual deity who is half Vishnu and half Shiva and carries the attributes of each.

temple looks quite large, much of the interior space is taken up by heavy masonry walls and a central masonry core surrounding the sanctuary, which was necessary to support the dome and shikhara.

Harihara, ***c. 900–1000 CE*** A large devotional image of Vishnu once graced the shrine and other freestanding images were set into niches in both the ambulatory and on the exterior. These sculptures were removed by a German engineer in the 1890s and taken to Berlin. The only original decorations remaining in the temple are the stucco relief images of Vishnu in his various manifestations, which were modeled over a brick armature. One of these depicts ***Harihara*** (Figure 7.7) a Hindu dual god who is, at the same time, both Vishnu (Hari) and Shiva (Hara). The relief image is a composite of the two deities, with the left half being Vishnu and the right, Shiva. The Vishnu half holds in his three hands a conch shell (front), mace (center), and discus. Shiva holds sword, bow, and trident in the same order. Remaining traces of blue paint indicate that the temple images were once brightly colored.

Ananda Temple, Bagan, Myanmar c. 1091–1105 CE A little more than a century after the Nathlaung Kyaung was built, King Anawrahta (r. 1044–1077), conquered the southern port city of Thaton, bringing most of what is today Myanmar under Bagan rule. Anawrath converted to Theravada Buddhism and encouraged his people to do so. He is known to have inaugurated a program of pagoda and temple building in the capital that was continued by his successors until the Mongol conquest in 1287 CE. Legend asserts the king and his successors built ten thousand shrines; all but 2,200 were torn down to defend against the Mongols. Historical accounts suggest the actual number built was only 4,446. The majority of these were small, bell-shaped or Pyu-style cylindrical stupas and the remainder were *Gu* temples. During the Bagan period Gu shrines grew quite large and evolved from single-face (single entry) like the Nathlaung Kyaung to four-faced (four entry) temples with projecting porches and four interior shrines as was the Ananda temple.

The Ananda Temple (Figure 7.8) named for the Buddha's cousin, was built under the patronage of King Kyanzittha (r. 1084–1113 CE), who may have been a younger son as he was not Anawrahta's immediate successor. The Ananda is a massive structure designed in the

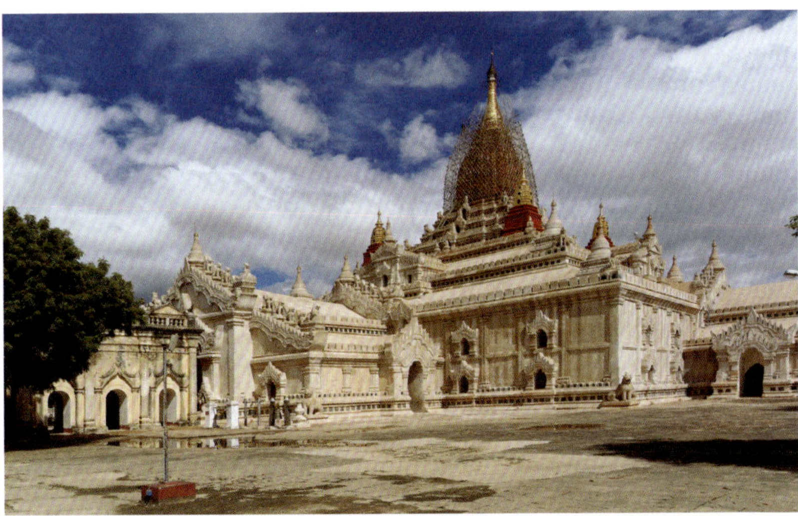

◀ 7.8 Myanmar, Bagan, Ananda Temple, c. 1091–1105.

The Ananda Temple is dedicated to the Buddha's cousin Ananda and was built by King Kyanzittha. It is a Greek-cross plan temple with a shikhara-like tower at the crossing.

form of a Greek cross with four portals and corridors leading to four shrines set into the central masonry core, each with its own devotional image. The four corridors are intersected by two ambulatories providing access to the shrines and entrance vestibules. The walls of the ambulatories are inset with niches housing images of the Buddha and reliefs of Jataka tales. Interior illumination was provided by clerestory windows in the outer walls. The temple roof rises in three steps to form a base for the tower. The lower section closely resembles the northern-style Hindu shikhara both in shape and the use of compressed bhumis but with the addition of a central lancet on each side, into which are set five stupa-shaped niches of receding scale, each housing an image of the Buddha. Topping the shikhara is a bell-shaped stupa surmounted by a slender, elongated steeple ending in a "crown" and finial. In 2005 the tower was gilded in honor of the temple's nine hundredth anniversary.

***Kahusandha Buddha, Ananda Temple, c. 1091–1105* CE** In each of the Ananda's four shrines is a gilded, teak-wood image of a standing Buddha; the figures are 31 feet (9.44 m) high. The four statues represent Buddhas of the past and present, and are associated with the cardinal directions. The Kahusandha (Figure 7.9) or north shrine sculpture, is one of two surviving original images; the other being the south image of the Buddha Kassapa. The two Bagan era sculptures show the strong stylistic influence of the Gupta era Sarnath School. Kahusandha wears the typical Gupta skin-hugging sanghati with a crinkled fold pattern along the double hem, has the same mango pit chin, long earlobes, smiling full lips, and he displays the Dharmachakra or "Turning the Wheel of Dharma" mudra. Where Kahusandha differs from his Indian prototypes is in the round face, more stylized scorpion-sting curls, and lower ushnisha.

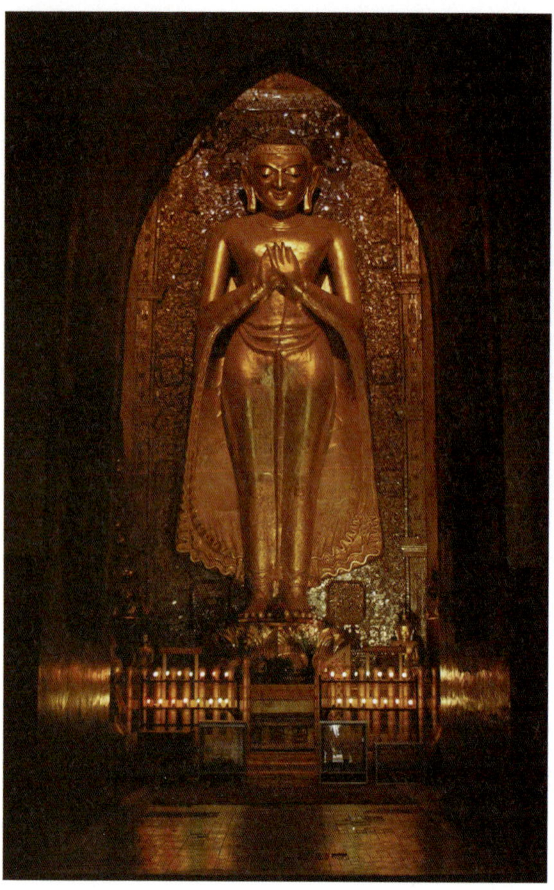

▲ 7.9 Myanmar, Bagan, Ananda Temple, Kahusandha (North) Buddha, c. 1091–1105 CE. Gilded teakwood, 31 ft. high.

One of two surviving original sculptures, this Buddha-image shows strong Gupta influence.

The Khmer Empire, Cambodia (802–1431 CE)

Chinese historical chronicles mention several cultures in early Cambodia: the Khmer, Chenla, and Funan, but very little is known about these early societies or about their political organization. The Funan kingdom is mentioned in the early Chinese accounts; in the seventh century Liang Shu described them as having been naked, tattooed, long-haired savages. The Funan port of Oc Eo was a stop on the sea route from India to China, and by the fifth century CE both Hinduism and Buddhism had been established in the kingdom as a result of Indian contact. The last Funan king was Rudravarman (r. 514–539 CE); in the mid-sixth century the state was conquered by the Chenla Kingdom, a former vassal state of Funan. The Chenla kingdom ruled for about 130 years and then fractured politically into a number of localized states, setting the stage for the rise of the Khmer kingdom.

The Khmer Empire was established in 802 CE when Jayavarman II (r. 790–835), in a solemn ritual atop the mountain known as Phnom Kulen, claimed the title of *chakravartain*, usually defined as a "universal ruler," which was justified by the empire he had constructed. Jayavarman II had conquered all of the Cambodian, Laotian, and Thai states as well as parts of Vietnam and the Malay Peninsula. He also claimed the title of ***devaraja*** or "god king." Under the concept of devaraja the Khmer king was seen as a living god, usually as manifestation of either Shiva or Vishnu, depending upon whether they were Shaivite or Vaishnavite devotees, but later it came to encompass other Hindu gods and even Buddhist bodhisattvas depending on the particular faith of the ruler. The ruler's divine status endured for his lifetime and when he died his essence returned to the god. The sacred image in the sanctuary embodied the divine power of the living king. After the death of the ruler, his state temple served as his mortuary temple, receiving the ashes of the king. The grandest of all the Khmer temples is Angkor Wat built by the sixteenth Khmer king, Suryavarman II.

Angkor Wat (c. 1113–1145 CE)

Suryavarman II (r. 1113–c. 1150) began work on his state temple, Angkor Wat (Figure 7.10) shortly after he ascended the Khmer throne. It is thought to have taken fifty thousand workmen some thirty years

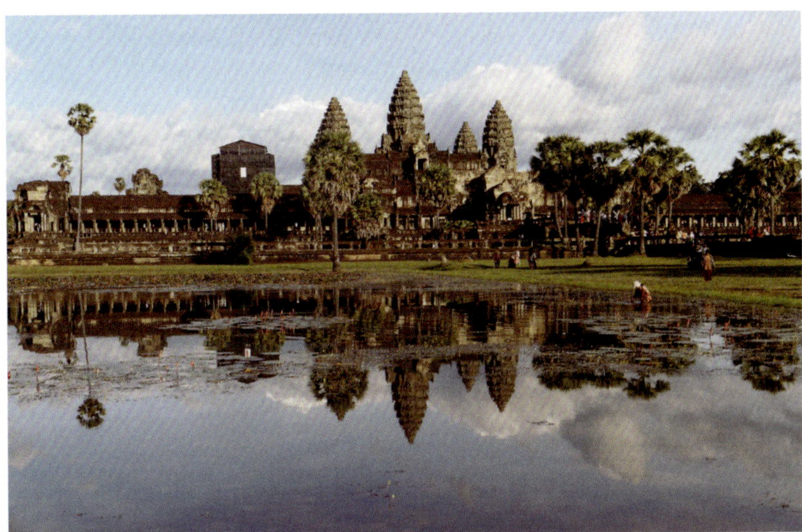

◀ 7.10 Cambodia, Angkor Wat, c. 1113–1145.

Suryavarman II began building this great mountain temple shortly after he took the throne. The cosmic symbolism was carried out across the site from the surrounding moat "ocean" to the mathematical proportions of the structure and its parts.

to construct. The Indian archetypes for Suryavarman's great temple can be found in the Nagara style monumental temples built by the Chandela dynasts at Khajuraho, in particular, the eleventh century Visvanatha and Kandariya Mahadeva temples. Like those, Angkor Wat was conceived as a temple-mountain, replicating in stone the cosmic mountain of Hindu mythology, Mount Meru. However, the cosmic symbolism did not end with the temple. The entire complex was intended as a model of the universe: the laterite wall enclosing the 500-acre compound represented the mountains at the edges of the earth beyond which the cosmic oceans were evoked by the 623 foot (190 m) expanse of the moat.

Angkor Wat rises from the center of the symbolic earth upon three stepped terraces, which are enclosed by covered galleries with towers at the corners. Each of the three platforms is smaller and rises higher than the preceding one. Traditionally, only the Khmer king and Hindu priests could ascend to the top level and enter the temple. Following its Khajuraho prototypes, the sandstone temple sits atop a raised platform or plinth, called a ***jagati***. It is constructed of massive stone laterite blocks, face with sandstone; the latter were laid-up without mortar and often were not keyed together, resulting in vertical joints being stacked on top of each other instead of staggered. Occasionally, blocks were joined using metal cramps. The temple takes the form of a Greek cross with four columned halls contained within a square gallery. Symbolizing the five peaks of Mount Meru, are graduated-tier towers, known as **lotus bud towers**. They were arranged to form a **quincunx** or a layout where the five towers form a square with one at each corner and one in the center. The tallest tower was positioned over the sanctuary which once held a bronze devotional image of the Hindu god, Vishnu to whom it was dedicated.

The temple itself rises to a height of 137 feet (42 m), but combined with the three terraces, the overall height is an impressive 213 feet (65 m).

Suryavarman II Holding Court, Angkor Wat, c. 1113–1145 CE The concentric terrace galleries contain thousands of square feet of bas-relief sculpture, including some images that were only rough-chiseled into the surface in the manner of a sketch before work ceased at the temple. The large-scale reliefs, generally about 7 feet (2 m) tall, are cut directly into the stone blocks from which the wall was constructed. They depict stories from the Hindu creation myths, battles between gods and demons, episodes from the *Mahabharata* and *Ramayana* epics, parades of voluptuous apsaras or "celestial nymphs," and scenes of Suryavarman II at court and in battle.

The court scenes are the first such depictions in Khmer art. In one relief Suryavarman (Figure 7.11), relaxing in a posture of **royal ease**, sits on an ornately carved howdah or elephant carriage, suggesting that the ruler is traveling; the artist has attempted to show the left and right sides of the chair-like box but utilizes a reverse perspective, expanding them outward until the side rails appear to be in line with the front of the chair. Behind the hierarchically sized king is a lotus pond suggested by the tall stalks of the lotus pads, and the open and closed blossoms. Gathered closely around the king are the servants who fan the king; at first glance the servants seem to be identical but upon closer examination there are subtle differences in the details of their ornaments. One figure seated under a tree appears to be a court official, most likely a scribe, who reads to the king. The panel and others at Angkor Wat have traces of red and black pigment and occasional bit of gold leaf, suggesting that the scenes were originally painted and elements heightened with gilding.

Angkor Thom, c. 1181–1400 CE After the death of Suryavarman II, the Khmer dynasty was weakened to the point the throne was usurped

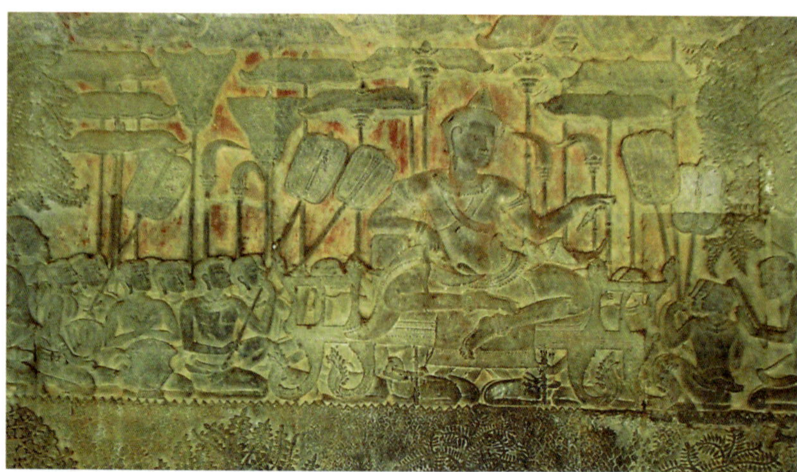

▶ 7.11 Cambodia, Angkor Wat, Gallery Relief showing Suryavarman II Holding Court, c. 1113–1145. Stone relief, pigment, and gold leaf.

In this scene Suryavarman has stopped while traveling and sits on an elephant chair in a position of royal ease.

by a court official who ruled for a decade. In 1177, the Cham attacked the capital and killed the usurper. During the four years they were in control of the capital, they sacked and destroyed much of it. The Cham takeover prompted Jayavarman VII (r. 1181–1220 CE) to return from the Champa kingdom, where he had been living in exile, and to claim the throne. Jayavarman VII is credited not only with restoring the empire but also with building the new capital of Angkor Thom about a kilometer north of the old city. The new "Great City" was designed to be unassailable. It was surrounded by a laterite wall 26 feet (8 m) high and a moat 328 feet (100 m) across. Inside the city walls were state temples, administrative buildings, the royal palace, and residences for monks, court officials, and the military. While many temples constructed by Jayavarman VII were stone, most of the other structures in the city, including the palace, were built of wood and have not survived.

The Bayon Temple, Angkor Thom, c. 1190 CE Jayavarman VII differed from earlier Khmer kings in that he was a follower of Mahayana Buddhism, so his temple-mountain, the Bayon, is a Buddhist shrine. Despite being a Buddhist temple, the Bayon (Figure 7.13) incorporates a number of Hindu design and cosmological elements. Like Angkor Wat, its prototype, the Bayon rises on three stepped platforms; the first two having galleries with a program of bas relief decoration. However, unlike the earlier temple, the Bayon has no outer wall or moat, those surrounding the city sufficing to complete the cosmological model. The third level contains the ruins of a circular temple with a central chamber and porched entrances marking the cardinal direction. The Bayon's fifty towers are a cross between Angkor Wat's lotus towers and the Nagara Shikhara. Each tower is carved with four

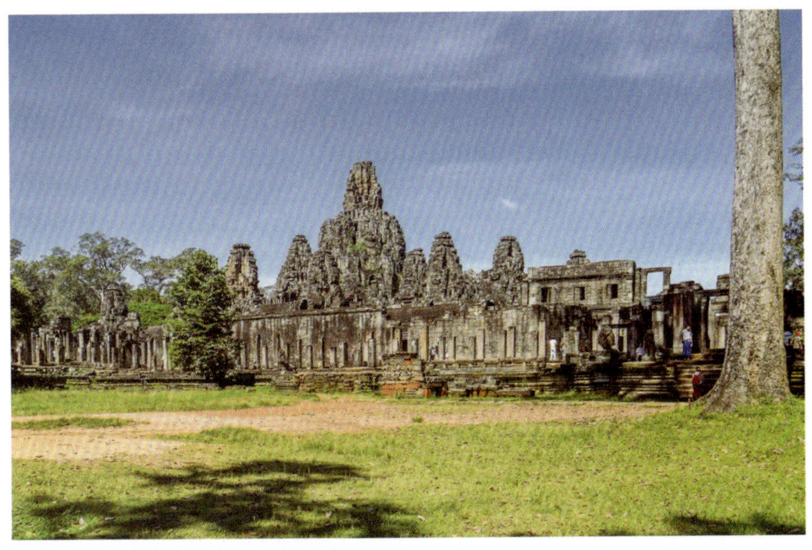

◀ **7.13** Cambodia, Angkor Thom, Bayon, c. 1190 CE.

Built by Jayavarman VII the Bayon is a Mahayana Buddhist temple dedicated to the Bodhisattva Lokeshvara, whose face decorate the sides of the temple's fifty towers.

bodhisattva faces, which look to the four directions and topped by an amalaka. Because Jayavarman VII considered himself to be the incarnation of the bodhisattva Lokeshvara, it is thought that the faces are portraits of the king. Compared to Angkor Wat, the Bayon appears more spatially constricted and lower; its towers only rise to a height of 75 feet (23 m).

Tonle Sap Naval Battle Scene, Bayon, Angkor Thom, c. 1190 CE Only the galleries of the Bayon's first two platform levels are decorated with bas-relief sculpture cut directly into the stone blocks of the wall. In many cases the relief is more deeply cut than at Angkor Wat but the quality of the carving seems to vary according to the skill of the artist; differences in style and degree of completion, suggests that the scenes were roughed in by one team of artisans and then finished by another. The walls are divided into three registers, sometimes separated by a

VISUAL COMPARISON
The Angkor Temples

The Khmer rulers used the architecture of their state temples in the capitals of Angkor and Angkor Thom to recount, in carved and painted reliefs, the defining events of their reigns and to reinforce, in visual terms, the religious philosophies of devaraja ("god king") or Buddharaja (Buddha king) under which they governed.

In the early twelfth century, Suryavarman II built the world's largest Hindu temple, Angkor Wat and dedicated it to the Hindu god, Vishnu. Around 1190 CE, Suryavarman II's first cousin once removed, Jayavarman VII, began construction of the Bayon, the last state temple to be built before the Angkor Thom capital was abandoned. Jayavarman VII's Bayon was dedicated to the compassionate bodhisattva Avalokiteśvara (locally Lokitesvara). Although the two rulers adhered to different religious traditions, the two temples have much in common. Both sit atop trilevel platforms, signifying Mount Meru, which in both Buddhist and Hindu cosmology stands at the center of the universe. To create a sense of Meru rising from the cosmic ocean, the temple compound at Angkor Wat was enclosed by a wall and moat. The Bayon compound is not surrounded by a separate wall and moat but uses those of the city to complete the cosmic mandala. The platform levels of each temple are bounded by long galleries containing carved stone reliefs recording historical events of the builder's reign and stories from Hindu and Buddhist mythology.

Where the buildings differ markedly is in the design of their summit temples. Hindu Angkor Wat follows a cruciform arrangement with a crowning central tower rising above the sanctuary and four lower spires at the corners to form a quinçunx. Buddhist Bayon features a circular pinnacle temple, subtly referencing a stupa form, and is surrounded by fifty towers, each bearing four faces of the Bodhisattva Lokeshivara. A final distinction is in the orientation of the temples. Angkor Wat faces west, suggesting a possible mortuary context, while the Bayon faces east, the direction faced by the Buddha when he achieved enlightenment under the Bodhi tree.

(Continued)

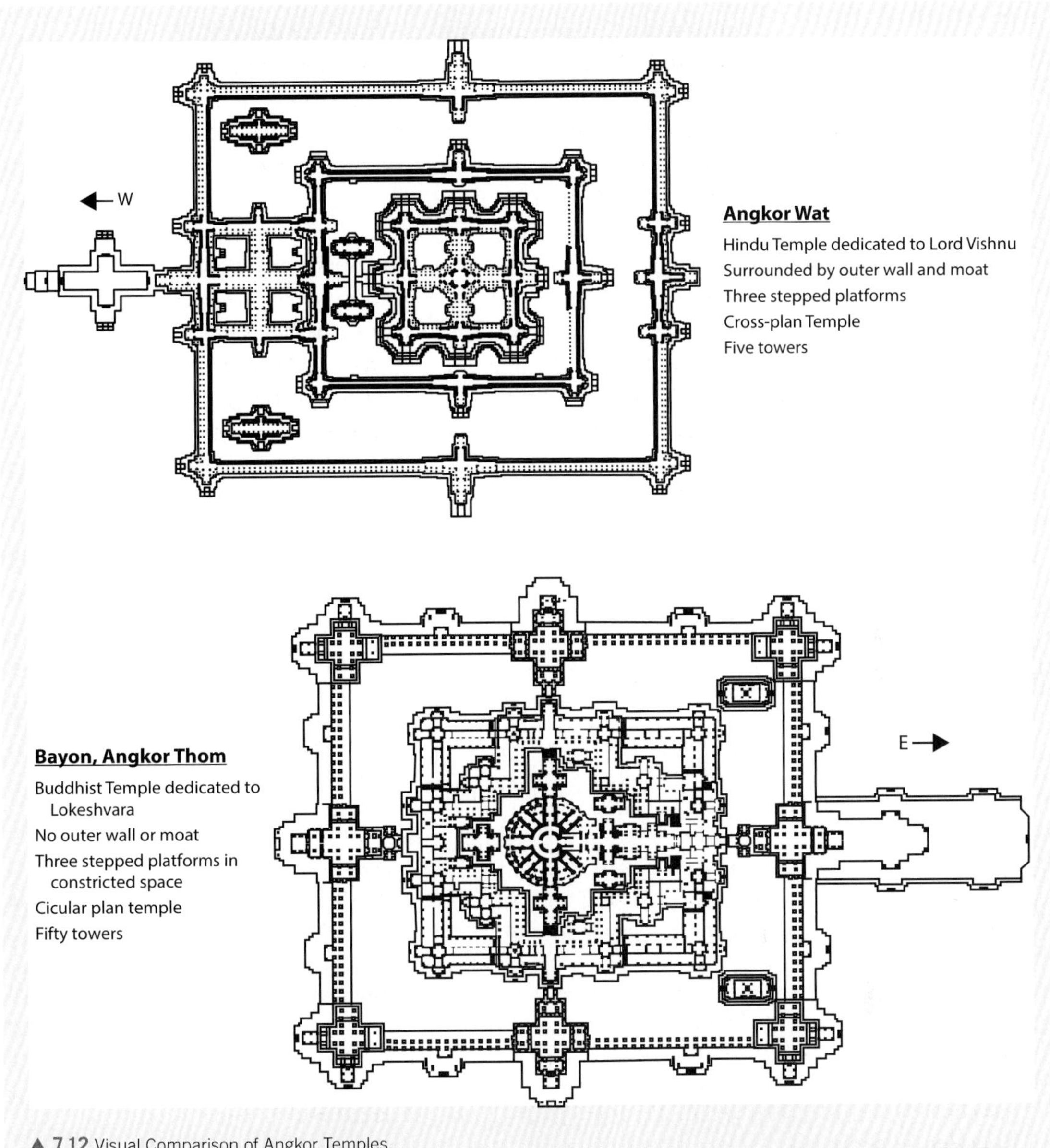

▲ **7.12** Visual Comparison of Angkor Temples.

Both temples, although representing different religions, conceptualize the temples as Mount Meru and serve as cosmic diagrams or mandalas.

ground band. The friezes show scenes of military processions in which Jayavarman VII is shown riding on a war elephant, the 1177 naval battle on Tonle Sap, a large lake to the south of Angkor (Figure 7.14), and scenes from everyday life, showing people fishing, women fishmongers dealing with customers, midwives attending childbirth, people at festivals, cockfights, and hunting scenes, among others. Regardless of the subject, these scenes show animated interactions between human

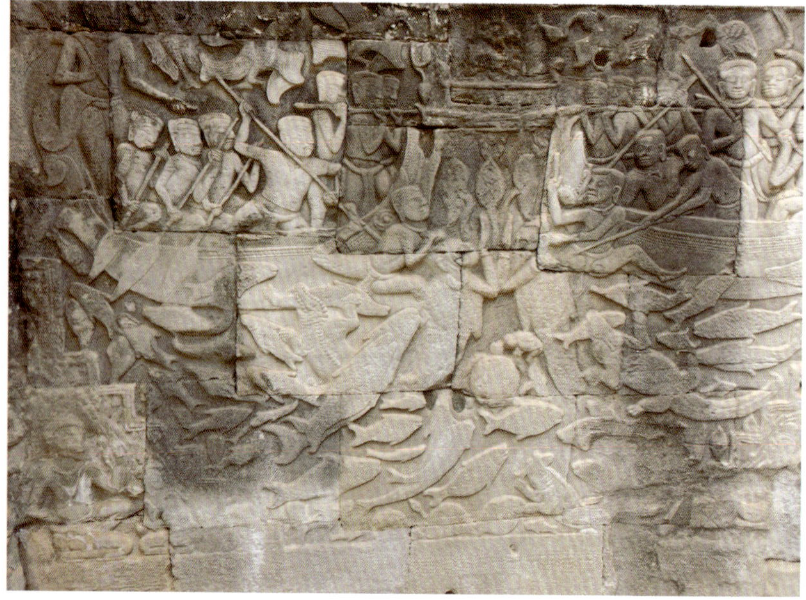

▶ 7.14 Cambodia, Angkor Thom, Bayon, *Tonle Sap Naval Battle Scene*, c. 1190 CE.

In this scene of a naval battle fighters fall into a lake filled with fish and hunting crocodiles.

and animal participants. Like the reliefs of Angkor Thom, these were probably enlivened with pigment.

Kingdom of Sukhothai, Thailand (1238–1438 CE)

The modern history of Thailand begins with the arrival of the Tai from southern China in the tenth century CE. Their ancestral homeland is believed to have been in what is today Hunan province. Beginning early in the current era, Tai groups began moving southward into the northern reaches of Southeast Asia, first into Vietnam and from there westward into the mountainous regions of northern Laos and Thailand. These migrations brought the Tai into conflict with the Khmer empire, which subdued them and made them vassals. In 1238, a Tai chieftain, Sri Intraditya, renounced his allegiance to the Khmer king and established the independent kingdom of Sukhothai in north central Thailand. Sri Indraditya's followers took the name Thai meaning "free" at this time to distinguish themselves from those Tai still subjects of the Khmer. The Sukhothai kings converted to Theravada Buddhism and, in sponsoring the building of temples, developed a unique style of architecture and sculpture.

Wat Mahathat, c. 1292–1347 CE The ruins of the ancient city of Sukhothai show it to have been fortified, enclosed on four sides by masonry walls and earthen ramparts. In the center of the city, surrounded by additional brick walls and a moat, were the royal palace and a Buddhist sanctuary known as Wat Mahathat (Figure 7.15). The Wat Mahathat ("old relic" temple) compound started out as a main ***chedi*** or stupa, encircled by eight smaller chedi to invoke Mount Meru, a viharn or sermon hall, an ***ubsot*** or ordination hall, and three-square shrines called ***mondops***, each of which house a Buddha statue. An extraordinary 26 foot (8 m) bronze Buddha originally stood in the viharn but it was removed to Bangkok by King Rama I in 1808 CE.

The main chedi sits on a square base, ornamented with 168 stuccoed figures of striding monks and pilgrims, all rendered in Gupta style (Figure 7.16). These striding figures, derived from study of the Pali Canon, are a characteristic of Sukhotai style in both relief and full-round sculpture. The Pali Canon gives several descriptions of the power and majesty with which the Buddha walked, even being specific in the statement that he led with the right foot. Despite the obvious importance of the theme of walking in the life story of the Buddha, before the Sukhothai period, he was generally rendered in art as a static figure. The Wat Mahathat relief figures are one of the earliest examples of this new type of Buddha image. Although the impression of movement is given, the mechanics of movement are not present. Like early Egyptian striding statues, the illusion of movement is accomplished by simply lengthening the nonengaged leg.

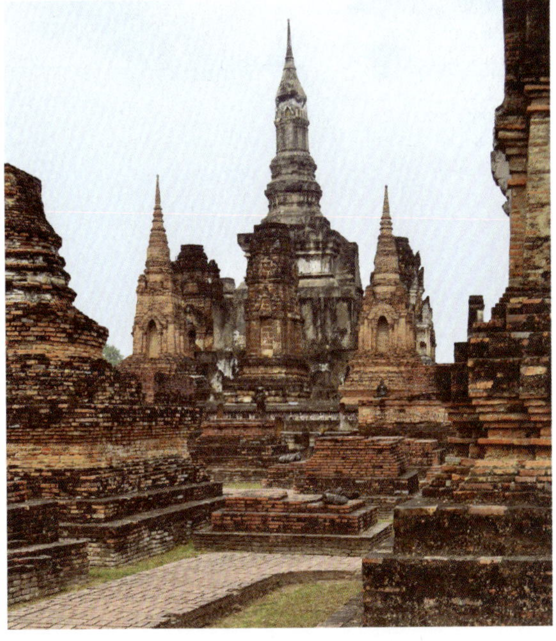

▲ 7.15 Thailand, Sukhotai, Wat Mahathat, Main Chedi, c. 1292–1347 CE.

Built on the grounds of the royal palace and surrounded by a moat, Wat Mahathat also drew on cosmic mountain imagery. The complex had several monumental Buddha images including a 26 ft. bronze Buddha.

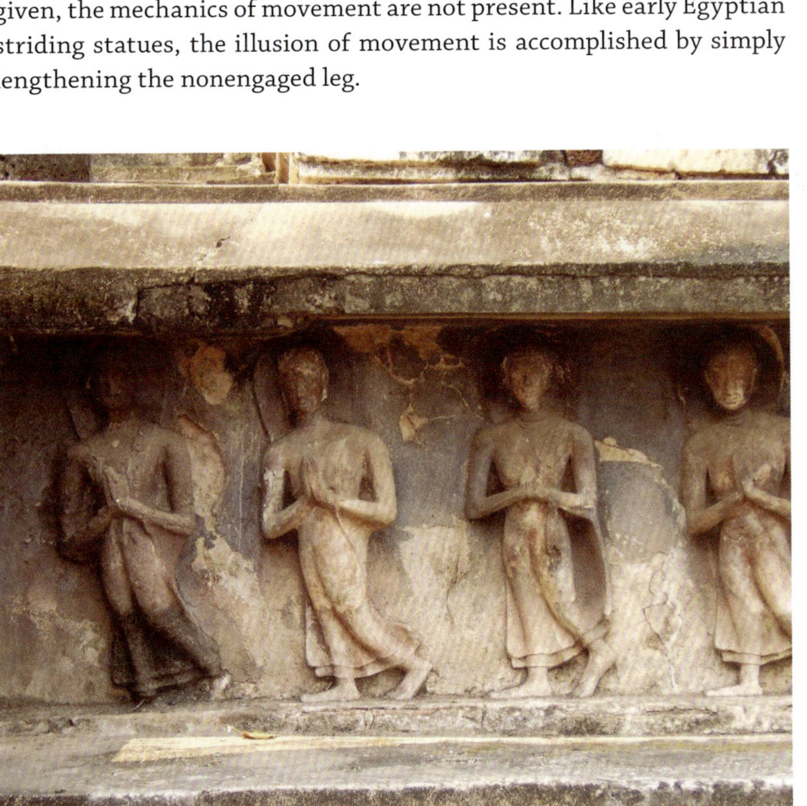

◀ 7.16 Thailand, Sukhotai, Wat Mahathat, Base Frieze of the Main Chedi, c. 1292–1347 CE.

Walking figures are a characteristic of the Sukhotai style in sculpture. However, the illusion is not based on body mechanics but achieved by simply lengthening the forward leg.

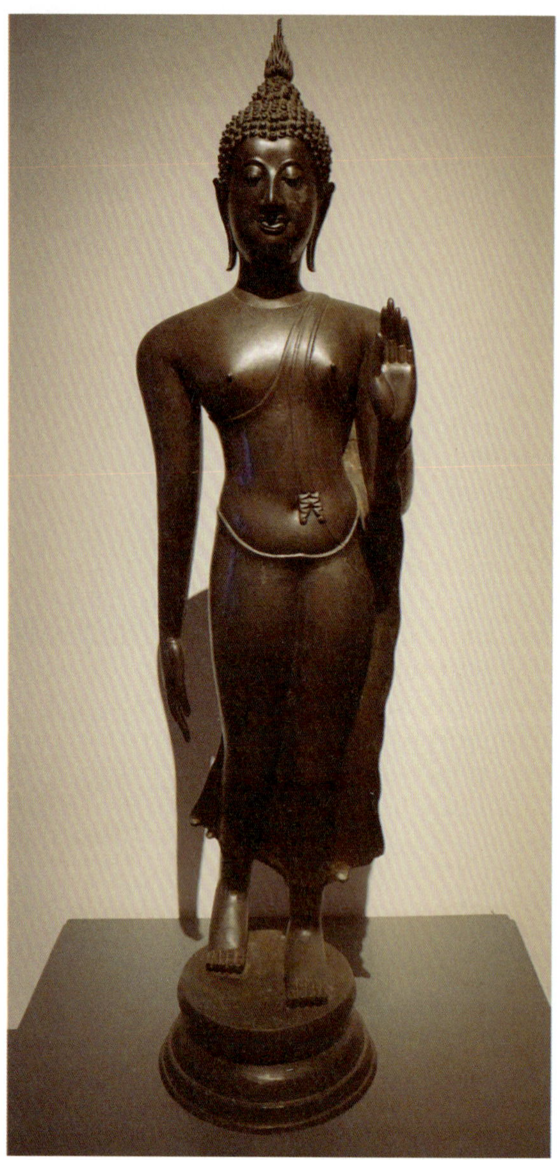

▲ **7.17** Thailand, Sukhotai Walking Buddha, c. fourteenth century CE.

Sukhotai walking Buddhas come in a range of sizes with the largest reaching over 39 ft. high. Based on the metaphoric descriptions of the Buddha in the Pali Canon, they are remarkably consistent. The striding Buddha image is unique to Sukhotai art.

The lower level of the stupa proper is ornamented with niches housing seated and standing images of the Buddha; the upper level has scenes from the life of Shakyamuni Buddha. A tall lotus bud steeple, unique to Sukhotai style, surmounts the main chedi. Subsequent Sukhothai kings enlarged Wat Mahathat, adding some two hundred small chedis in a variety of regional styles, reflecting the cosmopolitan nature of the kingdom.

Sukhotai Walking Buddhas (fourteenth–fifteenth century ce) The art of Sukhothai was inspired by the state adoption of Theravada Buddhism and its emphasis on the serene and compassionate nature of the Buddha Shakyamuni. In creating sculptures for the many temples built under royal patronage, Sukhothai artists based their interpretation of metaphors used to describe the Buddha's physical appearance in the Pali Canon. The Pali text lists the thirty-two ***lakshana*** (primary characteristics) and eighty ***anubyanjana*** (secondary characteristics), which became the standards for representations of the Buddha. Following the canon, Sukhothai artists created sitting, standing, and reclining Buddha images in bronze, stone and stucco, some of which were quite large. The Phra Attharot standing Buddha at Wat Mahathat, for example, is more than 39 feet (12 m) tall.

Stylistically Sukhothai Buddhas are indebted to the India Gupta style with its body-hugging garments and tight curls. Gupta conventions were brought to Thailand by Singhalese Theravada monks recruited to staff the monasteries and temples of the new Buddhist state. However, in the hands of Thai artists the old style was revitalized, becoming supple, curvaceous, cylindrical, boneless, and serenely elegant as they interpreted the old Pali canons in new poetic ways.

The bronze Walking Buddha (Figure 7.17) illustrates, in an abstracted and fluid form, the many flora and fauna analogies of the Pali Canon: arms like elephant's trunk, torso like a king lion, thighs like a banana palm, parrot's beak nose, and level feet. The Buddha raises his left hand in the fear-dispelling Abhaya mudra. A flame rises from the top of the Buddha's ushnisha, a common element in Thai art. The flame is a sign of the light of supreme knowledge resulting from the Buddha's enlightenment.

Kingdom of Ayutthaya, Thailand (1351–1767 CE)

In 1350 CE, Ramathibodi, prince of U Thong, a Mon state in central Thailand, established a new capital on an island in the Chao Phraya River, and named it Dvaravati Sri Ayudhya; the following year he was crowned king of Ayutthaya, called Siam by its neighbors. U Thong had long been a center of Khmer culture and Brahmanic Hinduism, especially among the elite classes. The name of Ramathibodi's capital and kingdom was inspired by the Hindu classic, the *Ramayana*. In the epic, Ayudhya was the home of Lord Rama, Vishnu's seventh avatar. In taking this name for his state, Ramathibodi was invoking devaraja as his kingdom's ruling principle. Under Ramathibodi and his successors Ayutthaya grew rapidly into a rich and powerful state. In 1431, they attacked and sacked the capital of the Khmer Empire and made it a vassal state. Seven years later, Sukhothai was subsumed into Ayutthaya. Having conquered both, the Siamese kings saw themselves as heirs to both the Sukhothai and Khmer traditions and this is especially evident in the art and architecture of Ayutthaya.

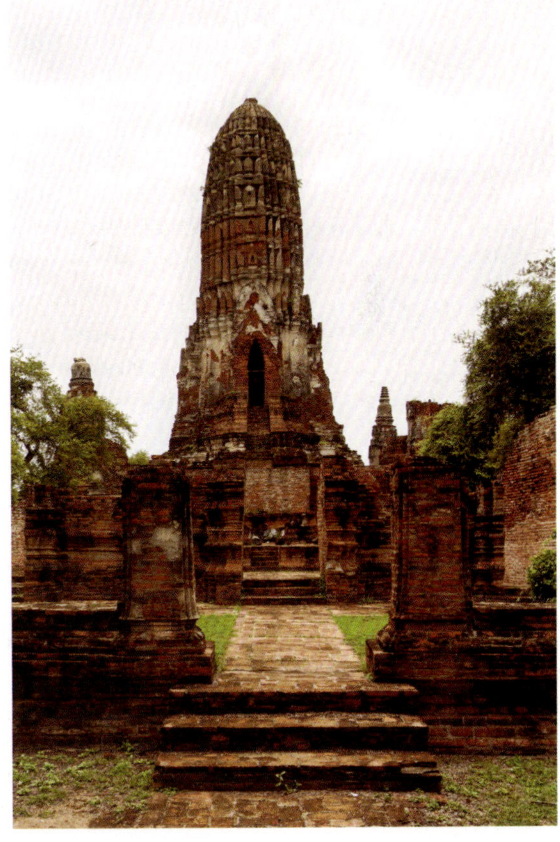

▼ 7.18 Thailand, Ayutthaya, Wat Phra Ram, c. 1369 CE.

Wat Phra Ram is one of the earliest of more than two hundred wats constructed by the Ayutthayan kings. It was built on the royal palace grounds to mark the cremation spot of the dynastic founder, King Ramathibodhi I.

Wat Phra Ram, Ayutthaya, c. 1369 The early Ayutthayan rulers were prolific builders; they are credited with more than two hundred wats. Unfortunately, many of these temples were damaged or destroyed in repeated Burmese invasions. The ruins of one of the earliest, Wat Phra Ram, stands on the grounds of the Siamese royal palace. According the early Siamese chronicle, the Luang Prasoet, written in 1681 CE, Wat Phra Ram (Figure 7.18) was constructed in 1369 to mark the cremation site of King Ramathibodhi I who died in that year. The shrine was restored and enlarged by later kings who added pillared halls and twenty-eight Sukhothai-style chedis.

Wat Phra Ram shows the Khmer influence in Siamese architecture as it draws heavily on Cambodian prototypes. The main shrine is a tall, round-topped, vertically grooved tower-form shrine known as a ***prang***. Some Siamese prangs are quite tall, reaching heights in excess of 130 feet (40 m). As is typical of early Ayutthaya Wats, the main tower is accompanied by four smaller prangs set up in a quincunx arrangement atop a high platform. The prang complex was originally enclosed within a walled court. The central Phra Ram prang has a small reliquary chamber which is accessible by means of a very steep stair on the east side. Unlike Khmer prangs, which were usually built of laterite blocks, the Siamese shrines were brick structures sealed with a coat of white plaster.

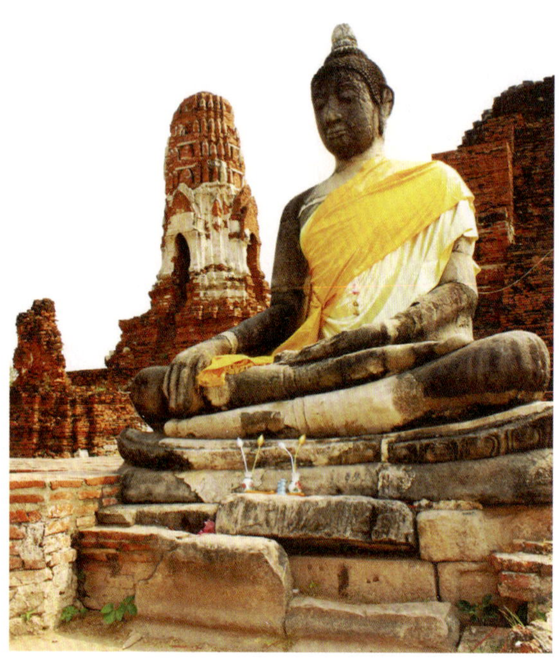

▲ 7.19 Thailand, Ayutthaya, Seated Buddha, c. fourteenth–fifteenth century CE.

This early Buddha shows, in its squarer body type, the influence of Khmer art. The Buddha has a rounder face and his ushnisha ends in a lotus bud. The statue has been draped in the saffron silk worn by Thai Buddhist monks.

Seated Buddha, Ayutthaya The seated stone Buddha (Figure 7.19) on the grounds of the Ayutthaya Historical Park shows the squarer, more substantial bodies that characterize Siamese sculpture. Early Ayutthaya sculpture drew on the Khmer conventions of U Thong art, creating erect bodied Buddhas with blocky heads crowned by diadems and conical ushnishas. After Sukhothai was incorporated into the Siamese kingdom, its style began to exert influence on the developing Siamese style, resulting sculptures with longer faces, hair formed into small, bead-like curls, and ringed ushnishas ending in lotus buds, as in this example, or later in flame-shaped finials. As an act of devotion, Buddha images and also Hindu divinities are often clothed. The Seated Buddha has been draped in the saffron yellow cloth worn by Thai Buddhist monks but underneath the silk, the Buddha's carved sanghati is rendered in typical Gupta fashion. Ayutthaya's location and control of trade in the region made it very wealthy. As the kingdom prospered the size of its stone images increased with some later ones reaching heights over 65 feet (20 m). Some of the smaller scale stone images were covered entirely in gold leaf and dressed in sheet-gold regal attire and crowns encrusted with jewels. Siamese artisans also produced bronze images, many of which were small scale votive images, rather than the large temple images of the Sukhothai era.

Maritime Southeast Asia: Indonesia (700–900 CE)

Hinduism and Buddhism were both introduced into the Indonesian archipelago in the early centuries of the Common Era. Hindu and Buddhist kingdoms arose on several islands but the best preserved and largest temples, among them Chandi Prambanan and Borobudur are found in Java. The golden age of temple building in Central Java began in the early ninth century CE under the patronage of two dynasties, the Sanjaya (c. 732–929), and the Sailendra (c. 750–850 CE). By the early tenth century both Borobudur and Prambanan had been abandoned, possibly in response to the eruption of the Merapi volcano.

Chandi Prambanan, Java, c. 856 CE Prambanan (Figure 7.20), dedicated to the Trimurti, is the largest Hindu temple complex in Indonesia. In the ***Trimurti*** or "Hindu trinity" Brahma, Vishnu, and Shiva represent the modalities of creation, preservation, and destruction respectively as aspects of the Hindu supreme god, Brahman. The trinity is represented within the inner compound at Prambanan by three temples and three associated shrines, once believed to house images of each god's animal mount and gatekeeper but this is no longer accepted. The largest temple is the central Shiva temple which rises to a height of 154 feet (47 m). It is the only temple to have four entrances oriented to the cardinal directions. The east entrance leads to the main Shiva sanctuary and cult statue; the others lead to secondary chapels dedicated to Durga, Ganesha, and Agastya.

Early Sanjaya temples appear to have been inspired by Dravidian style temples, such as those at Mamallapuram; they were square stone shrines raised up on low plinths and capped by three-stepped pyramidal towers. The Shiva temple at Prambanan is an elaboration and enlargement of this basic form. The low plinth has been replaced by a terraced platform ascended by a stair with an ornate Makara-form balustrade that continues around the terrace to form an outer gallery. The sanctuary has been heightened and projecting additions added on all four sides giving an accordion-fold effect to the corners. The surface of the exterior walls are divided by a string course into two tall registers,

▼ **7.20** Java, Chandi Prambanan, c. 856 CE.

Prambanan is dedicated to the Trimurti or Hindu Trinity of Brahma, Vishnu, and Shiva. Each of the three gods has a main Dravidian style temple and a smaller temple for his sacred animal. The three main temples were surrounded by 224 guardian temples.

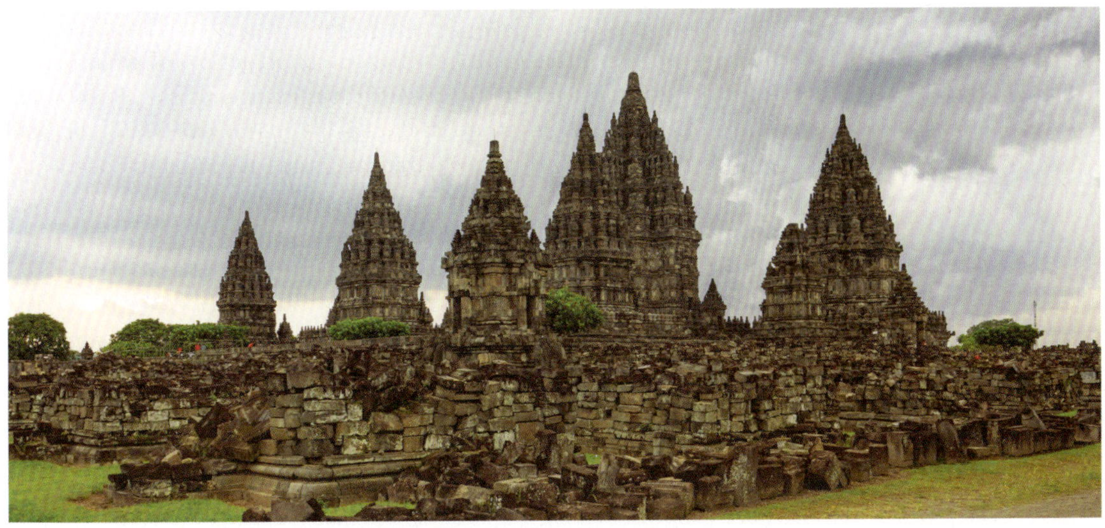

and enriched with sculpture or architectural elements such as pilasters and blind windows. Finally, the low pyramidal roof is taller, having the number of tiers increased to six, each lined with stupa-form shrines. To lessen the weight of the massive towers on the corbelled vaults of the sanctuary, the Prambanan architects developed an ingenious system of stacked "attic" voids or "rooms" within the masonry of the tower.

Set into the niches of the lower walls of the Shiva temple are twenty-four relief panels representing the four Lokapalas of the cardinal directions; images of Hindu gods and goddesses, and figures of Brahmin sages. The outer balustrade wall features reliefs of celestial musicians and dancing apsaras. On the inner surface are scenes from the Ramayana depicting the story of Sita's abduction by Ravana, King of Lanka. The Ramayana narrative is continued in the relief panels of the Vishnu (north) and the Brahma (south) temples. The Rama story is intended to be read as a manifestation of the Trimurti in the physical world.

Javanese temples have a symbolic tripartite arrangement derived from the Indian *Shilpa-shastras*, which compared the elevation of a temple to a standing figure. Thus, the base became the foot, the main part of the structure was the body, and the tower was the head. These divisions corresponded to the levels of the universe with the foot being the realm of desire (***kama-dhatu***); the body being the form world where enlightenment is attainable (***rupa-dhatu***), and the head being the formless realm of the gods and universal understanding (***arupa-dhatu***).

Between the inner sanctuary wall and the outer wall were 224 guardian shrines standing 45.5 feet (14 m) high. These were arranged in four concentric rows and faced away from the inner court toward the cardinal directions. Beyond the second wall, and what may have been a third, was an area originally having wooden structures where the priests and attendants are thought to have resided.

Borobudur, Java, c. 778–850 CE Around 778 CE, the Mahayana Buddhist Sailendra princes of central Java began construction of what would become the largest Buddhist monument in the world, Borobudur (Figure 7.21). Although the Sailendra kingdom was small, it was wealthy and could afford to build Buddhist temples as acts of devotion. The massive temple-mountain, measuring 113 feet (34.5 m) high, was built in four stages over a period of sixty-six years. Unlike earlier, solid brick or earthen-fill stupas, Borobudur was constructed around the terraced core of a natural hill.

Viewed from the air Borobudur is a ***mandala*** or sacred diagram of the cosmos rendered in stone. At the pinnacle of Borobudur is a bell-shaped stupa 26 foot (8 m) high with a diameter of 49 feet (15 m); it is surrounded by three concentric terraces supporting a total of 72 openwork stupas, each containing a seated, Gupta-style Buddha. The lower platform has six rectangular terraces which are lined with 2,672

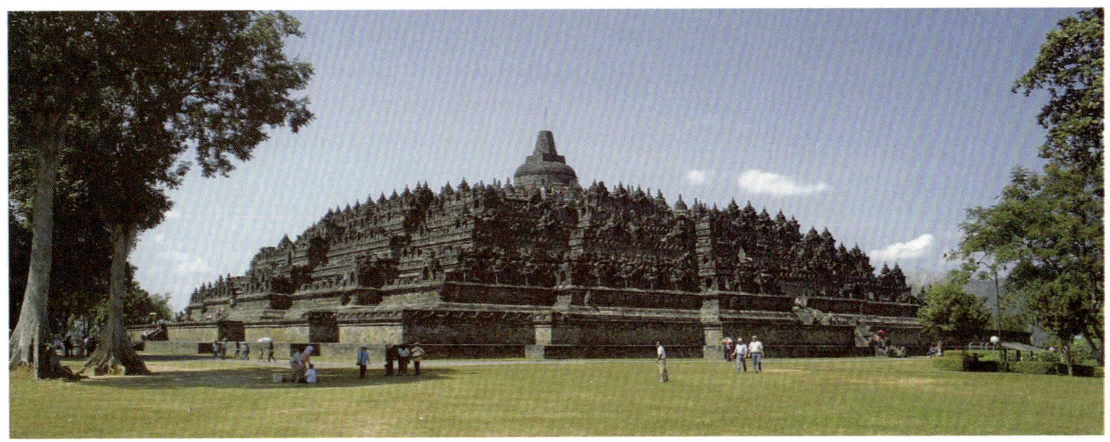

▲ 7.21 Java, Borobudur, c. 778–850 CE. 113 ft. high.

This massive temple mountain was built by terracing a natural hill and encasing it in a veneer of stone reliefs. The faithful venerated the Buddha at Borobudur by circumambulating through the galleries of each of the six levels of the lower terrace and the three levels of the upper terrace.

relief panels depicting Jataka tales, and 386 seated Buddhas once inhabited niche-like stupas set into the terraces. The Borobudur Buddhas are all identical except for variations in their mudras associated with the cardinal directions. Those on the east platform terraces perform the ***Bhumisparsha*** or "touch the earth" gesture; those on the south exhibit the ***Varada mudra*** in which a hand, palm out, is extended as a sign of bestowing charity; those on the west overlap their hands as a sign of meditation in the ***Dhyana mudra***, and those on the north raise their right hand in a gesture of fearlessness known as the ***Abhaya mudra***. The Buddhas in the openwork stupas of the three inner circles rotate their hands, giving motion to the ***Dharmachakra*** or "turning the wheel of law," which is associated with "center."

From the ground Borobudur replicated the cosmic mountain, Mount Meru in the center of both the Buddhist and Hindu universes. In addition to the didactic message of the reliefs, the structure is intended to give physical form to Buddhist teachings. As the devotee begins his journey at the eastern stair and circumambulates clockwise through these nine platform levels, following a path some 3 miles (5 km) long, he is physically and symbolically moving up through the illusory world of desire and the senses toward that of enlightenment and nirvana. The nine levels are broken into three groups to suggest the spheres of Buddhist teaching: the kama-dhatu (the realm of desire and feeling), the rupa-dhatu (the realm of form and materiality), and finally, the arupa-dhatu (the realm of formlessness or anti-materiality) in which detachment from the physical world comes with enlightenment. Thus, the tenth level with its single large stupa signifies attainment and the entry into nirvana.

Islam in Southeast Asia

Islam was established in Southeast Asia by seagoing Indian Sufi traders beginning perhaps as early as the tenth century CE. **Sufism** was a less formal, more personal and mystical version of Islam that emphasized a close personal relationship with Allah that made it more accepting of existing religious practices in the regions where it was introduced. As it spread, Sufic Islam often adapted to local practices, transforming local heroes into Islamic ones, and turning a blind eye to native gambling and gaming practices such as cockfighting. Although Islamic populations could be found in mainland port cities, the religion found its greatest acceptance in Malaysia and Indonesia, where it appears to have become established early. When Marco Polo stopped on the island of Sumatra (Lesser Java) in 1292, he noted the presence of a Muslim community in the port city of Ferlec.

Masjid Agung Demak, Java, c. 1466–1474 CE Located in the center of the ancient city of Demak, capital of the Demak Sultanate, the Masjid Agung Demak (Figure 7.22) or "Grand Mosque of Demak" is the oldest surviving mosque in Indonesia. Legend attributes its founding to the hero, mystic, and diplomat, Sunan Kalijaga (Raden Mas Said), one of the nine ***Wali Songo*** or Muslim saints. The Masjid Demak is the oldest mosque in Indonesia and the prototype for many others across the islands built in what is known as the Javanese style.

Javanese style mosques are very different from those of the Middle East or Moghul India; instead of stone they are timber-frame structures, inspired by the local ***joglo*** vernacular architecture. Joglo houses were typically elevated, square-plan structures with a high peaked-gable roof. To this basic design was added a central tower with a tiered-roof derived from Buddhist and Hindu temples also built of wood. In this type of construction, the tower is supported by four massive teak posts, known as ***soko guru*** or main posts. The soko guru are surrounded by a perimeter colonnade of smaller posts that support the main roof of the prayer hall; the design allows for a maximum of space and a minimum of visual obstruction. The space of the main hall is often extended by veranda or ***serambi*** at the front or on either side. The front wall of the masjid is decorated with porcelain tiles from

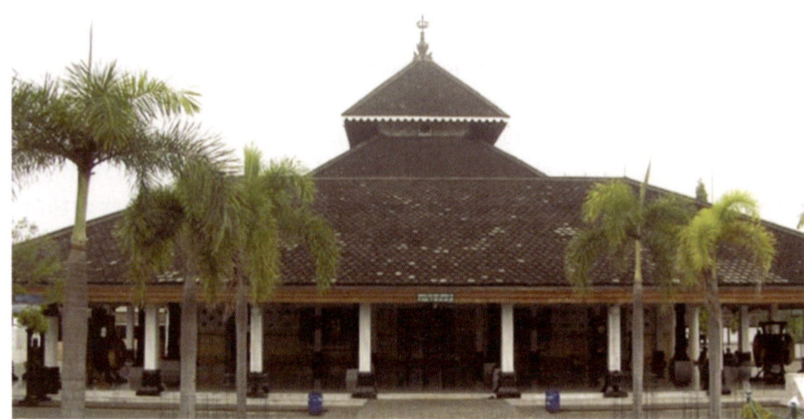

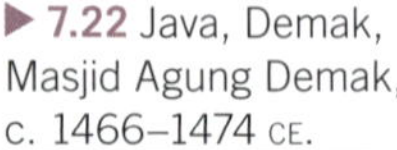

▶ **7.22** Java, Demak, Masjid Agung Demak, c. 1466–1474 CE.

This mosque is the oldest surviving mosque in Indonesia as was a prototype for the Javanese style mosque. It was inspired by vernacular building practices rather than replicating West Asian or Indian mosque types.

Vietnam. Originally, the masjid did not have a minaret, although today it has a rudimentary one on a scaffold. Instead, the call to prayer was announced by beating a wooden drum, called a ***kentong***, from one of the mosque verandas.

Sinification in Vietnam

Whether through direct contact with Indian culture or Indianized neighbors, much of mainland and maritime Southeast Asia was influenced to some degree by the cultural and religious traditions of India. The exception was northern Vietnam which experienced an intense Sinification. As early as 221 BCE, the Chinese Qin dynasty looked to northern Vietnam as it expanded southward. Qin Shi Huang sent his armies into Vietnam and established a Chinese commandery or military province. This initial foray into Vietnam ended with the collapse of the Qin. A little more than a century later, during the Han dynasty, three military provinces were established in northern Vietnam. China retained control of *Annam* or "the pacified South," as they called the region, for more than a thousand years. During this period Chinese language, writing, art, architecture, irrigation technology, Buddhism and Confucian philosophy, as well as Chinese administrative and military systems, were introduced into Vietnam. However, the Vietnamese never accepted Chinese supremacy as did the Koreans. In 939 CE, taking advantage of the political instability in China during the Five Dynasties and Ten Kingdoms period (907–960 CE), Vietnam rebelled and wrested its independence from China. Free of Chinese domination, the Dai Viet state pushed southward, ultimately defeating their Indianized Cham neighbors in 1471, and taking the Mekong Delta from the Khmer in 1749. During this time the Vietnamese kingdom was ruled in succession by the Later Ly dynasty (1009—1225 CE), Tran (1226—1400 CE), Le (1428—1788 CE), and Nguyen (1802—1945 CE). The instability of these dynasties brought on by rebellions, invasions, famine, and internal political strife, set the stage for the French takeover of the country in 1873 CE.

Tan Quoc Pagoda, Hanoi, Vietnam, c. 541–545 CE Almost three decades of war, first with France and then with the United States, destroyed many ancient monuments; some, like the Hindu seventy-temple site of Mỹ Sơn, were carpet bombed into piles of rubble. One of the few surviving early Chinese style pagodas is Tan Quoc Pagoda in Hanoi (Figure 7.23). It was built by Ly Nam De, founder of the Early Ly Dynasty (544–602 CE). Ly Nam De was the magistrate for the district of Giao Chau, in northern Vietnam. Although of Chinese descent, he was incensed by the corruption evident in the Chinese administration of the province. He led a rebellion, which successfully liberated the region from Chinese rule for more than sixty years. When the pagoda

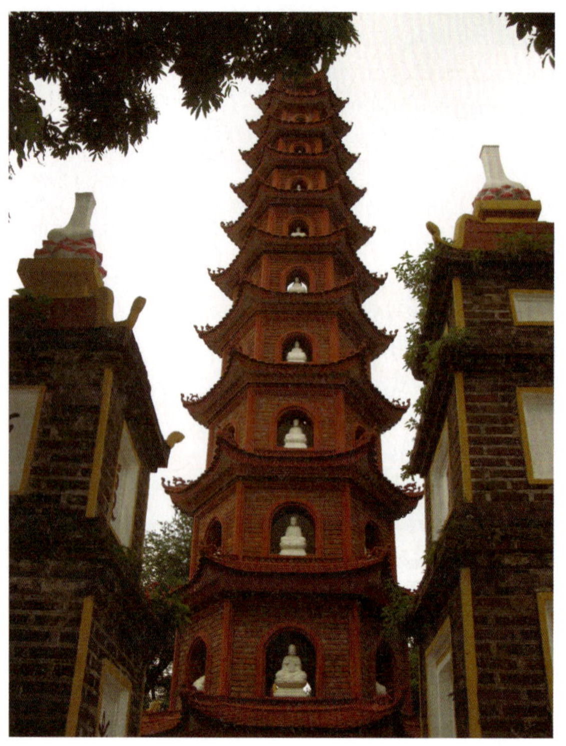

▲ **7.23** Vietnam, Hanoi, Tan Quoc Pagoda, c. 541–545 CE. 49 ft. high.

Tan Quoc is an eleven-level hexagonal pagoda, seated Buddha figures fill the niches of every level.

was dedicated, it was called "Khai Quoc," meaning "opening a country," a reference to the establishment of the independent state, and its six-sides a symbol of good fortune for the nation. In the seventeenth century the pagoda was moved to an island in the West Lake as its original location on the bank of the Red River was eroding away. After it was moved, it was renamed Tan Quoc Pagoda, meaning "Protecting the country." Tan Quoc is a hexagonal brick pagoda which rises from a six-step base to a height of 49 feet (15 m). The pagoda is divided into eleven levels by tiered-roofs with flying eaves. Seated stone sculptures of Amitabha Buddha are set into niches in each of the pagoda's six faces on every level. It is surmounted by a ringed steeple ending in a lotus finial. Its design is derived from Chinese stone pagodas of the era. Standing on the grounds of the pagoda is a Bodhi tree grown from a cutting from the tree at Bodh Gaya in India.

VIETNAMESE CERAMICS

The influence of Chinese styles and technologies on the development of Vietnamese ceramics was profound and continued long after the Dai Viet threw off Chinese domination. Beginning as early as the first century BCE, Vietnamese potters adopted Chinese vessel forms, glaze technologies, and stoneware clays. During the Chinese Yuan and Ming dynasties, the technique of underglaze painting was introduced into Annam perhaps through direct contact with Chinese potters. However, the first Vietnamese underglaze wares were produced using iron-black. It was not until the fourteenth century that cobalt-blue underglaze ceramics appeared in Vietnam. Enamel over-glaze techniques were introduced from Ming Dynasty China soon afterward.

Plate with Leaping Deer, My Xa Kilns, Le Dynasty, c. 1400–1500 CE The Plate with Leaping Deer motif (Figure 7.24) shows the influence of China in its form, composition, and use of cobalt underglaze and enamel overglaze techniques. The deer bounds across a mountainous landscape toward a flowering branch at the upper left; the sky around the deer is filled with red and green cloud forms, while the outer band is filled with fluidly painted floral motifs. The artist began by outlining the forms in blue underglaze and then adding details to the figure and ground with red and green enamel overglazes. What is distinctive about the Vietnamese approach to the motif is the whimsicality of the buck

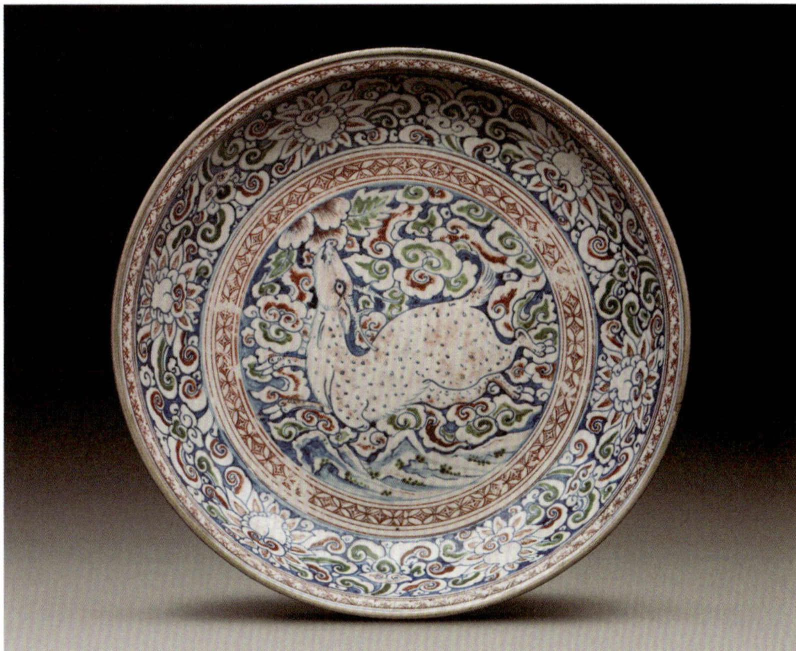

◀ 7.24 Vietnam, Plate with Leaping Deer, My Xa kilns, Le Dynasty, c. 1400–1500 CE. Cobalt underglaze and enamel overglaze technique.

Vietnamese porcelains often have a sense of whimsy in their decoration as, in this case, with a running buck stopping to smell the flowers.

seemingly smelling the flowers. As the Ming rulers of China became more xenophobic and closed off foreign trade, the Vietnamese took advantage of the situation and began exporting their imitation porcelain wares to Indonesia and the Philippines.

Colonialism, Nationalism, and Modern Art in Southeast Asia (1511–1947)

In the sixteenth century spices such as pepper, cinnamon, cloves, nutmeg, and ginger drew Europeans to India and Southeast Asia. The Portuguese were the first to arrive, capturing Malacca in 1511, but losing it in the seventeenth century to the Dutch, who came in 1605 under the auspices of the Dutch East India Company. Like their English counterpart, the Dutch East India Company had little interest in administering colonies and that mission was taken on by the Dutch government in 1825. The British moved into "Further India" in the early nineteenth century, after conquering Burma and making it a province of British India. The British acquired maritime trading settlements at Penang, Singapore, and Malacca, and used them as a base to expand into the Malay Peninsula. The French entered Vietnam in 1858 and the following year took Saigon, using it as a base while expanding north and west to conquer the rest of Vietnam, Laos, and Cambodia. These colonial states were administered as French Indochina.

Independent Thailand: The Rattanakosin Kingdom (1782–1932 CE)

The only Southeast Asian nation to escape European colonialization was Thailand. After the Burmese invasion of 1767 in which the Ayutthayan capital and dynasty were destroyed, a resistance movement against the invaders was led by a former Ayutthayan general and provincial governor, Phraya Taksin, who was of Chinese and Thai descent. Successfully repelling the Burmese, Taksin established a new capital at Thonburi and declared himself king. Taksin sent his armies, led by his general Chaophraya Chakri, to restore and expand the empire. In the late 1770s Chakri led armies into Vientiane (Laos) and brought back the Emerald Buddha, considered Thailand's most sacred Buddha image. By the end of the decade Taksin's rule had become increasingly fanatical and he was overthrown and executed. The factions that had led the uprising against Taksin offered the throne to General Chakri.

Chakri took the throne as Rama I (r. 1782–1809 CE), establishing the Rattanakosin kingdom with Bangkok as the capital. Rama and his successors restored the national economy, ended slavery, expanded education, and successfully deflected repeated colonization attempts by European powers but not without the loss of some of its conquered territories to the French (Laos and Cambodia) and British (Malay Peninsula). In 1932 dissatisfaction with the pace of modernization and poor economic conditions resulted in Thailand replacing the absolute monarchy with a constitutional one under which the Chakri dynasty continues to rule.

Wat Phra Kaew, c. 1785 The centerpiece of Rama I's new capital was the Wat Phra Kaew (Figure 7.25) or Phra Sri Rattana Satsadaram, meaning "residence of the holy jewel Buddha." The temple was built on the palace grounds specifically to house the Emerald Buddha, recovered by Rama I from Vientiane, Laos. Unlike other Buddhist temples, Wat Phra

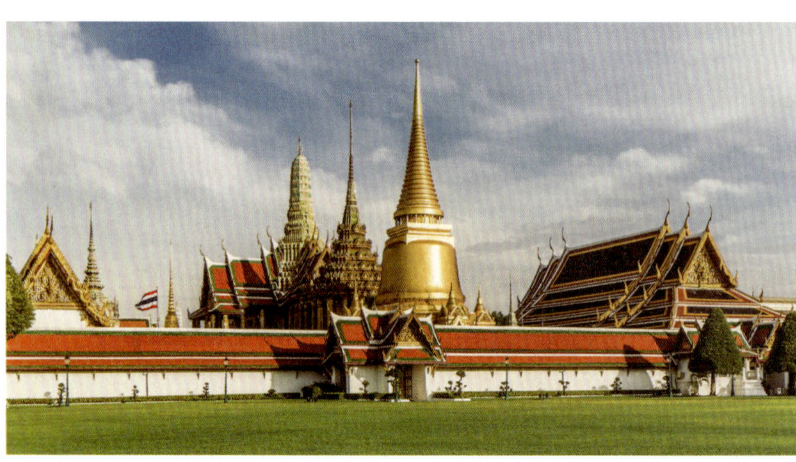

▶ **7.25** Thailand, Bangkok, Wat Phra Kaew, c. 1785.

This temple, on the palace grounds, was built to house the Emerald Buddha, a symbol of the nation, which the founder of the Rattanakosin dynasty retrieved from Laos. Unlike other Buddhist temples this one does not have a monastery.

Kaew does not have a monastery. The main sanctuary is the carved and gilded wooden ubosot in which the Emerald Buddha is displayed atop a thirty-foot-high platform. As the residence of the Emerald Buddha, a symbol of the nation, Phra Kaew is considered to be the most sacred temple in Thailand and as a result has never been allowed to fall into disrepair.

The Emerald Buddha, c. 1434 The Emerald Buddha (Figure 7.26) is a small statue, only 26 inches (66 cm) high, carved from a green stone, possibly jade or serpentine. Legend has its origin place as the northern city of Pataliputra in 43 BCE, although this is unlikely given its Gupta-derived style. The Buddha sits with right leg resting over the left rather than crossed; this pose is common to southern India, Sri Lanka, and Southeast Asian sculpture. The statue's hands rest palm-up, right over left in its lap, forming the Dhyana mudra of concentration. The torso is tapering and shows the slight swelling of the belly with prana. The face of the Buddha is egg-shaped; nose and mouth are small and the eyes are downcast, giving it a placid appearance. The Buddha's urna is marked in gold. Beneath his golden helmet, with its five prayer wheels symbolizing the turning of the law of Dharma, the sculpted head of the Buddha has a smooth ushnisha that ends in a blunted point.

Buddha images carved from semiprecious stones or rock crystal, known as jewel Buddhas, are believed to have special powers. In addition to bringing prosperity to the nation and legitimizing kingship, the Emerald Buddha is ascribed the ability to end drought and to ward off epidemics. During times of plague or drought these special Buddha images were brought out from their shrines and carried in procession through

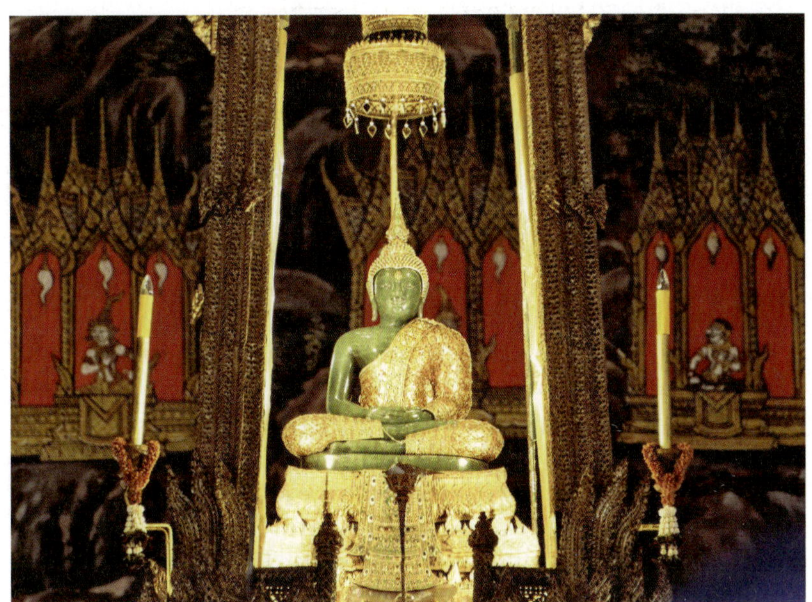

◀ **7.26** Thailand, Wat Phra Kaew, *The Emerald Buddha*, c. 1434. Green stone, 26 in. high.

The Buddha, shown here in his hot season costume is Thailand's most sacred icon. Three times a year the Thai king changes the Buddha's robes as appropriate to the season.

the city. The Emerald Buddha last left its shrine during the 1820 cholera epidemic. King Rama IV (r. 1851–1868) ended the custom of removing the Emerald Buddha for fear of it being damaged. At that time a sacred cord was attached to the image so that it could participate in ceremonies outside of the temple without being removed from its shrine.

Three times a year, at the changing of the seasons, the King of Thailand ceremonially changes the Buddha's robes; he is the only person allowed to touch the image. Two of the Emerald Buddha's robes, a golden, diamond-and-gemstone-studded tunic for the hot seasons, and one flecked with blue for the rainy season date from the time of Rama I. The third garment is a robe of solid gold for the cool season provided by Rama III (r. 1824–1851).

Academies in Colonial Southeast Asia

The French established the first art school in Saigon in 1913 and then, a little more than a decade later, opened the École de Beaux-Arts d'Indochine in Hanoi, both of which promoted European styles. However, British colonial officials did not establish art academies in Burma and Malaysia as they had in India, perhaps because those areas were administered by the viceregal government of India. Across Southeast Asia native artists, for the most part, leaned from traditional masters and worked under royal patronage in indigenous styles. As a result, European modernism had less impact on art in Southeast Asia than contemporaneous Meiji-era Japan. European artists did come to Burma, Malaysia, and French Indochina, and a few of them did take native students for instruction. The most active group of European artists was in Burma, where they founded the Burma Art Club in 1913, and through their instruction of local artists gave rise to the so-called "Rangoon School."

U Ba Nyan (1897–1945),* Portrait of U Ba Oo, *1933 The most prominent member of the Rangoon School was the realist painter U Ba Nyan from the Irrawaddy region of Myanmar. U Ba Nyan was the first Burmese artist to be accepted for study at the Royal College of Art in London in 1921. There he received training in Western style painting, specializing in portraiture and landscape painting. Upon his return he helped to advance Burmese painting as a teacher, training a new generation of artists in Western techniques. He is known to have been a successful portrait painter, receiving commissions to do portraits of colonial governors and even King George V. Unfortunately, U Ba Nyan died in 1945 as he was fleeing the Japanese army during World War II, and only six of his works survived destruction in the war.

The *Portrait of U Ba Oo* (Figure 7.27), the artist's father, is a sensitive study of a mature man, rendered primarily in tones of brown, the single pop of color being the cream of his head cloth. U Ba Oo sits in a position reminiscent of the "royal ease" posture of bodhisattvas and kings, a bowl of tea rests on the floor in front of him. His bare upper torso is taut and muscular, revealing a physical strength despite his advanced age. The portrait is a casual one, having the quality of a genre scene, rather than the stiffness of a formal portrait. The setting in which U Ba Oo has been placed is vague and shadowy; several blades of light, seeping from unseen shutters above and to the figure's left, rake across the subject's body, alternately revealing and obscuring the form. The painting is not only a highly realistic likeness, but also a tour de force of atmospheric rendering.

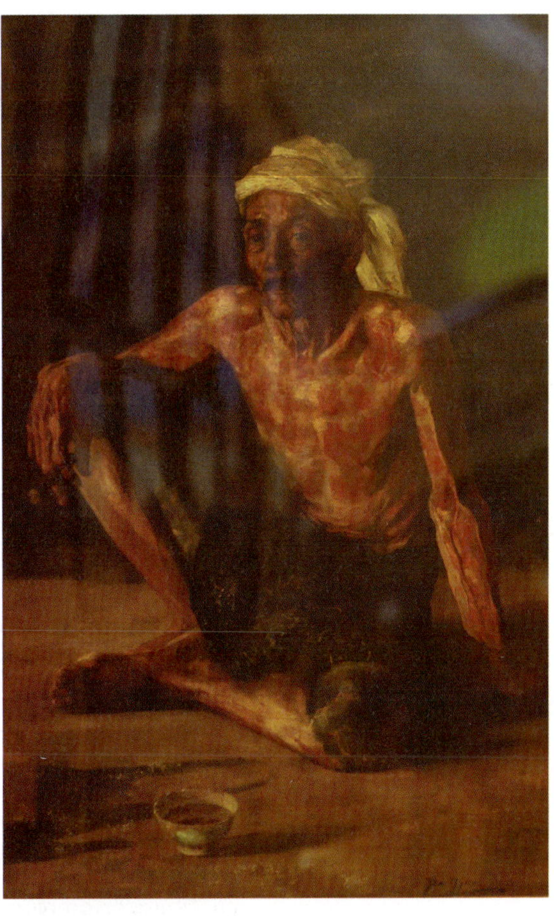

▲ **7.27** Myanmar, U Ba Nyan (1897–1945), *Portrait of U Ba Oo*, 1933 CE.

This portrait of the artist's father is considered to be a masterpiece. It is unusual in its casual, genre quality in contrast to the often more formal portraits of the Colonial Era.

Colonial Architecture

Where colonial European influence appears to have had the greatest impact was in architecture. Whether built by the British, Dutch, or French, colonial architecture in Southeast Asia was an eclectic mix of Western architectural styles, reflecting not only Victorian enthusiasm for historical revivals but also the prevailing aesthetic imperialism of the nineteenth and early twentieth centuries. John Begg (1866–1937), consulting architect to the government of India, and designer of the government telegraph and the government press buildings in Rangoon (Yangon), expressed the sentiment of the age when he compared the British Empire to that of Rome and suggested Britain should plant its architecture, system of laws and justice, and culture in all the far parts of the empire. In most cases this is exactly what the colonial powers did, bringing in architects like John Begg, James Ransome, and Harry Hoyne-Fox to design and construct government buildings, hospitals, and schools.

Despite the preference for Western architects and purely Western historical styles, there were some successful native architects who built important buildings during the Colonial era. Often their buildings are a fusion of indigenous and European styles. For example, the Burmese architect Sithu U Tin merged Buddhist elements with Neo-Classicism in his designs for the Yangon City Hall and the Central Railway Station. Slightly earlier in French colonial Vietnam, Tran Triem (1825–1899) combined Chinese Buddhist temple architecture with French Gothic in his Phat Diem Cathedral complex in Ninh Binh province.

Sithu U Tin (1890–1972), Yangon City Hall, 1925–1940 In Burma, after World War I, there was a growing nationalist sentiment with native legislators calling for an architecture that was responsive to the culture and religious traditions of the country. One of the first Burmese architects to receive a commission to design a civic building under the British Raj was Sithu U Tin, who had studied in Bombay. In 1925 he was selected to design the Yangon City Hall (Figure 7.28). This was an especially significant commission because the location chosen for the building was across from the Sule Pagoda in the center of the city. U Tin designed an Art Deco inspired edifice that while modern, responded to the Buddhist traditions and style of the stupa. Yangon City Hall is a four-story structure built around an interior courtyard. It has a fortress-like feeling because of the towers that mark the corners of the enormous structure. The central entrance block steps out in stages toward the street and features three tall windows set in Mughal style arches. It is also flanked by towers and crowned by an elaborate tri-level temple gateway. All of the City Hall towers are topped by traditional Burmese tiered-pyramidal roofs, known as pyatthat. A pair of large bronze ***nagas*** or Buddhist-Hindu serpent beings, an element usually found on temples, flank the entrance.

Contemporary Art in Southeast Asia

Independence came to Southeast Asia after World War II when the European colonial powers began, more or less willingly, to divest themselves of their overseas territories. Indonesia, the Philippines

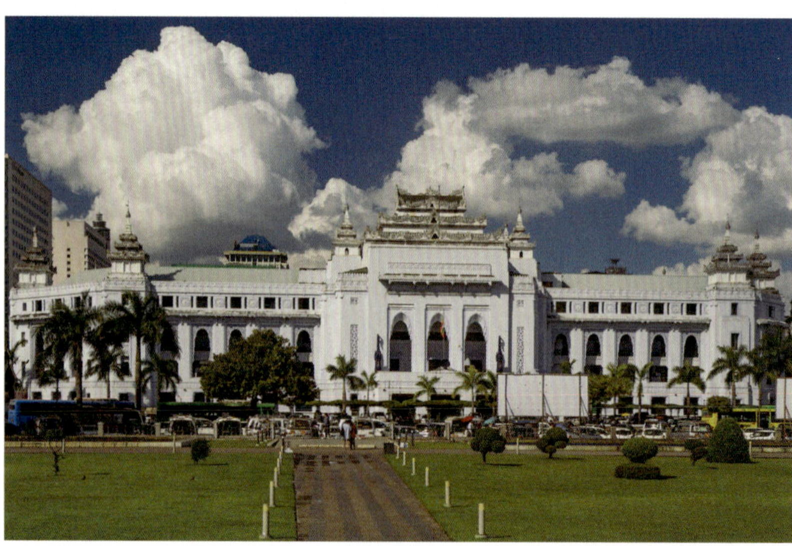

▶ **7.28** Myanmar, Sithu U Tin (1890–1972) Yangoon City Hall, 1925–1940 CE.

Built by a native Burmese architect during the British Colonial Era, the building blends traditional Burmese pyatthat roof towers and Mughal inspired window framing with an Art Deco–style structure.

(a U.S. possession), Burma, Malaya, Singapore, Cambodia, and Laos achieved independence within a decade of the end of the war. Vietnam was a different story, however, as the French wanted to retain control of their colony, a possibility rejected forcibly by the Vietnamese. The Vietnamese briefly achieved home rule on the battlefield after defeating French forces in the battle of Dien Bien Phu but in the ensuing peace negotiations (Geneva Conference 1954) the country was left divided, leading to the Second Indochina War. It was not until 1972 that Vietnam became a unified state.

Nowhere is the fallacy of a unified Southeast Asian region more evident than in the arts of the post–World War II era. Some artists embraced Western movements and the international art market, some went abroad, while others remained in country; some continued to work in traditional manners for traditional patrons, and still others had working styles and subject matter imposed by repressive governments. All of this creates a problem for art history, especially when written by foreign academics with preconceptions about the importance of modernism and regional coherence. The contemporary arts of this geographic region are as diverse as the experiences and practices of its artists; it is a living art filled with variety and contradiction.

Jirapat Tatsanasomboon (b. 1971), Thailand,* Forbidden Fruit: Rama versus Obama, *2009 A consistent theme in the work of Thai artist Jirapat Tatsanasomboon is the contest between East and

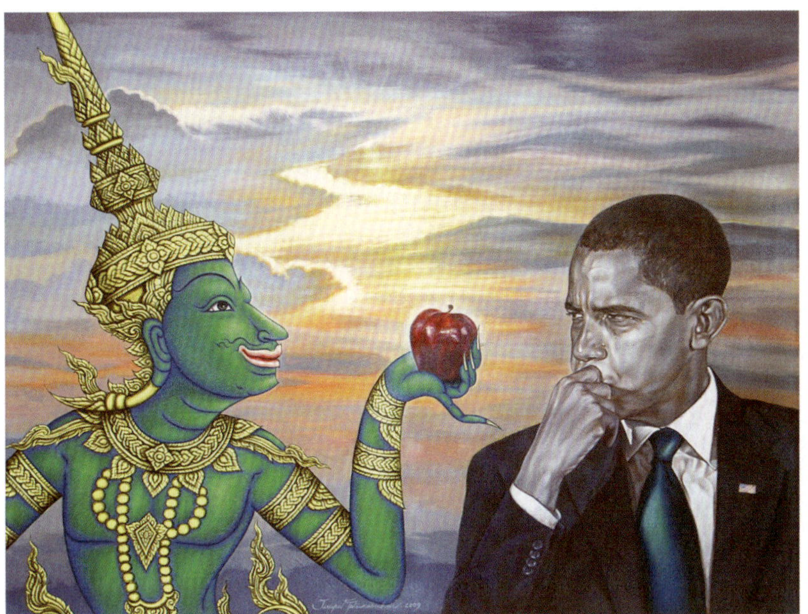

7.29 Thailand, Jirapat Tatsanasomboon (b. 1971), *Forbidden Fruit: Rama versus Obama*, 2009. Acrylic on canvas.

A theme in many of Jirapat's paintings is the struggle between East and West. In this painting he presents a symbolic clash of titans on many different levels from the crass to the profound.

West, between traditional Thai values and rampant Western consumerism. For much of the twentieth century Western modernism was a dominant influence on Thai artists. Jirapat challenged the presumed superiority of Western art in a series of pop art paintings that appropriate iconic works by artists such as Vincent van Gogh, Andy Warhol, Robert Indiana, Roy Lichtenstein, Fernando Botero, Frida Kahlo, and Georgia O'Keeffe, reinterpreting them as narratives from the *Ramakein*, the Thai version of the Ramayana. Jirapat deals with the impact of American popular culture in a series of paintings in which comic heroes such as Wonder Woman, Spiderman, Superman, Captain America, and even villains like the Green Goblin are pitted against characters such as Malyarap that are drawn from games. The almost religious worship of fame and celebrity in American life is fodder for a series of paintings featuring Hollywood icons like John Wayne, Elvis Presley, and Marilyn Monroe, juxtaposed against Buddhist prayer tablets and amulets.

In *Forbidden Fruit* (Figure 7.29), Jirapat takes a subtler approach to exploring the dichotomies of East and West by staging an interaction between the newly elected American president, and Rama, a manifestation of the god, Vishnu. As the hero of the Ramayana, Rama is considered to be the "Perfect Man" and "Lord of Virtue" because he followed his dharma. Here, however, Rama seems to take on the attributes of another of Vishnu's manifestations, the Buddha, specifically the Thai national protector, the Emerald Buddha in his rainy season tunic. The cartoonish Rama proffers an apple, suggesting the fruit of the tree of knowledge in the Garden of Eden, to a photo-realistic Obama. Obama stares intently at the forbidden fruit as if trying to decide whether or not to take the offering. Behind them the clouds part and the sun rises. Jirapata sets up some amusing oppositions and a few implied parallels in this painting: the perfect ruler of mythology versus the leader of the modern world, Thai superhero versus U.S. superpower, cartoon character versus real character, Eastern tradition versus Western capitalism, Hinduism/Buddhism versus Christianity, old beginnings (Genesis) versus a new day (current era) and between all is the apple with its own symbolic opposition in this case of the known versus the forbidden unknown.

Sopheap Pich (b. 1971), Cambodia,* Buddha 2, *2009 Sopheap Pich was born in Battambang in northwest Cambodia where his father was a farmer. When he was four years old the Khmer Rouge came to power. As the regime became more brutally oppressive, Pich's family left Cambodia, first living in a Thai refugee camp and them ultimately immigrating to the United States. Pich studied painting at the Art Institute of Chicago, graduating with a master's degree in 1999. He returned to Cambodia in 2002.

Pich began working with rattan and bamboo after his return because those were readily available materials in a country where there were no art supply stores. He liked the idea of these nontraditional, natural materials because it seemed to him that he was making his art out of nothing. His large-scale sculptures and installation pieces are far removed from the idea of simple basketry or porch furniture commonly evoked by rattan.

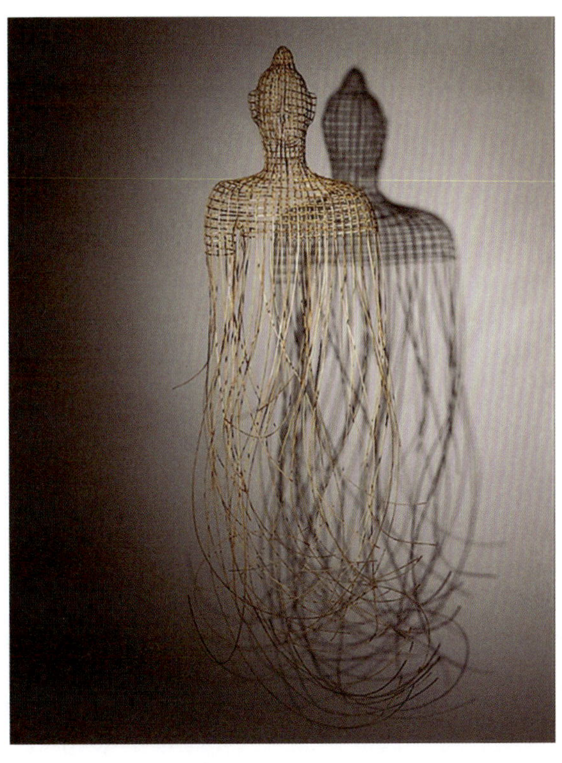

▲ **7.30** Cambodia, Sopheap Pich (b. 1971), *Buddha 2*, 2009.

Pich uses rattan and bamboo in his sculptures because they are readily available in a country with few art supply stores. *Buddha 2*, his first Buddha sculpture, was inspired by the blood-spattered floor of a neighborhood temple he had seen as a child during the Pol Pot era.

In *Buddha 2* (Figure 7.30) Pich presents a large, 100 inches (254 cm) long, rattan Buddha sculpture consisting of a skeletal-frame head and shoulders, and long streamers of unwoven rattan. The piece was inspired by childhood memories of a temple called Wat Ta Mim that was across from his family home. The Khmer Rouge had slain the monks and Pich remembered the temple floor was bloodstained, and so he dipped the ends of the rattan in ink to symbolize that blood. The construction seems transient and fragile but also allows for the natural play of light and shadow through the work; the second Buddha being the shadow of the first. The subject makes the work open to interpretation as a comment on religion and culture; in this case, perhaps, it is as much a statement about the fragility of human life and the loss of peace.

Nann Nann (Hnin Yin Nwe) (b. 1974), Myanmar,* Chaw Ei Thein, *n.d. The child of artists, Hnin Yin Nwe, also known as Nann Nann, grew up in an environment that nurtured her talents. In addition to her own studio practice, she is an art educator and furniture designer in Yangon. Having been raised in devoutly Buddhist Myanmar, religion is an element in her work as it is for many contemporary Burmese artists. However, instead of taking Buddhist monks, nuns, and temples as her subjects, she focuses on the spirituality of the religion in her work, making her paintings into a form of meditation.

Chaw Ei Thein (Figure 7.31) is an unusual work by Nann Nann, combining a portrait of the painter, performance artist, sculptor, singer and anti-junta activist Chaw Ei Thein, known for painting her face with lace-like patterns, with Nann's signature gold leaf squares. In this work the white crescent into which the gold squares seem to fall represents the artist's meditation seat; the gold squares represent acts of merit. In Buddhist practice the devout often make offerings of gold leaf to the temple and receive blessings in return, which the

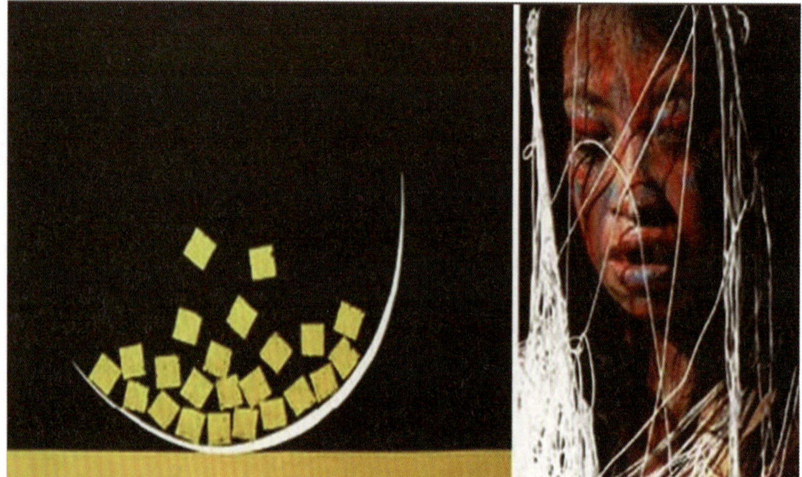

▶ 7.31 Myanmar, Nann Nann (b. 1974), *Chaw Ei Thein*, n.d.

The subject of this portrait is Chaw Ei Thein, a performance artist, sculptor, singer, and anti-junta activist who was known for painting her face with lace-like patterns. The gold squares are sheets of gold leaf, a signature element in Nann's work.

monks sometimes made concrete by binding the recipient's wrist with a string. The gold gifts individually are small acts but they add up to something important in the re-gilding of the pagoda. Nann has used gold leaf in her works for several years and sees each one has having a specific place in her works. There are a specific number of squares used in each work; too few or too many squares and the balance and harmony of the work is lost.

Chapter Quick Review

Neolithic Southeast Asia (4,000 BCE–300 CE)

- Ceramic making began at several sites in Southeast Asia during the third millennium BCE. Early forms ranged from elaborately painted jars and footed vessels to utilitarian plain wares, including lidded burial jars.
- Around 1500 BCE metalworkers in the region began casting copper and bronze vessels and drums and smelting iron for tools and weapons.

Indianization and Sinification in Medieval Southeast Asia (c. 500–1500 CE)

- Buddhism and Hinduism were introduced into Southeast Asia during the last centuries BCE and the first century CE. Both religions contributed significantly to the development of art and architecture in Southeast Asia, bringing styles, rituals, and works of literature such as the *Ramayana* to the region, which were adapted locally. Many temples built during this era showed a fusion of both Buddhist and Hindu architectural elements.
- After conquering various kingdoms in Cambodia, Laos, Thailand, and parts of Vietnam and the Malay Peninsula, Jayavarman II founded the Khmer Empire in 802, declared himself chakravartin, and established his rule under the principle of devaraja.

- New interpretations of the Buddha's image, based on the Pali Canon, appeared in the Kingdom of Sukhothai with the adoption of Theravada Buddhism.
- Chinese cultural and political dominance in northern Vietnam ends in 939 CE after more than a thousand years. Sufi Islam was introduced into Southeast Asia by Muslim traders sometime after 900 CE. Its impact on the mainland was small but it found ready acceptance in parts of Indonesia and the Malay Peninsula.
- The defining monuments of the period are Shwedagon Pagoda, Angkor Wat, Angkor Thom, Prambanan, and Borbudur, and the masjid Agung Demak.

Colonialism, Nationalism, and Modern Art in Southeast Asia (1511–1947)

- Portuguese, Dutch, and English traders arrived in the sixteenth and early seventeenth centuries, and began establishing outposts. The British expanded east from India, conquering Burma and adding parts of the Malay Peninsula to the empire.
- The French arrived in the mid-nineteenth century and began the conquest of Vietnam, Laos and Cambodia. Only Thailand under the Chakri Dynasty remained independent.
- The French established the first European emphasis art schools in Saigon and Hanoi, although European modernism had less impact in Southeast Asia than in other regions.
- Architecture during the Colonial Era followed prevailing European styles and was largely designed by European architects and engineers.

Contemporary Art in Southeast Asia

- With the exception of Vietnam, the former Southeast Asian colonies achieved their independence within a decade of the end of World War II. Vietnam's independence was delayed by the First Indochina War (1946–1954) and the Vietnam War (1956–1975).
- The post-war years were difficult for many newly independent Southeast Asian nations with civil war, communist takeovers, genocide, and military dictatorships taking a toll. Under the more repressive regimes, the production of art in other than Socialist Realist styles was suppressed.
- Today artists across Southeast Asia are actively engaged in the production of art in both traditional and contemporary styles.

Chapter Questions

1. Define the terms "Indianization" and "Sinification." Explain how the geographic position of Southeast Asia, as south of China and east of India, has both influenced and limited perceptions of its cultures and arts.
2. Describe how the Khmer, Sukhothai, and Ayutthayan rulers used art, concepts of chakravartin, devaraja, and buddharaja, or stories from the Ramayana to define their national and individual identities.

3. Southeast Asian artisans created unique Buddha forms such as Walking Buddhas and jewel Buddhas. Describe the characteristics of each and discuss how they differ from earlier Indian Gupta prototypes.
4. While derived from Indian stupa forms, the pagoda has been interpreted and elaborated in different ways across Southeast Asia. Using the Shwedagon as an example, describe the developments that are unique to Burmese pagoda forms.

Key Terms and Figures

Key Terms

Abhaya mudra "Have no Fear" mudra or hand gesture in which the Buddha or Bodhisattva raises his right hand to shoulder height with his palm facing outward to dispel fear and signal to his followers that they are welcome to approach.

Anubyanjana Eighty secondary characteristics of the Buddha described in the Pali Canon.

Arupa-dhatu "Formless Space" or the highest realm of existence in Buddhism.

Bhumisparsha mudra "Touch the earth" or "earth witness" mudra in which the fingers of the Buddha's right hand touch the earth to symbolize his enlightenment under the Bodhi tree.

Bicephalous Two-headed.

Chedi A stupa form unique to Sukhotai that sits on a square base and is crowned by a lotus bud tower. Wat Mahathat is an example.

Dharmachakra mudra Hand gesture in which the Buddha's hands seem to grasp and turn the wheel of Dharma, which the Buddha set into motion with his Sermon at the Deer Park.

Gu Artificial "cave temple" intended for meditation or devotional rituals.

Harihara Dual Hindu god who is both Vishnu (Hari) and Shiva (Hara), often represented in sculpture as a vertically divided figure, with each half wearing the costume and jewels and carrying the attributes of its god.

Jagati A raised platform, plinth, or terrace that serves as a base for a Hindu or Buddhist temple.

Joglo A form of Javanese vernacular architecture in which elevated, square-plan houses are topped with high peaked-gable roofs.

Kama-dhatu In Buddhism the desire realm, one of the three form realms into which beings may be reborn.

Kentong A type of wooden slit drum sometimes used in Javanese mosques to call the faithful to prayer.

Lakshana The thirty-two primary characteristics of the Buddha described in the Pali Canon.

Lotus bud tower A type of graduated-tier tower unique to Sukhotai architecture with a bud-shaped element below the crowning finial.

Mandala In Hinduism and Buddhism symbolic diagram of the universe; it may be a two-dimensional form such as a geometric pattern, or rendered in three dimensions like a temple such as Borobudur.

Nagas The Nagas were semidivine human-cobra hybrid beings common to Hindu, Buddhist, and Jain mythology. In art they may be represented a half human and half serpent or as fully human or fully serpent, and are associated with bodies of water.

Prang A Khmer temple tower form that is often richly ornamented with sculpture or in Thai examples, may be vertically grooved. Such towers are common elements of both Hindu and Buddhist Khmer and Khmer-influenced architecture.

Pyatthat A type of multitiered pyramidal roof, originating in Bagan architecture and common to Burmese Buddhist temples. The Ananda Temple in Bagan is an example. Typically, pyatthat have an odd number of levels.

Quincunx In architecture an arrangement of five towers with four marking the points of a square or rectangle and the last occupying the center point of the design.

Royal ease pose A less formal seated pose common to the depiction of bodhisattvas and kings in which one leg is raised while the other is relaxed and one arm is draped over the upright knee. See the depiction of Suryavarman II (Figure 7.11) for an example.

Rupa-dhatu Realm of form above the desire realm in which beings are freed from the distractions of physical sensation and can exist in a constant state of meditation.

Serambi A type of veranda derived from Javanese vernacular architecture.

Soko guru In Javanese architecture the soko guru are the main supporting posts.

Sufism A mystical form of Islam that evolved from early ascetic practices in which the adherent seeks the experience of divine love and wisdom through a close personal relationship with Allah.

Trimurti The Hindu trinity of Brahma, Vishnu, and Shiva.

Varada mudra A downward gesture of the left hand in which the palm is up and the fingers extended, symbolizing the giving of charity. It is commonly seen in Buddhist statues in Southeast Asia, often in conjunction with a right hand Abhaya mudra.

Wali Songo Nine revered Muslim saints credited with bringing Islam to Indonesia, particularly venerated on the island of Java.

Wat In Cambodia and Thailand the word "wat" designates a temple.

Key Figures

Anawrahta—Eleventh century king of Bagan who converted to Theravada Buddhism and encouraged his people to convert as well. He and his successors are said to have built ten thousand temples.

Chaophraya Chakri—The Ayutthaya general chosen to succeeded Taksin. He founded the Rattanakosin Kingdom, taking the throne as Rama I and establishing his capital at Bangkok. He retrieved the Emerald Buddha from Laos and enshrined it in Wat Phra Kaew.

Hsinbyushin—Eighteenth century king of the Burmese Konbaung Dynasty who raised the Shwedagon Pagoda to its current height of 326 feet.

Jayavarman II—Founder of the Khmer Empire.

Jayavarman VII—Khmer king who built Angkor Thom and the Bayon Temple.

Kyanzittha—King of Bagan and patron of the Ananda Temple.

Phraya Taksin—Chinese-Thai general of Ayutthaya who usurped the throne, reunited Thailand after the Burmese invasion, but became an increasingly despotic ruler. He was deposed and executed.

Ramathibodi I—Founder of kingdom Ayutthaya using the Ramayana as a model

Shinsawbu—Fifteenth century queen of the Burmese Kingdom of Hanthawaddy who donated her weight in gold to gild the Shwedagon pagoda.

Sri Intraditya—Founder of independent kingdom of Sukhotai.

Suryavarman II—Khmer king who built Angkor Wat.

Bibliography

Brown, Robert L. "God on Earth: The Walking Buddha in the Art of South and Southeast Asia." *Artibus Asiae* 50, no. 1–2 (1990): 73–107.

Chapman, William. *A Heritage of Ruins: The Ancient Sites of Southeast Asia and their Conservation*. University of Hawai'i Press, 2013.

Church, Peter. *A Short History of South-East Asia*. 5th edition. Singapore: John Wiley & Sons (Asia) Pte. Ltd., 2009.

Degroot, V. , and M. J. Klokke, editors. *Unearthing Southeast Asia's Past: Selected Papers from the 12th Conference of the EurASEAA*. Vol. 1, 64–75. Singapore: National University of Singapore Press, 2012.

Fontaine, Henri. "On the Extent of the Sa-Huynh Culture in Continental Southeast Asia." *Asian Perspectives* 23, no. 1 (1980): 67–69.

Higham, Charles, and Rachanie Thosarat. *Prehistoric Thailand: From Early Settlement to Sukhothai*. Bangkok: River Books, 1998.

Hla Tin Htun. *Old Myanmar Paintings in the Collection of U Win*. Bangkok: Thavibu Gallery, 2006.

Hodges, Ian. "Time in Transition: King Narai and the Luang Prasoet Chronicle of Ayutthaya." *Journal of the Siam Society* 87, nos. 1–2 (1999): 33–44.

Kempers, A. J. Bernet. *Ancient Indonesian Art*. Cambridge MA: Harvard University Press, 1959.

Kerlogue, Fiona. *Arts of Southeast Asia*. World of Art Series. London: Thames and Hudson, 2004.

Lippe, Aschwin. "A Dvaravati Bronze Buddha from Thailand." *Metropolitan Museum of Art Bulletin* 19, no. 5 (January 1961): 125–132.

Mourer, Cécile, and Roland Mourer. "Prehistoric Research in Cambodia During the Last Ten Years." *Asian Perspectives* 14 (1971): 35–42.

Nguyen Quan, and Duong Tuong. "Western Culture in Vietnam." *Journal of Decorative and Propaganda Arts* 20 (1994): 224–235.

O'Reilly, Dougald J. W. *Early Civilizations of Southeast Asia*. Lanham, MD: AltaMira Press, 2007.

Osborne, Milton. *Southeast Asia an Introductory History*. 11th edition. Sydney: Allen & Unwin, 2013.

Pettifor, Steven. "Cultural Confrontations." *Asian Art News* (September/October 2008): 114–117.

Rooney, Dawn. *Angkor: Cambodia's Wondrous Khmer Temples*. Hong Kong: Odyssey, 2007.

Sharif, Harlina Md., and Hazman Hazumi. "The Vernacular Mosques of the Malay World: Cultural Interpretations of Islamic Aspirations." https://www.academia.edu/8057262/The_Vernacular_Mosques_of_the_Malay_World_Cultural_Interpretation_of_Islamic_Aspirations

Sireekan, Rathsaran. *Intercultural Journey: The Art of Jirapat Tatsanasomboon.* Bangkok: Thavibu Gallery, 2014.

Strachan, Paul. *Imperial Pagan: Art and Architecture of Burma.* Honolulu: University of Hawai'i Press, 1989.

Taylor, Nora A., and Boreth Ly, editors. *Modern and Contemporary Southeast Asian Art: An Anthology.* Ithaca, NY: Cornell Southeast Asia Program Publications, 2012.

Wei Yan Aung. "Influential Artist Honored 70 Years after Death." *The Irrawaddy Newsletter.* July 27, 2017. https://www.irrawaddy.com/culture/influential-artist-honored-70-years-death.html

White, Joyce C. *Ban Chiang.* Philadelphia: University of Pennsylvania Press, 1982.

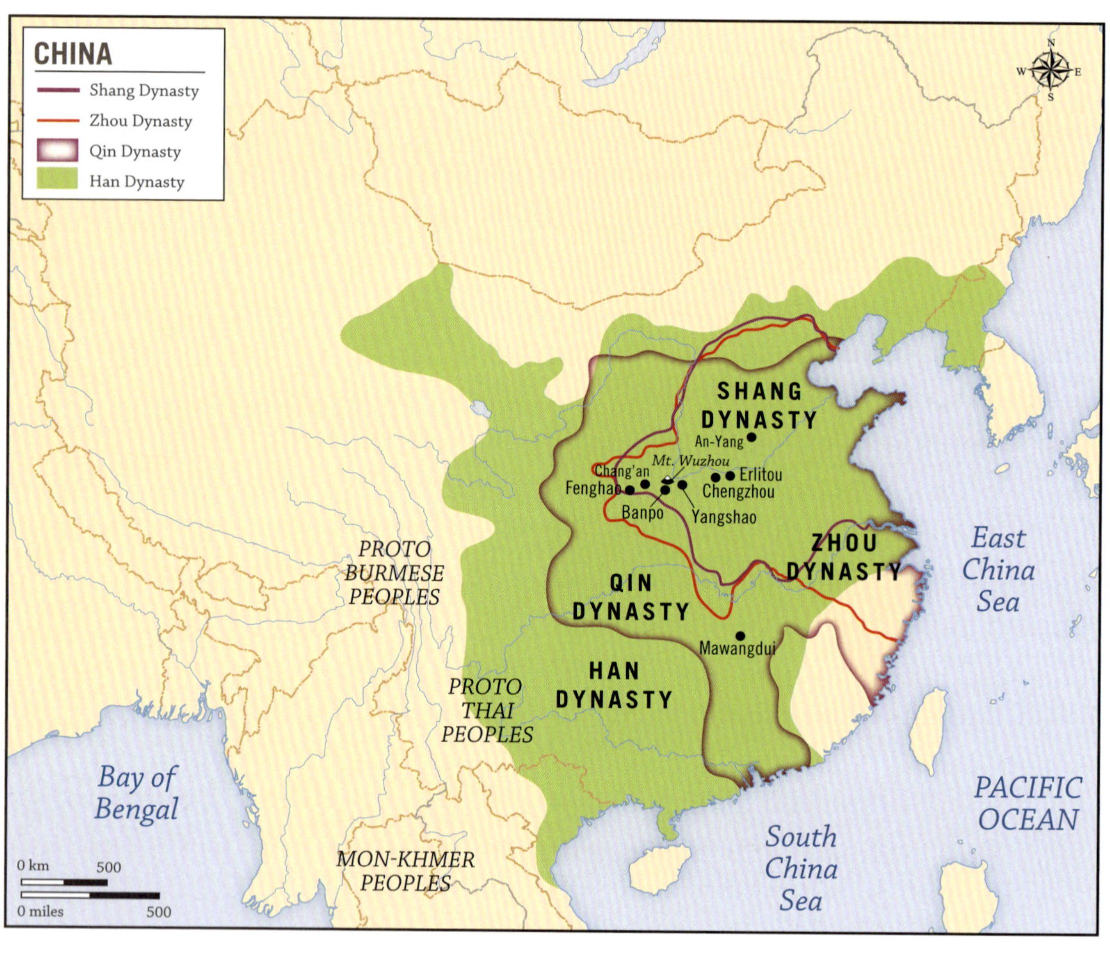
CHINA
Shang Dynasty
Zhou Dynasty
Qin Dynasty
Han Dynasty
N
W
E
S
SHANG DYNASTY
An-Yang
Mt. Wuzhou
Chang'an
Erlitou
Fenghao
Chengzhou
Banpo
Yangshao
ZHOU DYNASTY
QIN DYNASTY
Mawangdui
HAN DYNASTY
PROTO BURMESE PEOPLES
PROTO THAI PEOPLES
MON-KHMER PEOPLES
East China Sea
PACIFIC OCEAN
South China Sea
Bay of Bengal
0 km 500
0 miles 500

China

8

Brief Overview

The "Middle Kingdom," as China has been known for more than three thousand years, boasts the world's longest continuous civilization and art history. Pottery-making began earlier in China than anywhere else. In 1961, pottery sherds dating to 18,000 BCE, were discovered at Xianrendong Cave in Jiangxi Province and more recently, in 2009, pottery fragments dating to 16,000 BCE were found at Yuchanyan Cave in Hunan Province. By the time permanent agricultural settlements sprang up along the Yellow and Yangtze rivers, Chinese artisans working at Yangshao and other sites were producing beautifully painted wares in which vessel form and decorative motifs were fully and aesthetically integrated. Although not well-known in the West, numerous early rock art sites, some dating back to 12,000 BCE, have been found, which show that painting has also had a long history of practice in China. In the fourth millennium BCE Chinese artisans using stone tools began the tradition of jade carving, creating ritual Bi and Kong as well as ceremonial weapons for use in mortuary contexts.

Chapter Objectives

1. Recognize and be able to describe stylistic characteristics, media, and technologies from key periods in Chinese art history, including the Shang, Zhou, Han, Song, Yuan, and Ming.
2. Understand and be able to provide examples of how Buddhism, Confucianism, and Daoism traditions influenced the development of Chinese art.
3. Trace the development of tradition Chinese landscape painting from the Han Dynasty to modern times.
4. Describe the impact of the period of communist rule, the Cultural Revolution, and the post-Mao liberalizations on the art in modern China.

The beginning of the Bronze Age in China was marked by the rise of state level societies, the development of writing, and the association of art production with state rituals. Chinese rulers and feudal lords commissioned works of jade and cast bronze to propitiate the gods and ancestors, and for their own use in the afterlife. Artists and artisans working under court patronage went on to invent papermaking, the potter's wheel, silk-weaving, lacquer ware, and ink painting in a variety of artistic genres. Indigenous philosophies such as Confucianism and Daoism, and the introduction of Buddhism from India further enriched Chinese art, adding new themes and subjects. Over time, artists in China were accorded status, not on the basis

timeline

DATE	TYPE	EVENT
		BCE
c. 18,000	Art	First ceramics, Xianrendong Cave, Jiangxi Province
c. 16,000	Art	Second oldest ceramics, Yuchanyan Cave, Hunan
c. 8000	History	First settlements established along the Yellow and Yangtzi
c. 5000	Art	Yangshao pottery
c. 3400	Art	Liangzhu jade working began
c. 2700	Art	Silk-making began
c. 2100	History	Xia Dynasty founded
c. 1600	History	Xia overthrown by Shang
	Culture	Oracle bones used for divination; earliest writing
	Art	Piece mold bronze casting invented
c. 1066	History	Zhou conquer Shang; Western Zhou capital at Haojing
	History	Mandate of Heaven formulated to justify Zhou rule
	Culture	I Ching used for divination
c. 771	History	Western capital lost to Quanrong; Eastern Zhou period started
c. 722	History	*Spring and Autumn Annals* written
c. 700	Art	Lost wax casting developed in China
c. 600	Culture	Laozi, founder of Daoism, born
c. 551	Culture	Confucius, founder of Confucian philosophy, born in State of Lu
c. 544	Culture	Sun Tzu, general who wrote *The Art of War*, born
c. 500	Art	*Kao Gong Ji "Book of Diverse Crafts"* studio practice manual written
	Art	Metal inlay and depletion gilding practiced
c. 475	History	Start of Warring States Period
433	Art	Marquis Yi of Zheng buried with 10,000 musical instruments
c. 390	Culture	Shang Yang, formulator of Legalism as political theory, born
c. 296	Culture	*Bamboo Annals* written
256	History	Zhou capital captured and last Zhou king murdered
c. 246	Art	Manufacture of Terracotta Warriors begun
221	History	Qin Dynasty established by Qin Shi Huang

DATE	TYPE	EVENT
BCE		
	History	Writing, money, weights, width of cart axles standardized
220	History	Great Wall of China built
213	Culture	Confucian and Daoist scholars purged;
		Buddhism banned; history books before the Qin burned
206	History	Liu Pang established Han Dynasty
c. 168	Art	Lady Dai (Xin Zhui) buried in Mawangdui
150	Art	Paper invented in China
c. 109	Culture	Sima Qian's *Records of the Grand Historian* written *Classic of History* written
CE		
c. 9	History	Beginning of fourteen-year Wang Mang interregnum (Xin dyasty)
c. 68	Culture	Han Mindi welcomed first Buddhist missionaries to China
105	Art	Cai Lun improves paper with addition of hemp, rags, and fishnets
220	History	Han dynasty collapsed
	History	Three Kingdoms of Wei, Shu and Wu established
222	History	Six Dynasties begun in the south
265	History	Western Jin Dynasty founded
304	History	Sixteen Kingdoms formed in north China
317	History	Fall of Western Jin dynasty
c. 338	Art	Gilt-Bronze Shakyamuni Buddha created in China
c. 345	Art	Gu Kaizhi born
386	History	Northern Wei Dynasty established
c. 400	Culture	*Admonitions of the Instructress* painted by Gu Kaizhi
402	Culture	Introduction of Pure Land Buddhism
420	History	Southern and Northern Dynasties begin
428	History	Sixteen Kingdoms collapsed
c. 440	Art	Yungang Cave 20 Buddha carved
453	Art	Emperor Wencheng commissioned Imperial caves at Yungang

(*Continued*)

timeline *continued*

DATE	TYPE	EVENT
		CE
535	History	Northern Wei collapsed
589	History	Six Dynasties period ended; China united under the Sui dynasty
c. 600	Art	Woodblock printing invented in
		China Chan Buddhism introduced
618	History	Tang dynasty established
624	History	Wu Zetian born
c. 650	Art	*The Thirteen Emperors Handscroll* painted by Yan Liben
652	Art	Great Wild Goose Pagoda built by Emperor Gaozong
690	History	Wu Zetian took throne as empress
	Art	Vairocana Buddha of Fengxian Grotto carved
704	Art	Wu Zetian rebuilt Great Wild Goose Pagoda, adding five stories
706	Art	Qianling Mausoleum; Prince Zhang Huai tomb murals painted
c. 750	Art	Dunghuang Cave 172 cut and decorated
751	History	Tang armies defeated at Battle of Talas River in Central Asia
782	Art	Nanchan Temple Great Buddha Hall built
c. 850	History	Gunpowder invented
907	History	Start of Five Dynasties and Ten Kingdoms period
960	History	Sung dynasty established
	Art	Fan Kuan born about this time
1007	History	First paper money printed
1020	Art	Painter Guo Xi born
1041	Art	First moveable type (clay) invented
1072	Art	Guo Xi painted *Early Spring*
1101	History	Emperor Huizong acceded to the Song dynasty throne
	Art	Finches and bamboo painted by Huizong
	Art	Huizong invents shoujinti script
	Art	Huizong founded first Imperial Art Museum; catalogued collection
1126	History	Northern Sung territory lost to the Manchurian Jin Dynasty
1127	History	Zhao Gou established Southern Sung Empire

DATE	TYPE	EVENT
CE		
1140	Art	Ten Thousand Volume Hall constructed by Shi Zhengzhi
1195	Art	May Yuan Southern Sung court painter active
1246	Art	Liang Kai painted *Sixth Chan Patriarch Chopping Bamboo*
1206	History	Genghis Khan (Tenujin) became leader of the Mongols
1279	History	Kublai Khan defeated the Sung, declares Yuan dynasty
1296	Art	Zhao Mengfu painted *Groom and Horse*
1308	Art	Guan Dao Sheng painted *Bamboo Groves in Mist and Rain*
1335	Art	Wu Zhen painted *Crooked Pine*
1347	Art	Huang Gongwang painted *Dwelling in the Fuchun Mountains*
1351	Art	First Cobalt Blue underglaze porcelains made in China
1368	History	Ming Dynasty founded by Emperor Hong Wu
1372	Art	Ni Zan painted *Rongxi Studio*
1378	Art	Wang Meng painted *Forest Grotto in Juqu*
1402	Art	Construction of Forbidden City begun in Beijing
1467	Art	Shen Zhou painted *Lofty Mount Lu* for his teacher
1617	Art	Dong Qichang completed *The Qingbian Mountains*
1644	History	Qing dynasty established
1660	Art	Shitao active as a painter; avoided Qing court
1765	Art	Ten Thousand Volume Hall restored and renamed Master of the Fishing Nets Garden by Song Zongyuan
1864	History	Dowager Empress Cixi in control of China
1899	History	Boxer Rebellion begun
1911	History	Wuchang Uprising; Qing overthrown
1912	History	Republic of China declared; Sun Yat Sen first president
1937	History	Japanese invasion
1942	Art	Mao Zedong's Yenan Forum speech: art must service the party
1946	History	Mao Zedong established the Peoples' Republic of China Republic of China re-established in Taiwan
1966	History	Cultural Revolution begun

(*Continued*)

timeline *continued*

DATE	TYPE	EVENT
		CE
1976	History	Cultural Revolution ended with death of Mao
1979	Art	Xingxing or "Stars" Group
1985	Art	'85 New Wave movement
1986	Art	Xiamen Dada Group founded

of the type of art produced, but whether or not they accepted monetary payment. Those who worked for pay were considered "professional" artists and remain largely unknown; those associated with the courts, who did not sell their works, constituted an elite class of "scholar-artists," whose names and works fill the pages of Chinese art history.

In the modern era the Peoples' Republic of China is not only the most populous nation on earth but the world's second largest art market. Contemporary China has a vibrant and diverse art scene that has garnered considerable international attention. Chinese artists work in a variety of traditional Asian and modern Western media and styles, creating a wide range of paintings, sculpture, graphic arts, digital media, photography, and performance art.

Neolithic China (c. 18,000–2000 BCE)

Between the sixth and third millenniums BCE several advanced pottery-making and stone-working cultures appeared in China. These early potters were producing fine hand-built ceramics in a variety of forms, some of quite large size, and decorated with incised or painted designs featuring geometric and organic motifs. What is especially remarkable about these early wares is that they seem to express a well-developed aesthetic in which form and decoration are intrinsically integrated, ornamental motifs perfectly enhancing and following vessel forms. In addition to ceramics, by 4900 BCE, Chinese jade-workers were carving elegant ***Bi*** disks, representing the circle of the heavens and ***Kong*** forms, symbolizing the square of the earth.

Yangshao Culture (c. 5000–3000 BCE)

Some of the most spectacular Neolithic ceramics come from the Yangshao culture, in Henan, Shaanxi, and Shanxi provinces. Terracotta wares found in Yangshao (1921) and Banpo (1953) came from burials, suggesting that they were ritual rather than utilitarian or everyday vessels. Yangshao pottery is remarkable for its wide variety of forms: amphorae, pedestal bowls, jars, and pitchers. Although hand-built before the invention of the potter's wheel, Yangshao coil-constructed and scraped vessels are astonishingly symmetrical and thin-walled. Decoration was done by brushing red and brownish-black mineral "inks" onto a cream clay body. The most common designs were geometric patterns but occasionally stylized human, animal, and floral motifs have also been found.

Painted Earthenware Jar, c. 3900–3000 BCE The symmetry of form and uniformly thin walls of the 4 inch (12.2 cm) high globular Painted Earthenware Jar (Figure 8.1) are impressive. The shoulder of the jar is decorated with a band of cream daisy-like flowers, defined by a negative ground. Because the vessel was painted with pigment inks rather than clay slips, it has a flat matte finish. The vessel's rim was painted in a similar manner to define a cream square, enclosing the dark circle of the opening, a combination that seems to suggest the circle-in-square design and earth-sky symbolism of jade kongs.

The Three Dynasties Period (2070–221 BCE)

Early Chinese accounts, the *Bamboo Annals* (c. 296 BCE), *Classic of History*, and the *Records of the Grand Historian* (both c. 109 BCE), begin the story of Chinese history with the rule of the Yellow Emperor, the mythical ancestor of the Chinese people and bringer of civilization. He was succeeded by four legendary sage-kings before the formation of the first historical dynasties of the Xia, Shang, and Zhou.

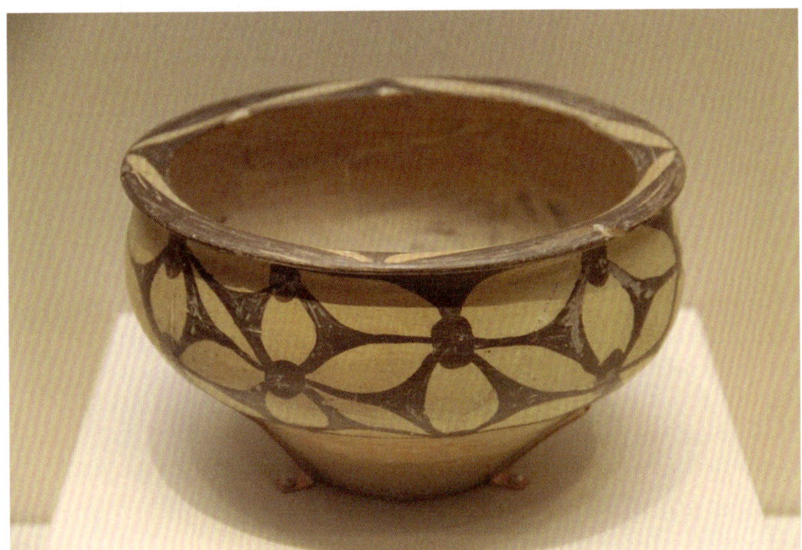

◀ **8.1** Yangshao Miaodigou type, c. 3900–3000 BCE. Negative painted brown pigment on buff clay, 4 in. × 8 in.

The matt surface of Yangshao pottery is a result of the use of pigment inks rather than clay slips.

TAKE A CLOSER LOOK

Chinese Jade Kong and Bi

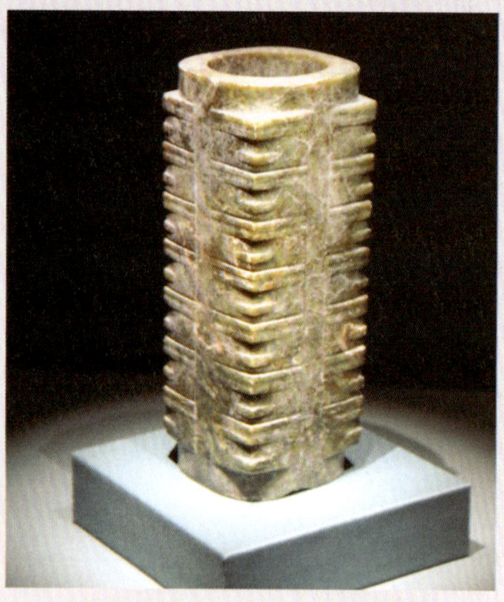

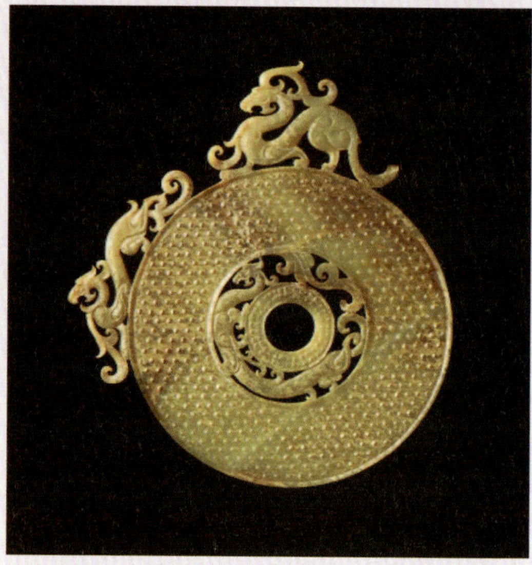

▲ **8.2** *Left: Jade Kong, Liangzhu Culture, c. 3200–2250 BCE ; Right: Jade Bi Disk with Dragons, Zhou Period, c. 771–256 BCE*

Jade working began during the Neolithic period in China but continued as a highly prized craft through subsequent periods into modern times. Chinese jade is nephrite, often called "soft jade," but it was still a remarkably hard stone, harder than any metal known to the ancient Chinese. It comes in a variety of colors, some, such as white jade, being more highly prized than others. To create objects of jade, Chinese lapidaries laboriously cut nephrite into rough forms and then ground down the stone using sand or quartz grit abrasives. Central openings were drilled using hollow tubes filled with abrasives, while fine cutwork, sometimes seen on Bi disks, was done using a string saw.

Chinese jade comes in a range of natural colors – green, white, lavender, red, black, and yellow. Certain colors were associated with the heavens, earth, cardinal directions, and by Confucius with the virtues of a gentleman. Throughout Chinese history jade was considered more valuable than gold and silver and thus conveyed rank and status; it was also believed to protect the wearer from injury and illness and to ensure immortality when buried with the dead.

The two most common forms found in burials are the Kong (above left) and Bi (above right). Kongs are thought to represent the square of the earth; their hollow cylindrical center suggests the place of the axis mundi, often symbolized as a pole or world tree at the center of the universe. The circular Bi represented the heavens.

By the Zhou period jade carving had reached technical perfection as seen in the *Bi Disk with Dragons*, which has been ground down to an exceptional thinness to enhance the translucency of the stone. Along the outer edge of the disk parade a pair of sinuous dragons; a third dragon, trailing a plume of smoke, curves around the center opening of the disk. Chinese dragons are hybrid creatures created from parts of nine animals and they appear in five colors, each with its own symbolic significance. Dragons were capable of flight and so were considered to be messengers between the heavenly realm and the earth, where they resided beneath the surface or in rivers and oceans. The positioning of dragons on the inner circle and outer rim of the Bi disk may reflect the two realms the mythical beast inhabited.

The Xia Dynasty (c. 2070–1600 BCE)

Sima Qian in his *Records of the Grand Historian* describes the rule of seventeen Xia kings before the last despotic king was overthrown by the Shang. Western scholars have long dismissed the Xia as a legendary dynasty, as they once did the Shang. The problem is that many supposed Xia cities, including the presumptive capital at Erlitou, were subsequently occupied by the Shang, making it difficult to ascertain where one culture ends and the next begins, particularly because the artifacts of both cultures are similar. Although the question of the Xia is far from resolved, what are believed to be Xia-era tombs were found at Lao Niu Po, Shaanxi province in 2010. While containing artifacts of a type consistent with probable Xia materials excavated at Erlitou, the four Lao Niu Po tombs did not contain any admixture of identifiably Shang materials (People's Daily Online 2011).

The Shang Dynasty (1766–1111 BCE)

The Shang Dynasty was founded by Zi Lu, a tribal warlord, who took the throne as Cheng Tang and established the first dynastic capital at Shang near the modern city of Zhengzhou. Over the six-hundred-year history of the Shang, its capital was moved at least five times, the last capital being Yin near Anyang. Excavations, begun at the site in 1928, revealed eleven Shang royal tombs, some 30 feet (9.1 m) to 60 feet (18 m) deep. These pit-type tombs typically had a wooden mortuary chamber and several adjoining offering rooms, often arranged in a cruciform pattern. During construction and furnishing of the tombs, they were accessed by means of a long ramp. The treasuries of these tombs contained some of the earliest known examples of Chinese writing in the form of thousands of animal bones and tortoise shells inscribed with archaic pictographic characters. The bones and carapaces were used for divination, and hence are known as **oracle bones**. The ruler's questions concerning military strategy, the ancestors, or perhaps the birth of an heir were inscribed onto the bones and then cast into a fire. The crack patterns resulting from the heating of the bones were then interpreted by diviners to answer the king's questions. The Shang royal tombs also contain offerings of worked jade and thousands of cast bronzes, ranging from small tripod vessels for heating wine to large cooking urns weighing as much as 400 pounds.

SHANG BRONZES

Shang bronze foundries produced at least twenty-four distinct vessel forms using a unique method of casting, known as piece-mold casting. Early Shang piece-mold cast bronzes are easy to identify by their flanges, which are a result of the molten bronze seeping between the mold sections. Because the complete removal of flanges was especially

TAKE A CLOSER LOOK
Piece-Mold Casting

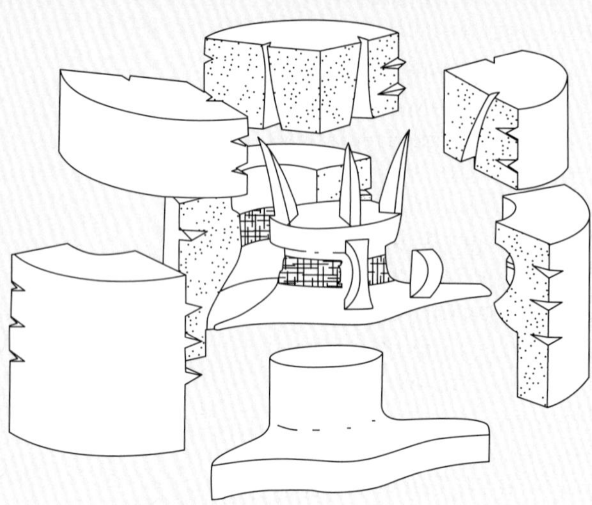

▲ 8.3 *Diagram of mold sections needed to cast a bronze tripod vessel.*

In most of the ancient world bronze casting was done using the lost wax process; however, the earliest bronze casting in China was done without wax using a complex piece-mold process instead. The reasons for this deviation might be related to the difficulty of obtaining beeswax as the practice of beekeeping in China can only be traced back to the second century CE with any reliability. Prior to this time and well into the seventeenth century honey and wax were primarily collected from wild bees (Pattinson 2012, 236–237). Although the lost wax casting process is thought to have been known during the Shang Dynasty, it was little used before the seventh century BCE.

- The process of piece-mold casting began with the creation of a clay original (center of diagram), complete with applied decoration.
- The clay original was allowed to dry leather-hard before it is encased in fresh clay to create the mold. When the added clay reached the correct dryness, it was sliced into sections and the mold removed from the original. Large or complex pieces might have required several molds stacked in sections (see diagram).
- The clay original was then shaved down (see bottom center) to serve as the core and provide the interior space of the vessel.
- The clay mold was reassembled around the core, the joints sealed on the outside with fresh clay, and the molten bronze poured into the mold. Stacked molds might require repeated bronze pours.

difficult on the highly decorated surfaces, Shang artists typically incorporated them into the overall design of the vessel. Typical Shang decoration was zoomorphic, featuring both real animals (deer, rams, elephants, and birds), and mythical beasts such as dragons. The animals were often arranged on the surface of the vessel to form the elements of a taotie mask. Although sometimes difficult to see on the densely ornamented surfaces, the taotie monster can be recognized by its prominent eyes; once the eyes have been located the other elements, often dragons, come into focus as the creature's nose, eyebrows, fangs, and ears. Later advances in mold-making and casting techniques reduced the problem of bronze seepage eliminating the flanges.

The Shang were not the only early peoples in China to discover a method of bronze casting. Some scholars believe that casting may have begun prior to the Shang Dynasty. Stone casting molds are known from the Xia era. The 1986 excavations at Sanxingdui, near Chengdu in southern China revealed the existence of another bronze-working culture that was contemporaneous with the late Shang. The Sanxingdui Culture (c. 1200–1000 BCE) bronze casters added higher amounts of lead to the copper and tin mix to create an alloy that allowed them to construct monumental bronze sculptures using multi-stage molds and sequential bronze pours.

Guang*, c. 1200–1050 BCE** A Shang ***guang or ritual wine vessel (Figure 8.4), probably from Anyang, is a fine example of Shang-style piece-mold bronze work. This type of vessel was used for pouring wine offerings over the altars of ancestors. It takes the form of a horned dragon with a humorous bug-eyed face and toothy grin, whose body is completely covered with a complex decorative scheme that combines both modeled and higher-relief zoomorphic forms, some twenty different dragons and birds, together with a geometric low-relief background pattern. Two large taotie or monster masks appear on the sides of the pitcher and two smaller ones are found under the chin and tail of the large dragon. The handle is another animal.

A four-part mold was used to form the pitcher and a two-part one for the lid. The artist has incorporated the mold flanges, formed in the pouring of the bronze, into the design scheme, using them to create the spine of the dragon on the lid and the noses of the taotie masks on the sides. Shang bronze casters are known to have manipulated the surface color and sheen with addition of gold, silver, lead, or arsenic to the

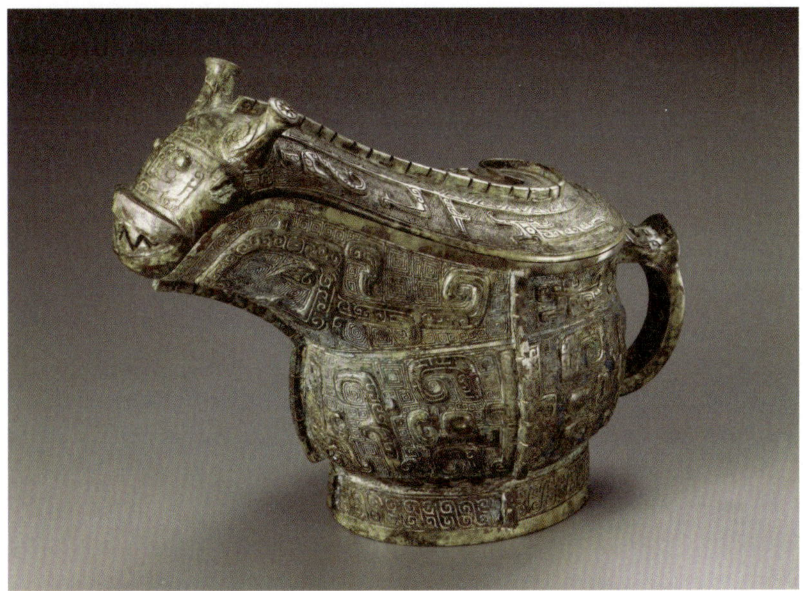

◀ **8.4** Shang, Ritual Wine Vessel (Guang), c. 1200–1046 BCE. Bronze, 6.50 in. × 3.25 in. × 8.50 in.

The surface of this wine serving vessel is decorated with dragons that swim against a low-relief background pattern. On the belly of the vessel the flange resulting from the piece-mold casting process forms the nose of a taotie mask with the dragons forming its eyebrows and horns. Circles on either side of the nose form eyes.

melting crucible. The silvery gray surface of this guang was the result of the addition of lead to the alloy.

The Zhou (1100–221 BCE)

The Zhou had once been vassals of the Shang but after a long period of misrule, they overthrew the Shang. They justified their takeover by advancing the concept of the **Mandate of Heaven**. As a political theory the Mandate of Heaven suggests that the power to rule is divinely given and maintained for as long as the rule is just and virtuous.

The Zhou referred to their kingdom as ***Zhongguó***, meaning "Middle Kingdom" to suggest a cultural core that distinguished them from their less advanced neighbors. To govern their territory, the Zhou created a feudal system, the ***fengjian***, which distributed grants of land to be administered by nobles and court officials loyal to the king. Feudalism allowed the Zhou to administer a vast territory but ultimately it brought down the state. The first Zhou capital was at Fenghao, but after the loss of its western territories in 771 BCE, the government was moved east to Chengzhou. The relocation of the capital marks the historical division of the Zhou into the Western and the Eastern periods.

WESTERN ZHOU PERIOD (1100–771 BCE)

The Western Zhou period was a time of economic prosperity and cultural advancement. During this era the sciences of astronomy, physics, and mathematics advanced, a working calendar was developed, and the arts flourished under Imperial and feudal patronage. The Early Zhou were not stylistically progressive. They adopted Shang religion, philosophy, and aesthetics, and employed artists who had worked for the Shang. Thus, their early bronzes are nearly indistinguishable from those of the Shang. However, by the ninth century BCE, the Zhou began to define a unique style.

A Matched Pair of Western Zhou Hu, c. 1046–771 BCE This remarkable pair of bronze ***hu*** or wine vessels (Figure 8.5) illustrates the increasing refinement of bronze casting during the Western Zhou period. Although the surfaces of these large vessels are not as crowded as examples from the Shang era and there are no apparent flanges, these squared pear-shaped vessels seem heavy and clumsy in comparison to the earlier forms. The ornamental scheme divides each face of the hu into four quadrants separated by wide crossed bands. In the center of each side is a raised diamond-shaped boss. The prominent taotie masks of the Shang have been greatly reduced, consisting in these vessels only as pairs of circular "eye" motifs bracketed by stylized dragons. These dragons, so prominent on Shang vessels, have been reduced to little more than a series of hooked elements on these vessels. The long-nosed dragons, modeled as loops on either side of each wine container, form the horns of the taotie monster. As the Shang animal mask lost

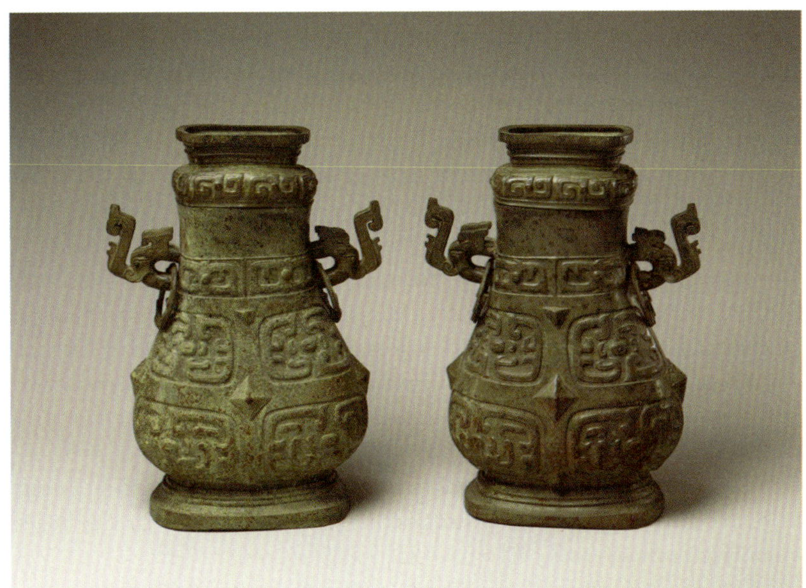

◀ **8.5** Western Zhou, Matched Hu or Wine Vessels, c. 1046–771 BCE. Bronze, 21.75 in. × 14.75 in.

The taotie monster masks on these vessels are subtler than under the Shang. The diamond boss forms the nose and the eyes are found in the center of the upper quadrants, while the handles form the horns of the mask.

its symbolic meaning under the Zhou, it dissolved into an ornamental pattern, as here, where an "eye" is encircled by curving hooked lines

EASTERN ZHOU PERIOD (770–221 BCE)

The Western Zhou era ended in 771 BCE when a foolish king, Zhou You, became infatuated with a young concubine named Baosi, who persuaded him to depose his queen and the crown prince Xuan Jiu, and to put her and her son in their places. The Zhou queen was the daughter of the Marquis of Shen and he responded to her ouster and his resulting loss of power by gathering his allies, including the nomadic ***Quanrong*** (non-Han Chinese), and attacking Fenghao, the Western Zhou capital, intending to set things right. However, the Quanrong ended up killing the king and his concubine, sacking the capital, and taking territory from the Zhou state. Xuan Jiu took the throne and established a new capital at Chengzhou inaugurating the Eastern Zhou Period.

SPRING AND AUTUMN PERIOD (771–476 BCE)

The Eastern Zhou era is traditionally subdivided into the *Spring and Autumn* and the *Warring States* periods, each of which takes its name from a literary work. The first is derived from the *Spring and Autumn Annals*, the chronicles recorded in the State of Lu from 722 to 481 BCE, and thought to have been edited by Confucius (551–479 BCE). "Spring and autumn" was a way of expressing the concept of "year" and the annals were one of the first histories recorded on a yearly basis; prior to this, history was written down only when major events happened. The Warring States period takes its name from the *Strategies of the Warring States*, attributed to Su Qin (380–284 BCE), reflecting a time of almost continual military conflict.

The events recorded in the Spring and Autumn Annals show that the murder of King Zhou You and the loss of the western territories considerably weakened the authority and power of the Zhou state. During the Spring and Autumn period military skirmishes between various Zhou states were a common occurrence, and many began to construct defensive walls around their territories. After 500 BCE these regional conflicts escalated to the point of almost continual warfare.

Despite the turmoil of the era, the Eastern Zhou period was one of continuing advances in the arts and sciences. Progress was made in bronze-working with new technologies for gilding and inlaying metals, lost wax casting, and the introduction of pattern blocks to regularize and speed up the process of bronze decoration. These new methods allowed Zhou artists to create new and larger vessel forms that were elegantly proportioned and aesthetically refined. Bronze coinage, kites, and corbel brackets (*dougong*) in architecture were some of the other inventions of the era.

The uncertainties of the times inspired the development of new schools of philosophy including Confucianism, Daoism, and Legalism, all of which attempted to understand human behavior as a cause of social and political problems, and to offer solutions that would bring about order. The first and most culturally significant of these was Confucianism.

▼ **8.6** Eastern Zhou, Spring and Autumn period, Hu Wine Container, c. 770–476 BCE. Bronze inlaid with copper, 15.4 in. high.

Three bands of intertwining dragons decorate the belly of this bronze vessel while at the mouth an inlay of copper, now oxidized, would have created a color contrast. The lid was the serving vessel for the wine.

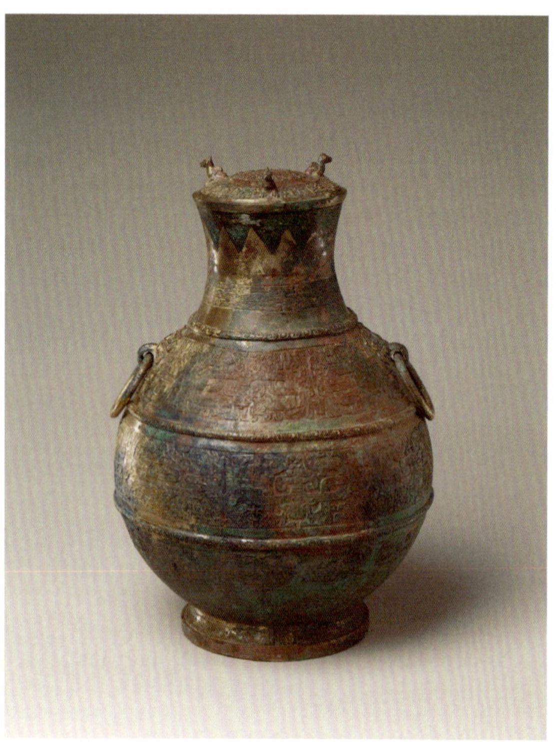

Bronze Hu Inlaid with Copper, c.770–476 BCE During the Spring and Autumn Period one of the first studio practice manuals, the *Kao Gong Ji* or *Book of Diverse Crafts* was written. The book provided information on technological processes and alloys used in bronze-working and tool manufacturing, lost wax casting, metal inlaying and gilding, dye preparation and dying processes, as well as information about other arts. A good example of the advancements recorded in the Kao Gong Ji is a Bronze Hu with Inlaid Copper in the collection of the Metropolitan Museum of Art.

Compared to earlier Western Zhou forms, the *hu* or wine container (Figure 8.6) is considerably more sophisticated in concept and execution. The gracefully rounded vessel is divided horizontally into registers of extremely shallow relief, which were pressed into the original using pattern blocks or carved stamps. The three bands feature interlaced horned dragons as mirrored pairs. Bands on the neck and foot of the vessel are decorated with cloud patterns, suggesting the intertwined dragons are ***tian-long*** or heavenly dragons. Around the

RELIGION AND PHILOSOPHY
Confucianism and later Neo-Confucianism

In order to understand how the various Chinese religions and philosophies influenced the arts, it is important to know basic tenets of each. **Confucianism** is a philosophy of life, scholarly tradition, social code, and a political ideology, more than a religion. It was promulgated by Kongqiu, known to his students as Kongfuzi (Great master Kong), who based it on his interpretation of elements of religious practices from the Zhou era. In essence it is the earliest form of humanism in that its basic principles, as enumerated by Master Kong, are ***Jen***, humaneness or benevolence; ***Li***, proper conduct in formal social roles; ***Yi***, innate moral sense, doing what is the right thing to do, and ***Hsiao***, filial piety or reverence. Although his followers, particularly Mencius, added other virtues to Confucianism, Master Kong saw these human-centered values as the glue that held the social order together. If every person understood and followed his proper role in the family, in the community, and in the state, society could be reformed and perfected. His teachings and saying were anthologized as the *Analects of Confucius*.

During the Sung Dynasty, the philosopher Zhou Dunyi (1017–1073 CE), realizing that Confucianism lacked a strong metaphysical system to explain the nature of existence, created a synthesis of Buddhism and Daoist ontological thought and incorporated it into Confucianism. This was further elaborated by Zhu Xi (1130–200 CE) in the following century. This new or **Neo-Confucianism** takes from Buddhism, particularly Chan Buddhism, constructs of the nature of the soul and its relation to the cosmos as well as concepts of a higher morality. From Daoism Neo-Confucianism derived ideals of individual self-cultivation and self-examination as a means of aligning oneself with nature and thereby achieving order and harmony.

In Confucian philosophy the practice of the arts was seen as a means of self-cultivation and moral improvement. Because many Confucian scholar-artists worked for the Imperial courts, the arts could also be seen as a form of service to the state through the exposition of moral exemplars. Yan Liben's *Thirteen Emperors Handscroll*, painted during the Tang Dynasty, offers portraits of thirteen emperors from the Han to the Sui Dynasties as models of kingship to either emulate or avoid. In each portrait, the artist provides clues, in terms of expression and posture, to the character of the ruler. Confucian painters used character analogies to convey similar information in non-figural works. For example, pine trees, because of their upright growth pattern, symbolized moral integrity, steadfastness, and self-discipline; bamboo, by virtue of its flexibility, epitomized strength and endurance in times of adversity, and orchids represented nobility, integrity, friendship, and the scholarly life, while the depiction of weeds expressed treachery and wrongdoing.

The philosophy and religion of **Daoism** is credited to Li Er or Laozi (Master Lao) a sixth-century BCE philosopher and scholar at the Zhou court, who is credited with writing the *Daodejing* or *Classic of the Way of Power*. However, the work is more likely a compilation of early philosophical writings by several authors. The *Daodejing* was intended as a guide not for the ordinary person but for the Zhou sovereign, who as the "Son of Heaven," stood at the center of the civil universe; his self-cultivation of ***wu wei*** or "non-doing" would naturally result in an orderly and prosperous society. The idea was not that the leader did nothing, but that he did nothing that was forced; instead he must act in a way that is spontaneous, effortless, and in harmony with the flow of nature, which is the Dao. From the Daoist point of view humans are only a small part of the natural world and their actions only make sense when they work in accord with nature instead of in opposition to it. Unnatural action that is contrary to the Dao was believed to be the cause of all society's problems. Daoists advocated going into nature to meditate and cultivate the ***de***, the conscious awareness of the Dao, which enables humans to act in a virtuous manner.

The influence of Daoist philosophy in the arts can be seen not only in depictions of Daoist pantheons, paradises, and land of immortals but also in the development of landscape painting and garden design, especially during the Sung Dynasty when increasing urbanization made withdrawing into nature for meditation more difficult. Works such as *Travelers among Mountains and Streams,* by Fan Kuan, a Daoist recluse, illustrate the Daoist emphasis on the transcendence of the natural world over man and his transitory works. Fan Kuan's mountain embodies *qi* or cosmic energy, which like the mountain itself cannot be contained even by his monumental painting. Kuan lovingly details every element of the natural world, even differentiating each type of leaf on the trees covering the middle ground hills, while the traveler and his mule train are reduced to the size of ants.

Legalism was a philosophy expounded during the late Warring States period by Shang Yang (c. 390–338 BCE) and furthered by Li Si (c. 280–208 BCE) and Han Feizi (c. 280–233 BCE). All three worked for the Dukes of Qin and the philosophy they formulated became the basis for the first Chinese empire under Qin Shi Huangdi. Legalism was a pragmatic philosophy that saw human nature as venal, egoistic, covetous, and generally incapable of moral behavior. Therefore, the role of government was to create a socio-political system that channeled these human tendencies in ways that benefited the state by increasing its power, wealth, and territory. For Legalists this meant a strong military and a system of laws that enforced harsh punishments for even minor crimes as well as rewarding behaviors desired by the state; both had the goal of preserving order and the authority of the ruler. Legalism was not a philosophy that inspired new themes or aesthetic approaches in art. Its influence is shown most directly in the forced labor of more than 1.5 million workers used by the Qin state to construct the Great Wall and Shi Huangdi's monumental mausoleum. The major art commission of the Qin Empire was the creation of the terracotta army, for which eighty master potters were brought in from all parts of the empire to mass produce and paint the clay soldiers. Unfortunately, upon completion of the tomb, these talented individuals were buried alive to preserve the interests of the state.

mouth of the vessel is a zigzag pattern, where copper was inlaid into the bronze to create an area of color contrast. Three birds are modeled onto the lid of the vessel; these were the feet for a shallow bowl that was used to serve the wine.

THE WARRING STATES PERIOD (476–221 BCE)

Toward the end of the Spring and Autumn period (circa 550 BCE), four Zhou states rose to dominate all the others. These were the Qin in the west, the Jin in the center, the Chu in the south, and the Qi in the east. In 497 BCE a civil war destroyed the Jin state, and its lands were partitioned among the Han, Wei, and Zhao clans. The Jin division marks the beginning of the Warring States Period. The political situation was even more turbulent that in the preceding period. However, artistic production at the feudal courts continued unabated.

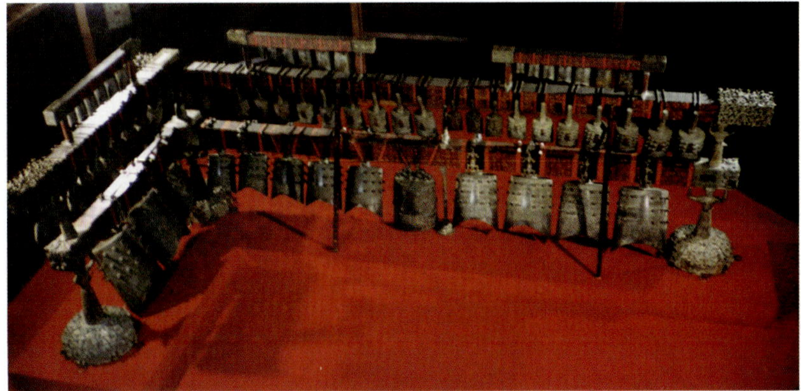

8.7 Eastern Zhou, Warring States period, Yongzhong of Marquis Yi of Zheng, c. 433 BCE. Bronze, 25 ft. long.

Bell sets such as these would be played by five musicians standing, kneeling, or sitting to reach their section of bells. Each bell produced two notes depending upon where it was struck.

Yongzhong of Marquis Yi of Zheng, c. 433 BCE Bronze items continued to be commissioned by the provincial rulers not only for use in their courts but also as furnishings for their tombs. Even the rulers of the smallest states commissioned an amazing number of works of bronze, gold, and jade. In 1978, Chinese archaeologists excavated the tomb of Marquis Yi, ruler of the small state of Zheng, who was buried in 433 BCE. The four-chambered tomb had a central room containing over 10,000 items. In addition to vessels of gold and bronze and pieces of worked jade, the tomb contained a wide array of musical instruments, including bronze bells, stone chimes, drums, lutes, and sets of reed and bamboo pipes. Confucian philosophers of the age held music in high regard, believing it brought harmony and purity of mind to the listener. Music played an important role at the Zhou courts; many rulers of the era were buried with their musical instruments as well as their court musicians.

The Yongzhong of Marquis Yi (Figure 8.7) is a set of sixty-five bronze chime-bells suspended from a triple bronze frame measuring some 25 feet in overall length. Each row had bells of different sizes and diameters and each elliptical bell could produce two notes: one, when struck with a wooden mallet in the center and another, when struck on the side. The total range of the bell set was eight and a half octaves. The Yongzhong required five musicians to play it. Depending upon their assigned bells, they stood, knelt, or sat. Each bell has nine raised bosses; nine is considered to be a lucky number. Above the rim of each bell is a decorative band of interlaced dragons.

The Qin Empire (221–207 BCE)

In 256 BCE, armies of the state of Qin captured the Zhou Capital and killed the last Zhou king. The loss of the Zhou king was of little importance to the provincial rulers as they had their own problems with the warlike Qin. In 221 BCE, Ying Zheng, Marquis of Qin, conquered the last of the old Zhou provincial states and declared the Qin Dynasty.

He took the title of Qin Shi Huang meaning "First August and Divine Emperor of Qin." Although reviled in Chinese history for his brutal methods and paranoid rule, Qin Shi Huang (r. 221–210 BCE), laid the foundations of the Chinese nation. He expanded the boundaries of his empire beyond those of the old Zhou state, sending his armies southward to the border of what is now Vietnam. Qin Shi Huang introduced a number of reforms to facilitate the smooth functioning of the empire. He divided the state into prefectures which were administered jointly by nonhereditary officials who were part of a centralized Imperial bureaucracy, decreed a uniform system of weights and measures, a single currency, standardized the writing of Chinese characters, and imposed Legalism, a philosophy promoting strict compliance to the rule of law.

The Great Wall c. 220 BCE Of all Qin Shi Huang's accomplishments, he is best known for commanding the building of the Great Wall of China. During the Warring States Period, the Zhou states had built defensive walls around their territories as protection against their bellicose neighbors. Qin Shi Huang ordered internal walls torn down, and the sections along the northern border joined up to create a great defensive wall against invasion by nomadic barbarians. Thousands of soldiers, convicts, and peasants were conscripted to build the Great Wall.

The Qin-era Great Wall was less impressive than the iconic Ming period reconstruction that features prominently in travel brochures. Depending upon the terrain and available materials, the first walls were made either of rammed earth or dry laid stone, and rose only to heights of between 10 and 20 feet (3.2 and 6 m). Guard towers were placed at intervals along the wall and, in some areas, the wall was overlapped to provide greater security. The wide ramparts atop the walls allowed quick movement of troops along the border, especially in areas of difficult terrain. Repairs to the wall were made by the Han, Sui, and Northern Dynasties but the most extensive repairs, and embellishments, such as carved reliefs, were made during the Ming dynasty.

Qin Shi Huang's Great Tomb, c. 215–210 BCE A second massive project of the First Emperor was his monumental mausoleum, which took 720,000 workers thirty-six years to complete. The tomb lies under an artificial mountain rising to a height of 247 feet (76 m), and according to historian Sima Qian, it contains a replica of the Qin kingdom and palace, with rivers and lakes of liquid mercury, and the stars of the night sky replicated with pearls on the ceiling of the vault. Of course, Sima Qian's account was written during the Han Dynasty, a century after the death of Qin Shi Huang, and may be entirely fictitious. The mound was set within two earthen-walled courts, an arrangement that reflected Zhou concepts of city design, which located the palace of the ruler within a walled court at the center of the city around which the outer city walls defined a second court.

The Terracotta Warriors, c. 215–210 BCE East of the mound and outside the enclosing walls is a garrison of several thousand terracotta warriors. It is possible that Qin Shi Huang believed his vanquished enemies were waiting for him in the afterlife as he placed his soldiers facing east toward the conquered Zhou states. Unlike the rulers of the preceding dynasties, Qin Shi Huang prepared for the battles of eternity, not by having soldiers killed to accompany him in death, but by having them replicated in terracotta.

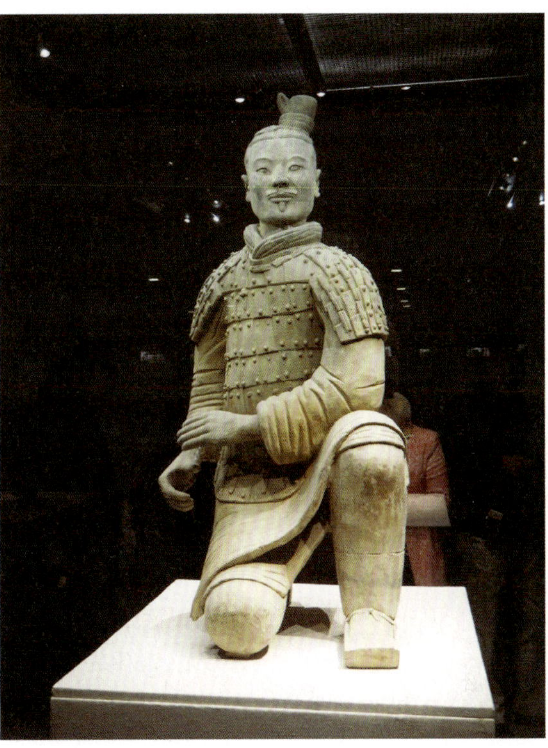

▲ **8.8** Qin, Tomb of Qin Shi Huang, Terracotta Warrior, c. 215–210 BCE.

The Qin Emperor was accompanied into the afterlife by an army of several thousand terracotta warriors. These were mass-produced using molds and the finished pieces assembled and painted to make them more lifelike.

The soldiers (Figure 8.8) were mass-produced, using section molds for the legs and torso. The assembled figures were brightly painted with colored lacquers, which, unfortunately, crumbled to dust when the figures were exposed to dry air. Heads were modeled separately and pegged into the neck. They are so individualized that it has been suggested that they are actual portraits. It is more probable that they meant to depict peoples from different regions of the empire. The terracotta warriors would have been a formidable army. Infantrymen stood between 5 feet 8 inches (1.7 m) and 6 feet 2 inches (1.8 m) while generals were 6 feet 5 inches (2 m), tall even by modern standards. Originally, each soldier was equipped with weapons appropriate to his military function, but these were looted by peasant rebels during the insurrection that ended the Qin Empire.

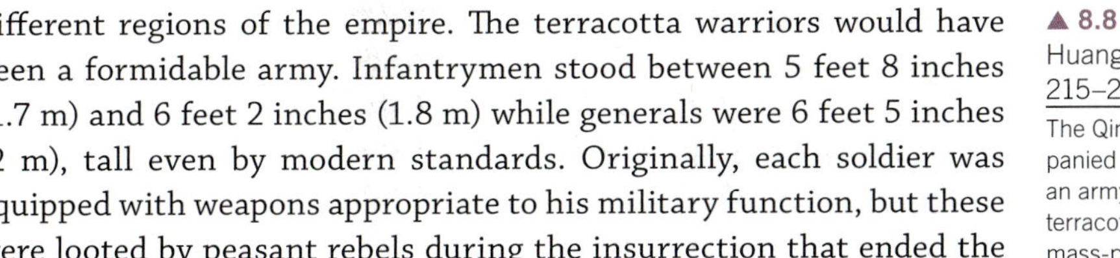

The Han Dynasty (206 BCE–220 CE)

The revolts that brought down the Qin Dynasty were led by a peasant general named Liu Pang. The former farmer was such an effective and courageous leader that his fellow rebels elected him emperor. Liu Pang took the regnal name of Han Gaozu, meaning "exalted ancestor." Emperor Gaozu was an effective ruler, consolidating the advances of the Qin while repairing some of Shi Huangdi's worst abuses. Gaozu welcomed to his court the Confucian scholars and Daoist philosophers, whose writings had been suppressed during the Qin, and put them to work transcribing from memory the texts that Shi Huangdi had burned.

HAN TOMBS

Han buildings were often constructed in wood, and thus, have not survived to modern times. What is known about the architecture of this era comes from ceramic house models found in tombs. Unlike the wood-chambered vaults of earlier periods, Han tombs were built with more durable and less porous brick and stone walls, which dramatically reduced air and moisture infiltration. These improved materials resulted in the contents of many Han tombs being extraordinarily well-preserved. The Han buried their elite dead with everything that they might need or enjoy in the afterlife. Burial goods, known as ***mingqi***, included utensils, weapons, musical instruments, food items, cosmetics, human and animal figurines, and ceramic house models ranging from palaces to farm outbuildings.

Tower Model, c. 25–220 CE The larger ceramic building models, especially the towering, multi-storied palaces, were created and fired in sections. The units were then assembled in the tomb to create ceramic models sometimes exceeding 6 feet (2 m) in height. This *Tower Model* (Figure 8.9) features four levels, three rising above the roof of the first which served as lookout posts, a guard on duty peers out of a window on the top level. The model provides a wealth of architectural information in its details, from the dougong brackets supporting the first, second, and fourth levels, to the differing lattice patterns of the third and fourth levels.

▼ **8.9** Han, Watch Tower, c. 25–220 CE. Earthenware with green lead glaze, 41 in. × 22.62 in. × 11.75 in.

Han tomb house models illustrate a wide variety of period architecture from palaces to pig pens. The larger pieces were constructed in floor sections and assembled after firing.

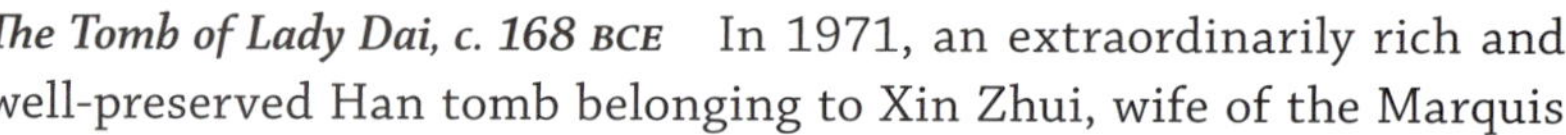

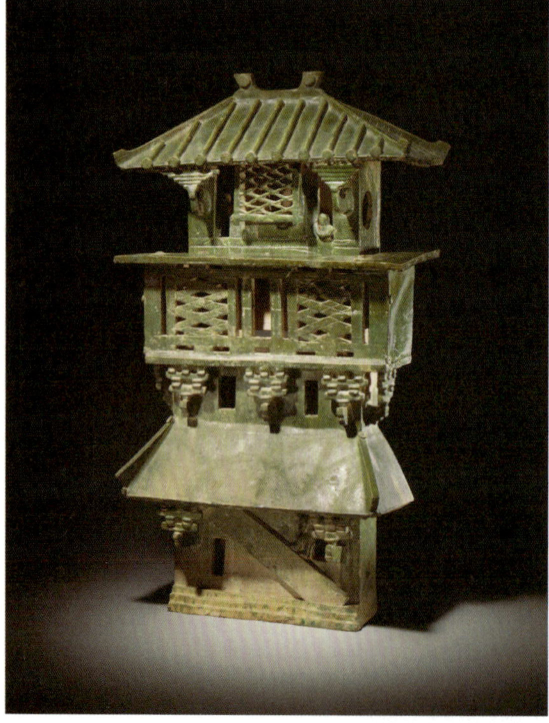

The Tomb of Lady Dai, c. 168 BCE In 1971, an extraordinarily rich and well-preserved Han tomb belonging to Xin Zhui, wife of the Marquis of Dai was discovered at Mawangdui. When archaeologists opened the innermost of Lady Dai's four nested wooden coffins, they were astonished to find no signs of decomposition. Her skin was elastic, limbs bendable, internal organs intact and the blood in her veins was still red more than two millennia after her death. Her body was so well preserved that pathologists were able to conduct an autopsy, which determined she had died of a heart attack at approximately fifty years old. Lady Dai's tomb contained more than a thousand items: cosmetics, food delicacies, silk textiles, books, lacquerware, and a small army of carved wooden figurines representing the servants who would tend to Lady Dai's every need in the afterlife.

Silk Funerary Banner of Lady Dai, c. 168 BCE After all the offerings were in place Lady Dai's tomb was filled with some five tons of charcoal and then sealed with white kaolin clay (Higgins 2016). The resulting extremely dry conditions allowed readily perishable goods such as food items and fine silk to be preserved. One of these rare survivals was a large T-shaped painted silk banner (Figure 8.10) carried in Lady Dai's funeral procession, and afterward draped over the innermost of her four nested coffins. The banner is divided vertically into the three cosmological realms of heavens, earth, and the underworld, and horizontally into Yin (female) on the left side and Yang (male) on the right. The banner illustrates Lady Dai's journey from the world of the living through the underworld and ultimately into the heavenly realm of the ancestors.

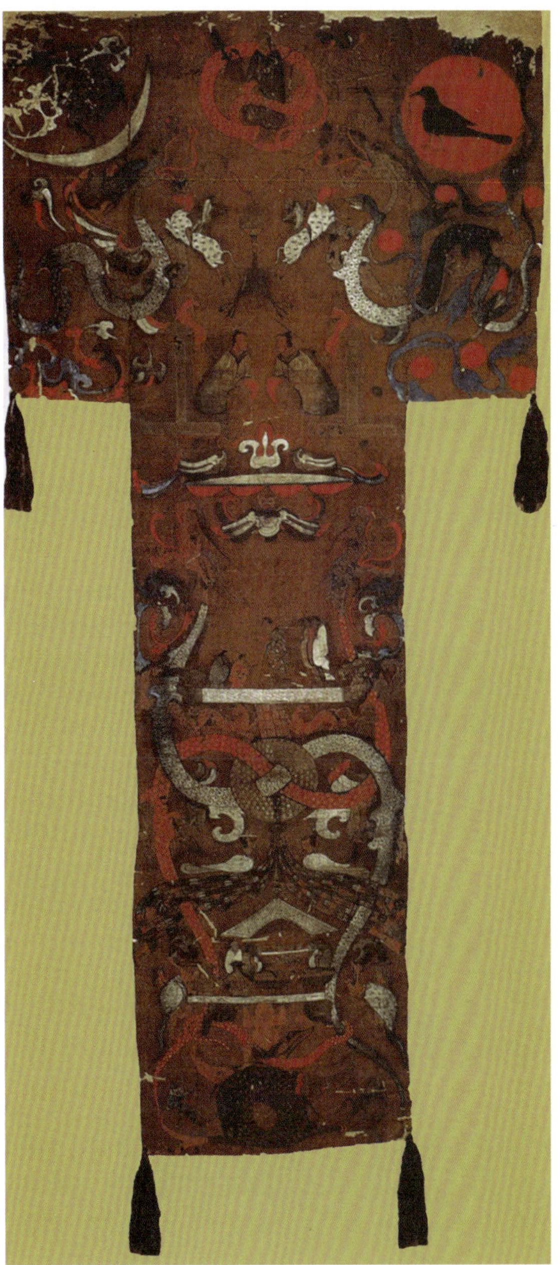

▲ **8.10** Han, Mawangdui, Funeral Banner of Lady Dai (Xin Zhui), c. 168 BCE. Ink on silk, 80.7 in. × 36.2 in. × 18.7 in.

The banner, which was laid over the innermost of Lady Dai's four nested coffins, shows her journey through life through the underworld and into the heavenly realm of the ancestors.

Lady Dai's image on her funerary banner is one of the earliest known portraits in Chinese art. She is shown in the middle section, standing on a dais and supporting herself with a cane that is similar to one actually found in the tomb. She is attended by three court ladies and receives the kowtows of two mourners. Beneath this scene is a Bi disk with two dragons intertwining through its center opening. This common tomb object is a symbol of immortality. In the bottom of the banner, Lady Dai's funerary feast has been set up under a canopy; her presence here is suggested by the coffin and offerings. Depicted on the horizontal part of the banner is the celestial realm, which is entered through a gateway guarded by two court officials. In the middle of this celestial realm the cup of immortality is held up by a pair of riders who are flanked by dragons and felines. In the center top sits Xi Wangmu, the goddess of immortality and personification of Yin or femininity. To her left is the crescent moon with the Moon Toad and Hare. To her right are the Sun with its Raven and eight small suns, referencing the nine suns of the Archer Yi myth and symbolizing the masculine or Yang.

The Period of Disunity (220–581 CE)

The final collapse of the Han, in 220 CE, ushered in a four-centuries-long era of almost continual civil war, and frequent regime change, generalized as the Period of Disunity. The first states to rise after the fall of the Han were the Three Kingdoms of Wei, Shu, and Wu (220–256 CE); the strongest of these, the Wei, managed, briefly, to reunite the whole of China under their rule as the Western Jin Dynasty (265–317 CE). However, the invasion of northern China by the Xiongnu, Xianbei, and related barbarian groups forced the Jin dynasty to flee south. The invaders divided the conquered north into Sixteen Kingdoms (304–438 CE). In 386 CE, northern China was reunited by the Xianbei under the Northern Wei Dynasty (386–535).

The kingdoms that rose in the south after the fall of the Han were as transitory as those of the north. In 220 CE, the Eastern Wu became the first of six dynasties that would rule the south in succession; each made Nanjing their capital. As had happened during the Warring States Period, the arts flourished in the various kingdoms of the north and south, especially as the new religion of Buddhism gained widespread acceptance.

The Northern Wei (396–589 CE)

The Northern Wei Dynasty was founded in 396 CE by the Xianbei leader Tuoba Gui. During the reign of Emperor Wencheng (r. 453–459), Buddhism was adopted as the state religion. As an act of devotion, the emperor commissioned the first five cave temples at Yungang on Mount Wuzhou. The site was near enough to the Northern Wei capital of Pengcheng for the emperor to make personal visits there. The carving of caves 16 through 20, known as the Imperial Caves, had been suggested to the emperor as an act of devotion and of atonement for his predecessor's persecution of Buddhism, by the monk and master carver Tan Yao. Little is known about the artist other than he came from Gansu Province, where several Buddhist cave sites were known around the Silk Road center of Dunhuang. Northern Wei patronage at Yungang continued until 494 CE when the capital was moved to Luoyang.

Yungang Cave 20 Buddha, c. 453 CE The focal point of each cave was a monumental Buddha image, the smallest of these being more than 32 feet (10 m) high. The walls of the grottos were also densely carved with relief images of the Buddha, some only a few inches tall. The style of the five Imperial Buddhas owes much to earlier Gandharan prototypes brought from India.

The largest of the Tan Yao sculptures is the 45.5 foot (14 meter) Buddha of Cave 20 (Figure 8.12). The immense, square-shouldered Buddha sits in a posture of meditation, attended by two standing Buddhas, one of which has been damaged by spalling. To heighten the realism of the face, the irises of the eyes are deeply incised and the pupils indicated with an inlay of black stone. The most distinctive feature of this and other Imperial Buddhas are large pendulous ears which almost touch the shoulders.

VISUAL COMPARISON
Gandharan Influences on Early Chinese Buddhist Art

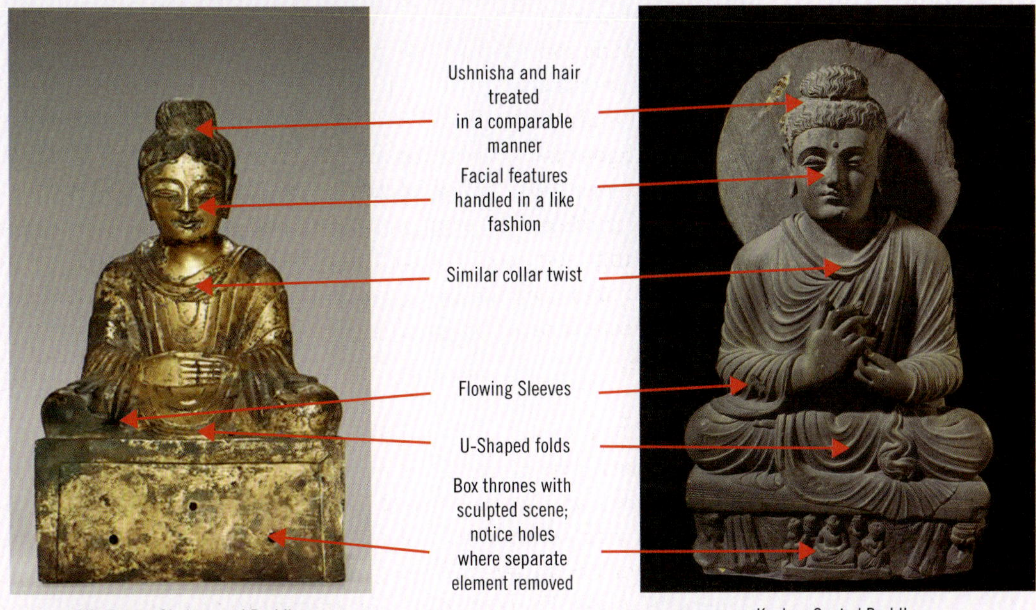

▲ **8.11** *Comparison Gilt Bronze Chinese Buddha from the Period of Disunity with a Kushan schist Buddha in the Gandharan style.*

In addition to luxury goods and spices, the Silk Road was also the vehicle for the transmission of technologies, philosophies, religions, and associated art styles to early China.

One of the earliest known examples of Chinese-made Buddhist art is the gilt-bronze image of Shakyamuni Buddha from Hebei province. It is inscribed with a date of 338 CE. The cast bronze image is quite small, only 15 inches (38.1 cm) high.

A comparison of the Gilt-Bronze Shakyamuni Buddha from Hebei province with the Kushan Seated Buddha from Gandhara shows a strong similarity in the treatment of tousled hair and ushnisha, proportions of the face, breadth of shoulder, and the treatment of the neck and folds of the sanghati, and the Buddha's throne. The Chinese version differs from the original only in the length of torso, positioning of the Buddha's hands in the representation of the dhyana mudra, and the lack of the scene on the front of the throne, although the holes in the front of the bronze suggested it may have once had such a scene pegged into the throne.

As indicated by the double-row of square mortise holes in the cave wall, just above and on either side of the Buddha's head, a shielding wooden roof was once raised over the sandstone figures. Also, as a protective measure, and to heighten the naturalism of the image, the projecting central Buddha was originally covered with a layer of plaster and presumably painted, although no traces of pigment remain. The rows of drill-holes evident in spalled areas once held wooden pegs used to anchor the plaster to the stone core.

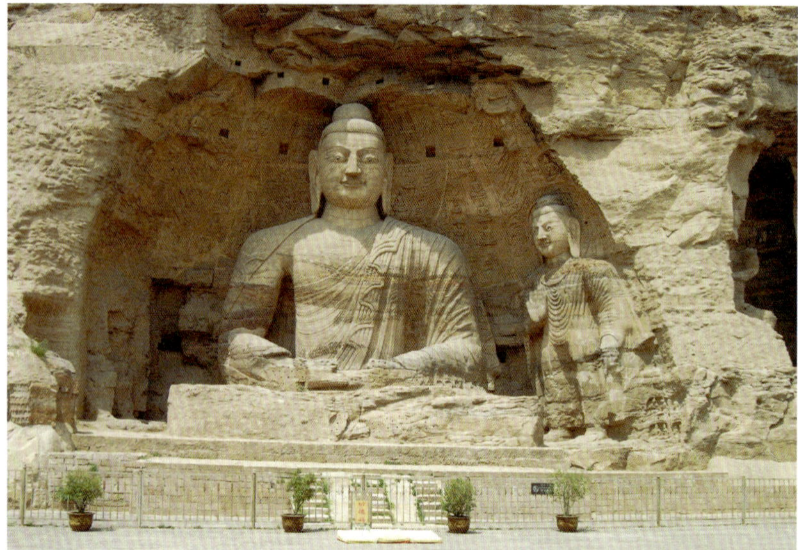

▶ 8.12 Northern Wei, Yungang Caves, Buddha of Cave 20, c. 453 CE. 45.5 ft. high.

The Buddha and his attendants were originally covered with a layer of burnished lime plaster, still visible in the brighter areas, which protected the soft limestone from spalling. This covering was anchored to the stone by wooden pegs, some of the holes for these are still visible on the sculpture.

The five Imperial Buddhas are thought to have depicted rulers of the Tuoba dynasty in the guise of living Buddhas. The Cave 20 Buddha is believed to a portrait of Crown Prince Jigmu, Emperor Wencheng's father. The identification of the Cave 20 Buddha is a matter of some debate. Various Buddhas have been suggested, including Shakyamuni Buddha in the company of Buddhas of the Past and Future, and Amitabha Buddha, the Buddha of the Western Paradise. The latter is a central figure of Pure Land Buddhism, which was introduced into China in the second century CE (Corradini 2003, 200).

The Six Dynasties (222–589 CE)

The Six Dynasties Period was a time of political instability, as six successive dynasties ruled briefly in the south of China. Yet, it was also a time when the arts prospered in the Nanjing courts and artists began to garner individual attention for their work. One of those was Gu Kaizhi (c. 344–c. 406), a painter at the Eastern Jin court and the first Chinese artist whose name is known to history. Additionally, the first art historical works were written during this era, the best known being Xie He's *Record of the Classification of Old Painters*, in which he outlines six criteria for evaluating and appreciating paintings, according to their creativity, brushwork, naturalism, use of color, composition, or accuracy in copying old master works.

Gu Kaizhi,* Admonitions of the Instructress to the Palace Ladies, *Scene 4:* Lady Feng and the Bear, *c. 500–700 CE based on original c. 400 CE Very little is known about Gu Kaizhi's life other than he was born in Wuxi, Jiangsu, and that he was the son of a government official. He is recorded as having been a prolific painter, producing more than seventy paintings, but only three have survived in the form of later Tang and Sung copies: *Admonitions of the Instructress to the Palace Ladies*, *Nymph of the Luo River*, and *Wise and Benevolent Women*. Gu Kaizhi is especially known for his portraits and figure paintings rendered with a fine classical line and a keen sense of character.

Gu Kaizhi's *Admonitions Scroll* takes its story from Zhang Hua's satirical account of life at the Western Jin court during the reign of Emperor Hui. The emperor was not of sound mind and his wife Jia Nan Feng was the de facto ruler of the empire from 291 to 300 CE. In a world governed by Confucian philosophy, Jia Nan Feng's behavior was considered inappropriate; women, even empresses, were expected to be submissive and meek, not murderous and power-hungry.

In keeping with Confucian ideals of the arts presenting moral exemplars, the scenes included in the *Admonitions Scroll* are intended as behavioral models to either emulate or avoid. They are presented as a series of lessons by the court instructress, whose job it is to teach proper conduct to the court ladies. The handscroll was divided into nine scenes separated by moralizing couplets. The scroll is now incomplete, missing its first three scenes and some of its inscriptions, presumably lost when it was looted from the Imperial treasury during the Boxer Uprising in 1900.

The first surviving scene is the fourth, which shows Lady Feng stepping into the path of an escaped black bear, sacrificing herself to prevent it from attacking the emperor Han Yuandi, while his other concubine runs away (Figure 8.13). Lady Feng's heroic, self-sacrificing act is intended to serve as a model of correct female behavior. The setting for this scene is minimal, the space implied rather than defined; that the event is taking place in the palace is assumed rather than shown

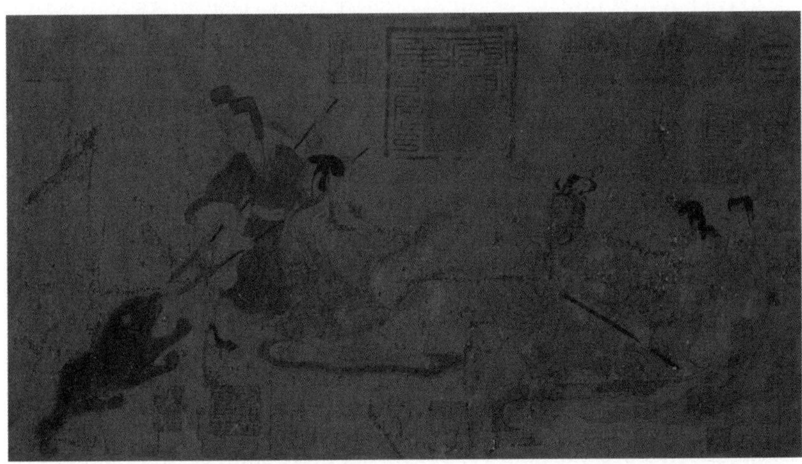

◀ **8.13** Six Dynasties, Gu Kaizhi (c. 344–c. 406), *Admonitions of the Instructress to the Palace Ladies* handscroll, Scene 4: *Lady Feng and the Bear* (copy), C. 600–700 CE. Ink on silk.

Gu Kaizhi's painting originally included eleven scenes based on a satirical text by Zhang Hua (c. 232–300 CE.) The scenes were intended to show correct female behavior according to Confucianism.

by the artist. With the possible exception of the emperor, the scene has no true portraits. The faces of the soldiers as well as those of the ladies are depictions of generic type, rather than individuals. The scene demonstrates the use of hierarchical scale with each person being sized in accordance with their rank and importance.

The Tang Dynasty (618–907 CE)

In 589, after almost three hundred years of political chaos, China was reunited under the short-lived Sui Dynasty. The first Sui Emperor, Wendi, was an able ruler who instituted a number of reforms that strengthened the nation; however, his son and successor, Emperor Yang, was not. In 618 CE Li Yuan, Duke of Tang and governor of Shaanxi province under the Sui overthrew Emperor Yang and founded the Tang Dynasty. Taking the throne as Emperor Gaozu, he established his capital at Chang'an (modern Xi'an), which was an important hub of the Silk Road. Under the Tang, Chang'an became a cosmopolitan city, its streets filled with foreign traders, artisans, and the embassies of China's far-flung trading partners.

▼ **8.14** Tang, Tomb Figure of a Neighing Horse, c. 700–800 CE. Earthenware with sancai glaze, 30 in. × 33 in. × 11 in.

The Ferghana horses depicted in Tang era tombs are much different from the cobby-bodied ponies in Shi Huang Di's tomb; they had longer legs and more powerful chests and were thought to be the finest horses of their time.

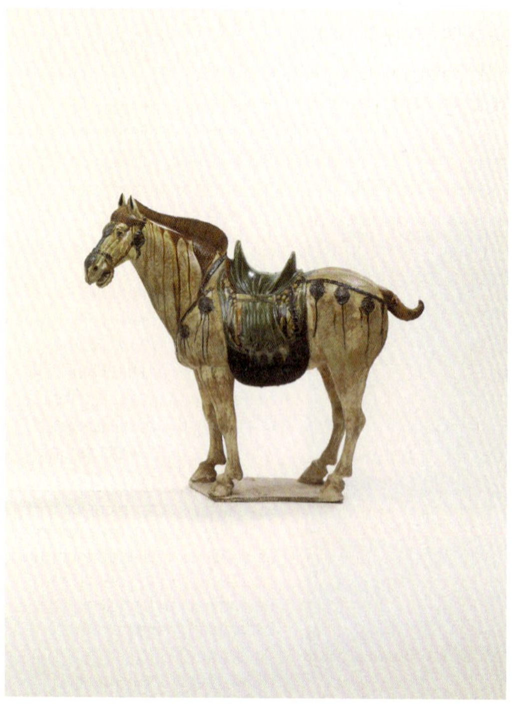

TANG CERAMICS

The diversity of Tang culture is reflected in the mingqi recovered from its tombs. Such burial offerings included colorfully glazed ceramic sculptures, some quite large, representing imported Ferghana horses, Arabian and Bactrian camels, court officials, and exotic foreigners from Persia and the Byzantine Empire. These low-fired ceramic statuettes were made exclusively as tomb offerings. Although decorated ceramics were known during the Han Dynasty, Tang potters invented new lead-glazes by adding copper, iron, and cobalt oxides to produce deeper and richer colors. Ceramics decorated with these vibrant new glazes were known as **sancai** or three-color wares.

Tomb Figure of a Neighing Horse, c. 700–800 CE
Among the more impressive Tang tomb mingqi are figures of the Ferghana horses the Chinese were importing from Central Asia (Uzbekistan). These animals were prized for their speed and endurance. The Chinese called them "Horses of Heaven" and believed that they were so powerful they sweated blood; this phenomenon is thought to have been a parasitic response in the breed. This is suggested in the *Neighing Horse* (Figure 8.14) by allowing the brown sancai glaze

streaming from the horse's mane and trappings. Tang tomb figures were mold-made in sections and then assembled. In glazing these works the artist has taken care to control the natural tendency of the sancai to drip and run. Prior to glazing the clay figure was lightly scored to position and control the flow of the glazes.

TANG PAINTING

It is not until the Tang Dynasty that the full spectrum of Chinese painting is revealed in the range of surviving examples, which include landscapes, figure studies, and Buddhist images. Chinese paintings of the Tang Dynasty, whether on the walls of tombs, or as portable works, such as hanging and hand scrolls, display an appreciation of the expressive quality of line, and purity of form. While color is a frequent element in murals, the majority of painted scrolls were done in monochrome. Chinese artists regarded color as a distraction, preferring to emphasize brushwork and the almost calligraphic contrast of ink and ground.

Foreign Ambassadors Received at Court, Tomb of Prince Li Xian, Qianling Mausoleum, c. 706 Tang tombs paintings offer glimpses into life at the Tang Court. Some of the best examples come from the Qianling Mausoleum on Liangshan Mountain, a complex of Li family tombs. Among the royal tombs are those of Crown Prince Zhang Huai (653–686 CE), Crown Prince Yide (682–701 CE), and Princess Yongtai (684–701 CE), all victims of their mother and grandmother respectively, Empress Wu Zetian (r. 684–705 CE).

A scene from the Tomb of Crown Prince Zhang Huai (Figure 8.15), shows Chinese ministers in bright orange robes, tall hats, and upturned "cloud shoes" leading three foreign emissaries to an official

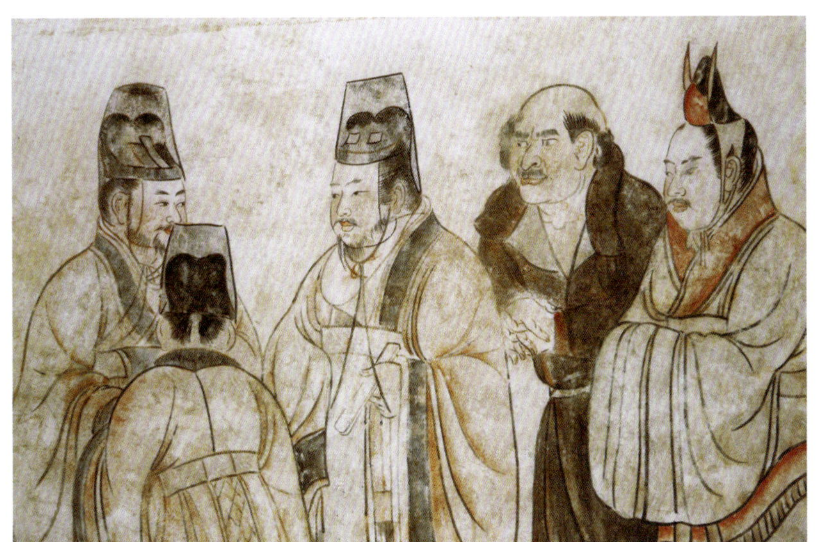

◀ **8.15** Tang, Xian, Qianling Mausoleum, Tomb of Prince Li Xuan, *Mural of Foreign Ambassadors Received at Court*, c. 706 CE.

The scene shows three court officials leading foreign emissaries to an audience with the prince; one of the foreigners is a Nestorian Christian monk from the Byzantine Empire.

audience; two of the ambassadors are Korean while the third one, dressed in a brown robe and black boots, is a Nestorian Christian monk from the Byzantine Empire. As in the *Thirteen Emperors Scroll*, the space is implied by the location of the figures as there are no details of the settling. While the artist who painted these murals uses the same conventions and styles found in scroll painting, tomb paintings were done by "professional" artists who were paid for their work, and thus were considered to be nothing more than skilled craftsmen.

Yan Liben (c. 600–673 CE), Thirteen Emperors Handscroll:* Emperor Guangwu of Han, *c. 650 CE Yan Liben, was a scholar, poet, architect, and artist who served as minister of public works and Imperial painter during the reigns of Emperors Taizong and Gaozong. He was elevated to Baron of Boling by Gaozong. He is best known as a painter of portraits and figures that epitomized Confucian ideals, but is also recorded as having created paintings of animals and birds, and Buddhist and Daoist subjects.

His most famous surviving work is the *Thirteen Emperors Handscroll* (Figure 8.16), which depicts thirteen successive emperors beginning with Emperor Han Liu Fulin (94–74 BCE) and ending with Emperor Sui Yang (569–618 CE). The rulers are depicted in hierarchical scale, towering over all others in their scenes whether standing or seated, to show their magnificence by virtue of the contrast. Yan Liben is especially interested in showing the essence of each emperor's character and personality; some appear wise, others foolish; some wrathful and others benevolent. While the emperors are individualized and appear to be portraits; the other figures are stereotypes of people of various stations, their importance indicated by the details of their clothing and their relative scale. Yan builds his figures with hard, consistent-width

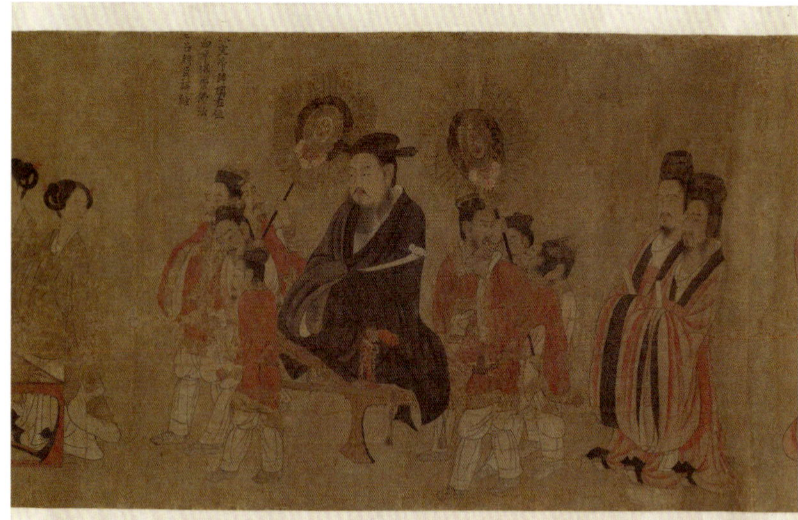

▶ **8.16** Tang, attrib. Yan Liben (c. 600–673 CE), Thirteen Emperors Handscroll: Emperor Guangwu of Han, c. 650 CE. Ink and color on silk, overall 20.18 in. × 209.06 in.

The only distinct individual in the scene is the emperor; the ladies, litter bearers, and court officials are stereotypes of their roles.

lines known as **iron-wire lines**; these lines are most obvious in the white garments of the litter-bearers where they are not obscured by the Yan Liben's strong color.

Buddhist Art in the Tang Dynasty

Taizong and Gaozong espoused Confucianism and placed Confucian scholars into administrative positions. Although Buddhism had been steadily gaining acceptance in China, its importance at the Imperial court increased during the rule of Wu Zetian. Wu Zetian came to the Imperial court as a thirteen-year-old to serve as one of Emperor Taizong's concubines. After Taizong's death, she spent a brief period at a Buddhist Temple before being recalled by Emperor Gaozong. Ambitious and ruthless, Wu Zetian engineered the ouster of the empress and took her place on the throne. When Gaozong was incapacitated by a stroke, she became regent, and after his death she ruled as emperor, the only woman in Chinese history to do so. When her rule was opposed by the Confucians at court, Wu Zetian turned to Buddhism and sponsored the building of temples and shrines to win the favor of the people. Among the many projects she patronized was the Fengxian Grotto (Ancestor Worshiping Cave) at Longmen (Dragon's Gate), overlooking the Yi River.

The Vairocana Buddha of Fengxian Grotto, c. 672–676 The central image at Fengxian Grotto a colossal, 56 foot (17 m) high image of the Cosmic Buddha, Vairocana (Figure 8.17). In Mahayana Buddhism, Vairocana is the embodiment of the generative force of the universe. He is shown seated on a lotus throne of one thousand petals. Each petal represents

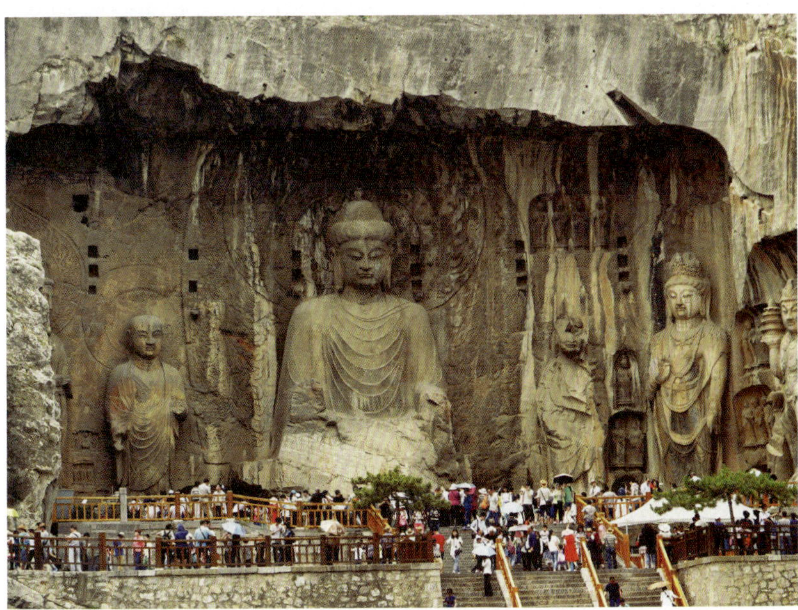

◀ **8.17** Tang, Fengxian Grotto, Vairocana Buddha, c. 672–676 CE, main figure 54 ft. high.

Empress Wu Zetian, the only female to rule China in her own name, personally sponsored the cutting of this grotto. The face of the cosmic Buddha Vairocana is thought to have the features of the empress.

a separate universe of one hundred million Buddhist worlds. On either side of the Buddha are attending bodhisattvas, disciples, and guardians, whose relative importance is shown through the use of hierarchical scale; the bodhisattvas stand 42 feet (13 m) tall, while the disciples are only 34 feet (10.5 m) high. Carved into the walls of the cave are lokapalas and figures of monks set into shallow niches between the larger figures.

Although inspired by the earlier Northern Wei style, the Fengxian Buddha has a more Sinicized appearance and less obtrusive ears. The body is less massive and more feminine. In contrast to the Buddha of Yungang Cave 20, the Fengxian Buddha wears a heavier, closed sanghati. The folds of the garment, so crisp and detailed at Yungang, are now schematized as a necklace of U-shaped lines across the Buddha's chest. The face of the Buddha also has a feminine quality and may be a portrait of Wu Zetian.

Dunhuang, Mogao Cave 45, c. 750 CE During the Tang Dynasty several Buddhist cave complexes were carved in the vicinity of Dunhuang; all were cut without royal patronage by pilgrims and merchants traveling the Silk Road. The 492 Mogao Caves range from tiny shrines to more elaborate temples filled with sculpture and paintings.

Some of the larger caves, including Cave 45 (Figure 8.18), feature alcoves filled with paintings and Buddhist sculptures. Unlike the limestone and sandstone cliffs of Longmen and Yungang, the escarpment at Mogao is a gravel conglomerate unsuitable for monumental sculpture. Instead local artisans modeled life-size sculptures out of mud and straw, using bundles of branches and reeds as an armature. These earthen figures were then covered with a coat of plaster and painted. The resulting figures are fluid in pose and gesture and seem capable of movement. In addition to sculpture, the walls of Cave 45 are decorated

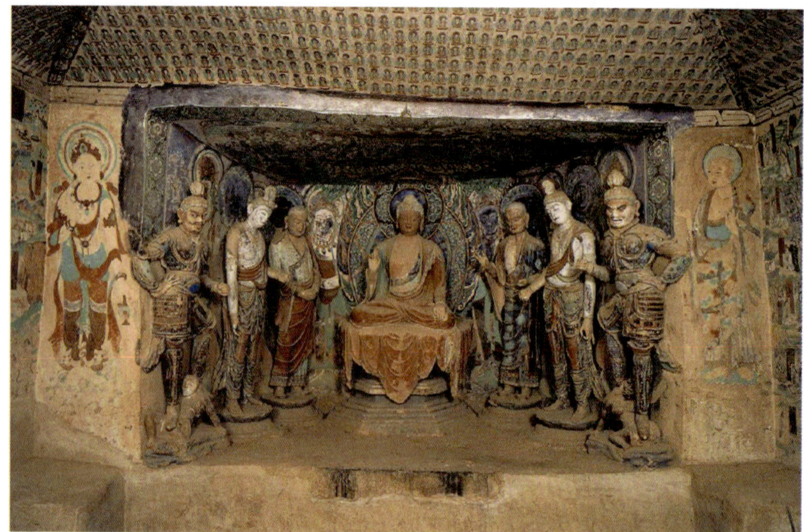

▶ **8.18** Tang, Dunhuang, Mogao Cave 45, Alcove with Buddha and Attendant Sculptures, c. 750 CE. Clay, straw, reed, plaster, and pigment.

The stone in the Dunhuang area was not suitable for carving so local artists modeled sculptures on straw and reed armatures, resulting in more natural figures that appear capable of movement.

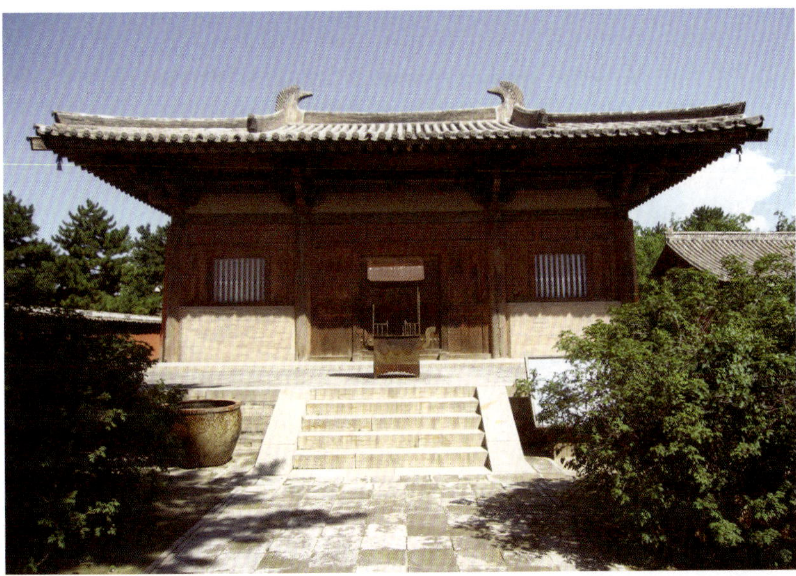

◀ 8.19 Tang, Mount Wutai, Great Buddha Hall of Nanchan Temple, 782 CE.

This timber-frame building features three bays built on a modular system and is one of the earliest surviving examples of the raised-beam roof construction that allowed the development of upswept rooflines in Chinese architecture.

with mural paintings of bodhisattvas, disciples, and guardian figures, reflecting the growing popularity of Pure Land Buddhism.

Nanchan Temple, 782 CE The Great Buddha Hall of Nanchan Temple (Figure 8.19) on Mount Wutai is one of the few examples of Tang architecture that survived the Buddhist Purges of 845 CE. An inscription on one of the beams dates the building to 782 CE, making it the oldest timber-frame building in China. The hall is a simple three bay structure, measuring 32.5 feet (10 m) deep by 38.2 feet (11.75 m) wide. As is typical in such post and beam structures, the exterior walls are non-load-bearing and simply enclose space. The roof-line shows the beginning stages of the "sweeping" upturned eaves that characterize Chinese architecture from the Tang era onward. This shape is achieved using a construction technique known as "raised-beam." In **raised-beam construction** the ridge beam sits on a stepped, box-like framework of beams and purlins which allow greater flexibility in the roof profile.

The Sung Dynasty (960–1279 CE)

The Tang dynasty collapsed in the early tenth century and China again was divided. The interregnum was another chaotic period of warring states known as the Five Dynasties and Ten Kingdoms (907–960 CE). Finally, Zhou Kuangyin, who had been a general of the Later Zhou Dynasty (951–960 CE) in the North, succeeded in reunifying the country, taking the throne as Emperor Taizu and establishing the Sung Dynasty. The Sung is divided historically into the Northern and Southern periods; the first ending with the loss of the northern territories in 1126 to Jurchen invaders.

Northern Sung Painting (c. 960–1126 CE)

The early Sung rulers were able rulers and effective military leaders who brought peace and prosperity to China. They revived the civil bureaucracy and instituted the Imperial Painting Academy under whose auspices the best artists from across China were brought to work at the Sung court. The result was an academic style that focused on representing the natural world in a highly descriptive, realistic manner. In particular, Chinese landscape painting reached its zenith during the Sung dynasty in the works of masters such Fan Kuan and Guo Xi.

▼ 8.20 Northern Sung, Fan Kuan (c. 960–1030 CE), *Travelers amid Mountains and Streams*, c. 990–1020 CE. Ink and color on silk, 81.22 in. × 40.66 in.

This monumental hanging scroll depicts a narrow slice of a vast mountain to express Daoist concepts of harmony in nature.

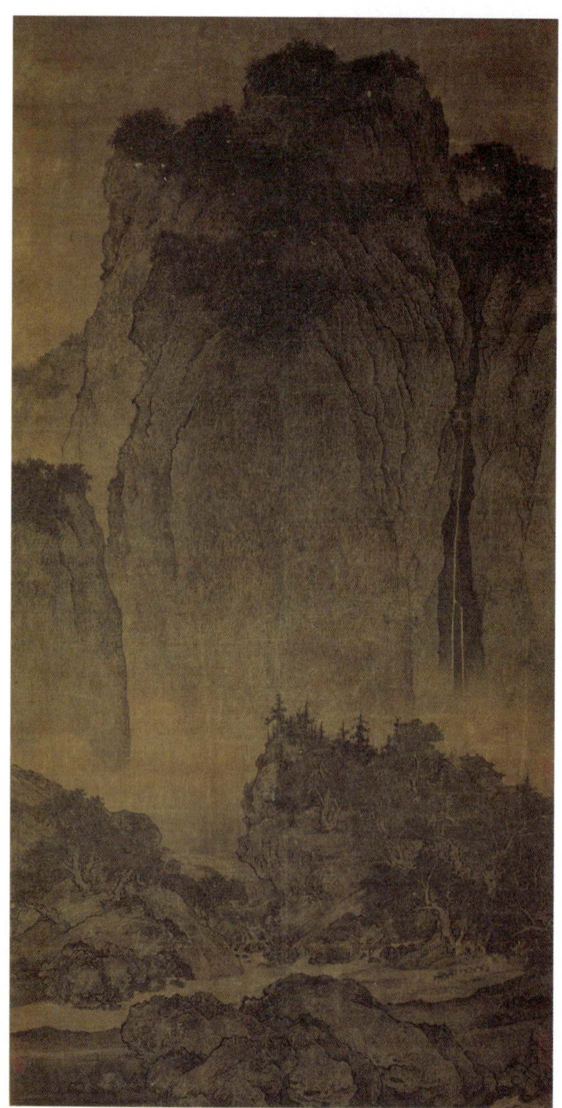

Fan Kuan (c. 960–1030 CE),* Travelers amid Mountains and Streams, *c. 990–1020 CE Perhaps the greatest master of the Northern Sung dynasty was Fan Kuan. Very little is known about the artist's life, except that he spent much of it as a Daoist recluse in the Shaanxi Mountains. His *Travelers amid Mountains and Streams* (Figure 8.20) is a Daoist meditation on nature and living in harmony with it. The large monochrome ink painting expresses the immenseness of nature by showing only a narrow slice of the massive mountain in the middle distance, making it clear that the landscape extends far beyond the edges of the scroll. Fan Kuan establishes a high vantage point in the foreground so that the viewer looks down onto a distant path cutting through low hills. Along this path an ant-size mule train moves, its miniscule scale in the landscape denoting the relative unimportance of man compared to nature. As is typical of Chinese painting, the viewer's vantage point shifts as the eye looks across to the middle ground and then up to the massive mountain in the distance.

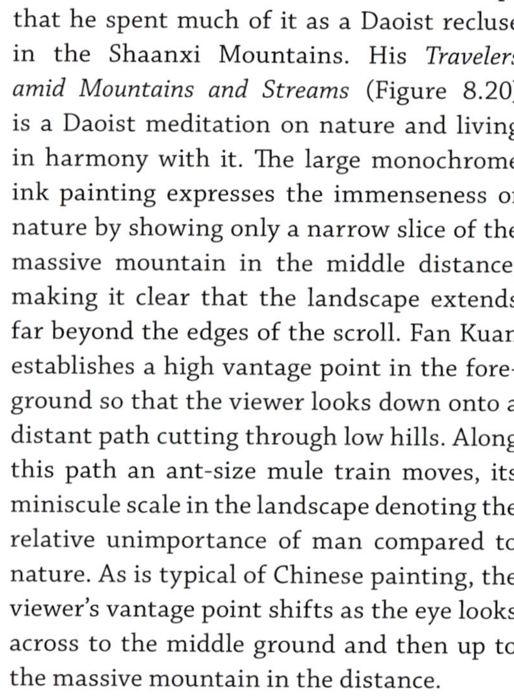

The large scale 6.75 feet (2 m) by 2.5 feet (0.8 m) of *Travelers amid Mountains and Streams* obscures some of the finer points of the scene, such as the Daoist temple on the hill above the mule train or the wealth of detail in the trees. As if stating that the essence of nature is in its particulars, Fan renders each individual leaf so exactly that at least three, perhaps four, different species of trees can be identified. Equally impressive is the skill with which the artist has drawn the tree trunks, using a single bold brush line to define form and shadow.

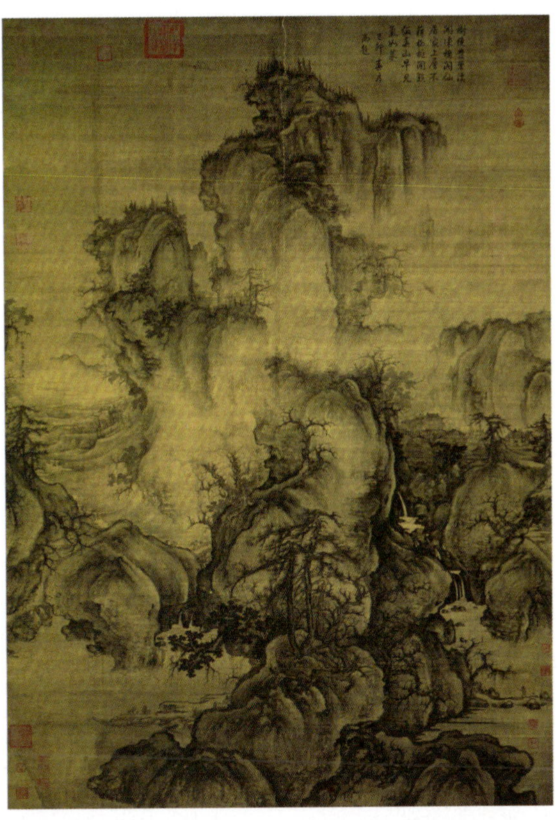

▲ 8.21 Northern Sung, Guo Xi (1020–1090 CE), *Early Spring*, 1072 CE. Ink and color on silk, 60.35 in. × 42.55 in.

In this monumental landscape Xi tries to give the viewer the experience of walking through the mountains by presenting, in shifting views, the totality of the peak.

Guo Xi (1020–1090 CE),* Early Spring, *1072 CE Guo Xi, like Fan Kuan, painted large-scale "monumental landscapes." However, unlike Daoist Fan, Guo did not withdraw from the world. He was a scholar-artist and theorist who worked in the academy of Emperor Shenzong (r. 1068–1085). He wrote an important treatise on landscape painting, *The Lofty Message of Forest and Streams*, in which he laid out his theories for creating landscape paintings that are considered from diverse perspectives within the work.

Early Spring (Figure 8.21), is a good example of Guo's unique approach to the landscape. In contrast to the prevailing view that a landscape should be painted from a single fixed vantage point, Guo favored a multipoint approach that mimicked a traveler's movement through a physical landscape. In the natural world the appearance of fixed objects in the landscape changes as the viewer shifts position from one location to the next. In an approach that seems to prefigure analytic cubism, Guo incorporated multiple views of the landscape as seen from different vantage points. He called this approach the "angle of totality" or **floating perspective**.

Guo also incorporated elements of Confucian character analogies into his landscapes. He is used three forms of trees in the landscape to describe to human nature. Upright trees represented individuals who were scholarly and approachable; bent trees suggested those who self-interested, hiding their knowledge, while gnarled trees were closed off and secretive. Guo was a master of the brush, deftly turning it from fat to thin, to define light and dark areas, create texture, and fashion the claw-like winter twigs, which were a signature element of his style. He built up chiaroscuro by layering ink washes, sometimes as many as eight over a single area.

Huizong (1082–1135 CE),* Finches and Bamboo, *c. 1100–1125 CE The eighth Sung Emperor, Huizong (r. 1101–26), was a master painter and calligrapher, who was little interested in the affairs of state. He left the task of running the empire to his mandarins and eunuchs so he could devote himself to the arts. Huizong is known for establishing the first Imperial Museum, filling it with some six thousand works collected from across the empire, and devising a system of classification for the museum holdings. He is also credited with inventing a type of script called ***shoujinti*** (slender gold script). As a painter he specialized in

TAKE A CLOSER LOOK
Painting Formats in East Asia

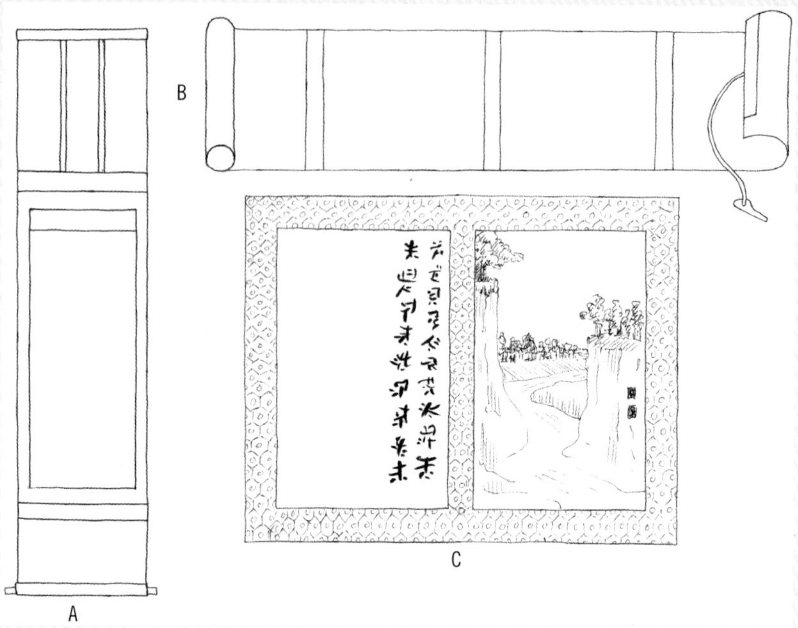

▲ **8.22** Chinese Painting Formats, A. Hanging Scroll, B. Hand Scroll, C. Album Leaf.
While painters in the West typically painted on wooden panels and later on canvas, the preferred supports in the East were silk and paper, formatted as hanging scrolls for paintings to be displayed on the walls, handscrolls for images in text or panoramic landscapes, and album leaves for more intimate works that would be held in the hand.

Unlike painters in the West who, at this time, were using tempera to create paintings on wooden panels and to illuminate manuscripts on vellum, traditional Chinese painters worked on silk and paper and used inks to create their paintings. Completed paintings were mounted to cloth backings in one of three standard formats: hanging scroll (A), handscroll (B), or album leaf (C).

Hanging scrolls are the closest in concept to Western painting. They were hung on the wall for viewing and featured a range of subjects, including calligraphy, figures, animals, floral studies, and landscapes, the last often being created in sets of four and changed out according to the seasons.

Handscrolls, by contrast, were meant to be laid out on a table for viewing in sections. Panoramic views of landscapes were frequently painted in the handscroll format so that the viewer unrolling the scroll moves through space and time as if traveling through the landscape.

Album leafs consisted of single sheet images and were often small in scale for hand viewing. Their subjects were the same as hanging scrolls but rendered in a more intimate manner. The images were commonly mounted in an accordion format, as in example C, and paired with a poem or blank page.

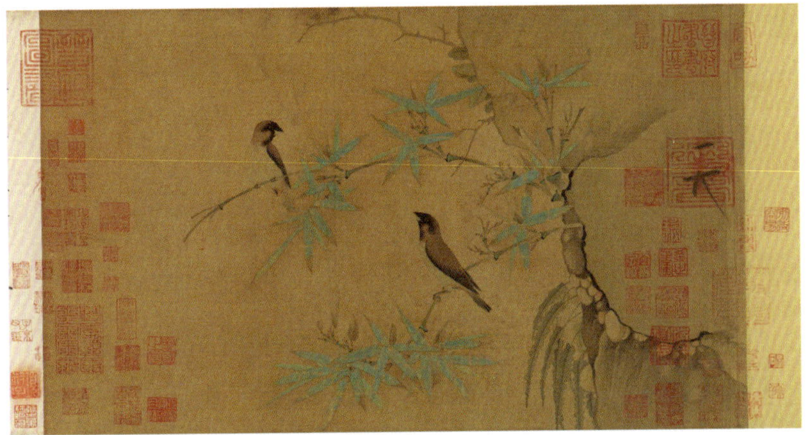

◀ **8.23** Northern Sung, Huizong (1082–1135 CE), *Finches and Bamboo*, c. 1100–1125 CE. Ink and color on silk, 13.25 in. × 21.81 in.

The images in this work are done in the mogu style, using color, rather than line, to define the forms.

scenes of court life, bamboo, flowers, and birds. He was also a poet who sought to capture the spirit of his subjects by incorporating poetry in his paintings.

Finches and Bamboo (Figure 8.23), attributed to Huizong, shows a pair of male finches alertly eyeing each other from different branches of the same bamboo stalk, as if poised to fight over mating territory. Unlike works of the monumental or panoramic styles of landscape painting where line conveyed the essence of the form, the finches and bamboo are painted in a style called ***mogu*** (boneless) in which the shape is defined by color without the use of an outline. As a final enhancement to the realism of the painting, Huizong added a single drop of clear lacquer to each bird's eyes to give them a glassy, lifelike sheen. Huizong did not sign his name to his paintings. His work is identified by the inscription *Yubi yiren* or "The Sovereign of the Imperial Brush" written at the end of the scroll (www.britishmuseum.org).

The Southern Sung Painting (c. 1127–1279 CE)

In 1125 CE the Jurchen Jin Dynasty attacked northern China and Emperor Huizong quickly abdicated in favor of his eldest son Zhao Huan. The last northern Sung emperor reigned for a single year before he, Huizong, and three thousand members of the court were taken prisoner. Huizong's ninth son, Zhao Gou, managed to flee to the south, where he established a new capital at Hangzhou, and took the throne of a greatly reduced Sung Empire, as Emperor Sung Gaozong (r. 1127–1162).

Gaozong gathered to his southern court all the Imperial administrators, scholars, and artists who had managed to evade the Jurchen, and tried to recreate the institutions of his father's northern court, including the Imperial Painting Academy. Painters of the restored academy continued to work in the same genres that had been staples of the Huizong era. Southern painters also produced more intimate works, often as album leafs, that seem to evoke a single transient moment in time.

Ma Yuan (c. 1160–1225),* On a Mountain Path in Spring, *c. 1190–1220

More than any other artist Ma Yuan's work exemplifies the spirit of the Southern Sung. He was born in Qiantang to a multi-generational family of artists, all of whom had worked in the Imperial Painting Academy. Ma Yuan served in the courts of Emperor Gaungzong and Emperor Ningzong as a painter in attendance.

Ma Yuan painted flowers, figures, and landscapes, the last being the genre in which he excelled. His hanging and hand scrolls often feature barren crags rising like shards of glass from fog-shrouded valleys. He preferred to paint in monochrome in an angular style, using iron-wire lines to define trees and rocks and ax-chop strokes to create the rough faces of mountains and boulders. In Daoist fashion his depictions of men and their works are often rendered in reduced scale compare to nature.

On a Mountain Path in Spring (Figure 8.24), a landscape in album leaf format, illustrates a foggy landscape through which a scholar and his servant pass. Most of the elements are placed in the lower left, leaving the remainder of the page to be interpreted as mist or cloud. This format was so often used by Ma that he was known as "one corner Ma." Also typical of Ma's work are the barren willow trees bending in the breeze; in this painting, the willow is a symbol of spring as well as the act of leaving. The scholar is followed by his servant, carrying a ***guzheng*** or Chinese zither, perhaps a reference to Confucian beliefs about the power of music. Startled by the passage of the men through the landscape, a bird takes wing. The path, branches, and bird all direct the viewer to the inscription, a poem written in the upper right-hand corner, which was composed by the Emperor Ningzong. The emperor, together with his empress, frequently wrote poems to accompany Ma's album leaf paintings. It reads "The wild flowers dance when brushed by my sleeves. Reclusive birds make no sound as they shun the presence of people."

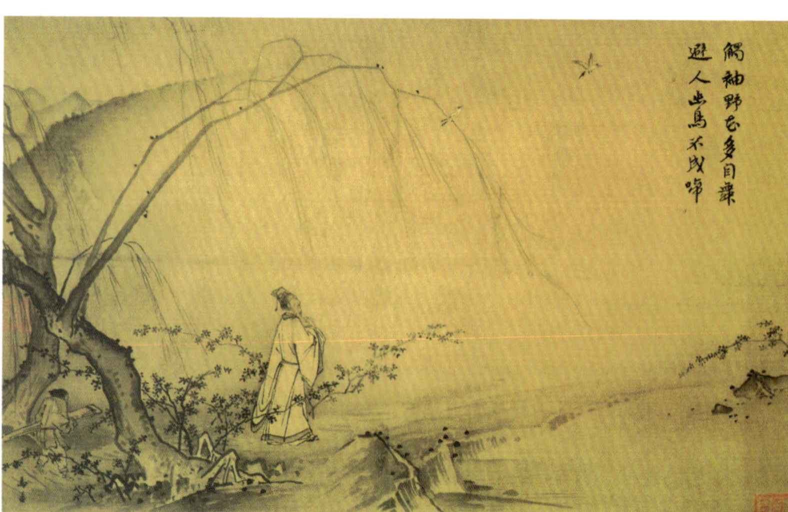

▶ **8.24** Southern Sung, Ma Yuan (c. 1160–1225 CE), *On a Mountain Path in Spring*, c. 1190–1220. Ink and color on silk, 10.78 in. × 17 in.

A scholar, followed by his servant, embarks on a journey on a foggy spring morning. The compositional elements direct the viewer to a poem Emperor Ningzong wrote to accompany the work.

Buddhist Art during the Southern Sung

During the late Tang and again during the Five Dynasties, many Buddhist sects were banned in China and the wealth of their temples seized. The exception was Chan Buddhism, which had been introduced in the sixth century CE by the Indian monk Bodhidarma, famous for his feats of meditation. Traditional Buddhist images were rejected by Chan devotes as worthless in achieving enlightenment. Instead, Chan Buddhism held that enlightenment could come as a spontaneous realization, often when engaged in menial, repetitive tasks, or as a gradual awakening through meditation.

Chan monks used monochrome brush painting as a form of meditation. In Chan Buddhist painting spontaneity was important, and paintings were begun with a few strokes or splashes of ink, and without any preconception of subject. In painting there was no attempt to model forms or create illusions of depth as that would be counterproductive to the goal of enlightenment, in essence adding illusion to the already illusionary world.

Liang Kai (c. 1140–1210 CE), Sixth Chan Patriarch Chopping Bamboo, _twelfth century CE_ Liang Kai began his artistic career by following the traditional path of the Imperial Painting Academy and ultimately rose to the rank of painter-in-attendance at the Imperial court. For unknown reasons he left court, and entered a Chan Buddhist monastery. *Sixth Chan Patriarch Chopping Bamboo* (Figure 8.25) is a simple, direct presentation of the Chan Patriarch Huineng engaged in the sort of mundane, repetitive activity that could lead to spiritual awakening. Indeed, Liang is showing us that very moment when the repetitive sound of the blade striking against the bamboo prompts the realization of the Patriarch's own enlightenment. Ironically, Chan Buddhist paintings are not much admired in China where the style originated. Many works by Liang Kai and other Chinese Chan Buddhist artists were exported to Japan where they influenced the development of Zen Buddhist painting.

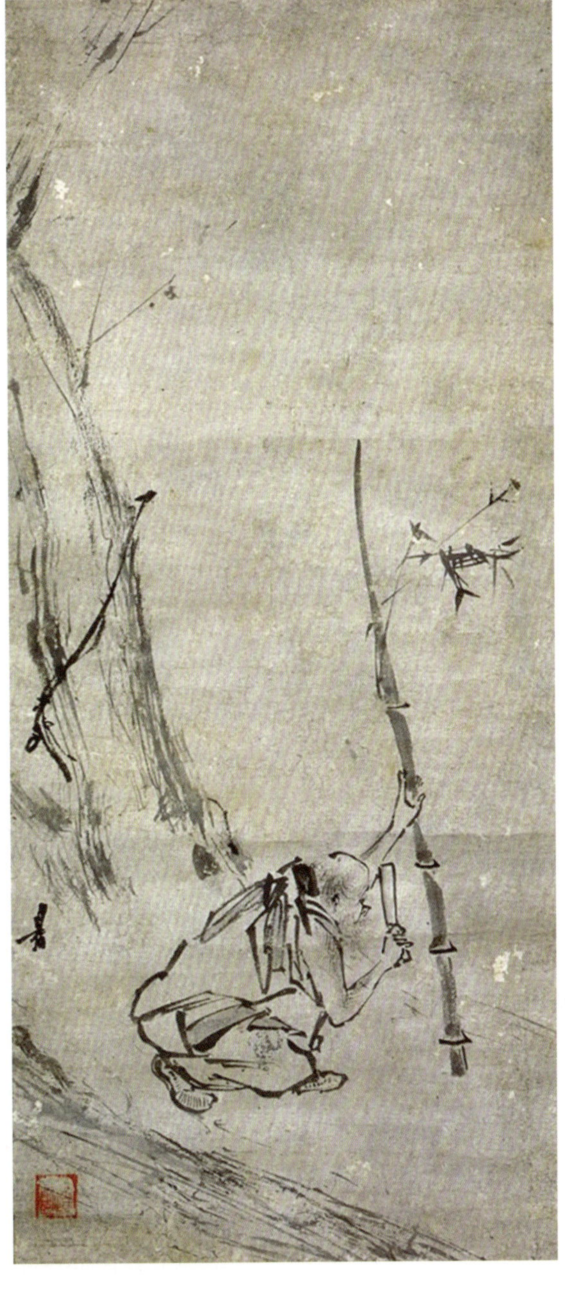

▼ 8.25 Southern Sung, Liang Kai (c. 1140–1210 CE), *The Sixth Chan Patriarch Chopping Bamboo*, twelfth century CE. Ink on paper.

Chan Buddhist paintings were a form of meditation and executed spontaneously. It shows the patriarch Huineng doing an activity that led to his spontaneous enlightenment.

The Yuan (Mongolian) Dynasty (1279–1368)

In 1206, the Mongol chief Temujin, having consolidated all the warring tribes under his rule, was proclaimed leader of all Mongols, and took the title Genghis Khan, meaning "world ruler." The Mongol empire he founded would ultimately stretch from the Yellow Sea in the east to the Caspian Sea in the west.

The conquest of the Jurchen Jin Dynasty in 1234 CE brought northern China into the Mongol Empire, and in 1279, the defeat of the Southern Sung brought all of China under the rule of the Yuan Dynasty. Kublai Khan established his capital at Khanbalik (Beijing), and determined to make his court as glorious as those of the Sung. He called China's greatest scholars and artists to his service, but most refused him. In 1286, Zhao Mengfu, a descendant of the Sung dynasty, believing that his presence at court would allow him to advocate on behalf of the Chinese people, accepted the Mongol invitation. However, his reputation in Chinese history suffered as a result of his collaboration with the Mongols.

Zhao Mengfu (1254–1322 CE),* Groom and Horse, *1296 CE Zhao Mengfu, put aside the refined styles of the Sung, realizing that his Yuan masters, while admiring the Sung, did not understand the intellectual subtitles of their art. Zhao drew on the painting traditions of the Tang dynasty, which were considered more direct and virile, to create a style that would be appreciated by the nomadic Mongols. This less refined style would be a better vehicle for his message, advocating for better treatment of the Chinese people, particularly the Chinese scholars at court, who were often assigned to the most menial tasks.

Groom and Horse (Figure 8.26) is an example of Zhao's subtle activism. Zhao depicts the powerful horse in an abstracted foreshortened pose with an economy of line, minimal modeling, and no color. The animal has grown fat from long hours in the stable. In contrast the groom is rendered frontally and is taller than the horse; both elements give him

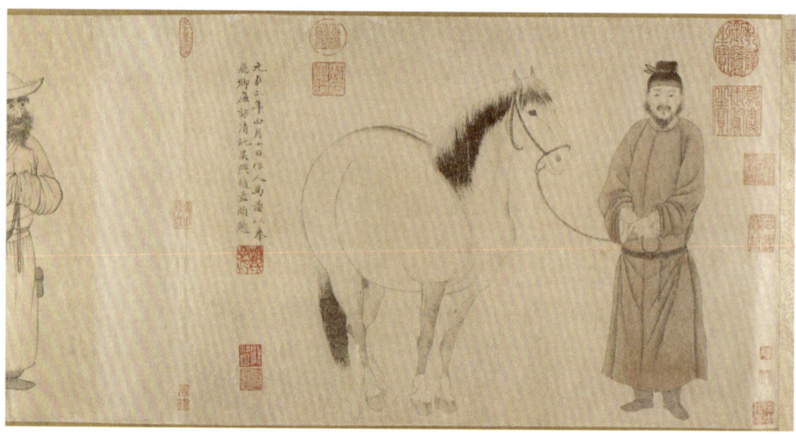

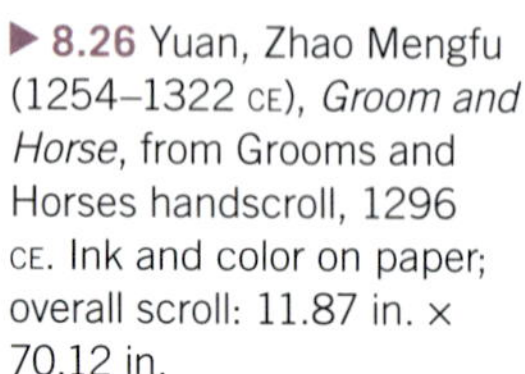

▶ **8.26** Yuan, Zhao Mengfu (1254–1322 CE), *Groom and Horse*, from Grooms and Horses handscroll, 1296 CE. Ink and color on paper; overall scroll: 11.87 in. × 70.12 in.

Zhao painted this work to advocate for better treatment of Chinese at the Yuan court, suggesting that they, like the horse, suffer from disuse.

greater visual importance. He is well-modeled, giving him a realism and dimensionality lacking in the horse. His face is an individualized portrait, possibly that of the artist, rather than a generalized type. The work was inspired by a saying attributed to the Tang era philosopher, Han Yu (762–824): "There are always excellent steeds, but not always a Bole, the excellent judge of horses." The reference is to a farmer Bo Le who is credited with the invention of equine physiognomy or judging horses by their appearance. In comparing the horse, highly valued by the Mongols, to the Chinese groom, the work can be read as a commentary on the Mongol ruler's failure to properly value Chinese scholars. The inspription tells us that the painting was created for Surveillance Commissioner Feiqing, who is thought to have been a government recruiter.

Guan Dao Sheng (1262–1319 CE),* Bamboo Groves in Mist and Rain, *1308 CE

Zhao Mengfu was accompanied to the Mongol court by his wife, Lady Guan Dao Sheng. While her husband painted to please his Yuan masters, Lady Guan was free to paint in the more literary style of the Sung era. She is especially known for her studies of bamboo and for her treatise on the subject, *The Bamboo in Monochrome*, which remains a standard reference on the art and philosophy of painting bamboo.

Bamboo Groves in Mist and Rain (Figure 8.27) depicts an entire grove of bamboo spread across a natural landscape, rather than the more typical solitary stalk against a blank ground. The level vantage point, shallow depth, obscuring mist, and calligraphic treatment of the bamboo reflect the influence of the Southern Sung School of painting. Guan DaoSheng skillfully moves the viewer through the composition without using the earlier Sung trope of a pathway. Instead, she uses the clumps of bamboo to lead the eye into the landscape and the fog bank to block and redirect visual movement.

THE LITERATI PAINTERS

The invitation to work at the Mongol court was refused by many scholar-artists who had served the fallen Sung. Instead, they elected to become recluses living far from the Mongol capital and spending

▼ **8.27** Yuan, Guan Dao Sheng (1262–1219 CE), *Bamboo Groves in Mist and Rain*, 1308 CE. Ink on paper, overall size: 9.12 in. × 44.87 in.

Lady Guan was a master of bamboo painting and wrote the standard treatise on the subject. In this scroll she skillfully moves the viewer through the landscape using fog banks to direct the eye.

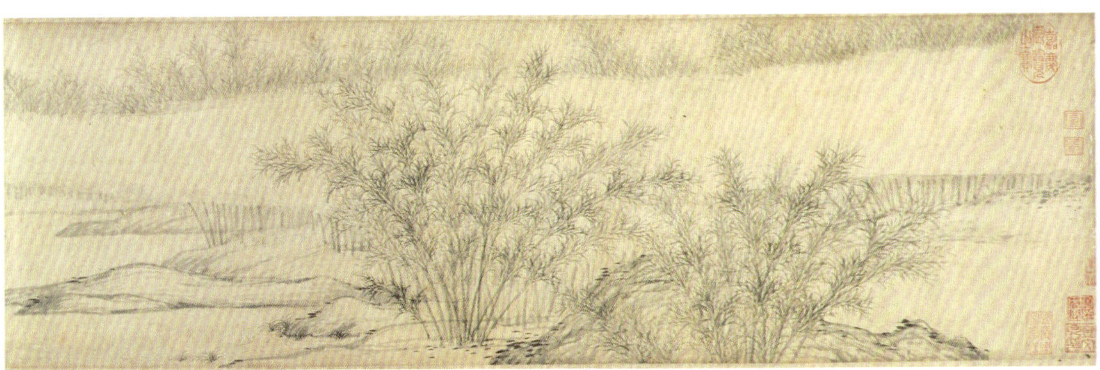

their time in scholarly pursuits, writing poetry, practicing calligraphy, and ink painting. Freed from the dictates of Imperial service, they developed art styles which emphasized individuality and self-expression. These artists became known as Literati painters, and four, Huang Gongwang, Wu Zhen, Ni Zan, and Wang Meng, are considered to be the Four Great Masters of Yuan Painting.

Huang Gongwang (1269–1354 CE),* Dwelling in the Fuchun Mountains, *1347–1350 CE Huang Gongwang was born Lu Jian in Changshu. A child prodigy and orphan, he was renowned for reading the Confucian classics at a young age. His talents attracted the attention of Huang Le, an elderly childless man, who adopted the boy to carry on his family's name. Lu Jian's adopted name reflects the circumstances of his adoption; it means "Old Man Huang's Longing." Huang Gongwang was brilliant but wayward. He easily passed the civil service exam but was quickly dismissed for malfeasance. For a time he made a living as a fortune-teller before ending up in prison in mid-life. When Huang was released from prison he retired to Zhejiang province in eastern China, took up residence along the banks of the Fuchun river, and devoted himself entirely to painting. His masterpiece *Dwelling in the Fuchun Mountains* was painted when the artist was seventy-eight years old.

Dwelling in the Fuchun Mountains (Figure 8.28) depicts the panorama of the mountains that rise west of Hangzhou. The colophon relates that the entire composition of mountains, hills, marshes, and river was sketched out in one sitting using light ink. Then as the spirit moved him, Huang added in features using a dry brush technique. The scroll is interesting in that it reveals that the artist reworked

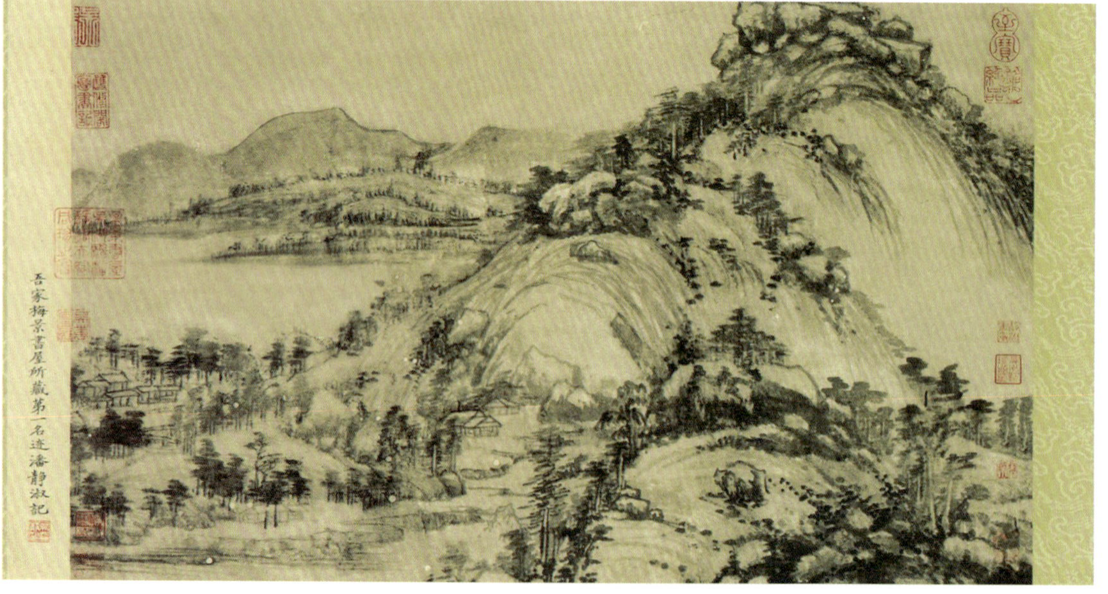

▼ 8.28 Huang Gongwang (1269–1354 CE), *Dwelling in the Fuchun Mountains*, 1347–1350 CE. Ink on paper.

Huang began his masterpiece when he was seventy-eight years old and worked on it for three years, off and on. In it he introduces a dry brush technique to give texture and form to his mountains.

parts of the composition, redrawing forms, darkening contour lines, and adding long **hemp-fiber** brush strokes to create texture on the hill-and-mountain-sides. Today the scroll exists in two sections, the longer one known as the *Master Wu Young Scroll* (in Taipei) and the smaller *Remaining Mountain* (in Hangzhou). In the seventeenth century the painting was owned by wealthy Wu Hongyu who ordered it to be burned as a ritual sacrifice at his death. The scroll was duly tossed into the flames by his relatives but it was rescued by a niece, who concealed her act by thowing another, less significant, scroll into the fire.

Wu Zhen (1280–1354 CE), Crooked Pine, 1335 CE Wu Zhen (1280–1354 CE) was born in Jiaxing and spent his life as a hermit in the mountains of Zhejiang province. Wu's paintings are more than depictions of their subjects—pine trees, rocks, fishermen; they are filled with symbols that reference the adversities of the time. Fishermen, for example, speak of the discrimination of Mongol rule, when Chinese scholars were often unemployed. Pine trees, long a Confucian analogy for the moral integrity and steadfastness of the Chinese scholar or gentleman, are another frequent subject.

Crooked Pine (Figure 8.29) depicts an ancient pine tree beside a rock. It is placed close to the picture plane with only the suggestion of another distant tree lost in the fog. While the lower portion of the tree trunk is upright, suggesting a past period of good conditions, the top is bent and twisted by adversity. By bending and twisting the upper trunk but not breaking it, Wu is suggesting the ability to withstand the travails of more recent times. In the hands of the Literati painter, pine trees became a metaphor for enduring the discrimination and hardships of the Mongol rule. The roots of the tree are wedged between the barren rock and weeds, a further suggestion of difficult times.

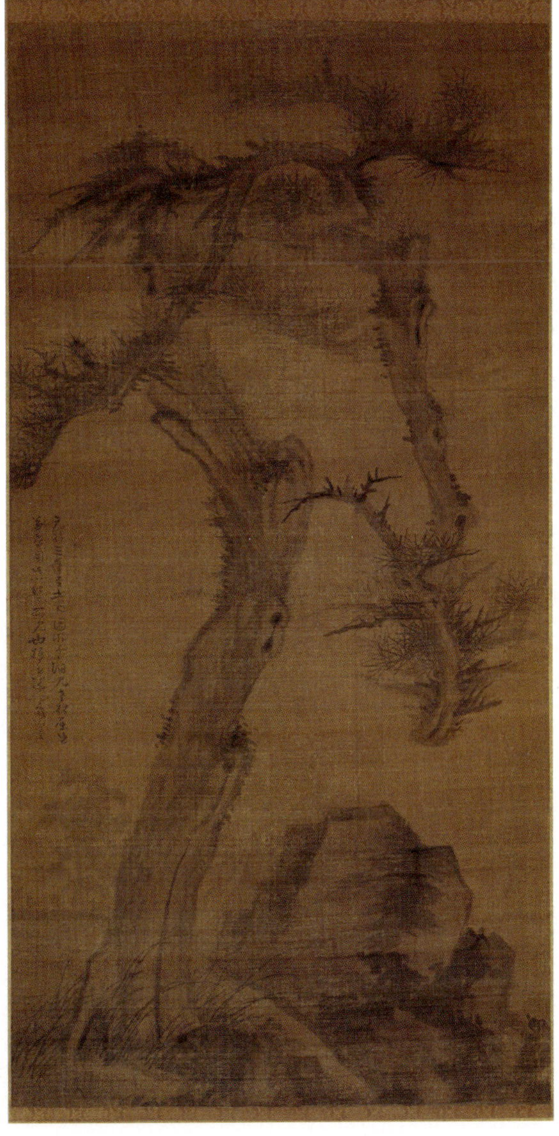

▼ **8.29** Yuan, Wu Zhen (1280–1354 CE), *Crooked Pine*, 1335 CE. Ink on silk, 65.37 in. × 32.50 in.

Wu Zhen's paintings often feature a few stalks of bamboo or a pine tree next to a mossy rock and are intended to express Confucian attributes that allow the Chinese scholar to endure the hardships of Mongol rule.

The Ming or "Radiant" Dynasty (1368–1644)

Although rebellions were common during the Yuan, most were local and easily put down by the ruthless Mongol armies. It was not until

1352, that Zhu Yuanzgang, leader of the Red Turbans, was able to unite all the rebel factions and drive the Mongols out of China. In 1368, he took the throne as Emperor Hong Wu of the Ming "radiant" Dynasty. The new emperor instituted land reforms and public works projects such as the restoration of the Great Wall, and sponsored the revival of traditional arts such as bronze-casting and lacquer-working. He also invited artists and scholars to his court, offering them rank and income. However, they soon realized they would not be accorded the same respect they had enjoyed under the Sung. They were expected to perform duties they considered to be beneath their status, and those who challenged the emperor, even on aesthetic matters, found themselves exiled, imprisoned, or executed. When Hong Wu died, he was briefly succeeded by his grandson, Zhu Yunwen. But in 1402, the throne was usurped by Zhu Di, the fourth son of Hong Wu, who had been passed over because of questions about his parentage. Zhu Di took the throne as Emperor Yongle (r. 1402–1424), meaning "Perpetual Happiness."

The Forbidden City or Zijincheng Palace, 1406 Emperor Yongle's first act was to move the capital to Beijing. His selection of Beijing was based on the city's symbolic importance. The Chinese believed Beijng to be directly under the North Star, a star that was a fixed point in the heavens and had a purplish tint. Beijing was somethimes called the "purple city" because of its association with the Pole Star. Yongle's palace is known in Chinese as Zijincheng, which translates literally as "North Star (zi) forbidden (jin) walled city (cheng)." By placing his palace in the center of the polar city and painting its walls purple, Yongle was comparing himself to the Pole Star, a fixed point in the heavens around which everything else revolved.

The design of the palace complex was inspired by concepts of state organization originating in the *Zhou Li*, written probably in the

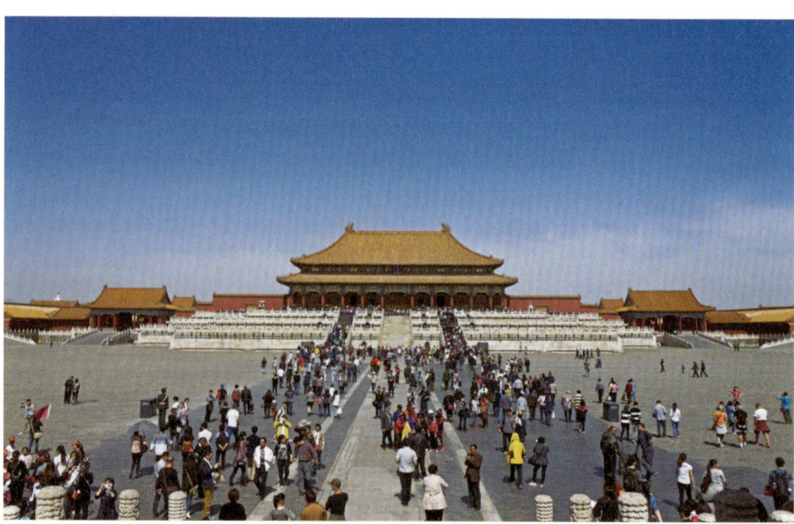

▶ 8.30 Ming, Beijing, Forbidden City, Outer Court and Hall of Supreme Harmony, 1406–1420 CE.

Begun by Emperor Yongle when he moved the capital to Beijing, construction of the city's 9,999 rooms was completed in only fourteen years by a labor force of 100,000 men.

first century BCE but attributed to the Western Zhou period and by the more practical Northern Sung dynasty architectural manual, the *Yingzao Fashi* or *Treatise on Architectural Methods* of Lie Zi. Both works argued for a hierachical arrangement of architecture, and this is clearly evident in the arrangement of public and private buildings within the greater complex. The Forbidden City encorporates within its walls and surrounding moat, an area measuring 3123 feet (961m) by 2447 feet (753 m). The palace is composed of several compounds with more than 2 million square feet of floor space divided into 9,999 rooms. The number nine symbolizes the quality of permanence or "everlastingness" in Chinese numerology. The palace buildings are formal, symmetrical, hierarchically ordered, and oriented according to the Chinese concepts of geomancy. Visitors entered through the meridian gate in the south wall, ascending one of the outer ramps according to their rank, and entered the first court, crossing over the canalized "Golden Waters" river. Dirt from the canal and moat excavations was used to construct an artificial hill on the north side of the compound opposite the Meridian Gate.

A second gateway provided access to the second court, the Wai Chao, where public ceremonies were held. The main feature of the second court was a large, tiered marble platform shaped like a capital letter "I," which supported a succession of three halls: the Hall of Supreme Harmony (Figure 8.30), the Hall of Central Harmony and the Hall of Preserving Harmony; the first two provided the stage for Imperial audiences and rituals, while the third was the site where the highest level of civil service exams were given. Within the third compound were the private residences of the emperor, empress, and chief concubines.

PAINTING IN THE MING DYNASTY

Painters of the revived Imperial Painting Academy were required to emulate the conservative, realistic, and often didactic styles of the Southern Sung as a means of demonstrating the virtue, grandeur, and beneficence of the Ming dynasty. Outside of the Imperial Academy two independent schools of painting evolved during the Ming. The first of these was the Zhe or Southern School. The name was derived from Zhejiang, the province of the Southern Song capital, Hangzhou; these painters also imitated the style of the Southern Sung. The second school was the Wu, located in the Wu county of Suzhou in Jiangsu province. The Wu school painters emulated the Literati painters of the Yuan and like them, saw art as a vehicle for personal expression and intellectual diversion.

Shen Zhou (1427–1509 CE),* Lofty Mount Lu, *1467 CE Shen Zhou, was born in Changzhou. His father was a tax collector under the Yuan and Ming Dynasties, a position that allowed the family to amass great wealth.

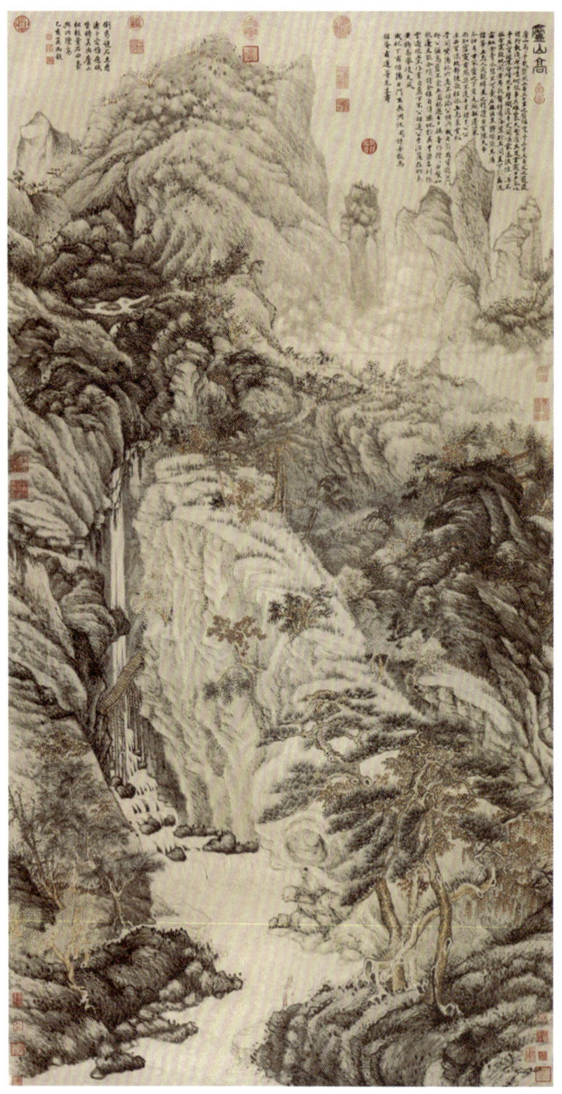

▲ 8.31 Ming, Shen Zhou (1427–1509 CE), *Lofty Mount Lu*, 1467 CE. Ink and color on paper, 76.29 in. × 38.62 in.

Shen painted this hanging scroll for his teacher on the occasion of Chen Kuan's seventieth birthday. In it he compares Chen's greatness to that of the sacred mountain from his master's home province. To give the viewer a sense of scale, Shen included a tiny figure in the foreground.

Although Shen Zhou expected to follow in his father's footsteps, when the elder Shen died, the son invoked Confucian filial duty, and remained at home to care for his widowed mother, devoting himself to his art. Shen Zhou spent his time collecting the art of the four Yuan masters and collaborating with like-minded painter-scholars to create works combining the arts of poetry, painting, and calligraphy. He is credited with founding the Wu or Southern School of painting.

Lofty Mount Lu (Figure 8.31), as indicated in the inscription, was painted as a seventieth birthday gift for Chen Kuan, Shen Zhou's teacher. The subject of the painting is Mount Lu, the sacred mountain where Huiyuan founded the first Pure Land Monastery. Shen intends the mountain as a learned allusion to the virtue and character of his teacher. Early in his career Shen greatly admired the structural complexity of Wang Meng's paintings. The influence of the Yuan master is evident in the way Shen Zhou builds up the dense masses of the mountain with long hemp-fiber strokes done in light brown ink, and then adds layers of darker inks to produce texture and pattern, and to energize his forms. To give the viewer a sense of the scale of the mountain, and by analogy the stature of his teacher, Shen Zhou includes a figure standing so that he is silhouetted against the river. Poetic inscriptions were an important part of Wu School painting and Shen fills the sky with a long poem of praise dedicated to his teacher, describing the mountain as low in comparison to the heights of his teacher's eminence (Edwards 1962, 84).

Dong Qichang (1555–1636 CE),* The Qingbian Mountains*, 1617 CE Dong Qichang was a child prodigy who passed the metropolitan civil service exam at age twelve. Five years later he took the Imperial exams but placed second because of his poor calligraphy. Undaunted by his failure, Dong spent the next few years mastering calligraphy. When he finally passed the Imperial exams, he began an undistinguished career as a civil servant. Dong seems to have had considerable difficulties dealing with the people. There are stories of student rebellions when he was at the Imperial Academy and of disputes with local townspeople ending in his house being set afire when he was a magistrate.

Despite his difficult personality, he was repeatedly called to service by the Emperor Guangzong. In 1634, at the age of seventy-nine, Dong retired, determined to devote himself entirely to his art.

The Qingbian Mountains (Figure 8.32) shows Dong's intellectual approach to painting. In it he compresses foreground, middleground, and background into a single vertical space that negates illusions of distance. Dong relies on the expressive power of his brushstrokes to abstract the landscape into austere patterns of negative and positive space, evoking the same stark contrasts of black ink and white paper valued in calligraphy. His scenes are not burdened with unnecessary detail, painterly excesses, or distracting narrative; instead, they are alive with the energy of nature.

In his writings Dong Qichang insisted on the importance of studying the work of past masters as a means of enhancing one's own work, not through imitation but as an aid to finding one's artistic voice. His works were often inspired by those of earlier painters. The first of two inscriptions at the top of the painting identifies the it as being of the Qingbian Mountains in manner of Dong Yuan (a painter of the Five Dynasties and Ten Kingdoms period), and as painted for Tung Hsuan-tsai (whose seal appears on the work), in the summer of 1617. The second inscription is a poetic description of the scene of mountains amid rustling streams as a worthy place to spend an autumn day, book in hand, meditating on the Dao (Way).

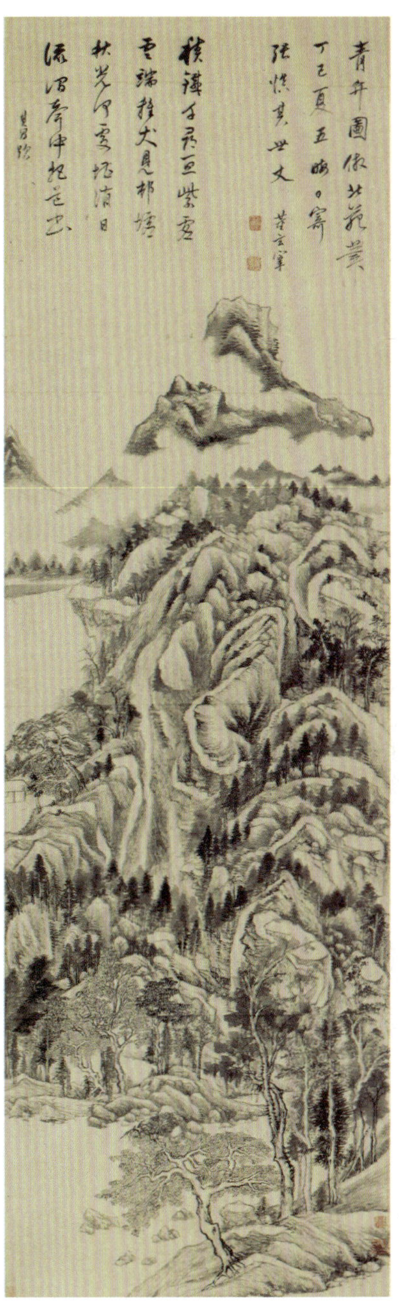

▲ **8.32** Ming, Dong Qichang (1555–1636 CE), *The Qingbian Mountains*, 1617 CE. Ink on paper, 88.38 in × 26.45 in.

Dong uses the contrast of black ink on white paper to build an abstracted landscape of negative and positive spaces.

The Qing Dynasty (1644–1911 CE)

In 1616, Nurhaci, a Jurchen chieftain, proclaimed the Later Jin Dynasty and declared himself emperor. Two years later, citing "Seven Great Vexations" allegedly perpetrated by the Ming against his family, his throne, and his state, he attacked China. The conquest of the Ming Empire was completed by his son, Huang Taiji (r. 1626–1643 CE). In 1635 Huang Taiji changed the name of his people to Manchu, and the following year, the name of the dynasty was changed to Qing.

The Qing dynasty was a time of increased contact with the West. Jesuit missionaries were allowed into China and some brought to the Imperial court to advance science, mathematics, and astronomy. Jesuit artists also came but ideas of Western perspective had little effect on Chinese artists who did view European art as significant. Chinese painters at the Imperial court, known as Orthodox Painters, worked in an extremely conservative style, which imitated the Yuan Literati painters but did not embrace their philosophy of personal expression.

At the other extreme were the Individualist Painters. who following the spirit of the Yuan Literati Masters, and chose not to work for foreign overlords. They lived as hermits and abided by the Yuan principles of personal expression, improvisation, and nonconformity in their art. The greatest of the Qing individualist painters was Zhu Ruoji, known as Shitao, a descendant of Ming Emperor Hong Wu.

Shitao (1642–1707 CE),* Man in a House beneath a Cliff, *c. 1660–1707

Shitao (Monk of the Bitter Gourd) lived most of his life in a Buddhist monastery far from Beijing. In 1693, he converted to Daoism and spent the last years of his life in Yangzhou. Shitao was an unconventional artist, rejecting the norms of the time, which valued imitation over innovation. Although Shitao was influenced by his Yuan Literati predecessors and the Ming artist Shen Zhou, his art breaks dramatically with theirs. Shitao often complained the obsession for imitating the old masters made it impossible for people to appreciate work that was original and innovative.

In his treatise "Collection of Sayings on Paintings," Shitao advocated the use of a single brushstroke or **primordial line** as the foundation of all painting. In *Man in a House beneath a Cliff* (Figure 8.33), he uses a bold contour line stroke to build up his forms, suggest contrasts of light and shadow, and create atmospheric perspective. After establishing his forms, Shitao added bold areas of washes and impressionistic **dian** or "dots" of pale pink and blue, to suggest the light refracting quality of mist.

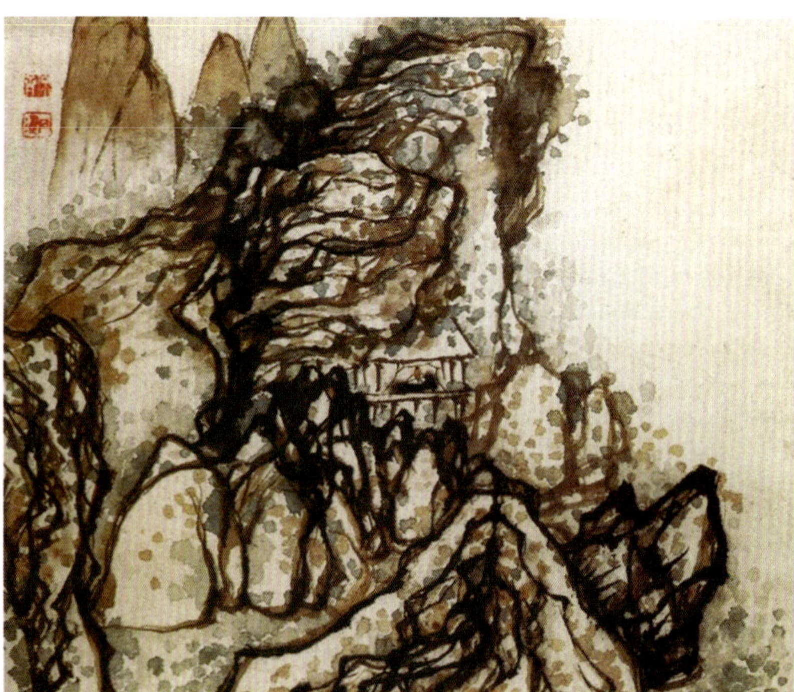

▶ 8.33 Qing, Shitao (1642–1707 CE), *Man in a House beneath a Cliff*, c. 1660–1707 CE. Ink and color on paper, 9.50 in. × 11 in.

In this work Shitao builds line and the illusion of space through the use of atmospheric contour or "primal" lines and dots of color.

The People's Republic of China (1949–)

After a series of revolts and rebellions, which necessitated foreign intervention, the Qing Dynasty fell in 1912. Under the leadership of Dr. Sun Yat-sin, a Western-style Republic of China (1912–1949) was instituted. During this brief period, Chinese artists were free to travel for study in the West. When they returned, they brought knowledge of Western modernism and media to China. This experiment in democracy was brought down after World War II during a civil war with Chinese communists led by Mao Zedong. The leaders of the republic fled to Taiwan and reestablished a democratic China there.

Under Mao Zedong the arts had only one purpose: to serve the propaganda needs of the Communist Party. In his 1942 speech at the Yenan Forum, Mao stated: "There is no such thing as art for art's sake, art that stands above the classes, or art that is detached from or independent of politics." Following the Soviet model, the only acceptable style under Mao was socialist realism. Traditional ink painting was seen as manifesting the bourgeois tastes of the oppressive regimes of the pre-Communist era. Artists working in traditional or Western styles, introduced during the brief republican era, risked public censure, imprisonment, torture, the destruction of their artwork, and loss of their homes and property. During the Cultural Revolution (1966–1976), many artists, particularly those who were teachers, were denounced and sent to reeducation camps while their work was ridiculed in "black painting" shows reminiscent of the Nazi exhibitions of "degenerate art."

Ye Yushan (b. 1935),* Rent Collection Courtyard, *1965 Ye Yushan is an artist whose work won favor under Mao. He studied at the Sichuan Institute of Fine Arts and the Central Academy of Fine Arts, and later served as the director of the Sichuan Institute of Fine Arts. In 1965, he was commissioned to create a multi-figure, site-specific work by the Sichuan Ministry of Culture. The work was a large propaganda piece that would be placed on the property in Dayi that had been owned by Liu Wencai (1881–1949). Under the Maoist regime, Liu Wencai was vilified as an example of the evils of the old regime, and of Republican era capitalism. His alleged crimes included abuses of the peasants such as imprisonment and murder. Although popularly portrayed as a monster, Liu was far from evil; during the Japanese invasion, he was credited with saving the lives of many Red Army soldiers.

The enormous sculpture group *The Rent Collection Courtyard* (Figure 8.34), originally included 114 life-size figures, and was the realization of Mao's call for a new revolutionary art that would depict the struggles and achievements of the proletariat. Mao believed this could only be achieved if artists lived and learned from the people, so Ye Yushan, along with a group of teachers and students from the

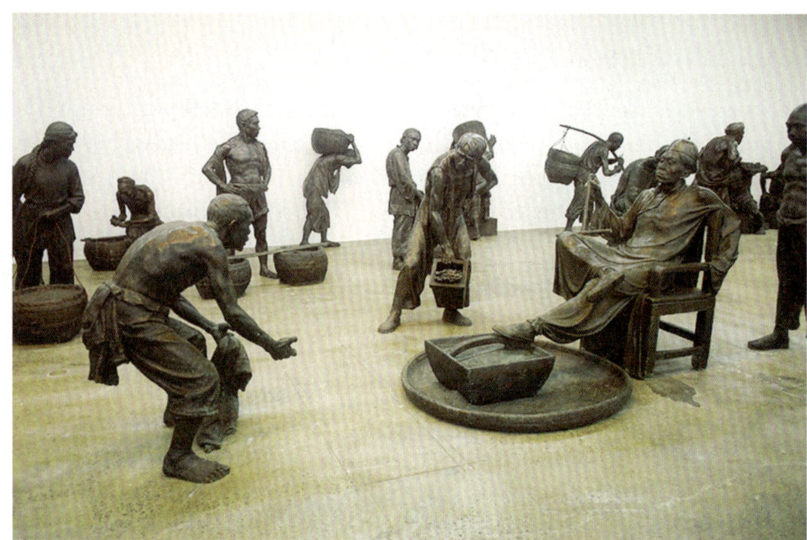

▶ **8.34** Ye Yushan (b. 1935), *Rent Collection Courtyard*, 1965. Copper-plated fiberglass replicas.

The original 114 sculptures were made using wooden armatures and modeled using clay and straw, then stained and given black glass eyes. They told the story of the alleged abuses of a wealthy landowner during the Qing and Republican eras.

Sichuan Fine Arts Institute, went to Dayi, where they worked with local folk artists to create the pieces, using "peasant" materials. In a technique reminiscent of the Mogao Buddhist sculptures near Dunhuang, the artists began by building wooden armatures over which the figures were modeled with a compound of clay and straw. The surface was then coated with a finer mixture of clay, sand, and cotton, with black glass added to give a life-like quality to the eyes. These original sculptures were completed in less than five months. *The Rent Collection Courtyard* proved so popular that 103 of its figures were replicated in copper-plated fiberglass for durability and use in traveling educational exhibitions across China.

Art after Mao (1976–)

When Den Xiaoping took the reins of government after the death of Chairman Mao, he began a program of reform and modernization that included opening a dialogue with the West. The mandate for social realist art was rescinded, allowing artists to experiment with previously banned traditional Chinese and Western modernist styles. As early as 1978 the first contemporary artists' groups, Xingxing or "Stars Group" (1979–1983) and the Xiamen Dada (1986–1988) appeared in China. The relative freedom of post-Mao China saw the rise of avant-garde movements, including the post-1970s Ego Generation, consisting of artists born after 1970, who returned to the self as subject in reaction to the one-child policy, and the conceptual and anti-socialist realism group '85 New Wave (1985–1989). Culturally and politically critical styles, Political Pop and Cynical Realism, also appeared during this period.

Ai Weiwei (b. 1957),* Dropping a Han Dynasty Urn, *1995 CE Ai Weiwei spent the first sixteen years of his life living in a dug-out hut while his parents endured reeducation under Mao. After Mao died, the family

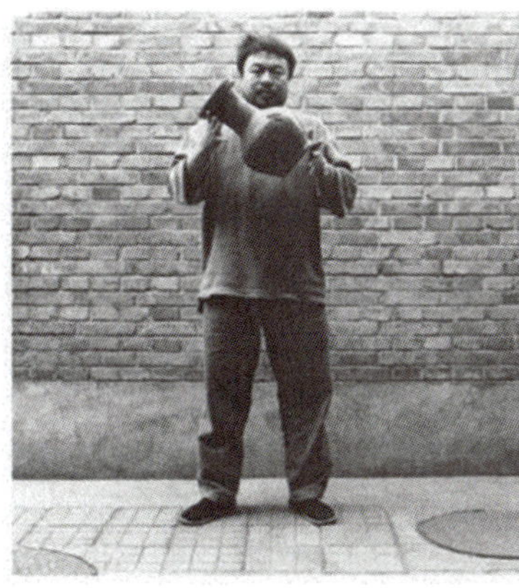
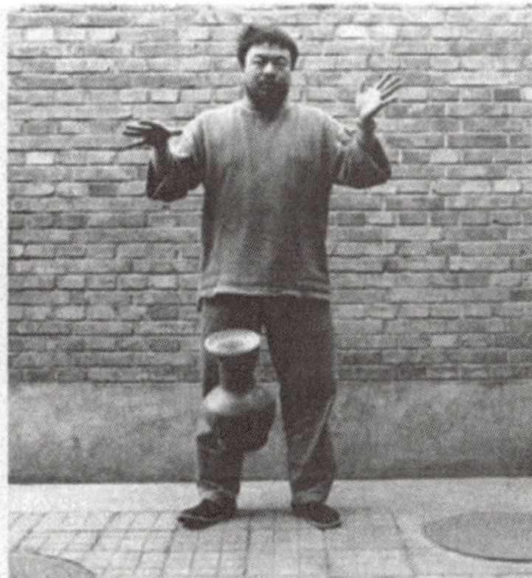
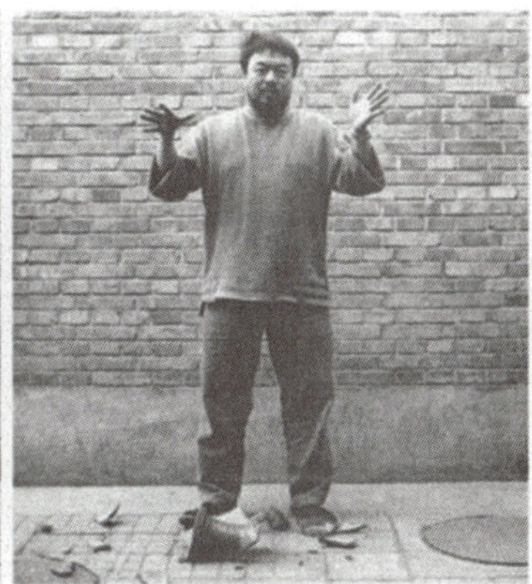

▲ **8.35** Ai Weiwei (b. 1957), Dropping a Han Dynasty Urn, 1995. Gelatin silver print triptych, each print 49.62 in. × 39.25 in.

Chinese antiquities are a frequent prop in Ai's performance and installation pieces, where they symbolize Chinese culture. Their destruction or defacement illustrates the loss of culture through communism and commercialism.

was allowed to return to Beijing and Ai Weiwei enrolled at the Beijing Film Academy. In 1981 he left for New York City, where he attended the Parsons School of Design and took classes at the Art Students' League. During this time, he explored a wide range of media, making films, doing installation and performance pieces, sculpture, and designing architecture (Aloi 2006). Ai Weiwei returned to China in 1993 to attend to his father, who was terminally ill.

In China, Ai began exploring the local antique markets and buying antiquities to use in installations, performance pieces, and as pop/conceptual art ready-mades. In *Dropping a Han Dynasty Urn* (Figure 8.35) Ai documents a performance piece in which a Han dynasty vessel is purposely dropped and destroyed. This seemingly wanton act was meant to highlight not only the destruction of traditional Chinese culture under communism but also the concept of creation through destruction. Antiquities have provided a base for many of Ai's works on the theme of cultural loss not only during the Cultural Revolution but also from the influence and predation of Western capitalism.

***Zhang Xiaogang (b. 1958),* Bloodline: Big Family No. 2, 1993** Zhang Xiaogang was another of the millions of Chinese youth sent for rural reeducation. After Mao's death, he studied oil painting at the Sichuan Academy of Fine Arts in Chongqing, and became involved with the '85 New Wave avant-garde movement. Zhang's Bloodlines Series was inspired by a box of old photographs found during a visit to his parents' home after the Tiananmen Square (1989) uprising.

Bloodlines: Big Family No. 2 (Figure 8.36) like others in the series, was painted in grisaille to evoke the feel of old black and white photographs; occasionally Zhang adds patches of color

▼ **8.36** Zhang Xiaogang (b. 1958), *Bloodline: Big Family No. 2*, 1993. Acrylic.

Zhang's large-scale paintings were inspired by a box of old photographs he found in his parents' house that were taken during the Cultural Revolution.

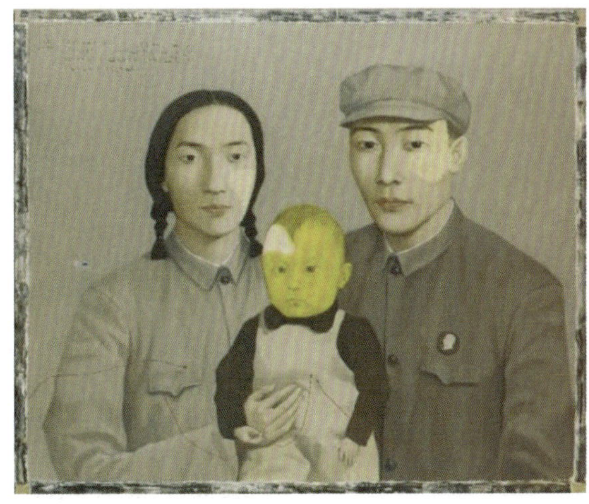

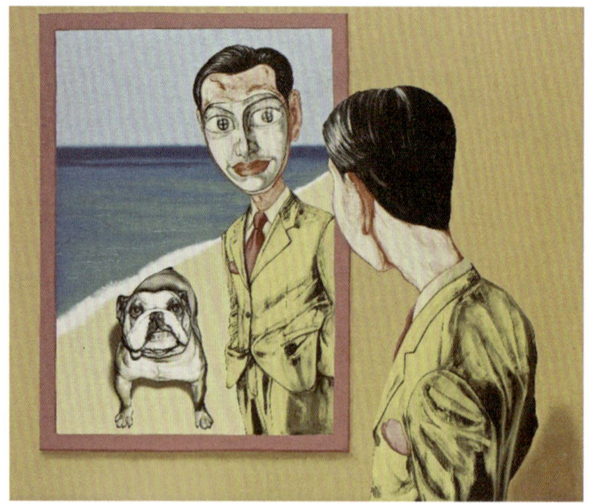

▲ 8.37 Zeng Fanzhi (b. 1964), *Mask Series No. 26*, 1998. Acrylic.

Zeng's paintings express feelings of isolation and alienation in a society where cordiality seemed to be an artifice.

such as the golden face of the eldest son in this work. All three figures have splotches on their faces suggesting the blemishes common in old photos as well as the metaphorical wounds and traumatic memories of the Maoist era. In this painting the three figures are also connected by a thin red line, a "bloodline" representing genealogical lines of decent. The scale of these images, often 6 feet (1.5 m) high and as much as 8 feet (1.8 m) wide, eliminates the nostalgic preciousness of actual family album images.

Zeng Fanzhi (b. 1964),* Mask Series No. 26, *1998 Zeng Fanzhi grew up during the Cultural Revolution. He studied at the Hubei Academy of Fine Arts, where he was fascinated by German art, especially Albrecht Durer, and later, by the German Expressionists, the latter being especially influential in Zeng's development of Cynical Realism. In 1993, Zeng moved to Beijing, then enjoying an economic boom, in the hope of finding a warmer reception for his art. However, far from his family and friends in Wuhan, Zeng felt isolated and alienated. As he observed the daily interactions of people in the city around him, Zeng sensed that seemingly cordial exchanges masked artifice and deception, and reflected a superficial environment filled with people hiding their true selves. Building on the artificiality of social relations, Zeng began a series of paintings of masked figures in 1994.

Mask Series No 26 (Figure 8.37) shows a well-dressed man apparently looking into a mirror. What the mirror reflects is very different from the ambiguous bland space in which the man stands with his back to the viewer and his hands thrust into his pockets in a contrived casualness. In the mirror the man wears a white mask with red lips and TV test-pattern eyes; he stands on a beach with a bulldog. The stylish suit with red pocket square seems out of place on a beach and the incongruity is purposeful. Zeng intends the suits as another form of mask; they were inspired by party officials, during the period of economic reform, changing their Zhongshan "Mao" jackets for Western business suits and ties. The suits and masks reflect the pretension, artificiality, and deception of life in Beijing and his own anxiety, isolation, and discomfort there.

Chapter Quick Review

Neolithic China (c. 18,000–2,000 BCE)

- The Neolithic began in China earlier than elsewhere with the first ceramics dating to 18,000 BCE. Neolithic ceramics were hand-built wares smoothed by scraping. Decoration was painted on with red and black pigment inks in floral, geometric, and sometimes figural designs. Design and form were aesthetically integrated.

- Jade carving began in the fourth millennium BCE with Bi disks and Kongs being the most common forms found in burial contexts. Jade was thought to ensure the immortality of the deceased. Kong represented the square of the earth and Bi, the dome of the heavens.

Three Dynasties Period (2070–221 BCE)

- The first stratified states appeared in China during the Three Dynasties Period. These, according to Chinese history, were the Xia (c. 2070–1600 BCE), Shang (1766–1111 BCE), and Zhou (1100–221 BCE).
- Chinese writing began with oracle bones found in Shang tombs. Later during the Zhou, the first annualized history, the *Spring and Autumn Annals*, were written in the State of Lu.
- Bronze casting begins in the late Xia–early Shang period, using the piece-mold process. The first studio manual, the *Book of Diverse Crafts*, was written. Lost wax casting began to be used in China during the seventh century BCE; gilding and metal inlay was used in bronze casting.
- Advances were made in the sciences, mathematics, astronomy, papermaking, silk-weaving, and architecture during the period. The philosophies of Confucianism, Daoism, and Legalism were advanced.

The Qin Empire (221–207 BCE)

- The Qin Dynasty was established in 221 BCE when the Ying Zheng, Marquis of Qin, conquered the last of the Zhou states and declared himself Shi Huangdi, "First August and Divine Emperor." Shi Huangdi was a brutal and authoritarian ruler but many of his reforms laid the foundation for the Chinese nation.
- Shi Huangdi linked up the northern border wall sections of the old Zhou states, creating the Great Wall of China.
- Shi Huangdi's monumental tomb was guarded by more than eight thousand terracotta soldiers. The soldiers were sized according to rank, with the officers standing 6 feet 5 inches (2 m) tall.

The Han Dynasty (206 BCE–220 CE)

- Han Gaozu, the first emperor of the Han Dynasty, retained some of the advancements of the Qin era while trying to repair much of the damage done by Shi Huangdi. He invited Confucian and Daoist scholars to his court and put them to work rewriting ancient texts from memory. Buddhism was introduced from India during the reign of Han Mingdi.
- Han tombs often contained models of Han palaces, houses, and farm buildings which provide important information about Han architecture.
- The silk funerary banner from Lady Dai's tomb not only presents Chinese cosmological views but also includes the first known portrait in Chinese art.

The Period of Disunity (220–581 CE)

- Earliest known examples of Chinese Buddhist art date from this period and were modeled after Gandharan examples. During the Northern Wei five Imperial Caves were cut at Yungang. Each featured a monumental Buddha, whose image was based on those of the Tuoba rulers.

- The first art history and theory, *Record of the Classification of Old Paintings*, was written by Xie He, in which he formulates six canons of Chinese art. Gu Kaizhi paints *Admonitions of the Instructress to the Palace Ladies* scroll.

The Tang Dynasty (618–907 CE)

- The early Tang period was one of openness in China as foreign traders were regularly seen in the capital of Chang'an. Figures of foreigners, exotic animals such as camels, and prized Ferghana horses were modeled in clay as offerings or mingqi to be placed in the tombs of Tang elite. New lead-based glazes called *sancai* were developed for ceramics.
- Buddhism was patronized by Wu Zetian, who commissioned Fengxian Grotto with its monumental statue of Vairocana Buddha. Buddhist caves were cut at Dunhuang by traders traveling the Silk Road. Many of these contained sculptures and murals featuring Pure Land Buddhism.
- Tang Emperor Wuzong began purges of Buddhist and other foreign religions in 845 CE, confiscating temple wealth and property.

The Sung Dynasty (960–1279 CE)

- The arts, particularly landscape painting, flourished in both the Northern and Southern Sung Dynasties. Fan Kuan and Guo Xi painted their monumental landscapes. Guo presented the "angle of totality" viewpoint in his paintings; he also wrote his treatise on landscape painting, *The Lofty Message of Forest and Streams*.
- Emperor Huizong built the first Imperial Museum, and catalogued its collection. An artist and calligrapher himself, he painted in the mogu style and invented Shoujinti a new type of calligraphy.
- Chan Buddhist painting, which stressed spontaneity as a means of achieving enlightenment, gained importance during the Southern Sung.

The Yuan (Mongolian) Dynasty (1279–1368)

- The Mongols conquered Jurchen-controlled northern China and moved on to defeat the Southern Sung, bringing all of China into the Mongol Empire.
- Many Chinese artists, with the exception of Zhao Mengfu, refused to work for the Mongol Yuan Dynasty. Instead they retired to the countryside, continuing to develop the art of landscape painting as Literati painters. These paintings often use Confucian and Daoist analogies to represent the suffering of the Chinese gentleman in the elements of landscape painting.
- The Mongols brought officials and artists from other parts of the empire to serve them in Khanbalik. In particular, these foreign artists brought new methods and materials to China, which facilitated the development of Chinese cobalt underglaze porcelain.

The Ming or "Radiant" Dynasty (1368–1644)

- A peasant uprising, led by Zhu Yuanzgang and the Red Turbans, brought down the Mongol Empire in 1368. Zhu Yuanzgang took the throne as Hong Wu, first emperor of the Ming Dynasty. Determined to make his reign as glorious as that of the Sung, he invited artists to his court, sponsored the revival of bronze casting and lacquer working, and inaugurated public works projects such as rebuilding the Great Wall. The Third Ming Emperor, Yongle, moved the capital to Beijing, building there the great palace complex known as the Forbidden City.

- Ming painting embraced a wide range of genres from portraiture to landscape. Painters of the Imperial Academy and Zhe School emulated the styles of the Southern Sung while painters of the Wu School sought inspiration from the Literati painters of the Yuan as exemplars of self-expression.
- Inspired by Daoism and by landscape painting, Chinese garden design enjoyed a renewal.
- Ming blue and white porcelain is perfected at the Jingdezhen kilns.

The Qing Dynasty (1644 CE–1911 CE)

- In 1644 the Manchu Qing established their rule over China. Increased contact with Jesuit missionaries introduced Western science and astronomy, resulting in improvements in the accuracy of the calendar. Jesuit artists also arrived but had little long-lasting impact on Chinese art. Painters during the Qing worked either in orthodox styles, which imitated the forms but not the individualism of the Literati painters, or were individualist painters like Shitao who sought personal expression in their art.
- Potters at the Jingdezhen kilns perfected enamel overglaze techniques to create multi-color wares.

The People's Republic of China (1949–)

- After the overthrow of the Qing in 1912, there was a brief, unsuccessful experiment with Western-style democracy under the leadership of Dr. Sun Yat-sen. This Republic of China was brought down after the Second World War by the Communists under Mao Zedong.
- Under Mao, traditional Chinese and Western modernist styles were suppressed. The only purpose of art was to serve the propaganda needs of the state and the only acceptable style was Socialist Realism.

Art after Mao (1976–)

- After the death of Chairman Mao brought the Cultural Revolution to an abrupt end, a period of cultural and political openness brought renewed contact with the West.
- This period of openness allowed artists to explore tradition styles of Chinese painting as well as various forms of Western modernism.

Chapter Questions

1. How did Daoism and Neo-Confucianism philosophies and increasing urbanization influence the development of landscape painting and garden design?
2. In almost every period China has had major women artists. What cultural or philosophical explanations can you find for women to have been so successful?

3. Explain the perceived difference between "professional" artists and "scholar" artists. Identify one work each made by professional and scholar artists during the same period. Discuss how they are similar or dissimilar in terms of style, technique, themes, and medium.
4. What is propaganda art and how was it used during the Maoist era?

Key Terms and Figures

Key Terms

Bi Jade disk with a central circular opening, thought to represent the heavens or sky.

De In Daoism, de refers to humans acting in accord with nature.

Dian Dots of color was used by Shitao to convey the atmospheric effects of mist.

Fengjian A system of decentralized governance used by the Zhou King in which members of the royal family were enfeoffed with grants of land that became the Zhou states.

Floating perspective Floating perspective or "angle of totality" is a type of perspective advanced by Guo Xi in which several views of a subject are presented simultaneously.

Guang A type of ritual wine vessel shaped like a pitcher with a handle and projecting lip or pouring.

Guzheng A Chinese zither or plucked string instrument.

Hemp-fiber stroke Relaxed medium-width strokes, often with a slight wave, which are used to define rocks and mountains in landscape painting.

Hu A ceremonial wine vessel with a low, pear-shaped form.

Iron-wire line An often thick, rigid line with sharp angles.

Kong A squared tube-like item of jade with a circular opening through the center, possibly representing the earth. These were common burial offerings in the Liangzhu culture.

Mandate of Heaven Political theory originating with the Zhou in which the emperor's right to rule was bestowed by heaven for as long as he governed well.

Mingqi Burial goods or tomb offerings including food, cosmetics, figurines, house models, etc.

Mogu A term meaning "boneless" that refers to a style of painting, either in monochrome or color, where form is defined without outlining.

Oracle bones Also known as "dragon bones," these were inscribed animal bones and turtle shells that were used for divination by the Shang.

Primordial Line A single brushstroke contour line used to define forms developed by Shitao during the Qing dynasty.

Quanrong A tribe of peoples, speaking Sino-Tibetan languages, living on the northwestern border of Zhou China, and who claimed descent from two white dogs or wolves.

Raised-beam construction In Chinese wood construction a system of framing the roof in which the ridge beam is supported by a stepped, box-like framework, rather than trusses as in the West. This system allows greater flexibility in shaping the roofline.

Sancai A term meaning "three glazes." During the Tang lead-based glazes colored with iron, copper, and cobalt were used to decorate ceramics, especially Ferghana horses.

Shoujinti "Slender gold wire" style of elegant calligraphy invented by Emperor Huizong during the Northern Sung Dynasty.

Taotie A motif common to the Shang and Zhou dynasties consisting only of a zoomorphic mask.

Tian-long In Chinese mythology these were flying, sky, or heavenly dragons.

Zhongguó The "Middle Kingdom"; what the Zhou called their kingdom.

Key Figures

Cheng Tang—Regnal name of Zi Lu, founder of the Shang Dynasty.

Dong Qichang—Ming Dynasty painter who advocated for the arts as a means of self-expression.

Fan Kuan—Northern Sung painter of monumental landscapes and Daoist recluse.

Guan Dao Sheng—Painter who wrote treatise on bamboo painting; wife of Zhao Mengfu.

Gu Kaizhi—Painter of the Six Dynasties period; first recorded artist in Chinese history.

Guo Xi—Northern Sung landscape painter who originated floating perspective.

Huang Gongwang—One of the Four Masters of Literati painting.

Huizong—Artist, calligrapher, poet, and eighth emperor of the Sung dynasty.

Liang Kai—Chan Buddhist painter of the Southern Sung.

Liu Pang—Rebel leader who founded the Han dynasty and took the name Han Gaozu.

Ma Yuan—Southern Sung landscape, portrait, and flower painter.

Ni Zan—One of the Four Masters of Literati painting.

Qin Shi Huang—"First August and Divine Emperor"; founder of the Qin Empire.

Shen Zhou—Founder of Wu or Southern School of Painting during the Ming Dynasty.

Shitao—Monk Bitter Gourd, Qing painter who saw primordial line as the foundation of painting.

Sima Qian—Chinese historian of the second century BCE who wrote *Records of the Grand Historian.*

Tan Yao—Buddhist monk who oversaw the cutting of the Imperial Caves at Yungang.

Tuoba Gui—Founder of the Northern Wei Dynasty.

Wang Meng—One of the Four Masters of Literati painting.

Wu Zetian—Ruled China as its only woman emperor; patron of Fengxian Grotto.

Wu Zhen—One of the Four Masters of Literati painting.

Yan Liben—Tang Dynasty painter of the Thirteen Emperors handscroll.

Zhao Gou—Established the Southern Sung dynasty and reigned as Emperor Gaosong.

Zhao Mengfu—Painter who worked at the Mongol court.

Zhou Kuangyin—Founder of the Sung dynasty; took the throne as Emperor Taizu.

Zhou You—Last king of the Western Zhou dynasty, killed by the Quanrong.

Zhu Yuanzgang—Rebel Leader who drove out the Mongols and founded Ming dynasty as Hong Wu.

Bibliography

Abe, Stanley K. "Provenance, Patronage, and Desire: Northern Wei Sculpture from Shaanxi Province." *Ars Orientalis* 31 (2001): 1–30.

Aloi, Daniel

"Ai Weiwei Literally Smashes China's Traditions in Art and Architecture," Cornell Chronicle, (November 15, 2006) http://news.cornell.edu/stories/2006/11/ai-weiwei-smashes-chinas-traditions-art-and-architecture

Anon.

"Xi'an Discovers Westernmost Xia Culture Site," People's Daily Online, (January 2011)

http://www.kaogu.cn/html/en/backup_new/new/2013/1026/42763.html

Barnes, Gina L. *Archaeology of East Asia: The Rise of Civilization in China, Korea and Japan.* Oxbow Books, 2015.

Campbell, Duncan. "Transplanted Peculiarity: The Garden of the Master of the Fishing Nets." *New Zealand Journal of Asian Studies* 9, no. 1 (June 2007): 9–25.

Caswell, James O., and Spencer P. M. Harrington. "Buddhas of Cloud Hill." *Archaeology* 49, no. 5 (September–October 1996): 60–65

Chang, Kwang-Chih. *Shang Civilization.* New Haven, CT: Yale University Press, 1980.

Clark, John. *Modern Asian Art.* Honolulu: University of Hawai'i Press, 1998.

Clunas, Craig. *Art in China.* New York: Oxford University Press, 1997.

Corradini, Piero. "Notes on the Establishment of the Tuoba Power in North China and on the Tan Yao Caves of Yungang." *Rivista degli studi orientali* 77, Fasc. 1–4 (2003): 187–207.

Cotter, Holland. "Buddha's Caves." *New York Times.* July 6, 2008. http://www.nytimes.com/2008/07/06/arts/design/06cott.html

Dupree, Nancy Hatch. "T'ang Tombs in Chien County, China." *Archaeology* 32, no. 4 (July–August 1979): 34–44.

Edwards, Richard. *The Field of Stones: A Study of the Art of Shen Chou (1427–1509).* Washington, DC: Smithsonian Institution, 1962.

Fairbank, Wilma. "Piece-Mold Craftsmanship and Shang Bronze Design." *Archives of the Chinese Art Society of America* 16 (1962): 8–15Higgins, Lisa

"The World's Best Preserved Mummy: The Lady of Dai is Soft to the Touch, Has Bendy Arms...and is 2,100 Years Old." *The Sun*, November 30, 2016.

https://www.thesun.co.uk/living/2299057/the-worlds-best-preserved-mummy-the-lady-of-dai-is-soft-to-the-touch-has-bendy-arms-and-is-2100-years-old/.

Hyland, Alice R. M. *The Literati Vision: Sixteenth Century Wu School Painting and Calligraphy.* Memphis Brooks Museum of Art, 1984.

Kesner, Ladislav. "Likeness of No One: (Re)presenting the First Emperor's Army." *Art Bulletin* 77, no. 1 (March 1995): 115–132.

Lee, Yun Kuen. "Building the Chronology of Early Chinese History." *Asian Perspectives* 41, no. 1 (Spring 2002): 15–42.

Lim, Lucy. *Six Contemporary Chinese Women Artists: Their Artistic Evolution.* Chinese Cultural Foundation of San Francisco, 1991.

Palmer, Jason. "'Oldest Pottery' Found in China." *BBC News.* June 1, 2009. http://news.bbc.co.uk/2/hi/science/nature/8077168.stm

Pattinson, David"Pre-modern Beekeeping in China: A Short History," Agricultural History, 86, no. 4 (Fall 2012): 235-255.

Pekarik, Andrew J., and Stephanie Stokes. "The Cave Temples of Dunhuang." *Archaeology* 36, no. 1 (January/February 1983): 20–27.

Rawson, Jessica. "Late Western Zhou: A Break in the Shang Bronze Tradition." *Early China* 11/12 (1985–1987): 289–296.

Shen, Chen. *The Warriors Emperor and China's Terracotta Army.* Royal Ontario Museum, 2010.

Shiff, Richard. *Zeng Fanzhi: Every Mark Its Mask.* Germany: Hatje Cantz, 2010.

Tregear, Mary. *Chinese Art.* London: Thames and Hudson World of Art, 1997.

Tsiang, Katherine R. "Changing Patterns of Divinity and Reform in the Late Northern Wei." *Art Bulletin* 84, no. 2 (June 2002): 222–245.

Valenstein, Suzanne G. *Chinese Ceramics: Revised and Enlarged Edition.* New York: Metropolitan Museum of Art, 1989.

Xu, Yiyu. "The Knowledge System of the Traditional Chinese Craftsman." *West 86th: A Journal of Decorative Arts, Design History, and Material Culture* 20, no. 2 (Fall–Winter 2013): 155–172.

Zhimin, An. "Archaeological Research on Neolithic China." *Current Anthropology* 29, no. 5 (December 1988): 753–759

Zhixin, Sun. "The Liangzhu Culture: Its Discovery and Its Jades." *Early China* 18: 1–40.

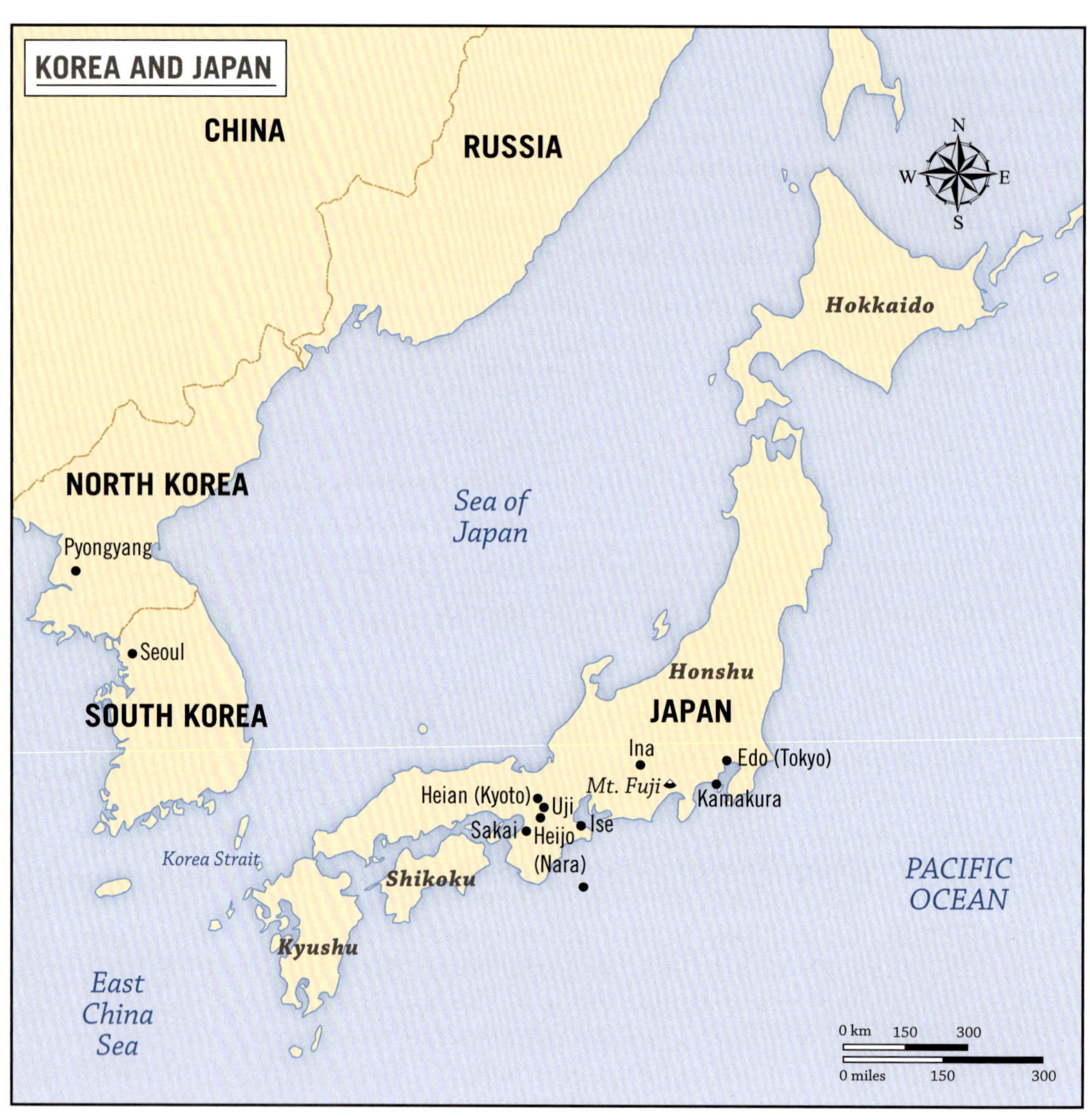
KOREA AND JAPAN
CHINA
RUSSIA
N
W
E
S
Hokkaido
NORTH KOREA
Sea of Japan
Pyongyang
Seoul
Honshu
SOUTH KOREA
JAPAN
Ina
Edo (Tokyo)
Mt. Fuji
Heian (Kyoto)
Kamakura
Uji
Sakai
Heijo (Nara)
Ise
Korea Strait
Shikoku
PACIFIC OCEAN
Kyushu
East China Sea
0 km 150 300
0 miles 150 300

Korea and Japan

9

Brief Overview

Since the earliest times Korea and Japan have shared a connection: Korea frequently serving as the conduit for the movement of peoples and ideas from the mainland to the islands. Both have long histories of art-making, beginning with the appearance of pottery during the Neolithic. The earliest ceramics outside of China belong to the Jomon culture of Japan. Excavations conducted in 1998 at the Odai Yamamoto I site, Aomori Prefecture in northern Honshu, found pottery fragments dating to 14,500 BCE. The earliest known pottery in Korea comes from the site of Gosan-ni on Jeju-do Island, where plain and applique-decorated Yunggimun ware sherds, dating to 8000 BCE or earlier, were found.

Chapter Objectives

1. Understand the unique character of Korean and Japanese arts, cultures, and histories and be able to discuss how each was influenced from China as well as by each other.
2. Explain how the introduction of Buddhism and Confucian philosophy shaped the development of the arts in each country.
3. Show how each nation took what it had borrowed from Chinese culture and adapted it to its particular needs.
4. Describe how each nation was impacted artistically by the events and aftermath of the Second World War.

Beginning in the late second century BCE in Korea and the first centuries CE in Japan, China became a dominant cultural influence on the artistic, cultural, and political lives of each nation. From China both received writing, metal casting, the potter's wheel, stoneware, versions of the dragon or climbing kiln, silk-weaving, papermaking, lacquerware, ink painting, Confucianism and Buddhism. During the succeeding centuries each took these Chinese gifts and refined them to suit their particular cultural needs. For example, both received literacy from the Chinese, initially using Chinese logographic systems but ultimately adapting them to create writing forms such as Korean Hangul and Japanese Kanji, which more closely expressed the nuances of their languages.

In the sixteen century Korea was repeatedly plundered by Japanese pirates and invaded by Japanese forces as the first step in Shogun Toyotomi Hideyoshi's plan for the conquest of the Asian mainland. Although the Japanese were repulsed by the Koreans at this time, the peninsula was annexed by Japan after the Russo-Japanese War. Japan controlled Korea until the end of the Second World War. Japanese rule in Korea was both repressive and oppressive. This dark period in

Korean history has been a continuing point of discord in Korean and Japanese relations to the present day.

In modern times Japan and Korea each have dynamic art scenes. In both nations contemporary artists approach art-making work in a variety of ways, including traditional ink painting, printmaking, and pottery; Western influenced modernism featuring oil and acrylic media; and unique new forms like anime, manga, and webtoons.

Neolithic Korea (8000–1500 BCE)

The first Korean pottery, termed Yunggimun for its raised-clay decoration, appears around 8,000 BCE, at several sites along the southeastern coast. These were simple, hand-built earthenware vessels fired in open pits at low temperature. However, it is the later Jeulmum pottery that typifies the Neolithic in Korea. The term Jeulmum means "comb-patterned" and specifically describes a style of conical vessels decorated by combing and cord-wrapping techniques, dating from 7000 to 1500 BCE. Jeulmum wares were utilitarian and have been found in pit-house excavations rather than in tombs.

Jeulmum Conical Vessel from Amsa-dong, c. 4000 BCE The village of Amsa-dong, one of many Jeulmum sites, was settled around 4500 BCE. The manufacture of coiled pottery begins at that time and continues without interruption until about 1500 BCE when it ceased entirely. Typical Amsa-dong vessels (Figure 9.1) are conical in shape with a pointed foot for anchoring in the coals of a cooking fire. Repeated heating caused these low-fired wares to crack so many vessels show ancient repair holes, where the vessel was lashed together with twine to stabilize the break. Typical decoration consists of bands of punctuation and diamond shapes around the mouth, and comb marks in several directions on the body of the vessel.

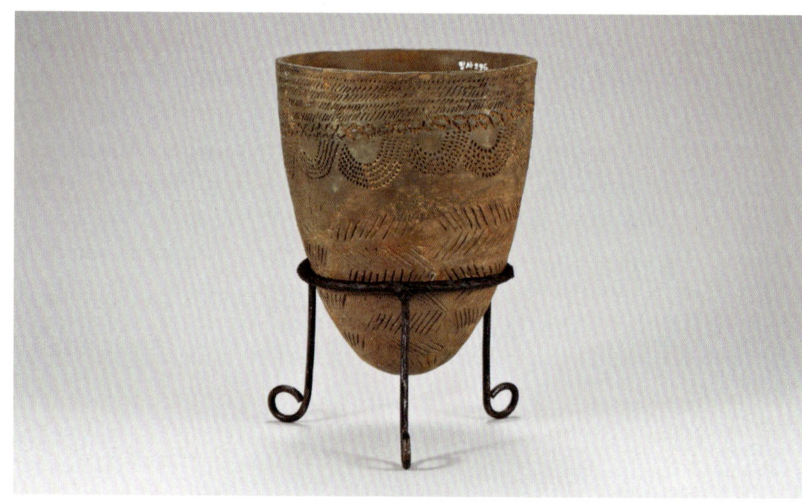

▶ 9.1 Korea, Jeulmum Conical Vessel from Amsa-dong, c. 4000 BCE. 8.18 in. high.

Jeulmum wares were utilitarian wares that often show ancient repairs, the typical combed and punctate decoration probably had practical as well as aesthetic purposes.

timeline

DATE	TYPE	EVENT
		BCE
c. 30,000	History	First peoples entered Korean peninsula and Japanese islands
c. 12,000	Art	Jomon pottery culture established in Japan
c. 8000	Art	Yunggimun pottery began in Korea at coastal sites
c. 4000	Art	Jeulmum corded pottery began at Amsa-dong
c. 2500	Art	Middle Jomon potters began making flameware
2333	History	Legendary founding of Gojoseon kingdom in Korea
c. 1500	Art	Mumum plain wares replaced Jeulmum pottery
c. 300	History	Yayoi people settled in Japan
	Art	First Dotaku made in Japan
	History	Likely date for the establishment of Gojoseon kingdom
108	History	Han Chinese conquered Gojoseon
	History	Chinese Lolang colony established
57	History	Silla Kingdom founded; Three Kingdoms Period started
	Art	Iron-working, the potter's wheel, the climbing kiln, stoneware introduced into Korea
	Culture	Buddhism and Confucian philosophy introduced to Korea
	History	Chinese system of writing brought to Korea
37	History	Kingdom of Goguryeo founded in Korea
18	History	Kingdom of Baekje founded in Korea
4	Art	Establishment of the Ise Jingu in Japan
		CE
c. 250	History	Kofun "Old Tombs" Period began in Japan
	History	Chinese writing system adopted at Japanese court
	Culture	Confucianism and Buddhism introduced to Japan
c. 391	Art	Janggunchong or "General's Tomb" begun in Korea
c. 399	Art	Emperor Nintoku buried in Daisen Kofun, Japan
c. 400	Art	Tomb of the Dancers painted, Korea
	Art	Hwangnam Daechong Tombs built in Silla kingdom, Korea
523	Art	Geumjegwansik diadems made for Baekje king Muryeong's
	History	Prince Shotoku appointed regent in Japan

(*Continued*)

timeline *continued*

DATE	TYPE	EVENT
		CE
c. 538	History	Asuka Period began in Japan
552	Culture	Buddhism introduced into Japan
604	History	Prince Shotoku wrote first Japanese constitution
607	Art	Horyu-ji founded and first temple built in Japan
623	Art	Tori Busshi created *The Shaka Triad* for Horyu-ji
629	Art	First rebuilding of the Ise Jingu, Japan
632	Art	Chomsongdae observatory built by Queen Sondok of Silla
645	History	Taika reforms in Japan; Fujiwara took power as regents
660	History	Combined Silla and Tang Chinese forces conquered Baekje
c. 670	Art	The Kondo rebuilt at Horyu-ji in Japan
668	Art	Silla and Tang Chinese forces conquered Goguryeo
	Art	Silla Kingdom became Unified Silla
710	History	Empress Genmei established capital at Heijo-kyo, Japan
742	Art	Construction of Sokkuram Grotto began in Korea
745	Art	Construction of Todai-ji began in Japan
774	Art	Sokkuram Grotto dedicated
794	History	Start of Heian Period in Japan
	History	Emperor Kammu established capital in Heian-kyo (Kyoto)
	History	Katakana and hiragana writing systems developed in Japan
c. 900	History	Unified Silla fractured back into its three component states
918	History	Wang Geon took throne of Goguryeo, conquered Baekje, and Silla; shortened name of kingdom to Goryeo
995	History	Fujiwara no Michinaga became *Nairan*
c. 1000	History	Lady Murasaki Shikibu wrote *The Tale of Gengi*
1053	Art	Fujiwara no Yorimici built Phoenix Hall at his Uji estate
	Art	Jocho created the Amida Nyorai for the Phoenix Hall
1126	History	First movable bronze type created in Korea
1145	History	*Samguk Sagi* (History of the Three Kingdoms) written
1168	Culture	Myoan Eisai traveled to China, brought tea and Zen Buddhism to Japan
1192	History	Minamoto Yoritomo's established his *bakufu* in Kamakura, Japan

DATE	TYPE	EVENT
		CE
b. 1207	Art	Kosho created his Kuya Shonin
1231	History	Mongol invasion of Korea
1240	Art	The *Heike monogatari* painted in Japan
1274	History	Mongols attempted to invade Japan but failed
1280s	History	*Samguk Yusa* (Memorabilia of the Three Kingdoms) written in Korea
1281	History	Mongols fail to invade Japan a second time
1310	Art	Water Moon Avalokitesvara painted at Korean court
1333	History	Emperor Go-Daigo seized control of government in Japan
1336	History	Muromachi Period began in Japan Ashikaga bakufu established
1337	History	Emperor Go-Daigo established Southern Court
1339	Art	First Zen Garden created at Saiho-ji
1392	History	Great Joseon Dynasty founded in Korea
	History	Unification of Northern and Southern Courts in Japan
1444	Culture	Hangul adopted as writing system in Korea
1447	Art	Korean artist Ahn Gyeon painted *Dream Journey to the Peach Blossom Land*
1467	History	Onin Wars began in Japan and continued for ten years
1477	History	Oda Nobunaga became first shogun
	Culture	Buddhism suppressed; Catholic missionaries arrived in Japan
1582	History	Oda assassinated; Toyotomi Hideyoshi took control as shogun
1583	Art	Toyotomi built Osaka Castle
	Art	Kano Eitoku painted *Chinese Lions* screen for Toyotomi
	Art	Sen no Rikyu created the Taian Teahouse
1588	History	Toyotomi instituted "Great Sword Hunt" to disarm peasants
1590	Culture	Catholic missionaries expelled from Japan
1592	History	Toyotomi invaded Korea
1600	History	Toyotomi died and Tokugawa Ieyasu seized power as shogun
1603	History	Edo Period began with establishment of Tokugawa bakufu
1620	Art	Hachijo-no-Miya Toshihito began work on Katsura Rikyu

(*Continued*)

timeline *continued*

DATE	TYPE	EVENT
		CE
1627	History	First Manchu invasion of Korea
1636	History	Second Manchu invasion of Korea
1734	Art	Jeong Seon painted *General View of Mt. Geumgansan* in Korea
1765	Art	Suzuki Harunobu created *Evening Bell at the Clock* in Japan
c. 1805	Art	Shin Ka-gwon painted *A Scenery on Dano Day* in Korea
1826	Art	Hokusai began *Thirty-Six Views of Mount Fuji* series in Japan
1828	Art	Takahashi Yuichi born in Japan
1853	History	Commodore Perry demanded access to Japanese ports
1866	Art	Kuroda Seiki born in Japan
1868	History	Meiji Restoration returned control to the Emperor Push for modernization began in Japan
1873	Art	Takahashi founded Tenkai Gakusha Western painting school in Japan
1874	Art	Hishida Shunso born in Japan
1910	History	Japan annexed Korea
1912	History	Prince Yoshihito took throne as Emperor Taisho
1913	Art	Kenzo Tange born in Japan
1921	History	Prince Hirohito served as regent for his father
1926	History	Prince Hirohito took the throne as Emperor Showa
1941	History	Japanese attacked Pearl Harbor
1945	History	Atomic bombs dropped on Hiroshima and Nagasaki World War II ended
		Korea is divided into North and South
1950	History	Korean War began
1953	History	Korean War halted by Armistice Agreement
1954	Art	Gutai Art Association formed in Japan
1960	Art	Metabolist Movement began in Japanese architecture
1968	Art	Mono-ha Art Movement began in Japan
1989	History	Prince Akihito took the throne as Emperor Heisei
2001	Art	Neo-Nihonga founded by Tenmyouya Hisashi
		Japanese Neo-Pop movement
		SuperFlat movement founded by Takashi Murakami

Three Kingdoms Period (c. 57 BCE–668 CE)

According to the thirteenth century *Samguk Yusa*, the first Korean kingdom was that of the Gojoseon founded by the legendary Dangun Wanggom in 2333 BCE. Scholars are uncertain as to the actual date of the kingdom's founding; the earliest mention of it in the Chinese Historical Records mention the state being in existence in 222 BCE, and it certainly was in 108 BCE, when the Han defeated the Gojoseon and established their colony of Lelang (Liaoning Province). About a half-century after the fall of the Gojoseon, the early tribal polities of the peninsula had coalesced into three states: the Kingdom of Goguryeo in the north, and those of Silla and Baekje in the south.

Kingdom of Goguryeo (37 BCE–668 CE)

The largest of these three kingdoms, the Goruryea was founded in 37 BCE according to the twelfth century *Samguk Sagi*, by Prince Jumong from Buyeo (Manchuria), who had fled conflicts at the royal court. During the reign of King Gwanggaeto (r. 391–412 CE), Goguryeo advanced northward into Manchuria, conquering most of it. As Goguryeo expanded it came into increasing conflict with neighboring China but Goguryeo's strong army and cavalry enabled it to repel repeated attempts at invasion. In times of peace it prospered culturally through its friendly relations with Han, Sui, and Tang China, receiving knowledge of silk-making, the Chinese writing system, the potter's wheel and climbing kiln, mural painting techniques and motifs, Buddhism, and Confucian philosophy.

Tomb of the Dancers, c. fifth century CE Han Chinese influence on the art of Goguryeo is most evident in the decoration of a group of mural tombs located in the necropolis on the Tonggou Plain (today Ji'an, China), which were painted long after the end of the Han Dynasty in China. Some 10,000 tombs make up the necropolis, which is located near the ancient ruins of Kuknaesong, the second capital of Goguryeo. Several types of tombs are found in the necropolis, including stone cairns, stone-chambered tombs that are covered by earthen mounds, and large stone-pile tombs, the most famous of which is the stepped-pyramid Tomb of the General, thought to be the mausoleum of the twentieth Goguryeo ruler, King Jangsu (r. 413–491).

The Tomb of the Dancers (Figure 9.2) is modest in scale and consists of two rooms: a small front room and a main chamber connected by a passageway. The stone walls of both rooms were covered with a plaster mix of seaweed and slaked lime and then the murals were added in the wet fresco technique. The figures were outlined in black

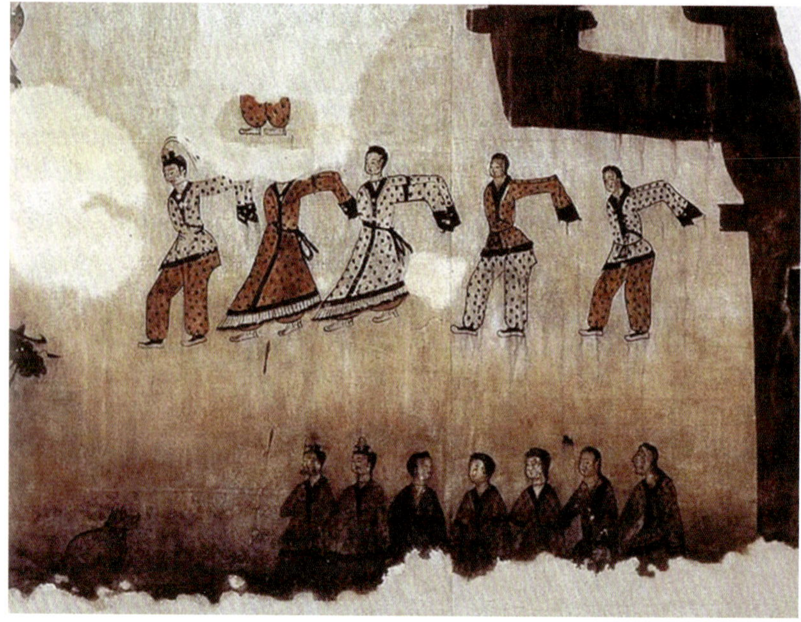

▶ 9.2 Korea, Three Kingdoms, Goguryeo, Tonggou Necropolis, Tomb of the Dancers, fifth century CE.

The murals on this tomb's walls showed activities ranging from hunting to feasting that were enjoyed by the occupant during his lifetime. The views of the different activities were broken by the painted architecture of a pavilion; notice the post and bracket at the right side of the image.

and then filled in with a somber palette consisting of dark red, brown, and yellow. The murals of the front room include scenes of houses and trees on the east wall and horse saddles to suggest a stable on the west. The occupant of the tomb and two male guests, possibly monks, are depicted on the north wall. Within the main chamber are scenes of activities that the decedent enjoyed in life. The entire west wall is a hunting scene in which five bowmen on horseback chase deer and tigers through a mountainous landscape. The north wall shows the decedent enjoying a banquet while an acrobat performs the "rolling lights" act around a burning lamp. The tomb takes its name from the entertainment depicted on the east wall: a scene of two female and three male dancers engaged in an animated line dance in front of an attentive audience. The male dancers wear loose trousers and jackets while the women wear long robes over ballooning pants. Elsewhere on the wall musicians and singers provide accompaniment for the dancers, and servants bring out food from a pavilion to the banquet on the north wall. In each corner of the room is a tromp l'oeil column with ornate corbelled brackets extending up to a beam at the ceiling, giving the effect of being within a pavilion looking out at the various scenes. The domed ceiling of the chamber is painted with astronomical and celestial images drawn directly from those used in Chinese tombs (Park 2002: 11–26).

Baekje (18 BCE–660 CE)

The Kingdom of Baekje was founded in 18 BCE by King Onjo, a prince of Goguryeo. Baekje was the most international of the three kingdoms having diplomatic relations with both China and Japan. Baekje architects were sent to Asuka Japan to construct the first Buddhist temples there. Although they adopted Buddhism in 384 CE, the Baekje kings continued to construct tumulus-style mausoleums on Mount Songsan. The most famous of these is the tomb of King Muryeong (r. 501–523 CE) and his queen, discovered in 1971. The tomb held nearly three thousand burial offerings including gold and silver items, Chinese celadon ceramics, and stone mirrors.

Geumjegwansik Diadems, c. 501–523 CE Unique among the gold items in Muryeong's tomb are a pair of diadems (Figure 9.3) in the form of flowering trees with an overall flame shape. It is thought that these pieces originally would have been hooked through rings at the base of the tree trunk to the left and right sides of king's black silk headpiece. The two openwork ornaments, known collectively as *Geumjegwansik*, were found stacked one on top of the other near the ruler's head in the tomb. The diadems differ slightly in size; the larger measuring approximately 12 inches (30 cm) by 5.5 inches (14 cm), and the second being about a half inch shorter and a quarter inch narrower; both were cut from gold sheets only seven-hundredths of an inch (2 mm) thick. To increase the play of light and perhaps add an element of sound, the diadems were decorated with small gold danglers.

Silla and Unified Silla Kingdoms (57 BCE–935 CE)

The Silla kingdom was formed in 57 BCE when the leaders of the six confederated Saro-guk villages decided on a power-sharing plan that rotated kingship among the heads of the three strongest clans: the Park, Kim, and Seok. The arrangement continued for four centuries until the

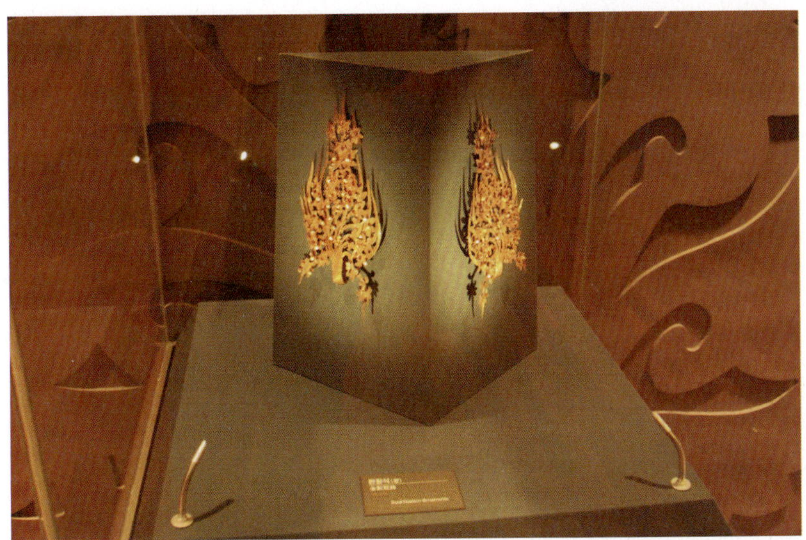

◀ 9.3 Korea, King Muryeong Tomb, Geumjegwansik Diadems, c. 501–523 CE. Gold, 12 in. high.

These fragile gold ornaments would have been attached to the sides of the ruler's black silk cap.

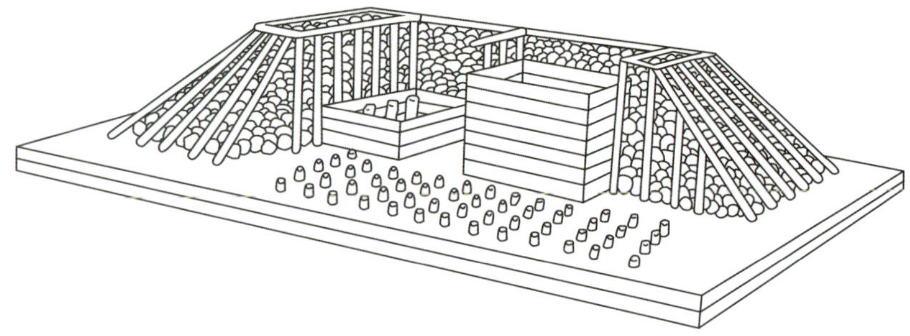

▶ 9.4 Korea, Construction of Hwangnam Daechong Tombs, fifth century CE.

This double tomb held the log tombs of a king on the south end and a queen in the north.

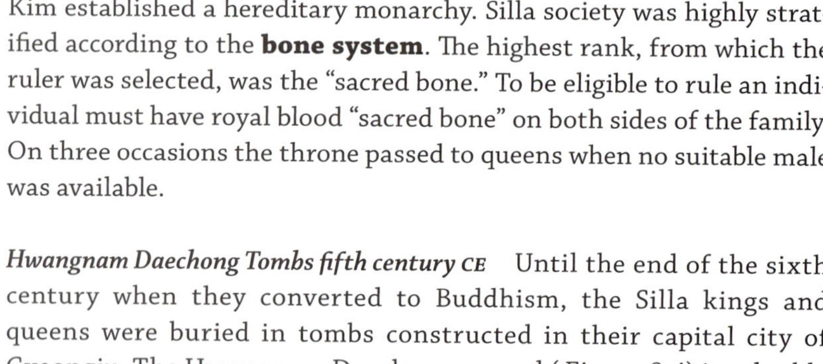

Kim established a hereditary monarchy. Silla society was highly stratified according to the **bone system**. The highest rank, from which the ruler was selected, was the "sacred bone." To be eligible to rule an individual must have royal blood "sacred bone" on both sides of the family. On three occasions the throne passed to queens when no suitable male was available.

Hwangnam Daechong Tombs fifth century CE Until the end of the sixth century when they converted to Buddhism, the Silla kings and queens were buried in tombs constructed in their capital city of Gyeongju. The Hwangnam Daechong mound (Figure 9.4) is a double tomb with the burial of a king in the south mound and that of a queen, buried later, in the north mound. Both tombs were constructed similarly; each began with the laying out of a stone perimeter wall that defined the size of the mound. In the center of that space a log chamber was constructed for the entombment of the king. Around the burial vault more posts were sunk into the tumulus floor to serve as stabilizing piers for the fill mass. Once the posts were in place and adjusted in height to correspond to the desired shape of the mound, stone rubble was added and then a final layer of earth.

▼ 9.5 Korea, Silla, Hwangnam Daechong, North Tomb, Gold Crown, fifth century CE. Gold with jade jewels, 10.75 in.

The elements of this crown symbolize the ruler's role as an intermediary between the celestial and terrestrial realms.

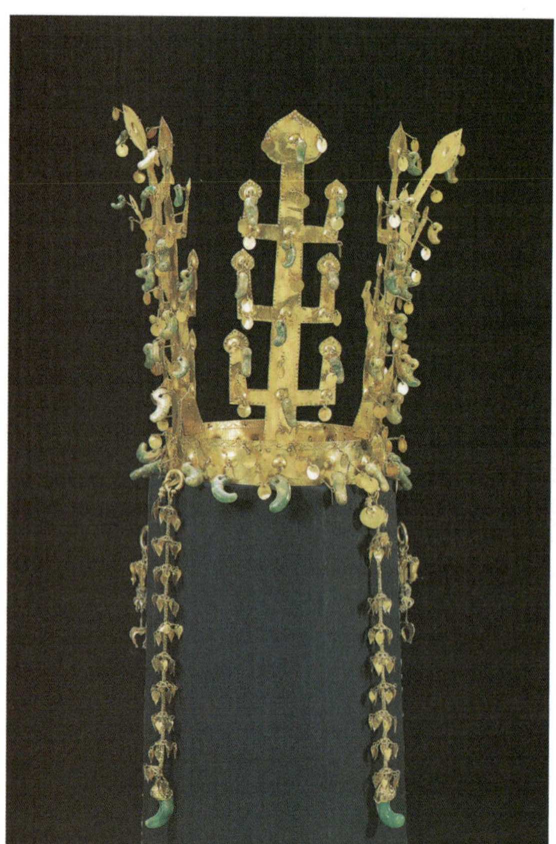

Silla Gold Crown, fifth century CE The *Silla Gold Crown* (Figure 9.5) excavated from the North (Queen's) tomb of the Hwangnam Daechong is the most elaborate diadem yet found in Korea. Prior to the adoption of Buddhism as the state religion, the Silla rulers practiced shamanism. Elements of the crown reflect those beliefs. At the center point of the crown's gold band is a vertical element with three horizontal branches, representing the world tree or axis mundi. Flanking the tree are pairs of antler-shaped elements and two wing-like extensions. The crown is decorated with claw-shaped jade jewels called *gogok* and circular gold danglers. Suspended from the side of the band, and set to frame the wearer's face, are gold chains ornamented with gogok or with leaf-like gold elements.

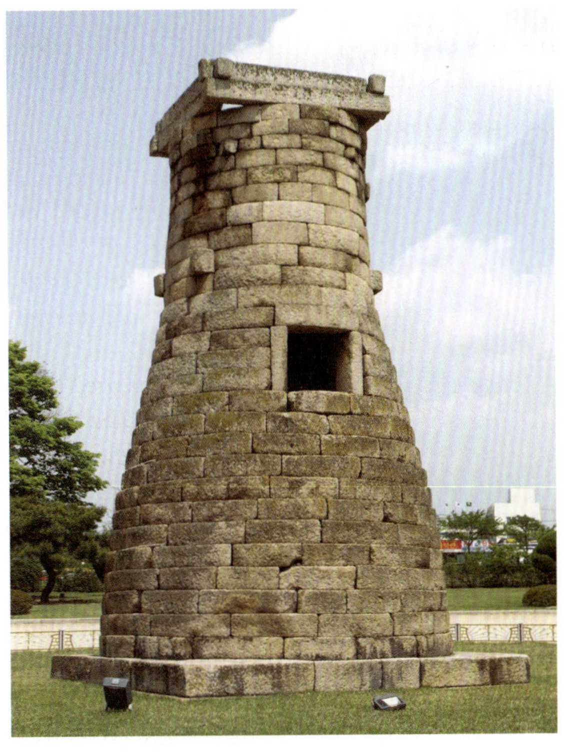

▲ **9.6** Korea, Gyeongju, Chomsongdae observatory, c. 632–647 CE. 30 ft. (9.17 m) high.

This first Asian observatory was built on the palace grounds by Queen Sondok who was keenly interested in astronomy.

Chomsongdae, Gyeongju, c. 632–647 CE One of the great Silla monarchs, Queen Sondok (r. 632–647 CE) was keenly interested in astronomy and during her reign built the Chomsongdae observatory (Figure 9.6) on the palace grounds in Gyeongju. The 30 foot (9.17 m) high, milk-bottle-shaped tower sits on 17.6 foot (5.36 m) square base made up of twelve stones arranged three to a side. These represent the four seasons and twelve months of the lunar year. The tower rises in twenty-seven tiers referencing the number of days required for the moon to orbit the earth as well as Queen Sondok's position as the twenty-seventh monarch in the line of succession. A total of 362 granite blocks were used in the construction of the cylinder; this number equals the number of days in the lunar year. The tower was filled with gravel up to the level of the entry door to create a floor for the interior ladder up to the viewing platform. The platform is only large enough to accommodate one seated adult at a time.

The Unified Silla (668–935 CE)

The Three Kingdoms despite their familial relations did not coexist peacefully, frequently attacking each other until in the mid-seventh century when Silla, with the assistance of Tang China, conquered the kingdoms of Baekje (660 CE) and Goguryeo (668 CE). However, when the victories had been achieved the Chinese refused to withdraw. Together with its recently conquered neighbors, Silla repelled the Tang and established the Unified Silla kingdom, the first state to unite the peninsula.

Kim Tae-song (active c. 740–774 CE), Sokkuram Grotto, c. 742–774 CE After their conversion to Buddhism, the Silla monarchs sponsored the building of numerous Buddhist temples and shrines around their capital. These buildings were located according to **geomancy**

to lock in place protective forces in nature. The Silla kings believed that by securing these powerful energies they would keep the city safe from attack by their enemies. The architect Kim Tae-song designed two of the most important Buddhist shrines of the United Silla era. Few facts are known about Kim Tae-song's life other than he was an official in the court of King Kyongdok (r. 742–765) and that he died in 774 CE. The two temples Sokkuram Grotto and Bulguksa were said to have been built to honor his parents in his previous and current lives respectively. Unfortunately, the original Bulguksa Temple was destroyed in the Japanese invasion of 1592. The Sokkuram Grotto, while looted of some of its sculptures during Japanese rule, fared better.

Sokkuram Grotto is a unique structure in the history of Buddhist architecture. It combines the idea of the mountain temple in its location, the rock-cut cave temple in concept, and the Indian stupa in its hemispherical form. The temple is located on Mount Tohan, one of the five protective mountains surrounding the capital; the mountain's granite flanks made leveling a space for a mountain temple or excavating a traditional cave temple impractical. Instead, Kim Tae-song created a built cave, using massive granite blocks to construct the chamber and entrance corridor. The stone structure was then covered with a layer of earth to give it the essence of a cave. The site selected for the temple offered the additional problem of moisture rising from underground springs so Kim Tae-song designed a series of channels under the floor to increase air circulation and keep the chamber dry. Sokkuram was oriented so that the rays of the sun, on the morning of the spring equinox, entering through the east doors, illuminate the Buddha statue in the center of the rotunda.

▼ 9.7 Korea, Sokkuram Buddha, c. 750–775 CE. Granite, 11 ft. high.

Stylistically, this monumental Buddha is a mix of Indian Gupta and Chinese Northern Wei elements.

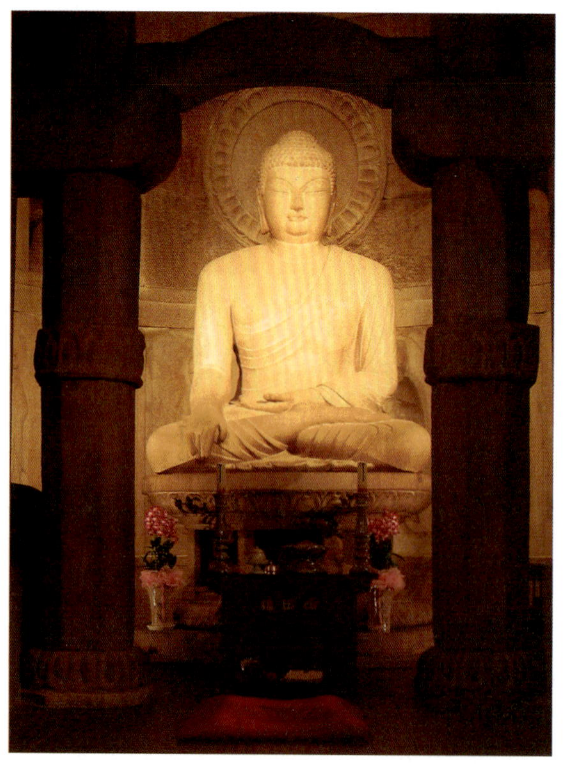

Sokkuram Buddha*, *c. 750–775 CE Regrettably, the name of the sculptor who carved the *Sokkuram Buddha* (Figure 9.7) from a single block of white granite was not recorded. The statue measures slightly more than 11 feet (3.5 m) tall and rests on a 4 foot (1.34 m) high pedestal. Stylistically the Sokkuram Buddha is a mix of Indian Gupta elements, such as scorpion-sting curls and fan-fold hem pleats, with Northern Wei interpretations derived from Gandharan prototypes. The Chinese influence is seen in the heavier torso and more rounded face.

Which Buddha is enshrined in Sokkuram is a matter of debate. As he seems to be performing the Touching the Earth Mudra, he is sometimes identified as Shakyamuni Buddha, but considering the Korean concepts of geomancy, Korean scholars see this gesture as one of protecting the land. If the story of Kim Tae-song's creation of the shrine as a memorial of filial piety is correct, then the Buddha would most likely represent Amitabha Buddha, the Buddha of the Western Paradise. Kim Tae-song's connection to nearby Bulguksa temple offers a third possibility that the figure represents Vairocana, the Cosmic Buddha who is venerated there. Little resolution of the Buddha's intended identity is offered in the associated images. On the lower walls of the chamber are low relief figures of ten disciples and five bodhisattvas including the eleven-headed Kwanum (Avalokitshivara), associated with Amitabha Buddha. However, the figures in the niches on the upper wall are figures of devas associated with the cardinal directions and constellations, suggesting Vairocana.

The Later Three Kingdoms and the Goryeo Dynasty (918–1392 CE)

At the end of the ninth century the Unified Silla fractured when Baekje and Goguryeo reasserted their independence becoming the Later Baekje and Later Goguryeo. This short-lived Later Three Kingdoms period ended when Wang Geon, who had usurped the throne of Goguryeo, conquered Silla in 935 CE and Backje the following year. Ruling over the entire peninsula as King Taejo, he shortened the name of the kingdom to Goryeo, from which the name "Korea" was later derived.

The Goryeo kings were enlightened rulers, abolishing slavery, reforming the government, and promoting the arts and literature, including the writing of the first Korean histories, the *Samguk Sagi* (History of the Three Kingdoms) and the *Samguk Yusa* (Memorabilia of the Three Kingdoms), and they sponsored the carving of the Tripitaka, a collection of wood blocks for the printing of all known Buddhist texts. When the palace library was burned in 1126 CE, King Injong (r. 1122–1146 CE) had the casters at his royal mint adapt coin casting techniques to produce bronze type, creating the first movable metal type some three hundred years before Europeans. In 1231 the Mongols invaded Korea and the Goryeo became a vassal state of the Yuan Empire.

Maebyeong Vase with Cranes and Clouds, thirteenth century CE Under Goryeo patronage celadon or "Chongja" ceramics reached perfection. The first **celadon** wares are thought to have been introduced from China with Chan Buddhism and tea. Korean celadons are high-fired,

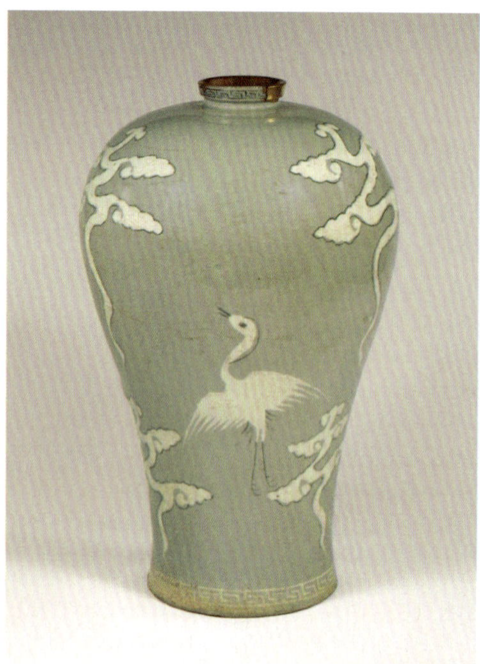

▲ 9.8 Korea, Goryeo dynasty, Maebyeong Vase with Cranes and Clouds, thirteenth century CE. Stoneware with inlaid designs and celadon glaze, 11.50 in. high.

While celadon glazes were introduced from China, Korean potters perfected them. The inlaid cranes on this vase are auspicious symbols.

light gray or buff colored stoneware vessels coated with a feldspathic glaze that turns various shades of bluish-green when reduction fired. Korean ceramic artists invented a number of decorative techniques for celadon that are unknown elsewhere, including reticulated openwork designs and ***sanggam*** or inlaid decoration.

The *Maebyeong Vase with Cranes and Clouds* (Figure 9.8) is a form derived from China. This type of tall vessel with a small mouth was used for displaying a single branch of blossoming plum. The cranes and clouds, traditional symbols of longevity, decorating its surfaces look to be fluidly painted but they are actually inlaid. Using the technique known as sanggam, the artist incised the design into vessel when the clay reached a leather-hard consistency. The excavated areas were filled with either white clay as in the cranes or reddish-brown clay that would turn black when fired as in the legs and beaks of the birds and the outlines of the clouds. After bisque-firing, the vessel was given a transparent celadon glaze that allowed the inlaid colors to show through. Goryeo potters also used copper-oxide underglazes to add touches of red to their designs.

Water Moon Avalokitesvara, 1310 Several genres of painting flourished at the cosmopolitan Goryeo court. Close relationships with Song China inspired Korean nobles to imitate their Chinese counterparts in taking up painting as a means of meditation and intellectual cultivation. Unfortunately, very few Goryeo paintings have survived to the present day. Only 160 examples are known, mostly Buddhist subjects, and a majority of those are in Japan.

A popular subject of the era was the *Water Moon Avalokitesvara* or *Gwanseeum-bosal* (Figure 9.9); thirty-eight examples are known. Among the surviving works is a monumental 16 foot (4.8 m) by 9 foot (2.7 m) silk hanging scroll in the Kagami Jinjya (Shinto) Temple in Karatsu, Japan. The scroll was created by a team of painters working at the court of King Chungseon (r. 1308–1313), under the direction of Queen Kim. The painting depicts the Bodhisattva seated on his mountain island home of Potalaka. In his right hands he holds the blue lotus that identifies him. In China and Korea Avalokitesvara often appears feminine since compassion was believed to be a characteristic of that gender but the Bodhisattva is capable of manifesting in any form necessary to teach a particular supplicant. The painting is based on a story from the *Flower Garland Sutra* in which the youth Sudhana seeks enlightenment through visits to fifty-three great sages. In the scroll,

Sudhana is the childlike figure in the lower right who is approaching the Bodhisattva. The scroll is thought to have been commissioned as a supplication to the Bodhisattva to release Korea from Mongol domination. Not long after this scroll was painted, it was taken by marauding pirates to Japan.

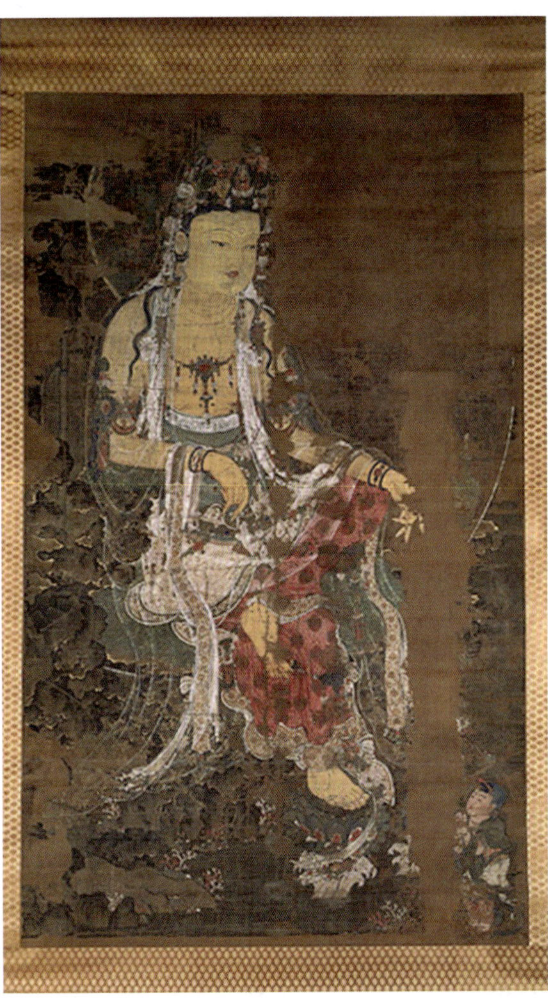

▲ **9.9** Korea, Goryeo, Water Moon Avalokitesvara, 1310 CE. Ink and color on silk, 16 ft. × 9 ft.

This monumental scale painting was the work of several court artists who painted it as an offering to the Bodhisattva and a request for his protection of the country.

Great Joseon Dynasty (1392–1910)

The fall of the Chinese Yuan Dynasty in 1368 also ended Mongolian control of the peninsula, and the Goryeo king moved quickly to remove Mongol officials and military officers who had been installed by the Yuan emperors. Despite the return of political autonomy, the last years of the Goryeo dynasty were beset with political strife, philosophical animosity between Buddhists and Neo-Confucians, and persistent incursions by Manchus and Japanese pirates. After successfully repulsing the Japanese, the Goryeo General Yi Seong-gye was ordered to attack Ming China, which had announced its intent to seize some of Korea's northern territories. However, instead of engaging the Ming,General Yi marched on the capital and executed a coup d'état. Taking the throne as King Taejo, he moved quickly to solidify his rule, eliminating nobles who had supported the Goryeo king, suppressing Buddhism, embracing Confucianism, and establishing relations with Ming China.

Ahn Gyeon (active c. 1440–1470) Dream Journey to the Peach Blossom Land, 1447 CE Painting flourished at the Joseon court, particularly during the reign of King Sejong (r. 1418–1450 CE), who is best known for inventing the Korean alphabet known as *hangul*. One of Sejong's court artists was Ahn Gyeon. In his contemporaneous *Record of Painting*, the Confucian scholar Shin Suk-ju praised Ahn Gyeon as a master of landscapes. The *Mongyudowon do* handscroll or *Dream Journey to the Peach Blossom Land* (Figure 9.10) is the only work by Ahn Gyeon that has survived. According to the painting's **colophon** or explanatory inscription, the work was inspired by a vivid dream Prince An-pyeong had in the spring of 1447 CE. In the dream the prince and his friend, Bak Paeng-nyeon, were walking through a landscape of forests and

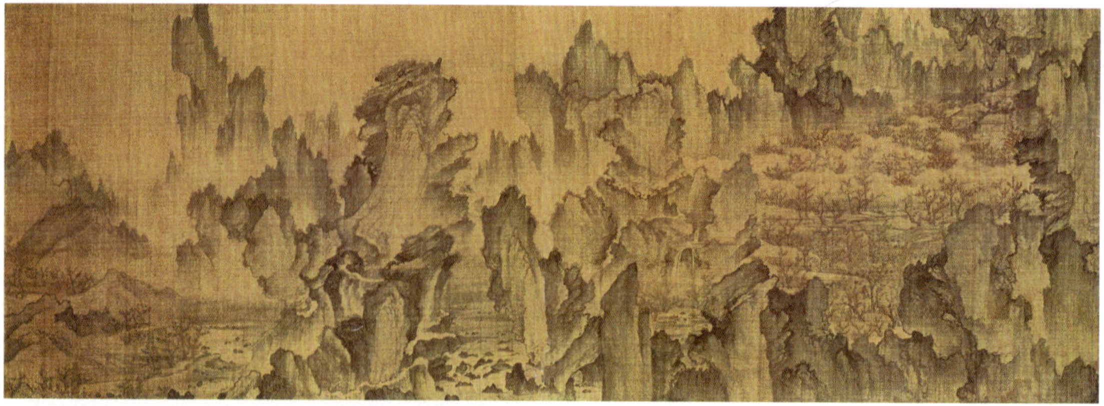

▲ 9.10 Korea, Ahn Gyeon (active c. 1440–1470 CE), *Dream Journey to the Peach Blossom Land*, 1447 CE. Ink and color on silk, 15.25 in. × 41.75 in.

Inspired by the dream of a prince, this painting blends views of the real world with those of an imaginary one.

mountains. On their journey they met a man who showed them the way to a peach orchard, a symbol associated with good fortune and longevity. When the prince woke, he summoned the painter, described his dream, and commanded the artist to paint it, which Ahn did in just three days.

As much as the prince's dream, Ahn Gyon's northern Song style painting may have been inspired by the story of *Peach Blossom Spring* by the Six Dynasties poet Tao Qian who told a story about a great peach orchard discovered by a simple fisherman; at the end of the grove he finds a community of people who had been hidden away from the world since the Qin period. In his painting Ahn leads the viewer from the realistically depicted world of the valley in the lower left through the progressively craggy and surreal mountains, suggesting a dream or otherworldly state, to the idyllic peach orchard in the upper right. Although the orchard is ringed by mountains, it appears to be an immense space; this effect was achieved by placing it on middle ground slope and allowing it to extend upwards to a distant range of mountains. The positioning of the orchard in this way counterbalances the deep perspective of the valley in the lower left.

Silhak Movement

In 1592, the Japanese army invaded Korea as the first step in Toyotomi Hideyoshi's plan for the conquest of Asia. The Joseon navy, equipped with "turtle ships," the world's first ironclads, defeated the Japanese at the battle of Hansan-do, forcing their withdrawal from the peninsula. The Joseon were less successful in rebuffing the attack of the Manchu Qing, who forced Korea into a tributary relationship in 1637. In an effort to rebuild Korean society after the invasions, the Neo-Confucian ***yangban*** (scholarly officials), instituted the ***Silhak*** Movement. Silhak stressed practical learning as the means to solve the country's economic and social problems. In the arts, Silhak encouraged Korean painters to look for indigenous subjects and scenes rather than continuing to imitate Chinese models.

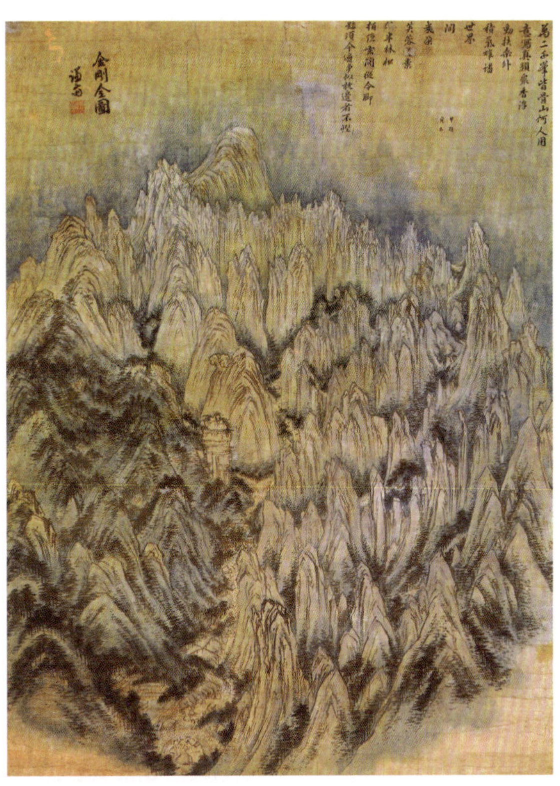

▲ **9.11** Korea, Jeong Seon (1676–1759), General View of Mt. Geumgangsan, 1734 CE. Ink and color on paper, 51.5 in. × 37 in.

Inspired by the Silhak movement, Jeong painted this accurate landscape of the especially craggy Korean mountain.

Jeong Seon (1676–1759),* General View of Mt. Geumgangsan, *1734 Jeong Seon was born into an aristocratic family and served as a local magistrate. He took up painting at the age of thirty-five and worked as an artist until his death. Although initially imitating Chinese paintings, under the influence of Silhak, Jeong devised a new highly realistic approach to landscape painting, which he termed ***jingyeong sansuhwa*** or "true-view painting." True-view painting required the artist to go out into the countryside and paint directly from nature, essentially painting *en plein air* almost a century before the Barbizon painters in Europe. Jeong is best known for his many ink and watercolor paintings of Mount Geumgangsan in the Taebaek range that runs along the eastern coast of the peninsula. In his famous painting of the mountain, *General View of Mt. Geumgangsan* (Figure 9.11), Jeong details in firm contour lines the thousands of Geumgangsan's shard-like granite peaks, which erupt from verdant valleys. Blue washes suggest mist rising from distant parts of the mountain. In a manner reminiscent of An Gyon, Jeong contrasts the large barren sharps rising on the right side of the mountain with a section on the left of softer, foliage-covered peaks. Separating the two is a narrow valley in which an almost unseen Buddhist monastery is nestled.

Shin Ka-gwon (1758–c. 1813),* A Scenery on Dano Day, *after 1805 Shin Ka-gwon, commonly known as Shin Yun-bok, was also inspired by the Silhak movement to create an indigenous Korean art. Shin came from a family of court painters and he was himself a member of the *Dohwaseo* (government office of painting) for a time before being expelled for obscenity. His offense was in treating the upper-class yangban not as the paragons of virtue they purported to be but as fallible humans susceptible to ordinary vices. In many of his paintings, Shin portrays the yangban enjoying the company of lower class *gisaeng* (female entertainers); such fraternization was considered to be extremely vulgar in Joseon society. An even greater offense was found in his drawing the women the same size as the yangban.

A Scenery on Dano Day (Figure 9.12) shows women performing the rituals associated with the Dano festival. In a scene reminiscent of the story of Susannah and the Elders, the women are shown in various stages of undress as they wash their hair in iris water and rinse in the stream before redressing for the festivities. While the women engage

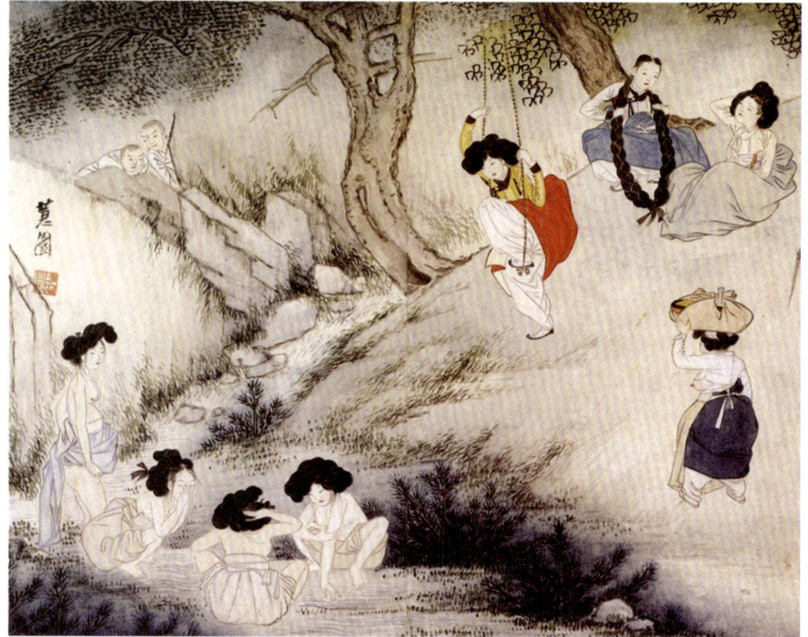

▶ 9.12 Korea, Shin Ka-gwon (1758–c. 1813), *A Scenery on Dano Day*, c. 1805. Ink and color on paper.

Painting under the name Hyewon, Shin focused his art on scenes of contemporary life in Korea often in a satirical manner.

in these innocent activities, they are being spied on by two men, drawn smaller in scale, who are hiding behind rocks. The men have removed their hats but appear to be dressed in the white *hanbok* coat worn by the yangban scholars.

Korean Art in the Modern Era

In 1910 Japan forced the abdication of the last Joseon monarch and annexed Korea. Japanese rule was repressive and socially disruptive; the Korean language was prohibited, farms and businesses were appropriated by the Japanese, and Korean traditional culture and arts were suppressed. During the occupation, the only art schools open to Koreans were those in Japan. This was an especially difficult time in Korea and as a result, the arts of this era have been little studied. The years after World War II saw the revival of traditional ink painting and celadon in South Korea as well as efforts to create a fusion of the traditional media with Western expressive modes such as abstraction. In North Korea, the approved art style was and remains socialist realism with its primary goals being the celebration of the leader and the revolution (Ksenija 2016).

Yi Kwae-dae (1913–1970),* Self-Portrait in Traditional Coat, *1948–1949 Yi Kwae-dae was born during the Japanese occupation. After high school in Seoul, he studied at the Imperial Art School in Japan, where he specialized in ***yôga*** or Western painting. Returning to Korea in the 1930s he organized the New Artists' Association, which, like the earlier Silhak movement, encouraged artists to produce works that were authentically Korean instead of following Japanese styles. Such ideas did not find favor with the Japanese colonial authorities.

When, after the war, the Korean peninsula was divided by United States and Soviet forces into north and south, Yi Kwae-dae actively protested the partitioning of his country. His activism and his brother's defection to the north put him under intense police scrutiny. When the Korean War broke out, he was arrested and sent to a prisoner-of-war camp. In 1953, he defected to North Korea.

Yi's Self-portrait in Traditional Coat (Figure 9.13) was painted after his brother's defection when Yi's own loyalty was being repeatedly questioned. In his self-portrait Yi Kwae-dae seems to be making a statement that goes beyond conflicting ideologies and the politics of partition. He looks directly at us, clench-jawed and determined, holding his palette and brushes like a shield as though he is making a statement that his allegiance is to Korean art. He wears a fedora and a traditional hanbok, while in the fauvist colored landscape behind him Korean women walk through the countryside carrying water pots and food baskets on their heads.

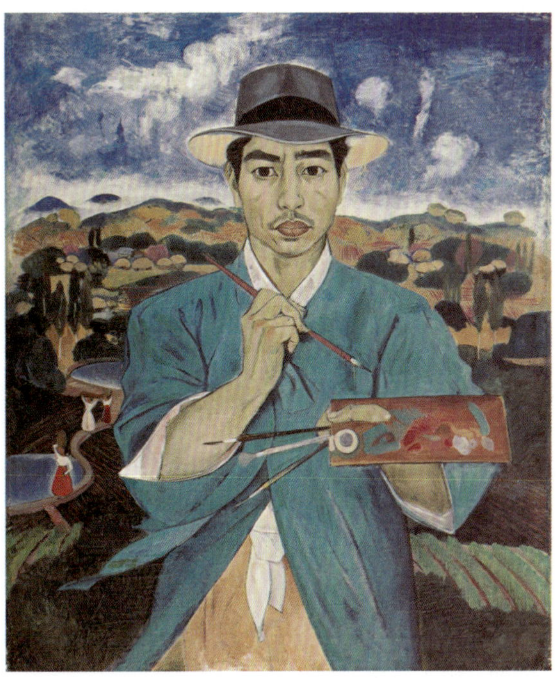

▲ **9.13** Korea, Yi Kwae-dae (1913–1970), *Self-Portrait in Traditional Coat*, 1948–1949. Oil on canvas.

In this self-portrait Yi expresses his search for a Korean identity after having grown up during the Japanese occupation.

Song Soo-nam (1938–2013),* Summer Trees, *1979 Song Soo-nam was also born during the Japanese occupation. He attended Hongik University, where he began as a student of Western art but in his senior year switched to traditional ink painting. He was one of the founders of the *Sumukhwa* or "Oriental Ink Movement," which advocated for the revival of traditional monochrome ink painting as a contemporary medium.

In *Summer Trees* (Figure 9.14) broad vertical strokes of diluted ink bleed and blend into each other, creating a monochromatic curtain that stops short of the bottom of the page to suggest a shallow clearing at the edge of a dense forest. A few abrupt strokes, added when the paper was dry, define trunks along the front edge of the grove. *Summer Trees* exudes a quiet meditative spirituality, recalling the long tradition of Daoist landscape painting. Yet at the same time its subtle blending of blacks and grays evokes Western color field paintings, particularly Morris Louis' *Veil Series* of the 1950s. Indeed, many of Song's pieces, while rooted in tradition, have an almost abstract quality.

Neolithic Japan (12,000–300 BCE)

The Neolithic begins in Japan with the submersion of the land bridges connecting it to the mainland, isolating its first settlers. The culture of this era came to be known as "Jomon" for the "cord-marked"

▶ 9.14 Korea, Song Soo-nam (1938–2013), *Summer Trees*, 1979. Ink on paper, 25.6 in. × 40.5 in.

Song's paintings exude the inner tranquility and spirituality that he felt were in danger of being lost in the modern world with its focus on technology and gadgets.

decorative patterns of their early pottery. The first Jomon wares were discovered in 1877 by an American zoologist, Edward S. Morse who, as one of the Meiji era foreign advisors, excavated the examples from the Omori shell mound. Recent excavations at Odai Yamamoto I site, Aomori Prefecture in northern Honshu found pottery sherds dating to 14,500 BCE. While the Jomon did live in small settled communities, they continued to use stone tools and survived by hunting, fishing, and gathering. The resource-rich islands allowed the Jomon to satisfy their needs without having to develop the intensive grain agriculture that characterized the Neolithic in other parts of the world.

Jomon Flameware Vessel, c. 2500 BCE Jomon ceramics are one of the longest-lived pottery traditions in history, continuing to evolve over the course of 13,000 years before ceasing around 1500 BCE. All of their pots were built up by coiling and then the surfaces were smoothed by scraping. Pots were wrapped with cordage to slow down the drying process of the clay. While many of the Jomon forms are practical utilitarian wares, some are so dramatically ornamented as to be impractical for most purposes. Beginning around 2500 BCE, the Jomon produced a type of pottery known as "flameware" (Figure 9.15), for the often flame-like flanges around the rims of vessels. Unlike earlier conical or round bottom forms, flameware vessels generally had flat bottoms, and cylindrical bodies. The sculptural elaboration of these vessels may indicate they were intended for ritual purposes.

The Yayoi Period (900 BCE–300 CE)

The first waves of settlers from Korea began arriving in western Kyushu around 900 BCE (Curry 2008: 18). These people, named Yayoi for the street in Tokyo where the first examples of their ceramics

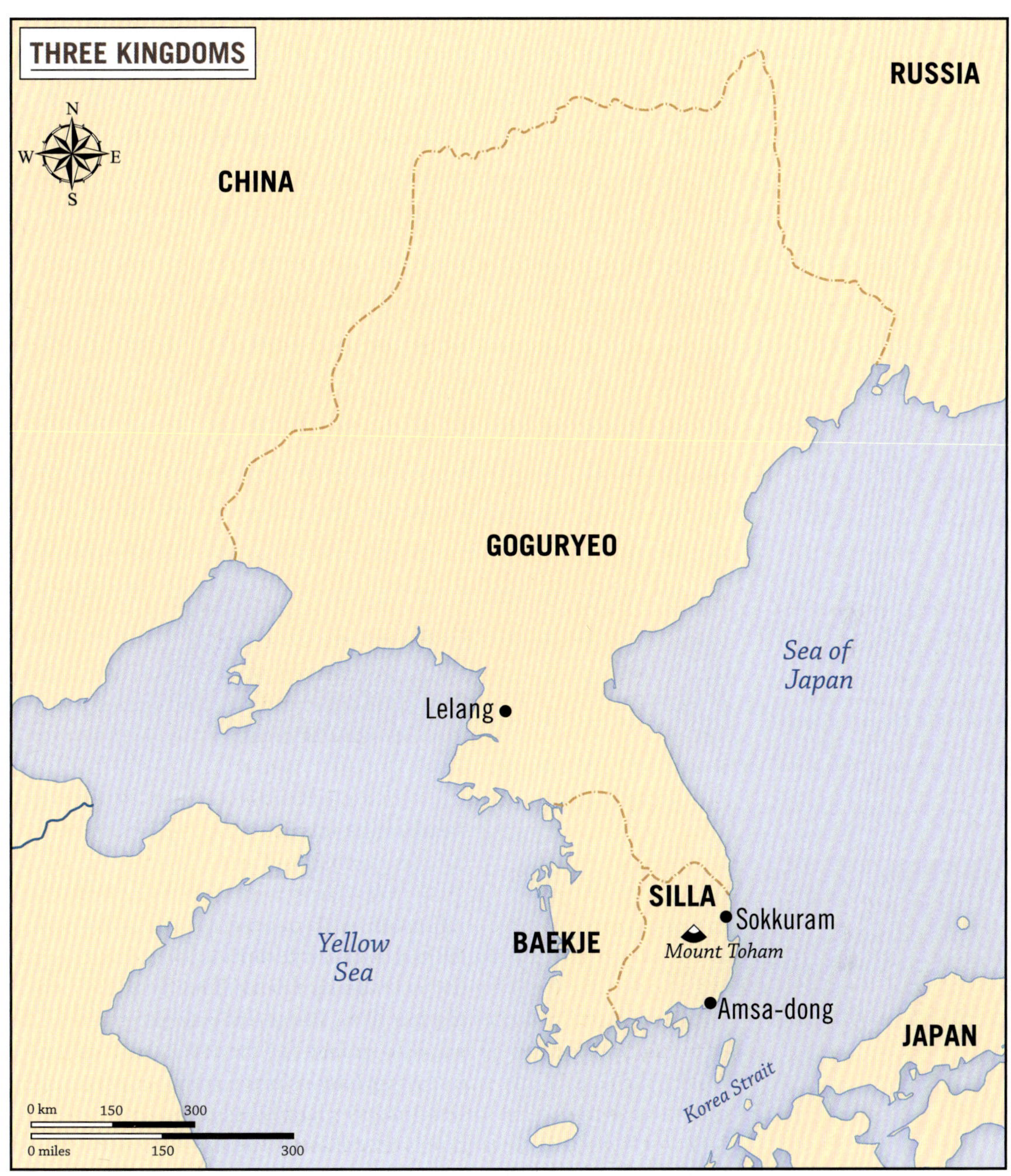

were found, are considered the ancestors of the modern Japanese people. The Yayoi period was one of rapid technological and social advancement. Intensive rice cultivation and irrigation systems were introduced along with bronze casting, iron-working, raised-floor architecture, and Shintoism, a religion of gods, nature-spirits, and rituals. It is also during this period that the first descriptions of the *Wa* (Japanese) appear in the Chinese Jin Dynasty chronicle, the *Wei Zhi*.

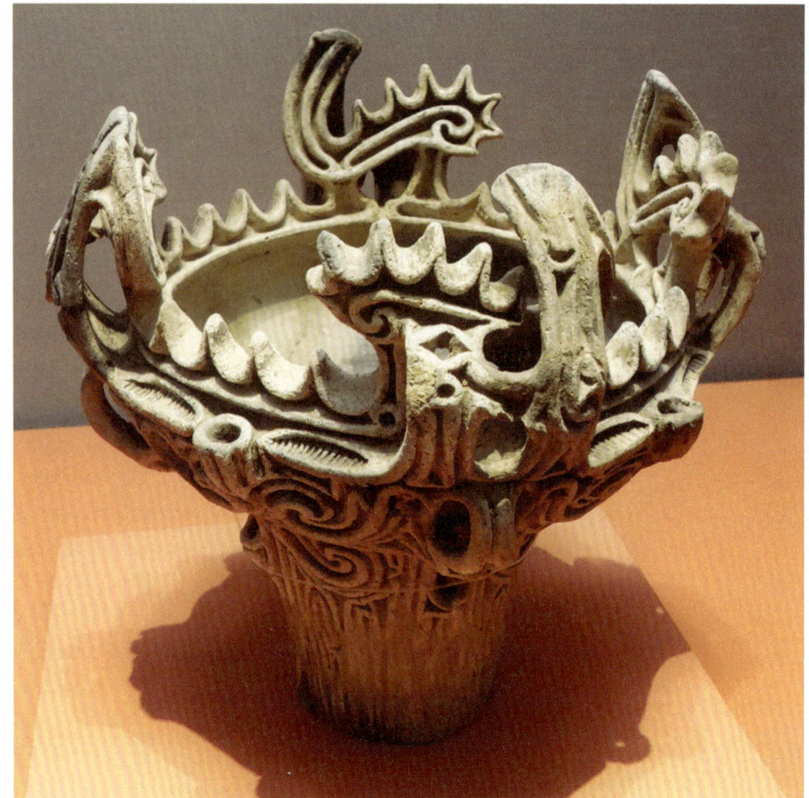

▶ **9.15** Japan, Jomon Flameware Vessel, c. 2500 BCE.

This Jomon flameware vessel is so dramatically ornamented around the rim with flame-like appendages that it could only be intended for ritual or funerary use.

▼ **9.16** Japan, Yayoi, Dotaku, c. 1–100 CE. Bronze, 43.50 in.

These bells come in a range of sizes from small to large and are thought to have been inspired by Korean bells. They are often found buried in caches on hillsides. The bells generally lack clappers and some are too thin to have resonated. Their function is unknown.

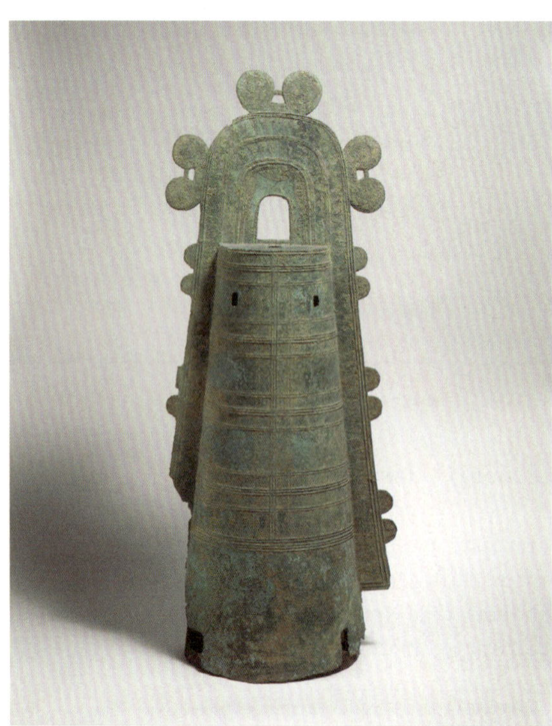

Dotaku, c. c. 1–100 CE The Yayoi brought both bronze casting and iron-working to Japan. They made their tools and other utilitarian items out of iron or stone, reserving bronze almost exclusively for ritual objects including mirrors, swords, and bells called ***dotaku*** (Figure 9.16). The earliest dotaku were quite small, 4 inches (10 cm) high and were cast using two-piece stone molds. Larger dotoku, up to 51 inches (129 cm), were cast in fired-clay molds. Dotaku do not have clappers nor do they appear to have been struck in the manner of Chinese bells. It is not entirely clear how they were used, as most of the more than four hundred that have been discovered were found buried far from habitation sites; they were often buried in pairs or even-numbered caches, sometimes with bronze weapons (Hudson 1992, 153–55). The bodies of the dotaku are typically divided horizontally into two, three, or more registers, crossed in the center by a vertical band. The resulting compartments might be undecorated, have linear slash and cross-hatching patterns, or have designs of animals—primarily deer, but also turtles, fish, birds, lizards, and dragonflies, or they have human figures, generally shown in profile. Based on descriptions in the *Wei Zhi* of the use of bells in Korean rice planting and harvesting festivals, it has been suggested that the Japanese dotaku may have had a similar agricultural function.

The Kofun Period (250–538 CE)

This period takes its name from the more than 30,000 ***kofun*** or "old tombs" built during the era for emperors, members of the royal family, lesser nobles, and the leaders of powerful clans. The tombs come in a range of sizes and shapes from round mounds about 30 feet (10 m) in diameter, to square mounds running 104 feet (32 m) on a side, octagonal mounds measuring 124 feet (38 m) per side, and combination forms such as the massive keyhole-shaped (square and round mound) tombs, which regularly exceed 300 feet (100 m) in length. The ability to command the large numbers of laborers required to build these large tombs was facilitated by the uniting of many the southern Honshu and the Kyushu clans under the leadership of the Imperial yamato government.

The Daisen Kofun of Emperor Nintoku, ***c. 313–399 CE*** The largest of all the keyhole tombs is the *Daisen Kofun of Emperor Nintoku* (Figure 9.17);

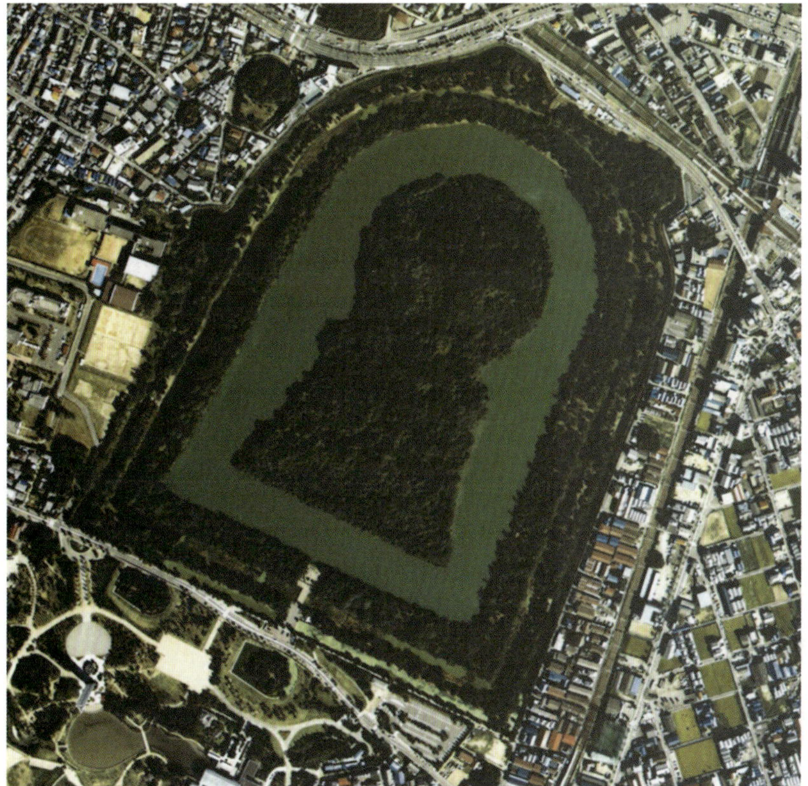

◀ **9.17** Japan, Kofun, Tomb of Emperor Nintoku, c. 313–399 CE. Overall length 2,700 ft.

This is the largest of all of the Kofun era tombs; it takes it characteristic keyhole shape from the merging of square and circular tomb types.

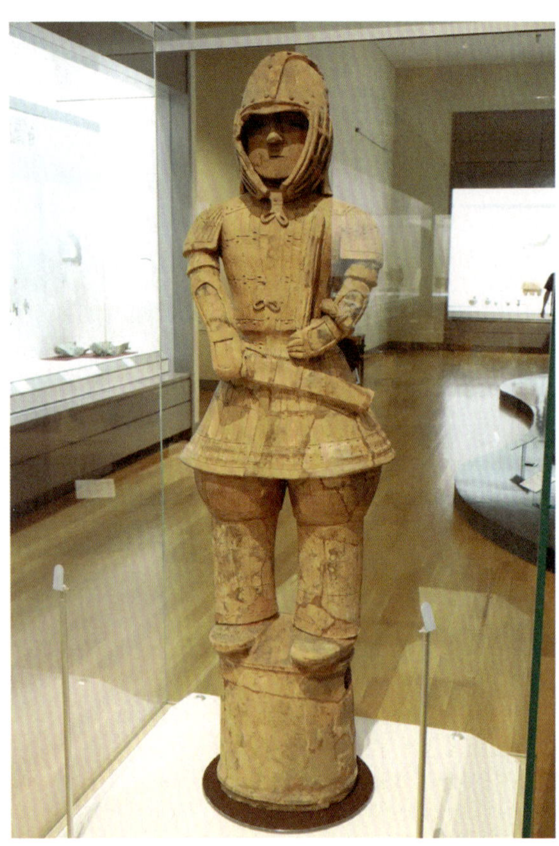

▲ 9.18 Japan, Kofun, Haniwa Warrior in Keiko Armor, c. sixth century CE. Terracotta, 51.8 in (131.5 cm).

Haniwa were set up as offerings on Kofun era tombs and modeled in the form of animals, objects, and humans of various classes and occupations.

it has an overall length including moats and levees of 2,700 feet (823 m). The mound itself is 1,579 feet (481.27 m) long, 1000 feet (305 m) wide, and 114 feet (35 m) high. Although it is difficult to see through the mound's covering vegetation, it is a three-tiered structure with spaces for rituals at the juncture of the square and round sections. As a presumed Imperial tomb, it has not been excavated; however, archaeology conducted on nonroyal tombs suggest that a megalithic chamber, containing house-shaped stone or terracotta sarcophagi, should be located beneath the circular section.

Haniwa of a Warrior in Keiko Armor and Helmet, ***c. sixth century CE,*** The burial mounds of the Kofun period were often decorated with terracotta sculptures known as ***haniwa***, literally "clay ring." Early in the period, haniwa were simple low-fired, clay cylinders which probably served as supports for offering bowls. Later sculptures of animals, men and women of various occupations, houses and other items were modeled on the tops of these cylinders. The figures were constructed by the coiling method with arms and legs often being formed separately and attached. Ribbons and beads of clay were appliqued to the figures to create clothing and jewelry details. None of the haniwa were ever glazed but a few examples have surviving pigment which suggest that at least some may have been brightly colored.

Among the highly detailed haniwa is the more than 4 foot (121.5 cm) tall figure of a warrior (Figure 9.18). He wears elaborate *keiko* armor made up of narrow iron plates that have been joined together with rivets and leather thongs, and an iron helmet with large cheek plates. His pose is cautious, one hand rests on the hilt of his sword while the other holds the tiller of a crossbow. A quiver with bolts hangs on his back. Every detail of his equipment, helmet, and armor has been exactingly detailed in contrast to the warrior's flat face, which stares mask-like from under the helmet; the eyes are simple almond-shaped holes, the mouth a slit, and the nose, a triangle of clay. The disparity in detail would seem to suggest that roles in society are more important than the individual.

The Asuka Period (c. 538–710)

The Asuka Period, as well those that follow, takes its name from the city that served as the Imperial capital. The Japanese emperors frequently changed palaces and even cities after the death of their predecessor as

RELIGION AND ART
Shinto, the Way of the Gods

Japanese culture is strongly influenced by Shinto, the indigenous religion of the country, so an understanding of its basic concepts is important to the understanding of Japanese art. As a religion it is unique in that adherence to Shinto does not preclude the practice of other religions such as Buddhism. In fact, many Japanese traditionally practiced both religions, turning to Shinto for certain rites, such as weddings, and Buddhism for others, such as funerals. There are also syncretic forms of Buddhistic Shinto.

In Shinto, rituals are held for ***kami***, the spirits that are believed to be the animating essence of all life. Kami inhabit a variety of natural phenomena, including mountains (Mt. Fuji in particular), seas, waterfalls, fire, ancient trees, earthquakes, storms, large interestingly shaped rocks, humans, and animals such as deer. These kami were worshiped in their natural settings, in sanctuaries or ***jinja*** that were often little more than clearings marked by a circle of stones or by a ***torii*** gateway to separate sacred space form the everyday world. In addition to wonders of nature, family ancestors and auspicious dead, such as soldiers who died in war, can be kami. The kami most closely associated with the Imperial family and the Japanese nation is Amaterasu, the sun goddess, whose temple is in Ise.

Shinto's influence on Japanese art and architecture is subtle and can be found in an artist's approach to craft and respect for materials rather than in a particular set of motifs. Until the Heian Period, Shinto had no sculptural tradition as the kami were not usually represented in anthropomorphic form. During the eighth and ninth centuries syncretic forms of Shinto-Buddhism emerged, which regarded the kami as local manifestations of Buddhas. These images, usually carved in wood and representing clan kami, were depicted in the guise of Buddhist monks.

bad luck was associated with places where a ruler had died. The period was one of significant change in Japan, beginning with the introduction of Buddhism from Korea and ending with the institution of a Chinese-style centralized government of ranked officials, and Japan's first charter, the Seventeen Article Constitution, in 604 CE. The guiding force behind these reforms was Shotoku Taishi, a son of Emperor Yomei, who served as prince regent during the reign of Empress Suiko (r. 593–628 CE). During Shotoku's regency Buddhism became a state religion but Shinto remained important, especially to the Imperial family, and the two religions coexisted peacefully with most Japanese adhering to the traditions of both.

Shintoism in Japan

The earliest Shinto shrines, circa 400–500 CE, were simple rustic structures built of natural materials. As they did not require interior space for a congregation, most were small buildings, modeled after traditional rice storehouses, which served as temporary dwellings for kami, usually represented by sacred objects shielded from common view within the structure. Typically, early shrines were built of debarked and unpainted cypress logs and roofed with Eulalia grass, water reed, or rice straw thatch. After the official introduction of Buddhism, Shinto shrines became progressively larger and more refined; the heavy log walls that had been capable of carrying the weight of wet thatch were planed down to the point that wooden posts had to be placed at the gable ends to support the ridge beam and weight of the thatch. By the beginning of the Nara period, newly built Shinto shrines were painted and had upturned tile roofs.

The Ise Jingu The most sacred of all Shinto shrines is the Ise Jingu or "Great Shrine" (Figure 9.19), founded in the late fifth century CE. It is home to Amateratsu, who is both the sun goddess and the divine ancestress of the Imperial family. Access to the shrine is limited to Shinto priests and the emperor; contained within are the three sacred objects: the jewel, the sword, and the mirror. These items represent the goddess and the divine authority she gave to the first emperor, Jimmu, her thrice great-grandson.

In 692 CE, Empress Jito sponsored the first *sengu* or "rebuilding" of the Ise shrine. Since it is built of natural and perishable materials, the shrine is reconstructed every twenty years. The process of rebuilding is a long one and it can take up to eight years from the time the first ancient trees are felled until the last bit of thatch is put into place. To facilitate the rebuilding cycle, two *kodenchi* or precincts, east and west, make up the compound so that as the construction can begin in one as the existing structure nears the end of its lifespan. When the new shrine has been readied, the sacred objects are transferred, and the old building removed except for the heart post which will serve as the center post of the next rebuilding. It is concealed in a small shed and the ground is purified with white pebbles.

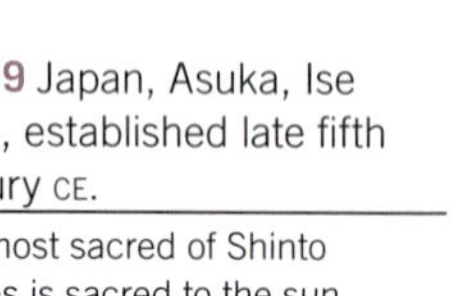

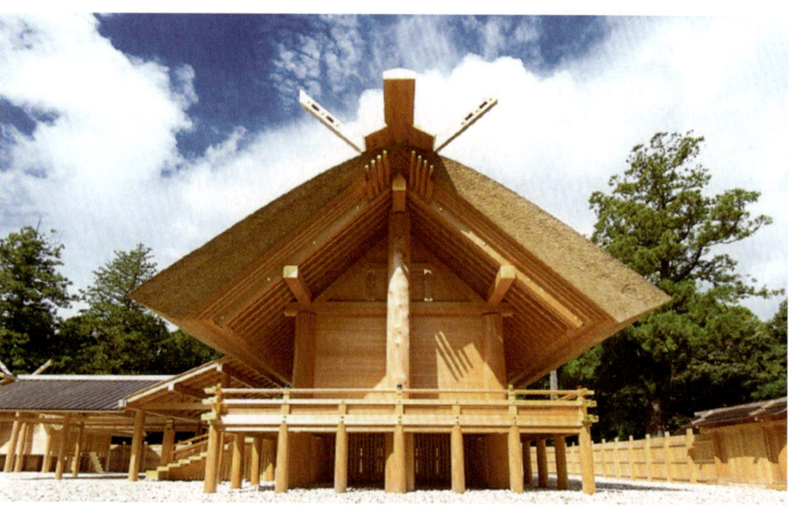

▶ 9.19 Japan, Asuka, Ise Jingu, established late fifth century CE.

This most sacred of Shinto shrines is sacred to the sun goddess Amateratsu, who is the divine ancestor of the Imperial family. The wooden shrine buildings have been rebuilt every twenty years since the sixth century CE.

Buddhism in Japan

Buddhism was introduced in the first half of the sixth century from Korea. Reception of the new religion was mixed until it was embraced by Prince Shotoku and Empress Suiko, who made it the state religion and sponsored the building of Buddhist temples, monasteries, and the creation of Buddhist images. Prince Shotoku is credited with establishing forty-six Buddhist temples across Japan and upon his death was declared to be an ***arhat*** or one who has achieved nirvana.

Horyu-ji, The Kondo and Pagoda, Ikaruga-cho, Nara Prefecturec, 670 CE The most important of the temples built by Prince Shotoku is Horyu-ji or "Temple of the Flourishing Law" (Figure 9.20), founded in 607 CE. The temple was dedicated to the Yakushi Nyorai, or Buddha of healing in fulfillment of a promise made by his father, Emperor Yomei. To build Horyu-ji and the other temples, the prince appealed to the king of Baekje to send skilled craftsmen, designers, and monks to Japan. Unfortunately, many of the original buildings, constructed under the prince's patronage, were lost to fire in 670 CE and subsequently rebuilt. Among the first rebuilt were the ***kondo*** or "golden hall," which houses the main Buddha images, and the pagoda. The Horyu-ji Kondo is considered to be the oldest existent wooden building in the world.

Both the kondo and the pagoda buildings are raised above ground level on low podiums. Each has four sets of cardinally oriented stairs that provide access to outer ambulatories for performing the act of circumambulation. Although the kondo is a single-story structure, the building's multiple rooflines give the impression that it has more levels; this is done as a means of visually demonstrating the importance of the structure. Inside, the walls of the kondo were originally

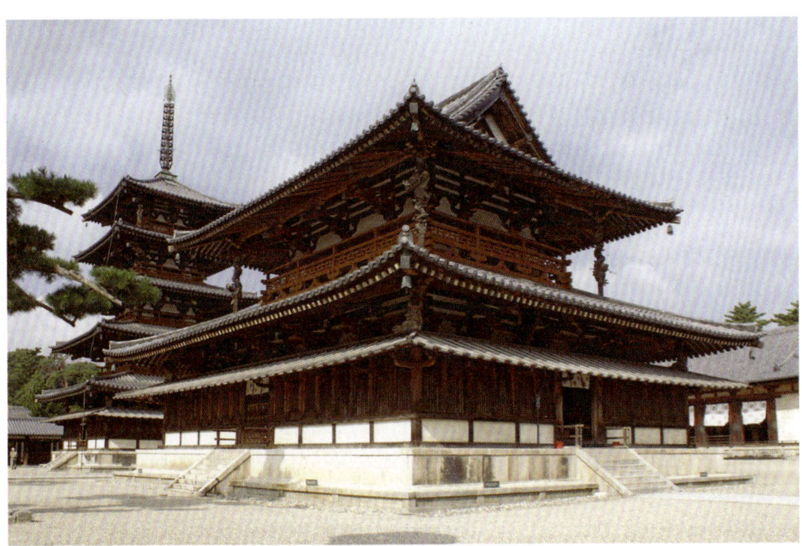

◀ **9.20** Japan, Asuka, Horyu-ji, Kondo and Pagoda, 670 CE.

Horyu-ji was founded by Prince Shotoku in 607 CE and rebuilt after a fire in 670 CE, making the temple buildings the oldest existing wooden buildings in the world. The original buildings were constructed by Korean artisans brought from the peninsula to build the monastery.

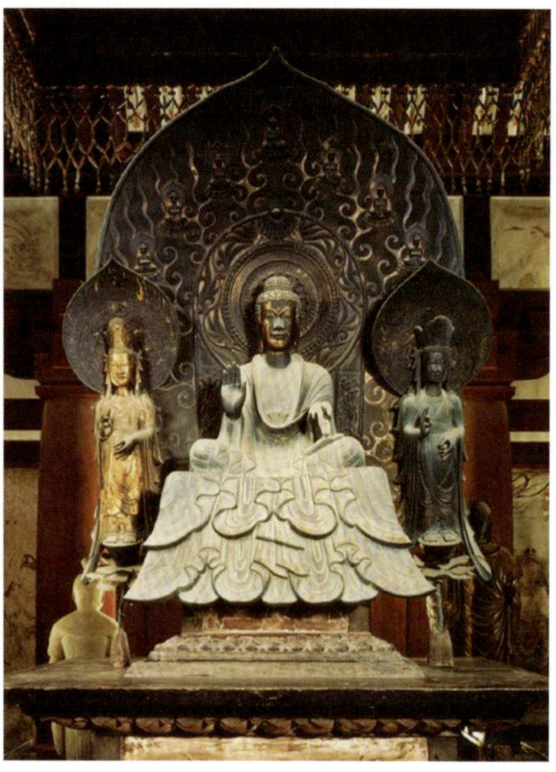

▲ 9.21 Japan, Kuratsukuri no Tori, Shakya Triad, Horyu-ji, Late sixth to seventh century CE.

Empress Suiko commissioned Tori to create in honor of Prince Shotoku, who died in 622.

decorated with 9-foot-high murals showing the Western Paradise of Amida (Amitabha) Buddha. Unfortunately, the original murals were damaged by fire in 1949 and only fragments remain today.

The rebuilding of Horyu-ji Pagoda is thought to have been completed around 708–710 CE; making it is the oldest wooden pagoda in Japan. Like all pagodas, it has an odd number of levels, in this case five, a common number for Japanese pagodas. Each of the Horyu-ji Pagoda's stories is slightly more slender than the previous one, creating the illusion of greater height. The ornate railings around the pagoda's levels suggest the possibility of magnificent views from the top of the 106.6 foot (32.5 m) high tower, but there are no floors within the structure nor stairs to ascend to those balconies. On the mainland, pagodas often filled the space of their hollow core with an enormous image of the Buddha that was the patron of the monastery; however, the Horyu-ji Pagoda has a unique construction that while making the structure earthquake resistant, allows little room for monumental sculpture. Inside, running from a foundation stone to the finial of the spire, is an octagonal cypress heart pillar, which is flanked by four columns at the corners and then, spaced to create an inner ambulatory, an additional twelve pillars. It is these sixteen wooden posts that support the weight of the pagoda that was built around, but not attached, to the heart pillar. In the same manner as the early Shinto shrines, the kondo and pagoda at Horyu-ji were constructed without the use of nails, all components being assembled with mortise and tenon joints, or in some parts of the structure cantilevered arms are slotted into brackets to allow the structure to shift and sway during quakes.

Kuratsukuri no Tori (late sixth–seventh century CE), Shakya Triad, 623 CE

The art of monumental bronze sculpture begins during the Asuka period with Kuratsukuri no Tori. He was the grandson of a Chinese saddle-maker, Shiba Tatsuko, who had immigrated to Japan in 522 CE. As professions were passed down through lineages in Japan, Tori, also known as Tori Busshi, a title meaning that he was a master Buddhist sculptor, was trained to model, cast, and gild bronze ornaments for horse saddles. A devout Buddhist, he is credited with creating the first Japanese Buddha image in 606 CE, the almost 16-foot (4.8m) high bronze Shakya Nyorai (the historical Buddha) for the Asuka-dera (Hoko-ji) Temple in Asuka.

VISUAL COMPARISON
Korean Influence on Tori Busshi's Shakya Triad

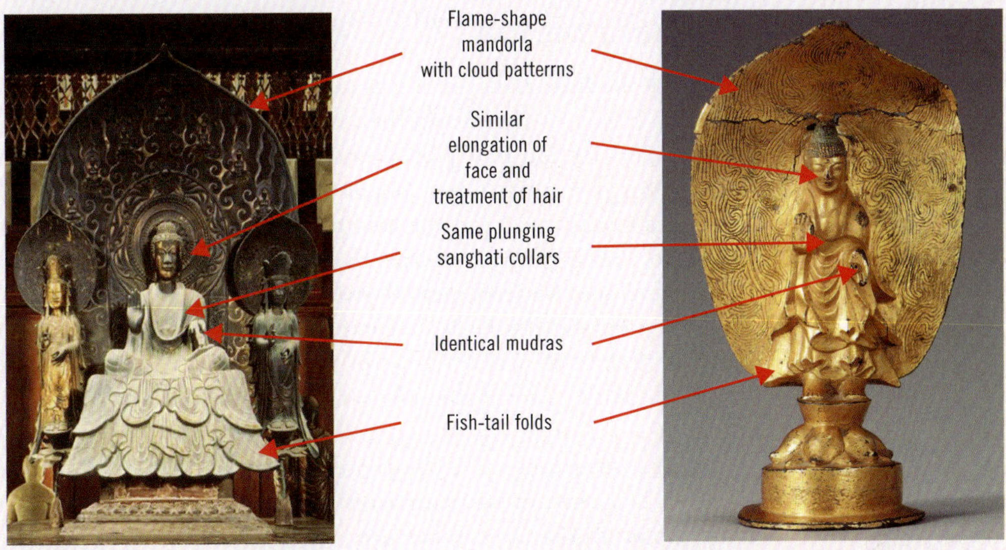

▲ **9.22** Korean influence on Tori Busshi's Shakya Triad. Korean Baekje and Goguryeo sculptures were obvious prototypes for the first Japanese bronze Buddhas

According to tradition Buddhism was introduced in 538 or 552 CE by a delegation from Korea, which brought among other gifts for the emperor a gilt bronze Buddha, Buddhist sutras, and a letter from the Korean ruler, praising Dharma. A plague erupted across the land after these gifts were accepted and it was determined that their acceptance had angered the kami so the statue and sutras were thrown into a canal.

Although this first Korean Buddhist image in Japan was lost, subsequent Korean Baekje and Goguryeo sculptures were obvious prototypes for the first Japanese bronze Buddhas cast by Kuratsukuri no Tori, known as Tori Busshi. As can be seen in the comparison of the Shakya Buddha with the Yeon-ga Buddha, believed to have been cast in Goguryeo in 539 CE, the two pieces have many points of similarity. Each has a slender, long face in contrast to the rounder Chinese faces of Northern Wei Buddhas, and each has a rounder, less blocky torso than Chinese types. Other similarities are found in the heavy U-shaped folds and side fish-tails of the drapery, the cloud patterns in the almond-shaped mandorlas, and in the mudras displayed.

In 622 the Empress Suiko commissioned Tori to create the Shakya Triad,(Figure 9. 22) a life-size bronze of Shakya Buddha with two attendant bodhisattvas, for Horyu-ji. According to tradition the face of the Buddha was modeled on that of Prince Shotoku, who died that year, and those of the two bodhisattvas, on his mother, and his principle wife. While the ultimate source of Tori Busshi's Shakya Nyorai and Shakya Triad is the Buddhist art of the Northern Wei Period, it appears that the style was filtered through Korea before being introduced into Japan. When compared to the Buddha of Yungang Cave 20 (see Figure 8.12), Tori's figures have leaner faces, less exaggerated ears, and more cylindrical torsos.

The Nara Period (710–784 CE)

In 710 CE the Imperial capital was moved to the new city of Heijo-kyo (modern Nara), inaugurating the Nara Period. The Nara was a time of rapid Sinicization in Japan. Chinese literature, art, law, and urban design provided models for Japanese development. The new capital Heijo-kyo closely followed the grid plan layout of the Tang capital of Chang'an, and like its counterpart was a cosmopolitan city with merchants and monks from across Asia walking its streets. Buddhism flourished during the Nara, becoming increasingly important in the political life of the nation. Emperor Shomu (r. 724–749 CE), himself a devout Buddhist, saw in the religion not only a means of ensuring the safety of the nation but also an instrument for the strengthening of the central government. He sponsored the building of the Kokubun-ji, a network of temples and monasteries connecting each province to a main temple in the capital, Todai-ji.

The Diabutsu and Daibutsuden, Todai-ji, begun 743 CE The nexus of Emperor Shomu's Kokubun-ji system was the "Great Eastern Temple" or Todai-ji in Heijo-kyo. As the Imperial temple, no expense was to be spared in the building of Todai-ji, and indeed, the costs of constructing the 500 ton, 52 foot (16 m) high gilt bronze Vairocana Buddha almost bankrupted the nation. The immense bronze sculpture was cast using a process adapted from the piece-mold system used by the Shang and early Zhou, but on a considerably larger scale. Once the site was chosen for the Daibutsu or "Great Buddha," a great cedar pole was set up to establish the height of the finished statue, and then, a wooden armature was constructed around the pole to support the weight of the clay original. When the statue was completed and had dried sufficiently, a mold was constructed around it, using a molding mixture of sand, clay, and rice husks. The finished mold was removed in sections, and the clay original reduced to allow for space between it and the reassembled mold. The actual casting was done in eight stages beginning with the base of the statue; the head and neck were cast separately and set into place. In each stage, the mold would be reassembled around the core and then held in place with a surrounding mound of earth that also served as scaffolding and smelting platform as the work progressed. The mound was leveled as the finishing work on the statue proceeded from the top down (Piggott 1990, 464). Unfortunately, the Daibutsu has suffered considerable damage from fires and the toppling of the head; currently the statue is only 49 feet (15 m) high after its 1692 restoration.

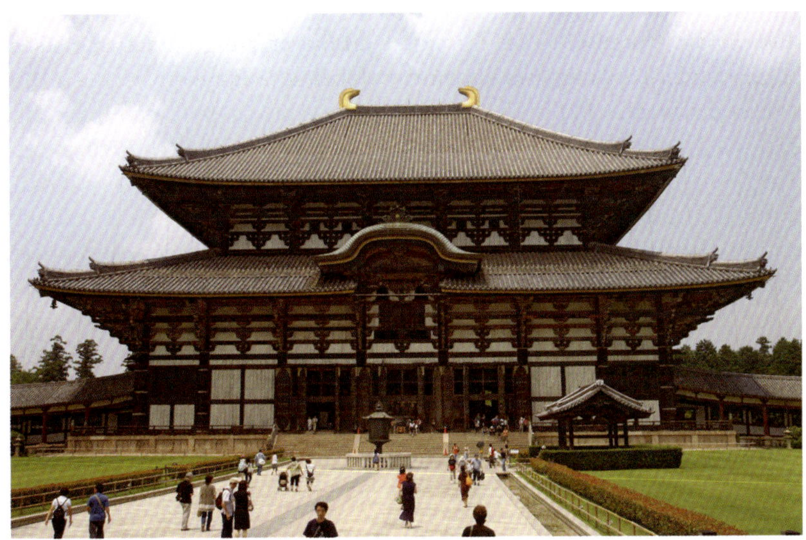

◀ 9.23 Japan, Nara, Todai-ji, Daibutsuden, 1709 CE.

Todai-ji was built by Emperor Shomu as the central temple of a network of Buddhist temples throughout Japan. The original building held a 52-foot-tall bronze Buddha image. The current kondo is considerably smaller than the original structure but was still the largest wooden building in the world until 1998.

Once the Daibutsu was completed in 751 CE, construction of its kondo began. The Todai-ji Daibutsuden (Figure 9.23) was a wooden building of unprecedented scale, measuring 282 feet (86 m) by 164 feet (40 m). The building of such a large wooden structure was possible during the Nara because Japan's old growth cypress forests had not yet been felled; those resources were no longer available when the building was reconstructed in 1195 and again in 1709, resulting in a much-reduced scale. The Daibutsuden's design and construction replicated that commonly used for Buddhist main halls in Tang China (see the Nanchan Temple, Figure 8.19, for example). Like its Chinese prototypes it was a timber frame structure supported on eighty-four massive cypress pillars that formed a basic three-bay module, surrounded by a single bay ambulatory under the lower roof. This basic module was replicated along the length of the structure until a building of the desired size was achieved. The Daibutsuden's hipped tile roof utilized the Tang raised-beam system, which resulted in a single incline with minimal upsweep of the eaves. At either end of the gable are golden horse-head ornaments. The current Daibutsuden, rebuilt in 1709, is considerably smaller than the original building at 164 feet (50 m) by 187 feet (57 m) and a height of 154 feet (47 m). . Even so it was still the largest wooden structure in the world until 1998, when it was surpassed by the Nipro Hachiko Dome in Akita, Japan.

Heian Period (794–1185 CE)

In 794 CE, Emperor Kammu established a new Chang'an style capital at Heian-kyo (modern Kyoto), ushering in the Heian period. The move to a new capital was a response to the growing influence in government of the Nara temples, which had grown in wealth and power under the

Kokunun-ji system. While the change of capitals did reduce monastic interference, it did little to lessen the jockeying for power between the rival clans at court. Ultimately the Fujiwara family rose to dominate the Imperial government at all levels. Where other clans had acquired power and prestige through their military abilities, the Fujiwara, beginning in the reign of Emperor Shomu, achieved status by giving their daughters as consorts to the emperors. The dominant figure of the age was Fujiwara Michinaga, who as regent (995–1027 CE), had the power to appoint and depose emperors at will. Despite the intrigues of the era, the Heian was a time of exceptional aesthetic and literary accomplishments as the court aristocrats transformed Chinese writing, art, and literature into uniquely Japanese forms, resulting in yamato-e painting, ***kanji*** and ***hiragana*** writing systems, and the world's first full length novel, *The Tale of Genji*, written by Lady Murasaki Shikibu around 1007 CE.

Lady Murasaki Shikibu (c. 973–c. 1020/31 CE),* Tale of Genji: Azumaya (Eastern Cottage) Chapter, *c. 1120–1140 CE Lady Murasaki was the daughter of Fujiwara no Tametoko, a renowned scholar of the Chinese classics, who was appointed a provincial governor in 996. As a child she showed great intellectual potential, so her father, breaching the social norms of the period, allowed her to study Chinese with her brother. In her mid-to-late twenties she was married to Fujiwara Nobuitaka, an older second cousin, with whom she had a daughter in 999 CE. After the death of her husband in 1001 CE, she was invited to the Imperial court, by Fujiwara no Michinaga, to serve as a lady-in-waiting to his daughter, Empress Shoshi.

Lady Murasaki's novel, *The Tale of Genji*, was inspired by her observations and experiences at the Imperial court. The hero of the story, Prince Genji, is the son of the emperor by one of his consorts. Because his mother's family was not powerful, Genji has no hope of becoming crown prince. He fills his days with aesthetic pursuits, political alliances, and amorous dalliances with all manner of women, including one of his father's consorts. One of the earliest surviving copies of the Genji-Monogatari is a set of early twelfth century handscrolls in the Tokugawa Art Museum. The scrolls were copied by court calligraphers in the elegant hiragana phonetic script that was used in vernacular writing. A painting illustrating a key event began each chapter of the novel.

The scene for the Azumaya or "Eastern Cottage" chapter (Figure 9.24) provides a glimpse into the lives of women during the Heian era. The painting shows Nakanokimi having her long hair combed while a lady reads to her from a book. The space in the scene is intimate; a fusuma or sliding screen closes off the background from view. The work is done in a painting style known as ***yamato-e***, meaning "Japanese Style." Yamato-e differed from Chinese painting in several important ways. First, yamato-e relied on the subtle use of fine line, brilliant colors and bold pattern rather than on virtuoso brush work. Second, instead of the shifting vantage points found in Chinese styles, yamato-e typically

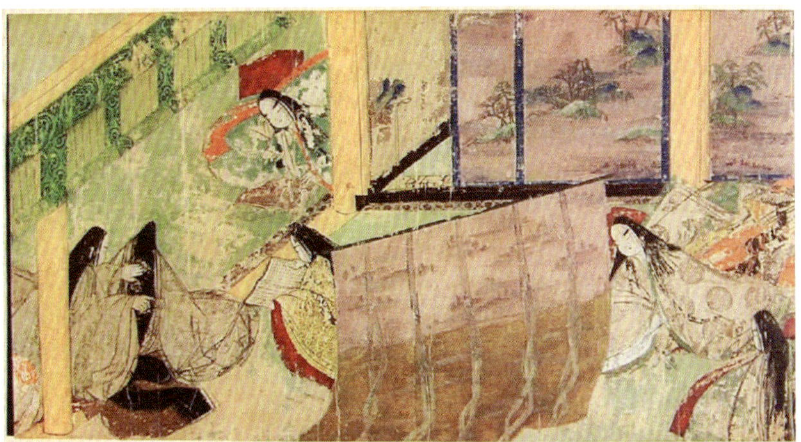

◀ **9.24** Japan, Heian, Lady Murasaki Shikibu (c. 973–c. 1020/31 CE), *Genji monogatari emak: Azumaya Chapter*, c. 1120–1140 CE. Ink and color on paper, 8.62 in.

An early example of "Japanese" or yamato-e painting, the scenes beginning the chapters focused on dramatic events in the story, removing walls and roofs if necessary to view the action.

uses an aerial perspective so that the viewer looks down on the scene as though flying over it. Third, Japanese artists removed obstacles such as walls and roofs that would interfere with the view, giving rise to what is known as the "open-roof" or ***fukinuki yatai*** technique. The fourth and greatest distinction between yamato-e and Chinese painting, however, is the Japanese preference for moments of high emotional drama between individuals rather than on the character analogies and exemplars of moral virtue common in Chinese art.

Fujiwara no Yorimici (990–1074 CE),* Hōōdō or Phoenix Hall, *1053 CE
Fujiwara no Yorimici succeeded his father as regent, continuing Fujiwara control over the Imperial government. In 1052 Fujiwara no Yorimici began converting his father's villa at Uji, across the river from Kyoto, into a Pure Land Buddhist temple, Byōdō-in. The centerpiece of the complex, and only remaining original building, is the *Phoenix Hall* or *Hōōdō*, built in 1053 (Figure 9.25). The name is derived from

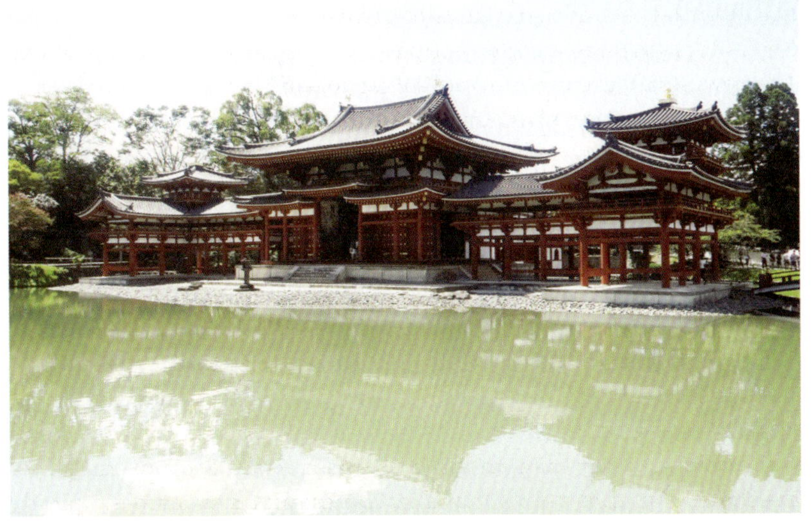

◀ **9.25** Japan, Heian, Byōdō-in, Phoenix Hall, 1053 CE.

Fujiwara no Yorimici converted his father's estate into a Pureland Buddhist temple and built this Amida hall which takes its name from its bird-like plan.

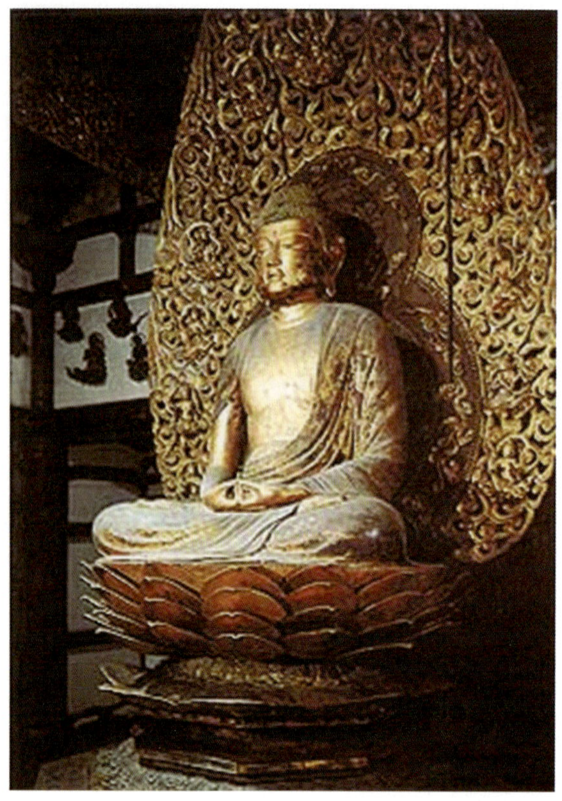

▲ **9.26** Japan, Heian, Jōchō (d. 1057), *Amida Nyorai*, 1053 CE. Gilt wood, 116 in.

Jōchō created this large sculpture using the joined block technique in which the blank form was constructed from several pieces of wood to reach the desired size.

the layout of the building as a hall with wing and tail corridors, giving it the aspect from above, of a bird, wings spread and tail streaming, landing on the island in the pond. A pair of gilt bronze phoenixes at the gable ends reinforces the name. The design of the building is unique in Japan but bears a close resemblance to the depiction of a Tang palace in the Paradise of Amitabha mural in Cave 172 at Dunhuang, China.

Jocho (d. 1057),* Amida Nyorai*, Byōdō-in, Uji, 1053 CE Enshrined in the *Phoenix Hall* is a great, gilt wood image of Amida Buddha (Figure 9.26) seated on a lotus throne, carved by the master sculptor, Jōchō. Jōchō and his father, Kōshō (active 990–1020 CE) were favorites of Fujiwara no Michinaga and Empress Shoshi. After the death of Kōshō, Jōchō worked almost exclusively for the Fujiwara family creating Buddhist sculptures for the temples they patronized.

Despite what must have been a prodigious output from his atelier, the Byōdō-in Amida Buddha is the only surviving work by the master. The statue was carved from Japanese cypress in a technique pioneered by Jōchō and known as *yosegi* or "joined-block" technique. Instead of carving a statue out of a single block of wood, the joined block technique began by halving wood blocks, hollowing them out, and then rejoining them with additional pieces of wood as needed to create a sculpture of the desired size and form. Several pieces of wood might be joined together like puzzle pieces to create more complex forms. This technique allowed Jōchō to create larger sculptures with more elaborate poses than were possible in solid wood. Sculptures produced with joined-block were also lighter and less prone to checking and cracking. However, since these sculptures were hollow, the surface carving had to be shallower than that of traditional solid wood figures; this is most obvious in the rendering of drapery, which while fluid is thin compared to earlier examples, and in the simplified anatomy. The finished carving was coated with black lacquer, and then painted to make it more lifelike, or in the case of the Amida Buddha covered with gold leaf.

The more than 9 foot (3 m) tall sculpture is especially noteworthy for the tenderness of the Buddha's expression. Unlike the Buddhas of earlier periods, Jōchō's Amida looks down to meet the gaze of the faithful and, in that acknowledgment, offers the promise of salvation and rebirth in his Western Paradise. Jōchō is credited with devising a

TAKE A CLOSER LOOK

Single Block and Joined-Block Carving

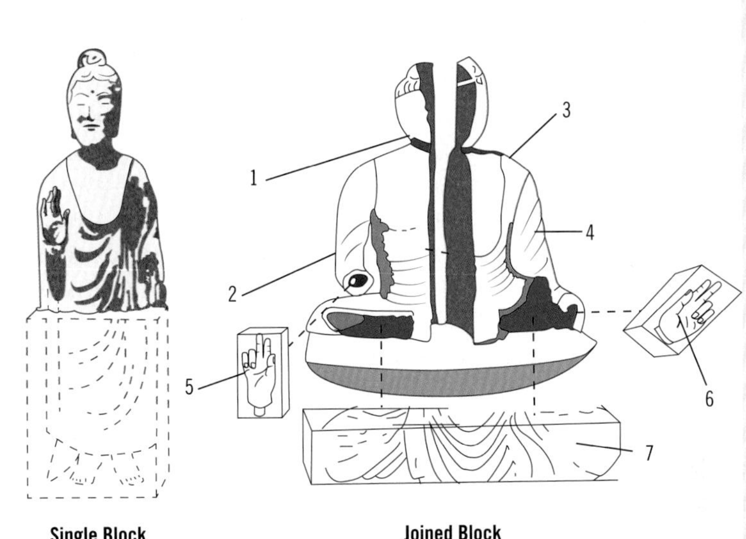

▲ 9.27 Japan, Left: Single Block; Right: Joined Block Carving.
The earliest Buddhist statues were carved out of a single block of wood. As old growth forests were cut, the carving of large figures became difficult. The solution was to assemble carving blanks from several joined blocks of wood.

Early Japanese wooden sculptures were carved in the single block techniques. The scale of carved works was limited by the diameter of the tree; this often resulted in tall, columnar sculptures. The chief advantage of this style of carving was the ability to cut deeply into the wood to create drapery folds and anatomical details. The disadvantages included the weight of the finished sculpture, and the high potential for checking and cracking as the solid wood dried.

By the late Heian period, many of the old growth forests had been cut, making it more difficult to find wood of sufficient diameter for large works, especially seated figures. Jocho's solution was the joined block process in which the block of wood for the torso of the figure was split and hollowed out and additional pieces added as needed for torso scale and for the creation of the arms and legs in seated poses. This allowed artist to create large, lightweight pieces that could move in three dimensions.

new sculptural canon of proportion in which the height of the figure was based on a unit of measurement equal to the distance from a figure's hairline to its chin, and the width of its seated pose, from knee to knee, was equal to the measurement from the hair to the base of the figure, resulting in an overall pyramidal form. The elaborate openwork mandorla was carved separately and attached to the figure.

The Kamakura Period (1192–1333 CE)

During the Heian, the number of Imperial relatives living at court periodically swelled to levels that threatened to bankrupt the treasury. At these times emperors would be forced to cut off relatives past a certain degree of kinship and demote them to noble status, including at times even some of the emperor's own children. The first Heian emperor to practice **dynastic shedding** was Emperor Saga (r. 809–823 CE), who had fathered forty-nine children. The demoted royals were given one of two family names, Minamoto (Genji) or Taira (Heike). These two noble clans grew branches as the names were awarded by successive emperors. Typically, these former royals went out into the countryside, acquired large landholdings, hired samurai retainers, and became feudal lords or daimyo. As the government had no standing army, the clans were called upon to fight its battles. The emperors used the clans to suppress rebels and barbarian tribes, defend the nation against Mongol invasions, and occasionally take sides in court intrigues or succession disputes. The system worked well, keeping the power of each in check, until the Taira defeated the Minamoto in the Heiji War of 1159 CE, and Taira Kiyomori took control of the government. When Taira died in 1181 CE, Minamoto Yoritomo led a successful uprising against the Taira, and took the reins of power as ***shogun***, and established his military government or ***bakufu*** at Kamakura on Sagami Bay. Although the Imperial government continued to claim authority, a series of bakufu governments would hold political and military power in Japan until the Meiji restoration at the end of the nineteenth century.

▼ **9.28** Japan, Kamakura, Heike monogatari emaki: *Night Attack on the Sanjo Palace*, c. 1240 CE. Ink and color on paper, 16.25 in. × 275.68 in.

In contrast to Chinese painting which prized brushwork, Japanese paintings of the Kamakura valued scenes of dramatic action and accurate detail.

Night Attack on the Sanjo Palace, *Heike monogatari emaki, c. 1240 CE*
Minamoto Yoritomo established his bakufu at Kamakura to remove his samurai from the corrupting influence of the luxury and overly-refined aesthetic pursuits of the Imperial court. Instead members of the warrior classes were encouraged to live frugal, disciplined lives and to place the utmost value on bravery, duty, loyalty, and honor. The art of the Kamakura period reflected these ideals in realistic depictions

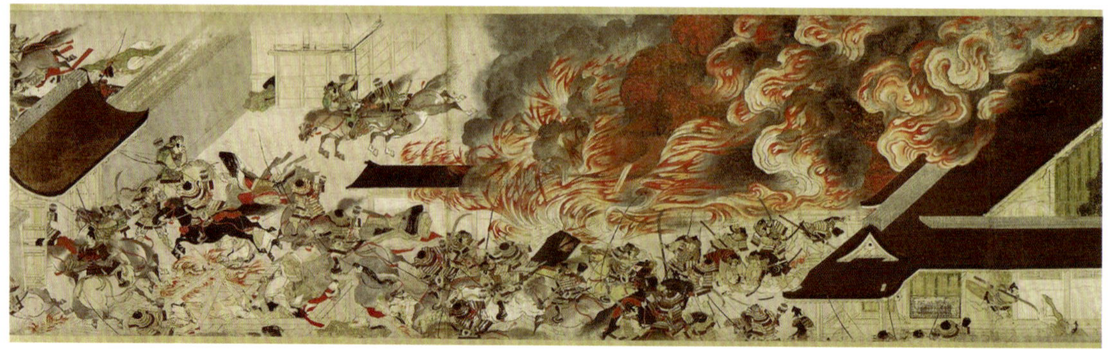

that glorified famous warriors and heroic battles. One of the popular works of the era was the *Heike monogatari emaki* or "*Tale of the Heike*, detailing the battles between the Heike and the Minamoto clans in the Genpei War (1180–1185 CE).

The illustrations that accompany the text are painted in traditional yamato-e style, with considerable emphasis placed on dramatic action and tension rather than brushwork. In *Night Attack on the Sanjo Palace* (Figure 9. 24), architectural elements expand outward from the viewer's aerial vantage point to form diagonals that bracket the frenzy of the battle: soldiers clash and samurai horsemen charge while flames and billowing smoke pour from the burning structure. Since the scene takes place at night, it is rendered primarily in gray scale with the red of the flames and occasional touches of blue, green, and tan. A great deal of attention has been paid to the details of armor and weapons, but above all it is the sort of action-oriented, historically accurate scene that would have appealed to the samurai classes.

The Muromachi Period (1336–1573 CE)

In 1333, the Kamakura bakufu was toppled and Emperor Go-Daigo (1288–1339 CE) briefly took control of the government. However, after only three years the emperor was overthrown and Ashikaga Takauji took over as shogun. The Muromachi district of Kyoto, where Ashikaga established his bakufu, lent its name to the period. The dethroned Emperor Go-Daigo and his followers established a new court south of Nara, and for the next fifty-six years Japan had two capitals and two emperors. This portion of the Muromachi period is known as the *Nambokucho* or Southern and Northern Courts.

Zen Buddhism

The Heian era Buddhist monk, Myoan Eisai (1141–1215 CE), is credited with introducing both tea drinking and Zen (Chan) Buddhism to Japan. Zen, with its emphasis on meditation and self-discipline, was particularly suited to the ethos of the warrior classes. Traditionally, Chan Buddhism had placed little value on Buddha sculptures and paintings as a means to achieving enlightenment. Instead, painting was cultivated as a form of meditation and a means of achieving the sudden awakening to one's true self and Buddha nature. As a result, Zen Buddhist painters were not interested in creating realistic illusions, but rather sought to render the essence of the thing in a few brushstrokes or splashes of ink.

Through the practice of Zen, Japanese artists developed a new aesthetical system called ***wabi-sabi***, which finds beauty in the transient, imperfect, and incomplete. Wabi-sabi profoundly shaped the practice of painting, sculpture, ceramics, garden design, and even Noh Theater. The concept of wabi can be described as rustic simplicity, unpretentiousness,

TAKE A CLOSER LOOK

Sen no Rikyu, *Taian Teahouse*, c. 1582–1583 CE

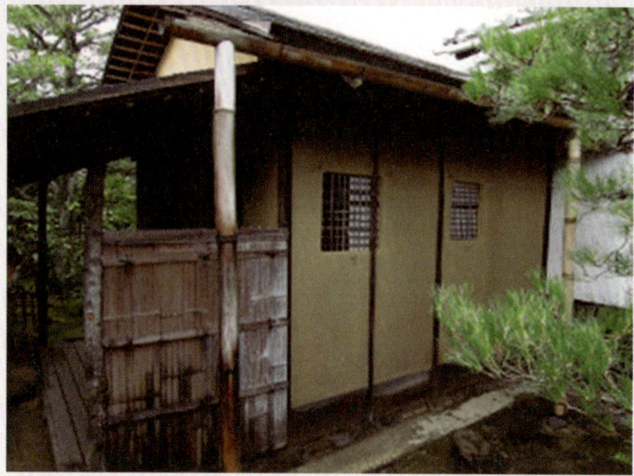

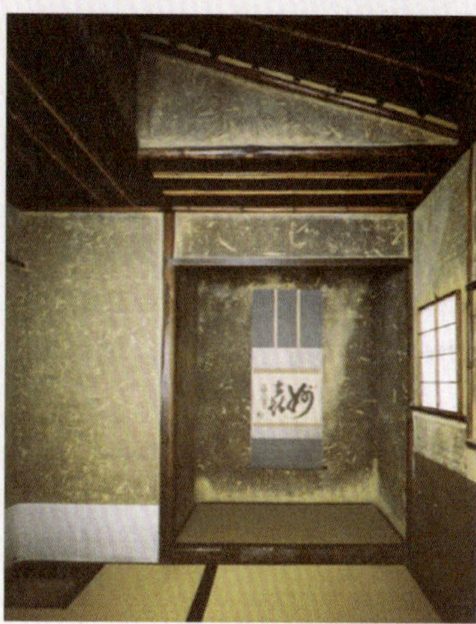

▲ **9.29** Japan, Sen no Rikyu, Taian Tea House, Myokian Temple, c. 1582—1583 CE.

Through the practice of Zen Buddhism, Japanese artists developed a new aesthetical system called wabi-sabi. It is expressed in the tea house as rustic simplicity and appreciation of the innate qualities of materials.

Sen no Rikyu (1521–1591) was born in Sakai to a merchant class family. Sakai is closely associated with the development of the tea ritual or ***chanoyu*** in Japan. Sen no Rikyu is known to have begun studying with a local master when he was sixteen. When Oda Nobunaga became shogun, he brought the already renowned tea master into his service to enhance his own status. Sen no Rikyu also served Toyotomi as a tea master and advisor until the shogun ordered him to commit ritual suicide for an unspecified offense. Sen no Rikyu is best known as a proponent, not of the elaborate reception hall tea rituals such as he would have conducted for Toyotomi, but of a simplified tea ceremony performed as a Zen meditation and discipline. This form of tea ritual reflects the ***wabicha*** (wabi + cha or tea) aesthetic.

Today the Taian Teahouse exists only as a reconstruction based on a description by Sen no Rikyu's student, Yamanoue Sojiki. The original teahouse was constructed in 1582 on the grounds of one of Toyotomi's castle estates. The Taian is a study in simplicity, humbleness, and the perfection of imperfection. It was a small, rustic wooden building, consisting of a passageway, preparation room, and a two-mat tearoom with an alcove or tokonoma meant to hold a tea scroll or small flower arrangement. Everything was plain and rustic from the soot-blackened walls to the ***raku*** fired tea bowls as the building was intended to create a sense of intimacy and equality among the participants regardless of their rank.

humbleness, or even plainness in that the materials used are not manipulated to appear as something other than they are. Sabi refers to the appreciation of the beauty of age and wear as expressed in the natural patinas and oxidation on metals, the weathering of woods, and the fading of the colors on fabrics and papers. In art wabi-sabi is expressed through seven principles: asymmetry, plainness, agedness or timeworn, naturalness, subtlety, unconventionality, and tranquility.

Sesshu Toyo (1420–1506), **Haboku-Sansui or Splashed Ink Landscape,** *1495* Born into the samurai class Oda family, Sesshū Tōyō was one of the great Zen painters of the Muromachi era. When he was ten or twelve years old, he was sent to be educated at the local temple in Hofuku-ji, Bitchu province, and there was given the name Tōyō, meaning willow-like. In 1440 CE he went to Shōkoku-ji in Kyoto, where he studied Sung landscape painting with the traditional master, Tensho Shubun. Sesshū became a master of ***sumi-e*** or "black ink" painting, which has affinities with calligraphy in that it relies on strong brushstrokes and the contrast of ink and paper. After two decades at Shōkoku-ji he went to Unkoku-ji in western Honshu where he served as the abbot. It was at this time that he began using the name Sesshū meaning "snow boat." In 1468, he made the journey to Ming China for further study. In Beijing he was received at the Imperial court and honored with the title, "First Seat of Mt. Tiantong." There he became familiar with the styles of the Ming Dynasty including that of the Zhe School which attempted to fuse Sung court styles with those of the Yuan Literati painters.

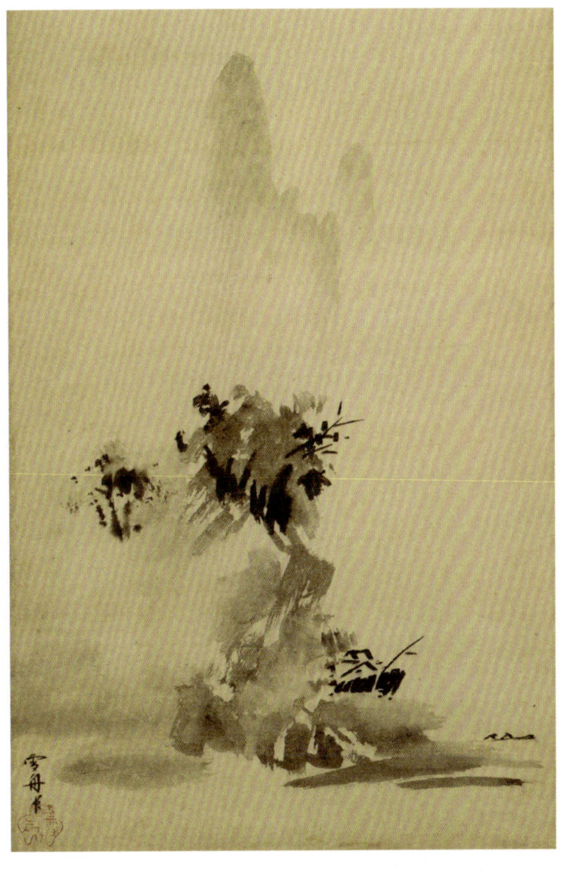

▲ 9.30 Japan, Muromachi, Sesshu Toyo (1420–1506 CE), *Haboku-Sansui or Splashed Ink Landscape*, 1495. Ink on paper, 43.9 in. × 29.84 in.

Sesshu was a master of sumi-e or "black ink" painting which is similar to calligraphy in its use of strong brushstrokes and the contrast of ink on paper.

Sesshū pioneered the ***haboku*** or "broken ink" and ***hatsuboku*** or "splashed ink" painting technique; the former relies on contrasts between white paper and black and gray ink washes, while the latter uses splashes of ink wash to define elements of landscape. His *Splashed Ink Landscape* (Figure 9.30) presents a scene of distant mountains shrouded in fog, while in the foreground a tree and a house at the edge of the water are suggested by areas of ink wash. There are no hard outlines defining these natural forms; however, the details of the house, fence, and boat are drawn with bold, calligraphic brushstrokes of black ink as if to highlight the contrast between the elements of nature and the works of man.

Kogaku-Sōkō (1464/5–1548), **Mountains and Dry Cascade,** *Daisen-in, Kyoto, 1509–1513* The Chinese concept of the garden as a three-dimensional landscape painting was introduced to Japan during the Asuka era. In the following Heian period, the walled Sung-style meditation gardens, featuring ponds and streams edged with interestingly shaped rocks or boulders grouped to represent the mountain home of the Eight Immortals, became popular with Japanese aristocrats. Although

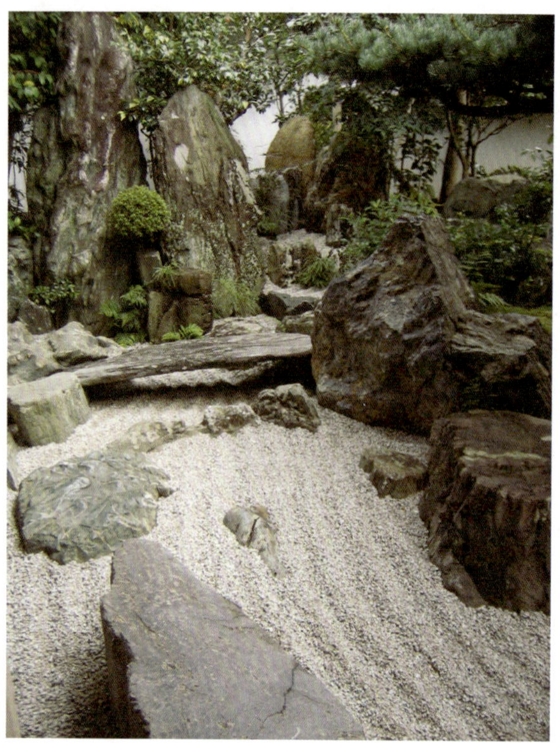

▲ 9.31 Japan, Muromachi, Kogaku-Soko (1464/5–1548 CE), Daisen-in, Mountains and Dry Cascade, 1509–1513 CE.

Chinese-style gardens as three-dimensional landscapes were introduced during the Asuka Period but in the Muromachi, the first Zen gardens, where gravel or sand replaced water, were introduced.

paradise gardens were an established feature of Pure Land Japanese Buddhist temples, the first Zen dry gardens, in which gravel replaced water features, were not constructed until the early Muromachi period, one of the first being the upper garden at Saihō-ji designed by the Zen Buddhist monk Musō Soseki in 1339. By the early sixteenth century, Zen gardens had become more abstract and less referential to the landscape. Most, such as those at Daisen-in (Figure 9.31), were small, enclosed by walls, had limited color palettes, and consisted mainly of rocks, gravel, and a few shaped pine trees or shrubs. This style of garden was meant to be viewed from a single vantage point while seated.

The Daisen-in temple in Kyoto is a sub-temple of Daioku-ji and was founded by the Zen monk Kogaku Sōkō, who established the dry landscape gardens or ***karesansui***. The Daisen-in gardens form two L-shaped brackets around the abbot's quarters and audience hall or ***shoin***. Together the gardens present a metaphorical journey, following the flow of "water" from the mountains and waterfall through the gravel river to the sea, and ultimately to the great ocean of sand, the largest and most austere space. The flow of water is suggested by patterns raked into the gravel.

Azuchi-Momoyama Period (1573–1603 CE)

The Azuchi-Momoyama period is defined by the two shoguns, Oda Nobunaga and Toyotomi Hideyoshi, who, in succession, ruled Japan. The Ashikaga bakufu was an ineffectual regime, unable by 1467 even to maintain order within Kyoto. The clan wars that began in Kyoto escalated into ten years of civil war, known as the Onin War. Order was finally restored in 1573 when Oda Nobunaga, with the help of Toyotomi, brought the warring clans under control, and deposed the last Ashikaga shogun. Oda died in 1582 and was succeeded by Toyotomi Hideyoshi. The double name of the period, Azuchi-Momoyama, is derived from the districts where Oda built his castle (Azuchi) and where Toyotomi planted a peach tree (Momoyama).

Oda and Toyotomi were not men of great refinement, but they valued and patronized the arts as a means of demonstrating and reinforcing their political power. Architecture was profoundly affected by the character of the time and the introduction of firearms. The shoguns and military elite constructed large castle complexes with stone walls designed to protect against rifle and cannon fire. The shoguns employed artists of the Kano school, particularly Kano Eitoku, to decorate the huge spaces within these castles with folding screens and sliding fusuma. These often-large-scale works were enriched with lavish amounts of gold and silver leaf. The extravagance of the shogunal courts of this era was unprecedented; Toyotomi not only had a portable golden tea room in which the walls and ceiling were gold, but also a solid gold tea service.

Toyotomi Hideyoshi (1537–1598), Osaka Castle, 1583 In 1583, Toyotomi Hideyoshi built his castle in Osaka (Figure 9.32) a little more than 25 miles (41 km) from the capital of Kyoto. Later as he anticipated his retirement, he built a second castle, Fushimi, in Kyoto. Like their European counterparts, medieval Japanese castles were surrounded by stone and earthen walls and moats. They also had a series of concentric inner walls and moats and a succession of courts and bottleneck gateways that were often set at right angles from the entry point, the purpose of these being to slow down and thin the lines of attackers within the walls. Typically, castles were located on hilltops, or if necessary artificial mounds were built as a base for the castle. The elevation of the buildings served military purposes but also made the castles seem more imposing. The stronghold or keep of the Japanese castle was the towering tenshu, often set on an even higher mound within the compound, and sometimes surrounded by an additional inner moat. The earliest Japanese mountain castles were built with log plank lower walls but the introduction of firearms in 1542 necessitated adaptions to the designs. The bottom levels of castles of the Momoyama period

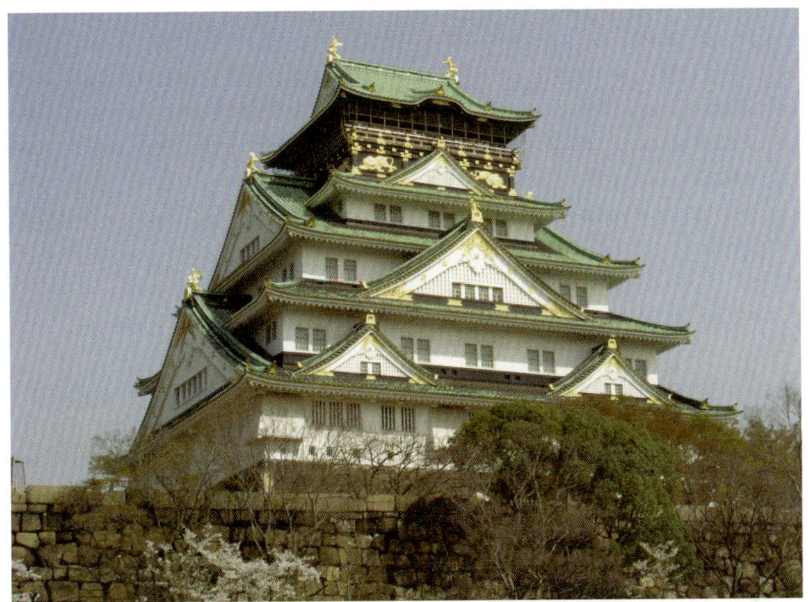

◀ **9.32** Japan, Azuchi-Momoyama, Osaka, Toyotomi Hideyoshi (1537–1598), Osaka Castle Tenshu, 1583 CE.

Japanese castles were surrounded by concentric moats and walls with the final stronghold being the tenshu, which had lower floors encased in stone for protection against cannon and rifle shot. The topmost level contained a lookout post.

had dry stacked stone walls laid up to create sweeping profiles that made them harder to climb.

Toyotomi's Osaka tenshu had seven floors although only five are visible above the stone base. The pristine white upper levels, like pagoda towers, are progressively smaller as the building rises; alternating levels have sweeping gables with lattice ornamentation and inset window bands. The gable barge boards feature elaborate decoration at the peaks and ends, including rosette medallions and roof finials all covered in gold. The sweeping lines of the gables give a remarkable lightness to the upper stories and the effect is often compared to a flock of white cranes taking flight. Just under the uppermost gable is an open watchtower from which archers could fend off attackers; emblazoned in gold on its dark walls are a pair of golden lions, a favored motif of Toyotomi's.

The Edo Period (1603–1867)

The Edo period begins in 1603 with the establishment of the Tokugawa bakufu in Edo (modern Tokyo) by Tokugawa Ieyasu. Tokugawa, a man well into his sixties when he seized control, had served Oda and Toyotomi. Although Tokugawa Ieyasu encouraged foreign trade, his grandson, Iemitsu, closed off Japan to all but Dutch traders. The country remained isolated until the threat of bombardment by U.S. naval warships led by Commodore Matthew Perry forced open Japanese ports in 1853.

During the Edo period new forms of art were introduced that appealed to prospering middle classes in the cities. These newly wealthy merchants and artisans had surplus income to spend on entertainments in the pleasure districts, such as Yoshiwara in Edo, where there were teahouses, restaurants, kabuki theaters, geisha houses, and brothels. New developments in woodblock printing during the Edo allowed the diversions of these districts to be immortalized in multicolored prints known as ***ukiyo-e***, a term which translates as "floating world pictures." Originally ukiyo-e was a word used by Buddhists to describe the transitory nature of human life, but during the Edo, it described transitory sensual and sexual pleasures. Those who could afford to indulge in these pastimes, as well as those who could only wish to do so, provided a market for ukiyo-e prints.

Suzuki Harunobu (c. 1725–1770), **Evening Bell at the Clock,** *c. 1766* Suzuki Harunobu is best known for his ukiyo-e prints of beautiful young women (***bijin***), courtesans (***orian***), and geisha, all of whom are depicted as willowy, graceful, and delicate. He is credited with popularizing, if not inventing, the multicolor woodblock printing technique known as ***nishiki-e*** or "brocade print." The first Japanese woodblock prints were issued in black and hand colored. In the 1760s Suzuki perfected a printing technique that employed multiple single-color woodblocks to create prints with as many as ten different colors. The process began with the artist's design being carved into a "key" or master block. The proofs from this master then were used to carve the individual color blocks. The blocks were used sequentially to produce images that were rich in both color and texture. The resulting prints were often issued in series or sets of as many as thirty images.

In one of his better-known prints, *Evening Bell at the Clock* (Figure 9.33), from the series Eight Views of the Parlor, Suzuki shows a geisha or female entertainer on an exterior deck, assisted by an attendant, drying off after her bath. The maid checks the time by turning to look at a mechanical clock rather than listening for the temple bell to chime. Behind the women is the framework side of a ***fusuma***, which has on its front a traditional monochrome bamboo painting; a bit of the painting is visible in the glass of a large cheval mirror. The clock, mirror, and sliding screens are intended to show that the "floating world" in which these women live and work is a place of modern sophistication and high style.

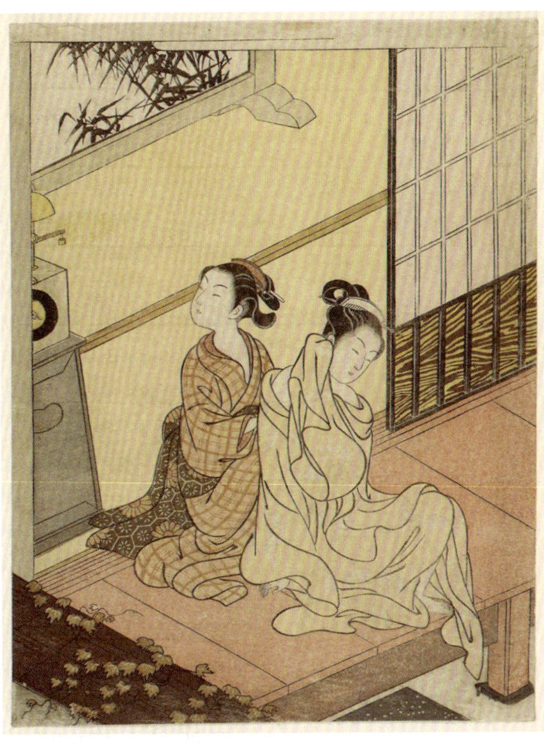

▲ 9.33 Japan, Edo, Suzuki Harunobu (c. 1725–1770 CE) *Evening Bell at the Clock*, c. 1766. Woodblock print, ink and color on paper, 10.87 in. × 8.12 in.

Suzuki pioneered multicolor or nishiki-e prints which required the use of separate blocks for each color.

Katsushika Hokusai (1760–1849), The Great Wave off Kanagawa, *1826–1833*

Another genre of print popularized during the Edo was the ***meisho-e*** or "pictures of famous places." The publication of the first Japanese travel guides and improved roads were enticements for townspeople to travel to view scenic places or to visit important shrines. As in the case of the ukiyo-e, the meisho-e prints were collected as souvenirs by those who had taken the trips as well as those unable to make the journey. Typically, meisho-e prints were issued in series that depicted famous places across the seasons and in various types of weather.

The undisputed master of meisho-e was Katsushika Hokusai, who was the son of an Edo mirror-maker. His artistic career began at age fourteen when he was apprenticed to a woodblock carver. At this time several people were involved in the creation of prints; in addition to the artist, who created the master image often at the suggestion of the print dealer, there were teams of carvers and printers who did the actual production work. After completing his apprenticeship, he spent the next decade in the studio of the ukiyo-e master Katsukawa Shunsho. Although Japan had been virtually closed off to the world for more than a century by the time Katsushika Hokusai was born, the

Dutch ships allowed to dock at the port of Nagasaki brought European copperplate engravings and new pigments such as Prussian blue (synthesized in 1704) to the country's artists. Intrigued by what he saw in these prints Hokusai began experimenting with linear perspective, chiaroscuro, and cast shadows, creating works that were radical compared to traditional Japanese and Chinese paintings with their vertical perspective, high horizon lines, flat picture planes, and bird's-eye vantage point. He abandoned ukiyo-e subjects and concentrated on combining landscape or cityscape views with genre scenes of ordinary Japanese people.

The Great Wave off Kanagawa (Figure 9.34), one of the prints from the series *Thirty-Six Views of Mount Fuji*, is the work most closely associated with Hokusai. The series shows Mount Fuji as seen from several locations, many in Edo itself but others from as far away as Nagano, Aichi, and Kanagawa, and in different weather conditions, times of day, and seasons of the year. The print captures a dramatic moment just before a great standing wave swamps the *oshiokuri* (cargo boats) laboring in the heavy seas. The viewer observes the scene from a low vantage point, suggesting a location in another boat farther out at sea. The great wave is made even more terrifying by the foam talons on its breaking edge and its dark Prussian blue color, which stand in marked contrast to the stillness of Mount Fuji in the distance. The dark horizon around Fuji-san suggests that the sun is rising behind the viewer, its first rays hitting the mountain's snowcap and turning the sky a golden color. In depicting Mount Fuji, Hokusai has taken some artistic liberties, reducing the mountain's scale and steepening the angle of its slope to create the sense of a greater distance between sea and mountain. By dressing the rowers in blue *samue* work clothes, Hokusai sets the

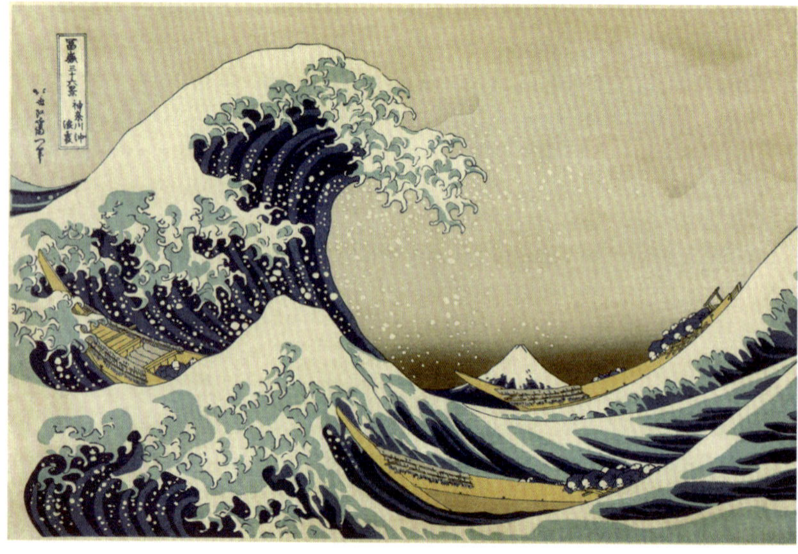

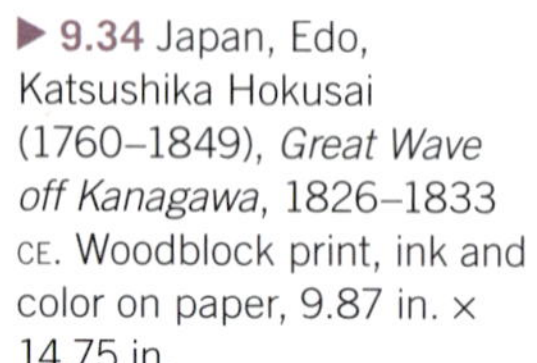

▶ **9.34** Japan, Edo, Katsushika Hokusai (1760–1849), *Great Wave off Kanagawa*, 1826–1833 CE. Woodblock print, ink and color on paper, 9.87 in. × 14.75 in.

Inspired by European prints coming into Japan, Hokusai combined traditional Japanese techniques with a European low horizon and the European pigment, Prussian blue.

season as springtime, which is also the time of year when large waves come rolling in from the south. The *Great Wave* is a blend of traditional Japanese elements: the flat patterning of waves, emphasis on seasonality and time of day, and dramatic subject, with Western concepts such as the low horizon, linear perspective, and use of Prussian blue.

The Meiji Period (1868–1912)

Japan's more than two centuries of isolation under the Tokugawa shogunate ended in 1853 with the arrival of nine American warships in Edo Bay. The concessions made to the Americans in 1854 and again in 1859 made the Tokugawa bakufu the focus of anti-government criticism and anti-foreign sentiment. Finally, in 1867, the last Tokugawa shogun resigned, and the following year power was restored to the emperor, ending almost seven centuries of military rule. Prince Mutsuhito took the throne as Emperor Meiji, inaugurating a new system of period naming based on regnal names. Emperor Meiji's reign saw the abolishment of the feudal system and the start of rapid modernization and Westernization in the arts, sciences, military, and government. Such reforms were seen as critical to maintaining Japan's independence from colonial rule.

As part of the Meiji push for modernization Japanese artists were encouraged to explore the new media, techniques, and modes of expression used in Western art. Western representational styles were considered more scientific and accurate as they sought to depict optical reality rather than the idealized world of yamato-e painting. European and American artists were recruited to teach in Japan and Japanese artists were encouraged to go abroad to study. The new Westernized style of painting was known as ***yôga***. In between the extremes of traditional yamato-e and Westernized yôga was a third style termed ***nihonga***. Nihonga was the inspiration of one of the visiting teachers, Dr. Ernest Fenollosa (1853–1908), an American art historian. Fenollosa was concerned that the push to modernize the arts would destroy centuries-old traditions of Japanese painting. His suggestion for nihonga painters was, essentially, to follow Hokusai's example and create a blend of traditional subjects and brushwork with Western perspective and chiaroscuro that would serve to heighten the realism of the painting.

Takahashi Yuichi (1828–1894),* Oiran *(1872) Takahashi Yuichi was one of the first Japanese artists to embrace Western style or yôga painting. Born in Edo to a samurai family, his early training was in the flamboyant style of the Kano school, but after seeing examples of European lithographs, he became interested in Western realism. He enrolled in the Bansho Shirabesho (Institute for Western Studies), and took further instruction in oil painting from Charles Wirgman, and Antonio Fontanesi. Takahashi was instrumental in promoting yôga painting to

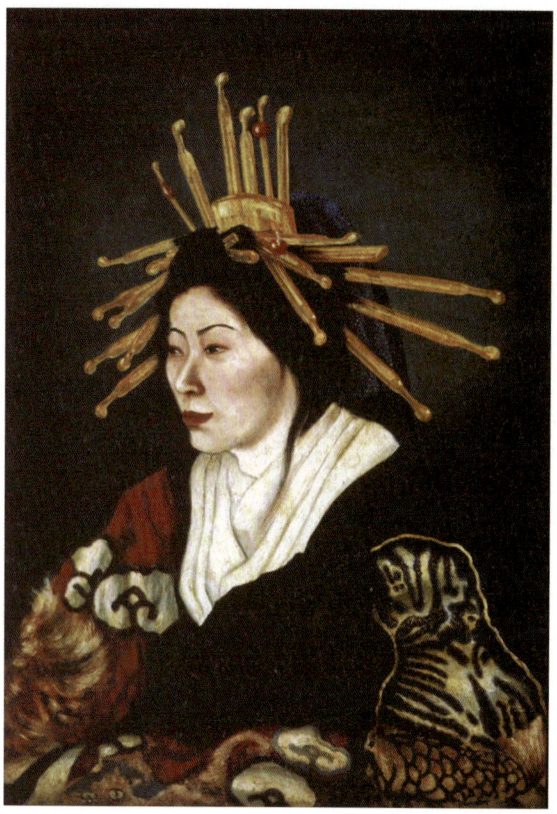

▲ **9.35** Japan, Meiji, Takahashi Yuichi (1828–1894), *Oiran*, 1872. Oil on canvas, 30.50 x 21.50 in.

In this painting Takahashi presents Japanese women as Europeans of the era saw them—exotic and charming—but not truly beautiful with their rice powdered faces.

other Japanese artists, opening the Tenkai Gakusha, a private school dedicated to teaching Western-oriented art, and founding the *Gayu Sekichin*, the first Japanese art journal.

In *Oiran* (Figure 9.35), Takahashi presents a portrait of a courtesan in traditional robes, make-up, and hair style. At first glance, she appears to be another example of the popular Japanese bijin or "beautiful woman"; however, closer examination reveals her lack of conformity with traditional Japanese aesthetics. In fact, one Japanese critic of the era described Orian as "exotic and grotesque." Nor does the Orian conform to contemporary Western ideals of feminine beauty; she is tired-looking, dull, and her white powdered face seems overly pasty, especially set against the dark gray background. What Takahashi seems to be trying to convey is not an ideal of either Eastern or Western beauty, but rather the Westerner's perception of Japanese women as charming but not aesthetically pleasing or particularly attractive.

Post-War Japan (1926–)

The character of the Japanese nation was profoundly changed by the events of the Second World War. By the time of the Japanese surrender most of the major cities had been destroyed by incendiary bombing and of course, the cities of Nagasaki and Hiroshima had been leveled by atomic bombs. Ordinary Japanese civilians and orphaned children endured enormous suffering: millions were starving amidst the devastation of the cities, thousands suffered physical and mental injuries without access to medical care, and the bodies of the dead and dying were lying everywhere. Even as living conditions improved under the military occupation, the at times authoritarian approach of America toward rebuilding Japanese law and society angered the Japanese. Japan's defeat and the paternalism of its post-war relationship with the United States have provided a continuing theme in Japanese art for much of the twentieth century. The last decades of the twentieth century saw the coming of age of a generation of artists who were born after the war and who had grown up with animated cartoons and short films (anime), comic strips (manga), video games, and early computers and cell phones. Popular culture, cuteness, consumerism, superficiality, artificiality, and the breaking down of the

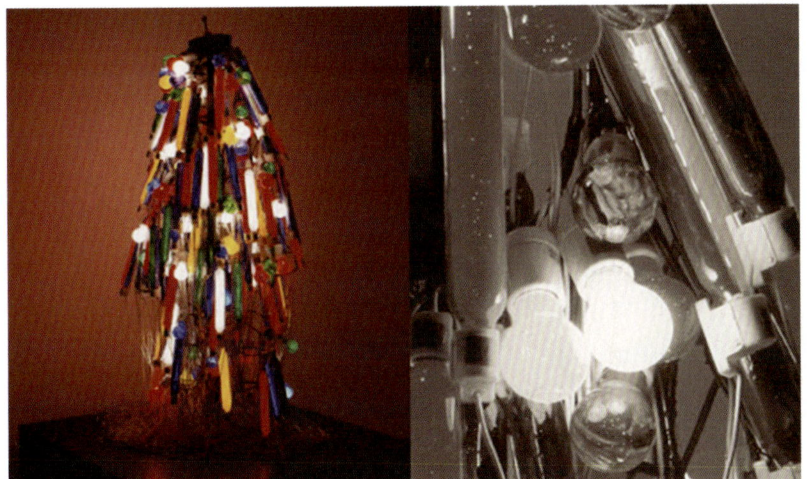

◀ 9.36 Japan, Tanaka Atsuko (1932–2005), *Electric Dress*, 1956 and 1986. Wire and colored incandescent bulbs.

The Electric Dress was created for a performance piece in which Tanaka staged a traditional Japanese wedding.

borders between high and low art are recurring themes in the works of this generation.

Tanaka Atsuko (1932–2005),* Electric Dress *(1956 and 1986) Tanaka Atsuko was born in Osaka and was a child during WWII. After the war she attended the Art Institute of the Osaka Municipal Museum of Art and then went for further study at Kyoto Municipal College. In the 1950s she was a member of the Gutai Art Association, an experimental group which rejected all traditional modes of art-making. Gutai members fired paint at canvases with cannons, staged performance pieces that included mud wrestling, throwing bottles of paint, or breaking through laminated rice paper screens, and they participated in the first "happenings."

Tanaka is best known for her installation and performance pieces, featuring nontraditional materials such as electric bells and light bulbs. Her Electric Dress (Figure 9.36) was created for a performance piece in which she staged a traditional Japanese wedding and wore a kimono constructed from hundreds of globular and tubular incandescent light bulbs, colored red, yellow, blue, green, and purple, and connected by hundreds of feet of electric cord. The bride wearing the Electric Dress is completely obscured by the materials used in the construction, suggesting the increasing isolation of people in the context of post-war reconstruction.

Tenmyouya Hisashi (b. 1966),* Japanese Spirit #3, *1997 Tenmyouya Hisashi was born in Tokyo. In elementary school he studied drawing with local masters but otherwise is self-taught. Early in his career he worked in a style he termed "Neo-Nihonga" as a counter to the revived Japanese painting styles, focusing on traditional materials and methods that

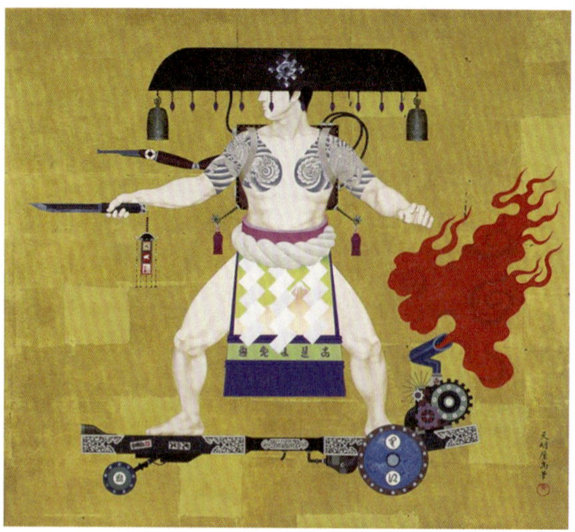

▲ **9.37** Japan, Tenmyouya Hisashi (b. 1966), *Japanese Spirit #3*, 1997. Acrylic.

In this work the artist holds up a mirror to American popular culture concepts of Japan as a land of Samuri, Yakuza, sumo wrestlers, Buddhist temples, and technology.

appeared after the war. Although his subject matter is Japanese, his Neo-Nihonga paintings used acrylic paints and mixed traditional themes and techniques with elements of popular culture. For example, his *Japanese Spirit #3* (Figure 9.37) depicts a samurai figure on a mechanical, fire-spitting, skateboard-like contraption. The figure is a metaphorical image of Japanese culture as seen through the eyes of Westerners. The skateboarding warrior wears the traditional straw hat of Buddhist monks, the *keshō-mawashi* loincloth of Sumo wrestlers, the tattoos of a Yakuza, and is armed with a samurai sword. Each of these motifs represents a stereotype of Japan derived from tourist brochures, movies, television, and the automobile industry.

Nara Yoshitomo (b. 1959),* Girl with a Knife in her Hand, *1991 Nara Yoshitomo was born in Hirosaki. He attended the Graduate School of Aichi Prefectural University of the Arts, and then went on for further study at the Kunstakasemie in Düsseldorf, Germany. His experience in Germany was one of profound loneliness due to his inability to master the language. Nara drew on his feelings of alienation in Germany and memories of childhood loneliness in developing his iconic otaku figures of lonely and isolated children.

Girl with a Knife in her Hand (Figure 9.38) depicts one of Nara's lonely children, a shojo or adolescent girl who stares wide-eyed at the viewer. At first glance she seems part of the Japanese cult of kawaii or "cuteness" like Yuko Shimizu's "Hello Kitty" character. Despite their cartoonish quality, there is often something disturbing about Nara's paintings of children: some smoke cigarettes, hold small toy-like weapons, or have glaring expressions suggesting anger or aggression. Even his more recent paintings where the expressions are more subtle, the ambiguity seems to present the possibility that there is deception behind the cuteness. Nara's childlike images have been interpreted as metaphors for the infantilization of a Japanese nation rendered impotent by its defeat in World War II, and by the continuing presence of the American military as protectors.

▼ **9.38** Japan, Nara Yoshitomo (B. 1959), *Girl with a Knife in Her Hand*, 1991. Acrylic on canvas, 59.25 in. × 55.12 in.

Nara's children do not fit comfortably into the cult of cuteness; there is something threatening in their expressions and the weapons they sometimes hold.

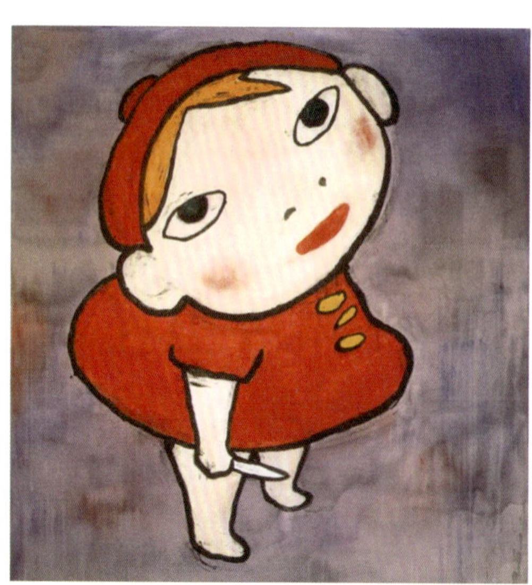

Chapter Quick Review

The Neolithic (14,500–1500 BCE) to the Iron Age (c. 300 BCE)

- The Neolithic in Korea is characterized by the development of Yunggimun, c. 8000 BCE, and Jeulmum, c. 7000–1500 BCE, pottery types and the development of rice agriculture.

Three Kingdoms Period Korea (c. 57 BCE–CE 668)

- The first organized states, the Kingdoms of Gojoseon, Baekje, and Silla are founded in Korea.
- Tombs were built in stacked block and tumulus forms, some, such as the *Tomb of the Dancer*, were ornamented with fresco paintings of the pursuits enjoyed by the tomb's occupant in life. Baekje and Silla rulers buried with elaborate gold crowns.

The Unified Silla (668–935 CE)

- With the aid of Tang China, the Silla Kingdom conquered its two neighbors and unified the peninsula as the Unified Silla.
- Sokkuram Grotto and Bulguksa Temple built by Korea's first great architect, Kim Tae-song.
- Sokkuram Buddha carved in a style that incorporates elements from Indian Gupta and Northern Wei.

The Later Three Kingdoms and the Goryeo Dynasty in Korea (918–1392 CE)

- The United Silla fractures into the Later Goguryeo and Later Baekje. Wang Geon usurps Goguryeo throne, shortens name to Goryeo, and reunites the peninsula under his rule.
- Celadon glazes are perfected in Korea; sanggam inlaid decoration is used to create areas of black and white on the vessels.
- In 1231 Mongols invade Korea and make it a vassal state. Water Moon Avalokitesvara painted at the court of King Chungseon as a plea for the Bodhisattva to release Korea from Mongol vassalage.

Great Joseon Dynasty (1392–1910)

- In 1392 Goryeo General Yi Seong-gye usurped the throne and established the Joseon Dynasty. He moved quickly to suppress Buddhism and to advance Confucianism. His actions ended the tradition of Buddhist painting and sculpture in Korea.
- Landscape painting following Chinese prototypes continued until the rise of the Silhak Movement in response to the Japanese invasion during the shogunate of Toyotomi Hideyoshi.
- The Silhak Movement was launched by Neo-Confucian scholars in an effort to rebuild Korea after the Japanese invasion. Artists were encouraged to paint scenes and subjects. Two of the more prominent Silhak artists were Jeong Seon and Shin Yun-bok.

Korean Art in the Modern Era

- In 1910 the Japanese forced the abdication of the last Joseon king and annexed Korea. The Japanese occupation was brutal and devastating to Korean culture; it continued until the end of World War II in 1945 when the peninsula was divided into North and South Koreas.
- Artists who came of age during the occupation were not allowed to practice traditional Korean forms or styles and were only allowed to receive art training in Japan, which during the Meiji promoted Western styles and media.
- After the end of the occupation some artists, such as Song Soo-nam, encouraged the recovery and modernization of traditional Korean media such as ink painting.

Neolithic Japan

- In Japan the natural richness of the environment did not necessitate the development of intensive agriculture but the Jomon people did invent ceramics around 14,500 BCE. Jomon pottery continued to develop new forms throughout its 13,000 year sustained history.

The Yayoi Period

- Korean settlers begin arriving in Japan around 900 BCE, inaugurating the Yayoi Period and bringing metalworking, rice agriculture, Shinto, and new housing styles. The Yayoi made tools of iron and cast bronze ritual items such as the bells known as dotaku.

The Kofun Period Japan (250–538 CE)

- Political centralization of the Imperial yamato government begins; contact with Korea continues.
- Large keyhole-shaped tombs, such as the Daisen Kofun of Emperor Nintoku, built for Imperial burials; smaller tumulus-type tombs build for individuals of lesser aristocratic rank.
- Haniwa evolve from simple clay cylinders placed on the sides of tomb mounds to hold offering bowls to works of sculpture featuring figures of humans, animals, and everyday items.

The Asuka Period Japan (c. 538–710)

- Imperial capital is moved Asuka and Japan's first charter, the Seventeen Article Constitution, is written in 604 CE by Prince Shotoku, regent of Empress Suiko.
- Buddhism is introduced and becomes state religion, coexisting with Shinto. Prince Shotoku founds Horyu-ji in 607 CE and forty-five others during his lifetime. Empress Suiko commissioned Tori to create the bronze Shakya Triad for Horyu-ji to honor Prince Shotoku, who died in 622 CE.
- In 692 CE, Empress Jito sponsored the first rebuilding of the Shinto Ise Jingu.

The Nara Period Japan (710–784 CE)

- Imperial capital is moved to Heijo-kyo (Nara) and the new city is laid out in imitation of Chang'an the capital of Tang China.

- Emperor Shomu institutes the Kokubun-ji network of Buddhist monasteries and temples; builds Todai-ji in the capital as the system's main temple.
- *Diabutsu*, a 500-ton, 52 foot (16 m) tall bronze Buddha cast, using massive piece-mold system and multiple bronze pours, and the *Daibutsuden*, its immense *kondo* was constructed around the statue.

Heian Period Japan (794–1185 CE)

- Emperor Kammu established a new Chang'an style capital at Heian-kyo, modern Kyoto.
- Myoan Eisai introduces Chan (Zen) Buddhism and tea drinking but Japan severs diplomatic ties with China after Tang Emperor Wuzong initiates Buddhist purges in 845 CE.
- Yamato-e or Japanese painting are developed and *kanji* and *hiragana* writing systems formulated to better express the Japanese language. Lady Murasaki Shikibu writes the Tale of Genji.
- Fujiwara no Yorimici succeeds his father as regent; converts his father's estate to a Pure Land Buddhist temple and builds the Phoenix Hall. Jocho creates the joined-block Amida Buddha for the hall.

Kamakura Period Japan (1192–1333 CE)

- Minamoto Yoritomo takes the reins of government in 1181 and becomes the first Shogun establishing his bakufu or tent government in Kamakura.
- Painting and sculpture become more realistic, focusing on historical events and personages in an effort to appeal to the ruling shoguns of the era.

Muromachi Period Japan (1336–1573 CE)

- Ashikaga Takauji took over as shogun, establishing his bakufu in the Muromachi district of Kyoto.
- *Wabi-sabi* aesthetic becomes important in the arts.
- Sesshu Toyo becomes master of *sumi-e* painting, works in "splashed ink" and "broken ink" techniques.
- Kogaku-Sōkō creates *Mountains and Dry Cascade*, Zen garden at Daisen-in, Kyoto

Azuchi-Momoyama Period (1573–1603 CE)

- Oda Nobunaga becomes shogun and builds his castle in the Azuchi district; is succeeded by Toyotomi Hideyoshi in 1582. The following year Toyotomi builds Osaka Castle.
- Sen no Rikyu creates Zen Taian teahouse; promotes wabi-cha aesthetics.

The Edo Period (1603–1867)

- Tokugawa Ieyasu becomes shogun; under the rule of his grandson Japan is closed off to all but the Dutch. Matthew Perry forces ports open in 1868.
- Japanese merchants prosper and have money to spend on entertainments of the Floating World; *ukiyo-e* prints are developed and a system of multi-color printing is devised using several blocks, one for each color.
- Improved roads encouraged travel and *meisho-e* or pictures of famous places become popular.

The Meiji Period (1868–1912)

- The restoration of power to the emperor in 1868 brought rapid Westernization, seen as modernization, to Japan. Teachers were imported from Europe and America and students were encouraged to study abroad. In the arts this meant adopting Western styles, techniques, media and even Western aesthetics. Western painting was known as Yôga.
- The rapid Westernization of Japanese arts concerned some of those teachers who had come to Japan; one of these, Dr. Ernest Fenollosa, proposed a hybrid of traditional Japanese and Western styles called *nihonga*.

Post-War Japan (1926–)

- After the Second World War, Japan was occupied by allied forces as the process of rebuilding the nation began. Artists working since the war have dealt with a number of themes, including the destruction of the war and the effects of American paternalism on Japanese society.
- Other artists experimented with new styles of Western modernism, participating in avant-garde movements such as Gutai.
- Japanese artists who came of age after 1970 grew up watching anime, reading manga, and playing video games on computers. Many of these artists take their themes from popular culture, dealing with rampant consumerism, personal isolation, artificiality, and the crumbling of distinctions between what is considered "high" and "low" art.

Chapter Questions

1. The connections between Korea and Japan are rooted deep in the history of these two lands. What was the role played by Korea in the development of Japanese art and culture?
2. Japan and Korea both were long-influenced by China. Characterize what each nation received from contact with China. How were these Chinese loans assimilated by each country?
3. Explain the Neo-Confucian concept of Silhak and why it came about. How did this movement impact the arts of Joseon Korea? Who are some artists associated with the movement?
4. What is Zen Buddhism and how did its practice inspire new art forms in Japan? Explain the terms *hatsuboku* and *haboku*. How are they used in ink painting?

Key Terms and Figures

Key Terms

Arhat Sanskrit: one who is worthy; in Buddhism a person who, having achieved enlightenment and nirvana, will not be reborn.

Bakufu A shogun's administration or government; tent headquarters.

Bijin In Japan a beautiful, charming, well-dressed woman.

Celadon A transparent jade green glaze invented by the Chinese but perfected by Korean potters during the Goryeo dynasty.

Chanoyu Japanese tea ceremony; the ritualized preparation and service of matcha or powdered green tea; seen as a form of meditation in Zen Buddhism.

Colophon A brief statement in calligraphy at the end of a handscroll that gives details about the creation of the scroll.

Dotaku Ritual bronze bells, cast in stone or clay piece-molds, and usually lacking clappers. They were made during the Yayoi period in Japan, but their use is unknown; they have been found buried in pairs or even numbered caches far from habitation sites.

Fukinuki yatai "Open roof" technique in which obstacles to an interior view such as walls and roofs are removed.

Fusuma In Japanese architecture these are sliding panel screens used to divide rooms.

Geomancy A belief in the ability to secure powerful protective forces of nature emanating from a particular place by building a temple or shrine on the spot.

Haboku "Broken ink," a style of Zen painting in which wash areas were broken by the addition of deeper or lighter tones while the first application of ink was still wet.

Haniwa Unglazed, although sometimes pigment-painted, clay cylinders and hollow that were placed on and around mounded tombs during the Kofun period in Japan.

Hatsuboku "Splashed ink," a style of Zen painting in the artist splashed and spontaneously applied ink and washes resulting in saturated areas of wash, blobs, and strokes.

Hiragana Japanese phonetic-based system of writing developed during the Heian period.

Jingyeong sansuhwa "True view" painting, painting done in the open air during the Joseon period in Korea.

Jinja A Shinto sanctuary usually marked by a Torii gate.

Kami In Shinto kami are nature spirits that dwell in rocks, trees, or animals.

Kanji Chinese logographic script adopted by the Japanese and used as a part of their system of writing.

Karesansui Japanese dry landscape or Zen garden; it suggests mountains and sea using only rocks, gravel, and sand.

Kondo In Japanese Buddhist architecture the kondo houses the main devotional image of the temple and includes an ambulatory for circumambulation.

Meisho-e Literally "pictures of famous places," a type of landscape print, often done as seasonal views produced during the Edo period in Japan.

Nihonga A style of modern Japanese painting proposed by Dr. Ernest Fenollosa in which traditional Japanese ink painting was enriched by Western perspective and chiaroscuro techniques.

Nishiki-e "Brocade picture," a technique for creating multicolor prints through the use of different carved blocks for each color ink in addition to a key block which produced the black outlines.

Orian In the Yoshiwara district of Edo, a high-class courtesan who was an entertainer.

Raku A type of Japanese hand-built pottery that is fired at a relatively low temperature, removed hot from the kiln, and placed in easily combustible materials such as sawdust or paper that ignite and create patterns on the surface of the vessel.

Sanggam A process of decorating ceramics in which the design is incised into the leather-hard clay body and the excavated area filed with clays that fire white or black.

Shogun "Barbarian Conquering General," a title bestowed on the military dictator who ruled Japan during the Kamakura through Edo periods.

Silhak "Practical Learning" movement promoted by Neo-Confucian scholars during the Joseon period in response to the Japanese invasion; it encouraged artists to focus on Korean scenes and culture.

Sumi-e Japanese ink painting rooted in Zen Buddhism.

Torii Traditional Japanese wooden gate having two posts and a double lintel, and sometimes painted red; used to mark the line of demarcation between sacred and profane spaces in Shinto.

Ukiyo-e "Floating world" prints, a type of Japanese print produced from the seventeenth through nineteenth centuries that featured the entertainments of the Yoshiwara district in Edo.

Wabi-sabi A Zen aesthetic that values the transient, imperfect, and natural qualities of materials.

Yamato-e Japanese style painting relying on fine lines and color over virtuoso brushwork.

Yôga Western-style painting.

Key Figures

Ahn Gyeon—Landscape painter at the court of King Sejong.

Emperor Shomu—Created the Kokubun-ji, a system of Buddhist temples under the control of the main temple of Todai-ji in the capital; sponsored the building of the Diabutsu Buddha and Daibutsuden.

Fenollosa, Ernest—American art historian responsible for Nihonga style painting in Japan.

Fujiwara Michinaga—Powerful regent during the Heian period and head of a clan that rose to power by marrying their daughters to the emperors.

Fujiwara no Yorimici—Son of Fujiwara Michinaga and successor as regent; built the Phoenix Hall at Byōdō-in.

Jeong Seon—Silhak painter who devised *Jingyeong sansuhwa* or "true view painting."

Jocho—Japanese sculptor who created the joined-block sculpture method.

Katsushika Hokusai—Edo period printmaker famous for his pictures of famous places.

Kim Tae-song—Korea's first recorded architect; built Sokkuram Grotto.

King Injong—Goryeo king who commissioned first bronze, movable type.

Minamoto Yoritomo—First Kamakura shogun.

Murasaki Shikibu—Author of the Tale of Genji.

Queen Sondok—Silla queen who built the first Asian observatory, the Chomsondae.

Sen no Rikyu—Renowned tea master who worked for Oda Nobunaga and Toyotomi Hideyosi; promoted the Wabi-sabi aesthetic; forced to commit suicide by Toyotomi.

Sesshu Toyo—Zen Buddhist painter of splashed ink and broken ink paintings.

Shin Ka-gwon—Also known as Shin Yun-bok, Korean painter of genre scenes.

Shotoku Taishi—Prince regent of the Asuka era who promoted Buddhism, patron of Horyu-ji and forty-five other temples, and wrote Japan's first constitution and first history.

Suzuki Harunobu—Edo period printmaker who invented the multicolor "brocade print."

Tori Busshi—Japanese sculpture of the sixth and seventh centuries who created the first monumental bronze sculptures in Japan, including the Shakya Triad at Horyu-ji.

Toyotomi Hideyoshi—Shogun of the Momoyama period who built Osaka Castle and launched an invasion of Korea.

Wang Geon—Founder of the Goryeo Dynasty; took throne as King Taejo.

Yi Seong-gye—Founder of Joseon Dynasty.

Quick Pronunciation Guide

Baekje (Pek-chyeh)
Goguryeo (Ko-gur-yo)
Goryeo (Gur-yae-yo)
Joseon (Cho-son)
Silla (Shih-lah)

Bibliography

Anderson, Jennifer L. "Japanese Tea Ritual: Religion in Practice." *Man* 22, no. 3 (September 1987): 475–498.

Akiyama, Terukazu. "The Door Paintings in the Phoenix Gall of the Byodoin as Yamatoe." *Artibus Asiae* 53, no. 1–2 (1993): 144–167.

Barnes, Gina L. "Mounded Tomb Cultures (2–5c AD)." In *Archaeology of East Asia: The Rise of Civilization in China, Korea and Japan*, 331–360. Oxbow Books, 2015.

Beynon, David. "From Techno-Cute to Superflat: Robots and Asian Architectural Futures." *Mechademia* 7 (2012): 129–148.

Butler, Kenneth Dean. "The Heike monogatari and the Japanese Warrior Ethic." *Harvard Journal of Asiatic Studies* 29 (1969): 93–108.

Chiyonobu, Yoshimasa, and Chiyo Yanhui. "Recent Archaeological Excavations at the Todai-ji." *Japanese Journal of Religious Studies* 19, nos. 2–3 (June–September 1992): 245–254.

Chong Pil Choe, and Martin T. Bale. "Current Perspectives on Settlement, Subsistence, and Cultivation in PreHistoric Korea." *Artic Anthropology* 39, no. 1–2 (2002): 95–121.

Curry, Andrew. "Turning Japanese: Radiocarbon Dates Fuel a Debate Over the Origins of an Ancient Asian Culture." *Archaeology* 61, no. 1 (January–February 2008): 18, 64–65.Elisséeff, Serge

"The Bommokyo and the Great Buddha of the Todaiji," *Harvard Journal of Asiatic Studies*, vol. 1, no.1 (Apr. 1936): 84-95.

Fang, Hui. *Sesshū Tōyō's Selective Assimilation of Ming Chinese Painting Elements.* Thesis. University of Oregon, 2013.

Farris, William Wayne. "Ancient Japan's Korean Connection." *Korean Studies* 20 (1996): 1–22.

Ford, Barbara Brennan, and Oliver R. Impey. *Japanese Art from the Gerry Collection in The Metropolitan Museum of Art.* New York: Metropolitan Museum of Art, 1989.

Fujimori, Terunobu. "Two for Tea." *Japan Journal* (August 2007). http://www.japanjournal.jp/tjje/show_art.php?INDyear=07&INDmon=08&artid=f163e1f847cf981422ef0f1ccc93168b

Guo, Qinghua. "From Tower to Pagoda: Structural and Technological Transition." *Construction History* 20 (2004): 3–19.

Harrell, Mark. "Sokkuram: Buddhist Monument and Political Statement in Korea." *World Archaeology* 27, no. 2 (October 1995): 318–335.

Hudson, Mark J. "Rice, Bronze, and Chieftains: An Archaeology of Yayoi Ritual." *Japanese Journal of Religious Studies* 19, nos. 2–3 (June–September 1992): 139–189.

Hong, Wontack. "Yayoi Wave, Kofun Wave, and Timing: The Formation of the Japanese People and Japanese Language." *Korean Studies* 29 (205): 1–29.**Hung, Wu.** "Rethinking East Asian Tombs: A Methodological Proposal." *Studies in the History of Art* 74 (January 2009): 138–165

Ikawa-Smith, Fumiko. "Current Issues in Japanese Archaeology." *American Scientist* 68, no. 2 (March–April 1980): 134–145.

Ivy, Marilyn. "The Art of Cute Little Things: Nara Yoshitomo's Parapolitics." *Mechademia* 5, Fanthropologies (2010): 3–29.**Jeon, Ho-Tae**

"Artistic Creation, Borrowing, Adaptation, and Assimilation in Kogiryo Tomb Murals of the Fourth to Seventh Century," *Archives of Asian Art*, vol. 56 (2006): 81-104.

Johei, Sasaki. "The Era of the Kano School." *Modern Asian Studies* 18, no. 4 (1984): 647–656.

Kee, Joan. "Points, Lines, Encounters: The World According to Lee Ufan." *Oxford Art Journal* 31, no. 3 (2008): 405–424.

Contemporary Korean Art: Tansaekhwa and the Urgency of Method. Minneapolis: University of Minnesota Press, 2013.

Kim, Won-Yong, and Richard Pearson. "Three Royal Tombs: New Discoveries in Korean Archaeology." *Archaeology* 30, no. 5 (September 1977): 302–313.**Lippit, Yukio.** "Of Modes and Manners in Japanese Ink Painting: Sesshu's 'Splashed Ink Landscape' of 1495." *Art Bulletin* 94, no. 1 (March 2012): 50–77.

Looser, Thomas. "Superflat and the Layers of Image and History in 1990s Japan." *Mechademia* 1 (2006): 92–109.

Moran, Sherwood F. "Early Heian Sculpture at its Best: Three Outstanding Examples." *Artibus Asiae* 34, no. 2–3 (1972): 119–161.

Morse, Samuel C. "Jocho's Statue of Amida at the Byodo-in and Cultural Legitimization in the Late Heian Japan." *RES: Anthropology and Aesthetics*, no. 23 (Spring 1993): 96–113.

Nakane, Shiro. "Structure in the Japanese Garden." *Antioch Review* 64, no. 2 (Spring 2006): 217–220.

Oyler, Elizabeth. "The Heike monogatari and Narrating the Genpei War." In *Swords, Oaths, and Prophetic Visions*, 1–28. Honolulu: University of Hawai'i Press, 2006. Pantelić, Ksenija (Silka P)

"What do we Know about North Korean Art?" *Widewalls*, September 6, 2016 https://www.widewalls.ch/north-korean-art/

Park, Ah-Rim. *Tomb of the Dancers: Koguryo Tombs in East Asian Funerary Art*. Dissertation. University of Pennsylvania, 2002.

Parkes, Graham. "The Eloquent Stillness of Stone: Rock in the Dry Landscape Garden." In *Japanese Hermeneutics: Current Debates on Aesthetics and Interpretation*, 44–59, edited by Michael F. Marra. Honolulu: University of Hawai'i Press, 2002.

Piggott, Joan R. "Mokkan: Wooden Documents from the Nara Period." *Monumenta Nipponica* 45, no. 4 (1990): 449–70.

Rhee, Song-Nai, and Choi Mong-Lyong. "Emergence of Complex Society in Prehistoric Korea." *Journal of World Prehistory* 6, no. 1 (March 1992): 51–95.

Sadler, A. L. "The Heike Monogatari." *Transactions of the Asiatic Society of Japan* 46, part 2 (1918).

Sample, L.L. "Tongsamdong: A Contribution to Korean Neolithic Culture History." *Artic Anthropology* 11, no. 2 (1974): 1–125.

Shin, Sook-Chung, Song-Nai Rhee, and C. Melvin Aikens. "Chulmun Neolithic Intensification, Complexity, and Emerging Agriculture in Korea." *Asian Perspectives* 51, no. 1 (Spring 2012): 68–109.

Smith, Judith G. editor. *Arts of Korea*. Metropolitan Museum of Art, 2000.

Stanley-Baker, Joan. *Japanese Art*. London: Thames and Hudson, 2000.

Steinhardt, Nancy Shatzman. "Liao Archaeology: Tombs and Ideology along the Northern Frontier of China." *Asian Perspectives* 37, no. 2 (Fall 1998): 224–244.

Tadashi, Hasegawa "The Early Stages of the Heike Monogatari," *Monumenta Nipponica*, vol 22, no. ½ (1967): 65-81.

Weiss, Allen S. "The Limits of Metaphor: Ideology and Representation in the Zen Garden." *Social Analysis: The Internation Journal of Social and Cultural Practice* 54, no. 2 (Summer 2010): 116–129.

Yoon, Hong-Key. "Human Modification of Korean Landforms for Geomantic Purposes." *Geographical Review* 101, no. 2 (April 2011): 243–260.

Yiengpruksawan, Mimi Hall. "What's in a Name? Fujiwara Fixation in Japanese Cultural History." *Monumenta Nipponica* 49, no. 4 (Winter, 1994): 423–453.

Yoshimoto, Midori. "Bye Bye Kitty!!!" *Impressions*, no. 33 (2012): 118–127.

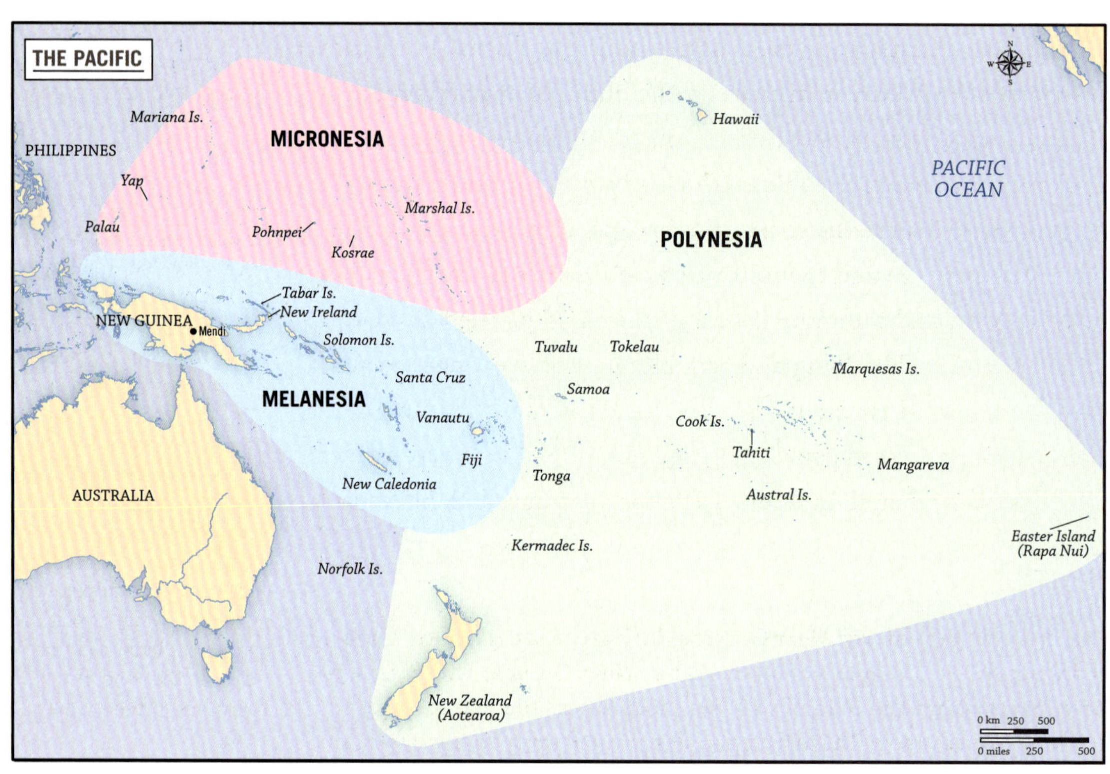
THE PACIFIC
N
W
E
S
Mariana Is.
PHILIPPINES
MICRONESIA
Yap
Palau
Pohnpei
Kosrae
Marshal Is.
Hawaii
PACIFIC
OCEAN
POLYNESIA
Tabar Is.
New Ireland
NEW GUINEA
Mendi
Solomon Is.
Santa Cruz
MELANESIA
Vanautu
Fiji
New Caledonia
Tuvalu
Tokelau
Samoa
Tonga
Cook Is.
Tahiti
Marquesas Is.
Mangareva
Austral Is.
AUSTRALIA
Kermadec Is.
Norfolk Is.
Easter Island
(Rapa Nui)
New Zealand
(Aotearoa)
0 km 250 500
0 miles 250 500

Oceania

10

Brief Overview

Oceania, a region of the Pacific encompassing the islands of Melanesia, Micronesia, Polynesia, and Australasia, offers an amazing diversity of arts made to propitiate the gods, venerate ancestors, placate spirits, and demonstrate rank and status. These arts are made even more remarkable by the limits of available materials and technology on most of the islands. Despite limited media and Stone Age tools, Oceanic artists were able to produce works of great beauty to serve the societal and religious needs of their communities. They created monolithic stone sculptures, carved wood into practical and ceremonial items, made and painted barkcloth for garments and bedding and as a medium of exchange, created elite featherwork garments, plaited pandanus into clothing and wall coverings, carved gourds, worked bone, shell, and greenstone into ornaments, and in some societies, decorated their bodies with tattoos.

Chapter Objectives

1. Understand how the arts in Oceania were limited by locally available means and materials, or what could be obtained through regional trade exchanges such as the *kula* in Melanesia.
2. Recognize how artists were trained in some of the societies of Oceania and how that training differed from one region to the next. Understand how their works, made to honor ancestors or placate gods and spirits, were defined by societal needs or patrons rather than concepts of free expression.
3. Show how the arrival of Europeans impacted the arts in both positive and negative ways not only at the time of contact but in the modern era.

The first settlers entered Near Oceania during the last glaciation, more than 35,000 years ago when Australia, New Guinea, the Bismarck Archipelago, and the Solomons were more accessible due to substantially lower sea levels. These first peoples arrived prior to the invention of pottery-making and metalworking. A second wave of immigrants, the Lapita, who began moving across Near Oceania between the fourth and second millennia BCE, did have knowledge of ceramics as demonstrated by finds of their pottery across Melanesia and into western Polynesia demonstrate, but apparently they did not find the resources necessary to sustain production or to develop metalworking. Indeed, island resources, including plants and animals, decline dramatically from western to eastern Oceania. For example, Easter Island offered settlers on a few species of sea birds, two kinds of lizards, and only a few varieties of trees. The final wave of colonizers, Europeans, began moving into the Pacific in the sixteenth century CE and their arrival profoundly changed the lives, cultures, and arts of the peoples they encountered. In some cases, the arrival of Europeans brought new metal tools that enabled island artists to carve works that would have been impossible with stone tools. However, in many others, European trade goods contributed to the loss of traditional art forms, such as barkcloth and featherwork. The most devastating effect of European arrival was missionization. Under the auspices of the London Missionary Society, many central Polynesian sculptures were destroyed as idols or emasculated as obscenities.

Although Europeans began making contact with Oceanic cultures more than five hundred years ago, the art of this region has not received the full attention of art history. This may have been due in part to European collectors' inability to see these works as anything other than ethnographic examples because they did not conform to the accepted media and styles of "high art" in the West, and even the most commonly recognized crafts, ceramics and metalworking, were not present in Oceania.

Australia

The oldest evidence of humans in Australia is found in the Arnhem Land region of the Northern Territories, where the Malakinanja II rock shelter site has yielded dates as early as 59,000 BCE, suggesting

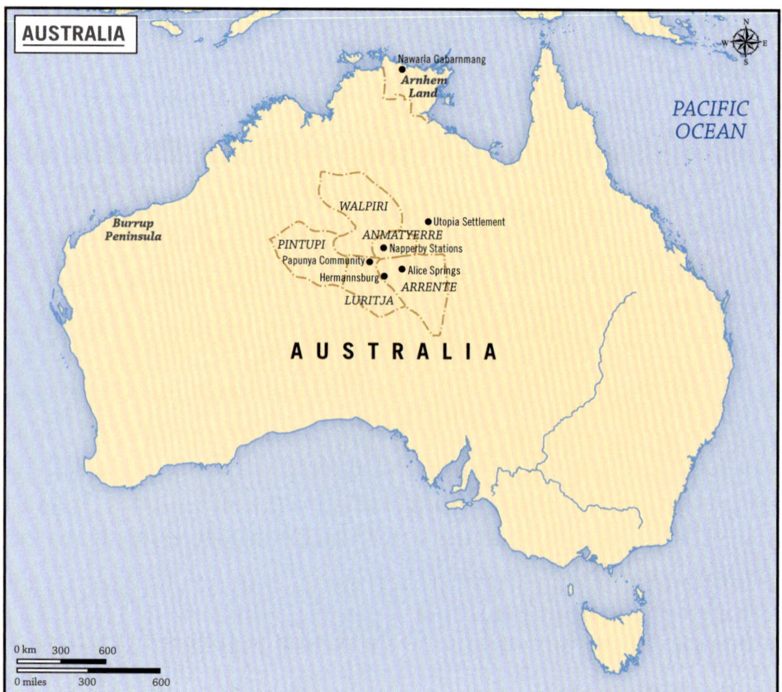

timeline

DATE	TYPE	EVENT
		BCE
c. 60,000	History	First settlers arrive in northern Australia and New Guinea
c. 50,000	Art	Hematite pigments first used at Nauwalabila I and Malakunanja II (Australia)
c. 40,000	Art	Burrup Peninsula rock art engravings
c. 28,000	Art	First paintings at Nawarla Gabarnmang (Australia)
	History	New Ireland settled
c. 15,000	Art	Laura, Queensland, petroglyphs incised (Australia)
c. 2000	Art	X-ray-style paintings first appeared in Arnhem Land (Australia)
	History	Settlers from Taiwan or the Philippines arrived in Micronesia
c. 1800	History	Melanesians arrived in Fiji
c. 1600	History	Lapita migrants landed in the Bismarck Archipelago
c. 825	History	Tonga settled
c. 800	History	Samoa settled
		CE
c. 500	Art	Work began in Temwen Lagoon, Pohnpei
c. 800	History	Settlers arrived in Cook Islands
1025–1170	History	Society Islands settled
c. 1100	Art	Construction of Nan Madol began on Pohnpei and Leluh on Kosrae
c. 1200	History	Hawaii, Rapa Nui, and New Zealand settled
1550	History	Carving of Moai on Rapa Nui declined
1592	History	Spain claimed the Marshall Islands
1616	History	Dirk Hartog sailed along coast of Western Australia
1623	History	Jan Carstensz stopped along Asmat coast of New Guinea
1642	History	Abel Janszoon Tasman visited New Zealand's South Island
1643	History	Tasman visited Fiji
1688	History	William Dampier arrived on west coast of Australia
c. 1700	Art	Construction of Bai-ra-Irrai began on Palau
1722	History	Jacob Roggeveen visited Rapa Nui, christens it Easter Island
1769	History	James Cook visited New Zealand
1770	History	Cook attacked by Asmat warriors in New Guinea

(Continued)

timeline *continued*

DATE	TYPE	EVENT
		CE
1778	History	Cook visited Hawaiian island of Maui
	History	Botany Bay penal colony established in Australia
1815	History	English missionaries arrived in New Zealand
1840	History	Maori rebelled against British rule
c. 1860	Art	Massim carver Mutuaga born
1877	History	Hermannsburg Mission founded in Australia
1880	Art	Whare Whakairo Ruatepupuke II commissioned, Tokomaru Bay, North Island, New Zealand
1884	History	Southeastern New Guinea became British protectorate Germany annexed the northeastern part
1902	Art	Albert Namatjira born at Hermannsburg Mission
c. 1910	Art	Emily Kame Kngwarreye born at Utopia Station, Australia
1912	Art	Walter Baldwin Spencer made first collection of Aboriginal bark paintings
c. 1930	Art	Asmat carver Matjemos born
c. 1932	Art	Clifford Possum Tjapaltjarri born at Napperby Station
1934	History	Gold discovered in Prince Alexander Mountains of New Guinea; Maprik established in Abelam territory
	Art	Reginald "Rex" Battarbee taught watercolor painting to Aboriginal men at Hermannsburg Mission; established Hermannsburg School
1939	History	Dutch colonial outpost established in Asmat territory
c. 1944	Art	Kauage Mathis born in Chimbu area of Papua New Guinea
1947	History	New Zealand achieved independence
1950	History	Asmat region pacified
1970	History	Tonga and Fiji achieved independence
1972	Art	Western Desert Art Movement began at Papunya; Papunya Tula Artists Pty Ltd. artist's collective founded at Papunya, Australia
1975	History	Papua New Guinea achieved independence
1979	History	Gilbert and Marshall Islands achieved independence
1980	History	Vanuatu achieved independence
1986	History	Australia gained full independence
1994	History	Palau achieved independence

that the first settlers arrived more than 60,000 years ago when New Guinea and Tasmania were still connected to the continent as part of the greater Sahul land mass. Because of the early arrival of humans and their subsequent isolation after sea levels rose, Australian Aboriginal rock art, including rock engravings and paintings, have generally been presumed to be the world's oldest, depicting an ancient and ongoing imagery. However, rock art is notoriously difficult to reliably date as many pigments contain no dateable organic components. The oldest currently known Australian example, a fragment of a charcoal painting found at the Nawarla Gabarnmang shelter in Arnhem Land, is only 28,000 years old. The next oldest reliably dated examples are the petroglyphs of Laura, Queensland, which are 13,000 to 15,000 years old. Hematite sticks, showing signs of use, recovered from the Nauwalabila I and Malakunanja II sites, and dating to over 50,000 ago suggest that some sort of art has been produced in Australia since the first peoples arrived.

From the Northern Territories the first peoples of Australia spread out across the continent and on to what is now the island of Tasmania, defining some 250 original homelands of the Aboriginal peoples. Traditionally, the Aboriginal peoples are thought to have been hunters and gatherers without fixed settlements. Recent excavations on Rosemary Island in the Dampier Archipelago have revealed circular stone house foundations dating from 7,000 BCE, suggesting that some groups may have lived a more sedentary lifestyle.

Early Rock Art

Australian rock art includes dry pigment drawings, paintings, and rock engravings. Dry pigment sticks of hematite, ocher, and charcoal were among the earliest rock art media. True paintings were made by adding water to pigments, such as white kaolin, and mixing in the mouth. These water-based paints were applied with brushes, which traditionally were made by chewing the end of a twig from the stringybark tree. Painted images were outlined with the brush and then the insides were done; often the fill paint was applied with the fingers. In some cases, pigments were mixed with binders such as blood, beeswax, or plant resins.

The Nawarla Gabarnmang In southwestern Arnhem Land is a large natural rock shelter formed by millennia of erosion known as the Nawarla Gabarnmang (Figure 10.1). Nawarla Gabarnmang translates from the local Jawoyn Aboriginal language as "place of the hole in the rock." Countless generations of Aboriginal artists decorated the rock shelter's ceiling and thirty-six pillars with images of spirits from the time of creation, humans, and animals. While the oldest Nawarla Gabarnmang paintings date back 28,000 years, new art continues to be added to the shelter to this day.

MIMI PAINTINGS

The earliest paintings, in the Nawarla Gabarnmang and other shelters across Australia, are believed to be the stick-like monochrome or "old red paintings," done in red ocher, blood, or a mixture of both. These red, or sometimes white, yellow, and black, figures represent primordial spirits known as ***mimi***. The Aborigines recognize mimi images as the oldest style of painting and they claim that the paintings were done by the spirits themselves. Mimi are often rendered in dynamic postures suggesting leaping or running with weapons; frequently multiple figures are shown in what appear to be ritual dances and kangaroo hunting scenes. Mimi style figures have been found in rock shelters across the continent. In some areas of the continent this painting style continues in modern times.

X-RAY STYLE PAINTINGS

The pillars and ceiling of the Nawarla Gabarnmang also show paintings done in a second and better-known style, termed x-ray style because internal anatomy, bones, and organs are rendered in a "see through" manner like that of a modern x-ray. X-ray style rock paintings are known only from Arnhem Land sites and the earliest are thought to date from 2000 BCE. These paintings are rendered as partial silhouettes painted in red with some internal hatching; spinal column, rib cage, and digestive tract are sometimes depicted. Over time more organs, accurately depicted, appeared, including gill rakers in fish, heart, lungs, liver, diaphragm, and intestines in animals, and the trachea and esophagus in humans (Brandl 1973, 168). The more elaborate paintings feature a polychrome palette of red, white, yellow, black, and, occasionally, blue-green. As the Nawarla Gabarnmang and other Arnhem Land shelter paintings show, the x-ray style is a living

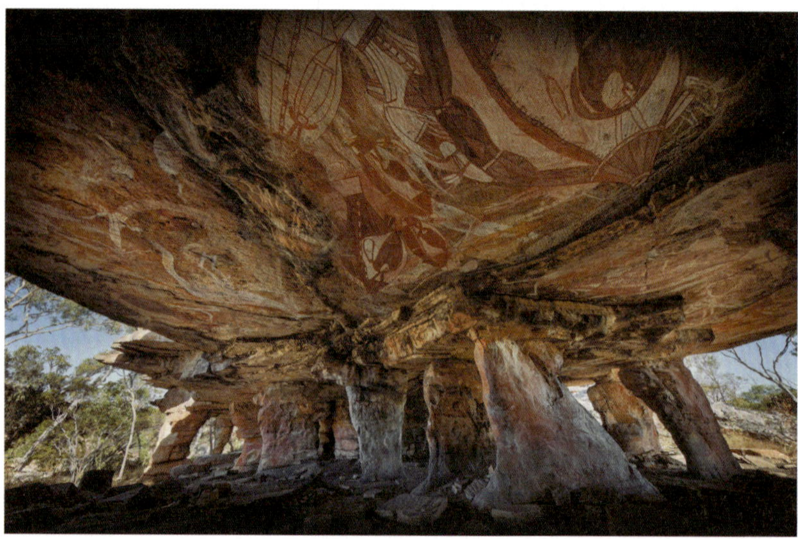

▶ **10.1** Australia, Nawarla Gabarnmang, c. 28,000 BCE.

The Nawarla Gabarnmang caves have been in use for thousands of years with new images still being added. The oldest sold red figures represent mimis or primordial beings from the time of the Dreaming.

tradition. New x-ray style paintings are still being created on rock shelter surfaces as well as on bark sheets. In some cases, these recent paintings are easily identified by their incorporation of modern elements such as rifles.

A ROCK ENGRAVINGS

Although rock engravings or petroglyphs (Figure 10.2) are known from sites across the Australian continent, the Burrup Peninsula in northwestern Australia is a particularly art-rich area; the estimated number of images from the more than 2,300 Burrup sites is well over a million. The dating of exposed rock art images is particularly difficult since they are created by incising, pecking, pounding, or abrading rock surfaces, a process that utilizes harder rocks and abrasives; however, the first Burrup engravings may date to around 40,000 BCE. Engravings that have been buried under occupational debris have been reliably dated by radiocarbon testing of charcoal samples found at the same depth. The oldest that have been dated in this manner are in Laura, Queensland, and are approximately 15,000 years old. Others have been dated based on what is depicted, for example, images of three and four masted sailing ships would, at most, be a little more than four hundred years old, since the first contact with Europeans was in 1606. Engravings are done in both linear and solid fill styles. Subjects depicted are consistent with those found in mimi-style paintings: spirits, humans, and animals, including some that are thought to represent extinct megafauna.

BARK PAINTINGS

The tradition of Aboriginal bark painting is probably of great antiquity although the nature of the material leaves very little evidence

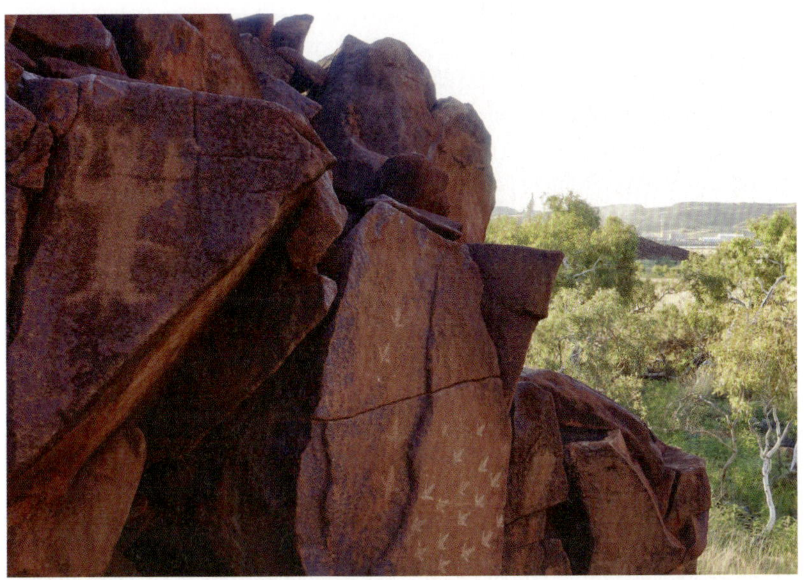

◀ **10.2** Australia, Murujuga National Park, Petroglyphs.

The oldest engravings at the site are thought to be around 40,000 years old but the site was still in use in the seventeenth century CE, when Aboriginal artists recorded images of European sailing ships.

of the practice. The earliest record of the use of bark painting dates from the first years of the nineteenth century when explorers trekking across inland Australia noted that the Aborigines made simple lean-to shelters or *gunyah* of sapling frames covered with decorated sheets of stringybark. Mention is also made of bark paintings being set up as markers over Aboriginal graves. Few examples of bark paintings were collected by these early explorers or settlers. The first major collection was amassed during the first decades of the twentieth century by Walter Baldwin Spencer, an ethnographer, who encouraged Aboriginal artists to produce paintings. Spencer made several trips into central and northern Australia, ultimately collecting some two hundred paintings.

Among most Aboriginal groups, bark painting was the province of male artists who underwent a long apprenticeship to learn to properly paint ancestral subjects. Before the 1990s few women painters were known; this began to change as a direct result of the active intervention of art advisors in response to the global art market. Women began to learn to paint from their husbands and fathers who guided them toward images with the fewest ceremonial restrictions (Taylor 2008, 870–71).

The creation of a bark painting begins with stripping a horizontal section of bark from a stringybark (eucalyptus) tree. After the outer bark has been scraped off, the bark sheet is dried and flattened over a fire and then buried in hot sand for several days to allow the sheet to set. The designs are painted employing the same pigments used in rock art: pipe clay for white, red, and yellow ochers, and charcoal for black. Traditionally the pigments were mixed with water and various weak binders, determined by what is locally available, but the most common were beeswax and honey, sea turtle egg yolk, and sap obtained from the bulbs of orchids. Since the 1960s these natural binders have largely been replaced by commercial wood glues, which offer greater permanence. The pigments are applied using brushes made from stringybark twigs, human hair, feathers, or more recently, commercially available artists' brushes. The bark sheets are laid flat on the ground and given a base coat of red or yellow ocher before the designs are added. The bark panel remains flat during painting so the artist can move around it. As a result, traditional bark paintings have no particular orientation as to up or down. The motifs on bark paintings had meanings and were not selected at random. Images, cross-hatching or ***rarrk*** patterns, and even some colors were considered to be the property of certain clans; artists from other groups could not use these proprietary designs without permission of the owners. Traditional bark painting designs were either figurative or geometric. Depending on the manner in which the motifs are handled, the paintings may be secular or ceremonial.

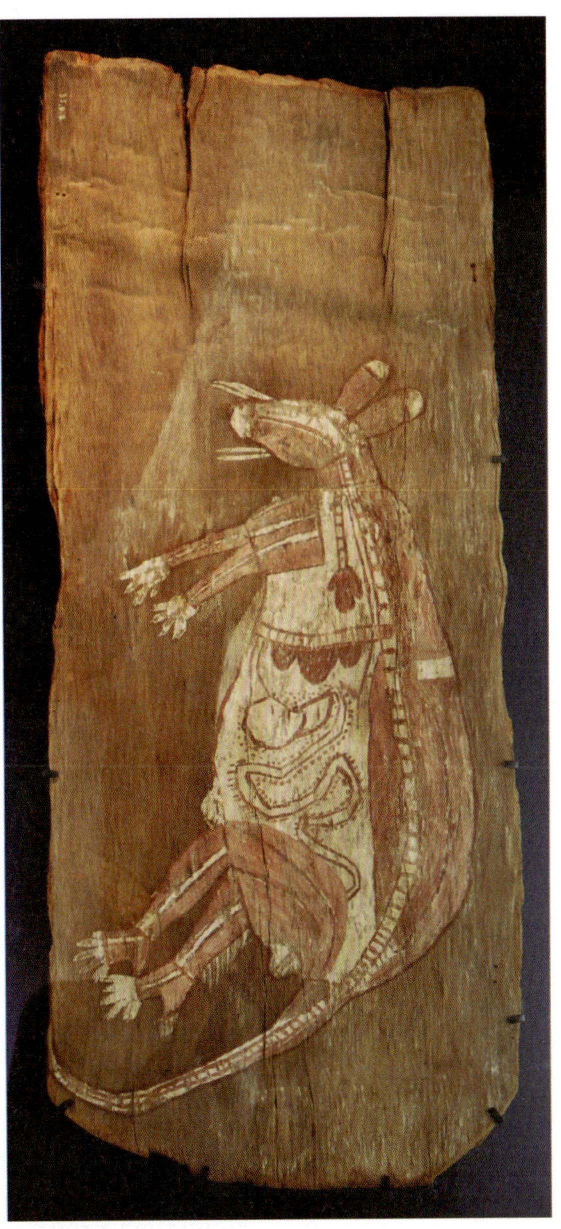

▲ **10.3** Australia, X-Ray-Style Bark Painting, nineteenth to early twentieth century CE. Pigment on eucalyptus bark.

X-ray style paintings take their name from the artist's depiction of the animal's bones and organs.

Geometric paintings were typically ceremonial and featured lines, circles, and dots, often on a framework of diamonds, rectangles, or triangles. The designs reference and manifest in the present creation stories that recount the action of ancestral spirits during **the Dreaming**. These spirits formed the land and traveled across it creating the rivers, waterholes, and mountain ranges. The elements in the paintings reference these features and the ***songlines*** or paths that the ancestors took as they moved over the land. At the same time the designs also reference body painting motifs worn in related ceremonies or painted on sacred wooden sculptures.

Female Kangaroo, X-Ray Style, Arnhem Land, c. 1915 Figurative designs include depictions of animal and human forms. These representations can be either secular or ceremonial depending upon how the infill is handled. Anthropomorphic figures may represent ancestral beings who have transformed from their animal to human form, the lightning spirit, water spirits, lesser spirits such as mimi, and ordinary humans. Zoomorphic images typically describe four categories of animals: fish, birds, crocodiles, and marsupials as well as others classified as "meat." The proper rendering of these forms requires that care be taken to master the iconic outline of the animal as well as anatomical peculiarities that identify species and gender. Animals that have typical x-ray features, such as the female kangaroo (Figure 10.3), or those divided to show the favored portions of flesh, represent game animals. Those that have white outlines and no color or show only bones are dead. Animals infilled with geometric designs represent ancestral beings in zoomorphic form as well as ceremonial dances related to the species.

Modern and Contemporary Aboriginal Art (1930–)

As more of the Australian outback was taken over by cattle stations, Aboriginal peoples were relocated to missions, government-sponsored settlements, and Aboriginal stations. It was in these locations and through contact with Euro-Australian artists and patrons, beginning in the second half of the nineteenth century that Aboriginal artists were first introduced to media such as drawing pencils, watercolor, and paper and to Western modes of expression. The work of some early twentieth century Aboriginal artists, for example Albert Namatjira, was initially dismissed as derivative because of his use of Western materials and styles, but nevertheless, the work of many modern and contemporary Aboriginal artists has been well received by the intenational art market.

THE HERMANNSBURG PAINTERS (1934–1960)

The Hermannsburg Mission 75 miles (120 km) west of Alice Springs in the Northern Territory was established in 1877 by two German Lutheran missionaries. The mission was set up to convert the local Arrente people to Christianity and frequently served as a sanctuary against local ranchers and police who regularly massacred Aborigines suspected of killing cattle. The completion of a railroad spur line from Alice Springs in the 1930s brought tourists and artists to the region to see and record its scenic landscapes. Among those artists was Reginald "Rex" Battarbee, whose views of the local landscapes fascinated the Aborigines at the mission. After several painting expeditions during the 1930s, Battarbee settled permanently in the area and began teaching the basics of watercolor to the Aboriginal men at Hermannsburg. His students included Albert Namatjira and his five sons; the three Pareroultja brothers, and Walter Ebatarinja. Battarbee promoted their work, arranging exhibitions and sales of their paintings.

Albert Namatjira (1902–1959), Ghost Gum, c. 1945 One of the first Hermannsburg painters to receive national and international recognition was Albert Namatjira. Born Elea at the mission, he was later baptized Albert when his parents converted to Christianity. At thirteen he underwent the traditional Arrente initiation rites and four years later he married Rubina, a woman from the neighboring Luritja community. He was thirty-two when he met Rex Battarsbee and served as his guide on the first of what would become several painting expeditions in the Northern Territory. After Battarsbee's exhibition of his work at Hermannsburg, Namatjira asked him for paints and paper so he could make his own paintings. On subsequent painting trips, Battarsbee taught Namatjira to paint and was astonished by his aptitude. In 1936 Battarsbee arranged Namatjira's first exhibition in Melbourne, followed by others in Sydney and Adelaide. The successful sale of his paintings brought Namatjira a good income and in 1951 he attempted to build a house in Alice Springs but was prevented under the terms of the Aboriginals Ordinance, which prohibited Aboriginals from owning land. In 1957 Namatjira became the first Aborigine to be granted full citizenship; he could then live where he wished, vote, purchase alcohol, and maintain rights to his children. The following year he was charged with giving alcohol to Aborigines, a crime, and sentenced to two months in prison. He appealed the sentence but a higher court denied his appeal. He died of a heart attack in 1959.

In works such as *Ghost Gum* (Figure 10.4), Namatjira responds to the stark desert landscape of the Northern Territories with the keen sensitivity of a person for whom the environment is not just an everyday reality but a spiritual experience. Much has been written about the Aborigines' connection to the land and their art as an expression of the Dreaming, and while Namatjira's work is certainly grounded in his life experience and beliefs, he is also a highly competent watercolorist with a keen understanding of composition and color. The brilliant white trunk of the *Ghost Gum* dominates the foreground, while in the distance, purple hills and valleys roll across the bright, light-filled land. Namatjira's detailed handling of form, light and shade, atmosphere, and perspective equal or exceed the handling of the same elements by Euro-Australian artists working in this genre during the period. However, because of his ethnicity, his work was often criticized as being inauthentic and derivative because he worked in a medium and realist style seen as the province of European artists.

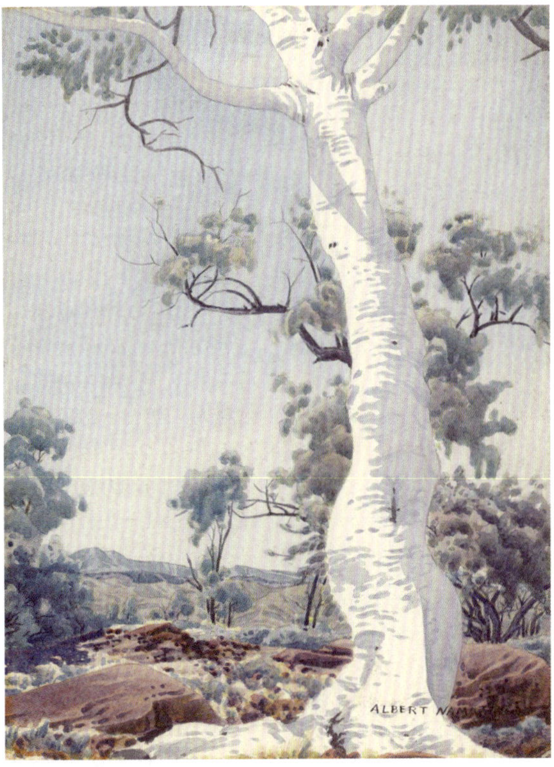

▲ **10.4** Australia, Albert Namatjira (1902–1959), *Ghost Gum*, c. 1945. Watercolor over pencil.

Namatjira learned to paint in watercolors from European artists visiting the Hermannsburg Mission. His paintings reflect an understanding of the landscape as something far beyond scenery.

THE WESTERN DESERT ART MOVEMENT (1972–)

The Western Desert Art Movement, also known as the "dot painting school," originated in the Papunya resettlement community, located in a remote area some 149 miles (240 km) to the northwest of Alice Springs. Papunya had been established by the government in 1960 as a place to warehouse and assimilate Aboriginal peoples from the Pintupi, Luritja, Walpiri, Arrente, and Anmatyerre groups whose traditional lands were wanted by Euro-Australian cattle ranchers. The groups sent to Papunya spoke different languages and had different customs; what they seemed to share was the disheartening effect of having been ripped from the ancestral lands that were an integral part of their personal and ceremonial identity.

The catalyst for change at Papunya was Geoffrey Bardon, who arrived in 1971 to take a post as an elementary art teacher. Prior to studying art education, Bardon had studied law. Bardon encouraged his students to paint a mural based on traditional sand painting and body painting designs. When the elders of the community saw the students' work, they decided that the project was more appropriate for the senior men. The men created a mural depicting the Honey Ant Dreaming, which was related to the Papunya area as the place where ancestral songlines converged. The government administrators had the mural painted over as a way of countering the resurgence of Aboriginal identity and pride that it inspired. Bardon was later dismissed by the administrators, but not before he helped the men form the Papunya Tula Artists Pty Ltd, an Aboriginal artists' collective, and to market their work. The works of the Papunya painters arrived on the Australian art scene just as Abstract Expressionism, Conceptualism, Minimalism, and Op Art were dominating the art market in Australia and elsewhere. The Papunya works, painted in acrylic on board and canvas, and often recounting multiple Dreaming narratives on one work, resonated with Australian collectors (Sayers 2001, 202–203).

▼ **10.5** Australia, Clifford Possum Tjapaltjarri (1932–2002), *Bush-fire II*, 1972. Synthetic polymer paint on composition board, 24 in. × 17 in.

In this painting the artist uses the colors of traditional bark painting to tell the story of Lungkata, the blue-tongued lizard.

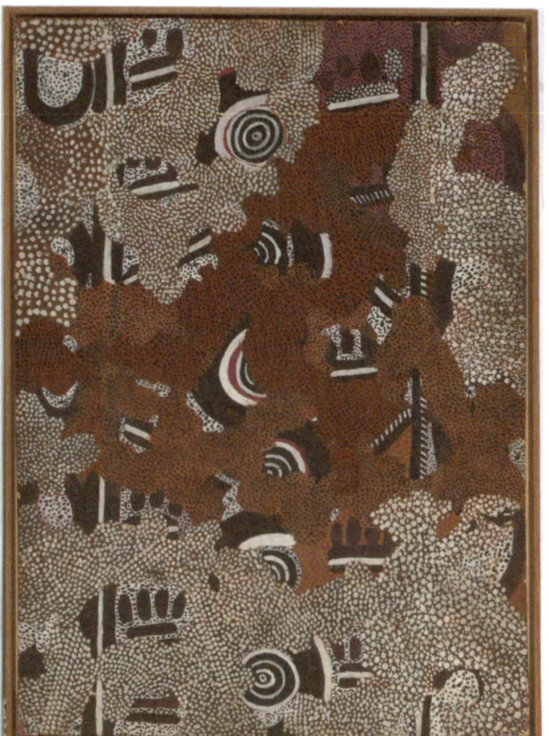

Clifford Possum Tjapaltjarri (c. 1932–2002), Bush-fire II, 1972 Clifford Possum Tjapaltjarri, a member of the Anmatyerre people, was born at Napperby Station, about 125 miles (200 km) northwest of Alice Springs in the Northern Territories. He began working as a stockman at age twelve, moving between several stations in the territories, and in the process learning six native languages and some English. In the 1970s he was living at Papunya station where he was a founding director of the Papunya Tula Artists collective, and served as its chairman into the early 1980s.

Although painted with acrylic paints on canvas, *Bush-fire II* (Figure 10.5) uses the colors of traditional bark painting to tell the story of Lungkata, the blue-tongued lizard, who, to punish his sons for eating a sacred kangaroo, started the ancestor of all bush fires at Warluglong (a site about 300 km northwest of Alice Springs). Tjapaltjarri inherited the right to this Dreaming through his mother's family. The painting depicts the origin point of the fire and its spread to the south and southwest. Concentric circles represent camp sites, some of which have been burned; arrangements of black bars are used to form the tracks across the land of an ancestral possum. In this way the painting functions not only as a narrative painting but also as a map of the landscape. Areas of brown dots represent the smoke and scorched land of the burned areas, while white dots suggest the clouds of ash thrown up by the fire. In addition to animating the surface of the painting, the dot patterns shield the sacred parts of the story from uninitiated males, women, and outsiders, revealing to them only the secular elements. Under traditional Aboriginal law, sacred Dreaming knowledge was to be shared only with initiated men. Tjapaltjarri's dot screen solution was adopted by other Papunya painters and ultimately by other Aboriginal artists across Australia.

UTOPIA SETTLEMENT AND WOMEN PAINTERS (1988–)

The success of the Papunya Tula Artists Pty Ltd. inspired other Aboriginal communities to form painting cooperatives. One such group was started in the Utopia region in the late 1980s; with few exceptions its members were women. In the 1970s Indonesia silk batik techniques were taught to the Utopia women as part of a program to combat poverty. The batik program received critical acclaim but did little to boost the local economy. In the late 1980s acrylic paints and canvas were brought to Utopia. The paintings produced by the women drew on their experience with batik designs and on body painting patterns used in the *Awelye* or "Women's" ceremonies. As was the case of the Papunya artists, the paintings were enthusiastically received by the mainstream art community in the major Australian cities and internationally.

Emily Kame Kngwarreye (c. 1910–1996), Emu Woman, 1989 The best known of the Utopia painters was Emily Kame Kngwarreye, a member of the Eastern Anmatyerre, who lived all her life at the isolated station, some 142 miles (230 km) northeast of Alice Springs. Although she had participated in the batik project at Utopia, the labor-intensive process was unsuited to the spontaneity of her art. In 1988 when she was in her late seventies, she began working with acrylic paints on canvas. In the eight years that she worked with the medium, she produced more than three thousand paintings, some more than 20 feet (6 m) long and 9 feet (2.7 m) wide. In her short eight-year career she had two one-woman shows and participated in more than fifty group exhibitions.

Emu Woman (Figure 10.6) is a good example of Knwarreye's early dot style before her work shifted toward bold, swirling stripes. The dabs of paint are laid down on the canvas in lace-like patterns to build up layers of intensely colored dots and lines that create the batik-derived effect of looking through several translucent veils of color. Although the colors of this painting are more somber and traditional, as was fitting to

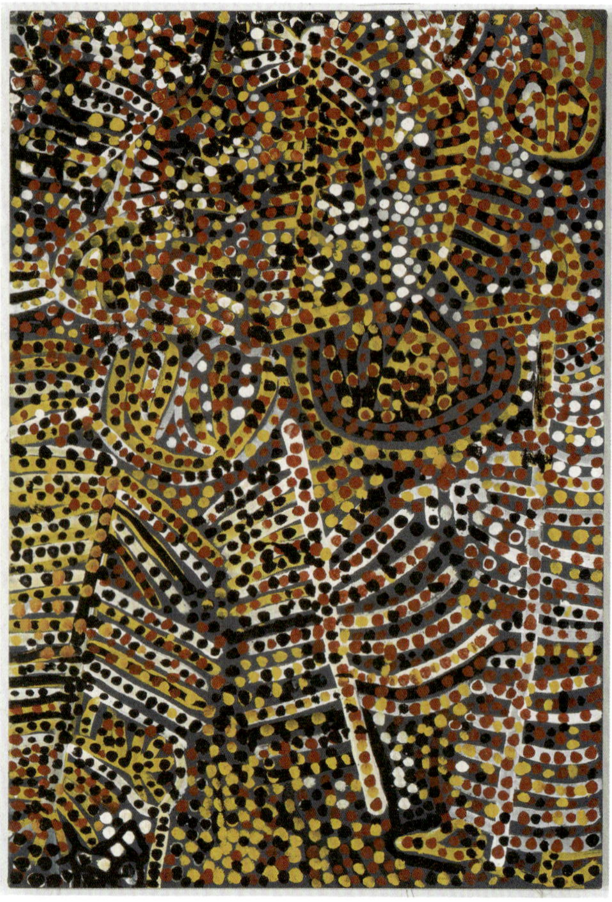

▲ **10.6** Australia, Emily Kame Kngwarreye (c. 1910–1996), *Emu Woman*, 1988–1989. Synthetic polymer paint on canvas, 36 in. × 24 in.

This painting recounts the Dreaming story of Bohra the Kangaroo and his emu wife, Dinewan, and how he created daylight.

its Dreaming subject, she often worked with vibrant, vigorously applied colors that gave her canvases a jewel-like glow. The left side of the canvas appears to be covered with frond-like leaves, while hidden in the foliage on the right is the emu. The painting relates to the sacred Emu Dreaming to which the Knwarreye family holds custodial rights. In one version of the story, Dinewan the emu was wife to Bohra the Kangaroo and at that time the world was in darkness because daytime had not been created. Bohra was happy to sleep but Dinewan was restless and began to complain about the darkness and her husband's laziness. She began to root around in the leaves on the ground, tossing them about, so that they sometimes they fell on Bohra's face, waking him. Finally, Bohra led his wife off through the bush in the darkness until they came to a clearing, where he told her to wait. He then set about rolling back the darkness until daylight appeared and the emu ran around happily.

Melanesia

Melanesia is a series of large and small islands which extend for some 2,500 miles, between the equator and the tropic of Capricorn, to the northwest, north, and northeast of Australia. The first settlers arrived in New Guinea when it was still part of "Greater Australia." However, New Guinea and the other Melanesian islands were not isolated like Australia when sea levels rose at the end of the last glaciation. These islands appear to have been along the main maritime route for peoples migrating from the mainland as well as from other island regions into near and remote Oceania.

New Guinea

The large, bird-shaped island of New Guinea is the most culturally diverse of the Melanesian islands; today it is divided politically between Indonesia and Papua New Guinea. It is home to more than seven hundred linguistically distinct peoples, each with a unique art style that was used in rituals to propitiate its ancestors, deities, and spirits, to ensure good harvests, or to mark important milestones in human life. Although none of these peoples seemed to have had a concept of "art" in the Western

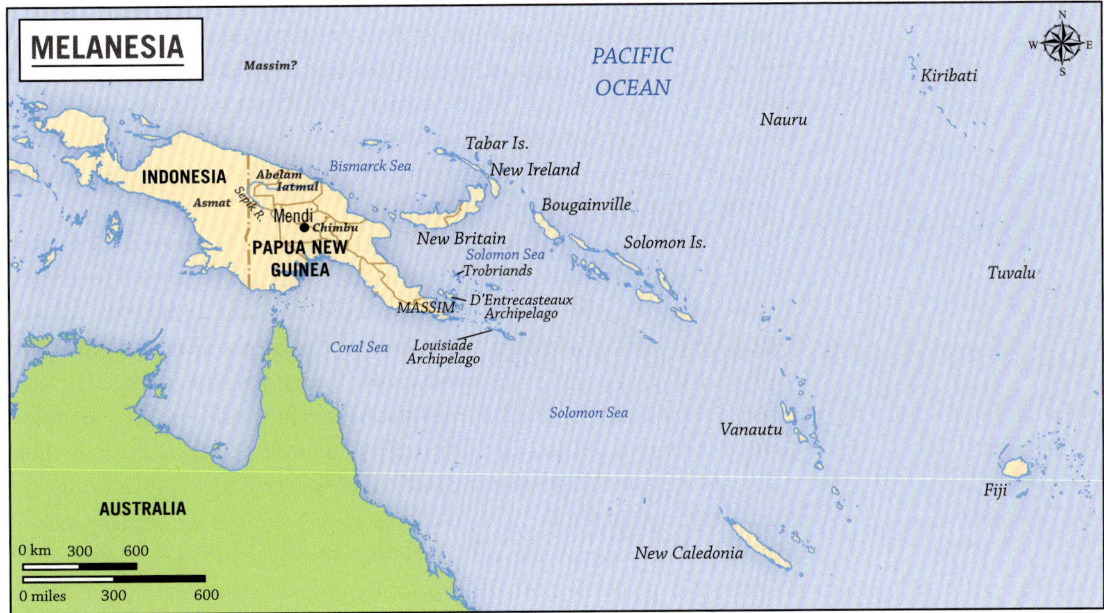

sense, every object, whether utilitarian or ceremonial, was beautifully crafted and decorated. By far the dominant form of expression was sculpture, typically in wood, and often enlivened, or in some cases animated, with the application of red, black, white, and yellow pigments.

Despite the wealth of art production in New Guinea, the island's art has been little studied. Many of its peoples live in inaccessible areas, some so remote as to be yet unexplored; while other regions, the territories of headhunters and cannibals, were dangerous to traverse well into the second half of the twentieth century. Among the cultures that have received some degree of scholarly attention are the Asmat, Abelam, and Massim peoples.

THE ASMAT

Although a few artifacts were collected in the late nineteenth and early twentieth centuries, the true richness of Asmat artistic production was little known before the second half of the last century. The Asmat homeland is located in southwestern Papua province on the Indonesia side of the island. This area of the Casuarina Coast is generally described as "inhospitable," being a mix of mosquito-infested marshlands and mangrove swamps through which upland rivers empty into the Arafura Sea. The first encounters between the Asmat and Europeans occurred in 1623 when Jan Carstensz was exploring the southern coast of New Guinea for the Dutch East India Company; finding the natives hostile and possessing nothing of value, he quickly moved on. James Cook experienced an equally bellicose reception when he stopped in Asmat territory in 1770 to take on fresh water; he and his sailors were attacked by a large party of Asmat warriors who chased them back to their vessel. Ships were warned not to stop along the Casuarina Coast due to the fearsome nature of its headhunting cannibal inhabitants. The first Dutch colonial administrative post in Asmat territory was established in 1939 but it was quickly abandoned at the start of World War II. It was not until the 1950s that the process of pacification, the joint effort of the Dutch government and Catholic missions, made the region safe for anthropologists and art collectors to do their work.

In Asmat society ***wowipits*** or master woodcarvers are highly respected. Their prestige is explained in Asmat creation stories about the hero *Fumeripits*, who was the first wood carver. Fumeripits carved the first Asmat ancestors from the sacred banyan tree and brought them to life with the sound of a sacred drum, which he also carved. For this reason, the Asmat refer to themselves *as-asmat,* meaning "tree-people." Asmat carvers are seen as continuing the work of Fumeripits in their carvings of ancestor images. The wowipits traditionally worked on their carvings in the men's house or ***jeu***. This long, rectangular, raised post-and-beam structure was the center of village life, where elder men decided village affairs, where headhunting parties were planned, initiation rites and other ceremonies were held, and important works of art, ancestor skulls, and ritual paraphernalia such as sacred drums were stored away from the eyes of women and the uninitiated. Inside the jeu, the supporting posts were frequently carved to embody figures of important ancestors; these carvings were seen as imbuing the jeu with the protective power of those forebears (Smidt 1993, 22).

Prior to the pacification of the Asmat region, much of the art produced was associated with warfare and headhunting rituals. The Asmat saw all deaths as resulting from the malicious sorcery of enemies. Consequently, the relatives of the deceased were required to retaliate against those enemies by organizing a headhunting party. Prior to the launch of the raid, the Bisjmam Asmat of the Central Coast would carve ***bis*** (also *bisj*) poles with figures representing those who had died. The completed bis poles would be erected in front of the jeu as visual reminders of the relatives' duty to avenge the dead. Despite the considerable labor that went into carving bis, they were intended for a one-time ceremonial use; afterward they were discarded in the sago palm groves or ritually destroyed.

Asmat Bis Pole from Omadesep, before 1950 During the 1950s, Michael C. Rockefeller collected several bis poles from villages around the Asmat territory; those poles now grace the Metropolitan Museum of Art in New York City. The collection includes an interesting and atypical example from the village of Omadesep, in the Faretsj region (Figure 10.8). The 18-foot-high (5.5 m) pole features two hierarchically scaled male figures, which instead of being stacked in the usual manner, face in opposite directions. The position of tsjemen is eccentric as well in this example. Normally this pennant-like appendage rises from the chest of a *bis* pole's topmost figure, but in this example the tsjemen emerges from the shaft of the pole between the two figures. Additionally, the lower

TAKE A CLOSER LOOK

Anatomy of an Asmat Bis Pole

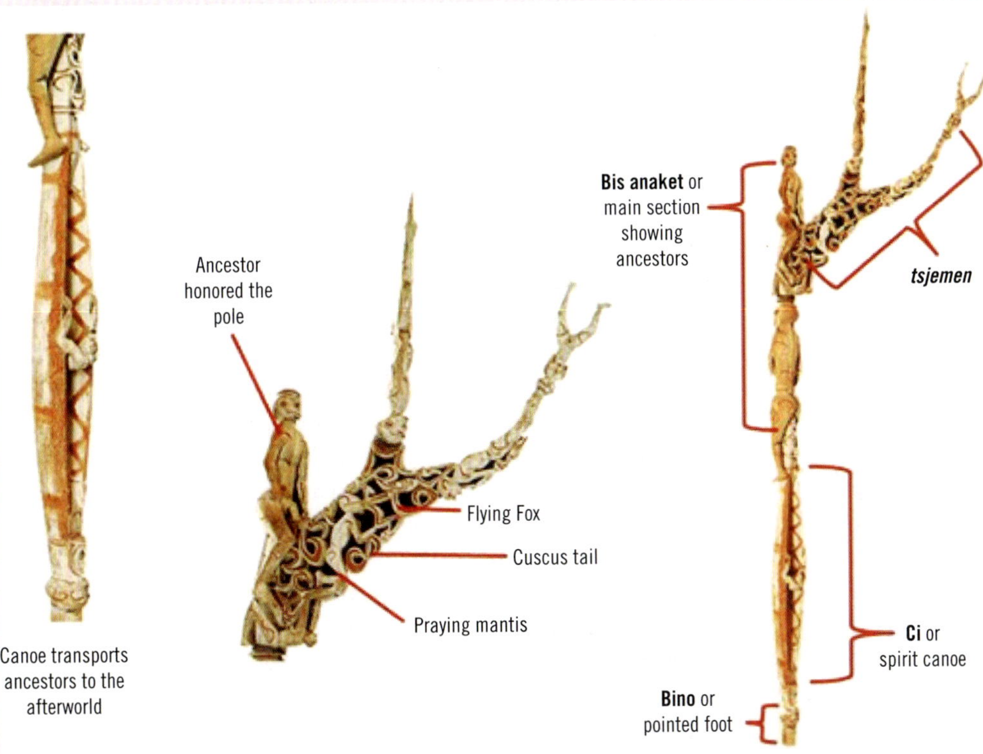

▲ 10.7 Anatomy of a Bis Pole.

The bis pole typically divides into three main sections: the foot with a spirit canoe, the man section with ancestor figures, and the tsjemen, wing-like projection that is usually carved in a openwork pattern.

The carving of a bis pole began with the selection of a mangrove tree of the appropriate size, the poles range from 12 to 26 feet (3.7 to 7.9 m) in height, depending upon the number of commemorative figures carved upon it. In selecting the tree for a bis pole the wowipits looked for one with a large buttress root, which, when the pole was inverted, served as the ***tsjemen*** (*cemen*) or symbolic penis of the pole. Before contact with the West, the poles were typically carved with stone and bone tools and smoothed with clam shells; now metal tools are used.

Generally, two stacked figures were carved on a pole, although there are some single figure examples. The figures are more or less naturalistically rendered and depict specific individuals whose deaths are pledged to be revenged; however, the figures are not actual portraits. The faces and bodies are generalized; they are distinguished by the surface decoration, which suggest body painting designs or scarification patterns worn by the deceased. Secondary figures may denote family members of the deceased. Additionally, zoomorphic forms with headhunting associations, such as flying foxes (bats) and praying mantises, typically decorate the openwork tsjemen.

The completed bis poles were enlivened with paint; typical colors being white, red, and black. Traditionally, the pigments, made from

(Continued)

ingredients found in the local environment, black from charcoal and soot, white from lime obtained by calcinating shells, and red from ocherous or from iron-rich clays, would be mixed with water and applied. However, increased contact with the Western world has led to the increased use of oil paints by the Asmat and other peoples. Very little research has been done on the symbolism of these color choices but in general white is seen as the color of death, human brains, sperm, fresh human skulls, and the staple food sago, red signified human blood and therefore life, and the black was used to indicate hair and to outline areas (Meyer 1996, 47–48). The paint was applied with the fingers, sticks, or bits of fiber used as a brush.

▼ **10.8** New Guinea (Irian Jaya), Omadesep, Asmat Bis Pole, before 1950. Wood and pigment, 216 in. × 39 in. × 63 in.

Traditionally, bis poles were erected in front of the men's house as a pledge to revenge the death of a relative. Once the vow had been fulfilled the poles would be taken down and left to rot in the sago palm groves.

figure stands on the prow of a canoe in which are seated two small personages. While unusual, the inclusion of the canoe is not unique to this pole. The canoe is most likely intended to be read as a ***wuramon*** or "soul-ship" and its passengers as the souls of the dead. Wuramon were carved for the *emak cem* or "bone house" ceremony, which had an aspect of avenging the dead and the initiation of boys into adulthood, since traditionally this required that the initiates take an enemy head. The incorporation of the wuramon on this pole may indicate that it was erected as part of male initiation rites.

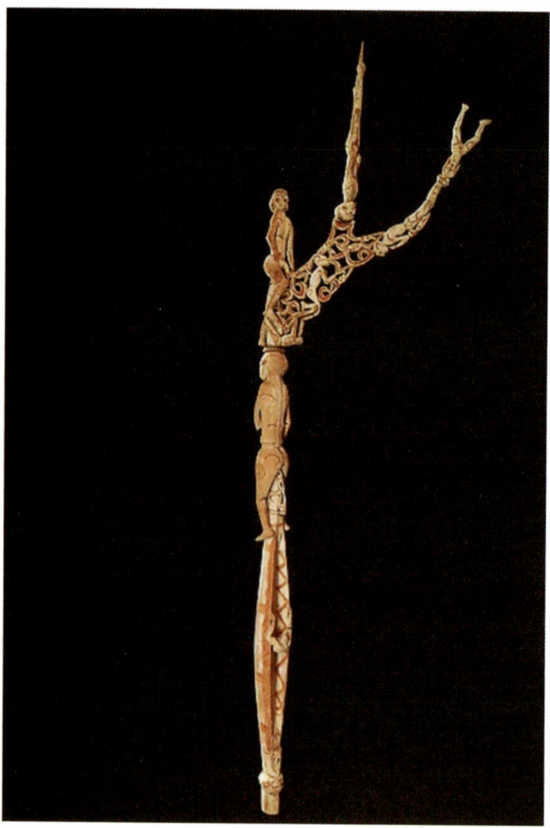

Matjemos (born c. 1930?), Hand-Drum with Praying Mantis Handle Matjemos was an extremely talented and original wood carver working in the village of Amanamkai on the southwest coast of New Guinea. His art was documented by ethnographer Adrian Gerbrands during the early 1960s, and while Gerbrands described his working technique in some detail, even filming Matjemos carving a drum, he gives very few details about the artist's life. When Gerbrands encountered him, Matjemos was a man of about thirty with a wife named Sèwos. When Matjemos was still a boy, his father and then, his mother were killed and he was raised by his maternal uncle Taunam. The details of his art training were not recorded but he probably learned from Bapmes and Bishur, two older wowipits active in the village. When Matjemos reached the age of initiation, he exacted revenge for the death of his mother by taking the head of a man from the village where she was murdered. Because his mother and father had been members of two different polities, Matjemos was able to carve for both the Amman and Awok jeus in his village (Gerbrands 1967, 53–81).

The 24.6 inch (62.5 cm) high *Hand-Drum with Praying Mantis Handle* (Figure 10.9) is the one created by Matjemos for Gerbrands' documentary film, Matjemosh (1963). Although not carved for ritual use, the drum follows the traditional hourglass form with a cutout handle. In Asmat society drums are sacred objects; Fumeripits carved the first drum and used it to play the wooden first ancestors to life. The drum's only decoration is the carving on the handle, which features three animals traditionally associated with headhunting: praying mantis, black cockatoo, and hornbill. The praying mantis is one of the more important headhunting symbols because the female of the species bites off the head of her partner after mating. The cockatoo and hornbill are fruit eaters, the fruit serving as a substitute

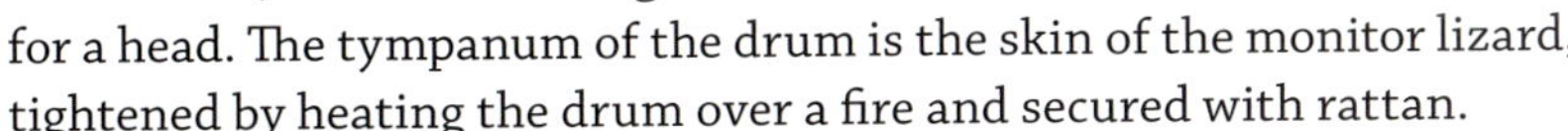

for a head. The tympanum of the drum is the skin of the monitor lizard, tightened by heating the drum over a fire and secured with rattan.

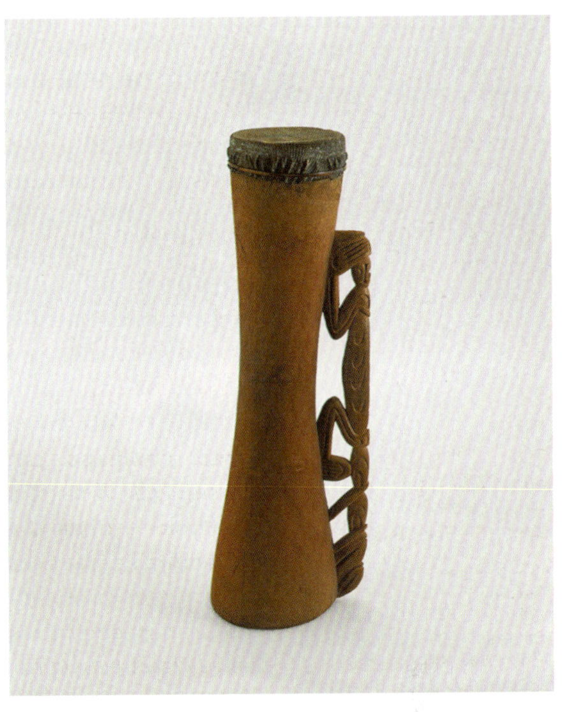

▲ **10.9** New Guinea (Irian Jaya) Asmat, Amanamkai Village, Matjemos (born c. 1930?–), Hand-Drum with Praying Mantis Handle, 1961. Wood and monitor lizard skin, 24.6 in. × 7.8 in. × 6.3 in.

The drum is the traditional Asmat hourglass type with a praying mantis handle.

THE MASSIM AREA

In the second half of the nineteenth century, the discovery of gold in far northeastern New Guinea spurred a great deal of interest in the peoples occupying the Milne Bay area of the "bird's tail" and the adjacent islands making up the Louisiade and D'Entrecasteaux archipelagoes, and the Trobriands. It was at this time that the culturally and linguistically related peoples of the region came to be known as "Massim," a term thought to be a probable corruption of the word "misima" or island (Young 1983, 4).—The point being that the name was not an indigenous self-designation but assigned by Western explorers and ethnographers who romanticized the Massim as argonauts and seafaring merchants engaged in a complex, long-distance exchange system known as the ***kula***. Fascination with the marine skills of the Massim and with the mechanics of the kula system has often resulted in the art and archaeology of the Massim area receiving less attention than might be desired. For example, many of the islands in the Massim area contain prehistoric stone arrangements, some associated with trenches, but relatively little is known about them.

Canoe Splashboard, Trobriand Islands, c. 1900 Massim carvers ornamented a wide range of items that were part of daily life and ritual practice, but seem to be mainly known for the decoration of the canoes used in the kula, a ritual exchange of white Conus shell arm bands for red Chama shell necklaces. The vessels used in the kula were often richly carved to show the prestige and importance of the trader. In particular the prows and splashboards were covered with bas-relief designs of extraordinary intricacy and delicacy, which were further enriched with the careful application of red, black, and white pigments.

The Massim recognize two levels of carvers: master carvers who have been initiated in the ritual systems associated with creative learning and uninitiated carvers who do not possess this sacred knowledge. Boys who exhibit talent in creating model huts and canoes and want to become artists may be trained by their fathers if he has been initiated. Artistic training includes both technical knowledge, acquired through observation and practice, and ritual or magical systems of knowledge or *sopi*, which must be taught to the initiate by a master carver. Even the master artist is not free to create whatever he wishes; the form a work is to take is decided by the person commissioning it. Additionally, each category of carving has its own traditional practices and associated patterns, some of which may be restricted according to the status of the person commissioning the work. Massim design motifs have been little studied or illustrated but they are thought to represent plants and animals as well as cloud formations and sea phenomena (Mosuwadoga and Beran 2006, 15–21).

Massim carving, whether in two or three dimensions, tends toward the symmetrical, although most works are not strictly bilateral; the two halves seldom reach the precision of mirror imagery due to small differences in the way motifs are expressed. The Canoe Splashboard or ***lagim*** (Figure 10.10), for example, deviates in that the pierced-work, interlacing "wave" band on the proper right side does not duplicate the position or exact motif of its companion on the left. The decorative scheme of the board is richly intricate and somewhat difficult to discern. The dominant motif of the lagim is a large pair of opposite-facing, stylized reef heron heads and necks which are connected by a central U-shape. The beaks of the birds have been recurved to form what the Massim consider a more aesthetically pleasing design. A second, smaller pair of birds, with beaks curving upward and back, interlock with the larger pair in a manner reminiscent of an M. C. Escher drawing. Contained within the U formed by the larger bird necks are rows of shell currency disks. Beneath this are a canoe-shaped motif and then a double spiral motif which replicates the basic shape

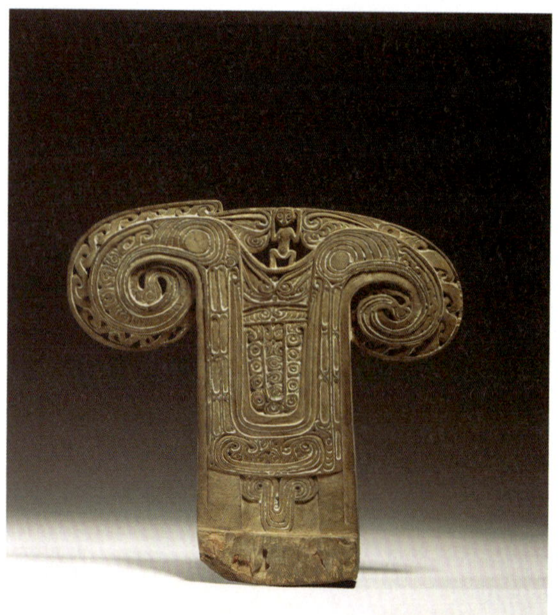

▼ **10.10** New Guinea, Trobriand Islands, Massim Area, Canoe Splashboard, c. 1900. Carved wood and pigment, 18 in. × 16.6 in. × 1.5 in.

Although the eye is immediately drawn to the easily recognizable human in the top center, the more significant motifs are the two sea birds with curving beaks on either side of the figure.

of the lagim itself. A single frontal anthropomorphic figure stands in the top center of the board; the figure may represent a clan ancestor. If the lagim is inverted, its rounded top replicates the form of an ocean-going canoe with a single mast and sail, creating a pairing with the carved canoe at the base of the lagim. In this way the lagim is reminiscent of the Massim ***gobaela*** or spondylus shell-currency presentation scepter, which depending upon the way it is turned may appear as single-masted canoe, as a stylized male being, or as male genitalia.

Mutuaga (c. 1860–c. 1920), Lime Spatula with Seated Drummer, c. 1880–1920 CE

The Massim carvers produced works of great aesthetic quality that were eagerly sought by collectors almost from the moment the area was opened to the West in the second half of the nineteenth century. The names and life histories of the artists who created these masterpieces are largely unknown. Their absence from the art historical record is a result of both colonial era bias and the presumption that history exists only in the written word. Had those pioneering ethnographers and anthropologists asked, they would have found that master artists, their styles, and their works were known to their Massim communities and that their stories had been passed down for some generations in oral accounts. One exception to the almost universal anonymity of early artists is Mutuaga, a master carver from the village of Dagodagoisu, South Cape, who was active from the last quarter of the nineteenth century into the second decade of the twentieth. Very little is known of Mutuaga's life other than he was married twice, the second time to Gaiomina, with whom he had a son born about 1915; that he walked with a limp, and never adopted Christianity despite his friendship with Charles Abel of the London Missionary Society (Beran 1996, 16–19). Likewise from whom Mutuaga received his artistic training is unknown, but based on stylistic affinities it is believed that he may have learned his craft from an earlier nineteenth century artist known as "The Master of the Prominent Eyes," or at the very least was familiar with that artist's work (Beran 1996, 126). Mutuaga left a corpus of more than 120 carvings, some made for the local community, but many more the result of commissions from Europeans due to the active promotion of his work by Abel.

▼ **10.11** New Guinea, Milner Bay, Mutuaga (1860–1920), *Lime Spatula with Seated Drummer*, c. 1880–1920 CE. Carved wood, 24.5 in. high.

This oversized spatula was probably made for ritual rather than daily use.

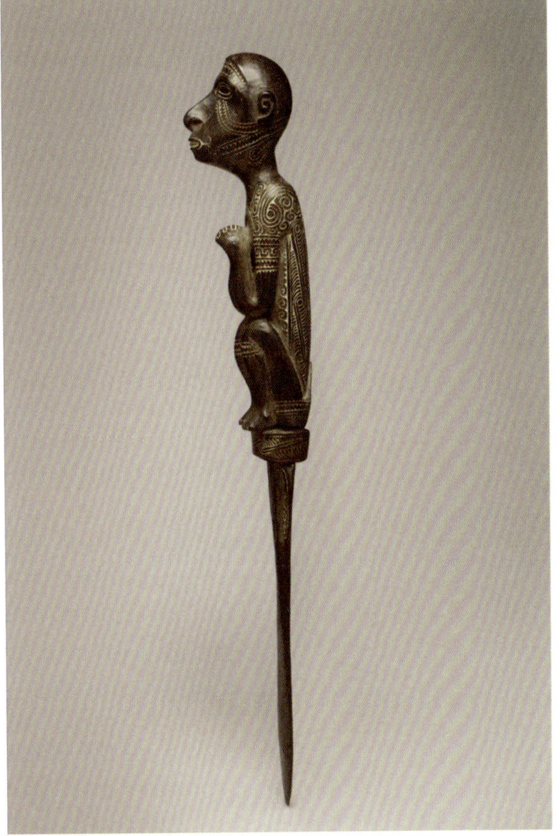

Mutauga's work is distinguished by a highly realistic and particularized rendering of both human and animal forms that reveals both a close observation of his subjects and an understanding of their basic anatomy. The seated figure that serves as the handle of the *Lime Spatula with Seated Drummer* (Figure 10.11) reveals a wealth of physical details such as prominent eyes, pierced septum, philtrum or vertical groove between nose and upper lip, well-defined helix and concha of the ear, supraorbital ridge, the bony prominences of the wrists and ankles, individualized fingers and toes, musculature of the limbs, posterior median furrow, and intergluteal cleft. Mutuaga has also taken care to render the drummer's shell armbands and body painting patterns. The depiction of the figure as seated on a stool is a new form that seems to have been originated by Mutuaga, perhaps as a result of interest from European collectors. Beneath the stool is a finely carved "gobaela" form, which serves as a stylized face for the blade of the spatula. The spatula, at 24.5 inches (62.2 cm) long, is a larger example and may have been made as a ceremonial object.

THE SEPIK RIVER CULTURES

Sepik River art first came to world attention in the early years of the twentieth century when the first German steamboat expeditions began exploring New Guinea's longest river, discovering its cultures, and collecting artifacts. Apparent stylistic similarities in the architecture, sculpture, and painting collected by early ethnographers and missionaries led to the definition of a "Sepik River Art Style" presumably based on a shared mythology and iconography. The style was characterized by the use of tall, gable-roofed ceremonial houses, phallic noses on the faces of figures, masks, and shields, and the tradition of over-modeling of human skulls. More recently, as the Sepik River and other New Guinea cultures have become better known, the construct of a regional Sepik style has been questioned as an overgeneralization.

IATMUL

The dominant art-producing center of the middle course of the Sepik River is a group of twenty-five autonomous villages, whose approximately 12,000 inhabitants speak some dialect of the Iatmul-Iambonai language. In the 1930s the British ethnographer Gregory Bateson appropriated the name "Iatmul" and used it as a cultural designation, implying an overarching socio-political cohesion among the villages that their inhabitants would have not recognized; some of the villages were allies while others were considered enemies.

Traditionally, much of Iatmul artistic production was focused on the ngaigo, either in the ornamentation of the structure itself or in the creation of the cult objects contained within. Additionally, everyday items were artistically embellished, often with the intent of making them more effective in use. Despite the wealth of art created by the

Iatmul, there does not seem to have been a class of master artists as among the Massim. Instead, every initiated man, at some point in his life, carved something; often with the oversight and commentary of elder men.

Ngaigo or Men's House, twentieth century Prior to the suppression of headhunting among the Iatmul and their subsequent adoption of Christianity, the ngaigo (Figure 10.12) or men's house (generalized in pidgin *Tok Pisin* as *Haus Tambaran*) was the ritual and spiritual focus of each Iatmul village. Traditionally, the men's house was where initiated men gathered to debate matters of importance to the village, plan rituals, curate sacred objects, and spend their leisure time. These massive boathouse-like structures sometimes exceeded 80 feet (25 m) in length and reached heights of 60 feet (18 m). Like the smaller domestic houses, ngaigo were raised up on stilts some 10 to 15 feet (3 to 4.6 m) off the ground to protect the inhabitants as well as sacred objects from river flooding during the six months of the wet season.

The traditional Iatmul ngaigo is often conceptualized as a crocodile. Its combination of projecting gable over a shed-roof appears to replicate the upper and lower jaws of a gaping crocodile. Additionally, some houses have woven triangular patterns on the sago palm leaf and bamboo walls that seem to imitate the bony external plates (scuta) on the crocodile's skin. Directly under the gable peak usually was a figure or mask, representing the face of the ngaigo. The lower level of the ngaigo was usually left open, the space defined by the heavy posts that framed the upper level. Each level of the house was divided longitudinally into two moieties with spaces assigned to each clan.

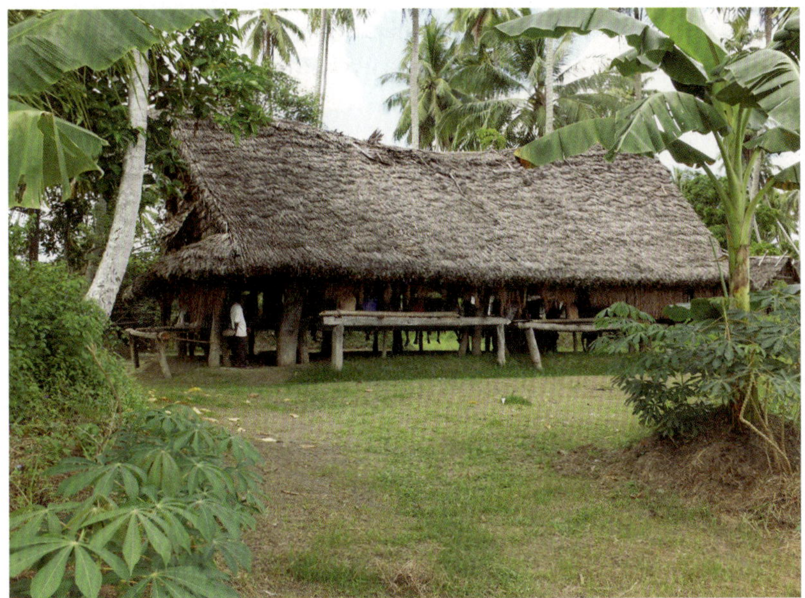

◀ **10.12** New Guinea, Tambunum Village, Iatmul Men's House, c. 2010.

The men's house of Haus Tambaran was the ritual and spiritual focus of the Iatmul village, where men gathered to debate matters of importance to the community.

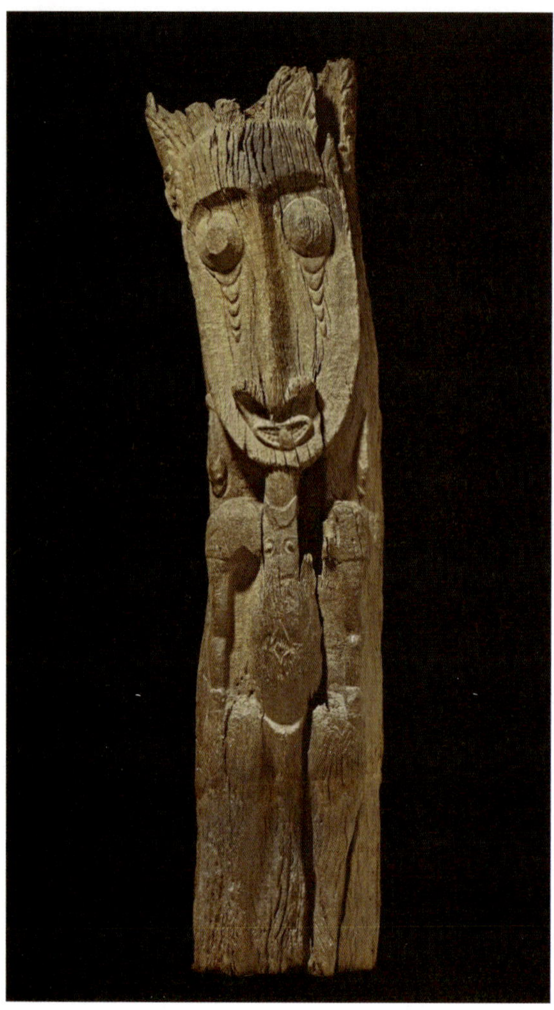

▲ 10.13 New Guinea, Ambunti area, Iatmul Ngaigo Post, c. 1880–1930 CE. Carved wood, 100 in. × 21.25 in. × 15 in.

Elaborately carved anthropomorphic posts representing ancestor spirits decorated the upper floors of traditional Iatmul men's houses. The animals carved around the figure were associated with the clans in the village.

The upper level was the sacred area of the house where the drums and flutes were stored, and the skulls of ancestors, sometimes mounted atop anthropomorphic food hooks, were displayed. Women and uninitiated men were not allowed to enter the ngaigo.

Ambunti Village Ngaigo Post, c. 1880–1930 CE The carved wooden post (Figure 10.13) from Ambunti Village is one of several that once decorated the upper level of an early twentieth century ngaigo; the notch in the top would have received a cross-timber. The principal motif on the post is a large human face, with round eyes, prominent nose, and open mouth; it is a type of image known as a ***ngwail*** or "ancestor spirit." In Iatmul carving anthropomorphic forms are often combined with those of animals, generally representing totemic clan animals. The Ambunti post has the remains of a pair of carved fish on either side of the face and another animal, possibly a turtle under the chin, At the end of the ngwail's chin is a serpent head, suggesting this ngwail is a wood spirit. Originally the post would have been enlivened with charcoal and ocher pigments.

Kawa Rigit or Orator's Stool The *kawa rigit* (seat of leaves) or orator's stool (Figure 10.14) was one of the most important carvings within the ngaigo; although resembling a chair, the orator's stool was not a seat but functioned more in the manner of a podium. Carved from a single large piece of wood, the orator's stool, along with the sacred slit gongs, usually occupies the central neutral area (belonging to neither moiety) on the lower floor of the ngaigo. As each debater takes the floor to express his thoughts, he carries a bundle of dracaena leaves, which he uses to emphasize his points by striking the chair with the leaves. As the speaker makes his points, he also recites the names of the clan ngwail, making a reference to past events, and then places a leaf on the seat of the stool for each pair of names. The figure carved as the "back" of the stool represents the ***wagen***, the paramount ancestor in the village pantheon (Silverman 1993, 395).

Although the orator stool figures may differ in style from one village or even one artist to the next, the head of the figure is typically rendered as overlarge, creating a proportional ratio of one-to-three or less in some cases. During debates the wagen is believed to temporarily occupy the stool, and the large scale of the head identifies it as the dwelling-place of the spirit. The head in this example is broad and flat as if intended to suggest an anthropomorphized crocodile spirit. The elements of the face are emphasized with charcoal outlining. The features are a mixture of human and animal elements: prominent stalk-like eyes, long phallic nose pierced for an ornament, and applied boar's tusks. The markings on the chest and shoulders of the figure replicate the scarification marks given to initiates to transform them into "crocodile men." The wrists and ankles of the figure are ornamented with raffia bands and around its waist is a raffia skirt covering its penis.

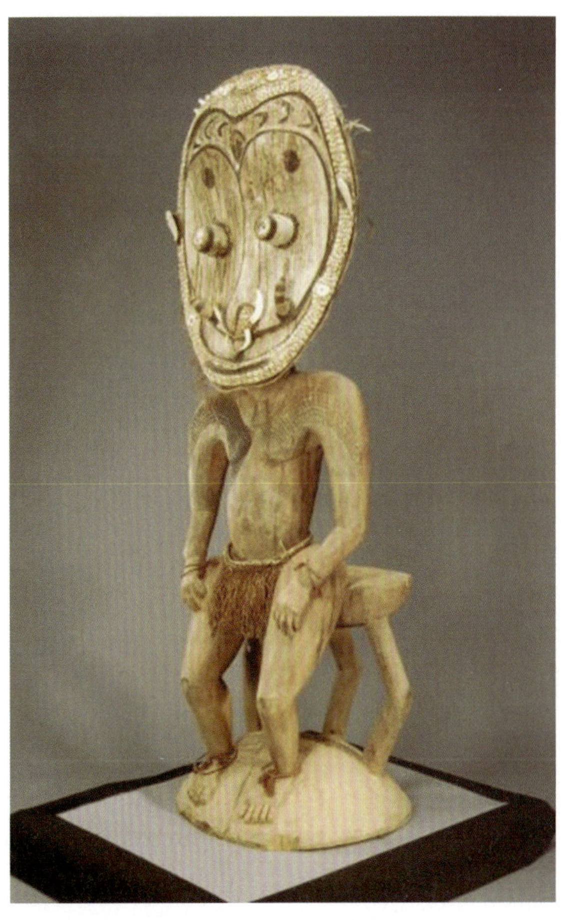

▲ **10.14** New Guinea, Iatmul Orator's Debating Stool or Kawa Rigit, twentieth century CE. Wood, clay, cowrie shells, paint.

These stools were not for sitting but were rather a podium used during debates in the men's house. As each speaker made a point he would strike the stool with a bundle of dracaena leaves.

THE ABELAM

Today, some 40,000 Abelam live in small villages on the plains and in the foothills of the Prince Alexander Range far to the north of the Iatmul and the middle course of the Sepik. Despite their current distance from the river, the Abelam are considered a Sepik culture. Abelam oral history and language suggest that they moved from territories along the river sometime in the first millennium BCE. As with the Iatmul, at the time of contact the Abelam lived in autonomous villages, each of which independently engaged in trade, formed alliances with other communities, and waged war against enemies. The Abelam had little contact with the outside world before the discovery of gold in the Prince Alexander Mountains in the 1930s, when the government post at Maprik was established to accommodate the short-lived rush of prospectors to the region. The town was abandoned during the Second World War in advance of the Japanese invasion. It was not until the early 1970s that Maprik was reoccupied and the government began a program of pacification in the region aimed at suppressing headhunting and warfare among the Abelam.

The Korambo or House of Spirits The Abelam ***korambo*** (Figure 10.15) is often generalized as a "men's house" or Haus Tambaran but it neither looks nor functions in the same way as the Iatmul *ngaigo*. The korambo is a dwelling place for ancestral and cult spirits (ngwalndu) rather than a meeting house for initiated men. The design of the korambo

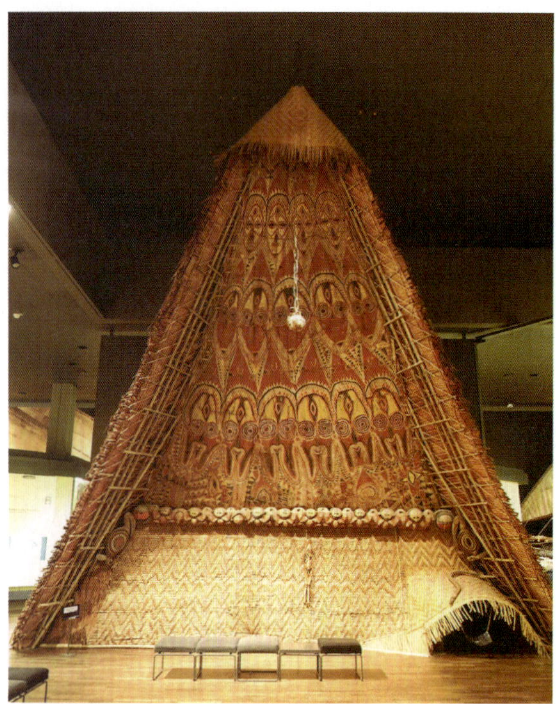

▲ 10.15 New Guinea, Maprik, Abelam Korambo or House of Spirits, twentieth century.

The Korambo is an A-frame house for ancestral and cult spirits rather than a meeting house for village men. Sacred figures used in male initiation rituals are stored in the structure's small interior space.

is distinct from that of the typical Haus Tambaran. Instead of an elevated post-and-lintel construction, the korambo is a modified A-frame structure built directly on the ground. It has a single, forward-leaning front gable and triangular façade. The largest korambo occasionally have reached heights of 90 feet (27.43 m) but the average is 50 to 60 feet (15 to 18 m).

The korambo's unique profile, which resembles that of an altitude obtuse triangle, is a function of its long, sloping ridgepole. Instead of being supported by a second gable of equal height at the rear, the ridgepole is supported by curved timbers or "crucks" as it slopes downward toward the ground, eliminating the need for center posts. Despite its open interior plan, there is very little space within the walls of the korambo as compared to the Iatmul ngaigo.

The korambo functions as a house for the major clan ***ngwalndu*** figures and other sacred objects and as a place for male initiation rites. Since the thatched roof serves as the building's sidewalls, the only exterior decoration is found on the façade. Typically the façade is divided by a carved and painted lintel into a gable zone, composed of painted bark strip panels that have been lashed together over a cane frame, and a base zone screened by a geometrically patterned, woven rattan mat; the entrance, usually a low tunnel, is covered with the same woven material.

Korambo Gable "Ngwalndu" Painting The painted decoration of the upper façade of the korambo gable (Figure 10.16) is one of the most important activities undertaken by the men of an Abelam village and the work is often taken on as part of the ritual preparation for initiation ceremonies. The triangular façade may reach monumental proportions with more than 900 square feet (274.32 m^2) of surface to be painted. Such large projects may require two or more senior artists to plan and draw out the design as well as the labor of eight to ten assistants, including apprentices, per master. While many of the men engaged in the project may be members of the clan owning the korambo, aspiring artists from other villages may also take part in the project as a way of learning their craft. All work together for the duration of the project under the direction of a supervising artist or master in an arrangement that is reminiscent of the atelier or workshop system (Forge 1962, 13).

In decorating the façade with ngwalndu (benevolent spirit) faces, flying foxes, and other standard motifs, inventive designs are not encouraged; the success of the painting rests upon how closely the artist's images follow the community's established pattern of designs; a work that does so is deemed to be "correct." The sail-like façade panel will be laid out on the ground and given a base coat of mud, either gray or black in color depending upon the locality; the mud serves as an absorbent foundation for the paint. While the mud dries the master artist will plan out the design, often using split cane to measure the sections and space the motifs in each façade row. If the façade is of sufficient size to require the service of more than one senior artist, the artists will divide the space up among themselves, taking care that their abutting sections blend together into a harmonious design. The master painter begins laying down the design at one side of the panel and working across, drawing in the component elements in white paint applied with a narrow chicken feather that gives a fine, fluid line. As he completes each portion of the layout, he will assign one of his more advanced assistants to add successive outlines, particularly around the eyes, in red, black, or yellow. Less skilled assistants are then set to work adding white dots or painting in the solid areas. Should a mistake be made, the offending area is covered with mud and repainted (Kaufmann 2010, 5–14). When the painting is completed the façade is hoisted into place on the front of the korambo.

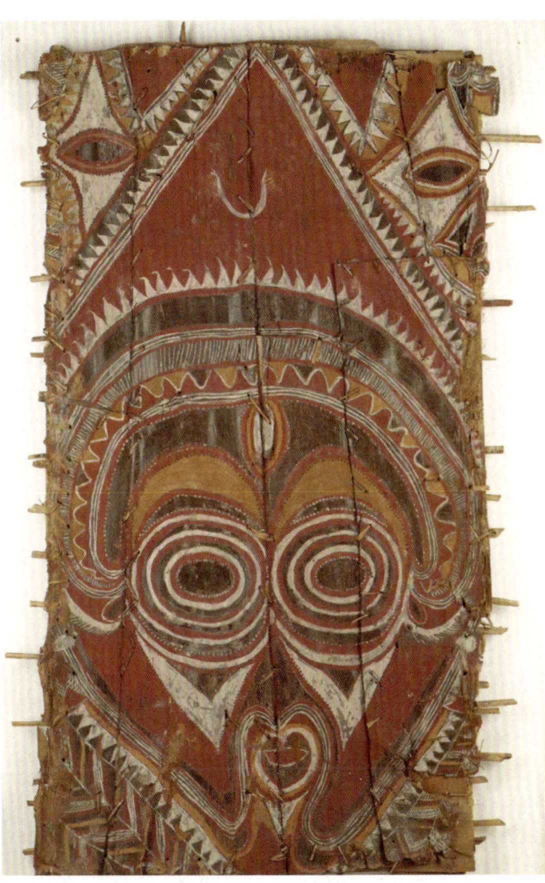

▲ **10.16** New Guinea, Abelam, Korambo Gable Painting, twentieth century. Bark and pigment, 73 in. × 33 in. × 3 in.

The designs on the façade include spirit faces and flying foxes. In painting the façade the introduction of new motifs is not encouraged.

Abelam artists typically work only in four colors: red, yellow, white, and black. The first three of these are derived from minerals: red and yellow from ochers and the white from calcitic stone or kaolin clays. These are crushed into powder and mixed with water and lime juice to make paint. Black is a different matter. If the undercoating mud is black, then the areas in the painting that are to be black will be left unpainted and glazed with tree sap. When the local mud is gray, a black pigment is made by chewing the scrapings from the bottoms of cooking pots with the sap and leaves of the native breadfruit tree; this task usually falls to the most junior apprentice who will spit the resulting paint into a coconut paint pot as needed by the artists (Forge 1962, 12–13).

Yam Mask One of the more unusual Abelam arts is associated with the growing, display, and competitive exchange of long yams (*Dioscorea alata*). The long yams are a distinct variety from the common food yam.

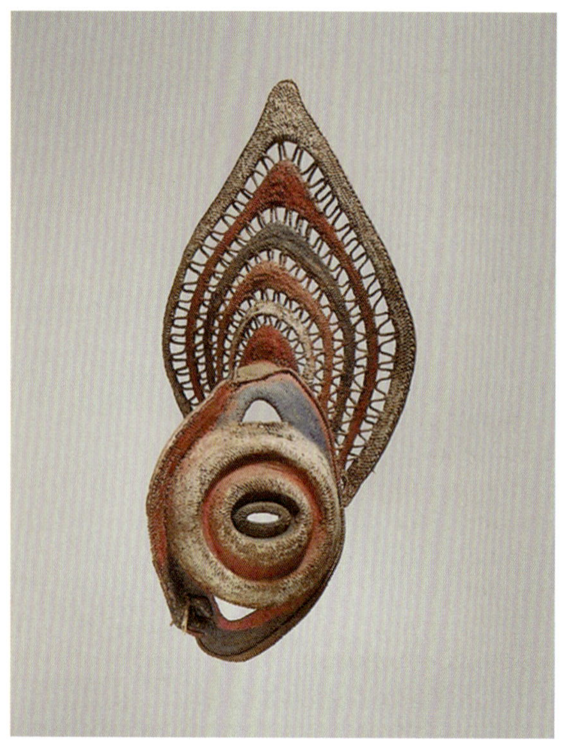

▲ **10.17** New Guinea, Abelam Yam Mask, twentieth century. Fiber and paint, 25 in. high.

These masks decorate long yams when displayed in front of the korambo during rituals of exchange; they are not worn by humans.

These massive tubers can reach lengths exceeding 12 feet (3.6 m) and can weigh as much as 140 pounds (63.5 kg). After the yams are harvested, they will be ceremonially displayed in front of the korambo before they are given to each man's exchange partner. Later the grower will receive his partner's yams and the man who has grown the largest yam gains the greater prestige.

Prior to the display the yams are decorated in secret by the men of the grower's lineage with cassowary and lesser bird of paradise feathers, brightly colored fruits, shell and boar tusk ornaments, and freshly repainted wooden or woven masks. The largest yam is topped with a triangular wagnen headdress, identifying it as embodying a particular clan spirit, and is given the name of that ngwalndu. Lesser yams receive a round disc-shaped headdress called *noute* and are given the name of a lesser spirit or more recently deceased ancestor (Hauser-Schäublin 2016, 124). Additionally, the surface of the yam may be painted with designs similar to those the Abelam use to decorate their own bodies (Losche 1982, 21). In the display the long, thick yams, considered to be male, are lined in the most prominent place while those that are bifurcated, and thus considered to be female, are set up around the periphery.

The basketry Yam Masks (Figure 10.17) are made by men from a variety of local materials including large grasses, palm spathe, and varieties of vine-like lygodium fern. These are woven into complex designs that include human and bird-like faces, with round, bulbous, or tubular eyes. The triangular crests of the masks often feature delicate filigree-like patterns. Traditionally, masks were painted in red, yellow, black, and white utilizing standard Abelam pigments. However, commercial acrylic and enamel paints acquired from traders have occasionally been used along with other commercial flotsam such as twist-ties and colored thread raveled from grain bags. The yam masks are only used to decorate the tubers and are never worn by the men.

New Ireland and the Tabar Islands

New Ireland is located in the Bismarck Archipelago to the northeast of the "bird tail" of Papua New Guinea. It is a 220 mile (350 km) long, extremely narrow island, which ranges in width from 5 miles (8 km) wide at its narrowest to 30 miles (48 km) at its widest point in the southeast. Rugged mountain ranges occupy much of the interior of the island.

Excavations in the Namatanai rock shelters suggest that the island was settled by at least 28,000 BCE and although the peoples of New Ireland were engaged in regional trade, the island remained relatively isolated until 1616 when Dutch explorers first sighted it. In the subsequent centuries the island was regularly visited by whaling ships, which brought the first metal tools. Metal tools made a significant impact on the art of New Ireland, particularly in the carvings made for the malangan. The majority of the carvings produced in New Ireland were made for funerary and initiation ceremonies.

THE MALANGAN

The memorial ceremonies that comprise the ***malangan*** originated on the Tabar Islands and spread from there to northern and central areas of New Ireland. The term is used to refer to the ceremonies, individual figures representing the deceased or other spirits, masks created for it, and the art style of these works. Traditionally, the family or clan of the deceased began preparations to host a malangan ceremony soon after the burial, but the process of planning the dances, collecting the food, and commissioning the carvings could take months or even years depending upon the financial resources of the family. The purpose of the malangan was to memorialize and honor the dead and also to help their souls to move on to the spirit world. At the same time, the malangan often presented an opportunity to initiate young men into adulthood; they would symbolically replace the dead in the community of the living. The intense missionizing efforts of the late nineteenth and early twentieth century negatively impacted the malangan and by the 1930s anthropologists working in New Ireland regarded the practice as dying. In the last fifty years the malangan has largely been replaced by concrete burial markers (Edgerly 1982, 554). Today malangan carvers are more likely to create carvings for the art market than for a malangan ceremony.

The creation of a malangan memorial figure began with the felling of a tree of sufficient trunk diameter to accommodate the carving of the image. The log was then cut to the required length and transported to a thatched hut for carving. The carving process was lengthy as the carving would cease periodically to allow the wood to dry out. Although the carvings were largely single-block pieces, additional elements, for example outstretched arms, might be carved separately and pegged into the sculpture. Many sculptures and masks had inset eyes of sea snail (*Turbo petholatus*) shell. The final stage was to energize the figure with an application of paint, beginning with a coat of white (powdered lime) and then red ocher. Other colors used included black (charcoal), yellow, and blue the last two being derived from plant sources (Bodrogi in Lincoln 1987, 25). Fibrous plants were used to make brushes but fine details were applied with a leaf stalk cut at an angle in the manner of a pen nib. Rattan, pandanus fruit fibers, or even short sticks might be used to suggest hair.

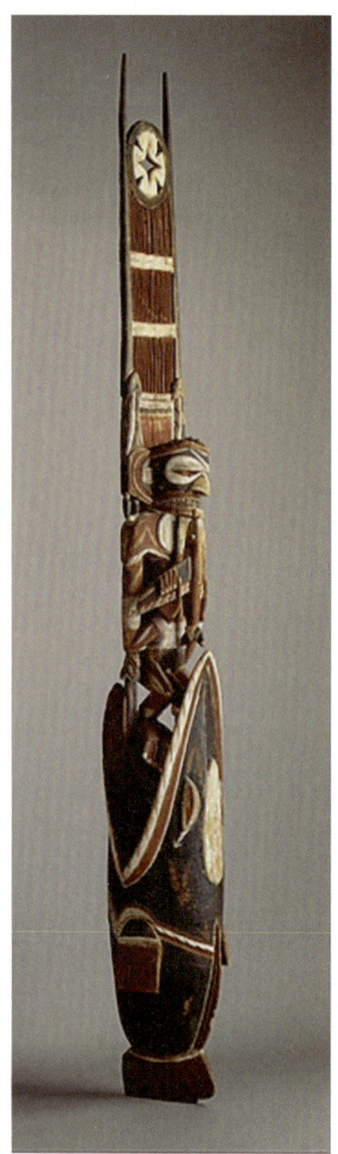

▲ 10.18 New Ireland, Malangan Funerary Carving, Malanggatsak type, late nineteenth–early twentieth century. Wood, fiber, and paint, 108 in.

This tableau figure shows a man being swallowed by a fish and is thought to reference not the manner of death but that of burial.

The malangan tableau may include several different types of figures, some representing important ancestors or mythic figures, and one or more representing the dead for whom the ceremony is being held. The figures of the deceased were physical portraits but identified the individual through the depiction of items referencing events in his or her life. The figures often have associated animal elements such as birds perched on the head, snakes along the sides of the body, or sharks which seem to be swallowing the figure. During the period of the malangan festival the souls of the deceased were believed to inhabit their representational figures and so were treated with the utmost respect. However, at the end of the ceremony when these familial spirits moved on to the land of the dead, the figures might be burned, taken to the woods to rot away, or sold to collectors. The carved masks, however, were stored for future use.

Malanggatsak Funerary Carving, c. late nineteenth to early twentieth century This *malanggatsak* type sculpture (Figure 10.18) stands 9 feet (2.74 m) high and is an example of the common "man swallowed by fish" theme in malangan art. Rather than depicting an event in the life of the dead man or his manner of death, the motif is thought to reference burial at sea. Cremation, symbolized by a hearth, and sea committal were traditional funerary practices in New Ireland. The man in this carving crouches within the mouth of an enormous fish, presumably a shark, while holding a smaller fish up to his mouth by its the wing-like fins as though he were speaking to the small fish. The figure's face is painted with black and white forms that divide the face diagonally above a grimacing mouth with blackened teeth. An elaborate openwork crest, decorated at the bottom with a pair of black and white snakes, rises from the man's head. The black and white snakes are New Guinea death adders (*genus Acanthophis*), an extremely poisonous viper identifiable by its triangular head, thick banded body and short thin tail (the skinny loops touching the shoulders of the figure). Two additional adders are found along the sides of the figure where they appear to be biting his elbows. The figure is painted to show ornaments that mark his importance. On his chest is a large *kapkap* worn by men in leadership positions and he wears shell bead bands at the ankles, wrist, upper arms, and around his waist.

Contemporary Art in Melanesia

After almost a century of colonial rule by German, British, and then Australian governments, Papua New Guinea achieved sovereignty in 1975. Although many artists in the new nation continued to work in traditional ways and materials, the first examples of modernism appeared in the late 1960s in the work of semi-traditional artists such as

Kauage Mathias, and then blossomed in the generation of young artists who came of age after independence. Many of these artists came from village backgrounds and made their way to the capital of Port Moresby to seek training from professional expatriate artists living in the city or to attend newly established schools such as the National Arts School or the Center for Creative Arts at the University of Papua New Guinea (PNG); still others went abroad to study in Australia or New Zealand. These first professional artists often incorporated elements of traditional community life and culturally relevant themes in their work but used Western media and modes of expression to explore changing concepts of identity and nation.

Kauage Mathis (1944–2003), Burial, 1990 Kauage Mathias was born and grew up in the Chimbu tribal area of highland Papua New Guinea, and after a brief stint at a Catholic mission school, he went to work as a laborer on a coffee plantation. As a young man in the late 1960s, he made his way to Port Moresby, where he found work as a cleaner. In the city he was fascinated by the cars, buses, helicopters, and airplanes but also frustrated by the menial jobs that were the only work he could get as an uneducated and unskilled man. His desire to work as an artist was ignited in 1969, when he saw an exhibition of drawings by Timothy Akis, a member of the Maring people from the Simbai Valley. The exhibition at the University of Papua New Guinea had been arranged by Georgina Betts Beier, an English expatriate artist. Beier helped Kauage to develop his skills as an artist first in drawing and then with repoussé reliefs done in copper and aluminum. In the 1970s, he began working as an artist and is credited for showing that being a professional, full-time artist was a viable career choice. Among the artists he taught were his brother-in-law John Siune and Chris Kauage (no relation). His achievements in the arts were acknowledged in 1998 when he was awarded the Order of the British Empire by Queen Elizabeth II.

▼ 10.19 New Guinea, Kauage Mathis (1944–2003), *Burial*, 1990.

Mathis drew on mythology and village life to find subjects for his paintings. In *Burial*, Mathis depicts the funeral of a village head man or chief.

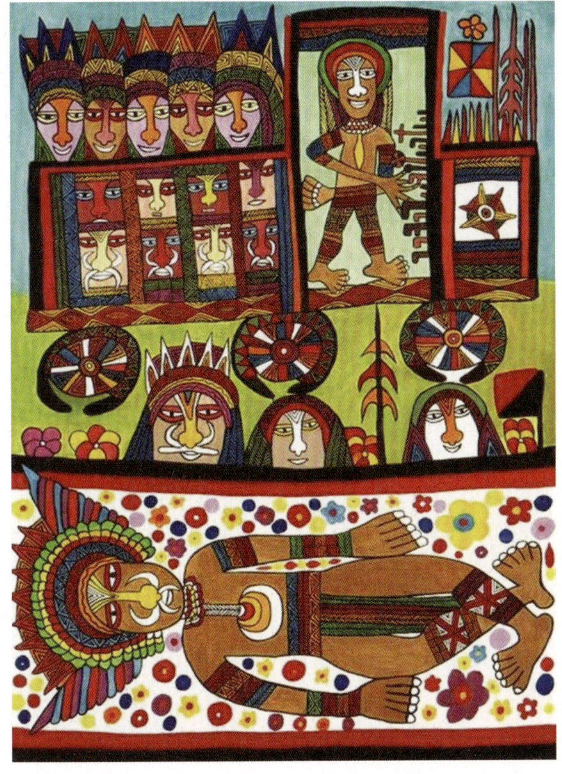

In *Burial* (Figure 10.19) Kauage depicts the funeral ceremonies of a village leader or “big man”; the dead man’s status is suggested by his elaborate headdress and shell ornaments. The body has been laid out on a flower-covered funeral bier; standing alongside the high platform are three individuals, perhaps family members of the deceased. Across a green expanse stands a structure containing shields, clubs, and axes, suggesting it might be a ceremonial men's house. A fourth figure watches from the doorway of that structure. While fascinated by the vehicles he saw in Port Moresby and the pageantry of Independence, Kauage often drew upon personal experience in his paintings, depicting stories from Chimbu myths and events in traditional village life, which for him expressed important social values.

Daniel Waswas (b. 1973), Look Within 2, 2007 Daniel Waswas was born in Mendi in the Southern Highlands of Papua New Guinea; his mother was a native woman and his father, whom he never knew, was Australian. He began his course of study in the fine arts at the University of Papua New Guinea and then went for further study in Auckland, New Zealand, ultimately earning a master of fine arts from the University of Auckland. Being mixed race in a country and time when tribal background was a large part of an individual's identity, Waswas was very aware of how Papua New Guineans perceived themselves and the impact of that mindset on the development of the country. His art advocates for national unity and the bridging of the divisions and tensions created by the extraordinary cultural diversity of the island.

In *Look Within 2* (Figure 10.20) the image of a young New Guinea girl in brightly colored tribal body paint, headdress and beads is repeated four times, creating two pairs of figures who turn to look deeply into their own eyes as if standing before their reflection in a mirror. Waswas uses highly realistic eyes as a means to draw the viewer into the painting and its subjects. In the background is the woven panel design from the lower section of the Parliament Building of Papua New Guinea

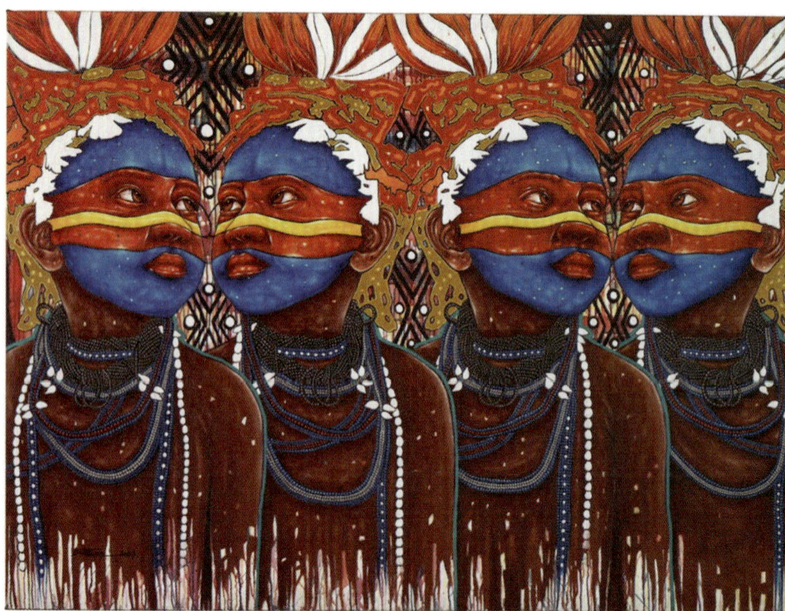

▶ **10.20** New Guinea, Daniel Waswas, *Look Within 2*, 2007. Acrylic on canvas, 77.8 in. × 59 in.

Four images of the same young girl seem to be looking into their own eyes in a moment of self-reflection.

in Port Moresby. In juxtaposing these young girls, who seem to be on the verge of becoming women, with the suggestion of a building that reflects the country's heritage and evolving future, Waswas is commenting on the fragility of traditional identities in a transitioning culture.

Micronesia

The region of relatively small islands, known as Micronesia, is located to the north of Melanesia and the equator. While Australia, New Guinea, and many of the Melanesian islands were thought to have been populated very early in prehistory, the first peoples arrived in Micronesia only in the third millennium BCE. Those first settlers are thought to have come from the Philippines, or possibly Taiwan, and to have brought potterymaking technologies with them to the Marianas. In the second millennium BCE they moved onto the islands of Palau and Yap in the Carolines. New migrants from eastern Melanesia began moving into the Caroline Islands in the first centuries CE and by the second millennium CE communities had been established on Pohnpei, Kosrae, and in the Marshalls. European contact was initiated in 1521 CE with the arrival of Ferdinand Magellan in the Marianas, and in 1565 the Marinas and the Carolinas were incorporated along with the Philippines into the Spanish East Indies. After the Spanish American War, Guam and the Philippines became territories of the United States and the remaining Spanish possessions in Micronesia were sold to the German Empire. Today, Micronesia is divided politically into the Federated States of Micronesia, the Republics of Marshall Islands, Kiribati (Gilbert Islands), and Nauru, and the American territory of Guam.

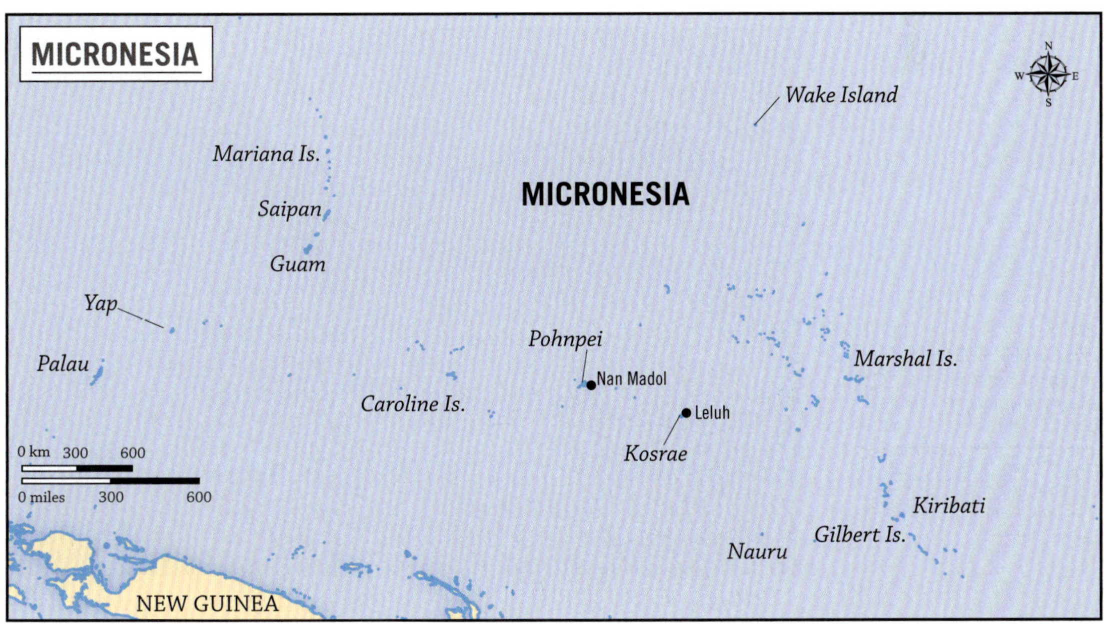

In all there are some two thousand Micronesian islands, ranging in size from less than one square mile (1.6 square km) to 212 square miles (341 square km) for the largest island, Guam. These include high volcanic islands, low coral islands, and coral atolls. The main groups are the Caroline, Gilbert, Mariana and Marshall Islands. Taken altogether the Micronesian islands constitute a land area of only 1,000 square miles (2,700 km^2).

The particular resources and geography of each island, or island group, are reflected in the materials, methods of construction, and designs of its architecture and the media of its associated sculpture, if any. In western Micronesia large rectangular meeting houses, for example the Palauan *bai* and the Yapese *pebacy*, were typically wood and thatch structures. Wooden buildings were also common in the Marianas but on Guam they were raised up 7 to 8 feet into the air on stone columns with inverted bell-shaped capstones, known as *latte*. Farther east on the islands of Pohnpei and Kosrae where prismatic basalt and coral stone were available, native architects built the monumental stone cities of Nan Madol and Lelu.

The Palauan Bai-ra-Irrai, c. eighteenth century In the traditional Palauan village, the ***bai*** (Figure 10.21) or meeting house was the most important structure. Here the men who were the elders of the ten clans met in council to discuss matters of importance to the community. Paired rows of stone pillars on Badrulchan Island and the similarly paired latte in the Marianas suggest that the bai's architectural form may be an ancient one. Unfortunately, very few village bai have survived into modern times; one of the few remaining bai is the

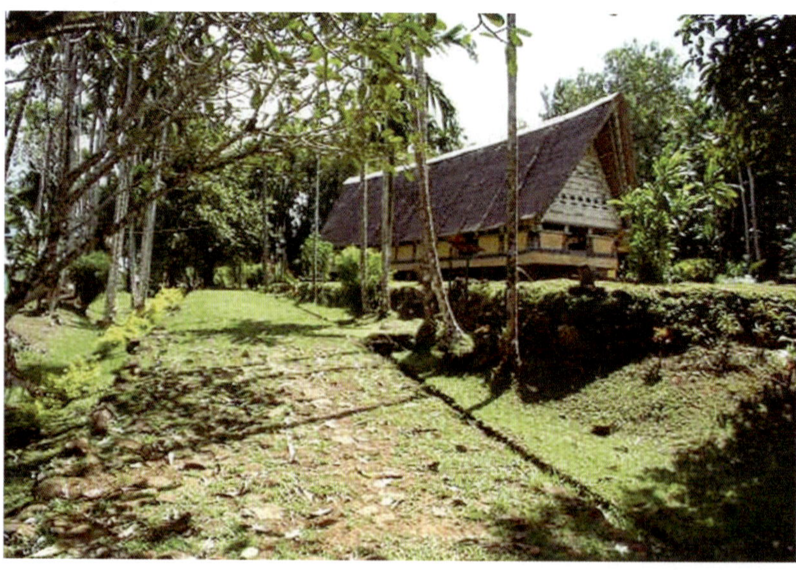

▶ 10.21 Palau, Babeldaob Island, *Bai-ra-Irrai*, Airai Village, eighteenth century.

The bai was a communal house where the elders of the village met to discuss issues of importance to the community. The bai at Airai is oldest of the surviving Palauan bai.

three-hundred-year-old *Bai-ra-Irrai*, Airai village, Babeldaob Island. *Bai-ra-Irrai* is the largest of three bai that originally stood on a 111foot (34 m) by 136 foot (40 m) stone-lined, earthen platform. Each building was raised up from the platform on an individual stone podium some 19 inches (48.25 cm) high. The two secondary bai, one of which was a rare two-story form, were lost during the twentieth century. Having multiple bai was a mark of a village's wealth and prestige since the villagers did not construct their own bai but paid workmen from another village to fabricate, assemble, and decorate their village bai.

Like the prehistoric examples, *Bai-ra-Irrai* was built on two rows of paired stones, at intervals of 6 feet (2 m) down the almost 70 foot (20.72 m) length of the building; the stones served as piers supporting the ends of eight massive ironwood floor beams, each measuring 8 inches (20 cm) by 30 inches (76 cm) and extending the entire 20 foot (6 m) width of the building. An equally massive sill, notched to lock the floor beams into place, brought the floor level of the bai to approximately 4 feet (1.2 m) above the podium. Rising from the sill are eight pairs of posts that support the rafters. Upper and lower tie beams stabilize the rafters and provide space for narrative pictorial decoration that visually recorded community histories and traditions. While most of the structural members were connected with mortice-and-tenon joinery, the roof stringers of the bai were lashed together so that each side of the thatched roof could be lowered, like a sail, during typhoons. Inside the bai the space was unobstructed except for two stone fire pits in the floor; there were no benches or partition walls. Access was provided by a wide door in each gable end and pairs of narrower doors on each long side. Additional illumination was provided by a foot-high gap between the lower wall and roof eave that ran all the way around the building (Morgan 1988, 20–25).

The gable ends and exterior walls of the bai provided large surfaces for painted decorations with both symbolic and narrative content. Four colors were traditionally used in painting: white derived from powdered lime, red and yellow from ochers, and black from soot or wood ash; these were mixed with parinarium nut oils as a binder. Once the elders of the bai had selected the stories to be depicted, a master artist would sketch out the designs and delegate their incising and painting to assistants. The decoration of the lower walls seems to be somewhat standardized, typically featuring bands of *udoud* or Palauan money (black crosses within a circle), Tridacna clam shells, roosters, demigods, and money birds (marked by holding or excreting money symbols). Decoration of the individual boards, called storyboards, that make up the gable facades is more varied. The images depicted on these boards reference legendary and historical events particular to that village and its clans. Bai-ra-Irrai's storyboards contain depictions of sharks, surgeonfish, human figures, canoes, houses, and trees; zigzag lines between figures represent conversations.

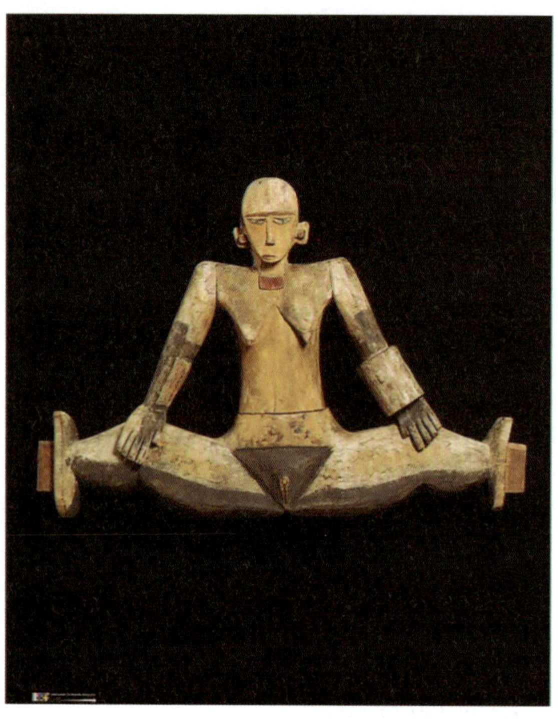

▲ **10.22** Palau, Caroline Islands, *Dilukai*, late nineteenth to early twentieth century. Wood and pigment, 25.68 in. × 38 in. × 7.87 in.

Many bai had Dilukai at the top of their gables, supposedly as a warning to village women to be chaste.

Dilukai, ***Palau, late nineteenth to early twentieth century*** In addition to incised and painted designs, some Palauan bai had three-dimensional carved images of nude females, called Dilukai (Figure 10.22), on their gable ends. A fine example from the Metropolitan Museum of Art depicts the Dilukai with her hair pulled back, wearing large ear ornaments, a valuable *bachel* pectoral, *derual* armband of stacked tortoise shell bangles, and tattoos on her arms and legs, which show her to have been a woman of high status. She is posed provocatively with her legs splayed to reveal her pubic triangle and labia majora; her hands are placed on her thighs as though she is opening her legs. The approximately 26 inches (65.2 cm) by 38 inches (96.5 cm) figure, like the bai itself, is a masterpiece of the woodworker's art. The head and upper torso were carved from one piece of wood, the lower body and legs from a second, and the arms from additional pieces, and then all were assembled with mortice-and-tenon joints. Local legends, probably influenced by Christian missionization, suggest that the image of Dilukai's in this displayed pose was placed on the bai either to shame her for her promiscuous behavior or to drive her brother Atmatuyuk from the village and prevent him from returning as it was forbidden for a brother to look upon his sister's genitalia. Other interpretations suggest that the figure is protective and is placed on the bai to protect the health and crops of the villagers and to bring wealth. This last explanation may be a sanitized reference to *mongols*. Traditionally, women were prohibited from entering the bai, except for the mongol or "consort of the bai," usually a young woman from another village whose family sold her into service at the bai (Kjellgren 2014, 129–131).

Nan Madol, ***Pohnpei, c. 1100–1600 CE*** On the eastern Caroline islands of Pohnpei and Kosrae stand two of the most impressive examples of Micronesian megalithic architecture and land art, Nan Madol and Leluh, respectively. The building of these administrative, ceremonial, funerary, and residential compounds coincided with the introduction of a new highly stratified and centralized form of governance in contrast to the earlier localized village or territorial rule on the islands. On Pohnpei Island construction of artificial islets in the lagoon of adjacent Temwen Island began around 500 CE with the quarrying of large prismatic basalt columns, weighing between 25 and 40 tons each, from sites such as *Pwisehn Malek* on the northwest side of the main island.

The stone shafts were separated from the volcanic plug by repeatedly fire heating and water shocking the rock. The large stones were then transported to Temwen lagoon and stacked in crisscross fashion atop the coral reefs to form the retaining foundation walls of each of Nan Madol's ninety-eight artificial islands (Figure 10.23). The resulting spaces were filled with rubble and coral debris to a height at least three feet above sea level at high tide. In all, these artificial islands comprise more than 200 acres (83 hectares) of reclaimed land with some of the larger islands measuring as much as 300 feet (91 m) on a side.

Construction of the monumental buildings on Nan Madol is thought to have begun in the twelfth century CE when the *Saudeleur Dynasty*, or "Lords of Deleur," conquered Pohnpei and established their seat at Nan Madol. According to Pohnpei oral histories, the dynasty was founded by two brothers, Olisihpa and Olosohpa, who came from *Katau Peidi*, a mythic foreign land. The brothers were said to have been powerful sorcerers who created Nan Madol through the use of magic. During the period of Saudeleur rule some 130 structures and twelfth seawalls were constructed at Nan Madol.

One of the largest and most impressive structures is the royal tomb complex on Nandauwas islet; the double walled compound encompasses an area some 262 feet (79.85 m) by 196 feet (59.74 m) or roughly the same size as a football field. The central structure is a prismatic basalt mausoleum over a subterranean burial vault thought to have been that of the first Saudeleur king, Olosohpa. Construction of the complex is thought to have begun around 1180 CE. Like the foundation walls of the islets, the tomb and its enclosing walls are laid in alternating header and stretcher courses, a pattern that both provides

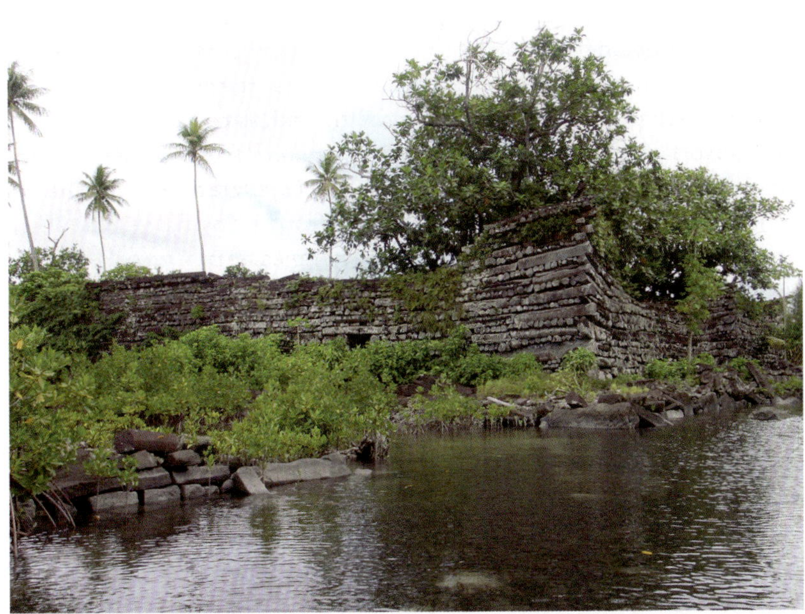

◄ **10.23** Pohnpei, Nan Madol, c. 1100–1600 CE.

Nan Madol was a complex of ninety-eight artificial islands that served as royal residence, temple, and burial sites. The island group was protected from storm surges by high, stacked granite sea walls.

structural stability and visual interest. Measured on the exterior, the walls of the mausoleum are approximately 21 feet (6.4 m) square, and rise to a height of 10 feet (3 m); the space inside the megalithic structure is much smaller, approximately 10 feet (3 m) by 13 feet (3.9 m) and 7 feet (2.13 m) high. The chamber seems to have functioned as a shrine or treasury; the accounts of nineteenth century visitors to Nan Madol describe its floor as having been covered by a large mass of shell ornaments and stone tools as well as later offerings, which included a gold crucifix and a silver-handled dagger. The tomb platform and its court were enclosed by a basalt wall 13 feet (3.9 m) high with its single opening to the west. The last four courses of the wall were cantilevered out to form a decorative cornice beneath its columnar basalt cap. A second larger wall, 26 feet (7.9 m) high, defined a large second court set some 18 inches (45.72 cm) lower than the level of the inner court and the same measurer higher than the outer walkway between the wall and the canal. Three smaller tombs of similar style but without enclosing walls were built in the outer court, one each to the north, south, and east of the main shrine. A unique feature of the outer perimeter wall was its upswept corners and entry opening. This effect was achieved by introducing extra stretchers and headers at the ends of the upper course to create the rise (McCoy et al. 2016; MacDonald 2016; Morgan 1988, 68–70). Although Nan Madol continued to be occupied, the Saudeleur Dynasty collapsed in 1628 CE after its defeat by a force from Kosrae.

Polynesia

Polynesia was the last region of Oceania to be settled. Its more than five hundred islands are scattered across some 800,000 square miles (2 million km^2) of the Pacific in a triangular configuration with the vertices being Hawaii, Easter Island (Rapa Nui), and New Zealand (Aotearoa). Early theories on the peopling of Polynesia proposed that its first settlers were a people known as the Lapita, named for the site on New Caledonia where shards of their pottery were first found. It was believed that the Lapita began moving into the Pacific around 1600 BCE but new research shows that they arrived in western Polynesia much later than originally thought, reaching Tonga around 826 BCE and Samoa around 800 BCE (Burley 2012).

While the Lapita may have continued to explore the Pacific and locate habitable islands, the movement of colonists into the eastern Pacific appears to have been a post-Lapita event. New dates, obtained using accelerator mass spectrometry (AMS) radiocarbon dating, place the arrival of the first colonists in the Society Islands around 1025 to 1120 CE, with the final push into the far eastern Pacific beginning between 1190 and 1290 CE and largely completed by 1460 CE (Wilmshurst et al. 2011). The rapidity of this last diaspora may account for the high

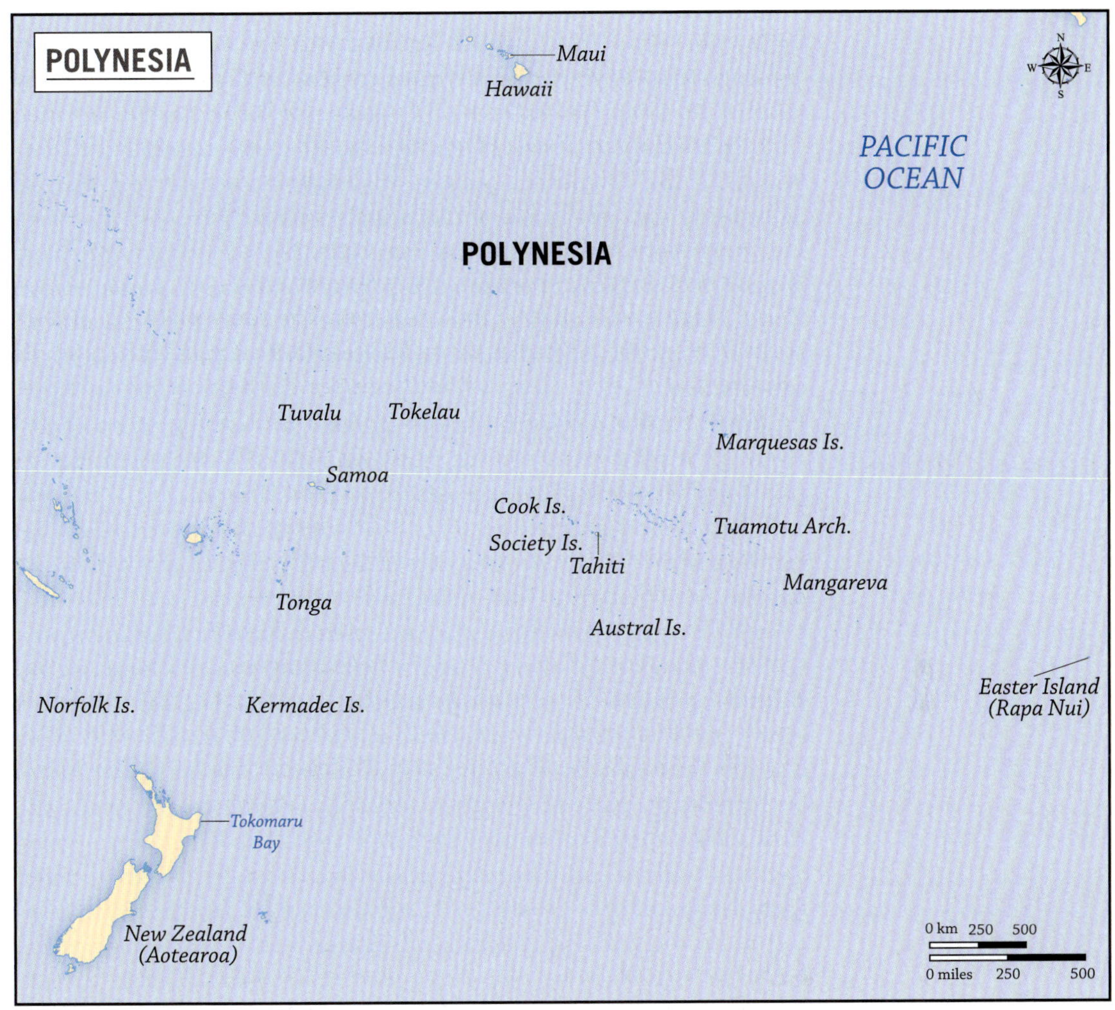

degree of societal and artistic uniformity found across Polynesia. In their canoes, these settlers brought with them not only tools, plants, and animals but also a highly evolved religious system with a pantheon of sky, earth, sea, war, and creator gods as well as local deities, the concepts of *mana* and *tapu*, and a highly stratified society headed by hereditary elite. Much of the art and architecture created in Polynesia was made for elite use and although local styles and media evolved to accommodate local resources, there are many motifs that are widespread across the region, such as geometric decorative patterns, stylized flora and fauna elements, and anthropomorphic figures. These were used in a variety of media, including carving, painting, featherwork, and on barkcloth.

Samoa and the Art of Barkcloth

Among the plants that were carried in the outrigger canoes moving out of western and central Polynesia into the eastern Pacific were paper mulberry seedlings. The inner bark of this tree was used in the production of barkcloth, generalized as with the Tahitian word *tapa*, although that term typically referred to cloth in its undecorated state; each island group had its own designation for the painted or finished cloth. With the exception of New Zealand where the tree did not flourish, all of the Polynesian peoples originally made barkcloth for use as bedding and clothing, for ritual and funerary purposes, and as a medium of ceremonial exchange. The production of barkcloth on many islands ceased after the arrival of Europeans and manufactured cotton cloth. Today barkcloth is made primarily in Tonga where the decorated cloth is known as *ngatu* and to a lesser extent in Samoa, where it is called ***siapo***.

The manufacture of barkcloth is done by women, often collectively, although men carved the tools and might help with planting the paper mulberry trees (*Broussonetia papyrifera*). The process of making the cloth begins with the cutting of saplings of the desired thickness (about 2 inches in diameter) and peeling off the bark and separating out the inner bark from that of the outer which is discarded. The strips of inner bark are soaked to soften the fibers before beating them on a wooden anvil with mallets. During the beating process the strips are thinned and spread until they are about twice their original width. The strips are joined together to form sheets of several layers, often using the starch of *kumara* (sweet potato) or manioc (cassava) as a binder; both plants are native to South America. Depending on the size of the cloth, the joining and layering process may take several hours or even days to complete. The cloth is then laid out on a work surface covered with design stencils (*kupesi* in Tonga or *upeti* in Samoa) made from coconut frond midribs. A light reddish brown *koka* (*Bischofia javanica*) bark dye is dabbed over these stencils to transfer the design pattern to the sheet. When the pattern has been transferred the sheet will be laid out to dry and a darker brown pigment, made from mangrove bark, will be used to accent the stencil design or to paint in freehand elements. Occasionally, yellow, red, and purple dyes are also used in Samoa and Tonga; however, black is rarely used except in tapa produced in Melanesia (Fiji).

Siapo with Banana Pod and Trochus Shell Motifs, twentieth century Few early examples of Polynesian tapa cloth have been preserved, in large part, due to the nature of the material, which is, in essence, a heavy paper, and considerably less durable than woven cloth. Traditionally thirteen basic patterns were used in Samoan siapo painting but each pattern could be elaborated in different ways. In addition to wavy line and net patterns, siapo designs were inspired by common animals: sandpiper, starfish, Trochus shells, worms and centipedes, and plants: banana, breadfruit, pandanus leaf, frangipani flowers.

The design of the *Siapo with Banana Pod and Trochus Shell Motifs* (Figure 10.24) was created by laying the tapa over a upeti or stencil

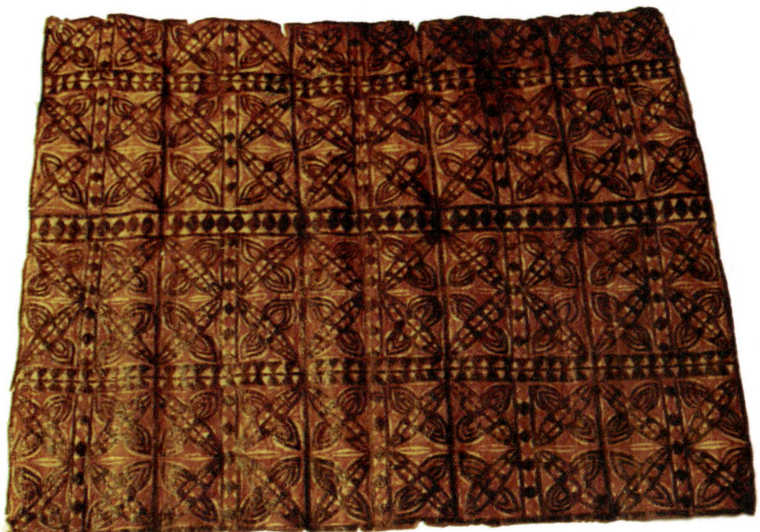

◀ 10.24 Samoa, Siapo with Banana Pod and Trochus Shell Motifs, twentieth century. Approx. 6 ft. × 8 ft.

At one time barkcloth was made on most of the Polynesian islands for clothing, bedding, funerary use, and as items of prestige and elite exchange. The introduction of European cloth and missionaries led to elimination of barkcloth on many islands.

featuring blocks of blooming banana pods (*Fa'a tumoa or Fa'a moa fai*) separated by rows of triangular Trochus shells (*Fa'a 'ali'ao*). Certain parts of the design were emboldened with darker brown pigment such as the alternating light on dark and dark on light bands of Trochus "diamonds." The blooming banana pod design was especially popular in the first half of the twentieth century (Pritchard 1984, 44).

Hawaii and the Art of Featherwork

While all classes in Polynesian society wore tapa cloth garments for daily use, albeit those of elites tended to be finer and softer than those of commoners, individuals of the highest status in eastern Polynesia were distinguished by their use of featherwork garments, helmets, staffs, and standards. Unfortunately, relatively few of these fragile items have survived into the modern era; many of those that have, were collected in the late eighteenth and early nineteenth centuries by early explorers, including Captain Cook and his officers. Both the production of featherwork and tapa declined rapidly with missionization and political change after European contact. The best known feathered garments are the colorful circular cloaks (*'ahu'ula*) and helmets (*mahiole*) of Hawaii, but trapezoidal capes were also made in Hawaii, New Zealand, and in the Society Islands, where they were part of the Tahitian mourning costume.

Feathers, particularly red ones, were difficult to obtain in many areas of Polynesia, and were highly valued because red was seen as a color suitable for chiefly and divine use (Hiroa 1944, 9). In Hawaii, red was associated with the manifestations of the god Ku, yellow with Kane, and black with Lono (Valeri 1985, 12). In Tahiti, red and yellow were associated with Ta'aroa, who is described in myth as an anthropomorphized bird that, by shaking out the red and yellow feathers from his plumage, created the island's covering flora. Birds and their feathers are often used annalistically in Hawaiian chants and stories to describe the qualities of individuals, particularly chiefs in their featherwork cloaks (Caldeira et al. 2015, 132–4).

The creation of a feathered garment was a process that took many months, if not years, to complete. The collection of the desired feathers from forest songbirds (honeycreepers), itself could take several seasons. Yellow feathers were collected from the *o'o* and *mamo* birds (both now extinct) during molting season, when the birds would be caught, a few yellow feathers plucked out and the bird released. The red feathers were taken from the *'i'iwi* and *'apapane*, which were killed, plucked, and eaten (Hiroa 1957, 218–291). Black feathers were taken from all of these bi-colored birds. The creation of a single cape required thousands of feathers; a recreation of King Kamehameha I's yellow cape required 250,000 much larger pheasant feathers and the equivalent of 511 days' work (Hamm 2014). The original is estimated to contain between 450,000 and 500,000 *mamo* feathers. Once sufficient feathers had been collected, they were attached in rows, beginning at the bottom, to a foundation of netting made from the inner bark of the *olona* (*Touchardia latifolia*) shrub. Several sections of netting might be joined together to form the shape of the cloak or other garment. The small feathers were gathered into bunches of eighteen feathers and the quills tied together with a piece of olona fiber. These small bunches were then tied, or in some cases glued, to the netting in overlapping rows so that the resulting surface resembles a plush velvet (Hiroa 1944, 10–16). Little is known about the makers of these garments; the assumption in the literature has been that they were made by men. Men were certainly employed in the collection of feathers and making the netting, but the fine handwork of sorting feathers, tying them into bunches, and perhaps sewing them onto the netting could have been performed by women as there was no prohibition against their handling feathers. High ranking women were also known to have owned and controlled feather cloaks (Brigham 1899, 55; Linnekin 1988, 266–274).

Hawaiian Cloak or 'Ahu'ula, eighteenth century This *ahu'ula*, literally "red garment" (Figure 10.25), is one of two Hawaiian cloaks believed to have been collected by Charles Clerke, captain of the *H.M.S. Discovery* during Captain Cook's third voyage of discovery (1776–1780). The cloak is recorded as having been presented to Captain Clerke in 1778, by Kahekili II (c. 1737–1794), King of Maui. After Clerke's death in 1779, his collection passed to Sir Joseph Banks and, through him, into the British Museum in 1780.

Feathered cloaks were highly valued and often passed down through the generations as a means of legitimating authority. The

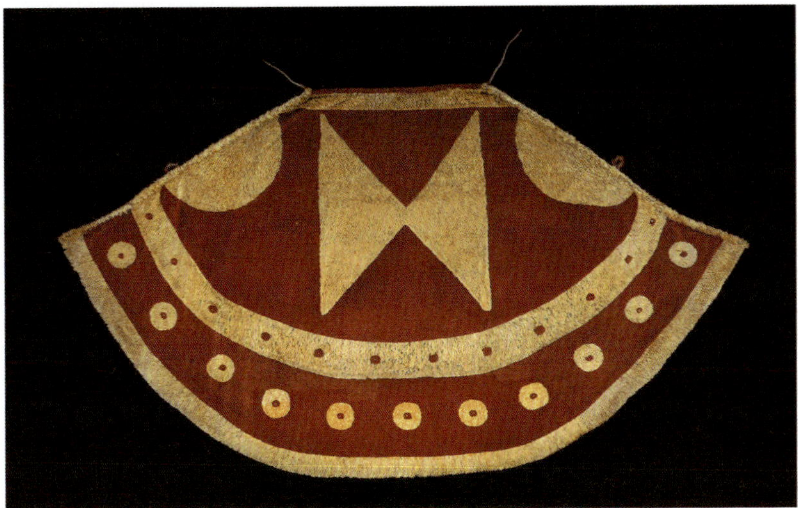

◀ 10.25 Hawaii, Hswaiian Cloak or 'Ahu'ula, eighteenth century. Olona fibre, honeyeater and honeycreeper feathers, 66 in. × 116 in.

Feather garments were highly valued by the kings and nobles of Hawaii and were passed down through the generations as symbols of power and authority. This is one of two cloaks collected on Captain Cook's voyage.

gifting of such an important elite garment suggests the enormous respect afforded to Captain Clerke by King Kahekili; it may well have been a cloak that was taken as a war prize and was unsuitable for the king's own use because its design was associated with another chiefly lineage. The length of the cloak and its use of rare red and yellow feathers marked it as the property of a wealthy *ali'i*; chiefs of lesser rank had shorter capes, often worked with large quantities of domestic fowl feathers and smaller numbers of the rare mamo and i'iwi plumes. The pattern of this cloak is an unusual one, featuring a prominent bow tie motif of congruent yellow triangles set into a red field between yellow half-moon shapes. When the cloak was worn, the half-moons formed a full circle on the chest of the wearer. Below these large geometric elements is a yellow band with a dozen red dots in a row, a red band with eleven yellow rings, and finally a plain yellow band at the hem. 'Ahu'ula motifs have been little studied, but the elements on this cloak are reminiscent of the trochus shell and rolled pandanus leaf patterns of Samoan sipao. Other common motifs found on the 160 surviving cloaks and capes include circles, triangles, diamonds, stripes, and especially crescents with a high central peak; less common were self-colored pieces such as King Kamehameha's yellow cloak.

Rapa Nui and the Moai

Rapa Nui, christened Easter Island by the Dutch explorer Jacob Roggeveen in 1722, is a triangularly shaped, volcanic island that marks the easternmost point of Polynesian colonization of the Pacific. Recent radiocarbon dates place the arrival of the first settlers during the period between 1200 and 1253 CE, when increased El Niño activity facilitated movements to more remote islands (Wilmshurst et al. 2011, 1817–18). According to the traditional histories of Rapa Nui, its first settlers arrived in two double-hulled canoes led by the great chief

Hotu Matu'a who landed at Anakena beach. The island they found was covered with palm and *toromiro* forests but supported little indigenous animal life other than two varieties of lizards and several species of mainly marine birds.

Socio-political organization and the production of art on Rapa Nui followed traditional Polynesian prototypes. The island was divided among ten clan lineages or mata, each led by a chief or *ariki*, who claimed one of the sons of Hotu Matu'a as founding ancestor. Supreme over these was the *ariki mau* or paramount chief who was considered a living god. The ariki mau was usually the highest ranking *Honga* chief of the royal *Miru* clan. Each of these chiefs, according to his rank and wealth, commissioned elite goods and artworks as displays of his personal prestige. However, the greatest effort seems to have gone into the production of religious architecture and art in the form of the burial and ceremonial platforms known as *ahu* and monumental stone statues or ***moai*** erected on them.

The Rapa Nui moai were first noted in the journals of Admiral Roggeveen, who, in 1722, recorded seeing many standing stone idols ringing the island. When Captain Cook visited a half century later some of the statues had fallen but most were still standing. Through a Tahitian interpreter, Cook determined that each moai had a name and that the moai represented important ariki or clan chiefs (Beaglehole 1961, 359). The period of ahu building and moai carving seems to have commenced soon after the first settlers arrived on Rapa Nui; intensified after 1400 CE, and then declined after 1550 CE or perhaps slightly later. In all some 887 moai were carved by the Rapa Nui masters but only a quarter of that number were erected on coastal ahus where they look inland toward the lands and gardens of the erecting clans.

Most moai were carved from the volcanic tuff of Raro Raraku on the eastern side of the island; a few others were sculpted from basalt, trachyte, or red scoria. Two characteristics made tufa rock the preferred medium. The first was its distinctive yellow-red color when first quarried; the color was similar to that used for elite body painting. The second was the ease with which the material could be worked. Only a few artisans, utilizing basalt tools, were needed to carve even a very large moai. The process began with a large rectangular block of stone being carved from the rock wall and partially undercut and braced to keep it from breaking free. A master artist would then establish the details of the head and face, and establish a median line running from the figure's nose to navel to ensure bilateral symmetry in the finished moai. After the sculpture was removed from the quarry, the final detailing was done and the surface polished with coral abraders (Kjellgren 2001, 26–28).

The average moai stands about 13 feet (3.9 m) high and weighs between 8 and 11 tons. The largest ever erected was Moai Paro at Ahu Te Pito Kura; it is 32.63 feet (9.8 m) high and is estimated to weigh 70 tons with its topknot adding another estimated 10 tons. The enormous size and substantial weight of the moai has inspired a number of theories about the methods used to move the sculptures to their final locations. The smaller, earlier moai could have been moved feasibly on sleds and rollers and some of the later and larger pieces may have been "walked" upright by opposing teams of men who rocked the statue from side to side by alternately heaving on ropes lashed around the top of the statue; a third team stabilized the moving stone from behind to keep it from falling forward. Placement of the statues on their ahu platforms was probably achieved using log stacks and levers.

Moai at Ahu Nau Nau, c. 1250–1400 CE Typically, the moai were carved as monolithic half-length sculptures in the round; in only one case is a moai known to have had legs. Most have arms hanging close to the body at the sides with long fingered hands turned to rest on the waist. Three carving styles seemed to have evolved over the four centuries of moai production on Rapa Nui. The earliest are the seven moai of Ahu Nau Nau on Anakena beach (Figure 10.26); these are the most naturalistic, having rounded bodies and only slightly elevated, square faces; the features and ears are well-defined and proportional. The back view shows the line of the posterior median furrow above the loop of the figure's loincloth. Four red scoria topknots or headdresses were recovered from the ocean and replaced on their moai. Also discovered during excavations at the site were white coral eye inserts with red scoria irises. Topknots seem to have been a marker of particular distinction; it is thought that only about a hundred moai ever had headdresses. Even fewer are believed to have been fitted with eye pieces; it may well be that the Rapa Nui priests inserted eyes into statues only when they needed to enliven a particular ancestor (Noble 1978).

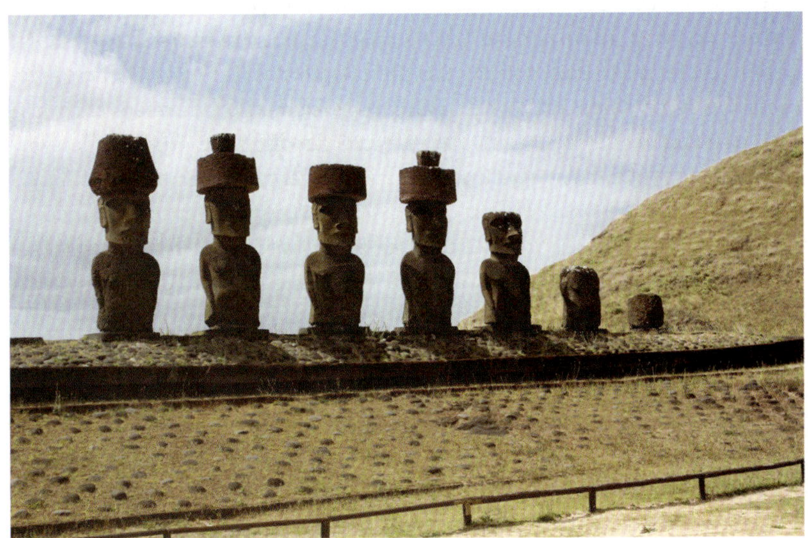

◄ **10.26** Easter Island, Moai at Ahu Nau Nau, c. 1250–1400 CE.

The moai or ancestor statues at Ahu Nau Nau are the oldest and the most naturalistically carved of the Easter Island moai. The statues were carved out of basalt and given topknots of red scoria. Shell eyes were added to enliven particular statues.

The second style of moai appears after 1400 CE and is exemplified by the fifteen moai of Ahu Tongariki. The figures tend to be larger and more rectangular overall especially the heads, which tilt more noticeably upward. The final style is represented by the moai on the slopes of Rano Raraku. These are among the largest moai and are much more abstracted than those of Ahu Nau Nau or Ahu Tongariki. The back-sloping heads are trapezoidal in shape, narrower at the forehead than the chin with elongated noses, pursed lips, and minimal ear detail. Many of the moai fell or were toppled during the nineteenth century and at least two were carried off by ships of exploration visiting the island. Many theories have been proposed to explain the fallen moai including factional wars but there is little hard evidence to support these claims. If the Rapa Nui toppled their moai, it may well have been because of their failure to protect the people from the ravages of European contact: disease, slave raids, and missionization.

Aotearoa (New Zealand) and the Art of the Maori Marae

Aotearoa, the "Land of the Long White Cloud," was settled during the last great push of Polynesian peoples into the remote Pacific. In oral tradition Aotearoa was discovered by a Polynesian explorer named Kupe who came from Hawaiki. Upon his return seven great voyaging canoes, loaded with the ancestors of the Maori, were sent to colonize the two islands known to the Maori as Te Ika-a-Maui or the "Fish of Maui" (North Island) and Te Wai Pounamu or "The Water of Greenstone" (South Island). The Maori people trace their lines of descent back to particular members of those original canoes.

Some four hundred years later in 1642, the first European contact was made when Dutch ships led by Abel Janszoon Tasman happened upon the South Island. Although Tasman's interests were in trading his encounter with the Maori turned hostile when he ordered his ship's cannon to be fired. When Captain Cook arrived in 1769 the initial encounter between British and Maori proved no more amicable but with persistence and the assistance of Tupaia, Cook's Tahitian interpreter, relations improved. Cook's journals provide the first glimpses into traditional Maori life; in them are descriptions of enormous war canoes, fortified hill towns or *pa*, and elaborately carved and decorated "assembly" buildings.

The Maori **marae** is an enclosed compound, 2 to 5 acres in size, which includes ritual spaces and buildings such as a dining hall, washrooms, and a meeting house or *Wharenui*, which is sometimes called a carved house or *Whare Whakairo*. This meeting house is considerably more than a building; it is considered *taonga*, a visualization of the body of an important progenitor or legendary hero and as such is referred to as "he." Conceptually the ancestor is seen as lying face down on the ground. Each structural element of the building is analogous to a corresponding part of the human body. The carved mask at the peak of the gable is his face, the barge boards are his arms, and the parts of the boards that extend beyond the two porch posts or *amo* represent his fingers; the deep space porch is his brain, the door is his mouth, and the window is his eye. Inside the house the ridge beam is his spine, and the rafters symbolize his ribs; the pillars supporting the ridge beam are his heart, and conceptually, the interior space of the building is his womb. Within the Whare are additional ancestors represented by the carved *poupou* or wall panels (Skinner 2016, 12–17).

***Whare Whakairo Ruatepupuke II*, Tokomaru Bay, 1881** The *Whare Whakairo Ruatepupuke II* (Figure 10.27) was commissioned by the Te Whanau-a-Ruataupare chief, Mokena Romio Babbington in 1880. The *Wharenui* is a large one measuring over 56 feet (17 m) long, 22 feet (6.7 m) wide, and rises to a height of 13.83 feet (4.21 m). He was built to honor the hero *Ruatepepuke*, who is credited in Maori myth with bringing the art of woodcarving to the people. He stood upon the spot where an earlier Whare to Ruatepupuke had been before being dismantled in the 1820s so his carvings could be hidden to protect them from marauding Ngapuhi warriors; unfortunately, when the Mangahauini River changed course the carvings were lost. The Ngati Porou mastercarver Hori (also Hoani or Hone) Ngatai (c. 1850–1910) of Rangitukia created the carvings for the new meeting house. *Ruatepupuke II* opened on September 23, 1881, but within a few years it had fallen into disrepair. The house was purchased by a local curio dealer named Hindmarsh, who, in turn, sold the disassembled house to the J. F. G. UmLauff Company, an ethnographic materials and artifact firm in Hamburg, Germany. In 1905, the Field Museum purchased the house for $5,000 (equivalent to about $150,000 today).

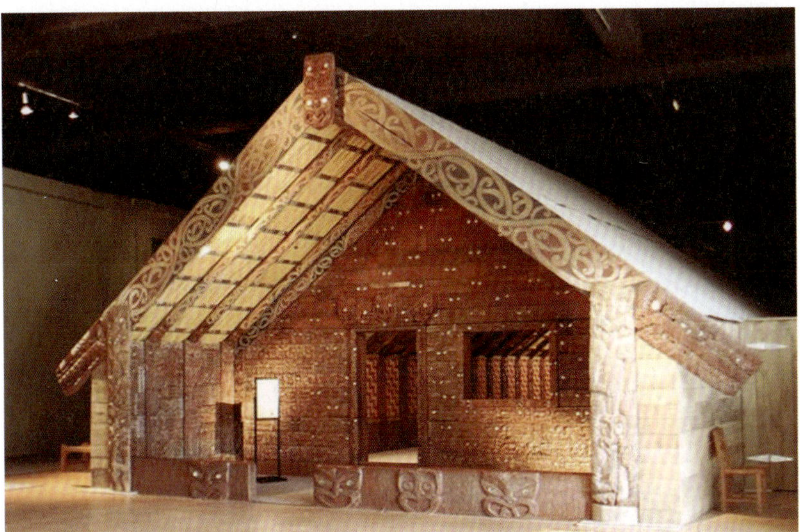

◀ **10.27** New Zealand, Tokomaru Bay, *Whare Whakairo Ruatepupuke II*, 1881 CE.

This ancestor house was commissioned by the Te Whanau-a-Ruataupare chief to replace one that had been lost when it was hidden in the river during the Maori wars.

A traditional east coast style carved house, *Ruatepupuke II* is fronted by a richly carved and painted gabled porch that extends across the entire façade. The ends of the porch are framed by carved upright posts that overlap the bargeboards, marking the point of separation between the painted *kowhaiwhai* designs and the carved *raparapa* finger ends of the boards. Depicted on each amo is a pair of highly stylized anthropomorphic figures, known as **tiki**: a large one, in an aggressive stance, stands on the shoulders of a half-figure at the base of the post. The surfaces of both forms are covered with intricate low relief spiral and linear designs that may represent tattoo patterns. The upper figure has a beak-like mouth and thrusts out his tongue in challenge, suggesting the ritual challenge performed by Maori warriors when visitors approach the marae. The eyes of the amo figures are inlaid with iridescent *pāua* (abalone) shell eyes, a reference to the origin of carving in the realm of the sea god Tangeroa. The most unusual feature of the porch is the decoration of the façade wall; more than a hundred bas-relief faces, with inlaid abalone shell eyes, decorate the boards.

Ruatepupuke II's bargeboards, rafters, and ridgepole are painted with ***kowhaiwhai*** designs in traditional red, black, and white colors. Kowhaiwhai were originally used to decorate paddles and war canoes but over time were added to wharenui as expressions of tribal identity. There are twenty-nine kowhaiwhai commonly used on Maori structures and while they are elegant decorations, they have particular meanings to the peoples who use them. The pattern used on *Ruatepupuke II* is the *koiri*; the word means "to bend or sway" and is an apt description of the flow of the design across the boards. The basic element in this pattern is the *koru* or "curled shoot" (fiddlehead) of an unfolding fern. The artist has divided and mirrored this simple motif to create a visually complex form. The pattern is rendered in white against alternating red and black grounds. Red ocher, charcoal, and pipeclay (burnt and ground) pigments were mixed with shark liver oil to make traditional paints.

Inside *Ruatepupuke II* (Figure 10.28) is a single open communal space, unobstructed except for the two "heart" posts supporting the ridgepole; the two figures forming the base of the poles are rendered in a highly naturalistic style, although the scale of the heads has been slightly exaggerated. The walls of the room are lined with alternating *poupou* panels, carved in the same abstracted style as the porch posts, and *tukutuku* or latticework panels. The panels are done in the *poutama* pattern, one of the earliest used in *tukutuku*; it symbolizes levels of attainment and advancement. The panels were formed on paired latticework frames made from native toetoe grass stalks. The panels were stitched by women working together to lace the designs from materials such as strands of golden sedge, native flax, and dyed kiekie leaves.

Maori Modernism

The British colonization of New Zealand began with the arrival of the first white settlers in January 1840, and despite wars with the Maori,

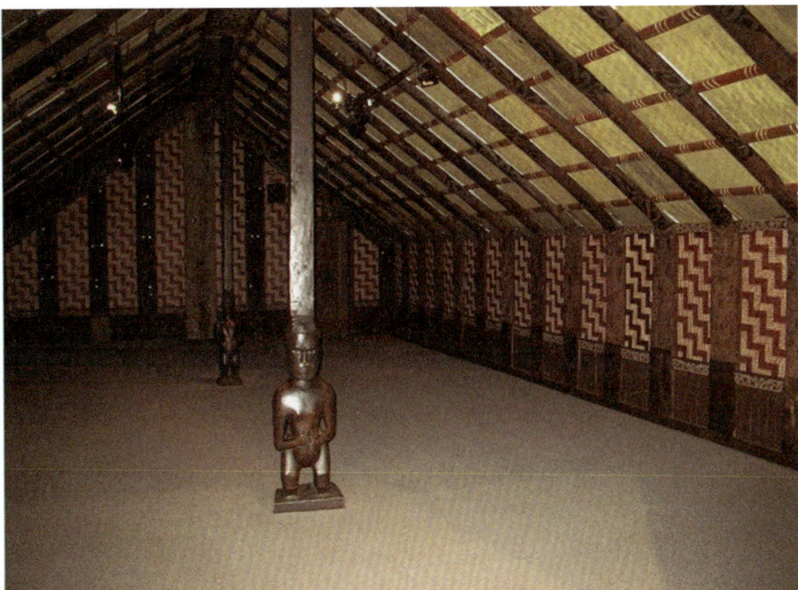

◀ **10.28** New Zealand, Tokomaru Bay, *Whare Whakairo Ruatepupuke II*, 1881 CE.

The house honors the hero Ruatepepuke who brought the art of woodcarving to the Maori. The carved figures inside the house are the work of the Maori master carver Hori Ngatai.

thousands of European immigrants poured into the country. In the nineteenth century "settler art," consisting primarily of landscape sketches and ethnographic studies of the Maori people, dominated. While traditional Maori artists continued to produce carvings and weavings, the quality of production, as well as the Maori culture itself, was seen as declining due to European pressure. In the early twentieth century a Maori revitalization movement was led by Sir Apirana Turupa Ngata (1874–1950), a prominent Maori barrister and politician. One outcome of the movement was the establishment of the Rotorua School of Maori Arts in 1927. Although it was in operation for only a decade, the school trained a generation of young Maori carvers in traditional woodworking techniques. At the same time government educational policies, with a focus on improving New Zealand arts, provided access to Western artistic training for both Maori and *Pakeha* (non-Maori) students. By the 1950s, this generation of well-educated young Maori artists had begun producing works that combined traditional Maori concepts of symbolic geometry with Western media and modes of expression.

Chapter Quick Review

Australia

- The first settlers arrived in Australia more than 60,000 years ago when New Guinea and Tasmania were still connected to the continent as part of the greater Sahul landmass.
- The oldest Aboriginal painting at Nawarla Gabarnmang dates back 28,000 years; new art continues to be added to the shelter to this day. The earliest images are red ocher paintings of spirit beings known as mimis. Rock engravings on the Burrup Peninsula may date as early as 40,000 BCE.

- In Arnhem Land a more recent style known x-ray paintings date from 2000 BCE. The name x-ray refers to a style in which profile drawings of animals and humans may show the esophagus, heart, spine, or other organs. This x-ray style works are also painted on bark but because of the material it is not certain how far back this tradition goes in history. The designs and Dreaming stories used in painting are owned by particular clans and cannot be used by others without permission.
- During the twentieth century several Aboriginal artists have adopted Western media to express their traditional stories; many, including Albert Namatjira, Clifford Possum Tjapaltjarri, and Emily Kame Kngwarreye have been internationally successful.

Melanesia

- Melanesia is a series of large and small islands that stretch for some 2,500 miles between the equator and the tropic of Capricorn; the largest and most culturally and artistically dense is the island of New Guinea, north of Australia. More than seven hundred different languages are spoken on the island.
- The Asmat of the Casuarina Coast of New Guinea are master carvers of shields, bis poles, and other items of wood. The large bis poles were created as a visible vow to avenge the death of a relative by taking the head of an enemy believed to have caused the death through sorcery.
- The maritime Massim of New Guinea participated in the long-distance kula exchanges by which white shell was traded for red shell. They carved elaborate canoe prows and splash guards that were symbols of the wealth and prestige of the canoe owner.
- The defining feature of Iatmul life was the ngaigo, the ceremonial men's house which was conceptualized as an ancestral crocodile. The house was divided to represent the moieties and clans of the village and sacred ritual items, drums, flutes and the skulls of ancestors were stored in the ngaigo. The upper posts were often carved in the form of ancestor figures.
- The Abelam created large spirit houses known as korumbo with elaborately painted gables featuring clan ancestors called ngwalndu. The Abelam also grow gigantic yams for exchange which are decorated with painting, ornaments, and woven or wooden masks.
- In New Ireland, elaborate memorial and initiation rituals called malangan were held to assist the recently deceased to move on to the world of spirits. In addition to feasts and masked dances, ritual tableaux were carved with figures representing the deceased and other spirits.
- In the modern era artists in New Guinea have worked both in traditional arts, for example the Massim carver Mutuaga, as well as experimenting with new media and traditional imagery as in the case of Kauage Mathis and Daniel Waswas.

Micronesia

- Limit resources on the tiny islands of Micronesia determined the type and scale of works that were produced.
- In western Micronesia where forest resources were more readily available, wood was used for important buildings such as community men's meeting houses or bai. These were often decorated with symbols representing wealth such as money symbols and money birds as well as sculptures of female Dilukai figures.

- In eastern Micronesia on the islands of Pohnpei and Kosrae, stone was used to construct artificial islands and buildings such as royal mausoleums, temples, and palaces for the ruling dynasty.

Polynesia

- The first settlers to arrive in Polynesia were the Lapita who began moving into the region during the second millennium BCE. A second wave of migrants arrived and began spreading out to the farthest islands beginning around 1100 CE.
- These last settlers brought paper mulberry, yams and other plant resources, stratified societies ruled by hereditary elite, and a common pantheon of gods.
- Depending on the local resources the Polynesians made barkcloth, feather garments, carved bone and greenstone ornaments, wood and monolithic stone sculpture, such as the moai of Rapa Nui, and built architecture, often highly decorated as in the case of the Maori marae.
- In the modern era Polynesian artists work in a variety of traditional and Western media, including oil and acrylic painting and multimedia sculpture as well as barkcloth, bark painting, and various forms of carving.

Chapter Questions

1. Explain how the environment in which an Oceanic artist lived affected the arts that he or she produces. How did the introduction of modern media change this?
2. Ancestor images play a large role in the corpus of Oceanic art. Cite some specific examples of such works and describe the different ways they were used in art and architecture. What characteristics define ancestor images in Australia, in Melanesia, and in Polynesia?
3. Most societies have some sort of communal house. Describe two examples of how these structures are conceptualized. By whom and how are they used?
4. Discuss how contact with the West impacted the arts and culture of this region, especially in modern times.

Key Terms and Figures

Key Terms

Bai In Palau the bai is a traditional men's meeting house.

Bis pole Asmat carved memorial pole originally set up in front of the men's house as a vow to avenge the death of a relative.

Dreaming or Dreamtime In Aboriginal belief, a time during which mythic creator beings created the land, animals, and people, and established the social order.

Gobaela Massim presentation scepters for shell currency.

Jeu Asmat ceremonial men's house.

Korambo Abelam spirit or ancestor house.

Lagim Massim canoe splash guard.

Malangan New Ireland memorial rituals which involve setting up figural tableaux representing spirits as well as the recently deceased whose spirits are encouraged to move on to the realm of spirits.

Marae In New Zealand a marae is an enclosed communal area that includes the meeting house, representing the clan ancestor of the Maori tribe to which it belongs.

Mimi In Aboriginal mythology the mimi are spirit people.

Moai The monolithic statues carved on Rapa Nui.

Ngaigo Iatmul men's house.

Ngwail Iatmul ancestor spirit.

Ngwalndu Abelam clan ancestor spirits.

Songlines Songlines are the paths taken across the land by creator beings during the Dreaming.

Siapo Samoan term for barkcloth.

Tiki In Polynesia, a wooden or stone anthropomorphic sculpture.

Tsjemen The openwork wing element of the bis pole.

Wagen Iatmul ancestral crocodile.

Wowipits Term for an Asmat master carver.

Key Figures

Babbington, Mokena Romio—Te Whanau-a-Ruataupare chief, who commissioned the *Whare Whakairo Ruatepupuke II.*

Bardon, Geoffrey Robert—Australian teacher who inspired the Western Desert Movement.

Bateson, Gregory—English anthropologist, ethnographer, and linguist who designated a group of peoples living along the middle Sepik river as "Iatmul" based on linguistic affiliations.

Battarbee, Reginald "Rex"—Australian watercolor artist who taught Albert Namatjira to paint.

Beier, Georgina Betts—English expatriate artist who taught Kauage Mathis to paint.

Cook, Captain James—Eighteenth century British explorer, who visited many of the Pacific islands including Hawaii, New Zealand, Easter Island, Tahiti, and Tonga.

Kngwarreye, Emily Kame—Australian Aboriginal artist associated with the Utopia Station painters.

Namatjira, Albert—Australian Aboriginal landscape watercolor painter associated with the Hermannsburg Mission painters.

Ngata, Sir Apirana Turupa—Prominent Maori lawyer and politician in New Zealand who helped to found the Rotorua School of Maori Arts in 1927.

Ngatai, Hori—Ngati Porou mastercarver who created the carvings for *Whare Whakairo Ruatepupuke II.*

Spencer, Walter Baldwin—English-Australian anthropologist and biologist who built one of the first collections of Aboriginal bark paintings at the begin ning of the twentieth century.

Tjapaltjarri, Clifford Possum—Australian Aboriginal artist associated with the Western Desert Movement.

Tupaia—Tahitian man who served as interpreter for Captain Cook.

Quick Pronunciation Guide

Abelam [UHBUH-luhm]
Aotearoa [OH-tee-ah row-ah]
Iatmul [YAHT-mool]
Kngwarreye [War-eye]
koru [pooru]
kowhaiwhai [KOH-phi-phi]
malangan [mal-AHN-gan]
Marae [mah-RYE]
Namatjira [Nama-jeer-ah]
ngaigo [NYE-oh]
poupou [po-po]
taonga [TAOH-mah]
Tjapaltjarri [Jappal-jar-ree]
tsjemen [cemen]
Whare Whakairo [Pah-rae Pah-KAI-doh]
Wharenui [PAH rae nui]

Bibliography

Anon. "About the Artist: Daniel Waswas." *Contemporary Pacific* 21, no. 2 (Fall 2009): VI-414. https://muse.jhu.edu/article/316472

"Bairairrai." http://pacificworlds.com/palau/native/native3.cfm

Addison, David J., and Elizabeth Matisoo-Smith. "Rethinking Polynesian Origins: A West-Polynesia Triple-I Model." *Archaeology in Oceania* 45, no. 1 (April 2010): 1–12.

Aijmer, Göran. "The Warawara Malanggan in Lesu: The Historical Anthropology of a New Ireland Society." *Anthropos*, Bd. 99, H. 2 (2004): 519–534.

Arbeit, Wendy. *Tapa in Tonga*. Honolulu, HI: Palm Frond Productions, 1982.

Athens, J. Stephen. "Pottery from Nan Madol, Ponape, Eastern Caroline Islands." *Journal of the Polynesian Society* 89, no. 1 (March 1980): 95–99.

Arthur, Linda Boynton. *The Hawaiian Quilt*. Waipahu, HI: Island Heritage Publishing, 2010.

Ayres, William S. "Mystery Islets of Micronesia." *Archaeology* 43, no. 1 (January–February 1990): 58–63.

Barrow, Terence. *The Art of Tahiti*. London: Thames and Hudson, 1979.

Maori Art of New Zealand. Paris, A. H. & A. W. Reed and the UNESCO Press, 1978.

Bateson, Gregory. *Naven*. 2nd edition. Stanford University Press, 1958.

"Social Structure of the Iatmul People of the Sepik River." *Oceania* 2, no. 3 (March 1932): 245–291.

"Social Structure of the Iatmul People of the Sepik River (Concluded)." *Oceania* 2, no. 4 (June 1932): 401–453.

Beaglehole, John C., editor. *The Journals of Captain James Cook on His Voyages of Discovery 2: The Voyages of the Resolution and Adventure (1772–1775)*. Hakluyt Society Extra Series, no. 35. Cambridge, UK: Cambridge University Press, 1961.

Beran, Harry. *Mutuaga, A Nineteenth-Century New Guinea Master Carver*. Wollongong, NSW: University of Wollongong Press, 1996.

Brandl, E. J. *Australian Aboriginal Paintings in Western and Central Arnhem Land.* Canberra, Australia: Australian Institute of Aboriginal Studies, 1973.

Brigham, William T. *Hawaiian Feather Work.* Honolulu, HI: Bishop Museum Press, 1899, 1–86.

Brown, Paula. *The Chimbu: A Study of the Change in the New Guinea Highlands.* Cambridge, MA: Schenkman Publishing Company, Inc., 1972.

Burley, David. "New Dating Pinpoints Tonga's Lapita Settlement." *Radio Australia.* November 12, 2012. http://www.radioaustralia.net.au/international/radio/program/pacific-beat/new-dating-pinpoints-tongas-lapita-settlement/1044482

Caldeira, Leah, Christina Hellmich, Adrienne L. Kaeppler, Betty Lou Kam, and Roger G. Rose, Stacy L. Kamehiro, editors. *Royal Hawaiian Featherwork: Nā Hulu Ali'i.* Honolulu: University of Hawai'i Press, 2015.

Clark, Geoffrey. "Radiocarbon Dates from the Ulong Site in Palau and Implications for Western Micronesian Prehistory." *Archaeology in Oceania* 39, no. 1 (April 2004): 26–33.

Caruana, Wally. *Aboriginal Art.* 3rd edition. New York: Thames and Hudson World of Art, 2012.

Cochrane, Susan. *Contemporary Art in Papua New Guinea.* Sydney, Australia: Craftsman House, 1997.

Cordy, Ross. "Lelū, The Stone City of Kosrae: 1978–1981 Research." *Journal of the Polynesian Society* 91, no. 1 (March 1982): 103–119.

Craib, John L. "Micronesian Prehistory: An Archaeological Overview." *Science* 219, no. 4587 (February 25, 1983): 922–927.

D'Alleva, Anne. *Arts of the Pacific Islands.* New York: Harry N. Abrams, Inc., 1998.

David, Bruno, Bryce Barker, Fiona Petchey, Jean-Jacques Delannoy, Jean-Michel Geneste, Cassandra Rowe, Mark Eccleston, Lara Lamb, and Ray Whear. "A 28,000-Year-Old Excavated Painted Rock from Nawarla Gabarnmang, Northern Australia." *Journal of Archaeological Science* 40 (2013): 2493–2501.

Dickson, T. Elder. "An Unusual Ceremonial Lime-Spatula from British New Guinea." *Man* 42 (May–June 1942): 49–51.

Dinerman, Ina R. "Iatmul Art as Iconography (New Guinea)." *Anthropos*, Bd. H. 5–6 (1981): 807–824.

Edgerly, John E.

"Surviving Traditional Art of Melanesia," *Journal of the Polynesian Society*, vol. 91, no.4 (December 1987): 543-579.

Evans, Miriama, and Ranui Ngarimu. *The Art of Maori Weaving.* Wellington, NZ: Huia Publishers, 2005.

Flood, Josephine. *Archaeology of the Dreamtime: The Story of Prehistoric Australia and Its People.* Revised Edition. New Haven, CT: Yale University Press, 1983.

Forge, Anthony. "The Abelam Artist." In *Social Organization: Essays Presented to Raymond Firth*, edited by Maurice Freedman. Chicago: Aldine Publishing Company, 1967.

"Art and Environment in the Sepik." *Proceedings of the Royal Anthropological Institute of Great Britain and Ireland*, no. 1965 (1965): 23–31.

"Paint: A Magical Substance." *Palette* 9 (1962): 9–16.

Gathereole, Peter, Adrienne L. Kaeppler, and Douglas Newton. *The Art of the Pacific Islands.* Washington, DC: National Gallery of Art, 1979.

Gerbrands, Adrian A.

Wow-Ipits: Eight Asmat Woodcarvers of New Guinea, The Hague: Mouton and Company, 1967.

Goldbarth, Albert. "Wuramon." *Iowa Review* 36, no. 1 (Spring 2006): 62–77.

Greub, Suzanne, editor. *Art of the Sepik River, Papua New Guinea.* Basel, Switzerland: Tribal Art Centre, 1985.

Art of Northwest New Guinea. New York: Rizzoli, 1992.

Hakiwai, Arapata, and John Terrell. *Ruatepupuke: A Maori Meeting House.* Chicago: Field Museum Press, 1994.

Hall, Nicholas. "Building Blocks and Stepping Stones: Some Key Foundations in the Development of Rock Art Conservation in Australia." *Archaeology in Oceania* 34, no. 3 (October 1999): 161–170.

Hamm, Catherine. "Hawaii: Replicas of Royal Garb Go on Display." *Los Angeles Times*. June 11, 2014. http://www.latimes.com/travel/deals/la-trb-hawaii-replica-of-royal-cape-20140610-story.html

Hardy, Jane. "Battarbee, Reginald Ernest (Rex) (1893–1973)." *Australian Dictionary of Biography*. National Centre of Biography. Australian National University, 1993. http://adb.anu.edu.au/biography/battarbee-reginald-ernest-rex-9453/text16625

Hauser-Schäublin, Brigitta. *Ceremonial Houses of the Abelam, Papua New Guinea: Architecture and Ritual—A Passage to the Ancestors*. Adelaide, Australia: Crawford House Publishing, 2016.

Hiroa, Te Rangi (P. H. Buck). "Samoan Material Culture." *Bernice P. Bishop Museum Bulletin 75*. Honolulu, 1930. Kraus Reprint, 1971.

Arts and Crafts of Hawaii: Clothing. Honolulu, HI: Bishop Museum Press, 1957.

"The Local Evolution of Hawaiian Feather Capes and Cloaks." *Journal of the Polynesian Society* 53, no. 1 (March 1944): 1–16.

Holt, John Dominis. *The Art of Featherwork in Old Hawai'i*. Honolulu, HI: Topgallant Publishing Co., 1985.

Hunt, Terry L. "Rethinking the Fall of Easter Island: New Evidence Points to an Alternative Explanation for a Civilization's Collapse." *American Scientist* 94, no. 5 (September–October 2006): 412–419.

Isaacs, Jennifer. *Australian Aboriginal Paintings*. New York: Dutton Studio Books, 1992.

Kaberry, Phyllis M. "The Abelam Tribe, Sepik District, New Guinea: A Preliminary Report." *Oceania* 11, no. 3 (March 1941): 233–258.

"The Abelam Tribe, Sepik District, New Guinea: A Preliminary Report (Continued)." *Oceania* 11, no. 4 (June 1941): 345–367.

Kaeppler, Adrienne L. *The Pacific Arts of Polynesia & Micronesia*. Oxford: Oxford University Press, 2008

Kaufmann, Christian. "Painting's Changing Role in Shaping our Understanding of Sepik Art (Part II)." *Pacific Arts* 9, no. 1 (2010): 5–14.

Kaufmann, Christian, and Oliver Wick. *Nukuro: Sculptures from Micronesia*. Fondation Beyeler. Basel: Hirmer Publishers, 2013.

Kjellgren, Eric. *How to Read Oceanic Art*. New York: Metropolitan Museum of Art, 2014.

Splendid Isolation: Art of Easter Island. New York: Metropolitan Museum of Art, 2001.

Kooijman, Simon. *Polynesian Barkcloth*. Shire Publications, 1988.

Kupka, Karel. "Australian Aboriginal Bark Painting." *Oceania* 27, no. 4 (June 1957): 264–267.

Lincoln, Louise. *An Assemblage of Spirits: Idea and Image in New Ireland*. New York: George Braziller, 1987.

Linnekin, Jocelyn. "Who Made the Feather Cloaks? A Problem in Hawaiian Gender Relations." *Journal of the Polynesian Society* 97, no. 3 (September 1988): 265–280.

Losche, Diane. *The Abelam, a People of Papua New Guinea*. Australian Museum, 1982.

"The Impossible Aesthetic: The Abelam, the Moa Bird and Me." *Oceania* 66, no. 4 (June 1996): 305–310.

"The Sepik Gaze: Iconographic Interpretation of Abelam Form." *Social Analysis: The International Journal of Social and Cultural Practice*, no. 38 (September 1995): 47–60.

MacDonald, Cheyenne. "The First King: 1200 AD Tomb Reveals Ancient City Invented New Kind of Society and Was the First of the Pacific Islands to Be Ruled by a Single Chief." *Daily Mail*. October 19, 2016. http://www.dailymail.co.uk/sciencetech/article-3853556/The-king-1200-AD-tomb-reveals-ancient-city-invented-new-kind-society-Pacific-Islands-ruded-single-chief.html

McCoy, Mark D., Helen A. Alderson, Richard Hemi, Hai Cheng, and R. Lawrence Edwards. "Earliest Direct Evidence of Monument Building at the Archaeological Site of Nan Madol (Pohnpei, Micronesia) Identified Using 230 TH/U Coral Dating and Geochemical Sourcing of Megalithic Architectural Stone." *Quaternary Research* 86 (2016): 295–303.

McLintock, A. H., editor. "Painted Designs." *An Encyclopaedia of New Zealand*, 1966. Te Ara—the Encyclopedia of New Zealand. http://www.TeAra.govt.nz/en/1966/maori-art/page-8

Malinowski, Bronislaw. *Argonauts of the Western Pacific.* Long Grove, IL: Waveland Press, Inc., 1922 (reissued 1984).

Mead, Hirini Moko. *The Art of Maori Carving.* Auckland, NZ: Libro International, 2015.

Meyer, Anthony J. P. *Oceanic Art.* 2 volumes. Knickerbocker Press, 1996.

Morgan, William N. *Prehistoric Architecture in Micronesia.* Austin: University of Texas Press, 1988.

Mosuwadoga, Geoffrey, and Harry Beran. "Art and Artistic Training in Boyowa Island, Trobriand Archipelago, Papua New Guinea." *Pacific Arts* 1 (2006): 12–26.

Mulholland, Malcolm. *Maori Carving: The Art of Recording Maori History.* Wellington, NZ: Huia Publishers, 2015.

Mulvaney, John, and Johan Kamminga. *Prehistory of Australia.* Washington, DC: Smithsonian Institution, 1999.

Newell, Jenny. *Pacific Art in Detail.* Cambridge, MA: Harvard University Press, 2011.

Newton, Douglas. *Massim: Art of the Massim Area, New Guinea.* New York: Museum of Primitive Art, 1975.

The Metropolitan Museum of Art: The Pacific Islands, Africa, and the Americas. New York: Metropolitan Museum of Art, 1987.

Arts of the South Seas: Island Southeast Asia, Melanesia, Polynesia, Micronesia. Munich: Prestel, 1999.

Noble, Joseph Veach. "Easter Island Heads Had Inlaid Eyes." *Archaeology* 31, no. 5 (September–October 1978), 53.

Pritchard, Mary J. *Bark Cloth Art of Samoa.* American Samoa Council on Culture, Arts and Humanities, Special Publication Number 1, 1984.

Powdermaker, Hortense. *Life in Lesu: The Study of a Melanesian Society in New Ireland.* London: Williams & Norgate, 1933.

Rainbird, Paul. "Prehistory in the Northwest Tropical Pacific: The Caroline, Mariana, and Marshall Islands." *Journal of World Prehistory* 8, no. 3 (September 1994): 293–349.

Sayers, Andrew. *Australian Art.* New York: Oxford University Press, 2001.

Scaglion, Richard. "Yam Cycles and Timeless Time in Melanesia." *Ethnology* 38, no. 3 (Summer 1999): 211–225.

Servaes, Caroline D., and Hew D.V. Prendergast. "Out of the Museum Darkness: A Mid-19th Century Bark Drawing from Victoria, Australia." *Economic Botany* 56, no. 1 (January–March 2002): 7–9.

Silverman, Eric Kline

Tanbunum: New Perspectives on Eastern Iatmul (Sepik River, Papua New Guinea) Kinship, Marriage and Society, Volumes I and II, Doctoral Thesis, University of Minnesota, 1993

Skinner, Damian. *The Maori Meeting House: Introducing the Whare Whakairo.* Honolulu: University of Hawai'i Press, 2016.

Smidt, Dirk A.M. (editor)

Asmat Art: Woodcarvings of Southwest New Guinea, New York: George Braziller, 1993.

Smith, DeVerne Reed. "The Palauan Storyboards." *Expedition Magazine* 18, no. 1 (September 1975). https://www.penn.museum/sites/expedition/the-palauan-storyboards/

Taylor, Luke. *Seeing the Inside: Bark Painting in Western Arnhem Land.* Oxford: Clarendon Press, 1996.

"'They May Say Tourist, May Say Truly Painting': Aesthetic Evaluation and Meaning of Bark Paintings in Western Arnhem Land, Northern Australia." *Journal of the Royal Anthropological Institute* 14, no. 4 (December 2008): 865–885.

Thomas, Frank R. "The Precontact Period." In *The Pacific Islands: Environment and Society,* revised edition, 125–137, edited by Moshe Rapaport. Honolulu: University of Hawai'i Press, 2013.

Thomas, Nicholas. *Oceanic Art*. London: Thames and Hudson, 1995.

Tuzin, Donald. "Art and Procreative Illusion in the Sepik: Comparing the Abelam and the Arapesh." *Oceania* 65, no. 4 (June 1995): 289–303.

Van Tilburg, Jo Anne. "Symbolic Stratigraphy: Rock Art and the Monolithic Statues of Easter Island." *World Archaeology* 19, no. 2 (October 1987): 133–149.

Wardwell, Allen. *Island Ancestors: Oceanic Art from the Masco Collection.* Seattle: University of Washington Press, 1994.

Williams, Christine. "Albert Namatjira: The Rich Heritage of Our Desert Earth Painter." *Australian Humanities Review*, no. 43 (December 2007).

Wilmhurst, Janet M., Terry L. Hunt, Carl P. Lipo, Atholl J. Anderson, and James O'Connell. "High-Precision Radiocarbon Dating Shows Recent and Rapid Initial Human Colonization of East Polynesia." *Proceedings of the National Academy of Sciences of the United States of America* 108, no. 5 (February 1, 2011): 1815–1820.

Young, Michael W."The Massim: An Introduction," *Journal of Pacific History*, vol. 18, no. 1 (January 1983): 3-30.

CREDITS

Chapter 1

Figure 1.1: Photo by Alfonsobouchot - Own work, Public Domain.

Figure 1.2: Parque-Museo de La Venta, Villahermosa, Tabasco (PMV–033). Photo: Consejo Nacional para la Cultura y las Artes–Instituto Nacional de Antropologia e Photo: National Council for Culture and the Arts – National Institute of Anthropology and History – Mexico – Javier Hinojosa, photographer

Figure 1.3: Photo by Glysiak, distributed under a CC BY-SA 4.0 license.

Figure 1.4: age fotostock / Alamy Stock Photo; LAS.org

Figure 1.5: Jim and Carole Cook

Figure 1.6: Photo by Diego Delso, distributed under a CC BY-SA 3.0 license.

Figure 1.7: Photo by Jack Hynes — uploaded on 25. Jul. 2006 to english wikipedia by author. Public Domain.

Figure 1.8: Photo courtesy of Dr. Karen Olsen Bruhns

Figure 1.9: Photograph by author; Image by HJPD distributed under a CC BY-SA 3.0 license.

Figure 1.10: Photo by Diego Delso, distributed under a CC BY-SA 3.0 license.

Figure 1.11: Photo courtesy of Dr. Karen Olsen Bruhns

Figure 1.12: Photograph by author

Figure 1.13: Foto © Jorge Pérez de Lara

Figure 1.14: Photo by Greg Willis (originally posted to Flickr as tikal-14) distributed under a CC BY-SA 2.0 license.

Figure 1.15: Photo by yogi (Flickr) distributed under [CC BY-SA 2.0 (https://creativecommons.org/licenses/by-sa/2.0)], via Wikimedia Commons

Figure 1.16: Photo by Raymond Ostertag distributed under a CC BY-SA 2.5 license.

Figure 1.17: LAS.org

Figure 1.18: Photo courtesy of Dr. Karen Olsen Bruhns

Figure 1.19: Photo by tato grasso, distributed under a CC BY-SA 2.5 license.

Figure 1.20: Photo by Jan Harenburg , distributed under a [CC BY 4.0 license. Ns]

Figure 1.21: Photo by By AlejandroLinaresGarcia distributed under a CC BY-SA 4.0 license.

Figure 1.22: LAS.org

Figure 1.23: LAS.org

Figure 1.24: LAS.org

Figure 1.25: Photo by runt35, distributed under a CC BY 3.0 license.

Figure 1.26: Courtesy of Dr. Karen Olsen Bruhns

Figure 1.27: Photo by Arian Zwegers from Brussels, Belgium (Tula, Pyramid B, atlantes) distributed under a CC BY 2.0 license.

Figure 1.28: Photo courtesy of Dr. Karen Olsen Bruhns

Figure 1.29: Photo by Miguel Alvarez - https://www.flickr.com/photos/miguelalvarez/4095977415/ distributed under a CC BY-SA 2.0 license.

Figure 1.30: Photo by Citlaltec distributed under a CC BY-SA 4.0 license.

Figure 1.31: [Public domain], via Wikimedia Commons

Figure 1.32: Photo by Nicojs distributed under a CC BY-SA 3.0 license.

Figure 1.33: [Public domain], via Wikimedia Commons

Figure 1.34: Photo credit: Jim Frank. Rufino Tamayo, *Woman Spinning*, 1943. Oil on canvas, 43 x 32 inches, Collection Friends of the Neuberger Museum of Art, Purchase College, State University of New York, gift from the Estate of Roy R. Neuberger. © Jim Frank

Chapter 2

Figure 2.2: Photo by DEA / G. DAGLI ORTI/De Agostini/Getty Images

Figure 2.4: Jesse Kraft / Alamy Stock Photo; Drawing by Rick Rishaw

Figure 2.5: Photo by Martin St-Amant (S23678)distributed under a CC BY 3.0 license.

Figure 2.6: Mark Green / Alamy Stock Photo

Figure 2.7: Mantle Peruvian, Paracas, South Coast, Early Intermediate Period, Phase 1, 0–A.D. 100

Wool plain weave embroidered with wool in stem-stitch, 142 x 241 cm (55 7/8 x 94 7/8 in.). Museum of Fine Arts, Boston. William Alfred Paine Fund, 31.501.

Figure 2.8: Paracas, Rattle Bowl with Oculate Deity, 3rd – 1st BCE, 6.75 in. (17.15 cm) Diameter. Metropolitan Museum of Art, New York, Gift of Nathan Cummings, 1963

Figure 2.9: Photo by Ingo Mehling distributed under a CC BY-SA 3.0 license.

Figure 2.10: Photo by Diego Delso distributed under a CC BY-SA 4.0 license https://commons.wikimedia.org/w/index.php?curid=42787827

Figure 2.11: Metropolitan Museum of Art, New York, Purchase, Arthur M. Bullowa Bequest, 1996

Figure 2.12: Restricted gift of Mrs. Edwin A. Seipp. Art Institute of Chicago, 1956.75.

Figure 2.13: Photo courtesy of Dr. Karen Olsen Bruhns

Figure 2.14: Photo by en:User:Chiwara – "Taken on site by me in July 2004." - en:User:Chiwara Via English Wikipedia en:-File:Cerro Blanco and Huaca de la Luna.JPG, distributed under a CC BY-SA 3.0 license.

Figure 2.15: Photo by Martin St-Amant (S23678) distributed under a CC BY 3.0 license.

Figure 2.16: The Cleveland Museum of Art, Gift of John Wise 1947.172

Figure 2.17: © The Trustees of the British Museum

Figure 2.18: Fowler Museum at UCLA, Photograph by Susan Einstein

Figure 2.19: Photo by Mhwater at Dutch Wikipedia - Transferred from nl.wikipedia to Commons., Public Domain.

Figure 2.20: Drawing by Rick Rishaw

Figure 2.21: Photo by Mhwater - Transfered from nl.wikipedia, Public Domain.

Figures 2.22 and 2.23: Overall: 202.6 x 112 cm (79 3/4 x 44 1/8 in.). The Cleveland Museum of Art, John L. Severance Fund 2007.179

Figure 2.24: Photo by Karolyn Aroca distributed under a CC BY-SA 3.0 license.

Figure 2.25: Photo by author.

Figure 2.26: Photo by Diego Delso distributed under a CC BY-SA 4.0 license.

Figure 2.27: Photo by Martin St-Amant (S23678) distributed under a CC BY-SA 3.0 license https://commons.wikimedia.org/w/index.php?curid=8450312

Figure 2.28: Photo courtesy of Dr. Karen Olsen Bruhns

Figure 2.29: Photo courtesy of Dr. Karen Olsen Bruhns

Figure 2.30: Photo by Again Erick distributed under a CC BY-SA 3.0 license.

Figure 2.31: Storage Jar (Aryballos). 15th–early 16th century. H. 8 5/8 x W. 7 3/8 x D. 5 3/4 in. (21.9 x 18.8 x 14.6 cm). Metropolitan Museum of Art; The Michael C. Rockefeller Memorial Collection, Purchase, Nelson A. Rockefeller Gift, 1961. Accession Number: 1978.412.68.

Figure 2.32: The Metropolitan Museum of Art, Purchase, The Rogers Fund, 1982

Figure 2.33: Circle of Diego Quispe Tito (Peruvian (Cuzco), 1611-1681). Virgin of Carmel Saving Souls in Purgatory, late 17th

century. Oil on canvas, 41 x 29 in. (104.1 x 73.7 cm). Brooklyn Museum, Museum Expedition 1941, Frank L. Babbott Fund, 41.1275.178 (Photo: Brooklyn Museum, 41.1275.178_SL1.jpg
Figure 2.34: New Orleans Museum of Art, Museum Purchase and Gift of Mr. and Mrs. Arthur Q. Davis and the Stern Fund
Figure 2.35: Brooklyn Museum, Gift of Dr. John H. Finney
Figure 2.36: Mark Green / Alamy Stock Photo

Chapter 3

Figure 3.1: Drawing by Rick Rishaw
Figure 3.2: Poverty Point Station Archaeology Program; data courtesy of FEMA and the state of Louisiana; data distribution courtesy of "ATLAS: The Louisiana Statewide GIS," LSU CADGIS Research Laboratory, Baton Rouge, Louisiana.
Figure 3.3: Photo by Jenny Ellerbe
Figure 3.4: Photograph by author
Figure 3.5: By Unknown - Scanned from Mills, William C. Archaeological Atlas of Ohio, page 71A, Public Domain.
Figure 3.6: Courtesy of the Ohio History Connection
Figure 3.7: Photo by Eric Ewing distributed under a CC BY-SA 3.0 license.
Figure 3.9: © The Field Museum, Image No. A110024c, Cat. No. 110132, Photographer Ron Testa.
Figure 3.10: Photo by Cacophony distributed under a CC BY-SA 3.0 license.
Figure 3.11: Photo by Skubasteve834 - EN.Wikipedia distributed under a CC BY-SA 3.0 license.
Figure 3.12: Photo by Herb Roe distributed under a CC BY-SA 3.0 license.
Figure 3.13: Photo courtesy of the Sam Noble Oklahoma Museum of Natural History, The University of Oklahoma, Norman, Oklahoma
Figure 3.14: Photo by Herb Roe distributed under a CC BY-SA 3.0 license.
Figure 3.15: Photo by Heironymous Rowe at en.wikipedia distributed under a CC BY-SA 3.0 license.
Figure 3.16: Photo by Tobi 87 distributed under a CC BY-SA 4.0 license.
Figure 3.17: Photo by WV Bailey at the English Wikipedia distributed under a CC BY-SA 3.0 license.
Figure 3.18: Photo by US National Park Service, Public Domain.
Figure 3.19: Metropolitan Museum of Art, New York, Gift of Kate Wells, 1892
Figure 3.20: National Parks Service, Historic Photos, Casa Grande Ruins National Monument, circa 1900 (CG-6333-1)
Figure 3.21: The Art Institute of Chicago, gift of Edward and Betty Harris, Reference Number 2004.1134.
Figure 3.22: Metropolitan Museum of Art, New York, The Michael C. Rockefeller Memorial Collection, Bequest of Nelson A. Rockefeller, 1979
Figure 3.23: By Jenny Hughes - Brooklyn Museum, No restrictions.
Figure 3.24: Cadzi Cody (Cosiogo) (Shoshone, 1866-1912). Painted Elk Hide Robe, ca. 1900. Elk hide, pigment, 81 x 78 in. (205.7 x 198.1 cm). Brooklyn Museum, Dick S. Ramsay Fund, 64.13. Creative Commons-BY (Photo: Brooklyn Museum, 64.13_detail_edited_SL1.jpg)
Figure 3.25: Photo by C. D. Arnold (1844-1927); H. D. Higinbotham - The Project Gutenberg EBook of Official Views Of The World's Columbian Exposition - site file, Public Domain.
Figure 3.26: Photo by The original uploader was Lordkinbote at English Wikipedia. - Transferred from en.wikipedia to Commons by SchuminWeb using CommonsHelper, distributed under a CC BY-SA 2.5 license.
Figure 3.27: Photo by Edward S. Curtis, Public Domain.
Figure 3.28: Anisalaga "Mary Ebbets Hunt" (1823-1919), Chilkat Dowry Blanket, c. 1880, Wool and Cedar Bark.
Figure 3.29: Photo by Edward S. Curtis, Public Domain.
Figure 3.30: Chilkat Blanket , Haida Gwaii, c. 1900, Wool and cedar, 68.50 x 35.43 in. (174 x 90 cm)
The British Museum, Donated by St. George Littledale, 1929
Figure 3.31: North Wind Mask (Negakfok). Alaska; Yup'ik. Early 20th century. Wood, paint, feathers, 45 1/4 x 21 3/8 x 17 7/8 in. (114.9 x 54.3 x 45.4 cm). The Michael C. Rockefeller Memorial Collection, Purchase, Nelson A. Rockefeller Gift, 1961 (1978.412.76a, b).The Metropolitan Museum of Art, New York, NY, USAART362943. Photo Credit: Image copyright © The Metropolitan Museum of Art. Image source: Art Resource, NY
Figure 3.32: Cherokee Booger Dance mask, ca. 1910, North Carolina Gourd, fox fur, cordage, 29 x 17 x 17 cm. Exchanged from John White 23/7839, Smithsonian National Museum of the American Indian, Exchanged from John White.
Figure 3.33: Photo courtesy of the US National Park Service By NPS - NPS, Public Domain.
Figure 3.34: Smithsonian National Museum of the American Indian
Figure 3.35: Jaune Quick-To-See Smith, State Names, 2000, oil, collage and mixed media on canvas, Smithsonian American Art Museum, Gift of Elizabeth Ann Dugan and museum purchase, 2004.28. Smithsonian American Art Museum, Washington, DC, U.S.A. Photo credit: Smithsonian American Art Museum, Washington, DC/Art Resource, NY.

Chapter 4

Figure 4.1: Courtesy of State Museum of Namibia or Trust for African Rock Art (TARA)
Figure 4.2: TARA/David Coulson
Figure 4.3: Photo by Fondazione Passaré distributed under a CC BY-SA 3.0 license.
Figure 4.4: Photo by Francesco Raffaele - http://xoomer.virgilio.it/francescoraf/hesyra/Hierakonpolis-tomb100.htm distributed under a CC BY-SA 3.0 license.
Figure 4.5: Egyptian Museum Cairo
Figure 4.6: Photo by Max Gattringer, Public Domain.
Figure 4.7: Photo by Jon Bodsworth (http://www.egyptarchive.co.uk/html/dahshur_08.html) [Copyrighted free use], via Wikimedia Commons
Figure 4.8: Photo by Ricardo Liberato - All Gizah Pyramids, distributed under a CC BY-SA 2.0 license
Figure 4.9: Photo by MusikAnimal distributed under a CC BY-SA 3.0 license.
Figure 4.10: Photo by A. Parrot distributed under a CC0, 1.0 Universal Public Domain Declaration license; Photo by Djehouty distributed under a CC BY-SA 4.0 license; Photo by Einsamer Schütze distributed under a CC BY-SA 3.0 license.
Figure 4.11: King Menkaura, the goddess Hathor, and the deified Hare nome, Egyptian, Old Kingdom, Dynasty 4, reign of Menkaura, 2490–2472 B.C. 43.5 x 84.5 x 49 cm, 187.8 kg (17 1/8 x 33 1/4 x 19 5/16 in., Museum of Fine Arts, Boston. Harvard University—Boston Museum of Fine Arts Expedition, 09.200.
Figure 4.12: By Olaf Tausch - Own work, CC BY 3.0 license.
Figure 4.13: Metropolitan Museum of Art, New York, Rogers Fund, 1930
Figure 4.14: Photo by Ad Meskens distributed under a CC BY-SA 3.0 license.
Figure 4.15: Photo by Alexander Baranov from Montpellier, France, distributed under a CC BY 2.0 license.
Figure 4.16: Photo by Gerbil from de.wikipedia - Own work, Public Domain.
Figure 4.17: Photo by Philip Pikart distributed under a CC BY-SA 3.0 license.
Figure 4.18: Conical eggshell-ware bowl, Nubian, Terminal A-Group, 3100–3000 B.C. Findspot: Sudan (Nubia), Pottery Height x rim diameter: 19 x 21 cm (7 1/2 x 8 1/4 in.) Museum of Fine Arts, Boston, Gift of Dr. George A. Reisner, 19.1540.
Figure 4.19: UNESCO under Creative Commons Attribution-ShareAlike 3.0 IGO license, Ron Van Oens, photographer
Figure 4.20: Photo by Ondřej Žváček distributed under a CC BY 2.5 license.
Figure 4.21: Photo by Bernard Gagnon distributed under a CC BY-SA 3.0 license.
Figure 4.22: Photo by Janice Bell distributed under a CC BY-SA 4.0 license.

Figure 4.23: Photo by Daderot distributed under a CC0, 1.0 Universal Public Domain Declaration license.
Figure 4.24: National Museum, Lagos, Nigeria, 79.R.4. Photo by Dirk Bakker
Figure 4.25: The British Museum, Funded by the Art Fund (as NACF), 1939.
Figure 4.26: The Metropolitan Museum of Art, New York, The Michael C. Rockefeller Memorial Collection, Bequest of Nelson A. Rockefeller, 1979.
Figure 4.27: Photo by MAREK SZAREJKO from CLONMEL, IRELAND - POLAND - Flickr, distributed under a CC BY-SA 2.0 license; CC BY-SA 2.5 license; IMG41624 © Aga Khan Trust for Culture; Photo by Andy Gilham - from [1] JCarriker (304322 bytes) (used with the permission of Andy Gilham of www.andy-gilham.com, distributed under a CC BY-SA 3.0 license.
Figure 4.28: Metropolitan Museum of Art, New York, Gift of Paul and Ruth Tishman, 1991; Museo Nazionale Prehistorico e Etnograpfico Luigi Pigorini, Rome; Seattle Art Museum, Acc # 68.31, Salt cellar, Sierra Leone. ca. 1490-1530, Ivory, 8 1/8 x 2 9/16 x 2 11/16 in. (20.7 x 6.5 x 6.8 cm). Nasli and Alice Heeramaneck Collection.
Figure 4.29: The Metropolitan Museum of Art, New York, Gift of Lester Wunderman, 1987. Masquerade Hood (Kanaga). Dogon peoples, Mali. 19th-20th CE. Wood, fiber (sanseveria), hide, pigment, H. 18 1/8 x W. 22 13/16 in. (46 x 57.9 cm). Front. Gift of Lester Wunderman, 1987 (1987.74h). Location: The Metropolitan Museum of Art, New York, NY, USA Photo Credit: Image copyright © The Metropolitan Museum of Art. Image source: Art Resource, NY.
Figure 4.30: The Metropolitan Museum of Art, New York, Purchase, Lila Acheson Wallace Gift, 1996.
Figure 4.31: Linguist Staff Finial Representing Two Men Sitting on Stools, c. 1945-1960 (wood and gold leaf), Bonsu, Osei (1900-1977) / Museum of Fine Arts, Houston, Texas, USA / Gift of Alfred C. Glassell, Jr. / Bridgeman Images.
Figure 4.32: Courtesy of the artist and Jack Shainman Gallery, New York
Figure 4.33: Courtesy of the artist

Chapter 5

Figure 5.1: Photographer Richard T. Bryant
Figure 5.2: Photo by Reinhard Dietrich - Own work, Public Domain.
Figure 5.3: Archaeological Museum, Amman, Jordan. Photo Credit: Erich Lessing / Art Resource, NY
Figure 5.4: Drawing by Rick Rishaw
Figure 5.5: Museum of Ankara
Figure 5.6: Photo by User:Roweromaniak - Archiwum "Roweromaniaka wielkopolskiego" No_B19-36, distributed under a CC BY-SA 2.5 license.
Figure 5.7: National Museum, Baghdad Iraq, Photo credit Scala/ Art Resource, NY, ART88144
Figure 5.8: By Unknown - Marie-Lan Nguyen (2005), Public Domain.
Figure 5.9: The British Museum, Ur Excavation 1927-1928
Figure 5.10: University of Pennsylvania, Museum of Archaeology and Anthropology, Philadelphia.
Figure 5.11: Photo by Rama distributed under a CC BY-SA 2.0 fr license.
Figure 5.12: Photo by Hardnfast distributed under a CC BY 3.0 license.
Figure 5.13: The British Museum, Purchase 1919
Figure 5.14: Photo by Mbzt distributed under a CC BY 3.0 license.
Figure 5.15: Photo by user:Rmashhadi - user:Rmashhadi, Public Domain.
Figure 5.16: The British Museum, Excavated 1856
Figure 5.17: By Radomir Vrbovsky - Own work, CC BY-SA 4.0 license.
Figure 5.18: Photo by Pentocelo distributed under a CC BY-SA 3.0 license.
Figure 5.19: Photo by user:Rmashhadi - user:Rmashhadi, Public Domain.
Figure 5.20: Photo by Bernard Gagnon distributed under a CC BY-SA 4.0 license.
Figure 5.21: By Unknown – "Wonders of the Past" vol. 2, Public Domain.
Figure 5.22: Photo by Andrew Shiva / Wikipedia, CC BY-SA 4.0 license.
Figure 5.23: Photo by Bernard Gagnon distributed under a CC BY-SA 3.0 license.
Figure 5.24: Photo by Aladdin distributed under a CC BY-SA 4.0 license.
Figure 5.26: Science History Images / Alamy Stock Photo
Figure 5.27: Photo by Jpbazard Jean-Pierre Bazard distributed under a CC BY-SA 3.0 license.
Figure 5.28: The Metropolitan Museum of Art, New York, Bequest of George D. Pratt, 1935
Figure 5.29: Freer/Sackler Gallery of Art, Smithsonian Institution, Washington, D.C.
Figure 5.31: Photo by Patrickringgenberg distributed under a CC BY-SA 3.0 license.
Figure 5.32: Photo by Self - Own work distributed under a CC BY-SA 3.0 license.
Figure 5.33: Shirazi Art Gallery PTY LTD
Figure 5.34: Courtesy Pi Artworks and the artist.
Figure 5.35: The British Museum, Funded by Brooke Sewell Permanent Fund

Chapter 6

Figure 6.1: Photo by Saqib Qayyum distributed under a CC BY-SA 3.0 license.
Figure 6.2: Photo by Ismoon (talk) 12:06, 20 February 2012 (UTC) distributed under a CC0 1.0 Universal Public Domain Dedication license.
Figure 6.3: AKG Images
Figure 6.4: By unknown Indus Valley Civilization sealmaker from Mohenjodaro archaeological site - http://www.columbia.edu/itc/mealac/pritchett/00routesdata/bce_500back/indusvalley/protoshiva/protoshiva.jpg, Public Domain.
Figure 6.7: By Chrisi1964 - Detail of this file:, CC BY-SA 4.0, license.
Figure 6.8: Photo by AmitNimade distributed under a CC BY-SA 4.0 license.
Figure 6.10: Photo by Biswarup Ganguly distributed under a CC BY 3.0 license.
Figure 6.11: Photo by Kevin Standage (kevinstandage1@google-mail.com) INDIAN TRAVEL PHOTOGRAPHY - Licensed through agreement by e-mail on 5 October 2017: Kevin Standage AN INDIAN TRAVEL PHOTOGRAPHY BLOG, under a CC BY-SA 2.0 license. By SMU Central University Libraries; Permission: SMU Central University Libraries @ Flickr Commons - Detail of, No restrictions, h.
Figure 6.12: The British Museum
Figure 6.13: National Museum of Scotland
Figure 6.14: Photo by June Coomaraswamy - June Coomaraswamy Origin of the Buddha Image, published 1927, Public Domain
Figure 6.15: Archaelogical Museum of Sarnath
Figure 6.16: Photo by Biswarup Ganguly distributed under a CC BY 3.0 license.
Figure 6.17: Photo by Youri distributed under a CC BY-SA 3.0 license.
Figure 6.18: Photo by csgautham distributed under a CC BY-SA 4.0 license.
Figure 6.19: Photo by Nittavinoda distributed under a CC BY-SA 4.0 license.
Figure 6.20: Photo by Rajaraja_mural.jpg: Original uploader was Venu62 at en.wikipediaderivative work: Keyan20 (talk) - Rajaraja_mural.jpg, Public Domain
Figure 6.21: Photo by Vbmindia distributed under a CC BY-SA 4.0 license.
Figure 6.22: Photo by KennyOMG distributed under a CC BY-SA 4.0 license.
Figure 6.23: The Metropolitan Museum of Art, New York, Gift of R. H. Ellsworth Ltd., in honor of Susan Dillon, 1987. Image copyright © The Metropolitan Museum of Art. Image source: Art Resource, NY

Figure 6.24: Photo by Balaji distributed under a CC BY-SA 3.0 license.
Figure 6.25: Photo by © Asitjain / Wikimedia Commons, distributed under a CC BY-SA 3.0 license.
Figure 6.26: Photo by Dennis Jarvis from Halifax, Canada - India-5740, distributed under a CC BY-SA 2.0 license
Figure 6.27: Photo by Afifa Afrin distributed under a CC BY-SA 4.0 license. By ampersandyslexia - originally posted to Flickr as India, Day 3, CC BY-SA 2.0.
Figure 6.28: Photo by Bikashrd distributed under a CC BY-SA 4.0 license.
Figure 6.29: The Victoria and Albert Museum
Figure 6.30: Attributed to: Mansur, Indian, active about 1590–1625, Zebra, Indian, Mughal, Mughal period, about 1621. Object Place: Northern India, Opaque watercolor and gold on paper, 18.9 x 27 cm (7 7/16 x 10 5/8 in.). Museum of Fine Arts, Boston, Francis Bartlett Donation of 1912 and Picture Fund, 14.659.
Figure 6.31: Freer Gallery of Art, Smithsonian Institution, Washington, DC.
Figure 6.32: Photo by Willard84 distributed under a CC BY-SA 4.0 license. Photo by Suraj rajiv distributed under a CC BY 4.0 license. Photo by Dennis Jarvis from Halifax, Canada - India-0155 - Humayun's Tomb (medical update - bottom) Uploaded by Ekabhishek, distributed under a CC BY-SA 2.0 license. Photo by Willard84 distributed under a CC BY-SA 4.0 license. Photo by Suraj rajiv distributed under a CC BY 4.0 license.
Figure 6.33: Attributed to Narsingh. Maharaja Jaswant Singh II of Marwar, ca. 1880. Opaque watercolors and gold on paper, sheet: 15 1/2 x 11 5/8 in. (39.4 x 29.5 cm). Brooklyn Museum, Gift of Mr. and Mrs. Robert L. Poster, 87.234.6 Photo: Brooklyn Museum
Figure 6.34: National Gallery of Modern Art, New Delhi
Figure 6.35: Courtesy of Usha Mittal, Victoria and Albert Museum, London
Figure 6.36: Courtesy the artist and Hauser & Wirth.
Figure 6.37: © Rashid Rana; Courtesy Lisson Gallery.

Chapter 7

Figure 7.1: Metropolitan Museum of Art, New York, Gift of Cynthia Hazen Polsky, 1987
Figure 7.2: The Metropolitan Museum of Art, New York, Samuel Eilenberg Collection, Bequest of Samuel Eilenberg, 1990
Figure 7.3: By Own work, Public Domain
Figure 7.4: Photo by Jakub Hałun distributed under a CC BY-SA 4.0 license.
Figure 7.5: Photo by Bjørn Christian Tørrissen distributed under a CC BY-SA 4.0 license.
Figure 7.6: Photo by Lionslayer distributed under a CC BY-SA 4.0 license.
Figure 7.7: Photo by Hybernator distributed under a CC BY-SA 3.0 license.
Figure 7.8: Photo by Jakub Hałun distributed under a CC BY-SA 4.0 license.
Figure 7.9: Photo by Gerd Eichmann distributed under a CC BY-SA 3.0 license.
Figure 7.10: Photo by Jakub Hałun distributed under a CC BY-SA 4.0 license.
Figure 7.11: Image by User:Markalexander100 distributed under a {{GFDL}} license.
Figure 7.13: Photo by Krzysztof Golik distributed under a CC BY-SA 4.0 license.
Figure 7.15: Photo by Shyamal distributed under a CC BY-SA 3.0 license.
Figure 7.16: Photo by Hartmann Linge distributed under a CC BY-SA 3.0 license.
Figure 7.17: Photo by Media lib distributed under a CC BY-SA 4.0 license.
Figure 7.18: Photo by Photo Dharma from Sadao, Thailand - 069 Walking Buddha, 14c, Sukhothai, distributed under a CC BY 2.0 license.
Figure 7.19: Photo by Diego Delso distributed under a CC BY-SA 3.0 license.
Figure 7.20: Photo by Kjfmartin. Original uploader was Kjfmartin at [http://en.wikip...Photo https://commons.wikimedia.org/w/index.php?curid=31321180
Figure 7.21: Photo by CEphoto, Uwe Aranas or alternatively © CEphoto, Uwe Aranas, distributed under a CC BY-SA 3.0 license.
Figure 7.22: Photo by Gunawan Kartapranata distributed under a CC BY-SA 3.0 license
Figure 7.23: Photo by Astayoga at English Wikipedia - Transferred from en.wikipedia to Commons by aboalbiss., Public Domain.
Figure 7.24: Photo by Caitriana Nicholson from 北京 ~ Beijing, 中国 ~ China - Tran Quoc Pagoda, Hanoi, distributed under a CC BY-SA 2.0 license.
Figure 7.25: Dish with deer, Vietnamese, Le dynasty, 15th–16th century, Object Place: Vietnam, Stoneware with underglaze cobalt blue and overglaze polychrome-enamel decoration, My Xa kilns 9 x 44 cm (3 9/16 x 17 5/16 in.) Museum of Fine Arts, Boston, Charles Bain Hoyt Fund, 1985.334.
Figure 7.26: Photo by Ninara from Helsinki, Finland. Edit: TSP - Own work based on File:Wat_Phra_Kaew_by_Ninara_(33271955941).jpg, distributed under a CC BY 4.0 license.
Figure 7.27: By Credit Jan S. Peterson. Cropped from original image and lighting balanced by DxO. This file has been extracted from another file: Emerald Buddha, August 2012, Bangkok.jpg distributed under a CC BY-SA 3.0 license.
Figure 7.28: Myanmar National Museum
Figure 7.29: Photo by Marcin Konsek / Wikimedia Commons, distributed under a CC BY-SA 4.0 license.
Figure 7.30: Courtesy of Jirapat Tatsanasomboon and Thavibu Art Advisory
Figure 7.31: Metropolitan Museum of Art, New York, Purchase, Friends of Asian Art Gifts, 2012. © Sopheap Pich
Figure 7.32: Photo courtesy of River Gallery

Chapter 8

Figure 8.1: Professor Gary Lee Todd, Sias International University, Xinzheng, Henan, China
Figure 8.2: Professor Gary Lee Todd, Sias International University, Xinzheng, Henan, China; Nelson-Atkins Museum of Art, Kansas City.
Figure 8.4: Brooklyn Museum, Gift of Mr. and Mrs. Alastair B. Martin, The Guennol Collection
Figure 8.5: The Metropolitan Museum of Art, Charlotte C. and John C. Weber Collection, Gift of Charlotte C. and John C. Weber through the Live Oak Foundation, 1988
Figure 8.6: The Metropolitan Museum of Art, Rogers Fund, 1999
Figure 8.7: Photo by Zzjgbc at Chinese Wikipedia distributed under a GNU Free Documentation License, Version 1.2 license.
Figure 8.8: Photo by Laika ac from UK distributed under a CC BY-SA 2.0 license.
Figure 8.9: The Metropolitan Museum of Art, Purchase, Dr. and Mrs. John C. Weber Gift, 1984
Figure 8.10: Changsha Hunan Provincial Museum
Figure 8.11: Asian Art Museum of San Francisco, Avery Brundage Collection, Object # B60B1034; The British Museum
Figure 8.12: Photo by Marcin Biatek distributed under a CC BY-SA 4.0 license.
Figure 8.13: The British Museum
Figure 8.14: Victoria and Albert Museum, London, Gift of Mrs. Robert Solomon, 2009, Museum no. C-50-1964
Figure 8.15: Photo by Wolfgang Kaehler/LightRocket via Getty Images
Figure 8.16: Attributed to: Yan Liben, Chinese, about 600–673. The thirteen emperors, Chinese, Tang dynasty, second half of the 7th century A.D. Ink and color on silk, 51.3 x 531 cm (20 3/16 x 209 1/16 in.). Museum of Fine Arts, Boston. Denman Waldo Ross Collection, 31.643.
Figure 8.17: Photo by Anagoria distributed under a CC BY 3.0 license.
Figure 8.19: Photo by Zeus1234 distributed under a CC By-SA 3.0 license.
Figure 8.20: National Palace Museum, Taiwan, Republic of China
Figure 8.21: National Palace Museum, Taiwan, Republic of China

Figure 8.23: The Metropolitan Museum of Art, John M. Crawford Jr. Collection, Purchase, Douglas Dillon Gift, 1981
Figure 8.24: National Palace Museum, Taiwan, Republic of China
Figure 8.25: Tokyo National Museum
Figure 8.26: The Metropolitan Museum of Art, Gift of John M. Crawford Jr., 1988
Figure 8.27: National Palace Museum, Taiwan, Republic of China
Figure 8.28: Zhejiang Provincial Museum in Hangzhou
Figure 8.29: The Metropolitan Museum of Art, Purchase, The Dillon Fund Gift, 1985
Figure 8.30: Photo by Daniel Case distributed under a CC BY-SA 3.0 license.
Figure 8.31: National Palace Museum, Taiwan, Republic of China
Figure 8.32: Cleveland Museum of Art
Figure 8.33: The Yorck Project (2002) 10.000 Meisterwerke der Malerei (DVD-ROM), distributed by DIRECTMEDIA Publishing GmbH.
Figure 8.37: Hauser and Wirth

Chapter 9

Figure 9.1: National Museum of Korea. Found here: https://readtiger.com/wkp/en/Korean_art. Under CC license
Figure 9.2: Dancers (closeup). Muyong Tomb, 5th century A.D. Ji'an city, Jilin province, China
Figure 9.3: Photo by J.T. Williams distributed under a CC BY-SA 2.0 license.
Figure 9.5: National Museum of Korea
Figure 9.6: Photo by Zsinj distributed under a CC BY-SA 4.0 license.
Figure 9.7: Photo by Richard Fabi distributed under a CC BY-SA 3.0 license.
Figure 9.8: The Metropolitan Museum of Art, Fletcher Fund 1927
Figure 9.9: Kagami Jinjya Temple, Karatsu, Japan
Figure 9.10: National Museum of Korea
Figure 9.11: Ho-Am Art Museum
Figure 9.12: Gansong Art Museum, Seoul
Figure 9.13: Museum of Modern and Contemporary Art, Korea
Figure 9.14: The British Museum
Figure 9.15: Photo by Daderot distributed under a CC0 1.0 Universal Public Domain Declaration license.
Figure 9.16: The Metropolitan Museum of Art, Rogers Fund, 1918
Figure 9.17: National Land Image Information (Color Aerial Photographs), Ministry of Land, Infrastructure, Transport and Tourism
Figure 9.18: Photo by Daderot distributed under a CC0 1.0 Universal Public Domain Declaration license.
Figure 9.19: Ise Jingu
Figure 9.20: Photo by user 663highland distributed under a CC BY 2.5 license.
Figure 9.23: Photo by user 663highland distributed under a CC BY 2.5 license.
Figure 9.24: Tokugawa Art Museum
Figure 9.25: Photo by ういき野郎 distributed under a CC BY-SA 4.0 license.
Figure 9.26: Phoenix Hall, Byodin
Figure 9.28: Night Attack on the Sanjō Palace, from the Illustrated Scrolls of the Events of the Heiji Era (Heiji monogatari emaki). Japanese, Kamakura period, second half of the 13th century. Handscroll; ink and color on paper. 41.3 × 700.3 cm (16 1/4 × 275 11/16 in.). Museum of Fine Arts, Boston. Fenollosa-Weld Collection, 11.4000.
Figure 9.30: Tokyo National Museum
Figure 9.31: https://commons.wikimedia.org/w/index.php?cu
Figure 9.32: https://commons.wikimedia.org/w/index.php?curid=105421
Figure 9.33: Suzuki Harunobu, Japanese, 1725–1770. Evening Bell of the Clock, from the series Eight Views of the Parlor (Zashiki hakkei), Japanese, Edo period, about 1766 (Meiwa 3), Woodblock print (nishiki-e); ink and color on paper, Vertical chûban; 27.6 x 20.6 cm (10 7/8 x 8 1/8 in.). Museum of Fine Arts, Boston, William S. and John T. Spaulding Collection, 21.4606.
Figure 9.34: The Great Wave off Kanagawa, from the series '36 Views of Mt. Fuji' ('Fugaku sanjuokkei') pub. by Nishimura Eijudo (woodblock print), Hokusai, Katsushika (1760-1849) / Private Collection / Bridgeman Images
Figure 9.35: University Art Museum, Tokyo University of the Arts
Figure 9.36: Atsuko Tanaka, Electric Dress (1956).Vinyl paint on light bulbs, electric cords and control console. Courtesy Takamatsu City Museum of Art, Copyright Ryoji Ito

Chapter 10

Figure 10.1: John Gollings
Figure 10.2: Photo by Marius Fenger distributed under a CC BY-SA 4.0 license.
Figure 10.3: Musée due Quai Branly
Figure 10.4: National Gallery of Australia, Gift of Gordon and Marilyn Darling, celebrating the National Gallery of Australia's 25th Anniversary, 2009. Donated through the Australia Government's Cultural Gifts Program. Accession no NGA 2009.992. Image rights: © Namatjira Legacy Trust/ Copyright Agency. Artists Rights Society, 2019. www.namatjiratrust.org. Ghost gum, c.1945 (w/c over pencil on paper), Namatjira, Albert (1902-59) / National Gallery of Australia, Canberra / Gift of Gordon and Marilyn Darling, celebrating the National Gallery of Australia's 25th Anniversary, 2009. Donated through the Australia Government's Cultural Gifts Program / Bridgeman Images
Figure 10.5: Australia, Clifford Possum Tjapaltjarri (1932-2002), Bush-fire II, 1972, synthetic polymer paint on composition board, (61 x 43 cm), Collection of the National Gallery of Australia.Image rights© the estate of the artist licensed by Aboriginal Artists Agency Ltd
Figure 10.6: The Holmes à Court Collection, Heytesbury.
Figure 10.8: The Metropolitan Museum of Art, Michael C. Rockefeller Memorial Collection, Bequest of Nelson A. Rockefeller, 1979
Figure 10.9: Tropenmuseum Amsterdam
Figure 10.10: The British Museum, Funded by Christy Fund, Field collection by Dr. Bronislaw Malinowski
Figure 10.11: Artokoloro Quint Lox Limited / Alamy Stock Photo
Figure 10.12: Photo by EK Silverman distributed under a CC BY-SA 4.0 license.
Figure 10.13: The British Museum
Figure 10.14: Denver Art Museum, Gift of the Center for International Cultural Exchange
Figure 10.15: Photo by Daderot distributed under a CC0 1.0 Universal Public Domain Declaration license.
Figure 10.16: The Brooklyn Museum
Figure 10.17: The Metropolitan Museum of Art, The Michael C. Rockefeller Memorial Collection, Purchase, Nelson A. Rockefeller Gift, 1965
Figure 10.18: Metropolitan Museum of Art, The Michael C. Rockefeller Memorial Collection, Gift of Nelson A. Rockefeller, 1972
Figure 10.19: Glasgow Museum of Art
Figure 10.20: The Museum of New Zealand
Figure 10.21: ©RDK Herman, Pacific Worlds, 2002
Figure 10.22: Gable Figure (Dilukai). Republic of Palau, Caroline Islands Belauan, late 19th-early 20th CE. Wood, paint, H. 25 11/16 x W. 38 x D. 7 7/8 in. (65.2 x 96.5 x 20 cm). The Michael C. Rockefeller Memorial Collection, Gift of Nelson A. Rockefeller, and Purchase, Nelson A. Rockefeller Gift, 1970 (1978.412.1558a-d). Image source: Art Resource, NY
Figure 10.23: Photo by CT Snow from Hsinchu, Taiwan distributed under a CC BY 2.0 license.
Figure 10.24: Author's photograph
Figure 10.25: © The Trustees of the British Museum
Figure 10.26: Photo by Arian Zwegers distributed under a CC BY 2.0 license.
Figure 10.27: Field Museum Chicago
Figure 10.28: Field Museum Chicago

INDEX